The 20th Century

1901-1940

Great Events from History

The 20th Century

1901-1940

Volume 5
1930-1937

Editor

Robert F. Gorman
Southwest Texas State University

SALEM PRESS

Pasadena, California   Hackensack, New Jersey

Editor in Chief: Dawn P. Dawson

Editorial Director: Christina J. Moose *Production Editor:* Andrea E. Miller
Acquisitions Editor: Mark Rehn *Design, Layout, and Graphics:* James Hutson
Research Supervisor: Jeffry Jensen *Additional Layout and Graphics:* William Zimmerman
Manuscript Editors: Judy Selhorst, *Photo Editor:* Cynthia Breslin Beres
Andy Perry, Anna A. Moore *Editorial Assistant:* Dana Garey
Research Assistant Editor: Tim Tiernan

Cover photos (pictured clockwise, from top left): Marlene Dietrich in *The Blue Angel*, 1930. (The Granger Collection, New York); Orville Wright in flight, 1909. (The Granger Collection, New York); Hammer and Sickle. (The Granger Collection, New York); Gold coffin of King Tut, photographed in 1922. (The Granger Collection, New York); Picasso's *Guernica*. (The Granger Collection, New York); American troops landing in France, 1918. (The Granger Collection, New York)

Some of the essays in this work originally appeared in the following Salem Press sets: *Chronology of European History: 15,000 b.c. to 1997* (1997, edited by John Powell; associate editors, E. G. Weltin, José M. Sánchez, Thomas P. Neill, and Edward P. Keleher); *Great Events from History: North American Series, Revised Edition* (1997, edited by Frank N. Magill); *Great Events from History II: Science and Technology* (1991, edited by Frank N. Magill); *Great Events from History II: Human Rights* (1992, edited by Frank N. Magill); *Great Events from History II: Arts and Culture* (1993, edited by Frank N. Magill); *Great Events from History II: Business and Commerce* (1994, edited by Frank N. Magill), and *Great Events from History II: Ecology and the Environment* (1995, edited by Frank N. Magill). New material has been added.

Library of Congress Cataloging-in-Publication Data

Great events from history. The 20th century, 1901-1940 / editor, Robert F. Gorman.

    p. cm.

Some of the essays in this work originally appeared in various Salem Press publications.

Includes bibliographical references and index.

ISBN 978-1-58765-324-7 (set : alk. paper) -- ISBN 978-1-58765-325-4 (v. 1: alk. paper) -- ISBN 978-1-58765-326-1 (v. 2 : alk. paper) -- ISBN 978-1-58765-327-8 (v. 3 : alk. paper) -- ISBN 978-1-58765-328-5 (v. 4 : alk. paper) -- ISBN 978-1-58765-329-2 (v. 5 : alk. paper) -- ISBN 978-1-58765-330-8 (v. 6 : alk. paper) 1. Twentieth century. I. Gorman, Robert F. II. Title: 20th century, 1901-1940. III. Title: Twentieth century, 1901-1940.

D421.G629 2007
909.82'1—dc22

2007001930

First Printing

CONTENTS

1930 *(continued)*

1931

1932

1933

CONTENTS ·

1934

1935

1936

CONTENTS

1937

KEYWORD LIST OF CONTENTS

LIST OF MAPS, TABLES, AND SIDEBARS

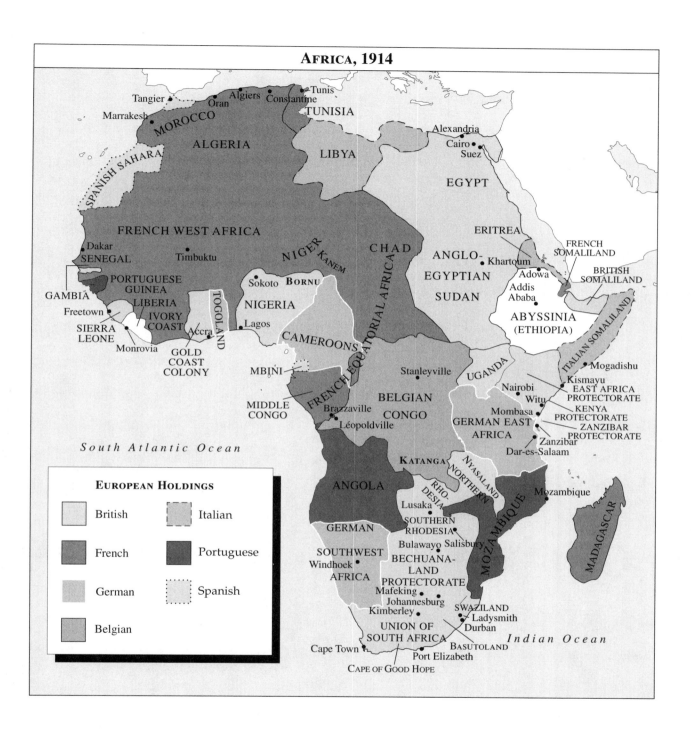

AFRICA, 1914

Tangier
Marrakesh
MOROCCO
Oran
Algiers
Constantine
Tunis
TUNISIA
ALGERIA
LIBYA
SPANISH SAHARA
Alexandria
Cairo
Suez
EGYPT
FRENCH WEST AFRICA
Dakar
SENEGAL
Timbuktu
NIGER
KANEM
CHAD
ERITREA
ANGLO-EGYPTIAN SUDAN
Khartoum
FRENCH SOMALILAND
BRITISH SOMALILAND
PORTUGUESE GUINEA
GAMBIA
LIBERIA
Freetown
SIERRA LEONE
Monrovia
IVORY COAST
Accra
GOLD COAST COLONY
TOGOLAND
Sokoto
BORNU
NIGERIA
Lagos
CAMEROONS
FRENCH EQUATORIAL AFRICA
Adowa
Addis Ababa
ABYSSINIA (ETHIOPIA)
ITALIAN SOMALILAND
Mogadishu
MBINI
MIDDLE CONGO
Brazzaville
Léopoldville
Stanleyville
BELGIAN CONGO
UGANDA
Nairobi
Witu
Mombasa
GERMAN EAST AFRICA
Zanzibar
Dar-es-Salaam
Kismayu
EAST AFRICA PROTECTORATE
KENYA PROTECTORATE
ZANZIBAR PROTECTORATE
South Atlantic Ocean
KATANGA
ANGOLA
NORTHERN RHODESIA
NYASALAND
Mozambique
MOZAMBIQUE
MADAGASCAR
Lusaka
SOUTHERN RHODESIA
Bulawayo
Salisbury
GERMAN SOUTHWEST AFRICA
Windhoek
BECHUANALAND PROTECTORATE
Mafeking
Johannesburg
Kimberley
SWAZILAND
Ladysmith
Durban
Indian Ocean
UNION OF SOUTH AFRICA
BASUTOLAND
Cape Town
Port Elizabeth
CAPE OF GOOD HOPE

EUROPEAN HOLDINGS

British	Italian
French	Portuguese
German	Spanish
Belgian	

EUROPE, 1914

Arctic Ocean

Iceland

Atlantic Ocean

Northern Ireland

IRELAND

GREAT BRITAIN

North Sea

DENMARK

NETHERLANDS

BELGIUM

GERMAN EMPIRE

NORWAY

SWEDEN

Baltic Sea

RUSSIA

FRANCE

SWITZER-LAND

AUSTRO-HUNGARIAN EMPIRE

ROMANIA

Black Sea

BULGARIA

Thrace

PORTUGAL

SPAIN

Corsica

ITALY

Adriatic Sea

MONTE-NEGRO

SERBIA

ALBANIA

GREECE

OTTOMAN EMPIRE

Sardinia

Sicily

Cyprus

ALGERIA

TUNISIA

Mediterranean Sea

Crete

MOROCCO

AFRICA

LIBYA

EGYPT

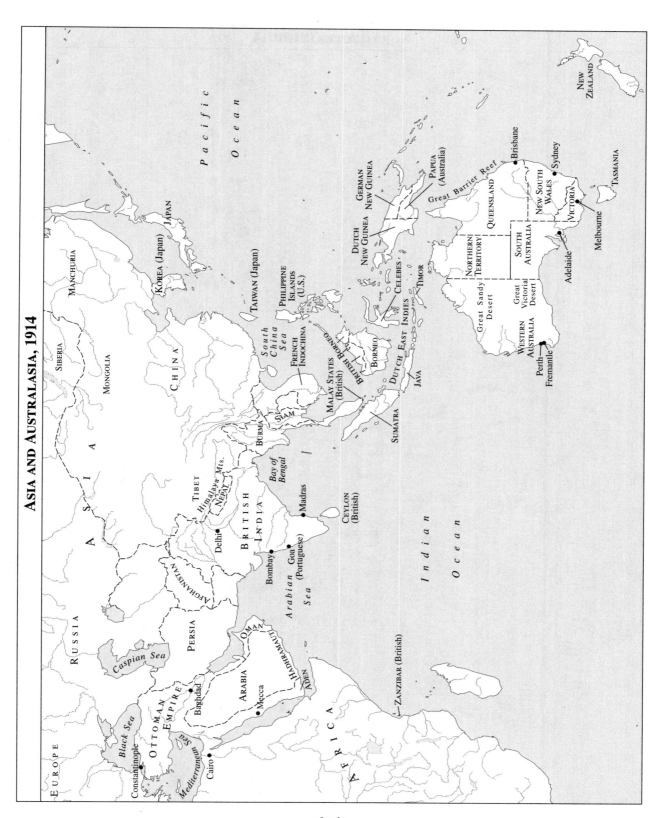

ASIA AND AUSTRALASIA, 1914

NORTH AMERICA, 1914

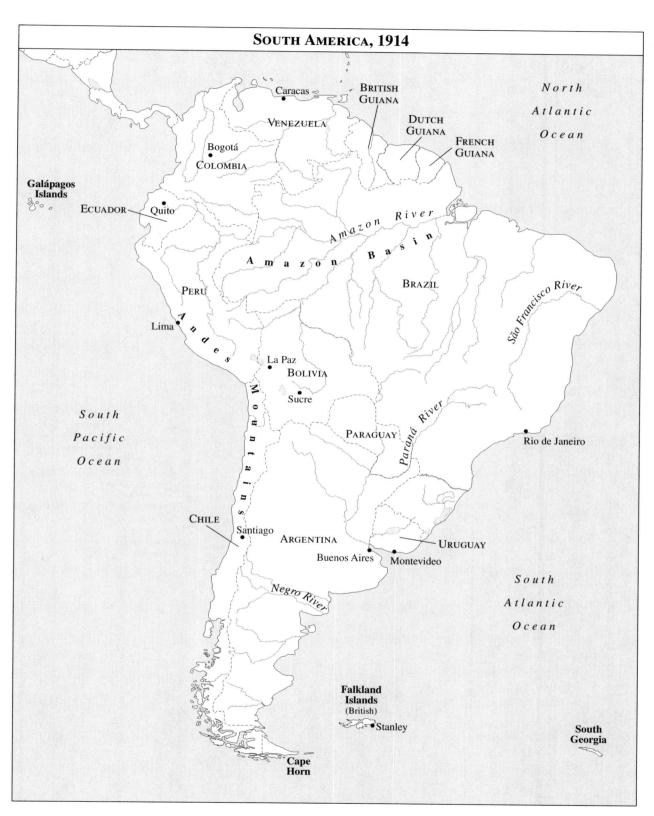

SOUTH AMERICA, 1914

Caracas
BRITISH
GUIANA
VENEZUELA
DUTCH
GUIANA
FRENCH
GUIANA
*North
Atlantic
Ocean*

Bogotá
COLOMBIA

**Galápagos
Islands**

ECUADOR
Quito

Amazon River

A m a z o n   B a s i n

BRAZIL

São Francisco River

PERU

Lima

A n d e s

*South
Pacific
Ocean*

La Paz
BOLIVIA
Sucre

M o u n t a i n s

Paraná River

PARAGUAY

Rio de Janeiro

CHILE
Santiago

ARGENTINA

URUGUAY

Buenos Aires
Montevideo

*South
Atlantic
Ocean*

Negro River

**Falkland
Islands**
(British)
Stanley

**South
Georgia**

**Cape
Horn**

cdxxxi

The 20th Century

1901-1940

February 18, 1930
TOMBAUGH DISCOVERS PLUTO

Clyde William Tombaugh, a self-educated astronomer, discovered Pluto, which was then regarded as the ninth planet in Earth's solar system.

LOCALE: Lowell Observatory, Flagstaff, Arizona
CATEGORIES: Science and technology; astronomy

KEY FIGURES
Clyde William Tombaugh (1906-1997), American amateur astronomer
Percival Lowell (1855-1916), American astronomer

SUMMARY OF EVENT

In 1920, Clyde William Tombaugh purchased a 2.2-inch (5.7-centimeter) telescope through the mail from the Sears, Roebuck catalog and taught himself the science of astronomy by reading everything he could on the subject. In 1924, he was impressed with Latimer Wilson's article "The Drift of Jupiter's Markings" in *Popular Astronomy*. Wilson's article included drawings he had made after observing the planet Jupiter with a homemade telescope. Tombaugh learned how to make telescopes through correspondence with Wilson. After Tombaugh built his telescope, he observed Jupiter and Mars, and in 1928 he recorded these observations in drawings. Fascinated with drawings of Mars released by the Lowell Observatory in Flagstaff, Arizona, and published in *Popular Astronomy*, Tombaugh sent his 1928 drawings to the observatory's director, Vesto Melvin Slipher, for some advice.

The Lowell Observatory was founded by Percival Lowell in 1894. Lowell was fascinated with the maps of the "canals" of Mars made popular by the Italian astronomer Giovanni Virginio Schiaparelli from 1877 to 1888. Lowell's observations extended the few dozen canals mapped by Schiaparelli to several hundred. He later popularized his speculations on Mars and alien civilizations in several books: *Mars* (1895), *Mars and Its Canals* (1906), *The Evolution of Worlds* (1909), and *Mars as the Abode of Life* (1908). Although Lowell's theories excited the public and inspired science-fiction writers, astronomers were not convinced. In an attempt to improve his credibility, Lowell initiated a search for a ninth planet in Earth's solar system.

Neptune, the eighth planet, had been discovered in 1846 based on the gravitational effect it was having on the orbit of its neighbor, Uranus. In the same way, the orbit of Neptune was different from what had been predicted, and this led astronomers Lowell and William

Pickering to suspect a yet more distant planet. Lowell called this object "Planet X"; Pickering called it "Planet O." Lowell reasoned that if he could predict the orbit of a ninth planet beyond Neptune and then find the planet, the discovery would enhance his professional status and thereby gain respect for his theory of Martian canals.

Lowell began searching with a special camera in 1905, confident of the planet's location and brightness. In 1911, he obtained a new research tool, a Zeiss blink-microscope comparator, to examine the photographic plates. With this device, two photographic plates of the same star region taken at different times are alternately seen or "blinked" in the viewer. Stellar objects, at their great distances, do not appear to move in the time between exposures. Closer objects, such as planets or asteroids, shift on the photographic plate and appear to "blink."

After ten years of searching, Lowell became discouraged. Ironically, Planet X appeared on two separate pho-

Clyde William Tombaugh. (NARA)

SEARCHING FOR PLANET X

In many ways, Clyde Tombaugh was like his astronomer hero William Herschel, who discovered Uranus unexpectedly during a routine sky survey in 1781. Both were dedicated amateur astronomers and skilled telescope makers who devoted hours to tedious observations. Tombaugh, however, was only twenty-four years old when he discovered Pluto, whereas Herschel was in his early forties when he made his discovery. Furthermore, Tombaugh's yearlong search for Planet X lasted much longer than that of either Herschel or Johann Galle, who discovered Neptune in 1846 on the first night he looked for it, lying less than 1 degree from its predicted position.

The search for Pluto was complicated by the fact that its orbit is highly eccentric—sometimes even passing inside the orbit of Neptune—and has a large inclination of about 17 degrees from the mean plane of the other planets. It is now known that Percival Lowell's predictions for the position of Pluto were based on faulty calculations, and its discovery within 6 degrees of the predicted location was only a coincidence. Fortunately, Tombaugh did not limit his observations to the predicted area of the sky or to the region close to the mean orbital plane of the planets.

When James Christy discovered Pluto's moon, Charon, in 1978, it was conclusively demonstrated that the mass of Pluto was far too small to cause observable deviations in the orbits of Uranus and Neptune; thus the two larger planets' orbits could not be used to predict Pluto's position. In the 1990's, several icy objects much smaller than Pluto were discovered just beyond Pluto's orbit in the Kuiper comet belt with periods of about 300 years, compared to Pluto's 248-year period.

tographic plates taken before his death in 1916. The planet was camouflaged by the Milky Way background between the constellations Taurus and Gemini. In 1919, Pickering, at the Mount Wilson Observatory, captured the planet on four different photographic plates yet failed to identify it.

In February, 1929, the Lowell Observatory resumed the quest for Planet X with the completion of a 13-inch (33-centimeter) telescope-camera. Tombaugh's letter and drawings of 1928 could not have arrived at a better time. His observations and drawings caught the attention of Slipher, who was looking for a talented amateur to operate the new photographic telescope. When Slipher offered Tombaugh the job, he accepted.

Initially, Slipher told Tombaugh to search the Gemini region. It took about a week for Slipher and his brother, Edward, to blink the Gemini plates, without result. Disappointed, Slipher directed the research eastward through the zodiac and in June of 1929 asked Tombaugh to take over the task of plate blinking. Tombaugh found plate blinking tedious and was often distracted by other objects in the photographs.

Frustrated with this Herculean task, Tombaugh devised a technique for photographing a region of the zodiac when it was "at opposition"—that is, on the side of Earth opposite the Sun. Having done so, he noticed several things. At opposition, asteroids shifted about 0.28 inch (7 millimeters) per day. Neptune, being farther from Earth and from the asteroid belt, shifted less, about 0.08 inch (2 millimeters) per day. Tombaugh then reasoned that any undiscovered planet beyond Neptune ought to shift less than Neptune. If he could find such a planet, it would truly be Planet X.

In early 1930, Tombaugh resumed plate blinking, but the proximity to the Milky Way slowed his progress. It was then that Tombaugh realized that the Sliphers had blinked through the 1929 Gemini plates in only about a week. He suspected that the Sliphers, in rushing the job, had missed something. Therefore, on the basis of his earlier theory, he decided to rephotograph the region, this time near opposition. The first exposure of the Gemini region on January 21, 1930, was disturbed by wind gusts that shook the observatory, disturbing the telescope and blurring the image. He rephotographed this region on January 23 and 29 and began the tedious blink procedure.

Tombaugh retrieved the poor January 21 plate, compared it with the January 23 plate, and found Planet X exactly where it should be. Using a hand magnifier, he then compared the plates with another taken by a smaller camera. The object was in the same corresponding position on all three plates. Tombaugh then called Carl O. Lampland and Slipher to the blink comparator to confirm his find. Both agreed that the object could be Planet X, and Slipher asked Tombaugh to rephotograph the region as soon as possible. Based on photographs shot on February 18, 1930, Lampland, Slipher, and Tombaugh were able to confirm the presence of Planet X.

SIGNIFICANCE

Slipher was aware of the impact of the discovery and carefully prepared for the public announcement and the questions that would result. The observatory's reputation was in question over the Martian canal research, and the researchers had to be very sure not only of their data but also of the protocol involved in the announcement.

When the discovery became known, thousands of letters arrived suggesting names for the planet. Because planets were usually named after mythological deities, three names headed the list: Minerva, Pluto, and Cronus. The first person to propose the name Pluto outside the Lowell group seems to have been Venetia Burney, an eleven-year-old child living in Oxford, England. Pickering, who had predicted a trans-Neptunian planet in 1908, also suggested Pluto, the name of the Greek god of darkness, who was able at times to render himself invisible. Without doubt, all involved in the search would agree this quality of invisibility was appropriate for the new planet.

The Lowell group proposed the name Pluto to the American Astronomical Society and the Royal Society, and both societies accepted it unanimously in 1930. In 1931, the Associated Press declared the discovery of the planet Pluto to be one of the top news stories in the world for 1930.

From the mid-1990's onward, new discoveries made possible by improvements in technology led to debates among astronomers concerning whether particular bodies in our solar system should be classified as planets. In 2006, the members of the International Astronomical Union voted to reclassify Pluto as a "dwarf planet," reducing to eight the official number of bodies in the solar system defined as true planets. The decision was itself the source of controversy, and the debate concerning Pluto's status continued.

—*Richard C. Jones*

FURTHER READING

Freedman, David H. "When Is a Planet Not a Planet? Arguments for and Against Demoting Pluto." *Atlantic Monthly*, February, 1998. Reviews the debate that arose in the mid-1990's regarding the status of Pluto as a major planet, given new discoveries.

Hoyt, William G. *Planet X and Pluto*. Tucson: University of Arizona Press, 1980. Comprehensive volume documents the transition between Lowell's work and Tombaugh's. A good source for the interested reader.

Tombaugh, Clyde William. "The Discovery of Pluto: Some Generally Unknown Aspects of the Story." *Mercury* 15, no. 3 (1986): 66-72; 15, no. 4 (1986): 98-102. Tombaugh describes his experiences on becoming an astronomer and the events leading to the discovery.

_____. "Reminiscences of the Discovery of Pluto." *Sky and Telescope* 19 (1960): 264-270. Tombaugh's own summary of the people and events surrounding the discovery.

Tombaugh, Clyde William, and Patrick Moore. *Out of Darkness: The Planet Pluto*. Harrisburg, Pa.: Stackpole Books, 1980. Provides a good review of all aspects of the search for planets and the personalities surrounding the events of the Pluto discovery. Accessible to the general reader.

Whyte, A. J. *The Planet Pluto*. New York: Pergamon Press, 1980. A relatively technical work for readers who wish to dig into the details of the discovery of Pluto. Provides an objective view of the process. Includes a historical review.

SEE ALSO: Aug., 1905: Lowell Predicts the Existence of Pluto; 1912: Slipher Obtains the Spectrum of a Distant Galaxy; Early 1920's: Slipher Presents Evidence of Redshifts in Galactic Spectra.

1930

March 12-April 5, 1930
GANDHI LEADS THE SALT MARCH

Mahatma Gandhi organized the Salt March in 1930 to protest British actions in India and to start a mass campaign of noncooperation that would inspire many future leaders, including American civil rights activist Martin Luther King, Jr.

LOCALE: India

CATEGORIES: Civil rights and liberties; colonialism and occupation; indigenous peoples' rights; social issues and reform; independence movements

KEY FIGURES

Mahatma Gandhi (1869-1948), Hindu leader of the Indian nationalist movement

Subhas Chandra Bose (1897-1945), radical member of the Indian National Congress who saw that opposition to Gandhi was impossible

Lord Halifax (Edward Frederick Lindley Wood; 1881-1959), viceroy of India, 1926-1931

Jawaharlal Nehru (1889-1964), Indian socialist and believer in Western science and technology

Motilal Nehru (1861-1931), founder of the Nehru dynasty who gave up his moderate politics to join Gandhi in the Salt March

SUMMARY OF EVENT

Mohandas Karamchand Gandhi was released from prison in 1924 after having been incarcerated for nearly two years for his part in the illegal activities of the noncooperation movement, which he started in 1920 in a successful attempt to arouse opposition to British rule. Gandhi (known as Mahatma, or "Great Soul") retired from politics upon his release and returned to his ashram (a spiritual retreat or commune) to devote himself to spinning *khadi* (homespun cloth) and to fostering Hindu-Muslim unity and the moral and economic uplift of village life. As a result, politics in India entered a lull and the Indian nationalist movement, which had gathered strength during the last part of the nineteenth century and became strong during the early twentieth century, was left without an active national leader. Nevertheless, all members of the Indian National Congress, the most important political party in India, knew that Gandhi was the most widely accepted leader in the country. Even during his period of retirement, political leaders constantly kept in touch with him and exchanged a voluminous correspondence. Party officials urged him to return to active politics and to resume leadership of the nationalist move-

ment. New leadership was taking control of the Congress party: Jawaharlal Nehru and Subhas Chandra Bose wanted to start a new noncooperation movement, but Gandhi was the only person who could lead such a movement.

The nationalist movement had not been very vigorous since Gandhi's retirement from politics, and many Indians had cooperated with the British and now served in government legislatures and agencies. As a result of this lack of active opposition by Indian politicians, the British continued to ignore Indian rights. Indians did not, for example, have control of the legislative councils that the British had introduced in 1923; instead, the councils were dominated by the British and their appointees. British judges controlled the legal system, and all the senior police and army officers were British. On a daily basis, the British continued to show disrespect to Indians by barring them from almost all British social clubs and by shunning their company except on special occasions. In short, Indians were treated as foreigners in their own land and kept down by a British *raj* (rule) that was backed up by a strong police force and army that Indians had to finance through taxes.

The situation would change only if Indians actively opposed it. The occasion for the resurgence in the nationalist movement came with the appointment of the Simon Commission in 1928. The commission was made up entirely of British politicians who had been sent to India to assess how the constitution of 1919 was working and to decide how the next step of reforms should take place. The British had sparked Indian anger by not appointing a single Indian to the commission, an action that was perceived as a racist slight. To show their disapproval, members of the Indian National Congress refused to attend the first session of the Round Table Conference, which was held in 1930 in London in order to allow Indians of various religious and other interest groups to discuss with the British how a new constitution should be written. In the meantime, the Congress party had, in fact, produced its own draft of a constitution (Motilal Nehru's *Nehru Report* of 1928) and threatened that if the British did not give India dominion status—which would have made India as free as Australia, Canada, and New Zealand—India would demand complete independence. These developments were on many Indians' minds when Gandhi resumed active participation at the end of 1928.

The Congress party and Gandhi met in December,

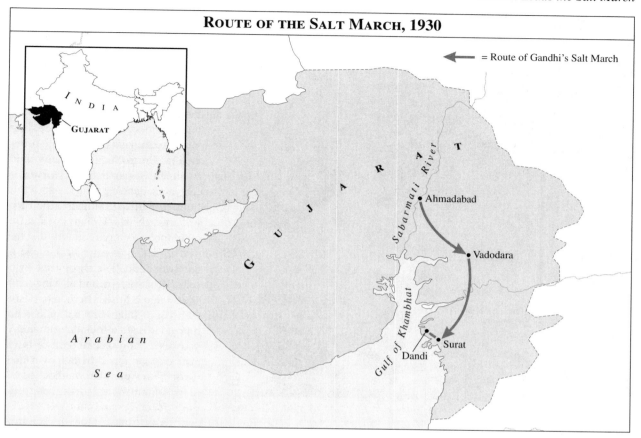

ROUTE OF THE SALT MARCH, 1930

⟵ = Route of Gandhi's Salt March

I N D I A

GUJARAT

G U J A R A T

Sabarmati River

Ahmadabad

Vadodara

Gulf of Khambhat

Dandi

Surat

A r a b i a n

S e a

1929, and decided to start a civil disobedience campaign similar to the noncooperation movement of 1920. This campaign would, they hoped, force the British to take notice of Indian demands for rights and freedom. It was left to Gandhi to decide how and when the campaign would start, and he decided that the central issue would be salt. Many were amazed that Gandhi chose this as the issue over which to oppose imperial rule, but salt was a heavily taxed government monopoly, and therefore all Indians would understand protests against its taxing. Before Gandhi began the movement, he offered peace to the government through his Eleven Points, a series of demands that included social reforms and economic reforms such as reduction of military expenditures. The British rejected these demands.

On March 5, Gandhi announced to his ashram that he and a group of his followers would march to the coast carrying copies of the Bhagavad Gita (a Hindu holy book). Once they arrived at the sea, they would break the law by making salt, deliberately undermining British rule in India. Gandhi informed the viceroy, Lord Irwin

(also known as Lord Halifax), that he proposed to start a civil disobedience campaign based on the issue of the salt laws, and on March 12, he and seventy-nine followers began their trek to the sea. They made the 240-mile trip in twenty-five days, arriving at Dandi, on the Indian Ocean, on April 5, 1930. Early the following morning, they went to the beach and picked up some salt-encrusted mud and boiled it to make salt, thus breaking the salt laws. Salt had now become the symbol of India's fight for freedom.

The salt campaign that began with Gandhi's month-long march lasted another two months, until the beginning of the monsoon season. At first the British did not respond to Gandhi's breach of the law, but when he wrote to the viceroy and informed him of plans to raid the nearby Dharsana Salt Works, Gandhi and all the Congress leaders were arrested on May 5. Gandhi was incarcerated under an 1827 regulation that did not require a trial or a fixed sentence. He was held in prison until January 26, 1931.

The Salt March and the noncooperation movement that followed coincided with the commencement of a

1930

Mahatma Gandhi with some of his followers during the Salt March in 1930. (Hulton Archive/Getty Images)

Salt was the symbol of the campaign, but it was not the only part of the civil disobedience movement. The salt campaign was localized along the coast, but the boycott of foreign cloth gathered steam across the entire country. Protesters pressured vendors and buyers by sealing foreign cloth stocks and by using their bodies to block merchants who attempted to move them. The major centers of India's foreign cloth trade came to a virtual halt for most of the year, and there was a dramatic drop in imports.

The salt movement catalyzed a number of smaller campaigns, which varied from province to province and were related to local grievances. In the west of India, in Gujarat, people refused to pay their land-revenue tax and started a social boycott of government workers. Many of those workers resigned from their positions. In the central provinces, people burned trees and cut grass in defiance of forestry regulations, and in Bihar people broke liquor laws. In the city of Bombay, the Congress party practically took control of the city. As the government official responsible for domestic affairs noted, "The numbers, the discipline, the organization and the brushing aside of the ordinary functions of police control of traffic have combined to produce a vivid impression of the power and the success of the Congress movement." The British administration hovered on the brink of collapse for months.

worldwide depression. Importers could not sell their stocks, tenant farmers could not earn enough from their crops to pay their rents, landlords and cultivating owners could not cover their land revenue, and even the government had to cut back staff and reduce salaries. The Salt March inspired a civil disobedience movement that was joined by large numbers of these disaffected people.

The Salt March, also known as the salt *satyagraha* (nonviolent civil disobedience campaign), affected almost every province in the country. People even went to local rivers to boil the water in a symbolic gesture of solidarity with Gandhi. The government was put on the defensive; volunteers surrounded the people making salt so that it became impossible to arrest the lawbreakers without resorting to great violence, and the Congress party publicized any violent event in great detail. As a result, a tremendous amount of enthusiasm for the movement and contempt for the government were generated through this campaign. Gandhi had once again seized the political initiative for the Congress party, and all of India was motivated to fight for freedom.

SIGNIFICANCE

Gandhi had inspired and started a mass movement in a manner never before seen in India. The British imprisoned sixty thousand people, but millions more heard of the campaign, avoided buying foreign cloth, made donations to the Congress party, or attended one of innumerable meetings. Some soldiers in the army refused to obey orders to fire on unarmed demonstrators. The government was concerned that, for the first time, protest had become a rural movement as well as an urban one. They also saw great significance in the fact that Gandhi's campaign had inspired upper-class and educated women to participate in politics for the first time in history. Women continued the work of husbands or male members of the family who went to prison. Some of them even went to prison themselves. This reflected an incredible change in attitude: Before Gandhi led the nationalist movement, going to prison would have been a mark of terrible shame, but now people were willingly defying the police and committing crimes in the name of freedom. Further, the movement involved people of all ages, including children, who became active participants in the movement.

With the involvement of so many people of all classes and ages, the prestige of the Indian National Congress grew immensely, and people proudly called themselves followers of Gandhi. The public began to sense that independence was near, and Indians began to talk about what would happen after the British left. Those politicians who had not supported the movement and who were cooperating with the British to reform the constitution were embarrassed to be seen as collaborators and were pushed—often against their will—into opposition to the British. At this juncture, Mohammed Ali Jinnah, one of the most important Muslim leaders in the country and one who had always opposed Gandhi's tactics, left India and settled in England.

The Salt March and the movement it started were an enormous success. The British government increasingly had to use force to maintain law and order, and this use of force put it more and more in the wrong with the Indian people. Slowly, the British lost all moral authority in the land. The Congress party increasingly came to be identified as the nation's most representative political body. The Salt March also had a major impact on the nation's psychology. Indians of all classes and ages became willing to stand up for their rights. Large numbers of women were involved in a political movement for the first time in history. The whole nation had been mobilized, and the image of Gandhi marching to the sea in defiance of the British Empire became front-page news in all the major newspapers of the world. Gandhi became a hero to nationalists everywhere; even in England, he received the admiration of many people.

By 1931, the movement had exhausted both the British and the Indians. After Gandhi and the leaders of the Congress party had been released from prison, Gandhi wrote to the viceroy, asking for a meeting and a truce. Lord Irwin agreed, and the result was the Gandhi-Irwin Pact (also known as the Delhi Pact) of March 5, 1931. As a result of the Gandhi-Irwin Pact, Gandhi was invited to attend the Second Round Table Conference. He did so as the sole representative of the Congress party. Although Gandhi ultimately considered the conference a failure, the Government of India Act of 1935 (which emerged from the meeting) gave virtual independence to the provinces and foreshadowed the arrival of national independence. The British still ruled India, but Gandhi had mobilized the Indians to such an extent that the days of foreign dominance over this vast land were clearly numbered.

Gandhi's philosophy of nonviolent resistance would live on in other major human rights and civil rights campaigns. It was perhaps most successful in the American Civil Rights movement, in which Martin Luther King, Jr., employed Gandhi's tactics in the 1960's. These tactics were less successful, however, in the 1989 Tianamen Square protest in China, which was brutally repressed.

—*Roger D. Long*

FURTHER READING

Brown, Judith M. *Gandhi and Civil Disobedience: The Mahatma in Indian Politics, 1928-1934*. Cambridge, England: Cambridge University Press, 1977. For the most detailed account of the Salt March available, this is the book to read. It is an almost week-by-week chronicle of Gandhi's activities during the period 1928-1934.

_____. *Gandhi: Prisoner of Hope*. New Haven, Conn.: Yale University Press, 1989. This is not a detailed account of the Salt March, but it does discuss the period and places it in broader context. Brown has dedicated her academic career to studying Gandhi, and her book is an authoritative and fundamental work on his life.

Copley, Antony. *Gandhi: Against the Tide*. London: Basil Blackwell, 1987. To place the accounts of the Salt March in context and within an understanding of Gandhi's life work, this is a short and handy reference.

Erikson, Erik. *Gandhi's Truth: On the Origins of Militant Nonviolence*. New York: W. W. Norton, 1969. Gandhi's aim during the Salt March was not only to mobilize Indians against the British but also to raise the people's level of consciousness and to give them a psychological lift. Erikson is a psychoanalyst who describes Gandhi's attempts during the Salt March to change the psychology of Indians and to make them less passive.

Fox, Richard G. *Gandhian Utopia: Experiments with Culture*. Boston: Beacon Press, 1989. Gandhi was aiming not only at freedom for Indians; he also wanted to influence India's cultural and social life.

1930

Fox is an anthropologist who discusses the cultural dimensions of Gandhi's work during the Salt March.

Gandhi, M. K. *An Autobiography: The Story of My Experiments with Truth*. Boston: Beacon Press, 1957. Gandhi stops his autobiography when he reaches the year 1920, but this book is essential to understanding Gandhi's ideas as he developed them in his early life.

Haksar, Vinit. *Rights, Communities, and Disobedience: Liberalism and Gandhi*. 2d ed. New York: Oxford University Press, 2003. A discussion of Gandhi's influence on modern philosophy. Focuses on the relevance of the Salt March and other events as models for resolution of conflicts between individual and group rights and between the rights of competing groups.

Nehru, Jawaharlal. *Toward Freedom: The Autobiography of Jawaharlal Nehru*. 1941. Reprint. Boston: Beacon Press, 1963. Nehru, an internationalist who was considered a radical, was very different from Gandhi, yet for a variety of reasons he became one of Gandhi's most devoted followers. This autobiography reveals the remarkable power Gandhi had over Indians and how modernists such as Nehru were flabbergasted when Gandhi came up with the idea of the Salt March. Later, however, they conceded that Gandhi had chosen the exact symbol with which to arouse opposition to the British. This is a classic, firsthand account.

Wolpert, Stanley. *Gandhi's Passion: The Life and Legacy of Mahatma Gandhi*. New York: Oxford University Press, 2001. More of a history of the anticolonial and independence movements in India than a biography. Wolpert places special emphasis on exploring Gandhi's interest in nonviolent resistance.

SEE ALSO: June 6, 1903: Founding of the Weekly *Indian Opinion*; Mar., 1915: Defense of India Act Impedes the Freedom Struggle; Apr. 13, 1919: British Soldiers Massacre Indians at Amritsar; 1920-1922: Gandhi Leads a Noncooperation Movement; Aug., 1921: Moplah Rebellion; 1925-1935: Women's Rights in India Undergo a Decade of Change; Mar. 5, 1931: India Signs the Delhi Pact; Sept. 25, 1932: Poona Pact Grants Representation to India's Untouchables.

March 31, 1930-1931
HAWK'S NEST TUNNEL CONSTRUCTION LEADS TO DISASTER

The construction of the Hawk's Nest Tunnel to supply water to a hydroelectric complex led to the nation's deadliest industrial accident, in which hundreds of workers died from acute silicosis.

LOCALE: Gauley Bridge, West Virginia
CATEGORIES: Health and medicine; environmental issues; business and labor

KEY FIGURES
O. M. Jones (fl. early twentieth century), chief engineer for the New Kanawha Power Company
Robert M. Lambie (fl. early twentieth century), director of the West Virginia Department of Mines
Cora Jones (fl. early twentieth century), West Virginia homemaker and wife of a tunnel worker
Leroy Harless (fl. early twentieth century), West Virginia physician

SUMMARY OF EVENT
On March 31, 1930, ground was broken for the three-mile-long Hawk's Nest Tunnel. The tunnel was planned to divert water from the New River to a dam and hydro- electric plant that would supply electricity to the metallurgical works at Glen Ferris, West Virginia. From the first, the project was clouded by a disregard for the law and for human safety.

The tunnel was constructed through a mountain formed of sandstone and silica rock; the silica mined from the mountain was said to be more than 90 percent pure. During the drilling, blasting, and cleaning of rock debris out of the tunnel, safety precautions were not followed, and many men were stricken with acute silicosis, the filling up and scarring of the lungs with silica dust nodes. The companies involved covered up the facts of the industrial disaster. The passivity of the federal government and the negligence of the companies involved in the construction of the tunnel resulted in the slow and painful deaths of several hundred workers.

The exploitation of hydroelectric resources in the Gauley Bridge area dates back to 1899, when the Wilson Aluminum Company had received permission from the secretary of war to construct a temporary timber dam at Kanawha Falls, just downstream from Gauley Bridge. By 1901, the company had completed the dam, which exploited the eight-foot natural falls to drive the first hydro-electric plant in the state. Six years later, the Electro-Metallurgical Company absorbed Wilson Aluminum and expanded the temporary dam without seeking the necessary permission. Early operations were only moderately successful, as local industrial markets were limited. In 1917, the Electro-Metallurgical Company merged with other companies to form the Union Carbide and Carbon Corporation (commonly known as Union Carbide).

One of the first acts of this corporation was to increase the size of the dam at Kanawha Falls again. This plan met resistance from the U.S. Army Corps of Engineers, which in 1913 told Congress that the enlarged dam would block navigation on the New River. As early as 1812, inland rivers were seen as transportation routes, and control of them, including the New River, therefore belonged to the federal government.

Union Carbide found a way to circumvent this problem: Company officials simply did not inform the Corps of Engineers about construction that was under way. One year later, two hundred feet of concrete on the dam and a new powerhouse had been constructed at Glen Ferris. Later, Union Carbide informed the corps of the improvements and asked for an extension of the dam permits. Although permission was denied, no action was taken to remove the structures, and Union Carbide's exploitation of waterpower on the New River did not end.

A new metallurgical works was proposed five miles below Glen Ferris, at Boncar. It was to be larger than the one at Kanawha Falls and would require greater resources of power. The New Kanawha Power Company was chartered in 1927 with the purpose of constructing public utilities in West Virginia. New Kanawha Power was formed by Union Carbide as a dummy company, set up to develop and produce power for general public sales and commercial use. During the company's brief history, it had only one customer, Union Carbide.

Later in 1927, the New Kanawha Power Company filed a declaration of intent to develop the New River with two dams, two tunnels, and two power stations in addition to the complex at Boncar. The site chosen for one of the tunnels and dams was at Hawk's Nest. Upstream, the New River was more than one thousand feet wide, but it narrowed to less than one hundred feet wide as it began its descent to Gauley Bridge. A three-mile-long tunnel with a 162-foot descent would divert the New River through the mountain and create a rapid river flow. The State Public Service Commission gave its approval to the project in 1928.

Effects on river navigation were questioned by a local

coal company, but such concerns were not brought to the attention of the Corps of Engineers. The State Public Service Commission dismissed the complaint. Even though Union Carbide openly admitted that New Kanawha Power was a wholly owned subsidiary and that the power it produced was meant solely for use by Union Carbide, permission was granted. The need for a water-driven power supply increased in 1929 with the collapse of the U.S. economy in the Great Depression: Many West Virginia coal mines closed, and coal production dropped as a result. A new, cheap energy source was needed. Electric power, dubbed "white coal" by some, was a potential replacement for coal-based power; indeed, it would become the focus of many of the New Deal's public works projects.

Union Carbide's project went forward. The Rinehart and Dennis Company of Charlottesville, Virginia, a company well known for its experience in building dams and other waterworks projects, was the low bidder on the tunnel construction contract, which it was awarded on March 13, 1930. Eighteen days later, ground was broken for the tunnel. The tunnel was bored from different directions: There was a main intake where the New River would enter the tunnel and a tunnel exit where the water would enter the river again. There was also an adit to the surge basin within the tunnel, for an excess or overflow of water to enter. Drilling commenced at all these openings.

From the beginning, the Rinehart and Dennis Company used questionable practices. Many local white people who were laid off from the mines were hired, but African American migrant workers from the South were encouraged to travel north to work inside the tunnel. White workers were given better—and often safer—jobs, whereas black workers were usually hired as common laborers at the face of the tunnel. The African American workers were paid lower wages than the white workers, and their company-provided living quarters were inadequate, with as many as ten or twelve people sharing one four-room shack. White workers were paid in cash, but black workers were paid in company scrip, with deductions taken out for coal, linens, food, and other essentials that they could purchase only at the company stores.

The African American workers were expected to do the most grueling jobs. The foreman and assistant foreman positions were held by white workers, and much of the work outside the tunnel was performed by white employees. A few of the white workers worked inside the tunnel, but only a few worked the face of the tunnel. When drilling or blasting, the workers were not provided

1930

with respirators or masks to shield their faces from the silica dust. The laborers were not supposed to be in the mine while the blasting occurred, but the foremen would allow the workers to retreat only a few feet from the blasting site and would direct them to start clearing the debris as soon as the blasting was completed.

These practices were unorthodox and unnecessarily dangerous even by the standards of the time, especially by international standards. Wet drilling, a process in which fluids are used to help control airborne debris, was introduced in England in 1897. Dry drilling had been strictly forbidden by 1911 in many European, South American, and African countries. In the United States, silicosis and its causes were widely known before 1930. The U.S. Public Health Service had published an official bulletin in 1917 describing silicosis studies performed on zinc miners in Joplin, Missouri. In 1915, the first workers' compensation laws provided implicit regulations regarding silicosis. Nevertheless, many Hawk's Nest tunnellers used dry drills, raising clouds of dangerous silica dust.

In the United States, the control of occupational diseases had proceeded more slowly than it had in Western Europe. The delay was a result of limited enforcement rather than a failure to recognize occupational diseases. Federal agencies were restricted in their involvement in occupational disease control, and state regulations were relatively toothless. Inspectors from the West Virginia Department of Mines, which was run by Robert M. Lambie, wrote citations for the infractions they witnessed. The Rinehart and Dennis Company simply ignored the citations and continued business as usual. It posted lookouts to warn of the arrival of inspectors and stopped work or detained the inspectors while conditions were improved in the tunnel.

Men working in the tunnel complained that they could see only a few feet in front of them, and they collided with parked machinery in the thick dust. Instead of drilling with water to suppress the dust, they were required to drill dry because it was faster. Sixteen drills were operating at one time, and fewer than half of them used water to hold down the dust. Normally, battery-powered locomotives would run cars to the face of a tunnel to remove blasted rock and silica. The Rinehart and Dennis Company, however, brought gasoline-powered machinery to the tunnel site, and the gasoline engines caused a carbon monoxide buildup. Workers who complained that they could not breathe or who became sick or sleepy from the dust and fumes were beaten and run off the job. If they could not work, they could not stay in company housing.

Many workers were carried from the tunnel and left to die. Many men lasted a maximum of two months, and only 2 percent worked from the beginning of the project to its completion. When a worker could no longer work, he was fired.

There are many reasons that the events at Hawk's Nest Tunnel were allowed to continue, and legislation was created at the state and federal levels as a result of lawsuits and investigations that followed. The fact that the disaster happened in a rural setting helped to conceal it. The disease that killed so many workers was not well understood at the time. Silicosis was believed to be a disease that took from twenty to thirty years to kill its victim. The men in the tunnel, however, breathed pure silica in great quantities, so their deaths were comparatively fast and painful; many died in a matter of months from acute silicosis. Many doctors labeled the cause of death "tunnel pneumonia" or "tunnelitis." They knew it was a lung disease, but they were unaware, for the most part, of its true nature. Only after Dr. Leroy Harless did autopsies on several victims did he realize that the scarring in the lungs was killing their laborers.

Construction on the tunnel was completed in 1931. Cora Jones filed suit in circuit court in 1932 against the Rinehart and Dennis Company after her three sons, all between the ages of nineteen and twenty-four, died as a result of their work on the tunnel; her husband was also stricken. Harless saved the fibrous lungs of Jones's youngest son as evidence of what happened to workers who were subjected to pure silica dust. Compensation was awarded after the company was found to be at fault.

SIGNIFICANCE

The companies running the Hawk's Nest project acknowledged 109 deaths of workers on the tunnel, but the actual total was much higher. A congressional investigation determined that 476 people died; in his 1986 book *The Hawk's Nest Incident*, Martin Cherniack set the figure at 764 deaths and estimated that 1,500 surviving workers suffered from silicosis. It was difficult to keep track of the deaths because many men had been buried in unmarked graves, different causes of death had been recorded, and many migrant workers had left the area, making it virtually impossible to account for their fates.

The U.S. House of Representatives conducted an investigation into the conditions of workers employed in the construction of public utilities in January and February of 1936. Many people associated with the Hawk's Nest Tunnel were called to testify before the committee about events that took place during construction of the tunnel. Several positive steps were taken as a result of the hearings.

The authority of the Bureau of Mines was expanded to give the agency jurisdiction over a broad range of underground work. The Bureau of Mines was not believed to have authority at Hawk's Nest because the tunnel was a construction project, not a mine. The Bureau of Mines also expanded its dust investigation practices; dust sampling was expanded to include analysis of the composition, particle size, and concentration of airborne dusts. Surveys were conducted to determine the exposure of industrial workers to various dust conditions and the effect of such conditions on the workers. New methods of dust control were developed, and studies in removing dust from work areas were conducted. Other cooperative ventures with the Public Health Service involving dust and its effect on workers were launched.

In the decades following the Hawk's Nest incident, many state and federal agencies were created to ensure that workers in the United States would not be subjected to the kind of work environment that existed at Gauley Bridge between 1930 and 1931. Agencies at both the state and federal levels would check and recheck working conditions above and below ground to ensure provision of safe workplaces for all ranks of workers. Although hundreds of people died as a consequence of their work on the Hawk's Nest Tunnel, their deaths helped prompt the creation of a bureaucracy that has protected generations of laborers.

—*Larry N. Sypolt*

FURTHER READING

Cherniack, Martin. *The Hawk's Nest Incident*. New Haven, Conn.: Yale University Press, 1986. An investigation into the cover-up of working conditions at Hawk's Nest. Cherniack asserts that the death toll from the project was substantially higher than earlier estimates.

Comstock, Jim. "476 Graves: The Story of Hawk's Nest Tunnel." In *West Virginia Heritage*. Vol. 7. Richwood: West Virginia Heritage Foundation, 1972. Provides a transcript of the House of Representatives hearings regarding the Hawk's Nest Tunnel tragedy.

Fishback, Price V. "Workplace Safety During the Progressive Era: Fatal Accidents in Bituminous Coal Mining, 1912-1923." *Explorations in Economic History* 23, no. 3 (1986): 269-298. A look at the mining industry's safety record in the period leading up to the Hawk's Nest disaster. Useful historical perspective.

Serrin, William. "The Wages of Work." *The Nation* 252, no. 3 (January 28, 1991): 80-82. A jarring look at contemporary worker safety. Serrin reports that, despite regulatory and other improvements, about three hundred Americans die every day from work-related injuries or diseases. He views the scant attention paid such incidents as a consequence of class bias.

Skidmore, Hubert. *Hawk's Nest: A Novel*. Knoxville: University of Tennessee Press, 2004. Fictionalized account of the tragedy based on detailed research and including bibliographic references to nonfiction sources.

Wallace, Michael. "Dying for Coal: The Struggle for Health and Safety Conditions in American Coal Mining, 1930-82." *Social Forces* 66, no. 2 (1987): 336-364. Suggests that labor activism and market factors have had more to do with safety improvements than have government regulations. Somewhat technical.

Williams, John Alexander. *West Virginia: A History*. 2d ed. Morgantown: West Virginia University Press, 2001. Includes a chapter on the Hawk's Next incident and its effects on West Virginia and the United States. Bibliographic references and index.

SEE ALSO: Mar. 25, 1911: Triangle Shirtwaist Factory Fire; 1934-1939: Dust Bowl Devastates the Great Plains.

1930

April, 1930
MIDGLEY INTRODUCES DICHLORODIFLUOROMETHANE AS A REFRIGERANT GAS

Thomas Midgley, Jr., introduced dichlorodifluoromethane as a safe refrigerant gas for domestic refrigerators, leading to rapid growth in the acceptance of refrigerators in homes.

LOCALE: Dayton, Ohio
CATEGORIES: Science and technology; chemistry

KEY FIGURES
Thomas Midgley, Jr. (1889-1944), American engineer and chemist
Charles Franklin Kettering (1876-1958), American engineer and inventor
Albert Leon Henne (1901-1967), American chemist
Frédéric Swarts (1866-1940), Belgian chemist

SUMMARY OF EVENT
The growing availability of reliable refrigerators, freezers, and air conditioners had major impacts on the way Americans lived and worked as the twentieth century progressed. People could live more comfortably in hot and humid areas. Greater varieties of perishable foods could be transported and stored for extended periods. As recently as the early nineteenth century, the foods most regularly available to most Americans were salted meats and bread. Vegetables, fruits, and dairy products—items now considered essential to a balanced diet—were produced, purchased, and consumed only in small amounts. Commercial refrigeration became a necessity and a reality in the United States during the nineteenth century, when the population became concentrated in towns and cities. Through the early part of the twentieth century, the pattern of food storage and distribution evolved to make perishable foods more available. Farmers shipped dairy products and frozen meats in mechanically refrigerated railroad cars or in refrigerated ships. Wholesalers had large mechanically refrigerated warehouses. Smaller stores and most American households used iceboxes to keep perishable foods fresh. The iceman, who delivered large blocks of ice regularly, was a familiar figure on the streets of American towns.

In 1930, domestic mechanical refrigerators were still relatively uncommon, although they were being produced in increasing numbers. Most of them were vapor compression machines, in which a gas was compressed in a closed system of pipes outside the refrigerator by a mechanical pump and condensed to a liquid. The liquid was pumped into a sealed chamber in the refrigerator and allowed to evaporate to a gas. This evaporation cooled the interior of the refrigerator.

The major mechanical problems in designing an efficient home refrigerator had been solved by 1930; small and quite efficient electric motors had been developed to power the compression cycle, and compact and reliable automatic temperature controllers had become available. The remaining source of difficulty was the material constituting the working gas of the refrigerator. This gas had to have particular properties: It had to boil at a fairly low temperature, preferably between about –1.1 degrees Celsius and 4.4 degrees Celsius, and had to have an appropriate heat of vaporization—meaning that, in its evaporation from liquid to gas inside the sealed chamber of the refrigerator, it had to abstract a reasonable amount of heat energy from the inside of the refrigerator.

The gases in use in domestic refrigerators in 1930 included ammonia, sulfur dioxide, and methyl chloride. These gases were acceptable if the refrigerator's gas pipes never sprang a leak. In actual operation of refrigerators, however, leaks sometimes occur; at such times, these refrigerant gases posed serious problems because all were toxic. Ammonia and sulfur dioxide both had unpleasant odors; if they leaked, at least they would be detected rapidly. Methyl chloride could form a dangerously explosive mixture with air, and it had only a very faint, and not unpleasant, odor. In a hospital in Cleveland during the 1920's, a refrigerator with methyl chloride leaked, resulting in a disastrous explosion of the methyl chloride/air mixture. After that, methyl chloride for use in refrigerators was mixed with a small amount of a powerfully unpleasant-smelling compound to make leaks detectable. (The same method is used today with natural gas.)

General Motors, through its Frigidaire division, had a substantial interest in the domestic refrigerator market. Frigidaire refrigerators used sulfur dioxide as the refrigerant gas. Charles Franklin Kettering, director of research for General Motors, was an engineer and inventor with an impressive record of solving problems. Among his major successes had been his collaboration with Thomas Midgley, Jr., a mechanical engineer and self-taught chemist, in discovering that tetraethyl lead is an effective antiknocking agent for gasoline. Kettering decided that Frigidaire needed a new refrigerant gas for its household refrigerators, a material that would have the good thermal properties of methyl chloride or sulfur dioxide, but that would be nontoxic and nonexplosive. In early 1930, he sent Lester S. Keilholtz, chief engineer of the General Motors Frigidaire division, to Midgley, who was working at Dayton, Ohio, with the challenge to develop such a new gas.

Midgley's chemist associates Albert Leon Henne and Robert McNary researched what types of compounds might have been reported already that fit Kettering's specifications. Apparently, an inaccuracy in a reference source made them think about compounds containing fluorine as possible refrigerants. The reference listed the boiling point of carbon tetrafluoride as –15 degrees Celsius, in the acceptable range for a refrigerant. When they checked other research articles, they found that the reference was incorrect; the actual boiling point was -127.8 degrees Celsius, far too low for the compound to be useful. That library search suggested, however, that the right compound might be found among carbon compounds containing both fluorine and chlorine.

Only a few such compounds had been reported; the Belgian chemist Frédéric Swarts had done pioneering basic research on them in the late nineteenth and early twentieth centuries, but no applications had resulted. Midgley, Henne, and McNary worked with Swarts's data and concluded from their calculations that dichlorodifluoromethane, a compound whose molecules each contain one carbon atom, two chlorine atoms, and two fluorine atoms, should have ideal thermal properties and the right boiling point for a refrigerant gas. The great unknown was the toxicity of such a compound; they would have to prepare it in order to test it.

Preparation of the compound involved reaction between carbon tetrachloride (a common solvent used, at that time, in the dry-cleaning industry) and antimony trifluoride. The chemists prepared a few grams of dichlorodifluoromethane and put it, along with a guinea pig, into a closed chamber. They were delighted to see that the animal seemed to suffer no ill effects at all and was able to breathe and move normally. They were briefly puzzled when a second batch of the compound, made with another sample of antimony trifluoride, killed a second guinea pig almost instantly, but soon they discovered that an impurity in the antimony trifluoride had produced a potent poison in the refrigerant gas. A simple washing procedure completely removed the poisonous contaminant.

Experiments confirmed their calculations: Dichlorodifluoromethane was ideally suited to be a refrigerant gas, being nontoxic, nonflammable, and possessing excellent thermal properties. Its boiling point of –5.6 degrees Celsius was in the required range. This astonishingly successful research project was completed in three days. A few months later, Midgley announced the discovery at a meeting of the American Chemical Society held in Atlanta, Georgia, in April, 1930. When Midgley was awarded the Perkin Medal for industrial chemistry in 1937, he gave the audience a graphic demonstration of the properties of dichlorodifluoromethane. He inhaled deeply of its vapors and exhaled gently into a jar containing a burning candle. The candle flame promptly went out. This provided visual evidence that dichlorodifluoromethane was not poisonous and would not burn.

In order to produce the new refrigerant in commercial quantities, General Motors arranged to form a new company with Du Pont, which was the established supplier of sulfur dioxide to Frigidaire. The new product, dichlorodifluoromethane, was given the shorter trademarked name of Freon. The Du Pont laboratories undertook extensive toxicity testing, the results of which confirmed the safety of Freon, and Kinetic Chemicals arranged with the Interstate Commerce Commission to allow interstate transport of Freon and anhydrous hydrogen fluoride, which was needed to make Freon in large quantities.

Thomas Midgley, Jr. (Library of Congress)

1930

Within a year of the original discovery by Midgley and his associates, Freon was being manufactured and shipped not only to Frigidaire but also to most other major manufacturers of refrigeration and air-conditioning equipment.

SIGNIFICANCE

Because of its desirable properties, Freon quickly became the preferred refrigerant gas for refrigerators and air conditioners. The availability of this safe refrigerant gas gave a major impetus to the production and sale of small and medium-sized refrigerators and freezers; it led to the patterns of food production, distribution, and consumption that became standard in the late twentieth century.

Air-conditioning was developed early in the twentieth century for industries such as printing and pharmaceutical companies that needed climate control in factories. By 1930, a few theaters, motion-picture houses, and hospitals were air-conditioned. Freon made small, safe air conditioners practical for houses and automobiles. By the late 1970's, most American cars and residences were equipped with air-conditioning, and automakers and housing designers in other countries with hot climates followed suit. Consequently, major relocations of populations and businesses became possible. After World War II, the U.S. population experienced steady migration to the Sun Belt—the states spanning the United States from southeast to southwest—because these areas became much more livable with air-conditioning.

Dichlorodifluoromethane was later designated "Freon 12" to distinguish it from other chlorofluorocarbons. During World War II, when U.S. servicemen were fighting in areas where diseases such as malaria were endemic, there was a need for an easy way to spray insecticides. The aerosol can was invented for this purpose, and the propellant chosen was a Freon, because of its volatility and inertness. After the war, aerosols became popular, and spray cans were used to deliver paints, shaving cream, and many other products. A new product developed at the same time was foamed plastic—Styrofoam is a familiar example. Plastic foams are good insulators, especially when they are made with a Freon blowing agent; they are used in insulation for buildings, beverage cups, and other insulated containers. As a result of these novel applications, worldwide production of chlorofluorocarbons increased during the 1960's and 1970's. Production of Freon 12, for example, peaked at 473,000 tons in 1974.

In 1974, scientists began to ask whether there might be a serious effect on the environment from the release of chlorofluorocarbons into the air. They speculated that, because these compounds were so unreactive, they would persist and slowly migrate into the stratosphere, where they might be decomposed by the intense ultraviolet light from the Sun, which does not reach Earth's surface because it is absorbed by a thin, but vital, layer of ozone in the stratosphere. The decomposition products of the chlorofluorocarbons would include reactive free chlorine atoms, which are known to have the capability of destroying large amounts of ozone. Thus, in the judgment of the scientists who raised these questions, continued release of chlorofluorocarbons into the air could greatly reduce the ozone layer, permitting more ultraviolet radiation from the Sun to reach Earth's surface. In addition to possible adverse climatic effects, this would raise the incidence of skin cancers, which can be initiated by overexposure of the skin to ultraviolet radiation.

Impressed by the plausibility of these arguments, the Environmental Protection Agency banned the use of chlorofluorocarbons as aerosol propellants in the United States in 1978. They are being used still as refrigerant gases and as blowing agents for foamed plastics. International conferences on the environmental effects of chlorofluorocarbons have been held, and the major industrial nations have agreed to stop producing chlorofluorocarbons that are believed to affect the ozone layer. Chemical manufacturers have worked to develop alternative refrigerant gases that are slightly broken down by sunlight in the lower portions of the atmosphere so that they will not survive to interfere with ozone in the stratosphere.

—Harold Goldwhite

FURTHER READING

Anderson, Oscar Edward. *Refrigeration in America.* Princeton, N.J.: Princeton University Press, 1953. Valuable survey of the history of refrigeration in the United States devotes eight chapters to changes between the pre- and post-Freon eras.

Benarde, Melvin A. *Our Precarious Habitat: Fifteen Years Later.* New York: John Wiley & Sons, 1989. Assesses environmental risk factors, including chlorofluorocarbons, and their potential impact on human health. Presents a reasonably balanced, nontechnical discussion.

Christie, Maureen. *The Ozone Layer: A Philosophy of Science Perspective.* New York: Cambridge University Press, 2001. Presents the history of human knowledge about stratospheric ozone in a manner accessible to lay readers. Includes brief discussion of the impact of refrigerants on the ozone layer.

Haynes, Williams. "Thomas Midgley, Jr." In *Great Chemists*, edited by Eduard Farber. New York: Interscience, 1961. Detailed biography of Midgley by a major contributor to the history of industrial chemistry in the United States. Includes accounts of Midgley's life and of his major discoveries.

Parson, Edward A. *Protecting the Ozone Layer: Science and Strategy*. New York: Oxford University Press, 2003. Comprehensive technical discussion of efforts to protect the ozone layer undertaken through international cooperation. Includes information about refrigerants.

Schufle, Joseph A. "Thomas Midgley, Jr." In *American Chemists and Chemical Engineers*, edited by Wyndham D. Miles. Washington, D.C.: American Chemical Society, 1976. Brief biography of Midgley

focuses on his chemical discoveries and training.

Spiro, Thomas G., and William M. Stigliani. *Environmental Issues in Chemical Perspective*. Albany: State University of New York Press, 1980. Presents a moderately technical, balanced view of the chlorofluorocarbon problem.

Thevenot, Roger. *A History of Refrigeration Throughout the World*. Translated by J. C. Fidler. Paris: International Institute of Refrigeration, 1979. Broad overview of refrigeration worldwide, with major sections on the changes brought about by the introduction of Freons.

SEE ALSO: Aug. 30, 1901: Booth Receives Patent for the Vacuum Cleaner; 1904-1912: Brandenberger Invents Cellophane; 1910: Electric Washing Machine Is Introduced; May 20, 1915: Corning Glass Works Trademarks Pyrex; 1917: Birdseye Invents Quick-Frozen Foods.

April 2, 1930
HAILE SELASSIE IS CROWNED EMPEROR OF ETHIOPIA

Haile Selassie (born Tafari Makonnen) emerged as the undisputed ruler of the ancient kingdom of Ethiopia, beginning a forty-four-year reign interrupted by war and exile that ended in a Marxist coup. Haile Selassie's ascension to the Ethiopian throne marked the end of feudal decentralization and the emergence of a relatively modern and centralized national government dominated by an absolute monarch.

LOCALE: Addis Ababa, Ethiopia
CATEGORY: Government and politics

KEY FIGURES

Haile Selassie I (Tafari Makonnen; 1892-1975), emperor of Ethiopia, r. 1930-1974
Zauditu (Zawditu; 1876-1930), empress of Ethiopia, r. 1916-1930, under whom Tafari served as regent and heir apparent
Menelik II (1844-1913), the architect of modern Ethiopia, r. 1889-1913
Lij Iyasu (1896-1935), grandson of Emperor Menelik and successor to the Ethiopian throne, deposed in 1916
Ras Makonnen (1852-1906), father of Tafari and governor of Harar province
Fitawrari Habte Giorgis (d. 1926), Ethiopian minister of war and a staunch supporter of the old order

Ras Gugsa Welle (1887-1930), Empress Zauditu's husband and governor of Begemdir who continued to resist Tafari's power until his death in battle in March of 1930

SUMMARY OF EVENT

On November 2, 1930, Tafari Makonnen was formally crowned emperor of Ethiopia. Following the tradition in which Ethiopian monarchs take a new name following their coronation, Makonnen adopted a new name, Haile Selassie (which means "power of the trinity"). Affixed to this name was the customary title for Ethiopian emperors: king of kings, conquering lion of Judah and the elect of God. Although an ascension to the Solomonic throne had always been an occasion of great celebration, the pomp and weeklong extravaganza that followed Haile Selassie's coronation was probably the most splendid in Ethiopian history. In a way, this event was skillfully staged by Haile Selassie to help him achieve several political objectives. First and foremost, the new emperor used the occasion to send a clear message to his own people that the old feudal order, in which power was shared among a number of competing grandees, had been replaced by a new centralized bureaucratic system under the authority of a strong monarch. The ceremony provided Haile Selassie an opportunity to demonstrate his

1930

own elevated position and the diminished status of the traditional nobility, who were required to attend the event literally at the feet of the emperor.

Haile Selassie also used the occasion to win recognition and respect for the "new" Ethiopia that he had labored to create during the first two decades of the twentieth century, when he was still a regent. Although Ethiopia had successfully fended off European imperialism, its survival as the only independent African state was continuously challenged. Britain, France, and Italy, whose empires completely surrounded Ethiopia and had completely cut the country off from the sea, were not fully reconciled to the idea of Ethiopian independence. The coronation pageantry was designed to maximize international publicity for Ethiopia and its new ruler, and the ceremony was delayed for seven months after the death of the previous ruler, Empress Zauditu, to ensure the largest possible number of foreign representatives. Meticulous preparations were carried out to impress foreign dignitaries and the hundreds of journalists who came to Addis Ababa from all over the world. Several of the leading nations of Europe and North America sent representatives to the coronation.

Haile Selassie had been patiently preparing for this day ever since he was chosen as regent and heir apparent in 1917, when the youthful but reckless Lij Iyasu was overthrown and Empress Zauditu was placed on the throne. A grandnephew of Emperor Menelik II and the son of Ras Makonnen, Tafari was perhaps the most progressive and agile politician in the capital when he was appointed regent. He made himself the power behind the throne by effectively isolating the empress and moving shrewdly and decisively against the bulwarks of the old system. The death of the minister of war and powerful lord Fitawrari Habte Giorgis in 1926 and the removal of Dejazmach Balcha Saffo from power in 1928 brought Tafari close to the pinnacle of power. The defeat and death in March of 1930 of Ras Gugsa Welle, Empress Zauditu's husband and the last paragon of the old guards, removed the last obstacle to the consolidation of Tafari's personal power. The empress died two days later, leaving Tafari as the undisputed master of the Ethiopian throne on April 2, 1930.

Once he secured the throne, Haile Selassie continued to push his program to create a unitary state—the dream of all Ethiopian emperors since the mid-nineteenth century. Haile Selassie placed loyal supporters in key government positions and provincial posts, and he banned the regional lords from importing arms or maintaining armies outside the central government's command. As a result, the central government monopolized key sources of revenue. These efforts to centralize the state and consolidate Haile Selassie's autocratic control were greatly assisted by the selected program of modernization, and new schools opened to produce the next generation of state cadres. A new constitution providing a legal framework for the consolidation of the emperor's absolute power was proclaimed in 1931.

These reforms were, however, interrupted by the Italian invasion of the country in 1935. After the disastrous defeat of his army at the Battle of Maichew in April of 1936, the emperor fled into exile in England, where he remained until the end of 1940. The outbreak of World War II provided Haile Selassie with a fresh opportunity to win British military support and to join his warriors, who

ETHIOPIA, 1930

had continued the resistance against fascist Italy. Haile Selassie regained his throne on May 5, 1941, and once again resumed his attempts to modernize the country and aggrandize his personal power. Despite his apparent success in changing the country's traditional institutions and his enormous international standing, these changes were not fundamental enough to transform the country. The emperor lacked the commitment to meet the growing expectations that his own reforms had engendered.

Emperor Haile Selassie I (right) with an interpreter in February, 1941, during his exile. (AP/Wide World Photos)

SIGNIFICANCE

The coronation of Emperor Haile Selassie was one of the most pivotal events in the history of modern Ethiopia. It heralded the political demise of the hereditary nobility that had hitherto limited the power of the monarchy. Haile Selassie transformed Ethiopia from an antiquated feudal polity into a relatively modern and centralized bureaucratic state. He carried out a series of reforms that gave the country the facade of modernity. Unfortunately for Ethiopia, most of these reforms were carried out selectively, with the view of aggrandizing the emperor's personal power and prestige both at home and abroad. As time passed, the emperor grew more isolated and detached from the many complex problems that beset the country in the second half of the twentieth century. Few were surprised when, in 1974, the emperor who had wielded absolute power for half a century was overthrown by a military coup led by junior officers. Haile Selassie died in detention on August 27, 1975; some said he was killed by a military junta.

—*Shumet Sishagne*

FURTHER READING

Bahru Zewde. *A History of Modern Ethiopia*. London: James Currey, 1991. One of the most authoritative works on modern Ethiopia. Provides succinct analysis of the development of the absolutist state under Emperor Haile Selassie.

Haile Selassie. *My Life and Ethiopia's Progress, 1892-1937*. Edited and translated by Edward Ullendorff. Oxford, England: Oxford University Press, 1976. The emperor's autobiography is particularly interesting for its vivid description of the coronation ceremony.

Henze, Paul. *Layers of Time: A History of Ethiopia*. New York: Palgrave, 2000. A readable general work that has utilized some of the most important contemporary accounts to provide an interesting description of the rise of Haile Selassie and the transformation of the Ethiopian polity in the twentieth century.

Marcus, Harold. *A History of Ethiopia*. Berkeley: University of California Press, 1994. One of the best standard works on Ethiopia by an author with a profound grasp of Ethiopian history.

Spencer, John H. *Ethiopia at Bay: A Personal Account of the Haile Sellassie Years*. Algonac, Mich.: Reference Publications, 1987. An intimate account of Haile Selassie's personality and style of rule by an American adviser who worked with the emperor and his ministers beginning in the 1930's.

SEE ALSO: Early 1920: Britain Represses Somali Rebellion; Oct. 11, 1935-July 15, 1936: League of Nations Applies Economic Sanctions Against Italy; Aug. 3, 1940-Mar., 1941: Italy Invades British Somaliland; Sept. 13, 1940: Italy Invades Egypt.

1930

May 30, 1930
CANADIAN NATIONAL PARKS ACT

The Canadian National Parks Act of 1930 removed the nation's national parks from the authority of the Dominion Forest Reserves and Parks Act and stated that the parks should be used but preserved for the enjoyment of future generations.

LOCALE: Ottawa, Ontario, Canada
CATEGORIES: Laws, acts, and legal history; environmental issues

KEY FIGURES

James Bernard Harkin (1875-1955), first Canadian commissioner of national parks
William Wallace Cory (1865-1943), Canadian deputy minister of the interior
John Edward Brownlee (1884-1961), premier of Alberta, 1925-1934
William Lyon Mackenzie King (1874-1950), prime minister of Canada, 1921-1926, 1926-1930, and 1935-1948

SUMMARY OF EVENT

The National Parks Act of 1930 changed the purpose of Canada's existing national parks. Previously, the parks had been areas in which resource exploitation was encouraged; after the act, the parks became places to be preserved for future generations. Between 1887 and the passage of the legislation in 1930, fourteen national parks had been established. In addition to removing the parks from the authority of the Dominion Forest Reserves and Parks Act, the National Parks Act also stated that only an act of Parliament could establish a new park or change the boundaries of existing parks.

The act resulted from compromise among national ministries and the provinces. It was passed concurrently with the Manitoba Natural Resources Act, the Saskatchewan National Resources Act, the Alberta Natural Resources Act, and the Railway Belt and Peace River Block Act. These acts transferred natural resources within the boundaries of their respective provinces from the national government to the provinces themselves. With this legislation, land, including valuable resources that had been contained within some already existing national parks, was given to the provinces, and new national park boundaries were drawn.

Canada's first national park had been established in 1887 in Banff, Alberta, as Rocky Mountains Park. The park owed its origins to transcontinental railroad work-

ers who discovered hot springs in the area in 1883. The area and the springs were recognized as a natural treasure, valuable for sanitary purposes (the mineral baths) and as a potential tourist attraction, and therefore worthy of protection for all Canadians. The Canadian government officially preserved the springs and the surrounding land in a series of steps that led to the Rocky Mountains Park Act of June 23, 1887, establishing this first national park.

Although the park's primary purpose was to promote tourism and recreation, another major objective was to use the wilderness for economic development. Mining, grazing, and lumbering were allowed with permission from the minister of the interior, but preservation was encouraged by prohibiting activities that would inhibit public enjoyment and recreation. The establishment of Rocky Mountains Park encouraged members of Parliament and officials of the Canadian Pacific Railway, the builder of the transcontinental railroad, to act to preserve other lands of western Canada. The five preservations established from 1887 to 1895 would later become the national parks of Yoho, Kootenay, Glacier, Waterton Lakes, and Mount Revelstoke.

The development of these early reserves and parks was intertwined with legislation passed by the Canadian parliament, including the Dominion Forest Reserves and Parks Act of 1911. This law provided for the administration of forest reserves and dominion (national) parks and allowed dominion parks to be established from forest reserves. The Dominion Parks Service, created as a new branch in the Department of the Interior, became the first distinct bureau of national parks in the world. James Bernard Harkin served as the organization's commissioner from its inception in 1911 until 1936.

Harkin worked not only to separate the administration of the parks from that of the forests but also to emphasize resource preservation. Deputy Minister of the Interior William Wallace Cory called for the drafting of legislation changing the administration of the parks. The legislation included giving the proposed new park branch exclusive control of all waters in the parks. The debate over water control continued through the 1920's.

The proposed national parks bill required the permission of Parliament to dispose of any resources within the parks. Because the Canadian government was planning to transfer to the provinces natural resources found within the provinces but outside the national parks, the boundaries of the parks became critical. The premier of Alberta, John Edward Brownlee, suggested that the parks be surveyed to identify natural resources necessary for the industrial development of the province. Prime Minister William Lyon Mackenzie King agreed. In the summers of 1927 and 1928, Deputy Minister of the Interior R. W. Cautley traveled through Rocky Mountains Park and Jasper Park, and he suggested removing valuable commercial areas from the parks and giving them to the province.

In its final form, the National Parks Act of 1930 dedicated the parks to the benefit, education, and enjoyment of the people of Canada and stated that the parks should be maintained to leave them unimpaired for the enjoyment of future generations. The act also changed the name of Rocky Mountains Park to Banff National Park. Its boundaries and those of Jasper National Park were changed, removing economically valuable waterbeds, grazing lands, and other resources, including coal. The act stated that the lands and minerals within the boundaries of the parks belonged to and would be administered by the federal government. Animals, plants, and minerals were to be protected, and violators would be subject to legal action, but the rights of holders of existing mineral grants were not rescinded. Provincial taxes would apply within the parks.

The act permitted, under government regulation, the granting of leases in town sites for lots for residence and trade, as well as for the provision of public works and utilities. The national parks were to be places where plants and animals could be protected but also places where human beings could live and work.

The act expanded the role of the national parks by permitting the establishment of national historic parks to commemorate historic events and to preserve historic landmarks or any object deemed to be of national importance. The act also abolished three national parks—Fort Howe, Mennissawok, and Vidal's Point—which were considered unworthy of national park status and were returned to their local governments.

SIGNIFICANCE

The full impact of the National Parks Act of 1930 was limited until the 1960's. Federal appropriations for the national parks declined sharply with the Great Depression and World War II. Federal funds were, however, used for unemployment relief projects, including highway, building, and campground construction in the western parks. From 1930 to 1969, four parks were established: Cape Breton Highlands in Nova Scotia in 1936, Prince Edward Island in 1937, Fundy in New Brunswick in 1948, and Terra Nova in Newfoundland in 1957.

The legislation that had been passed concurrently with the National Parks Act allowing transfer of natural resource ownership to the provinces led to new policies in park formation in the western provinces. It slowed establishment of new national parks because the provincial governments had to agree to all transfers of control and administration to the federal government, and the provinces and the national government did not always have the same needs or goals. The change in transfer policy did, however, lead to the development of provincial park systems in the provinces of Alberta, Manitoba, and Saskatchewan. Prior to passage of the act, only the provinces of Ontario, Quebec, and British Columbia had provincial parks.

With land set aside as national parks, natural resources outside the parks could be extracted, thus helping the economic development of the country. The resources inside the parks remained attractive, however,

A campsite near Banff, Alberta, in the 1940's. Canada's first national park was established in 1887 in Banff as Rocky Mountains Park. (AP/Wide World Photos)

1930

perpetuating decades of conflict over the relative values of preservation and exploitation of natural resources. Many of the national parks operated more as recreation areas than as areas of natural conservation, however, and the law was modified in later years to address the concerns of preservationists.

Since the act of 1930, Canada has formed more than twenty new national parks or national park reserves, spanning all ten provinces and the two northern territories. Conflicts in management and long-range planning remain. Although the lands within the parks are protected from development, many parks contain towns and the concomitant human activities and natural disruptions. Many parks have highways running through them. The highways bring visitors and serve as vital components of major transportation routes. In the northern parks, indigenous peoples are permitted to use resources as part of their traditional ways of life. Regardless of what activities are prohibited within the parks, the lands outside are sometimes areas of resource development. Activities such as logging and mining affect wildlife and contribute to air and water pollution within and around the parks.

Since its passage, the act has been responsible not only for the creation of more federal parks but also for the growth of provincial parks and preserves. National parks cover more than 220,000 square kilometers of Canada. The act's emphasis on resource preservation over resource use continued and expanded after 1930. As wilderness in the parks became threatened, the act was amended to permit the designation of wilderness areas within national parks. Within these areas, visitor activities and facilities were designed to be compatible with wilderness and thus were fairly primitive. Motor access was not allowed. In reflection of the need to save wilderness, four mountain national parks—Banff, Jasper, Kootenay, and Yoho—merged to compose the Rocky Mountain World Heritage Site, one of several areas around the world affording special natural protection.

Without the National Parks Act, much of Canada's natural beauty would not have been protected from development or preserved for future generations. Its influence continues, both in Canada and around the world.

—*Margaret F. Boorstein*

FURTHER READING

Bella, Leslie. "John A. Macdonald's Realism Saved Banff." *Canadian Geographic* 97 (October, 1978): 20-27. Traces the history of Banff from its origins to the late 1970's. Traces the effects of the National Parks Act of 1930 and of government actions during the 1960's and 1970's on the entire national park system. Discusses how the doctrine of usefulness has been involved in national park policy.

Eidsvik, Harold K., and William D. Henwood. "Canada." In *International Handbook of National Parks and Nature Preserves*, edited by Craig W. Allin. New York: Greenwood Press, 1990. An excellent review of the history of national parks in Canada. Discusses the impact of the National Parks Act of 1930 on the evolution of the park system and examines issues facing the parks.

Lothian, William Fergus. *A Brief History of Canada's National Parks*. Ottawa, Ont.: Parks Canada, 1987. Provides fascinating details about the evolution and growth of the Canadian national parks. The book discusses the history of individual parks and contains tremendous amounts of information, including many noteworthy names and dates. Photographs illustrating the early days of the parks enhance the book.

_____. *History of Canada's National Parks*. Vol. 2. Ottawa, Ont.: Parks Canada, 1977. One part of a four-volume series providing a detailed account of the history of Canadian national parks. Extremely useful in providing information not easily available elsewhere.

Nicol, John I. "The National Parks Movement in Canada." In *Canadian Parks in Perspective*, edited by J. G. Nelson. Montreal: Harvest House, 1969. Provides a succinct history of the national parks movement and of national parks in Canada from 1867 to 1968. Discusses the situation and problems in the parks in the 1960's and suggests new policy for Canadian parks and outdoor recreation as a whole.

Searle, Rick. *Phantom Parks: The Struggle to Save Canada's National Parks*. Toronto: Key Porter Books, 2000. Details the status of Canada's national parks at the turn of the twenty-first century, including threats to the parks and measures designed to preserve them. Bibliographic references and index.

SEE ALSO: May, 1903: Roosevelt and Muir Visit Yosemite; May 13-15, 1908: Conference on the Conservation of Natural Resources; Aug. 25, 1916: National Park Service Is Created; Feb. 26, 1917: Mount McKinley National Park Is Created; Feb. 1, 1919: Lenin Approves the First Soviet Nature Preserve; Nov. 19, 1929: Serengeti Game Reserve Is Created; Sept., 1933: Marshall Writes *The People's Forests*; Oct. 19, 1934: Marshall and Leopold Form the Wilderness Society.

June 6, 1930-August 27, 1934
FIRST MANNED BATHYSPHERE DIVES

William Beebe and Otis Barton pioneered the exploration of the ocean depths, contributed to the knowledge of deep-sea life, and provided a model for the further development of deep-sea diving vehicles and for the scientific observation of the seas.

LOCALE: Atlantic Ocean, near Bermuda
CATEGORIES: Science and technology; earth science; exploration and discovery

KEY FIGURES

William Beebe (1877-1962), American naturalist and curator of ornithology
Otis Barton (b. 1899), American engineer
John Tee-Van (1897-1967), general associate with the New York Zoological Society
Gloria Hollister Anable (c. 1901-1988), research associate with the New York Zoological Society
Jocelyn Crane Griffin (1909-1988), technical associate with the New York Zoological Society
Gilbert Hovey Grosvenor (1875-1966), National Geographic Society director, 1899-1966, president, 1920-1954, and chairman, 1954-1966

SUMMARY OF EVENT

The first half of the twentieth century was an age of exploration. On land, both the North and South Poles were conquered, and the most remote portions of Africa, Asia, and South America were revealed to explorers, paleontologists, and archaeologists. In the air, humans traveled in airplanes and dirigibles and assaulted the heights of the atmosphere in balloons. Until the 1930's, however, the vast depths of the oceans remained largely unexplored.

People did know something of the oceans' depths. Soundings and nettings of the ocean bottom had been made many times since the 1870's. Diving helmets had allowed humans to descend more than 90 meters below the surface, and the submarine allowed them to reach a depth of nearly 120 meters. There was no firsthand knowledge, however, of the deepest reaches of the submarine world.

The person who gave the world the first account of life at the great depths was William Beebe. When he announced in 1926 that he was attempting to build a craft to explore the ocean, he was already a well-known naturalist. Although his only advanced degrees were honorary doctorates, Beebe had graduated as a special student in

the Department of Zoology of Columbia University in 1898. He had begun his lifelong association with the New York Zoological Society in 1899. His first specialty had been in ornithology, and he had made his name in that field through a four-volume monograph on pheasants, which he studied in the field for many years. The events of his many trips and expeditions were recounted in a number of popular books and articles.

It was during a trip to the Galápagos Islands that Beebe turned his attention to oceanography. He became the first scientist to use a diving helmet in fieldwork, swimming in the shallow waters. He continued this shallow-water work at the new station he established in 1928, with the permission of English authorities, on the tiny island of Nonesuch in the Bermudas. Beebe realized, however, that he had reached the limits of the current technology and that studying the animal life of the ocean depths would require a new approach.

While he was considering various cylindrical designs for a new deep-sea exploratory craft, Beebe was introduced to Otis Barton. Barton, a young New Englander who had been trained as an engineer at Harvard University, had turned to the problems of ocean diving while doing postgraduate work at Columbia University. Although he had begun designing a spherical diving device as early as 1926, the reports of Beebe's forthcoming attempts temporarily dissuaded Barton from pursuing its development. By December, 1928, however, Barton had heard nothing further of Beebe's work, so he brought his blueprints to Beebe. Beebe immediately saw that Barton's design was what he was looking for, and the two went ahead with its construction.

The bathysphere, as Beebe named the device, weighed 5,000 pounds, with a diameter of 1.45 meters and steel walls 3.8 centimeters thick. The door, weighing 400 pounds, would be fastened over a manhole with ten bolts. Four windows, made of fused quartz at the suggestion of Edwin Elway Free, a New York physicist and lecturer, were ordered from the General Electric Company at a cost of five hundred dollars each. A 250-watt water spotlight, loaned by the Westinghouse Company, provided exterior illumination, and a telephone, loaned from the Bell Telephone Laboratory, provided the means for communicating with the surface. The breathing apparatus consisted of two oxygen tanks that allowed two liters of oxygen per minute to escape into the sphere. During the dive, carbon dioxide and moisture were removed from

1930

the interior by a tray containing, respectively, soda lime and calcium chloride. A winch using steel cable would lower the bathysphere.

On June 3, 1930, Beebe and Barton tested the completed bathysphere. They lowered the unmanned craft to a depth of 610 meters. When the craft was raised, the communications line was tangled around the cable. An unperceived twisting had occurred in transferring the cable from its original spool onto the winch, and this twisting undid itself under water. Three days later, a second unmanned test dive was made. This time, all went well, and only about a quart of water had seeped into the sphere when it returned from a depth of 457 meters.

Thus, at 1:00 P.M. on June 6, the first manned dive commenced. Beebe and Barton descended to a depth of 244 meters. A small leak had started through the door at 91 meters, but it was no worse than during the test dive. A short circuit in one of the switches showered them with sparks momentarily, but the descent was largely a success. Beebe and Barton had descended farther than had any human before.

Two more days of diving yielded more minor inconveniences and a final dive record of 435 meters below sea level. On these dives, Beebe and the other members of his staff (ichthyologist John Tee-Van and zoologist Gloria Hollister Anable) saw many species of fish and other marine life that previously had been seen only after being caught in nets. These first dives proved that an undersea exploratory craft had potential value, at least for deep water.

Beebe's group, joined by a new associate, Jocelyn Crane Griffin, set out once again with the bathysphere in the fall of 1932. Two unmanned test dives initially yielded only a bathysphere full of cold seawater: A new window had been improperly installed. After draining the craft and fixing the window, the group prepared for another round of manned dives. The most dramatic of the dives came on September 22. The National Broadcasting Company (NBC) had arranged to do a live broadcast on a Sunday afternoon. The first attempts had to be postponed because of weather and other technical problems, but on that afternoon, even though the seas would normally have been too rough, Beebe and Barton made a descent. The last several hundred meters of the descent were carried live, and a large audience heard Beebe's conversation with Anable. Several new species of fish were tentatively identified. A new depth record was set at 671 meters; Beebe decided to come up at that point because of the buffeting the bathysphere was taking as the mother ship was tossed by waves. After the 1932 dives, the

bathysphere went on display at the Century of Progress Exhibition in Chicago.

In late 1933, Gilbert Hovey Grosvenor, president of the National Geographic Society, offered to sponsor another series of dives. Although a new record was not a stipulation of sponsorship, Beebe was determined to set one. Beebe still considered the primary purpose of the dives to be scientific. He had thought to include cosmic ray analysis experiments on the dives, but Robert Andrews Millikan, the Nobel Prize-winning physicist, responded to his queries by saying that the bathysphere would not be submerged long enough for any useful data to be obtained. Similarly, spectrographic data could not be gathered because the smallest spectroscope could not fit through the door of the bathysphere.

The bathysphere was completely refitted before the new dives. Again, many companies donated the equipment Beebe needed. Notable was a more modern breathing apparatus donated by the Air Reduction Company. The outer sphere also was altered. An unmanned test dive to 920 meters was made on August 7, 1934, once again off Nonesuch Island. Minor adjustments were made, and on the morning of August 11, the first manned dive commenced, attaining a depth of 765 meters and recording a number of new scientific observations. Several days later, on August 15, the weather was again right for a dive.

This dive also paid rich dividends in the number of species of deep-sea life observed. Finally, with only a few turns of cable left on the winch spool, a record depth of 923 meters—almost a kilometer below the ocean's surface—was attained. The ascent was marred by the breaking of a guy rope used to spool the incoming cable, but this was scarcely noticed by Beebe and Barton.

Later dives included the other members of the group. Anable descended to a depth of 368 meters, a record for a woman. Griffin reached a depth of 351 meters. Tee-Van descended to 457 meters on August 27, 1934. After these dives, Beebe turned his focus to shallow-water dives in the Pacific Ocean.

SIGNIFICANCE

The work of Beebe and Barton with the bathysphere marked both an end and a beginning. It marked an end in the sense that although it showed that undersea exploration was a scientifically profitable enterprise, it also pointed out the limitations of the bathysphere in pursuing that enterprise. Beebe had originally sought to build a new exploration craft because he saw the limitations of what was then the best method of exploration: the rigid diving suit or diving helmet. Although the bathysphere solved the immediate problems of diver mobility and depth limitations, it did not cut the "umbilical cord"—the bathysphere was still dependent on a surface vessel. Further, there were inherent problems with the basic design. The bathysphere had no fail-safe contingency should the sphere become separated from the cable. The danger of such a catastrophic failure was always a possibility. Technologically, the bathysphere was near its design limits: The deeper one went, the more steel cable was needed; the more cable that was needed, the heavier the combined weight of the cable and bathysphere, thus calling for larger and larger winches and mother ships and raising the cost of the expedition. The inability to maneuver horizontally also limited the bathysphere's scientific effectiveness.

Barton continued to work on the bathysphere design for some years. It was not until 1948, however, that

William Beebe (left) and John Tee-Van in November, 1934, with the bathysphere in which Beebe plunged to record ocean depths. (AP/Wide World Photos)

his new design, the benthoscope, was finally constructed. It was similar in basic design to the bathysphere, but the walls were strengthened to withstand greater pressures. Other improvements were made, but the essential strengths and weaknesses of the original bathysphere remained. On August 16, 1949, Barton, diving alone, broke the record he and Beebe had set fifteen years earlier, reaching a depth of 1,372 meters off Santa Cruz Island in Southern California.

The bathysphere effectively marked the end of the tethered exploration of the deep, but it pointed the way to other possibilities: In 1943, Jacques Cousteau and Émile Gagnan developed the Aqualung underwater breathing apparatus, allowing unfettered and largely unencumbered exploration down to about 60 meters. This was by no means deep-sea diving, but the development of true shallow-water mobility was clearly a step along the lines that Beebe had envisioned for underwater research.

A further step came in the development of the bathyscaphe by Auguste Piccard, the renowned Swiss physicist who, in the 1930's, conquered the stratosphere in high-altitude balloons. The bathyscaphe itself was a balloon but operated in reverse. A spherical steel passenger

cabin was attached beneath a large float filled with gasoline for buoyancy. Several tons of iron pellets held by electromagnets acted as ballast. The bathyscaphe would sink slowly to the bottom of the ocean, and when its passengers wished to return to the surface, the ballast would be dumped. Although bathyscaphes were constructed before the benthoscope in 1948, early tests were partial failures. In 1953, however, both the French navy's *FNRS-3* under the command of Georges Houot and Pierre-Henri Willm and the *Trieste* under the command of Piccard and his son Jacques set new records. On August 14, Houot and Willm dove to 2,099 meters without touching bottom off Provençal. The Piccards touched bottom off Capri on September 30, some 3,000 meters below the surface.

Finally, spheres of any kind were surpassed by improved submarines designed for deep-sea exploration. A craft that existed when Beebe began his deep-sea research became the design that would ultimately conquer the ocean's depths. It cannot be denied, however, that all of these further attempts owed something to the courageous and scientific spirit of Beebe and Barton.

—George R. Ehrhardt

1930

FURTHER READING

Barton, Otis. *The World Beneath the Sea.* New York: Thomas Y. Crowell, 1953. Barton tells the story of his life from shortly before his first meeting with Beebe up to the period after his record-setting dive. The account is heavy with anecdotes and opinions and should be used only to supplement Beebe's account (cited below). Photographs.

Beebe, William. *Half Mile Down.* New York: Harcourt, Brace, 1934. Beebe's definitive popular account of the dives, some of which had been published earlier in *National Geographic* and other popular magazines. Includes technical appendixes by Barton, Tee-Van, Anable, and Griffin, as well as photographs, illustrations, and an index.

Gould, Carol Grant. *The Remarkable Life of William Beebe: Explorer and Naturalist.* Washington, D.C.: Island Press/Shearwater Books, 2004. Exhaustive study of the life and career of Beebe, from his early work as a naturalist, through his deep-sea explorations, to his later jungle expeditions. Bibliographic references and index.

Guberlet, Muriel L. *Explorers of the Sea: Famous Oceanographic Expeditions.* New York: Ronald Press, 1964. Popular, episodic account of a number of ocean explorers, loosely defined. A bit too enthusiastic, but a good story. Bibliography and an index.

Matsen, Brad. *Descent: The Heroic Discovery of the Abyss.* New York: Pantheon Books, 2005. Recounts the design, construction, and expeditions of Beebe and Barton's bathysphere. Bibliographic references and index.

Piccard, Jacques, and Robert S. Dietz. *Seven Miles Down: The Story of the Bathyscaph Trieste.* New York: G. P. Putnam's Sons, 1961. Piccard, pilot on all dives of the *Trieste* and son of its inventor, and Dietz, the first American to make a dive in the bathyscaphe, tell the story of the dives made from 1948 to 1960. Useful for comparisons between the crafts and their descents. Photographs and an index.

Soule, Gardner. *The Greatest Depths: Probing the Seas to Twenty Thousand Feet and Below.* Philadelphia: Macrae Smith, 1970. A popular account, written by a reporter, that covers all aspects of deep-sea study. Quotes freely from many other works and includes a few interesting comments from Beebe's second wife. Photographs, bibliography, and an index.

Welker, Robert Henry. *Natural Man: The Life of William Beebe.* Bloomington: Indiana University Press, 1975. An unconventional biography of Beebe that delves into critical analysis. Indispensable for understanding Beebe. Scholarly, but very readable. Photographs, notes, and an index.

SEE ALSO: Aug. 4, 1906: First German U-Boat Is Launched; 1907: Haldane Develops Stage Decompression for Deep-Sea Divers; Sept. 22, 1914: Germany Begins Extensive Submarine Warfare; Oct., 1915-Mar., 1917: Langevin Develops Active Sonar.

June 17, 1930
HOOVER SIGNS THE HAWLEY-SMOOT TARIFF ACT

The Hawley-Smoot Tariff Act raised protectionist tariffs in the United States. It sparked foreign retaliation against American products and helped bring on a temporary collapse of the international trading system, exacerbating the financial troubles caused by the onset of the Great Depression.

ALSO KNOWN AS: Smoot-Hawley Tariff Act
LOCALE: Washington, D.C.
CATEGORIES: Diplomacy and international relations; trade and commerce

KEY FIGURES

Willis C. Hawley (1864-1941), U.S. representative from Oregon, 1907-1932, and chairman of the House Ways and Means Committee, 1927-1930

Reed Smoot (1862-1941), U.S. senator from Utah, 1903-1932, and chairman of the Senate Finance Committee, 1923-1932

Herbert Hoover (1874-1964), president of the United States, 1929-1933

William Lyon Mackenzie King (1874-1950), prime minister of Canada, 1921-1926, 1926-1930, 1935-1948

Richard Bedford Bennett (1870-1947), Canadian leader of the Conservative Party, 1927-1938, and prime minister, 1930-1935

Ramsay MacDonald (1866-1937), prime minister of Great Britain, 1924, 1929-1935

Stanley Baldwin (1867-1947), prime minister of Great Britain, 1923-1924, 1924-1929, 1935-1937

SUMMARY OF EVENT

The Hawley-Smoot Tariff raised average U.S. tariff rates by approximately 18 percent. The largest increases were on agricultural products, on which average tariff rates increased by about 57 percent. President Herbert Hoover's signing of the tariff bill on June 17, 1930, climaxed a political struggle that had lasted more than a year. Proponents of higher tariff rates had hoped in particular to give relief to farmers, whose incomes generally had lagged during the prosperity of the 1920's. More generally, they hoped that protection from foreign competition would allow U.S. producers to avoid production cutbacks and layoffs as the Great Depression began to unfold.

Opponents of higher tariffs had three main concerns. First, they feared that higher tariffs would end up protecting inefficient domestic producers and thereby result in higher prices for consumers. Second, they were afraid that an increase in U.S. tariffs would spark foreign retaliation, hurting the U.S. export sector. Finally, opponents were afraid that if the United States reduced its purchases of goods from other countries (particularly in Europe) that were heavily indebted to the United States, then it would become difficult for those countries to continue to make payments on their debt. The result might be the undermining of the international financial system.

While serving as secretary of commerce during the Warren G. Harding and Calvin Coolidge administrations, Hoover had become known as a strong proponent of protective tariffs. The 1928 Republican Party platform called for increased duties on agricultural products, and Hoover made this promise a central part of his presidential campaign. Although Hoover himself did not come out in favor of a general increase in tariff rates, he did state during the campaign that the United States should confine its imports largely to those products that could not be produced domestically. This position makes more understandable Hoover's eventual willingness to accept a general increase in tariff rates.

Shortly after assuming office, Hoover called a special session of Congress to convene on April 15, 1929, for the express purpose of raising tariff duties on agricultural products. Because it was a measure dealing with revenue, the bill the president required was constitutionally required to originate in the House of Representatives. The House quickly passed a tariff bill raising agricultural duties as the president wished. As a result of political trading during the legislative process, the bill contained substantial increases in duties on nonagricultural products as well. The bill was known

formally as the Hawley-Smoot bill after its two congressional sponsors, Willis C. Hawley of Oregon—the chairman of the House Ways and Means Committee—and Reed Smoot of Utah, the chairman of the Senate Finance Committee. Hawley's name came first in the bill's formal name because he was the first to introduce it, but given Smoot's greater political prominence, the measure was more popularly known as the Smoot-Hawley bill.

Despite Smoot's sponsorship of the bill, the Senate was much slower to act on it than the House had been, and the special session of Congress concluded in November without the passage of a new tariff law. When Congress reconvened in April, 1930, a compromise was worked out. The final version of the bill passed in Congress on June 14. The final version of the bill achieved passage in the House fairly easily, by a vote of 222 to 153. It was largely a party-line vote, with 208 Republicans voting for the bill and only 20 against it; 133 Democrats voted against the bill, and only 14 voted for it. The vote in the Senate was much closer—44 to 42 for passage—as a group of eleven so-called Republican Insurgents led by Senators William E. Borah, George W. Norris, and Robert M. La Follette voted against the bill.

Because the increase in tariff rates embodied in the bill went well beyond Hoover's initial call for an increase in agricultural duties, there was some hope among the bill's opponents that the president might veto it. Among those arguing in favor of a veto were prominent members of the banking and financial community, some leading industrialists (including Henry Ford), the editors of many prominent newspapers (including *The New York Times*), and, perhaps most famously, a group of more than one thousand economists who signed a petition urging a veto. Prominent among those arguing in favor of signing the bill were most farm organizations and the American Federation of Labor.

Hoover's decision to sign the bill was probably most dependent on three considerations. First, as his statements during the 1928 presidential campaign had made clear, he had a strongly protectionist philosophy. Second, he doubted that a better bill could be procured from Congress, and he believed that the failure to pass any tariff bill would be seen, particularly by farmers, as a failure to carry through on an important campaign promise. Finally, he managed to get included in the bill a provision allowing the U.S. Tariff Commission to modify tariff duties in the future. Hoover expected that this provision would put an effective end to congressional tariff making. Hoover signed the Hawley-Smoot Tariff Act into law on June 17, and the law went into effect with the new fiscal year that began on July 1, 1930.

Hoover, Smoot, Hawley, and their proponents hoped that the tariff act would lead to increased income and employment in the United States. This hope was dependent on other nations failing to respond to the measure in kind, and as a result it was not realized. At the time Hoover took office, the Canadian government, under Liberal prime minister William Lyon Mackenzie King, was committed to lower tariffs. There is some reason to believe that King might have planned to include tariff reductions in his budget announcement of March, 1929, but this possibility was foreclosed by anticipation of Hoover's announcement of the special session of Congress to consider tariff increases. As time passed and the likelihood of general tariff increases in the United States increased, King came under increasing pressure from Conservative Party leader Richard Bedford Bennett. Bennett argued in favor of using tariffs to shift Canada's economic relations away from the United States and toward the British Empire. In a widely publicized speech in November, 1929, King warned that if tariff increases adversely affecting Canada were passed by the U.S. Congress, some reaction would surely follow. King still hoped either that no new tariff bill would make it through Congress or that if one did pass, Hoover would somehow manage to shield Canada from its worst effects.

By the spring of 1930, King felt obliged to include in his budget tariff adjustments that reflected the changing political realities. The duties on 270 goods imported from within the British Empire were reduced, and there were small increases in duties on certain imports from the United States. The budget included countervailing duties on 16 products, under which the Canadian duty would be raised to match any increase in duties on those products levied by other countries.

Perhaps buoyed by the initially favorable domestic response to the new budget, King announced that a general election would be held in July. Most observers believed the key issue in the campaign to be the proper Canadian response to the Hawley-Smoot Tariff Act. Bennett accused the United States of attempting to steal the jobs of Canadian workers through tariff increases and reiterated his view that Canada should adjust its tariff structure so as to encourage trade with other countries in the British Empire at the expense of the United States. On the defensive, King attempted to play up what he claimed was the alarm in the United States over the mild tariff increases enacted by Canada in May.

Although many expected the election to be close, the Conservatives won a large victory, securing their only majority in the Canadian parliament in any election between 1911 and 1958. The key to the size of the Conservatives' victory was their unexpectedly strong showing in Quebec, where resentment against increased U.S. duties on dairy products was very strong, and in the provinces of Alberta, Manitoba, and Saskatchewan, where increased U.S. duties on wheat led to a strong political reaction. Once in power, Bennett fulfilled his promise to increase duties on U.S. products and reorient Canadian trade toward the British Empire.

The reaction of the British government and public to Hawley-Smoot is somewhat difficult to disentangle from general developments in British politics at the time. From the middle of the nineteenth century, Britain had been strongly committed to free trade. As the Great Depression began, Prime Minister Ramsay MacDonald's Labor government attempted to maintain this commitment to free trade. Rising unemployment, however, helped reinforce calls for a turn toward protectionism. The passage of Hawley-Smoot further undermined support for free trade, particularly within the Conservative Party.

The Conservative Party had been home to a substantial protectionist wing dating back at least to Joseph Chamberlain's 1903 campaign to raise British tariffs and to negotiate reciprocal tariff preferences with members of the British Empire. However, the majority view within the party, probably reflecting the majority view of the British public, remained in favor of free trade. The Conservative defeat in the 1929 general election was attributed by some to the party's failure to adopt an aggressive protectionist policy as an offset to the Labor Party's natural appeal during a time of rising unemployment. It was only following the passage of the Hawley-Smoot Act and increases in tariffs in several British dominions, notably Canada, that Stanley Baldwin, the leader of the Conservative Party, came out in favor of increased British tariffs. Baldwin said that although he remained opposed to protectionism, he had become convinced that only by raising its own tariffs would Britain obtain the bargaining power necessary to negotiate successfully a multilateral reduction in tariff rates.

In September, 1931, Ramsay MacDonald, having lost much of the support of his own party, formed a coalition government, relying heavily on Conservative support. Running on a platform that included pledges of higher tariffs, the coalition won a large victory in October, 1931. A general increase in tariffs was then passed by the

House of Commons in February, 1932. This was followed by further tariff increases following the Ottawa Conference of July, 1932, at which Britain and its dominions and colonies agreed to further tariff increases on non-Empire imports and reductions in tariffs on imports from within the British Empire.

SIGNIFICANCE

It is not possible to determine with certainty whether the passage of the Hawley-Smoot Tariff Act led directly to an increase in tariffs in other nations. For example, the situation in Britain might well have led to increased tariffs regardless. On the other hand, given Prime Minister King's general philosophy, it is almost certain that Canadian tariffs would at worst have remained the same and might have decreased had not the American law been passed. The tariff war with Canada cost U.S. exporters dearly. In 1929, 18 percent of U.S. merchandise exports had gone to Canada, and the United States had enjoyed a $445 million merchandise trade surplus with Canada. By 1933, only 13 percent of U.S. merchandise exports were going to Canada, and the United States ran a surplus of only $26 million with Canada.

Overall, the net negative impact on the U.S. economy from the unraveling of the world trade system in the face of retaliatory tariff increases was considerable. Measured in constant 1982 dollars, the United States had a trade surplus in goods and services of $4.7 billion in 1929. By 1933, it had a trade deficit of $1.4 billion. The League of Nations estimated that the volume of world trade declined in real terms by more than 65 percent between 1929 and 1933. Not until the General Agreement on Tariffs and Trade was successfully negotiated in 1947 was the world trading system restored to a sound footing. Willis C. Hawley, Reed Smoot, and Herbert Hoover were all defeated in the 1932 elections.

—*Anthony Patrick O'Brien*

FURTHER READING

Ball, Stuart. *Baldwin and the Conservative Party: The Crisis of 1929-1931*. New Haven, Conn.: Yale University Press, 1988. Includes a discussion of the debates within the British Conservative Party between protectionists and free traders.

Eichengreen, Barry. "The Political Economy of the Smoot-Hawley Tariff." In *Research in Economic History*, edited by Roger Ransom. Vol. 12. Westport, Conn.: JAI Press, 1989. The most complete recent discussion of the passage of the bill and its economic implications. Notable for being skeptical of the extent of foreign retaliation and for arguing that Hawley-Smoot may actually have mitigated the impact of the Depression on the United States.

Hoover, Herbert. *The Memoirs of Herbert Hoover: The Cabinet and the Presidency, 1920-1933*. New York: Macmillan, 1952. Chapter 41 contains Hoover's discussion of the background to Hawley-Smoot and his reasons for signing the bill.

Irwin, Douglas A. "From Smoot-Hawley to Reciprocal Trade Agreements: Changing the Course of U.S. Trade Policy in the 1930's." In *The Defining Moment: The Great Depression and the American Economy in the Twentieth Century*, edited by Michael D. Bordo, Claudia Goldin, and Eugene N. White. Chicago: University of Chicago Press, 1998. Originally published as a pamphlet by the National Bureau of Economic Research, this essay traces the evolution of the U.S. government's attitude toward tariffs and trade during the 1930's. Bibliographic references and index.

Jones, Joseph M., Jr. *Tariff Retaliation: Repercussions of the Hawley-Smoot Bill*. Philadelphia: University of Pennsylvania Press, 1934. Classic discussion of foreign retaliation against Hawley-Smoot. The largely nontechnical discussion goes into too much detail for most readers but remains the best available account. Chapter 6 discusses Canada, and chapter 7 discusses Great Britain.

Kindleberger, Charles P. *The World in Depression, 1929-1939*. Berkeley: University of California Press, 1975. Discussion of the contribution of problems in the world trade and financial systems to the deepening of the Depression.

Overbeek, Johannes, ed. *Free Trade Versus Protectionism: A Source Book of Essays and Readings*. Northampton, Mass.: Edward Elgar, 1999. Anthology of primary documents in the debate between protectionism and free trade; includes selections from Smoot and Hawley. Bibliographic references and indexes.

Pastor, Robert A. *Congress and the Politics of U.S. Foreign Policy, 1929-1976*. Berkeley: University of California Press, 1980. Argues that the passage of Hawley-Smoot can be explained by Republican predilections to turn to tariffs during times of economic stress. Provides a good, nontechnical discussion of evolution of tariffs after Hawley-Smoot.

Schattschneider, E. E. *Politics, Pressures, and the Tariff*. New York: Prentice-Hall, 1935. Classic and very influential argument that the final version of the

Hawley-Smoot bill was the result of the influence of special interests and lobbyists. Long and rather heavy going for the general reader, but worthwhile for those interested in a still-relevant inside look at the legislative process.

SEE ALSO: Sept. 8, 1916: United States Establishes a Permanent Tariff Commission; June 15, 1929: Agricultural Marketing Act; Sept. 8, 1930: Canada Enacts Depression-Era Relief Legislation; July 21-Aug. 21, 1932: Ottawa Agreements.

Summer, 1930
NATION OF ISLAM IS FOUNDED

The Nation of Islam, a religious organization, worked to inculcate black pride and help elevate African Americans' social and economic status.

ALSO KNOWN AS: Black Muslim movement
LOCALE: Detroit, Michigan
CATEGORIES: Organizations and institutions; religion, theology, and ethics

KEY FIGURES
Wallace D. Fard (c. 1877-1934), first prophet of the Nation of Islam
Malcolm X (1925-1965), Nation of Islam minister and spokesperson
Elijah Muhammad (1897-1975), founder and spiritual leader of the Nation of Islam

SUMMARY OF EVENT
The Nation of Islam (NOI), also known as the Black Muslim movement and the Lost-Found Nation of Islam in the Wilderness of North America, is a religious organization that has successfully melded orthodox Islam, black nationalism, and a set of social and economic principles to produce a highly structured way of life for its African American membership. A religious sect founded in 1930 in Detroit, Michigan, the NOI borrowed from earlier movements as it crystallized around three leaders: Wallace D. Fard, Elijah Muhammad, and Malcolm X.

Orthodox Islam was started in the city of Mecca, in what is now Saudi Arabia, by the Prophet Muḥammad (570-632 C.E.). A major world religion, Islam may have arrived in the Americas with the Spanish explorers. In 1888, Alexander Russell Webb established an Islamic community in the United States. Members of the Islamic religion are known as Muslims. To distinguish between orthodox Muslims and members of the Nation of Islam sect, theologian C. Eric Lincoln coined the term Black Muslims. Although the NOI considers itself a branch of orthodox Islam, the majority of the organization's earliest members were affiliated with Christianity.

The Nation of Islam embraces the essential teachings of orthodox Islam: prayer five times daily; belief in one God, named Allah; acceptance of the sacred Islamic book, the Qur'ān; the coming of the "guided one," known as Mahdī; and pilgrimage to the holy city of Mecca. Both groups stress cleanliness and a strict moral code, and both shun alcohol, drug abuse, and the eating of pork. Early NOI leaders, however, expanded orthodox Islam because of the historic oppression of African Americans. The Nation of Islam is orthodox Islam customized for the African American experience, with membership solidarity and racial pride being key added features. Black Muslims are required to drop their European last names, which are associated with enslavement, and adopt the "X" until they earn an Islamic surname. Additional elements, such as advocating a separate nation for its members and teaching about the racist deeds of the "white man," were the source of much outside criticism and prevented the NOI's acceptance into the official fold of orthodox Islam.

During the first half of the twentieth century, African Americans were treated as second-class citizens in the United States. Institutionalized racism made it difficult for many African Americans to rise above poverty and oppression. In the midst of Great Depression woes and the past specter of slavery, many African Americans were disillusioned and susceptible to philosophies and leaders who promised improvements. Consequently, a number of black nationalistic and religious movements developed during this period. The Nation of Islam includes principles that were embedded in two of these movements: Noble Drew Ali's Moorish Science Temple, founded in 1913, and Marcus Garvey's Universal Negro Improvement Association.

Timothy Drew, known as Noble Drew Ali, introduced Islam to African Americans. He and his followers adopted the Qur'ān and called themselves Moors, after an ancient North African people. Ali's church had thousands of members in northern U.S. cities before his unexplained death in 1929. Subsequently, many of Ali's followers joined Wallace D. Fard's group, which emerged a year later.

The Nation of Islam espoused the political nationalism of Jamaican-born Marcus Garvey, who amassed thousands of followers in the United States from 1916 until his imprisonment in 1923 and subsequent deportation. Garvey advocated a separate African American nation, economic and political solidarity, and racial pride. When Fard appeared on the American scene during the summer of 1930, the conditions that fostered the acceptance of the ideas of Garvey and Ali were still present, although the original founders were not. Consequently, Fard soon filled a void that, after setbacks, developed into a viable religious sect. The Nation of Islam grew out of informal visits Fard paid to the homes of African Americans in Detroit, where he peddled silk products and discussed orthodox Islam, the African heritage, and the misdeeds of the "white man."

The first prophet of the Nation of Islam is shrouded in mystery. Although he is believed to be from Mecca, his national origins, his real name, and the circumstances of his 1934 disappearance are not known. In addition to being known as W. D. Fard, Wallace D. Fard, and Wallace Fard Muhammad, he is referred to as Wali Farrad, F. Mohammad, and other names. Fard's achievements, however, are well documented. In four years during the Great Depression, he established the church's basic philosophy, created a security force known as the Fruit of Islam, opened the University of Islam, built its first temple, and amassed about eight thousand followers. Many of his followers, including Elijah Muhammad, thought Fard to be Allah reincarnated as well as the promised Mahdī. After Fard's sudden disappearance, Elijah Muhammad became the group's leader.

Elijah Muhammad, born Elijah Poole in Sandersville, Georgia, was respectfully known as the Honorable Elijah Muham-

WHO WAS WALLACE D. FARD?

The first prophet of the Nation of Islam is shrouded in mystery: His national origins, his real name, and the circumstances of his 1934 disappearance are not fully known, but an FBI memorandum from Special Agent Edwin O. Raudsep, dated March 8, 1965 (approximately three decades after Fard's death), rehearses the known facts about Fard at that time.

[Wallace] Dodd arrived in the United States from New Zealand in 1913, settled briefly in Portland, Oregon. He married but abandoned his wife and infant son. He lingered in the Seattle Area as Fred Dodd for a few months, then moved to Los Angeles and opened a restaurant at 803 W. Third Street as Wallace D. Ford. He was arrested for bootlegging in January, 1926; served a brief jail sentence (also as Wallace D. Ford)—identified on record as white.

On June 12, 1926, also as Ford, was sentenced to San Quentin for sale of narcotics at his restaurant; got 6-months to 6-years sentence—released from San Quentin May 27, 1929. Prison record lists him as Caucasian.

After release, went to Chicago, then to Detroit as a silk peddler. His customers were mostly Negro and he himself posed as a Negro. He prided himself as a biblical authority and mathematician.

When Elijah Muhammad (Poole) met him, he was passing himself off as a savior and claiming that he was born in Mecca and had arrived in the U.S. on July 4, 1930.

In 1933 there was a scandal revolving about the sect involving a "human sacrifice" which may or may not have been trumped up. At any rate, the leader was arrested May 25, 1933, under the name Fard with 8 other listed aliases (W. D. Farrad, Wallace Farad, Walt Farrad, Prof. Ford, etc.). The official report says Dodd admitted that his teachings were "strictly a racket" and he was "getting all the money out of it he could." He was ordered out of Detroit.

[In a] newspaper article which appeared in the *San Francisco Examiner* and the *Los Angeles Examiner* on July 28, 1963, reporter Ed Montgomery . . . claimed to have contacted Dodd's former common law wife. . . . According to this account, Dodd went to Chicago after leaving Detroit and became a traveling suit salesman for a mail order tailer [*sic*]. In this position he worked himself across the midwest and ultimately arrived in Los Angeles in the spring of 1934 in a new car and wearing flowing white robes. He tried to work out a reconciliation with the woman, but she would not agree to one. . . . He stayed in Los Angeles for two weeks, frequently visiting his son. Then he sold his car and boarded a ship bound for New Zealand where he said he would visit relatives.

On Sunday, February 28, 1965, Ed Montgomery wrote a rehash of the above in which he said the Muslims claim "police and San Quentin Prison records dating back to the early 1920's had been altered and that fingerprints identifying Farad as Dodd had been doctored." Elijah Mohummad [*sic*] said he would have posted $100,000 reward "for any person who could prove Farad and Dodd were one and the same person." Ten days later Muhammad's office in Chicago was advised Farad's common law wife and a blood relative were prepared to establish the truth of Farad's identity. The $100,000 never was placed in escrow and the matter was dropped forthwith.

1930

Elijah Muhammad addresses the national convention of the Nation of Islam in 1966.
(AP/Wide World Photos)

operated a major printing press; and had a membership of more than 100,000. Much of Muhammad's success, however, can be attributed to one of his ministers, Malcolm X.

Malcolm X was born Malcolm Little in Omaha, Nebraska. His parents, Earle and Louise Little, were organizers for Marcus Garvey's Universal Negro Improvement Association. Because of their views, the Littles were forced to move away from Omaha. They eventually settled in East Lansing, Michigan, where Earle apparently was murdered and Louise had a breakdown. Malcolm then lived with his sister and foster families. Later, he wandered between odd jobs and engaged in petty crime. He was imprisoned from 1946 to 1952, and he married Betty Shabazz in 1958.

In prison, Malcolm became self-educated and converted to Islam. After his release, he met Elijah Muhammad, received his X, and trained for the NOI ministry. He headed temples in several cities before becoming the primary spokesperson for the Nation of Islam. His frank speeches and numerous public appearances catapulted the NOI into the national forefront. Membership swelled because of Malcolm's visibility, but the number of his enemies increased as well. For unauthorized remarks he made about President John F. Kennedy's assassination, Malcolm was suspended from the NOI. Around that time, he changed his name to El-Hajj Malik el-Shabazz. He left the NOI in March, 1964, and formed two new organizations, the success of which was curtailed by his murder on February 21, 1965.

After Elijah Muhammad's death, his son, Warith, also known as Wallace, became the NOI leader. Warith's changes forced another NOI split, spearheaded by Louis Farrakhan. The NOI expanded under Farrakhan, a controversial figure in part because of his adamant and at times incendiary statements. In October, 1995, the nondenominational NOI-sponsored Million Man March in Washington, D.C., added immensely to Farrakhan's visibility and to some extent mitigated his controversial image.

—*Linda Rochell Lane*

mad, the Messenger of Allah. His parents had been slaves and sharecroppers. His father was a Baptist minister. While a teenager, Muhammad moved to Atlanta. He married Clara Evans in 1919, and during the 1920's he and his family migrated to Detroit. It was in Detroit that Muhammad met Fard and became one of his most devoted converts. He was rewarded by being chosen as Fard's successor, and he transformed Fard's sincere project into a thriving organization.

SIGNIFICANCE

After Fard's disappearance, rivalry caused some factionalism and a sharp decrease in NOI membership. Muhammad, often the victim of harassment and death threats, was imprisoned. Consequently, Muhammad moved the NOI headquarters from Detroit to Chicago. Although still confronted with adversities, Muhammad was able to rebuild and strengthen the organization. When Muhammad died in 1975, the Nation of Islam had temples and schools from coast to coast; owned a string of restaurants, apartments, and other businesses and real estate;

FURTHER READING

Carson, Clayborne. *Malcolm X: The FBI Files*. New York: Carroll & Graf, 1991. Extracts data from Federal Bureau of Investigation files and provides information on Malcolm X, his family, and the Nation of Islam from 1919 to 1980. Arranged in time-line format.

Clark, John Henrick, ed. *Malcolm X: The Man and His Times*. Trenton, N.J.: African World Press, 1990. Collection of essays by scholars as well as personal acquaintances of Malcolm X and a chapter in his own words. Includes documents in an appendix.

Frazier, E. Franklin. *The Negro Church in America*. 1963. Reprint. New York: Schocken Books, 1974. Reprint volume also includes Eric C. Lincoln's *The Black Church Since Frazier*. Together, these works provide critical background on African American religion.

Lincoln, C. Eric. *The Black Muslims in America*. 3d ed. Grand Rapids, Mich.: Wm. B. Eerdmans, 1994. Revised and updated edition of a classic work, the first complete academic analysis of the Nation of Islam, which was published in 1961.

Lippman, Thomas W. *Understanding Islam: An Intro-* *duction to the Muslim World*. 2d rev. ed. New York: Penguin Books, 1995. Useful introduction to orthodox Islam. Includes glossary, bibliography, and index.

Malcolm X with Alex Haley. *The Autobiography of Malcolm X*. 1965. Reprint. New York: Ballantine Books, 1992. Classic work tells the story of the African American revolutionary and Black Muslim leader.

Muhammad, Elijah. *The Supreme Wisdom*. 2 vols. Brooklyn: Temple of Islam, 1957. The Nation of Islam's founder explains the organization's tenets.

Walker, Dennis. *Islam and the Search for African American Nationhood: Elijah Muhammad, Louis Farrakhan, and the Nation of Islam*. Atlanta, Ga.: Clarity Press, 2005. Examines the history of the Nation of Islam and the organization's standing among African Americans. Written by an expert on Muslim minorities.

SEE ALSO: July 11, 1905: Founding of the Niagara Movement; 1910-1930: Great Northern Migration; May, 1917: Universal Negro Improvement Association Establishes a U.S. Chapter; 1920's: Harlem Renaissance; 1932-1940: Development of Negritude.

August, 1930
LAMBETH CONFERENCE ALLOWS ARTIFICIAL CONTRACEPTION

Reversing past ecclesiastical pronouncements that condemned birth control, Anglican bishops declared that Christians might sometimes legitimately use methods of "conception control" other than abstinence.

LOCALE: London, England
CATEGORIES: Religion, theology, and ethics; social issues and reform; women's issues

KEY FIGURES
William Cosmo Gordon Lang (1864-1945), archbishop of Canterbury, 1928-1942
Pius XI (Ambrogio Damiano Achille Ratti; 1857-1939), Roman Catholic pope, 1922-1939
Marie Stopes (1880-1958), British leader of a movement to promote birth control

SUMMARY OF EVENT
From the beginning of history, some members of every society have sought to control childbearing through con-

traceptive methods. The acceptability of such methods to religious and moral authorities has varied over time. Saint Augustine, the fifth century bishop of Hippo, set the rationale for the official Christian position, which opposed contraception under all circumstances. This position prevailed in Christianity throughout the medieval and early modern periods. How much the rule influenced ordinary people's lives is unknown, but as long as the birthrate stayed high, few questioned it openly.

When the rate of births in Western Europe began to drop at the end of the eighteenth century, religious and political leaders tried to limit the availability of contraceptives. Eventually, restrictive measures such as the so-called Comstock law in the United States (an 1873 measure forbidding the mailing of advertising or information about contraceptives) were enacted in several countries. They had little effect, however, on either birthrates or average family size, both of which continued to decline during the late nineteenth and early twentieth centuries. Meanwhile, a rationale for birth control was advanced by

1930

philosophers Jeremy Bentham and James Mills, who saw it as a way to ensure that families would have the resources to support every child born to them—an argument that surely paralleled many parents' own concerns.

The religious objection to contraception was based on the Catholic Church's model of marriage, which considered procreation to be marriage's primary purpose. Any "artificial" interference with this purpose was held to be wrong. Protestant reformers, including Martin Luther and John Wesley, followed the same model of moral theology, as did the Church of England. In 1908 and 1920, the Lambeth Conferences (meetings of all the bishops of the worldwide Anglican Communion, convened approximately every ten years since 1867 by the archbishop of Canterbury) reaffirmed the Church of England's opposition to birth control.

By the twentieth century, however, a new ideal of marriage—as a partnership for mutual support and companionship between spouses—was coming to replace the procreative-only rationale in much of Western society. Birth control advocates such as Margaret Sanger in the United States and Marie Stopes in England opened clinics, held lecture tours, and publicized the plights of women who wrote to them, desperate for help in limiting their childbearing. Sanger and Stopes framed their appeals in terms of families' emotional as well as material well-being. They argued that the relationship at the heart

of family life, that between husband and wife, cannot flourish if the wife lives in constant fear of unwelcome pregnancies. This argument carried additional weight in an era when divorce was viewed as a burgeoning threat to the family. Stopes, in fact, deliberately launched a major press campaign for contraception in advance of the upcoming 1930 Lambeth Conference. By 1930, with the worldwide Great Depression taking a toll on family life, the old arguments against contraception were inoperative even for many Christians.

The agendas of the Lambeth Conferences cover a wide range of topics, although at each conference one issue is often "hot" enough to draw the lion's share of news coverage. The 1930 conference, for example, issued seventy-five resolutions on subjects ranging from "the unity of the church" to "the ministry of women." The resolutions issued by the Lambeth Conferences take the form of statements that represent the consensus of the bishops' thought and are meant to provide guidance for Christians.

At the time of the 1930 Lambeth Conference, William Cosmo Gordon Lang was the archbishop of Canterbury. A Scot, Lang had been a "slum priest" in his youth and had served twenty years as archbishop of York before moving to Canterbury in 1928. The 1930 conference was his first opportunity to preside over the gathering of bishops, each of whom brought his own experience and national and cultural preoccupations to the deliberations. One of Lang's important aims was the achievement of agreement among the conference participants. Unlike the pope, the archbishop of Canterbury does not have the power to rule on theological or moral matters by fiat.

The 1930 Lambeth Conference put forth twelve resolutions concerning marriage. These were accompanied by a background paper that acknowledged the strong tradition that had made contraception unlawful for Christians. It went on to note that this tradition was not based on anything in the New Testament or on any ruling by an ecumenical council. The paper reaffirmed that the first obligation of married people is to parenthood, but it added that when a birth would cause a mother's health, or the whole family, to suffer unduly, the use of contraceptives is an allowable choice.

The conference adopted Resolution 15, which reflected these points, by a vote of 193 to 67, with 46 participants abstaining. The tone of the resolution was extremely moderate—it confirmed abstinence as the primary option for limiting births and emphasized the need for married partners to make all decisions concerning contraception in the light of Christian conscience.

RESOLUTION 15

Among the twelve resolutions concerning marriage issued by the Lambeth Conference of 1930, Resolution 15 attracted the greatest attention because of its groundbreaking stance on contraception. The full resolution reads as follows:

Where there is clearly felt moral obligation to limit or avoid parenthood, the method must be decided on Christian principles. The primary and obvious method is complete abstinence from intercourse (as far as may be necessary) in a life of discipline and self-control lived in the power of the Holy Spirit. Nevertheless in those cases where there is such a clearly felt moral obligation to limit or avoid parenthood, and where there is a morally sound reason for avoiding complete abstinence, the Conference agrees that other methods may be used, provided that this is done in the light of the same Christian principles. The Conference records its strong condemnation of the use of any methods of conception control from motives of selfishness, luxury, or mere convenience.

Nonetheless, the statement met with a burst of outrage and shock from many religious quarters. This was the first time a Christian group had publicly spoken in favor of contraception. In actuality, world reaction was mixed, but the protests gained more press coverage than did reactions of approval.

On December 31, 1930, the Roman Catholic pontiff, Pope Pius XI, released the encyclical *Casti Connubii*. This papal statement was at least in part a reply to the Lambeth resolution. It restated the traditional Catholic condemnation of "artificial" birth control, calling it a "sin against God," regardless of the couple's circumstances. The terms were thus set for a divide that would continue within Christianity indefinitely, stemming as it did from incompatible basic principles.

Why did the Lambeth resolution come in 1930, when the conference of a decade before still supported the opposite view? Some chance factors may have contributed; for example, most of the bishops attending in 1930 were married men, whereas a decade earlier most attendees were bachelors. The presence of William Inge, dean of St. Paul's Cathedral, an influential churchman, and an enthusiastic supporter of Margaret Sanger, may have helped. However, compassion and sincere conviction surely also played a part. In addition, Anglican and other Protestant clergy were quite aware that, as the conference's background paper said, contraception methods were by then widely used in every class of society. The conference participants likely reasoned that they would look ridiculous if they continued to fulminate against a practice that most parishioners—including the clergy—were going to continue in any case. It is worth noting that only the Roman Catholic Church had a workable mechanism for enforcing a ban on contraception, in the requirement of confession to a priest before communion.

SIGNIFICANCE

As the first statement by a Christian body in support of contraception, the Lambeth Conference's 1930 resolution gave moral support to couples who might have been troubled about using birth control. The resolution showed that Christian teachings, even in the highly charged arena of social and sexual behavior, might be reevaluated under some circumstances. By doing so, it opened the way for further discussion within Christianity on other controversial social issues.

Such discussion was not long in coming. As the century went on, new issues kept challenging traditional church teachings. Divorce, female clergy, abortion, and

homosexuality were among the most problematic of these. The Anglican Communion was not always foremost in dealing with new social mores. Indeed, it came late to the recognition of both divorce and women priests, and not all member national churches accepted these. However, because of the Lambeth Conference's pioneering role in the controversy concerning contraception as well as the Anglican Church's historic position as a church with both Protestant and Catholic heritage, when an Anglican council addressed such issues, the rest of Christianity took note.

—*Emily Alward*

FURTHER READING

McKibbin, Ross. *Classes and Culture: England, 1918-1951.* New York: Oxford University Press, 1998. Topical treatment of British customs and attitudes notes variations among the upper, middle, and working classes. Points out that as the state church, the Church of England had to reflect the basically Protestant outlook of the majority, despite the Anglo-Catholic sentiments of many of its clergy.

McLaren, Angus. *A History of Contraception.* Cambridge, Mass.: Basil Blackwell, 1991. Wide-ranging study by a historian, based largely on documentary evidence. Recognizes the existence of women's networks and folk methods of contraception, but only glancingly. Includes copious source citations.

Maguire, Daniel C., ed. *Sacred Rights: The Case for Contraception and Abortion in World Religions.* New York: Oxford University Press, 2003. Collection of essays by specialists on contraception in various cultures. Especially valuable for its coverage of non-Abrahamic points of view; includes discussion of Hindu, Buddhist, and American Indian traditions.

Tobin, Kathleen A. *The American Debate over Birth Control, 1907-1937.* Jefferson, N.C.: McFarland, 2001. Readable scholarly study documents the shift from disapproval to grudging acceptance of birth control in Protestantism over three decades. Asserts that Roman Catholic outspokenness against birth control worked in reformers' favor by mobilizing latent anti-immigrant and antipapal fears.

SEE ALSO: 1915-1919: National Birth Control League Forms; Oct. 16, 1916: First American Birth Control Clinic Opens; Nov. 11-13, 1921, and Mar. 25-31, 1925: Sanger Organizes Conferences on Birth Control.

1930

August, 1930-1935
BENNETT ERA IN CANADA

Canadians elected a Conservative government after nine years of Liberal rule, but the government, under the leadership of Prime Minister Richard Bedford Bennett, proved unpopular, damaging the reputation of the party and condemning it to another twenty-two years in the minority from 1935 to 1957.

LOCALE: Canada
CATEGORY: Government and politics

KEY FIGURES

Richard Bedford Bennett (1870-1947), prime minister of Canada, 1930-1935
Robert Laird Borden (1854-1937), prime minister of Canada, 1911-1920
Herbert Hoover (1874-1964), president of the United States, 1929-1933
William Lyon Mackenzie King (1874-1950), prime minister of Canada, 1921-1926, 1926-1930, and 1935-1948
Arthur Meighen (1874-1960), prime minister of Canada, 1920-1921 and 1926

SUMMARY OF EVENT

Although Richard Bedford Bennett played an active role in Canadian politics throughout the first third of the twentieth century, historians generally believe that he was an uninspired politician who accomplished little during his five years of service as prime minister of Canada. His ineffectiveness as prime minister made his Conservative Party so unpopular with Canadian voters that the Conservatives would not win another general election in Canada until 1957, when the Conservative John Diefenbaker succeeded the Liberal Louis St. Laurent as prime minister.

Bennett was born in the small town of Hopewell, New Brunswick, in 1870, the son of farmers. He studied law at Dalhousie University in Halifax, Nova Scotia. After his admission to the bar, he moved to Calgary, Alberta, where he became a successful lawyer, and his investments in real estate and various Calgary companies made him a millionaire by the first decade of the twentieth century.

Like his principal political rival, William Lyon Mackenzie King, Bennett never married: Law, business, and politics were Bennett's sole interests. After having served for thirteen years, first in the legislature of the Northwest Territories and then in the legislature in Al-

berta, Bennett was elected in a Calgary district as a Conservative member of Canada's national parliament. He earned the nickname Bonfire Bennett because he often spoke in public at more than two hundred words per minute. Prime ministers Sir Robert Laird Borden and Arthur Meighen both recognized his adminstrative and legal skills. In Borden's government, Bennett served as the director-general of National Service, responsible for encouraging enlistment in the Canadian armed forces during World War I. In 1921, Meighen named Bennett his minister of justice. Bennett was an ethical and effective public servant, which led the Conservatives to conclude that he would lead their party to victory in the general election of 1930.

When the Great Depression began with the U.S. stock market crash on October 29, 1929, the Canadian economy suffered greatly. Businesses failed throughout Canada, and unemployment exceeded 25 percent in many provinces. Canadian voters expected Prime Minister King to do something about this economic and social crisis, but, like U.S. president Herbert Hoover, King believed that the Depression would not last long. Both leaders also felt that the Depression would worsen if their governments increased spending on social programs. Just before the July, 1930, general election, King made an incredible blunder. During debate in the House of Commons, he stated his unwillingness to send even "a five-cent piece" in unemployment assistance to provincial governments controlled by the Conservative Party. During the election campaign of 1930, Conservative candidates repeatedly referred to King's injudicious remark and suggested that a Conservative prime minister such as Bennett, who already had created many jobs through his Calgary companies, would be more successful than the Liberals in dealing with Canada's economic problems. This argument proved persuasive with Canadian voters, who gave the Conservatives a solid majority in the House of Commons.

Once Bennett assumed power in August, it became clear that he did not intend to share it, even with fellow Conservatives. In addition to his responsibilities as prime minister, he assigned to himself the posts of secretary of state for foreign affairs and minister of finance. Canadian political commentators of the day drew cartoons depicting Bennett alone and suggested that he was holding a cabinet meeting with himself. His unwillingness to listen to advice from such respected Conservative leaders as former prime ministers Borden and Meighen caused a precipitous decline in the standing of his party in the minds of Canadian voters. His one solution to the economic depression was to impose stiff tariffs on foreign products imported into Canada in an attempt to protect Canadian companies from foreign competition. Other countries retaliated, and the export of Canadian products decreased significantly. The resulting loss of jobs worsened an already alarming unemployment problem throughout Canada.

During his five years as prime minister, the wealthy Bennett lived in an elegant suite in the Chateau Laurier, Ottawa's finest hotel. He spoke repeatedly of the need for personal initiative and hard work in order to solve Canada's economic problem. A strong work ethic had helped Bennett to become a millionaire, and he firmly believed that it sufficed to cure Canada's economic and social problems. He was opposed philosophically to increased spending on social programs because he believed that the main responsibility of the federal government in Ottawa was to avoid deficits. Although Canadians admired Bennett's integrity and his personal generosity—as shown by his large contributions to charitable organizations— they came to believe that he had no practical ideas for solving Canada's economic and social problems.

Starting in 1932, Bennett spent less time on domestic issues and more on international concerns. At the 1932 Imperial Conference in Ottawa, he persuaded the British government to modify the British North America Act of 1867, which had created Canada as a British dominion, in order to increase Canada's political independence from Great Britain. This was a major accomplishment, but in the minds of Canadian voters, it did not make up for Bennett's unwillingness to recognize the extreme seriousness of the Great Depression. The Liberals, under the leadership of King, argued for the need for increased federal spending to deal with homelessness and unemployment, but such proposals were consistently rejected by the Conservative majority in the House of Commons.

Just before the general election of 1935, Bennett suddenly changed his position and argued in favor of increased federal spending on social programs. He presented his new proposals as a Canadian version of Franklin D. Roosevelt's New Deal, but Canadian voters were suspicious of this sudden change in the domestic program of Bennett's Conservative government. The Liberals, under King, won 173 of the 244 seats in the House of Commons, bringing the Bennett era to an end.

SIGNIFICANCE

Bennett reacted bitterly to his defeat. In 1938, he left Canada permanently for England and transferred his allegiance to Great Britain. Thanks to the help of his friend Lord Beaverbrook, Bennett was appointed to the British House of Lords. When he died in 1947, he had been almost forgotten by Canadians, who never understood why a former prime minister of their country would emigrate from Canada. Canadian historians often have compared Bennett to Herbert Hoover, but the comparison is unfair. Neither Bennett nor Hoover succeeded in ending the economic depression, but Hoover was never considered arrogant, and he remained in the United States after his term in office and continued to serve his country as a respected adviser to both Democratic and Republican presidents.

Canadian prime minister Richard Bedford Bennett (left) with U.S. president Franklin D. Roosevelt and U.S. secretary of state Cordell Hull in 1933. (Library of Congress)

1930

If Bennett was forgotten, however, his effect on his party was not. As party leader for eleven years, five of which he spent as prime minister, Bennett helped to define the image of the Conservative Party for a generation. The nation's reaction to that image is to be seen most clearly in its refusal to elect another Conservative government for more than two decades after Bennett's defeat.

—*Edmund J. Campion*

FURTHER READING

Bothwell, Robert, Ian Drummond, and John English. *Canada, 1900-1945.* Toronto: University of Toronto Press, 1987. A well-documented history of the Great Depression in Canada and Bennett's problems in dealing with economic issues.

Bothwell, Robert, and J. L. Granatstein. *Our Century: The Canadian Journey in the Twentieth Century.* Toronto: McArthur, 2000. Places Bennett's ministry in the context of twentieth century Canadian history. Bibliographic references.

Creighton, Donald. *Canada's First Century, 1867-1967.* Toronto: Macmillan of Canada, 1970. Describes the terrible effects of the Depression in Canada, especially in Alberta and Saskatchewan, which experienced both high unemployment in private industry and drought conditions in farming regions.

Glassford, Larry. *Reaction and Reform: The Politics of the Conservative Party Under R. B. Bennett, 1927-1938.* Toronto: University of Toronto Press, 1992. Contains a thoughtful analysis of the reasons for Bennett's popularity within the Conservative Party during his six years as leader of the opposition and five years as prime minister.

Hutchison, Bruce. *Macdonald to Pearson: The Prime Ministers of Canada.* Don Mills, Ont.: Longmans Canada, 1967. The chapter on Bennett describes his successful career in business and discusses his inability to understand that Canadians wanted him to spend more money on social programs during the Great Depression.

Taylor, M. Brook, and Doug Owram, eds. *Canadian History: A Reader's Guide.* 2 vols. Toronto: University of Toronto Press, 1994. Contains an annotated bibliography of important studies on the domestic and foreign policies of Bennett.

SEE ALSO: July 10, 1920-Sept., 1926: Meighen Era in Canada; 1921-1948: King Era in Canada; June 17, 1930: Hoover Signs the Hawley-Smoot Tariff Act; Sept. 8, 1930: Canada Enacts Depression-Era Relief Legislation; July 21-Aug. 21, 1932: Ottawa Agreements.

August 29, 1930
JAPANESE AMERICAN CITIZENS LEAGUE IS FOUNDED

The Japanese American Citizens League was founded to advocate for the acceptance of Japanese Americans by portraying the members of this population as loyal mainstream Americans. Despite early legislative victories, the league's cooperation with World War II internment and its promotion of assimilation and Americanization rendered it controversial within the Japanese American community.

LOCALE: Seattle, Washington

CATEGORIES: Organizations and institutions; social issues and reform

KEY FIGURES

Clarence Takeya Arai (1901-1964), lawyer who convened the first national meeting of the Japanese American Citizens League (JACL)

Thomas T. Yatabe (1897-1945), cofounder of the San Francisco American Loyalty League and the JACL

James Y. Sakamoto (1903-1955), newspaper publisher and early supporter of the JACL

Tokie Slocum (b. 1895), JACL lobbyist for the Nye-Lea Bill granting citizenship to Issei veterans of World War I

Suma Sugi (b. 1906), first Nisei lobbyist and JACL lobbyist for amendment of the Cable Act

Mike Masaru Masaoka (1915-1991), JACL official and lobbyist who promoted Nisei patriotism

Dillon S. Myer (1891-1982), director of War Relocation Authority during World War II

Wayne Mortimer Collins (1899 or 1900-1974), attorney who defended Japanese American civil rights during and after World War II

SUMMARY OF EVENT

In the words of its own historian, Bill Hosokawa, the Japanese American Citizens League (JACL) originated as "a civic and patriotic organization concerned with the well-being and political and economic progress of American citizens of Japanese ancestry." Responding to widespread anti-Asian sentiment in the United States, the JACL promoted assimilation and Americanization as the most effective way for the Nisei (second-generation Japanese Americans) to gain the approval of the general public. Initially a loose federation of loyalty leagues, the JACL had minimal influence until 1941, when it cooperated with the federal government in carrying out President Franklin D. Roosevelt's Executive Order 9066, which ordered the internment of Japanese Americans in restricted camps during World War II. Because of that cooperation, the league lost the respect of many Japanese Americans. After World War II, the JACL achieved a positive public profile as it lobbied for civil rights legislation; however, it remained controversial for its insistence on accommodation rather than confrontation in the political arena. Now the largest and most influential Japanese American political organization, the JACL must deal with conflicts within its own ranks regarding its basic goals.

The roots of the JACL can be traced to 1918 in San Francisco, when Thomas T. Yatabe and a small group of his college-educated friends met to discuss the future of the Nisei in the United States. Calling themselves the American Loyalty League, they were well aware of the racism blocking the economic progress of Asian immigrants and their families at that time. The Issei (first-generation Japanese Americans) hoped their children, the Nisei, would have opportunities for economic and social advancement. However, as scholar Ronald Takaki has documented, widespread discrimination made it very difficult for them to find employment other than manual or menial labor. Yatabe and his friends were among the fortunate few who had achieved professional success; a recent dental school graduate, Yatabe drew into his circle another dentist, a doctor, and an attorney. They realized that Nisei in general still faced an uncertain future. In their view, the best way to gain acceptance by the general public was to define themselves first and foremost as loyal Americans dedicated to advancement of democratic ideals. Individual enterprise, fair play, and respect for law and order were cornerstones of this philosophy.

In 1922, James Y. Sakamoto founded a similar group, the Seattle Progressive Citizens League. In 1923, Yatabe established the Fresno American Loyalty League, the first statewide league. In 1928, he and Saburo Kido founded the San Francisco New American Citizens League. All of these groups shared a commitment to being "100 percent American" in their outlook. Realizing how much more effective they would be if they joined together, Clarence Takeya Arai, who was elected president of the Seattle

group in 1928, proposed a national meeting of delegates. He envisioned the formation of a national council of Japanese American citizens' leagues that would present a positive public profile. This four-day meeting, called to order by Arai on August 29, 1930, in Seattle, Washington, became the founding convention of the JACL, the first national political organization of Japanese Americans.

The Nisei leadership at the convention represented a special group of college-educated professionals with economically secure, middle-class, urban backgrounds. Mostly in their late twenties and early thirties, they were strikingly unlike the majority of Nisei in the United States at that time, who were younger (with an average age of seventeen) and from rural, working-class backgrounds. Moreover, they were distinctly different from the Issei, who still held political, economic, and social power in local Japanese American communities through the Japanese Associations, which provided legal aid and other services for immigrants.

The Issei usually chose (or were forced by racism) to remain within their own communities; their English skills often were minimal, and their direct interactions with outsiders were limited. Through the Japanese Associations and other local organizations—such as prefectural associations, merchants' and farmers' mutual-aid societies, vernacular newspapers, and Japanese-language schools—the Issei maintained their communities as best they could within the larger American society. The Nisei leadership of the JACL, however, insisted on a completely different approach to finding a secure place for Japanese Americans in the United States. Above all, they stressed assimilation, not ethnicity, underscoring their American aspirations rather than their Japanese heritage.

Therefore, one of the first items of business at the founding convention was to remove the hyphen from "Japanese-American," on the basis that any Japanese aspect of Nisei identity had to be subordinated to the group's American destiny. More than one hundred delegates from five states (Washington, Oregon, California, Illinois, and New York) and the territory of Hawaii approved resolutions asking that Congress address two timely issues: the constitutionality of the 1922 Cable Act and the eligibility of Issei veterans of World War I for citizenship. Suma Sugi became their lobbyist for amendment of the Cable Act, which stripped citizenship from any American woman who married an "alien ineligible to citizenship"; through Sugi's efforts and those of the League of Women Voters, Congress changed the law in 1931, so that citizenship could not be revoked by marriage. Tokie Slocum became the JACL lobbyist for vet-

1930

eran citizenship, which finally was secured by the Nye-Lea Bill in 1935.

SIGNIFICANCE

The Japanese American Citizens League helped pass two important pieces of legislation within five years of its foundation. These laws prevented American women from losing their citizenship if they married Japanese men and allowed Japanese men who had fought for the United States to become U.S. citizens. Despite these accomplishments, however, the JACL had little direct effect on the Japanese American community at large during the first decade of the group's existence. This situation changed dramatically in 1941, when President Roosevelt issued Executive Order 9066, authorizing the internment of Japanese Americans during World War II.

Under Roosevelt's order, the federal government imprisoned virtually all Issei leaders of businesses, schools, and churches on the West Coast. The JACL then took over, directing Japanese Americans not to resist relocation. In fact, the JACL cooperated with the War Relocation Authority (WRA) in identifying community members who might be subversives. Dillon S. Myer, WRA director, worked closely with JACL official Mike Masaru Masaoka in administering the camps—a relationship intensely resented by the majority of Japanese Americans. Attorney Wayne Mortimer Collins, who stood against popular opinion to defend Japanese American civil rights during and after World War II, went so far as to blame the JACL for much of the suffering that internees endured.

The JACL succeeded in building a positive public profile after the war by lobbying for civil rights legislation such as amendment of the McCarran-Walter Act in 1952, thereby guaranteeing the right of all Issei to naturalized citizenship. To this day, however, the JACL has remained a controversial organization, especially because of its conservative political stance. The JACL now must deal with interfactional conflicts between its "old guard" and younger members who question the league's basic goals.

—*Mary Louise Buley-Meissner*

FURTHER READING

Chan, Sucheng. *Asian Americans: An Interpretive History.* Boston: Twayne, 1991. Carefully researched investigation of Asian American socioeconomic, political, educational, and cultural realities. Provides contexts for assessing JACL achievements. Extensive bibliography, index, and black-and-white illustrations.

Drinnon, Richard. *Keeper of Concentration Camps: Dillon S. Myer and American Racism.* Berkeley: University of California Press, 1987. Painstakingly researched revisionist history of Myer's administration of the War Location Authority, including his collaboration with Mike Masaoka and the JACL. Extensive bibliography, index, and black-and-white illustrations.

Hosokawa, Bill. *JACL in Quest of Justice.* New York: William Morrow, 1982. History book commissioned by the JACL to record its accomplishments. Mainly covers the 1930's and 1940's, emphasizing the organization's patriotic nature. Index, black-and-white illustrations.

Ichioka, Yuji. *Before Internment: Essays in Prewar Japanese American History.* Edited by Gordon H. Chang and Eiichiro Azuma. Stanford, Calif.: Stanford University Press, 2006. Detailed study of Japanese Americans in the first four decades of the twentieth century. Bibliographic references and index.

Niiya, Brian, ed. *Japanese American History: An A-to-Z Reference from 1868 to the Present.* New York: Japanese American National Museum and Facts On File, 1993. Invaluable resource including narrative historical overview, chronology of Japanese American history, and dictionary entries for that history. Scholarly research accessible to general audience. Index.

Spickard, Paul R. "The Nisei Assume Power: The Japanese Citizens League, 1941-1942." *Pacific Historical Review* 52, no. 2 (May, 1983): 147-174. Argues that early JACL leadership represented Nisei who seized the historical moment to wrest political, economic, and social power from Issei.

Takahasi, Jere. "Japanese American Responses to Race Relations: The Formation of Nisei Perspectives." *Amerasia Journal* 9, no. 1 (Spring/Summer, 1982): 29-57. Analyzes three major self- and group-concepts developed between 1920 and World War II: cultural bridge, American ideal, and progressive. Discusses JACL history in that context.

Takaki, Ronald. *Strangers from a Different Shore: A History of Asian Americans.* New York: Penguin Books, 1989. Groundbreaking investigation of Asian American contributions to socioeconomic and political development in the United States. Provides contexts for assessing JACL achievements. Index, black-and-white illustrations.

SEE ALSO: Mar. 14, 1907: Gentlemen's Agreement; May 20, 1913: Passage of the First Alien Land Law; Nov. 13, 1922: *Ozawa v. United States.*

September, 1930
AUDEN'S POEMS SPEAK FOR A GENERATION

The publication of W. H. Auden's Poems *in 1930 immediately established him as the spokesman for the interwar generation in Great Britain.*

LOCALE: London, England
CATEGORY: Literature

KEY FIGURES

W. H. Auden (1907-1973), English poet
T. S. Eliot (1888-1965), American poet and essayist
Christopher Isherwood (1904-1986), American writer
C. Day Lewis (1904-1972), Irish poet
Louis MacNeice (1907-1963), Anglo-Irish poet
Stephen Spender (1909-1995), English poet

SUMMARY OF EVENT

The University of Oxford in the late 1920's was a breeding ground for poets. When W. H. Auden entered Christ Church College in 1925, he soon met John Betjeman, C. Day Lewis, and Rex Warner, all of whom would make their marks as poets—and all of whom were impressed by the intelligence and talent of this eighteen-year-old from York. Subsequently, Auden and Day Lewis jointly edited the 1927 edition of *Oxford Poetry*. A year after Auden entered, Louis MacNeice enrolled at Merton College; although he and Auden were not close friends at Oxford, the two would be viewed as confederates a few years later.

Also in 1927, Auden submitted his first book of poems to Faber & Gwyer (later Faber & Faber), the London publisher whose poetry editor, T. S. Eliot, had leaped into prominence a decade before with the publication of his *Prufrock and Other Observations* (1917) and had attained the status of a major modern poet with *The Waste Land* (1922). Eliot rejected the book but, as Auden judged, offered encouragement.

Following his graduation in 1928, Auden issued a book of poems that was privately printed by another Oxford friend, Stephen Spender, then an undergraduate at University College. Thereafter, Auden left England to spend a year in Berlin, where he continued to read and write and incidentally witnessed the profound German unrest of the time. Violence between Communists and the police erupted on May Day, 1929, not far from where Auden lived. "All this time was anxiety at night,/ Shooting and barricade in street," he wrote. Both the violence and the anxiety would become characteristic Auden themes. Returning to England two months later, Auden

found employment in London as a tutor; the following year, he secured a position teaching English and French in a private boys' school in Scotland. Around this time, Faber accepted for publication Auden's *Poems* (1930), a collection totally different from the 1927 submission, although containing some poems from the 1928 effort.

By 1930, the errors of the World War I settlement were becoming obvious. A worldwide economic depression had set in, and "communism," "fascism," and "Nazism" were becoming household words. It was a time when young artists and intellectuals could hardly have escaped preoccupation with social and governmental ills, and Auden's early poetry, despite its obscurity, ushered in a period in which young poets expressed the bitterness and frustration of a failed economic order and—as became increasingly clearer—a failed peace.

According to Spender, Auden did not think of himself as the leader of a movement or as a public figure. In his poetry, he was trying to apply the techniques he had learned from such older poets as Eliot and William Butler Yeats to the composition of poems that spoke to a generation embittered by the economic breakdown, by the drift toward dictatorial regimes in some European countries, and by the complicity of free nations. A number of the poetic movements of recent generations, such as French Symbolism, "art for art's sake," and Imagism, had produced a private poetry of interest mainly to sophisticated coteries; Auden and his companions—particularly Spender, Day Lewis, and MacNeice—wanted to bring poetry within the orbit of people distressed by the political and social evils of the time.

Insofar as Auden and his contemporaries had a literary hero, it was Eliot; despite the older poet's bold new voice, however, he seemed too conservative to be a model. The year of Auden's first commercially published book was also the year of *Ash Wednesday* (1930), the first of Eliot's religious poems signaling his growing Church of England sympathies. Although Auden saw that wasteland imagery effectively symbolized aspects of the modern world, Eliot seemed too detached, too much a part of the older generation that had inflicted that world on those in the new century. To Eliot, the modern city was "unreal"; to Auden (in a poem that came to be called "Family Ghosts"), it was "assaulted." *The Waste Land* is populated by merchants, habitués of pubs, and bored lovers; Auden's 1930 poems are populated by spies, secret agents, and vengeful proletarians. Eliot had heaped scorn on decadents; Auden now warned against enemies.

The 1930 volume contained thirty-nine poems bearing roman numerals rather than titles, a feature that encouraged readers to regard them collectively as a kind of sequence rather than as an assortment from which one might pick and choose favorites. The first lines of the poems often projected urgency, even alarm: "Control of the passes was, he saw, the key" (VIII), "Consider this and in our time" (XXX), "Get there if you can and see the land you once were proud to own" (XXXI), "Doom is dark and deeper than any sea-dingle" (XXXVII). Auden's voice differed distinctly from any heard before in English poetry.

SIGNIFICANCE

It would be a mistake to assume that Auden's book, despite its publisher, made a large impact on the literary establishment of 1930. *The Times Literary Supplement* found the poems "eccentric," and *The Listener* professed an inability to understand them at all. The favorable reviews came from Auden's Oxford friends Spender, MacNeice, and Day Lewis, more or less obscure young men who would, in time, be recognized as among the most important writers of their generation.

The impact on young activists in England, however, was immediate and profound. They took such lines as "Get there if you can and see the land you once were proud to own" as signifying the necessity of transforming a failed society. Auden had articulated in *Poems* what such activists had been feeling all along. Some joined the New Party, formed by a few parliamentary dissidents in February of 1931 in opposition to the Labour Party, which had had little success in dealing with the massive unemployment caused by the 1929 stock market crash. Later that year, *Action*, a weekly radical newspaper, began publication. Auden did not contribute to the paper, but his friend Christopher Isherwood did. Hopes of engineering change by political means faded, however, when the New Party, some of whose spokesmen clearly frightened voters with assorted fascist and communist sentiments, won no seats in the general election of October, 1931.

The young people motivated by Auden were attempting not just political but also social reform. Formal education, seen as denying students the chance of developing free personalities, came under attack. Young radicals scorned marriage as an unnatural and immoral institution; they urged sexual freedom, including homosexual and bisexual relationships.

Auden's second book, *The Orators*, issued by Faber in 1932, created more of a stir in the literary establishment. Almost impossible to describe, the book is a mélange: hortatory prose, poems, diagrams, and journal entries. The first part, heavily indebted to the thought of the recently deceased D. H. Lawrence, consists of four diverse "orations" united by a theme Auden referred to as "the failure of the romantic conception of personality." The second part, which critics found most interesting, expresses the plans of a dedicated but mentally disordered revolutionary leader. The third part consists of six odes that dramatize, ambiguously and often parodically, the sentiment for a leader who can "save" England.

As often happens with the second book of a previously neglected author, the new work drew attention back to the earlier one. Although few critics professed any great understanding of Auden's poetry, they agreed on the brilliance with which he had caught the perspective of his generation. He spoke for an embittered, confused, and worried generation with no settled views but with a sense of the need for action to remedy a civilization sinking deeper into a mire. Faith in democracy, capitalism, and traditional religion were all fast waning; the most committed people were either communists or fas-

W. H. Auden. (© Jill Krementz)

cists. Neither the obscurity of the book nor the apparent incoherence of its author's philosophy were regarded as flaws.

Not only did reviewers for *Criterion* and *The Times Literary Supplement* praise the book, but influential men of letters on both sides of the Atlantic also took notice. Edmund Wilson began advising his literary friends to read *The Orators, Poems*, and Auden's 1933 play *The Dance of Death*. The influential editor of *Scrutiny*, F. R. Leavis, chose to attack Auden's work, a sure sign of Auden's growing importance. In retrospect, much of the criticism both pro and con looks imperceptive or even irrelevant, but it made Auden a very famous man while he was still in his twenties.

Auden was essentially a private man much more interested in doing his own work than in leading a movement, but by force of his intellectual interests he was leading one anyway. No other poet could match his command of Freudian psychology, Marxist political theory, and general scientific knowledge. His formidable poetic vocabulary and the exceptionally wide range of his allusions confounded efforts to interpret individual poems, but collectively, they communicated an indelible impression of a poet fully engaged with the world and society of his time. Isherwood pointed out in 1937 that when Auden contemplated a ruin, it was not that of an ancient abbey such as Sir Walter Scott, William Wordsworth, or even Eliot might celebrate, but of an abandoned factory or mill. Auden's poetry accommodated subject matter outside the ken of other poets.

Many of the young Auden enthusiasts rushed off to support the Republican cause in the Spanish Civil War against General Francisco Franco, and some lost their lives there. Auden himself went to Spain for a few weeks early in 1937, presumably with the intention of driving an ambulance. He attributed the fact of his finding little to do there to his having failed to join the Communist Party.

When, later that year, Auden accepted the King's Medal for Poetry for his 1936 collection of poems *Look, Stranger!* some of his support among young radicals fell away, but his general readership had increased greatly. Also in 1937, Geoffrey Grigson devoted one issue of his *New Verse* (which had been featuring Auden's poetry since its inception in 1932) entirely to articles about Auden.

An assessment of the impact of Auden's early poetry must take into account its effect on the poet. A comparison of Edward Mendelson's edition of *Collected Poems* (1976), including only those poems that Auden wished to

preserve, and the same editor's *The English Auden: Poems, Essays, and Dramatic Writings, 1927-1939* (1977) demonstrates how many early poems Auden later rejected, including some of the incendiary ones that had excited his early champions. Whether dissatisfied with these poems or afraid that they distorted the body of his work by implying a Marxist outlook to which he never committed himself (although he was for a time in the 1930's taken up enthusiastically by Marxist critics), Auden did much throughout the 1930's to modify the impression that his poems of the late 1920's and very early 1930's had made on the reading public.

Finally, in a celebrated 1939 poem, Auden repudiated a conviction that, rightly or wrongly, both friendly and unfriendly critics had widely attributed to him. "In Memory of W. B. Yeats," following within weeks of the death of the great Irish poet, asserts that "poetry makes nothing happen." His point was not that poetry has no effect on people—quite the contrary—but that poetry is a celebration of its subject matter and of language itself. It is not propaganda, not a blueprint for a program.

Like Eliot before him, Auden turned religious, disappointing followers who, for the most part, continued to admire him immensely. He continued to write forcefully for more than three decades, until his death in 1973, but by 1940 he seemed less the leader of a poetic generation than the imposing individual he had always been. Auden settled in the United States in 1939 and acquired U.S. citizenship in 1946, although he served as professor of poetry at Oxford from 1956 to 1961.

—*Robert P. Ellis*

FURTHER READING

Auden, W. H. *The English Auden: Poems, Essays, and Dramatic Writings, 1927-1939.* Edited by Edward Mendelson. New York: Random House, 1977. The works that established Auden in their complete and original versions as edited by Auden's literary executor. Meticulously re-creates a body of work, some of which Auden, from the perspective of his maturity, sought to suppress.

Bozorth, Richard R. *Auden's Games of Knowledge: Poetry and the Meanings of Homosexuality.* New York: Columbia University Press, 2001. Argues that Auden's work was directly influenced by his homosexuality and his efforts to understand how to be a homosexual poet.

Carpenter, Humphrey. *W. H. Auden: A Biography.* Boston: Houghton Mifflin, 1981. Comprehensive and extensively documented life of the poet. Does a thor-

1930

ough job of tracing reviews of, and reactions to, Auden's early poems. Chronological narrative features considerable information about Auden's literary friends. Includes many photographs and a good bibliography.

Fuller, John. *W. H. Auden: A Commentary*. Princeton, N.J.: Princeton University Press, 1998. Designed to help readers understand Auden's poetry and other works by placing them in the context of the times in which they were written, explaining allusions, paraphrasing passages, and providing information on sources, publication history, and so on.

Hynes, Samuel. *The Auden Generation: Literature and Politics in England in the 1930's*. New York: Viking Press, 1976. Scrupulously scholarly and nonpartisan work (in contrast to the Spender and Symons books cited below) with a firm and balanced sense of historical context. Illuminates the often neglected subject of the influences of Auden's contemporaries on his own development.

Spears, Monroe K., ed. *Auden: A Collection of Critical Essays*. Englewood Cliffs, N.J.: Prentice-Hall, 1964. Excellent essays include Christopher Isherwood's "Some Notes on Auden's Early Poetry" and G. S. Fraser's "The Career of W. H. Auden." Isherwood's essay, originally printed in Geoffrey Grigson's 1937 Auden issue of *New Verse*, represents the best in 1930's criticism of Auden.

Spender, Stephen. *The Thirties and After: Poetry, Politics, People, 1933-1970*. New York: Random House, 1978. Collection of Spender's essays includes reminiscences of Auden and Louis MacNeice as well as somewhat edited versions of Spender's early pronouncements on the relationship between poetry and revolutionary thought and on his espousal of communism. The final essay is the memorial address delivered at Oxford in 1973.

Symons, Julian. *The Thirties: A Dream Revolved*. 1960. Reprint. North Yorkshire, England: House of Stratus, 2001. Quotes from a variety of literary and journalistic sources, many of them leftist, and comments on them to convey a sense of the intellectual, social, and political background of a decade in which the author himself was young, leftist, and thoroughly imbued with Auden's poetry. Deftly evokes the period with well-chosen photographs of social, artistic, and theatrical subjects.

SEE ALSO: 1911-1923: Rilke's *Duino Elegies* Redefines Poetics; Oct., 1912: Harriet Monroe Founds *Poetry* Magazine; 1917: Yeats Publishes *The Wild Swans at Coole*; 1922: Eliot Publishes *The Waste Land*; Feb., 1930: Crane Publishes *The Bridge*.

September 8, 1930
CANADA ENACTS DEPRESSION-ERA RELIEF LEGISLATION

The Canadian government sought relief from the Great Depression by implementing new policies aimed at improving the economy and putting people back to work.

LOCALE: Canada
CATEGORIES: Trade and commerce; diplomacy and international relations

KEY FIGURES

Richard Bedford Bennett (1870-1947), prime minister of Canada, 1930-1935
William Lyon Mackenzie King (1874-1950), prime minister of Canada, 1921-1926, 1926-1930, and 1935-1948
Herbert Hoover (1874-1964), president of the United States, 1929-1933
Edward Beatty (1877-1943), president of the Canadian Pacific Railroad

SUMMARY OF EVENT

On September 8, 1930, the Canadian parliament passed new tariff laws designed to help Canada weather what became the Great Depression. The laws were designed to exclude the importation into Canada of types of articles already being produced domestically, as well as products that Canadians might produce in the future. The 1930 laws by themselves were not critical; they were merely the first in a series of tariff laws passed between 1930 and 1932. The cumulative effect of these laws mitigated the Depression somewhat. For the most part, however, it was not until the onset of World War II that Canada recovered from the Depression.

Virtually every aspect of the Canadian economy went into a long-term tailspin starting in 1929. The worldwide economic downturn had a particularly adverse effect on the country's balance of trade, because Canada was highly dependent on exports to fuel its economy. In fact, prior to the stock market crash in 1929, exports accounted for more than one-third of the country's national income. The fact that many foreign countries, most notably the United States, reacted to their individual economic problems by curbing imports and raising tariffs hurt Canada enormously. Entire export-driven Canadian industries shut down. For example, industries based on lumber and pulp, commercial fishing, and mining practically ceased operations, throwing thousands of employees out of work. These displaced people flocked to the cities looking for work, only to meet competition from thousands of unemployed factory workers. To make matters worse, prices in the Canadian wheat market collapsed.

Price was only one of the farmers' worries, however, as nature compounded their problems. A drought that affected Canada for almost ten years began around 1930. Making matters worse, clouds of grasshoppers destroyed the little grain that grew. The drought and the grasshoppers caused wheat to shrivel, cattle to die, and wind to pick up dirt and blow it in raging dust storms that could be seen for hundreds of miles.

The Canadian government had few, if any, social programs in place, in part because of constitutional limitations that prohibited the federal government from enacting unemployment insurance legislation. Paradoxically, judicial decisions in the 1920's left the provinces with heavy responsibilities in social arenas and the federal government with access to the largest sources of revenue. This situation presented a quandary for Canada throughout the 1930's. A small old-age pension fund scheme had been started in 1927, but little else existed to help the unemployed, sick, or destitute. Out-of-work Canadians had to rely on the charity of private and public institutions for support, and that was something to which Canadians simply were not accustomed.

Even though the Depression affected the entire country, citizens had to deal with it as best they could on a community-by-community basis. Even the provincial governments found themselves on the verge of bankruptcy. In Saskatchewan, for example, two-thirds of the province's rural population was forced to seek public assistance. More than 95 percent of the province's rural municipalities were at the brink of bankruptcy, and the provincial government could offer very little relief. Farmers lined up for a monthly allowance of flour and money to buy other food. As Canadians dependent on small-scale relief provided by communities and private charities searched desperately for a better answer, Richard Bedford Bennett offered some solutions.

Bennett, a self-made multimillionaire and member of the Conservative Party, was a New Brunswick native who had made his fortune as a lawyer and businessman, first in western Canada and later in the central section of the country. He became prime minister in 1930. Backed by worried eastern Canadian industrialists, Bennett campaigned on the promise that he would provide tariff protection for industry and badly needed jobs for workers. He also promised farmers that he would help Canada blast its way into the markets of the world. Once elected, he made good on his first promise, raising protective tariffs. Bennett moved partly to combat similar tariffs instituted in the United States, in particular the Hawley-Smoot Tariff Act of 1930, which imposed the highest tariffs in U.S. history. That tariff made the devaluation of foreign currencies almost inevitable and made it impossible for European nations to earn the dollars they needed to continue making payments on their World War I debts to the United States. These conditions helped bring on financial collapse in Europe in 1931. As Canada was inextricably tied to England as a member of the British Empire, the U.S. actions had a major impact on the Canadian economy.

Economists had pointed out to President Herbert Hoover all the drawbacks of the Hawley-Smoot Tariff. They suggested that the act would cause higher prices for consumers, destroy international trade, and make it difficult, it not impossible, for other countries to sell their goods to the United States. Additionally, they claimed, it would not help U.S. farmers, who were producing great surpluses at the time. Hoover ignored a petition, signed by a thousand economists, that asked him to refuse to sign the act.

Hoover believed that he could use the flexible provision the Hawley-Smoot Act contained to raise or lower rates up to 50 percent, on advice of the Tariff Commission. Other countries saw no alternative but to implement high tariffs of their own, the route Bennett chose. Bennett based his 1930 campaign for prime minister in part on the need for new tariffs. The Canadian Conservative Party argued that higher levels of protection were needed to preserve the Canadian market for Canadian businesses until other countries, primarily the United States, lowered their tariffs. The incumbent Liberals, on the other hand, led by longtime prime minister William Lyon Mackenzie King, advocated tariff adjustments designed to reduce duties on a few items while raising them on others. The difference in the two parties' approaches to protectionism had a major impact on the outcome of the election.

1930

Once elected, Bennett wasted little time implementing his protectionist program. He placed new duties on agricultural products and granted increased protection to virtually every industry of any importance. Overall, Bennett raised the general tariff level almost 50 percent. He also employed a series of special devices such as arbitrary valuations for customs purposes and arbitrary fixing of exchange rates in the case of depreciated foreign currencies. The end result was the most sweeping change ever in the Canadian tariff system. The results, however, were mixed.

The protectionist policy led to a heavy reduction in imports and increased Canadian manufacturers' share of the domestic market, which eased unemployment. It did little, however, to increase domestic purchasing power and imposed higher costs on large groups of both producers and consumers. The tariff was of little help to the country's basic producers unless used not as a barrier but as a lever to force trade concessions from other countries. Unfortunately for the Canadian government, such concessions were hard to come by, as most nations were experiencing economic downturns of their own. Bennett hoped, however, that protectionism would stimulate the Canadian economy in the short run. He was less concerned about the long term.

In general, Canadians did not believe the financial downturn prompted by the 1929 stock market crash would last long. For example, Edward Beatty, president of the Canadian Pacific Railroad, suggested that once the temporary adverse effects of economic problems had run their course, Canadian economic conditions would be more soundly based, with the way cleared for a vigorous forward movement. The economic downturn proved to be much more than temporary. Beatty, like many Canadians, failed to recognize just how widespread the problem was. Perhaps the country's economy could have survived with minimal disruption if only one major sector had been hit. Because both the industrial and agricultural sectors were affected at the same time, the country as a whole suffered.

Grains, particularly wheat, provided Canada with one of its largest overseas markets in the early 1920's. By the mid-1920's, however, most European countries, in an effort to save their own farmers, began to raise tariffs. To make matters worse for Canadians, the Soviet Union began exporting wheat again after a suspension that began during World War I. The combination of protective tariffs and the Soviet Union's reentry into the wheat exporting business drove wheat prices down and presaged problems for Canadian farmers. Prices dropped by more than half in some cases.

Canadian manufacturers were not as dependent on exports as were farmers; nevertheless, they could not absorb price reductions of more than half for pulp, paper, and mining products that beset them between 1929 and 1933. These four years were particularly trying as export markets shrank dramatically in the face of increasing tariffs imposed by other countries. Shrinking exports led to decreased purchasing power in Canada. Manufacturers cut back on production and started laying off their workers.

By the summer of 1930, more than 390,000 people were out of work in Canada, nearly 13 percent of the country's labor force. The percentage doubled by 1933 and remained high for the rest of the decade; it returned to the 1933 level only once before 1939. A concomitant drop in income occurred: Between 1928 and 1933, Canadians' annual per-capita income declined by 48 percent, from $471 to $247. The highest declines occurred in the prairie wheat belt. For example, Saskatchewan's per-capita income dropped by 72 percent, Alberta's by 61 percent, and Manitoba's by 49 percent.

SIGNIFICANCE

In addition to higher tariffs, Bennett established work camps in British Columbia to control moving gangs of unemployed men who were "riding the rails" across the country in search of work. Thousands of these men joined the Communist-sponsored Relief Camp Workers' Union and began to march to Ottawa, the nation's capital, to seek relief from the chronic unemployment plaguing the country. When they reached Regina, Saskatchewan, Royal Canadian Mounted Police arrested the group's leaders. In the ensuing riot, one police officer was killed and several others were wounded. That effectively ended the work camp experience.

Bennett increased payments to the provinces for the relief of unemployment and sponsored legislation establishing the Bank of Canada, which added an important weapon to the central government's fiscal and monetary policy arsenal. On the international front, he worked with Great Britain and other countries in the British Empire to establish an imperial free trading area protected against the rest of the world. He achieved some success in this attempt, securing the Ottawa Agreements in 1932, but nowhere near enough to right the foundering Canadian economy.

There were a few signs of abatement in the world's economic problems in the mid-1930's. In Canada, between 1932 and 1937, the wholesale price index rose by nearly one-third, and exports increased from $500 million to more than $1 billion. The minor improvements were not enough, and Bennett continued to seek ways to right the country's economy.

As the Depression dragged on, Bennett revised his strategies. In 1935, without consulting his cabinet, he went on the radio to talk directly to Canadians. He revealed a new approach to ending the economic downturn, one patterned after Franklin D. Roosevelt's New Deal. After addressing the nation, he presented Parliament with a package of hastily prepared legislation that provided for unemployment insurance, minimum wages and maximum hours for work, legislation for fair trade, and the establishment of a grain board to regulate prices. Unfortunately for Bennett, many Canadians thought of the measures as too little, too late. Later that year, Canadians ousted Bennett from office and returned William Lyon Mackenzie King.

King had no immediate easy answers either. He did refer Bennett's new social legislation to the Canadian Supreme Court, which determined that most of its important provisions were unconstitutional. King's government ratified a new trade agreement with the United States, the negotiation of which Bennett's Conservatives had initiated. King did not push for any new social initiatives, but he did succeed in winning the approval of the provinces for a constitutional amendment giving the federal government the power to enact unemployment insurance legislation.

Canada's economy did not improve as the 1930's dragged on; in 1937, it worsened as a new depression materialized. The amount of personal suffering and the number of institutional bankruptcies grew. In response, King appointed the Royal Commission on Dominion-Provincial Relations, also known as the Rowell-Sirois Commission, to examine the distribution of constitutional powers and the financial arrangements of the federal system. The commission's main task was to find a new constitutional equilibrium that would distribute revenues and responsibilities in conformity with the needs of an industrial society. It took three years for the commission to make recommendations, which were ultimately rejected by the larger provinces in 1940.

In the interim, under King's guidance, the federal government became more active in setting up social programs. By 1938, it was financing a variety of work projects, supporting a costly training program for youth, and contributing substantial subsidies to house building and other construction projects. By themselves, neither the increased number of social programs nor the Rowell-Sirois Commission's efforts had much impact on ending

the Depression. Government programs did not bring an end to the lengthy Depression; the end came only when war broke out again.

The onset of World War II did for Canada what nothing else had been able to: It spurred the economy and created a demand for Canadian products. Bennett and King perhaps had done the best they could under trying circumstances, but the depth of the Depression stymied them as much as it did their counterparts throughout the world. The war may not have been the solution that most governments wanted, but it did put the worldwide economy back on track. Canada regained its economic strength and put to rest the most frustrating decade in its history.

—*Arthur G. Sharp*

FURTHER READING

Brebner, John Bartlett. *Canada: A Modern History*. Rev. ed. Ann Arbor: University of Michigan Press, 1970. A comprehensive, readable history of Canada.

Brown, Craig, ed. *The Illustrated History of Canada*. 4th ed. Toronto: Key Porter Books, 2003. Easy-to-follow history of Canada features numerous photographs and other illustrations.

Creighton, Donald Grant. *Dominion of the North: A History of Canada*. Rev. ed. Toronto: Macmillan of Canada, 1972. Focuses on significant events in Canadian history. Provides useful context and background for the events of the Depression years.

McInnis, Edgar. *Canada: A Political and Social History*. 4th ed. New York: Holt, Rinehart and Winston, 1982. Focuses on the sociological impacts of historical events in Canada.

McMenemy, John. *The Language of Canadian Politics: A Guide to Important Terms and Concepts*. 3d ed. Waterloo, Ont.: Wilfrid Laurier University Press, 2001. Collection of more than five hundred brief essays on a wide range of topics related to the Canadian system of government, Canadian political history, Canadian laws and legal history, and more.

Riendeau, Roger. *A Brief History of Canada*. 2d rev. ed. New York: Facts On File, 2006. Concise history includes discussion of Canada's difficulties during the Great Depression.

SEE ALSO: 1921-1948: King Era in Canada; June 17, 1930: Hoover Signs the Hawley-Smoot Tariff Act; Aug., 1930-1935: Bennett Era in Canada; Dec. 11, 1931: Formation of the British Commonwealth of Nations; July 21-Aug. 21, 1932: Ottawa Agreements; Aug. 1, 1932: Canada's First Major Socialist Movement; Nov. 11, 1936: Reciprocal Trade Act.

1930

September 27, 1930
FIRST GRAND SLAM OF GOLF

When amateur golfer Bobby Jones won all four of the world's major golf tournaments in a single year, he became a popular national hero in the United States, and coverage of his success helped increase the popularity of recreational golf throughout the world.

LOCALE: St. Andrews, Scotland; Hoylake, England; Edina, Minnesota; Ardmore, Pennsylvania
CATEGORY: Sports

KEY FIGURE
Bobby Jones (1902-1971), American amateur golfer

SUMMARY OF EVENT
In the history of competitive golf, 1930 marked the first ever "grand slam," the winning of all four of the world's major golf championships in the same calendar year by a single player. The tournaments considered to be part of the grand slam have changed over time. In 1930, they were the British Amateur, the British Open, the United States Open, and the United States Amateur championships, and American amateur golfer Bobby Jones won all four.

Golf historians believe that Jones knew 1930 would offer him his only chance to achieve wins in all four major tournaments during a single year. Traveling across the Atlantic Ocean by ocean liner was time-consuming and expensive. The Walker Cup amateur team competition between the United States and Great Britain was held that spring in England, so the United States Golf Association named Jones to be its playing captain and, therefore, paid his travel expenses. The trip gave Jones a chance to fine-tune his skills and then extend his stay for the British Amateur and the British Open in May and June as well as to lead the American side to victory in the Walker Cup competition.

The first tournament of Jones's grand slam was the British Amateur Championship, held May 26-31 at the famous Old Course at St. Andrews in Scotland. It was a match play competition; that is, the scores of individual players were compared on each individual golf hole, with the overall winner being the player who won the greatest number of holes. Jones won matches against eight different players, three of them by a narrow one-up margin, and defeated the defending British Amateur champion, Cyril Tolley, in the fourth match. In the thirty-sixth hole final match, Jones closed out the 1923 champion, Roger Wethered, by a clear margin with five holes left to play.

The second tournament of the grand slam was the Open Championship of the British Isles, commonly known as the British Open, held June 18-20 at the Royal Liverpool Golf Club in Hoylake, England. Jones did not play well in the qualifying competition but still qualified to play. After the first two eighteen-hole rounds of the tournament, Jones was in first place by one shot, and after the third eighteen-hole round he was one shot behind Archie Compton. Jones won the tournament after the fourth round by a slim two-shot margin over Macdonald Smith and Leo Diegel. It was his third British Open title in four tries, a very noteworthy achievement. On July 2, on his return to the United States after winning the two British championships, Jones was celebrated in a ticker-tape parade through Manhattan streets.

The grand slam's third tournament was the U.S. Open Championship, held July 10-12 at the Interlachen Country Club at Edina, Minnesota. Jones was ahead of the field by five shots after the third eighteen-hole round and won the tournament by a two-shot margin over Macdonald Smith. It was a nervous final eighteen holes for Jones; he scored poorly on the seventeenth hole and then made a remarkable forty-foot putt for a birdie (a score of one stroke less than par) on the eighteenth hole.

By this time, the world media and the golfing world were intensely following Jones's quest for the grand slam. The fourth and final tournament that would complete his accomplishment was the U.S. Amateur Championship, held September 22-27 at the Merion Cricket Club in Ardmore, Pennsylvania. Jones won the match play tournament in rather convincing fashion. He finished the two qualifying rounds in first place, and he won his first two match play victories by a comfortable five-hole margin, first defeating the Canadian Amateur champion, Sandy Sommerville. The last three matches, consisting of thirty-six holes each, were a severe test of endurance for Jones. He won by six holes in the final eight-player quarterfinal and then defeated Jess Sweetster by nine holes in the four-player semifinal. During the last match, Jones defeated Eugene Homans, who conceded at the twenty-ninth hole.

Newspaper accounts of the final tournament of the grand slam emphasized the huge crowds of spectators lining the fairways of each hole played by Jones and the presence of a security guard detail to protect him from being engulfed by joyous fans at the completion of his victory. O. B. Keeler, a writer for the *Atlanta Journal*

Bobby Jones. (Library of Congress)

golf. He played golf competitively only from age fourteen to age twenty-eight, but during those fourteen years he won thirteen major championships: four U.S. Opens, three British Opens, five U.S. Amateurs, and one British Amateur. In 1926, he was the first player ever to win the U.S. and British Open tournaments in the same year.

Jones practiced law and pursued business dealings from 1928 onward, and after he retired from competitive golf he was paid about $250,000 to make a series of golf instructional films. With A. G. Spalding and Company, he designed and manufactured the first set of matched golf clubs. He was among the thirteen original members inducted into the World Golf Hall of Fame in 1974.

SIGNIFICANCE

By 1930, golf was rapidly evolving into a sport dominated by professional players. Jones's chief rivals in the "open" championships (meaning that they were open to both amateur and professional players) were professionals, including the great Walter Hagen. Many historians believe that the publicity generated by Jones's accomplishments in these tournaments helped to increase the popularity of recreational golf, leading to greater numbers of players, more courses, and mass production of equipment.

Jones was the primary founder of the Masters golf tournament at the Augusta National Golf Club in 1933, a tournament that later became part of golf's grand slam. Jones retired from competitive golf in 1931, and by 1932 he had helped design and build the Augusta club. Jones served as the host of the Masters all the way through 1968, personally presenting the ceremonial green jacket to the winner each year.

—*Alan Prescott Peterson*

newspaper in Atlanta, Georgia, accompanied Jones throughout his adult golf career. Keeler is credited with first using the phrase "grand slam" to describe the winning of all four major tournaments; he also referred to the accomplishment as the "impregnable quadrilateral."

Most golf historians agree that Jones's grand slam stands as the greatest achievement in golf history because Jones truly was an amateur player, balancing a career in law and business with family responsibilities and competitive golf. He played in an era when amateur sport was more esteemed than professional sports. After he completed the grand slam, Jones appeared on the cover of *Time* magazine and received another New York City ticker-tape parade.

Jones had a truly remarkable career in competitive

FURTHER READING

Frost, Mark. *The Grand Slam: Bobby Jones, America, and the Story of Golf.* New York: Hyperion, 2004. Very detailed, research-based biography relies on thorough analysis of newspaper accounts and first-person accounts. Provides readers with a sense of the significance of Jones's accomplishment and the degree of his fame. Includes photographs.

1930

Jones, Bobby. *How I Play Golf* [DVD]. Burbank, Calif.: Warner Bros., 2004. After he retired from competitive golf, Jones made a series of instructional films that were shown in movie theaters. These are now available in DVD format.

Lewis, Catherine M. *Bobby Jones and the Quest for the Grand Slam.* Chicago: Triumph Books, 2005. Biography places Jones's golfing accomplishments within the context of his life and times. Includes bibliography and index.

Rapoport, Ron. *The Immortal Bobby: Bobby Jones and the Golden Age of Golf.* New York: John Wiley & Sons, 2005. Carefully researched and readable guide to Jones's life and accomplishments. Includes bibliography and index.

SEE ALSO: Jan., 1901: American Bowling Club Hosts Its First Tournament; June, 1922: New Wimbledon Tennis Stadium Is Dedicated; Sept. 17, 1938: First Grand Slam of Tennis.

December, 1930
DU PONT INTRODUCES FREON

In response to a growing need for such chemicals, the Du Pont Corporation introduced a class of nontoxic, nonflammable chemicals called chlorofluorocarbons for use as refrigerants, which they trademarked under the name Freon. Despite the advance in health and safety that Freon seemed to represent, it later was shown to harm the earth's ozone shield, potentially creating a greater long-term hazard than did the more toxic chemicals it replaced.

LOCALE: Wilmington, Delaware

CATEGORIES: Environmental issues; inventions; science and technology; earth science

KEY FIGURES

Thomas Midgley, Jr. (1889-1944), engineer, scientist, and president of the American Chemical Society

Charles Franklin Kettering (1876-1958), American engineer and automotive pioneer

Albert Leon Henne (1901-1967), chemistry professor at Ohio State University

F. Sherwood Rowland (b. 1927), chemistry professor at the University of California at Irvine

Richard S. Stolarski (fl. late twentieth century), physicist at the University of Michigan

SUMMARY OF EVENT

The history of mechanical refrigerators can be traced to the late eighteenth century, but the earliest devices relied on steam power and were large and cumbersome. Nevertheless, some refrigerators were used for ice-making and for industrial cooling in the nineteenth century. The source of the cooling effect was the evaporation of a volatile substance (the "refrigerant") in a closed system. The evaporation cooled saltwater or air that circulated around the outside of the closed system. In order to achieve continuous cooling, the refrigerant would be reliquefied by a compressor, with the accompanying heat being rejected to the outside through air cooling. In effect, the refrigerator acted to pump heat from the interior of the unit to the outside, causing its surroundings to become warmer and creating a cold zone inside.

Household refrigerators became practical after electricity and small electrical motors became available, eliminating the need for steam power. In 1913, the first home refrigerator went on sale in the United States. It used sulfur dioxide as a refrigerant, but it required the owner to keep a compressor in the cellar; the compressor would be connected by tubes to an icebox upstairs in the kitchen. This arrangement was considered necessary because of the possibility of leakage of obnoxious fumes from the compressor. In the 1920's, some household refrigerators appeared in which ammonia—a toxic, flammable substance—was used as a refrigerant. These appliances were successful enough to show that an enormous potential market existed, but it was necessary for manufacturers to achieve greater safety and reliability before refrigerators could become commonplace.

In response to this need, Charles Franklin Kettering, an executive at General Motors Corporation, asked Thomas Midgley, Jr., an engineer, to look into the development of a safe, effective refrigerant for use in consumer products. After talking to Lester Keilholtz, the chief engineer at the Frigidaire Corporation, Midgley went to work in the library, along with coworkers Albert Leon Henne and Robert MacNary. They became familiar with the physical and chemical properties of the known useful refrigerants described in chemical and engineering literature. All such materials contained one or more of the elements carbon, hydrogen, oxygen, or nitrogen, elements that occur in the first part of the chemist's periodic table. The element fluorine, adjacent to oxygen in the periodic table, was known to form many compounds with low boiling points that might be suitable refrigerants. The possible toxicity of such compounds was of concern, however, as several fluorine compounds, such as hydrogen fluoride, are hazardous to breathe.

At the time of Midgley's work, organic fluorine compounds were not yet available commercially, but they could be made in the laboratory by fluorination procedures worked out by the Belgian fluorine pioneer Frédéric Swarts. Swarts's methods depended on the replacement of chlorine atoms in carbon-chlorine compounds by fluorine through the use of metal fluorides, such as antimony trifluoride, as fluorine carriers. Midgley obtained several bottles of antimony trifluoride, which he later described as probably the entire U.S. supply of the compound. He did not know that only one of the samples was pure and free of water. Fortunately, and quite by accident, the pure sample was used in the first fluorocarbon preparation and afforded a pure, nontoxic fluorocarbon, harmless to experimental animals. The less-pure antimony fluoride released toxic gases in addition to the desired fluorocarbon.

Encouraged by the preliminary experiment, Midgley and Henne made a thorough study of possible organic fluorides for use as refrigerants, and they published their findings in 1930. General Motors and the Du Pont Corporation formed a new company, Kinetic Chemicals, to manufacture dichlorodifluoromethane (Freon 12), and production began in December, 1930. The company trademarked the term Freon, which came to refer to a category of fluorocarbons or chlorofluorocarbons used as refrigerants, rather than to a particular chemical. During 1931, more than one million pounds of Freon 12 were sold. In 1935, a U.S. patent was granted to General Motors for the use of Freon as a refrigerant.

SIGNIFICANCE

The increasing production and use of chlorofluorocarbons (CFCs) had many and diverse effects in the United States. An enormous increase in sales of home refrigerators began in the 1930's and escalated after World War II. According to one source, there were 35 million households with refrigerators by 1950 and 51 million by 1960. The use of CFCs in these refrigerators made them more appealing to the consumer. Later, home and automobile air conditioners were also sold in vast numbers. The convenience and portability of these appliances re-

sulted partly from the use of CFC refrigerants.

At major chemical companies such as Du Pont, chemists began to foresee other uses for CFCs. Soon, CFC solvents were developed and became increasingly important in electronic applications, such as the removal of grease from printed circuits. Volatile fluorocarbons and chlorofluorocarbons began to be used as aerosol propellants. In this application, their low toxicity and lack of flammability gave them an advantage over such propellants as butane or nitrous oxide. Foam plastic manufacturers began to use fluorocarbon gases as "blowing agents" to create bubbles in plastic. Bromine-containing fluorocarbons were developed for use as fire-extinguishing materials such as Halon. As the uses of fluorocarbons expanded, more corporations began to manufacture them, not only in the United States but also in Europe and Japan. By 1969, production of fluorocarbons reached 700 million pounds, of which about half was dichlorodifluoromethane. By 1974, world production of fluorocarbons was almost 2 billion pounds. This expansion was not an unmixed blessing, as events were to show. The fluorocarbons, CFCs, Freons, and their chemical cousins that were being so copiously manufactured were ultimately escaping into the atmosphere.

In June, 1974, F. Sherwood Rowland and M. Molina published a paper in the British journal *Nature* describing the possible fate of CFCs in the earth's atmosphere. They theorized that, after diffusing slowly into the stratosphere, CFCs would undergo irradiation by highly energetic ultraviolet light from the Sun. This radiation, upon absorption by a CFC molecule, would produce a temperature increase and, at the same time, would cause some CFC molecules to break up, forming highly reactive chlorine atoms. Earlier in 1974, Richard S. Stolarski and Ralph J. Cicerone had shown that chlorine atoms from rocket exhaust could cause ozone decomposition in the stratosphere.

The stratosphere, an atmospheric layer of about ten to fifty kilometers in altitude, is the site of the earth's protective ozone layer. Ozone is a form of oxygen containing three oxygen atoms rather than the two atoms present in ordinary oxygen. Ozone exists at low pressures and is continually forming and decomposing under the influence of solar radiation and through encounters with other constituents of the atmosphere. Although ozone is highly irritating and toxic and is regarded as a threat to health when it occurs near the earth's surface, it has at least two beneficial effects when in its proper concentration and location in the stratosphere: It absorbs potentially dangerous ultraviolet radiation that might otherwise pene-

1930

trate to the earth's surface, and it helps to regulate the temperature of the stratosphere.

Health effects of ultraviolet radiation include damage to skin and eyes, damage that can lead to skin cancer and cataracts. Although these effects are well known, it is difficult or impossible to predict the increased incidence of cancer or cataracts as a function of solar ultraviolet radiation. The effects are of a statistical nature, and many other environmental and hereditary factors may be involved in the incidence of such problems. Most scientists agree that degradation of the ozone layer presents a health hazard, but estimates of the magnitude of the threat vary widely.

The story of the CFCs has shown the importance of considering the long-term environmental effects of each new product, particularly those that are manufactured and discarded in large quantities. The unique international cooperation shown in response to the threat to the ozone layer has been based on the recognition that, as the atmosphere has no political boundaries, the rules to protect it must also transcend such distinctions.

—*John R. Phillips*

FURTHER READING

Benedick, Richard E. *Ozone Diplomacy: New Directions in Safeguarding the Planet.* Cambridge, Mass.: Harvard University Press, 1991. Presents the text and a list of signers of the Montreal Protocol of 1987 and a detailed account of the negotiations that led to it. Authored by the head U.S. negotiator.

Biddle, Wayne. *A Field Guide to the Invisible.* New York: Henry Holt, 1998. Discussion of the practical effects of fifty-eight unseeable entities, including Freon. Other entities discussed range from radio waves to bad breath to God. Bibliographic references and index.

Derra, Skip. "CFC's: No Easy Solutions." *Research and Development* 32 (May, 1990): 56-66. The applications of CFCs are discussed, and attempts to find replacements are outlined. Provides a list that shows the uses of individual CFCs and their effects on the ozone layer. Includes an account of steps being taken in various countries toward compliance with the Montreal Protocol.

Gillespie, Alexander. *Climate Change, Ozone Depletion, and Air Pollution: Legal Commentaries Within the Context of Science and Policy.* Boston: M. Nijhoff, 2006. Extensive legal analysis of the chemical threat to the ozone layer, synthesizing scientific knowledge on the subject with policy analysis. Bibliographic references and index.

Gribbin, John. *The Hole in the Sky.* Rev. ed. New York: Bantam Books, 1993. An introduction to the ozone shield and its problems. Describes the discovery of the Antarctic ozone hole.

Midgley, T. M., Jr. "From the Periodic Table to Production." *Industrial and Engineering Chemistry* 29 (1937): 241-244. Midgley gives a vivid account of the events leading up to the development of chlorofluorocarbon refrigerants. This account is either paraphrased or quoted from in most historical works that treat the subject.

Midgley, Thomas, and A. L. Henne. "Organic Fluorides as Refrigerants." *Industrial and Engineering Chemistry* 22 (May, 1930): 542-548. Originally read as a paper at a 1930 meeting of the American Chemical Society, this paper announces the development of CFCs as refrigerants.

Roan, Sharon. *The Ozone Crisis: The Fifteen-Year Evolution of a Sudden Global Emergency.* New York: John Wiley & Sons, 1989. Follows the complicated story of the ozone crisis, starting from the Rowland-Molina publication of 1974. All the political maneuverings and scientific evidence are recounted in a historical-journalistic approach.

Rowland, F. Sherwood. "Stratospheric Ozone in the Twenty-first Century: The Chlorofluorocarbon Problem." *Environmental Science and Technology* 25 (April, 1991): 622-628. Clear, well-illustrated article that discusses the Antarctic ozone hole and the role of CFCs and ozone in the greenhouse effect.

Schwartz, A. Truman, et al. *Chemistry in Context.* Dubuque, Iowa: William C. Brown, 1994. The first three chapters of this college-level chemistry book deal with the earth's atmosphere. Discusses global warming and the effects of CFCs on the ozone layer. Basic scientific background for an understanding of atmospheric chemistry. Color illustrations and list of references.

Stolarski, Richard S. "The Antarctic Ozone Hole." *Scientific American* 258 (January, 1988): 30-36. Describes how ice crystals in stratospheric clouds may facilitate the breakdown of chlorine compounds, leading to ozone destruction. Considers whether the ozone hole of 1984 was an anomaly or whether such holes might reappear in the Antarctic and perhaps elsewhere.

SEE ALSO: 1917: Birdseye Invents Quick-Frozen Foods; Apr., 1930: Midgley Introduces Dichlorodifluoromethane as a Refrigerant Gas.

December 11, 1930
BANK OF UNITED STATES FAILS

The failure of the Bank of United States aggravated the country's slide into the Great Depression and strengthened pressures to reform banking and the securities business.

LOCALE: New York, New York
CATEGORIES: Banking and finance; economics

KEY FIGURES

Bernard Marcus (1890-1954), president of the Bank of United States, 1927-1930
Saul Singer (1881-1948), vice president of the Bank of United States, 1926-1930
Joseph Broderick (1881-1959), New York State superintendent of banking, 1929-1934
Amadeo P. Giannini (1870-1949), head of San Francisco's Bank of Italy, 1904-1936

SUMMARY OF EVENT

The Bank of United States was closed by order of the New York State banking authorities in December, 1930, at a time when the country was already sliding into severe depression. In terms of the dollar volume of deposits, it was the largest bank to fail in the United States up to that date. It was the twenty-eighth largest bank in the country in 1929, with $238 million in deposits and more than four hundred thousand depositors.

The Bank of United States was established in 1913 by Joseph Marcus, an immigrant from Russia. Some criticized the bank's choice of name, saying that it implied a nonexistent connection with the government, but in general the bank was honestly if aggressively managed. Catering especially to New York City's Jewish merchants, it grew rapidly. As its profits increased, the market value of its stock increased rapidly. Part of this increase reflected investors' high opinion of New York bank stocks in general. Several New York banks had succeeded in boosting their profits and stock values by creating "securities affiliates." These affiliates were legally separate corporations owned by the same people who owned stock in the bank. The affiliates were free to speculate in securities and to engage in profitable financial services such as underwriting new securities issues and brokering existing shares. In New York, both First National Bank and National City Bank created highly profitable affiliates. Printing stock certificates of banks and their affiliates back-to-back ensured that both would be owned by exactly the same people. Although the parent banks were

subject to regular bank examination by state or federal authorities, the affiliates were not until, in 1929, New York State bank superintendent Joseph Broderick extended the inspections to include affiliates.

In 1927, Joseph Marcus died, and the management of the Bank of United States came under the control of his son, Bernard Marcus, working closely with vice president Saul Singer. They observed the rapid rise of most stock prices, which took bank stock prices to especially high multiples of earnings. They apparently were impressed by the operations of Bancitaly, an affiliate organized by California's Amadeo P. Giannini and closely linked with the Bank of Italy, forerunner of the Bank of America.

In the late months of 1927, Marcus and Singer embarked on a three-pronged strategy designed to raise the market value of stock in the Bank of United States. They invested heavily in the stock, using money borrowed from their own bank. The first part of the strategy involved expansion through mergers and bank purchases. Within a year following May, 1928, they merged with or acquired five other banks. Usually these combinations involved giving stock in the bank or its affiliates in exchange for stock of the acquired bank. In several cases, the bank promised to repurchase its stock if its market value fell below the level at which these exchanges were made. These agreements exposed the bank to heavy losses when its stock did in fact fall.

The second element of the Marcus-Singer strategy involved the creation of securities affiliates. This process began with the creation of City Financial Corporation in August, 1927. In December, 1928, Marcus and Singer established the Bankus Corporation, which then absorbed City Financial. Shares of Bankus were linked one to one with those of the Bank of United States and sold together as "units." Another securities affiliate, Municipal Finance, joined the group through merger in April, 1929. City, Bankus, and Municipal in turn became investors in a second layer of affiliates, which included by 1929 an insurance company, a mortgage company, and three safe deposit companies. The affiliates also made extensive purchases of the bank's stock or made loans with that stock as collateral.

The third element of the strategy was a heavy commitment to real estate finance in New York City, even though the nation's real estate markets were showing signs of trouble and banks were being warned against

Irate and bewildered customers crowd around the closed doors of the Bank of United States on December 11, 1930. (AP/Wide World Photos)

such involvements. Because banking law severely restricted real estate lending and direct ownership, the bank organized its real estate involvements through a bevy of additional affiliates. A typical affiliate would own and operate an apartment building using funds obtained from City, Bankus, Municipal, or the second-line affiliates, which in turn were obtaining money by borrowing from the Bank of United States. Many of the real estate ventures involved heavy risk exposure, as the bank's affiliates either were the owners of heavily indebted property or held junior mortgages. In 1929, bank examiners were critical of the real estate involvements.

The Marcus-Singer efforts to raise the value of the bank's stock and thus enrich themselves were not successful. Even as the general stock market rose in 1929, the bank's "units" began to decline in value. From $242 in April, 1929, the price fell to $207 in early July. This decline led to a frenzy of effort by the bank's management to sell shares to depositors. The bank's employees were instructed to promise depositors that the bank would repurchase its shares if they fell below $198; about $6 million of additional stock was sold under this unwritten promise. The various affiliates were also buying the bank's stock to try to prop up its price. Despite these efforts, the bank's stock continued to decline, and it fell even more in the general market collapse in October, 1929. By December, the stock had fallen to $75 a share. Very few investors got the bank to stand behind its promise to buy back shares. The market decline meant a sharp fall in revenues from financial services, and capital losses replaced capital gains in the affiliates' accounts. The bank's earnings were disappearing, a process aggravated by neglect of honest and competent administration of mainstream banking operations.

A thorough government examination of the bank began in July, 1930, and lasted until September. The authorities concluded that the bank was in serious trouble and that it could be saved only through merger. Various merger proposals were explored with the aid of federal and state officials, but excessive demands by the bank's management prevented successful completion of a merger. In late November, a four-bank merger appeared to be firm, but the partners feared heavy deposit withdrawals and insisted that other New York banks stand ready to lend to them. These guarantees from other New York banks could not be secured. As withdrawals of deposits accelerated with news of the merger failure, Superintendent Broderick reluctantly agreed to close the bank, effective December 11, 1930. The bank's assets were impaired partly because of the decline in the value of its stock, which was extensively pledged as collateral, and of its real estate assets.

SIGNIFICANCE

The immediate effect of the bank's failure was to aggravate the country's slide into serious depression. The bank's stockholders sustained double losses. Not only did the stock in the bank and its affiliates become worthless, but also, under the "double liability" law in force at the time, stockholders were liable for an additional $25 per share to cover depositors' claims. About $10 million was collected from stockholders.

At the time the bank closed, its deposits totaled about $160 million, and this purchasing power was temporarily unavailable to depositors. As soon as the bank closed, intense efforts were made to collect its loans. Thousands of small businesses that counted on continuation of their lines of credit from the bank found themselves cut off. These developments caused a direct drop in consumer spending in New York, as measured by sales of department stores and chain stores.

Ultimately, depositors received most of their money back. Collecting loans, selling assets, and suing stockholders and directors enabled depositors to regain about three-fourths of their funds. The bank's affairs were not settled, however, until 1944.

Although there were no other major bank failures in New York City in 1931 and 1932, the intense publicity attending the bank's failure and liquidation undoubtedly added to public distrust of the banking system. This was reflected in heavy sustained withdrawals of currency from banks in 1931. These withdrawals reduced bank reserves and obliged banks to reduce their lending, adding force to the deflationary process.

The failure of the Bank of United States was an early and dramatic part of the massive wave of bank failures that swept the United States from 1930 to 1933. The lesson was learned that bank failures could be a major source of deflationary damage, aggravating depression and unemployment. From this lesson emerged several important policy measures.

In 1932, Congress created the Reconstruction Finance Corporation, an emergency lending agency charged particularly with making emergency credit available to distressed banks, even to the point of lending to suspended banks so that they could accelerate their payouts to depositors. A more permanent result was the establishment, through the Banking Act of June, 1933, of federal deposit insurance. The Federal Deposit Insurance Corporation (FDIC) began operations in 1934. A major purpose of the FDIC was to ensure that even if a bank failed, the rank and file of household and small-business depositors would receive their deposit funds without loss or delay. Despite problems with deposit insurance in the 1980's, it has remained an important reason why no serious depression has afflicted the United States since the 1930's.

The bank's failure, coming so soon after the stock market crash of 1929, added to the public's anger directed toward financial speculators and manipulators. Bernard Marcus and Saul Singer were indicted, convicted, and sentenced to prison terms for fraudulent actions. Politically, this anger led to the passage of the Securities Act of May, 1933, and the Securities Exchange Act of June, 1934, regulating securities trading and requiring much more complete reporting of corporate financial conditions.

Outrage was particularly directed toward the securities affiliates, which were blamed for banking difficulties. The Bankus experience was important evidence leading to the provisions of the Banking Act of 1933, which forbade banks to act as underwriters or dealers in securities or to be affiliated with such activities. Public anger was also directed at regulatory officials who let banking mismanagement go on so long. Superintendent Broderick was indicted for negligence in failing to close or reorganize the bank, but he was acquitted of the charges in 1932. Because of similar experiences throughout the country, bank regulators began to take much more aggressive attitudes toward ousting misbehaving bank managers. The newly created FDIC took on a forceful regulatory role toward banks not already under federal supervision.

—Paul B. Trescott

1930

FURTHER READING

Friedman, Milton, and Anna Jacobson Schwartz. *A Monetary History of the United States, 1867-1960*. Princeton, N.J.: Princeton University Press, 1963. Definitive and sometimes quite technical scholarly work makes brief mention of the failure of the Bank of United States, placing it in the context of the monetary crisis and showing how it led to increased withdrawal of currency from other banks. Presents controversial assertions about the causes and consequences of the failure.

Kindleberger, Charles P. *Manias, Panics, and Crashes: A History of Financial Crises*. 4th ed. New York: John Wiley & Sons, 2000. General survey of financial speculation and monetary crises from the eighteenth century to the late twentieth century.

Peach, W. Nelson. *The Security Affiliates of National Banks*. Baltimore: The Johns Hopkins University Press, 1941. Scholarly work examines the evolution of securities affiliates and describes their role in the stock boom and bust of the 1920's. Describes the hostility toward affiliates resulting from the stock market crash and assesses the resulting reform legislation.

Pecora, Ferdinand. *Wall Street Under Oath*. 1939. Reprint. New York: Augustus M. Kelley, 1973. Pecora was a major participant in the investigation of stock market scandals and recounts many of these in colorful if not entirely objective fashion. The securities affiliates receive much attention.

Temin, Peter. *Did Monetary Forces Cause the Great Depression?* New York: W. W. Norton, 1976. Refutes arguments by Friedman and Schwartz (cited above) about the causes of the bank's failure and asserts that the failure did not have important economic consequences in worsening the Great Depression.

Trescott, Paul B. "The Failure of the Bank of United States, 1930." *Journal of Money, Credit, and Banking* 24 (August, 1992): 384-399. Examines the bank's relationships with its affiliates, explains the causes of its failure, and shows evidence of the failure's impact on currency withdrawals and on consumer spending.

Werner, Morris Robert. *Little Napoleons and Dummy Directors: Being the Narrative of the Bank of United States*. New York: Harper & Brothers, 1933. Detailed narrative of the bank's failure is full of valuable details drawn in large part from the numerous civil and criminal court proceedings attending the failure. Colorful and melodramatic but not very analytic. Some of the material also appeared in a *Fortune* magazine article in March, 1933.

Wicker, Elmus. *The Banking Panics of the Great Depression*. New York: Cambridge University Press, 1996. Examines the origins, magnitudes, and effects of five individual banking panics. Includes discussion of the Bank of United States failure. Features figures, tables, references, and index.

SEE ALSO: Oct.-Nov., 1907: Panic of 1907; Dec. 23, 1913: Federal Reserve Act; Feb. 25, 1927: McFadden Act Regulates Branch Banking; June 16, 1933: Banking Act of 1933 Reorganizes the American Banking System; Aug. 23, 1935: Banking Act of 1935 Centralizes U.S. Monetary Control.

1931
KARLOFF AND LUGOSI BECOME KINGS OF HORROR

Bela Lugosi in the motion picture Dracula *and Boris Karloff in* Frankenstein *created the archetypes for two of the most famous monsters in the horror film genre.*

LOCALE: Hollywood, California
CATEGORIES: Motion pictures; entertainment

KEY FIGURES
Boris Karloff (1887-1969), British American film actor
Bela Lugosi (1882-1956), Hungarian American film actor
James Whale (1889-1957), British-born film director
Tod Browning (1880-1962), American film director

SUMMARY OF EVENT
No two performers have been more associated with a particular motion-picture genre than Boris Karloff and Bela Lugosi. Lugosi's chilling portrayal of the vampire in *Dracula* and Karloff's sensational incarnation as the monster in *Frankenstein* left Hollywood with a legacy of definitive performances that established a standard for horror films to come.

Dracula and *Frankenstein*, both released in 1931, were the first horror films produced by Universal Pictures. The genre of the horror film, however, dates back to the beginnings of cinema and to the work of such directors as Georges Méliès and Thomas Alva Edison. Edison produced an extraordinary one-reel version of *Frankenstein* in 1910, the first attempt to transfer to film Mary Wollstonecraft Shelley's 1818 novel *Frankenstein: Or, The Modern Prometheus*. Universal's horror hits of the 1930's and 1940's, however, remain the classics of the genre. The enduring popularity of horror films is to a great extent a result of the performances of Lugosi and Karloff in these early productions.

In 1930, Universal bought the film rights to a play by Hamilton Deane that was based on the 1897 Bram Stoker novel *Dracula*. In the play's successful run on Broadway in 1927, Hungarian-born actor Bela Lugosi played the title role. Lugosi had fled his homeland in 1919 after a period of political unrest there and had made his way to New York, where he joined the Hungarian community and began working in Hungarian-language theater productions.

The director of the film version of *Dracula*, Tod Browning, had a talent for the macabre. His direction of Lon Chaney, a master of grotesque disguises, resulted in several notable melodramas in the 1920's, including *The*

Unholy Three (1925), *The Big City* (1928), and *West of Zanzibar* (1928). Originally, Universal had chosen the play as a vehicle for Chaney; when Chaney died of cancer in 1930, Browning considered several other actors for the lead. Lugosi, who had not yet mastered English, badly wanted the part and was finally hired—perhaps because he had successfully played the role on Broadway.

The tremendous impact the film had on audiences was in part due to Lugosi's exotic and mysterious presence. His halting command of English, his long black cape, and his refined manners created a stir among women, some of whom actually fainted during showings of the film. In the credits, however, Lugosi was merely listed along with the other players.

In the film, Lugosi plays the part of Count Dracula, a five-hundred-year-old vampire whose thirst for human blood cannot be quenched. As the undying vampire constantly in search of new victims, he moves from his castle in Transylvania to the ruins of an abbey in England. While attending an opera one evening, he meets two young women from polite society. Using his cultivated charm and mysterious gaze, he begins stalking them, apparently with the aim of turning them into vampires also, but a famous vampire killer, Dr. Van Helsing (Edward Van Sloan) comes to the rescue. After some psychic struggle between the two, Van Helsing tracks Dracula to his coffin lair and drives a stake through his heart, thus breaking the spell.

Because *Dracula* was being filmed during the Depression, when Universal operated under rather severe budget restraints, every effort was made to save money. In one scene, Universal even used footage cannibalized from one of its other films. Most of the four hundred thousand dollars it cost to make *Dracula* went into the fantastic sets of Dracula's castle; Lugosi was paid a mere thirty-five hundred dollars for his performance.

Universal was at first unsure of the impact *Dracula* would have on the public. Fearing that the film might be rejected as too horrible or disgusting, the studio had its publicity department advertise the film as "the story of the strangest passion the world has ever known."

Dracula was released on Valentine's Day, 1931, and was an instant success. The popularity of the film owed as much to Lugosi's sinister charisma as to Tod Browning's direction and the magnificent sets. The role of Count Dracula was Lugosi's greatest success, and he became permanently typecast as a player of vampires, monsters, and fiends. His "Count Dracula" was copyrighted by Universal, and virtually all subsequent movie vampires were modeled after him in name or in style.

So successful was *Dracula* that Universal immediately set out to make another horror film. Choosing the right material was a challenge; however, Mary Shelley's gothic novel *Frankenstein* was considered a likely follow-up to *Dracula*. Although an early treatment was prepared by writer-director Robert Florey, the studio finally gave the picture to director James Whale.

Whale, a theatrically trained director, selected Boris Karloff, an established character player in Hollywood films, to test for the part of the monster. Karloff saw the role as a dramatic challenge and had Jack P. Pierce, Universal's greatest makeup artist, design the monster's image for his audition. When Whale saw the result, he immediately gave the part of Karloff. Oddly enough, the part of the monster had originally been offered to Lugosi. Lugosi, who was not interested in a nonspeaking part and who did not like having to wear the heavy makeup, turned down the role.

As adapted for film, *Frankenstein* is the story of a slightly mad scientist, Dr. Frankenstein (Colin Clive), who attempts to create a living man by stitching together parts of cadavers. His final and most important step in the process is to find a suitable brain. Frankenstein's assistant, Fritz (Dwight Frye), a half-witted hunchback, mistakenly brings his master a criminal brain rather than a normal one. After being subjected to electrical current from bolts of lightning, the monster comes alive. Although Frankenstein is thrilled at the success of his work, the monster is so hideous that he is kept hidden from view in a dungeon-like cell. After being tortured by Fritz and finally escaping, the monster accidentally kills a child and is pursued by an angry mob of villagers. Dr. Frankenstein joins the mob in search of the monster. During the night, the monster grabs his creator and seeks refuge in an old windmill. The villagers finally surround the windmill and set fire to it, apparently killing the monster in the process.

Jack Pierce's artistry transformed Karloff into a truly horrible creature, with hinged skull, electrodes protruding from his neck, and a stiff-legged, lurching walk. So fearful were studio

managers that Karloff would terrify audiences that a prologue was added to warn the audiences that the film was capable of frightening and shocking them.

When *Frankenstein* premiered in Santa Barbara, California, on December 6, 1931, it created a huge sensation. Karloff, who was not even invited to the premiere, became an overnight horror superstar. In choosing Karloff to play the monster, Whale had made a brilliant choice. Karloff, who had served a lengthy apprenticeship both on the stage and in films, gave the monster a sympathetic quality. Although the character had no dialogue, Karloff was able to convey a wide range of emotions, from childlike innocence to terrified bewilderment. The poignant performance confirmed Karloff's ability as a first-rate actor.

SIGNIFICANCE

Not only are *Frankenstein* and *Dracula* the most famous of the Universal horror films of the 1930's and 1940's, but they also influenced the development of the entire genre. One of the most significant results of the success of the films has been the enduring popularity of Bela Lugosi and Boris Karloff. Both men were highly regarded actors who had already established their careers well before becoming involved in horror films. Because of their definitive performances, however, Lugosi and Karloff became typecast in the horror genre. For better or worse, their names became forever linked in the minds of the public to films that evoke fear and terror.

Bela Lugosi in character as Count Dracula. (AP/Wide World Photos)

Frankenstein was quickly followed by *Murders in the Rue Morgue*, which was released in 1932. Based on the short story by Edgar Allan Poe (but drastically altered), the film starred Lugosi as Dr. Mirakle. This odd and disappointing melodrama is notable mainly for the presence of Lugosi as the mad scientist intent on proving his bizarre theory of evolution.

Two other Universal films of 1932, *The Old Dark House* and *The Mummy*, starred Karloff. In the first film, Karloff's performance was both brief and undistinguished. A much better film is *The Mummy*, which was directed by Karl Freund and starred Boris Karloff in the dual roles of Im-ho-tep, a mummy, and the resurrected Egyptian high priest Ardath Bey. Karloff plays Ardath Bey with an articulate charm and sense of style that resulted in one of his finest performances. *The Mummy*, noted for its excellent script, cast, and direction, is also famous for the incredible makeup by Jack Pierce. A unique and intelligent horror film, *The Mummy* spawned such lookalike films as *The Mummy's Hand* (1940) and *The Mummy's Tomb* (1942) and maintains a place alongside Universal's two great horror films of 1931. Universal followed *The Mummy* with *Secret of the Blue Room* (1933) and *The Invisible Man* (1933). *The Invisible Man*, directed by James Whale and starring Claude Rains, was adapted from H. G. Wells's 1897 novel *The Invisible Man: A Grotesque Romance*. Because of the innovative special effects devised to convey the illusion of invisibility, *The Invisible Man* is considered a unique film in Hollywood history.

Lugosi and Karloff made their first joint appearance in a Universal film in *The Black Cat* (1934). Based loosely on a story by Poe, the film is a catalog of depravity, with various episodes of sadism, torture, mutilation, and murder acted out in a loosely woven tapestry of melodramatic sensationalism. In the film, archenemies Dr. Vitus Werdegast (Lugosi) and Hjalmar Poelzig (Karloff) go at each other almost immediately upon reuniting in Poelzig's mountaintop home. Werdegast accuses Poelzig of having killed his wife while Werdegast served time as a prisoner of war. In the years since their last meeting, Poelzig has been conducting monstrous experiments involving the preservation of the dead bodies of beautiful women. When Poelzig shows Werdegast the preserved body of his wife, Werdegast goes berserk, unleashing the forces of murder and mayhem that result in the death of both protagonists. Although *The Black Cat* was recut extensively prior to its release in order to placate studio chiefs who felt the film was too grisly, it remains a fascinating and bizarre horror film.

Lugosi and Karloff were to be paired again in the 1930's in another Universal adaptation of a Poe tale, *The Raven* (1935). Karloff was to re-create his role as the monster in two *Frankenstein* sequels, *The Bride of Frankenstein* (1935) and *Son of Frankenstein* (1939), which also featured Lugosi. Among the other memorable films of those years are *Dracula's Daughter* (1936), *The Wolf Man* (1941), and *The Mummy's Tomb*. The studio even successfully rereleased *Frankenstein* and *Dracula* on a double bill in 1938.

Although Lugosi was perhaps as talented an actor as Karloff, he did not select his roles carefully, and he went on to make a number of forgettable, even embarrassing, films. In later years, marital and health problems took their toll, and by the mid-1950's he was broke and addicted to drugs. He died practically destitute in 1956. Karloff, although also typecast as a horror film star, had a busy and varied career in other areas of show business, including television and the stage. In 1941, he achieved critical success in the Broadway production of *Arsenic and Old Lace*. Karloff's gentle nature and quiet refinement were in stark contrast to the fiendishness of the ghouls he played in films.

By the end of the 1930's, although fans still turned out to see the latest Universal tales of horror, many of the studio's films were mere remakes that exploited earlier films. The result was that each new title seemed to parody the horror genre.

Although *Dracula* and *Frankenstein* are far from perfect films, horror fans continue to consider them minor masterpieces. The films may have lost much of their power to frighten, but the monsters created by Lugosi and Karloff remain definitive horror performances.

—Francis Poole

FURTHER READING

Bojarski, Richard. *The Complete Films of Bela Lugosi.* New York: Citadel Press, 1980. Comprehensive survey of all Lugosi's film appearances, including his earliest films made in Hungary and Germany. Carol Borland, who played the female vampire Luna alongside Lugosi in *Mark of the Vampire* (1935), contributes a wonderful introduction. Brief biography precedes the catalog of films. Includes many rare photographs.
Brunas, Michael, John Brunas, and Tom Weaver. *Universal Horrors: The Studio's Classic Films, 1931-1946.* Jefferson, N.C.: McFarland, 1990. A critical examination of every horror film produced by Universal in the 1930's and 1940's, presented chronologically.

Features insightful commentary presented with a nice touch of humor. Includes photographs and informative appendixes.

Lennig, Arthur. *The Immortal Count: The Life and Films of Bela Lugosi*. Lexington: University Press of Kentucky, 2003. Extensively researched biography seeks to expand the public's view of Lugosi beyond his image as the Count. Draws on interviews, studio memos, and other primary documents. Includes numerous photographs.

Lindsay, Cynthia. *Dear Boris*. New York: Alfred A. Knopf, 1975. Intimate, readable biography of Karloff by a longtime friend. Carefully explores Karloff's early years in England and his moves to Canada and then to the United States. Quotes Karloff extensively and features excerpts of letters to Karloff from such friends as Vincent Price and Ronald Reagan. Includes photographs, family tree, and filmography.

Nollen, Scott A. *Boris Karloff: A Critical Account of His Screen, Stage, Radio, Television, and Recording Work*. Jefferson, N.C.: McFarland, 1991. Scholarly historical and critical analysis of Karloff's body of work, well organized and well documented. Features an assessment of Karloff's artistic contributions writ-

ten by Ray Bradbury in 1969. Includes filmography, list of television and radio performances, and bibliography.

_____. *Boris Karloff: A Gentleman's Life*. Baltimore: Midnight Marquee Press, 2005. Biography written with the cooperation of Karloff's daughter includes coverage of all aspects of the actor's life. Features appendixes listing all of Karloff's many performances, including those in radio and television as well as those on stage and in film.

Underwood, Peter. *Karloff: The Life of Boris Karloff*. New York: Drake, 1972. Biography effectively recalls Karloff's struggle to become an actor, first on the stage and then in films. Offers a detailed, anecdotal account of the making of *Frankenstein*. Includes photographs, selected bibliography, discography, and filmography.

SEE ALSO: 1920: Premiere of *The Cabinet of Dr. Caligari*; May 11, 1928: Sound Technology Revolutionizes the Motion-Picture Industry; 1930's: Hollywood Enters Its Golden Age; 1930's-1940's: Studio System Dominates Hollywood Filmmaking; 1931-1932: Gangster Films Become Popular.

1931
ULTRAMARES CASE ESTABLISHES LIABILITY FOR AUDITORS

The 1931 New York case of Ultramares Corporation v. Touche *set a precedent in establishing auditor liability to third-party users of audited financial statements.*

LOCALE: New York, New York
CATEGORIES: Business and labor; laws, acts, and legal history

KEY FIGURES

Benjamin N. Cardozo (1870-1938), chief justice of the Upper New York Court of Appeals
George A. Touche (1861-1935), founder and partner of Touche, Niven, and Company
John Ballantine Niven (1871-1954), founding partner of Touche, Niven, and Company

SUMMARY OF EVENT

The 1931 court case *Ultramares Corporation v. Touche* set a precedent in establishing auditor liability to third parties. The case established that auditors were not liable to "unknown" third-party users of financial statements

for ordinary negligence. The New York Court of Appeals held, however, that auditors could be liable to "known" third parties for ordinary and gross negligence and liable to "unknown" third parties for gross negligence when the negligence equated with "constructive" fraud.

In January, 1924, Fred Stern and Company hired a public accounting firm, Touche, Niven, and Company (founded by George A. Touche and John Ballantine Niven), to audit its balance sheet for December 31, 1923. Touche performed the audit and rendered a "clean" opinion. Touche, Niven, and Company attached to the balance sheet a certificate dated February 26, 1924, that read as follows:

> We have examined the accounts of Fred Stern & Co., Inc., for the year ending December 31, 1923, and hereby certify that the annexed balance sheet is in accordance therewith and with the information and explanations given us. We further certify that, subject to provision for federal taxes on income, the said statement, in our opin-

ion, presents a true and correct view of the financial condition of Fred Stern & Co., Inc., as at December 31, 1923.

After the opinion by Touche was rendered, Stern presented the balance sheet and certificate in its financial dealings. The balance sheet indicated assets of $2,550,671, liabilities of $1,479,956, and net worth of $1,070,715. In reality, the corporation was insolvent, with liabilities exceeding assets by about $200,000.

Stern normally borrowed large sums of money to finance its operations. In March, 1924, the company approached Ultramares, a lending corporation, to borrow money. Based on the information contained in Stern's audited balance sheet and certificate, Ultramares granted Stern three loans, for $100,000, $25,000, and $40,000, in December of 1924. Soon thereafter, on January 2, 1925, Fred Stern and Company declared bankruptcy. In November of 1926, Ultramares Corporation brought suit against Touche, Niven, and Company to recover the losses from the uncollectible loans. The company sued on the grounds of negligence and fraudulent misrepresentation.

The balance sheet audited by Touche showed approximately $1,350,000 of accounts receivable, of which more than $700,000 was fictitious. These fictitious receivables were recorded in Stern's books by a late entry on February 3, 1924, made by a Stern employee. The auditors accepted the adjustment and did not perform tests on the fictitious receivables. If they had, they would likely have discovered the fraud. Other suspicious discrepancies also existed in the balance sheet. For example, the auditors discovered mistakes totaling $303,863 in Stern's inventory account, which was originally reported at $347,219.

The *Ultramares* case made its way through three courts. The initial court hearing was a trial by jury that resulted in a ruling in favor of Ultramares Corporation on both counts, of negligence and of fraud. On appeal, the Lower New York Court of Appeals ruled again that negligence had occurred, but it found no fraud. The court based its decision on the 1922 case of *Glanzer v. Shepard*. The *Glanzer* decision stated that if a service was rendered primarily for the benefit of a third party, a company is potentially liable to the third party. Furthermore, the court stated that negligence, no matter how gross, was not equivalent to fraud.

The Upper Court of Appeals reversed the lower court opinion. It made an important distinction between the *Glanzer* and *Ultramares* cases: The service provided by Touche was primarily for the benefit of Fred Stern and Company, not a third party. For a third party to collect based on ordinary negligence, it must be a primary beneficiary, one that the auditor had been informed about prior to conducting the audit. If so, then there is "privity of contract" between the two parties.

Chief Justice Benjamin N. Cardozo wrote about privity that "if there has been neither reckless misstatement nor insincere profession of an opinion, but only honest blunder, the ensuing liability for negligence is one that is bounded by the contract, and is to be enforced between the parties by whom the contract is made." He stated that if accountants were liable for ordinary negligence, then "a thoughtless slip or blunder, the failure to detect a theft or forgery beneath the cover of deceptive entries, may expose accountants to a liability in an indeterminate amount for an indeterminate time to an indeterminate class."

The court went on to say that this finding did not free Touche from the consequences of fraud. Cardozo stated that negligence, when considered gross or extreme, can be construed to be equivalent to fraud, even though there is no intent to deceive or to do harm. The court believed that gross negligence existed in the *Ultramares* case, because by "certifying to the correspondence between balance sheet and accounts the defendants made a statement as true to their knowledge, when they had . . . no knowledge on the subject." As a result of the court's finding, Cardozo ordered that a new trial be granted to Ultramares concerning fraudulent misrepresentation.

SIGNIFICANCE

The 1931 *Ultramares* case brought to the forefront the issue of auditor liability to third parties. Liability can extend to include both "known" and "unknown" third-party users depending on the type of negligence. In recent years, some courts have broadened the *Ultramares* doctrine to include recovery for ordinary negligence by "unknown" third-party beneficiaries. The Restatement of Torts, an authoritative compendium of legal principles, allows recovery by a reasonably limited and identifiable group whose members rely on the auditor's work, known as "foreseen" users. The *Credit Alliance* court case (1985) further extended liability to "foreseeable" users. Under this concept, users that the auditor should have been able to foresee have the same rights as those in privity of contract.

As a result of *Ultramares* and other legal cases, accountants have become increasingly vulnerable to litigation. If an audited business experiences financial difficulties, and if a plaintiff can prove reliance on financial statements, the auditor may be subject to legal action no matter how professionally he or she conducted the audit. Investors and creditors with monetary losses sometimes have difficulty distinguishing between audit failure and business failure. Unable to recover money from a bankrupt business, they turn to auditors for compensation.

The cost of defending against such litigation has become extremely high. As a result, many accountants will settle out of court even if not guilty. In order to counter potential litigation, the accounting profession responded by setting up auditing standards and a code of professional conduct. The first authoritative auditing pronouncement, issued in 1917, was described as a "memorandum on balance sheet audits" and was intended to promote "a uniform system of accounting." At the time of the *Ultramares* case, audit work was preformed primarily to assure the owner that the accounting within his or her business had been handled properly. The *Ultramares* court ruling, however, extended liability beyond that of the owner. Furthermore, in the late 1920's, operating performance and net income became equally as important as the balance sheet. As the complexity and scope of business changed, the auditor's role shifted from certifying the correctness of the balance sheet to reviewing the accounting system and gathering evidence to render an opinion on the fair presentation of financial statements.

A 1936 bulletin, "Examination of Financial Statements by Independent Public Accountants," changed the accountant's role from simple verification of the balance sheet to examination of the financial statements as a whole. Auditing standards concerning the auditor's new role began to be issued. In 1947, the national professional accounting organization, the American Institute of Certified Public Accountants (AICPA), released its ten "generally accepted auditing standards" (GAAS). These represented general guidelines to aid auditors in fulfilling their professional audit responsibilities. The ten GAAS were divided into three categories: general standards, standards of fieldwork, and standards of reporting. With a few minimal changes, these standards continued to govern auditors' work into the twenty-first century.

In brief, the general standards require auditors to be trained and proficient, to be independent in mental attitude, and to exercise due professional care. The standards of fieldwork require audit planning, the study of internal control, and the gathering of evidence. The reporting standards provide guidelines on matters to be addressed in the audit report. This discussion must include the client's conformity with and consistent application of generally accepted accounting principles, full disclosure, and the rendering of an audit opinion.

As the number of third-party users of financial statements increased, the AICPA adopted its Code of Professional Ethics in 1973 to give further guidance regarding professional conduct. Certified public accountants were to conduct their affairs in a manner meriting public trust. The code of conduct consisted of general statements of ideal conduct and specific rules of unacceptable behavior. The code included discussion concerning topics such as independence, integrity and objectivity, and compliance with standards and principles. The code, now called the Accountant's Code of Professional Conduct, was revised in 1988.

In further response to an increasingly litigious society, the AICPA updated the auditor reports in 1988 to define more clearly the roles of the auditor and management in the audit. Furthermore, at the beginning of an audit, accountants provide engagement letters to their clients that clearly outline the nature of the audit, the client's responsibilities for the financial statements, and the meaning of the auditor's report. Generally, accountants carry liability insurance to provide for payment of court defenses and claims. In addition, as another way of maintaining high quality within the accounting profession, the AICPA and some states require all public accounting firms providing attestation services to participate in periodic quality control reviews.

Ultramares was the first of many legal cases that affected the accounting profession and its development. As a result of the ruling in that case, auditors began to take a defensive approach when conducting audits. They became aware of the potential risk of litigation, and organizations of accounting professionals began working to maintain high standards for their members' conduct.

—*Marsha M. Huber*

FURTHER READING

American Institute of Certified Public Accountants Staff. *AICPA Professional Standards*. Chicago: Commerce Clearing House, 1992. Volume B contains the Accountant's Code of Professional Conduct.

Cook, John W., and Gary M. Winkle. *Auditing*. 4th ed. Boston: Houghton Mifflin, 1988. Well-written textbook on auditing principles. Chapter on legal liability provides both historical and more current perspectives on the impacts of legal cases and government regulation on the auditing profession.

Guy, Dan M., and D. R. Carmichael. *Wiley's Student GAAS Guide*. 2d ed. New York: John Wiley & Sons, 2000. A presentation of the AICPA's standards for auditing aimed at accounting students.

Hubbard, Thomas D., et al. *Readings and Cases in Auditing*. 6th ed. Houston: Dame, 1989. Collection of writings explaining and critiquing the auditing profession.

Nielsen, Oswald. *Cases in Auditing*. Homewood, Ill.: R. D. Irwin, 1965. Contains legal opinions from all major court cases affecting the auditing profession.

Strawser, Jerry R., and Robert H. Strawser. *Auditing: Theory and Practice*. 9th ed. Houston: Dame, 2001. College textbook includes excerpts from newspaper and journal articles relating to developments in the accounting profession.

SEE ALSO: 1914: U.S. Government Begins Using Cost-Plus Contracts; Sept. 19, 1916: American Institute of Accountants Is Founded; Oct. 3, 1917: U.S. Congress Imposes a Wartime Excess-Profits Tax; 1925: McKinsey Founds a Management Consulting Firm.

1931-1932
GANGSTER FILMS BECOME POPULAR

Emerging out of the depths of the Great Depression, the gangster film revealed much about Americans' frustrations and proved one of the most popular and resilient of film genres.

LOCALE: United States
CATEGORIES: Motion pictures; entertainment

KEY FIGURES
Edward G. Robinson (1893-1973), American film actor
Mervyn LeRoy (1900-1987), American film director
William Wellman (1896-1975), American film director
James Cagney (1899-1986), American film actor
Howard Hawks (1896-1977), American film director
Paul Muni (1895-1967), American film actor

SUMMARY OF EVENT
The years 1931 and 1932 launched Hollywood's time of the gangster. Caught in the widening Great Depression, the American people were disillusioned and angry. The national dream of economic opportunity had become a nightmare, and society's institutions, especially the federal government under President Herbert Hoover, seemed unable to do anything except utter hollow, optimistic nostrums. The film industry, itself suffering from sagging attendance, discovered that tapping this mounting public discontent would bring people back to the theaters. In addition to normal escapist fare, the studios began offering productions dealing with corrupt politicians and businessmen, shady lawyers, dishonest journalists, and women driven to prostitution by economic necessity. These pictures showing the United States in a bleak, unsavory light were popular, but it was the gangster film

that most caught the public's interest and offered the deepest insights into the troubled national psyche. Few gangster films were produced before the Depression; now they would proliferate, and the screen mobster, especially as he appeared in *Little Caesar* (1931), *The Public Enemy* (1931), and *Scarface* (1932), would offer himself as a new, disturbing hero.

Little Caesar, directed for Warner Bros. by Mervyn LeRoy in late 1930 and released in January, 1931, broke the ground. It is a simple tale of a small-time hoodlum, Rico (played by Edward G. Robinson), who joins a mob and quickly gains power by being tougher, more relentless, and more ferocious than anyone else. Eventually, he becomes the second most important boss in the city. Rico is extremely ruthless, although ultimately not ruthless enough. He falls because he cannot bring himself to kill an old friend who wants to leave the mob. Rico stays his hand, the friend betrays him to the authorities, and Rico's organization crumbles. Alone, on the run, he is finally gunned down by the police in an unfair fight. The police kill Rico, yet they really have little to do with his actual destruction. His doom stems from his going soft over friendship.

Little Caesar was an instant hit. The film is not particularly well made or well plotted; its effectiveness comes from its violent action and the character of Rico as realized by Robinson. Rico is a compelling figure who, despite his murderous nature, emerges as a somewhat sympathetic protagonist.

Rico's prime ambition is to get ahead, to make something of himself. He wants wealth and control; even more, he desires status. He seeks to be somebody. A few decades earlier, he might have aspired to be a robber baron. Totally devoted to his ambition and rather puritanical in his personal behavior, he does not drink, involve himself with the easy women of the underworld, or do anything else that he thinks might distract him from his goals. For most of the film, Rico is successful. Through Rico, *Little Caesar* suggests that, given the shambles of American society, crime is perhaps the only way left to secure at least some of the American Dream.

Warner Bros. quickly followed up *Little Caesar* with *The Public Enemy.* Made by veteran director William Wellman, the new picture surpassed *Little Caesar* in its realism and complexity of story and in its indictment of American society. *The Public Enemy* chronicles the career of Tommy Powers, a young man from a poor working-class district who savors the lifestyle of the wealthy mobster. Tommy, played with ebullient energy by James Cagney, takes up crime as a boy and then, with brutal efficiency, moves up the ranks of organized crime. He never obtains as much control or status as Rico, but he has more fun. Tommy likes alcohol, parties, and women. He is witty and engaging and, despite the fact that he also shoots people, he is presented as a hero. In *The Public Enemy*, those who have honest jobs and play by the legal rules fail. If you want to win, the film seems to say, be like Tommy Powers.

Tommy enjoys his life immensely; nevertheless, he too dies, murdered by rival hoodlums while lying helpless, recovering from wounds. The gangsters of these films meet violent ends because Hollywood was unwilling to risk the wrath of censors by letting screen criminals get away with their crimes completely. Significantly, however, the film gangster's death usually does not illustrate a crime-does-not-pay moral or occur in order that justice be upheld. Rarely does a protagonist's demise have much to do with the nature of his crimes. He succumbs because of a personal weakness—in Rico's case, affection for an old buddy—or, like Tommy, as a result of power struggles within the underworld. In facing death, the film gangster is often given stature and nobility; he becomes a tragic hero.

The primary focus of the gangster film, however, is on these men's lives, not their deaths, and their lives are sagas of achievement. In the midst of the economic chaos and spiritual malaise of the Great Depression, they make money in adventurous ways and enjoy great material comfort. They are common men, men of the city, men often of immigrant roots. In other words, they are men with whom millions can identify. They advance by their own talents and without hypocrisy. In a society in which the stock market crash of 1929 had revealed many business,

James Cagney and Jean Harlow in a scene from The Public Enemy. (AP/Wide World Photos)

professional, and political leaders as frauds, the screen gangsters do not cover up what they are. Although they break the law, the law as presented in these films is either corrupt or irrelevant. In *Little Caesar*, the top criminal in the city, the only man more powerful than Rico, is clearly an established member of the upper-class governing elite. There are no courts in the gangster film, and the police, when they appear, are ineffectual at best. The police may show up at the end of a film to kill the gangster, as they do in *Little Caesar;* however, such an ending is usually a tacked-on resolution that has little to do with the logic of a film's plot. By the time the police appear, the protagonist is already finished. In *The Public Enemy*, neither law nor government exists. The society belongs to those who seize control.

The box-office triumphs of *Little Caesar* and *The Public Enemy* generated a host of similar films. From *Little Caesar*'s release through 1932, the film industry produced dozens of gangster films. Americans wanted to see gangster pictures; the individualistic criminal as a culture hero and the savage portrayal of American society struck responsive chords. There were other reasons, too, for the outlaw's fascination. Gangsters were part of the daily scene, not simply creations of Hollywood's imagination. Every major city had its colorful mobsters, and their contemporary notoriety must have enhanced the genre's attraction. Moreover, Prohibition was still the law. Gangsters provided alcohol for the average citizen, and many Americans were willing to accept them as long as they only killed one another and kept the booze flowing. The gangster films, by the nature of their subject matter, also included a good deal of sex and violence, which have always been popular with audiences. During the Depression, such escapist elements seemed especially popular.

Although the gangster film helped to revive Hollywood's fortunes, many in American society were outraged by the new genre. Religious and other groups that sought to monitor community standards complained loudly about the films' level of sex and violence, glorification of criminals, and disparaging view of law and order. That the mobsters were killed off in the end did not satisfy them. As protests mounted, independent producer Howard Hughes released *Scarface* in March, 1932.

Directed by Howard Hawks, who, like Wellman, was an established filmmaker, *Scarface* purportedly deals with Al Capone, the best-known gangster in 1930's America. Capone, whose nickname was "Scarface," supposedly was the model for Tony Camonte, the film's protagonist. Actually, little of Capone's career or personality is portrayed in the film. Capone was an ugly, bestial, thug of a man. Tony Camonte, as played by Paul Muni, is good-looking, somewhat boyish, and occasionally naïve. Hardly a brute, although certainly murderous, Tony is almost a composite of Rico and Tommy Powers. Determined to get to the top and merciless in his methods, Tony does take over the city. As he does so, however, he indulges himself with women and spends his ill-gotten gains along the way. Muni's Tony is a man with a gun in his hand and a twinkle in his eye, a likable killer.

Although the film's story is the familiar one of a hood's progress, Hawks's direction makes *Scarface* special. Hawks utilizes a fast pace, goes well beyond the normal gangster film in both body count and sexual suggestiveness, and wraps the whole film in an absorbing, impressionistic visual style. Tony, of course, dies at the end; he is one of those with a weakness. Hawks, however, makes Tony's flaw singularly different: Tony has

incestuous feelings for his sister. When he discovers his best friend has gone off with his sister, he kills the man. The sister informs on Tony, and the police, who have spent the film doing little besides occasionally bemoaning their powerlessness, show up at the end to kill Tony. It takes large numbers of them, and a huge shootout scene, to get Tony Camonte, who goes down with almost operatic grandeur.

SIGNIFICANCE

Scarface was the last of the seminal gangster films of the 1930's. By 1933, the cycle was ending. The election of Franklin D. Roosevelt was a major factor; as Roosevelt's New Deal took hold, Americans felt that the government was finally doing something to help them. The angry national mood that had sustained the gangster films' appeal diminished considerably. Roosevelt also ended Prohibition, eliminating any need for most people to feel grateful to organized crime. Most important, outcries against films depicting the United States as sick, films with too much sex and killing—especially mobster films—became deafening. Church and civic groups threatened boycotts, censors raged at state and local levels, and possible federal intervention loomed. Hollywood panicked. After *Scarface*'s release, the studios began curtailing gangster film production and moved to a self-censoring system to ensure that they would maintain control of their films. Theoretically, Hollywood had regulated itself since the 1920's, but the program was feeble. In 1933 and 1934, the studios accepted a tougher production code that was to keep sex, excessive violence, severe disrespect for society, and glorification of such nasty people as gangsters out of films for decades.

The new code at first kept the mobster off the screen, but soon he began a slow comeback. He had been so popular, had made the studios so much money, that they were loath to part with him. By 1935, Hollywood decided to make gangster films again, although with differences. There would be less violence and no sex. The moral message of the films must be clear: Crime does not pay. Government and the law, particularly the federal government in the person of the Federal Bureau of Investigation (FBI) agent, or "G-man"—and not the criminals—must be presented as admirable.

With these changes, the gangster returned. His hard edge gone, he was no longer the gutsy protagonist making his way in a lawless world. The spirits of Rico, Tommy Powers, and Tony Camonte, however, were hard to bury. As the years went by, the gangster subtly and incrementally took control of films. Although law-

and-order themes prevailed through the World War II years (1939-1945), the screen gangster emerged increasingly as a more potent, attractive character, and in postwar America, he once more came into his own. The once-tough production code atrophied, and the crime film again became popular at the box office. Many of the same themes seen in the early 1930's reappeared: sex, violence, a corrupt and lawless society, and the mobster as success story. Shaken by such issues as the Vietnam War, the Watergate scandal, urban problems, and economic stagnation, Americans remained troubled, and the film gangster continued to serve as a representative of people disillusioned by the distance between the American Dream and its actuality. Many of the numerous films noirs of the late 1940's and the 1950's, as well as films of later decades such as *The Godfather* (1972) and its sequels, *GoodFellas* (1990), and *Bugsy* (1991), are heirs of the early 1930's, and their protagonists are often similar to those of *Little Caesar, The Public Enemy,* and *Scarface.*

—*Clarke Wilhelm*

FURTHER READING

Bergman, Andrew. *We're in the Money: Depression America and Its Films.* 1971. Reprint. Chicago: Ivan R. Dee, 1992. Excellent study of the Depression through its films provides an analysis of the gangster genre and also looks at other film types that reveal discontent with American society. Includes bibliography and index.

Clarens, Carlos. *Crime Movies: From Griffith to "The Godfather" and Beyond.* New York: W. W. Norton, 1980. Comprehensive history of the crime film is accessible to both film buff and serious cinema scholar. Examines most of the major crime films and provides full and insightful discussion of the gangster genre.

Includes photographs, bibliography, and index.

McCarty, John. *Bullets over Hollywood: The American Gangster Picture from the Silents to the "The Sopranos."* New York: Da Capo Press, 2004. Comprehensive history of gangster films addresses the various elements that make up the genre and analyzes the films' appeal. Includes select bibliography and index.

Mast, Gerald. *Howard Hawks, Storyteller.* New York: Oxford University Press, 1982. Biography and study of Hawks's films is a valuable source of information on the making of *Scarface* and the film's multiple layers of meaning. Includes bibliography, filmography, and index.

Roffman, Peter, and Jim Purdy. *The Hollywood Social Problem Film: Madness, Despair, and Politics from the Depression to the Fifties.* Bloomington: Indiana University Press, 1981. Scholarly study of pivotal Depression-era films includes brief discussion of the gangster film. Features select bibliography, filmography, and index.

Warshow, Robert. *The Immediate Experience: Movies, Comics, Theatre, and Other Aspects of Popular Culture.* Enlarged ed. Cambridge, Mass.: Harvard University Press, 2002. Collection of essays on popular culture includes "The Gangster as Tragic Hero," which is generally considered one of the most important and original analyses of the meaning of the early gangster films.

SEE ALSO: Aug., 1912: Sennett Defines Slapstick Comedy; Aug., 1926-Sept., 1928: Warner Bros. Introduces Talking Motion Pictures; May 16, 1929: First Academy Awards Honor Film Achievement; 1930's: Hollywood Enters Its Golden Age; 1930's-1940's: Studio System Dominates Hollywood Filmmaking; 1931: Karloff and Lugosi Become Kings of Horror.

1931-1935

CHANDRASEKHAR CALCULATES THE UPPER LIMIT OF A WHITE DWARF STAR'S MASS

Subrahmanyan Chandrasekhar developed a mathematically rigorous theory of the structure of white dwarf stars that placed their maximum mass at 1.4 solar masses.

LOCALE: India; England
CATEGORIES: Science and technology; astronomy

KEY FIGURES

Subrahmanyan Chandrasekhar (1910-1995), Indian-born and British-trained theoretical astrophysicist
Arthur Stanley Eddington (1882-1944), English astrophysicist
Ralph H. Fowler (1889-1944), English astrophysicist
Walter Sydney Adams (1876-1956), American astronomer

SUMMARY OF EVENT

White dwarf stars have challenged and perplexed astronomers since their accidental discovery in the mid-nineteenth century. The German astronomer Friedrich Wilhelm Bessel noted a wobble in the path of the star Sirius as it moved across the sky. After eliminating recognizable sources of error, in 1844 he concluded that a small companion star must be affecting the motion of the larger, brighter Sirius. From the wobble in the motion of the larger star, the mass of the smaller star was calculated to be that of the Sun.

In 1915, Walter Sydney Adams managed to channel the light from the companion star into a spectrograph. The light from the star, now called Sirius B, indicated that the surface of the star was almost as hot as Sirius. From the temperature and the brightness of Sirius B, astronomers calculated that Sirius B had a radius of about 24,000 kilometers (approximately 14,913 miles—about twice that of Earth). Packing a mass nearly that of the Sun into a volume fifty thousand times smaller yielded densities that were much larger than astronomers had ever known: One cubic centimeter (about 0.06 cubic inch) of the star—less than the size of a throat lozenge—would weigh 100 kilograms (about 220 pounds).

Sir Arthur Stanley Eddington, the foremost astrophysicist of his time, was not completely convinced that these very small but bright stars, later called white dwarfs, were indeed so dense. Many other skeptics, however, were convinced by the 1925 measurement of the "redshift" of Sirius B. Light trying to escape from a white dwarf is strongly affected by the extreme gravitational force arising from the large mass of the white dwarf. The photons of light lose energy as they struggle against the intense gravity. The frequency of the light is "shifted" toward the red end of the spectrum (reflecting the loss of energy) as the light struggles to escape. Albert Einstein's general theory of relativity predicts that light will be affected in this manner by gravity. The amount of "shift" was equal to that predicted by Einstein's theory.

Eddington's influential *The Internal Constitution of the Stars* (1926) attempted to bring together fifty years of work involving the mechanical and physical conditions of stellar interiors. When it came to white dwarfs, his theory ran into problems. In his theory, most of a star's lifetime was spent balancing the outward pressure of the escaping heat of nuclear reactions with the inward pressure of gravity. Eventually, the store of nuclear fuel would be depleted and the star would collapse into itself, becoming a white dwarf. The atomic nuclei, which make up the mass of the white dwarf, would then keep cooling and the electrons that had been ripped from the nuclei would be able to reattach themselves to the nuclei in the star. The problem was that the amount of energy required to reform the atoms of the star would be more than that available in the star. In effect, the star would not have enough energy to cool down. This paradox puzzled Eddington.

Eddington believed that the pace of work in the field was quickening and that the newly developed field of quantum mechanics might be able to cast light on the theory of stellar interiors. He was correct on both counts. The paradox introduced by Eddington was resolved shortly after it was stated. Ralph H. Fowler resolved the paradox using the recently developed quantum mechanics, but he showed that white dwarf stars were even stranger than anticipated. The pressure that kept the star from contracting indefinitely was the result not of the temperature of the star but of "electron degeneracy." In the intense heat and pressure of a star's interior, electrons are torn away from nuclei and move about freely. In the classical theory, the electrons can move about unrestricted. According to quantum theory, however, the electrons are restricted to a discrete set of energies. In a normal star, electrons typically occupy many of the higher allowed energy levels.

In the interior of a white dwarf star, however, the electrons enter a special energy state. Electrons occupy all the lower energy levels. In this special case, the pressure exerted by the electrons becomes independent of the temperature. The star, according to Fowler, can no longer contract. The electrons cannot be forced into lower energy levels. The electrons are said to be "degenerate" because the electrons have become "neutralized"—they are no longer a factor in determining the resistance to gravitational collapse. Fowler resolved Eddington's paradox by showing that a white dwarf can resist the force of gravity through electron degeneracy. The temperature of the star no longer matters. White dwarfs can live out their lives slowly cooling off.

A SURPRISING SNUB

In 1935, Subrahmanyan Chandrasekhar was scheduled to present his radical new theory of stellar evolution before the meeting of England's Royal Astronomical Society. Shortly before the meeting, Chandrasekhar received a program. He noticed that Arthur Stanley Eddington was also giving a paper. Chandrasekhar's findings contradicted those of Eddington.

At the meeting, Chandrasekhar discussed his results, which indicated that the lifetime of a star of small mass must be essentially different from that of a star of large mass. Edward Arthur Milne, also attending the meeting, said that he had achieved similar results using a cruder method. Eddington then launched into a personal attack on Chandrasekhar and his theory. Eddington was convinced that Chandrasekhar's method was faulty because it was based on a combination of relativistic mechanics and nonrelativistic quantum theory. He argued that his own result could still be obtained after suitable modifications of Chandrasekhar's theory. Although Eddington admitted that he could find no fault with the technical details of Chandrasekhar's approach, he was compelled to challenge the results because of the unexpected result that large stars will continue to contract. The depth of Eddington's objections and the way in which they were made surprised and upset Chandrasekhar: "Eddington effectively made a fool of me," he later recalled.

The dispute with Eddington lasted years, yet the two remained cordial. Chandrasekhar left England in 1937 for Chicago. In 1939, he summed up his work on stellar structure. In 1974, Chandrasekhar accounted for the delay in the acceptance of his theory, stating that his conclusions "did not meet with the approval of the stalwarts of the day." He noted the irony of Eddington's position: Eddington argued against the continual collapse of stars with a mass over the Chandrasekhar limit because such stars would "go on radiating and radiating and contracting and contracting until, I suppose, it gets down to a few [kilometers'] radius when gravity becomes strong enough to hold the radiation and the star can at last find peace."

Chandrasekhar was describing what is now called a "black hole," which Eddington thought was an absurdity. Nevertheless, years later black holes were accepted as the final fate of stars that were so massive that their gravity even prevented light from escaping. Chandrasekhar's "foolishness" was ultimately proved correct.

Subrahmanyan Chandrasekhar followed the latest developments in astrophysics during his studies in theoretical physics in India. Upon graduation in 1930, he went to Trinity College, Cambridge, on a scholarship. He won a physics contest, for which he received a copy of Eddington's *The Internal Constitution of the Stars*. He began to question Eddington's conclusions concerning white dwarfs and Fowler's calculations concerning electron degeneracy. He calculated that electrons in the dense core of a white dwarf would be moving at a velocity nearly that of light, so corrections must be made to the classical formulas describing the behavior of matter.

Chandrasekhar made the necessary corrections and realized that the effect was dramatic. For stars with a mass greater than about 1.4 times that of the Sun, the "pressure" exerted by electron degeneracy would not be enough to overcome the force of gravity. Instead of a long, slow cooling off, such stars would continue to contract, apparently indefinitely. Chandrasekhar did not speculate on the ultimate fate of stars of more than 1.4 solar masses. Calculations done years later by others showed that those stars form either neutron stars or black holes.

From 1931 to 1935, Chandrasekhar published a series of papers of his findings. During this time, he worked with Fowler and Eddington. By 1935, Chandrasekhar had developed a detailed, quantitative, mathematically rigorous theory of white dwarf stars, and he fully expected Eddington to accept his theory. Eddington gave no indication to Chandrasekhar that he had any doubts about the surprising results Chandrasekhar's theory predicted. In 1935, Chandrasekhar was scheduled to present his results to the Royal Astronomical Society. Eddington also presented a paper, but to Chandrasekhar's surprise it included an attack on Chandrasekhar's theory.

However, work on white dwarfs continued, and further evidence was presented in support for his calculations. Chandrasekhar's ideas gained gradual acceptance in the 1940's and 1950's as more white dwarfs were discovered and as spectrographic evidence mounted.

SIGNIFICANCE

Chandrasekhar's theory introduced the notion that not all stars behave as benignly in their old age as white dwarfs. He did not speculate what would happen to a star with a mass above the limit. For stars with masses below the limit, he devised a complete theory to account for their properties. He won the Nobel Prize in 1983 for his theoretical studies on the structure and evolution of stars.

Chandrasekhar's limit is the dividing line between the strange but benign white dwarfs and the truly exotic black holes, pulsars, and neutron stars. It established the possibility that the strange behavior of stars nearing the end of their lives as white dwarfs could get stranger. Chandrasekhar's legacy is the mathematical order that he brought to the theory of white dwarfs. He continued to bring mathematical order to other areas of astrophysics, including black holes.

—*Roger Sensenbaugh*

FURTHER READING

Asimov, Isaac. *The Collapsing Universe.* 1977. Reprint. New York: Pocket Books, 1986. Engagingly written volume, intended for a wide audience, takes particular care to emphasize the immense range of stellar phenomena. Excellent introduction to astrophysics for the lay reader.

Chandrasekhar, Subrahmanyan. *Eddington: The Most Distinguished Astrophysicist of His Time.* Cambridge, England: Cambridge University Press, 1983. Slim volume presents two Sir Arthur Stanley Eddington Centenary Lectures, encapsulating both Chandrasekhar's personality and his relationship with Eddington. Reviews Eddington's contributions to astrophysics with grace and style and politely points out where Eddington was incorrect. Moderately technical.

Cooke, Donald A. *The Life and Death of Stars.* New York: Crown, 1985. Discusses the life history of stars in clear language, with minimal use of technical terms (which are carefully introduced in the early chapters). Profusely illustrated with both color and black-and-white photographs, charts, and diagrams. Highly recommended as a general introduction to stellar astronomy.

Cropper, William H. *Great Physicists: The Life and Times of Leading Physicists from Galileo to Hawking.* New York: Oxford University Press, 2001. Presents portraits of the lives and accomplishments of important physicists and shows how they influenced one another with their work. Chapter 28 is devoted to Subrahmanyan Chandrasekhar. Includes glossary and index.

Miller, Arthur I. *Empire of the Stars: Obsession, Friendship, and Betrayal in the Quest for Black Holes.* Boston: Houghton Mifflin, 2005. Provides background on the history of the idea of black holes and describes the debate between Chandrasekhar and Eddington concerning the nature of black holes as well as the implications of that debate for twentieth century science.

Shipman, Harry L. *Black Holes, Quasars, and the Universe.* 2d ed. Boston: Houghton Mifflin, 1980. Written for nonastronomers and for use as a supplemental text in university courses for nonscientists. Includes discussion of black holes and white dwarfs. Provides summaries throughout.

Tierney, John. "Subrahmanyan Chandrasekhar: Quest for Order." In *A Passion to Know*, edited by Allen L. Hammond. New York: Charles Scribner's Sons, 1984. Interview with Chandrasekhar accompanied by some additional biographical information. Provides an interesting perspective on Chandrasekhar's personality and work habits; gives minimal attention to the technical details of his theories.

SEE ALSO: 1916: Schwarzschild Solves the Equations of General Relativity; July, 1926: Eddington Publishes *The Internal Constitution of the Stars*; 1934: Zwicky and Baade Propose a Theory of Neutron Stars.

1931-1941
THE GROUP THEATRE FLOURISHES

The Group Theatre, founded in 1931 as a permanent theater company, flourished during the Great Depression before folding in 1941 after the United States entered World War II.

LOCALE: New York, New York
CATEGORY: Theater

KEY FIGURES

Harold Clurman (1901-1980), cofounder and director of the Group Theatre
Cheryl Crawford (1902-1986), cofounder and director of the Group Theatre
Lee Strasberg (1901-1982), cofounder and director of the Group Theatre
Stella Adler (1902-1992), American actor
Morris Carnovsky (1897-1992), American actor
Paul Green (1894-1981), American playwright
Clifford Odets (1906-1963), American actor and playwright

SUMMARY OF EVENT

Harold Clurman, Cheryl Crawford, and Lee Strasberg founded the Group Theatre as a permanent acting company in 1931, when the United States was in the depths of the Great Depression. Clurman had been a play reader for the Theatre Guild, where Crawford was a casting director. Lee Strasberg was an actor who had learned the Stanislavsky method at the American Laboratory Theater.

American theater grew rapidly during the 1920's. Eugene O'Neill had emerged after World War I as a towering theatrical figure in a country that had little high-quality indigenous drama to stage until O'Neill began writing plays. A new freedom of language and outlook affected the emerging drama.

Most of the American theater of the early century consisted of dramas by European playwrights or by such canonical playwrights as William Shakespeare. Broad Jewish comedies in Yiddish or "Yinglish," as the dialect that combined Yiddish and English came to be called, were also popular. Earlier American playwrights such as George H. Boker, Robert Montgomery Bird, Dion Boucicault, and Clyde Fitch made little artistic impact on American theater. Their plays were mere vehicles for the stars, who dominated the theater. The star system was sufficiently entrenched that Eugene O'Neill's father, James, could spend most of his acting life playing one

character: the count in the stage version of Alexandre Dumas's novel *Le Comte de Monte-Cristo* (1844-1845; *The Count of Monte-Cristo*, 1846).

Most plays revolved around stars of legendary proportions. Stages were filled with supporting cast members—sometimes large supporting casts—but all attention was focused essentially on one or two actors (male or female) who dominated. The Theatre Guild, founded in 1918 to support living theater, bowed to the star system.

One of the Theatre Guild's experiments during 1929 involved its Studio Program, which was intended to produce special Sunday performances of serious dramas. Crawford, Strasberg, and Clurman were all involved in putting on the first—and only—performance of the Studio Program. The play was a Russian drama, and it brought all sorts of communist sympathizers to the theater.

After the Studio Program collapsed, Clurman dreamed of organizing an acting company unlike any in the United States. He wanted to develop a permanent—but not a repertory—company that would have its own cadre of actors, playwrights, and directors. Clurman knew that Strasberg could help in the implementation of this dream, but he knew as well that Strasberg was not a good organizer and that, despite his intelligence and talent, Strasberg could be devastatingly tactless. Clurman needed Strasberg, but he also needed a practical, down-to-earth organizer to carry on the day-to-day operation of the theater he envisioned. Crawford's handling of the production for the Studio Program convinced Clurman that she could offer his project precisely the skills required.

During the next months, the three worked toward establishing a theater company with the express aim of scrapping the star system. Its plays, written by various playwrights associated with the company, would have fewer than ten characters, with each as equal in prominence as the playwrights could manage. Actors would play lead roles one week and smaller roles or no roles the next. The favored acting technique was the Stanislavsky method of affective acting.

Everyone associated with the group would share equally in any profits—again a blow to any vestigial thoughts the members might have about a star system. The playwrights were not to be stars either; rather, the plays were viewed as instruments for the expression of ideas and the formulation of philosophies. The playwrights received an equal share of the meager profits the Group Theatre's plays usually generated.

ODETS AND THE GROUP THEATRE

Out of the work of the Group Theatre came one of the most important American playwrights of the twentieth century, Clifford Odets, whose major works of drama are listed below. The Group Theatre produced all of Odets's plays through Night Music *in 1940.*

- *Waiting for Lefty* (pr., pb. 1935)
- *Till the Day I Die* (pr., pb. 1935)
- *Awake and Sing!* (pr., pb. 1935)
- *Paradise Lost* (pr. 1935, pb. 1936)
- *I Can't Sleep* (pr. 1935, pb. 1936)
- *Golden Boy* (pr., pb. 1937)
- *Rocket to the Moon* (pr. 1938, pb. 1939)
- *Night Music* (pr., pb. 1940)
- *Clash by Night* (pr. 1941, pb. 1942)
- *The Russian People* (pr. 1942, pb. 1946; adaptation of Konstantin Simonov's play *The Russians*)
- *The Big Knife* (pr., pb. 1949)
- *The Country Girl* (pr. 1950, pb. 1951)
- *The Flowering Peach* (pr., pb. 1954)

By late 1930, Clurman's dream was in the first stages of becoming a reality. He and his two fellow founders enticed many theater people to meet with them in strategy sessions. Actors including Franchot Tone, Morris Carnovsky, J. Edward Bromberg, Phoebe Brand, Dorothy Patten, and Stella Adler and her brother Luther became interested in the concept of the Group Theatre. Clurman held meetings every Friday night to draw Broadway people into his scheme. When these meetings grew too large to fit into Clurman's room at the Hotel Meurice, they were moved to Crawford's apartment. When the enthusiastic crowd overflowed the apartment, the Friday night sessions moved to Steinway Hall.

By June, 1931, the Group Theatre company—twenty-eight actors, along with their various spouses, children, and others—left New York for the compound Crawford had found for them at Brookfield Center, near Danbury, Connecticut, where they undertook preparation for the theater's initial summer of operation. The first play scheduled for production was *The House of Connelly* (pr., pb. 1931), by Paul Green of North Carolina.

Clifford Odets was among the actors at Brookfield Center for the Group Theatre's first summer together. He remained with the Group Theatre for most of its existence, leaving only to accept a tempting offer to write for Hollywood. Such an act meant that Odets was prostituting himself in his own eyes, but he did so to make money

he could send back to Clurman to keep the financially strapped Group Theatre afloat.

The summer over, the Group Theatre returned to New York. Its members rented a ten-room apartment on West Fifty-seventh Street for fifty dollars a month, and the Group Theatre continued to operate during the winter. During its first few years, the organization presented important new plays by Group Theatre playwrights and also provided excellent experience for actors.

In 1935, Odets burst upon the dramatic scene with the January production of his *Waiting for Lefty* (pr., pb. 1935), a tour de force that was precisely right for its time. By summer, Odets had two more plays on Broadway, *Till the Day I Die* (pr., pb. 1935) and *Awake and Sing!* (pr., pb. 1935). In the autumn, his *Paradise Lost* (pr. 1935) was brought to Broadway, transforming an unknown actor who claimed to live on ten cents a week into a playwright who was the toast of New York.

The Group Theatre produced all Odets's subsequent plays through *Night Music* (pr., pb. 1940). Its financial problems intensified when the United States entered World War II, a development that reduced the size of audiences. The Group Theatre was finally disbanded in 1941. With its disappearance, a significant chapter in the history of American drama ended.

SIGNIFICANCE

The Group Theatre affected American drama in many ways. Even with the emergence of Eugene O'Neill as a full-fledged, high-quality American playwright, American theater was somewhat without a compass until the Group Theatre redefined the place of drama in society. Much of the drama of the 1920's—excluding that by O'Neill—was a drama of manners. It did not seek to engage its audiences in penetrating thought along socioeconomic lines, nor, in the roaring 1920's, could it have.

The Group Theatre productions staged in the grim years of the Great Depression, however, raised thorny social questions relating to economics, the place of the individual in society, the role of government, pacifism and conscientious objection to war, and ethnically generated social injustice. One did not come to Group Theatre productions with the expectation of laughing, of being lulled into complacency, or of being amused. Nevertheless, people came, perhaps to have their consciences tweaked, their awareness of daunting economic problems raised.

The social backdrop against which Group Theatre productions played was one of poverty, joblessness, insecurity, and social alienation. The plays the Group

Theatre presented dealt with all these problems, although they played to audiences who certainly had the financial means to rise above the immediate problems that surrounded them. Theatrical audiences obviously have enough disposable income to enable them to attend plays; the theatrical audiences of the early 1930's seemed as well to have enough social conscience to encourage and patronize the kind of drama the Group Theatre favored.

That the Group Theatre changed permanently the structure of American drama cannot be denied. By moving away from the star system and encouraging playwrights whose plays had a balance of significant roles, the philosophy of the Group Theatre opened new possibilities to playwrights, particularly to such later practitioners of the art as Arthur Miller, Tennessee Williams, William Inge, and Edward Albee. It is interesting to note that in a work such as Albee's *Who's Afraid of Virginia Woolf?* (pr., pb. 1962), for example, the play's four characters—Martha, George, Honey, and Nick—have virtually equal dramatic stature, even if Martha's mouth gives her a slight advantage.

The same can be said of plays such as Miller's *Death of a Salesman* (pr., pb. 1949), Inge's *Come Back, Little Sheba* (pr., pb. 1950), and Williams's *The Glass Menagerie* (pr. 1944). In *Death of a Salesman*, the characters Willy and Linda Loman and their two sons, Happy and Biff, are virtually dramatic equals; Lola, Doc, Marie, and Turk are almost equivalent characters in the Inge play; Amanda, Tom, Laura, and Jim are essentially equals in *The Glass Menagerie*.

The Group Theatre was also largely responsible for emphasizing method acting in the United States. The technique had been taught previously by such organizations as the American Laboratory Theater, but the Group Theatre made it clear that this was the most effective way to act, and its mandate to advance "the Method" in its training sessions stuck.

The countless actors produced by the Group Theatre included Franchot Tone, Stella Adler, Luther Adler, Jacob Adler, Morris Carnovsky, J. Edward Bromberg, Lee J. Cobb, Katharine Cornell, John Garfield, Frances Farmer, Luise Rainer, and Brock Pemberton. An even greater legacy, however, accrued to the next generation, to actors such as Marlon Brando, James Dean, Marilyn Monroe, and others whose training, often with individuals who had been part of the Group Theatre experience, emphasized method acting.

Among those who act and write plays, the work of the Group Theatre remains well known, and its impact is readily acknowledged. Although the Group Theatre existed for only a decade, it forged professional relationships and encouraged approaches to drama that were, until the company's existence, all but unimaginable.

—*R. Baird Shuman*

FURTHER READING

Bordman, Gerald. *American Theatre: A Chronicle of Comedy and Drama, 1930-1969*. New York: Oxford University Press, 1996. Survey of every nonmusical play produced on Broadway (and some off-Broadway productions) during the period covered. Includes synopses and other details on many Group Theatre productions.

Brenman-Gibson, Margaret. *Clifford Odets: An American Playwright—The Years from 1906 to 1940*. 1981. Reprint. New York: Applause Books, 2002. First volume of a comprehensive biography of Odets includes many entries for the Group Theatre in its index. Unusually well-documented biography goes far beyond the narrow limits of one person's life and embraces an entire period of great change in American drama. A treasure trove for the scholar.

Clurman, Harold. *The Fervent Years: The Story of the Group Theatre and the Thirties*. 1945. Reprint. New York: Da Capo Press, 1983. Authoritative history of the Group Theatre by one of its founders and directors. Warm narrative discusses the people who made the Group Theatre possible. One of the most important books available on the topic.

Cohn, Ruby. *Dialogue in American Drama*. Bloomington: Indiana University Press, 1971. Examines the proletarian drama of the 1930's, much of which was dialect drama. Relates the lyricism of such playwrights as Clifford Odets and Thornton Wilder to the use of language of later playwrights such as Arthur Miller, Tennessee Williams, and Edward Albee. Written to be accessible to nonspecialists with a general interest in drama.

Gassner, John. *Dramatic Soundings: Evaluations and Retractions Culled from Thirty Years of Dramatic Criticism*. New York: Crown, 1968. Collection of critic Gassner's essays and theatrical reviews from 1935 through 1965. Includes perceptive insights into the work of the Group Theatre and its playwrights, particularly Clifford Odets, Paul Green, Philip Barry, and Maxwell Anderson. Focuses specifically on the Group Theatre, the Actors Studio, and the Theatre Guild.

Herr, Christopher J. *Clifford Odets and American Political Theatre*. Westport, Conn.: Praeger, 2003. Places Odets's works in the context of the time of social, political, and economic change in which they were written. Includes many references to his work with the Group Theatre.

Krutch, Joseph Wood. *The American Drama Since 1918.* Rev. ed. New York: George Braziller, 1957. Engaging overview of American drama between the world wars includes discussion of playwrights associated with the Group Theatre and the Group Theatre itself. An essential resource for anyone who wishes to understand the drama of the period in which the Group Theatre flourished.

Odets, Clifford. *The Time Is Ripe: The 1940 Journal of Clifford Odets.* New York: Grove Press, 1988. The Group Theatre figures centrally in this journal, which Odets kept at a time when his life was changing drastically. His marriage to Luise Rainer was deteriorating, his artistic integrity was on the line, and the Group Theatre, whose members formed his surrogate family, was dissolving. Includes many cogent references to the Group Theatre and what it meant to him.

Smith, Wendy. *Real Life Drama: The Group Theatre and America, 1931-1940.* New York: Grove Press, 1990. History of the Group Theatre discusses the personalities of the individuals involved and the social and political context of the times. Includes a list of the plays produced by the theater.

Williams, Jay. *Stage Left.* New York: Charles Scribner's Sons, 1974. Engaging examination of radical theater in the United States is almost an informal history of the Group Theatre. Focuses on several of the Group Theatre's playwrights—Green, Odets, Sidney Kingsley—and addresses the shift in American society that made proletarian drama, the mainstay of the Group Theatre, possible.

SEE ALSO: 1905: Baker Establishes the 47 Workshop at Harvard; Oct. 29, 1929-1939: Great Depression; Feb. 19, 1935: Odets's *Awake and Sing!* Becomes a Model for Protest Drama; Aug. 29, 1935-June 30, 1939: Federal Theatre Project Promotes Live Theater.

January 2, 1931
LAWRENCE DEVELOPS THE CYCLOTRON

Ernest Orlando Lawrence's development of the first successful magnetic resonance accelerator for protons marked the beginning of the modern era of particle accelerators.

LOCALE: Berkeley, California
CATEGORIES: Science and technology; physics; inventions

KEY FIGURES
Ernest Orlando Lawrence (1901-1958), American nuclear physicist
M. Stanley Livingston (1905-1986), American nuclear physicist
Niels Edlefsen (b. 1893), American physicist
David Sloan (b. 1905), American physicist and electrical engineer

SUMMARY OF EVENT
The invention of the cyclotron by Ernest Orlando Lawrence was a first step toward the modern era of high-energy physics. Although the energies have increased steadily, the principles incorporated in the cyclotron have been fundamental to succeeding generations of accelerators, many of which were also developed in Law-

rence's laboratory. The care and support of such machines have also given rise to "big science": the massing of scientists, money, and machines in support of experiments to discover the nature of the atom and its constituents.

Lawrence received his undergraduate degree in physics at the University of South Dakota and studied under W. F. G. Swann, an expert in electromagnetic theory and experiment at the Universities of Minnesota and Chicago and at Yale University, where he received his Ph.D. in 1925. Lawrence was an assistant professor until 1928, when he was lured to the University of California by an associate professorship, the opportunity to teach more graduate courses, and the university's new physics research laboratory.

At the University of California, Lawrence took an interest in the new physics of the atomic nucleus, which had been developed by Ernest Rutherford and his followers in England. This work was attracting increasing attention as the development of quantum mechanics seemed to offer an explanation of the problems of atomic physics that had long preoccupied physicists.

In order to explore the nucleus of the atom, however, suitable probes were required. Rutherford had used alpha particles ejected from radioactive substances to make his early studies, but these were not energetic enough to penetrate the nuclei of most atoms. An artificial means of accelerating ions to high energies was needed. During the late 1920's, a variety of means were tried to accelerate alpha particles, protons (hydrogen ions), and electrons, but none had been successful in causing a nuclear transformation when Lawrence entered the field. The high voltages required stressed the resources available to physicists. It was believed that more than one million volts would be required to accelerate an ion to sufficient energies to penetrate even the lightest atomic nuclei. At such voltages, insulators broke down, releasing sparks across great distances. European researchers even attempted to harness lightning to the task, with fatal results.

Early in April, 1929, Lawrence chanced on an article in *Archiv für Electrotechnik* by Rolf Wideroe, a German electrical engineer, describing a linear accelerator of ions that worked by passing an ion through two sets of electrodes, each of which carried the same voltage and increased the energy of the ions correspondingly. By spacing the electrodes appropriately and using an alternating electrical field, this "resonance acceleration" of ions could speed subatomic particles up to many multiplies of the energy applied in each step, overcoming the problems presented when one tried to apply a single charge to an ion all at once. Unfortunately, the spacing of the electrodes would have to be increased as the ions were accelerated, because they would travel farther between each alternation of the phase of the accelerating charge, making an accelerator impractically long in those days of small-scale physics.

Lawrence knew that a magnetic field would cause the ions to be deflected and form a curved path. If the electrodes were placed across the diameter of the circle formed by the ions' path, they should spiral out as they were accelerated, staying in phase with the accelerating charge until they reached the periphery of the magnetic field. This, he reasoned, would afford a means of producing indefinitely high voltages without using high voltages by recycling the accelerated ions through the same electrodes. Many doubted that such a method would be effective. No mechanism was known that would keep the circulating ions in sufficiently tight orbits to avoid collisions with the walls of the accelerating chamber. Others tried to use resonance acceleration without success. Lawrence waited nearly a year before encouragement from Otto Stern, a visitor in the University of California physics department from the University of Hamburg, persuaded him to try the method.

Ernest Orlando Lawrence. (The Nobel Foundation)

In the spring of 1930, Lawrence put one of his graduate students, Niels Edlefsen, to work on reducing his idea to practice. Edlefsen used glass flasks coated with silver or copper with a diametrical gap to serve as their electrodes. A filament introduced through one aperture in the flask produced protons from hydrogen introduced through another. When the flask was placed between the poles of a 10-centimeter (3.9-inch) electromagnet and radio frequency current was applied to the metallic electrodes, Edlefsen thought he saw evidence of particle acceleration. Unfortunately, he left Berkeley before this could be confirmed.

Another graduate student, M. Stanley Livingston, took up the project. He decided quickly that resonance could not be achieved with Edlefsen's apparatus. For his dissertation project, he used a brass cylinder 10 centimeters in diameter sealed with wax to hold a vacuum, a half pillbox of copper mounted on an insulated stem to serve as the electrode, and a Hartley radio frequency oscillator producing 10 watts. The shape resembled the letter D. The box itself constituted the other electrode: A brass bar was placed across it parallel to the straight side of the D with slots corresponding to those in the D. The hydrogen molecular ions were produced by a thermionic cathode mounted near the center of the apparatus from hydrogen gas admitted through an aperture in the side of the cylinder after a vacuum had been produced by a pump. Once formed, the oscillating electrical field drew them out and accelerated them as they passed through the gap between the bar and the D. The accelerated ions spiraled out in a magnetic field produced by a 10-centimeter electromagnet to a collector. By November, 1930, Livingston observed peaks in the collector current as he tuned the magnetic field through the value calculated to produce acceleration.

Borrowing a stronger magnet and tuning his radio frequency oscillator appropriately, Livingston produced 80,000-electronvolt ions at his collector on January 2, 1931, thus demonstrating the principle of magnetic resonance acceleration.

SIGNIFICANCE

Demonstration of the principle led to a succession of large cyclotrons, beginning with a 25-centimeter (9.8-inch) cyclotron developed in the spring and summer of 1931, which produced million-electronvolt protons. Lawrence succeeded in winning support for his device from Frederick Cottrell's Research Corporation and the Chemical Foundation, which were interested in its applications to the production of high-voltage X rays. Lawrence also developed a linear accelerator for heavy ions with the help of David Sloan, another of his graduate students. Sloan built a million-volt X-ray tube as well. With the support of the Research Corporation, Lawrence was able to secure a large electromagnet that had been developed for radio transmission and a disused civil engineering laboratory to house it. This was the Radiation Laboratory. The 69-centimeter (27.2-inch) cyclotron built with the magnet was used to explore nuclear physics. Rather than ordinary hydrogen ions, it accelerated deuterons, ions of heavy water or deuterium that contain, in addition to the proton, the neutron, which was discovered by Sir James Chadwick in 1932. The accelerated deuteron, which injected neutrons into target atoms, was used to produce a wide variety of artificial radioisotopes, which had been discovered by Frédéric Joliot and Irène Joliot-Curie. Many of these, like technetium and carbon 14, were discovered with the cyclotron and found applications in medicine and tracer research.

The 69-centimeter cyclotron was enlarged to 94 centimeters (37 inches) in diameter in 1937. By 1939, Lawrence had built a 152-centimeter (59.8-inch) cyclotron for medical uses, including therapy with neutron beams. In that year, he won the Nobel Prize in Physics for the invention of the cyclotron and the production of radioisotopes. He also received $1.15 million from the Rockefeller Foundation in 1940 to build a 467-centimeter (183.9 inch) cyclotron, designed to produce 200-million-electronvolt deuterons. World War II interrupted this effort, and Lawrence and the members of his Radiation Laboratory developed electromagnetic separation of uranium ions to produce the uranium-235 required for the atomic bomb. After the war, the 467-centimeter cyclotron was completed as a synchrocyclotron, which modulated the frequency of the accelerating fields to compensate for the increase of mass of ions as they approached the speed of light. The principle of synchronous acceleration, invented by Lawrence's associate Edwin Mattison McMillan, became fundamental to proton and electron synchrotrons, just as the linear accelerator was developed by another member of the Radiation Laboratory staff, Luis W. Alvarez.

The cyclotron and the Radiation Laboratory were the center of accelerator physics throughout the 1930's and well into the postwar era. The invention of the cyclotron not only provided a new tool for probing the nucleus but also gave rise to new forms of organizing scientific work and to applications in nuclear medicine and nuclear chemistry. Cyclotrons were built in many laboratories in the United States, Europe, and Japan, and became standard tools of nuclear physics.

—Robert W. Seidel

FURTHER READING

Childs, Herbert. *An American Genius: The Life of Ernest Orlando Lawrence, Father of the Cyclotron.* New York: E. P. Dutton, 1968. Details the life of the cyclotron's inventor in anecdotes, relying heavily on interviews with his colleagues. Includes photographs, bibliography, and index.

Heilbron, J. L., and Robert W. Seidel. *Lawrence and His Laboratory: A History of Lawrence Berkeley Laboratory.* Berkeley: University of California Press, 1989. Describes in detail the development of accelerator technology in the 1920's and 1930's and the impact of these developments on nuclear physics up to World War II. Includes illustrations, bibliography, and index.

Lee, S. Y. *Accelerator Physics.* 2d ed. Hackensack, N.J.: World Scientific Publishing, 2004. Text intended for college physics majors or graduate students begins with a chapter on the history of the development of particle accelerators.

Livingston, M. Stanley. *Particle Accelerators: A Brief History.* Cambridge, Mass.: Harvard University Press, 1969. Describes for the general reader the early attempts to produce high voltages for nuclear physics, the invention of the cyclotron and the electrostatic generator, the development of the betatron, and the origin and growth of the principles of synchronous acceleration and alternating gradient focusing. Includes illustrations, references, and index.

_____, ed. *The Development of High-Energy Accelerators.* New York: Dover, 1966. Collection of twenty-eight classic articles and an introduction written by the coinventor of the cyclotron. Depicts the evolution of direct voltage, resonance, linear, synchronous, and strong-focusing accelerators. Includes illustrations and index.

Livingston, M. Stanley, and John P. Blewett. *Particle Accelerators.* New York: McGraw-Hill, 1962. Clas-sic technical reference on particle accelerators offers a comparative critical analysis of the capabilities of various types of accelerators as well as a brief historical essay on each. Includes illustrations, references, and indexes.

Mann, Wilfred Basil. *The Cyclotron.* 4th ed. New York: John Wiley & Sons, 1953. Describes the cyclotron's history and development. Well illustrated, with sketches of the components of cyclotrons. Features an introduction by Lawrence. Includes references and index.

Wilson, Edmund. *An Introduction to Particle Accelerators.* New York: Oxford University Press, 2001. Moderately technical text devotes first chapter to the history of particle accelerators, including brief discussion of the Lawrence's work on the cyclotron.

SEE ALSO: May 14, 1913: Rockefeller Foundation Is Founded; Apr., 1932: Cockcroft and Walton Split the Atom; Jan.-Sept., 1937: Segrè Identifies the First Artificial Element.

March 5, 1931
INDIA SIGNS THE DELHI PACT

Mahatma Gandhi and the British viceroy of India agreed to the Delhi Pact, which ended a civil disobedience campaign and provided for talks between the Indian National Congress party and the British.

ALSO KNOWN AS: Gandhi-Irwin Pact
LOCALE: India
CATEGORIES: Indigenous peoples' rights; diplomacy and international relations; independence movements

KEY FIGURES
Mahatma Gandhi (1869-1948), Hindu leader of the Indian National Congress
Lord Halifax (Edward Frederick Lindley Wood; 1881-1959), viceroy of India, 1926-1931
Jawaharlal Nehru (1889-1964), president of the Indian National Congress

SUMMARY OF EVENT
In 1928, Mahatma Gandhi and the Indian National Congress party decided to mount vigorous opposition to the appointment of the Simon Commission, which the British sent to India to decide how the next step of constitutional reforms should take place. Gandhi decided that the opposition would take the form of a noncooperation movement. This would be a movement of civil disobedience begun with deliberate breaking of the salt laws, which gave a monopoly on salt production to the British government. Accordingly, on March 12, 1930, Gandhi and his followers started a twenty-five-day march to the sea to collect salt and thus break the law. The Salt March started off a nationwide protest over a wide variety of issues involving millions of Indians of all ages, classes, and religions. On May 5, Gandhi and the leaders of the Indian National Congress were arrested and imprisoned. Eventually, the British incarcerated more than sixty thousand people in their efforts to stop this protest movement, which led people to block streets, disobey police orders, and march through city centers curtailing business and disrupting all normal activities.

The Congress leaders were held in prison for nearly a year, until January 26, 1931, when they were released by the viceroy, Lord Irwin (also known as Lord Halifax). They were set free because the British wanted a truce with the Congress. The British were anxious to bring the Congress into the ongoing constitutional discussions—the Second Round Table Conference, to be held in London at the end of the year—so that Indians would accept the new constitution the British wanted to introduce into India. Because of this, they needed an end to the civil disobedience movement and Gandhi's participation and cooperation.

The Congress saw the noncooperation movement as a success, achieving a response never before seen in India, but many people, including Gandhi, were exhausted and ready for peace with the government. The rank-and-file members of the Congress who had led the demonstrations against the government were tired, and Indian businesspeople, who had in some cases lost a substantial sum of money because they were stopped from selling British products, wanted an end to disruptive practices. At this time, one of the most radical members of the Congress, Jawaharlal Nehru, came firmly under Gandhi's influence after the death of his father, Motilal Nehru. In addition, many of the more moderate politicians in India wanted an end to illegal activities. The result was that Gandhi responded positively to the viceroy's January 17 invitation to talks.

The formal meetings between Gandhi and Lord Irwin began in New Delhi on February 17, 1931. There was a total of eight meetings over a period of three weeks. Gandhi and Irwin got along well together, as both men were very religious and appreciated that quality in each other. The talks represented the highest point of Gandhi's political career and led to the Delhi Pact (popularly known as the Gandhi-Irwin Pact) of March 5, 1931.

The meetings did not meet with everyone's approval. Many Indians, including one of the most radical and forceful advocates of violent opposition to the British, Subhas Chandra Bose, wanted total opposition to British rule instead of talks and cooperation. Even they saw that opposition to Gandhi, who was immensely popular among the elite politicians as well as among the masses, would weaken their own position. Many conservatives in England were also strongly opposed to the meetings. Winston Churchill, the leading opponent in the Conservative Party, made the most famous comment when, referring to Gandhi, he complained about "the nauseating and humiliating spectacle of this one-time Inner Temple lawyer, now seditious fakir, striding half-naked up the steps of the Viceroy's palace there to parley on equal terms with the representative of the King-Emperor."

This comment revealed the new reality of the political situation in India and the significance of the Delhi Pact: An Indian was talking as an equal with the British viceroy for the first time in history. Through their noncooperation and their mass opposition, Indians, under the leadership of Gandhi, had forced the British to establish a

new relationship with the colonized people. Gandhi had aroused significant opposition to the British *raj* (rule), and India was no longer the docile and profitable country it had once been. The British knew they could no longer ignore Indian public opinion or ride roughshod over Indians' civil rights. As a result, they seriously planned to hand over the government of India to the Indians. The end of nearly two hundred years of foreign rule was clearly near.

Gandhi and the viceroy discussed a large number of issues. In the end, they came to an agreement on most and agreed to disagree on the others. The agreement began over the salt laws. The salt laws were not repealed, but local residents of areas where salt was made were allowed to produce some for domestic consumption and for sale within their villages. They were not, however, allowed to sell or trade their salt outside their villages. An amnesty was given to the many thousands of people arrested during the noncooperation movement who were not guilty of violent crimes, and all special ordinances passed to control the campaign were withdrawn. Those properties that were confiscated, forfeited, or attached because of a failure to pay fines and had not yet been sold by the government were restored to their owners. People were given back their government jobs if they had resigned from them as part of the noncooperation movement, provided that the jobs had not been offered to someone else in the meantime. Gandhi demanded an inquiry into police behavior during the campaign, but Irwin refused. Gandhi gave in on this point.

Gandhi agreed that civil disobedience would be stopped. In particular, organized defiance of any law, the movement for the nonpayment of land-revenue and other legal fees, the publication of news sheets in support of civil disobedience, and attempts to influence civil and military officials or to persuade them to resign were to cease. Gandhi also agreed that Congress would attend the second meeting of the Round Table Conference, to be held in London in the fall, to discuss a new constitution. Gandhi's comment after the talks were over was that Indians now had proof that the British were serious about giving them freedom and self-government.

The Delhi Pact was an important breakthrough with regard to the rights of Indians. Gandhi and the Congress, which represented the majority of Hindus in India, had in the past been the major opponent of British rule. Previously, the British had ignored this opposition as much as they could. This was no longer possible. The Delhi Pact, which resulted from the Salt March and the noncooperation movement, created a new relationship between

Indians and the British. The British had to respect Indians' civil rights in a way they never had in the past.

SIGNIFICANCE

As a result of the Delhi Pact, the Indian National Congress changed its policy of noncooperation with the British to one of working with them to write a new constitution and taking part in the government under that constitution. The pact also increased the determination of the British to work out a constitution that would be acceptable to Indians and would prevent any reoccurrence of noncooperation.

Gandhi attended the second session of the Round Table Conference, which opened in September, 1931, as the sole representative of the Congress. He did not get everything he wanted, but the Government of India Act of 1935, which followed from the conference, provided for representative government in the provinces and planned for independence at the center as well. One British concession at the conference was that minorities such as the Muslims were given special representation in regional parliaments and the national assembly. This increased their civil rights considerably. The pact established a new relationship between Indians and the British—they were now partners and not master and servant in the government of India.

The Government of India Act of 1935 called for general elections to be held in all the provinces of British India. These were held at the end of 1936 and the beginning of 1937. The Congress scored a major triumph, securing power in most of the provinces, and essentially ran the country from 1937 to 1939. The Congress members resigned from their government positions then because the British had declared war on behalf of India without consulting them. This had the unforeseen result of alienating elite Muslims, who believed they were excluded from government positions and contracts by the Hindus, who now had most of the power and patronage. In March, 1940, the leading Muslim political party, the All-India Muslim League, called for the creation of a separate country for Muslims. When India received its independence in 1947, the country was split into the Hindu area of India and the Muslim area of Pakistan.

The Delhi Pact was a turning point in Indian history because it established a new relationship between the British and the Indians. The agreement of a viceroy of the world's most powerful empire with Gandhi, a small man who dressed and acted as a saint, symbolized the triumph of Gandhi's ideas of nonviolence and civil disobedience.

—Roger D. Long

FURTHER READING

Brown, Judith M. *Gandhi and Civil Disobedience: The Mahatma in Indian Politics, 1928-34.* New York: Cambridge University Press, 1977. Provides an excellent detailed account of the events surrounding the signing of the Delhi Pact.

_____. *Gandhi: Prisoner of Hope.* New Haven, Conn.: Yale University Press, 1990. Places the Delhi Pact within the context of Gandhi's long and complex political life.

Copley, Antony. *Gandhi: Against the Tide.* 1987. Reprint. New York: Oxford University Press, 1997. Brief biography shows the place of the Delhi Pact within the framework of the Indian struggle for freedom. A useful quick reference.

Erikson, Erik. *Gandhi's Truth: On the Origins of Militant Nonviolence.* 1969. Reprint. New York: W. W. Norton, 1993. Psychoanalyst looks at the psychology of Gandhi's actions and the psychological dimensions of his relationship with the British. Analyzes Gandhi's decision to enter into negotiations with the British and the reasons for the Delhi Pact.

Fox, Richard G. *Gandhian Utopia: Experiments with Culture.* Boston: Beacon Press, 1989. Anthropologist shows how Gandhi was not only attempting to come to political decisions with the viceroy through the Delhi Pact but also trying to define the Indian nationalist movement in cultural terms congruent with traditional Indian culture.

Gandhi, M. K. *An Autobiography: The Story of My Experiments with Truth.* 1957. Reprint. Boston: Beacon Press, 1993. Essential source shows how Gandhi's coming to terms and negotiating with his opponents had its origins in his experiences in South Africa. Covers only up to 1920, so does not include discussion of the Delhi Pact.

_____. *Mohandas Gandhi: Essential Writings.* Edited by John Dear. Maryknoll, N.Y.: Orbis Books, 2002. Collection of Gandhi's writings is organized thematically, with topics including nonviolent resistance, the search for God, and the pursuit of truth. Includes a chronology as well as a list of sources and recommended readings.

Nehru, Jawaharlal. *Toward Freedom: The Autobiography of Jawaharlal Nehru.* 1941. Reprint. Boston: Beacon Press, 1963. An insider's account of the events surrounding the signing of the Delhi Pact by one of Gandhi's most loyal followers. A classic work, essential for its firsthand account of the Indian nationalist movement of the 1920's and 1930's.

Parekh, Bhiku. *Colonialism, Tradition, and Reform: An Analysis of Gandhi's Political Discourse.* Rev. ed. Thousand Oaks, Calif.: Sage, 2000. Examines Gandhi's political technique and explains how Gandhi was careful to use Indian symbols during his negotiations that led to the Delhi Pact. A rich analysis by a renowned Indian thinker.

Rudolph, Susanne Hoeber, and Lloyd I. Rudolph. *Gandhi: The Traditional Roots of Charisma.* Chicago: University of Chicago Press, 1983. Analyzes Gandhi's appeal and his use of all kinds of symbols—political, religious, and traditional—to impart his message.

Wolpert, Stanley. *Gandhi's Passion: The Life and Leg-*

acy of Mahatma Gandhi. New York: Oxford University Press, 2002. Biography of Gandhi and evaluation of his life's work inspired in part by India's seeming abandonment of his vision of nonviolence in the late twentieth and early twenty-first centuries. Includes bibliography and index.

SEE ALSO: Mar., 1915: Defense of India Act Impedes the Freedom Struggle; Apr. 13, 1919: British Soldiers Massacre Indians at Amritsar; 1920-1922: Gandhi Leads a Noncooperation Movement; 1925-1935: Women's Rights in India Undergo a Decade of Change; Mar. 12-Apr. 5, 1930: Gandhi Leads the Salt March; Sept. 25, 1932: Poona Pact Grants Representation to India's Untouchables.

March 19, 1931
NEVADA LEGALIZES GAMBLING

Nevada governor Fred B. Balzar signed two bills that would have major impacts on the state's image and economy. The first bill legalized most forms of gambling within the state, and the second made divorce easier in Nevada than in other states by cutting the necessary period of residency to six weeks.

LOCALE: Carson City, Nevada

CATEGORIES: Laws, acts, and legal history; social issues and reform; trade and commerce

KEY FIGURES

Phil M. Tobin (1901-1976), Nevada state assemblyman who sponsored the bill to legalize gambling in Nevada

Fred B. Balzar (1880-1934), governor of Nevada, 1927-1934

Raymond I. Smith (1887-1967), entrepreneur who promoted the Harold's Club around the world

SUMMARY OF EVENT

Nevada's legalization of gambling followed a tradition that predated clanging slot machines or glittering casinos. Its roots lay in the state's frontier past, when the first white settlers—cattlemen, sheepherders, miners, and the mountain men of the wilderness—came to northern Nevada. Gambling and liquor were always available to fill lonely workers' idle hours in the mining camps and boom towns that sprang up around the state. Frontier conditions also bred a libertarian attitude toward personal behavior that not even the state's strong Mormon influence could shake.

Nevada gained statehood in 1865. Two years later, the first state governor, Henry G. Blasdel, vetoed an act to legalize gambling. His objection was based on moral grounds, but in 1869 the state legislature overrode Blasdel's veto. Gambling remained legal in Nevada for the next forty years, and the state also had some of the era's most liberal divorce laws, which required a residency of only six months before papers were filed.

In 1910, under pressure from Progressives and other reformers both in and outside of Nevada, gambling was outlawed. Over the next few years, the legislature ventured a few changes around the edges of the gambling laws—exempting private card games, for example—but the legislation remained largely intact. However, this did not mean that gambling stopped. "Key clubs" flourished in Reno, and they had guarded entries and other subterfuges. Almost any town large enough to support an undercover gambling den had one, or several, and police generally overlooked them (with or without a bit of bribery).

By 1931, the Progressive Era had waned, and both the Great Depression and Prohibition had taken hold on the national scene. Nevada was especially hard hit when, in 1930, the production of silver—still one of the state's major industries—and other minerals fell to less than half the previous year's figures. Livestock production also began a downward slide in the late 1920's, and although Nevada had not yet felt the full force of the Depression by 1931, businessmen and politicians were aware of the need for other economic stimuli to replace the losses.

George Wingfield, a leading banker and Reno hotel owner, and Thomas H. Carroll, an influential Las Vegas real estate agent, were outspoken in their belief that legalized gambling and an even more liberalized divorce law could bring tourist dollars into the state. Almost as important in changing the climate of opinion, however, was the public's disillusion with the results of prohibiting gambling. The 1910 law was unenforceable, and despite frequent efforts to strengthen its regulation, gambling flourished in back rooms all over the state, and most police and officials were indifferent to it. Of course, by this time the United States had also adopted Prohibition, which had similar results. One state alone could not change the Eighteenth Amendment (1917), but the Nevada statute forbidding gambling could be overturned by one session of the legislature.

By the time that body met in 1931, both legislators and public were ready to end Nevada's prohibition of gambling. There had been low-key discussion in local newspapers, but the only strong voices opposing legalization came from women's clubs and some religious groups, and they were a minority. Finding a representative to sponsor a bill, however, was not easy. Although many thought legalizing gambling was a good idea, few politicians wanted to "own" the bill. Finally, on February 13, Phil M. Tobin, a freshman assemblyman from Humboldt County, introduced Assembly Bill 98. Winnemucca, Tobin's hometown, had recently polled its chamber of commerce members about legalized gambling. All but one of the sixty-nine members favored legalization, a fact that provided some cover for Tobin.

The bill sailed through Nevada's assembly and senate with very little opposition. On March 19, it was signed by Governor Fred B. Balzar and was slated to take immediate effect. On the same day, Balzar also signed a bill that lowered the residency period for divorce to an unprecedented six weeks. The new divorce legislation went into effect on May 1, 1931. Provisions of the gambling law were fairly simple. Licensing was done by city or county officials, who imposed a modest fee that was similar to building and other business licenses. Only some years later, when gambling mushroomed into a giant enterprise and shady characters from outside the state made inroads into casino ownership, did the state's modern complex of laws, licenses, and regulations develop.

The law's immediate economic impact was underwhelming. The Bank Club in Reno, the city's largest casino, remodeled in anticipation of the new law and held a gala grand opening on the night the law took effect. However, most card clubs and other establishments were used to keeping a low profile, and there was confusion at first about just what legal licensing entailed. Most gambling stayed in the back rooms where it had previously operated. Advertising was mostly by word of mouth.

Reno, the state's largest city, expected to prosper from the law. It did so, but for the first five years, the economic impact of the divorce legislation was much larger than that of gambling. The was because divorce was difficult to get in many jurisdictions. The only grounds allowed for divorce in New York State were adultery, and in booming California, just across the mountains, there were still rigorous provisions. As a result of its lenient policies, Reno gained a growing reputation as a glittering "big little city" visited by celebrities, surrounded by dude ranches and spectacular scenery.

In 1931, Las Vegas had a population of only around five thousand people. It was much more focused on the Boulder Dam project, which was just getting under way some few miles south, than it was on legalized gambling as a route to prosperity. Smaller cities, especially Elko and

Gamblers play roulette in a Nevada casino in 1939. (AP/Wide World Photos)

Sparks, had mixed feelings toward the new law, and they tried to minimize its impact by denying licenses. In general, Nevada officials maintained a cautious approach for several years; they feared that the Puritan influence of other states might prompt federal interference that would kill the infant industry.

This began to change with the advent of Harold's Club, which opened in 1936 on Reno's Virginia Street. Harold Smith, the owner, and his father, Raymond I. "Pappy" Smith, a public relations genius, put the casino and the city on the map through advertising and clever innovations. The elder Smith had "Harold's Club or Bust" signs placed all over the nation's highways and even in other countries, and this made people around the world curious about the little casino. The Smiths also designed a roulette game that was operated by mice. A little mouse ran around and around the wheel, and whichever hole he dived into was the winning number. This created valuable buzz and helped end the taboo against women in casinos; women could now use the excuse of going in to watch cute little mice. With these two advertising innovations and a customer base that included both sexes, legalized gambling was able to become a tourist attraction and economic engine for Nevada.

SIGNIFICANCE

The two bills signed by Governor Balzar in March of 1931 had significant effects. Legalized gambling ultimately led to giant, corporate-managed casinos, with the Las Vegas Strip drawing visitors from the entire world. Because of its economic impact, that city and its suburbs became some of the fastest-growing cities in the United States. Furthermore, Nevada's success with legal gambling led to its demystification and its acceptance by a wide segment of the U.S. population. Atlantic City, New Jersey, the Mississippi Gulf Coast, and Native American tribes became the most notable investors in casinos, which brought prosperity to depressed areas and peoples.

In addition, many states adopted lotteries (still forbidden in Nevada by the state constitution) as a revenue source.

The significance of the liberalized divorce legislation is harder to assess. For several decades it did contribute to Nevada's influx of tourists and gave rise to dude ranches and other western-themed attractions in northern Nevada. Since the 1970's, when no-fault divorce became available in most states, few of Nevada's visitors came to the state simply to get a divorce. In fact, Las Vegas's wedding chapels became more of a draw. The six-week residency requirement did not have a major influence on other states' divorce requirements.

—*Emily Alward*

FURTHER READING

Barker, Thomas, and Marjie Britz. *Jokers Wild: Legalized Gambling in the Twenty-First Century.* Westport, Conn.: Praeger, 2004. Topical treatment, with analysis of gambling as legitimate industry, gangster involvement, state-run lotteries, and gambling's effect on communities.

Hulse, James W. *The Silver State: Nevada's Heritage Reinterpreted.* 3d ed. Reno: University of Nevada Press, 2004. Overview of Nevada history, from original Native American inhabitants to the late twentieth century population boom. Photographs, maps, and extensive bibliography.

Laxalt, Robert. *Nevada: A Bicentennial History.* Reno: University of Nevada Press, 1977. Nevada history told in an informal style, with emphasis on colorful people and bizarre events that shaped the state. Chapter on "The Sin State" traces the state's reputation back to an 1897 prizefight.

SEE ALSO: Jan. 16, 1920-Dec. 5, 1933: Prohibition; Mar. 5, 1923: Nevada and Montana Introduce Old-Age Pensions; Mar. 11, 1936: Boulder Dam Is Completed.

Spring, 1931
LE CORBUSIER'S VILLA SAVOYE EXEMPLIFIES FUNCTIONALIST ARCHITECTURE

Le Corbusier used his design for a weekend house to demonstrate that functionalist rules for architecture could produce a new style and a great work of art.

ALSO KNOWN AS: Les Heures Claires
LOCALE: Poissy-sur-Seine, near Paris, France
CATEGORY: Architecture

KEY FIGURES
Le Corbusier (1887-1965), Swiss-born French architect and city planner
Pierre Jeanneret (1896-1968), French engineer
Mme Pierre Savoye (fl. mid-twentieth century), Frenchwoman who commissioned Le Corbusier to design a weekend house near Paris

SUMMARY OF EVENT

The Villa Savoye, also known as Les Heures Claires, is the most beautiful, rigorous, and subtle building designed during the tumultuous developing years of modern architecture, 1919-1930. When the building's architect, Le Corbusier, undertook its design in 1928, he had been the leading spokesman for the modern movement in architecture for five years. His aphorism "A house is a machine for living," published in his 1923 book *Vers une architecture* (*Towards a New Architecture*, 1927), articulated the beliefs of many radical architects in the decade after World War I. Architecture, Le Corbusier declared, could be a living art only if architects ceased to copy past artistic styles and worked toward a simple expression of functional needs. The bare white walls and relentlessly regular streets in Le Corbusier's drawings of as-yet-unbuilt designs, and his praise of automobiles, steamships, and mass-produced cheap goods, gave him a reputation as a farsighted but extreme propagandist for functionalism. Because of the broad scope of his proposals, he was much better known as a theorist of urban planning than as an architect.

In 1928, Le Corbusier's office was busy with several large-scale commissions, including a hostel for Swiss students in Paris and a government office complex in Moscow. He had built a few low-budget houses around Paris for artists and patrons. In the fall of that year, the wife of wealthy Parisian Pierre Savoye asked him to design a three-bedroom weekend villa on some twelve acres above the Seine valley; Le Corbusier later described Mme Savoye as without preconceptions for or

against modernism. The building budget—approximately 350,000 francs—was far greater than any of his previous house budgets.

The house was to be built on a gently domed hill in the middle of a field. As presented in October, 1928, the plans for the project called for a square reinforced-concrete dwelling unit with four long strip windows, lifted a story above ground level on twenty-five slim concrete pillars (*pilotis*). Within the open ground-floor space was a driveway curved around a glass-walled entry chamber. On the top floor was another curved-wall space enclosing Mme Savoye's bedroom. When this project was rejected as too expensive (758,000 francs), Le Corbusier presented a second, less elegant proposal in November, 1928; thereafter, however, he fought to return to the layout of the first concept. Optimistic budget estimates and the elimination of the top-floor bedroom (its curved wall remained as a roof-garden screen) led the Savoyes to approve the project in December, 1928, at a budget of 487,000 francs. Construction began in April, 1929. The Savoyes moved into the villa in the spring of 1931, but Le Corbusier began featuring the house in his writings and lectures as early as October, 1929. For the architect, it represented the culmination of all his work and theories to date.

The Villa Savoye's design owed much less to the Savoyes' specific requirements than to the "five points of a new architecture" formulated by Le Corbusier and his cousin and design partner Pierre Jeanneret in 1926. These "points" were a list of functional requirements for buildings in the machine-age city that would become a universal stylistic vocabulary for architecture. The first point called for the elevation of the building on concrete posts, separating human-made buildings from the landscape and making the space under them accessible to nature and human circulation. The second point called for the creation of roof gardens, replacing the light, air, and greenery eliminated by a building by making them part of the building itself. The third point concerned the "open plan," the separation of load-bearing pillars (concrete or steel) from walls that were to act only as screens—a requirement of structural honesty. The fourth point, the strip window, was intended to give the interior uniform light and the outside a sense of horizontal repose. The fifth, the "free facade"—the construction of

The Villa Savoye. (The Granger Collection, New York)

the outside wall as a thin screen, not a bearing wall— would allow building fronts to be composed for aesthetic effect. The sense of overlapping thin walls, punctuated by windows and cutouts, would create an abstract, cubist aesthetic for the building.

The Villa Savoye fulfills all five points masterfully in a complex yet integrated whole. The principle of the "open plan" separates the structural *pilotis* from the enclosure, made of taut, thin concrete walls finished in smooth white stucco. Resting on its white *pilotis*, the house rises from its field as the image of abstract reason in harmony with nature. The "open plan" also turns practical circulation into dramas of spatial experience—first as one drives up to and under the house by car, then as one climbs the interior ramp or the adjacent spiral staircase from the entry to the free-form living floor. This floor wraps around an open terrace, from which another ramp climbs to the steamship-funnel-like roof screen. The terrace represents the principle of the roof garden inserted into the mass of the building. The ribbon windows are uniform on all four sides, even where they cut through the wall that encloses the terrace. The house thus com-

bines symmetry and repose with an exciting intermingling of closed and open spaces.

The Villa Savoye is a "machine" for beauty and harmony with nature. Le Corbusier declared that the Savoyes, "who will have come here because this countryside was beautiful . . . will contemplate it, preserved intact, from the height of their suspended garden or from the four sides of the long window. Their domestic life will be inserted into a Virgilian dream."

SIGNIFICANCE

Le Corbusier himself saw the Villa Savoye as the climax of his ideas of the 1920's, but not as a new starting point. His designs soon began to change radically. The house's critical success, however, forced reconsideration of the nature of Le Corbusier's achievement and provided justification on several levels for adopting his methods.

For critics, the house disproved the common estimation of Le Corbusier as an art-hating functionalist who could conceive utopian cities but not real buildings. In reality, as the Villa Savoye proved, Le Corbusier saw architecture as an art before anything else. The white, recti-

2487

linear style in which he worked symbolized for him the marble classical architecture of the Mediterranean world, the exotic stucco architecture of the Arabs, and the vision-transforming planes of cubist painting. (The architect was himself a painter; he called his orderly version of cubism "Purism.") Functionalism was only the twentieth century's means toward architecture's eternal purpose: to give walls and space vivid emotional impact.

The Villa Savoye realized this purpose in a new, abstract way. In its geometric purity, it could be read as a contemporary version of the perfect harmony of the classical temple or the Renaissance country mansions of Andrea Palladio. The interplay of wall screens, solid geometrical shapes, and half-hidden open spaces gave the house an abstractness unknown to classical architecture, as did the way in which functional elements became part of the composition. Modernity and technology, in Le Corbusier's hands, could call up the whole past history of the architectural art without ceasing to be the tools of "the machine for living."

The Villa Savoye's aesthetic success seemed to bear out the inevitability of the "five points of a new architecture." With the very limited repertory of the points—white freestanding walls, exposed supports, ribbon windows, unornamented right-angle forms, flat roofs—Le Corbusier had created a structure that seemed to meet all possible requirements of modern building, practical, urbanistic, ideological, and aesthetic. Younger architects who had come to doubt the usefulness of classic and Gothic Revival styles took Le Corbusier at his word and declared that his manner was a perfected style—in fact, the only possible style. This was the argument made by the Museum of Modern Art in New York in its seminal "International Style" exhibition of 1932, which showed the work of Le Corbusier and others in order to prove that such a new style existed. The argument was taken up by such architects as Wallace Harrison and Edward Durrell Stone in America, Bertold Lubetkin and the Tecton Group in England, and Oscar Niemeyer in Brazil. Despite angry disclaimers by modernists with different approaches, such as Frank Lloyd Wright, the "white box" style canonized in the Villa Savoye came to seem mandatory for contemporary architecture.

The Villa Savoye also proved that functionalist beliefs did not necessarily lead to low-budget, utilitarian decisions in design. A sensitive artist could transform a type or program—in this case, the modern house—into a personal, unique work. That Le Corbusier had transformed functionalism into art was a crucial point in the arguments over modernism in the period from 1928 to

1931. His own earlier writings had given the (mistaken) impression that he saw modern architecture as a cheap form of social planning, not an aesthetic discipline. The idea that functionalism could be the means of building a new visual and social world economically had been even more strongly advanced by Walter Gropius, the founder of the Bauhaus design school in Germany, and by German municipal housing architects. To such designers at the beginning of the Depression, preoccupation with art in preference to society seemed blinkered, willfully individualist, and reactionary. By putting art, in the form of the Villa Savoye, before social reform, Le Corbusier seemed to be breaking with this position.

Supporters of the modernist aesthetic who feared that social planning would replace artistic judgment in a social revolution were relieved to see that the greatest practitioner of the modern style was not a revolutionary. This sense of relief was essential to the Museum of Modern Art's encouragement of the Villa Savoye's style and helped lead to the adoption of Le Corbusier's manner (and that of the equally art-conscious German modernist Ludwig Mies van der Rohe) as the style of the corporate establishment after World War II. The power of Le Corbusier's earlier urban-renewal arguments, however, made his approach equally acceptable to the architects of government housing projects during and after the Depression. After World War II, urban-renewal architects tended to confuse his arguments with those of Gropius.

By the time Les Heures Claires was completed in 1931, Le Corbusier himself had begun to transform the elements of the "five points," especially the *piloti*, box, and free wall, into heavier and more earthbound terms. His Swiss Pavilion in Paris (1931) used massive concrete *pilotis* with sculptural shapes and stone facings on the hostel block. The De Mandrot house of the same year rested on the ground, not on posts, and used fieldstone and rough plywood. Having proved in the Villa Savoye that machinelike abstract geometry could be used to make great buildings, Le Corbusier began to explore organic shapes and materials toward the same end. It would be some two decades before his followers took up this path themselves, and still longer before architects and critics realized that his ideal had been the freedom of the artist, not the necessity of machine functionalism.

—*M. David Samson*

FURTHER READING

Benton, Tim. "The Villa Savoye and the Architect's Practice." In *Le Corbusier*, edited by H. Allen Brooks. Princeton, N.J.: Princeton University Press, 1987.

Traces how Le Corbusier developed the Villa Savoye's design, using the architect's preliminary drawings and his lectures about the house. Discussions of budget and the clients' complaints illuminate the practical problems of Le Corbusier's art. Includes illustrations and index.

_____. *The Villas of Le Corbusier, 1920-1930*. New Haven, Conn.: Yale University Press, 1987. Chronological catalog describes the circumstances, characteristics, and importance of all the architect's house designs before 1930. Presents little discussion of non-residential work of the same years. Provides a full list of surviving architectural drawings of Le Corbusier buildings.

Blake, Peter. *The Master Builders: Le Corbusier, Mies van der Rohe, Frank Lloyd Wright*. Rev. ed. 1976. Reprint. New York: W. W. Norton, 1996. Provides an accessible and entertaining account of Le Corbusier's life and principles. Somewhat dated; chapters written during the subject's life were not revised after his death, and the book reflects little of the widespread dissatisfaction with modernism after 1960. Includes index.

Curtis, William J. R. *Modern Architecture Since 1900*. 3d ed. London: Phaidon Press, 1996. A general textbook that devotes much attention to Le Corbusier and defends his achievements against contemporary and later critiques. Synthesizes the insights of other authors and critics while stressing the classical features of the Villa Savoye and other Le Corbusier work of the 1920's. Includes endnotes and index.

Jencks, Charles. *Le Corbusier and the Continual Revolu-tion in Architecture*. New York: Monacelli Press, 2000. Biography by a noted architectural historian covers Le Corbusier's personal life as well as the development of his work. Includes endnotes and index.

_____. *Le Corbusier and the Tragic View of Architecture*. Cambridge, Mass.: Harvard University Press, 1973. Presents an often complex analysis that convincingly links the biographical, artistic, and theoretical in the architect's work. More inclusive than Benton's account (cited above), but more speculative. Includes index.

Le Corbusier. *Precisions: On the Present State of Architecture of City Planning*. Translated by Edith Schreiber Aujame. Cambridge, Mass.: MIT Press, 1991. Collection of the 1929 Buenos Aires lectures in which Le Corbusier explained the Villa Savoye as the synthesis of his principles. Illustrated by the architect's own sketches.

Rowe, Colin. *The Mathematics of the Ideal Villa, and Other Essays*. Cambridge, Mass.: MIT Press, 1976. The title essay introduced the idea that Le Corbusier's architecture had classical as well as functionalist sources. This and the other essays illuminate how architects can be inspired by the past in indirect ways, but Rowe often relies more on hunches than on scholarship.

SEE ALSO: 1905: Hoffmann Designs the Palais Stoclet; 1910: Gaudí Completes the Casa Milá Apartment House; Oct., 1932: Wright Founds the Taliesin Fellowship; 1937: Prouvé Pioneers Architectural Prefabrication; 1937-1938: Aalto Designs Villa Mairea.

March 25, 1931-July, 1937
SCOTTSBORO TRIALS

The trials of nine young African Americans on trumped-up rape charges mirrored both entrenched southern bigotry and antiliberal sentiments. The U.S. Supreme Court's decision to grant the defendants a new trial expanded the rights of the accused to adequate counsel and due process of law.

LOCALE: Scottsboro and Decatur, Alabama
CATEGORIES: Laws, acts, and legal history; civil rights and liberties

KEY FIGURES

Ruby Bates (1915-1976), and
Victoria Price (1911-1982), American professed rape victims
Olen Montgomery (b. 1914),
Clarence Norris (1912-1989),
Haywood Patterson (1913-1952),
Ozie Powell (b. 1916),
Willie Roberson (b. 1915),
Charlie Weems (b. 1911),
Eugene Williams (b. 1918),
Andy Wright (b. 1912), and
Roy Wright (1918-1959), African Americans accused of rape
James E. Horton (1878-1973), American judge
Thomas E. Knight, Jr. (1898-1937), attorney general of Alabama
Samuel Leibowitz (1893-1978), American defense counsel

SUMMARY OF EVENT

On March 25, 1931, nine young African Americans were pulled off a freight train in Scottsboro, Alabama, after an alleged fight with a group of white youths. As the African Americans were being rounded up by sheriff's deputies, two women passengers told onlookers that they had been raped by the entire group. Within a month, the boys had been tried in Scottsboro, and eight of them had been convicted and sentenced to death; the case of the youngest boy, only thirteen years of age, was declared a mistrial. Because of the speed of the convictions, the questionable nature of much of the testimony, and the hostile atmosphere in which the trial had been held, the case soon attracted widespread attention. Both the International Labor Defense (ILD), an arm of the Communist Party, and the National Association for the Advancement of Colored People (NAACP) expressed concern about the

possibility of injustice and launched an appeal for a new trial. The boys and their parents chose the ILD to manage their defense.

The consolidated appeals reached the U.S. Supreme Court as *Powell v. Alabama* (1932), and the Court overturned the boys' convictions and ordered that they be given new trials. The Court's seven-to-two decision was based on the fact that the defendants had had access to counsel only immediately before the trial, preventing them from mounting an adequate defense. It also involved the lack of due deliberation in the overly speedy trial and the racial makeup of the jury.

Only three of the defendants were retried immediately. Their trials took place in Decatur, Alabama, from March to December, 1933. All three received convictions and death sentences, but the U.S. Supreme Court again sustained their appeal, this time on the basis of irregularities in the selection of jurors: The apellants pointed out that Decatur's voting rolls showed no African Americans registered to vote in the county in spite of a very large population of qualified African Americans residing there. This issue was to reappear on several occasions over the course of the Scottsboro trials.

In January, 1936, a third group of trials, held in Decatur, resulted in the conviction of Haywood Patterson, who was sentenced to seventy-five years in prison. After more than a year of delay and behind-the-scenes negotiations between Alabama state officials and a group of the defendants' supporters, the remaining eight were tried in the summer of 1937. One received the death penalty, three were sentenced to long prison terms, and the other four were released without charges. Although the one death sentence was later commuted to life imprisonment, the five convicted Scottsboro boys were unable to obtain any further reversals of their convictions. One of them was paroled in 1943, two more in 1946, and a fourth in 1950. The final prisoner escaped from a work gang in 1948 and managed to reach Michigan, whose governor refused to extradite him back to Alabama. The former defendant quickly found himself in trouble, however, committing a murder and being sentenced to Michigan's worst prison. He was unable to escape the environment in which he had spent most of his days, the prison.

It was not simply the length of the Scottsboro trials that accounted for the vast amount of publicity they attracted throughout the 1930's. Most observers outside Alabama and an increasingly large number of people within the state came to believe that the defendants were innocent and were, therefore, the victims of southern racial injustice. One of their two accusers, Ruby Bates, had retracted her testimony by 1934 and admitted that she had lied in her original accusations. The other, a prostitute named Victoria Price, presented testimony so full of contradictions that one of the judges in the 1933 trials, Alabamian James E. Horton, overruled the jury's guilty verdict and declared a mistrial. At least one of the defendants was ruled physically incapable of rape, and a physician testified that a medical examination of Bates and Price, performed shortly after the presumed attack, did not support their claims. Although both women were found to have had recent sexual intercourse, there were no contusions or other injuries that would have matched their stories about brutality at the hands of the nine men. None of this had any appreciable effect on the juries, the prosecutors, or Judge William W. Callahan, who presided after Horton was removed from the case. Even the milder sentences meted out in 1937 resulted as much from a desire to end the unfavorable publicity surrounding the trials as from any reevaluation of the evidence. That is why four of the defendants were eventually released on the same testimony that convicted the other five.

SIGNIFICANCE

Aside from serving as a symbol of southern bigotry, the Scottsboro trials attracted attention because of the efforts of the Communist Party to identify the cause of the defendants with their own. Working through the ILD, the Communist Party was one of the first groups to protest the verdicts in the 1931 trials, and it was the only group to offer direct aid at that time. For several years, the party engaged in a running battle with the NAACP and an "American Scottsboro Committee" over the right to manage the boys' defense. The effect of these struggles was to unite many Alabamians against all "reds and foreigners" and make it more difficult to revise the verdicts.

The chief defense counsel after 1931 was Samuel Leibowitz, a Jewish attorney from New York who became the target of scurrilous attacks from the prosecutors. Even he, along with Judge Callahan and part of the

Defendant Haywood Patterson (center) appears in court in April, 1933. (NARA)

Alabama press, came to regard the defendants' Communist support as a liability, and Leibowitz sought to dissociate the ILD from the case. In 1935, the NAACP, the American Civil Liberties Union, and the ILD joined to form the Scottsboro Defense Committee (SDC), which was designed to coordinate support for the defendants and seek cooperation from moderate Alabamians. Although the ILD played a much smaller role in the case from that point on, there remained enough hostility toward outside interference in Alabama to frustrate the SDC's efforts.

The Scottsboro case mirrored many of the important social currents of the 1930's. Although it illustrated the extent to which white southerners would go to defend a system of white supremacy, it also marked a change from the not-too-distant era when the defendants might well have been summarily lynched. The hysterical attitude with which many Alabamians reacted to outside interest in the case underlined a regional insecurity that had been intensified by the unsettled conditions of the Great Depression. It was common for both men and women to hop onto freight trains, which the nine men had done, as had the two alleged victims. The Scottsboro boys had gotten into a fight with several white men. In Scottsboro and Decatur, race was on trial, not nine boys and men, much to the lasting chagrin of the state of Alabama. The episode would not end until 1976, when the Alabama Board of Pardons and Paroles granted Clarence Norris a full pardon. It thus took forty-five years for justice to be served.

—Courtney B. Ross and John Jacob

FURTHER READING

Carter, Dan T. *Scottsboro: A Tragedy of the American South*. Rev. ed. Baton Rouge: Louisiana State University Press, 1979. Reprint. Delanco, N.J.: Gryphon Editions, 2000. Analyzes the trials and treatment of the nine African Americans and discusses the impact of the events on the South.

Chalmers, Allan Knight. *They Shall Be Free*. Garden City, N.Y.: Doubleday, 1951. An account of the Scottsboro trials from the perspective of one of the defense attorneys who also argued before the U.S. Supreme Court.

Khan, Lin Shi, and Tony Perez. *Scottsboro, Alabama: A Story in Linoleum Cuts*. Edited by Andrew H. Lee. Foreword by Robin D. G. Kelley. New York: New York University Press, 2002. A fascinating primary source, this collection of 118 linocuts was unearthed by an NYU librarian. Originally created in 1935, they tell the story of the Scottsboro trials as a parable of the working classes resisting the tyranny of the ruling class. Bibliographic references.

Levy, Leonard, et al., eds. *Encyclopedia of the American Constitution*. 4 vols. New York: Macmillan, 1986. Volume 3 provides ancillary but detailed analysis of decisions made by the Supreme Court in these cases.

Norris, Clarence, and Sybil D. Washington. *The Last of the Scottsboro Boys*. New York: Putnam, 1979. The last and most literate of the defendants presents his case. Valuable for its perspective and the view of prison conditions over many years.

Patterson, Haywood, and Earl Conrad. *Scottsboro Boy*. Garden City, N.Y.: Doubleday, 1950. The first book to shed personal light on the plight of the nine, it remains a powerful testament to a decade of injustice.

SEE ALSO: Feb. 12, 1909: National Association for the Advancement of Colored People Is Founded; 1940: Wright's *Native Son* Depicts Racism in America.

April, 1931
FIRST ELECTRON MICROSCOPE IS CONSTRUCTED

Replacing light rays and optical lenses, respectively, with electron beams and "electron lenses," a group of German engineers pioneered electron microscopy.

LOCALE: Berlin Institute of Technology, Berlin, Germany
CATEGORIES: Science and technology; physics; inventions

KEY FIGURES

Ernst Ruska (1906-1988), German engineer and inventor
Max Knoll (1897-1969), German engineer
Hans Busch (1884-1973), German physicist
Louis de Broglie (1892-1987), French physicist
Reinhold Rüdenberg (1883-1961), German engineer

SUMMARY OF EVENT

A number of the most important inventions of the twentieth century had scattered origins, as did the first electron microscope, constructed by Ernst Ruska and Max Knoll in 1931. The electron microscope's history can be traced along three lines: motivation, theory, and technology. Scientists who look into the microcosmic world always demand microscopes of higher and higher resolution, or resolving power—that is, the ability of an optical instrument to distinguish closely spaced objects. As early as 1834, George Airy, the eminent British astronomer, theorized that there should be a natural limit to the resolution of (optical) microscopes. In 1873, two Germans, Ernst Abbe, cofounder of the Karl Zeiss Optical Works at Jena, and Hermann von Helmholtz, the famous physicist and philosopher, independently published papers on this issue. Both arrived at the same conclusion as Airy.

When it was proved that the wavelength of the light is the ultimate obstacle in raising the resolving power of the microscope, scientists and engineers began to consider electromagnetic radiations of shorter and shorter wavelengths. At the beginning of the twentieth century, Joseph Edwin Barnard experimented on microscopes using ultraviolet light. Such instruments, however, only modestly improved the resolution. In 1912, Max von Laue considered trying X rays. At the time, however, it was hard to turn "X-ray microscopy" into a physical reality. The wavelengths of X rays were exceedingly short, but they mostly penetrated material objects. It was thus made clear in the early 1920's that, in terms of resolving power, the optical microscope was approaching its limit.

In a new microscopy, light—even electromagnetic radiation in general—as the traditional medium that carries image information, had to be replaced by a new medium. At the same time, progress in physics—theoretical as well as experimental—began to offer a prospective medium. In 1924, the French theoretical physicist Louis de Broglie advanced a startling hypothesis. His insight into the analogues between dynamic and optical phenomena and their mathematical formalities—a profound analogy first disclosed by Sir William Rowan Hamilton in the 1830's—led him to state that there was something of a wave nature associated with material particles, particularly light microcosmic particles, such as electrons. His quantitative conclusions included a formula relating the particle's motion—more exactly, momentum—to the wavelength of the particle's associated wave. The faster the particle moves, the shorter the wavelength is.

Before the first electron microscope had been built, the technological possibility of electron microscopy occurred to some theoreticians along the line of the "matter wave." According to Dennis Gabor, in 1928 Leo Szilard suggested to him that an electron microscope should be made. Gabor, however, dismissed the idea with a forceful yet hypothetical statement: "Everything under the electron beam would burn to a cinder!" The electron microscope is another case of technological breakthrough that illustrates an interesting historical theme: Those who knew too much theory did not make the thing; those who made it were not aware of the latest theory.

When Knoll and Ruska built the first electron microscope in 1931, they had never heard about de Broglie's "matter wave." Ruska recollected that when, in 1932, he and Knoll first learned about de Broglie's idea, he became "extremely disappointed" but then "was immediately heartened" because he realized that those matter waves "must be around five orders of magnitude shorter in wavelength than light waves." It was based on two other lines of physical study—oscillography and electron optics—that Knoll and Ruska accomplished their invention. The core component of the two new subjects was the electron beam, or the cathode ray, as it was usually called then. Although for a long time the physical nature of the beam was not clear, some nineteenth century physicists succeeded in controlling and focusing it. As early as 1858, the mathematician and physicist Julius Plücker noticed that magnetic fields could deflect the "electric glow discharge." Later, in 1869, Johann Wilhelm Hittorf performed more and better experiments in controlling the cathode rays. In 1891, Eduard Riecke, using Hittorf's results and carrying out his own calculations, conjectured about the ultimate corpuscular nature of the phenomena involved. Five years later, in 1896, Olaf Kristian Birkeland, a Norwegian physicist, after experimenting with axially symmetric magnetic fields, arrived at a very encouraging conclusion: "Parallel light rays are not concentrated better to the focal point by a lens than are cathode rays by a magnet."

From around 1910, the German physicist Hans Busch was the leading researcher in this field. In 1926, he published his theory on the trajectories of electrons in magnetic fields. His conclusion was that magnetic or electric fields possessing axial symmetry act as lenses for electrons or other charged particles. In 1927, he conducted experiments verifying his own theory with a magnetic lens. With these contributions, Busch has been recognized as the founder of a new field later known as electron optics. His theoretical study showed, among other things, the exactness of the analogy between light rays

and optical lenses on one side and electron beams and electromagnetic lenses on the other. One logical consequence thus should be the feasibility of electron microscopy. Busch's experimental verification, however, was not a complete success. Ruska noticed that there existed an "order-of-magnitude discrepancy between the size of cathode image that he [Busch] found experimentally and that required by the imaging equation," in short, between theory and measurement.

From 1928, Ruska, as a graduate student at the Berlin Institute of Technology, belonged to a group engaged in studying and building cathode-ray oscilloscopes, an instrument much in demand in the industry of electric power. Knoll and Ruska worked hard to find the physical laws of focusing electron beams by magnetic or electric fields. Ruska's first project was the "bundling" of electron rays in the coaxial magnetic field of the short coil. On one hand, he had to find a method of calculation for the optimal design; on the other, he tried to build "powerful and compactly built oscillographs." Because of this task, he was concerned with the discrepancies in Busch's result. At this juncture, the difficulty of Busch became Ruska's motivational force. Ruska carried out accurate measurements, especially with regard to the "lens theory of the short coil." By doing so, he identified the major problem in Busch's work, that is, the nonuniformity of the energy of the electrons in the beam. Beginning with certain nonuniformity, everything thereafter became increasingly diffused.

Knoll and Ruska's effort ended in a series of successes: verification of Busch's theory, design and materialization of a concentrated electron "writing spot," and the actual construction of the electron microscope. By April, 1931, they established a technological landmark with the "first constructional realization of an electron microscope," although when Knoll lectured about their work in June, he avoided the term "electron microscope" because he did not want to be "accused of showmanship."

SIGNIFICANCE

The world's first electron microscope, which took its first photographic record on April 7, 1931, was rudimentary. Its two-stage total magnification was only sixteen times. Since that time, however, progress in electron microscopy has been spectacular. It is one of the prominent examples that illustrate the historically unprecedented pace of science and technology in the twentieth century. One comparison in the field of microscopy is that it took centuries for the simple magnifier, or the "burning

Ernst Ruska. (The Nobel Foundation)

glass," to become the compound microscope, but the equivalent transition in the transmission electron microscope took only two years.

Ruska and Knoll's achievement immediately motivated others to study further and experiment, although electron microscopes with better-than-light-microscope resolution seemed in 1932, according to many experts at the time, a pipe dream. Ruska had set his goal to create an electron microscope that would have a resolution better than that of the best optical microscope and that could observe every kind of specimen that had been observed previously in the light microscope. After Knoll left the team to work on the developing technology of television, Ruska found new coworkers and stimulated more. Reinhold Rüdenberg was then the chief of the scientific department of the Siemens-Schuckent-Werke. At the end of May, 1931, he applied for a patent in electron microscopy; later, after Knoll and Ruska's first paper was published in 1932, he stated that similar work had been ongoing for some time at Siemens. According to Ruska, Rudenberg could not substantiate such claims with actual results.

In 1935, for the first time the electron microscope surpassed the optical microscope in resolution. The problem of damaging the specimen by the heating effects of the electron beam proved to be more difficult to resolve. In 1937, a team at the University of Toronto constructed the first generally usable electron microscope. In 1942, a group at the Radio Corporation of America (RCA) headed by James Hillier produced its commercial transmission electron microscopes. From 1939 and 1940, research papers on electron microscopes began to appear in Sweden, Canada, the United States, and Japan; from 1944 to 1947, papers appeared in Switzerland, France, the Soviet Union, the Netherlands, and England. Following research work in laboratories, commercial transmission electron microscopes using magnetic lenses with short focal lengths also appeared in these countries.

Despite some priority disputes, Ruska's personal contribution has been generally recognized. In 1960, Ruska and Hillier were jointly presented the Albert Lasker Award in Medical Research for "their major contribution to the design, construction, development and perfection of the electron microscope, which led to the creation of an unique and much used research instrument." In 1986, Ruska received the Nobel Prize in Physics with Gerd Binnig and Heinrich Rohrer, two IBM physicist-engineers, for inventing the scanning tunneling microscope in the early 1980's. Although the scanning tunneling microscope is a different microscope from Ruska's

transmission electron microscope, both types use the quantum mechanical characteristics of the electron beam.

The electron microscope has been described as one of the most important inventions of the twentieth century, and the long-range impacts of the instrument on science and engineering are self-evident. About Ruska's work, John Reisner of RCA stated: "While electron-optics people knew of the idea after the work by Busch on electron trajectories, Ruska did it. It was tough technology, and his was the step that got everyone going."

—*Wen-yuan Qian*

FURTHER READING

Bradbury, S. *The Evolution of the Microscope.* Elmsford, N.Y.: Pergamon Press, 1967. Detailed examination of the evolution of microscopy as a whole; ends with a history of the electron microscope.

Burton, E. F., and W. H. Kohl. *The Electron Microscope.* New York: Reinhold, 1942. Although dated, explains the physics and technology of the electron microscope in a manner accessible to lay readers. Chapters titled "The Dual Theory of the Electron" and "The History of the Electron Microscope" are particularly informative.

Hawkes, Peter W., ed. *The Beginnings of Electron Microscopy.* Orlando, Fla.: Academic Press, 1985. Substantial anthology covers the history of electron microscopy. Most of the contributions discuss its development in various nations, fields, and laboratories. Includes a preface by Ruska.

Marton, Ladislas. *Early History of the Electron Microscope.* 2d ed. San Francisco: San Francisco Press, 1994. Brief historical introduction by an original contributor in the development of electron microscopy. Includes a preface by Dennis Gabor, the major constructor of the first electron lens and oscilloscope.

Rasmussen, Nicolas. *Picture Control: The Electron Microscope and the Transformation of Biology in America, 1940-1960.* Stanford, Calif.: Stanford University Press, 1997. Discusses the rapid impact of the availability of the electron microscope on the direction of biological research in the United States. Includes index.

Ruska, Ernst. *The Early Development of Electron Lenses and Electron Microscopy.* Translated by Thomas Mulvey. Stuttgart, Germany: S. Hirzel, 1980. Historical introduction by the acknowledged inventor himself begins with the ancestry of the optical microscope. Aware of his special position in the overall development, Ruska is careful to acknowledge other researchers' contributions. This account extends to around 1940, when Ruska's major contributions (magnetic lens with short focal lengths and the prototype transmission electron microscopes) still exerted significant influence.

Wyckoff, Ralph W. G. *Electron Microscopy*. New York: Interscience, 1949. Although dated, provides an in-

formative historical introduction to the technique and the applications of the electron microscope.

SEE ALSO: 1902: Zsigmondy Invents the Ultramicroscope; 1923: De Broglie Explains the Wave-Particle Duality of Light; 1936: Müller Invents the Field Emission Microscope.

April 14, 1931
SECOND SPANISH REPUBLIC IS PROCLAIMED

The Second Spanish Republic was proclaimed after the abdication of the king and the election of a constituent Cortes. The moderate and left-wing republicans formed a coalition government, but after five years of pressure from the far Right and the far Left, the government collapsed into civil war.

LOCALE: Madrid, Spain
CATEGORY: Government and politics

KEY FIGURES

Niceto Alcalá-Zamora y Torres (1877-1949), president of the Second Spanish Republic, 1931-1936

Julián Besteiro (1870-1940), president of the Cortes, 1931-1939

Manuel Azaña y Díaz (1880-1940), founder and leader of the Republican Action Party and prime minister of Spain, 1931-1933 and 1936-1939

Alejandro Lerroux (1864-1949), leader of the Radical Party and prime minister of Spain, 1933-1935

Alfonso XIII (1886-1941), king of Spain, r. 1886-1931

Francisco Largo Caballero (1869-1946), leader of radical elements in the Socialist Party

Indalecio Prieto (1883-1962), leader of moderate elements in the Spanish Socialist Party

José María Gil Robles y Quiñones (1898-1980), journalist and leader of the moderate Catholic party

Miguel Maura y Gamazo (1887-1971), minister of the interior of Spain, 1931

José Sanjurjo (fl. early twentieth century), leader of an attempted coup by the right wing

SUMMARY OF EVENT

By 1931, Alfonso XIII of Spain was a bankrupt monarch. In addition to his failure to provide Spain with the leadership necessary to solve its problems, he had approved the 1923 coup d'état of Miguel Primo de Rivera y Orbaneja, which had established a dictatorship. When the dictator

had resigned in 1930, Alfonso had hoped to provide a transitional regime that would prepare the way for a return to constitutional government.

The reformist parties, however, had gained great strength since the mid-1920's. The Socialist Party, led by Indalecio Prieto and Francisco Largo Caballero, and the Republican Radical Party, led by Alejandro Lerroux, joined newly established liberal parties and groups under Manuel Azaña y Díaz and Niceto Alcalá-Zamora y Torres to demand the establishment of a reform republican government. When the king announced municipal elections in April, 1931, to test this republican sentiment, the results indicated that the Crown had lost. On April 14, 1931, the republican politicians proclaimed the Second Spanish Republic, and Alfonso went into exile.

In July, 1931, elections were held for the constituent Cortes, or parliament, and a liberal Republican-Socialist coalition was formed to govern Spain. The first cabinet reflected the overwhelming support of the electorate for Republican and Socialist deputies. Right-wing Republicans, the majority of whom were from the Radical Party of Alejandro Lerroux, and left-wing Republicans under Manuel Azaña y Díaz held more than half of the seats in the Cortes, while Socialists, led by Largo Caballero and Prieto, held an additional 115 seats. Alcalá-Zamora was chosen as prime minister, but became the first president of the republic later that year, after Azaña was selected to be prime minister of the governing coalition. Other members of the first government included Miguel Maura y Gamazo, minister of the interior; Lerroux, foreign minister; and Azaña, who also served as minister of war.

The Cortes wrote a constitution incorporating many liberal reforms and providing regional autonomy for those provinces that desired it, thereby solving the Catalan problem. It provided for reform of the military and action against the Roman Catholic Church, which had been one of the supporters of the old regime. The Church

Some of the important figures of the Second Spanish Republic (front row, left to right): Manuel Azaña y Díaz, Álvaro de Albornoz, Niceto Alcalá-Zamora y Torres, Miguel Maura y Gamazo, Francisco Largo Caballero, Fernando de los Ríos, and Alejandro Lerroux. (NARA)

was disestablished, the clergy's salaries were abolished, the Jesuit order was dissolved, and provisions were made to prevent the clergy from teaching. This attack on the Church, however, precipitated a crisis that brought down the first cabinet. When Article 26 of the constitution went into effect, many excellent schools operated by Jesuits and Augustinians closed; there were no state schools immediately available to take their place. This action angered both devout Catholics and members of the middle class whose children's schooling was disrupted.

Other reforms established machinery for wide and sweeping land reform, because solving Spain's agrarian problems was critical to the new government. These reforms did not do enough to satisfy many peasants, and incidents in several small villages led to riots and murder. The government's actions began to polarize the country. Liberal reforms satisfied many moderates, but practicing

Catholics were unhappy. Furthermore, extremist elements opposed the Republican-Socialists. On the right, the monarchists schemed with the military to restore Alfonso. General José Sanjurjo led a coup against the Republic in 1932, but he and his followers were arrested. Anarchists of the Left called the reforms too moderate. They countered with strikes and industrial violence and tried to provoke the clergy by burning churches and monasteries.

SIGNIFICANCE

In 1933, the first phase of the Second Spanish Republic ended, as the Republican-Socialist coalition fell, and the election was won by Confederación Española de Derechos Autónomos (CEDA), the moderate Catholic party led by José María Gil Robles y Quiñones, and the Radicals, then becoming more conservative under their leader Lerroux. Because the CEDA had unsavory monarchist connections, the Republican-Socialists in the newly elected Cortes rejected Gil Robles's bid for power. Instead, Lerroux became prime minister with CEDA backing.

CEDA-Radical ministries governed Spain from 1933 to 1935. As the CEDA's main concern was revision of the anticlerical legislation and the Radicals had no reform plans, little action was taken during these years. Most of the Republican-Socialist reform legislation was allowed to lapse or was not implemented, causing the parties of the Left to refer to the period as the "Two Black Years." The Anarchists protested and, along with certain Republicans and Socialists, revolted against the government in 1934. The revolt was put down, and many of the proletarian party leaders were imprisoned. Finally, in late 1935, Alcalá-Zamora dissolved the Cortes and ordered new elections in order to break the parliamentary impasse.

In the elections of early 1936, the forces of the Left—Liberals and Socialists, with the tacit approval of the Anarchists—joined in a coalition known as the Popular Front. They defeated the disunited rightists and gained control of the Cortes. The Republican-Socialist reforms were once again implemented, but there was so much opposition from both extremes that public order was gravely compromised, thus provoking a military uprising by the right wing in July, 1936. This marked the beginning of the Spanish Civil War, as the forces of the Right battled the leftist government for control of the country until 1939, when the Fascists achieved victory with the support of Germany's Nazi Party. The Second Spanish Republic was at an end, and the inability of the extreme Right and Left to accept a middle-leftist coalition had ultimately led to the establishment of an authoritarian right-wing regime.

—*José M. Sánchez and James A. Baer*

FURTHER READING

Brenan, Gerald. *The Spanish Labyrinth: An Account of the Social and Political Background of the Civil War.* Canto ed. New York: Cambridge University Press, 1990. Gives an excellent background to the civil war, and provides much information on the most important political forces in Spain.

Carr, Raymond. *Spain, 1808-1939.* Oxford: Clarendon Press, 1961. A comprehensive history of Spain with a chapter on the period of the Second Spanish Republic.

Crow, John A. *Spain, the Root and the Flower: An Interpretation of Spain and the Spanish People.* 3d ed. Berkeley: University of California Press, 1985. Offers a cultural history of Spain, with chapters 12 and 13 specifically on the background and events of the Second Spanish Republic.

Jackson, Gabriel. *The Spanish Republic and the Civil War, 1931-1939.* Princeton, N.J.: Princeton University Press, 1964. Political analysis sympathetic to the Second Republic and critical of "extremist" elements on both the left and the right.

Lewis, Norman. *The Tomb in Seville: Crossing Spain on the Brink of Civil War.* New York: Carroll & Graf, 2005. Travel memoir of a British writer's journeys in Spain during the Second Republic and his observations of the situation on the ground leading up to the civil war.

Madariaga, Salvado de. *Spain: A Modern History.* New York: Frederick A. Praeger, 1958. A history of Spain and the events of the Second Republic from a minister of Education in the Republican government. Author states in Introduction that he does not treat Nationalist side evenly because he did not know these men and was sympathetic to those he knew in the Republican government.

Payne, Stanley G. *The Collapse of the Spanish Republic, 1933-1936: Origins of the Civil War.* New Haven, Conn.: Yale University Press, 2006. Comprehensive study of the crux-years of the republic and the causes of its instability and collapse. Bibliographic references and index.

Smith, Rhea Marsh. *Spain: A Modern History.* Ann Arbor: University of Michigan Press, 1965. General history of Spain from prehistoric times to the twentieth century includes clearly written chapters on the dictatorship of Primo de Rivera and the Second Republic.

Thomas, Hugh. *The Spanish Civil War.* New York: Harper & Row, 1961. A classic study of the background of the civil war and its major events from a political as well as military perspective.

SEE ALSO: July 17, 1936: Spanish Civil War Begins; Jan. 6, 1937: Embargo on Arms to Spain; Apr. 26, 1937: Raids on Guernica; July, 1937: Picasso Exhibits *Guernica*.

May 1, 1931
EMPIRE STATE BUILDING OPENS

The opening of the Empire State Building expressed the state of the art of skyscraper technology and introduced to the world an enduring symbol of American ingenuity and progressiveness.

LOCALE: 350 Fifth Avenue, New York, New York
CATEGORIES: Architecture; science and technology; economics

KEY FIGURES
John Jakob Raskob (1879-1950), American financier
William F. Lamb (1883-1952), American architect
Alfred E. Smith (1873-1944), former governor of New York and president of the Empire State Corporation
Lewis W. Hine (1874-1940), American photographer

SUMMARY OF EVENT
On August 29, 1929, *The New York Times* headlined an announcement that the Empire State Corporation would begin construction on an important commercial venture at Thirty-fourth Street and Fifth Avenue, site of the famous Waldorf-Astoria Hotel. The five New York financiers involved intended to erect the world's tallest building on the two-acre site. Their plan was to offer prestigious rental office space in a skyscraper that would embody the richness and achievement of New York, the Empire State. When it opened during the Great Depression, the Empire State Building represented an image of strength and spirit of which New Yorkers and, by extension, all Americans could be proud.

The building was the inspiration of John Jakob Raskob, an influential New Yorker who was head of the Empire State Corporation and a vice president and shareholder in the General Motors Corporation. Politically active, he served as the Democratic National Chairman and acted as campaign manager for presidential candidate Alfred E. Smith, New York's popular four-time governor. Smith lost to Herbert Hoover in the 1928 election, providing Raskob with the opportunity to offer him the position of president of the Empire State Corporation and manager of the proposed Empire State Building. Raskob's shrewd decision to hire the charismatic Smith proved to be crucial to the success of the project. In late October of 1929, the stock market crashed, plunging the United States into the Great Depression. Many construction and skyscraper projects planned at the time were criticized as frivolous, given the severe economic slump. The Empire State Building project survived, however,

largely as a result of Smith's association with it. The man's powerful identification with New York, his obvious pride in the city, and his immense personal appeal and reputation for integrity helped to secure a loan of $27.5 million from the Metropolitan Life Insurance Company.

The architectural firm of Shreve, Lamb, and Harmon was hired to design the Empire State Building. It was a young partnership with excellent credentials and a reputation for taking a practical, functional approach to commercial building. Together with chief architect William F. Lamb, Raskob calculated that 36 million cubic feet of rentable space would be needed to make the venture a profitable one. It soon became clear to Lamb that the skyscraper mass would be shaped primarily by practical matters: the size of the site (200 feet by 425 feet), a fixed budget of $60 million, a May 1, 1931, deadline, and city zoning laws. Adherence to the deadline date was of particular concern to Raskob, who wanted to avoid financial loss by ensuring immediate availability of rental space on the customary day for signing commercial leases.

Of all the practical elements involved in the design of the Empire State Building, the restrictions imposed by New York City's 1916 zoning law contributed most significantly to the building's final shape. Aimed at protecting the city from overbuilding and ensuring sufficient light and air for all streets and offices, the law required street setbacks above the thirtieth floor for any building mass and required that no floor be more than one quarter the area of the site. The pyramidal style common to many New York City skyscrapers clearly was a reaction by local architects to these restrictions.

Lamb designed from the top down. His sixteenth attempt (Plan K) at shaping the skyscraper resulted in the final design for the Empire State Building. Following the form of the classical column, the mass was divided into three parts: a five-story base topped by a sixty-foot terrace (meeting the required setback restriction), a limestone office tower that soared to the eighty-sixth-floor observation deck, and a cap composed of a rounded fourteen-story glass and metal mooring mast for dirigibles. It was Raskob's intent that with the continuation of transatlantic dirigible travel, the top floor of New York City's tallest building would make the ideal international arrival lounge. The style of the building was restrained Art Deco and blended traditional motifs with the streamlined look of the machine age. Fully conceived, the image of the Empire State Building was sleek, glamorous, and uplifting.

The construction firm of Starrett Brothers and Eken was engaged, and an elaborate strategy was mapped out in minute detail, complete with a set of overlapping monthly schedules. By October 1, 1929, the demolition of the Waldorf-Astoria was begun. The hotel would relocate to a chic uptown location. On March 30, 1930, excavation for the Empire State Building was under way. The speed with which the structure rose was surprising even to those who worked on the project.

Lamb planned to meet the May 1 deadline by doing away with hand-work wherever possible, instead using glass, stone, and steel elements capable of being accurately mass produced and speedily assembled. A new method of fenestration was used that cut time and costs as well as saved office space: Glass for the sixty-five hundred windows was applied to the outside wall, or skin, of the skyscraper with metal brackets, rather than setting each pane into an individual stone frame. This also created the building's characteristic smooth and shimmery exterior. Another timesaving innovation involved a temporary miniature railway that made tightly scheduled runs to each floor, carrying needed tools and materials.

On April 11, 1931—having broken several construction records—the completed Empire State Building towered 1,250 feet and 102 stories above New York City's busy avenues. Built in one year and forty-five days at a cost of approximately $41 million, the world's tallest skyscraper had, incredibly, been finished ahead of schedule and under budget.

The building officially opened at 11:15 A.M. on May 1, 1931. Standing before a festive crowd of onlookers, Alfred E. Smith assisted his two young grandchildren in a traditional ribbon-cutting ceremony at the magnificent Fifth Avenue entrance. At 11:30 A.M., President Herbert Hoover pushed a button in Washington, D.C., and the main corridors of the Empire State Building were bathed in light. Later, at a luncheon celebration on the eighty-sixth-floor observation deck, Governor Franklin D. Roosevelt noted that, as a creation of vision and faith, the

---

THE EMPIRE STATE BUILDING: FACTS AND FIGURES

- *Completion time:* 410 days
- *Architect:* Shreve, Lamb & Harmon Associates
- *Contractor:* Starrett Brothers and Eken
- *Construction man-hours:* 7,000,000
- *Cost including land:* $40,948,900
- *Cost of building alone:* $24,718,000
- *Site area:* 79,288 square feet
- *Foundation:* 55 feet below ground
- *Basement:* 35 feet below ground
- *Lobby:* 47 feet above sea level
- *Height to top of lightning rod:* 1,453 feet, 8 9/16 inches
- *Floors:* 103
- *Steps:* 1,860 from street to 102d floor
- *Volume:* 37 million cubic feet
- *Weight:* 365,000 tons
- *Windows:* 6,500
- *Elevators:* 73
- *Exterior materials:* 200,000 cubic feet of Indiana limestone; 10,000 square feet of rose famosa and estrallante marble; 300,000 square feet of Hauteville and Rocheron marble for interiors
- *Plumbing:* 70 miles of pipe
- *Electricity:* 2,500,000 feet of electrical wire

Empire State Building "is needed in the city of New York. It is located at a strategic center. . . . It is needed by the whole nation."

SIGNIFICANCE

The Empire State Building is as much an icon as it is an outstanding example of architectural achievement. Since its opening in 1931, it has become an important and dramatic source of identity for the people of New York and an internationally recognized symbol of the wealth and strength of the American nation. As such, the Empire State Building remains one of New York City's biggest tourist attractions. More than 65 million visitors flock to the eighty-sixth-floor observation deck annually. They go to experience the dizzying sensation of height, to see the magnificent views (more than fifty miles on a clear day), and to buy millions of souvenirs. Pencils, pens, postcards, glasses and mugs, key chains, spoons, snow-globe paperweights, and at least nine different variations of the Empire State Building in miniature serve to carry its famous image to even the most remote areas of the world.

Architecturally, the Empire State Building represents the culmination of the American skyscraper race of the

1920's and 1930's, when monumentality was expressed by hugeness of mass and soaring height. This notion of height, which became an overriding concern among New York architects in particular, gave New York City a distinctive skyline and a progressive image that applied not only to it but also to other American cities of maturity. The building signified the nation's vitality. It became a symbol of skyscrapers everywhere and of a force that would forever change the American urban environment. Its sheer size served to heighten controversy about the potential dangers of populating modern cities with densely packed high-rise buildings. Some perceived the great American skyscrapers as symbols of greed and profit. As the nation trudged along through the difficult Depression years, interest in the skyscraper movement waned.

From an artistic standpoint, the Empire State Building's restrained Art Deco style sent a message to the world about the successful marriage of art and technology in the machine age. It was a theme common to many major skyscrapers of that era. By blending progressive, eclectic, and traditional European stylistic elements, Art Deco skyscrapers such as the Empire State Building expressed the forces of motion, energy, and life, integrating these with the streamlined nature of the machine. The move away from the manual way of doing things was

projected, and the future of technology was glorified. American skyscrapers became linked symbolically to national dreams and expectations.

During the Depression, construction of the Empire State Building provided positive images to the suffering populace. In May of 1930, American photographer Lewis W. Hine was commissioned to chronicle the rise of the building. He took more than one thousand photographs, concentrating on the energy and fearlessness of the thousands of workers involved. The photographs collected in Hine's 1932 book *Men at Work: Photographic Studies of Modern Men and Machines* portrayed the workers as heroes. The collection revealed heartening images of courage, tenacity, and teamwork at a time when Depression hardships seemed almost insurmountable.

The Empire State Building remains a focal point for New Yorkers. In the 1930's, a television antenna was mounted on the top of the building and, in a pioneering effort, images of Mickey Mouse and Felix the Cat were transmitted to homes within a fifty-two-mile range. Later, topped by a sixty-foot metal pole, the building was transformed into an immense lightning rod so that scientists could study the phenomenon of lightning. Tragically, the famed building received national attention in 1945, when a B-25 bomber became lost in Manhattan's foggy maze of skyscrapers and crashed into the seventy-ninth floor.

Lives were lost, yet only one steel beam in the entire structure was damaged. The accident briefly renewed negative comments about the continued construction of skyscrapers.

The Empire State Building is an easily identifiable image and a part of American lore. Over the years, it has played a part in many motion pictures, including *King Kong* (1933), *An Affair to Remember* (1957), and *Sleepless in Seattle* (1993). Artists such as Georgia O'Keeffe and photographers such as Alfred Stieglitz have incorporated it into their works. Suicidal individuals and celebrities alike have been drawn by the mystique and majesty of the towering structure. Visitors have included Albert Einstein, Winston Churchill, Queen Elizabeth II, and Helen Keller.

The Empire State Building is about many things—glamour, identity, commerce, entertainment, technology, op-

A construction worker high above Manhattan streets on the framework of the Empire State Building. This photograph by Lewis W. Hine is one of many he created to document the courage of those who constructed the building. (NARA)

portunity, and, most important, achievement. Although it was surpassed in height when New York's World Trade Center towers opened in 1972, and later by the Sears Tower in Chicago and the Petronas Towers in Kuala Lumpur, Malaysia, its image and symbolism endure. With the destruction of the World Trade Center towers in the terrorist attack of September 11, 2001, the Empire State Building once again came to dominate the New York skyline.

—*Cynthia L. Breslin*

FURTHER READING

Goldberger, Paul. *The Skyscraper*. New York: Alfred A. Knopf, 1981. Excellent discussion of the skyscraper movement in Chicago versus that in New York. Chapter 5 focuses on the skyscraper races of the 1930's that produced the Chrysler, Chanin, and Empire State Buildings. Includes photographs, endnotes, and index.

Goldman, Jonathan. *The Empire State Building Book*. New York: St. Martin's Press, 1980. Brief, entertaining history presents facts and anecdotes. Includes excellent photographs and an interesting collection of postcard pictures, artists' renditions, and other memorabilia.

Huxtable, Ada Louise. *The Tall Building Artistically Reconsidered: The Search for a Skyscraper Style*. 1984. Reprint. Berkeley: University of California Press, 1992. Treatise on the history, aesthetics, politics, and economics of tall office building—what the Pulitzer Prize-winning author calls the "drama of the skyscraper." Chronicles the search for a skyscraper style from the time when architects looked to the architectural styles of the past for inspiration to the newer varied styles of the late twentieth century.

James, Theodore, Jr. *The Empire State Building*. New York: Harper & Row, 1975. Exuberant, almost emotional, history includes many unusual facts and anecdotes. Features photographs (many taken by Lewis W. Hine), appendix of interesting facts, bibliography, and index.

Macauley, David. *Unbuilding*. Boston: Houghton Mifflin, 1980. Author/illustrator combines meticulous and playful pen-and-ink drawings with a unique fantasy tale about the dismantling of the Empire State Building in the year 1989. The story provides a vehicle for a technically accurate explanation of the building's structure and engineering. Enjoyable for both juvenile and adult readers. Includes glossary.

Messler, Norbert. *The Art Deco Skyscraper in New York*. Rev. ed. New York: Peter Lang, 1986. Sophisticated treatment of the cultural and historical significance of New York City's Art Deco skyscrapers of the 1920's and 1930's. Highlights and interprets the architectural elements unique to this style and discusses the American focus on technology and the machine age. Includes photographs, extensive notes, and index.

Reynolds, Donald Martin. *The Architecture of New York City: Histories and Views of Important Structures, Sites, and Symbols*. Rev. ed. New York: Macmillan, 1994. Interesting and informative chronological survey of New York City architecture from the seventeenth century to the end of the twentieth century. Provides details about a wide range of significant buildings and structures. The Empire State Building is covered in Chapter 12, which is devoted to a study of the Art Deco skyscrapers. Includes glossary, bibliography, and index.

Roth, Leland M. *American Architecture: A History*. 2d ed. Boulder, Colo.: Westview Press, 2003. Discussion of the history of architecture in the United States examines the many different forces that have influenced styles and trends. Places the design of the urban skyscraper within the larger national context. Includes many illustrations, chronology, glossary, and index.

Schleier, Merrill. *The Skyscraper in American Art, 1890-1931*. Ann Arbor, Mich.: UMI Research Press, 1986. Discusses the significance and meaning of skyscraper imagery in the arts as a direct reflection of the effects of skyscraper technology on American culture. Highlights artists such as photographers Alfred Stieglitz and Margaret Bourke-White and painter Georgia O'Keeffe. Includes bibliography and index.

Tauranac, John. *The Empire State Building: The Making of a Landmark*. New York: Scribner, 1995. A thorough history of the building and its place in the history of architecture as well as the history of New York City. Includes photographs, bibliography, and index.

SEE ALSO: May-June, 1925: Paris Exhibition Defines Art Deco; Spring, 1931: Le Corbusier's Villa Savoye Exemplifies Functionalist Architecture; Oct., 1932: Wright Founds the Taliesin Fellowship; 1937-1938: Aalto Designs Villa Mairea; May 27, 1937: Golden Gate Bridge Opens; Nov. 1, 1939: Rockefeller Center Is Completed.

May 8, 1931
CREDIT-ANSTALT BANK OF AUSTRIA FAILS

The first of a series of European bank failures and restructurings, the failure of the Credit-Anstalt Bank shook international financial markets and led to a worsening of the worldwide depression.

LOCALE: Vienna, Austria

CATEGORIES: Banking and finance; economics

KEY FIGURES

Montagu Norman (1871-1950), governor of the Bank of England

Lionel Walter Rothschild (1868-1937), chairman of the Austrian Credit-Anstalt creditors' committee

Alexander Spitzmüller (1862-1953), director of the reorganization of the Credit-Anstalt

Adrianus Johannes van Hengel (1886-1936), general director of the Credit-Anstalt

SUMMARY OF EVENT

The failure of the Credit-Anstalt Bank of Austria, of which the Austrian government was informed on May 8, 1931, was announced to the world on May 11, 1931. The Credit-Anstalt was one of the leading banks of Austria, both before and after World War I. Its failure precipitated a rush by international lenders to repatriate loans made during the heady days of the late 1920's. The repatriation of foreign loans, intricately linked to one another, forced the entire delicate financial structure of Europe into crisis, deepened the depression that had begun the preceding year, and contributed to the rise of radical political movements in Central Europe.

Prior to World War I, the Credit-Anstalt had been part of a network of Austrian banks that had provided much of the credit used by business and commerce in Eastern Europe. The number of banks needed to finance the businesses of an empire was far larger than the number needed simply to finance the businesses of the small Austrian republic that emerged from the peace treaties settling World War I. During the 1920's, this oversupply of financial institutions was gradually corrected by the merger of a number of Viennese banks, often under pressure from the Austrian government. One of the chief mergers was that of the Credit-Anstalt with the Boden-Kredit-Anstalt (Farm Credit Institute) in 1929. As the accountants of the Credit-Anstalt struggled to incorporate the loans and deposits of the Farm Credit Institute into their own portfolio, they were appalled to discover that the Farm Credit Institute had a negative net worth, a

strain that, in the existing conditions, it was difficult for the Credit-Anstalt to absorb.

The Credit-Anstalt of 1931 was substantially an international bank. It had major equity interests in the states created from the Austrian Empire, having invested in eleven banks and at least forty industrial firms, including a Romanian sugar refinery. Besides the equity investments, the bank provided credit for many of the firms in which it had invested. Most of these firms were producers of primary products, a sector that experienced severe overcapacity in the late 1920's. A highly competitive world market put a severe squeeze on profits, to the point at which the profitability of many of the bank's investments was questionable.

The Credit-Anstalt crisis began on Friday, May 8, 1931. The bank discovered a shortfall of 166 million schillings in its cash position. This information was provided to the Austrian government, with a request that the government guarantee the bank's liabilities. After an intense weekend of negotiation, during which the bank sought to pressure the government with the argument that it was "too big to fail," it was agreed that the government would guarantee the bank's liabilities. In return, the bank's shares would be devalued by 25 percent, the government would receive shares amounting to one-third of the total, and the Austrian National Bank would become a 10 percent shareholder. It was the government's intention to place its shares on the market at the earliest opportunity.

The financial difficulties of the Credit-Anstalt were revealed to the world on May 11, 1931. Even though the Austrian government announced that it was providing a guarantee of the bank's liabilities, depositors rushed to withdraw their funds, many of them purchasing foreign exchange, which the bank discounted at the Austrian National Bank. These losses forced the Austrian National Bank to seek an international loan through the Bank for International Settlements (BIS) in Basel, Switzerland. The BIS brokered a loan underwritten by twelve national banks, but in return it required that the Austrian National Bank guarantee the entire Credit-Anstalt operation. The Austrian government put two-thirds of its annual budget on the line in this guarantee.

The run on the Credit-Anstalt was so large that the first BIS loan of 100 million schillings (about $14 million) was used up by early June. The Austrian National Bank asked for a second loan, to be arranged by the BIS.

This loan contained the additional requirement that the Austrian government itself should obtain from foreign sources a longer-term loan, with a maturity of two to three years, in the amount of 150 million schillings. The French exhibited substantial reluctance about this project, particularly because they were concerned about a proposed Austro-German customs union that had recently been proposed. Meanwhile, the Bank of England's governor, Montagu Norman, came to the rescue with a seven-day loan to the Austrian government. This loan was extended several times and was replaced in the fall by a loan brokered by the League of Nations.

The effective insolvency of the Credit-Anstalt required reorganization of the bank. Discussions over reorganization began in May and continued throughout the summer and fall. A committee was formed from representatives of the bank's creditors, the Austrian government, and the Austrian National Bank. The head of the committee was Lionel Walter Rothschild, representing the creditors. The Rothschild family owned about one-third of the bank's shares. English interests, chiefly the Bank of England and the Anglo-Austrian Bank of London, owned another third. American interests, including Kuhn, Loeb and Company and the Guarantee Trust Company of New York, also had large positions. The principal government representative on the reorganization committee was Alexander Spitzmüller, briefly a director of the Credit-Anstalt before the war and also a former finance minister of the Austrian Empire. He had presided over the liquidation of the old Austro-Hungarian National Bank in the early 1920's.

The task of reorganization, in which Spitzmüller appears to have played the most active role, was to liquidate the assets of the bank, in the form of its industrial investments and credits, with some residual falling to the bank. Generally the reorganization was gentle to debtors, refusing to advance further credit but allowing extended payment opportunities.

A further obligation of the reorganization committee was to determine the extent to which the stockholders would suffer losses. The original plan, in which the foreign creditors' shares would lose 25 percent of their value, was no longer acceptable to the international bankers. Negotiations continued into the next year, when it was finally agreed that, in return for a further devaluation of the foreign creditors' shares, some of the losses would be made good by annuities that would be paid by the Austrian government over a seven-year period. No payments were made in 1934 and 1935, and in 1936 the Austrian government refused to make any payments. A new agreement was reached. The reorganized Credit-Anstalt loaned the Austrian government cash to compensate, in part, the annuity claimants. In return, the government agreed to pay the sum back in annual payments over forty years while also paying residual annuities to the foreign creditors over a twenty-year period.

During the summer and fall of 1931, aided by increased interest rates on deposits, the Credit-Anstalt was able to resume normal operations, decreasingly relying on discounting with the Austrian National Bank. The appointment of a Dutchman, Adrianus Johannes van Hengel, as the bank's director in February, 1932, restored confidence in the bank. It was able to function in normal fashion, although its sphere of activity had been essentially restricted to Austria.

SIGNIFICANCE

The effects of the failure of the Credit-Anstalt were far-reaching. The countries of Eastern Europe, which for decades had relied on Viennese banks for credit, were deprived of a major source of finance. Those of the bank's assets outside Austria that did not have to be liquidated were turned over to a new company, organized in Monaco. The proceeds of this latter operation were intended to help pay off investors in the Credit-Anstalt.

Of much greater importance, however, was the international financial crisis precipitated by the failure of the Credit-Anstalt. The run on the Credit-Anstalt frightened depositors throughout Central Europe, particularly in Germany, where large banks began to lose deposits at an alarming rate in June of 1931. Most of these withdrawals were either in the form of foreign currency credits, particularly British pounds, or gold. The banking crisis in Germany was made worse by restrictions placed on the German central bank, the Reichsbank, by the Allies, in conjunction with the revisions of reparations payments in 1924 and 1929-1930. These rules made it impossible for the Reichsbank to rediscount notes issued by the other commercial banks.

The run on German banks continued into the summer, precipitating the failure of the Darmstaedter Bank in July. The German government responded in the same manner as the Austrian government. It guaranteed the deposits at the Darmstaedter and subsequently forced its merger with another large bank, the Dresdner. These commitments, combined with large withdrawals from most of the large German banks, put the Reichsbank itself in jeopardy. The Reichsbank appealed to the central banks of England, France, and the United States for help.

These central banks supplied several loans of several hundred million dollars to prevent the depletion of the Reichsbank's stock of gold and foreign credits. Strict exchange controls were imposed that continued in effect throughout the 1930's.

The crisis in the banks and the precarious position of the Reichsbank's foreign credits and gold supply made it obvious that the major foreign currency transactions required by the various reparations agreements would not take place. President Herbert Hoover had proposed a moratorium on reparations payments as early as mid-June. Because he did not simultaneously offer a moratorium on inter-Allied debts, substantial negotiations were required before the moratorium could take effect. The French agreed to the moratorium on July 6, in return for a commitment that a proposed Austro-German customs union would not form.

The banking crisis also had implications internally for most of the countries of Europe. In order to attract deposits, the banks had to raise the interest rates they were offering. They then had to charge higher interest rates on loans to pay the cost of interest on deposits. These higher rates had the usual effect of severely restricting the credit available to small businesses, which in turn were constrained in the amount of business they could do. Many were obliged to lay off workers, adding to the rapidly growing level of unemployment.

The international banking crisis was also responsible for forcing the British to abandon the gold standard. After suspending conversion of paper money into gold during the war, the British government had returned to the gold standard in 1925 in the hope of restoring Great Britain's position as the economic and financial center of the industrialized world. When the future of the European banks became suspect, and when the Bank of England made substantial loans to shore up the Central European currencies, suspicion was transferred to the soundness of the pound. Those who had deposits in London sought to convert them to gold, and a severe run on the Bank of England's gold supply followed. On September 30, 1931, the British government suspended payment in gold.

The United States was not immune to the effects of the Credit-Anstalt failure. The general contraction of foreign credits affected U.S. banks, many of which had made a significant number of international loans to various European banks. The resultant contraction of the money supply produced deflation in both Europe and the United States, making the depression in the United States worse than it might otherwise have been.

The worsening depression had political consequences. In Central Europe, it provoked a sharp increase in voting for radical political parties and almost certainly contributed to the growing support for the Nazis among disillusioned German voters. A similar development occurred in Austria. Even in countries that remained democratic, the lack of funds available for borrowing forced budgetary policies that precluded deficit financing to lessen the impact of unemployment. Both Germany and Great Britain cut back on public subsidy of the unemployed. Governments throughout Europe hewed to balanced budgets in the face of a downward spiral in tax revenues. The depression was made worse worldwide by the ramifications of the failure of the Credit-Anstalt Bank of Austria.

—*Nancy M. Gordon*

FURTHER READING

Bennett, Edward W. *Germany and the Diplomacy of the Financial Crisis, 1931.* 1962. Reprint. Cambridge, Mass.: Harvard University Press, 1981. Classic study of the 1931 financial crisis.

James, Harold. *The German Slump: Politics and Economics, 1924-1936.* New York: Oxford University Press, 1986. Primarily focuses on the economic crisis in Germany but also discusses the contribution of the Credit-Anstalt failure to the development of the international financial crisis. Provides insight into the larger implications of the Credit-Anstalt collapse.

Kindleberger, Charles P. *The World in Depression, 1929-1939.* Rev. ed. Berkeley: University of California Press, 1986. Relates the antecedents of the Credit-Anstalt failure and provides a broad discussion of the ramifications of the failure. Includes a brief summary of the events leading up to the crisis of May, 1931.

Schubert, Aurel. *The Credit-Anstalt Crisis of 1931.* New York: Cambridge University Press, 1991. Thorough analysis includes examination of the causes of the crisis as well as the responses to it. Features tables, bibliography, and index.

Spitzmüller, Alexander. *Memoirs of Alexander Spitzmüller, Freiherr von Harmersbach (1862-1953).* Translated and edited by Carvel de Bussy. New York: Columbia University Press, 1987. Provides numerous details of the reorganization of the Credit-Anstalt. Given that Spitzmüller was a man with a very large ego, this account should be read with some caution.

Stiefel, Dieter. "The Reconstruction of the Credit-Anstalt." In *International Business and Central Europe, 1918-1939*, edited by Alice Teichova and P. L.

Cottrell. Leicester, England: Leicester University Press, 1983. Provides a balanced and detailed account of the collapse of the Credit-Anstalt. Commentary by other scholars following the chapter offers insight into some of the more controversial issues surrounding the crisis.

SEE ALSO: Oct. 24-29, 1929: U.S. Stock Market Crashes; Oct. 29, 1929-1939: Great Depression; Dec. 11, 1930: Bank of United States Fails; June 16, 1933: Banking Act of 1933 Reorganizes the American Banking System; 1936-1946: France Nationalizes Its Banking and Industrial Sectors.

May 27, 1931
PICCARD TRAVELS TO THE STRATOSPHERE BY BALLOON

Auguste Piccard piloted a balloon through an extended ascent into the stratosphere, presaging the space age with his pioneering use of a controlled-environment cabin.

LOCALE: Augsburg, Germany; Ober-Gurgl, Austria
CATEGORIES: Space and aviation; science and technology; physics

KEY FIGURES
Auguste Piccard (1884-1962), Swiss physicist, aeronaut, and engineer
Paul Kipfer (b. 1905), Swiss physicist

SUMMARY OF EVENT
In the early 1930's, the last of Earth's physical frontiers were slowly being understood and conquered. Stories of humankind pushing its limits regularly qualified for the front pages of major newspapers. When Auguste Piccard and Paul Kipfer ascended to 15,781 meters (approximately 51,775 feet) to break the world altitude record in a balloon of Piccard's own design, the world was enthralled and the scientific community gained new venues for exploration.

The stratosphere remained as one physical barrier that had been touched previously only barely. In 1902, Léon Teisserenc de Bort discovered the stratosphere, a layer in the atmosphere above the troposphere. There, the temperature does not decrease with altitude but is approximately constant at −55 degrees Celsius. The altitude of the lower boundary of the stratosphere varies greatly; a useful average is 12 kilometers (about 7.46 miles). Because barometric pressure decreases with altitude, the ambient pressure at such an altitude is about one-sixth that at Earth's surface; at 16 kilometers (9.94 miles), the fraction is only about one-tenth.

Prior to 1931, only two humans0 had been able to penetrate beyond 12 kilometers, and neither had available to them technology that would sustain life at that al-

titude for extended periods of time. In 1927, U.S. Army captain Hawthorne Gray made two flights to 12.7 kilometers (7.89 miles) utilizing an open gondola. Neither flight, however, set an official altitude mark; the first ended in a bailout and the second in Gray's death from lack of oxygen. In 1930, U.S. Navy lieutenant Apollo Soucek flew successfully to the lower reaches of the stratosphere in an airplane with the aid of heated goggles, gloves, and oxygen mask, setting a record of 13.16 kilometers (8.18 miles).

In the two decades preceding Piccard's flight in 1931,

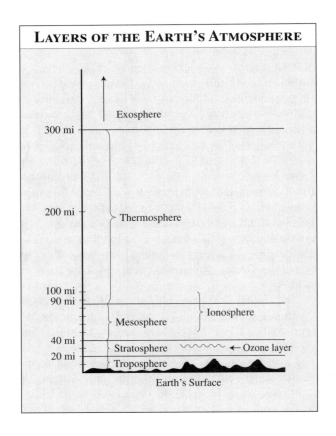

LAYERS OF THE EARTH'S ATMOSPHERE

Exosphere

300 mi

Thermosphere

200 mi

100 mi
90 mi
　　　　　　　　　　Ionosphere
Mesosphere

40 mi
Stratosphere　～～～ ← Ozone layer
20 mi
Troposphere

Earth's Surface

the realm of high-energy physics saw unexpected developments. Victor Franz Hess of Austria made a scientific balloon flight in 1912 in which he discovered a source of ionizing radiation that increased with altitude. Robert Andrews Millikan of the California Institute of Technology named the radiation "cosmic rays," although it had not been generally agreed yet that these rays were celestial in origin. Into this setting entered Auguste Piccard. Piccard, a native of Switzerland, was trained in mechanical engineering and became a professor of physics at the University of Brussels. His scientific interests included radioactivity and electricity in both laboratory and natural environments. He also actively pursued an interest in aeronautics, first learning his practical ballooning skills in the Swiss Aero-Club, and later serving in the Swiss Army Observation Balloon Corps. His complement of skills and interests led him, as early as 1926, to work on a balloon enve-

Auguste Piccard enters his balloon before one of his attempts to ascend to the stratosphere on January 1, 1932. (Hulton Archive/Getty Images)

lope and gondola capable of ascending to extremely high altitudes. He saw the balloon as a platform from which he could conduct cosmic-ray research far away from the radioactive elements of Earth, which would otherwise bias any measurements.

The balloon Piccard designed incorporated several innovative features. Most notably, the gondola was to be sealed and airtight, so that air pressure inside the gondola would not be lost as the balloon ascended to regions of lower and lower pressure. Piccard chose to construct the gondola out of aluminum, a material that had been under development only recently. Because the flight would be many hours long and the gondola relatively small, there needed to be a source of oxygen as well as a way of detoxifying exhaled air. For these purposes, Piccard imported technology used in German submarines, a filtering system known as a Draeger apparatus. It utilized alkaline compounds to absorb unwanted gases. The oxygen supply was stored in liquid form; it restored the cabin air as it slowly vaporized.

The balloon envelope was spherical, as was usual for hydrogen-filled balloons. The constraints of a high-altitude flight, however, dictated some adjustment. To

prevent the lightweight rubberized cotton balloon from bursting as it ascended into the low pressures of the stratosphere, the balloon was only partially inflated at takeoff. The balloon, which was pleated for storage, would unfold and expand of its own accord as it ascended. To ensure that the fabric unfolded safely, Piccard devised a way to hang the gondola to the envelope from points on a horizontal band attached to the envelope, rather than from a net that enclosed the envelope.

Piccard applied for funding from the Belgian science agency, the Fonds National de Recherches Scientifique (FNRS), founded by King Albert I. As the king was eager to promote Belgium's reputation as a leading nation in scientific and industrial endeavors, and given that he was a balloon enthusiast himself, he was happy to provide the necessary funds. The craft, named the *FNRS*, was ready in the fall of 1930. Piccard scheduled an ascent for September 14, from Augsburg, Germany. The weather changed, however, and Piccard reluctantly called off the flight at the last moment. Weather conditions were not suitable again until the next spring. An ascent was finally planned for 5:30 A.M. on May 27, 1931. During the night, the wind began to rise; in anticipation of worsening weather, the crew prepared for a hastened launch. Suddenly, at 3:57 A.M., the ground crew somehow let go of the ropes without communicating the designated warning signal. Piccard and his assistant Kipfer found themselves in the air and rising quickly. A few minutes later, Piccard discovered a leak in the gondola caused by a broken seal; the damage had been done when the gondola was accidentally dropped during takeoff procedures. Piccard had prepared a supply of petroleum jelly mixed with fibers in case of just such accidents, and the mixture proved its worth.

As the day progressed, Piccard and Kipfer discovered a problem with the gas exhaust valve. This was the valve with which they were to let gas out of the balloon, a principal component of their altitude control. Their eventual landing would be problematic if they could not control the valve. The only way to proceed was to wait until sundown, when the lower temperature would cause the balloon envelope to shrink, thereby reducing the lift sufficiently for a landing. Piccard and Kipfer tied down the instruments in anticipation of a difficult landing. Hours passed, and the balloon drifted southward over Bavaria and into Tyrol. Finally, around 9:00 P.M., the gondola touched ground on a glacier in the Tyrolean Alps, in the region of Ober-Gurgl. The two aeronauts spent the night on the glacier and the next morning hiked toward the village of Gurgl. A patrol sent up from the valley met them around noon and led them to safety.

Piccard had planned several scientific activities for the ascent of the *FNRS*. The quick rate of ascent, the emergency leak that had to be taken care of, and the uncertain landing all conspired to prevent any measurements from being made while the balloon was at any other but top altitude. Piccard and Kipfer thus lost their opportunity to obtain many useful data, such as information on cosmic-ray altitude-intensity curves. One approximate observation was made, however, that suggested cosmic rays were indeed more intense in the stratosphere than below it; this, in turn, lent support to the theory that cosmic rays are in fact extraterrestrial.

For their achievements, Piccard and Kipfer were knighted by the King of Belgium, and Piccard received nominations for the Nobel Prize in Physics in both 1932 and 1933. Their altitude record of 15,781 meters stood for more than a year, until it was surpassed by Piccard and Max Cosyns.

SIGNIFICANCE

The flight of the *FNRS* made its mark on a wide cross section of the scientific world, less by resolving scientific

controversies than by preparing the way for further exploration. The data obtained on the flight were encouraging. Piccard and Kipfer measured cosmic radiation apparently 2.5 times more intense at 16 kilometers (9.94 miles) than that measured by Werner Kolhörster at 9 kilometers (5.59 miles). This piece of information was only marginally useful, however; because only one measurement was taken, it could not be calibrated with data from previous flights at lower altitudes, and its accuracy was not absolutely certain.

Nevertheless, this first flight gave subsequent balloonists a resource of experience and technology from which to draw. In fact, the next stratospheric ascent, with Piccard and Cosyns piloting the *FNRS* in August, 1932, was quite successful scientifically as well as logistically, bringing back data to fill in the Hess-Kolhörster cosmic-ray altitude-intensity curve between 9 and 16 kilometers. A 1934 flight in *Explorer II* by Americans Albert Stevens and Orvil Anderson returned cosmic-ray data that physicists Robert Andrews Millikan and his rival Arthur Holly Compton both considered useful for their respective theories. In addition, the flight carried interesting experiments in other branches of science. For example, Stevens and Anderson measured ozone distribution in the atmosphere, photographed Earth from very high altitudes, and demonstrated an increased mutation rate in fruit flies. Piccard's vision of the balloon as a platform from which to conduct scientific research thus did prove moderately productive.

Ascents subsequent to those of the *FNRS* retained many of Piccard's innovations. For example, American balloons such as *Explorer* used bands also rather than nets to attach the gondola. Most significant, however, was the sealed gondola. As late as 1956, balloons such as *Stratolab* were still using a gondola of essentially the same design as that of 1931.

The flights of the *FNRS* preceded the space age by only three decades. During those years, stratospheric ballooning evolved from a matter of rising in open-air baskets to one of orbiting Earth in space capsules. Pressurized passenger airplane cabins and the modern-day space shuttle trace their ancestry to the sealed cabin that Piccard devised for his *FNRS*. Although the impact of Piccard and Kipfer's ascent into the stratosphere reaches beyond the glory that their achievement brought, the glory itself was instrumental in promoting ballooning to the public and to policy makers. Proponents of aeronautic exploration in the United States in the following decades pointed to the flights of the *FNRS* to convince major funding agencies that research in high-altitude flight was feasible and that the symbolic value of accomplishing such flights was worth the expense. Both technologically and sociologically, it was only a small step between the *Stratolab 5* balloon flight in 1961 and the Mercury, Gemini, and Apollo space missions of the same period. To those who came after Piccard, his flights stood as vital inspiration and encouragement.

—Joyce Tang

FURTHER READING

DeVorkin, David H. *Race to the Stratosphere: Manned Scientific Ballooning in America.* New York: Springer-Verlag, 1989. Excellent history of ballooning and analysis of science policy by the curator of the Smithsonian Institution's National Air and Space Museum. Focuses on ballooning in the United States, but Piccard and his twin brother, Jean-Felix, figure prominently in the story. Well-researched and highly readable resource. Includes reference notes and extensive bibliography.

Piccard, Auguste. "Ballooning in the Stratosphere." *National Geographic* 63 (March, 1933): 353-384. Consistent with its calling to promote exploration, the National Geographic Society supported scientific ballooning from the start, publishing reports of projects such as Piccard's in its popular magazine.

_____. *Earth, Sky, and Sea.* Translated by Christina Stead. New York: Oxford University Press, 1956. First-person account of Piccard's voyages into the stratosphere and later, in a bathyscaphe, into the depths of the sea. Provides a personal perspective on his work.

Sekido, Yataro, and Harry Elliot, eds. *Early History of Cosmic Ray Studies: Personal Reminiscences with Old Photographs.* Boston: D. Reidel, 1985. Anthology of writings by leading cosmic-ray researchers provides a depiction of the birth of the field that is balanced and thorough. Acknowledges and describes the roles of manned and unmanned balloons, underwater observations, and developments in theory. Often technical, but aimed at the general science reader. Includes photographs, illustrations, notes, and index.

Stehling, Kurt R., and William Beller. *Skyhooks.* Garden City, N.Y.: Doubleday, 1962. Details the stories of fifteen historic balloon flights from the birth of ballooning in 1783 to the early 1960's in a manner accessible to the general reader. Chapter on the flight of the *FNRS* contains some minor inaccuracies. Includes a chronology of important ascents.

SEE ALSO: Aug. 7 and 12, 1912: Hess Discovers Cosmic Rays; 1920-1930: Millikan Investigates Cosmic Rays; 1927: Lemaître Proposes the Big Bang Theory; 1934: Discovery of the Cherenkov Effect.

July, 1931
YELLOW RIVER FLOOD

Apart from epidemics and famines, the Yellow River flood was the deadliest natural disaster of the twentieth century. Between three and four million perished, and tens of millions were displaced. International relief efforts prevented even greater losses.

ALSO KNOWN AS: Huang He flood; Yangtze River flood; North China flood

LOCALE: North China Plain and eastern Yangtze lowland, northeastern China

CATEGORIES: Agriculture; geography; disasters; environmental issues

KEY FIGURES

Chiang Kai-shek (1887-1975), Nationalist Chinese military and political leader, 1927-1949, and president of the Republic of China, 1949-1975

Harry Virden Bernard (1879-1968), flood relief organizer

Charles A. Lindbergh (1902-1974), American aviation pioneer

SUMMARY OF EVENT

The Yellow River flood occurred when the waters of several rivers commingled across the low-lying plains that stretch from Tianjin, on the North China Plain near the Yellow River, to Nanjing (China's capital in 1931), which sits on the floodplain of the Yangtze River. These two rivers were the main sources of the flood, so some historical sources refer to the deluge as the Yellow River flood; others call it the Yangtze River flood.

The North China Plain is a low-lying platform of sediment built relatively recently (at least in geological terms) by four east-flowing rivers—the Yellow (Huang), Hai, Huai, and Yonglin—that come from the western uplands and fill the western rim of the pouch-shaped Bohai Sea. The Yellow River is the largest stream: It carries

THE YELLOW AND YANGTZE RIVERS

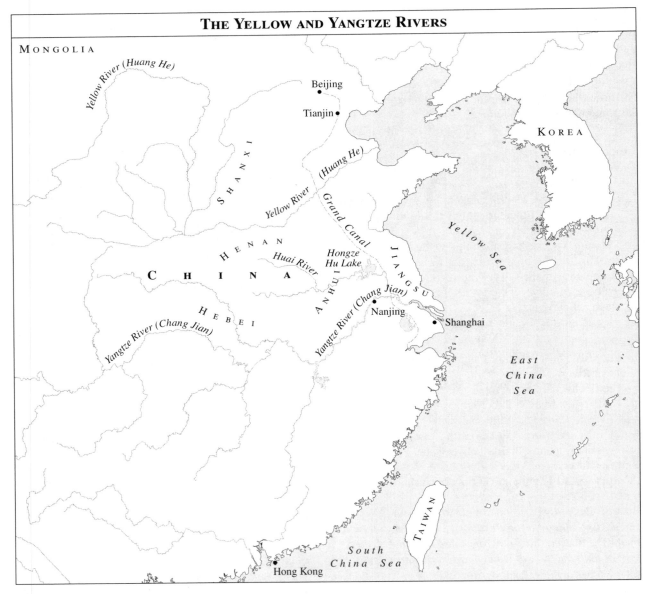

about 1.6 billion tons of silt annually, and its floodwaters created a gigantic delta that spans about 96,525 square miles. The river is notorious for flooding its lower reaches: Huge amounts of silt clog the stream's channel and raise the elevation of the river's streambed, and this causes the river to flow over its banks and onto the floodplain. The extraordinary height of the streambed above the adjoining floodplain raises the risk of rapid, deep, and widespread flooding in the densely populated delta.

The drainage area of the Yangtze River is more than two and one-half times the size of the Yellow River, and its average discharge is more than seven times greater. The Yangtze formed a large delta during the Pleistocene ice age, but it changed course about four thousand years ago, and this delta is now the Jiangsu Plain, which lies north of the city of Shanghai. In 1931, Shanghai was China's largest city, and that year's flood covered parts of the Yangtze's delta, its broad inland floodplains, and the Jiangsu Plain.

July is the peak month for precipitation in northern China, and the rain that occurs from early or mid-June to early or mid-July is called "plum rain" by local people in the Yangtze and Huai valleys because it arrives when the flowers of plum and other deciduous fruit trees in these valleys are in bloom. Plum rain occurs because a polar front, the transitional boundary between polar and tropical air masses, hovers over these two valleys. Typically, moisture-laden southeastern monsoon winds push against newly arrived northwestern cold air, and the colder air wedges under the approaching monsoon air, lifting the monsoon air upward in a violent corkscrew spiral that spawns frontal cyclonic storms. The weather is continuously rainy and provides good conditions for rice paddies. On average, two slow-moving cyclonic storms pass over the region in July, but July of 1931 saw a series of seven storms in rapid succession.

On July 28, dikes on the north side of the Yangtze River broke, sending waters rushing north onto the Jiangsu Plain and south into the delta and the city of Shanghai. At about the same time, the Yellow River tore at its confining banks and sent some of its flow gushing south into the channel it had abandoned nearly eighty years earlier. Effectively, the two rivers' floodwaters converged. The most serious flooding took place in the convergence zone, which was supposed to be drained by the Huai River, a tributary of the Yellow River.

The floodwaters of the three rivers blended and covered low-lying areas in the provinces of Henan, Hubei, Anhui, and Jiangsu. Additionally, the Grand Canal, which runs south to north across the eastern boundary of the usually gentle divide between the Yangtze and Yellow Rivers, ruptured and flooded the provinces. Floodwaters in this zone and in floodplains bordering the middle course of the Yangtze covered a total of 47,000 square miles (an area the size of New York State). Widespread flooding also took place over the North China Plain. The flooding continued unabated until mid-August, and in many areas the floodwaters did not recede for six months, making farming impossible. In the colder northern areas around Tianjin, vast lakes of frozen floodwaters did not thaw and drain completely until early April, 1932, nine months after the flood.

Initially, the disaster did not receive much attention around the world, partly because the flood itself caused a massive breakdown in communications. News reporters underestimated the scale of the deluge, and torrents isolated Nanjing and Shanghai, where foreign journalists got most of their news about China. The flood also paralyzed the country's two main seaports, Shanghai and Tianjin. In addition, a bloody civil war between General Chiang Kai-shek's Nationalist army and Mao Zedong's Communist forces preoccupied the nation. (At the time of the flood, Chiang was suffering heavy casualties in his fight against Communists in Shanxi Province.) Japan's September invasion of the Chinese territory of Manchuria only added to China's concerns.

The Chinese Nationalist government hastily organized the National Relief Commission in an attempt to care for the refugees and to repair 7,000 miles of dikes. Over the next two years, the United States lent China $59 million to buy wheat and cotton (two major crops destroyed by the flood), to rebuild roads, and to pay wages for flood refugees rebuilding the dikes. Chiang appointed Harry Virden Bernard, an American businessman, as head of the Shanghai district of the National Flood Relief Commission, and Bernard held this position until 1934. In 1938, the International Red Cross chose him to head its program to aid Chinese refugees from the 1937-1945 Sino-Japanese War.

Charles A. Lindbergh and his wife provided a valuable record of how widespread the devastation was in the Yangtze and Huai River basins. They were in Shanghai in late September, while the floodwaters were still extensive, and they flew over the area and took aerial photographs of the devastation. The photographs later appeared in a government report on the flood.

SIGNIFICANCE

The Yellow River flood occurred in the heartland and granary of Chiang's struggling Republic of China. The flood destroyed rice and wheat crops and spawned severe food shortages in one of the world's most populous regions. Some 200 million people lived in the middle and lower sections of the Yangtze Valley, and 80 million people lived in the North China Plain, which meant that the flood affected 14 percent of the world's total 1931 population of 2 billion.

Initial reports of the deluge and its aftermath were as murky as the lingering, silt-laden waters. Estimates of drowning deaths published in foreign newspapers varied between 40,000 and 150,000, and the estimates of people rendered homeless ranged from 10 million to 50 million. According to the modern-day death estimate, 3.7 million people perished, although this larger figure includes deaths that accrued over the next two or three years from diseases (mainly cholera) and starvation. This estimate makes the 1931 flood in China the deadliest natural disaster on record.

Efforts to curb the threat of floods that were undertaken immediately following the Yellow River disaster included the building of large flood-retention reservoirs and improvements on existing dikes. After China's com-

munist government came to power in 1949, emphasis was placed on building dams in higher sections of the Yellow and Yangtze Rivers in order to control their flow.
— *Richard A. Crooker*

FURTHER READING

Buck, J. Lossing. *The 1931 Flood in China: An Economic Survey by the Department of Agricultural Economics, College of Agriculture and Forestry, the University of Nanking, in Cooperation with the National Flood Relief Commission.* Chicago: University of Chicago Press, 1932. This survey attempted to pinpoint the population affected by the 1931 flood.

Buck, Pearl S. *The Good Earth.* New York: John Day, 1931. Fictional work describes a peasant family's trials with flood, drought, and famine in the Huai River area.

Chetham, Deirde. *Before the Deluge: The Vanishing World of the Yangtze's Three Gorges.* Brookline, Mass.: Palgrave Macmillan, 2002. Provides a balanced perspective on the pros and cons of the world's most controversial dam-building project.

National Flood Relief Commission. *Report of the National Flood Relief Commission, 1931-1932.* Shanghai, China: Comacrib Press, 1933. Provides a summary of relief efforts in the immediate aftermath of the flood.

Silver, Sylvia Cochrane. "Memories of North China Flood." *Asia Survey* (May, 1933): 309-313, 317. Recounts the author's personal experiences of the flood.

Sinclair, Kevin. *The Yellow River: A Five Thousand-Year Journey Through China.* London: Weidenfeld & Nicolson, 1987. Well-written description of the evolving relationship between the people and the land along the Yellow River.

Winchester, Simon. *The River at the Centre of the World.* London: Picador, 2004. Includes historical information about the river's floods and how they have affected people's lives.

Woodhead, H. G. W., ed. *The China Year Book, 1932.* Shanghai, China: North China Daily News Herald, 1932. Among the data are a chapter on climate of China and a special chapter on the flood.

Zhao Songqiao. *Geography of China: Environment, Resources, Population and Development.* New York: John Wiley & Sons, 1994. Excellent source of information about the climate, weather patterns, soil, and agriculture of the area affected by the flood.

SEE ALSO: 1926-1949: Chinese Civil War; June 7, 1938: Chinese Forces Break Yellow River Levees.

July 26, 1931
INTERNATIONAL BIBLE STUDENTS ASSOCIATION BECOMES JEHOVAH'S WITNESSES

When Joseph Franklin Rutherford, president of the Watch Tower Bible and Tract Society, addressed a convention assembly of the society's London-based affiliate, the International Bible Students Association, he presented a stirring discourse and resolution that called for a distinctive name—Jehovah's Witnesses—to be given to those who claimed to be servant-witnesses of God.

LOCALE: Columbus, Ohio
CATEGORIES: Religion, theology, and ethics; organizations and institutions

KEY FIGURES

Joseph Franklin Rutherford (1869-1942), second president of the Watch Tower Bible and Tract Society, 1917-1942

Charles Taze Russell (1852-1916), founder of the Bible Student movement that later incorporated as the Watch Tower Bible and Tract Society

Nathan Homer Knorr (1905-1977), third president of the Watch Tower Bible and Tract Society, Jehovah's Witnesses, 1942-1977

SUMMARY OF EVENT

In 1872, in Allegheny, Pennsylvania (now part of Pittsburgh), Charles Taze Russell founded the religious sect that would later become known as the Watch Tower Bible and Tract Society. Russell successfully advanced the new movement's presence through far-ranging speaking tours and extensive publication and distribution of his writings. The organization's growth led to the relocation of its headquarters to Brooklyn, New York, in 1909.

One of the more prominent doctrines that Russell and his Bible Student movement espoused was the belief that the year 1914 marked the end of the "gentile times." Before 1914, Russell said, Christ had ruled in heaven on his throne of authority, but the time had come for him to cleanse the earth of its wickedness by defeating evil, personified as Satan, at the Battle of Armageddon. Following this cataclysmic event, the earth would be restored to paradise. Russell also promised that a "little flock" of 144,000 faithful, "born-again" Christians would rule with Christ in heaven while a great multitude of the righteous would live forever in a peaceful post-Armageddon earthly kingdom. Although the Bible's chronology does not reveal the exact year of Armageddon, Russell admitted, biblical prophecy indicated that humankind had been living in the "last days." As a result of this belief, the concept of an imminent end of time was often obvious in the organization's activities and doctrines.

After Russell's death in 1916, Joseph Franklin Rutherford (nicknamed "Judge"), who had been serving as the society's chief legal counsel, was elected in January of 1917 to become the organization's president. Challenges to Rutherford's election and Rutherford's own determination to squelch opposition within the society's board of directors created a bitter schism that resulted in a significant drop in membership. Another challenge to the president's leadership came in 1918, when Rutherford and several close associates from the society were arrested and charged with sedition under the terms of the Espionage Act (1917). These charges stemmed from the society's opposition to U.S. involvement in World War I. Rutherford and his associates were found guilty and sentenced to lengthy prison terms, but they were released after nine months. After his release, Rutherford continued to exert tremendous influence on the society's doctrines through his extensive writings in Watch Tower publications and numerous speaking appearances. Under Rutherford's leadership, the organization became significantly more doctrinally orthodox and autocratic.

From the inception of Russell's movement, the members were commonly referred to as Bible Students, but they were also called Russellites, Watch Tower Bible people, Rutherfordites, and Millennial Dawn people. The 1931 convention of the Watch Tower Bible and Tract Society and the International Bible Students Association, the organization's London-based affiliate, was held in Columbus, Ohio, from July 24 to 30. Attendees noticed the prominent display of the initials "J. W." on the program and other convention literature, but the meaning of these letters was not revealed until the gathering's third day.

At noon on Sunday, July 26, Rutherford addressed the convention with a discourse titled "The Kingdom, the Hope of the World." In the talk, he referred to Jehovah's Witnesses as the proclaimers of the kingdom of God, and he presented the resolution "Warning from Jehovah," in which he asserted that existing governments were un-

righteous and would be judged accordingly by Jehovah (God). The true hope of the world, Rutherford said, was the righteous kingdom of God that had Christ as its head.

The speech received an enthusiastic response from the audience, and at 4:00 P.M. that afternoon, Rutherford again addressed the assembly. He followed his earlier "warning" by engaging the audience with a second discourse that focused on the need for a distinctive name for the organization. Rutherford believed that such a title would help define the true loyalties of the various Bible Student groups as well as provide a rallying point for expanding the organization's evangelism. To provide biblical support for the new name he was about to introduce, Rutherford read several passages from the Scriptures that address the religious duty of being a witness of Jehovah. He placed special emphasis on Isaiah 43:8-12, the concluding passage for his stirring presentation.

Rutherford presented a resolution declaring that the group's name should not be tied to any specific person (including founder Charles Taze Russell) or derived from any of the titles of the society's various affiliates. The resolution also declared that Bible Students was an unsuitable name, although that name had been long associated with Russell's movement. Finally, Rutherford concluded his resolution by stating that the new name, which had been ordained by God, would be Jehovah's Witnesses. Rutherford's dramatic speech was broadcast around the world via radio, and millions of print copies were distributed in a booklet titled *The Kingdom, the Hope of the World*.

SIGNIFICANCE

The Old Testament prophet Isaiah issued the imperative for adopting the name Jehovah's Witnesses; the Book of Isaiah indicated that Jehovah is the personal name of God and that his chosen servants are to be witnesses who give testimony to their sovereign and his purpose for creation. On a more practical level, however, adopting this name afforded Watch Tower supporters recognition and differentiated them from others who remained aligned with the Bible Student movement still closely identified with Russell. Rutherford's bold move was, in effect, an effort to distinguish his followers from the many disaffected Bible Students who had left the society during Rutherford's tenure as president. This event enabled Rutherford to centralize his authority in the society, the structure of which had shifted from somewhat democratic to increasingly theocratic.

Following Rutherford's death in 1942, Nathan Homer Knorr, who had served as vice president of the Pennsyl-

1931

vania affiliate (the Watch Tower Bible and Tract Society of Pennsylvania), became the third president of the organization. During Knorr's twenty-five-year tenure as president, the Jehovah's Witnesses increased attention to public relations, published a translation of the Bible in modern English called *The New World Translation of the Holy Scriptures, Rendered from the Original Languages by the New World Bible Translation Committee* (1961), and undertook a significant international expansion of the Witnesses' message. In 1943, Knorr helped establish "theocratic ministry schools" in local congregations and a missionary training school called Gilead at South Lansing, New York. Knorr's presidency also saw the last great international convention of Jehovah's Witnesses in one place, an event held in 1958 in New York City.

—*David L. DeHart*

FURTHER READING

Holden, Andrew. *Jehovah's Witnesses: Portrait of a Contemporary Religious Movement.* London: Rout-

ledge, 2002. Well-researched analysis of the Jehovah's Witnesses from a sociologist's viewpoint.

Penton, M. James. *Apocalypse Delayed: The Story of the Jehovah's Witnesses.* 2d ed. Toronto: University of Toronto Press, 1997. A readable, comprehensive overview of the sect by a former member.

Stroup, Herbert Hewitt. *The Jehovah's Witnesses.* New York: Russell & Russell, 1967. Detailed study and analysis of the Witness movement from its beginning to the early 1940's.

Watchtower Bible and Tract Society of New York. *Jehovah's Witnesses: Proclaimers of God's Kingdom.* Brooklyn: Author, 1993. The Jehovah's Witnesses' own detailed account of their history and culture.

SEE ALSO: Oct. 31, 1904-1906: Welsh Revival Spreads Pentecostalism; Apr., 1906-1908: Azusa Street Revival; 1919: Founding of the World Christian Fundamentals Association; Summer, 1930: Nation of Islam Is Founded.

November 17, 1931
WHITNEY MUSEUM OF AMERICAN ART OPENS IN NEW YORK

The Whitney Museum helped to give American artists public importance and gained international recognition for American art as a distinct and viable movement.

LOCALE: New York, New York
CATEGORIES: Arts; organizations and institutions

KEY FIGURES

Gertrude Vanderbilt Whitney (1875-1942), American heiress and artist
Juliana Rieser Force (1876-1948), first director of the Whitney Museum
Robert Henri (1865-1929), American artist
John French Sloan (1871-1951), American artist
Forbes Watson (1880-1960), American art critic and public relations expert
Alfred Stieglitz (1864-1946), American photographer and art gallery owner

SUMMARY OF EVENT

In a short statement at the ceremony inaugurating the museum named in her honor, Gertrude Vanderbilt Whitney noted that she had been collecting American art for twenty-five years not only because she thought it worthwhile but also because she believed in American creative

talent. The struggle to achieve recognition for American art, and for modernism in general, had been difficult and was far from over.

When Whitney, at the beginning of the twentieth century, had sought to escape the stifling social atmosphere into which she was born and to seek an identity for herself, she had no thought of establishing a museum. Turning to sculpture, for which she had some talent, she hired instructors and took classes. For the first time, she became aware of the struggles and often bleak world of the average American artist. American art, particularly modern American art, had no official recognition. The artistic establishment was firmly under the control of conservatives who saw merit in contemporary art only to the extent that it imitated the past.

In 1906, Whitney by chance met Robert Henri, a member of a group of avant-garde artists seeking to escape the regimentation of existing artistic standards, especially as to subject matter. Henri believed firmly that American art should be indigenous and free of foreign influence. Even though the United States was undergoing tremendous social change in the face of increasing industrialization and urbanization, Americans did not generally tolerate "social realism" in art. Henri was so persuasive that when Whitney organized a 1907 art exhibition in honor of the opening of the Colony Club, a fashionable social club for women, she included works from his group. Seeking to identify herself further with the avant-garde, Whitney at the time of the exhibit also acquired a studio in New York's Greenwich Village. During the same period, she hired Juliana Rieser—an action that would change the lives of both. Exuberant, gregarious, efficient, and dedicated, Rieser gave focus and direction to her employer's artistic development and objectives.

The Colony Club exhibit set the stage for the mounting of an exhibit the following year that many consider to be the real beginning of the Whitney Museum of American Art. As one of the judges for the annual spring exhibit of the National Academy of Design, Henri wanted to enter works by six of his colleagues. To his chagrin, all but one were refused by the academy's jury because of the "inappropriateness" of the works' subject matter. The fallout resulted in the controversial *Exhibit of Eight* mounted in the Macbeth Gallery in 1908. The artists involved were Henri, George Luks, William Glackens, John French Sloan, Everett Shinn, Ernest Lawson, Maurice Prendergast, and Arthur B. Davies. Because of the novelty of the new work, viewers flocked to the exhibit largely to express their disapproval. The artists were dubbed the "Apostles of Ugliness" and the "Black Gang." The name that stuck was the "Ashcan School."

Another, more comprehensive exhibit was immediately planned. Under the guidance of the cosmopolitan Davies, it was decided that the exhibit would be dedicated to modernism in general and would include the works of leading European artists. The result was the Armory Show of 1913, which included more than a thousand works by nearly four hundred artists. Americans were exposed to movements such as Fauvism, with its emphasis on pure color, and cubism. For the first time, the American public saw works by Paul Cézanne, Pablo Picasso, Paul Gauguin, and Vincent van Gogh. What was also painfully obvious to many American artists was how immature their work seemed in comparison to that of their European counterparts.

Gertrude Whitney was the largest purchaser of works from the *Exhibit of Eight*, and she subsidized the group organizing the Armory Show. With her capable new assistant (who had in the meantime married and changed her name to Juliana Force), Whitney was determined to play a more direct role in American art largely through her sizable financial resources. In 1913, she acquired a town house that abutted her studio and established the Whitney Studio to show the works of artists who could not exhibit elsewhere. Seeking to assist artists further, Whitney acquired another property and established the Whitney Studio Club, which enabled artists not only to display but also to work on the premises.

With no formal entrance requirements, the club grew to an unmanageable size, and both the studio and the club faced the possibility of becoming little more than forms of artistic charity. Under the direction of Juliana Force and with the advice and guidance of John Sloan and Forbes Watson, both began to give greater focus and selectivity to exhibitions and to purchases. Watson, as editor of an art magazine and with newspaper connections, not only was a capable adviser and discerning critic but also was able to manage the increasingly necessary publicity. A model for the Whitney group's objectives was the famous 291 New York gallery of the pioneer photographer Alfred Stieglitz. Limiting himself to a relatively small number of artists of promise, Stieglitz had promoted both American art and his artists, resulting in increasing sales and commissions.

During the 1920's, the Whitney group staged a number of exhibitions of works by artists who later became famous, including George Bellows, Jo Davidson, Edward Hopper, Rockwell Kent, Charles Demuth, Gaston Lachaise, and Elie Nadelman. To accommodate the increased activity, Whitney acquired two buildings adjoining the studio building. The financial drain, however, began to be a burden even for Whitney, who was beginning to think about the eventual disposition of her by then considerable collection of American art. A solution seemed to be to place the collection in an endowed separate wing of the Metropolitan Museum of Art. The museum, however, summarily rejected Whitney's offer, so strong still was the prejudice against modern or experimental American art.

Whitney was more disturbed by the rejection than was Force, who had been charged with making the offer. Force had always hoped that the Whitney collection would keep its separate identity; she believed that even if the Metropolitan were to accept the offer, the museum would not give modern American art the respect and attention it deserved. The decision was made to create a separate museum. A building on West Eighth Street in New York City was acquired for the project; the new building's facade was decorated with a picture of an American eagle with outspread wings. This, the first of three homes to the Whitney Museum of American Art, opened its doors on November 17, 1931. Subsequent moves were necessitated by the growth and importance of the museum's collection.

SIGNIFICANCE

The primary impact of the establishment of the Whitney Museum of American Art was the legitimation of American art. The museum's existence encouraged the recognition of American art as one of the world's great art movements, on par with and soon to surpass that of Europe. This outcome had been a planned objective. In her speech at the opening, Juliana Force, in her role as the museum's first director, noted that the Whitney would be devoted to the difficult but important task of gaining for modern American art the prestige that previously had been reserved for the art of foreign countries and the art of the past.

An important step in validating the kind of art the Whitney promoted was the recognition of the free creative spirit of the nonacademic artist. Much of the battle waged by the founders of the Whitney had been against the narrow restrictions imposed by academic institutions such as the National Academy of Design. One of the consequences of increasing artistic freedom was the evolution of abstraction, which was central to the development of perhaps the first important American school of art, the New York school that developed in the decades after 1945. Central to the movement were abstract expressionists such as Arshile Gorky and Jackson Pollock. Force was attracted to abstraction, and the Whitney purchased a Gorky work in 1937. The museum would later become a major repository for American abstract art.

The opening of the Whitney Museum also gave a major impetus to twentieth century art and to modern art in general. In the 1910's and 1920's, the Whitney Studio and the Whitney Studio Club were among the few places where so-called modern art could be seen in the United States. In the years 1929 to 1931, an artistic explosion of a sort took place with the openings of the Museum of Modern Art and the Albert E. Gallatin Gallery of Living Art as well as the beginnings of the Solomon R. Guggenheim Museum of Non-Objective Painting and the Peggy Guggenheim Gallery.

The opening of the Whitney also did much to raise the prestige of American artists. Gone were the days when the artist John Sloan could pessimistically observe that the pioneering American artist was like a roach—not wanted, not encouraged, yet present. One of Gertrude Whitney's major objectives, from which she never deviated, was to assist artists. Therefore, her emphasis was on encouraging living artists, and the exhibits at both the Whitney Studio and the Whitney Studio Club were primarily staged to enable artists to promote and sell their works.

An adjunct to the prestige gained by the artist and the growing value of artworks was the growth of the art industry, which became a vital part of the economies of such American cities as New York, Chicago, and San Francisco. When the Whitney Studio first opened, only a handful of American galleries existed, and almost none was willing to exhibit nonacademic works. By the time the Whitney Museum opened, dozens of galleries were operating, and the number kept growing. Art indeed had become big business.

Perhaps the most pervasive impact of the opening of the Whitney Museum was its influence on the American public's awareness and appreciation of art. Appropriate publicity was part of the museum's operation from the beginning, and the Whitney was among the first art museums to arrange traveling exhibits both in the United States and abroad. Just as Gertrude Vanderbilt Whitney predicted in her address at the museum's opening, the Whitney Museum of American Art grew and increased in importance as its public also grew. In the twenty-first century, it is considered one of the world's great museums.

—*Nis Petersen*

FURTHER READING

Ashton, Dore. *The New York School: A Cultural Reckoning.* 1972. Reprint. Berkeley: University of California Press, 1992. Stresses the beginnings of the modern American art movement, discussing its maturation in the form of the New York school associated with Surrealism and abstract expressionism. Includes little mention of the Whitney Museum, however, even in relation to the artistic life of Greenwich Village.

Berman, Avis. *Rebels on Eighth Street: Juliana Force and the Whitney Museum of American Art.* New York: Atheneum, 1990. One of the best works available on the founding of the Whitney Museum. Stresses the role of Force, possibly because the author is persuaded that Force has not been given the credit she deserves. Includes excellent bibliography and index. Illustrations, all in black and white, are meager for a work on an art museum.

Biddle, Flora Miller. *The Whitney Women and the Museum They Made: A Family Memoir.* New York: Arcade, 1999. Chronicle of the founding and nurturing of the Whitney Museum, written by Gertrude Vanderbilt Whitney's granddaughter.

Doss, Erika. *Twentieth-Century American Art.* New York: Oxford University Press, 2002. Examines art movements in the United States in the twentieth century, with emphasis on the relations among artists, museums, and art audiences. Includes illustrations, time line, list of museums, and index.

Friedman, B. H. *Gertrude Vanderbilt Whitney*. Garden City, N.Y.: Doubleday, 1978. May be viewed as the history of the museum from the standpoint of Whitney. Most valuable is part 3, "Alone Again," which focuses on the death of Whitney's husband in 1930 as a motivating factor in her work to establish the museum.

Goodrich, Lloyd. *Pioneers in Modern Art in America: The Decade of the Armory Show, 1910-1920*. New York: Praeger, 1963. The "Exhibit of Eight" in 1908 and the Armory Show of 1913 were instrumental in establishing the environment for the founding of the Whitney Museum and the Museum of Modern Art. Goodrich, the third director of the Whitney, shows how an indig-

enous American art movement began to coalesce after the cultural vacuum of the early part of the century.

Sims, Patterson. *Whitney Museum of American Art*. 1985. Reprint. New York: Whitney Museum of Art, 1992. Contains reproductions of many of the Whitney's outstanding works, all in color. Two of the more interesting paintings are a portrait of Gertrude Vanderbilt Whitney by Robert Henri and George Bellow's *Dempsy and Firpo*, which greeted visitors when the Whitney opened its doors in 1931. Includes an excellent overview of the history of the museum and short biographies of its major artists.

SEE ALSO: Feb. 17, 1902: Stieglitz Organizes the Photo-Secession; Feb. 17-Mar. 15, 1913: Armory Show; 1921: Man Ray Creates the Rayograph; Feb. 12, 1935: Exhibition of American Abstract Painting Opens in New York.

December 11, 1931
FORMATION OF THE BRITISH COMMONWEALTH OF NATIONS

In the 1920's, the self-governing former colonies of the British Empire, known as dominions, wanted to encode in law their growing political autonomy from Great Britain. The Balfour resolution, created at the Imperial Conference of 1926, asserted the dominions' right to govern themselves independently.

ALSO KNOWN AS: Balfour resolution; Statute of Westminster

LOCALE: London, England; Canada; Australia; New Zealand; South Africa; Newfoundland; Irish Free State

CATEGORIES: Laws, acts, and legal history; colonialism and occupation; government and politics; independence movements

KEY FIGURES
Arthur Balfour (1848-1930), British prime minister, 1902-1905, first earl of Balfour after 1922, and lord president of the council in the British cabinet after 1925

William Lyon Mackenzie King (1874-1950), Canadian prime minister, 1921-1926, 1926-1930, and 1935-1948

SUMMARY OF EVENT
By the beginning of World War I, several British colonies settled by European immigrants—Canada, Austra-

lia, New Zealand, South Africa, Newfoundland, and the Irish Free State—had acquired a measure of self-government. The British North America Act of 1867 had given Canada the right to govern its internal affairs and had laid the foundation for its federal system. The six colonies of Australia had gained some measure of independence in the nineteenth century, and the 1901 Australia Act combined these regions into the Commonwealth of Australia, which operated under a federal system similar to Canada's. Likewise, the 1909 South Africa Act bound the four provinces of that country, which had been united after the Boer War (1899-1902). The Irish Free State had been formed in 1922 as a compromise between two sides: one that wanted to sever ties with Great Britain and one that wanted to remain part of the United Kingdom. New Zealand and Newfoundland had also gained the right to internal self-government as unitary entities. In 1907, the British government recognized the former colonies' status by forming a Dominions Section in its Colonial Office.

The dominions had raised and paid for forces to aid the Allies in World War I. As a result, at the Paris Peace Conference in 1919 the dominions had been recognized as independent countries and were allowed to sit at the negotiating table. Each country signed the Treaty of Versailles and became a founding member of the League of Nations. However, this de facto independence was not necessarily encoded in law. At first, some thought that the United Kingdom would develop a single foreign policy based on consultation, but this idea disintegrated in 1923, when Britain requested unilateral support from its dominion partners to help settle a dispute between Turkey and Greece. The resulting confusion made it obvious that constant consultation over foreign policy was neither practical nor desired. In the meantime, however, British officials in London were becoming increasingly conscious of the strength of the empire as a whole and of the individual countries within it. No longer were the dominions dismissed as simply places for emigration, exports, and cheap foodstuffs.

At the 1926 Imperial Conference of Prime Ministers, the dominions, led by William Lyon Mackenzie King of Canada, pressed the British government to make a formal statement on dominion independence. Arthur Balfour, the British lord president of council, issued a statement that came to be called the Balfour resolution (not to be confused with the 1917 Balfour Declaration, which expressed British approval of the Zionist philosophy). The resolution had a number of significant clauses, the first of which stated that the dominions and the United Kingdom were to be seen as equal in status as well as independent from each other. The second clause assured that there would be a common acknowledgment of the British crown as head of state, although each dominion would be allowed to choose its own governor-general as its representative. The third clause stipulated that the laws of Great Britain would be applied only to each dominion by express agreement and that all laws passed by each dominion would receive the governor-general's approval.

The Crown and the dominions officially agreed that the dominions and other colonies would be called the British Commonwealth of Nations. There were, however, two notable exceptions to the rule on including British colonies in the Commonwealth. India, the "jewel in the British Empire's crown," had not yet achieved complete internal independence, even though it retained

The state opening of Parliament, 1931. (NARA)

a separate seat at the League of Nations and had sent troops to World War I. The 1935 Government of India Act gave the nation further freedoms, but it was not until 1947 that complete independence was achieved by three separate countries: India, Pakistan, and Burma. The second exception was Southern Rhodesia, whose white settlers—but not its large native African population—had become self-governing in 1923. When the colony tried to achieve independence unilaterally in the 1960's, it was promptly expelled from the Commonwealth. Not until the white minority had ceded power to the African majority were sanctions against Southern Rhodesia dropped and it was allowed to rejoin the Commonwealth.

The legal groundwork necessary to put the Balfour resolution into practice was drawn up during the period 1926-1931. In each country, Britain started to appoint high commissioners; the individuals in these positions were ambassadors required to represent the British view, and they were seen quite separately from the governors-general. In 1931, Australia was the first Commonwealth country to appoint its own governor-general, even though King George V of England disapproved. The adoption of the Balfour resolution meant that the Colonial Laws Validity Act of 1865 was declared irrelevant, and so each country gained the power to legislate the actions of its citizens regardless of whether they lived in that particular dominion.

An intervening Imperial Conference in 1930 dealt more with trade, and it was here that the possibility of "Commonwealth preference"—advantageous trading terms between the Commonwealth countries—was discussed. After some discussion and compromise, these terms were established in 1932 in Ottawa, Canada. In 1931, the Commonwealth nations pegged their currencies to the British pound and thus became known as the sterling area. That same year saw the promulgation of the Statute of Westminster, which had to be passed by both the British parliament and by each Commonwealth country. Until the statute was approved by a dominion, the older acts of Parliament remained in effect there, and the dominion government remained based in London.

THE STATUTE OF WESTMINSTER

In the Statute of Westminster, delegates from the dominions of Australia, Canada, New Zealand, South Africa, Ireland, and Newfoundland laid the foundation for their own self-government. The statute's first four sections read as follows:

1. In this Act the expression "Dominion" means any of the following Dominions, that is to say, the Dominion of Canada, the Commonwealth of Australia, the Dominion of New Zealand, the Union of South Africa, the Irish Free State and Newfoundland.
2. (1) The Colonial Laws Validity Act, 1865, shall not apply to any law made after the commencement of this Act by the Parliament of a Dominion.
   (2) No law and no provision of any law made after the commencement of this Act by the Parliament of a Dominion shall be void or inoperative on the ground that it is repugnant to the law of England, or to the provisions of any existing or future Act of Parliament of the United Kingdom, or to any order, rule, or regulation made under any such Act, and the powers of the Parliament of a Dominion shall include the power to repeal or amend any such Act, order, rule or regulation in so far as the same is part of the law of the Dominion.
3. It is hereby declared and enacted that the Parliament of a Dominion has full power to make laws having extra-territorial operation.
4. No Act of Parliament of the United Kingdom passed after the commencement of this Act shall extend or be deemed to extend, to a Dominion as part of the law of that Dominion, unless it is expressly declared in that Act that that Dominion has requested, and consented to, the enactment thereof.

1931

SIGNIFICANCE

The Statute of Westminster was part of a much longer evolution from colony to independent country. It allowed the dominions to be more independent while retaining links with the United Kingdom, and it enabled the dominions to adopt fresh approaches to legislation. No other colonial empire had managed such a process in such a completely legislative manner.

A number of dominions, including Canada and New Zealand, chose not to act immediately. In Australia, the Statute of Westminster Adoption Act was not passed until 1942, during World War II, when Australia was threatened by invasion from Japan and realized it needed help from the United States as well as Great Britain. Up to that point, Australia had been content to have Great Britain determine its foreign policy. In dominions more hostile to Britain, such as the Irish Free State and South Africa, the Statute of Westminster was quickly approved. In fact, the Irish withdrew from the Commonwealth entirely in 1947, and South Africa's apartheid policies forced it to withdraw (rather than be expelled) for a time in the 1970's and 1980's. During the years of the Great Depression, Newfoundland found that its economy was not strong enough to allow it independent existence, and it was reincorporated as a British colony and administered by the Colonial Office in London until 1949, when the residents of Newfoundland decided to make it Canada's tenth province. Canada did not introduce its own citizenship requirements until 1947, and it did not take full control over its constitution until 1982.

After World War II, new Commonwealth members were allowed to move to a republican system of democracy: They could elect their own leaders and were no longer required to recognize the British crown as head of state. India and Pakistan were the first nations to take advantage of this freedom, and South Africa followed suit. Ghana (formerly the Gold Coast) was the first nonwhite African country to become independent when it joined the Commonwealth in 1957. Other colonies had to fight fierce wars to achieve their independence, including Kenya, Malaya, and Cyprus. A few former colonies, such as Burma (present-day Myanmar), formerly part of India, chose not to become members of the Commonwealth, and others have left and returned, as Pakistan did in 1989.

The Statute of Westminster allowed the British Commonwealth of Nations to grow and develop. The Commonwealth lost some cohesion as countries exited and entered, but its members continued to share a commitment to democracy (through constitutional monarchy or republican forms of government) and many cultural ties (including language). The British monarch makes regular tours through Commonwealth nations, Commonwealth prime ministers still meet every four years, and there is still a considerable amount of immigration to Commonwealth countries from the United Kingdom.

—*David Barratt*

FURTHER READING

Darwin, John. "The Dominion Idea in Imperial Politics." In *The Twentieth Century*, edited by Judith M. Brown. Vol. 4 in *The Oxford History of the British Empire*, edited by W. Roger Louis. New York: Oxford University Press, 1999. Presents a solid account of the establishment of the British dominions.

Judd, Dennis, and Peter Shinn. *The Evolution of the Modern Commonwealth, 1902-1980*. London: Palgrave Macmillan, 1982. A good account of the evolutionary processes involved in the change from dominions to Commonwealth.

Kitchen, Martin. *The British Empire and Commonwealth: A Short History*. London: Palgrave Macmillan, 1996. Focusing on the nineteenth and twentieth centuries, explains how Britain came to have the only true empire in the Victorian era and how it emerged victorious in two world wars.

Lloyd, T. O. "The Defeat of the Imperial Idea, 1922-1945." In *The British Empire, 1558-1995*. 2d ed. New York: Oxford University Press, 1996. Discussion places the Statute of Westminster in a fuller context of British history.

Rose, J. Holland, A. P. Newton, and E. A. Benians, eds. *The Cambridge History of the British Empire*. 8 vols. Cambridge, England: Cambridge University Press, 1929-1963. The definitive history of the Commonwealth, although it has become somewhat dated.

SEE ALSO: Jan. 1, 1901: Commonwealth of Australia Is Formed; May 31, 1910: Formation of the Union of South Africa; 1920-1921: Ireland Is Granted Home Rule and Northern Ireland Is Created; 1921-1948: King Era in Canada; May 1, 1925: Cyprus Becomes a British Crown Colony; July 21-Aug. 21, 1932: Ottawa Agreements; Aug. 16, 1940: Ogdensburg Agreement.

1932

BERLE AND MEANS DISCUSS CORPORATE CONTROL

Adolf A. Berle, Jr., and Gardiner C. Means drew national attention to emerging corporate centralism in the United States with their book The Modern Corporation and Private Property, *setting the stage for the development of new ideas and mechanisms to protect individuals' property rights and interests.*

ALSO KNOWN AS: *The Modern Corporation and Private Property*

LOCALE: New York, New York

CATEGORIES: Business and labor; economics; publishing and journalism

KEY FIGURES

Adolf A. Berle, Jr. (1895-1971), American corporate finance scholar

Gardiner C. Means (1896-1988), American economist

Michael C. Jensen (b. 1939), American professor of business administration

William H. Meckling (1922-1998), American professor of business administration

SUMMARY OF EVENT

The 1932 publication of *The Modern Corporation and Private Property* by Adolf A. Berle, Jr., and Gardiner C. Means recognized and documented the corporate system that was gradually replacing the free enterprise system in the United States. The pioneering book brought to national attention the existence of a forceful trend that already had resulted in concentration of power and control. Such concentration of power within corporations was taking place at the cost of alienating a diverse group of owner-managers, innovators, and entrepreneurs, the same group of individuals who had made Adam Smith's laissez-faire philosophy so workable. The thesis developed in the book has since become known as the paradigm of separation of ownership and control. According to this theory, the structure of corporate ownership, with numerous stockholders putatively owning companies that in fact were controlled by managers, led to owners' having little control over their property.

Berle and Means's claims regarding the emerging economic, social, and political order fell on deaf ears for some time. Theirs was not the message that economists, and possibly other scholars, wanted to hear. The separation of ownership and control, and the consequential conflict of interest between managers and owners, meant that there was something very wrong with prevailing economic theories and practices. Accepted knowledge among economists, legal scholars, and policy makers was that corporate managers were hired by shareholders and therefore they would do their best to maximize shareholders' wealth and welfare. The direct implication was that stockholders held real power as well as real wealth. They could hire and fire quickly and effectively without any adverse consequences on the company's operations. Shareholders were assumed to be fully represented by their elected representatives on a corporation's board of directors. Such boards were supposed to be free of any influences, threats, and possible manipulations that might be initiated by the managing directors.

Berle and Means, however, discovered a different picture. Shareholders did not appear to be exerting the natural control that would accompany the holding of property, in this case shares of common stock. Stockholders had become passive investors who did not—and in practice could not—have any say in the operation of the companies that they owned. It appeared that Adam Smith's worst nightmare was in the making. He had warned about the potential conflict of interest in diversely owned corporations. Managers of other people's money, rather than of their own, Smith wrote, are unlikely to exercise full care and vigilance because they will neither receive the benefit from such care nor suffer the losses resulting from poor management.

The statistical evidence and conclusions provided by Berle and Means regarding the emerging separation between ownership and control and the resultant changes in the structure of private ownership were irrefutable. Aside from the many changes occurring at the time in intellectual, judicial, and policy-making circles, the new trend toward a corporate state was gathering momentum.

The main thesis advanced in *The Modern Corporation and Private Property* was based on two major statistical observations. First, the American economic system showed trends of increasing concentration of wealth. Second, separation between ownership and control in the public corporation appeared to be expanding. Both developments seemed to be incompatible with the spirit of the free enterprise system.

It took more than a quarter of a century for the warnings and thoughts expressed by Berle and Means to sink in. Eventually, researchers and practitioners from the fields of economics and law started addressing the issues of ownership and control. Publication of "Theory of the

Firm: Managerial Behavior, Agency Costs, and Owner-ship Structure" by Michael C. Jensen and William H. Meckling in the mid-1970's elevated the separation of ownership and control paradigm to a new level of recognition, sophistication, and interest. This paper integrated elements from the fields of property rights, corporate finance, and agency relations to build a new theory of ownership structures of business enterprises. Jensen and Meckling based their work on the insights and realities recognized and outlined in *The Modern Corporation and Private Property* and provided new insights into changing relationships in ownership structure. Jensen and Meckling's work resulted in numerous other studies on the subject. Almost all such studies tried to both downplay and justify the separation of management and control. For example, Eugene F. Fama introduced the idea of a "managerial labor market" as a mechanism for disciplining nonloyal and nonabiding managers. He assumed that such markets were efficient, and that shareholders therefore should not be concerned about any conflict of interest. Berle and Means's work did not allow for any such mechanism.

SIGNIFICANCE

At least two major contributions to the U.S. and world economies can be attributed to the publication of *The Modern Corporation and Private Property*. First is the fundamental impact the study had on the passage, as well as strengthening and modification, of U.S. federal legislation concerning corporate securities. Berle and Means's book became the foundation for the 1933 Securities Act and the 1934 Securities Exchange Act. The 1933 act dealt with full and truthful disclosure of material information concerning new securities sold in primary markets, and the 1934 act provided federal rules governing the sale of securities sold in secondary markets, including organized markets such as the New York Stock Exchange and the over-the-counter (OTC) markets. The 1934 act created the Securities and Exchange Commission (SEC) to operate as a watchdog for the securities industry.

More important, *The Modern Corporation and Private Property*, along with similar studies it inspired, provided justification for the SEC to institute further regulations to protect the interests of stockholders against the discretionary power of managers. The role of the SEC in protecting stockholders' interests became obvious when a frenzy of management-led special buyout arrangements surfaced in the 1980's. Such deals, generally known as management buyouts (MBOs) or leveraged buyouts (LBOs), were not all in the best interests of shareholders. In an MBO, the ruling management buys enough of the company's shares from other investors to take control of the company. To finance the purchase, management may borrow needed funds from financial institutions. In such a case, the managers or other buyers leverage their capital by using the company as collateral for loans—thus the term "leveraged buyout" for this kind of takeover. A problem arises because the buying management has full and free access to all available information within the corporation, giving management an advantage over the selling parties, the shareholders. The buying management has a much better idea of the true worth of the company.

The second major contribution of *The Modern Corporation and Private Property* was the fact that the study acted as a forceful advocate for the free enterprise system in the United States and elsewhere. The book aroused awareness and curiosity among scholars and the general public. As part of the awareness exercise, Berle and Means explained the new corporate form as "a commercial instrument of formidable effectiveness, feared because of its power, hated because of the excesses with which the power was used, suspect because of the extent of its political manipulations within the political State, admired because of its capacity to get things done."

The major concerns expressed by Berle and Means turned out to be justified. Transformation of the American economy to one of corporate dominance came close to becoming reality. *The Modern Corporation and Private Property* prompted systems of checks and balances to be designed and put in place, so that a complete change to insider control of American business never materialized.

One of the resultant movements was the formation in the United States of the United Shareholders Association (USA) in the 1980's. This association of stockholders was built on the theses and principles discovered by Berle and Means in the early 1930's. USA became a powerful voice in shaping public opinion regarding the massive power held by management in large corporations. It mobilized and united shareholders across the United States and educated them about how to watch after their interests in publicly held corporations. As a result, many combative corporate managers had no choice but to cooperate with shareholders or launch expensive proxy fights to keep their jobs. The shareholder revolt did not stop at the level of individual investors. Institutional investors such as pension funds and insurance companies, which by the 1980's held a majority of outstanding common stock, also became active participants in running the companies in which they invested.

A drive toward entrepreneurialism and innovation beginning in the 1970's also aided in taking power from large corporations and their management teams. That trend, which surfaced with full power in the late 1970's in the United States, gathered strength, and its effects were seen through the end of the twentieth century and into the twenty-first. Corporate monoliths became susceptible to attack from such entrepreneurial companies as Apple Computer and Novell. This apparent reversal of power made traditional corporate power much more vulnerable and less secure. Managers in large corporations had greater reason not to ignore their fiduciary responsibility to shareholders, as executive jobs were not as well protected as they once were.

Berle and Means found an intellectual ally in Thomas Peters. In 1992, Peters published *Liberation Management: Necessary Disorganization for the Nanosecond Nineties*. The message of this book is very clear: Large corporations are a thing of the past. To stay competitive and agile, businesses must disorganize, shedding bureaucracy and allowing individual innovation and entrepreneurship. Top management should become much closer to the production lines—that is, it should be subject to close scrutiny by workers, owners, and other stakeholders. In such a world, the power of the corporate manager comes from below.

In large part as a result of awareness initiated by *The Modern Corporation and Private Property*, the trend toward corporate centralism was reversed. According to statistics published by the U.S. Small Business Administration, about 41 percent of all U.S. private sales in the early 2000's were under management by smaller companies. In addition, small firms produced more than half of U.S. output and employed half of the private workforce. Trends appeared to favor smaller and entrepreneurial firms, which have relatively few problems with conflicts of interest.

—*Rassoul Yazdipour*

Further Reading

Berle, Adolf A., and Gardiner C. Means. *The Modern Corporation and Private Property*. Rev. ed. New York: Harcourt, Brace, & World, 1968. This revised edition of Berle and Means's classic work includes an introduction written by the authors in 1967. Appropriate for general readers as well as readers with background in economics.

Brown, Courtney C. *Putting the Corporate Board to Work*. New York: Macmillan, 1976. Presents a form of organization and practice—along with suggested reforms—that could correct shortcomings of the board-of-directors form of corporate control. Intended for corporate managers.

Freeland, Robert F. *The Struggle for Control of the Modern Corporation: Organizational Change at General Motors, 1924-1970*. New York: Cambridge University Press, 2001. Examines the nature of the modern corporation and how corporations have changed by focusing on the specific case of General Motors.

Herman, Edward S. *Corporate Control, Corporate Power*. New York: Cambridge University Press, 1981. A reassessment of Berle and Means's work in the light of changes that occurred following World War II. Asserts that the power of government to restrict or limit corporate action is exaggerated and that corporations have remained faithful to their basic objective of profit maximization.

Jensen, Michael C., and William H. Meckling. "Theory of the Firm: Managerial Behavior, Agency Costs, and Ownership Structure." In *The Modern Theory of Corporate Finance*, edited by Michael C. Jensen and Clifford W. Smith. New York: McGraw-Hill, 1984. Original publication of this pioneering work in the mid-1970's effectively rejuvenated and placed in a new framework the principles and theses developed by Berle and Means. Successfully took the issues to a wider audience and developed new interest in the area. Recommended for readers with some background in economics and business.

Mason, Edward S., ed. *The Corporation in Modern Society*. Cambridge, Mass.: Harvard University Press, 1959. Collection of readings contains interesting pieces from both legal and economics scholars. The main purpose of the collection is to shed new light on issues related to ownership and control. Most contributions are accessible to general readers.

Mueller, Dennis C. *The Modern Corporation*. Lincoln: University of Nebraska Press, 1986. Discusses different frameworks and models in the theory of the firm and addresses some negative aspects of managerial capitalism. Intended for readers with background in business administration.

Peters, Thomas. *Liberation Management: Necessary Disorganization for the Nanosecond Nineties*. New York: Alfred A. Knopf, 1992. Envisions the future of corporations and management. Aimed at readers with ties to the business world.

Putterman, Louis, and Randall S. Kroszner, eds. *The Economic Nature of the Firm: A Reader*. 2d ed. New York: Cambridge University Press, 1996. Collection of classic papers on the topic of the economic nature of firms includes Jensen and Meckling's "Theory of the Firm." Intended for readers with backgrounds in business and economics.

SEE ALSO: Oct. 24-29, 1929: U.S. Stock Market Crashes; Dec. 11, 1930: Bank of United States Fails; June 6, 1934: Securities and Exchange Commission Is Established.

1932
CÉLINE'S *JOURNEY TO THE END OF THE NIGHT* EXPRESSES INTERWAR CYNICISM

Louis-Ferdinand Céline's novel Journey to the End of the Night *radiated an earthy vigor and alternately shocked and inspired readers with its exuberant expressions of disgust for civilization.*

LOCALE: Paris, France
CATEGORY: Literature

KEY FIGURES
Louis-Ferdinand Céline (1894-1961), French novelist
Émile Zola (1840-1902), French novelist
Fyodor Dostoevski (1821-1881), Russian novelist

SUMMARY OF EVENT
The son of hard-pressed lower-middle-class Parisian shopkeepers, Louis-Ferdinand Destouches borrowed his pen name of Céline from his grandmother before making the transition from doctor to novelist in the 1930's. His maiden novel, *Voyage au bout de la nuit* (1932; *Journey to the End of the Night*, 1934), vaulted him into the front ranks of the French literary scene, typically eliciting polarized reactions of either enthusiastic praise or vehement criticism from reviewers. Supporters contended that Céline had squarely faced the hypocrisy and degradation of modern social life with unprecedented candor and sensitivity, whereas one of the many detractors who rejected the novel as lowbrow and morally corrupt wisecracked that a tax levied on each of the myriad obscenities in the book would make a major dent in France's ballooning budget deficit. Subsequent novels by Céline would differ from *Journey to the End of the Night* in various ways, but his maiden work established his lifelong pattern of writing darkly humorous picaresque novels featuring argot-peppered prose and a spirit of outspoken and often truculent pessimism.

Like other picaresque novels, *Journey to the End of the Night* follows the footloose peregrinations of a dominant protagonist. Ferdinand Bardamu doubles as narrator and protagonist, and the many resonances of his life story with Céline's make him at least a semiautobio-

graphical figure. Bardamu's life mirrors Céline's as follows: He suffers a serious injury while fighting against Germany as a volunteer in World War I and soon comes to dismiss war as a totally absurd and vain ritual; he goes to Africa, where he experiences revulsion at both European colonialism and native folkways; he voyages to America, where he works for a period in the intimidating atmosphere of mammoth auto plants and indulges in flings with American women of low repute; and he returns across the Atlantic to France, where he settles down as a doctor in a seedy working-class neighborhood of Paris. Although the careful reader cannot go so far as to assume a relationship of absolute identity between Céline and Bardamu, the close overlap between the life stories of author and protagonist has persuaded most reviewers and interpreters to identify the major attitudes and values of Bardamu with those of Céline, even if many of the minor details in Bardamu's life bear the mark of poetic license. Indeed, Céline's subsequent novels would continue to adopt the first book's strange mixture of plodding confessional autobiography and mercurial, hallucinatory disjunctiveness.

The hallucinatory quality of *Journey to the End of the Night* emerges early in the novel. After Bardamu startles a somewhat conservative interlocutor at a Paris café with an outspoken exposition of his cynical and pessimistic view of the ordinary citizen as but a galley slave for the rich at the top of the social pyramid, a parade of men enlisting for military service in World War I rounds a street corner in the two young men's direction. Supposedly overcome by the spectacle of a largely female crowd lining both sides of the street and cheering the marching men, Bardamu impulsively leaps up from his chair and hurries to join the procession of enlistees. Although the reader gradually becomes accustomed to the mercurial impulsiveness of Céline's picaro, Bardamu's cocksure rejection of his civilization as disgustingly corrupt and exploitative sits very uneasily beside the ebullient optimism with which he decides to defend his country. To say that this abrupt turn in attitude lacks verisimilitude would be understating the case, for Bardamu's apparent amnesia regarding what he has just been saying about a world of galley slaves reminds one more of a dream or hallucination than of a plausible state of waking consciousness.

After a war wound allows Bardamu to cheat the heavy odds against him at the battlefront and to return alive to convalesce in Paris, he has an affair with a young American woman, whom he eventually comes to despise. A subsequent trip to a French colony in sub-Saharan Africa seems to reinforce his jaundiced view of civilization as a whole, although he singles out a certain French petty official for adulatory praise, likening the man to an angel because of his selfless devotion to a young woman. Later on in the novel during Bardamu's wanderings in America, he briefly shows obeisance to another model of selflessness, on this occasion the familiar popular archetype of the prostitute with a heart of gold, specifically the elusive and hastily sketched figure of Molly. Céline's view of the human condition thus shows itself as highly polarized: The narrator views himself and the great majority of fellow humans as despicably selfish exploiters, while a tiny minority of saintlike and selfless characters such as Molly and the French official stand in stark contrast to the malevolent multitude. Given the relish with which Céline describes the failings of the majority and the brevity and sketchiness with which he portrays the tiny angelic minority, however, one can only conclude that the novelist attributes far more vitality and genuine significance to the wretched and ignoble majority.

Although Bardamu takes Molly as his lover and seems satisfied with her as a partner, his wanderlust knows no bounds, and both he and his American paramour soon agree that the two of them must part for no other reason than his yearning for the road. Soon back in France, Bardamu takes up the practice of medicine in the same seedy neighborhood that houses Léon Robinson, his old war buddy and fellow pessimistic cynic.

Robinson comes across as something of an alter ego or double for Bardamu. Robinson abruptly veers in and out of the narrative from beginning to end as Bardamu's companion in avoiding the front lines in war, sampling American factory life in Detroit, and hustling jobs and approachable women in a grim working-class Parisian neighborhood. Both men harbor too much bitterness toward their society to take the step of partially integrating themselves with it by settling down and raising families. As the two escort their paramours on a double date to a cheap amusement park, the reader encounters yet an-

other example of a coarse and callow sensibility bent on perpetually extending the joyful irresponsibility of adolescent drifting while indulging in paranoid fantasies about a cruel society forever victimizing the innocent. When Robinson's lover suspects that she means little more to him than one of the passing entertainments at the amusement park, she begins to insist that he show some commitment to their relationship of several months and talk about how it might be made permanent. Robinson merely scoffs at this idea with a cackle. When he notices how furious his lover has become, he tries to gloss over things by insisting that he has nothing personal against her but simply has an aversion to sullying himself with what he views as the hypocritical conventions of love and marriage. When he sinks into a sullen silence in response to her increasingly overwrought demands that he follow through with the implied commitment he has made to her over the past several months, she finally goes berserk and shoots him in the abdomen, at which point she flees the scene. Like many of Céline's characters, she abruptly slips out of the narrative, never to be heard of again.

Instead of rushing Robinson to a hospital, where inconvenient questions from the despised police might be asked, Bardamu and his paramour carry the bleeding and half-conscious man to a bed in the narrator's sanatorium ward. Simply assuming that Robinson has no chance of surviving, Bardamu holds his dying sidekick's hand while waiting for internal hemorrhaging to finish him off. The thoughts that run through Bardamu's mind at this point well represent the caustically antihumanistic tenor of Céline's pessimism, for Bardamu confesses that he feels less pity for the dying Robinson, his best friend, than he would have felt for a dying dog. After all, Bardamu muses, a dog is not sly, whereas Robinson was sly, as are humans in general. Were the word "sly" replaced with the word "sinful," Céline would appear much like one of the religious zealots who pontificate about the utter depravity of man and the impossible state of the world as a vale of tears. As Céline rules out the possibility of efficacious intervention on the part of either human or supernatural forces, however, his views wind up even more acridly bitter and negative. It is hardly surprising that he can find no more appropriate line with which to end *Journey to the End of the Night* than "Let us hear no more of all this."

SIGNIFICANCE

Heavily pessimistic fiction can hardly be considered rare, as any reader of Thomas Hardy's Wessex novels or Émile Zola's Rougon-Macquart series could attest.

Novels such as Hardy's and Zola's, however, offer the reader at least the possibility of a satisfactory resolution and also present the onset of disillusionment as a gradual development governed by intelligible relations of cause and effect. In contrast, *Journey to the End of the Night* does not even attempt to present an incremental rise in disillusionment of the protagonist; instead, the book offers the reader an antiheroic picaro who seems astonishingly free of "illusions" about wretched humankind from the very outset. Just a few pages into the novel, Bardamu self-assuredly likens the lot of both himself and the vast majority of humans to the miserable fate of galley slaves, who must row like the devil in a stinking ship's hold while the captain lounges on the breezy deck with a perfumed and nubile young woman on his lap. Rather than witnessing Bardamu's increasing understanding of human suffering over time, the reader of *Journey to the End of the Night* observes merely a repetitious piling up of anecdotes, vignettes, and pronouncements on the theme of human degradation and vileness.

The degree to which the disjointedly connected episodes in *Journey to the End of the Night* can be appreciated independently of what occurs before or after in the novel seems extreme even by the loose standards of the picaresque novel; the overall effect is somewhat like that of a series of vaudeville acts united only by the sameness of the lead performer. Céline draws on his mastery of the spoken idiom and theatrical exuberance to forestall the monotony that tends to result from repetitiousness of attitude and disjointedness of incident, but his racy argot and theatricality can rarely make up for the absence of a larger order in the scheme of his novel. In lieu of setting up a structural framework for his novels, Céline draws on the concept of "lacework" to explain his proclivity for articulating an intricate but predictable pattern or motif time and time again, as if he were weaving a piece of lace.

Céline's antisocial and partly hooliganish picaro stands as an important intermediary between Fyodor Dostoevski's underground man of *Zapiski iz podpolya* (1864; *Letters from the Underworld*, 1913; better known as *Notes from the Underground*) and the rebellious countercultural protagonists common in the works of Henry Miller and such Beat generation novelists as Jack Kerouac, Ken Kesey, and William S. Burroughs. Like Dostoevski's underground man, Bardamu angrily resents the civilization from which he hails, and he repeatedly lashes both it and himself with partially relevant but greatly overblown accusations of sickness and inequity. Céline goes a step further, however, in jettisoning the decorum of a somewhat restrained and literate narrative

persona. It was one thing to allow one's characters to brawl and spout obscenities, as many a character in Zola's novels did, but it was quite another to create a narrator who similarly exulted in mouthing expletive-laden argot and slapping defenseless women around.

Although the rough-and-tumble language and brutish antics of Céline's narrators scandalized many readers at first, more and more writers followed suit with narrative personae similarly contemptuous of decorum and delicate aesthetic sensibilities. As a result, the kind of narrator who had shocked Céline's readers in the 1930's became an increasingly familiar figure in European and American fiction by the 1960's. In more recent years, Céline's writings have become so accepted within the canon of major modern French writers that passages from his novels have made their way into the very pillar of cultural traditionalism, the national *baccalauréat* examination.

Céline often referred to his picaros as traveling the "night subway" through the seamy side of modern social life that more genteel writers ignored, falsified, or prettified. Although even many of his admirers have noted the dangers posed by his amoral stance and irrational and intolerant turns of thought, Céline's important stature and wide influence in the realm of twentieth century fiction can no longer be contested.

—Philip F. Williams

FURTHER READING

Booth, Wayne C. *The Rhetoric of Fiction*. 2d ed. Chicago: University of Chicago Press, 1983. Acknowledges Céline's literary talent in the concluding chapter, "The Morality of Impersonal Narration," but also emphasizes how the French author's hard-bitten distrust of virtually all human motivations contradicts his self-assured pronouncements on virtues and vices.

Bouchard, Norma. *Céline, Gadda, Beckett: Experimental Writings of the 1930s*. Gainesville: University Press of Florida, 2000. Scholarly work examines the writings of the three authors and argues that they contain the roots of what came to be known as postmodernism. Includes a close reading of *Journey to the End of the Night*.

Buckley, William K., ed. *Critical Essays on Louis-Ferdinand Céline*. Boston: G. K. Hall, 1989. One of the most comprehensive volumes of Céline criticism available in English. Contains a representative selection of positive, negative, and neutral evaluations of the novelist.

Céline, Louis-Ferdinand. *Journey to the End of the*

Night. Translated by John H. P. Marks. New York: New Directions, 1960. The standard English translation of Céline's first and most famous novel.

Hewitt, Nicholas. *The Golden Age of Louis-Ferdinand Céline*. Leamington Spa, England: Berg, 1987. Survey of Céline's work includes a chapter on the novelist's 1920's nonfiction writings about medical hygiene as significant influences on his fiction.

———. *The Life of Céline: A Critical Biography*. Malden, Mass.: Blackwell, 1999. Comprehensive biography includes substantial discussion of Céline's works, placing them within the context of his life and times.

Luce, Stanford L., and William K. Buckley. *A Half-Century of Céline: An Annotated Bibliography, 1932-1982*. New York: Garland, 1983. One of the most comprehensive bibliographies of Céline criticism available in English.

McCarthy, Patrick. *Céline*. London: Allen Lane, 1975. Excellent life-and-works study of Céline illuminates many connections between the author's major novels and French politics of the 1930's.

SEE ALSO: 1921-1923: Hašek's *The Good Soldier Švejk* Reflects Postwar Disillusionment; Feb. 2, 1922: Joyce's *Ulysses* Redefines Modern Fiction; 1924: Mann's *The Magic Mountain* Reflects European Crisis; 1925: Gide's *The Counterfeiters* Questions Moral Absolutes; Jan., 1929: *All Quiet on the Western Front* Stresses the Futility of War; Winter, 1932: Huxley's *Brave New World* Forecasts Technological Totalitarianism; Sept. 1, 1934: Miller's *Tropic of Cancer* Stirs Controversy.

1932

1932
GILSON'S *SPIRIT OF MEDIEVAL PHILOSOPHY* REASSESSES CHRISTIAN THOUGHT

Étienne Gilson's research in medieval history and his insistence that the Middle Ages played an important role in modern philosophy's development brought about major changes in the study of the Middle Ages and in attitudes about the roles of religion and philosophy.

LOCALE: Paris, France

CATEGORIES: Philosophy; historiography; publishing and journalism

KEY FIGURES

Étienne Gilson (1884-1978), French historian of philosophy and philosopher

Émile Bréhier (1876-1952), French historian of philosophy and Gilson opponent

Jacques Maritain (1882-1973), French neo-Thomist philosopher

SUMMARY OF EVENT

Étienne Gilson, who was to become one of the most important and influential medieval scholars and neo-Thomist philosophers of the twentieth century, received his early education in France's Roman Catholic schools and later in secular *lycées*. He then pursued a philosophy degree at the Sorbonne, where he became particularly interested in Cartesian and post-Cartesian philosophy; he wrote his dissertation on René Descartes. On the advice of his professor Lucien Levy-Bruhl, Gilson narrowed his topic to a study of the scholastic origins of Descartes's thought. In 1913, he completed his dissertation titled "La Liberté chez Descartes et la Théologie" (freedom in Descartes and theology).

While he was researching and writing his dissertation, Gilson developed new research interests: medieval philosophy and theology. Through study of the texts written by Saints Augustine, Thomas Aquinas, and Bonaventure, Gilson became convinced that the theologians of the Middle Ages (which lasted from 500 to 1500 C.E.) had made significant contributions to the field of philosophy by combining it with theology to create Christian philosophy.

In 1921, Gilson became a professor of medieval history at the Sorbonne. A devout Catholic, Gilson was also an independent thinker, and he introduced his ideas about medieval philosophers and the importance of studying original texts into his teaching, lectures, and publications. He soon gained a reputation as one of the best medieval scholars and historians of his time; medieval scholars considered his work on Thomas Aquinas, Augustine, and Bonaventure to be one of the field's standard reference works.

Gilson also gained an international reputation as a philosopher. In 1927, he received an invitation to be a guest lecturer at Harvard University; while he was there, he was asked to go to Toronto to establish an institute for medieval studies. In 1929, he founded the Pontifical Institute of Mediaeval Studies at Saint Michael's College of the University of Toronto; the institute was instrumental in disseminating Gilson's methods and approaches to medieval scholarship. The following school year (1930-1931), Gilson was invited to the University of Aberdeen in Scotland, where he gave a series of talks known as the Gifford Lectures. These were published as *The Spirit of Medieval Philosophy* in 1932.

As early as 1929, several important French philosophers, including Émile Bréhier, had begun to take issue with the idea of a Christian philosophy. Philosophers, historians of philosophy, and medievalists had generally accepted that the Middle Ages had been devoid of real philosophical thought, at least compared to the times of the Greeks and Romans. Bréhier insisted that philosophy slumbered during the Middle Ages and that it had been revived only when René Descartes began writing in the seventeenth century. Bréhier also insisted that it was absurd to talk about a Christian philosophy: Such a philosophy is no more possible than a Christian mathematics or a Christian physics. Philosophy, like mathematics or physics, requires the use of reason; revelation and faith belong to the discipline of theology. Maurice Blondel, Fernand van Steenberghen, Étienne Gilson, and Jacques Maritain all debated the issue with Bréhier, but Gilson was the chief spokesman for those opposing Bréhier.

The Gifford Lectures began Gilson's response to Bréhier. The first two lectures, which would become the first two chapters of *The Spirit of Medieval Philosophy*, dealt with Christian philosophy. The first lecture addressed the problem of Christian philosophy, and the second one dealt with the concept of Christian philosophy. In his first lecture, Gilson examined and refuted each objection to the idea of a Christian philosophy. He concluded that historical facts, the original works of the medieval theologian-philosophers, and the premises on which modern philosophers such as Descartes and Gottfried Wilhelm Leibniz elaborated their philosophies all supported the idea of a Christian philosophy. In his second lecture, he proposed a definition of Christian philosophy based on a close examination of the medieval thinkers who accepted Christian revelation and yet viewed reason as a way to understanding. He argued that for these scholars, faith served as an aid to reason. The rest of the Gifford Lectures examined original philosophical texts and their treatments of religion and philosophy.

During the years that followed, Gilson published many books and articles in which he continued to demonstrate the importance of the medieval thinkers and their influence on the development of philosophy in the seventeenth, eighteenth, and nineteenth centuries. In many of his writings, Gilson sought to correct what he saw as errors in the research methods used to evaluate the medieval writers' works, and his contributions to medieval scholarship and to philosophical thought earned him election to the French Academy in 1946.

SIGNIFICANCE

Étienne Gilson had a major impact on medieval history and philosophy. His lack of formal training in medieval philosophy helped him develop an original way of viewing medieval writers, and he found that study of the original texts revealed aspects of the authors that were different from those revealed by most critics. He revitalized medievalists' research methods by insisting on the use of original texts, and in the courses he taught he stressed that the Middle Ages were in fact times of significant intellectual activity. Through his founding and subsequent work with the Pontifical Institute of Mediaeval Studies, Gilson continued to encourage and facilitate research on the significant contributions made by medieval thinkers to the understanding of being and of moral philosophy. Gilson also created and developed the concept of Christian philosophy, and in *The Spirit of Medieval Philosophy* and later works he developed a convincing argument that theology and philosophy—faith and reason—are not mutually exclusive. His insistence that the medieval thinkers were philosophers as well as theologians and that their works created a Christian philosophy resulted in debates that reignited interest in these scholars and in philosophy in general.

—Shawncey Webb

FURTHER READING

Dulles, Avery. "Can Philosophy Be Christian?" *First Things: A Monthly Journal of Religion and Public Life*, April, 2000, 24-29. Definition and program of Gilson's philosophy. Links his ideas to Pope John Paul II's 1998 encyclical *Fides et Ratio*.

Gilson, Étienne. *The Spirit of Mediaeval Philosophy*. Translated by A. H. C. Downes. Notre Dame, Ind.: University of Notre Dame Press, 1991. Gilson's explanation of Christian philosophy as it was developed in the Middle Ages. This is the publication of his Gifford Lectures, which were given in 1930 and 1931.

Grogin, R. C. *The Bergsonian Controversy in France, 1900-1914*. Calgary, Alta.: University of Calgary

Press, 1988. Examines philosophical controversy about being, especially at the Sorbonne. Many quotes from Gilson on the subject.

McCool, Gerald A. *From Unity to Pluralism: The Internal Evolution of Thomism*. New York: Fordham University Press, 1999. Deals with four major Thomists. Chapter 8 discusses Gilson's work on the theologian philosophers of the Middle Ages in terms of Christian philosophy.

_____. *The Neo-Thomists*. Milwaukee, Wis.: Marquette University Press, 1994. Places Gilson among the Neo-Thomists and discusses the importance of his research and his creation of "existential Thomism."

Redpath, Peter A., ed. *A Thomist Tapestry: Essays in Memory of Étienne Gilson*. New York: Éditions Rodopi, 2003. Written by Gilson's students. Good survey of Gilson's method of philosophy and his scholarship.

Shook, Laurence K. *Étienne Gilson*. Toronto: Pontifical Institute of Mediaeval Studies, 1984. Provides accurate and complete biographical information on Gilson.

SEE ALSO: 1902: James Proposes a Rational Basis for Religious Experience; 1921: Wittgenstein Emerges as an Important Philosopher; 1923: Buber Breaks New Ground in Religious Philosophy; Sept. 30, 1925: Chesterton Critiques Modernism and Defends Christianity; May, 1926: Durant Publishes *The Story of Philosophy*; 1927: Heidegger Publishes *Being and Time*.

1932

1932-1935
DOMAGK DISCOVERS THAT SULFONAMIDES CAN SAVE LIVES

Gerhard Domagk developed the experimental procedures for testing the effectiveness of drugs and discovered that sulfonamides are effective in curing a large number of diseases caused by bacteria.

LOCALE: Elberfeld, Germany
CATEGORY: Health and medicine

KEY FIGURES
Gerhard Domagk (1895-1964), German physician
Paul Ehrlich (1854-1915), German chemist and
   bacteriologist

SUMMARY OF EVENT

Quinine was used to treat malaria for hundreds of years and had been purified by the French chemists Pierre Joseph Pelletier and Joseph Bienaimé Caventou around 1820. Nevertheless, Paul Ehrlich is usually credited with being the father of modern chemotherapy because he was responsible for discovering a number of useful drugs. Ehrlich was familiar with dyes used to stain microorganisms and suspected that some of them might specifically poison the microorganisms responsible for disease but not hurt the patient. He began a search of dyes for "magic bullets" that would destroy microorganisms and cure diseases. From 1906 to 1910, he tested compounds that had been developed by the German dye industry. He eventually found that a number of complex trypan dyes inhibited the protozoans that cause African sleeping sickness.

Ehrlich and his coworkers also synthesized hundreds of organic compounds that contained arsenic. In 1910, he found that one of these compounds, later named Salvarsan, was useful in curing syphilis, a disease caused by the bacterium *Treponema*. This was an important discovery because at that time the disease was killing large numbers of Europeans each year. Unfortunately, Salvarsan was very toxic to patients because it had to be taken in large doses for one to two years to effect a cure. Ehrlich's continued research resulted in a less toxic arsenic compound that was also effective against syphilis; this compound, Neo-Salvarsan, replaced Salvarsan in 1912.

In 1915, tartar emetic (a compound containing the metal antimony) was found to be useful in treating kala-azar, a disease caused by a protozoan. Kala-azar affected millions of people in Africa, India, and Asia, causing much suffering and many deaths each year. Two years later, it was discovered that injection of tartar emetic into the blood of persons suffering from bilharziasis killed the flatworms infecting the bladder, liver, and spleen. In 1920, suramin, a colorless compound developed from trypan red, was introduced to treat African sleeping sickness. It was much less toxic to the patient than any of the drugs Ehrlich had developed, and a single dose would give protection for more than a month. From the dye methylene blue, chemists made mepacrine (also called Atabrine and quinacrine), which was effective against the protozoan that causes malaria. This chemical was introduced in 1933 and used during World War II. Its drawback was that it caused the skin to become yellow.

Gerhard Domagk had been trained in medicine but turned to research in an attempt to discover chemicals that would inhibit or kill microorganisms. He became director of experimental pathology and bacteriology at the Elberfeld laboratories of the German chemical firm I. G. Farbenindustrie in 1927. Ehrlich's discovery that trypan dyes selectively poisoned microorganisms suggested to Domagk that he look for antimicrobials in a new group of chemicals known as azo dyes. A number of these dyes were synthesized from sulfonamides and purified by Fritz Mietzsch and Josef Klarer. Domagk found that many of these dyes protected mice infected with the bacteria *Streptococcus pyogenes*. In 1932, he discovered that one of these dyes was much more effective than any tested previously. This red azo dye containing a sulfonamide was named prontosil rubrum.

From 1932 to 1935, Domagk began a rigorous testing program to determine the effectiveness and dangers of prontosil at different doses in animals. Given that all chemicals injected into animals or humans are potentially dangerous, Domagk set about determining the doses that would harm or kill. In addition, he worked out the lowest doses that would eliminate the pathogen. The ratio of the smallest amount of drug that kills the patient to the minimum amount of drug that eliminates the pathogen is called the therapeutic ratio of the drug. Chemicals with low therapeutic ratios (near one) are not very useful; those with high therapeutic ratios (greater than ten) are usually the safest and the most effective drugs. The firm supplied samples of the drug to a select number of physicians to carry out clinical trials on humans. Animal experimentation can only indicate which chemicals might be useful in humans and what doses are required.

The synthesis and purification of a drug, its testing in animals, and then its testing in humans require the involvement of many scientists and technicians as well as expensive and appropriate facilities. Clearly, the discovery of a new group of useful drugs does not result from the discovery and work of a single person. The chemists, the animal researchers, and the physicians at clinics all contribute to the final conclusions.

From drug testing in animals, Domagk learned what doses were effective and safe. This knowledge saved his daughter's life. One day while knitting, Domagk's daughter punctured her finger with a needle and infected herself with virulent bacteria. The bacteria quickly multiplied and spread from the wound into neighboring tissue. In an attempt to alleviate the swelling, the infected

area was lanced and allow to drain. This did not stop the infection that was spreading into her lymph and blood, however. The child became critically ill because of the developing septicemia (blood poisoning). In those days, more than 75 percent of those who acquired blood infections died. Domagk realized that the chances for his daughter's survival were very poor. In desperation, he obtained some of the powdered prontosil that had worked so well on infected animals. He extrapolated from his animal experiments how much to give his daughter so that the bacteria would be killed but his daughter would not be poisoned. Within hours of the first treatment, her fever dropped. Complete recovery followed repeated oral doses of prontosil. Domagk's daughter was saved.

In 1935, Domagk published his results demonstrating that prontosil was useful in treating streptococcal infections in animals. German physicians, who had extensively tested prontosil on humans, reported that it was also extremely effective in treating streptococcal infections in humans. This announcement was an important first step in the battle against diseases caused by bacteria. Different strains of *Streptococcus pyogenes* are responsible for strep throat, rheumatic fever, scarlet fever, erysipelas (a spreading skin infection), cellulitis (a localized skin infection), puerperal sepsis (childbed fever), and septicemia. During the 1920's, puerperal sepsis, rheumatic fever, scarlet fever, and septicemia killed thousands of women, babies, and children every year.

The use of sulfonamides lowered the death rates of a number of diseases very quickly. Before 1935, the death rate for puerperal sepsis in England was 175 per 100,000 births. In 1937 and 1938, the rate fell to 80 per 100,000. The use of sulfanilamides saved the lives of more than one thousand English mothers in only two years.

SIGNIFICANCE

The publication of Domagk's 1935 paper stimulated extensive research in Germany, France, and England. French researchers found that the active portion of the azo dye prontosil was the colorless sulfonamide called sulfanilamide. Much later, it was discovered that bacteria are sensitive to prontosil if they are able to cleave the azo dye and release sulfanilamide. Sulfanilamide, as well as other sulfonamides, blocks the synthesis of a coenzyme bacteria needed to grow. The discovery that sulfanilamide was the actual antimicrobial agent spurred scientists to synthesize new classes of sulfonamides and test their effectiveness on other pathogenic bacteria.

Domagk demonstrated that some sulfonamides called

ulirons were effective against the bacteria that caused gonorrhea. The ulirons were the first drugs used in Germany to treat gonorrhea because prontosils were not effective. Soon after the introduction of ulirons, it was found that gonorrhea could be treated more effectively with a number of newly synthesized sulfonamides. By 1938, English researchers and physicians demonstrated that sulfapyridine was effective against a number of bacterial pathogens. It was used to treat gonorrhea, pneumonia, meningitis, and wound infections. Another sulfonamide called sulfathiazole was even more effective against these organisms. Because of its rapid excretion, sulfathiazole was replaced by sulfadiazine and sulfadimidine.

Research on the many different sulfonamides and their effectiveness on bacterial infections showed that bacterial species varied significantly in their sensitivity to a particular sulfanilamide. For example, some gonococci (bacteria that cause gonorrhea) were sensitive and effectively inhibited by low concentrations of a sulfonamide. Other bacteria of the same species were extremely resistant and would grow even when subjected to very high concentrations of the sulfonamide. It was found that a particular bacterium was not inhibited equally by all the different sulfonamides. Sulfathiazole, for example, might be more effective than sulfapyridine, which in turn might be more effective than uliron. Experiments showed that a particular sulfonamide was not equally effective when tested on different genera. For gonococcal infection, sulfathiazole was found to be the best sulfonamide. Nevertheless, sulfapyrimidines and sulfones were discovered to be more effective for streptococcal infections.

In 1940, Domagk observed that sulfathiazole and sulfathiodiazole inhibited the bacterium *Mycobacterium tuberculosis* that causes tuberculosis. In 1946, Domagk and the chemists working with him reported the development of a new group of compounds called thiosemicarbazones that were also effective against the mycobacteria that caused tuberculosis. Treatment of tuberculosis with the semicarbazones required more than one hundred days at a dose of one gram a day. The use of sulfonamides and semicarbazones beginning in 1945 caused a dramatic decline in the number of cases and deaths caused by tuberculosis. Because mycobacteria frequently develops resistance if treated with only one drug, tuberculosis is now treated with a combination of drugs that include streptomycin (1947), para-aminosalicylic acid (1950), isoniazid (1952), and rifampin (1963). Dapsone, a sulfone studied by Domagk, is used to treat leprosy (Hansen's disease), which is caused by *Mycobacterium leprae*.

Domagk's work also showed that sulfonamides were effective in treating gas gangrene caused by the anaerobic bacteria *Clostridium septicum, C. perfringens*, and *C. novyi*. Sulfonamides were not very useful in treating tetanus even though *Clostridium tetani* was inhibited. This results from the fact that the disease is caused by a toxin that binds to nerve cells. Killing the bacteria with sulfonamides after the toxin has caused its damage is like closing the barn door after the horses have escaped. A new sulfonamide, resembling sulfanilamide, was shown to be more effective on the clostridia than sulfanilamide, uliron, or sulfathiazole.

Spread on wounds and taken orally, sulfonamides saved thousands of lives during World War II. For example, the U.S. Army lost 8.25 percent of its wounded in World War I, but in World War II, thanks largely to the use of sulfonamides, the proportion of wounded who died was cut to 4.5 percent. The proportion of fatalities resulting from operations on perforated appendixes fell from 14 percent to 1 percent when sulfonamides were used.

Although Domagk was awarded the 1939 Nobel Prize, he was unable to accept the prize money or give his Nobel lecture because Europe had entered World War II. He gave his postponed lecture, titled "Further Progress in Chemotherapy of Bacterial Infections," after the war, on December 12, 1947. Much of the lecture concerned the relative effectiveness of the various sulfonamides, semicarbazones, and sulfones.

—*Jaime S. Colome*

FURTHER READING

Brock, Thomas D., ed. *Milestones in Microbiology*. 1961. Reprint. Washington, D.C.: American Society for Microbiology Press, 1998. Collection of original papers by scientists who contributed to the development of microbiology. Part 5 is concerned with chemotherapy. Papers by Ehrlich, Sir Alexander Fleming, and Domagk are worthwhile reading.

Edwards, David I. *Antimicrobial Drug Action*. Baltimore: University Park Press, 1980. Concise, clearly written resource for those interested in antimicrobial drugs. Includes a short history of antimicrobial chemotherapy, but most discussion is devoted to how the drugs inhibit and kill microorganisms as well as how microorganisms become resistant to drugs. Features a section on chemotherapeutic agents used to treat some cancers.

Franklin, T. J., and G. A. Snow. *Biochemistry and Mo-*

lecular Biology of Antimicrobial Drug Action. 6th ed. New York: Springer, 2005. Presents a concise history of the discovery of antimicrobial agents. Includes discussion of the mechanism of action of the sulfonamides.

Silverstein, Arthur M. *Paul Ehrlich's Receptor Immunology: The Magnificent Obsession.* New York: Academic Press, 2001. Focuses on Ehrlich's many contributions to the field of immunology, placing them in the context of their times. Includes appendixes and indexes.

Taylor, F. Sherwood. *The Conquest of Bacteria: From Salvarsan to Sulphapyridine.* New York: Philosophi-

cal Library, 1942. A history for the general reader of drug development before antibiotics were developed in the 1940's. Focuses on the discoveries that different sulfonamides were effective on a variety of pathogenic bacteria. Makes clear the roles played by Domagk and other researchers in the discovery of the effectiveness of the sulfonamides.

SEE ALSO: 1907: Plague Kills 1.2 Million in India; Apr., 1910: Ehrlich Introduces Salvarsan as a Cure for Syphilis; Sept., 1928: Fleming Discovers Penicillin in Molds; May, 1940: Florey and Chain Develop Penicillin as an Antibiotic.

1932-1940
DEVELOPMENT OF NEGRITUDE

Drawing influence from the Harlem Renaissance in the United States and their own experiences as men from France's colonies in Africa, Aimé Césaire of Martinique, Léopold Senghor of Senegal, and Léon-Gontran Damas of French Guyana discussed and wrote about the concept of negritude.

LOCALE: Martinique; Senegal; French Guiana; France
CATEGORIES: Literature; civil rights and liberties; psychology and psychiatry; social issues and reform

KEY FIGURES

Aimé Césaire (b. 1913), poet, playwright, and politician born in Martinique

Léopold Senghor (1906-2001), first president of Senegal, 1960-1981, and a poet and philosopher influential in formulating the concept of negritude

Léon-Gontran Damas (1912-1978), poet and political activist

Leo Frobenius (1873-1938), German scholar whose work promoted the value of African culture

SUMMARY OF EVENT

The negritude movement in Paris in the 1930's had much in common with the Harlem Renaissance in the United States. It grew out of Paris, a city that, like Harlem, had a diverse population of people of African descent, and it also evolved out of discussions and concepts that were eventually expressed in verse. Although the negritude movement drew some of its ideas from what had happened in Harlem ten to fifteen years earlier, there were clear differences between the two movements. The negri-

tude movement brought significant change to France's colonies of France: It produced political activists and political leaders as well as artists. Furthermore, it outlived the Harlem Renaissance, which faded into obscurity in the 1930's.

The negritude movement was grounded in a celebration of African heritage. It was developed by men and women of African descent who lived in white cultures that privileged European lineage and subjugated African heritage, a hierarchy that had become firmly ingrained in the English language. For example, as Malcolm X explains in *The Autobiography of Malcolm X* (1965), the word "white" is associated with innocence and purity, whereas the word "black" is associated with blindness and evil. In European and American educational systems early in the twentieth century, then, Africa was portrayed as a country that lived in darkness, without civilization, while Europe was the center of civilization. European culture was hailed by many as a civilizing influence on peoples from Africa and the Caribbean.

In Paris in the 1930's, college students Aimé Césaire, Léopold Senghor, and Léon-Gontran Damas all felt alienated by French society. In a famous description of his arrival in Paris, Senghor conveyed some of this feeling: "I disembarked one morning in Paris in a cold rain and October sky. And everything was gray, even the famous monuments. What a deception!" These men found that many of their colleagues shared their discontent, and they refused to be indoctrinated into the Eurocentric system. Instead, they valued, explored, and celebrated their African identities, and they were joined by others who

Former Senegal president and poet Léopold Senghor (standing) at the Académie Française in Paris in 1984. (AP/Wide World Photos)

also wanted to develop a sense of community. There were, however, a large number of people of other nationalities, and the realization of this fact helped Césaire, Senghor, and Damas develop a sense of cultural relativity.

Resistance to assimilation—an idea that would become one of negritude's essential tenets—developed partly as a result of the negative experiences Césaire, Senghor, Damas, and others had while living in poverty in Paris. They were underprivileged and wore tattered clothes, were often hungry, and worked long hours in order to remain in Paris and get a university education. While taking courses at three institutions, Damas worked various menial jobs: He was a day laborer, a dishwasher, and a bartender; at one point he worked all night at a market in Les Halles and attended school during the day. Recounting his experiences as a student in Paris during the 1930's, Césaire remembered, "It was a pretty unbalanced life. . . . I was sick. I suffered from headaches,

stomach aches, and that's when I lost perspective." Césaire eventually suffered a mental breakdown that rendered him incapable of continuing his university work. Senghor, who remembered Césaire's breakdown quite clearly, later wrote that the three were rebels whose marginalization helped them to value their heritage: "We lived our writing morally, even physically and metaphysically to the edge of dementia."

Damas was the first of the three to publish a volume of verse. By the time he got to Paris, he spoke English and had already read and embraced many of the writers of the Harlem Renaissance. His volume of poetry, *Pigment* (1937), became "a manifesto of negritude": It articulated many of the ideas that others in the group were just beginning to experience. This book continued to influence the movement for years to come. Even before Damas published *Pigment*, however, the negritude movement had begun to create visibility for students of African descent. In 1934, Césaire, Senghor, and Damas founded a literary journal for black students called *L'Étudiant noir* (the black student). The journal began the exploration of African roots and colonial alienation that would form the negritude movement's basis. *L'Étudiant noir*, which was published until 1940, was actually the continuation of an earlier college journal that celebrated African identity called *Légitime Défense*, which began in 1932 and was discontinued in 1934. *L'Étudiant noir*'s longer life span was probably due to the prominence its founders achieved in the literary world.

SIGNIFICANCE

Despite their early poverty and their cultural position, in Paris Césaire, Senghor, and Damas experienced opportunities not afforded to people of African descent in other parts of the world. In France, blacks had free access to libraries, museums, and galleries. Furthermore, they had access to a university education, something few blacks in the United States were able to experience in the 1930's. As a result, all three scholars had the opportunity to explore their cultural roots and to encounter writers such as Leo Frobenius, a German ethnologist who bucked the standard historical view that African culture was inherently uncivilized. All three negritude founders were heavily influenced by Frobenius, whose work Senghor described as "a sudden burst of thunder."

The negritude movement catalyzed a group of intellectuals whose articulation of a universal sense of African identity united people of African heritage around the world. The movement drew on and extended many of the ideas made famous by the Harlem Renaissance, and in the process it set the stage for liberation movements in

France and created ideas that would inspire the Civil Rights movement in the United States.

—*H. William Rice*

FURTHER READING

Bahri, Deepika. "Introduction to Postcolonial Studies." http://www.english.emory.edu/Bahri/Intro.html. Very good brief introduction to the issues and people in colonial France.

Jack, Belinda E. *Negritude and Literary Criticism.* New York: Greenwood Press, 1996. A study of people of African heritage writing in French from 1920 onward.

Kestelhoot, Lilyan. *Black Writers in French: A Literary History of Negritude.* Washington, D.C.: Howard University Press, 1991. A study of African American writers in French as examples of the worldwide explosion of African self-realization.

Wilder, Gary. *The French Imperial Nation-State: Negritude and Colonial Humanism Between the Two World Wars.* Chicago: University of Chicago Press, 2005. A study of the political milieu out of which the negritude movement developed.

SEE ALSO: July 11, 1905: Founding of the Niagara Movement; Feb. 12, 1909: National Association for the Advancement of Colored People Is Founded; 1910-1930: Great Northern Migration; May, 1917: Universal Negro Improvement Association Establishes a U.S. Chapter; 1920's: Harlem Renaissance; Aug. 7, 1925: West African Student Union Is Founded; Summer, 1930: Nation of Islam Is Founded.

January-February, 1932
EL SALVADOR'S MILITARY MASSACRES CIVILIANS

The massacre of up to thirty thousand peasants by the Salvadoran army ended a radical reform movement in the countryside and ushered in fifty years of repression and military rule in El Salvador.

LOCALE: El Salvador
CATEGORIES: Atrocities and war crimes; wars, uprisings, and civil unrest

KEY FIGURES
Agustín Farabundo Martí (1893-1932), principal leader of the Salvadoran Communist Party
Maximiliano Hernández Martínez (1882-1966), military dictator of El Salvador, 1931-1944
Arturo Araújo (1877-1967), president of El Salvador, March-December, 1931

SUMMARY OF EVENT
Social relations in El Salvador in the first decades of the twentieth century were characterized by a wide division in power. The peasant masses, who had once enjoyed communal property rights as part of an ancient landholding system, had seen these rights taken away in the late 1800's by a powerful clique of coffee planters. Behind a shield of "liberal" legislation, these growers had succeeded in expanding their holdings to encompass nearly all of the country's arable land. They modernized the economy by tying their fortunes to the exclusive cultivation of coffee, for which a large international market existed.

The peasants, most of whom were Pipil Indians, had an almost mystical reverence for their cornfields. The disestablishment of their communal system had a psychological as well as a material effect on their lives. Without access to land, they had no options other than to work on the coffee plantations as *colonos*, receiving in exchange tiny plots for their own subsistence along with miserable wages, often issued in kind. Once-independent peasants were thus reduced to debt peons.

For their part, the members of the coffee growers' oligarchy took advantage of a seemingly limitless world demand for their product. The coffee boom, which lasted throughout the 1920's, stimulated urbanization, brought railways and telegraph lines to the interior, and widened the economic gap between the oligarchs and the peasantry. The wealthy lived in regal splendor while the poor seethed in their poverty.

The rural environment of El Salvador had little in it of philanthropy. The planters kept wages low, and they paid almost no taxes that might support social services. As a consequence, discontent among the poor was widespread, and isolated uprisings occurred frequently. The rural constabulary and the national guard crushed all of these movements. As time went by, the oligarchs came to rely more and more on coercion to maintain the status quo in the countryside.

The coming of the Great Depression in 1929 provided the catalyst for a social explosion. The demand for coffee on the world markets collapsed. With prices falling, the *colonos* lost the opportunity to find work. Wages fell 60 percent. In the cities, the Depression gave rise to a period of intense political discussion, with younger members of the oligarchy expressing some doubts as to whether the traditional order could contain the social crisis. A few individuals looked to reformist solutions.

Among their number was Arturo Araújo, an admirer of Britain's Fabian Socialists. Araújo was something of a wild card in Salvadoran politics, and the Partido Laborista he founded reflected an eclectic blend of mysticism, anti-imperialism, and what was termed *vitalismo mínimo*–the idea that every citizen deserved a "vital minimum" of goods and services necessary to a happy life. Such sentiments appealed to many, especially in the cities, where trade unionists and middle-class professionals lent avid support to Araújo.

The Communist Party of El Salvador also favored this wayward son of the oligarchy. In this instance, however, the party's support was conditional, because the Communists, led by veteran activist Agustín Farabundo Martí, feared that Araújo's popularity might overshadow their own plans to carve a measure of power from the country's difficulties. As it turned out, they needed to fear something far more sinister.

Despite the misgivings of most oligarchs, the government held free elections in January, 1931. Five presidential candidates, most of whom represented conservative coffee interests, entered the field against Araújo. The latter went on to win anyway and took office at the beginning of March. Problems plagued Araújo from the beginning. The Depression hit the country people very hard. Although he had made vague promises as to land reform, the new president simply could not deliver on these while simultaneously safeguarding the privileges of the elite.

The lack of direction displayed by Araújo was evident from the beginning. The oligarchs, who had previously thought Araújo merely risky, now saw him as positively dangerous and looked to anyone who might deliver them from his influences. The peasants and the trade unionists also became disillusioned. Seeing that their support had brought them repression and not reform, they began to consider more radical solutions, particularly those espoused by Farabundo Martí and the Communists. Several strikes by *colonos* in April and May were brutally put down by forces under War Minister (and Vice President) Maximiliano Hernández Martínez. Widespread rebellion now seemed likely.

Of all the groups opposed to Araújo, clearly the most willing to act on its grievances was the military. The president had tried to reduce the army's budget by 25 percent and tried to retire a number of senior officers. Most crucial, however, was his inability to pay his soldiers. In normal times, export duties paid the greater part of government expenses, but with coffee exports at rock bottom, Araújo's administration was delinquent in its payments to all officials.

The end came swiftly. On December 2, 1931, army units loyal to General Hernández Martínez seized control of San Salvador and other major cities. Only Araújo loyalists initially condemned the attack. Most political parties, including the Communists, gave their tacit approval. They felt reassured when Hernández Martínez announced that municipal elections scheduled for January, 1932, would go forward. The Left then organized meetings and street demonstrations, distributed leaflets, and prepared for the elections. Few doubted that Hernández Martínez would keep his word.

The general, however, had his own ambitions. A man of a mystical frame of mind who would later conduct seances in the presidential palace, he felt certain that he acted with divine aid. Having identified all opposition organizers, he cancelled the elections and began a massive repression. Realizing that they were moving in the eleventh hour, the Communists launched an urban revolt on January 22, supposedly set to coincide with a rural insurrection in the western departments of Santa Ana, Ahuachapán, and Sonsonate. The Indian leaders of those areas had tenuous ties to Farabundo Martí, even though they had no use for Communists generally. They nevertheless decided that a revolt offered them their last chance of deliverance.

They were wrong, tragically so. The army quelled the urban uprising in a matter of hours, police agents having already penetrated the revolutionary cells. They had previously detained Farabundo Martí. A policy of summary execution began that included even suspected members of opposition groups. Martí received unusual treatment: He was given a brief trial before he faced the firing squad.

The rural districts experienced the full fury of the repression. The peasant rebels, armed with machetes, managed to hold out for forty-eight hours. They killed some fifty policemen. The army and the irregular forces set up by the landowners exacted an awesome revenge in what Salvadorans still refer to simply as *la matanza*, the massacre. The army regarded anyone with Indian features as being automatically guilty and liable for the ultimate penalty. Whole villages were razed. Hospitals were checked and the wounded dragged out and killed. Women, children, and dogs were shot along with men. The corpses soon became so numerous that they could not be buried and were simply left in ditches along the roads. As one witness later observed, only the vultures ate well that year. Before the violence had run its course in February, as many as thirty thousand people had died. The massacre left a legacy of violence in Salvadoran politics that was overcome only decades later.

SIGNIFICANCE

La matanza left a deep scar in Salvadoran society. Virtually every family in the western part of the country lost someone to the army terror. The effects of the repression went even further, however, than the loss of life. There were cultural losses. Because Hernández Martínez and the army chose to identify the Pipil Indians as part of a wide Communist conspiracy, most Indian survivors rushed to deny their Indian identity. They abandoned the use of native garb, which they saw as a provocative symbol of resistance likely to bring down the wrath of the police. Indians encouraged their children to avoid speaking Pipil except at home, and then only in hushed tones.

There were social losses. With the members of many families serving in the army or among the rebels, the repression could not help but have a divisive impact. It became impossible to trust anyone. All of the traditional foci of rural authority and trust—the church and, more important, the socioreligious brotherhoods (*cofradías*)—lost the popular support they once had enjoyed. Fear dominated the peasant landscape. Only the oligarchs could claim that *la matanza* had increased the level of solidarity in their ranks. It also taught them the false lesson that class solidarity outweighed national reconciliation and that their survival depended on the subordination of the peasants.

Finally, the repression brought political losses. General Hernández Martínez followed *la matanza* with a twelve-year dictatorship that brooked little opposition, even from the oligarchs. Although civilian vigilantes conducted much of the 1932 slaughter, that event's political outcome confirmed the army's claim on power. Hernández Martínez was only one of many military presidents who were to rule El Salvador during the twentieth century. As an institution, the Salvadoran armed forces consistently resisted pressures to make room for civilian participation in politics. When open application of force was inadvisable, the military acted in collusion with the oligarchs to create death squads.

For their part, the peasant masses in El Salvador became caught between two polar extremes in the late twentieth century. They could either join the ranks of the army and the elites, who perceived the struggle as an anti-Communist crusade, or they could join with the Farabundo Martí National Liberation Front (FMLN) guerrillas, the ideological descendants of Martí, and fight to establish the kind of Leninist regime that had been repudiated throughout the Eastern Bloc. In either direction, death threatened the average citizen. The greatest and most frightening legacies of *la matanza* were the effects that it left in the popular mind and the knowledge that it could happen again. However, a peace settlement reached in 1992 between the Salvadoran government and the FMLN paved the way for these fears to be alleviated in a spirit of national reconciliation and a new democratic process for a nation too long torn by civil war.

—*Thomas L. Whigham*

FURTHER READING

Anderson, Thomas P. *Matanza*. 2d ed. Willimantic, Conn.: Curbstone Press, 1992. Considered the classic English-language account of the repression. Thoughtful treatment draws on extensive interviews with participants and previously little-known manuscript materials. Includes map, footnotes, extensive bibliography, and index.

Dalton, Roque. *Miguel Marmol*. Willimantic, Conn.: Curbstone Press, 1987. Unique and fascinating account of *la matanza* based on extensive interviews with an active organizer of the Salvadoran Communist Party who was himself shot and left for dead in 1932 and who later spent many years in exile in the Soviet Union. Marmol's Stalinist attitude dates him, but his comments about sacrifice and struggle still ring true. Dalton, an important poet and member of the revolutionary underground, was murdered in 1975 by a rival leftist faction. Includes three letters from Marmol as well as an October, 1986, interview.

Holden, Robert H. *Armies Without Nations: Public Violence and State Formation in Central America, 1821-1960*. New York: Oxford University Press, 2004. Examines how Central American states have exercised public violence as a way of maintaining authority. Includes discussion of *la matanza* in El Salvador. Features photographs, endnotes, and index.

McClintock, Michael. *State Terror and Popular Resistance in El Salvador*. Vol. 1 in *The American Connection*. London: Zed Books, 1985. Thorough examination of U.S. military and economic aid to El Salvador contains some useful information on the 1932 massacre, including some of the comments of the American military attaché in San Salvador at the time. Includes endnotes, bibliography, and index.

Montgomery, Tommie Sue. *Revolution in El Salvador: From Civil Strife to Civil Peace*. 2d ed. Boulder, Colo.: Westview Press, 1995. Insightful history of the Salvadoran struggle for justice focuses more on the 1970's and 1980's than on *la matanza* but provides a detailed account of the antecedents of the quagmire of the 1990's, making it a key source for those seeking to understand modern El Salvador. Includes photos, maps, tables, bibliography, and index.

North, Liisa. *Bitter Grounds: Roots of Revolt in El Salvador*. 2d ed. Westport, Conn.: Lawrence Hill, 1985. Brief but concise treatment of Salvadoran politics in the twentieth century, especially strong concerning economic questions. Chapter 3 covers the 1932 peasant revolt and its bloody aftermath. Includes maps, tables, notes, bibliography, appendixes, and index.

Parkman, Patricia. *Nonviolent Insurrection in El Salvador: The Fall of Maximiliano Hernández Martínez*. Tucson: University of Arizona Press, 1988. Valuable, well-researched account of the Hernández Martínez regime focuses more on his ouster in the mid-1940's than on *la matanza*. Based largely on materials drawn from the archives of the U.S. Department of State and on interviews. Includes maps, illustrations, endnotes, and bibliography.

Russell, Philip L. *El Salvador in Crisis*. Austin, Tex.: Colorado River Press, 1984. Like most "committed" historical works, this study favors a leftist solution for the Salvadoran problem. Provides a thorough treatment of the 1932 bloodbath. Includes maps, tables, illustrations, graphs, endnotes, bibliography, and index.

SEE ALSO: Jan. 22, 1905: Bloody Sunday; Apr. 13, 1919: British Soldiers Massacre Indians at Amritsar; Aug. 11-13, 1933: Iraqi Army Slaughters Assyrian Christians; Apr.-May, 1940: Soviets Massacre Polish Prisoners of War.

1932

January 7, 1932
STIMSON DOCTRINE

Following Japanese military activity in Manchuria in 1931, Secretary of State Henry L. Stimson stated that the United States would not recognize any territorial changes accomplished through the use of force. Japan ignored the doctrine.

ALSO KNOWN AS: Hoover-Stimson Doctrine
LOCALE: Washington, D.C.
CATEGORIES: Diplomacy and international relations; government and politics; wars, uprisings, and civil unrest

KEY FIGURES
Henry L. Stimson (1867-1950), U.S. secretary of state, 1929-1933, and U.S. secretary of war, 1940-1945
Herbert Hoover (1874-1964), president of the United States, 1929-1933
William E. Borah (1865-1940), U.S. senator from Idaho, 1907-1940
Yōsuke Matsuoka (1880-1946), Japanese diplomat and president of the South Manchurian Railroad
Second Earl of Lytton (Victor Bulwer-Lytton; 1876-1947), British delegate to the League of Nations
Puyi (P'u-i; 1906-1967), last emperor of China, r. 1908-1912, and emperor of Manchukuo, r. 1934-1945
Franklin D. Roosevelt (1882-1945), president of the United States, 1933-1945
Hideki Tojo (1884-1948), Japanese general, later prime minister of Japan, 1941-1944

SUMMARY OF EVENT
In the late 1920's, Japan and the Soviet Union both clashed with the Chinese government over the construction and operation of the Chinese Eastern Railway, a section of the Trans-Siberian Railroad in Manchuria, the northeast region of China. By 1929, it seemed possible that the Soviet Union could go to war with China in order to control the Chinese Eastern Railway. War did not break out, but the dispute made it clear that the League of Nations and the Kellogg-Briand Pact of 1928 could not prevent military conflict. Even though it did not resort to warfare, the Soviet Union managed to bully China into allowing it to take control of the Chinese Eastern Railway, and the international community did nothing to prevent the Soviet actions.

Japan took note of the situation and began to exert greater control of the South Manchurian Railroad. By the

late 1920's, the Japanese military patrolled the railway, and Japan operated several armed military camps in Manchuria. Ostensibly, the Japanese sought to protect the railway they operated, but the Chinese government objected to the foreign military presence. However, the Chinese government was not strong enough to resist Japanese encroachment.

The situation turned into a crisis on September 18, 1931, when an explosion damaged a section of the South Manchurian Railroad operated by Japan. The Japanese leveled blame for the explosion, which became known as the Mukden incident, on Chinese saboteurs and moved greater numbers of soldiers into southern Manchuria. The Chinese put up little resistance, and the Japanese quickly began extending their influence. Although no formal accusations were proven, the speed of the Japanese response to the explosion made it plain to the international community that the Japanese military had planned the entire event.

The League of Nations responded to the incident by sending a commission to investigate; the commission was led by the British diplomat the second earl of Lytton. The Lytton Commission operated slowly, and several months passed before all of its members were appointed. A number of American officials wanted a more rapid response, but opinion in the United States was divided on how to handle the situation. President Herbert Hoover, however, made it clear that he did not favor imposing economic sanctions against Japan because he believed they would lead to war, which would cause further hardship to those Americans already suffering under the Great Depression. In the absence of any substantive international action opposing their efforts in Manchuria, the Japanese continued to expand their military influence throughout the region, and by the beginning of 1931 they had effectively stopped all Chinese resistance.

Hoover's secretary of state, Henry L. Stimson, believed that the United States could not sit by and watch Japan conquer Manchuria, and he responded by sending a letter to the Chinese and Japanese governments on January 7, 1932. The letter was sent on behalf of the U.S. government, but Stimson took this action on his own initiative, without President Hoover's consent. The letter stated that the United States would follow a policy of nonrecognition: It would not acknowledge any territorial changes between Japan and China that developed as the result of Japanese aggression. Stimson's letter quickly became known as the Hoover-Stimson Doctrine, or more simply as the Stimson Doctrine. However, President Hoover refused to implement the policy officially, because he believed that the doctrine would lead to economic sanctions against Japan that would create a war between Japan and the United States.

The Japanese ignored Stimson's letter. On January 29, they launched a major offensive against Shanghai and continued to expand their influence in Manchuria. Unable to take any action due to constraints placed on him by Hoover, Stimson responded by sending a letter to Senator William E. Borah. That letter, which immediately entered the public domain, outlined the treaties that Japan had violated in Manchuria. It also demonstrated that Stimson favored nonrecognition backed with military force, if necessary, in order to restrain Japan.

By defending his position through the Borah letter, Stimson generated support for his position, and the League of Nations gave him some vindication by passing a resolution with similar language in March of 1932. Seemingly cowed by the international response, Japan responded by removing most of its troops in May of 1932. The country followed this move by renaming Manchuria as Manchukuo, and it extended official diplomatic recognition to Manchukuo as a new independent

Henry L. Stimson. (Library of Congress)

nation in September of 1932. In theory, Manchukuo was independent, and the Japanese installed Puyi, the former emperor of China, as the head of state. However, Puyi ruled as a Japanese puppet, and most other nations did not recognize Manchukuo as a legitimate nation.

The Lytton Commission finally issued its findings to the League of Nations in October of 1932. Lytton named Japan as the aggressor in Manchuria, and, in early 1933, the League accepted the commission's findings and formally admonished Japan. Yōsuke Matsuoka, Japan's representative in the League of Nations, walked out of the negotiations, and Japan withdrew from the League soon thereafter.

SIGNIFICANCE

The Stimson Doctrine failed to restrain the Japanese conquest of Manchuria, and Japanese aggression continued when Japan initiated open warfare against China in 1937. The concept of the doctrine in American foreign policy might have disappeared after 1937, but President Franklin D. Roosevelt appointed Stimson as his secretary of war in 1940. Roosevelt made the appointment largely for political reasons: Stimson was a prominent Republican and could generate support for Roosevelt's foreign policies on the eve of American entry into World War II.

After his appointment, Stimson urged Roosevelt to accept his doctrine officially in order to halt the continued Japanese actions against China. As a result, the United States levied economic sanctions against Japan by embargoing the sale of military goods, notably oil, to Japan. The oil embargo, however, did not halt the Second Sino-Japanese War (1937-1945) any more than the Stimson Doctrine had halted Japanese aggression in Manchuria. Furthermore, the embargo fulfilled Hoover's predictions that economic sanctions would lead to war with Japan. Japan had become increasingly militaristic as General Hideki Tojo rose to power, and the oil embargo led directly to the Japanese attack on Pearl Harbor on December 7, 1941.

Even though the Stimson Doctrine's inability to stop Japanese aggression in Manchuria and China meant that it was generally regarded as a failed policy, the philosophy of nonrecognition had an impact on international relations long after 1932. A handful of treaties, such as the 1933 Anti-War Treaty of Nonaggression and Conciliation, incorporated the Stimson Doctrine's ideas, and the Roosevelt administration followed the doctrine's philosophy in 1940 when it announced it would not recognize the Soviet annexation of the Baltic states of Estonia, Latvia, and Lithuania. Officially, the United States continued to follow this policy toward the Baltic states until their independence in 1991.

—*John K. Franklin*

FURTHER READING

Cohen, Warren I. *Empire Without Tears: American Foreign Relations, 1921-1933*. Philadelphia: Temple University Press, 1987. Overview of American foreign policy from 1921 to 1933. Demonstrates that the 1920's were not merely a period of American isolationism.

Schmitz, David L. *Henry L. Stimson: The First Wise Man*. Wilmington, Del.: SR Books, 2001. Biography of Stimson that shows his importance to American foreign policy from the administration of Theodore Roosevelt through the administration of Harry S. Truman.

Tohmatsu, Haruo, and H. P. Willmott. *A Gathering Darkness: The Coming of War to the Far East and the Pacific, 1921-1942*. Lanham, Md.: SR Books, 2005. An overview of Japanese foreign policy and military actions, such as the Mukden incident, that led to World War II.

SEE ALSO: Feb. 9, 1904-Sept. 5, 1905: Russo-Japanese War; Aug. 22, 1910: Japanese Annexation of Korea; Feb. 24, 1933: Japan Withdraws from the League of Nations; Dec. 29, 1934: Japan Renounces Disarmament Treaties; July 7, 1937: China Declares War on Japan; Dec., 1937-Feb., 1938: Rape of Nanjing; Aug., 1940: Japan Announces the Greater East Asia Coprosperity Sphere; Sept., 1940: Japan Occupies Indochinese Ports.

January 22, 1932
RECONSTRUCTION FINANCE CORPORATION IS CREATED

Created to support ailing financial institutions during the Great Depression, the Reconstruction Finance Corporation was a government agency that provided capital for New Deal programs, war production, and undercapitalized private ventures.

LOCALE: Washington, D.C.

CATEGORIES: Banking and finance; business and labor; economics; government and politics

KEY FIGURES

Herbert Hoover (1874-1964), president of the United States, 1929-1933

Eugene Meyer (1875-1959), chairman of the Federal Reserve Board and first chairman of the Reconstruction Finance Corporation

Franklin D. Roosevelt (1882-1945), president of the United States, 1933-1945

SUMMARY OF EVENT

The Reconstruction Finance Corporation (RFC) functioned from its establishment on January 22, 1932, until its dissolution in 1954 as a federal agency that provided capital and credit for a wide variety of public and private ventures. Lending more than $51 billion during its existence, the RFC played an instrumental role in stabilizing the American financial system during the early years of the Great Depression by supporting banks and financing numerous New Deal programs. During World War II, the RFC served as a conduit through which the nation's eco-

nomic resources were shifted from civilian output to military production.

The stock market crash of 1929 and the onset of the Great Depression created a severe crisis for the nation's financial institutions. Facing a catastrophic decline in the value of assets and a rush of depositors anxious to recover their money, the American banking system teetered on the brink of collapse. Most vulnerable were institutions holding large amounts of unsecured loans made during the previous decade to finance speculative ventures in the securities, real estate, and construction industries. By 1931, nearly twenty-three hundred commercial banks and savings and loans faced insolvency.

The worldwide financial chaos of the period also contributed to the severity of the situation in the United States. At the beginning of the Depression, European banks began to withdraw substantial amounts of gold reserves held in American banks. Additionally, the Hawley-Smoot Tariff, enacted in 1930 with the intention of protecting American firms by increasing import duties, instead produced a worldwide protectionist movement that in turn created a further contraction of available capital and credit in the United States.

President Herbert Hoover, a disciple of voluntarism, initially suggested that those in the financial industry should pool their resources and make loans to ailing banks without governmental intervention. In October, 1931, the National Credit Corporation (NCC), a voluntary association that encouraged healthy banks to lend capital to weaker ones, began operation. As the Depression worsened, however, the NCC proved unable to cope with the increasing number of bank failures.

Recognizing the shortcomings of the NCC, on December 8, 1931, Hoover recommended the creation of a government agency with broad powers to issue bonds and extend credit to the financial industry. Congress moved quickly, and Hoover signed the bill creating the Reconstruction Finance Corporation on January 22, 1932. Capitalized at $500 million, the RFC was authorized to borrow an additional $3.3 billion to shore up the nation's financial infrastructure. The RFC initially was intended only to provide capital to ailing banks, but Congress soon extended its powers to lend money to a variety of public and private organizations. The major economic sectors that received RFC loans included banks and other financial intermediaries, railroads, agriculture, commercial and industrial businesses, mortgage lenders, public agencies, and national defense contractors.

The administrative structure of the RFC included a seven-member board of directors, including the secretary of the treasury and the chairman of the Federal Reserve Board, who served as ex officio members. Eugene Meyer, chairman of the Federal Reserve Board when the RFC was created, became the agency's first chairman. Meyer served until 1933, when President Franklin D. Roosevelt appointed Jesse H. Jones to head the agency. Jones was followed by Emil Schram and Charles B. Henderson.

During the New Deal, the RFC played a significant role in financing the nation's economic recovery programs. To alleviate the banking crisis of 1933, the agency purchased more than $1.3 billion of bank stocks, helping to bolster ailing institutions and restore public confidence in the financial system. The RFC also aided the agricultural sector through the creation of a subsidiary, the Commodity Credit Corporation, that gave farmers access to RFC funds. The agency also financed the Rural Electrification Administration and provided credit to tenant farmers for the acquisition of land.

Amendments to the RFC Act empowered the agency to finance home mortgages directly and to purchase the capital stock of mortgage lenders. The creation of the RFC Mortgage Company, which lent nearly $700,000 between 1935 and 1947, and the Federal National Mortgage Association (later known as Fannie Mae), which financed more than $3 billion in home loans between 1938 and 1950, played a crucial role in expanding the opportunity for home ownership in the United States and provided a much-needed boost to the construction industry.

The RFC was also active in supporting public works projects and helped to finance a variety of programs such as bridge and tunnel construction, public housing, natural resource development, and conservation projects. The RFC also organized and funded the Export-Import Bank to assist foreign economic development. Between 1934 and 1945, the agency loaned more than $500 million to various Latin American nations, Great Britain, Greece, Turkey, the Soviet Union, and Nationalist China.

In 1934, Congress authorized the RFC to make business loans, provided that they were "adequately secured" and that the companies could not otherwise obtain capital on the open market. Originally, the maximum amount available was $500,000 over a five-year term. Congress later liberalized both the amount ceiling and the maximum maturity. RFC administrators excluded certain industries. For example, no loans were extended to the oil and automotive industries, which were deemed sufficiently profitable to obtain capital without government assistance. The RFC also refused loans to newspapers and radio stations for fear of influencing editorial content.

During World War II, the RFC played a crucial role in shifting economic resources from the civilian to the defense sector. A variety of subsidiary corporations supervised the transfer of credit to defense-related industries. These corporations included the Defense Plant Corporation, the Defense Supplies Corporation, the Rubber Development Corporation, the Metal Reserve Corporation, the War Damage Corporation, and the United States Commercial Company. The largest subsidiary, the Defense Plant Corporation, constructed and equipped twenty-three hundred defense plants at a cost exceeding $9 billion.

Despite a series of damaging scandals during the postwar years, the RFC remained active until July 30, 1953, when President Dwight D. Eisenhower signed the Small Business Act, which officially terminated the RFC. The Small Business Administration assumed current RFC loans, and a number of the RFC's subsidiary corporations, including the Federal National Mortgage Association and the Export-Import Bank, became independent agencies. The RFC terminated its operations in June, 1954, and by 1957 all the agency's outstanding loans had been liquidated.

SIGNIFICANCE

During the early years of the Great Depression, the RFC played a significant role in stabilizing the U.S. financial

1932

system. By providing capital and credit to banks, the RFC enabled many otherwise insolvent institutions to continue operations. This had important psychological as well as economic benefits and mitigated the perception held by many Americans that the capitalist system was inherently flawed. The RFC helped ensure that the nation's economic infrastructure would continue to function and, through infusions of capital, prevented disruptions in one sector from initiating a chain reaction of economic chaos.

The RFC undoubtedly saved many banks, railroads, insurance companies, and farmers. Many historians have observed that the Great Depression would have been far worse without government intervention in capital markets to cushion the effect of declining demand and ease the impact of deflation and unemployment. The RFC failed to generate an economic recovery primarily because the decline in aggregate demand was simply too large to be offset by the RFC's limited resources. Governmental policy also impeded the potential effectiveness of the RFC during the late 1930's. In 1937, President Roosevelt tried to balance the budget for political reasons. He instructed the RFC to stop all lending, even though its loans did not appear in the budget. At the same time, the president reduced spending on public works and raised taxes, producing an economic contraction and increasing unemployment. RFC officials believed that this situation could have been avoided by increasing, rather than curtailing, available credit and by continuing public works projects.

The most enduring legacy of the RFC was the establishment of the Federal National Mortgage Association, which revolutionized home finance by providing long-term mortgages. Previously, home mortgages typically had been intermediate-term loans requiring large down payments. Although other factors were involved, home ownership statistics reveal the impact of RFC policies. Prior to 1929, one-third of American families owned homes; by the 1950's, nearly two-thirds were home owners.

The RFC also had a significant impact in marshaling the nation's economic resources for defense production during World War II. From 1940 to 1945, more than 80 percent of RFC loans went to support defense-related production, and more than half of all RFC financing occurred during the war years. Through its various subsidiary corporations, the agency constructed war plants, allocated strategic materials, and provided insurance for war-related assets against damage by military operations. As a result of its wartime activities, by the end of the war the RFC held substantial interests in a number of industries such as shipping, nonferrous metals, machine tools, synthetic rubber, and aviation.

During the postwar period, the RFC suffered from a series of scandals surrounding its involvement in providing capital for housing production. Congressional investigations revealed that the RFC had offered loans to highly speculative ventures supported by a number of senators and administration officials, in return for a promise of increased funding for the agency. The scandal tarnished the RFC's reputation and led to a reevaluation of its economic mission. With a strong postwar economy, many questioned the need for continued federal intervention in capital markets. Opponents of the agency also feared that it would contribute to inflation by raising aggregate demand and argued that private financial markets allocated capital more effectively without governmental interference.

As the need for the RFC diminished and as its political influence eroded after the taint of scandal, many who had been among the agency's most vocal supporters called for its termination. The RFC was formally dissolved in 1953 by the Small Business Administration Act, although the Federal National Mortgage Association and the Export-Import Bank survived as independent agencies. Throughout the twentieth century, the Export-Import Bank continued to provide loan guarantees to exporters of American products.

The Small Business Administration represented an evolutionary concept of governmental intervention by providing direct loans and loan guarantees to small firms to assist them in competing with larger enterprises. This more limited role retained the original RFC concept of providing access to capital for companies in need, although it restricted the government's ability to influence broad sectors of the economy unduly. Even this level of government intervention was controversial, however. Despite occasional calls for a revival of the RFC or the establishment of a similar organization to assist distressed sectors of the economy, prevailing economic theory at the beginning of the twenty-first century favors market allocation over governmental control of capital markets.

—*Douglas Knerr*

FURTHER READING

Bickley, James M. "An Evaluation of the Reconstruction Finance Corporation with Implications for Current Capital Needs of the Steel Industry." In *New Tools for Economic Development: The Enterprise Zone, Devel-*

opment Bank, and RFC, edited by George Sternlieb and David Listokin. Piscataway, N.J.: Rutgers University Press, 1981. Brief, highly informative overview of the background and achievements of the RFC. Provides analysis of the agency's strengths and weaknesses within the context of government stimulus of economic growth.

Ellis, Edward Robb. *A Nation in Torment: The Great American Depression, 1929-1939*. 1970. Reprint. New York: Kodansha International, 1995. Journalistic account of the Depression includes a chapter devoted to the Reconstruction Finance Corporation.

Gup, Benton E., ed. *Too Big to Fail: Policies and Practices in Government Bailouts*. Westport, Conn.: Praeger, 2004. Collection of essays includes discussion of the RFC, in particular the agency's assistance to the railroad industry during the Depression.

Himmelberg, Robert F. *The Great Depression and the New Deal*. Westport, Conn.: Greenwood Press, 2000. Discusses the causes of the Depression and the actions taken in the United States to alleviate its effects, including establishment of the RFC. Features chronology, glossary, and index.

Jones, Jesse H. *Fifty Billion Dollars: My Thirteen Years with the RFC, 1932-1945*. 1951. Reprint. New York: Da Capo Press, 1975. Personal recollections of the second chairman of the RFC, who was appointed to the board of directors at the time the agency was created. Presents a detailed account of the RFC's accomplishments. Especially informative regarding the personalities and political infighting at the RFC during a crucial period in its history.

Olson, James S. *Herbert Hoover and the Reconstruction Finance Corporation, 1931-1933*. Ames: Iowa State University Press, 1977. One of the best works available on the early years of the RFC. Presents a balanced view of the agency, its mission, and its accomplishments as well as a detailed account of the congressional battles surrounding the agency's creation.

_____. *Saving Capitalism: The Reconstruction Finance Corporation and the New Deal, 1933-1940*. Princeton, N.J.: Princeton University Press, 1988. Takes up where Olson's earlier study of the RFC (cited above) leaves off. Traces the agency's involvement in financing numerous New Deal programs.

Pusey, Merlo J. *Eugene Meyer*. New York: Alfred A. Knopf, 1974. Discusses the full span of Meyer's life and delineates the role he played in suggesting and designing the RFC. Although a political conservative, Meyer had no illusions regarding the problems in the U.S. economy that the RFC was created to correct.

Studenski, Paul, and Herman Edward Krooss. *Financial History of the United States: Fiscal, Monetary, Banking, and Tariff, Including Financial Administration and State and Local Finance*. 2d ed. 1963. Reprint. New York: Beard Books, 2003. An important general reference for financial research. Provides fundamental information as well as analysis of financial institutions and their place in the economic history of the United States.

SEE ALSO: Nov. 4, 1924: Coolidge Is Elected U.S. President; Oct. 29, 1929-1939: Great Depression; Dec. 11, 1930: Bank of United States Fails; Nov. 8, 1932: Franklin D. Roosevelt Is Elected U.S. President; Oct. 18, 1933: Roosevelt Creates the Commodity Credit Corporation; June 26, 1934: Federal Credit Union Act.

1932

February, 1932
CHADWICK DISCOVERS THE NEUTRON

James Chadwick discovered that there is a fundamental particle in the atom that has no electrical charge and has a mass approximately equal to that of the proton.

LOCALE: Cavendish Laboratory, Cambridge, England
CATEGORIES: Science and technology; physics

KEY FIGURES

James Chadwick (1891-1974), British physicist
Ernest Rutherford (1871-1937), English physicist
Frédéric Joliot (1900-1958), French physicist
Irène Joliot-Curie (1897-1956), French physicist
Walther Bothe (1891-1957), German physicist

SUMMARY OF EVENT

The word "atom" comes from the Greek *atomos*, meaning "indivisible," but discoveries in the late nineteenth century indicated that the atom has a divisible and very complex structure. By 1914, Ernest Rutherford, an English physicist, had developed a model of the atom based on his own work as well as on the work of many scientists before him. In this model, nearly all the mass of the atom and all the positive electrical charge are concentrated in an extremely small part of the atom, the nucleus. Rutherford estimated the diameter of the nucleus to be one ten-thousandth of the diameter of the atom. Consequently, the electrons associated with the atom occupied a much larger volume than the nucleus and carried all the negative electrical charge, but had very little mass. He named the carrier of the positive charge in the nucleus the "proton" (for the Greek word for "first").

At this point, then, there were two elementary particles: the proton, with a positive charge, and the electron, with a negative electrical charge of the same magnitude as the positive charge of the proton. The atom, therefore, had to be built up with only these two particles. Helium, for example, would have two protons and two electrons. However, because the mass of the helium atom was known to be four times the mass of the hydrogen atom (which has one proton and one electron), the nucleus of the helium atom needed two more protons to produce the appropriate mass. In order to keep the electrical charge of the nucleus equal to that of two protons, it was suggested there were also two electrons in the nucleus, which neutralized the charge of the additional two protons.

As early as 1920, Rutherford speculated that there might be another elementary particle with about the same mass as the proton, but with no charge. Perhaps it was somehow produced by the combination of a proton and an electron. In 1921, American chemist William Draper Harkins named this hypothetical particle the neutron, because it was electrically neutral.

English physicist James Chadwick began his search for the neutron at the Cavendish Laboratory under Rutherford's guidance. At first, his search was unsuccessful; however, he was not the only one searching. In 1930, Walther Bothe of Germany found that when beryllium and boron were bombarded by high-energy alpha particles, radiation with no electrical charge but with great penetrating power was produced. Only two years later, Irène Joliot-Curie and Frédéric Joliot reported that

James Chadwick. (The Nobel Foundation)

CHADWICK: FROM NEUTRONS TO CYCLOTRONS

James Chadwick majored in physics instead of mathematics because of a mistake in the registration procedure at the Victoria University of Manchester. However, after attending lectures on electromagnetism by Ernest Rutherford, the world leader in the investigation of radioactivity, he decided his major was no mistake, and he received a first-class honors degree in that subject in 1911. That year, Rutherford made one of the most important scientific discoveries of this century: the nuclear structure of the atom. In 1913, Chadwick received his master's degree as well as a scholarship that sent him to study radioactivity with Hans Geiger, in Germany. There he discovered that the spectrum of beta rays was continuous. World War I began, and Chadwick was interned in a camp for enemy aliens. Despite brutal conditions, he conducted experiments using a German brand of toothpaste.

After the war, Chadwick worked in the Cavendish Laboratory of Cambridge University under his old mentor, Rutherford. There they investigated elements by alpha-particle bombardment. A notable exception to this line of work was his confirmation in 1920 that the charge on the atomic nucleus was equal to the atomic number, as had been suggested by A. van den Broek and Henry Moseley several years before. Chadwick's most important scientific discovery was his identification of the neutron in 1932, for which he received the Royal Society's 1932 Hughes Medal and the 1935 Nobel Prize in Physics. The neutron not only explained the hitherto unresolved problem of just what particles composed the nuclei of atoms but also gave impetus to Enrico Fermi's studies in nuclear reactions in uranium, which led to the 1938 discovery of nuclear fission by Otto Hahn and Fritz Strassmann.

In 1935, Chadwick accepted the Lyon Jones Chair of Physics at the University of Liverpool, where he had the opportunity to create his own laboratory and build a cyclotron, a machine that accelerates nuclear particles to great energies and then directs the beam upon a target. After World War II began, Chadwick was influential in furthering the atom-bomb projects of both the British and U.S. governments. As head of the British mission in Washington, D.C., he formed a remarkable friendship with General Leslie Groves, an able but tactless man whom most scientists disliked. Their repoire helped minimize the inevitable policy differences any two nations would have. Chadwick left Liverpool in 1948 to become master of Gonville and Caius College, Cambridge University. A decade later he retired to a cottage in North Wales, and in 1969 he made his final move, back to Cambridge, where he died in 1974.

barded by the unknown radiation, that the radiation could not be gamma rays, as previously reported.

Chadwick then showed that his experimental results were completely consistent with the assumption that each proton ejected from the paraffin had undergone a collision with an unknown particle of approximately equal mass (very much like what happens when billiard balls collide). When Chadwick was unable to deflect this particle in a magnetic field, he concluded that it had no electrical charge. Given that it did not correspond to any previously known particle, it must be the long-sought neutron.

SIGNIFICANCE

The discovery of the neutron, in 1932, marked the beginning of nuclear physics—that is, the study of the nuclear structure of the atom. It was readily seen that, as the nuclei of most elements are extremely stable, there were forces of attraction hitherto unknown between the "nucleons" (the word coined to designate the particles in the nucleus). Until the discovery of the neutron, the only known forces in physics were those of gravity, electricity, and magnetism. After 1932, it was necessary to speak of a new kind of force: the nuclear force.

With the discovery of the neutron came a much clearer understanding of atomic structure, specifically the structure of the nucleus. German physicist Werner Heisenberg proposed that envisioning the nucleus of an atom as being constructed of neutrons and protons resolved a number of difficulties. These included the problem of the missing mass of the helium atom—the answer is that two neutrons make up the additional mass. Neutrons also provide an explanation for isotopes, which are atoms of the same element that have different atomic masses. Clearly, the additional mass is caused by the presence of more neutrons in the nucleus.

In 1939, it was discovered that when uranium atoms are bombarded by neutrons, they undergo fission. Shortly thereafter, physicists showed that this fission

this radiation could cause protons to be ejected from paraffin. These scientists concluded that the radiation was a type of gamma ray—that is, electromagnetic energy of very high frequency.

When Chadwick read the account of the experiments performed by the French scientists, he immediately decided to examine this phenomenon further. He found that when boron and beryllium were bombarded by alpha particles from polonium, the mysterious radiation from these two substances could eject protons from any materials that contained hydrogen. He also discovered, from calculating the energy acquired by nitrogen atoms bom-

would release considerable energy. When it was also discovered that the fission process produced additional neutrons, scientists realized that a chain reaction of great power was possible. Consequently, the discovery of the neutron ushered in the atomic age.

— *Wilfred Theisen*

FURTHER READING

Asimov, Isaac. *Mass and Energy: The Neutron, the Structure of the Nucleus.* Vol. 2 in *Worlds Within Worlds: The Story of Nuclear Energy.* Washington, D.C.: U.S. Atomic Energy Commission, Office of Information Services, 1972. Brief discussion on the history of atomic energy by a renowned science writer begins with the theory of relativity and concludes with the use of neutrons to bombard uranium. Nonmathematical and nontechnical presentation, with many fine illustrations and photographs.

Brown, Andrew. *The Neutron and the Bomb: A Biography of Sir James Chadwick.* New York: Oxford University Press, 1997. First full-length biography of Chadwick places his work within the larger context of his life and times. Features numerous extracts from his personal correspondence with other scientists. Includes index.

Crowther, J. G. *The Cavendish Laboratory, 1874-1974.* New York: Science History Publications, 1974. An excellent account for readers interested in the historical context in which the development of atomic theory took place. Describes how close Chadwick's contemporaries in France and Germany came to discovering the neutron.

Goldhaber, Maurice. "With Chadwick at the Cavendish." *Bulletin of the Atomic Scientists* 13 (December, 1982): 12-13. Lively brief account of Chadwick and some of his coworkers at the Cavendish Laboratory by a distinguished German physicist who worked with Chadwick. Of interest for its view of the personal side of scientific activity, as it shows how scientific ideas arise and how scientists are motivated and influenced by one another.

Hughes, Donald J. *The Neutron Story.* Garden City, N.Y.: Doubleday, 1959. Excellent historical perspective provided by an author who was directly acquainted with some of the physicists associated with the development of nuclear physics. The physics is presented in nontechnical language without passing over significant details. Includes index.

Oliphant, Mark. "The Beginning: Chadwick and the Neutron." *Bulletin of the Atomic Scientists* 15 (December, 1982): 14-18. Description of Chadwick's work by a close associate of Chadwick at Cavendish Laboratory. Demonstrates how scientists work closely with others concerned with the same problems.

Piel, Gerard. *The Age of Science: What Scientists Learned in the Twentieth Century.* New York: Basic Books, 2001. An overview of the scientific achievements of the twentieth century. Chapter 3 discusses Chadwick's work. Includes many illustrations and index.

Smyth, Henry De Wolf. *Atomic Energy for Military Purposes.* 1945. Reprint. Stanford, Calif.: Stanford University Press, 1990. The first published account of the Manhattan Project—the story of the development of the atomic bomb during World War II. As the bomb's production depended on the possibility of a chain reaction, the role of the neutron was crucial to the success of the project. Contains numerous helpful appendixes and an index.

SEE ALSO: Early 20th cent.: Elster and Geitel Study Radioactivity; Dec. 10, 1903: Becquerel Wins the Nobel Prize for Discovering Natural Radioactivity; Feb. 11, 1908: Geiger and Rutherford Develop a Radiation Counter; 1912-1913: Bohr Uses Quantum Theory to Identify Atomic Structure; Mar. 7, 1912: Rutherford Describes the Atomic Nucleus; 1914: Rutherford Discovers the Proton; Apr., 1932: Cockcroft and Walton Split the Atom.

March 9, 1932
DE VALERA IS ELECTED PRESIDENT OF THE IRISH DÁIL

When Eamon de Valera was elected president of the Irish Dáil, he became in effect the prime minister of the Irish Free State after the Fianna Fáil established a majority in the Irish parliament.

LOCALE: Dublin, Ireland
CATEGORY: Government and politics

KEY FIGURES

Eamon de Valera (1882-1975), head of Fianna Fáil
William T. Cosgrave (1880-1965), leader of Cumann na nGaedheal
Sean Lemass (1899-1971), Fianna Fáil official
James McNeill (1869-1938), governor-general of Ireland

SUMMARY OF EVENT

The elections of February, 1932, saw Eamon de Valera's Fianna Fáil become the majority party in the Dáil Éireann, the parliament of the Irish Free State. On March 9, de Valera, long a major figure in Irish life and lore, was chosen as president of the executive council of the Dáil, equivalent to the position of prime minister, and came to command the state he had violently opposed at the time of its birth in 1922.

Irish history is full of irony and paradox, much of it tragic, and de Valera's career exhibits those qualities to the fullest. He had been at the center of the Irish consciousness since the failed Easter Monday Rising against Britain in 1916. A number of leaders were executed but de Valera was spared, possibly because of the perception that the earlier executions had created sympathy for the rebels, or perhaps because de Valera had been born in the United States.

In 1919, war broke out between Britain and the Irish rebels, who were politically organized as Sinn Féin (ourselves alone) and militarily in the Irish Republican Army (IRA). De Valera, as head of Sinn Féin, and David Lloyd George, the British prime minister, agreed to a truce in the summer of 1921, but de Valera refused to participate in the subsequent negotiations, sending as head of the delegation his rival, Michael Collins. An "Irish republic" was never a possibility, as de Valera undoubtedly knew, and Collins and his associates accepted dominion status within the British Empire. Designated the "Irish Free State," the dominion would still have as its constitutional head the British monarch, who lacked substantive power but was a symbol of the British connection, represented

in Ireland by a governor-general. Supported by Collins but opposed by de Valera, the treaty was narrowly adopted. The result was a new civil war in Ireland, green against green, the Free State forces against Sinn Féin and the IRA, and before it ended with a Free State victory, Collins and numerous others on both sides were killed.

De Valera survived but was imprisoned by the Free State and ignored by the military leaders of the IRA. During the years that followed, the Free State government, led by William T. Cosgrave, got the fledgling state under way. The shadow of history and Britain lay heavily over the new nation, and the partition of Ireland into the Free State and Northern Ireland generated controversy. The greatest threat, however, came not from Britain or Northern Ireland but from the losers in the treaty debate: de Valera's Sinn Féin and the IRA.

One of the most brilliant politicians in Irish history—he was an avowed student of Niccolò Machiavelli's *Il principe* (1532; *The Prince*, 1640)—de Valera combined idealistic nationalism with ruthless self-interest. He was never as hard-line as many republicans, being willing to settle for what he called "external association" with Britain, but like everyone involved on both sides, he held symbols to be important. For de Valera, the required oath to the British crown remained a seemingly insurmountable obstacle. De Valera decided to disengage himself from the IRA's violence and use the mechanisms of the hated Free State to gain power, but when many of his Sinn Féin colleagues refused to follow, de Valera resigned as president of the organization and founded Fianna Fáil (warriors of destiny) in May, 1926. In the 1927 elections, Fianna Fáil became the second largest party, with Sinn Féin reduced to insignificance. To take one's seat in the Dáil, one had to sign one's name as evidence of subscribing to the oath. In a gesture worthy of Machiavelli, de Valera signed his name but denied he was taking the oath and entered the Dáil in 1927.

Cosgrave's Cumann na nGaedheal (League of the Gaels), as the largest party in the multiparty Dáil, dominated the political arena throughout the 1920's. Like its British and American counterparts, the government's economic philosophy tended toward classic liberalism: The less government involvement, the better. The coming of the Great Depression, however, made such attitudes less tenable. In addition, Cosgrave attempted to enlist the Catholic Church's support for his regime. The Catholic Church in Ireland was, if anything, more con-

Eamon de Valera. (Library of Congress)

servative than the Vatican in political and social matters. The Free State outlawed divorce and established a censorship board to search out any obscenities, including any reference to birth control. Suspicious of socialism and adamantly against the IRA's violence, the bishops were a political prize worth having. De Valera also needed the Church, or at least its neutrality. Sincere in his own Catholicism, de Valera had the barrier of his Sinn Féin connections to overcome, but he and Fianna Fáil did so by complaining that Cosgrave had not taken a firm enough approach to entrenching the Catholic Church into Irish life. Also, as the established newspapers largely supported Cosgrave, in 1931 de Valera founded his own daily newspaper, the *Irish Press*, which became and remained de Valera's political mouthpiece: He owned it, and he controlled it.

Cosgrave called an election for February 16, 1932, several months earlier than constitutionally required—with the economy worsening, early elections seemed the lesser evil. Predictably, the government said little about economic policy, relying in its platform on being the party of religion, law and order, and accusing Fianna Fáil of be-

ing crypto-communists with ties to the IRA. De Valera committed himself to abolishing the oath but stressed his economic programs that would increase welfare and reduce unemployment through public housing and other social programs. The Machiavellian de Valera's chief adviser, Sean Lemass, reassured the IRA of Fianna Fáil's friendship, Cosgrave's party was accused of being Masons and British unionists, and de Valera used every opportunity to identify himself with the Church.

The election results saw Fianna Fáil become the largest party in the Dáil with seventy-two seats, up fifteen from 1927. Cosgrave's party won only fifty-seven seats. Although his party lacked an absolute majority—Labour and other minor parties held the balance of power—it was understood that de Valera would head the new government. During the campaign he had assured the voters that in the event of a Fianna Fáil victory there would be no untoward measures taken against the party's political opponents. There were rumors that elements of the army would resort to a military coup in order to nullify Fianna Fáil's victory, but Cosgrave, committed to democracy, had consistently reduced the influence of the military throughout his long tenure.

On March 9, 1932, de Valera entered the Dáil, with his son Vivion at his side, armed with a revolver because of assassination rumors. There was no violence, however. Cosgrave did not even offer himself as a candidate, and thus de Valera, long a legend, as hero or villain, was elected president of the executive council by a vote of eighty-one to sixty-eight and came to preside over the state he had disowned at its birth.

SIGNIFICANCE

In a gesture of conciliation, Governor-General James McNeill took the initiative and went to the Dáil to confirm de Valera's election instead of requiring that de Valera travel to the Viceregal Lodge. McNeill was soon replaced, however, by a de Valera sycophant, much reducing the governor-general's position as an imperial symbol. De Valera also suspended land annuity payments that were owed to the British government, beginning an economic war that lasted until the eve of World War II.

Once in power, de Valera proved to be no friend to the IRA, cracking down on its activities as Cosgrave had before him. In 1937, a new constitution was promulgated that further weakened Free State ties with Britain, but it was not until 1947, ironically with de Valera briefly out of power, that the Irish Republic was established.

The election of 1932 was a crucial event in Irish history. It brought de Valera into office as head of the government, and through the peaceful transition of power between two groups that had been shooting at each other only a few years earlier, it proved to many that Irish democracy could be a reality.

—*Eugene Larson*

FURTHER READING

Coogan, Tim Pat. *Eamon de Valera: The Man Who Was Ireland*. New York: HarperCollins, 1995. Comprehensive biography places de Valera in the context of his times. Includes bibliography and index.

_____. *Ireland in the Twentieth Century*. New York: Palgrave Macmillan, 2004. History of twentieth century Ireland by a respected historian and biographer examines events, attitudes, and cultures. Includes bibliography and index.

Edwards, Owen Dudley. *Eamon de Valera*. Cardiff: University of Wales Press, 1987. Interpretive biography discusses de Valera's character and motives.

Foley, Conor. *Legion of the Rearguard: The IRA and the Modern Irish State*. London: Pluto Press, 1992. History of the IRA includes discussion of the 1932 election.

Lee, J. J. *Ireland, 1912-1985: Politics and Society*. New York: Cambridge University Press, 1989. Comprehensive account of economic, cultural, social, and political events in Ireland during the period examined. Includes maps, tables, selected bibliography, and index.

Longford, Frank Pakenham, and Thomas P. O'Neill. *Eamon de Valera*. London: Hutchinson, 1970. Authorized biography published before de Valera's death presents a sympathetic portrait.

SEE ALSO: Nov. 28, 1905: Sinn Féin Is Founded; Sept. 15, 1914: Irish Home Rule Bill; 1920-1921: Ireland Is Granted Home Rule and Northern Ireland Is Created.

1932

March 19, 1932
DEDICATION OF THE SYDNEY HARBOUR BRIDGE

When it was constructed, the Sydney Harbour Bridge was the second-longest steel-arch bridge in the world, and it remained both the third-longest steel-arch bridge and the world's widest steel-arch bridge through the end of the twentieth century. The bridge greatly improved transit between Sydney and North Sydney, and it also led to an increase in tourism and commerce in Sydney. The bridge's construction may have been the single most important factor in Sydney's rise to international prominence.

LOCALE: Sydney, New South Wales, Australia
CATEGORIES: Engineering; transportation; urban planning

KEY FIGURES
John Job Crew Bradfield (1867-1943), chief engineer and codesigner of the Sydney Harbour Bridge
Sir Ralph Freeman (1880-1950), consulting engineer for the British firm Dorman Long and codesigner of the Sydney Harbour Bridge
John Thomas Lang (1876-1975), premier of New South Wales, leader of its Labor Party, and former treasurer of New South Wales's labor government
Francis de Groot (1888-1969), member of the New Guard, an anticommunist paramilitary group

SUMMARY OF EVENT
On March 19, 1932, the Sydney Harbour Bridge was officially opened by John Thomas Lang, the premier of New South Wales. Several thousand people attended the dedication ceremony. Many anchored their sailboats and yachts in the harbor, and thousands more watched and listened from the beaches as Lang, chief engineer John Job Crew Bradfield, and many others spoke over a public-address system. There was clearly a great deal of interest in the event, and attendance numbers may have been boosted by the serious advertising effort undertaken by New South Wales's Urban Transit Authority. For example, the poster that Douglas Annand created for the event later became a valued piece of Australian art.

Before the ribbon was cut, several important speeches were made, including one from Bradfield, who predicted that the bridge, which now linked Sydney with the poorer area of North Sydney, would drastically improve the economic circumstances of many Australians. Before the bridge's construction, people and companies delivering and procuring goods had to drive cars and take trains for many miles around the bay or contract ferries across the bay in order to reach Sydney's industry and ports. This was often too expensive for common citizens and too inefficient for vibrant commerce, and economic development in Sydney was stifled for decades. Bradfield pointed out that the bridge would make it economically possible for more than a million people to reside in the North Sydney suburbs because they would have easy transportation to the city, an industrial powerhouse in New South Wales. The result of the bridge, Bradfield predicted, would be Sydney's progression as a city that would rival New York in commerce, industry, and urban development.

Those in attendance at the opening of the bridge observed a parade of sorts that included a cavalcade of cars carrying Lang, Bradfield, and city, regional, and provincial officials such as the British governor-general and the New South Wales minister of works. The cavalcade was accompanied by outriders, decorated soldiers in military dress who rode on horseback. In fact, one of the most humorous and confusing events of the bridge's opening concerned one of these outriders. Captain Francis de Groot, a furniture maker, dressed as a soldier, rode a horse, and even donned a sword and several war medals so that he could ride with the cavalcade. De Groot was a member of the New Guard, a paramilitary organization

that rebelled against communism and the Labor Party, of which Lang was a leader. De Groot was not recognized as he rode with the procession to the bridge, where he waited through several speeches. Before the ribbon-cutting ceremony, de Groot positioned himself very near Lang, who motioned for the ribbon to be cut after he finished his speech. Instead, however, de Groot cut the ribbon with his sword and declared the bridge to be open to all the deserving citizens of New South Wales. The ribbon was then retied, and Lang formally opened the bridge.

Lang was a controversial figure, although this was largely because he governed during a period of considerable tumult in the Australian economy, part of the Great Depression that engulfed the world. However, it was also due to disagreements over the bridge. Huge numbers of people were, in fact, wholeheartedly against the bridge's construction, mainly because the massive amount of money that it required could have been used to bolster the nation's railway systems. Also, many still believed that tunnels beneath the harbor would have been superior to a

The Sydney Harbour Bridge under construction in 1930. (Courtesy, National Library of Australia)

bridge, even though the construction of such tunnels was proved unfeasible by 1912. Finally, many were bitter about the way hundreds of people had been forced to leave their homes, which were to be demolished to make way for the bridge, without any compensation from the government.

By the time the bridge opened, the citizens of Sydney had seen the installation of the bridge's two enormous pylons, which anchored the force displaced by the dual metal arches (although the lower arch was more important as an anchor). Many onlookers were very impressed by the pattern of perfect symmetry offered by the web of steel girders that connected the arches to each other and the arches to the deck. Many were also awestruck by the fact that the crown of these arches hovered 440 feet above sea level and the deck rose 178 feet above sea level.

In 1922, when Bradfield and fellow designer Sir Ralph Freeman finalized their design, their bridge promised to be the longest, widest, and most massive in the world. At the time, the only project remotely similar to theirs was New York's Hell's Gate Bridge, which had been designed by Gustav Lindenthal in 1916. The Hell's Gate Bridge, however, was 977.5 feet long, whereas the Sydney Harbour Bridge spanned 1,650 feet. Although Bradfield had been to New York to study long-span bridges, he had not seen the Hell's Gate in person. Some said that he used the Hell's Gate as an example in his original design, but clearly he must have studied it from a secondary source.

The immense Bayonne Bridge, which linked Newark, New Jersey, to Staten Island, New York, was finished in 1931, but there is no evidence that Bradfield and Freeman's design referenced it. Although they are both steel-arch bridges, and although the Bayonne is three feet longer, the Sydney Harbour Bridge is more massive, and many argued that the Sydney bridge was designed with aesthetic value in mind, whereas the Bayonne's value is entirely functional. Bradfield and Freeman's task was further complicated by the need to include a connection to Sydney's railway system in the plan—an engineering feat in itself.

Significance

Although the Sydney Harbour Bridge created controversy, it allowed millions of Sydney residents to believe that things would get better during the devastating years of the Great Depression. It turned the world's attention to

Sydney, and it also gave the city a moral victory over the Australian cities of Victoria and Melbourne, with which Sydney was in constant competition. The bridge cost an estimated ten million pounds (paid for by loans), which very roughly translates to more than a billion American dollars in more modern terms. This amount was not paid off until 1988. However, the bridge's construction created fourteen hundred jobs on-site, and several thousand additional workers were needed to supply the site with materials. Given that Australia's economic depression largely ended by 1933, it is possible that the bridge's construction played an important role in the country's economic improvement.

Bradfield's predictions largely came true. The beautiful Sydney Harbor gradually became a huge tourist and business destination. Hundreds of office buildings and hotels were built to support and develop an increase in commerce and tourism after World War II, and the demand for housing around the Sydney Harbor continued to grow. In retrospect, the bridge was constructed at an opportune time—during a depression and before World War II—to help Sydney become one of the most important commerce centers in the world. The bridge made it easier for people and goods to move, but it also grew as a source of general interest: By the end of the twentieth century, approximately seven hundred tourists were paying each day to climb to its 440-foot crown.

—*Troy Place*

Further Reading

Johnson, Stephen, and Roberto T. Leon. *The Encyclopedia of Bridges and Tunnels*. New York: Facts On File, 2002. Provides historical background on tunnels and bridge types and a semitechnical analysis of these structures and how they function. Provides specifications of famous bridges and tunnels and ranks them by length.

Moorhouse, Geoffrey. *Sydney: The Story of a City*. New York: Harcourt, 1999. Discusses the history of Sydney in terms of cultural struggle, politics, urban planning, urban sprawl, shipping, and commerce.

Stephensen, P. R. *The History and Description of Sydney Harbour*. Adelaide, S.Aust.: Rigby, 1966. Provides an exceptionally thorough historical description of Sydney's harbor from 1788 to 1965.

SEE ALSO: May 27, 1937: Golden Gate Bridge Opens; Nov. 7, 1940: Tacoma Narrows Bridge Collapses.

1932

March 23, 1932
NORRIS-LA GUARDIA ACT STRENGTHENS LABOR ORGANIZATIONS

By curbing the use of injunctions in labor disputes, extending unions' exemption from antitrust laws, and prohibiting yellow-dog contracts, the Norris-La Guardia Act made it easier for labor unions to organize and operate.

LOCALE: Washington, D.C.
CATEGORIES: Laws, acts, and legal history; business and labor

KEY FIGURES

George W. Norris (1861-1944), U.S. senator from Nebraska, 1913-1943
Fiorello Henry La Guardia (1882-1947), U.S. congressman from New York, 1917-1933
Louis D. Brandeis (1856-1941), associate justice of the United States, 1916-1939
John L. Lewis (1880-1969), president of the United Mine Workers, 1920-1960

SUMMARY OF EVENT

The Norris-La Guardia Act of 1932 was passed in order to free labor unions from antiunion actions involving three related elements: the Sherman Antitrust Act, the injunction, and the "yellow-dog contract." As industry developed rapidly in the United States in the late nineteenth century, widespread efforts were undertaken to organize labor unions and to engage employers in collective bargaining. Many employers resisted these efforts. One instrument for such resistance was the Sherman Antitrust Act of 1890, which outlawed "every contract . . . or conspiracy, in restraint of trade or commerce." Union actions such as strikes and boycotts could be penalized through employer lawsuits for triple damages, as in the Danbury Hatters case (*Loewe v. Lawlor*) of 1908. Antiunion employers often were able to obtain court injunctions against union actions. An injunction is a court order primarily intended to forbid someone from taking actions that could cause severe injury to another. Courts had wide latitude in issuing injunctions. Violating an injunction could bring the offender under severe penalties for contempt of court, again with wide discretion for the court.

Another antiunion instrument was the so-called yellow-dog contract, whereby a worker was required, as a condition of employment, to agree explicitly not to join a union and to renounce any current union membership. Efforts by legislatures to outlaw such contracts had been overruled by the U.S. Supreme Court. A company whose

workers had signed such contracts could seek an injunction against any union organizer who might try to persuade workers to breach their contracts.

The Clayton Antitrust Act of 1914 ostensibly established the principle that the existence and operation of labor unions were not illegal under the Sherman Act. Further, the law forbade the federal courts to issue injunctions against a long list of union activities, vaguely worded but clearly referring to strikes and boycotts. Union jubilation that the Clayton Act would expand labor's scope of organized activity was short-lived. In 1917, the Supreme Court held in the *Hitchman Coal and Coke Company v. Mitchell* case that issuing an injunction was an appropriate remedy against a union organizer trying to persuade workers to breach their yellow-dog contracts. Even more striking was the *Duplex Printing Press Company v. Deering* case of 1921. The Duplex Company had attempted to obtain court action against a system of union boycotts intended to force it to become unionized. Federal district and appeals courts refused to uphold the Duplex claim, but the Supreme Court overruled them in 1921. The decision held that the union's actions could be in violation of the Sherman Act and did not constitute a "labor dispute" protected by the specific terms of the Clayton Act. Furthermore, issuing an injunction was appropriate to prevent harm to the employer. In a dissenting opinion, Justice Louis D. Brandeis pointed out that the majority opinion appeared to deny the intent of the Clayton Act.

A strong antiunion trend persisted in Supreme Court decisions during the 1920's. In 1921, the Court upheld use of an injunction against picketing when there were elements of intimidation and when "outsiders" to the direct dispute were involved, in *American Steel Foundries v. Tri-City Central Trades Council*. Also in 1921, the Court held unconstitutional an Arizona statute establishing the right to peaceful picketing in *Truax v. Corrigan*. The case of *Bedford Cut Stone Company v. Journeymen Stone Cutters' Association* (1927) involved concerted refusal by union stonecutters to work on the products of a nonunion firm. The Court held that this action could be considered a violation of the Sherman Antitrust Act and that an injunction was an appropriate form of relief. In a vigorous dissent, Justice Brandeis pointed out the lack of parallel between the union activities and the business monopoly actions against which the antitrust laws were directed.

The prosperous condition of the U.S. economy in the 1920's did not produce much union militancy; in fact, union membership showed a declining trend. After 1929, however, the economy headed into severe depression. As workers faced wage reductions, layoffs, or reduced hours, many perceived an increased need for the protection of union members and collective bargaining. Workers brought increasing political pressure to overrule the antiunion legal doctrines. In the U.S. Congress, their cause was taken up by Senator George W. Norris, a Republican progressive from Nebraska. With the aid of a panel of distinguished labor law experts, including Felix Frankfurter of Harvard Law School, Norris drafted a bill to achieve the intent of the Clayton Act. Congressman Fiorello Henry La Guardia of New York, also a progressive, introduced the bill into the House of Representatives. As the worsening depression created a sense of panic among many legislators who became eager to show concern for workers, the Norris-La Guardia Act passed both houses of Congress by overwhelming margins and became law on March 23, 1932.

Sections 3 and 4 of the law stated that contracts whereby workers agreed not to join a union were not to be enforced and could not be the basis for injunctions. Section 4 directed federal courts not to issue injunctions against concerted refusals to work (that is, strikes), joining or remaining in a union, giving financial or other aid to a union or strike, publicizing a labor dispute by picketing or other methods, or assembling peaceably to organize or promote a labor dispute. Further, such actions were not to be held to constitute violations of the antitrust laws. Section 13 gave a broad definition of a labor dispute, allowing disputes to involve persons other than an employer and his or her workers, thus broadening the range of union activities protected by the law. Section 6 provided that no union officer or member could be held liable for financial damages for the separate and independent actions of other union members or officers.

SIGNIFICANCE

The Norris-La Guardia Act removed obstacles to the formation of unions and to unions' activities, particularly organizing, striking, and boycotting. The law did not commit the government directly to the promotion of unions, but such promotion was soon forthcoming. After the election of 1932, Franklin D. Roosevelt's New Deal swept aside the Republican administration and many Republican members of Congress, including La Guardia. One of the first acts of the New Deal was passage of the National Industrial Recovery Act (NIRA) of 1933. Its

section 7a guaranteed workers the right to form and join unions of their own choosing and obliged employers to bargain with those unions. Similar provisions were contained in the Railway Labor Act of 1934. When the NIRA was held unconstitutional in 1935, Congress enacted the National Labor Relations Act (Wagner Act) of 1935, which affirmed a "right" to unionize and created the National Labor Relations Board (NLRB) to make this right effective. Whereas the Norris-La Guardia Act merely protected union activities from damage suits and injunctions, the Wagner Act protected unions from a long list of "unfair" labor practices. These included employer interference with union organizing activities or union operations, discrimination against union members, and refusal to bargain collectively "in good faith" with certified unions. The NLRB was authorized to conduct elections to determine if a group of workers should be represented by a union.

As a consequence of this legislation, much of the focus in labor relations shifted away from the private lawsuits with which the Norris-La Guardia Act was concerned. Union organizers undertook vigorous campaigns for new members, sparked by the Congress of Industrial Organizations (CIO) under the leadership of John L. Lewis. Union membership, which had fallen below three million in 1933, passed ten million in 1941. Organizing efforts continued to meet with strong opposition, and employers still tried to enlist the courts to assist them, without much success. In 1938, the Supreme Court upheld the constitutionality of the Norris-La Guardia Act in the case of *Lauf v. E. G. Shinner and Company*. The Court affirmed the legality of union picketing activities directed against a nonunion employer. In the case of *Apex Hosiery Company v. Leader*, the Supreme Court in 1940 refused to consider a union sit-down strike to be a violation of the antitrust laws. The case arose from a violent incident in 1937 when union members broke into the company's plant and physically took possession of it. The Court noted that the union's actions were clearly unlawful but argued that the appropriate remedies lay in channels other than the antitrust laws. In the case of *United States v. Hutcheson* (1941), the Supreme Court again refused to permit antitrust prosecution to be brought against union officials. The carpenters' union that was the target of the lawsuit was trying to use a boycott to induce Anheuser-Busch Brewing Company to reverse a decision that certain work should be performed by machinists. It was a no-win situation for the company, because it could be similarly attacked by the machinists if it reversed its decision. The Supreme Court simply af-

1932

firmed that the union actions should not be viewed as a violation of the Sherman Antitrust Act.

The great spread of unionization in the late 1930's helps explain why hourly wage rates in manufacturing increased about 30 percent between 1935 and 1941 at a time when more than 10 percent of workers remained unemployed. Some economists noted that while union workers were benefiting, their gains were raising business costs and thus slowing the rise of job openings for the unemployed.

Union membership continued to increase during World War II, but developments led many observers to believe that unions held too much power. Strikes by coal miners led by Lewis during the war were particularly damaging to the image of unions. In November, 1946, Lewis provoked a confrontation with the government, which was then nominally operating the mines under wartime legislation. A federal court issued an injunction against a work stoppage by the union and then imposed heavy fines on Lewis and the union when they did not comply. In March, 1947, the Supreme Court upheld the injunction, ruling that the Norris-La Guardia Act did not apply when the government was in the role of employer. In 1945, the Supreme Court established that some labor union actions could be considered to violate the Sherman Antitrust Act, if the union acted in collusion with employers in a manner that promoted monopoly conditions in markets for business products.

The belief that unions had gained too much power ultimately led to adoption of the Taft-Hartley Act in 1947. That act prohibited a long list of "unfair" practices by unions. By that time, many of the issues confronted by the Norris-La Guardia Act had faded from significance. Under the protection of the Wagner Act, unions had been organized and certified in most of the areas in which workers wanted them. Yellow-dog contracts had disappeared, and harassment of union organizers had diminished. A major consequence of the Norris-La Guardia Act was to shift the bulk of litigation involving labor union activities to state courts. Picketing and related activities associated with strikes and other labor disputes often primarily involved state laws, local ordinances, and local police. Private business firms largely lost the opportunity to bring civil lawsuits to halt or penalize nonviolent strikes and other labor union activities.

—Paul B. Trescott

FURTHER READING

Babson, Steve. *The Unfinished Struggle: Turning Points in American Labor, 1877-Present.* Lanham, Md.:

Rowman & Littlefield, 1999. Concise and comprehensive history of the American labor movement. Includes notes and index.

Bernstein, Irving. *The Lean Years: A History of the American Worker, 1920-1933.* 1960. Reprint. New York: Da Capo Press, 1983. First volume of two-volume history; see below.

_____. *Turbulent Years: A History of the American Worker, 1933-1941.* Boston: Houghton Mifflin, 1970. These two volumes provide an excellent detailed narrative of a colorful and dramatic period in labor history.

Breen, W. J. *Labor Market Politics and the Great War: The Department of Labor, the States, and the First U.S. Employment Service, 1907-1933.* Kent, Ohio: Kent State University Press, 1997. History of the federal government's involvement in labor issues during the critical period from before World War I through the early years of the Great Depression. Includes bibliography and index.

Daugherty, Carroll R. *Labor Problems in American Industry.* Boston: Houghton Mifflin, 1941. Deals at length with all aspects of labor relations, including the Norris-La Guardia Act and many court cases subsequent to it.

Gregory, Charles O., and Harold A. Katz. *Labor and the Law.* 3d ed. New York: W. W. Norton, 1979. Detailed, readable account of U.S. legislation and court actions relating to unions. Chapter 7 focuses on the Norris-La Guardia Act and related litigation.

Jacoby, Daniel. *Laboring for Freedom: A New Look at the History of Labor in America.* Armonk, N.Y.: M. E. Sharpe, 1998. Examines opposed ideas concerning freedom as manifested in labor history in the United States. Includes bibliography and index.

Lieberman, Elias. *Unions Before the Bar.* New York: Harper & Brothers, 1950. Devotes a chapter apiece to twenty-six major court cases involving unions. Excellent background on the events. Summarizes litigation at all court levels.

Limpus, Lowell M., and Burr Leyson. *This Man La Guardia.* New York: E. P. Dutton, 1938. Provides a good review of La Guardia's colorful career, including his tenure as mayor of New York City.

Mason, Alpheus Thomas. *Brandeis: A Free Man's Life.* New York: Viking Press, 1946. Detailed account of the life of the powerful liberal thinker and activist puts his Supreme Court role in a broad context. Includes discussion of his dissents in labor cases.

Norris, George W. *Fighting Liberal: The Autobiography*

of George W. Norris. 1945. Reprint. Lincoln: University of Nebraska Press, 1992. Demonstrates the impressive array of liberal causes Norris supported. Chapter titled "Yellow Dog Contract" gives a narrative of the evolution of the Norris-La Guardia Act.

SEE ALSO: Jan. 27, 1908: U.S. Supreme Court Ruling Allows Yellow-Dog Contracts; Oct. 15, 1914: Labor Unions Win Exemption from Antitrust Laws; May 20, 1926: Railway Labor Act Provides for Mediation of Labor Disputes; July 5, 1935: Wagner Act.

April, 1932
COCKCROFT AND WALTON SPLIT THE ATOM

John Douglas Cockcroft and Ernest Thomas Sinton Walton bombarded a lithium atom with protons, producing the first artificial nuclear disintegration with accelerated particles.

LOCALE: Cavendish Laboratory, Cambridge, England
CATEGORIES: Science and technology; physics

KEY FIGURES
John Douglas Cockcroft (1897-1967), English physicist and electrical engineer
Ernest Thomas Sinton Walton (1903-1995), Irish physicist
Marcus Laurence Oliphant (1901-2000), Australian nuclear physicist
Ernest Rutherford (1871-1937), English nuclear physicist
T. E. Allibone (1903-2003), English electrical engineer

SUMMARY OF EVENT
Sir John Douglas Cockcroft and Ernest Thomas Sinton Walton opened a new era in physics in 1932 when they successfully split the lithium nucleus using 500-kilovolt protons accelerated in a voltage multiplier. Modern nuclear and particle physics depends on subatomic particle accelerators for sources of probes to investigate the behavior of nuclei of atoms, their constituent particles, and the forces that influence them. Cockcroft and Walton's achievement made the heart of the atom accessible for nuclear physicists.

Following Ernest Rutherford's discovery of the atomic nucleus in 1910, his transformation of nitrogen into radioactive oxygen using natural radioactive substances in 1917, and his assumption of the directorship of the Cavendish Laboratory at Cambridge University in 1918, the importance of the atomic nucleus as a field of physical inquiry was well established. However, the nature of the nucleus could not be explored adequately with the projectiles placed at scientists' disposal by nature: alpha particles, electrons, and gamma rays. An artificial

means of producing high-energy particles was required to disintegrate the atomic nucleus; this was first supplied by Cockcroft and Walton.

Cockcroft was educated in physics at the University of Manchester and Cambridge University, and in electrical engineering at the Manchester College of Technology. At Metropolitan Vickers Company, one of the engineers, T. E. Allibone, had made the first attempts to produce nuclear disintegration with accelerated electrons produced by a modified tesla coil in 1927, thus inspiring Rutherford's call "for a copious supply of atoms and electrons which have an individual energy far transcending that of the alpha- and beta-particles from radioactive bodies."

Walton had earned his doctorate in physics at Cambridge University by investigating a variety of means of accelerating subatomic particles: electrons in a circular magnetic field similar to the one later successfully used by Ernest Orlando Lawrence in his cyclotron and by Donald Kerst in his betatron, and positive ions of the heavier elements in a linear accelerator.

Late in 1928, Cockcroft became aware of a theory propounded by Soviet theoretical physicist George Gamow. Using the wave mechanics developed by Erwin Schrödinger, Gamow had proposed that alpha particles escaped their parent atoms occasionally, not by attaining sufficient energy to overcome the potential barrier that surrounded the nuclei but by "tunneling" through it. The reverse process, Gamow argued, could account for a particle penetrating the nucleus with smaller energies than those of its potential barrier.

Cockcroft realized that several-million-volt subatomic particles were not required to penetrate the nucleus. Given enough subatomic particles, however, about six in one thousand particles with energies of about 300,000 volts should penetrate a boron nucleus. Cockcroft informed Rutherford of this prospect and immediately began to build an accelerator to test this hypothesis. Rutherford assigned Walton to assist Cockcroft in building a source of protons (positive hydrogen ions) and a vacuum tube to withstand several hundred kilovolts to accelerate them. Rutherford then arranged for the team to receive a grant to purchase a transformer and rectifiers to produce steady direct-current voltage for the experiments; these were provided by the Metropolitan Vickers Company. The 350-kilovolt transformer was custom-built to fit the room in which it was housed by B. L. Goodlet and was installed in December, 1928. The rectifiers were designed by Allibone to produce steady direct currents to accelerate ions from the transformer's alternating current. When the transformer failed in August, Cockcroft determined a new means of producing higher voltages than the 280 kilovolts they had achieved.

Cockcroft reinvented the "voltage multiplying" circuit in which condensers, which store electric charges like a battery, were linked alternately in parallel with rectifying diodes. The voltage was divided from the transformer, which had been applied to the first condenser in the series between it and the others, then separating the condensers as the first was charged up again, and reconnecting them so that it was possible to build up a charge equivalent to three times that of the source. With the 200-kilovolt transformer, four rectifiers, and four condensers, 800 kilovolts could be built up in this way.

Cockcroft and Walton also built an accelerating tube strong enough to bear this high voltage, basing their design on that of a high-voltage X-ray tube invented by W. D. Coolidge of General Electric in the United States. The particles to be accelerated were generated in a small glass chamber at its top, to which 60 kilovolts were applied. Then they entered two evacuated glass tubes placed end to end in which the electrodes, supported by a steel plate to withstand the stresses induced by the high voltages applied to them, supplied the energy to accelerate the tubes to 710 kilovolts.

At this point, Cockcroft and Walton's experiments were interrupted by the demands of the laboratory in which they had built their apparatus. They moved the apparatus to a larger laboratory in May of 1931 and resumed their experiments. By early 1932, 710-kilovolt protons had been produced by the tube. The two researchers, however, interrupted these studies to look for gamma rays that they expected to be produced when alpha particles struck beryllium, as Irène Joliot-Curie and Frédéric Joliot had observed in Paris. Although it had yet to be revealed by their colleague James Chadwick, these "gamma rays" were in fact neutrons, which Rutherford had predicted ten years earlier should exist in the nucleus.

Ernest Thomas Sinton Walton. (The Nobel Foundation)

After a fruitless search, Cockcroft and Walton returned to accelerating protons and measured their magnetic deflection in order to determine their energies. At this point, Rutherford intervened and reminded them of the fundamental technique for detecting alpha particles that had been developed by the Cavendish Laboratory: the use of a fluorescent screen, a paper or a card coated with zinc sulfide. He was convinced that when protons bombarded lithium, alpha particles must be produced. Rutherford believed they should give up their search for gamma rays to hunt them. On April 14, 1932, they inserted a lithium target in the tube, and Walton climbed into a darkened cabin built at its base to look for fluorescence. He saw them immediately and summoned Rutherford, who confirmed that the fluorescence was produced by alpha particles. This was the first human-made artificial disintegration of any atom: The proton had united with lithium and broken it up into two atoms of helium, releasing 17 million electronvolts of energy. This energy conformed to the difference between the masses of the lithium and hydrogen before the disintegration and the helium afterward. Mass had been converted to energy according to the formula $E = mc^2$, exactly as predicted by Albert Einstein's theory of special relativity.

SIGNIFICANCE

The disintegration of the lithium atom by Cockcroft and Walton unleashed the power of particle accelerators on the nucleus and led to the rapid development of the field of nuclear physics in the succeeding decades. Rutherford and Marcus Laurence Oliphant, who came to Cavendish in 1927 from Australia, developed a low-energy accelerator of protons to follow up the experiments of Cockcroft and Walton with 200-kilovolt protons in order to examine the thresholds of proton-induced nuclear reactions. They succeeded in producing the disintegration of lithium with only 100-kilovolt protons by February, 1933, and subsequently found that 20-kilovolt protons would suffice; boron required only 60-kilovolt protons.

Other accelerator developers, such as Lawrence at the University of California's Radiation Laboratory in Berkeley, Robert J. Van de Graaff at Princeton University, and Charles C. Lauritsen at the Kellogg High-Voltage Laboratory at the California Institute of Technology, quickly entered the field with more powerful particle accelerators. They had not paused to look for disintegration of atoms at the energies Cockcroft and Walton used because they were not as familiar with nuclear theory. Once they had developed the appropriate detectors, they were able to surpass the Cambridge experimenters, whose machine was not capable of much higher energies. Indeed, Cockcroft built a cyclotron at the Cavendish in 1937, after trying and failing to develop a larger machine of their design in collaboration with a physicist in the Netherlands. Lawrence's cyclotron easily outpaced direct-current accelerators in energy, although very significant scientific work was done with the accelerators developed at Cambridge in the mid-1930's.

The voltage multiplier remained, however, a very successful source of potentials around 1 million volts and has been used extensively as the first stage of many larger accelerators. Cockcroft and Walton received the Nobel Prize in Physics in 1951 for their pioneering work with this accelerator. By demonstrating that it was possible to disintegrate nuclei with artificially accelerated particles, they had opened up the new field of accelerator physics and demonstrated conclusively the conversion of mass to energy in nuclear processes.

Their achievement also reflected the new constella-

tion of interests that was to give rise to modern science. The involvement of industrial firms such as Metropolitan Vickers and General Electric with the Cavendish Laboratory in the investigation of nuclear physics presaged the industrial scale of the particle accelerators that were to be developed in the twentieth century. Allibone and Cockcroft needed engineering skills along with training in physics to accomplish the goal of artificially accelerating protons to energies sufficient to split the atom. The state of the art in high-voltage engineering had to be advanced for them to do this; therefore, industry benefited from the quest to understand the nucleus just as did physics. These early collaborations engendered gigantic efforts such as the construction of the Superconducting Super Collider, on which the U.S. government spent $2 billion before the partially completed project was ultimately canceled in 1993.

—Robert W. Seidel

FURTHER READING

Cathcart, Brian. *The Fly in the Cathedral: How a Group of Cambridge Scientists Won the International Race to Split the Atom.* New York: Farrar, Straus and Giroux, 2005. Relates the story of Cockcroft and Walton's work in an exciting way, focusing on the Cambridge physicists' struggle to split the atom ahead of competing scientists in the United States and Germany.

Cockburn, Stewart, and David Ellyard. *Oliphant.* Adelaide, S.Aust.: Axiom Books, 1981. Biography of Rutherford's associate chronicles aspects of nuclear physics at Cambridge during Oliphant's tenure there from 1927 to 1936 and his work with Rutherford in following up the Cockcroft and Walton experiment. Includes illustrations, bibliography, and index.

Crowther, J. G. *The Cavendish Laboratory, 1874-1974.* New York: Science History Publications, 1974. Anecdotal history of the Cavendish Laboratory is a well-illustrated introduction to its work. Includes references and index.

Hartcup, Guy, and T. E. Allibone. *Cockcroft and the Atom.* Bristol, England: Adam Hilger, 1984. Biography of Cockcroft, written in part by Allibone, who was a participant in the work, is an authoritative source of information on Cockcroft's life and work. Includes illustrations, appendixes, bibliography, and index.

Hendry, John, ed. *Cambridge Physics in the Thirties.* Bristol, England: Adam Hilger, 1984. Collection of retrospective accounts interspersed with historical

1932

commentary places the achievements of the 1930's in a broad context and illuminates many of the more obscure technical developments that ensured the Cambridge physicists' leadership in the field. Includes illustrations, selected bibliography, and name index.

Oliphant, Mark. *Rutherford: Recollections of Cambridge Days*. New York: Elsevier, 1972. Anecdotal account intended for a wide audience includes a chapter on the work of Cockcroft and Walton by a participant who knew them. Illustrated with contemporary photographs.

Piel, Gerard. *The Age of Science: What Scientists Learned in the Twentieth Century*. New York: Basic Books, 2001. An overview of the scientific achievements of the twentieth century. Chapter 3 discusses Cockcroft and Walton's work. Includes many illustrations and index.

Rutherford, Lord Ernest. *The Newer Alchemy*. 1937. Reprint. Whitefish, Mont.: Kessinger, 2003. A brief dis-

cussion of nuclear physics by its founder. Written for a general audience.

Wilson, David. *Rutherford: Simple Genius*. Cambridge, Mass.: MIT Press, 1983. Massive biography of the founder of nuclear physics summarizes what has been said in many other volumes on the "force of nature" who led the Cavendish Laboratory at the time of Cockcroft and Walton's work. Includes illustrations, bibliography, and index.

SEE ALSO: Dec. 10, 1906: Thomson Wins the Nobel Prize for Discovering the Electron; 1912-1913: Bohr Uses Quantum Theory to Identify Atomic Structure; Mar. 7, 1912: Rutherford Describes the Atomic Nucleus; 1914: Rutherford Discovers the Proton; Spring, 1925: Pauli Formulates the Exclusion Principle; Summer, 1928: Gamow Explains Radioactive Alpha Decay with Quantum Tunneling; Feb., 1932: Chadwick Discovers the Neutron; Dec., 1938: Hahn Splits the Uranium Atom.

April 23, 1932
STALIN RESTRICTS SOVIET COMPOSERS

Joseph Stalin's mandate that all Soviet music conform to the dictates of Socialist Realism was complicated by the inherent abstraction of music. This resulted in a situation in which composers were not merely expected to conform to socialist ideology—as were all Soviet artists of the period—but were also subject to the unpredictable dictates of subjective taste on the part of Communist Party leaders, as even the presence or absence of realist representation in a piece of music is an almost entirely subjective matter.

LOCALE: Moscow, Soviet Union (now Russia)
CATEGORIES: Music; civil rights and liberties; social issues and reform

KEY FIGURES
Joseph Stalin (Joseph Vissarionovich Dzhugashvili; 1878-1953), general secretary of the Central Committee of the Communist Party of the Soviet Union, 1922-1953
Karl Radek (1885-1939), Soviet Communist Party official
Andrei Zhdanov (1896-1948), Soviet Communist Party official
Sergei Prokofiev (1891-1953), Soviet composer
Dmitri Shostakovich (1906-1975), Soviet composer

SUMMARY OF EVENT
Socialist Realism was an outgrowth of basic Marxist-Leninist philosophy. "Realism," in the context of socialism, could better be defined as "idealism," given that the goal of socialism is the elusive concept of a perfect, harmonious life for all. The Bolshevik Revolution of 1917 established Marxist-Leninist socialism in what then became the Union of Soviet Socialist Republics. The result was the creation of a totalitarian society that provided a fertile ground for the forced application of socialist goals to all areas of life, including arts and culture.

In 1925, Soviet leadership was seized by Joseph Stalin, who wanted every aspect of Soviet life under his direct control; his massive ego led to the creation of the "Stalin cult" by 1929. This, in turn, allowed Stalin to begin enforcing his brand of socialism throughout the Soviet Union. His First Five-Year Plan (1928-1933) called for all Soviet artists, writers, and musicians, in their creative works, to support his socialist goals by glorifying the real and imaginary accomplishments of the workers and peasants.

From 1929 to 1932, the idea of Socialist Realism emerged. The term is attributed to Stalin himself. In an early definition of the idea, Karl Radek emphasized that reality, in socialist terminology, is not only what is but also what will be. All Soviet citizens involved in the creative arts were thus expected not only to portray the future but also to help create it. They were to become, again in Stalin's words, "engineers of the human mind." The result of that engineering was that the Soviet Union entered a cultural wilderness from which the country did not emerge until after Stalin's death in 1953.

As Stalin was an avid reader, it was natural that the first application of the doctrine of Socialist Realism should have been in the field of literature. Andrei Zhdanov, a top Stalinist official, led the efforts to silence Soviet writers who would not confess their past "errors" of espousing Western views and who would not conform to Socialist Realism. Zhdanov's efforts were soon felt in other cultural areas, including music. Soviet writers, musicians, and others were soon being compelled to produce works envisioning a glorious socialist future.

In the field of music, the major enemy of Socialist Realism was Western formalism. However, in music the distinction between realism (or any form of representation) and formalism (or any form of abstraction) is tenuous at best, lending itself to extremely subjective interpretations of given pieces as either realist or formalist. Unsurprisingly, then, "formalism" soon came to mean anything that Stalin and his top officials did not like or did not understand—and as Stalin rarely attended concerts and apparently knew little about music, the latter category was broad. Certain musical concepts, either correctly or incorrectly identified as Western, were soon officially banned. One of these concepts was atonality, the perceived absence of a tonal center in musical compositions.

The rich heritage of Russian music soon began to suffer. Earlier Russian composers such as Mikhail Glinka, Nikolay Rimsky-Korsakov, Modest Mussorgsky, and Peter Ilich Tchaikovsky had used the age-old themes of Russian nationalist folk music. Soviet composers laboring under Socialist Realism were expected not to renounce the folk traditions but to project them into the socialistic future. Of the earlier musicians, Mussorgsky was the most useful to the architects of Socialist Realism because of his belief that music had to be "true" as well as beautiful. Tchaikovsky was also useful as a model, because his music was international in its scope and thus conformed more readily to the vision of a socialistic world order.

Because music is more abstract than the other arts, it was less easily brought under government control. As long as Soviet composers paid lip service to the dogmas established by the Central Committee of the Communist Party, they were able to maintain more individuality than other artists. Music's inherent abstraction also meant that compositions that included vocal or narrative texts, such as opera or ballet, were best suited to Socialist Realism. Stalin enjoyed these forms because they could combine the nation's rich folk heritage with plots expressing socialistic goals. Even nonvocal music, however, was expected to project those same goals in some manner.

Long before the official proclamation of Socialist Realism, organs were in operation in the Soviet Union to support the ideological goals of the movement. On January 1, 1929, the journal *Proletarskii muzykant* (proletarian musician) began publication in Moscow. In the preface of the first issue, the editors declared that they would be opposing the decadent influence of Western bourgeois music, supporting the ideologically acceptable contributions of the past, and promoting new styles of proletarian music. The editors, however, had not yet been told what those new styles were.

In March, 1931, the Russian Association of Proletarian Musicians held its first convention in Moscow. This group, and similar groups in other cultural arts, was controlled by its own leaders, who were then to obey the dictates of the Central Committee. This arrangement, however, did not give the Central Committee members the immediate control they desired. On April 23, 1932, the Central Committee dissolved by decree the Russian Association of Proletarian Musicians and the other cultural organizations, an event that marked the official beginning of Socialist Realism. From that date until Stalin's death, cultural leadership was in the largely uncultured hands of the members of the Central Committee.

In September, 1934, the Soviet government decreed the amount of money that composers would get for their work; it thus became financially advantageous for composers to create works that supported Socialist Realism. The obvious result was that some musicians, especially the younger ones who were trained after the Bolshevik Revolution in 1917, began to channel their creativity in order to gain favor with Stalin and other government leaders. Sergei Prokofiev, an older composer, dared to remark that Socialist Realism in music really meant the writing of tunes that Stalin could whistle. Later, however, even Prokofiev helped to create those tunes.

SIGNIFICANCE

The first impact of Socialist Realism on music was its application to composers of worldwide fame. Because Stalin enjoyed the music of Ludwig van Beethoven, Beethoven was declared in conformity to Socialist Realism. In fact, some Soviet leaders classified Beethoven as the first Socialist Realist composer. The work of Johann Sebastian Bach, on the other hand, was respectfully rejected by Stalin; Stalin could not perceive the meaning of Bach's compositions. It is obvious that Igor Stravinsky, a Russian composer in exile, was a major factor in the rejection of Bach. Stravinsky sought to return to many of Bach's principles; Stalin interpreted this as an expression of preference for the past rather than for the bright future of socialism.

In 1934, when Stalin's bloody purges of the Soviet Union began, the avalanche of Socialist Realism buried the once-rich Russian culture. Replacing that richness was the ideologically uniform culture of the Communist Party. This new culture was molded around the personal-

Sergei Prokofiev. (Library of Congress)

ity of Joseph Stalin. The terror of the purges had a savage, sadistic twist when it was applied to cultural leaders. Writers and musicians were often forced to be the instruments in declaring their own condemnations. One by one, Soviet composers and other cultural greats either capitulated to the dictates of Socialist Realism or disappeared into the oblivion shared by many others who were a perceived threat to Stalin's tyranny.

Sergei Prokofiev provides a classic example of the impact of the constant and ever-increasing pressure of the state's mandate to conform to the values of Socialist Realism. After living and working in Paris during the 1920's, Prokofiev returned to the Soviet Union in 1934. He first tried to ignore the concept of Socialist Realism, but this soon proved to be impossible. Prokofiev's music then became more practical and even propagandistic. For the remainder of his life, Prokofiev fell in and out of favor with the leaders of Socialist Realism. The reasons for the periodic attacks on Prokofiev remained obscure to Western observers, given that most of his music appeared to conform to the dictates of Socialist Realism.

The government's reception of Dmitri Shostakovich provides the best example of the official cultural policy toward the younger Soviet composers who were trained after 1917. The starting point for the music of Shostakovich was Beethoven—which put Shostakovich in good favor with the government of Stalin. Shostakovich, however, soon exhibited a spirit of individuality that provoked official criticism. His famous opera *Ledi Makbet Mtsenskogo uezda* (1930-1932; *Lady Macbeth of the Mtsensk District*) is an intense satire that fell far short of Socialist Realism. Trouble for Shostakovich began when Stalin attended a performance of this opera. After being sharply attacked, Shostakovich tried, without immediate success, to redeem himself. Finally, his Fifth Symphony in 1937 sufficiently conformed to accepted standards, and Shostakovich settled down to produce a series of patriotic works with heroic themes. His later *Leningrad Symphony* (1941) expressed both the fury of the German invasion of the Soviet Union and the successful Soviet defense of the city and country.

Two other composers of the post-1917 generation, Aram Khachaturian and Dmitry Kabalevsky, were sufficiently able to uphold the ideals of Socialist Realism so as to avoid serious criticism. To some Western critics, however, the music of these men had a superficial character that might have been absent in a free environment. Fortunately for Soviet composers, the bloody purges of the late 1930's concentrated on perceived political and literary threats to Stalin. The purges were soon followed by World War II (called the "Great Patriotic War" in the Soviet Union), when all energies were directed toward survival.

The end of World War II in 1945, and the simultaneous advent of the Cold War with the West, initiated a revival of Socialist Realism in the Soviet Union. A pathetic scene was created in 1946 when Prokofiev, Shostakovich, and Khachaturian were forced to repent publicly for some of their earlier works that did not uphold the tenets of Socialist Realism. Soviet citizens were accustomed to seeing their political leaders publicly confess to imaginary crimes, but seeing their composers and other cultural leaders grovel at the feet of Stalin was a shock. For most of the remainder of his life, Prokofiev conformed, at least outwardly, to Socialist Realism, although not without criticism. Vocal texts were often added to his compositions to help achieve the desired goals. One of his last works, *On Guard for Peace* (1950), was widely hailed by Soviet leaders.

From 1946 to 1948, the revival of Socialist Realism was led by its earlier spokesman, Andrei Zhdanov. By then a secretary of the Central Committee of the Communist Party, Zhdanov demanded the total abolishment of Western cultural influences. Because independence was the greatest threat to Socialist Realism, the most independent-minded composer, Shostakovich, was specifically attacked. Shostakovich then performed the usual repentance and produced several works in honor of Stalin. Zhdanov's death in 1948 did not mean the end of his campaign. Although his replacement, Mikhail Suslov, preferred to work behind the scenes, the pressure to conform with Socialist Realism did not weaken. Once again, Prokofiev was attacked and forced to recant in a letter to the Central Committee.

The total impact of Socialist Realism on Russian culture becomes clear when it is realized that professional composers were compelled to produce their work according to the dictates of professional politicians who knew little or nothing about music. The very livelihood of the composers, who were under contract to the State Committee on Arts, depended on their conformity to those dictates. This did not mean that the composers were mere stooges of the Communist Party. The subtle nature of music, combined with the musical ignorance of most party leaders, meant that the good composers could still manifest their independence. One cannot help but wonder, however, what kinds of works Prokofiev, Shostakovich, and others would have produced if they had not been compelled to labor under the weight of Socialist Realism.

The death of Stalin in March, 1953, brought sighs of relief in many areas of Soviet life. One of these areas was culture. The full weight of Socialist Realism died with Stalin; Stalin's successors found milder means of cultural control. As the reality of this began to spread, musicians and others began to produce more independent works.

—Glenn L. Swygart

FURTHER READING

Bek, Mikuláš, Geoffrey Chew, and Petr Macek, eds. *Socialist Realism and Music*. Brno, Czech Republic: Institute of Musicology, Masaryk University, 2004. Proceedings of a conference on Socialist Realism in music held in Brno in 2001. Includes relevant sheet music from compositions discussed in the papers presented.

Dobrenko, Evgeny. *Aesthetics of Alienation: Reassessment of Early Soviet Cultural Theories*. Evanston, Ill.: Northwestern University Press, 2005. Study of Soviet aethetics, specific governmental groups and institutions, and their negotiations by individual artists. Includes a chapter on the Prolekult movement's effects on Soviet music and composition. Bibliographic references and index.

Fitzsimmons, Thomas, Peter Malof, and John C. Fiske. *U.S.S.R.: Its People, Its Society, Its Culture*. New Haven, Conn.: HRAF Press, 1960. Provides an excellent overview of Soviet life and culture. Published just seven years after Stalin's death, this book is valuable for readers who are not familiar with Stalin and the oppression of his regime.

Heller, Mikhail, and Aleksandr Nekrich. *Utopia in Power*. New York: Summit Books, 1985. Written originally in Russian by authors who were raised and educated in the Soviet Union, this book reveals the tragic effects of Marxist-Leninist socialism on Russia. Particularly valuable in showing the reader the progress of Socialist Realism after World War II.

Kulski, W. W. "The Party and the West." In *The Soviet Regime: Communism in Practice*. Syracuse, N.Y.: Syracuse University Press, 1954. This chapter by Kulski presents a detailed picture of Stalin's attempt to rid the Soviet Union of all Western influences, including music styles. The author defines what the Central Committee of the Communist Party meant in classifying Western music as "pathological." Readers familiar with composers such as Prokofiev and Shostakovich will better understand the pressure under which they labored.

1932

Randall, Francis B. "The Culture." In *Stalin's Russia.* New York: Free Press, 1965. Randall tries to analyze Stalin's personality in order better to understand Socialist Realism. He emphasizes the use of censorship and terror to discourage dissent by cultural leaders. Compares what Stalin called the "bourgeois realism" of the nineteenth century with the Socialist Realism of the twentieth century.

Salzman, Eric. "National Styles." In *Twentieth Century Music: An Introduction.* Englewood Cliffs, N.J.: Prentice-Hall, 1974. Salzman presents an excellent survey of twentieth century music styles. Himself a composer, the author in this chapter discusses the influence of Socialist Realism on Soviet composers and also describes the changes it produced in the Soviet Union's nationalist music styles.

Treadgold, Donald W. "Stalin's Cultural Policy, 1927-1945." In *Twentieth Century Russia.* 9th ed. Boulder, Colo.: Westview Press, 2000. In this chapter, the author, a respected scholar of Soviet studies, evaluates Socialist Realism in the light of Stalin's full totalitarian rule. Reveals the influence of the Communist Party and officials such as Zhdanov in determining what was or was not acceptable in music and other cultural areas.

SEE ALSO: Dec. 17, 1915: Malevich Introduces Suprematism; 1929-1930: *The Bedbug* and *The Bathhouse* Exemplify Revolutionary Theater; Apr. 23, 1932-Aug., 1934: Socialist Realism Is Mandated in Soviet Literature; 1934: Soviet Union Bans Abstract Art; Feb., 1934: Rivera's Rockefeller Center Mural Is Destroyed; Jan. 28, 1936: Soviets Condemn Shostakovich's *Lady Macbeth of the Mtsensk District.*

April 23, 1932-August, 1934
SOCIALIST REALISM IS MANDATED IN SOVIET LITERATURE

The Communist state regimented the Soviet literary world, reversing the encouragement of artistic innovation shown in the years immediately following the 1917 revolution.

LOCALE: Soviet Union (now Russia)
CATEGORIES: Literature; civil rights and liberties; social issues and reform

KEY FIGURES
Joseph Stalin (Joseph Vissarionovich Dzhugashvili; 1878-1953), general secretary of the Central Committee of the Communist Party of the Soviet Union, 1922-1953
Andrei Zhdanov (1896-1948), secretary of the Bolskevik Central Committee
Maxim Gorky (Aleksey Maksimovich Peshkov; 1868-1936), first president of the Soviet Writers' Union
Leopold Averbakh (1903-1939), Soviet literary critic and leader of the Russian Association of Proletarian Writers
Nikolay Ivanovich Bukharin (1888-1938), political rival of Stalin

SUMMARY OF EVENT
The year 1932 was a milestone in Russian literary history. Persecution of literary figures in the Soviet Union had begun before 1932, and it would worsen later, as part of an even more rigorous regimentation of the arts in general. It was in 1932, however, that the Soviet government officially eschewed pluralism and tolerance of differing literary ideologies. Instead, it was declared that Socialist Realism was to be the only school of Soviet literature; all other literary movements were prohibited.

Under Communism, the age of broadest freedom for Soviet writers before the late 1980's was the New Economic Policy era (1921-1928). Led by Vladimir Ilich Lenin, the Bolsheviks, victors in the Russian Revolution of 1917 and the subsequent civil war, did not at first try to enforce literary conformity. Indeed, they welcomed a plurality of viewpoints, in keeping with Karl Marx's ideal of the free expression of species-being. A spirit of experimentation flourished in poetry, fiction, drama, music, and cinema. Vladimir Mayakovsky, a fiery young poet and playwright who would commit suicide in 1930, ardently defended both the new regime and avant-garde literature. Exile was not yet permanent; the literary portrayer of late czarist Russia's urban poor, the novelist and playwright Maxim Gorky, left the Soviet Union in 1921 but was later allowed to return home. Writers were even permitted to maintain contacts with Western European publishing houses. In contrast with later periods, varied schools of literary thought were permitted.

Two principal types of Soviet writers coexisted in the 1920's: the proletarians, who glorified the new regime in works of fiction about the Russian Civil War (1918-1921) and the tasks of reconstruction, and the fellow travelers, who, although they did not make propaganda for the new regime, were non-Communist rather than anti-Communist. Proletarian novelists included Fedor Vasil'evich Gladkov, Aleksandr Aleksandrovich Fadeev, and Mikhail Sholokhov. The satirist Yevgeny Zamyatin, the short-story writers Boris Pilnyak and Isaac Babel, and the novelists Konstantin Aleksandrovich Fedin, Aleksey Nikolayevich Tolstoy, Yury Olesha, and Leonid Maksimovich Leonov were fellow travelers. Mediating between the two was Aleksandr Voronsky, a literary critic and editor of the journal *Red Virgin Soil*, who urged both government aid to and broad freedom for writers. In June, 1925, the Communist Party Central Committee, while explicitly encouraging proletarian literature, ordained continued freedom for other approaches as well.

Politics destroyed this climate of tolerance. After Lenin died in 1924, Nikolay Ivanovich Bukharin, Leon Trotsky, and Joseph Stalin vied for power; by the end of 1929, Stalin had won the upper hand. Stalin believed in agricultural collectivization and rapid industrialization, but not in freedom for the arts. In 1927, Voronsky had to resign the editorship of *Red Virgin Soil*. Mayakovsky's satirical plays *Klop* (pr., pb. 1929; *The Bedbug*, 1931) and *Banya* (pr., pb. 1930; *The Bathhouse*, 1963) were withdrawn from the stage after sharp official criticism. In August, 1929, the leader of the Russian Association of Proletarian Writers (RAPP), Leopold Averbakh, attacked Pilnyak and Zamyatin as traitors. Pilnyak's career was ruined; Zamyatin left Russia in 1931. RAPP seemed about to take over the Soviet literary world.

On April 23, 1932, the Communist Party suddenly called a halt to the strife by ordering that all competing literary associations be dissolved, to be replaced by a single Soviet Writers' Union. The term "Socialist Realism," first used by *Izvestia* editor Ivan Gronsky in a speech of May 20, 1932, was defined publicly by Stalin's spokesman Andrei Zhdanov at the First Congress of the Soviet Writers' Union held in August, 1934. Although this congress had a pro-Stalin majority, it was attended by writers of all viewpoints, including such mavericks as Babel, Olesha, and the poet Boris Pasternak, as well as by the out-of-favor Communist Bukharin, who praised Pasternak's poetry. Gorky, back from Italian exile, was named president of the new union; his novel *Mat* (1906; *The Mother*, 1906), about a woman converted to the revolutionary cause by her son, was now praised as a model of Socialist Realism. The adoption by the congress of So-

cialist Realism as an official creed was a bad omen, yet some writers, tired of the zealotry of RAPP, mistakenly thought that a new era of tolerance was at hand.

After Leningrad party boss Sergey Mironovich Kirov was assassinated in December, 1934, Stalin's purges began. In 1938, Bukharin was tried and executed. Vladimir Stavsky, who headed the Writers' Union after Gorky's death in 1936, ferreted out suspected anti-Stalinists among the literati. Artist victims of the purges included Ivan Katayev, who had once written a short story expressing doubts about agricultural collectivization, Pilnyak, Babel, the poet Osip Mandelstam, and the innovative theatrical director Vsevolod Yemilyevich Meyerhold. Ironically, Averbakh himself was purged as an alleged Trotskyite; fellow RAPP member Fadeev survived to become a key Soviet Writers' Union bureaucrat. The purge was the final stage in the regimentation of literature.

Socialist Realism may be viewed as mixing formal conservatism with ideological radicalism in its content, although many literary critics believe that ideology is inseparable from form, greatly complicating that formulation. Initially applied to fiction, it was later imposed on the theater, motion pictures, the visual arts, and music. The novel was seen as the highest expression of literature; its protagonist, according to the doctrine, should be a positive hero who fights for the goals of socialism and attains these goals despite stiff social or natural obstacles. A novel should pay heed to the Communist Party's role in guiding people toward a new society; its ending must be happy for the community as a whole, if not for individuals. Writers were urged to use a simple style, avoiding any experimentation that might make their works difficult for ordinary people to comprehend, yet they were also commanded to go beyond mere realism and to educate people toward socialism. Ironically, such "realist" literature often ended up sugarcoating some of the harsher realities of life in the Soviet state.

SIGNIFICANCE

Any discussion of the impact of the imposition of Socialist Realism on Soviet writers must treat both the effect on individual writers and the effect on those writers taken as a group. Even in the Stalinist era, not all writers who strayed from Socialist Realism were purged. Some, unwilling to produce literature of the approved type, simply stopped writing original work altogether. Olesha, who published nothing from 1934 until the 1950's, was one of these; so was Pasternak, who turned from poetry writing to translation. If permitted to remain writers, those literati who were judged to have deviated from the creed either revised their own works or saw them revised by others.

Loyalty to the creed of Socialist Realism was enforced with carrots as well as with sticks. After 1934, writers who became members of the Writers' Union and steered clear of Stalin's wrath were guaranteed a market for their writings; various material perquisites were also attached to membership in the Writers' Union. Those recognized as writers by the state came to enjoy both high social status and a privileged lifestyle, important considerations given the narrow range of white-collar occupations permitted in a socialist economy. Just how seductive the allure of privilege could be is indicated by the fact that some of the writers who did well under Stalin (such as Aleksey Tolstoy) had been fellow travelers rather than proletarian writers in the 1920's.

The enforcement of Socialist Realism as the state literary school was somewhat capricious. Once the creed was imposed, works published by first-time writers under official auspices adhered to Socialist Realism slavishly. Hence a book such as the autobiographical novel *Kak zakalyalas stal* (1932-1934; *The Making of a Hero*, 1937), by Nikolai Alekseevich Ostrovsky, about a boy from a poverty-stricken background who fights bravely for Bolshevism despite severe physical handicaps, is regarded as an example of Socialist Realism by both Russian and Western critics. However, some works published before 1932 that are cited by Russian literary critics as models of Socialist Realism are found by Western critics to deviate from that literary creed in some way.

Thus Sholokhov's *Tikhy Don* (1928-1940; translated in two parts as *And Quiet Flows the Don*, 1934, and *The Don Flows Home to the Sea*, 1940), the first two volumes of which were published in 1928-1929, is not only beautifully written but also remarkably impartial. In this novel of the civil war in the Don Cossack country, the Bolsheviks are not portrayed as plaster saints, nor are their enemies cartoon villains. The protagonist, no positive hero, switches back and forth between the Bolshevik and anti-Bolshevik sides, and the ending is not a happy one, yet because of the enormous popularity of the novel both in the Soviet Union and abroad, Communist critics praised it as a Socialist Realist classic. Sholokhov's fame may even have saved him from being purged in the 1930's. In his hurriedly produced novel about agricultural collectivization, *Podnyataya tselina* (1932; *Virgin Soil Upturned*, 1935), Sholokhov tried harder to glorify the role of the Communist Party without entirely glossing over the disruptions collectivization had imposed on the peasantry.

On the other hand, Leonov's *Doroga na okean* (1935; *Road to the Ocean*, 1944) was severely criticized for its pessimism, individualism, and emphasis on personal tragedy and death, and it was practically suppressed. Leonov, turning to the writing of plays, did not publish another novel until 1953. Fedin was not punished in the 1930's for his somewhat unorthodox (by 1934 standards) work of the 1920's; he did, however, try to ingratiate himself with Stalin's new order in art by writing a cliché-filled novel, *Pohkishchenie Evropy* (1933-1935; the rape of Europe). In the cases of Sholokhov, Fedin, and Leonov, one could argue that the contortions necessary to make their literary works politically acceptable stultified to some extent the creativity that all three had shown in the 1920's.

During World War II, controls were relaxed; the strictest enforcement of Socialist Realism came during the period between the end of the war in 1945 and Stalin's death in 1953. In 1946, the satirist Mikhail Zoshchenko, tolerated up to that time, was driven from his profession by Zhdanov, Stalin's cultural watchdog, for a story that seemed to compare Soviet man to an ape. Even Fadeev, a party literary stalwart, was compelled to rewrite his World War II novel *Molodaya gvardia* (1946; the young guard) because it did not sufficiently emphasize the role played in the war effort by the Communist Party. Writers were now expected to refrain from portraying either the less pleasant sides of Soviet society or the conflicts within it. During the period from 1945 to 1953, Socialist Realism was also imposed on the literary world in those Eastern European states on which Stalin had imposed Communist regimes. Thus it grew from the mandated literary school of the Soviet Union to become the mandated literary school everwhere the Communist Party held sway.

—Paul D. Mageli

FURTHER READING

Brown, Edward J. *The Proletarian Episode in Russian Literature, 1928-1932*. New York: Columbia University Press, 1953. This study of the rise and fall of Leopold Averbakh and RAPP emphasizes the diversity of viewpoints within the proletarian literary movement. Views proletarian writers not as mere fanatics but as defenders of artistic autonomy and victims of Stalin's regimentation of literature. Endnotes, selected bibliography, index.

Clark, Katerina. *The Soviet Novel: History as Ritual*. 3d ed. Bloomington: Indiana University Press, 2000. Using the tools of anthropology and literary criticism,

Clark, examining novels by various authors, outlines a prototypical Socialist Realist plot. Denies that Socialist Realism was simply imposed by bureaucrats; sees its roots in pre-revolutionary literature and its influence in the writings of post-1953 dissidents. Endnotes, bibliography, index.

Dobrenko, Evgeny. *Aesthetics of Alienation: Reassessment of Early Soviet Cultural Theories.* Evanston, Ill.: Northwestern University Press, 2005. Study of Soviet literary aethetics, specific governmental groups and institutions, and their negotiations by individual authors. Bibliographic references and index.

Ermolaev, Herman. *Soviet Literary Theories, 1917-1934: The Genesis of Socialist Realism.* University of California Publications in Modern Philology 69. Berkeley: University of California Press, 1963. A pathbreaking study, repeatedly cited by scholars of Communist-era Russian literature. Analyzes critical articles, speeches, resolutions, and debates. The treatment of the period from 1932 to 1934, when an official definition of Socialist Realism was hammered out, is especially good. Sees Socialist Realism as imposed by Stalin. Endnotes, bibliography, index.

Estraikh, Gennady. *In Harness: Yiddish Writers' Romance with Communism.* Syracuse, N.Y.: Syracuse University Press, 2005. Study of Yiddish writers in the Soviet Union, ending with a chapter on Socialist Realism in Soviet Yiddish literature. Bibliographic references and index.

Garrard, John, and Carol Garrard. *Inside the Soviet Writers' Union.* New York: Free Press, 1990. Contains two historical chapters that treat the Stalin era. The account of the 1934 Writers' Congress relies partly on survivors' testimony published in the 1980's. Tries to estimate exactly how many writers were purged by Stalin. No analysis of literary works. Endnotes, index.

Maguire, Robert A. *Red Virgin Soil: Soviet Literature in the 1920's.* Princeton, N.J.: Princeton University Press, 1968. A history not just of Voronsky's journal but also of literary politics in the 1920's. Suggests that writers' poverty spurred them to form associations to secure government help and argues that Socialist Realism combined Voronsky's reverence for past literary models with the activism of the proletarian writers. Footnotes, index, bibliography.

Simmons, Ernest J. *Russian Fiction and Soviet Ideology: Introduction to Fedin, Leonov, and Sholokhov.* New York: Columbia University Press, 1958. Shows how three writers who had made their reputations in the relatively liberal 1920's adapted to the literary dogmatism prevalent in the 1930's; the damage done to artistic integrity varied with each writer, being probably greatest with Leonov. List of works discussed, index, photographs of each writer.

Struve, Gleb. *Russian Literature Under Lenin and Stalin, 1917-1953.* Norman: University of Oklahoma Press, 1971. A useful survey. Nine chapters out of thirty treat the 1930's; the 1934 Writers' Congress gets an entire chapter. Sees proletarian writers as accomplices in, as well as victims of, Stalin's regimentation of literature. Discusses the influence of Socialist Realism on fiction, poetry, and drama. Bibliography, footnotes, index.

1932

SEE ALSO: Dec. 17, 1915: Malevich Introduces Suprematism; 1929-1930: *The Bedbug* and *The Bathhouse* Exemplify Revolutionary Theater; Apr. 23, 1932: Stalin Restricts Soviet Composers; 1934: Soviet Union Bans Abstract Art; Feb., 1934: Rivera's Rockefeller Center Mural Is Destroyed; Jan. 28, 1936: Soviets Condemn Shostakovich's *Lady Macbeth of the Mtsensk District.*

May 20-21, 1932
FIRST TRANSATLANTIC SOLO FLIGHT BY A WOMAN

Amelia Earhart, an American aviator, was the first woman to fly solo across the Atlantic Ocean, becoming a national hero and an ardent advocate for female independence. She died attempting to become the first female pilot to fly around the world.

LOCALE: Atlantic Ocean from Canada to Ireland
CATEGORIES: Space and aviation; transportation; women's issues

KEY FIGURES
Amelia Earhart (1897-1937), pioneer aviator and the first woman to fly solo across the Atlantic
Frederick Joseph Noonan (1893-1937), navigator on Pan-American Airlines's mapping flights in the Pacific and Earhart's navigator
George P. Putnam (1887-1950), Earhart's husband and publicist

SUMMARY OF EVENT
For decades after her death, Amelia Earhart remained the most famous female American aviator. During her brief career in aviation, she set many aviation records, including being the first female pilot to fly solo across the Atlantic. She actively promoted the growth of the air transportation industry and the role of women in aviation.

Earhart was born in Atchison, Kansas, on July 24, 1897. During World War I she lived in Toronto, Canada, where she served as a nurse at a military hospital. After the war, she enrolled as a premed student at Columbia University, but she did not finish the training. In 1920 Earhart moved to California and took her first flight in an airplane, a 10-minute ride over Los Angeles. She began taking flying lessons almost immediately, and her instructor, Anita Snook, was one of the world's first female pilots. Earhart bought her first airplane, a Kinner Airster that she named *The Canary*, on her twenty-fourth birthday. A few months later, in October, she set a new women's altitude record of 14,000 feet in *The Canary*.

Earhart moved to Boston, where she worked as a social worker, but she continued to be interested in aviation, and she publicized the role of women in aviation at a time when women had just been given the right to vote in the United States. Her activities brought her to the attention of George P. Putnam, the New York City publicist who had promoted Charles Lindbergh's book *We* (1927), which described Lindbergh's 1927 solo flight across the Atlantic Ocean. Putnam had been hired by Amy Guest, a wealthy American living in London, to identify someone suitable to be the first female to fly across the Atlantic Ocean. Guest had purchased Commander Richard Byrd's Fokker F7, a powerful three-engine airplane, and she had initially intended to be the first woman passenger on a transatlantic flight. Guest's family objected to the risk such a journey posed, however, and Putnam recommended Earhart for the flight.

Although Earhart was a licensed pilot, she had no experience flying an airplane that had more than one engine, and she had much more experience navigating with ground references than with more advanced navigational instruments. For these reasons, Earhart was a passenger on the flight, which was piloted by Wilmer Stultz and Louis Gordon. On June 18, 1928, the Fokker F7, named *Friendship*, took off from Trepassy, Newfoundland. Stultz, Gordon, and Earhart flew through dense fog for most of the trip, which made navigation difficult. They completely missed Ireland, their intended destination. After a flight that lasted 20 hours and 40 minutes, *Friendship* landed at Burry Port in South Wales with almost no fuel to spare.

The welcoming crowd paid little attention to Stultz and Gordon, since men had already flown the Atlantic. Instead, the media seized on Earhart's role as the first woman to cross the Atlantic in an airplane. Earhart, however, was uncomfortable with the acclaim she received, since she had only been a passenger on the flight. As a publicist, Putnam recognized the significance of being a record-breaker, and he began arranging Earhart's career. He organized a national speaking tour and a cross-country flight for Earhart, who described her first transatlantic flight in her book *Twenty Hours, Forty Minutes* (1928). Earhart married Putnam in 1931. She bought a new aircraft, a Lockheed Vega, and set several women's speed records in her new airplane.

Piloting a craft across the Atlantic remained a challenge for Earhart. On the evening of May 20, 1932, five years after Lindbergh left on his own solo flight across the Atlantic, Earhart took off from Harbor Grace, Newfoundland. This time she was both the pilot and the only occupant of her single-engine Lockheed Vega. She encountered good weather for several hours and was able to navigate using the moon's position in the sky. Then the altimeter, which displays the height of the aircraft above sea level, failed, and the Vega encountered a severe thunderstorm. Earhart struggled to keep the plane level in the

First Transatlantic Solo Flight by a Woman

Amelia Earhart's Final Flight, 1937

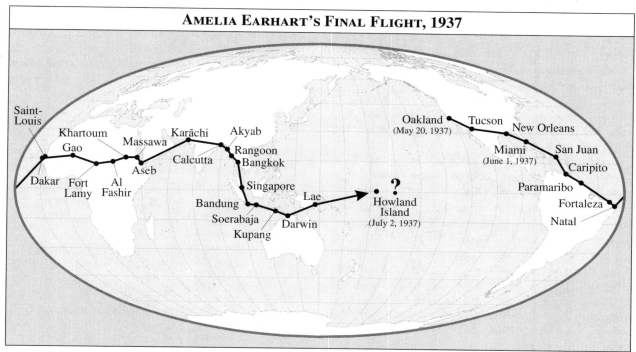

Amelia Earhart disappeared somewhere between Lae and Howland Island in July, 1937, while attempting to fly around the world.

storm as the updrafts and downdrafts stressed the plane's structure. It was night, and she saw flames coming from a cracked weld on the engine. Hours later, with her aircraft running low on fuel and flames continuing to come from the engine, Earhart saw the Irish coast. She landed in a field near Londonderry, Ireland, at 2:30 P.M. on May 21, where she was greeted by a surprised farm laborer.

Earhart set four world's records on the flight: The flight was the fastest crossing of the Atlantic by air (in 14 hours, 54 minutes) and the longest distance flown by a woman (2,206 miles), and Earhart became both the first woman to fly solo across the Atlantic Ocean and the only person to have flown across the Atlantic twice. When she returned to the United States, President Herbert Hoover presented her with a medal from the National Geographic Society, and she received a ticker-tape parade in New York City.

After her second transatlantic flight, Earhart became active in encouraging the development of commercial aviation. She served as vice president of Luddington Airlines,

Earhart Sets the Record Straight

In 1932, the National Geographic Society awarded Amelia Earhart its Special Medal in recognition of her transatlantic flight. In her acceptance speech, Earhart debunked some of the popular stories that had circulated about the flight:

Some features of the flight I fear have been exaggerated. It made a much better story to say I landed with but one gallon of gasoline left. As a matter of fact, I had more than a hundred. The exact quantity I remember because I had to pay a tax for every gallon imported into Ireland!

I did not land within six feet (2 meters) of a hedge of trees. I taxied to the upper end of a sloping pasture and turned my plane into the shelter of some trees, as a matter of course. It made a much better story the other way, I admit.

No flames were threatening to burn my plane in the air. I did have some trouble with my exhaust manifold, of which I shall tell you later. There was no extreme hazard from that cause, however.

I did not kill a cow in landing—unless one died of fright. Of course, I came down in a pasture and I had to circle many other pastures to find the best one. The horses, sheep, and cows in Londonderry were not used to airplanes, and so, as I flew low, they jumped up and down and displayed certain disquiet. I really was afraid that an Irishman would shoot me as I stepped out of the plane, thinking that I was just a "smart Alec" from some big town come down to scare the cattle.

which provided passenger service between New York and Washington, D.C., and wrote her second book, *The Fun of It* (1932). Three years after her solo transatlantic flight, Earhart became the first person to fly from Hawaii to the U.S. mainland, a 2,408-mile flight across the Pacific Ocean. Before her successful flight, ten pilots had died attempting this journey. Earhart's voyage had the further distinction of being the first time a civilian aircraft carried a two-way radio.

On May 20, 1937, Earhart set out from Oakland, California, in a twin-engine Lockheed Electra in an attempt to fly around the world. Fred Noonan served as navigator on the flight, the route of which went from Miami to Puerto Rico, South America, Africa, India, and Australia. On June 29, Earhart and Noonan reached New Guinea and had only 7,000 miles left to go. On July 2, they left New Guinea on the most difficult segment of the trip, a 2,556-mile flight to Howland Island, which was only 6,000 feet long and 1,500 feet wide. They carried a two-way radio, and their last confirmed position report was over the Nukumanu Islands, about 800 miles along their route. The Coast Guard cutter *Itasca* was at Howland Island to communicate with Earhart and help her locate the small island, but the *Itasca* never received a clear transmission from Earhart, and an intensive search found no trace of her, Noonan, or their plane. The disappearance became one of the unsolved mysteries of the twentieth century.

SIGNIFICANCE

Earhart used her fame as an aviator to promote two causes in which she strongly believed: She became an advocate for the developing industry of passenger air transportation, and she encouraged an increasingly prominent role for women in aviation. Earhart's second transatlantic flight demonstrated the growing safety of airplane flight. Prior to this flight, several pilots had perished on their first attempt to cross the Atlantic, but only a few years later, on March 26, 1939, Pan-American Airlines made its first trial transatlantic flight, from Baltimore, Maryland, to Foynes, Ireland, using a Boeing-314 Yankee Clipper. By the 1970's, jet airplanes had replaced ocean liners as the most common mode of transatlantic travel.

In 1929, Earhart cofounded the Ninety-Nines, an international organization of female pilots, and she served as its first president. The Ninety-Nines, which grew to more than five thousand members, continued to promote opportunities for women in aviation and offered the Amelia Earhart Memorial Scholarship to support female pilots trying to complete advanced pilot-training courses. As part of her support of women's rights, Earhart suggested that women be drafted to fight in wars just like men.

—*George J. Flynn*

FURTHER READING

Gilbert, James B., and Amelia Earhart. *Twenty Hours, Forty Minutes: Our Flight in the "Friendship."* Salem, N.H.: Ayer, 1979. Earhart's own account of her first transatlantic flight includes copies of pages from her flight log and many photographs.

Lovell, Mary S. *The Sound of Wings: The Life of Amelia Earhart.* New York: St. Martin's Press, 1989. A well-researched account of Earhart's life from her childhood to her consuming quest for aviation fame. Well illustrated; includes twenty-four pages of photographs.

Morrissey, Muriel Earhart, and Carol L. Osborne. *Amelia, My Courageous Sister: Biography of Amelia Earhart.* Santa Clara, Calif.: Osborne, 1987. Earhart's sister provides an account of the pilot's life and achievements in aviation. Includes many family pictures, letters, and documents.

Rich, Doris L. *Amelia Earhart: A Biography.* Washington, D.C.: Smithsonian Books, 1989. Account of Earhart's life includes discussion of her first flying experience, how she was selected to be the first woman to fly across the Atlantic, her marriage to Putnam, her support of women's rights, and her attempt to fly around the world.

Van Pelt, Lori. *Amelia Earhart: The Sky's No Limit.* New York: Forge Press, 2005. Brief account of the life and achievements of Amelia Earhart emphasizes her efforts to refuse all limits on the role of women in American society.

SEE ALSO: Dec. 17, 1903: Wright Brothers' First Flight; July 25, 1909: First Airplane Flight Across the English Channel; Aug. 26, 1920: U.S. Women Gain the Right to Vote; Sept. 8, 1920: U.S. Post Office Begins Transcontinental Airmail Delivery; May 20, 1926: Air Commerce Act Creates a Federal Airways System; May 20, 1927: Lindbergh Makes the First Nonstop Transatlantic Flight; June 25, 1936: The DC-3 Opens a New Era of Air Travel; June 30, 1940: Congress Centralizes Regulation of U.S. Commercial Air Traffic.

July 3, 1932
JOOSS'S ANTIWAR DANCE *THE GREEN TABLE* PREMIERES

Kurt Jooss's The Green Table, *a powerful commentary on the futility of war, extended the subject matter and technical range of modern dance.*

LOCALE: Théâtre des Champs-Élyseés, Paris, France
CATEGORY: Dance

KEY FIGURES
Kurt Jooss (1901-1979), German choreographer and
    dancer
Fritz A. Cohen (1904-1967), German composer
Hein Heckroth (1901-1970), German designer of
    theatrical sets and costumes

SUMMARY OF EVENT
The Green Table is a *danse macabre* in contemporary terms. Consisting of six scenes, a prologue, and an epilogue, the work presents the consequences of war and their related social results realistically in a stylized, unromanticized manner. Before the dance begins, discordant piano sounds foretell the ominous atmosphere of the ballet that will unfold. The music then changes into a light-hearted cabaret tango. The curtain opens to reveal a rectangular conference table covered in green; the table is lined on two sides by diplomats dressed in black morning coats and spats and wearing grotesque masks. The factions on either side of the table engage in rituals of diplomacy, making points and counterpoints, bickering among themselves, and almost coming to blows with the opposing group. A feigned mood of courtesy prevails as the arbiters gesticulate in puppetlike fashion. The scene concludes in response to the rising insurmountable tensions among the diplomats. Finding no solution to their discussion, they remove pistols from their vests, bow politely to one another, lift their arms upward, and shoot the pistols into the air, symbolically releasing a pattern of violence that will bring death, injury, and tragedy. The stage goes dark.

The grisly image of Death is then gradually revealed out of the blackness. Death, who dominates the work, is humanized as a skeleton and is garbed in the breastplate and helmet of Mars, the god of war. His menacing, repetitive, marchlike steps evoke a sense of doom.

The Standard-Bearer enters, holding a banner and rallying troops. Forces for battle are assembled, trained, and called to action. The combatants take leave of their sweethearts and mothers, and the story of war continues. The cunning Profiteer, a sleazy character whose pleasure

derives from the misfortunes of others, is portrayed. The hovering, ever-present Death claims his victims one by one and triumphantly leads them in a procession of the dead. The figure of Death fades into blackness. Pistol shots ring out, and the scene returns to the conference table. Friendly relations are resumed, and the politicians once more enact their charade, which freezes in a stalemate.

The conceptualization of the libretto for *The Green Table* grew gradually over a ten-year period. Kurt Jooss had seen a sequence of medieval drawings of individuals from various walks of life dancing with Death, personified as a skeleton. Jooss found the dance of death a fascinating subject and thought the idea could be a proposal for an actual dance work. He also interpolated memories of World War I and the Depression into the piece. Jooss was an avid reader of *Die Weltbühne*, a German periodical edited by Carl von Ossie. The magazine published political writings by Kurt Tucholsky that concerned moral integrity and the struggle for human decency; Tucholsky's work directly affected the political overtones of *The Green Table*.

Movement for the ballet stemmed, in part, from Jooss's study with Rudolf Laban, an innovative teacher and theorist of the style of "plastic rhythm," or motion for its own sake. This extremely different form of dance expression rejected the artificiality and structure of classical ballet that existed in German dance prior to World War I. Laban elaborated on the principles of anatomical expression and gesture set forth by François Delsarte in the mid-nineteenth century. In 1921, Jooss began to study with Laban at the National Theater in Mannheim, Germany, later becoming his assistant and principal dancer. Subsequently, Jooss founded Neue Tanzbühne (New Dance Stage), a separate entity of the state theater in Münster. The group included the dancers Sigurd Leeder and Aino Sümola, the composer and conductor Fritz A. Cohen, and the designer Hein Heckroth. The company toured throughout Germany for a two-year period presenting a repertoire of Jooss's works.

Jooss's search for expression in a personal manner led him to merge and reorganize new ideas in theater dance continually. He traveled to Paris and Vienna in the winter of 1926 with Sigurd Leeder to study, both in mind and body, the system of classical ballet. While gaining physical mastery of classical dance, Jooss examined its technique and pedagogy. He adapted some of these ideas into

1932

2569

Jooss's Antiwar Dance The Green Table *Premieres*   THE TWENTIETH CENTURY, 1901-1940

his choreographic endeavors as he sought to give clarity to performance. Jooss earned the hostility of his classical as well as his modern dance colleagues in 1928, when he candidly stated that the rivalry between the two dance forms was absurd.

The Green Table synthesizes these two forms of dance, combining the dramatic expression of modern dance with ballet technique. The choreography utilizes the range of everyday movement while adding strong distinctive patterns for the soldiers, diplomats, and other dancers. Identifying movements used only by the Profiteer and Death were created.

The music moves along with the dancing and does not influence the shape of the choreography or its movement. At times the score conveys the atmosphere, which ranges from foreboding to lyrical to plaintive.

The masks used for *The Green Table* evolved in response to practical considerations. With only sixteen dancers in the piece, requiring a quick change of the opening scene and a change of costumes, the possibility of applying makeup was negligible. As the dancers had to look grotesque for the prologue and epilogue, masks were designed to transform their appearance in a rapid fashion.

SIGNIFICANCE

The Green Table won first prize in a choreography competition organized by the Archives Internationales de la Danse in Paris, and the success led to an offer to participate in a season of innovative dance at the Casino de Paris in the fall of 1932. The event called for the inclusion of *The Green Table* and the competition's other prizewinners in a production during the dormant period between the casino's regular shows. When the Jooss dancers arrived in Paris, however, they learned that the other groups were unavailable and the casino was continuing to present its revues. The fall season's offering began with the casino's attractions of nudity, risqué songs, and other suggestive happenings. Following the intermission, *The Green Table*, with its sober commentary, was presented. The ballet, in sharp contrast to what went before it, was met with such commotion that the music could not be heard. In a short time, however, as the Parisian public learned of the performance, different types of audiences began to attend and gave their approval to the work.

A proper theater season in Paris and Europe was arranged for the following spring, and Ballets Jooss, as the company had become known, was firmly established. *The Green Table* was presented along with other works by Jooss.

Created a year before Adolf Hitler seized power, the ballet expressed a message that was comparable to those expressed in many antiwar novels of the time. Sentiments portrayed in *The Green Table* were not, however, in keeping with the views of Hitler and the Nazi Party. As a result of this and of Jooss's support of Jewish and partly Jewish colleagues, of necessity, Jooss and his company fled Germany.

During World War II, while Ballets Jooss was performing in England, Jooss made the decision to withdraw *The Green Table* from the repertoire. He believed that the effects of war were too near at hand and that those who attended the theater in wartime did so for relaxation. Audiences requested the ballet, however, and *The Green Table* was restored to the programs. With the final days of World War II approaching, Jooss again believed the end of *The Green Table*'s performance life was near, but he was proved wrong once more. Audiences continued to request the ballet, and so Ballets Jooss continued performing the work.

In 1948, Jooss was invited to Santiago, Chile, by former soloists of Ballets Jooss who had performed in the original production of *The Green Table*. There, Jooss staged *The Green Table* for the Chilean National Ballet, which his dancers had founded. During this production, Jooss made his final appearance as a dancer in the role of Death.

The enduring quality of *The Green Table* led to its incorporation into the repertoires of ballet companies worldwide. Productions have been staged by the City Center Joffrey Ballet in New York (March, 1967), the Tanz-Forum in Cologne (December, 1971), the Royal Winnipeg Ballet in Toronto (November, 1974), the Batsheva Dance Company in Tel Aviv (November, 1975), the José Limon Dance Company in New York (April, 1977), the Opernhaus in Zurich (May, 1978), the Suomen Kansallisbaletti in Helsinki (November, 1982), and the Bühnen der Stadt in Essen, Germany (March, 1985), among others. In addition, continued interest in *The Green Table* led to several televised productions of the ballet, including a German production in 1963, a British production in 1966 directed by Peter Wright, a Swedish production in 1977, and a Japanese production in 1979. In 1982, the Joffrey Ballet undertook a production for public television's *Dance in America* series.

The Green Table's significance extends beyond the ballet's message and reflects Jooss's innovative use of choreography, stagecraft, and lighting. A period of development during which Jooss formulated his beliefs and experimented in dance movement and in stagecraft preceded his creation of *The Green Table*. His dance technique negated many premises that were accepted by ballet choreographers of the time. To Jooss, a painted set, a corps de ballet, and the sound of an orchestra were nonessential; instead, the dramatic effect of dance was underlined by stagecraft. He placed emphasis on costume rather than on decor, using costumes to accentuate symbolism rather than for merely decorative purposes. Jooss also used costumes to make his dancers appear more vividly three-dimensional to the audience.

Jooss's unusually fluid use of lighting contributed to his three-dimensional concept. He altered the stage space by filling or emptying different areas, surfaces, and levels with light. He used lighting to mask, reveal, or emphasize a solo figure or group; the color, volume, and direction of Jooss's lighting were constantly changing to reveal the spaces necessary for action at any moment.

All aspects of Jooss's style of theatrical dance were first completely realized in *The Green Table*. Jooss blazed a trail in dance with *The Green Table*; until the piece's premiere, dance, with few exceptions, was escapist in its audience appeal. *The Green Table* is acknowledged as Jooss's greatest, most successful, and most enduring work. The ballet remains a powerful indictment of war.

—*Mary Pat Balkus*

FURTHER READING

Anderson, Jack. *Art Without Boundaries: The World of Modern Dance*. Iowa City: University of Iowa Press, 1997. Comprehensive chronological history of dance since the nineteenth century presents discussion of Jooss's work. Includes photographs.

Bergsohn, Isa, and Harold Bergsohn. *The Makers of Modern Dance in Germany: Rudolf Laban, Mary Wigman, Kurt Jooss*. Hightstown, N.J.: Princeton Book Company, 2003. Examines the connections and influences among the three choreographers considered to be the founders of German modern dance. Includes photographs and index.

Chujoy, Anatole, and P. W. Manchester, eds. *The Dance Encyclopedia*. Rev. ed. New York: Simon & Schuster, 1967. Provides brief accounts of *The Green Table*, Kurt Jooss, and Ballets Jooss. Includes a photograph of Jooss in the role of Death.

Clarke, Mary, and Clement Crisp. *The Ballet Goer's Guide*. New York: Alfred A. Knopf, 1981. Presents a capsule view of Jooss's career and a brief synopsis of *The Green Table*. Illustrations include photographs of the tableau that opens and closes the work and Jooss in the role of Death.

Coton, A. V. *The New Ballet: Kurt Jooss and His Work*. London: Dennis Dobson, 1946. Valuable work on Jooss presents discussion of the background of twentieth century ballet that places the development of Ballets Jooss in proper context. Includes excellent information on *The Green Table* and other selected Jooss works. Features photographs and line drawings.

Gruen, John. *The World's Greatest Ballets*. New York: Harry N. Abrams, 1981. Presents an account of Jooss's career and a vividly descriptive synopsis of *The Green Table*.

Markard, Anna, and Hermann Markard. *Jooss*. Cologne, Germany: Ballett-Buhnen-Verlag, 1985. Excellent resource, based on part of an exhibition for a 1981 Venice dance festival. Includes a biography of Jooss, a record of the tours of Ballets Jooss, and a list of Jooss's choreographic works. Features photographs of ballets and of soloists, some taken at productions of *The Green Table*.

Partsch-Bergsohn, Isa. *Modern Dance in Germany and the United States: Crosscurrents and Influences*. Chur, Switzerland: Harwood Academic Publishers, 1994. Discusses the progression of American and German modern dance over the course of the twentieth century, focusing on the similarities and differences in the art in the two nations. Includes discussion of Jooss's work and its influence. Features bibliography and index.

Williamson, Audrey. *Contemporary Ballet*. London: Rockliff, 1946. Provides a chapter of commentary on Ballets Jooss, which made its home in England during World War II. Critiques the major ballets of Jooss and presents insightful commentary on *The Green Table*.

SEE ALSO: Dec. 26, 1904: Duncan Interprets Chopin in Her Russian Debut; May 19, 1909: Diaghilev's Ballets Russes Astounds Paris; June 2, 1909: Fokine's *Les Sylphides* Introduces Abstract Ballet; June 25, 1910: *The Firebird* Premieres in Paris; May 29, 1913: *The Rite of Spring* Stuns Audiences; Summer, 1915: Denishawn School of Dance Opens; Jan. 26, 1936: Tudor's *Jardin aux lilas* Premieres in London.

1932

July 18, 1932
ST. LAWRENCE SEAWAY TREATY

The signing of the St. Lawrence Seaway Treaty in 1932 initiated a series of negotiations that spanned twenty-five years before the United States and Canada agreed on the conditions for constructing the seaway. The seaway's completion in 1959 established a new level of interaction between the two countries.

ALSO KNOWN AS: St. Lawrence Deep Waterway Treaty; Hoover-Bennett Treaty
LOCALE: St. Lawrence River watershed in both Canada and the United States
CATEGORIES: Diplomacy and international relations; laws, acts, and legal history; transportation

KEY FIGURES
Tom Connally (1877-1963), U.S. senator from Texas
Dwight D. Eisenhower (1890-1969), president of the United States, 1953-1961
Herbert Hoover (1874-1964), president of the United States, 1929-1933

SUMMARY OF EVENT

The story of the St. Lawrence Seaway began in 1909, when the United States and Canada signed the Boundary Waters Treaty, which created the International Joint Commission. The commission was charged with implementing joint development of all navigable boundary waters. The St. Lawrence River was first and foremost among these waters. Although most of the river flowed through Canada, it divided the two nations for a 44-mile stretch between the province of Ontario and the state of New York. The St. Lawrence had been an important communications route between Europe and North America since the time of European exploration of the American continent. Because it is the outflow of the Great Lakes, four of which also form the boundary between Canada and the United States (only Lake Michigan is wholly within the United States), it had become a major trade artery for both countries.

Before the nations could carry out the commitments expressed in the Boundary Waters Treaty, a number of engineering problems needed to be solved. One of these was passing Niagara Falls, which lies between Lake Erie and Lake Ontario. This problem was addressed by the Welland Canal, which was built in Canadian territory. In the 1820's, the canal had been dug to a depth of eight feet, and it had been progressively enlarged and deepened during the nineteenth and twentieth centuries. In its

course west of Montreal, Canada, the river contained a number of rapids that severely impeded navigation, and there were significant shoals in the section that formed the international boundary between the two countries. Finally, the river's massive flow offered substantial hydroelectric potential that would require dams or diversions to harvest.

Powerful interests lobbied on both sides of the issue. In favor were the agricultural interests of the Midwest, both in Canada and the United States, that wanted a water-based transportation system (as opposed to a rail system), which would be a cheaper way of sending bulk commodities such as grain. In the 1930's, the iron and steel industries, especially those in the United States, expected to mine the iron deposits of northern Minnesota's Mesabi range indefinitely, but by the end of World War II it was clear that these supplies were almost gone. The most promising replacement was the extensive deposits recently discovered in Labrador, and the steel industry realized that it could move these deposits to the plants of the Midwest if ships were able travel down the St. Lawrence River from the Atlantic Ocean and make it at least as far as Lake Erie. Until it became clear that this new source of iron was needed, the steel corporations were not interested in promoting the seaway.

Multiple interests were opposed to the seaway's development, partly because it would involve major government investments and partly because it would negatively affect their businesses. The railroads of both nations saw the seaway as a competitor and were strongly opposed to its development; prior to the seaway's completion, many exporters had used the railroads to transport their products to the coasts. The coal industry (of which the railroads were major customers) also opposed the seaway, since it would harm the railroad industry. Ports along the Atlantic coast opposed the seaway because it would enable ships to proceed from the Midwest directly to their destinations elsewhere in the world. Private utilities did not want to compete with government-funded facilities that produced hydroelectric power, and so they were also opposed.

Major political interests also opposed the seaway's development. In Canada, the dominant political forces in both Ontario and Quebec opposed ceding power to the federal government, arguing instead that Canada's constitution gave control over boundary waters to the provinces. In the United States, progress on the issue was stymied by senators from the South; these senators, notably Tom Connally of Texas, were able to prevent approval of the treaty, which required a positive vote of two-thirds of senators before it could go into effect. Despite the fact that every president from Herbert Hoover to Dwight D. Eisenhower supported the idea, opposition from the Senate could not be overcome for more than twenty years.

There was also the question of local versus federal control over any hydroelectric power developed in conjunction with the seaway's construction. In Canada, the federal government could not proceed with a plan to develop the seaway until the premier of the province of Ontario was brought on board. This issue was resolved by two 1941 agreements between Ontario and Canada's federal government, in which the federal government assumed responsibility for any navigational improvements in the St. Lawrence and Ontario was put in charge of any

hydroelectric capabilities that were developed in conjunction with the seaway.

Resolving the hydroelectric issue in the United States was harder, because New York State wanted its own power authority to control its share of the hydroelectric power, and it could do so only with the approval of the Federal Power Commission (FPC) in Washington, D.C. Opponents of the seaway remained in control of the FPC almost to the end of negotiations, but finally President Eisenhower overrode the FPC's opposition by arguing that the seaway could be a useful tool in the U.S. defense arsenal.

Once the Canadians had resolved their differences about the seaway, they became its chief proponents in the post-World War II era. As long as it was impossible to resolve congressional opposition to U.S. participation, the Canadians had to develop an alternative solution. They proposed that Canada should develop the seaway alone,

1932

A Great Lakes freighter passes through the Cornwall Locks of the St. Lawrence Seaway in Ontario, Canada, on the U.S. border, in 1955. (AP/Wide World Photos)

which became possible when most of the construction costs were shifted from the navigational improvements to developing the hydroelectric capabilities. Canada created its own St. Lawrence Seaway Authority, which was in charge of the development. Canadian officials agreed, however, that this was a less desirable solution than joint development, and it was hoped that this prospect would spur the United States to action.

SIGNIFICANCE

Efforts to build the St. Lawrence Seaway spanned the first half of the twentieth century in both the United States and Canada. The seaway's completion was a monument to a new level of cooperation between the two North American powers. Its construction indicated the shifting priorities of both countries, even though from a population standpoint Canada remained about one-tenth the size of the United States. The joint creation of the St. Lawrence Seaway inaugurated a series of cooperative ventures of the two largest North American powers, and its economic and political success led to the nations' increased regionalization.

The combination of shifting many of the costs to the hydroelectric development at last moved Congress to act, and in the spring of 1954, Congress voted to create the St. Lawrence Seaway Development Corporation, which would work jointly with Canada's St. Lawrence Seaway Authority in developing the project. FPC approval of the New York State Power Authority was also secured. Work immediately began on construction of the seaway improvements to navigation-related matters and the creation of the hydroelectric elements. The entire project was built in the period 1954-1958, and it opened on June 26, 1959, in a formal ceremony presided over by Queen Elizabeth of England, who represented Canada, and President Eisenhower, who represented the United States.

—*Nancy M. Gordon*

FURTHER READING

Bothwell, Robert. *A Short History of Ontario*. Edmonton, Alta.: Hurtig, 1986. Describes the negotiations by which Ontario and the Canadian federal government resolved their differences.

MacLennan, Hugh. *The Rivers of Canada*. Toronto: Macmillan of Canada, 1977. Describes the history of the St. Lawrence and clarifies its enormous strategic significance.

Rea, K. J. *The Prosperous Years: The Economic History of Ontario*. Toronto: University of Toronto Press, 1985. A thorough survey of economic developments in Ontario, the most developed part of Canada.

Willoughby, William R. *The St. Lawrence Waterway: A Study in Politics and Diplomacy*. Madison: University of Wisconsin Press, 1961. An exhaustive account of the attempts, on both sides of the border, to construct the waterway.

SEE ALSO: 1921-1948: King Era in Canada; Oct. 21, 1924: Halibut Treaty; Sept. 8, 1930: Canada Enacts Depression-Era Relief Legislation; Dec. 11, 1931: Formation of the British Commonwealth of Nations; July 21-Aug. 21, 1932: Ottawa Agreements; Apr. 15, 1935: Arbitration Affirms National Responsibility for Pollution; Oct. 23, 1935-Nov. 15, 1948: King Returns to Power in Canada; Nov. 11, 1936: Reciprocal Trade Act; Aug. 16, 1940: Ogdensburg Agreement.

July 21-August 21, 1932
OTTAWA AGREEMENTS

The Canadian government approved the Ottawa Agreements in an attempt to relieve pressures caused by the Great Depression. The agreements secured more favorable tariffs from Great Britain and other British dominions.

LOCALE: Canada
CATEGORIES: Trade and commerce; diplomacy and international relations; government and politics

KEY FIGURES

Richard Bedford Bennett (1870-1947), prime minister of Canada, 1930-1935
Ramsay MacDonald (1866-1937), prime minister of Great Britain, 1931-1935
William Lyon Mackenzie King (1874-1950), prime minister of Canada, 1921-1926, 1926-1930, and 1935-1948
Franklin D. Roosevelt (1882-1945), president of the United States, 1933-1945

SUMMARY OF EVENT

The worldwide Great Depression of the 1930's had a devastating impact on Canada, in part because Canada did not have an independent economy at the time. Instead, the country was linked inextricably to the economies of the United States, England, and the rest of Europe. Canada's domestic production was particularly dependent on trade with Europe. Unfortunately, many countries throughout the world, including the United States and Great Britain, raised tariffs and curbed imports during the 1930's to protect their own economies.

Early on, the Canadian government had little success in easing the Depression. Prime Minister Richard Bedford Bennett, who took office in 1930, instituted new tariffs to retaliate against other countries that had raised their own tariffs and to protect Canada's economy. He and other government leaders did not believe that much more needed to be done to help Canadians in the early days of the Depression; they expected it to be relatively short-lived. They made some attempts to enact social programs such as unemployment insurance but were stymied somewhat in their attempts by constitutional limitations on such programs.

Bennett soon recognized that England would have to help Canada survive the economic downturn. In 1930, he traveled to a conference in England to demand that the British Labour government permit the creation of a com-

monwealth that would provide protection for the dominions and would allow the dominions and England mutual preferences. At the conference, Bennett pleaded for a system of preferences, and he also made it clear that this system must be reconciled with the fullest protection for Canadian producers against competition from foreign nations as well as from Great Britain and the other dominions. Bennett announced that he stood solidly behind the doctrine of "Canada first," and he conceded that the other dominions would also believe that they should come first. Nevertheless, he said, they should all work together to hammer out a collective agreement that would benefit each nation.

Bennett offered specific solutions to the problem. He suggested that after Canada had decided on the level of tariff protection it needed, it would add an extra 10 percent against non-British companies, with a certain flexibility in this margin in the case of specific products. The ruling British Labour party, long proponents of free trade, scoffed at Bennett, but he was not deterred. Bennett believed that the British had both political and economic reasons for reaching some type of agreement with the other members of the Empire. England faced both a declining trade position and a growing crisis in international affairs. At Bennett's insistence, the conference participants agreed to meet in Ottawa in 1932 to continue their discussions. By 1932, England's economic picture had changed for the worse, strengthening Canada's demand for preferential treatment within the Commonwealth. Unfortunately, Canada's economy also had worsened, primarily as a result of other countries' protective actions.

From 1930 through 1932, Germany and Italy both levied tariffs against Canadian wheat. In 1930, the United States enacted its controversial Hawley-Smoot Tariff Act against Canadian lumber, cattle, and agricultural products. Even England, considered to be the home of free trade, instituted an emergency tariff in 1931. Moreover, British prime minister Ramsay MacDonald's government was in turmoil as a result of the impending collapse of the Bank of England and opposition from his own party for his inability to balance the nation's budget. These factors made Canada's economic status more tenuous and increased the need for concessions from England.

Bennett hoped that Great Britain and the dominions would agree to the establishment of an imperial free trade

1932

area protected against the rest of the world. He also wanted to exploit England's trading interests, which reached far beyond the Empire. The British were not particularly interested in satisfying either of Bennett's hopes, but as 1932 arrived, they were not in a position to deny him entirely. By 1932, the Conservatives were back in power in England, and one of their first acts was to institute protection. In February of 1932, the British government passed the Imports Duties Act, which imposed a 10 percent duty on many articles imported by England. The act exempted the dominions from the tax.

In 1932, the Commonwealth countries hammered out a series of twelve separate trade agreements, most of them five-year bilateral pacts, known as the Ottawa Agreements. In general, the agreements worked in Canada's favor. Representatives from each of the dominions needed to secure preferred markets for themselves, but none of them wanted to curtail individual levels of trade. It did not take long before the problems became obvious, and these problems were especially serious for England. About two-thirds of the country's exports went to countries outside Europe, and England also had the distinction of being the largest shipowner and international banker in the world. As a result, the British banking industry had huge amounts of long-term investments throughout the world. Understandably, England was not willing to jeopardize its banking and shipowning industries in order to create an uncertain unity among the dominions or raise the cost of living for its own citizens. England also had to deal with the Commonwealth countries' growing independence; many of these nations wanted to develop favorable trade agreements to benefit themselves at England's expense.

There was a certain amount of irony in Bennett's appeal to the British for economic help: His plea contradicted the idea that nationalism was alive and well in Canada. The majority of Canada's citizens believed in the concept of one country, even though the individual provinces were unsure as to the exact legal status of their federation. Moreover, there existed no formal agreement establishing Canada's position in the Commonwealth. The nearest thing to one was the Balfour resolution of 1926, which stated that the members of the Commonwealth "are autonomous communities within the British Empire, equal in status, in no way subordinate one to another in any aspect of their domestic or external affairs, though united by a common allegiance to the Crown, and freely associated as members of the British Commonwealth of Nations." This was affirmed by the 1931 Statute of Westminster, which declared that "no act of the

British Parliament shall apply to any dominion unless the latter requests it." Canada had taken its autonomy seriously.

The conference in July and August of 1932 was intended to be the British answer to the worldwide Depression. Nine countries participated, hoping to establish free trade within the Commonwealth while retaining or raising tariffs against nonmember countries. Protective tariffs played a big role in the economies of the dominions. The British delegation supported low tariffs on goods exchanged among the members of the Commonwealth, but Bennett, in accord with his party's protectionist philosophy, fought for high tariffs. He asked for preference in the British market for Canadian lumber, wheat, bacon, cheese, and butter. In return, he offered partial preference to British textiles and steel products, and none at all for boots and shoes. Bennett wanted to base preferential treatment on a general raising of tariffs on foreign nations' products. In the end, the British acceded to his demands. To the Canadians' delight, tariffs remained high.

The British government tendered generous trade privileges to the Canadians, granting a privileged market for Canada's principal exports without getting much in return for its own products, in order to maintain peace between the two countries. Canadian manufacturers continued to demand and receive protection, especially against the textiles that England wanted to export. The Canadians could not be blamed for their demands for protection, as they were concerned about Russian and Argentine competition in the British market for primary products.

SIGNIFICANCE

The Ottawa Agreements had mixed results. The cotton producers of the two countries held a side conference that broke down completely with no agreement, Canada's sheltered industries opposed any threats to their protected position, and England demanded reduced duties on textiles, iron, and steel products. That demand produced heated discussions, as did Canada's insistence that Great Britain impose an embargo on Russian lumber and other competing products. Progress was slow on any agreements, and the conference almost came to a premature halt. That was partly a result of personality conflicts, as participants accused Bennett of being too domineering and overbearing. However, England could not afford to end the talks without some sort of agreement.

At last, the countries compromised on several issues. England agreed to forgo tariffs on a substantial number of Canadian goods, including manufactured products, food, and raw materials. It also imposed duties of 10 to 33 percent on competing foreign products. Of primary importance to Canada was England's decision to grant preference to Canadian wheat. Great Britain also agreed to take effective steps against foreign dumping of products, particularly of Russian lumber.

Canada increased the margin of preference on 223 British products, either by lowering existing preferential rates or by raising the general tariff imposed on competitors. The chief beneficiaries were the textile, iron, steel, leather goods, coal, and chemicals industries. In addition, Canada agreed to restrict protection to industries that had a reasonable prospect of success. Finally, it allowed the British to be represented in a tariff board on the administration of tariffs or any proposed changes in rates. A series of bilateral agreements with the other dominions supplemented the arrangements with England and promised to give Canada wider access to Empire markets. Despite the fact that some historians saw the conference as a failure, Bennett's government won some important concessions.

In each year from 1927 through 1932, payments by Canada to the United Kingdom exceeded receipts, although the reverse was true from 1933 to 1939. Canadian product exports to England increased steadily after 1932, although values were lower because of lower prices. The proportion of Canada's exports shipped to England rose from 28 to 38 percent. For the Empire as a whole, the increase was from 36 to 48 percent. Conversely, Canadian imports from England did not rise above the 1932 level until 1935. Overall, the percentage of Canada's trade with England was slightly higher during the 1930's than it had been in the 1920's. That made the Ottawa Agreements worthwhile in the eyes of some Canadians.

The Canadian parliament vehemently argued about whether Canada had benefited from the conference. William Lyon Mackenzie King, the prime minister before 1930, seized on the agreements as a political issue. He criticized the agreements because they raised Canadian duties, granted only a slight concession to England, and made it more difficult to reach a new trade agreement with the United States. This last issue was particularly important to King.

Regardless of macroeconomic trends, many Canadians believed that it was vital to exchange goods freely with the United States. In the absence of such an arrangement, Canada would be forced to meet its heavy financial obligations to the United States through an increasing drain on its gold supply, a prospect that was extremely unappealing to many Canadians. Manufacturers and farmers also had mixed feelings about the conference and about Bennett himself.

There was some serious international political fallout from the Ottawa Agreements. Many non-Empire countries were affronted by the concessions Commonwealth members granted to one another. Ironically, the United States, which had imposed high tariffs of its own to combat the Depression, was one of them, and Americans felt slighted by the agreements. In the final analysis, the Ottawa Agreements gave Canadians the perception that free trade among the Empire's members was one step closer. On the other hand, however, the agreements heightened the dislocation of world trade and accentuated the trend toward anarchy. Overall, however, to Canadians, the Ottawa Agreements represented a step toward economic independence, which was perhaps the most welcome benefit of all.

—*Arthur G. Sharp*

FURTHER READING

Brown, Craig, ed. *The Illustrated History of Canada*. Toronto: Lester & Orpen Dennys, 1987. An easy-to-follow history of Canada replete with photos that give readers a visual image of the people and events that contributed to the country's history.

Creighton, Donald. *A History of Canada*. Boston: Houghton Mifflin, 1958. A lengthy history of Canada focusing on the most significant events in the country's past.

Ferguson, Linda W. *Canada*. New York: Charles Scribner's Sons, 1979. An overview of Canadian history. Offers a broad view of the people and events that have contributed to the country's history.

Hall, Walter Phelps, Robert G. Albion, and Jennie B. Pope. *A History of England and the Empire-Commonwealth*. 4th ed. Waltman, Mass.: Blaisdell, 1965. A textbook that provides insights into major events in Canadian history, from the British viewpoint.

McDiarmid, Orville John. *Commercial Policy in the Canadian Economy*. Cambridge, Mass.: Harvard University Press, 1946. A comprehensive history of the Canadian tariff.

McInnis, Edgar. *Canada: A Political and Social History*. New York: Holt, Rinehart and Winston, 1959. A readable book that focuses on the sociological impact of historical events in Canada.

McMenemy, John. *The Language of Canadian Politics: A Guide to Important Terms and Concepts*. 3d ed. Waterloo, Ont.: Wilfrid Laurier University Press, 2001. Collection of more than five hundred brief es-

1932

says on a wide range of topics related to the Canadian system of government, Canadian political history, Canadian laws and legal history, and more.

Miller, J. D. H. *Britain and the Old Dominions*. London: Chatto & Windus, 1966. Positive evaluation of the Ottawa Agreements.

Riendeau, Roger. *A Brief History of Canada*. 2d rev. ed. New York: Facts On File, 2006. Concise history includes discussion of Canada's difficulties during the Great Depression.

Safarian, A. E. *The Canadian Economy in the Great Depression*. Toronto: Toronto University Press, 1959. The role of the Depression in making the agreements possible.

Wittke, Carl. *A History of Canada*. 3d ed. New York: F. S. Crofts & Company, 1942. A concise history of

Canada. Contains marginal notes that make it easy for the reader to identify major events in the narrative.

Young, J. H. *Canadian Commercial Policy*. Ottawa: Royal Commission on Canadian Economic Prospects, 1957. Brief treatment of the agreements in the context of Canada's commercial policy.

SEE ALSO: 1911-1920: Borden Leads Canada Through World War I; July 10, 1920-Sept., 1926: Meighen Era in Canada; Oct. 21, 1924: Halibut Treaty; Oct. 29, 1929-1939: Great Depression; Aug., 1930-1935: Bennett Era in Canada; Sept. 8, 1930: Canada Enacts Depression-Era Relief Legislation; Aug. 1, 1932: Canada's First Major Socialist Movement; Oct. 23, 1935-Nov. 15, 1948: King Returns to Power in Canada; Nov. 11, 1936: Reciprocal Trade Act.

July 28, 1932
BONUS MARCH

At the beginning of the Great Depression, frustrated World War I veterans demanded a promised bonus. Although Congress attempted to meet the soldiers' demands, President Herbert Hoover and General Douglas MacArthur took a harder line, and the rebellion was silenced.

LOCALE: Washington, D.C.; Anacostia Flats, Maryland

CATEGORIES: Social issues and reform; government and politics

KEY FIGURES

Herbert Hoover (1874-1964), president of the United States, 1929-1933

Patrick J. Hurley (1883-1963), U.S. secretary of war

Douglas MacArthur (1880-1964), chief of staff of the U.S. Army

Walter W. Waters (1898-?), elected leader of the Bonus Army

SUMMARY OF EVENT

In the years following World War I (1914-1918), many of the more than three million U.S. veterans of that war joined the American Legion and other lobbying organizations. One of the benefits to be awarded as a result of these groups' lobbying efforts was a bonus that the American Legion called "adjusted compensation," which was the difference between the pay that was re-

ceived during military service and what soldiers could have earned outside the military. The first bonus bill passed Congress in 1922 and was vetoed by President Warren G. Harding. The Congress finally passed a bonus bill over the veto of President Calvin Coolidge in 1924. The bill provided for each veteran one dollar per day of military service inside the United States and a dollar and a quarter per day outside the United States, but payment was deferred to the year 1945.

Described as endowment insurance, 3.5 million interest-bearing compensation certificates were issued, to expire twenty years later. Each was worth about a thousand dollars, for a total value of $3.5 billion. Veterans were not satisfied, however, and they continued to pressure the government as the Great Depression intensified. In 1931, over President Herbert Hoover's veto, Congress passed a provision that stipulated that 50 percent of the individual cash value of a certificate could be borrowed at an interest rate of 4.5 percent.

The Great Depression created massive unemployment, and many of the unemployed were veterans. There had been agitation and some violent demonstrations in the early 1930's, and the role of the Communist Party in the United States and abroad was seen by some as significant. At another level, the role of the American Legion and other advocacy groups was also important.

Because of the deteriorating economic conditions, groups of veterans from all over the nation began to de-

Bonus Marchers and police battle in Washington, D.C. (NARA)

mand action. Some traveled great distances to the U.S. Capitol in Washington, D.C., where they lobbied for immediate payment of their bonus. A bill proposing full and prompt payment to veterans was introduced in the 1931 session of Congress, and as a result, approximately fifteen thousand veterans descended on Washington in the spring of 1932.

The elected leader of the veterans was Walter W. Waters. He organized the veterans into military-type units, each of which found or built makeshift housing all over the city. Some were housed in a group of abandoned government buildings, and others created an encampment consisting of more than two thousand tents and lean-tos across the Anacostia River in Maryland at Anacostia Flats. Many of the tents were provided by the U.S. Army.

During the spring and summer of 1932, the assembled veterans, called the Bonus Army or Bonus Expeditionary Force (BEF), exerted increasing pressure on Congress to pass a bonus bill that would providing cash payments to each eligible veteran. Such a bill was introduced by Congressman Wright Patman of Texas, and although it

passed the House of Representatives on June 15, it was defeated in the Senate. Congress adjourned, and most of the veterans left Washington. Some money was allocated to help veterans get home. About two thousand veterans remained.

Matters reached crisis level on July 28. A series of demonstrations began on Pennsylvania Avenue and Third and Fourth Streets Northwest. The Board of Commissioners of the District of Columbia asked President Hoover for assistance. By early afternoon, Secretary of War Patrick J. Hurley had ordered General Douglas MacArthur, chief of staff of the U.S. Army, to bring in previously prepared army units. MacArthur chose to lead the army units on horseback and dressed in full uniform with medals.

There was a great deal of confusion, and the marchers were driven out of the abandoned government buildings. There is some question about whether Hurley ordered MacArthur to pursue other marchers outside the District of Columbia. In any event, the army forces pursued the marchers across the river, using copious tear gas but not firing their guns. By midnight, the shantytown at Anacostia Flats had been burned. (Later tests confirmed that the tear gas used could initiate fires.) Two deaths and dozens of injuries resulted from the rioting.

SIGNIFICANCE

Studies of the Bonus March have emphasized two factors: MacArthur's ostentatious display and the role of the Communist Party of the United States. Although Communist Party organizers were present, Waters and others claimed that they had distanced themselves from the activists. In his memoirs and in partisan biographies, MacArthur insisted that the Communists had instigated the entire affair, and there was even talk that Communists had a list of officials who would be jailed after the revolution and that MacArthur's name allegedly led the list. Some hagiographic MacArthur biographers went gone so far as to link the Bonus March imbroglio with MacArthur's 1951 recall by President Harry S. Truman, claiming that the Communists were responsible for both. For his part, MacArthur claimed that only one in ten of the Bonus Marchers was a legitimate veteran. A survey by the Veterans Bureau, however, concluded that 94 percent were legitimate. At the time, President Hoover, Secretary Hurley, and especially General MacArthur were roundly criticized in the press for overreacting.

—*Eugene L. Rasor*

FURTHER READING

Daniels, Roger. *The Bonus March: An Episode of the Great Depression.* Westport, Conn.: Greenwood Press, 1971. Criticizes Hoover and MacArthur. Enumerates several myths: that the Army fired on and killed veterans, that the marchers had machine guns, and that the BEF was infiltrated by large numbers of Communists. Includes the controversial report MacArthur wrote summarizing his actions.

Hunt, Frazier. *The Untold Story of Douglas MacArthur.* New York: Devin-Adair, 1954. One of several hagiographic biographies of MacArthur. Describes the Bonus March as a plot of the U.S. Communist Party, which supposedly had been instructed by Moscow to bring about a bloody riot.

James, D. Clayton. *The Years of MacArthur.* 3 vols. Boston: Houghton Mifflin, 1970-1985. The standard and authoritative biography of MacArthur. The Bonus March is covered in volume 1.

MacArthur, Douglas. *Reminiscences.* Annapolis, Md.: Bluejacket Books, 2001. A self-serving memoir that should be read with caution. Declares that the Communist Party planned the riot and denies that he wore medals during the march.

Perrett, Geoffrey. *Old Soldiers Never Die: The Life of Douglas MacArthur.* Holbrook, Mass.: Adams Media, 2001. Very readable but sometimes inaccurate biography. Its clear bias toward its subject makes it less valuable than many other biographies of MacArthur.

Waters, Walter W. *B.E.F.: The Whole Story of the Bonus Army.* New York: John Day, 1933. A personal memoir by the most identifiable leader of the Bonus Marchers.

SEE ALSO: Mar. 15-May 9, 1919: Formation of the American Legion; June 28, 1919: Treaty of Versailles; Oct. 24-29, 1929: U.S. Stock Market Crashes; Oct. 29, 1929-1939: Great Depression; Dec. 11, 1930: Bank of United States Fails; Nov. 8, 1932: Franklin D. Roosevelt Is Elected U.S. President; Mar. 9-June 16, 1933: The Hundred Days.

August 1, 1932
CANADA'S FIRST MAJOR SOCIALIST MOVEMENT

The Cooperative Commonwealth Federation, led by James Shaver Woodsworth, was founded at a conference in Calgary, Alberta. The formation of the CCF, Canada's first democratic socialist movement, transformed the Canadian political scene and represented a serious challenge to political orthodoxy in the climate of the Great Depression.

ALSO KNOWN AS: Cooperative Commonwealth Federation; New Democratic Party
LOCALE: Calgary, Alberta, Canada
CATEGORIES: Government and politics; social issues and reform

KEY FIGURES
James Shaver Woodsworth (1874-1942), Methodist minister, social activist, and politician
William Irvine (1885-1962), Unitarian minister and politician
Francis Reginald Scott (1899-1985), poet and professor of constitutional law
Frank Underhill (1889-1971), historian and political theorist
James Coldwell (1888-1974), teacher and politician
Agnes Macphail (1890-1954), Canada's first female member of Parliament
Tommy Douglas (1904-1986), Baptist minister, politician and CCF premier of Saskatchewan, 1944-1961

SUMMARY OF EVENT

On August 1, 1932, a conference at Calgary, Alberta, launched a new force in Canadian politics: the Cooperative Commonwealth Federation (CCF). Socialist ideas as well as the interests of labor and farmers were represented at the conference, and the CCF combined previously distinct movements into a single party. A follow-up conference in Regina, Saskatchewan, in 1933 produced the Regina Manifesto, a sweeping document calling for overthrow of capitalism.

The formation of the CCF owed much to the climate of the Great Depression. The 1929 stock market crash dried up investment, and high tariffs led to shrinking world markets. Since a third of Canada's income came from exports, many Canadians lost their jobs, and 30 percent of the labor force was unemployed by 1933. On Canada's prairies, the situation was especially dire. Wheat prices declined sharply, from $1.60 per bushel in

the middle of 1929 to $0.50 by the end of 1930. More serious difficulties followed as Canada's Prairie Provinces—parts of Manitoba, Alberta, and especially Saskatchewan—faced the scourge of grasshopper plagues, hail, and drought. With successive years of inadequate rainfall, the prairies became a dustbowl, and valuable topsoil blew away. Two-thirds of Saskatchewan's population was dependent on government relief, and the prevailing capitalist system was not equal to the challenge. The solutions proposed by orthodox political parties were clearly inadequate; Richard Bedford Bennett, Canada's Conservative prime minister from 1930 to 1935, clung to the belief that tariffs would help Canada "blast a way" into world markets. Disillusioned people became more willing to entertain unconventional economic and political theories, and ideas such as communism and social credit—a complicated scheme of deficit spending through the distribution of dividends—received a more sympathetic hearing than they might have in better times. American populist ideas, which promoted antagonism toward "power elites," and British socialism were among the ideological currents to which the CCF owed some of its inspiration.

Chief among the CCF's first organizers was James Shaver Woodsworth, a former Methodist minister with roots in the Social Gospel movement. Woodsworth had worked among the poor, participated in the Winnipeg General Strike of 1919, and had been a Labour and independent member of Parliament for Winnipeg North Centre since 1921. True to his Social Gospel principles, Woodsworth focused his efforts on the salvation of society as a whole through political action. Sometimes called "the conscience of Canada," Woodsworth moved a resolution in each session of Parliament calling for the replacement of capitalism's competitive profit motive with public and cooperative ownership of the means of production and distribution. This idea became the core of the CCF.

The CCF, however, encompassed more than socialist ideals. Farmers' organizations had been active since early in the century, and a tradition of political activism grew out of Grain Growers Associations and cooperatives formed to market grain through collectively owned pools. A perception that Canada's National Policy tariffs served the interests of manufacturers at the expense of farmers also fueled political action. Provincial parties devoted to farmers' interests, such as the United Farmers

1932

of Ontario (UFO) and United Farmers of Alberta (UFA), had made rapid gains, and in the 1921 election the farmer-supported Progressive Party gained the second largest number of seats in Canada's federal parliament. These farmers' parties, however, did not function as truly disciplined political parties in the traditional sense; instead, they perceived themselves as interest groups that condemned the whole party system as inherently corrupt.

In 1924, a splinter group of more radical Progressives called the Ginger Group (to commemorate labor leader Ginger Goodwin, who had been killed by police) broke away to join with two Labour members of Parliament, James Shaver Woodsworth and William Irvine. Irvine, another devotee of the Social Gospel ideal, was a member of Parliament from Alberta and the author of *The Farmers in Politics* (1920). The Ginger Group would ultimately form the nucleus of the CCF.

Another key to the party's formation was the establishment in 1931 of the League for Social Reconstruction (LSR). The LSR consisted largely of left-wing intellectuals drawn from Canadian universities who were admirers of Woodsworth's ideals and who expressed skepticism about the future of the capitalist system. The most prominent members of the LSR were Frank Underhill, a historian from the University of Toronto, and Francis Reginald Scott, a poet and law professor from McGill University in Montreal. Underhill and Scott would be the authors of the CCF's 1933 Regina Manifesto. The *Canadian Forum*, a political periodical founded in Toronto in 1920, became a means of disseminating the league's ideas.

In May of 1932, Woodsworth met in Ottawa with a dozen or so others devoted to forming a "commonwealth party" that would unify labor, socialists, and farmers in a federation. William Irvine was among the group, as was Agnes Macphail, Canada's first female member of Parliament, who was elected under the Progressive banner in 1921. Other key organizers were Angus MacInnis, Woodsworth's son-in-law and a Vancouver Labour member of Parliament, and James Coldwell, a Saskatchewan teacher who would ultimately succeed Woodsworth as party leader. The leaders of this new political movement worked to bring together key radical groups. Several of these groups were holding their own conferences throughout the summer of 1932: the Western Conference of Labour Political Parties, the United Farmers of Canada, and the United Farmers of Alberta, who had formed the government in that province since 1921.

These groups, along with other labor and farmers' parties, answered the call from the Ottawa organizers to

come together at the Calgary conference on August 1, 1932. The delegates considered adopting such names as the Socialist Party of Canada or the United Workers Commonwealth, but at last they settled on the Cooperative Commonwealth Federation. Woodsworth was elected president of the new group. No definitive policy declaration was accepted at the Calgary conference, but ideas presented there ultimately found their way into the Regina Manifesto, which was produced in 1933 and represented a fundamental rejection of free market capitalism. There was broad agreement on a program drafted by James Coldwell, which included the need for socialization of production, distribution, and exchange. The federation favored public ownership of banking, credit, utilities, and natural resources, and social legislation was to be pursued, especially with respect to health and employment insurance. Socialization would not extend to landownership, however, and the land tenure of farmers was to remain secure. In this respect, the early CCF revealed a fundamentally conservative stripe that differed from communist ideology. The deep religious convictions held by many CCF adherents was another key point of distinction. Nevertheless, defenders of the status quo in the Canadian press raised the specter of Soviet-style forced collectivization and warned that the adoption of CCF principles would lead to the burning of churches.

SIGNIFICANCE

The 1932 formation of the CCF at the Calgary conference was followed the next year by a conference at Regina, Saskatchewan, that set out the party's manifesto. The Regina Manifesto boldly called for the replacement of the capitalist system "with its inherent injustice and inhumanity, by a social order from which the domination and exploitation of one class by another will be eliminated." But it rejected Communist-style violent revolution in favor of democracy. Under Woodsworth's leadership, the CCF functioned as a disciplined political party, an essential strategy to gain influence within the existing parliamentary system.

While the CCF alarmed the political right, it was also criticized by Communists, who called for more sweeping change. Woodsworth displayed his disavowal of such ideas by dissolving the Communist-dominated Ontario branch of the CCF in 1934. The CCF gained 8.9 percent of the popular vote in the 1935 federal election, winning seven seats. The presence of a viable socialist alternative arguably pushed mainstream parties into more progressive legislation. Under Tommy Douglas, the CCF formed the provincial government in Saskatchewan in

1944. The party would continue to be a force in Canadian federal and provincial politics, evolving into the New Democratic Party (NDP) in 1961.

—*Barbara J. Messamore*

FURTHER READING

Brennan, William J., ed. *Building the Co-operative Commonwealth: Essays on the Democratic Socialist Tradition in Canada*. Regina, Sask.: Canadian Plains Research Center, 1984. Essays by prominent scholars of Canadian socialist history consider such topics as the role of women in the CCF and the Saskatchewan CCF government of Tommy Douglas.

McNaught, Kenneth. *A Prophet in Politics: A Biography of J. S. Woodsworth*. 1959. Reprint. Toronto: University of Toronto Press, 2002. A frequently reprinted narrative of Woodsworth's life that reveals his centrality to the formation of the CCF and puts the events into the context of a life devoted to social reform.

Whitehorn, Alan. *Canadian Socialism: Essays on the CCF-NDP*. Toronto: Oxford University Press, 1992.

Written from a political-science perspective, these essays offer detailed analysis of the party's early history.

Young, Walter D. *The Anatomy of a Party: The National CCF, 1932-61*. Toronto: University of Toronto Press, 1969. A reliable and detailed account of the formation of the CCF. Young rejects the "party" label as applicable to capitalist organizations and prefers to consider the CCF a "movement."

SEE ALSO: Sept. 20, 1917: Canadian Women Gain the Vote; May 15-June 26, 1919: Winnipeg General Strike; July 10, 1920-Sept., 1926: Meighen Era in Canada; 1921-1948: King Era in Canada; Oct. 29, 1929-1939: Great Depression; Aug., 1930-1935: Bennett Era in Canada; Sept. 8, 1930: Canada Enacts Depression-Era Relief Legislation; Dec. 11, 1931: Formation of the British Commonwealth of Nations; July 18, 1932: St. Lawrence Seaway Treaty; July 21-Aug. 21, 1932: Ottawa Agreements; Oct. 23, 1935-Nov. 15, 1948: King Returns to Power in Canada.

1932

September, 1932
ANDERSON DISCOVERS THE POSITRON

Carl David Anderson discovered the first antiparticle, a particle with the same mass as an electron but with a positive charge. His discovery represented the first evidence that antimatter exists and confirmed a prediction of relativistic quantum mechanical theory.

LOCALE: Pasadena, California
CATEGORIES: Physics; science and technology

KEY FIGURES

Carl David Anderson (1905-1991), American physicist and professor
Paul Adrien Maurice Dirac (1902-1984), British physicist
Robert Andrews Millikan (1868-1953), American experimental physicist

SUMMARY OF EVENT

The first three decades of the twentieth century saw perhaps the most radical conceptual changes in the history of physics, especially at subatomic levels. To this period belong groundbreaking theoretical work on the quantum of energy (Max Planck), the quantum of light and the theory of relativity (Albert Einstein), the theory of atomic structure (Ernest Rutherford and Niels Bohr), the un-

certainty principle (Werner Heisenberg), quantum mechanics (Erwin Schrödinger), and relativistic quantum mechanics (Paul Adrien Maurice Dirac). The early twentieth century was also a period of great experimental discoveries, particularly of hitherto unknown constituents of matter. The electronic charge was measured by Robert Andrews Millikan, and the charge-to-mass ratio was measured by Sir Joseph John Thomson. The alpha particle was discovered by Ernest Rutherford, and the neutron was discovered by James Chadwick. It seemed as though the basic structure of matter was being completely unveiled, as though physicists had discovered a way to describe subatomic matter exhaustively in terms of Schrödinger's and Heisenberg's quantum mechanical theories.

Thus, by the mid-1920's, it had been established that matter consists primarily of heavy particles called protons, with a positive electric charge, and very light, negatively charged particles called electrons. The neutron—an electrically neutral particle, now known to be the third primary constituent of matter—had not been discovered yet. The neutron was discovered in 1932 by Chadwick.

Dirac, a physicist at St. John's College, Cambridge, was convinced that the quantum theory and the theory of

2583

relativity needed to be combined. This combination was accomplished in 1928, when Dirac formulated relativistic quantum theory. The mathematically elegant theory led to the conclusion that every particle had to have an antiparticle—a counterpart that was oppositely charged and that had an opposite "spin" (a property of every particle that is difficult to measure). This conclusion meant that there should be positive electrons and negative protons. It even led Dirac to expect there to be antineutrons, which, like neutrons, would have no charge, but would have a spin opposite to that of neutrons. Dirac's relativistic quantum mechanics thus predicted theoretically the existence of "antimatter." Antimatter particles, however, had yet to be observed.

In 1927, Carl David Anderson, a physicist at the California Institute of Technology (Caltech) in Pasadena, started to study elementary particles by investigating cosmic radiation. Cosmic radiation is a continuous stream of radiation, originating from nuclear reactions on the Sun and elsewhere in the cosmos, that flows into Earth's atmosphere. It was not yet clear if these "cosmic rays" contained particles in addition to high-energy radiation. Early experiments could not detect any particles. Anderson began his work at Caltech in the Norman Bridge Laboratory of Physics under Millikan, the physicist who had first measured the charge on an electron. Their research goal was to find the nature of cosmic radiation. As Millikan's junior research colleague, Anderson was first given the job of planning and directing the research.

The necessary experimental equipment was ready for operation in the summer of 1931. The technique used was to send up balloons containing instruments containing water vapor called cloud chambers. When a charged particle entered one of these chambers, it left a track. By studying the track, the mass and charge of the particle that caused the track were calculated. In addition, if a magnet was placed in the chamber so that the track was made in the presence of a magnetic field, the way the track curved would indicate whether the particle had a positive or negative charge.

Anderson and Millikan's equipment took photographs every fifteen seconds. A very strong electromagnet was incorporated into the cloud chamber. The photographs showed several tracks of particles with very high energies. They also seemed to indicate that there were as many positive as negative particles in cosmic radiation, in many instances originating from the same point. The first explanation of the physicists' empirical observations was that the positive particles whose tracks were

observed must be protons, and the negative ones must be electrons. Nevertheless, the experimental results seemed to show that the positive particles in the cosmic radiation showers had masses close or equal to those of electrons. (A proton has 1,835 times the mass of an electron.)

As Anderson stated in his 1936 Nobel lecture, the assumption that the positive particles had electronic mass "appeared very radical at the time." Further refined experiments, however, indicated that the positively charged particles observed in cosmic radiation had to be light particles, like electrons, rather than heavier protons. Anderson published a paper in September, 1932, announcing the existence of positive electrons, or positrons.

Experiments by Patrick M. S. Blackett and Giuseppe Occhialini at the University of Cambridge confirmed Anderson's findings in 1933. Blackett and his coworkers suggested that the positive particle they had found was the antiparticle of the electron that Dirac's theory had predicted. This discovery was the first evidence of the existence of antimatter. Dirac received the 1933 Nobel Prize in Physics (with Schrödinger) for his experimental confirmation of the theory. Anderson received the Nobel Prize in Physics in 1936 (with Victor Franz Hess) for his work on the positron. Anderson went on to win many other awards for his efforts, such as the Gold Medal of the American Institute of the City of New York (1935), the Elliot Cresson Medal of the Franklin Institute (1937), and the Presidential Certificate of Merit (1945).

The collections of positive and negative particles originating in the same point noted by Anderson now had an explanation. Some of the energy in the cosmic radiation was changing into particles, forming an electron-positron pair, which then sped off in opposite directions under the influence of the magnetic field. This was the first observation of what is known as "pair creation" (or pair production). It was also an example of the conversion of energy into matter, as predicted by Einstein's famous equation $E = mc^2$. The opposite of pair creation is annihilation: When equal amounts of matter and antimatter collide, they annihilate each other, with their mass being turned into pure energy.

Some of the theories of the early history of the universe involve the conversion of energy into matter through pair creation. According to the big bang theory of the creation of the universe, fifteen billion years ago a gigantic explosion took place that created substance from energy. As many antiparticles as particles would have been created at that moment. The question arises as to why Earth's part of the universe is predominantly composed of one type of particles (matter: protons, electrons, and neutrons) to the exclusion of the other type, antimatter. It is not known yet if there are galaxies that are predominantly composed of antimatter. Anderson's discovery was the first evidence that this is a possibility.

SIGNIFICANCE

The discovery of the positron—the first antiparticle to be discovered—furnished direct evidence supporting Dirac's theory of the existence of antimatter. Because antimatter is scarce on Earth, scientists began to produce antimatter under laboratory conditions. These experiments required particles at very high energies. At these energies, it was found that many new kinds of reactions occured and new kinds of particles were produced.

The entire field of "high-energy physics," for which large and expensive particle accelerators are required, can be considered to have started with Anderson's discovery of the positron. His discovery gave physicists a clearer understanding of elementary particles. Further, this branch of physics has led to the unveiling of a very complex set of particles and of new forces that operate in the subnuclear realm.

—*Indira Nair*

FURTHER READING

Charlton, M., and J. W. Humberston. *Positron Physics*. New York: Cambridge University Press, 2001. A lengthy treatise on the study of positrons and of positronium (an unstable form of matter consisting of an electron and a positron in orbit around each other).

Foot, Robert. *Shadowlands: Quest for Mirror Matter in the Universe*. Parkland, Fla.: Universal, 2002. An introduction for lay readers to antimatter, dark matter, mirror matter, and other "non-ordinary" types of matter that are predicted by quantum mechanics and rela-

tivity. Explains the evidence that such types of matter exist, as well as the implications of their existence.

Guillemin, Victor. *The Story of Quantum Mechanics*. New York: Charles Scribner's Sons, 1968. A general textbook discussion on the history of the development of quantum mechanics.

Heathcote, Niels H. de V. *Nobel Prize Winners in Physics, 1901-1950*. New York: Henry Schuman, 1953. Entries contain the details of the discoveries for which the Nobel Prizes were awarded and give lengthy extracts from the Nobel lectures.

Inman, Fred W., and Carl E. Miller. *Contemporary Physics*. New York: Macmillan, 1975. A modern survey of physics, this book divides physics into the classical and modern eras. The discoveries of the modern era, including that of the positron, are described.

Kim, S. K. *Physics: The Fabric of Reality*. New York: Macmillan, 1975. Starting with the idea of absolute and relative motion, this book attempts to give a simple description of the central concepts of modern physics, including Dirac's relativistic quantum theory, for the nonspecialist.

Trefil, James S. *The Moment of Creation: Big Bang Physics from Before the First Millisecond to the Present Universe*. New York: Charles Scribner's Sons, 1983. This book is a description of the theories of the starting point and development of the universe and includes a lengthy discussion of the role of matter and antimatter in this development.

SEE ALSO: Aug. 7 and 12, 1912: Hess Discovers Cosmic Rays; Spring, 1925: Pauli Formulates the Exclusion Principle; 1933-1934: First Artificial Radioactive Element Is Developed; Nov.-Dec., 1933: Fermi Proposes the Neutrino Theory of Beta Decay; Nov., 1934: Yukawa Proposes the Existence of Mesons.

1932

September 25, 1932
POONA PACT GRANTS REPRESENTATION TO INDIA'S UNTOUCHABLES

The Poona Pact was a compromise measure that rescinded an award of separate electorates to the untouchables but gave them reserved seats in an electoral college.

ALSO KNOWN AS: Yeravda Pact

LOCALE: Poona, India

CATEGORIES: Civil rights and liberties; indigenous peoples' rights; laws, acts, and legal history; diplomacy and international relations

KEY FIGURES

Bhimrao Ramji Ambedkar (1891-1956), leader of the depressed classes and founder of the All-India Depressed Classes Federation, a signatory to the Poona Pact

Mahatma Gandhi (1869-1948), leader of the Indian National Congress and signatory to the Poona Pact

Ramsay MacDonald (1866-1937), prime minister of Great Britain, 1931-1935

SUMMARY OF EVENT

The Second Round Table Conference was called both to frame a new constitution for British India and to establish gradual moves toward self-government that would lead to dominion status and then independence. It was held in London in 1932. At the conference, members of the British government, including Prime Minister Ramsay Mac-Donald and representatives of the Indian National Congress Party, met to discuss constitutional safeguards, the protection of minority communities in India, and the establishment of provisional and central legislatures. The All-India Muslim League had successfully convinced the British government that Muslims and other minority groups needed these types of safeguards to protect their political, economic, and educational interests.

As the need for constitutional safeguards became widely recognized, other communal groups—including Sikhs, Indian Christians, Mahrattas, Anglo-Indians, members of the European community, the so-called backward classes, and women—also petitioned the government for special representation in the 1935 Indian constitution. One such religious group was the untouchables, the Hindu "outcastes" (also known by their more political names of "scheduled castes" or "depressed classes"), whom Mahatma Gandhi referred to as Harijans, or "children of God." The untouchable classes were divided into three categories—untouchables, unap-

proachables, and unseeables. In 1962, the number of untouchables was estimated at about sixty million (out of three hundred million Hindus).

It was very difficult for the Congress Party to accept the idea that there were two communities in India—the Hindus and the largest minority, the Indian Muslims—whose interests diverged. The prospect of recognizing differences between caste Hindus and the group historically known as the untouchables was extremely daunting. When an August 4, 1932, decision made communal awards not only to Muslims but also to the depressed and other classes, Gandhi, who was in Yeravda Prison for his civil disobedience activities, reacted very strongly. He deeply opposed the creation of separate electorates for the depressed classes and the government's insistence that fundamental differences lay between them and caste Hindus. Prime Minister MacDonald tried to justify the decision, and in response Gandhi began a fast that he vowed would continue until his death if separate electorates were not lifted. In essence, Gandhi wanted one electorate that would include all classes, and he wanted caste Hindus to recognize their moral and social responsibilities toward eradicating untouchability and bringing "outcaste" persons into the fold.

In a September 16 statement announcing his fast, Gandhi said that he would begin eating as soon as the threat of separate electorates was removed once and for all. As a prisoner, he considered himself unfit to set forth his proposals, and he agreed to accept any accord that was made by a joint electorate composed of responsible caste Hindus and members of the depressed classes and was accepted by mass meetings of all Hindus. Essentially, Gandhi required the removal of the state-sanctioned inequality that had long been attached to untouchability.

The Poona Pact, also known as the Yeravda Pact, was reached on September 24 and signed on September 25, 1932. Dr. Bhimrao Ramji Ambedkar, a highly educated member and representative of the depressed classes, agreed to the pact on September 26. The pact was seen as a compromise: While it continued to recognize the special status of the depressed classes, it would not award separate electorates to them. Instead, an electoral college of members of the depressed classes would be created, and voters would elect four candidates to participate in primary elections. The general electorate would then vote on the winners of the primary elections. Although the provision was designed to last ten years, it could be abolished earlier.

In every province, the pact provided money for the establishment of educational facilities for members of the depressed classes, and it also required that members of the depressed classes be allowed as candidates for public-service jobs. The scheme for primaries, in which only the depressed classes would have a vote, was proposed by Sir Tej Bahadur Sapru; this feature made the compromise more palatable to Ambedkar.

The Poona Pact, which·later became part of the 1935 Indian Constitution, offered less to the depressed classes than had the 1932 communal decision. However, the fact that the pact established separate electorates secured Ambedkar's reputation as an effective voice for the untouchables. Crucially, the pact gave legitimacy to the idea that the caste system in India was unfair and certainly outdated, an idea that had strong religious as well as political implications. Gandhi himself said that he saw the division of castes as a religious matter and moral issue, and he believed that these matters could only be corrected by Hinduism itself rather than by what he called "political constitutions."

SIGNIFICANCE

The most immediate consequence of the Poona Pact's acceptance was the termination of the "epic fast" and the preservation of Gandhi's life. When he began fasting, Gandhi indicated that his actions were not a response to those who disagreed with him but rather a way to force his supporters to confront an issue—untouchability—that had disturbed him since he was a young man. Putting his life on the line over this matter was a way to show how deeply he was affected by it, although it is important to note that even Gandhi was unwilling for the caste system to be entirely abolished because it was so central to Indian history and culture. In contrast, however, some saw the removal of the caste system as the only way untouchability would disappear.

The Poona Pact did convince the Indian National Congress to put untouchability on its agenda, and as a result the issue became a cause for the reform movement. Other movements

---

THE POONA PACT

The Poona Pact created a special type of electoral college for India's depressed classes. Just as important, however, it ensured Bhimrao Ramji Ambedkar's place as a leader and ended Mahatma Gandhi's life-threatening fast. The full text of the pact follows:

1. There shall be seats reserved for the Depressed Classes out of general electorate seats in the provincial legislatures as follows: Madras, 30; Bombay with Sind, 15; Punjab, 8; Bihar and Orissa, 18; Central Provinces, 20; Assam, 7; Bengal, 30; United Provinces, 20. Total 148. These figures are based on the Prime Minister's (British) decision.

2. Election to these seats shall be by joint electorates subject, however, to the following procedure: All members of the Depressed Classes registered in the general electoral roll of a constituency will form an electoral college which will elect a panel of four candidates belonging to the Depressed Classes for each of such reserved seats by the method of the single vote and four persons getting the highest number of votes in such primary elections shall be the candidates for election by the general electorate.

3. The representation of the Depressed Classes in the Central Legislature shall likewise be on the principle of joint electorates and reserved seats by the method of primary election in the manner provided for in clause above for their representation in the provincial legislatures.

4. In the Central Legislature 18 percent of the seats allotted to the general electorate for British India in the said legislature shall be reserved for the Depressed Classes.

5. The system of primary election to a panel of candidates for election to the Central and Provincial Legislatures as herein before mentioned shall come to an end after the first ten years, unless terminated sooner by mutual agreement under the provision of clause 6 below.

6. The system of representation of Depressed Classes by reserved seats in the Provincial and Central Legislatures as provided for in clauses (1) and (4) shall continue until determined otherwise by mutual agreement between the communities concerned in this settlement.

7. The Franchise for the Central and Provincial Legislatures of the Depressed Classes shall be as indicated in the Lothian Committee Report.

8. There shall be no disabilities attached to anyone on the ground of his being a member of the Depressed Classes in regard to any election to local bodies or appointment to the public services. Every endeavour shall be made to secure a fair representation of the Depressed Classes in these respects, subject to such educational qualifications as may be laid down for appointment to the Public Services.

9. In every province out of the educational grant an adequate sum shall be earmarked for providing educational facilities to the members of Depressed Classes.

1932

had sought to ameliorate the situation of the depressed classes by eliminating subcastes, relaxing caste restrictions, or even abolishing caste altogether. After the pact was signed, Gandhi attempted to eradicate the debilitating social and religious effects of untouchability by opening Hindu temples to untouchables. He remained opposed to interdining and intermarriage, although these eventually took place as well. By not endorsing the interdining and intermarriages that were taking place even then—including private efforts to join the depressed classes and the Sanatanists, or orthodox Hindus, at the table—some said that Gandhi sent ambiguous signals to people who wished to follow his example.

In 1932, the All-India Anti-untouchability League, an organization to assist the untouchables, was founded. In 1933, Gandhi renamed the league the Harijan Sevak Sangh. That same year, a new weekly paper, *Harijan*, was also started. The paper published graphic drawings of the miserable habitations in which these "outcastes" lived. Their disabilities were listed at length: In some parts of the country they were denied access to village wells, schools, and post offices, and they were prevented from using umbrellas and wearing sandals. The Poona Pact could not end the curse of untouchability, which was more than three thousand years old, and the Harijans remained at the bottom of Indian society. In fact, after the fast and the signing of the Poona Pact, untouchability even lost some of its stigma: The debate had given the concept moral legitimacy.

—Nancy Elizabeth Fitch

FURTHER READING

Coupland, Reginald. *The Indian Problem: Report on the Constitutional Problem in India*. New York: Oxford University Press, 1944. Discusses British India's constitutions of 1919 and 1935 and the Round Table Conferences that led to the latter statute. Good background for the constitutional problems with untouchability, including itemization of political liabilities of the depressed classes.

Desai, A. R. *Crusade Against Untouchability: Social Background of Indian Nationalism*. 3d ed. Bombay: G. R. Bhatkal, 1959. Provides glimpses of the history of untouchability and what it means as a cultural principle as well as a brief history of reform movements that attempted to improve the situation of people who suffered under it. Also shows the economic basis of untouchability, which historically has favored caste Hindus.

Fischer, Louis. "Climax." In *The Life of Mahatma Gandhi*. New York: Harper & Brothers, 1950. A chapter in an interesting biography of Gandhi that gives a detailed analysis of Gandhi's fast.

Gandhi, M. K. *Mohandas Gandhi: Essential Writings*. Edited by John Dear. Maryknoll, N.Y.: Orbis Books, 2002. Collection of Gandhi's writings organized thematically, with topics including nonviolent resistance, the search for God, and the pursuit of truth. Includes a chronology as well as a list of sources and recommended readings.

Keer, Dhananjay. *Dr. Ambedkar: Life and Mission*. Bombay: Popular Prakashan, 1962. A biography of the leader of the depressed classes with a detailed account of the activities of Ambedkar and Gandhi during the second Round Table Conference. Particularly interesting for its recounting of pressures on Ambedkar to accept the Poona Pact and thus end Gandhi's fast.

Majumdar, R. C., ed. *Struggle for Freedom*. Vol. 11 in *The History and Culture of the Indian People*. Bombay: Bharatiya Vidya Bhavan, 1969. Good encyclopedic review of Indian nationalism with an interesting and slightly polemic view of Gandhi's motivations in fighting against untouchability. Lengthy discussion of pre-Gandhi social reforms against this practice.

Nanda, Bal R. "Harijans." In *Mahatma Gandhi: A Biography*. Boston: Beacon Press, 1958. The biographer strongly makes his point that Gandhi, throughout his life, was very much against untouchability. Nanda suggests that fasting might have been a form of coercion, but if so it was directed at Gandhi's followers rather than those wanting separate electorates—that it was "to sting the conscience of the Hindu community into right religious action."

Parekh, Bhiku. *Colonialism, Tradition, and Reform: An Analysis of Gandhi's Political Discourse*. Rev. ed. Thousand Oaks, Calif.: Sage, 2000. Examines Gandhi's political technique and explains how Gandhi was careful to use Indian symbols during his negotiations that led to the Delhi Pact. A rich analysis by a renowned Indian thinker.

SEE ALSO: June 6, 1903: Founding of the Weekly *Indian Opinion*; 1920-1922: Gandhi Leads a Noncooperation Movement; Aug., 1921: Moplah Rebellion; 1925-1935: Women's Rights in India Undergo a Decade of Change; Mar. 12-Apr. 5, 1930: Gandhi Leads the Salt March; Mar. 5, 1931: India Signs the Delhi Pact.

October, 1932
WRIGHT FOUNDS THE TALIESIN FELLOWSHIP

The great architect Frank Lloyd Wright invited apprentices to work with him during the third and most productive period of his career.

LOCALE: Spring Green, Wisconsin; Scottsdale, Arizona

CATEGORY: Architecture

KEY FIGURES

Frank Lloyd Wright (1867-1959), American architect

William Wesley Peters (1912-1991), American architect

Edgar Kaufmann, Jr. (1910-1989), American architect

Edgar Tafel (b. 1912), American architect

SUMMARY OF EVENT

In 1932, at the age of sixty-five, architect Frank Lloyd Wright had fallen on hard times. Taliesin, his home in Spring Green, Wisconsin, had been struck by lightning and burned. Having fallen in love with another woman during a messy divorce, he was hounded by police and forced to spend a night in jail before he could remarry. The Great Depression was making the money needed to create big buildings scarce. In nearly five years, Wright had created buildings for only two paying clients, one a cousin. With his new bride, he returned to Taliesin with plans to rebuild it and to write his autobiography.

Genius struck again, however—Wright decided to found the Taliesin Fellowship. He invited apprentices from around the world to live and work with him at Taliesin, where they could learn architecture from the ground up. It was a self-sufficient community: The Taliesin fellows generated electricity, grew their own food, cut their own lumber, quarried stone, and built buildings to live and study in. Having learned design and construction, the fellows helped to engineer and superintend construction of Wright's greatest buildings. Twenty-three fellows gathered at Taliesin in October, 1932. A few soon left, daunted by the work; others stayed a decade or more. The fellowship flourished, and the numbers of fellows doubled and tripled.

To escape the brutal winter of 1937, Wright led the fellows by caravan to Arizona, where they built winter quarters in Scottsdale at what became Taliesin West. A frontier camp at first, the new location had a drafting room that was lit by sunlight through a canvas roof. Based on Wright's principles of organic architecture, the headquarters was designed to blend with the desert land-

scape and was made mostly of materials that were readily at hand.

Wright remained young at heart, especially in old age, and he formed a natural bond with his young apprentices. He believed buildings should not be designed by politicians with grudges or old people with prejudices to preserve, but by fresh young minds. His own creative vigor was spurred by that of his fellows. The Taliesin Fellowship thrust Wright's career into a second golden age.

Among the first to join Wright at Taliesin was Edgar Kaufmann, Jr., who persuaded his father to commission a vacation home in the wild woods of western Pennsylvania. Wright visited the spot, and the result was Fallingwater, perhaps the most famous private home ever built for a person not of royal blood. Senior Taliesin fellows superintended the construction of Fallingwater. A boulder by a stream, which had been the family's favorite picnic spot, shoulders through the floor beside the hearth. Anchored to that rock, the house sweeps out horizontally over a waterfall on cantilevered, reinforced concrete balconies. Light and sound from the rippling waters reverberate on slabs of stone, glass, and concrete. Indoors and outdoors blend. United with nature organically, interior space seems unenclosed, reaching out from within.

In the same year, Herbert Johnson asked Wright and his fellows to make a new headquarters for his wax company. They presented him with one of the most astonishingly original, aesthetically pleasing commercial building ever erected. One newspaper reviewer said it was "like a beautiful naked woman bathing in a forest pool," a rare compliment for an office building. Fashioned on low horizontal curves without corners, the building is entered from behind and beneath, through a carport. Its windowless walls afford no view of drab downtown Racine, Wisconsin, yet there is no feeling of containment, for bands of glass tubing encircle the building, shedding natural daylight on a great communal workspace without cubicles or partitions. As the tubes of glass disperse consciousness of walls, so the ceiling is effaced by giant columns shaped like lily pads; the columns are twenty-four feet in diameter at the top, slimming down to a width of nine inches at the floor. Building code inspectors balked at this design, as each column had to support seven tons. Wright staged a public demonstration in which sixty tons was loaded on one column; the permit was issued, and the spectacle drew nationwide attention. Johnson de-

Frank Lloyd Wright (center) works with four Taliesin fellows (from left): Eugene Masselink, Edgar Tafel, John H. Howe, and Bennie Dombar. (AP/Wide World Photos)

clared the building was worth more than five times its cost in publicity alone; he gave the fellowship a twenty-thousand-dollar tip and renewed that donation every year.

One of the fellowship's first projects had been a scale model of Broadacre City, Wright's visionary plan for a community with a tillable acre of land for each family. The model had featured low-cost "Usonian" (American) homes incorporating Wright's functional concepts. Madison newspaperman Herbert Jacobs commissioned the first truly Usonian home actually built. Without plaster, radiators, attic, or cellar, the famous five-thousand-dollar house was built of concrete blocks and glass on a concrete slab heated by hot-water pipes. Jacobs also commissioned another home that made history, a rounded structure with a berm in back and glass in front for exposure to the sun. Called the solar hemicycle, it was the prototype for passive solar design.

One of the last great projects undertaken by Wright and his fellows proved their most controversial: the

Guggenheim Museum in New York City, an art gallery for nonfigurative art. Wright designed a circular structure that looked more like a concrete eggshell than a regular building. Inside, he coiled a walkway three-fourths of a mile long down from a glass skylight dome on a 3 percent grade. Visitors take an elevator up to the top and then stroll past paintings hung on luminous walls. A turn toward the center presents a prospect of the whole collection. One floor flows into another imperceptibly. Nowhere does the eye meet with any abrupt change of form; all lines flow together in unified harmony. The whole effect is quite serene. Unfortunately, Wright died just months before the museum was opened.

SIGNIFICANCE

The Taliesin Fellowship had impacts on Wright's own career, on the careers of the fellows, and on modern architecture in the United States and around the world. *Taliesin* is a Welsh word that means "the shining brow." Wright took it as the name for his sparkling house of rock and glass built on the brow of a hill in rural Wisconsin. Taliesin was also the name of a mythical Welsh bard who entertained King Arthur and his knights of the Round Table. For Wright, the name thus suggested artistic inspiration, and he used it to christen the fellowship that lifted him late in life with abundant inspiration. With his fellows around the drafting board, he could play King Arthur with his court. They built a new Camelot for themselves and enlivened architecture around the world.

The commission that relaunched the great architect's career came from the father of a Taliesin fellow. The worldwide acclaim that Fallingwater garnered was unprecedented and led to dozens of other residential commissions, the bread and butter of an architect whose scandalous private life had turned away many corporate and governmental customers.

The Taliesin Fellowship itself drew a significant amount of publicity. Its work-camp ethic appealed to American values during Depression years. Much was made of receiving visitors at Taliesin. For fifty cents, a visitor could receive tours of the house and grounds conducted by fellows, attend a performance of the Taliesin orchestra or chorus, and be greeted by Wright himself. The fellowship gained many clients and allies in this way, among them Herbert Johnson, Carl Sandburg, Adlai Stevenson, Henry R. and Clare Boothe Luce, and other influential shapers of public opinion.

The most immediate and long-range effect the Taliesin Fellowship had on architecture was to spread the fame and influence of Frank Lloyd Wright around the world. The successes of Fallingwater and the Johnson Wax headquarters early in the life of the fellowship reestablished Wright's professional reputation. In 1938, a special edition of the influential journal *Architectural Forum* was devoted to Wright's recent work, and his portrait appeared on the cover of *Time* magazine. In 1939, Wright was asked to lecture at the Royal Institute of British Architects. Taliesin fellows put together a major retrospective exhibition shown at the Museum of Modern Art in 1940. In the 1950's, Philadelphia architect Oscar Stonorov organized an exhibition of Wright's work titled *Sixty Years of Living Architecture* and presented it in several cities in the United States, Europe, and Mexico. Wright was the first American architect to gain worldwide fame and influence, and fascination with his work has hardly abated since his founding of the fellowship.

Individually and as an organization, many of the fellows carried on after Wright's death. The fellowship was transformed into Taliesin Associated Architects, a firm that extended Wright's organic principles of design

across the United States. The Frank Lloyd Wright Foundation and School of Architecture were also established to promulgate Wright's philosophy and provide professional education in architecture.

Taliesin Associates completed several important projects unfinished at the time of Wright's death: the buildings at Florida Southern College, the Marin County Civic Center complex, and the Grady Grammage Memorial Auditorium at Arizona State University. Some of Wright's designs were executed as late as the 1970's, such as the Pfeiffer House at Taliesin West, the Feldman House in Berkeley, California, and the Loveness Guest House in Stillwater, Minnesota.

Many fellows went on to achieve prominence in their own right in architecture and related fields, among them Edmund Thomas Casey, Bruce Gobb, Aaron Green, John deKoren Hill, John H. Howe, Edgar Kaufmann, Jr., Eugene Masselink, Charles Mantooth, Robert Mosher, William Wesley Peters, Ling Po, John Rattenbury, Paolo Soleri, and Edgar Tafel. Moreover, Taliesin Associated Architects was responsible for several significant structures erected in the decade after Wright's death, such as the Ascension Lutheran Church in Scottsdale, Arizona, designed by Peters; the Prairie School in Racine, designed by Mantooth; the Rocky Mountain National Park Center; the Lincoln Income Life Insurance Company in Louisville, Kentucky; the Spring Green resort development near Taliesin; and the Lescohier House in Madison, designed by Peters.

Wright regretted that his effects on architecture had been more imitative than emulative, but they were both. The course of modern architecture was charted by the possibilities of concrete, steel, and glass that he and his Taliesin fellows pioneered. Indeed, his concepts of the prairie house, the Usonian house, and passive solar design revolutionized residential architecture, especially in American suburbs. City planners, of course, never realized the concepts Wright envisioned for Broadacre City in full, but they did try to bring more of the country into the city. In the 1970's and 1980's, many downtowns were redesigned as pedestrian malls and gardens to minimize or eliminate the presence of private automobiles. Suburban shopping malls, with their wide-open spacing and horizontal sweep, reflect the massive indirect influence of Wright's Taliesin period.

If Wright had retired at sixty-five instead of founding the Taliesin Fellowship, he would be remembered as a daring experimentalist in residential architecture and interior design. The impact of his creative innovations and organic philosophy on subsequent architecture would

1932

have been marginal, however, as it was before 1932, and his impact on modern building would have been a fraction of what it became.

—*John L. McLean*

FURTHER READING

Costantino, Maria. *Frank Lloyd Wright*. New York: Crescent Books, 1991. Lavishly illustrated picture book of Wright's architecture, with brief commentary, covering all periods of his work in chronological order. Features numerous full-color photographs and black-and-white illustrations. Includes biographical introduction and index.

Levine, Neil. *The Architecture of Frank Lloyd Wright*. Princeton, N.J.: Princeton University Press, 1996. Examines Wright's life as well as his architectural career, addressing the ways in which each influenced the other. Includes many illustrations, bibliographical note, and index.

Smith, Norris Kelly. *Frank Lloyd Wright: A Study in Architectural Content*. Englewood Cliffs, N.J.: Prentice-Hall, 1966. An intriguing portrait of the architect; not a biography, but an analysis of his political, religious, social aesthetic, and philosophical beliefs. Asserts that Wright was a romantic spirit committed to the universal salvation of humankind, a fundamentally conservative and religious cause. Includes illustrations and footnotes.

Storrer, William Allin. *The Architecture of Frank Lloyd Wright: A Complete Catalog*. 3d ed. Chicago: University of Chicago Press, 2002. Provides photographs or sketches of all buildings known to have been designed by Wright, with brief, cogent commentary. Includes an introduction, floor plans for several structures, maps, and geographic and alphabetical indexes.

Tafel, Edgar. *Apprentice to Genius: Years with Frank Lloyd Wright*. New York: McGraw-Hill, 1979. Full and reliable account of the Taliesin Fellowship by one of Wright's greatest protégés. Lavishly illustrated with dozens of photographs, maps, and designs, many in color, including photographs of apprentices at work and buildings under construction. Includes list of Wright buildings that are open to the public and index.

Twombly, Robert C. *Frank Lloyd Wright: An Interpretive Biography*. New York: Harper & Row, 1973. Excellent interpretation of Wright's life, work, and thought for the general reader. Offers cogent commentary on the major designs and an appreciative yet balanced assessment of Wright's political and social ideas and their impact on his work. Marred somewhat by vituperative attacks on Wright's followers. Includes illustrations, notes, annotated bibliography, and index.

Wright, Frank Lloyd. *An Autobiography*. Rev. ed. New York: Horizon Press, 1977. Wright's own revelations of his amazing experiences and the overwhelming adversity he overcame remain lively, fresh, and intriguing. This edition incorporates corrections of earlier editions and eighty-two photographs of people and works built as late as 1976.

Wright, Olgivanna. *Frank Lloyd Wright: His Life, His Work, His Words*. New York: Horizon Press, 1966. Laudatory first-person account of the architect by his beloved third wife. Interesting as an insider's view of life at Taliesin and as a sampler of Wright's lectures to his Taliesin fellows. Includes many black-and-white photographs, a chronological list of Wright's architectural innovations, a catalog of his buildings and unfinished projects, and several sketches of later designs by Taliesin fellows.

SEE ALSO: 1905: Hoffmann Designs the Palais Stoclet; Oct., 1909: Completion of the AEG Turbine Factory; 1910: Gaudí Completes the Casa Milá Apartment House; 1919: German Artists Found the Bauhaus; 1925: Cranbrook Academy Promotes the Arts and Crafts Movement; Spring, 1931: Le Corbusier's Villa Savoye Exemplifies Functionalist Architecture; May 1, 1931: Empire State Building Opens; 1937-1938: Aalto Designs Villa Mairea.

November, 1932
ANTITRUST PROSECUTION FORCES RCA TO RESTRUCTURE

The Radio Corporation of America was restructured following an antitrust lawsuit, bringing an end to the "radio trust."

LOCALE: Washington, D.C.
CATEGORIES: Radio and television; trade and commerce; laws, acts, and legal history

KEY FIGURES

David Sarnoff (1891-1971), founder and leader of the Radio Corporation of America

Owen D. Young (1874-1962), founder of the Radio Corporation of America

Lee de Forest (1873-1961), American scientist and inventor

Warren Olney (1870-1939), assistant U.S. attorney general

SUMMARY OF EVENT

The action taken by the U.S. government to curtail monopolistic practices of the "radio trust" forced the Radio Corporation of America (RCA) to restructure its corporate organization in 1932, profoundly altering its status and its role in the growing home entertainment field. The U.S. government began to investigate RCA for violations of antitrust legislation in 1924, just five years after the government had played an important part in creating the Radio Corporation of America. In 1919, radio was used primarily for point-to-point transmission between stations and ships at sea. The federal government was concerned that this important service would come under the control of foreign hands, namely, the British Marconi Company. It used its influence to persuade Owen D. Young of the General Electric Company (GE) not to sell some important radio patents to Marconi. With government support, GE acquired the American Marconi Company and joined with the Westinghouse, American Telephone and Telegraph (AT&T), and United Fruit companies to form the Radio Corporation of America. Each of the founding companies held important patents in radio technology and received stock in the new organization in return for putting their patents into the RCA pool. AT&T and United Fruit sold their interest in RCA after a few years of operation, leaving GE and Westinghouse as the principal shareholders.

RCA was created on the foundation of radio-related patents—about two thousand of them in 1920—and given the mission to wrest control of wireless communi-

cation from Great Britain. It quickly achieved these goals and successfully acquired many more patents, until it dominated the technology of radio. In the early 1920's, the astonishing rise of radio as home entertainment brought immense wealth and power to RCA but also changed its relationship with the U.S. government.

David Sarnoff was the force behind RCA's move into radio as home entertainment. He had first brought the idea of a radio "music box" to the attention of the management of RCA and had directed the company's strategy of acquiring broadcasting stations and manufacturing radio receivers. Point-to-point transmission of radio messages was usually the preserve of monopolies, but the fledgling broadcast industry was a highly competitive business with hundreds of new companies. Sarnoff saw that RCA's pool of patents could bring order to this chaos. He encouraged energetic prosecution of patent infringers in the courts.

Once RCA's key patents had been upheld, the path was clear to establish a radio monopoly. The technology of wireless communication rested on numerous patents, but Sarnoff chose to use the vacuum tube as the means to enforce RCA's patent holdings and establish its monopoly. The vacuum tube detected and amplified radio waves and was a vital component of radio sets and many other valuable products, such as control devices for industry. RCA's patent position was especially strong in vacuum tubes, and its research laboratories were constantly producing new types of tubes that brought dramatic improvements in radio sets.

Sarnoff instituted a system of "package licensing" by which a company wishing to enter the radio field could get access to all necessary patents by acquiring one license from RCA. It was impossible to make radio equipment without infringing on RCA's patents, especially those related to vacuum tubes. In the early days of radio, in the first years of the 1920's, twenty-five large companies received licenses from RCA in return for substantial fees and a royalty paid on each radio set sold. The conditions of the license favored RCA's monopoly because the licensees had to agree to use only RCA vacuum tubes in their products. Independent producers of vacuum tubes, such as inventor Lee de Forest, who had created one of the pioneer tubes, opposed this restriction and took their case to the U.S. Congress. Independent radio manufacturers, such as the Grigsby-Grunow company, brought suits against RCA and kept the issue of the radio monopoly in the public eye.

As radio sets became one of the most popular consumer products of the 1920's and vacuum tubes were applied to many more products, RCA's patent holdings became more profitable. By the end of the 1920's, royalty income was running around $7 million annually and was the main source of revenue for the company. Although RCA allowed smaller companies to acquire licenses, it still held a stranglehold on the booming business of making radio receivers. It increased the amount of royalty payments and placed more restrictions on use of the licenses it issued. Soon, disgruntled radio companies were referring to RCA as the "radio trust."

Complaints from radio manufacturers led the Federal Trade Commission to launch a four-year investigation into RCA in 1924. That investigation brought many accusations that the company and its owners were restraining trade but no prosecution. In 1930, the U.S. Justice Department filed suit against RCA and its owners, alleging unlawful conspiracy to dictate the terms by which any potential competitor could use any of the patents held by RCA. In terms of the dollar amount of business covered by the prosecution, this was one of the largest antitrust suits ever initiated by the United States.

The announcement of an impending lawsuit against RCA quickly led to negotiations with the Justice Department to find a basis for dropping the prosecution. These negotiations continued through 1931 and 1932. The Justice Department was represented by Assistant Attorney General Warren Olney. The government's position was that the leading participants in RCA should take their patents back, thus removing the means of monopoly power in the radio field and restoring competition. They favored an open patent pool with no restrictive licenses. RCA argued that the patents were its greatest asset and that removing them would lead to the dissolution of the company. The Great Depression had already begun to take its toll in the radio industry, and RCA's common stock, which had once been priced at 114, reached its low point.

Several times during 1932, preliminary agreements on terms of the breakup of the radio trust were reached, but RCA backed out because it believed that the conditions were too severe. Many in the company believed that an open patent pool that gave free access to inventions was unfair to those who had worked to produce them, including RCA's own laboratories. Representatives of each side met daily in an effort to resolve their differences. Opinion within RCA was that no wrongdoing had occurred in their contracts with affiliates, but Owen D. Young argued for compromise to avoid a long

and potentially damaging lawsuit. In November, 1932, RCA gave way and agreed to the conditions demanded by the Justice Department two days before the trial was scheduled to begin. It signed a consent decree that did not admit guilt of any antitrust violations.

SIGNIFICANCE

The major result of the consent decree was that General Electric and Westinghouse had to divest themselves of stock in RCA. Their employees who sat on the board of directors of RCA had to resign their seats. Owen D. Young, who had been a founder of RCA and had played a major part in forging the agreement with the Justice Department, had to leave the board. GE and Westinghouse agreed to stay out of the business of manufacturing radio sets in competition with RCA for a period of thirty months, by which time RCA was expected to have weathered the transition from monopoly status and become fit to compete.

The agreement also made it possible for AT&T to re-enter the radio business and begin making its own sets. The telephone companies had been some of the first to investigate wireless transmission because it threatened their long lines. After playing an important part in the formation of RCA, AT&T had sold its shares in the organization in 1922 and in 1926 had abandoned its interests in radio broadcasting. It had exploited the work of its Western Electric laboratories to become a leading force in vacuum tube technology and had established itself as the major supplier of sound equipment for motion-picture studios. It now stood as a dangerous competitor to RCA in the new field of electronic equipment manufacture.

The conditions of the agreement between RCA and the Justice Department were not all unfavorable to the company. Under its old relationships, RCA had been obliged to buy vacuum tubes and transmitting apparatus from GE and Westinghouse and then use them in its own products. Now it was able to make its own tubes and use them in new businesses, such as industrial applications. This opened up several profitable new fields for the company.

The consent decree ended the practice of issuing exclusive licenses that forced radio manufacturers to use only RCA tubes. RCA could no longer pick and choose whom to allow into the radio business because it was forced to license any applicant. RCA no longer dominated the patent pool, and the independent radio manufacturers hoped that they would be able to secure licenses from General Electric or Westinghouse. They saw competition as a means of lowering license and royalty fees.

The open patent pool never materialized, and AT&T controlled many important patents. It was not until 1958 that RCA's licensing power was ended by a Justice Department antitrust suit.

Although the consent decree limited RCA's monopoly power in the radio field, it did not bring the company to bankruptcy, as many feared it would, nor did it hinder RCA's growth during the 1930's. The radio trust might have been broken, but by 1932 the great radio boom was over. Sales of receiving sets had reached the saturation point. David Sarnoff had correctly recognized that the time was right to diversify RCA's business. To this end, he had moved into the businesses of broadcasting, filmmaking, and the manufacture of phonographs and records.

As news of the impending antitrust suit was reaching RCA in the late 1920's, Sarnoff was already pressing the directors to turn the company into a self-contained concern that manufactured all the components used in its products. Sarnoff wanted to integrate the company fully by building up its research operation and by creating a strong manufacturing base. He also wanted to make RCA a force in technologies other than radio. Rather than undermining this strategy, the consent decree actually pushed RCA further along this path. RCA acquired several manufacturing facilities from GE and Westinghouse and embarked on the manufacture of a wide range of electronic products. Although the United States was in the grip of a serious depression, RCA continued to be a highly profitable concern. The company had sales of $100 million and profits of $6 million in 1936.

The government's antitrust suit helped turn RCA from an organization focused on collecting royalty payments into a broad-based manufacturing concern driven by the innovations emerging from its laboratories. The critical cross-licensing agreement that had been the basis of the original idea for the Radio Corporation of America was left untouched by the consent decree. RCA still had access to radio-related inventions produced in the laboratories of GE and Westinghouse and could share in the advance of radio technology. It also had acquired several of their development laboratories. RCA emerged from the antitrust suit as one of the most powerful research and development organizations in American business.

Although Sarnoff publicly mourned the breakup of the radio trust and predicted hard times for RCA after it had been separated from its powerful owners, he was actually pleased that he now had free rein to lead the company. Free from the restraints of operating within the larger corporate control of GE and Westinghouse, Sarnoff seized the opportunity to make RCA into a more flexible and innovative company. Under his tenure, research became one of the foundations of RCA's operations and the guiding force of its business strategies. Sarnoff's vision was of an enterprise based on technology, not necessarily the result of accumulating patents but the consequence of an ambitious research agenda. RCA was one of the first companies to investigate the technical and commercial opportunities of television, carrying out important research in the 1930's. Television became a bigger and more profitable business than radio after World War II and established RCA as the leader in the home entertainment field.

—Andre Millard

FURTHER READING

Aitken, Hugh G. *The Continuous Wave: Technology and American Radio, 1900-1932*. Princeton, N.J.: Princeton University Press, 1985. The definitive study of the early years of radio. Contains a detailed description of the founding of the Radio Corporation of America.

Bilby, Kenneth. *The General: David Sarnoff and the Rise of the Communications Industry*. New York: Harper & Row, 1986. One among many favorable biographies of Sarnoff, written by an RCA executive who worked with him. Reveals the inner workings of the company up to the 1960's.

Head, Sydney W., Thomas Spann, and Michael A. McGregor. *Broadcasting in America: A Survey of Electronic Media*. 9th ed. Boston: Houghton Mifflin, 2000. The standard introduction to the institutions of radio and television in the United States.

Maclaurin, W. Rupert, and R. Joyce Harman. *Invention and Innovation in the Radio Industry*. 1949. Reprint. New York: Arno Press, 1976. Although somewhat dated, still an excellent overall account of the formation and first decades of the radio industry. Includes illustrations and index.

Sarnoff, David. *Looking Ahead: The Papers of David Sarnoff*. New York: McGraw-Hill, 1968. Contains selections from Sarnoff's papers held at Princeton University. Focuses on technology but reveals Sarnoff's strategies and personality.

Sobel, Robert. *RCA*. New York: Stein & Day, 1986. Good overview of the history of the company, written by a leading business historian for the lay reader. Places the growth of RCA and its technology in the context of the times. Portrays Sarnoff in a more realistic and less flattering light than do other sources.

Sterling, Christopher H., and John Michael Kittross. *Stay Tuned: A History of American Broadcasting*. 3d ed. Mahwah, N.J.: Lawrence Erlbaum, 2001. The standard one-volume history of radio and television in the United States.

SEE ALSO: Oct. 15, 1914: Clayton Antitrust Act; 1920's: Radio Develops as a Mass Broadcast Medium; Mar. 1, 1920: *United States v. United States Steel Corporation*; Aug. 20-Nov. 2, 1920: Radio Broadcasting Begins; Sept. 9, 1926: National Broadcasting Company Is Founded; Feb. 21, 1927: Eastman Kodak Is Found to Be in Violation of the Sherman Act; Nov. 1, 1939: Rockefeller Center Is Completed; Sept. 1, 1940: First Color Television Broadcast.

November 8, 1932
FRANKLIN D. ROOSEVELT IS ELECTED U.S. PRESIDENT

Dissatisfied with President Herbert Hoover's response to the Great Depression, Americans voted for Franklin D. Roosevelt, who promised them a "New Deal." Roosevelt would become the only president reelected three times as well as the most famous and successful Democratic leader of the twentieth century.

LOCALE: United States
CATEGORIES: Government and politics; economics

KEY FIGURES
Franklin D. Roosevelt (1882-1945), governor of New York, 1929-1933, and president of the United States, 1933-1945
Eleanor Roosevelt (1884-1962), first lady of the United States, 1933-1945
Herbert Hoover (1874-1964), president of the United States, 1929-1933
James Aloysius Farley (1888-1976), chairman of the National Democratic Committee and Roosevelt's campaign manager
John Nance Garner (1868-1967), speaker of the House of Representatives, 1931-1932, and vice president of the United States, 1933-1941
Huey Long (1893-1935), Louisiana politician

SUMMARY OF EVENT
On July 2, 1932, Franklin D. Roosevelt boarded a trimotored airplane at Albany, New York, and flew to Chicago, where the Democratic National Convention had nominated him to be the party's candidate in the general election for president of the United States. It was a dramatic gesture. Breaking tradition, Roosevelt became the first presidential candidate ever to make an acceptance speech at a nominating convention. Previously, nominees had awaited official notification through the U.S. mail. In a personal appearance, he could both emphasize his determination to take vigorous action against the nation's economic ills and demonstrate his physical ability to handle the job. His plane bucked strong headwinds and twice had to land in order to refuel. When he at last stood before the sweating delegates in Chicago Stadium, he endorsed the party platform, promising relief for the unemployed, public works, repeal of Prohibition, agricultural reform, and tariff reduction. In a ringing conclusion he declared: "I pledge you, I pledge myself, to a new deal for the American people."

Three years of the worst economic depression in U.S. history, occurring under a Republican administration, had wrecked Republican chances to retain the White House in 1932. An unenthusiastic Republican convention had nominated President Herbert Hoover and his vice president, Charles Curtis, to run for a second term. Republican leaders were under no illusions. Only a sudden upturn in the economy could offer the ticket any hope.

Given the near certainty of a Democratic victory, the struggle within the Democratic Party's ranks for the nomination was intense. As governor of New York, Roosevelt had emerged as the early front-runner. He had support among both urban and rural Democrats, the two factions that had torn the party apart in recent elections, but he lost ground late in the primaries. Al Smith, the titular leader of the party and the 1928 presidential nominee, was the darling of the eastern political bosses. The most important favorite son was a Texan, John Nance Garner, who had the backing of powerful newspaper publisher William Randolph Hearst.

If the anti-Roosevelt coalition had stayed together, the nomination might have gone to a dark horse such as Newton D. Baker, secretary of war in the Woodrow Wilson cabinet. On the third ballot, the Roosevelt forces were stopped cold, about one hundred votes short of the necessary two-thirds majority. The bandwagon envisioned by Roosevelt's campaign manager, James Aloy-

U.S. ELECTORAL VOTE, 1932

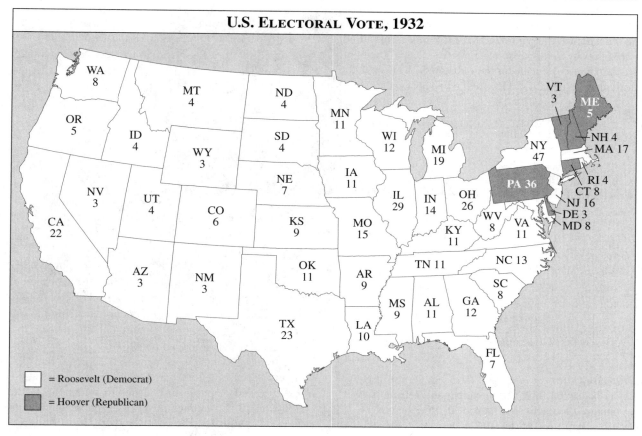

WA 8 · OR 5 · MT 4 · ID 4 · WY 3 · ND 4 · SD 4 · MN 11 · WI 12 · MI 19 · VT 3 · ME 5 · NH 4 · MA 17 · NY 47 · PA 36 · RI 4 · CT 8 · NJ 16 · DE 3 · MD 8 · NV 3 · UT 4 · CO 6 · NE 7 · IA 11 · IL 29 · IN 14 · OH 26 · WV 8 · VA 11 · CA 22 · AZ 3 · NM 3 · KS 9 · MO 15 · KY 11 · NC 13 · TN 11 · OK 11 · AR 9 · SC 8 · MS 9 · AL 11 · GA 12 · TX 23 · LA 10 · FL 7

□ = Roosevelt (Democrat)
■ = Hoover (Republican)

1932

sius Farley, had not materialized, and the prize seemed about to slip away. After a brief recess, Texas and California switched their votes to support Roosevelt, giving him the necessary majority. Garner himself had made the crucial decision. He was a loyal Democrat who feared the consequences of a deadlocked convention and the nomination of a weak compromise choice; to mollify his supporters and balance the ticket, he accepted the vice presidential nomination. Louisiana's governor, Huey Long, assisted Garner with southern delegations.

The flight to Chicago the next day set the tone of the Democratic campaign, but Roosevelt remained vague about the "new deal" he so casually had promised. He spoke in warm but sometimes contradictory generalities, always playing it safe; most of all, he wanted to keep his fractious party together and gather the enormous vote of protest against Hoover. His major farm address, at Topeka, Kansas, promised a national program of planned agricultural production without being explicit about how it would work. To the business community, he pledged a 25 percent reduction in federal spending and a balanced budget. The Hoover administration, he said at Pittsburgh, was "the most reckless and extravagant" peacetime government in history. This speech would haunt him later, but he was thoroughly serious. He left himself one loophole: People would not be allowed to starve, even if the government had to run a deficit. In his address before the Commonwealth Club at San Francisco, he came closest to spelling out his economic philosophy: that government must assume the role of regulator of the common good within the existing economic system.

Hoover's brutal use of the army against the Bonus Marchers that summer—in a demonstration that turned into the Anacostia Flats riots—confirmed the popular image of him as a man insensitive to suffering. On the hustings, Hoover hammered out his speeches without the aid of speechwriters, and his plodding performances contrasted with Roosevelt's ebullience. Sometimes Hoover and Roosevelt sounded strangely alike, but they had fundamental differences. Hoover argued that the causes of the Depression lay in Europe and thus far away from U.S. shores, whereas Roosevelt emphasized the

Depression's domestic origins. They also disagreed on tariff policy, the gold standard, Prohibition, and public utility regulation. Late in the campaign, Hoover panicked with the fear that U.S. institutions were in jeopardy. If Roosevelt had his way on the tariff, Hoover said, "The grass will grow in the streets of a hundred cities, a thousand towns; the weeds will overrun the fields of millions of farms."

Despite the lack of any real debate of the issues, voters understood that Roosevelt's election meant change, even if it was not clear exactly where he would lead them. Roosevelt amassed 22,821,857 votes to Hoover's 15,761,841, losing only six northeastern states; he overwhelmingly carried the electoral college with a vote of 472 to 59. The Socialist and Communist Parties polled less than a million votes in what should have been a golden opportunity to exploit discontent. Between election day and the inaugural lay another hard winter. While the nation awaited clarification of Roosevelt's "new deal," the Great Depression reached its nadir.

SIGNIFICANCE

Once Roosevelt took office, he began to turn his campaign references to a "new deal" into the reality of a series of social and economic reforms called the New Deal. He instituted programs to create jobs, to feed the starving, to help banks recover, and otherwise to fight the effects of the Great Depression. Roosevelt's administrations are remembered as the most successful incarnation of Democratic "big government," as he significantly expanded the federal government and used that government as a tool of what would later be called "social justice." At the time, the forces of the Right labeled Roosevelt a socialist and fought tooth and nail against many of his most famous and most popular programs. However, Roosevelt's eventual success in combating the Depression—arguably as much a function of the advent of World War II and the mobilization of a wartime economy as anything else—ensured that subsequent generations would portray him differently. By the 1980's, he was portrayed almost universally in the mainstream of American politics as a great leader (whatever might have been said about him in private), and such diverse political voices as Ronald Reagan and Lyndon LaRouche have claimed to be the authentic inheritors of the Roosevelt legacy.

—*Donald Holley and Joseph Edward Lee*

Franklin D. Roosevelt takes the oath of office from Chief Justice Charles Evans Hughes in 1933. (AP/Wide World Photos)

FURTHER READING

Alter, Jonathan. *The Defining Moment: FDR's Hundred Days and the Triumph of Hope*. New York: Simon & Schuster, 2006. Tightly focused study of the first one hundred days of Roosevelt's first term in office, during which he responded to the national crisis and defined his presidency and legacy for generations. Includes bibliographic references and index.

Bernstein, Michael. *The Great Depression*. New York: Cambridge University Press, 1987. A provocative study of the causes of the Great Depression.

Brinkley, Alan. *Voices of Protest*. New York: Vintage Books, 1983. Analyzes the criticism that was aimed at the New Deal by Huey P. Long and Father Charles Coughlin.

Friedel, Frank. *Franklin D. Roosevelt: A Rendezvous with Destiny*. Boston: Little, Brown, 1990. In a single volume, one of the most prolific Roosevelt experts examines the president's career.

Garraty, John A., ed. *The Great Depression*. San Diego, Calif.: Harcourt Brace Jovanovich, 1986. A collection of essays exploring the economic collapse from an international perspective.

Lash, Joseph. *Eleanor and Franklin*. New York: W. W. Norton, 1971. Documents the role played by Eleanor Roosevelt in her husband's march toward the White House.

Leuchtenburg, William E. *Franklin D. Roosevelt and the New Deal*. New York: Harper & Row, 1963. An excellent analysis of the implementation of Roosevelt's program.

Winkler, Allan M. *Franklin D. Roosevelt and the Making of Modern America*. New York: Pearson/Longman, 2006. A study of Roosevelt's administration, ar-

guing that Roosevelt's transformation of the federal government defined its role and functions in American life for the rest of the century and beyond.

SEE ALSO: Oct. 29, 1929-1939: Great Depression; 1930's: Americans Embrace Radio Entertainment; Jan. 22, 1932: Reconstruction Finance Corporation Is Created; Feb. 28, 1933: Perkins Becomes First Woman Secretary of Labor; Mar. 9-June 16, 1933: The Hundred Days; Oct. 18, 1933: Roosevelt Creates the Commodity Credit Corporation; Nov. 16, 1933: United States Recognizes Russia's Bolshevik Regime; May 27, 1935: Black Monday; July 5, 1935: Wagner Act; Aug. 31, 1935-Nov. 4, 1939: Neutrality Acts; Jan. 6, 1937: Embargo on Arms to Spain; Feb. 5-July 22, 1937: Supreme Court-Packing Fight; June 25, 1938: Fair Labor Standards Act; June 14, 1940: United States Begins Building a Two-Ocean Navy.

1932

December, 1932-Spring, 1934
GREAT FAMINE STRIKES THE SOVIET UNION

In the Soviet Union, forced collectivization and the seizure of foodstuffs by the central government resulted in the deaths of millions of peasants. Huge numbers of people were either murdered outright or died as a result of horrific conditions in state-run camps, although Joseph Stalin's government attempted to hide its crimes from the world.

ALSO KNOWN AS: Terror Famine

LOCALE: Ukraine, Russia, Kazakhstan, and the Soviet Union's North Caucasus regions

CATEGORIES: Agriculture; disasters; government and politics; human rights

KEY FIGURES

Joseph Stalin (Joseph Vissarionovich Dzhugashvili; 1878-1953), general secretary of the Communist Party in Russia and dictator in the Soviet Union, 1929-1953

Nikita S. Khrushchev (1894-1971), Soviet leader in the Ukraine

Pavlik Morozov (1918-1932), one of many young people who informed on their parents at the behest of the Soviet state

SUMMARY OF EVENT

In October of 1928, Soviet dictator Joseph Stalin rolled out the First Five-Year Plan for the Soviet Union's eco-

nomic transformation. The plan promised to ensure the comprehensive development of industry throughout the Soviet Union and included a plan to modernize Soviet agriculture, which remained largely unchanged from its days under the czars: Most peasants still lived in small villages and followed traditional methods of agriculture.

The Five-Year Plan was supposed to transform Soviet peasants into an agricultural proletariat. Although some would become direct employees of state-owned farms, the rural equivalent of factories, the majority were expected to join cooperative enterprises known as collective farms, in which they would pool their tools and labor and share in the proceeds. These new farms would be provided with modern farm machinery that would help bring Soviet agricultural productivity in line with that of industrialized Western nations.

In theory, the transition was supposed to be voluntary, and a great deal of publicity was devoted to the first few peasants who joined. However, only the poorest of peasants stood to gain anything under the new arrangement, and so most simply ignored the call to collectivize. Many resisted the government's attempts to compel their participation.

Stalin's response to attempts at resistance was brutal and coercive. The prosperous peasants, often known as kulaks (the Russian word for "fist"), were condemned as enemies of the people. Another group, known as subkulaks, was theoretically composed of peasants too prosperous to be grouped among the very poor and not prosperous enough to be kulaks, although in reality this group included anyone who objected to collectivization. Kulaks and subkulaks were arrested in huge numbers and sent to prison camps in obscure regions of Siberia, where many began building their own camps immediately after disembarking from the deportation trains. Thousands died of exposure within days of their arrival: Prisoners often wore nothing but the clothes they had on at the time of their arrest in the far warmer lands of Ukraine and the northern Caucasus.

Many of the peasants who were not arrested were accused of hoarding food. Arbitrary production quotas from the central planning agencies were enforced by the secret police, whose members operated under the assumption that peasants had plenty of food and that they were simply hiding it from the government. Agents regularly broke into peasant huts and barns to take whatever they found, and in response desperate peasants sought food wherever they could, often picking fallen grain from the fields. Stalin reacted by promulgating even harsher laws. A person could be shot for "stealing" as little as five heads of wheat. The mere possession of grain, even if it was being stored for the next year's planting, was considered evidence of hoarding, and the accused were often executed without even the pretense of a trial.

Children were encouraged to inform on their parents for hoarding grain or for otherwise resisting collectivization. The most famous case was that of Pavlik Morozov, a fourteen-year-old member of the Young Pioneers (the state-sanctioned youth organization) who turned in his father—who had been the head of the village soviet in Gerasimovka—and was subsequently murdered by a group of villagers led by his uncle. The Soviet government quickly made Morozov a martyr and erected a shrine to him in the house where his father's trial had been held. Stalin's background as a former seminarian was perversely expressed in the development of the cults centered on Morozov and others like him, including Kolya Myagotin, Kolya Yakovlev, Kychan Dzhalkylov, and Promya Kolibin. At least one mother who lost her son in the collectivization and resulting famine said that she would rather see her child killed than have him twisted into the type of person who would betray family to the government.

Whole families perished during the artificial scarcity: Some collapsed from exhaustion while in search of food, while others died quietly in their huts. Starving peasants who searched for food in the towns and cities were turned away, and some became so maddened by hunger that they filled their bellies with anything remotely edible, including tree bark and grass. Others were so desperate that they turned to preying on their fellow human beings, eating what little flesh remained on the bones of those who had already starved or murdering people outright. Nikita S. Khrushchev's memoirs grimly recounted the author's memory of finding a peasant woman ranting that she had already eaten her daughter and was now salting her son's flesh.

In March of 1930, Stalin issued a proclamation called "Dizzy with Success," a tactical retreat in which he criticized the "excesses" of collectivization, but this meager action did little to slow famine's rising tide, and the disruption of agriculture and widespread starvation continued for several years. Furthermore, Stalin refused to seek international aid and determinedly concealed the famine's extent. Western democracies were largely unaware of the massive numbers of deaths; Stalin did not want to give the world powers reason to doubt the First Five-Year Plan. In order to prevent the unauthorized flow of information, Stalin established strict controls on travel, and any contact between Soviet and foreign citizens was automatically suspect.

SIGNIFICANCE

Forced collectivization and the resulting famine dealt huge blows to Soviet agriculture. Agricultural productivity plummeted just as the Soviet Union was most in need of food to fuel the industrialization imposed by the First Five-Year Plan. Production would not return to pre-collectivization levels until 1940, just before the Nazi invasion inflicted further destruction on the Soviet Union's principal agricultural regions. The problems at the root of the Soviet systems of collective farming and central planning prevented the country's agricultural advancement and made it permanently incapable of feeding its citizens. Even Soviet president Mikhail Gorbachev's 1980's-era program of perestroika (restructuring) proved incapable of remedying the situation. Furthermore, Stalinist policies discouraged farmers' attempts to take any initiative, and this legacy continued to plague Russian farmers after the Soviet Union's fall.

The famine's human cost was enormous but could not be acknowledged under Stalin's inflexible policies. Noted Soviet writer Boris Pasternak suggested that the 1936-1937 Great Terror, in which thousands of Soviets suspected of opposing Stalin were killed, was the direct result of collectivization's failure: Because the catastrophe of collectivization could not be acknowledged, Soviet citizens were taught to ignore the evidence of their own experience and believe what they were told. This absurd situation spawned show trials in which the Bolshevik Revolution's founding fathers confessed to outlandish accusations that they had spied for foreign governments and had conspired to destroy the government that in reality they had risked everything to create.

—*Leigh Husband Kimmel*

FURTHER READING

Belov, Fedor. *The History of a Soviet Collective Farm.* New York: Frederick A. Praeger, 1955. A study of the experiences of a single collective farm through the 1930's and beyond.

Conquest, Robert. *The Harvest of Sorrow: Soviet Collectivization and the Terror-Famine.* New York: Oxford University Press, 1986. A comprehensive history of the period by the noted expert on the subsequent Great Terror.

Khrushchev, Nikita S. *Khrushchev Remembers.* Boston: Little, Brown, 1970. A revealing primary source, although it must be read with some skepticism given Khrushchev's complicity in many of the crimes he describes and his desire to minimize his own culpability.

Lewin, M. *Russian Peasants and Soviet Power: A Study of Collectivization.* New York: W. W. Norton, 1968. An in-depth scholarly study of collectivization.

Rayfield, Donald. *Stalin and His Hangmen: The Tyrant and Those Who Killed for Him.* New York: Random House, 2004. Carefully researched study of the relationship between Stalin and his chief henchmen. Describes Stalin's ability to manipulate those around him.

SEE ALSO: 1907: Famine Strikes Russia; 1921-1923: Famine in Russia Claims Millions of Lives; May 18, 1928: Shakhty Case Debuts Show Trials in Moscow; Oct. 1, 1928: Stalin Introduces Central Planning; Jan., 1929: Trotsky Is Sent into Exile; Dec., 1934: Stalin Begins the Purge Trials; Summer, 1939: Stalin Suppresses the Russian Orthodox Church.

1932

Winter, 1932

HUXLEY'S *BRAVE NEW WORLD* FORECASTS TECHNOLOGICAL TOTALITARIANISM

Aldous Huxley's novel Brave New World *titillated readers with a portrait of a dystopian world in which science and technology have satisfied every need at the expense of human freedom.*

LOCALE: England
CATEGORY: Literature

KEY FIGURES
Aldous Huxley (1894-1963), English novelist
John B. Watson (1878-1958), American psychologist

SUMMARY OF EVENT

By the time *Brave New World* was published early in 1932, Aldous Huxley was reaching the zenith of his fame as a novelist. Although he would publish much more over the next thirty years, he would turn increasingly to nonfiction.

Huxley grew up in the stimulating intellectual atmosphere of a family of prominent scientists and literary figures. His exposure to writing and matters of style came about as a natural consequence of his father's editorship of the influential *Cornhill Magazine*. Huxley's early writings included his contributions to the University of Oxford's respected *The Athæneum*. During World War I, while still a student at Oxford, he published two books of poetry. Another volume of poetry and a book of short fiction immediately preceded the 1921 publication of his first novel, *Crome Yellow*, which was a critical and popular success and established Huxley as a novelist of ideas and as a satirist.

Huxley's world, from the beginning of his literary career up until (and certainly after) the publication of *Brave New World*, was one in which satire seemed to be the writer's appropriate mode. The post-World War I era was crassly materialistic, skeptical, and cynical; at the same time, it was buoyantly optimistic owing to the explosion of research and knowledge in many areas of life. Huxley and his literary contemporaries also detected a moral and spiritual emptiness that focused their themes. Huxley's 1920's novels witheringly portrayed the same frivolous generation being explored and satirized in the works of Evelyn Waugh, W. Somerset Maugham, F. Scott Fitzgerald, and Sinclair Lewis. Disillusionment, loss of faith, and spiritual shallowness received equal although less satirical treatment by Ernest Hemingway,

D. H. Lawrence, Virginia Woolf, Ezra Pound, and T. S. Eliot. Over them all loomed the genius of James Joyce, who liberated style and form in the novel and strengthened Huxley's conviction that satirical fiction was the proper vehicle for the exploration of the modern human condition.

The beneficial effects of the literary atmosphere in which Huxley evolved as a writer were offset by some of the unpleasant social realities of the 1920's and early 1930's. England's postwar economic woes belied the feverish consumerism of the privileged classes. The "Roaring Twenties" were punctuated by the 1926 General Strike and the global 1929 stock market crash and ensuing Great Depression. In the new Soviet Union, power struggles unfolded that resulted in the ascent of Joseph Stalin. His aggressive totalitarianism was repeated in the equally ominous comings to power of Adolf Hitler, Benito Mussolini, and Francisco Franco. The eco-nomic disarray of their nations provided fertile ground for these dictators' relentless repression of individual and cultural freedom; the progressive breakdown of European nations signaled the inevitability of another global war.

At the same time, exciting developments in the sciences, both physical and social, were occurring. These stimulated both Huxley's intellect and his imagination. For example, mass production was revolutionizing industry (including arms production) through use of the assembly line, making inexpensive, mass-produced consumer goods widely available. Air travel technology, glamorized by the exploits of Charles A. Lindbergh and Amelia Earhart, was rapidly developing, and the pace of achievement in communications technology was stunning. Explorations in genetics and genetic mutation were stirring public debate. Behaviorist and conditioning theories, pioneered by American psychologist John B. Watson, were stimulating controversy and influencing theories of child care and education. In 1928, Margaret Mead published *Coming of Age in Samoa: A Psychological Study of Primitive Youth for Western Civilization*, forcing cultural anthropologists to redefine many ideas about human social behavior. Huxley's considerable scientific knowledge enabled him to consider these advances, carried to their satirical extreme, in *Brave New World*.

Because of Huxley's well-established literary fame, *Brave New World* provoked an immediate popular response when it appeared in the winter of 1932. In its first year, it sold a total of twenty-eight thousand copies in England and the United States. Eventually, it was translated into nineteen languages, and it continued to enjoy respectable sales throughout the remainder of the century. It evidently struck a chord in a population both fascinated by and fearful of the huge scientific and technological advances of an era beset by economic instability, the possibility of renewed global warfare, and a decline in traditional values.

As a novelist of provocative ideas and sophisticated style, Huxley viewed fiction as the vehicle through which the human experience, especially in his eventful times, could best be explored. Judging by the novel's continuing popularity, *Brave New World* was the work with which Huxley came closest to achieving his goal of examining the dilemma posed by hu-

Aldous Huxley. (AP/Wide World Photos)

THE BRAVE POSTNUCLEAR WORLD

In his foreword to the 1946 edition of Brave New World, *Huxley—from the vantage of one year after World War II and into the age of nuclear weapons— mused over the speed with which his predictions seemed to be coming true. From the perspective of the twenty-first century, his novel is eerily prophetic:*

All things considered it looks as though Utopia were far closer to us than anyone, only fifteen years ago [when the novel first appeared in 1932], could have imagined. I projected it six hundred years into the future. Today it seems quite possible that the horror may be upon us within a single century. That is, if we refrain from blowing ourselves to smithereens in the interval. Indeed, unless we choose to decentralize and to use applied science, not as the end to which human beings are to be made the means, but as the means to producing a race of free individuals, we have only two alternatives to choose from: either a number of national, militarized totalitarianisms, having as their root the terror of the atomic bomb and as their consequence the destruction of civilization . . . or else one supra-national totalitarianism, called into existence by the social chaos resulting from rapid technological progress in general and the atomic revolution in particular, and developing, under the need for efficiency and stability, into the welfare-tyranny of Utopia. You pays your money and you takes your choice.

mankind's equal impulses for good and evil, for creativity and self-destructiveness.

SIGNIFICANCE

Although all of Huxley's first four novels satirize contemporary life, *Brave New World* extrapolates the values and the scientific and technological achievements of that life into a world exactly six hundred years in the future. A global holocaust, the Nine Years' War, has reshaped the world. Its spokesman in 632 A.F. (After Ford) is the world controller, Mustapha Mond. Early in the novel, he expounds the principles on which the society, portrayed largely in a transformed London, is founded. Stability is its cornerstone; relentless elimination of human individuality through biological engineering and superficially benign totalitarianism is its most chilling achievement.

Life is orderly and tranquil, owing largely to the technological wizardry applied to its daily functions. The showpiece is the assembly-line production of the five types of humans, ranging from the intellectually superior Alphas to the semimoronic Epsilons. The novel opens with a tour of the Central London Hatchery and Conditioning Center. Huxley's wit and evocative descriptive style are at their best here, as the hatchery's director proudly describes the fetuses' inexorable nine-month journey by bottle through a twilight world, controlled and manipulated at every phase, to "decanting" into a life

already programmed and predestined. Although free of illness and old age, it is a sterile life without free will or emotional depth. All human endeavor is directed toward satisfying the population's carefully conditioned impulses for material consumption and immediate sexual gratification. As the novel progresses, every aspect of life is scrutinized and ultimately trivialized by the jingles and slogans that have replaced thought and idealism.

Little in the way of a satisfying alternative to this frighteningly shallow (some critics said misogynist) society is offered. In keeping with the traditions of satire, characters' names suggest to an alert reader the existing political and philosophical ideals that Huxley either rejects or admires. The central protagonists, everyday people through whose eyes the future society is mostly presented and who provide the measure of Huxley's satirical intent, are themselves flawed and hopelessly alienated. Short, dark Alpha-Plus Bernard Marx, a psychological counselor, is set apart by physical deviation from the handsome, strapping Alpha and Beta norm, represented, for example, by the "pneumatic," intelligent, but determinedly conformist Lenina Crowne.

Bernard abhors the casual, sterile sexual license that keeps the population docile. He also resists soma, the soporific drug carried by all citizens to provide them with an immediate "holiday" from any unpleasantness or stress, any pesky remnant of dissatisfaction or longing for a fuller life not quite bred out of the human psyche. Bernard consciously rejects the ideal of undisturbed, painless existence. Unfortunately, the courage he displays in doing this is offset by his tendencies toward egotism and whining. His eventual fate is exile to Iceland, suitably remote and cold for hopeless social deviants. John the Savage, nurtured (accidentally) on the poetry and humanism of William Shakespeare, also has been shaped by the degraded society of his birth, a New Mexican reservation where poverty, disease, brutality, and corrupted tribal tradition prevail. In England, to which Bernard brings John and his ruined Beta-Minus mother Linda, John is first an object of scientific interest and public fascination but finally a figure of fun. In both dystopian societies, he is an outcast from birth—indeed, by the very process of birth, natural reproduction being considered the most revolting of the old human habits known. Denied the nobility inherent in his Rousseau-esque life and name, his dignity, and his Shakespearean outlook, John's only possible response is suicide. The one protagonist clearly intended as sympathetic is Bernard's friend and confidant Helmholtz Watson, a peripheral character marked for exile from the outset.

Critical response to *Brave New World* was contradictory. Huxley's literary reputation caused the novel to command the immediate attention of a large group of intellectual heavyweights in whose circles Huxley had moved all of his life, and with whom he debated the heady ideas—literary, historical, philosophical, scientific, and religious—of the time. Much of the reaction was negative and focused on the novel's satirizing of current scientific thought and research. Influential novelist and historian H. G. Wells, for example, reportedly was deeply offended by what he regarded as Huxley's betrayal of science and the future. Critic Joseph Needham, a distinguished biologist, thought the novel would appeal only to special-interest readers such as biologists and philosophers. Other reviewers, unreceptive to the novel's satirical intent and tone, dismissed it as frivolous. Some reviewers thought that Huxley was promoting the ideals of his anti-Utopia and were disgusted. Perhaps the most telling observations came from such influential contemporary thinkers as Bertrand Russell, Rebecca West, and Hermann Hesse, who all recognized in *Brave New World* its application to the present world, the anxiety it expressed about the human condition, and the serious intent beneath the surface cleverness and playful wit. This latter view prevailed in successive generations of readers, especially as some of Huxley's projections about modern life seemed to come horribly true.

Brave New World was a watershed in Huxley's development as a writer and thinker. After his 1932 introduction to mystic Gerald Heard, his interest in the spiritual parameters of life led him to controlled experimentation with drugs, which colored his subsequent writing and thinking. He continued to ponder his achievement in *Brave New World* in a foreword to a 1946 edition and finally in the full-length *Brave New World Revisited* (1958). Paramount among the novel's weaknesses, Huxley believed, was his own failure to recognize the ominous potential of nuclear fission, "for the possibilities of atomic energy had been a popular topic of conversation for years before the book was written." Huxley came to believe, especially after the dropping of the atomic bomb, that individual freedom was much closer to extinction than he had suggested when he placed *Brave New World* six hundred years in the future. His fundamental optimism about humanity is also evident in the novel. Huxley observed, "The theme of *Brave New World* is not the advancement of science as such; it is the advancement of science as it affects human individuals." One artistic failure, he thought, was the character John the Savage, because he was not offered sanity as a possible alternative to the shortcomings of future life. Huxley hoped throughout his life that sanity would prevail to pull humankind back from the brink of annihilation.

Ironically, *Brave New World* is best described today by the adjective "Orwellian," coined after George Orwell's *Nineteen Eighty-Four* (1949) described the nightmare world of Oceania and its successful assault on individual freedom. In a 1959 review of both novels, influential novelist, playwright, and essayist C. P. Snow dismissed the two works on artistic grounds and especially for their pessimism about scientific progress and social purpose. Yet Huxley, like Orwell, simply tried to express the pervasive anxiety of the turbulent twentieth century, above all acknowledging the contradictory creative and destructive forces of humankind's most potent capability, that of free will.

—*Jill Rollins*

FURTHER READING

Brander, Laurence. *Aldous Huxley: A Critical Study*. Lewisburg, Pa.: Bucknell University Press, 1970. Exhaustive, readable study covering all of Huxley's writing except his poetry. Includes a short selected bibliography and an index of topics related to Huxley's works and thought.

Deery, June. *Aldous Huxley and the Mysticism of Science*. London: Palgrave Macmillan, 1996. Focuses on the roles of religion and science, and the relationship between the two, in Huxley's writings. Includes chronology and index.

Firchow, Peter Edgerly. *The End of Utopia: A Study of Aldous Huxley's "Brave New World."* Lewisburg, Pa.: Bucknell University Press, 1984. Examines the novel as literature, as prophecy of future science and technology, as consideration of future humankind, as political anti-Utopia, and in comparison to Orwell's *Nineteen Eighty-Four*.

Henderson, Alexander. *Aldous Huxley*. New York: Russell & Russell, 1936. Describes Huxley's life and assesses all of his writing to the mid-1930's. An interesting if a bit pedantic study of contemporary thought on Huxley's works.

Kuehn, Robert E., ed. *Aldous Huxley: A Collection of Critical Essays.* Englewood Cliffs, N.J.: Prentice-Hall, 1974. A variety of critical response reflected in ten essays and a critical symposium written for the *London Magazine* (1955). Includes chronology and selected bibliography.

Murray, Nicholas. *Aldous Huxley: A Biography.* New York: Thomas Dunne Books, 2002. Draws on previously unpublished material and interviews with Huxley's family members and friends to show the complexity of the author's life and place his work in context. Includes chronology and index.

Nance, Guinevera A. *Aldous Huxley.* New York: Continuum, 1988. Chapter titled "Heaven and Hell: The Utopian Theme in Three Novels" explores this aspect of *Brave New World.* Analyzes the progress of Hux-ley's vision from dystopian to positive, with hindsight offering a clear perspective. Interesting and readable.

Watt, Donald, ed. *Aldous Huxley: The Critical Heritage.* 1975. Reprint. London: Routledge & Kegan Paul, 1997. Indispensable collection of critical reviews of Huxley's writings from beginning to end, listed chronologically by title and date of work. Includes an intelligent biographical introduction, interesting appendixes, bibliography, and index.

SEE ALSO: 1915: *The Metamorphosis* Anticipates Modern Feelings of Alienation; Apr. 10, 1925: Fitzgerald Captures the Roaring Twenties in *The Great Gatsby*; Aug., 1928: Mead Publishes *Coming of Age in Samoa*; 1938: Hofmann Synthesizes the Potent Psychedelic Drug LSD-25.

1933
BILLIE HOLIDAY BEGINS HER RECORDING CAREER

Producer John Hammond's recording of Billie Holiday singing with Benny Goodman's band in 1933 brought her to the attention of jazz aficionados, and she gradually became a legendary singer.

LOCALE: New York, New York
CATEGORY: Music

KEY FIGURES

Billie Holiday (1915-1959), jazz and blues singer whose recordings and innovative techniques would prove widely influential

Lester Young (1909-1959), celebrated saxophonist who teamed with Holiday on many of her best recordings

Teddy Wilson (1912-1986), pianist who recorded with Holiday and helped to launch her career

John Hammond (1910-1987), Columbia Records producer who signed Holiday to her first recording contract

Benny Goodman (1909-1986), renowned bandleader with whom Holiday made her first recordings

Louis Armstrong (1901-1971), hugely influential trumpeter and jazz musician

SUMMARY OF EVENT

Billie Holiday was born Eleanora Fagan in Baltimore, Maryland, on April 7, 1915, to Sadie Fagan and guitarist Clarence Holiday, a guitarist in the renowned band led by Fletcher "Smack" Henderson. Her parents were later married, but only for a brief time. After they separated, Holiday was left with relatives while her mother went to New York to find work. Several stories have been told about the origin of the name "Billie," including that she was a tomboy, that her father called her "Bill," and that the actress Billie Dove was her idol.

When Holiday was ten years old, she was raped by a forty-year-old man. He went free, and she was sent to a Catholic "correctional" home. At thirteen, she went to live with her mother in Harlem. She smoked marijuana and was jailed as a prostitute. She said she ran errands for a madam so that she could hear the Bessie Smith and Louis Armstrong records played in the parlor of the brothel.

At seventeen, she began to sing professionally in Harlem at Monette Moore's speakeasy on 133rd Street for ten dollars a week. She soon began working at other Harlem clubs, and eventually Columbia Records producer John Hammond heard her. He arranged for her to record with Benny Goodman's band on Columbia in 1933. The two sides were "Riffin' the Scotch" and "Your Mother's Son-in-Law." In that same year, Teddy Wilson came to New York and signed with Brunswick Records. He played piano with Goodman's small group (Lionel Hampton was on vibes) and recorded pop tunes for Brunswick in 1935. Earlier, Wilson had been allowed to record with Goodman for Victor Records; in return, Goodman had agreed to record as a sideman with him for

Brunswick. Billie Holiday was chosen as the vocalist, and these recordings created a following among jazz musicians and jazz buffs.

In 1936, Count Basie's band came to New York City. "The Count" had a Decca Records contract and could not play on the Wilson-Holiday recordings, but his sidemen—Buck Clayton, Freddie Greene, Walter Page, and Lester "Prez" Young—could. Young is generally recognized as the person who gave Holiday the nickname "Lady Day" or "The Lady." In the jazz world, there was a Duke (Ellington), a Count, a "Prez"—short for "president"—and now a Lady.

In addition to Holiday, the 1936 recordings featured other fine musicians, including Jonah Jones, Johnny Hodges, Harry Carney, John Kirby, Cozy Cole, Vido Musso, Ben Webster, and of course, Teddy Wilson, whose ability to play with his left hand was far ahead of most other pianists. For eight months, Holiday was Count Basie's vocalist, and three airchecks—recordings of the Basie band live at the Savoy Ballroom in Harlem in 1937—made during this time were later released commercially. For a short time, she was also the vocalist for bandleader Artie Shaw, but a miserable trip on the band bus through the segregated South helped inform her decision to work on her own from that point.

In 1936, she began recording with her own group for Vocalion Records. Shaw was a sideman on one session along with Bunny Berigan and Joe Bushkin. She again recorded for Vocalion in 1938 and 1939 and also worked for Columbia as Wilson's vocalist and as the leader of a group called Billie Holiday and Her Orchestra. From 1939 through 1941, she recorded with her own band for OKeh Records and as vocalist with Teddy Wilson and his orchestra. On a number of the OKeh recordings, Lester Young, Walter Page, Freddie Greene, and Jo Jones joined her. Roy "Little Jazz" Eldridge played trumpet on several of the recordings, and Charlie Shavers also played on one. Lester Young, Eddie Heywood (on piano), and Kenny Clarke (on drums) were among the people who recorded "Georgia on My Mind" with Holiday in 1941.

In the late 1940's, some of the Teddy Wilson recordings were reissued by Commodore Records, including "Gloomy Sunday," which was more of a folk song than a piece of jazz or popular music but nonetheless became identified with Holiday. The recording was purportedly a version of a Hungarian "suicide song" that had, it was

Billie Holiday. (AP/Wide World Photos)

said, been banned from radio because some listeners had killed themselves—although a disclaimer toward the end of the song noted that the singer was "only dreaming."

Another song that was neither jazz nor pop belongs to Holiday alone. "Strange Fruit," a poem set to music, describes the contrast between the ugly violence of lynchings and the physical beauty of the South. She recorded it in 1939, a brave act at a time when the issue of such a racially charged song could have wrecked her career or led to physical harm. Southern writer Lillian Smith used the song's title as the title of a novel about racial violence in the South.

Holiday created some other songs that would always be identified with her, including "God Bless the Child," which has the structure of a pop tune but the feel of a blues lament and is still recorded by vocalists in many genres. Several original blues tunes that she performed have stayed in the jazz vocalist repertoire, including "Fine and Mellow," "Billie's Bounce," "Long Gone Blues," and "Billie's Blues."

Later, Holiday made other recordings of the tunes she had first sung in the 1930's and early 1940's, but the early recordings give the listener a strong, young Holiday at home within the structure of the song. Among these often-recorded early performances were "Them There Eyes," "Love Me or Leave Me," "I Cover the Waterfront," "I Can't Get Started," "These Foolish Things," "No Regrets," and "Some Other Spring." Other later songs also identified with Holiday include "Trav'lin' Light," "Don't Explain," "Good Morning, Heartache," and "Easy Livin'." Even some songs originally identified with blues giant Bessie Smith came to be known as Holiday's, including "Gimme a Pigfoot" and "Ain't Nobody's Business."

SIGNIFICANCE

In 1938, Holiday moved from Harlem into Manhattan. She began performing at the well-known Café Society, and until the late 1940's she worked at various Manhattan jazz clubs. In 1947, she appeared, dressed as a maid, in the film *New Orleans*. In that same year, however, she was arrested for possession of heroin and sentenced to a year and a day in a federal prison in Alderson, West Virginia. Ten days after her release, she performed to a sold-out crowd at Carnegie Hall. She could not, however, work in any jazz club in New York City; an archaic law required performers in establishments that sold liquor to obtain a "cabaret card" that permitted them to work there, and cabaret cards were unavailable to musicians with drug convictions. Holiday was thus prohibited from working in her own town, the center of live jazz performance in the United States at that time.

In the early 1950's, Steve Allen, the host of an early New York television variety show that would later become *The Tonight Show*, featured a number of notable jazz performers, including Holiday, on his program. In 1957, a television special with Lester Young and others let fans see and hear her one more time; the sound track to the special was released as the album *The Sound of Jazz*. In 1956, Holiday wrote her autobiography, *Lady Sings the Blues*, with coauthor William F. Dufty. A hit 1972 film based on the book starred Diana Ross as Holiday. Although Ross's music was very different from Holiday's, the film's sound track introduced another generation to Holiday's songs.

Holiday toured Europe in the last few years of her life and was enthusiastically received. Her last performance in New York City was a 1959 benefit performance at the Phoenix Theater. On May 31 of that year, she collapsed at her Manhattan apartment. In a coma, she was taken by a police ambulance to a private hospital, where she lay unattended for an hour. She was then taken to Metropolitan Hospital in Harlem. She lingered, under an oxygen tent, for more than two weeks, with a policeman outside her door. Authorities denied that the officer was waiting to arrest her, but rumors of Holiday's pending arrest continued, and the officer was removed by court order the day before Holiday died.

When Holiday collapsed, she had seventy cents in her bank account and $750 in cash taped to her leg. Three thousand people attended her funeral at St. Paul the Apostle Catholic Church in Harlem, and she was buried in Raymond's Cemetery in the Bronx. For some time, her grave was not marked by a headstone, a fact that resulted in an angry article in *Downbeat* magazine. (Ironically, she never won the top spot in any of *Downbeat*'s celebrated polls.)

The success of Holiday's music was entirely dependent on her much-discussed style. Despite the fact that many scholars have written about the way she altered the melodic line of a song, she did not, in fact, play around with melody very much—no more, for example, than the young Miles Davis, who played "Blue Room" almost note for note. Unlike other popular African American stars of the day such as Ella Fitzgerald, Fats Waller, the Ink Spots, and the Mills Brothers, Holiday's music was not featured on the jukeboxes in white establishments. She simply recorded the popular songs of the day, some of which became standards.

Others commented that Holiday sang "like a horn player," but this is not quite right. Holiday shared Louis Armstrong's ability to use vocals to play with the time, a skill she demonstrated on the "up" tunes on her 1930's recordings. On such songs, the last bars of the chorus that led into a musician's solo often anticipated the solo, inviting the instrumentalist into the tune. Holiday's talent, however, was not confined to the room she could make inside those four-beat rhythms. Sometimes it emerged from the spaces between the notes or in her accents on particular notes, words, or syllables. Although "percussive" is too strong a term to describe her technique, her work is almost percussive and almost syncopated. To her unique sense of timing she added bent, gliding notes in a voice that could seem both sweet and sassy. Although toward the end of her career—when both her health and breath were fading—she sometimes sounded like an imitation of herself, many people preferred her later style, which seemed to embody a universally held idea of suffering.

—*Katherine Lederer*

1933

FURTHER READING

Friedwald, Will. *Jazz Singing: America's Great Voices from Bessie Smith to Bebop and Beyond.* New York: Charles Scribner's Sons, 1990. An excellent illustrated overview of the contributions of great jazz vocalists, from Louis Armstrong and Bing Crosby through Betty Carter. The author contrasts Holiday's singing with that of Ella Fitzgerald, noting that the two singers "travel completely different ways to the same destination." Lucid, scholarly, and comprehensive.

Holiday, Billie, and William F. Dufty. *Lady Sings the Blues.* Garden City, N.Y.: Doubleday, 1956. Holiday's autobiography is frank in its presentation of details about her painful childhood and drug addiction, although some people who knew Holiday later in life have criticized the book as unreliable.

James, Burnett. *Billie Holiday.* New York: Hippocrene Books, 1984. A useful short biography of the singer produced as part of the "Jazz Masters" series. Illustrated; helpful selective discography.

Jones, LeRoi. *Blues People: The Negro Experience in White America.* 1963. Reprint. New York: William Morrow, 1999. Examines how blues and jazz evolved in white America, including valuable discussion of Holiday's work. Generally an important and useful study. Includes index.

Kliment, Bud. *Billie Holiday.* New York: Chelsea House, 1990. A profusely illustrated biography directed toward younger readers. Contains an introductory essay, "On Achievement," by Coretta Scott King.

Pleasants, Henry. *The Great American Popular Singers.* New York: Simon & Schuster, 1974. An interesting although somewhat dated overview of the topic. Useful, and somewhat unusual, in its discussion of Holiday and other jazz and blues artists alongside singers such as Elvis Presley and Hank Williams, who earned their fame in other genres. Illustrated, with a glossary of singing terms.

Southern, Eileen. *The Music of Black Americans: A History.* 3d ed. New York: W. W. Norton, 1997. Excellent scholarly account of the subject provides both background and important detail. Includes critical bibliography and discography as well as numerous selections from scores and an extensive index.

SEE ALSO: Feb. 15, 1923: Bessie Smith Records "Downhearted Blues"; Nov., 1925: Armstrong Records with the Hot Five; Dec. 4, 1927: Ellington Begins Performing at the Cotton Club; Dec. 1, 1934: Goodman Begins His *Let's Dance* Broadcasts; Jan. 2, 1939: Marian Anderson Is Barred from Constitution Hall; 1940: Wright's *Native Son* Depicts Racism in America.

1933
FORTY-SECOND STREET DEFINES 1930'S FILM MUSICALS

With film studios near bankruptcy at the height of the Great Depression, Busby Berkeley revitalized film musicals with new camera and staging techniques.

LOCALE: Hollywood, California
CATEGORIES: Motion pictures; dance; entertainment

KEY FIGURES

Busby Berkeley (1895-1976), Broadway dance director who created a musical form unique to film
Ruby Keeler (1909-1993), former Broadway performer who became a film star in *Forty-Second Street*
Dick Powell (1904-1963), actor who played Keeler's love interest in the film
Warner Baxter (1891-1951), distinguished character actor who played a Broadway producer in the film
Lloyd Bacon (1890-1955), former silent-screen actor who directed the nondancing part of the film

SUMMARY OF EVENT

In the late 1920's, when sound films began to replace silent films, Hollywood studios produced a flood of musicals. Early sound cameras were almost immobile, since any motion created noise that was magnified on the sound track; most early musicals were therefore photographed as if the camera were a member of the audience. Apparently, studio directors did not realize that sloppy dancing, tawdry sets, and poor costumes, while sometimes effective on the stage, would appear ridiculous when magnified many times over on the screen. As a result, the first musicals failed at the box office. In 1928, sixty were released, but in 1932, only fifteen were released, and only two of those made a profit. By then, the Depression had forced many studios near bankruptcy, and in 1933, some twenty-five hundred theaters had been forced to close.

Darryl Zanuck, then employed by Warner Bros., believed the musical still had a future, although he did not tell his bosses that he had a musical in mind when he brought Busby Berkeley to the studio. Berkeley had been dance director for twenty-one Broadway musicals, and as a soldier during World War I he had devised trick-drill patterns to allow the movement of masses of men in close formation. Both experiences would influence his Hollywood career. He had never had a dancing lesson, and he did not know much about cameras or photography when he was brought to Hollywood in 1930 to direct dance numbers for Eddie Cantor and Mary Pickford.

Berkeley had run out of work by the time he was assigned to *Forty-Second Street*. He directed production numbers at one site, while his colleague Lloyd Bacon worked with the rest of the script at another. Veteran cameraman Sol Polito was in charge of filming at both. The directors emphasized the Cinderella theme of this backstage musical, replacing the tearful sentimentality of many earlier musicals such as Al Jolson's *The Singing Fool* (1928), which had involved, among other things, a dying child. Both directors understood that the Depression audience needed hope, not more depression.

Still, the film's script and its first production numbers were fully grounded in the realities of the Depression. The threat of unemployment hangs over the characters who appear early in the film, from Julian Marsh (played by Warner Baxter), a Broadway producer who has lost his money and health, to the girlish Peggy Sawyer (played by Ruby Keeler). After being given a place in the chorus, Sawyer faints in rehearsal from hunger and fatigue. She and other chorus girls, desperate for work, stoically endure brutally crude sexual remarks and groping hands. Even the fictitious show's star endures the witless sexual aggression of the show's lecherous financial backer until, driven beyond her capacity, she rejects him. Shortly afterward, she is injured and must be replaced. Sawyer steps in, and in one grueling rehearsal scene, she is forced to prove her talent, courage, and capacity for hard work. At this point in the story, Berkeley inserted production numbers that reminded the Depression audience that bravery and a strong work ethic could make dreams come true.

The play's music and staging change when Sawyer becomes a star. She does not appear in the first major production number, "Young and Healthy," sung by Dick Powell, which introduced the moving platforms and geometric designs for which Berkeley became famous. The second major number, "Shuffle Off to Buffalo," depicts Sawyer as a young bride, but the Pullman sleeping car in which she is traveling surrealistically splits in half, and she finds herself surrounded by chorus girls wearing night cream and mouthing cynical asides about love and marriage. These numbers are dwarfed by "Forty-Second Street," which closes the film and made Berkeley's reputation.

As that number begins, Sawyer is dancing, as if on a stage. The camera pulls back, and she is seen on top of a taxi. She climbs down and is surrounded by New Yorkers—police officers, nursemaids, ordinary pedestrians—going about their everyday dramas. A woman appears in an upstairs window. Terrified, she flees from a man who pursues her into the street and stabs her. Her death attracts no more than a moment's attention, as Powell sings "Forty-Second Street" from an upstairs window. An instant later, both are forgotten as a chorus of precisely choreographed and beautifully costumed dancers tap along with the title song. They mount a staircase and, turning, reveal cardboard cutouts that form the Manhattan skyline. The skyline dances, stabilizes, and opens to reveal a skyscraper with Powell and Keeler embracing at the top. Berkeley had created a fairy-tale ending to a dazzling fantasy, and in doing so, he had built a world that could exist nowhere except on film and could be staged nowhere except huge Hollywood sound stages.

The techniques he used changed Hollywood musicals. He worked with a single camera rather than with the customary four, planning out each number so that its development was smooth. The camera's eye was the audience's eye, and Berkeley photographed from every possible angle. He respected the integrity of the production number and showed it without interruption. He demanded both beauty and intelligence of his dancers, and while critics complained about his tendency to focus on their bodies, he was careful to let his camera pause on their faces and especially on their eyes. He allowed greater variation of face and body types than was permissible later on, and he demanded precise movement, proud posture, and precision. By juxtaposing violence and musical exuberance, Berkeley reminded the audience of the world they were escaping even as they escaped it. His techniques would have their greatest effect on the Hollywood musical before the mid-1950's, when the decline of the Hollywood studio system virtually ended the production of these expensive films.

SIGNIFICANCE

The immediate effect of *Forty-Second Street* was that Berkeley was given a free hand and almost unlimited financial support at Warner Bros., which allowed him to

1933

develop his vision. The film's success motivated other Hollywood studios to produce equally popular pictures. Among the first of these was the Metro-Goldwyn-Mayer (MGM) production *Dancing Lady* (1933), which attempted to exploit the popularity of Clark Gable and Joan Crawford, neither of whom was suited for musical films. Crawford's dancing was strained and ungainly, but Fred Astaire, then new to Hollywood, played a bit part. MGM's 1936 *The Great Ziegfeld*, with its giant wedding cake and beautifully costumed tiers of girls, owed more to Berkeley than to anything the real Florenz Ziegfeld could have produced on the narrow confines of a Broadway stage.

RKO gave Astaire a role—along with Ginger Rogers, who had attracted attention with a bit part in *Forty-Second Street*—in its new film, *Flying Down to Rio* (1933), and the pair's famous partnership was formed. Berkeley's influence is evident in the spectacular aerial ballet that ends the RKO film and in the precision dancing of the "Carioca" production number that is the film's showpiece. Twentieth Century (later Twentieth Century-Fox) imitated Berkeley with *Stand Up and Cheer* and *George White's Scandals*, both in 1934, but it was not to find a successful formula until later in the 1930's, when it featured singer Alice Faye, child star Shirley Temple, and ice-skating champion Sonja Henie.

While being imitated, Berkeley polished the forms he introduced in *Forty-Second Street* and developed new ones. His *Gold Diggers of 1933* featured, among others, the spectacular "We're in the Money" number, in which Ginger Rogers led the Berkeley dancers, dressed in oversized gold coins, against a backdrop of gigantic coins. His "Shadow Waltz" in that film showed his chorus playing illumined violins and finally shaping themselves into the pattern of a lighted violin. In "Remember My Forgotten Man," a parade of World War I soldiers, filmed in silhouette, becomes a ragged procession of the unemployed, and an out-of-work drunk wearing a combat medal is arrested. In *Footlight Parade* (1933), Berkeley shot a water ballet from over, under, and around a specially designed pool, and he incorporated "Shanghai Lil," a number sung and danced by Keeler and James Cagney, which begins in barroom violence and ends, some time later, in one of the military formations that Berkeley frequently used. In *Roman Scandals* (1933), he filmed naked dancers.

In *Gold Diggers of 1935* (1935), Berkeley filmed what is generally considered his best work, "Lullaby of Broadway." In this production number, the audience sees the life and death of a Broadway party girl as an army of precision tap dancers paces out the cadence of her life. Singer Wini Shaw's face is first seen as a small white dot on a black screen. She sings "Lullaby of Broadway" as the camera moves gradually into close-up, and her face dissolves into a view of Manhattan. The audience sees her story: She arrives home after a night of fun, feeds her cat, sleeps all day, and sets out with Dick Powell for another night of entertainment. They go to an enormous nightclub, where two dancers begin the lullaby. Suddenly, the dancers become an army of men and women who engage in a dazzling display of precision dancing that does without musical accompaniment for many beats. The dancers become threatening and overpowering, and as they begin to engulf Shaw and Powell, Shaw flees to a balcony and then falls screaming to her death. The camera moves back to the New York scene. The cat waits to be fed. Shaw's face fades back to a tiny white dot and then disappears.

In the late 1930's, Berkeley moved to MGM, where his dance direction included *Ziegfeld Girl* (1941). His MGM credits also included *Lady Be Good* (1941), with dancer Eleanor Powell, and three of the most popular Mickey Rooney-Judy Garland musicals, *Babes in Arms* (1939), *Strike up the Band* (1940), and *Babes on Broadway* (1941), all backstage musicals that were variations on the Cinderella theme. He directed the eccentric dance by Scarecrow Ray Bolger, "If I Only Had a Brain," for *The Wizard of Oz* (1939) and designed spectacular swimming ballets for Esther Williams in *Million Dollar Mermaid* (1952) and *Easy to Love* (1953).

Although Berkeley was frequently imitated, some of his techniques were impossible to re-create. Far more than most dance directors, he stressed the precision movement of masses of people more than dance steps. No other director turned dancers into geometric patterns—flattening conventional perspective—as frequently as he did. At the same time, more than most other directors, he featured the dancers' faces; his stars had to work harder to prove themselves than did the stars of more conventional musicals, which often showed the star figure alone against a vaguely photographed background of anonymous bodies. His juxtaposition of violence and exuberance was often imitated but was never presented as forcefully as in Berkeley's own productions, in which Berkeley would not allow the use of mood music to signal the coming of tragedy. Berkeley's gift was to give his audience a reality that they understood, one in which violence and agony come without warning, while at the same time giving his Cinderella figures an escape even more fantastic than the most imaginative of his audiences could dream. He was best known for his camera angles, but these were more easily imitated than the other qualities that made him unique.

—*Betty Richardson*

FURTHER READING

Altman, Rick. *The American Film Musical.* Bloomington: Indiana University Press, 1989. Made unnecessarily difficult by scholarly jargon, this book contains both difficult chapters on theory and more readable ones. The latter can be read separately and provide an excellent categorization of folk musicals, fairy-tale musicals, and backstage musicals. The material on backstage musicals necessarily includes much about Berkeley.

Delameter, Jerome. *Dance in the Hollywood Musical.* Ann Arbor, Mich.: UMI Research Press, 1981. This scholarly but relatively readable work includes two chapters, "Dance in Film Before 1930" and "Busby Berkeley at Warner Brothers," which are useful for an understanding of Berkeley's importance. Delameter, primarily interested in technical dance, thinks little of Berkeley but rightfully associates him with the French Surrealism.

Kantor, Michael, and Laurence Maslon. *Broadway: The American Musical.* New York: Bulfinch, 2004. Comprehensive, lavishly illustrated volume on the history of musicals. Includes year-by-year list of significant shows, selected bibliography, and maps of the theater district at different periods. Companion book to a six-part PBS series.

Knapp, Raymond. *The American Musical and the Formation of National Identity.* Princeton, N.J.: Princeton University Press, 2004. History of the genre focuses on how themes in American musical productions relate to how Americans view themselves. Includes useful appendixes, notes, bibliography, and index.

Mordden, Ethan. *The Hollywood Musical.* New York: St. Martin's Press, 1981. Mordden's witty, opinionated, and readable work remains a standard starting place for students of the film musical; he offers a general overview of Berkeley's role in reviving musicals and influence on the genre.

Pike, Bob, and Dave Martin. *The Genius of Busby Berkeley.* Reseda, Calif.: Creative Film Society, 1973. This poorly produced book contains a lengthy interview with Berkeley, most of which is accessible in Tony Thomas's book (see below). Also includes a filmography, some review material, and a biography that largely repeats the interview.

Schatz, Thomas. *The Genius of the System: Hollywood Filmmaking in the Studio Era.* New York: Pantheon, 1988. Easily the best readily accessible source for information about the business side of filmmaking, including the making of *Forty-Second Street.* Provides an excellent list of archival sources and a reliable bibliography.

Sennett, Ted. *Warner Brothers Presents: The Most Exciting Years—From the "Jazz Singer" to "White Heat."* New Rochelle, N.Y.: Arlington House, 1971. Discusses Berkeley as a film director, a role in which he was relatively unsuccessful, as well as a dance director. Sennett gives an overview of Berkeley's creative use of cameras, his inventiveness, and his contribution to the revival of the studio.

Thomas, Tony, and Jim Terry, with Busby Berkeley. *The Busby Berkeley Book.* Greenwich, Conn.: New York Graphic Society, 1973. This is the single essential work for a study of Berkeley. Lavishly illustrated, it contains a foreword by Ruby Keeler, a biography, and a filmography.

SEE ALSO: Dec. 27, 1927: *Show Boat* Is the First American Musical to Emphasize Plot; 1929: *Hallelujah* Is the First Important Black Musical Film; 1930's: Hollywood Enters Its Golden Age; 1930's-1940's: Studio System Dominates Hollywood Filmmaking; 1931-1932: Gangster Films Become Popular; 1934: Lubitsch's *The Merry Widow* Opens New Vistas for Film Musicals; Sept. 6, 1935: *Top Hat* Establishes the Astaire-Rogers Dance Team.

1933

1933
KALLET AND SCHLINK PUBLISH *100,000,000 GUINEA PIGS*

Arthur Kallet and Frederick John Schlink's
100,000,000 Guinea Pigs *shocked Americans by
accusing well-known food, drug, and cosmetic
companies of gross irresponsibility in producing and
marketing their products. The public outcry led to
stricter regulation and increased powers for the FDA.*

LOCALE: United States
CATEGORIES: Publishing and journalism; trade and
commerce

KEY FIGURES
Arthur Kallet (1902-1972), American engineer and
consumer advocate
Frederick John Schlink (1891-1995), American
engineer, physicist, and consumer advocate
Harvey W. Wiley (1844-1930), chief chemist of the
U.S. Department of Agriculture, 1883-1912

SUMMARY OF EVENT
In 1933, Arthur Kallet and Frederick John Schlink collaborated to publish *100,000,000 Guinea Pigs: Dangers
in Everyday Foods, Drugs, and Cosmetics*, a shocking book in which the authors alleged that many of the
best-known U.S. consumer products of the day were either useless or dangerous. Products they warned against
included such heavily advertised brands as Listerine,
Pepsodent, Kellogg's All-Bran, Crisco, Lifebuoy,
Bromo-Seltzer, Mercurochrome, Absorbine Jr., and Ex-
Lax, as well as a number of others that were household
names but have since been forgotten. The public was astonished to learn that in the modern American marketplace, as in ancient Rome, it was still a matter of buyer
beware.

Kallet and Schlink warned that Ex-Lax, probably the
best-known laxative of the time, could produce laxative
dependency and had killed a child who ate a whole box
because the drug tasted like chocolate candy. In the case
of Kellogg's All-Bran, a cereal commonly believed to be
effective in relieving constipation, the authors charged
that harsh bran ingested in large quantities on a daily basis could cause serious damage to the intestines and even
lead to death from cancer.

Kallet and Schlink knew they were leaving themselves and their publisher open to libel suits from the
makers of the products they named. Nevertheless, these
two crusaders accused some of the biggest business firms
in the country of gross negligence in marketing their

products. They explained their charges in detail, and
their words had the ring of authority. For example, they
charged that Crisco, the best-known vegetable shortening of its kind, was dangerous because, although the normal human body temperature is 98.6 degrees, part of the
fats in most vegetable shortenings became liquefied only
at higher temperatures. This meant that a fatty residue
would remain in the intestines of consumers for several
days, causing indigestion and even more serious stomach
disorders over time.

Kallet and Schlink also charged that the cleaning
agent in Pepsodent toothpaste contained "large sharp angular particles" that were dangerous to tooth enamel. "Of
the thousands of drugs, medicines and other preparations
cluttering the shelves of every large drug store," wrote
Kallet and Schlink, "hundreds are potentially poisonous
or injurious." They also charged that many well-known
medications and antiseptics, though not actually dangerous, were vastly overrated in their advertising.

Americans had never seen such a wholesale indictment. Kallet and Schlink called Americans "guinea pigs"
because the food, drug, and cosmetic industries were experimenting on them just as if they were laboratory animals. The authors had nothing but contempt for the officials of the Food and Drug Administration (FDA), with
the exception of the courageous Dr. Harvey W. Wiley,
who had been forced to step down as head of that government agency because he had been too outspoken and too
zealous in prosecuting offenders. Kallet and Schlink
called for American consumers to take positive action.
They recommended boycotting offending firms, especially those that opposed stricter legislation or were
members of trade associations that opposed corrective
measures. Kallet and Schlink suggested that consumers
demand immediate dismissal of government officials
who made rulings that showed a lack of sensitivity to the
public interest. In particular, they asked their readers to
keep in constant contact with their representatives, senators, and state legislators on matters related to foods,
drugs, and cosmetics.

Another way consumers could be effective, according
to Kallet and Schlink, was in writing letters to newspapers and magazines in which they criticized publishers
for accepting advertising from known violators of the Pure
Food and Drug Act of 1906. They suggested that readers
could act more effectively by joining consumer-advocate
organizations, and they praised American women's clubs

for taking a leading role in matters related to the protection of their families. Kallet and Schlink also pointed out that lawyers could be utilized in cases of fraud or negligence, reminding readers that they could initiate civil suits for monetary compensation and criminal suits threatening violators with fines and imprisonment.

Kallet and Schlink called for consumers to demand radical changes in government supervision of the food, drug, and cosmetic industries. These changes would include licensing and bonding, on-site federal supervision of manufacturing plants, and drastic penalties for malpractice. They suggested that the burden of proof for compliance with regulations should be placed on the manufacturer and not on the FDA. They called for truthful and complete labeling and for the abolition of the advertising of "mystery ingredients" and "secret formulas." Their anger did not fail to transmit itself to their readers. They talked about padlocking firms that did not rate close to perfection in sanitation and observed that the FDA had "no right of entry into plants manufacturing foods and drugs, nor any right to supervise or to stop processes, even if an inspector should see rat poison being added to canned soup before his very eyes."

It is not surprising that *100,000,000 Guinea Pigs* raised a storm of controversy. It was the most shocking book to be published in the United States since *The Jungle*, Upton Sinclair's horrifying 1906 novel about the meatpacking industry. Many prestigious magazines and newspapers published caustic reviews of Kallet and Schlink's call to arms and charged the authors with recklessness, gross exaggeration, incompetence, and opportunism. A review of the book in *The Nation* called it

A MENACE TO HEALTH AND LIFE

In the first chapter of their book, titled "The Great American Guinea Pig," Kallet and Schlink set forth in shocking detail the dangers posed by U.S. manufacturers of foods and other consumer goods:

In the magazines, in the newspapers, over the radio, a terrific verbal barrage has been laid down on a hundred million Americans, first, to set in motion a host of fears about their health, their stomachs, their bowels, their teeth, their throats, their looks; second, to persuade them that only by eating, drinking, gargling, brushing, or smearing with Smith's Whole Vitamin Breakfast Food, Jones' Yeast Cubes, Blue Giant Apples, Prussian Salts, Listroboris Mouthwash, Grandpa's Wonder Toothpaste, and a thousand and one other foods, drinks, gargles and pastes, can they either postpone the onset of disease, of social ostracism, of business failure, or recover from ailments, physical or social, already contracted.

If these foods and medicines were—to most of the people who use them—merely worthless; if there were no other charge to be made than that the manufacturers', sales managers', and advertising agents' claims for them were false, this book would not have been written. But many of them, including some of the most widely advertised and sold, are not only worthless, but are actually dangerous. That All-Bran you eat every morning—do you know that it may cause serious and perhaps irreparable intestinal trouble? That big juicy apple you have at lunch—do you know that indifferent Government officials let it come to your table coated with arsenic, one of the deadliest of poisons? The Pebeco Toothpaste with which you brush your teeth twice every day—do you know that a tube of it contains enough poison if eaten, to kill three people? . . .

It is exceedingly likely that the poisons legally and systematically fed to the American public will, by disturbing the bodily functions, overtaxing the kidneys and other organs, and upsetting the digestive processes, bring the onset of old age and functional weakness and infirmity earlier than it would otherwise have come. . . . Such shortening of the average life can conservatively be estimated at from three to ten years. . . .

All of the propaganda agencies of business have skillfully conditioned the public to believe that the only safeguard needed is the integrity of the manufacturer. . . . But, on the whole, this first link in the chain of consumer protection is the weakest. In case after case, the manufacturers have demonstrated that their chief and most consistent interest is in profits; and we speak here not only of the small herb compounder and cancer quack, but also of the largest and most reputable drug and food houses. . . . Case after case demonstrates only too well that the average manufacturer will resist to the end any interference with his business, any attempt to deprive him of his vested interest, even when it has been proved beyond doubt that his product is a menace to health and life. . . .

The food and drug manufacturers also kill. Perhaps we should name a new crime for them and call it statistical homicide. But whatever we call it, they are responsible for the death of very large numbers of persons—death through premature old age, disease of stomach, bowels, and kidneys, which weakened organs cannot resist, and death because good medicine or medical care was needed, and a patent medicine for pneumonia or tuberculosis or cancer was taken instead.

Source: Arthur Kallet and Frederick John Schlink, *100,000,000 Guinea Pigs: Dangers in Everyday Foods, Drugs, and Cosmetics* (New York: Vanguard Press, 1933).

1933

"intemperate, misleading, and potentially pernicious." Newspapers and magazines, which were by and large heavily dependent on advertising for their existence, tended to reflect the probusiness sentiments of their owners. Kallet and Schlink charged that offenses against the public interest were often known but were ignored by the "venal press." When firms were penalized under the Pure Food and Drug Act or committed offenses that resulted in lawsuits, they alleged, such news was often overlooked or buried in the back pages, along with the weather news and the high school batting averages.

SIGNIFICANCE

Kallet and Schlink's work had a strong effect on the American public because the book was written in nontechnical language and referred to products used by millions of people every day. The book's impact was comparable to that of *The Jungle*; like Sinclair's novel, it led to an outcry for strict government intervention. In fact, *100,000,000 Guinea Pigs* has been credited with being largely responsible for the enactment of the Federal Food, Drug, and Cosmetic Act of 1938. The accusations in the book implied the need for stricter government control of business—and more government control was exactly what big business interests did not want. It was, however, exactly what the Franklin D. Roosevelt administration did want, and *100,000,000 Guinea Pigs* helped to turn the sympathies of many American voters in favor of greater bureaucratic control at the national level.

Kallet and Schlink's best seller appeared at a time when the United States was undergoing a dramatic social and political transformation. The year 1933 marked the beginning of Roosevelt's presidency and the introduction of his New Deal program, which proposed to revolutionize the influence of government in the lives of Americans. Roosevelt was to be elected president for four consecutive terms; during his lengthy administration, the federal government assumed unprecedented regulatory powers. Roosevelt's popularity can be seen as a reaction against the adulation of big-business tycoons that had dissipated with the stock market crash of 1929 and the Great Depression that followed it.

Kallet and Schlink called on American consumers to pressure the federal government to exercise far greater control over the manufacture and sale of potentially dangerous products. They also suggested that the federal government take much stronger control over advertising. Advertising would prove to be a sensitive area, given the First Amendment to the U.S. Constitution, which prohib-

its Congress from "abridging the freedom of speech, or of the press." It nevertheless became common practice for the government to force advertisers to stop making unprovable claims.

Moreover, *100,000,000 Guinea Pigs* gave lawyers the notion that considerable money might be made in civil actions under what insurance companies term "product liability." As the public at large had been alerted to the hidden dangers in familiar household products, many lawyers reasoned, it would be easier to persuade jurors to award generous damages to claimants. The triple threat of stricter government control, civil lawsuits, and mass boycotting by an outraged public motivated manufacturers to become more responsible about the food, drugs, and cosmetics they marketed and to become more circumspect about the claims they made in their advertisements. The fact that Americans now buy food, drugs, and cosmetics with greater confidence than they did in the 1930's is largely a result of the efforts of such individuals as Wiley, Sinclair, and Kallet and Schlink.

In the long term, *100,000,000 Guinea Pigs* was important because it helped change American consciousness. The book helped turn the American people against the idea that unrestricted competition inevitably leads to a better way of life for everyone, undermined Americans' naïve adulation of business tycoons, whose private lives were chronicled in the society pages, and persuaded Americans to think in terms of government regulation. This increase in consumer consciousness affected the public's general voting habits as well: By making Americans suspicious of big business, the book indirectly helped the Roosevelt administration enact legislative reforms, including reforms that had little to do with consumer goods.

—Bill Delaney

FURTHER READING

Anderson, Oscar Edward. *The Health of a Nation: Harvey W. Wiley and the Fight for Pure Food*. Chicago: University of Chicago Press, 1958. Biography of the courageous crusader for pure food and drug legislation. Wiley was singled out for special praise by Kallet and Schlink.

Chase, Stuart, and F. J. Schlink. *Your Money's Worth: A Study in the Waste of the Consumer's Dollar*. New York: Macmillan, 1927. Schlink collaborated with Stuart Chase to write this best-selling exposé of the sharp practices of certain American businessmen. The authors compare the value of products to their actual costs and suggest ways that consumers can protect themselves from unethical practices.

Fuller, John G. *200,000,000 Guinea Pigs: New Dangers in Everyday Foods, Drugs, and Cosmetics.* New York: Putnam, 1972. This excellent book, written in the same spirit as Kallet and Schlink's landmark and published nearly forty years later, was intended to show that there were still many abuses by the food, drug, and cosmetic industries and that the FDA still needed improvement.

Goodwin, Lorine Swainston. *The Pure Food, Drink, and Drug Crusaders, 1879-1914.* Jefferson, N.C.: McFarland, 1999. A study of the precursors of Kallet and Schlink and the important work done to educate consumers in the late nineteenth and early twentieth centuries. Bibliographic references and index.

Kallet, Arthur. *Counterfeit: Not Your Money but What It Buys.* New York: Vanguard Press, 1935. Discusses the ways in which manufacturers and retailers deceive the public. Contains many illustrations of popular products and copies of their advertisements. Calls for fundamental change in the U.S. economic system.

"New Food Labels: At Last, You Can Trust Them—Most of the Time." *Consumer Reports* 59 (July, 1994): 437-438. An article about the new food labels mandated by the U.S. Department of Agriculture. *Consumer Reports*, founded in 1936, accepts no advertising and strives to remain impartial in its evaluation of products and services.

Newman, Kathy M. *Radio Active: Advertising and Consumer Activism, 1935-1947.* Berkeley: University of California Press, 2004. A focused study of the effects on radio of the increased consumer consciousness brought about in part by the publication of *100,000,000 Guinea Pigs*. Discusses the use of radio as a tool of consumer activism, as well as the grassroots battle to regulate radio advertising. Bibliographic references and index.

Wiley, Harvey Washington. *The History of a Crime Against the Food Law.* 1929. Reprint. New York: Arno Press, 1976. Wiley's best-known publication. Provided strong evidence for Kallet and Schlink to use in *100,000,000 Guinea Pigs*.

SEE ALSO: Feb., 1906: Sinclair Publishes *The Jungle*; 1927: U.S. Food and Drug Administration Is Established; Jan.-Mar., 1936: Consumers Union of the United States Emerges; June 25, 1938: Federal Food, Drug, and Cosmetic Act.

1933-1934
FIRST ARTIFICIAL RADIOACTIVE ELEMENT IS DEVELOPED

Frédéric Joliot and Irène Joliot-Curie used alpha particles from polonium to bombard aluminum and create phosphorus 30, an artificial nucleus that is radioactive.

LOCALE: Radium Institute, Paris, France
CATEGORIES: Science and technology; physics

KEY FIGURES
Irène Joliot-Curie (1897-1956), French physicist
Frédéric Joliot (1900-1958), French physicist

SUMMARY OF EVENT
In 1930, a German team of scientists reported that beryllium bombarded by alpha particles emitted a new sort of penetrating radiation. In France, the husband-wife team of Irène Joliot-Curie and Frédéric Joliot confirmed the German results and in the process came close to proving the existence of the neutron, of which the new radiation was composed. This particle, which has no charge but has the same mass as the proton, joins the proton to form the nucleus of the atom. British physicist James Chadwick won a Nobel Prize in Physics for making the actual discovery of the neutron.

In 1932, the Joliot-Curies, studying cosmic radiation in the high Alps, observed the positron, a particle with the same mass as the electron but with a positive rather than a negative charge. They failed to follow up their observation, and that same year, an American physicist, Carl David Anderson, identified the positron, using equipment similar to that used by the Joliot-Curies.

By early 1933, the Joliot-Curies were using alpha particles produced from polonium to bombard boron, beryllium, fluorine, aluminum, and sodium. After the bombardment, these elements emitted neutrons and both positrons and electrons. The accuracy of the results of their experiments was questioned at the Seventh Solvay Conference, which was attended by most of the major physicists in Europe. They returned to Paris with damaged pride and a new determination to prove conclusively that neutrons and positrons were emitted at the same time from their irradiated targets.

To conduct the necessary experiments, they were forced to modify their experimental apparatus. Until now, the Geiger counter, which detected radioactivity, had been automatically turned off when the radioactive source (the source of the alpha particles) was removed. In the new arrangement, it would be left on after the source was removed. With this arrangement, they noticed that aluminum continued to emit positrons for some time after the removal of the radioactive source. This

meant that the aluminum target had been made artificially radioactive by bombardment with alpha particles.

The Joliot-Curies were certain that they had produced artificial radioactivity. In order to place their discovery beyond doubt, they needed to separate chemically the source of the new radioactivity and to demonstrate that it had nothing to do with the original aluminum target. On January 15, 1934, friends, including Irène's famous mother, Marie Curie, received frantic telephone calls from the young researchers and rushed to the laboratory. From makeshift apparatus scattered in apparent disarray over several tables, the Joliot-Curies bombarded aluminum with alpha particles and separated from the irradiated samples an isotope of phosphorus with a half-life of only three minutes and fifteen seconds. Marie Curie, who was dying of the leukemia produced by her lifetime work with radioactivity, was handed a tiny tube containing the first sample of artificially produced radioactivity. Her face expressed joy and excitement. Other colleagues filled the room with lively discussions.

The Joliot-Curies soon repeated their experiments with boron and magnesium, producing still other sources of artificial radioactivity. They promptly sent off a report of their discovery to the scientific press. Its publication opened a floodgate of new experiments on the transmutation of nuclei, which led directly to the discovery of "nuclear fission" five years later.

RADIOACTIVE ROMANCE

Irène Joliot-Curie was the daughter of the legendary Marie Curie, the physical chemist who twice won the Nobel Prize, and a member of the French scientific elite by birth as well as a brilliant physicist in her own right. As a teenager, she had worked alongside her mother, using X-ray equipment to treat soldiers wounded during World War I. She published her first paper in physics in 1921, and in 1932 she succeeded her mother as director of the Radium Institute.

Frédéric Joliot grew up in a middle-class family and attended the École de Physique et de Chimie Industrielle de la Ville de Paris rather than one of the prestigious French universities. Because of his unquestionable ability as an experimenter, he was recommended to Marie Curie as an assistant by a close friend, French physicist Paul Langevin. He joined the laboratory at the end of 1924 and gradually acquired the necessary degrees. Because of his background, he found it difficult to break into the inner circle of French science, despite his personal charm and ability.

The outgoing, charming, handsome Frédéric fell in love with the quiet, capable, socially awkward Irène. In 1926, they were wed, beginning a very happy marriage and an extremely successful scientific collaboration. During the first four years of the 1930's, they embarked upon a remarkable series of experiments in nuclear physics that led to the creation of radioactive elements in the laboratory. Their achievement led directly to nuclear fission, achieved in 1939.

The Joliot-Curies continued to lead a rich family life hampered only by poor health caused, in Irène's case, by her early work with large amounts of radioactive materials. Frédéric Joliot was now accepted as a member of the French scientific elite and not as an upstart who had married Madame Curie's daughter. As World War II loomed on the horizon, Frédéric Joliot was drafted into the military. Recognizing the possibility of a nuclear fission bomb, he took steps to secure uranium for France and began negotiations for a large supply of "heavy water" located in Norway. With the Nazis closing in, he and his colleagues smuggled the heavy water to Britain and hid the uranium in Morocco just ahead of Adolf Hitler's advancing troops. During the war, Joliot used the prestige of his Nobel Prize to conceal his activities in support of the French Resistance. Thus, in addition to being a major scientific contributor in his own right, Joliot helped tilt the war in the direction of the Allies.

SIGNIFICANCE

The report of the discovery of artificial radioactivity was published early in 1934, and in 1935 the discovery earned for the husband and wife a shared Nobel Prize in Chemistry. The scientific community almost immediately recognized the discovery as equal to that of the neutron or the positron. Physicist Enrico Fermi and his group in Rome quickly noted that neutrons were more effective in producing artificial radioactivity than the alpha particles used in the original experiments. The entire community, including the Joliot-Curies, began to study artificial radioactivity produced by bombarding different

King Gustav of Sweden congratulates Irène Joliot-Curie during the 1935 Nobel Prize presentation ceremony. Frédéric Joliot stands behind his wife. (AP/Wide World Photos)

elements with neutrons. Studies on uranium in Rome, Berlin, and Paris led to confusing results, which were finally interpreted as nuclear fission in 1939. (Nuclear fission is the splitting of an atomic nucleus into two parts, especially when bombarded by a neutron. When the nuclei of uranium atoms are split, great amounts of energy are released.)

—*Ruth H. Howes*

FURTHER READING

Biquard, Pierre. *Frédéric Joliot-Curie: The Man and His Theories.* Translated by Geoffrey Strachan. New York: Paul S. Eriksson, 1966. Biography by a scientific colleague who was an eyewitness to the discovery of artificial radioactivity. Marred somewhat by the author's extremely sentimental attachment to Frédéric Joliot.

Goldsmith, Maurice. *Frédéric Joliot-Curie.* London: Lawrence & Wishart, 1976. Readable biography written by a colleague of Joliot provides a clear account of the physics of the scientist's work but tends to idealize him. Includes discussion of Joliot's role in World War II that reads like a spy novel.

Jungk, Robert. *Brighter than a Thousand Suns: A Personal History of the Atomic Scientists.* Translated by James Cleugh. New York: Harcourt Brace, 1958. History of the Manhattan Project provides solid background on the physics of that time. Chapter titled "An Unexpected Discovery" provides a history of the discovery of artificial radioactivity in the context of the time during which it was made.

Opfell, Olga S. "Irène Joliot-Curie." In *The Lady Laureates: Women Who Have Won the Nobel Prize.* 2d ed. Metuchen, N.J.: Scarecrow Press, 1986. Readable account of the vital role Joliot-Curie played in the discovery of artificial radioactivity. Emphasizes her life as a wife and mother and as the daughter of a Nobel laureate.

Rayner-Canham, Marelene F., and Geoffrey W. Rayner-Canham. *A Devotion to Their Science: Pioneer Women of Radioactivity.* Philadelphia: Chemical Heritage Foundation, 2005. Collection of biographical essays on twenty-three women involved in atomic science research in the early part of the twentieth century includes essays on Irène Joliot-Curie and Marie Curie as well as on many lesser-known scientists whose stories are rarely told.

Rhodes, Richard. *The Making of the Atomic Bomb.* New York: Simon & Schuster, 1986. Excellent history of early twentieth century physics. Chapter titled "Stirring and Digging" provides a lively description of the discovery of artificial radioactivity set in the context of the physics community and the political events surrounding it.

SEE ALSO: Early 20th cent.: Elster and Geitel Study Radioactivity; Dec. 10, 1903: Becquerel Wins the Nobel Prize for Discovering Natural Radioactivity; 1905-1907: Boltwood Uses Radioactivity to Determine Ages of Rocks; Feb. 11, 1908: Geiger and Rutherford Develop a Radiation Counter; Summer, 1928: Gamow Explains Radioactive Alpha Decay with Quantum Tunneling.

January 2, 1933
COWARD'S *DESIGN FOR LIVING* EPITOMIZES THE 1930'S

Noël Coward kept a promise to Alfred Lunt and Lynn Fontanne and wrote a comedy that epitomized the laughter and despair of the 1930's.

LOCALE: Hanna Theatre, Cleveland, Ohio
CATEGORY: Theater

KEY FIGURES
Noël Coward (1899-1973), English playwright, composer, and actor
Lynn Fontanne (1887-1983), English actor
Alfred Lunt (1892-1977), American actor
Max Gordon (1892-1978), American theater producer

SUMMARY OF EVENT
Design for Living (pr., pb. 1933) resulted from an eleven-year-old promise. In 1921, actors Noël Coward, Alfred Lunt, and Lynn Fontanne were relatively unknown. They dreamed of stardom, and they agreed that, when fame arrived, Coward would write a play to star all three.

Coward had begun to perform in 1910; he had worked in Charles Hawtrey's company in 1911 and, among other appearances, had briefly acted in D. W. Griffith's film *Hearts of the World* (1918). His first major hit was the 1923 revue *London Calling*, based largely on his lyrics. He performed in it with Gertrude Lawrence. Fontanne made her English debut in a 1905 production of *Cinderella* before arriving in the United States in 1910. She met Lunt in 1917 and appeared with him for the first time on stage in 1919 in a play titled *A Young Man's Fancy*. In 1921, she made her reputation in George S. Kaufman and Marc Connelly's *Dulcy*. Lunt's first major recognition came for his Broadway performance as the title character in Booth Tarkington's *Clarence* (pr. 1919). After their marriage in 1922, Lunt and Fontanne achieved the kind of fame they desired with their appearance as a team in a 1924 Theatre Guild production of Ferenc Molnár's *The Guardsman* (Hungarian title *A testőr*, pr., pb. 1910).

Coward's major breakthrough came with his own serious drama *The Vortex* (pr. 1924), in which he played the role of Nicky. *The Vortex* provided a considerable and scandalous sensation, and it presented a theme that was to remain a constant in Coward's work: the struggles of post-World War I characters to work out their own values, as the values of the past had become outmoded or bankrupt. The principal characters in *The Vortex* are Nicky, who is addicted to drugs, and his mother, who is addicted to eternal youthfulness. She refuses to admit her maturity, takes lovers her son's age, and cannot relinquish her own pleasures to be a mother to her son. At the end, mother and son vow to reform, but they leave the audience with no particular reason to believe that they will.

This contrast between the meaningless lives of moderns and the values of the past that are lost underlies many of the Coward hits that followed. In *Cavalcade* (pr. 1931), a panorama of England from the Boer War to 1929, Coward ends by juxtaposing the weary song "Twentieth Century Blues" with the figures of six basket-weaving wounded World War I veterans as well as with a cacophony of noise from planes, jazz, and loudspeakers; these suddenly give way to a singing of the traditional "God Save the King." At the end of Coward's musical *Bitter Sweet* (pr., pb. 1929), heroine Sari Linden sings of the enduring loves and loyalties of the past only to find herself abandoned by her uncomprehending audience of Jazz Age young people. Most bitterly in *Post-Mortem* (pb. 1931), Coward shows his affinity with the great wave of revulsion that swept Europe, England, and, to some extent, the United States in reaction to the traditional values that had produced the devastation of World War I, with its aerial bombardment, gas and trench warfare, and millions of casualties. In *Post-Mortem*, young John Cavan, killed in action, returns from the dead to learn that his death, apparently, meant little. Attitudes have not changed; the platitudes and hypocrisy that made the war possible still conceal its brutal reality. Young people, survivors of the war, cannot accept these values but have nothing with which to replace them.

Design for Living moved to the Ethel Barrymore Theatre in New York City on January 24, 1933, after opening at the Hanna Theatre in Cleveland, Ohio, on January 2. Although the play is high comedy, indirectly it reflects the grim world of the 1930's, a world in which frivolous laughter barely conceals despair. The play reflects the decade's insecurity, recorded in Coward's autobiography and letters, about the Great Depression and the European situation that was to lead to World War II. Coward wrote *Design for Living* very quickly on his way back from Chile, where he had received a cable from the Lunts informing him that their Theatre Guild commitment was over and asking him about the play he had promised to write. He returned to California, the lone passenger on a Norwegian freighter, and completed the play two days before the ship docked at Los Angeles. Clearly, the play emerged from preoccupations, especially the idea, suggestive of George Bernard Shaw's beliefs, that moderns must overthrow traditional moral and social sanctions to create their own lives and values. Coward's play is light, seemingly frivolous, but its action points irrevocably to this single conclusion.

Gilda, Leo, and Otto are the play's principal characters. Leo (played by Coward in the original production) is a playwright, Otto (Lunt) is a painter, and Gilda (Fontanne) loves both. In the first act, Gilda lives with Otto in Paris. She and picture dealer Ernest Friedman (played in 1933 by Campbell Gullan) are talking as Otto returns from a trip. Leo emerges from the bedroom. Conventionally furious, Otto stalks off, feeling betrayed. In the second act, Gilda is living with Leo in London. Leo leaves for a country weekend but returns early to find Otto with Gilda. Disgusted with both men's reactions, Gilda stalks out. She marries Ernest, a merchant, not a creator, and tries to live a conventionally money-hungry life in New York. The third act takes place in their New York apartment, where their pictures and even their fur-

niture are for sale. Otto and Leo enter and scandalize some guests. Gilda walks out again. Ernest returns the next morning to find both Otto and Leo emerging from the bedroom, wearing his pajamas. They claim they want Gilda. Conventional Ernest is horrified and flies into a fury, mouthing the platitudes of an outraged moralist, when Gilda returns to say she is leaving with Otto and Leo. She cannot live without them both. It is Ernest's turn to stalk out, but he trips and falls flat, and the play ends with the laughter of Otto, Leo, and Gilda.

SIGNIFICANCE

Like many other Coward plays, *Design for Living* was a success, but critical reviews were mixed. Having exhausted himself during the run of *The Vortex*, Coward had promised himself that he would appear in no more than a three-month run, but *Design for Living* was so successful that he extended this to five months. According to Coward biographer Cole Lesley, during the final week of the play's run, police had to be called out to control the crowds. For the only time in his life, Coward had to hire a bodyguard. He had rented a secluded cottage and was receiving threatening letters, which may have been related to the play.

Critics, while praising *Design for Living*, often described it as decadent or amoral. The most famous still photograph from the 1933 production emphasizes a possible homosexual relationship between Leo and Otto; one man reclines in the arms of the other while reaching out to Gilda, who sits separately. Then, too, the play supports an aristocracy of the elite, whose duty is to live by its own precepts regardless of the conventional morality for which Ernest, as his name suggests, is the humorless spokesman. Finally, Gilda walks out on her marriage to Ernest, not for high principles, as was true of Henrik Ibsen's Nora in *Et dukkehjem* (pr., pb. 1879; *A Doll's House*, 1880), but simply because she wants to do so. In fact, problems with British censorship probably explain why the play was not performed in England until 1939. Paramount filmed the play in 1933, with Ernst Lubitsch as director, but screenwriter Ben Hecht threw out most of Coward's script. (The film starred Fredric March, Gary Cooper, Miriam Hopkins, and Edward Everett Horton.)

The popularity of Lunt, Fontanne, and Coward himself, however, was such that would-be censors had no power over the production, thus opening up hitherto questionable material for future playwrights, such as Coward's admirer Edward Albee. Of those involved, only theatrical producer Max Gordon's career was profoundly affected, and that positively. Coward had been

Noël Coward. (AP/Wide World Photos)

impressed by Gordon's frank critique of his performance in Coward's earlier play *Private Lives* (pr., pb. 1930). When Coward offered Gordon the opportunity to produce *Design for Living*, he apparently did not know that Gordon was having financial problems so severe that they had brought him near bankruptcy; he was suicidal and had been hospitalized. For Gordon, *Design for Living* was a lifeline; he became solvent again and went on to produce such hits as *Roberta* (1933), *The Great Waltz* (1934), *The Women* (1936), *My Sister Eileen* (1940), and *Born Yesterday* (1945). The Lunts, too, went on from this success to others such as *Reunion in Vienna* (1931), *Idiot's Delight* (1936), *Amphitryon 38* (1937), *There Shall Be No Night* (1940), and *The Pirate* (1942).

Coward's career was at its height with *Design for Living*. He followed it with *Conversation Piece* in 1934, written for French singer Yvonne Printemps, and in that year the first volume of his collected plays appeared. Of the many plays that followed, the two most important are *Tonight at 8:30* (a collective title for nine plays designed to be presented in various combinations of three bills of three plays; pr. 1935) and *Blithe Spirit* (pr., pb. 1941). In 1942, he gained wartime celebrity for writing and acting in the patriotic film *In Which We Serve*, which also starred John Mills and Michael Wilding. The film was a starkly realistic account of the German destruction of a British ship and its effects on the people involved.

In the post-World War II world, Coward lost critical favor but retained his popular audience. John Osborne's play *Look Back in Anger* (pr. 1956) introduced a new kind of realism, as shocking in its way as Coward's had been two decades earlier. Coward continued to write plays, but he rarely repeated his earlier successes. He continued entertaining as well. In 1953, for example, he appeared as King Magnus in a London production of Shaw's *The Apple Cart* (pr. 1929). Shaw's advice had been an early influence on him, and a continuing influence can be seen in the structure and dialogue of Coward's plays.

By the mid-1950's, the critical tide again turned, and Coward became celebrated as the grand old man of British theater. He appeared several times in the 1950's at London's Café de Paris, and in 1954 he gave a royal command performance at London's Palladium. In the following year, he wrote and directed *Together with Music*, a U.S. television review, for himself and Mary Martin. He also made other television appearances, including, in 1967, a role in a U.S. performance of Shaw's *Androcles and the Lion* (pr. 1913). A number of his own plays were adapted for television. In 1955, to his astonishment, he

was offered forty thousand dollars a week to appear at the Desert Inn in Las Vegas; that engagement was a personal triumph. Also in that year, he appeared in the film version of *Around the World in Eighty Days*. He followed this with a noteworthy performance in the 1959 film of Graham Greene's *Our Man in Havana*. A London revival of *Private Lives* led to major revivals of many of his other plays.

COWARD COMMENTS

In his introduction to one of the earliest volumes collecting several of his plays, Noël Coward offers these comments about Design for Living:

Design for Living has been produced, published, and reviewed. It has been liked and disliked, and hated and admired, but never, I think, sufficiently loved by any but its three leading actors. This, perhaps, was only to be expected, as its central theme, from the point of view of the average, must appear to be definitely antisocial. People were certainly interested and entertained and occasionally even moved by it, but it seemed, to many of them, "unpleasant." This sense of "unpleasantness" might have been mitigated for them a little if they had realized that the title was ironic rather than dogmatic. I never intended for a moment that the design for living suggested in the play should apply to anyone outside its three principal characters, Gilda, Otto, and Leo. These glib, over-articulate, and amoral creatures force their lives into fantastic shapes and problems because they cannot help themselves. Impelled chiefly by the impact of their personalities each upon the other, they are like moths in a pool of light, unable to tolerate the lonely outer darkness, and equally unable to share the light without colliding constantly and bruising one another's wings.

The end of the play is equivocal. The three of them, after various partings and reunions and partings again, after torturing and loving and hating one another, are left together as the curtain falls, laughing. Different minds found different meanings in this laughter. Some considered it to be directed against Ernest, Gilda's husband, and the time-honoured friend of all three. If so, it was certainly cruel, and in the worst possible taste. Some saw in it a lascivious anticipation of a sort of triangular carnal frolic. Others, with less ribald imaginations, regarded it as a meaningless and slightly inept excuse to bring the curtain down. I as author, however, prefer to think that Gilda and Otto and Leo were laughing at themselves.

Source: Noël Coward, "Introduction," in *Play Parade* (Garden City, N.Y.: Garden City, 1933).

In 1970, Coward was knighted in recognition of his contributions, and in 1971, he received an honorary Tony Award for his career achievements. In 1972, the Coward revue *Cowardy Custard* played in London, and the revue *Oh! Coward* played in New York in 1973; both shows were essentially anthologies of his lyrics.

—*Betty Richardson*

FURTHER READING

Castle, Charles. *Noël.* Garden City, N.Y.: Doubleday, 1973. Informal compilation of biographical notes, photographs, texts of songs, extracts from plays, and recollections of friends provides an interesting supplement to more formal biographies.

Coward, Noël. *Collected Plays.* Vol. 3. London: Methuen, 2000. Collection of plays includes *Design for Living, Cavalcade, Conversation Piece,* and three plays from the *Tonight at 8:30* cycle.

_____. *Noël Coward: Autobiography.* 1986. Reprint. London: Methuen, 2003. Contains his three autobiographies: *Present Indicative* (1937), *Future Indefinite* (1954), and *Past Conditional* (an unfinished work). Includes index.

Gordon, Max, with Lewis Funke. *Max Gordon Presents.* New York: Bernard Beis, 1963. Readable, generally anecdotal account of Gordon's rise from New York slums to prominence as a theatrical producer. Includes some coverage of his work with Coward.

Hoare, Philip. *Noël Coward: A Biography.* New York: Simon & Schuster, 1995. Comprehensive, thoroughly researched biography places Coward's work within the context of his life and times. Includes photographs and index.

Lahr, John. *Coward the Playwright.* 1982. Reprint. Berkeley: University of California Press, 2002. One of the earliest studies to take full account of Coward's homosexuality. Stresses that topic and Coward's desire for fame, sometimes at the expense of the plays' substance. Includes photographs, bibliography, and index.

Lesley, Cole. *Remembered Laughter: The Life of Noël Coward.* New York: Alfred A. Knopf, 1977. Well-written memoir is tipped slightly toward a personal, rather than professional, biography. First employed by Coward in 1936, Lesley remained his companion and assistant until Coward's death.

Levin, Milton. *Noël Coward.* Rev. ed. Boston: Twayne, 1989. Workmanlike study includes chronology, bibliography of Coward's works, and limited bibliography of works about him.

Mander, Raymond, and Joe Mitchenson. *The Theatrical Companion to Coward.* 1957. Reprint. London: Oberon Books, 1999. Extremely useful for information on Coward's early plays and other works. Includes a tribute to Coward by playwright Terence Rattigan as well as cast lists, production dates, synopses, a discography, and a list of individual songs.

Morley, Sheridan. *A Talent to Amuse: A Biography of Noël Coward.* Rev. ed. Boston: Little, Brown, 1985. Focuses slightly more on Coward's professional life than on his personal life. Includes a valuable chronology that lists his work as playwright, performer, composer, author, and director as well as major revivals of his work.

Peters, Margot. *Design for Living: Alfred Lunt and Lynn Fontanne.* New York: Alfred A. Knopf, 2003. Biography of the Lunts features considerable material about their relationship with Coward. Includes photographs, chronology, selected bibliography, and index.

SEE ALSO: Dec. 27, 1927: *Show Boat* Is the First American Musical to Emphasize Plot; 1931-1941: The Group Theatre Flourishes; 1934-1938: Production Code Gives Birth to Screwball Comedy; Feb. 19, 1935: Odets's *Awake and Sing!* Becomes a Model for Protest Drama; Aug. 29, 1935-June 30, 1939: Federal Theatre Project Promotes Live Theater; Oct. 10, 1935: Gershwin's *Porgy and Bess* Opens in New York; Feb. 4, 1938: *Our Town* Opens on Broadway.

1933

January 23, 1933
ITALY CREATES THE INDUSTRIAL RECONSTRUCTION INSTITUTE

As a response to the banking crisis of the 1930's, the Italian government created the Industrial Reconstruction Institute, which bought bank-owned shares of stock in failing companies.

LOCALE: Rome, Italy

CATEGORIES: Banking and finance; organizations and institutions; government and politics

KEY FIGURES

Alberto Beneduce (1877-1944), president of the Industrial Reconstruction Institute, 1933-1939

Donato Menichella (1896-1984), general manager of the Industrial Reconstruction Institute, 1933-1943

Benito Mussolini (1883-1945), dictator of Italy, 1922-1945

Giuseppe Toeplitz (1866-1938), director of Banca Commerciale Italiana, a major holder of industrial securities

SUMMARY OF EVENT

In the 1920's, Italian banks commonly purchased large blocks of stocks in firms to which they had lent money. By doing so, the banks could have an influence on management operations and, presumably, make sure that their financial interests were being handled responsibly. As a result of the worldwide economic depression of the 1930's, which was precipitated by the stock market crash of 1929, many Italian businesses became undervalued, and their stock prices plummeted. Three major banks in Italy—Banca Commerciale Italiana, Credito Italiano, and Banco di Roma—faced failure because of their holdings in such businesses. The Instituto per la Rico Struzione Industriale (the Industrial Reconstruction Institute, or IRI) was created as a temporary measure to keep these banks afloat through the purchase of their stock holdings. The IRI thus obtained great potential influence over Italian business. Eventually, the IRI developed into a permanent holding company owned by the state but independent of direct government control. The IRI became a major tool for implementing economic and industrial policy controls in Italy.

Although the Fascist government of Italy (led by dictator Benito Mussolini) supported the use of public funds to subsidize private business, it did not create the concept. Just prior to World War I, in 1914, the Italian government had established an industrial business cooperative to provide funds for the production of war materials.

In 1921, this cooperative was permitted to use Italian treasury funds to rescue two important businesses that had joint operations. These firms were the giant industrial company Ansaldo and the Banca Italiana di Sconto (the Italian Discount Bank). Two brothers who managed Ansaldo had earlier given Mussolini support for his newspaper, *Il Popolo d'Italia*. In 1923, partly to please the Vatican and partly to avert a major economic downturn, Mussolini worked directly to save the Banco di Roma through the use of public funds. Soon the Fascists were regularly transferring public money to private organizations. Of principal concern through this period was the survival of banks, on which consumer confidence and industrial development depended.

During the 1920's and 1930's, a small number of associations of industrialists and industrial organizations had formed and developed considerable power. The most influential, the CGII (General Confederation of Italian Industrialists), had assisted the Fascists when they attained power in October, 1922. Because of its close association with the government, it began to transform from a collection of private business interests to a powerful element of the public bureaucracy.

In November, 1931, it became clear that the banking community had more severe problems than could be solved by the methods used to help the Italian Discount Bank and others in the 1920's. The CGII became adamant that the government do something dramatic to avoid severe bank failures. As a response, the Italian Mobilization Institute (IMI) was created and given authority to collect funds from any source to rescue troubled banks. Although it continued to operate, the IMI did not satisfactorily accomplish its mission, in part because of an austere management style and in part because of the uncertainty of the private funds that were to be included in the mix of funds to be administered for failing banks.

The IRI was established as a last-resort response to the failure of the CGII. It was to use only public funds to directly purchase, from banks, shares of stock in failing companies that had been held in security. The creation of the IRI was an uneventful occasion, as most people regarded this extreme measure as only a temporary direct intervention of government into business affairs. The immediate need was to save three major banks from failure. Among them, only the Banca Commerciale Italiana was very reluctant to sell its industrial holdings to the newly created IRI. Giuseppe Toeplitz, director of the bank, finally gave his approval in 1933, and in doing so he firmly established the IRI's legitimacy.

At this stage, Mussolini was careful not to appoint people with strong stands either for or against fascism to management positions. The first president of the IRI, Alberto Beneduce, appeared to be the type of neutral person of whom Italy and the world at large would approve. Appearances, however, were somewhat deceiving. Beneduce had long been active in politics, and as a member of the moderate Social Democrat Party, he had served in several minor positions as statistician, and from 1921 to 1922 he served Italy as minister of labor and welfare. Mussolini and Beneduce developed a relationship of mutual respect despite their philosophical differences; both were technically competent and yearned for power, regardless of labels.

In 1935, Beneduce became convinced that the future of governmental intervention in business in Italy should take the form of managerial directives and strategies rather than direct financial subsidization. The IRI thus made no more loans or purchases of bank-held stocks. These functions were returned to the IMI in March, 1936. In June, 1937, the IRI became a permanent government agency, responsible for overseeing industrial production, management, and strategy of those companies in which it held major blocks of shares. The business community objected, but IRI prevailed, primarily through the vast amount of control, through stock ownership, it had obtained in earlier years from failing banks.

In those industries in which productivity and innovation had remained at relatively high levels, repurchase of ownership was possible, but the majority of companies were unable to regain ownership. The IRI, therefore, continued to have a significant amount of control of industrial operations, principally in industries that did not operate at a profit. It had controlling interests in a number of key industries, including electricity, machinery, shipping, and telephone systems.

Because stock purchases by the IRI were not complete takeovers (the institute did not buy all the shares of any one company), the resultant industrial model was that of a mixed economy, with ownership of manufacturing industries shared between the private and public sectors. The war years devastated Italy's production capacity, but the IRI survived largely through the efforts of its early leaders and the demand for the heavy industrial products created by large-scale warfare.

SIGNIFICANCE

The short-term impact of the IRI was to stabilize the Italian banking system through reorganization of industrial stock portfolios and the sale of such stabilized portfolios back to the banks. The IRI eventually became a permanent holding company and a major economic institution with direct influence on political and social institutions, and much of postwar Italy's cultural character was shaped by the IRI's presence and activities. In addition, by the end of the 1960's, Great Britain, France, Canada, Australia, Sweden, and Germany had all established state holding companies based on the IRI model.

For a time, the future of the IRI was in doubt. The war destroyed approximately 45 percent of Italy's production capacity, and much of the capacity that remained had to be reconstructed for the production of peacetime goods. The years immediately following the war saw uncertainty over the country's development, and a 1946 statute reaffirmed the 1937 legislation establishing the IRI as a permanent agency. That act was soon disavowed, but it was replaced by more permanent (but equally controversial) legislation in 1948. The Allies severely restricted the IRI's management, and although aid provided under the Marshall Plan was necessary for any economic redevelopment, such aid was highly controlled. The Christian Democrat Party, the ruling party of the postwar period, was undecided as to how much influence the IRI should have, and the government presented an ambiguous direction for the IRI.

Nevertheless, the IRI was permitted to grow for two primary reasons. First, there were economies of scale in large industries that could be exploited by the IRI's centralized administrative apparatus. Second, the IRI instituted policies that were perceived as humane, such as retaining employees who were not needed in order to prevent their deportation or conscription to Germany. By 1949, the IRI had achieved its prewar capacity. From the mid-1950's, it had an influence on virtually every aspect of Italian society. The Italian economy experienced remarkably rapid growth during the postwar period, and although a number of factors contributed to this growth—including the European Common Market, the Marshall Plan, foreign investments, and increased domestic consumption—the IRI is generally acknowledged as the single most important factor behind the Italian economy's expansion.

The IRI benefited private industry in important ways. Its operation reduced responsibility for unprofitable ventures, thus encouraging entrepreneurship and maximization of profit-producing investments. The IRI's decision

1933

to issue stock was particularly helpful to private industry: Businesses could buy shares of ownership in the holding company which, in turn, held ownership in their firms. In consequence, the IRI had more capital and could blur the lines between public and private sources of funds, which created an extremely strong cover for the "mixed" economy. The IRI thus posed no threat to private initiative but did provide for centralized economies of scale and protection against economic disaster.

Perhaps the most outstanding example of this influence was in the development of the Italian steel industry. For purposes of national security and to support the auto and other heavy industries, reduced dependence on imported steel was a high priority in postwar Italy. The country had very few deposits of iron ore, the basic material for the production of steel. The Italian steel industry, therefore, had always depended on steel scrap as a raw material. This approach, however, put the Italian industry at the mercy of worldwide supply and demand for scrap. Under the leadership and financial sponsorship of an IRI group called Finsider, a scrap-steel plant near Genoa was rebuilt to accommodate raw iron ore. Dredging operations produced channels that would permit oceangoing freight vessels to dock at the shore-based plant. Direct importing of raw iron began, essentially eliminating dependence on steel scrap. An immediate result of this was to ensure Italy's membership in the European Coal and Steel Community. This, along with a long-term contract with Fiat to supply auto-quality steel, ensured an adequate supply of raw iron ore and a demand for product.

Most researchers attribute a number of positive social consequences to the influence of the IRI. From 1948 to 1972, employment rose by 93 percent, sales rose a phenomenal 1,300 percent, and investment rose 1,500 percent. The result of these developments was creation of a highly productive economy that by the 1980's was among the world leaders. Such rapid growth meant wide availability of consumer goods, incomes with which to purchase them, and a comfortable standard of living.

The IRI's impacts beyond Italy were also substantial. The British Industrial Reorganization Corporation was established in January, 1966, followed in March, 1970, by the French Industrial Development Institute and the Canada Development Corporation, and in June, 1970, by the Australian Industries Development Corporation. All were modeled principally on the Italian IRI. What began as a temporary measure to save three banks from failure on the eve of World War II became a major

economic institution of Italy and a model for the institutional arrangements in the mixed economies of many other nations.

—*Steven K. Paulson*

FURTHER READING

Allen, Kevin, and Andrew Stevenson. *An Introduction to the Italian Economy.* New York: Barnes and Noble, 1975. A detailed and adequate reference on the Italian economy up to the 1970's. Chapters 1 and 7 present detailed discussions of economic developments in the 1930's and 1940's, with a focus on the state sector.

Clough, Shepard B. *The Economic History of Modern Italy.* New York: Columbia University Press, 1964. An extraordinarily thorough treatment of the economic history of Italy from the late nineteenth century through the mid-1960's. The Fascist period is discussed in chapters 7 and 8. Provides a helpful discussion of the context within which the IRI was created and developed.

De Grand, Alexander. *Italian Fascism: Its Origins and Development.* 2d ed. Lincoln: University of Nebraska Press, 1989. This relatively short book presents a very readable and concise history of Italian Fascism. The development and impact of the IRI are reviewed in several pages.

Holland, Stuart, ed. *The State as Entrepreneur.* London: Weidenfeld & Nicolson, 1972. Comprehensive analysis of the IRI as the prototype state holding company. Provides considerable factual information about the formative period of the IRI as well as its long-term impacts on other economies.

Kindleberger, Charles P. *Manias, Panics, and Crashes: A History of Financial Crises.* 4th ed. New York: John Wiley & Sons, 2000. General survey of financial speculation and monetary crises from the eighteenth century to the late twentieth century.

Posner, M. V., and S. J. Woolf. *Italian Public Enterprise.* Cambridge, Mass.: Harvard University Press, 1967. Brief examination of the role of state enterprises in Italy for the period 1952-1967. Devotes much attention to the role of the IRI and provides informative discussion of the IRI's origins. Also discusses the long-run impact of the IRI on the postwar economy of Italy.

Sarti, Roland. *Fascism and the Industrial Leadership in Italy, 1919-1940.* Berkeley: University of California Press, 1971. Brief but thorough analysis of the relationship between the Italian Fascists and economic developments of the period 1919-1940. Provides detailed insights into the personalities important to the creation and development of the IRI as a product of Fascist authority and, at times, the direct involvement of Mussolini.

Wicker, Elmus. *The Banking Panics of the Great Depression*. New York: Cambridge University Press, 1996. Examines the origins, magnitudes, and effects of five individual banking panics. Features figures, tables, references, and index.

SEE ALSO: Oct. 24-29, 1929: U.S. Stock Market Crashes; Dec. 11, 1930: Bank of United States Fails; May 8, 1931: Credit-Anstalt Bank of Austria Fails; June 16, 1933: Banking Act of 1933 Reorganizes the American Banking System; Aug. 23, 1935: Banking Act of 1935 Centralizes U.S. Monetary Control; 1936-1946: France Nationalizes Its Banking and Industrial Sectors.

January 30, 1933
HITLER COMES TO POWER IN GERMANY

Adolf Hitler's rise to power and his leadership of the Nazi Party marked the end of German democracy in the 1930's and ushered in political changes that led to World War II.

LOCALE: Germany
CATEGORIES: Government and politics; World War II; wars, uprisings, and civil unrest

KEY FIGURES

Adolf Hitler (1889-1945), chancellor of Germany, 1933-1945
Joseph Goebbels (1897-1945), Nazi leader of Berlin and later propaganda minister under Hitler
Hermann Göring (1893-1946), president of the Reichstag, 1932-1933, and minister in Hitler's cabinet
Paul von Hindenburg (1847-1934), president of the Weimar Republic, 1925-1934
Franz von Papen (1879-1969), chancellor of Germany, 1932, and vice chancellor under Hitler, 1933-1934
Ernst Röhm (1887-1934), chief of staff of the paramilitary Sturm Abteilung (SA)
Kurt von Schleicher (1882-1934), chancellor of Germany, 1932-1933

SUMMARY OF EVENT

On the morning of January 30, 1933, Adolf Hitler took the oath of office from Weimar Republic president Paul von Hindenburg. That evening, thousands of torch-bearing Nazi Brownshirts, members of the paramilitary Sturm Abteilung (SA), marched through the Brandenburg Gate past the new chancellor, celebrating their victory over the forces of German democracy. The Third Reich, which would bring the fanatical allegiance of the majority of Germans to Hitler and would lead to the vast holocaust of World War II, had begun.

Hitler's movement, the National Socialist German Workers' Party (NSDAP), also known as the Nazi Party, had begun with a handful of malcontents in Munich shortly after World War I. Many other racist-nationalist groups existed at the time, but Hitler's ruthless, brilliant leadership made the NSDAP a special case. Although Hitler had first tried to grasp power in 1923 in the Beer Hall Putsch, Weimar democracy had prevailed, and by the time of the 1928 elections the Nazis appeared to be no more than an annoying, inconsequential party from the radical right. Their combination of nationalism, anti-Marxism, anti-Semitism, anti-big business "socialism," militaristic agitation, and raucous oratory had gained them less than 3 percent of the popular vote. Yet, in less than five years, Hitler was chancellor of Germany, and he placed such key men as Hermann Göring and Joseph Goebbels in charge of the state. By the time of Hindenburg's death in August, 1934, Hitler had secured totalitarian control of the state.

Historians noted a number of reasons for the Nazi's rise. Few modern scholars accepted the early argument that Hitler's victory was made inevitable by the German intellectual traditions that venerated the authority of the state, lauded military virtues, and praised the greatness of the German people. Nevertheless, this background provided traditions that Hitler could pervert and exploit. The Great Depression, which hit Germany soon after the 1929 stock market crash in the United States, gave Hitler's movement its greatest boost. As business indicators fell and the unemployment lines grew, the Nazis scored impressive electoral gains.

Curiously, however, Hitler's votes did not come from the unemployed; most of those were working-class people devoted to Marxism. If they were moderates, they voted for Social Democrats, if they were radicals, they voted for Communists. While research supports the con-

1933

tention that the Nazi voters appear to have come largely from the ranks of the middle classes, including shopkeepers, managers, small farmers, white-collar workers, civil servants, and other members of petite bourgeoisie, some studies indicate that Hitler's support extended across a much broader section of society. For the most part, those who voted for Hitler's NSDAP feared Marxist rhetoric and had abandoned the traditional bourgeois parties in frustration.

Nationalistic appeals based on denunciation of the Treaty of Versailles (1919), which had been imposed on Germany after World War I, heightened levels of support. Hitler, portrayed through careful and manipulative propaganda as a humble soldier from the ranks and a member of the German "race" (although he was an Austrian by birth), appealed to the German sense of pride by calling for a greater Germany.

Adolf Hitler (second from right) and other members of his party raise their hands in the Nazi salute after winning elections in 1933. (Hulton Archive/Getty Images)

The German people were not as lacking in democratic traditions as some commentators (including Hitler) believed, but their feelings about the Weimar Constitution were pragmatic, and when unstable parliamentary coalitions proved incapable handling the economic crisis, they were fully prepared to try more authoritarian solutions. The Nazis, with their vigorous and aggressive (if somewhat ill-defined) program, stood out in stark contrast to the modesty and fatigue which characterized the other middle-class parties. Hitler's leadership, amplified by the Goebbels propaganda machine, brought many solid German burghers to his side.

The Nazis became the largest single power in the German multiparty system, but they never received an absolute majority in a free national election. It was the intrigues of reactionary politicians, rather than the votes of Germans, that put Hitler in power. In March of 1932, Hitler ran for president against the aging Hindenburg. Hitler received 30.1 percent of the votes to Hindenburg's 49.6 percent, with the remaining votes going to the Communist candidate (13.2 percent), and two minor candidates. Clearly, Hitler had lost, but a second ballot was necessary because no one had received an absolute majority. In April, Hindenburg beat Hitler, receiving 53 percent of the vote as compared to Hitler's 36.8 percent. Several state legislative elections followed, the most significant of which was in Prussia. The Nazis emerged as the largest single party there, with 36.2 percent of the votes.

In July, when the national parliament, the Reichstag, was elected, the Nazis won 37.3 percent of the vote. Together, the Nazis and the Communists—the antidemocratic forces, respectively, of the radical Right and the radical Left—held a majority of Reichstag seats. A government based on even the broadest coalition of the middle parties was impossible, so in November the German people voted again. This time the Nazi totals fell, giving Hitler and his party only 33.1 percent. The Nazi campaign coffers were depleted, and the flood of Nazi votes seemed to have crested and receded. Hindenburg refused to give Hitler the dictatorial powers he demanded as his price for supporting a government with Nazi votes in the Reichstag. Both Hitler and Goebbels became despondent.

Since midyear, the chancellorship had been held by Franz von Papen, a reactionary aristocrat once active in the Catholic Center Party. After the November elections, Papen found his position undermined not only by the Nazis but by General Kurt von Schleicher, army chief and an inveterate political manipulator. Hindenburg appointed Schleicher to serve as chancellor in December, 1932. The clever general tried to split the Nazi Party and form a coalition of left-wing Nazis, right-wing Social Democrats, and conservatives in order to keep Hitler from power. Schleicher's plan gathered little support, and Papen worked behind the scenes to unseat Schleicher and create a coalition of Nazis and Nationalists (German National People's Party) in which he would hold a key position. Papen assured Hindenburg and others on the traditional right that Hitler could be controlled by the conservatives in the cabinet. Indeed, only three Nazis—Hermann Göring, Wilhelm Frick, and Hitler himself—would be in the cabinet. Thus Hindenburg agreed to make the fatal appointment.

The first few months of Hitler's rule were crucial to his success: During that period he accomplished a revolution after coming to power. Rather than controlling Hitler as they had planned, Papen and the other conservatives found themselves outmaneuvered by him at every turn. Hitler skillfully dismantled the constitutional guarantees he had sworn to uphold and went on to establish a totalitarian dictatorship in the years that followed. Upon Hindenburg's death in August of 1934, Hitler assumed his powers as president and exacted an oath of personal loyalty from the military.

SIGNIFICANCE

After Hitler's rise to power, the Nazi revolution occurred in four phases. First, Hitler prevailed on Hindenburg to call new elections for the Reichstag. Nazis now controlled the police, so Brownshirt terrorism went unchecked while the opposition parties labored under severe handicaps. A few days before the election, a former Communist Dutch arsonist set fire to the Reichstag building. Quickly, the Nazis fabricated evidence of a Communist uprising and promulgated emergency decrees that suspended civil rights. The decrees were never lifted. Even with all the power of the state behind them, the Nazis missed a majority, receiving 43.9 percent of the votes on March 5, 1933.

The second phase was the forcing through the Reichstag of the Enabling Act (1933), which was written to give Hitler dictatorial powers for four years and required a two-thirds vote of the Reichstag for passage. The Communists had been forcibly excluded, and many Social Democrats had been threatened and did not appear. Nevertheless, Hitler needed the votes of the Catholic Center Party, so he combined honeyed words and threats to gain its support. When the vote came, only the Social Democratic Party voted against Hitler. As a result, his dictatorship was legitimated on March 23, 1933.

The third phase of the Nazi revolution was the policy of *Gleichschaltung* (coordination), which subordinated every organization to the Nazi state. All other political parties dissolved more or less "voluntarily" (that is, without being physically forced to do so). The mass media

and the arts were coordinated under Goebbels's leadership, and youth organizations, unions, professional societies, and even singing groups and garden clubs found it prudent either to amalgamate with the parallel Nazi organizations or simply to go out of business. Coordination was a process rather than a single action, so it overlapped other phases of the Nazi takeover, and its results were uneven. Within the churches, for example, pockets of independence continued to exist, although the vast majority of both Protestants and Catholics formally accepted Nazi dominance. Anyone who actively and publicly opposed coordination faced the prospect of joining thousands of dissidents in the concentration camps.

The fourth phase included two events in 1934 that placed the capstone on Hitler's control of the state. In late June, rumors of a putsch—an attempt to overthrow the government—by Ernst Röhm and certain other "radicals" within the SA provided an excuse for a bloody purge. During what has come to be known as the Night of the Long Knives or the Great Blood Purge, between 150 and 200 potential or real opponents of the regime were shot on Hitler's orders by the Schutzstaffel (SS), which was directed by Heinrich Himmler. Röhm and a number of other prominent conservatives were killed, including Schleicher. On August 2, 1934, the eighty-six-year-old Hindenburg finally died, and Hitler swiftly assumed the powers of the deceased president and had the military swear a personal oath of loyalty to him as führer (leader). He then arranged for a plebiscite in which 89.9 percent of the valid votes cast supported him.

—George R. Mitchell and Liesel Ashley Miller

FURTHER READING

Abel, Theodore. *Why Hitler Came into Power.* Cambridge, Mass.: Harvard University Press, 1986. Originally published in 1938, Abel's study remains an analytic cornerstone in the question of why Hitler was successful in becoming Germany's leader. This edition has a foreword by Thomas Childers.

Allen, William Sheridan. *The Nazi Seizure of Power: The Experience of a Single German Town, 1930-1935.* Chicago: Quadrangle Books, 1965. Allen's book shows the local impact of Nazism and how the grassroots organization and support of the party made possible Hitler's ultimate seizure of power.

Bullock, Alan. *Hitler: A Study in Tyranny.* New York: Harper & Row, 1962. Remains one of the best, most thorough standard biographies of Hitler. Shows how Hitler carried out his "revolution after power."

Childers, Thomas. *The Nazi Voter.* Chapel Hill: Univer-

1933

sity of North Carolina Press, 1983. In this statistical analysis of German voting behavior, Childers contends that Hitler's supporters came not simply from an indistinguishable middle class, but from very diverse backgrounds.

Flood, Charles Bracelen. *Hitler: The Path to Power.* Boston: Houghton Mifflin, 1989. An insightful addition to accounts of Hitler and his rise to power, this work provides an exhaustive bibliography of both primary and secondary sources.

Hamann, Brigitte. *Hitler's Vienna: A Dictator's Apprenticeship.* New York: Oxford University Press, 1999. Focuses on Hitler's years in Vienna. Includes photographs, select bibliography, and index.

Hamilton, Richard F. *Who Voted for Hitler?* Princeton, N.J.: Princeton University Press, 1982. In this controversial book, Hamilton rejects the traditional centrist argument—that of the dominant lower-middle-class support for the NSDAP—and suggests alternative explanations for the Nazi rise to power.

Hilberg, Raul. *The Destruction of the European Jews.* 3d ed. New Haven, Conn.: Yale University Press, 2003. Comprehensive account of the Nazi treatment of the Jews of Germany and Nazi-occupied Europe. Graphically illustrates how the ideas Hitler expressed in *Mein Kampf* led directly to unspeakable suffering for millions of people. Includes excellent bibliography and index.

Hitler, Adolf. *Mein Kampf.* Translated by Ralph Manheim. Reprint. New York: Mariner Books, 1998. No commentary can illustrate Hitler's ideas as well as *Mein Kampf* itself. Hitler's clumsy and often pompous prose does not prevent the reader from understanding that his program called for the destruction of many basic human rights, including freedom of the press, freedom of speech, freedom of association, free enterprise, and sexual freedom. Manheim's translation is among the best available.

Maier, Charles S., Stanley Hoffmann, and Andrew Gould, eds. *The Rise of the Nazi Regime: Historical Reassessments.* Boulder, Colo.: Westview Press, 1986. This collection of essays begins with an informative overview by Charles Maier, while subsequent contributors address the collapse of Weimar and the Nazi rise to power.

SEE ALSO: Nov. 8, 1923: Beer Hall Putsch; July 18, 1925-Dec. 11, 1926: *Mein Kampf* Outlines Nazi Thought; Feb. 27, 1933: Reichstag Fire; Mar., 1933: Nazi Concentration Camps Begin Operating; Mar. 23, 1933: Enabling Act of 1933; June 30-July 2, 1934: Great Blood Purge; Mar. 7, 1936: German Troops March into the Rhineland; Feb. 12-Apr. 10, 1938: The Anschluss; Sept. 29-30, 1938: Munich Conference; Nov. 9-10, 1938: Kristallnacht; 1939-1945: Nazi Extermination of the Jews; Aug. 23-24, 1939: Nazi-Soviet Pact.

February 24, 1933
JAPAN WITHDRAWS FROM THE LEAGUE OF NATIONS

In 1931, the Japanese military invaded Manchuria. By 1932, it had installed a puppet regime there, as well as a subservient civilian government at home. The League of Nations commissioned an investigation of the seizure of Manchuria, and when the investigation concluded with a report condemning the invasion, Japan formally withdrew from the League, destabilizing its diplomatic relations with most of the world powers.

LOCALE: Geneva, Switzerland

CATEGORIES: Diplomacy and international relations; organizations and institutions; colonialism and occupation

KEY FIGURES

Chiang Kai-shek (1887-1975), Chinese military and political leader

Yōsuke Matsuoka (1880-1946), chief Japanese delegate to the League of Nations

Inukai Tsuyoshi (1855-1932), prime minister of Japan, 1931-1932

Second Earl of Lytton (Victor Bulwer-Lytton; 1876-1947), British delegate to the League of Nations and president of the Commission of Inquiry into the Manchurian Incident

Puyi (1906-1967), former Chinese emperor and figurehead ruler of Manchukuo, 1932-1945

SUMMARY OF EVENT

On February 24, 1933, Yōsuke Matsuoka, the chief Japanese delegate to the League of Nations, read a long and impassioned plea to the General Assembly in Geneva. He implored the League not to give sanction to its own Lytton

Commission report, which criticized Japan's actions in the so-called Mukden incident of 1931 and its subsequent actions in relation to the establishment of the Japanese puppet regime in Manchukuo in 1932. When the League ignored his plea and voted to sustain the report, Matsuoka turned on his heel, summoned his Japanese colleagues to follow, and stalked dramatically out of the meeting hall. In so doing, he visibly dramatized Japan's eventual official withdrawal from the League and, some historians have argued, the beginning of World War II.

Without doubt, Japan's decision to withdraw from the League of Nations was a watershed event in Sino-Japanese relations and in the history of human rights in Manchuria as well. It was also an event that contributed to the destruction of civilian democratic government in Japan and drew a suffocating pall over the possibilities for democracy in China. Japan's withdrawal from the League can be traced directly to the Mukden incident, which occurred on the evening of September 18, 1931. In that incident, the Japanese Kwangtung Army stationed in Manchuria feigned a Chinese attack on the Japanese-owned South Manchuria Railroad as part of a strategy to overrun all of Manchuria and parts of northeast China.

The antecedents of the 1933 withdrawal can also be traced to Japanese attempts to win supremacy in Manchuria as early as the First Sino-Japanese War of 1894-1895. For the next thirty years, Japan attempted to wrest control of that mineral-rich area from China. By the time the Japanese Kwangtung Army precipitated the Mukden incident, Japan had come to believe that it possessed "special interests" and rights in the region. In fact, only three years before, the army had attempted to create cause for military intervention by assassinating its own military protégé, the Manchurian warlord Zhang Zuolin.

In the Mukden incident, when the Japanese army "responded" to the fabricated Chinese attack on the railroad, it was the culmination of a longstanding wish to separate Manchuria from China. Before the Japanese government could reestablish control over its own troops, the Kwangtung Army had driven before it most of the Chinese troops in the area as a "protective reaction." A week after the beginning of the incident, most of Manchuria and parts of North China were firmly in the possession of the Kwangtung Army. The army had in effect conducted its own foreign policy and now dared the Japanese civilian government to negate a victory for which the Japanese people showed great support and enthusiasm.

The government was confronted with a nearly impossible situation. On one hand, it faced a military that was split internally on many issues (including army versus navy and "old" army versus Young Officer Movement) but solidly united against the idea of returning Manchuria to a corrupt Chinese government. On the other hand, Japan's government was assailed by opposition parties that wished to use the crisis to further their own political objectives. Criticism of the government's weak foreign policies had been the time-tested weapon for opposition parties in Japan for half a century. To its credit, the government tried to manage the crisis by attempting to reach a compromise with Chinese military leader Chiang Kai-shek. The Kwangtung Army, however, continued to make matters worse. The army leadership recognized that if something were not done to destroy the chances for an agreement between the Chinese and Japanese governments, all their hard-won territory might be returned to Chinese sovereignty. Despite explicit government orders not to precipitate more problems, the army began to manuever to create a separate Manchurian regime that it could control.

China, like Japan, was a member of the League of Nations and therefore appealed to the League for redress. The League agreed to investigate the matter, and after nearly a year of preparation it appointed an investigatory commission led by its British delegate, the second earl of Lytton. Before the Lytton Commission could accomplish its tasks, however, in mid-December, 1931, the Japanese government collapsed. It was replaced by one led by Inukai Tsuyoshi, who five months later was gunned down by militarists in May, 1932, ushering in what one historian has called "government by assassination."

As busy as the military was coercing political change by threat and intimidation in Japan, its branch in Manchuria was equally intent on extending its power and control there as well. In a series of rapid strikes, it secured the strategic strongholds of the area. In March, 1932, it engineered a Kwangtung Army-inspired "spontaneous" native Manchu revolution and declared an independent state of Manchukuo. The army installed Puyi, the "last emperor" of the Chinese Qing Dynasty, as the "emperor of Manchukuo." Puyi had ruled as a child emperor from 1908-1912 and had then been made a mere figurehead, retaining only the title of emperor until 1924. His prior twelve years as a powerless ruler made him seem the perfect candidate to act as Japan's puppet. Inukai was assassinated in part because he refused to recognize this travesty of a government under Puyi. His successor extended full diplomatic recognition to Manchukuo in September, 1932, almost exactly one year after the Mukden incident.

As for the political and human rights of the Manchurians, the Japanese military already had an imperialist

1933

blueprint for the treatment of subjugated people. Like the Taiwanese in 1895 and the Koreans in 1910, Manchurians in 1931 became second-class citizens in their own homeland. The heretofore untapped major mineral and commercial sectors of their economy were controlled outright by the Japanese, and nearly all forms of political expression were brutally suppressed. Manchuria had been controlled previously by a mixture of feudal warlords, former members of the Chinese Imperial government, and members of the landed elite. Most of this leadership had fled with the retreating Chinese army in September, 1931. Those who had not were closely watched, imprisoned, or both. The Manchurian government, which mirrored Japan's own, was in fact totally controlled by Japanese "advisers," and all decisions were made by the commander of the Kwangtung Army. A few Manchurian collaborators were used as puppets, but the Manchurians were in the main relegated to subservient positions.

A second year went by as the Lytton Commission went about its task. Japan attempted to coerce the Chinese government into recognizing Manchukuo, but China preferred to await the final League disposition of the case. Finally, in late September, 1932, the Lytton Commission reported that "without any declaration of war, a large part of Chinese territory has been forcibly seized and occupied by Japanese troops." It recommended that the Kwangtung Army return to its position and function as of September 17, 1931, and that all actions taken subsequent to that date not be recognized or sanctioned by the League.

Japan's chief delegate to the League, Matsuoka, scrambled to try to have the report tabled pending a trilateral agreement between Japan, China, and Manchukuo (which he knew to be unlikely if not impossible). The League, after some deliberation, decided to vote on whether to accept the Lytton Commission's report. At this point, Matsuoka made a quixotic and impassioned speech to the General Assembly in which he implored it not to accept the report "for the sake of peace in the Far East and for the sake of peace in the world." Unconvinced, the General Assembly voted to accept the report by an overwhelming majority (forty-six to one, with Siam abstaining). Matsuoka and the Japanese delegation then made their dramatic and symbolic exit.

One month later, on March 27, 1933, the Japanese government officially notified the League of its intention to withdraw from that body. Manchukuo remained a nation in name only, with only Japan, Italy, Germany, and a few other nations extending it diplomatic recognition. It became part of Japan's wartime Greater East Asia Co-

Japanese diplomats gather their belongings as they leave their posts at the League of Nations. (NARA)

prosperity Sphere and was returned to Chinese control with the defeat of the Japanese Empire in August, 1945.

Significance

Once it had seized Manchuria, Japan began a concerted effort to colonize the country with nearly one-half million Japanese immigrants, who found ready employment as managers in companies "jointly owned" by Japanese financial interests and the government of Manchukuo. All political parties, with the exception of the Hsieh Ho Hui (Concordia Association), were outlawed. All other forms of political expression, including the few remaining Manchu-language newspapers, were tightly controlled or completely stifled.

By 1937, the country had become part of Japan's fancifully named Greater East Asia Coprosperity Sphere. A corporation was established in October, 1937, to help supply Japan with war materials. The corporation, like the government of Manchukuo, was under the complete control of the Kwangtung Army. The bulk of Manchuria's natural resources were exported to Japan for the war effort.

The government of Manchukuo was modeled on that of Japan, but in reality the organs of government were firmly in the hands of the Japanese. In fact, virtually every aspect of Manchurian society was controlled by the Kwangtung Army. "Emperor" Puyi was never allowed even the semblance of power. The thirty million Manchurian people were limited to working for Japanese-owned and -controlled companies, their every political, civil, and human right suppressed by the brutal military government. Hundreds of thousands of them were imprisoned or forced to work as slave laborers during the war. Estimates of Manchurian deaths by starvation, torture, malnutrition, and execution ranged between 80,000 and 100,000.

Between 1931 and 1945, Manchurians were denied the rights to own property, to assemble and speak freely, to vote, to a fair trial, to sue, to emigrate, and even to divorce their spouses. In short, Manchurians were denied virtually every conceivable human and civil right by their Japanese masters. At home, the Japanese military continued to threaten and assassinate its civilian and even its own military leaders. In mid-1937, a military-controlled Japan began another war with China, a conflict that would last until Japan's defeat in August, 1945.

Japan's political party system, which had been the first in East Asia and had showed promise, was dismantled. All political parties were coerced into "cooperating" with the military during the war. They disbanded and joined the Imperial Rule Assistance Association

(Taisei Yokusankai), which acquiesced in Japan's eventual extension of the war with China to include the United States, Great Britain, and the other Allies. Thousands of Japanese dissidents were rounded up and imprisoned without trial, and hundreds more simply disappeared, probably assassinated by the secret police forces of the army. Opposition newspapers were closed down and their editors imprisoned, political rallies of all sorts were outlawed, and legal and civil rights were suspended for the duration of the war.

It may be fairly said then that the Mukden incident of September 18, 1931, led directly to the establishment of Manchukuo. Both, in turn, contributed to withdrawal of Japan from the League of Nations. The incidents foisted on a hapless Japanese civilian government by the Kwangtung Army and its supporters in Japan helped to discredit, destabilize, and ultimately destroy the political party-style democratic government in Japan.

—*Louis G. Perez*

Further Reading

Borg, Dorothy. *The United States and the Far Eastern Crisis of 1933-1938.* Cambridge, Mass.: Harvard University Press, 1964. Concerned primarily with the effects of the crisis on American foreign policy. Excellent analysis and masterful integration of both Japanese as well as American sources. Valuable bibliography, especially for access to the Tokyo war crimes trial documents.

Byas, Hugh. *Government by Assassination.* New York: Alfred A. Knopf, 1942. Although suffering from a dearth of Japanese sources and a lack of objectivity (written by a journalist-turned-historian in the middle of the war), it is still valuable for the description of Japanese domestic politics.

Crowley, James B. *Japan's Quest for Autonomy: National Security and Foreign Policy 1930-1938.* Princeton, N.J.: Princeton University Press, 1966. A superb work that integrates the crises into the greater history of Japan's foreign policy. Chapter 3, "Withdrawal from the League," is truly masterful. Excellent bibliography.

Jones, Francis C. *Manchuria Since 1931.* London: Royal Institute of International Affairs, 1949. The best study of the effects of the crises on Manchuria. Excellent chapters on "Japanese Immigration and Settlement" and on "Treatment of Racial Minorities." Extensive charts, maps, and statistical tables.

League of Nations. *Official Journal, 1931-1933.* Geneva: Author, 1933. Contains official proceedings, deliberations, speeches, and the extensive Lytton Commission report. Wordy and difficult to use, but invaluable for particulars as well as detailed maps. No index.

Ogata, Sadako N. *Defiance in Manchuria: The Making of Japanese Foreign Policy, 1931-1932*. Berkeley: University of California Press, 1964. Valuable for its time, but superseded two years later by Crowley's work. Good use of Japanese documents. Valuable bibliography, well indexed.

Smith, Sara. *The Manchurian Crisis, 1931-1932: A Tragedy in International Relations*. New York: Columbia University Press, 1948. Dated, but still valuable as an example of the argument that the crisis exposed the League's weaknesses and led Mussolini and Hitler into their own foreign adventures. Uses no Japanese sources.

Thorne, Christopher. *The Limits of Foreign Policy: The West, the League, and the Far Eastern Crisis of 1931-1933*. London: Hamish Hamilton, 1972. Perhaps the definitive monograph of the subject from the Euro-American perspective. Relies heavily on the translated works of Japanese historians. Excellent bibliography.

Wilson, Sandra. *The Manchurian Crisis and Japanese Society, 1931-1933*. New York: Routledge, 2002. Study of the crisis, not from the point of view of international relations, but rather from the point of view of its domestic causes and effects. Bibliographic references and index.

Yoshihaski, Takehiko. *Conspiracy at Mukden: The Rise of the Japanese Military*. New Haven, Conn.: Yale University Press, 1963. Concerned with the crisis up to the fall of the Japanese government in December, 1931. Uses the crisis as a case study for the rise of militarism in Japan. Handy chronology, good bibliography and index.

Young, Louise. *Japan's Total Empire: Manchuria and the Culture of Wartime Imperialism*. Berkeley: University of California Press, 1998. Study of the Japanese expansionist military regime, its annexation of Manchuria, and its participation in World War II. Bibliographic references and index.

SEE ALSO: Jan. 30, 1902: Anglo-Japanese Treaty Brings Japan into World Markets; Apr. 28, 1919: League of Nations Is Established; May 5, 1925: Japan Introduces Suffrage for Men; Jan. 7, 1932: Stimson Doctrine; July 7, 1937: China Declares War on Japan; Dec., 1937-Feb., 1938: Rape of Nanjing; Aug., 1940: Japan Announces the Greater East Asia Coprosperity Sphere.

February 27, 1933
REICHSTAG FIRE

Adolf Hitler used the burning of the Reichstag, the German parliament building, as an excuse to limit civil and political liberties granted under the Weimar Constitution.

LOCALE: Berlin, Germany
CATEGORIES: Government and politics; civil rights and liberties

KEY FIGURES

Adolf Hitler (1889-1945), chancellor of Germany and leader of the Nazi Party
Hermann Göring (1893-1946), Prussian minister of the interior, president of the Reichstag, and prosecutor at the trial that followed the Reichstag fire
Joseph Goebbels (1897-1945), Nazi propaganda leader and German minister of propaganda after March 13, 1933
Marinus van der Lubbe (1909-1934), Dutch arsonist who burned the Reichstag building
Georgi Mikhailovich Dimitrov (1882-1949), Bulgarian defendant at the trial, later secretary-general of the Communist International
Ernst Torgler (1893-1963), German communist representative to the Reichstag and defendant at the trial
Ernst Hanfstaengl (1887-1975), German Nazi sympathizer and friend of Hitler
Franz von Papen (1879-1969), German chancellor, 1932, and vice chancellor under Hitler, 1933-1934
Paul von Hindenburg (1847-1934), president of the German Republic

SUMMARY OF EVENT

The years following World War I were chaotic ones for Germany. Defeat in war and the humiliation of the peace at Versailles made the populace bitter, frustrated, and angry. They vented their frustration on the Allies, on Jews and other non-German peoples, and above all on the

Weimar Republic, which had been created to replace the monarchy. The first wave of turmoil arose from 1918 to 1923, but it subsided as economic conditions improved in the second half of the 1920's. The Weimar Constitution appeared to be working very well, but the outbreak of a worldwide economic depression in 1929 led to a new swell of political agitation based on hatred of certain races and classes.

The turbulent years immediately after the war saw the rise of extremist parties on the left and right. From 1919 to 1923, the German Communist Party initiated three uprisings, and nationalist, anticommunist, and anti-Semitic groups also attempted to overthrow the republic and committed acts of terror against its officials. The most infamous uprising of the political right in those years occurred in Munich in November of 1923, when Adolf Hitler led the unsuccessful Beer Hall Putsch. The party did not fare well from 1925 to 1929, but the worldwide economic depression helped Hitler gain the support of many extremist organizations.

As conditions in Germany worsened and political haggling in the Reichstag (the German parliament) accomplished little, the aged and reactionary president of the republic, former Field Marshal Paul von Hindenburg, disregarded the principles of democratic government. He relied on rule by his aristocratic cronies, principally Franz von Papen, who assumed the chancellorship in 1932. The latter, however, found himself stymied by the Communists and the Nazis, whose strength in the parliament had increased with the Great Depression. Papen came to an agreement with Hitler, whom he hoped to control. After a number of backroom deals, on January 30, 1933, Papen convinced Hindenburg to appoint Hitler as the new chancellor of Germany.

Hitler's chancellorship did not come through a mass revolution or through the ballot box. Although the Nazi Party had grown rapidly in strength since 1929, Hitler had lost the presidential election to Hindenburg in 1932. Similarly, his Nazis won only 37 percent of the vote in the parliamentary elections of July, 1932, although they were able to gain a plurality. Without sufficient popular support, Hitler was forced to find a different way to free himself from Papen's restrictions.

In one of his first acts as chancellor, Hitler used emergency decrees provided by the constitution to replace the democratically elected government with one led by Hermann Göring, a Nazi minister without portfolio in the national cabinet. Hitler also took measures against the Communists, who were calling for resistance (but were not carrying out any overt acts). Göring raided Commu-

nist headquarters in Berlin and closed their printing presses. Up to this point, many had not seen Hitler's chancellery as a threat because the Nazis remained a minority in the government. The left now became alarmed, and apprehension spread.

On February 25, the day after Göring's raid, three attempts to start fires in government buildings were aborted. The next day, Hitler's astrologer, Erik Hanussen, predicted a building would soon go up in flames. On Monday, February 27, a Dutch arsonist, Marinus van der Lubbe, perpetrator of the February 25 attempts, purchased some incendiary materials and went to the Reichstag. After surveying the building from several directions, he entered a nearby structure to wait for dark. At 9:00 P.M., he scaled the wall to the balcony near a little-used entrance. Shortly afterward, a passerby, hearing breaking glass and seeing a person (presumably van der Lubbe) fleeing with a flame in his hands, notified the police. An officer went to the scene but could only watch, transfixed, as flames began to engulf the internal rooms.

By the time the firemen arrived, the building was already burning down. Ernst "Putzi" Hanfstaengl, an associate of Hitler's, saw the fire from his apartment and notified Goebbels, who was hosting a party that Hitler and others were attending. At first, neither Hitler nor Goebbels believed Hanfstaengl, who was known for his practical jokes, but as the fire progressed, even the revelers could see the red sky. One report states that Hitler yelled, "It's the communists!" Hitler and Goebbels went to the scene, where they found Göring distraught over the possible loss of the building's precious Gobelin tapestries. Göring also blamed the communists. He told Hitler that a number of communist deputies had been in the building shortly before the fire broke out and that one arrest had already been made. Hitler asked about other buildings, and Göring assured him that he had taken precautions to preserve them.

Hitler, Göring, and Papen then conferred on what action to take. Papen went to inform Hindenburg, and Hitler called a meeting of his cabinet and civic and police officials. The police inspector assigned to the case reported that the police had found van der Lubbe, who admitted that he committed the arson as a protest. Göring shouted, "This is the beginning of a communist uprising," and Hitler added, "Now we'll show them! Anyone who stands in our way will be mown down!" He threatened to hang or shoot communists, socialists, and even conservative opponents. When the police inspector revealed that van der Lubbe was not a communist and had carried out the deed alone, Hitler refused to believe it. "This is a

1933

Flames rise from the Reichstag in Berlin. (Hulton Archive/Getty Images)

ings. In fact, however, later research demonstrated that van der Lubbe set the fire alone. The International Communist Party to which he belonged was a small splinter group, more anarchist than Marxist in ideology and not part of the Communist International directed by Moscow. Indeed, van der Lubbe and the Communists loyal to Joseph Stalin had little use for each other.

Göring found four communists to indict in addition to van der Lubbe: Ernst Torgler, a leader of the German Communist Party and a member of the Reichstag, and three Bulgarian agents of the Communist International: Georgi Mikhailovich Dimitrov, Vasili Tanev, and Blagoi Popov. In a spectacular trial in which Hitler, Goebbels, and Göring (one of the prosecutors) hoped to prove to the world that a communist conspiracy actually did exist, the communist defendants, particularly Georgi Dimitrov, proved their innocence. In fact, Dimitrov even accused the Nazis of deliberately setting the fire themselves. He humiliated Göring in an unexpected courtroom confrontation that was broadcast and reported around the world. In other countries, communists and other antifascists organized protests. Nazi opponents convened a countertrial in London with a court of respected international jurists to show that the Nazis did indeed start the fire. Goebbels's propaganda ploy had backfired, and the government moved the trial from Berlin to Leipzig, where it concluded with little publicity.

The court acquitted the Communists but found van der Lubbe guilty, and he was executed shortly thereafter. Dimitrov, Tanev, and Popov were released and welcomed in the Soviet Union. Some said their acquittal and release came through pressure from Moscow, which threatened retaliation against German citizens living in the Soviet Union. Torgler was released several months after the Bulgarians. Even though the court ruled that the accused Communists were innocent, it said that the fire was part of a more general communist conspiracy.

SIGNIFICANCE

In 1935, Dimitrov became the secretary-general of the Communist International and the spokesperson for Moscow's new foreign policy, which was to be implemented

cunning and well-prepared plot," he said. The chancellor then went to the offices of the Nazi Party newspaper, *Voelkischer Beobachter* (people's observer), and immediately helped compose a version of the story that blamed the communists for the fire. Göring assisted in changing the report of the official Prussian press service to exaggerate the facts and imply that a conspiracy had been involved.

The fire was just the excuse Hitler needed to begin the drive for totalitarian power that would change the Weimar Republic into the Third Reich. Hitler argued that a single individual could not have perpetrated the arson and that van der Lubbe had been a member of the International Communist Party and had been arrested twice in Leiden, the Netherlands, for setting fires to public build-by world communist parties promoting antifascist coalitions (even at the expense of delaying the world socialist revolution). In 1948, Dimitrov became prime minister of communist Bulgaria. Popov also returned to Bulgaria after the war and served in a number of government posts. Tanev was killed in guerrilla warfare during World War II. Torgler, falsely accused of being a Nazi agent, was expelled by the German Communist Party. He settled in Hanover, where he retired from political life.

Even before Hitler became chancellor, economic crises and flaws in the Weimar Republic's constitutional government subjected Germany to stress and social disorientation. The constitution's provisions allowed President Hindenburg and Chancellor Papen to act in a high-handed manner. They were not concerned about parliamentary or democratic government in general and the Weimar Constitution in particular, and the spirit of the law fell victim to their disregard. The conservative government's favoritism toward right-wing nationalists allowed Nazi storm troopers to wreak havoc in the German cities and placed Jews, trade unionists, political moderates, and the political left in a state of jeopardy and fear. These events did not bode well for the civil and political freedom that the Weimar Constitution's drafters had hoped to bring to a recovering Germany.

Papen and Hindenburg's political manipulations brought Hitler to power, although he needed little excuse to begin antidemocratic and anticonstitutional actions such as the dismissal of state governments and raids on opponents. Nevertheless, the high-handed manner in which the Nazis dealt with power did not help them maintain relationships with aristocrats such as Hindenburg and Papen, who disliked the Nazis not so much because of their nationalist and anticommunist ideology but because of their lower-class origins and crudeness. Hitler's party may have had the plurality in the Reichstag, but it did not have the majority and had not demonstrated its ability to win a clear victory at the polls.

The Reichstag fire gave Hitler the opportunity to demand the enabling legislation that created his dictatorship. Whether he believed that the communists were conspiring to seize power is immaterial, just as it is immaterial whether, as the communists charged at the time, the Nazis deliberately started the fire to help them secure the passage of such legislation. Historical opinion considered the latter allegation true until the 1960's, when it was disproved. The fire was an opportune event for Hitler, but if it had not happened, he undoubtedly would have found another route to totalitarian power.

President Hindenburg enacted the enabling legislation on February 28, 1933, the day after the fire. He cited a constitutional provision that permitted the government to rule by decree in times of emergency. The justification was the need for "a defensive measure against communist acts of violence endangering the state." The decree read, in part: "Restrictions on personal liberty, on the right of free expression of opinion, including freedom of the press; on the rights of assembly and association; and violations of the privacy of postal, telegraphic, and telephonic communications; and warrants for house searchers, orders for confiscations as well as restrictions on property, are also permissible beyond the legal limits otherwise prescribed."

With the enabling legislation, Hitler outlawed the Communist Party and arrested its leadership. He harassed other opposition parties as well, closing their newspapers and outlawing their meetings. New elections were scheduled for March 5. The government tried to silence the opposition's campaigns, but the Nazis were still unable to gain more than 44 percent of the vote. Nevertheless, Hitler held full power. He used the legislation to break down the federal structure of the republic and take over all the state governments. Although originally perceived to be temporary, the decrees enacted under the enabling legislation were permanently applied to the Third Reich. Over the ensuing months, the government banned all political parties except the Nazis, and civil and political guarantees were effectively ended. Discriminatory legislation directed against the Jews was put into effect. Political opponents, some even within the Nazi Party, were arrested without cause, forced to emigrate, or even murdered extralegally. The Weimar Republic was dead, and the führer was dictator.

—*Frederick B. Chary*

FURTHER READING

Broszat, Martin, and Volker R. Berghahn. *Hitler and the Collapse of Weimar Germany*. Translated by Volker R. Berghahn. New York: Berg, 1987. A survey of the descent of the Weimar government through the period before Hitler was appointed chancellor. Bibliography and index.

Delmer, Sefton. *Trail Sinister: An Autobiography*. Vol. 1. London: Secker & Warburg, 1961. The autobiography of an Australian journalist born in Germany. It contains a very good eyewitness account of the Reichstag fire, the trial, and its consequences. Index.

Fest, Joachim C. *Hitler*. New York: Harcourt Brace Jovanovich, 1974. The best scholarly biography of Hitler, placing him in the context of German history

1933

and politics of the twentieth century. Fest tends to follow Tobias (below) on the issue of the Reichstag fire but does not absolutely reject the possibility of a Nazi plot. He believes the actual culprits are irrelevant and argues that the fire provided a convenient excuse to institute totalitarianism. Documented; bibliography, indexed.

Fischer, Klaus P. *A History of Nazi Germany*. New York: Continuum, 1995. The most recent comprehensive account of the Nazi regime, based on research up to the time of its publication. Concludes that the Reichstag fire most likely resulted from the efforts of van der Lubbe and unnamed accomplices.

Gilfond, Henry. *The Reichstag Fire, February, 1933: Hitler Utilizes Arson to Extend His Dictatorship*. New York: Franklin Watts, 1973. An unconvincing argument that the Nazis deliberately burned the Reichstag building in order to stampede Hindenburg into granting Hitler the power to suppress the anticipated Communist revolution.

Lee, Stephen J. *The Weimar Republic*. New York: Routledge, 1998. Overview of the Weimar Republic with a chapter on its collapse. Bibliography.

Leers, Johann von [Paulus van Obbergen, pseud.]. *The Oberfohren Memorandum*. London: German Information Bureau, 1933. An attempt by an official organ of the German government to refute the so-called Oberfohren memorandum. Ostensibly written by Ernst Oberfohren, a former leader of a German political party, and published in the *Manchester Guardian* on April 27, 1933, the memorandum accused the Nazis of setting the Reichstag fire.

Mommsen, Hans. *The Rise and Fall of Weimar Democracy*. Translated by Larry E. Jones and Elborg Forster. Chapel Hill: University of North Carolina Press, 1996. Examines the political, social, and economic developments of Germany in the period 1919-1933.

Reed, Douglas. *The Burning of the Reichstag*. New York: Covici-Friede, 1934. Concludes that van der Lubbe was not guilty, or at least did not act alone.

Spielvogel, Jackson J. *Hitler and Nazi Germany: A History*. Englewood Cliffs, N.J.: Prentice Hall, 1988. A widely used college text on the Nazi era which leaves open the question of responsibility for the Reichstag fire, but points out that Hitler gained much from the fire, while it cost the Communists dearly.

Tobias, Fritz. *The Reichstag Fire*. Introduction by A. J. P. Taylor. New York: G. P. Putnam's Sons, 1964. This controversial book first revealed the fact that the Nazis did not burn down the Reichstag, but that van der Lubbe did it alone. It is a well-researched refutation of the Brown Book's thesis (see next entry), although at times it sinks to an anticommunist polemic. Illustrations, bibliography, index.

_____. *The Reichstag Fire Trial*. Translated by Arnold J. Pomerantz. New York: G. P. Putnam's Sons, 1964. Argues that van der Lubbe was guilty of setting fire to the Reichstag building and did act alone. An introduction by famed British historian A. J. P. Taylor supports the author's position.

World Committee for the Victims of German Fascism. *The Reichstag Fire Trial: The Second Brown Book of the Hitler Terror*. 1934. Reprint. New York: Howard Fertig, 1969. A reprint of the 1934 edition published to demonstrate that the Nazis themselves actually burned down the Reichstag. Critics claim that it is communist propaganda, exaggerating and manufacturing facts and evidence. Presents the case against the Nazis which was believed universally until Fritz Tobias's research. Contains a list of about 750 victims of Nazi atrocities before March, 1934. Has illustrations but is not indexed.

SEE ALSO: Nov. 8, 1923: Beer Hall Putsch; July 18, 1925-Dec. 11, 1926: *Mein Kampf* Outlines Nazi Thought; Jan. 30, 1933: Hitler Comes to Power in Germany; Mar., 1933: Nazi Concentration Camps Begin Operating; Mar. 23, 1933: Enabling Act of 1933; June 30-July 2, 1934: Great Blood Purge; Mar. 7, 1936: German Troops March into the Rhineland; Feb. 12-Apr. 10, 1938: The Anschluss; Sept. 29-30, 1938: Munich Conference; 1939-1945: Nazi Extermination of the Jews; Aug. 23-24, 1939: Nazi-Soviet Pact.

February 28, 1933
PERKINS BECOMES FIRST WOMAN SECRETARY OF LABOR

The appointment of Frances Perkins as the first female secretary of labor proved that women could play a key role in national politics.

LOCALE: Washington, D.C.
CATEGORIES: Women's issues; business and labor; government and politics

KEY FIGURES

Frances Perkins (1880-1965), American social worker with a strong background in industrial and labor relations before her appointment as U.S. secretary of labor

Franklin D. Roosevelt (1882-1945), president of the United States, 1933-1945

Alfred E. Smith (1873-1944), governor of New York, 1919-1920 and 1923-1928, who gave Perkins her first significant appointive post

Martin Dies, Jr. (1900-1972), first chair of the House Committee on Un-American Activities

Harry Bridges (1901-1990), radical labor leader and target for deportation

SUMMARY OF EVENT

Franklin D. Roosevelt appointed Frances Perkins as secretary of labor on February 28, 1933. She took office on March 4, 1933, and served until July 1, 1945. For Perkins, the appointment was a recognition of almost thirty years of distinguished service as a social worker and civil servant whose expertise in labor relations was acknowledged throughout the country. For Roosevelt, appointing Perkins was a practical way to seek the support of female Progressive reformers, whose post-1920 (when woman suffrage was secured) political achievements were relatively few. By appointing Perkins, Roosevelt secured a cabinet member who had recognized national expertise in her department. She was a better choice than the male candidate recommended by the American Federation of Labor, since she possessed an independent background that allowed critical thinking and did not force allegiance to labor union's positions.

Perkins was the daughter of Fred and Susan Perkins, who anticipated that their talented daughter's primary career would be as wife and mother. They bucked tradition, however, by encouraging her to graduate from Worcester Classical High School in 1898 and Mount Holyoke College in 1902. The Perkinses provided financial assistance to their daughter in the early stages of her social

work career, although they would have been happier if she had remained a volunteer and not become a professional social worker. Perkins began to form an independent identity as a student at Mount Holyoke, where she researched factory conditions as part of a class project. More important, at Mount Holyoke Perkins was elected class president, and in that position she demonstrated potential as a political candidate. Perkins deserted the conservative Republican politics supported by her parents, who were successful and respected small-business owners. Perkins also deserted her parents' Congregational faith by becoming a devout Episcopalian, and her intense devotions to her faith contrasted sharply with the haphazard Episcopalianism of Franklin D. Roosevelt.

After college, Perkins did volunteer work and taught in Lake Forest, Illinois, where she met Graham Taylor, head of the Chicago Commons settlement house. Through Taylor, Perkins met social reformers Jane Addams, Ellen Gates Starr, and Grace Abbott. By 1907, Perkins lived at Hull House, worked at the Chicago Commons, and had decided on a career in social work. In September of 1907, Perkins became general secretary of the Philadelphia Research and Protective Association. She received a nominal salary of fifty dollars per month from this organization. At the association, Perkins worked with young female immigrants and African Americans who had migrated to Philadelphia from the South; both of these groups were often forced to work under extremely exploitive conditions or were recruited for brothels. Meanwhile, Perkins also attended classes in economics and sociology at the Wharton School of Finance and Commerce at the University of Pennsylvania.

After two years in Philadelphia, Perkins moved to New York in 1909 and used a five-hundred-dollar fellowship to attend the New York School of Philanthropy. While she lived in settlement houses, Perkins's thesis "A Study of Malnutrition in 197 Children from Public School 51" qualified her for a master's degree in political science at Columbia University on June 10, 1910. Despite the fact that her degree was granted in political science, most of the courses Perkins had taken were in economics and sociology.

In 1910, Perkins became general secretary of the National Consumers League. Through the Consumers League, Perkins formed a lasting friendship with its national director, Florence Kelley, and gained a national reputation for her surveys of industrial conditions. Con-

1933

ditions were unhealthy and dangerous in most occupations, and Perkins saw the Triangle Shirtwaist Factory fire on March 25, 1911, in which 146 women either burned or jumped to their deaths. Influenced by this fire, Perkins served from 1912 to 1917 as executive secretary of a committee on safety that was formed to press for better working conditions. The Triangle fire led to the creation of the New York State Factory Investigating Commission, and Perkins served as one of the commission's investigators in 1912 and 1913.

Perkins married Paul C. Wilson, an economist on the staff of New York City reformist mayor John Purroy Mitchell. This marriage lasted until Wilson's death in 1951, despite the fact that he was hospitalized for mental illness throughout most of the marriage. Perkins was the breadwinner for Wilson and their daughter Susanna, who was born in 1916. Both Perkins and her husband agreed that Perkins would keep her maiden name for professional purposes.

In 1919, Governor Alfred E. Smith, whom Perkins had known since 1911, appointed her to the State Indus-

trial Commission. She served from 1919 to 1920, and Smith reappointed Perkins after he began his second term as governor in 1922. She also served with the Industrial Board of the State Labor Department. In 1926, Smith recognized Perkins's increasing professional credibility as an expert in labor law by naming her chair of the Industrial Board. When Smith lost his presidential race in 1928, Franklin D. Roosevelt was elected governor of New York. Roosevelt appointed Perkins to be industrial commissioner of New York, a state-level position that helped prepare Perkins for her cabinet appointment.

Perkins's educational and professional background made her a highly qualified cabinet appointee, and no affirmative action was needed to advance candidacy. She was prepared to reorganize the Labor Department for Roosevelt and to participate in the passage of the Social Security Act of 1935. Martin Dies, Jr., and the House Un-American Activities Committee introduced impeachment action against her in 1938; Dies resented her refusal to deport radical longshoreman Harry Bridges. Despite this controversy, however, Perkins was generally seen as a successful cabinet member, and her appointment and service set a precedent for other women. Although Perkins did not favor an equal rights amendment—which she viewed as a threat to protective legislation for women—she must be viewed as a practical advocate of women's rights within the context of her times.

SIGNIFICANCE

Perkins's appointment had enduring consequences in several areas related to human rights. Like many successful, college-educated women of her day, Perkins broke important ground in proving that women could be competent professionals, and she devoted her career to alleviating the misery created by the excesses of industrial capitalism in diverse areas of public concern. Trained in social work, she sought practical measures to protect the dignity of American workers.

Perkins's success established the previously untested competence of women to hold cabinet-level positions. As the first female cabinet member, she helped make it possible for other women, such as Oveta Culp Hobby and Elizabeth Dole, to serve in future cabinets. Although Perkins supported protective legislation for women and opposed the idea of an equal rights amendment, her contributions greatly furthered women's search for equal participation in American politics.

Perkins was a consistent proponent of emerging unions and organized labor's right to organize and bargain collectively, even though as a social worker she had

Frances Perkins. (Library of Congress)

showed more interest in the rights of nonunion labor than the American Federation of Labor (AFL) would have liked. She supported pro-union legislation such as the Employment Stabilization Act of 1931, and she made impassioned pleas to industrial employers, asking them to recognize that their employees could not effectively negotiate as individuals. She believed, however, that social legislation needed to address the concerns of nonunion labor in an era when labor unions often considered collaboration with nonunion labor as counterproductive to their organizing efforts.

Perkins was also a consistent advocate of the emerging economic, political, and social interests of African American workers. She insisted that New Deal work-relief programs serve African American workers in the Deep South, and she symbolically integrated the Labor Department cafeteria in racially segregated Washington, D.C. She also worked to promote African American employees into higher-level professional positions in the Department of Labor. Perkins opposed the Federal Bureau of Investigation's proposal that all American citizens be fingerprinted, which she argued was a potentially totalitarian measure. Ultimately, she defeated J. Edgar Hoover on this issue, and her victory extended her influence beyond strictly labor-related matters.

Perkins fought to end the intimidation of resident aliens who were perceived as dangerous radicals, such as longshoreman leader Harry Bridges. She suffered great political and personal embarrassment over this issue, but she protected the civil rights of alien workers even while losing the Labor Department's traditional control of immigration enforcement to other agencies. Perkins's concerns for the rights of workers, minorities, and women left a significant human rights legacy in the United States. Her political achievements were formidable, and she broke with tradition in many arenas; for example, she consistently insisted on being addressed as "Miss Perkins," a decision that helped establish the right of women to retain their maiden names. An active lecturer at Cornell University until the 1960's, she was a unique combination of Christian idealist and practical politician who successfully applied the doctrines of the Social Gospel movement in a public context without breaching the separation of church and state.

—*Susan A. Stussy*

FURTHER READING

Babson, Steve. *The Unfinished Struggle: Turning Points in American Labor, 1877-Present.* Lanham, Md.: Rowman & Littlefield, 1999. Concise and comprehensive history of the American labor movement. Includes notes and index.

Braden, Maria. *Women Politicians and the Media.* Lexington: University Press of Kentucky, 1996. Discusses how women politicians have been scrutinized by the American media and how the media's treatment has influenced public perceptions of these women. Includes illustrations, bibliography, and index.

Cobble, Dorothy Sue. "A Self-Possessed Woman: A View of F.D.R.'s Secretary of Labor, Madame Perkins." *Labor History* 29 (February, 1988): 225-229. Cobble reviews the film *You May Call Her Madam Secretary* in this laudatory essay. She views Perkins as a successful pathbreaker for women.

Goldberg, Joseph P. "Frances Perkins, Isador Lubin, and the Bureau of Labor Statistics." *Monthly Labor Review* 103 (April, 1980): 22-27. Goldberg details how Lubin and Perkins modernized the statistical record-keeping system at the Department of Labor. Although the article focuses more on Lubin than on Perkins, it provides useful background to Perkins's career.

Guzda, Henry P. "Frances Perkins's Interest in a New Deal for Blacks." *Monthly Labor Review* 103 (April, 1980): 31-35. Guzda contends that Perkins made the welfare of African American laborers a priority at the Labor Department, and that she made a significant effort to include blacks in New Deal programs. Although her actions were minimal by post-Civil Rights era standards, Perkins attempted to see that blacks benefited from New Deal labor-relief programs.

Hardin, Patrick, and John E. Higgins, Jr., eds. *The Developing Labor Law.* 2 vols. 4th ed. Chicago: Bureau of National Affairs, 2002. Collection provides comprehensive coverage of rights under the National Labor Relations Act. Contributions are written by members of the American Bar Association's Section on Labor and Employment Law.

Martin, George. *Madam Secretary, Frances Perkins.* Boston: Houghton Mifflin, 1976. Provides a comprehensive and definitive scholarly account of Perkins's life. The author is clearly an admirer of Perkins and her work in the New Deal. It is notable that he gives fair attention to her religious motivations and to the interaction among Progressive Era women.

Mohr, Lillian Holmen. *Frances Perkins: That Woman in FDR's Cabinet.* Croton-on-Hudson, N.Y.: North River Press, 1979. Mohr provides a competent account of Perkins's life notable for its reticence in describing the nature of Paul C. Wilson's illness. Mohr, a professor at Cornell, knew Perkins during the last years of her life.

1933

SEE ALSO: Mar. 25, 1911: Triangle Shirtwaist Factory
Fire; Nov. 7, 1916: First Woman Is Elected to the U.S.
Congress; 1921: First Woman Elected to Australian
Parliament; Jan. 5, 1925: First Female Governor in
the United States; Oct. 29, 1929-1939: Great Depression; Aug. 14, 1935: Roosevelt Signs the Social Security Act; May 26, 1938: HUAC Is Established; June
25, 1938: Fair Labor Standards Act.

March, 1933
NAZI CONCENTRATION CAMPS BEGIN OPERATING

*The opening of Nazi Germany's first concentration
camps was an early step in a process of destruction
that culminated in the Holocaust.*

LOCALE: Germany
CATEGORIES: Atrocities and war crimes; human
rights; civil rights and liberties

KEY FIGURES
Adolf Hitler (1889-1945), Nazi Party leader named
German chancellor on January 30, 1933
Heinrich Himmler (1900-1945), second in power in
Nazi Germany who presided over the "final
solution"
Theodor Eicke (1892-1943), commandant of the
Dachau camp beginning in June, 1933, and chief of
Nazi concentration camps from July, 1934
Hermann Göring (1893-1946), Prussian minister of the
interior who played a leading role in organizing the
Gestapo
Rudolf Höss (1900-1947), SS officer who became
commandant of the death camp at Auschwitz
Ernst Röhm (1887-1934), leader of the Nazi storm
troopers
Paul von Hindenburg (1847-1934), president of
Germany, 1925-1934

SUMMARY OF EVENT

Although the Nazis never gained a majority in any freely
contested election, their control of Germany began on
January 30, 1933, when Adolf Hitler was named chancellor by Paul von Hindenburg, president of the Weimar
Republic. Six months later, the Nazis were the only legal
political party in Germany, Hitler's decrees were as good
as law, basic civil rights had been suspended, and thousands of the regime's suspected political opponents had
been interned in a growing number of concentration
camps. Before the Third Reich fell twelve years later,
millions of people—including two-thirds of the Jews in
Europe—would perish in concentration camps.

Nazi concentration camps disregarded the principle
that one should not be punished unless found guilty in a
fair trial. Instead, they removed people who could not be
confined through the normal workings of a state's criminal code. The Nazis did not invent the concept of a concentration camp, nor did they have a systematic design
for developing such places when they came to power in
Germany. Gradually, however, a deadly camp system
evolved. An early step in that process occurred at Dachau, a town about ten miles northwest of Munich, where
one of the first concentration camps was established. The
site of a vacated World War I munitions factory provided
the needed space for Dachau's first prisoners, who entered the camp in late March of 1933. Those early inmates were political opponents of the Nazis—mainly
Communists and Social Democrats—who were kept under "protective custody."

Heinrich Himmler established Dachau. In 1925, he
had joined the SS (Schutzstaffel), a small group of dedicated Nazis who served as Adolf Hitler's personal bodyguards. Hitler appointed Himmler head of the SS in
1929. At the time, the SS included about two hundred
members, but under Himmler's direction it eventually
numbered in the hundreds of thousands and formed an
awesome empire within the Nazi state. Meanwhile,
shortly after Hitler became chancellor in 1933, Himmler
gained important police powers in Munich and in the entire province of Bavaria. He used his authority to create
the Dachau camp.

Bavarian state police guarded the camp at first, but in
April, 1933, SS personnel took control. Theodor Eicke
became Dachau's commandant in June. As he regulated
camp life, including stating rules about work and punishment, Eicke ensured that Dachau's procedures would be
systematic and replicable as well as harsh. After Eicke
was appointed head of the Nazi network of concentration
camps in July, 1934, the system he had developed at
Dachau became standard. The SS personnel who trained
under him saw to it that his policies were established at
other camps as they rose to new positions of leadership
in the system. One who did so, for example, was Ru-

dolf Höss, whose Dachau training prepared him to become the commandant of Auschwitz in German-occupied Poland in 1940.

Although the Dachau model fostered by Himmler's SS leadership eventually dominated the Nazi camp system, that outcome was not a foregone conclusion in the early months of the Third Reich. By the end of July of 1933, Nazi Germany held nearly twenty-seven thousand political prisoners in protective custody. Dachau contained its share, but thousands more could be found in a variety of other detention centers. These centers, however, lacked overall coordination, and their only common trait was that the incarcerated people were "guilty" only in the sense that they were judged politically suspect by the Nazis.

An early pretext for arrests of the politically suspect was the fire that ravaged the German parliament building on February 27, 1933. Although Nazis were suspected of setting the blaze to serve their own purposes, Hitler blamed the Reichstag's destruction on arson by Communists. The next day, President Paul von Hindenburg signed the emergency decree that the Nazis wanted: By suspending basic rights guaranteed by the Weimar Constitution, and thereby allowing detention for persons suspected of hostility to the state, the decree opened the door for a policy of *Schutzhaft*, or protective custody, that would guard the Reich's security by imprisoning those who were suspected of threatening it. Taking advantage of this sweeping decree, the Nazis launched a wave of arrests throughout the country.

Many victims of this campaign were interned in camps quickly set up by the SA, the brown-shirted Nazi storm troopers led by Ernst Röhm. Others, especially in the state of Prussia, were imprisoned in detention centers created by Hermann Göring, the chief of the Prussian police, who was also organizing the Gestapo, a secret police force dedicated to maintaining the security of the Nazi state. Precisely how many of these camps existed in 1933 remains unclear, although informed estimates indicate that Prussia alone had twenty of them.

As part of their early program of making life as difficult as possible for German Jews, the Nazis began a boycott of Jewish businesses in 1933. The sign reads, "Germans, defend yourselves, do not buy from Jews." (NARA)

In a regime where terror loomed so large, anyone who could gain control of the Nazi concentration camps would wield immense power. Göring attempted to outdo his rivals, but his efforts were surpassed by Himmler. By early July, 1934, Himmler had not only established the SS camp at Dachau but had also gained control of the political police in the Reich's various states, including Göring's Gestapo in Prussia. In addition, he had masterminded a purge of the SA, and appointed Eicke, his SS subordinate, to supervise the concentration camps throughout Germany.

This consolidation of power eliminated most of the small camps that had sprung up in 1933. By September,

NAZI EXTERMINATION CAMPS

The Nazis operated several types of camps: prison camps, collection centers, transit centers, labor camps, and extermination camps. This table presents information on the ten extermination camps.

Name of Camp	Country (today)	Period of Operation	Number of Deaths (estimated)
Auschwitz-Birkenau	Poland	April, 1940-January, 1945	1.1 to 1.5 million
Bełżec	Poland	March, 1942-June, 1943	600,000
Chełmno	Poland	December, 1941-April, 1943 April, 1944-January, 1945	340,000
Jasenovac	Croatia	August, 1941-April, 1945	700,000
Lwów, Janowska Street	Ukraine	September, 1941-November, 1943	More than 40,000
Majdanek	Poland	July, 1941-July, 1944	78,000
Maly Trostenets	Belarus	July, 1941-June, 1944	200,000-500,000
Sobibór	Poland	May, 1942-October, 1943	250,000
Treblinka	Poland	July, 1942-November, 1943	At least 800,000
Warsaw	Poland	1942-1944	Up to 200,000

1935, the six official concentration camps in the Third Reich were at Dachau, Lichtenburg, Sachsenburg, Esterwegen, Oranienburg, and Columbia Haus (near Berlin). On the eve of World War II, in the late summer of 1939, even those camps—except for Dachau, which was reconstructed in 1937 and 1938—had been eclipsed by newer and larger installations at Sachsenhausen (1936), Buchenwald (1937), Flossenbürg (1938), Mauthausen (in Austria, 1938), and Ravensbruck (a concentration camp for women, 1939).

In the period from 1933 until the outbreak of World War II in 1939, there were changes in the concentration camp population. The number of prisoners fluctuated. Although mostly political prisoners were incarcerated at first, the concentration camps gradually engulfed many other types of people in addition to the Communists, Social Democrats, and trade unionists who had been initially targeted. By 1938, Jehovah's Witnesses, members of the clergy, and "asocial elements" (such as homosexuals and so-called habitual criminals) as well as Roma and Jews were among those in the camps. Treatment varied from person to person and place to place, but exhausting labor, severe punishment, poor food, filth, disease, and execution were all among the possible and persistent threats. Release from a concentration camp was possible, but death while in a camp was likely.

SIGNIFICANCE

Nazi concentration camps of the kind that began at Dachau in March, 1933, were only the beginning of an unprecedented twelve-year assault on human rights. Although all the Nazi camps derived partly from impulses and intentions that brought Dachau into existence, not every camp in the Nazi system was simply a holding pen for political detainees. After World War II began (with the German invasion of Poland on September 1, 1939) different but related institutions started to appear. There were, for example, labor camps, transit camps, prisoner-of-war camps, and, most destructive of all, extermination or death camps.

The Nazis violated human rights in virtually every possible way, but no group received more inhumane treatment than the Jews. In the early years, however, relatively small numbers of Jews were interned in concentration camps such as Dachau and Buchenwald. Not until the summer of 1938, and especially after the Kristallnacht pogrom in November, 1938, were large numbers of Jews imprisoned strictly on religious grounds. Even then, most of these Jewish prisoners were eventually released after paying a ransom or proving that they were about to emigrate from Germany. This practice would change catastrophically with the outbreak of World War II, however.

Nazi ideology held that Jews were the chief obstacle to the racial and cultural purity that Hitler craved for the Third Reich. Political opponents were dealt with ruthlessly to ensure Nazi domination, but the Jews were soon identified as an even more virulent threat. Their polluting presence, Hitler believed, had to be eliminated. For a time, the Nazis relied largely on punitive laws to segregate Jews, expropriate their property, and deprive them of their professions and other rights. The Nazi strategy was to make life so difficult that the German Jews would be forced to leave. This plan did not achieve its goals, and when Hitler went to war with the aim of expanding the German nation, Nazi policies aimed at population reduction had to change.

Hitler's conquests, especially in Eastern Europe, brought millions of Jews under German domination. What gradually evolved was a policy of mass murder—the "final solution"—that was implemented from late 1941 until late 1944. Its most devastating effects occurred in the gas chambers that operated at six death camps in occupied Poland: Chełmno, Bełżec, Sobibór, Treblinka, Majdanek, and Auschwitz-Birkenau.

Dachau and the other early concentration camps on German soil were never death factories like Treblinka and Auschwitz-Birkenau. The violations of human rights initiated at the first camps, however, were part of wide-ranging aims to stamp out every element of dissent and diversity that stood in the way of Nazi domination. Concentration camps such as Dachau helped to pave the way for other camps, which were even worse because they were specifically designed to remove unwanted lives, especially Jewish ones, through unrelenting mass murder. Six million Jews died in the camps, as well as millions of non-Jews, especially people from the Slavic countries occupied by Germany during the war.

—*John K. Roth*

FURTHER READING

Feig, Konnilyn G. *Hitler's Death Camps: The Sanity of Madness*. New York: Holmes & Meier, 1979. This detailed study gives an overview of the Nazi concentration and death camps and, focusing on their structure and function, a camp-by-camp analysis of many of them, including Dachau. Contains helpful maps and photographs.

Gutman, Israel, ed. *Encyclopedia of the Holocaust*. 4 vols. New York: Macmillan, 1990. Contains articles on many concentration camps as well as on the camp system as a whole. Provides surveys of the SS, SA, and Gestapo, as well as essays about individual SS leaders in the camp system. All of the essays in this extensive work have been carefully prepared by highly qualified scholars. Useful maps and illustrations included.

Hilberg, Raul. *The Destruction of the European Jews*. 3d ed. New Haven, Conn.: Yale University Press, 2003. An unrivaled study of the bureaucratic process of de-struction that the Nazis directed toward the Jews of Europe. Analysis situates the concentration and death camps within that systematic process. Focuses especially on developments that transformed the conventional concentration camps into centers of mass murder such as those at Treblinka and Auschwitz-Birkenau in German-occupied Poland.

Höhne, Heinz. *The Order of the Death's Head: The Story of Hitler's SS*. Translated by Richard Barry. New York: Ballantine Books, 1979. Offers a detailed study of the rise of the SS, its immense power in Nazi Germany, and its central role in administration of the concentration and death camps. Focuses on individual figures as well as on the overall organization of the SS.

Krausnick, Helmut, Hans Buchheim, Martin Brozat, and Hans-Adolf Jacobsen. *Anatomy of the SS State*. Translated by Richard Barry, Marian Jackson, and Dorothy Long. New York: Walker and Company, 1968. Supports a theory of concentration camp crimes and genocidal treatment of Jews as essential features of Nazism. Martin Brozat's "The Concentration Camps, 1933-1945" provides particularly effective documentation.

Laqueur, Walter, and Judith Tydor Baumel, eds. *The Holocaust Encyclopedia*. New Haven, Conn.: Yale University Press, 2001. Detailed, comprehensive survey of all aspects of the Holocaust. Includes more than 200 photos and many helpful research tools.

Rubenstein, Richard L., and John K. Roth. *Approaches to Auschwitz: The Holocaust and Its Legacy*. Atlanta: John Knox Press, 1987. An overview of the Holocaust. Discusses the emergence and development of the concentration and death camps that played a central role in the mass death unleashed by Nazi Germany. Focuses on the victims as well as on the perpetrators.

Wistrich, Robert S. *Hitler and the Holocaust*. New York: Random House, 2001. An authoritative work recounting the major issues of the Holocaust.

SEE ALSO: Nov. 8, 1923: Beer Hall Putsch; July 18, 1925-Dec. 11, 1926: *Mein Kampf* Outlines Nazi Thought; Jan. 30, 1933: Hitler Comes to Power in Germany; Mar. 23, 1933: Enabling Act of 1933; June 30-July 2, 1934: Great Blood Purge; Mar. 7, 1936: German Troops March into the Rhineland; Feb. 12-Apr. 10, 1938: The Anschluss; Sept. 29-30, 1938: Munich Conference; Nov. 9-10, 1938: Kristallnacht; 1939-1945: Nazi Extermination of the Jews; Aug. 23-24, 1939: Nazi-Soviet Pact; May 16, 1940-1944: Gypsies Are Exterminated in Nazi Death Camps.

1933

March 4, 1933-1945
GOOD NEIGHBOR POLICY

A new articulation of U.S. relations with Latin American nations replaced military interventionism with mutual respect and cooperation.

LOCALE: Western Hemisphere
CATEGORIES: Diplomacy and international relations; government and politics; laws, acts, and legal history

KEY FIGURES
Franklin D. Roosevelt (1882-1945), president of the United States, 1933-1945
Cordell Hull (1871-1955), U.S. secretary of state
Herbert Hoover (1874-1964), president of the United States, 1929-1933
Sumner Welles (1892-1961), U.S. assistant secretary of state and ambassador to Cuba

SUMMARY OF EVENT
In his first inaugural address, President Franklin D. Roosevelt promised that the United States would be a good neighbor. After he applied the term specifically to relations with Latin America and pledged his opposition to armed intervention, the phrase "good neighbor" came to be identified with his policies toward Latin America. Some questioned U.S. intentions, however, because of the country's interventionist history. The United States had used its military to intervene in Central American and Caribbean affairs after the Spanish-American War (1898). Asserting its right to exercise a police power in the Americas under the 1904 Roosevelt Corollary to the Monroe Doctrine, U.S. presidents sent troops into Cuba, Haiti, the Dominican Republic, Nicaragua, Mexico, and Panama to stabilize conditions, prevent European intervention, and protect the lives and property of U.S. citizens. After a brief incursion in 1909, a contingent of U.S. Marines was stationed in Nicaragua from 1912 to 1933.

Seeking to prevent future interventions, several Latin American jurists proposed the adoption of doctrines against intervention, the use of force, and the use of diplomatic recognition as means of protecting the interests of foreign nations in Latin America or changing Latin American governments. At the Sixth Inter-American Conference, held in Havana, Cuba, in 1928, the Latin American representatives tried, but failed, to obtain U.S. support for a nonintervention resolution. Meanwhile, in the United States, more and more citizens opposed the policy of sending troops to protect U.S. interests in Central America and the Caribbean.

In 1928, President-elect Herbert Hoover made a series of goodwill trips to Latin America, and in 1930 he repudiated the Roosevelt Corollary to the Monroe Doctrine. Resisting pressure to intervene to protect U.S. investors, Hoover prepared to withdraw troops from Haiti and removed the marines from Nicaragua. His goodwill gestures were undermined, however, by the Great Depression and the high duties imposed by the Tariff Act of 1930.

On March 4, 1933, in his inaugural address, Franklin D. Roosevelt declared that in foreign policy he wished to "dedicate this nation to the policy of the good neighbor . . . who respects himself and . . . the rights of others." After his inauguration, Roosevelt undertook specific measures to improve relations with Latin America and to stimulate economic recovery. In 1933, at the Seventh International Conference of American States, in Montevideo, Uruguay, Secretary of State Cordell Hull accepted the principle of nonintervention and signed a convention declaring that no state had the right to intervene in the internal and external affairs of other countries. Hull also proposed the reduction of tariffs and trade agreements to stimulate trade. In 1936, at the Inter-American Conference for the Maintenance of Peace in Buenos Aires, the United States signed an expanded resolution that renounced intervention and agreed to the principle of consultation in the event of a war between American nations or an external threat to the peace of the Americas.

In 1933, Roosevelt had also dispatched Assistant Secretary of State Sumner Welles to Cuba, where Welles orchestrated the resignation of dictator Gerardo Machado. When Welles's personally designated successor was overthrown by a sergeant's revolt, Welles persuaded Roosevelt to withhold recognition from the nationalistic government of Ramón Grau San Martín. With U.S. naval vessels offshore, this policy of nonrecognition encouraged a second revolt, and a series of presidents controlled by Colonel Fulgencio Batista was brought to office.

Despite his clear interference in Cuban politics, President Roosevelt had refrained from using armed force in Cuba, and in 1934 the United States and Cuba agreed to the removal of the Platt Amendment (1901), which, following the Spanish-American War, gave the United States the right to intervene in Cuba when its independence was threatened and the right to maintain a military base on the island. Similar agreements were created with Panama and the Dominican Republic. The United States and Cuba also signed reciprocal trade agreements that lowered duties on Cuban sugar, guaranteed access to the U.S. market for Cuban agricultural exports, and reduced duties on hundreds of U.S.-manufactured goods exported to Cuba.

When Bolivia, Mexico, and Venezuela threatened to nationalize their oil industries in 1937 and 1938, the Good Neighbor Policy faced a direct challenge. President Roosevelt resisted pressures to intervene, and he also accepted the right of these countries to seize the foreign companies' assets or increase government revenues from their operations as long as they made immediate and just compensation. Roosevelt continued to provide economic assistance and, after a brief suspension, signed new trade agreements with Bolivia and Mexico. By refusing to intervene to protect the oil companies, Roosevelt demonstrated his adherence to the principle of nonintervention and his Good Neighbor Policy. Furthermore, in addition to renouncing the use of military force in the Caribbean and Central America, the United States provided credits to struggling countries through the newly created Export-Import Bank and negotiated a series of reciprocal trade agreements to lower barriers to trade between the United States and Latin America.

By renouncing intervention and withdrawing its troops, the United States demonstrated its commitment to its Good Neighbor Policy and fostered an era of good relations and cooperation between Latin America and the United States. In a series of agreements drawn up at prewar conferences, nations of Latin America and the United States agreed to cooperate and form an alliance of mutual protection. Following the attack on Pearl Harbor, all Latin American countries except Argentina joined the Allied war effort, cracking down on Axis sympathizers and supplying strategic materials, airbases, and troops for the Allies. Although Argentina was eventually pressured to declare war on the Axis countries, public efforts by the U.S. ambassador to influence or change the government in Buenos Aires not only backfired but also raised the specter of past interventions.

While the unity and cooperation between the United States and Latin America survived the war, Roosevelt's death on April 12, 1945, and the departure of the architects of the Good Neighbor Policy from the State Department contributed to the policy's demise. Differences between Latin America and the United States had already surfaced at wartime and postwar conferences, and with the advent of the Cold War, the United States turned its attention to the economic recovery of Europe and the defense of the West.

SIGNIFICANCE

After 1945, therefore, Latin American requests for economic cooperation and assistance were ignored until the triumph of Fidel Castro's revolution in Cuba in 1959. When the Central Intelligence Agency conducted a covert action to overthrow the democratically elected government of Guatemala in 1954, it appeared that the United States had abandoned nonintervention in favor of military intervention and protection of U.S. companies. Subsequent attempts to overthrow Castro, U.S. invasions of the Dominican Republic, Grenada, and Panama, the overthrow of President Salvador Allende in Chile, and the support of military forces in Central America also violated the principle of nonintervention and the Good Neighbor Policy. However, with the collapse of communism in 1991, successive U.S. administrations decreased the nation's interventionist stance.

The Good Neighbor Policy did not promote freedom and democracy. After the removal of U.S. troops, the commanders of the national guards trained by the United States seized power and established long-term dictatorships. Since these regimes guaranteed stability, protected foreign investments, and were anticommunist, they received U.S. economic and military aid. Although the reciprocal trade agreements stimulated trade, they also reinforced a dependency on the U.S. market and prevented economic development through diversification. Nevertheless, the Good Neighbor Policy fostered a period of goodwill among the nations of the Western Hemisphere, as well as a sense of political hegemony against potential aggressors. The United States demonstrated its growing role in world affairs and safeguarded its long-range interests in both the economic well-being and political autonomy of its Latin American neighbors.

—*D. Anthony White*

FURTHER READING

Aguilar Monteverde, Alonso. *Pan-Americanism from Monroe to the Present: A View from the Other Side.* Translated by Asa Zatz. New York: Monthly Review Press, 1968. A Latin American view of Pan-Americanism and U.S. imperialism.

Blasier, Cole. *The Hovering Giant: U.S. Responses to Revolutionary Change in Latin America, 1910-1985.* Rev. ed. Pittsburgh: University of Pittsburgh Press, 1985. A study of U.S. reactions to revolutionary movements in Mexico, Bolivia, Guatemala, Cuba, Chile, Grenada, and Nicaragua.

Gellman, Irwin F. *Good Neighbor Diplomacy: United States Policies in Latin America, 1933-1945.* Balti-

1933

more: The Johns Hopkins University Press, 1979. A thorough study that emphasizes the significance and originality of Roosevelt's policy and the contributions of Cordell Hull and Sumner Welles.

Kirk, John M., and Peter McKenna. *Canada-Cuba Relations: The Other Good Neighbor Policy.* Gainesville: University Press of Florida, 1997. The United States tends to dominate most discussions of relations between Cuba and its northern neighbors, so this in-depth treatment of Canada's foreign policy is a welcome one.

LaFeber, Walter. *Inevitable Revolutions: The United States in Central America.* New York: W. W. Norton, 1984. A critical history of U.S. policy that views conflicts as a consequence of U.S. policy and externally imposed conditions of dependency.

Roorda, Eric Paul. *The Dictator Next Door: The Good Neighbor Policy and the Trujillo Regime in the Do-* minican Republic, 1930-1945. Durham, N.C.: Duke University Press, 1998. A thorough discussion of the complicated relationship between the Roosevelt administration and the brutal dictatorship of Rafael Trujillo.

Wood, Bryce. *The Dismantling of the Good Neighbor Policy.* Austin: University of Texas Press, 1985. Traces the gradual dismantling of the Good Neighbor Policy after the death of Roosevelt, ending with the U.S. intervention in Guatemala in 1954.

SEE ALSO: Dec. 2-5, 1902: Founding of the International Sanitary Bureau; May 22, 1903: Platt Amendment; June 3-Aug. 28, 1929: Tacna-Arica Compromise; Nov. 11, 1936: Reciprocal Trade Act; Dec., 1936: Inter-American Conference for the Maintenance of Peace; Mar. 18, 1938: Mexico Nationalizes Foreign Oil Properties.

March 9-June 16, 1933
THE HUNDRED DAYS

In its first days, the Franklin D. Roosevelt administration passed a series of acts aimed at bringing hope to millions of Depression-weary Americans.

LOCALE: Washington, D.C.
CATEGORIES: Social issues and reform; laws, acts, and legal history; government and politics

KEY FIGURES
Franklin D. Roosevelt (1882-1945), president of the United States, 1933-1945
Harry Hopkins (1890-1946), head of the Federal Emergency Relief Administration and later Roosevelt's second in command
Henry A. Wallace (1888-1965), U.S. secretary of agriculture, 1933-1940
Hugo L. Black (1886-1971), U.S. senator from Alabama, 1926-1937, and associate justice of the United States, 1937-1971
Raymond Moley (1886-1975), assistant secretary of state in 1933 and member of Roosevelt's Brain Trust
Rexford Guy Tugwell (1891-1979), economist from Columbia University and member of Roosevelt's Brain Trust

SUMMARY OF EVENT
On November 8, 1932, Franklin D. Roosevelt was elected president of the United States. Few people knew what to expect from Roosevelt, a consummate politician who once described himself only as "a Christian and a Democrat." One thing, however, was clear: Immediate action of some kind was imperative to stop the nation from slipping further into economic chaos. Voters had been impressed by the confidence evident in Roosevelt's inaugural address and his promises of immediate action. The problem facing the new administration was how to sustain this sense of movement and have confidence in a new order. On March 9, 1933, a special session of Congress met, and it sat until June 16. During that period, which became known as the Hundred Days, fifteen major resolutions became law, and the United States underwent a revolutionary change. The legislation was the product of no single person or particular group. In essence, the program was a series of emergency compromises, and Roosevelt was the mediator.

The immediate problem politicians faced involved the paralyzed banking system and the lack of confidence in American business. As a preliminary measure, Roosevelt issued an executive order that proclaimed March 6 the beginning of a national bank holiday. During the holiday, cash from the Federal Reserve replenished bank vaults. The closing of the banks convinced many people that the crisis had reached its bottom and things would begin to improve. On March 9, 1933, Roosevelt submitted to Congress the Emergency Banking Act (also known as the Emergency Banking Relief Act), which was immediately passed. The act gave the president power over gold transactions, outlawed hoarding, and provided for the gradual reopening of the banks under the supervision of the secretary of the treasury. This had been preceded by the Economy Act (1932), which initially caused some members of Congress to threaten revolt but ultimately drastically reduced federal expenditures by cutting government salaries and veterans' payments. On March 12, Roosevelt gave the first of many radio addresses that came to be known as "fireside chats." He emphasized that most of the banks were sound and would reopen in a few days. When the banks did reopen, people rushed to deposit money rather than to make withdrawals. The banking crisis subsided.

Next, Roosevelt attempted to eradicate some of the abuses in the nation's banking and financial practices. The Securities Act of May 27, 1933, called for close supervision by the Federal Trade Commission of the issue of new stock, and held those who sold stock liable if they provided false information. A complementary measure was the Banking Act of June 16, 1933, which differentiated between commercial and investment banking. An important corollary of this act was the creation of the Federal Deposit Insurance Corporation (FDIC), which insured individual bank deposits up to five thousand dollars. The creation of insurance on deposits was a significant step in restoring public confidence and bringing currency back into the banks.

Another pressing problem was agriculture. In preparing his legislation, Roosevelt relied heavily on the advice of his secretary of agriculture, Henry A. Wallace. A former farm editor and horticulturist, Wallace advocated a domestic-allotment plan designed to combat overproduction and declining prices by restricting acreage and leasing to government land that had been left idle. The scale of payments was aimed at establishing parity between farm prices and the cost of manufactured goods based on figures for the

years 1909 to 1914. Not all farming interests accepted this idea of production control, and many demanded cheap money as a remedy. When the Agricultural Adjustment Act (AAA) was finally signed into law on May 12, 1933, government leasing of idle land was not the only option provided for controlling production. Additional New Deal legislation provided for loans through the Farm Credit Administration, aid to very poor farmers through the Resettlement Administration, and a means for all rural areas to receive power through the Rural Electrification Administration.

One of the most successful programs of the Roosevelt administration was the enactment of the Tennessee

---

ROOSEVELT'S FIRST FIRESIDE CHAT

In the first of thirty national radio broadcasts—his "fireside chats"—on March 12, 1933, President Franklin D. Roosevelt spoke about the state of the country's banking system. In his other fireside chats, which continued until June 12, 1944, Roosevelt addressed such topics as the Dust Bowl and the war in Europe.

We had a bad banking situation. Some of our bankers had shown themselves either incompetent or dishonest in their handling of the people's funds. They had used the money entrusted to them in speculations and unwise loans. This was of course not true in the vast majority of our banks but it was true in enough of them to shock the people for a time into a sense of insecurity and to put them into a frame of mind where they did not differentiate, but seemed to assume that the acts of a comparative few had tainted them all. It was the government's job to straighten out this situation and do it as quickly as possible—and the job is being performed.

I do not promise you that every bank will be reopened or that individual losses will not be suffered, but there will be no losses that possibly could be avoided; and there would have been more and greater losses had we continued to drift. I can even promise you salvation for some at least of the sorely pressed banks. We shall be engaged not merely in reopening sound banks but in the creation of sound banks through reorganization. It has been wonderful to me to catch the note of confidence from all over the country. I can never be sufficiently grateful to the people for the loyal support they have given me in their acceptance of the judgment that has dictated our course, even though all of our processes may not have seemed clear to them.

After all there is an element in the readjustment of our financial system more important than currency, more important than gold, and that is the confidence of the people. Confidence and courage are the essentials of success in carrying out our plan. You people must have faith; you must not be stampeded by rumors or guesses. Let us unite in banishing fear. We have provided the machinery to restore our financial system; it is up to you to support and make it work.

It is your problem no less than it is mine. Together we cannot fail.

Valley Authority Act (TVA) on May 18, 1933. The act provided for a regional authority that would build dams designed to control disastrous flooding in the states of the Tennessee River basin, bring electricity to rural areas, and replant forests. Eventually, the TVA became the largest utility company in the United States. The unemployed and the middle class also received benefits under the new legislation, which later became known collectively as the New Deal. The unemployed were helped through the Civilian Conservation Corps (CCC), which was created by the Reforestation Relief Act, one of Roosevelt's most popular measures. The act, passed March 31, 1933, provided for a civilian army of young men to work in reforestation and conservation projects. In the CCC's nine-year life span, a total of 250,000 jobless men from the ages of eighteen to twenty-five were given an opportunity to move forward in life.

Enactment of the Federal Emergency Relief Act on May 12, 1933, and the subsequent creation of the Federal Emergency Relief Administration (FERA) provided direct federal grants to states and fostered cooperation between federal and state agencies. FERA, headed by Harry Hopkins, promoted the idea of work relief instead of the "dole" (as welfare was often called at the time) and stipulated that no discrimination toward recipients would be tolerated. Many middle-class home owners faced mortgage foreclosures, and the Home Owners' Loan Act, passed in June, 1933, provided for the exchange of defaulted mortgages for guaranteed government bonds, but it appeared to give more assistance to mortgage companies than to hard-pressed home owners. Home owners benefited later, when it became government policy to refinance loans where possible instead of taking possession of homes.

When organized labor demanded action to relieve unemployment, Senator Hugo L. Black of Alabama proposed a thirty-hour workweek, and his proposal received considerable support from labor interests. Roosevelt regarded the bill proposed by Black to be both unconstitutional and unworkable, but he had to meet the growing demand for relief by industry and industrial workers. He therefore ordered his advisers to prepare an omnibus labor and industry measure to attack the root causes of depression in those fields. A draft was prepared under the direction of Raymond Moley, economist and assistant secretary of state.

The National Industrial Recovery Act (NIRA), passed on June 16, 1933, provided for industrial self-government through the use of universal codes regulating production, wages, and hours, but negated enforcement of the antitrust laws. Although the program was short-lived, the wage and hour provisions of the codes benefited nearly four million women workers. The program did not, however, set up codes for agricultural or domestic laborers, three-fourths of whom were African Americans. The Roosevelt administration hoped that the act would eliminate inefficiency and raise prices.

The provision that all codes had to be submitted for government approval pleased advocates of government control, such as Rexford Guy Tugwell, a member of Roosevelt's Brain Trust, a group of distinguished individuals who served as advisers to the president. Organized labor received legal guarantees that all codes would have to provide for collective bargaining before they could be recognized. Finally, the unemployed were assured of aid from a vast program of public works connected with the NIRA and financed from additional money through increased federal spending.

SIGNIFICANCE
On June 16, 1933, Congress adjourned after its historic session. Never in the nation's history had so much new legislation been enacted in so short a time. With support from both houses, bills originating from the president's White House office were passed nearly every day in order to give the country help during the emergency of the Depression. The hasty legislation that was adopted during the Hundred Days helps to explain why so many measures subsequently had to be drastically amended or abandoned altogether.

—*George Q. Flynn and Marilyn Elizabeth Perry*

FURTHER READING
Davis, Kenneth S. *FDR: The New Deal Years, 1933-1937*. 1986. Reprint. New York: Random House, 1995. A chronicle of the New Deal years combined with the interactions of people and events and their effect on strategy.
Freidel, Frank. *Franklin D. Roosevelt: A Rendezvous with Destiny*. Boston: Little, Brown, 1990. A complete biography of Roosevelt, detailing the Depression and the measures taken to bring recovery.
Leuchtenburg, William E. *Franklin D. Roosevelt and the New Deal, 1932-1940*. New York: Harper & Row, 1963. A one-volume survey of the New Deal period. Excellent bibliography.
Morgan, Ted. *FDR: A Biography*. New York: Simon & Schuster, 1985. Emphasizes Roosevelt's private life and how that influenced his political decisions.
Schlesinger, Arthur Meier. *The Coming of the New Deal.*

Vol. 2 in *The Age of Roosevelt*. Boston: Houghton Mifflin, 1959. Re-creating the prevailing atmosphere, attempts to place the Hundred Days within the context of modern U.S. reform.

Sitkoff, Harvard, ed. *Fifty Years Later: The New Deal Evaluated*. Philadelphia: Temple University Press, 1985. Essays outlining the merits and pitfalls of the New Deal.

Watkins, T. H. *The Hungry Years: A Narrative History of the Great Depression in America*. New York: Henry Holt, 1999. Draws on oral histories as well as memoirs and other documents of the time to present a picture of the lives of Americans during the Depression. Includes index.

SEE ALSO: Oct. 24-29, 1929: U.S. Stock Market Crashes; Oct. 29, 1929-1939: Great Depression; Jan. 22, 1932: Reconstruction Finance Corporation Is Created; Nov. 8, 1932: Franklin D. Roosevelt Is Elected U.S. President; Apr. 5, 1933: U.S. Civilian Conservation Corps Is Established; June 16, 1933: Roosevelt Signs the National Industrial Recovery Act; Oct. 18, 1933: Roosevelt Creates the Commodity Credit Corporation; Apr. 8, 1935: Works Progress Administration Is Established; May 27, 1935: Black Monday.

March 23, 1933
ENABLING ACT OF 1933

The Enabling Act of 1933 ultimately doomed the Weimar Republic by granting Adolf Hitler unprecedented powers and lending his totalitarian ends the illusion of legitimacy.

ALSO KNOWN AS: Act for Ending the Distress of People and Nation

LOCALE: Kroll Opera House in Berlin, Germany

CATEGORIES: Laws, acts, and legal history; government and politics

KEY FIGURES

Adolf Hitler (1889-1945), chancellor of Germany, 1933-1945

Paul von Hindenburg (1847-1934), president of Germany, 1925-1934

Joseph Goebbels (1897-1945), German minister of propaganda

Ludwig Kaas (1881-1952), leader of the Center Party

Franz von Papen (1879-1969), chancellor of Germany, 1932, and Hitler's vice chancellor, 1933

Otto Wels (1873-1939), leader of the Social Democratic Party

Hermann Göring (1893-1946), chairman of the Reichstag, 1933

SUMMARY OF EVENT

Only two months after becoming chancellor, Adolf Hitler sought a legal foundation for dictatorship by proposing the Act for Ending the Distress of People and Nation, commonly known as the Enabling Act. In five short paragraphs, this bill transferred key legislative powers held by the Reichstag, or parliament, to Hitler's Nationalist Socialist (Nazi) Party for four years. Specifically, the act allowed Hitler and his cabinet to draft and pass laws without the Reichstag's consent, to propose amendments to the constitution and even to suspend it, to control the national budget, and to enter into foreign treaties. Although it contained reassuring phrases about not curtailing the power of either President Paul von Hindenburg or the parliament, the bill actually enabled Hitler to bypass all opposition. Because it modified the Weimar Constitution, however, Hitler needed a two-thirds majority in the Reichstag to enact the bill, which meant that more than two-thirds of the deputies had to be present, and at least two-thirds of those present had to vote for it so that it could pass into law.

The general elections of March 5, 1933, had given the Nazis 44 percent of the total vote and 288 out of the 647 seats in the Reichstag. After the elections, Hitler turned his attention to the task of obtaining the two-thirds majority in the Reichstag. First, he expelled the eighty-one Communist deputies: Those not arrested were threatened with arrest if they attempted to take their seats in the Reichstag. Second, Hitler persuaded the Center Party and the Nationalists to vote for the Enabling Act. The Center Party, under the leadership of Monsignor Ludwig Kaas, was pessimistic about blocking the bill and decided to support it in the hope of gaining Hitler's consideration for its own Catholic interests. Hesitant to trust Hitler's verbal pledge, however, the party demanded a written promise that Hitler would abide by the president's power of veto. Kaas never received such an assurance from Hitler, but he accepted a letter from President Hindenburg stating that he had been assured by Hitler that the Enabling Act would not be used without prior consultation with the president. Thus Kaas made the same error as his fellow Center Party member Franz von Papen, who had agitated for Hitler's installation after his own dismissal from the chancellorship because he hoped to share and profit from Hitler's power.

To win the support of the Nationalists and the army, Hitler and his newly appointed minister of propaganda, Joseph Goebbels, staged a well-planned ceremony in the Garrison Church at Potsdam. The ceremony was held on March 21 to mark the opening of the new Reichstag, two days before it was to consider the Enabling Act. Hitler and Goebbels selected Potsdam, the royal residence of the Hohenzollerns and seat of their dynasty (the Second Reich, which ruled Brandenburg-Prussia from 1415-1918 and imperial Germany from 1871 to 1918) and the Garrison Church, which housed the grave of Frederick the Great, to symbolically marry the past glories of Prussia to the new Nazi regime. Even the date of the ceremony had significance: Otto von Bismarck, chancellor of the German empire, had opened the first Reichstag on March 21, 1871.

At noon, Hitler entered the church beside the fading, eighty-six-year-old Hindenburg, who endorsed the simple former corporal's new government to the crowd; Hitler's own speech emphasized the national renewal evident since he had taken office. The two men's handclasp at the climax of the ceremony convinced many that Hitler stood for a restoration of the old order in Germany. The success of Hitler's policy was demonstrated when the Reichstag convened two days later in the Kroll Opera House in Berlin to vote on the Enabling Act. The building was surrounded by belligerent SS and SA troops. Hitler opened the session with a speech notable for its restraint: He pointed out that the new powers would be used only to carry out vital measures and that such occasions were unlikely to occur very often.

SIGNIFICANCE

The only deputy to speak out against the bill was Otto Wels, leader of the Social Democrats. Amid the menacing jeers of swastika-waving storm troopers, Wels began a speech condemning the Nazis' gangster mentality, but he was soon interrupted by Hitler. Infuriated by Wels's opposition, Hitler threw off all restraint. After savagely

Adolf Hitler, the newly appointed chancellor of Germany, rides with Reich president Paul von Hindenburg in a parade in May, 1933. (Hulton Archive/Getty Images)

attacking the Social Democrats, he told them that he did not need their votes: Germany would be free, he said, and its freedom would come despite the Social Democrats' efforts. Moreover, Hitler reminded Wels, the Nazis had merely observed legal niceties by seeking Reichstag approval for something that they could and would readily have taken through extralegal means, if necessary.

Despite this clue about Hitler's ruthlessness, the Enabling Act passed by a huge majority: 441 votes for and 94 votes against. The opposition votes were cast by the Social Democrats. When Hermann Göring, president of the Reichstag and Hitler's trusted henchman, made the votes known, the Nazi deputies sprang to their feet and sang the Nazi anthem, "Die Fahne Hoch" (also called the "Horst Wessel" song), while giving the Nazi salute. The Nazis had reason to be happy: Their leader had just freed himself from dependency on the Reichstag and the president. Hitler could now issues decrees without the president's approval, even if such legislation modified the Weimar Constitution. A provision introduced by Hindenburg on January 31, 1933, technically limited the Enabling Act's legislative powers to the particular cabinet in office, but Hitler soon flouted this restriction. He also seized on Hindenburg's death on August 1, 1934, using the event as a pretext for fusing the presidency and chancellorship and justifying his growing power by saying that Hindenburg's will had named him successor.

—*Harry E. Wade and Margaret Bozenna Goscilo*

FURTHER READING

Bracher, Karl Dietrich. "The Technique of Nationalist Socialist Seizure of Power." In *The Path to Dictatorship, 1918-1933*, edited by Theodor Eschenburg et al. New York: Frederick A. Praeger, 1966. The author analyzes how the concept of "legal revolution" led to the middle-class parties' naïve trust in Hitler and their consequent passage of the Enabling Act.

Burleigh, Michael. *The Third Reich: A New History.* New York: Hill & Wang, 2000. Not as accessible as Evans, but a thorough investigation of the rise of Nazism and the construction of the Enabling Act.

Evans, Richard J. *The Coming of the Third Reich.* New York: Penguin Books, 2004. A work of impressive and engaging scholarship that includes an in-depth discussion of the Enabling Act.

Fischer, Klaus P. *Nazi Germany: A New History.* New York: Continuum, 1995. Fischer's masterful study stresses the Nazi cynicism and terrorism underlying both the Potsdam ceremony and the ratification of the Enabling Act.

Hamann, Brigitte. *Hitler's Vienna: A Dictator's Apprenticeship.* New York: Oxford University Press, 1999. Focuses on Hitler's years in Vienna and how his experiences there influenced him. Includes photographs, select bibliography, and index.

Hamilton, Richard F. *Who Voted for Hitler?* Princeton, N.J.: Princeton University Press, 1982. Controversial book rejects the traditional centrist argument—that of the support for Hitler among the dominant lower-middle classes—and suggests alternative explanations for the Nazi rise to power.

Hoffmann, Peter. *The History of the German Resistance 1933-1945.* Translated by Richard Barry. Cambridge, Mass.: MIT Press, 1977. Convincingly argues that the lack of meaningful opposition to Hitler's pseudolegal seizure of power was rooted in terrorism, ignorance and denial about Nazi values, and weak democracy.

Kershaw, Ian. *Hitler, 1889-1936: Hubris.* New York: W. W. Norton, 1999. A comprehensive and well-documented examination of Hitler's rise to power.

Krausnick, Helmut. "Stages of 'Co-ordination.'" In *The Path to Dictatorship*, edited by Theodor Eschenburg et al. New York: Frederick A. Praeger, 1966. Krausnick views the Enabling Act as a decisive step in the "coordination" of German institutions to Hitler's will, second only to the February 28, 1933, decree suspending basic constitutional rights.

Redlich, Fritz. *Hitler: Diagnosis of a Destructive Prophet.* New York: Oxford University Press, 1999. Although mainly a behavioral study, this book does focus some attention on the Enabling Act as a psychological milestone in the Nazi dictator's obsessive quest for power.

Shirer, William L. *The Rise and Fall of the Third Reich: A History of Nazi Germany.* New York: Simon & Schuster, 1960. Shirer's account of the Enabling Act emphasizes Hitler's manipulation of Prussian patriotism—and the Social Democrats' weakness—in bringing the nation under the Nazi's control.

SEE ALSO: Nov. 8, 1923: Beer Hall Putsch; July 18, 1925-Dec. 11, 1926: *Mein Kampf* Outlines Nazi Thought; Jan. 30, 1933: Hitler Comes to Power in Germany; Feb. 27, 1933: Reichstag Fire; Mar., 1933: Nazi Concentration Camps Begin Operating; June 30-July 2, 1934: Great Blood Purge; Mar. 7, 1936: German Troops March into the Rhineland; Feb. 12-Apr. 10, 1938: The Anschluss; Sept. 29-30, 1938: Munich Conference; 1939-1945: Nazi Extermination of the Jews; Aug. 23-24, 1939: Nazi-Soviet Pact.

1933

April 5, 1933
U.S. CIVILIAN CONSERVATION CORPS IS ESTABLISHED

The Civilian Conservation Corps was established to put millions of unemployed people to work in beautification, forestry, and other natural resource projects. One of the first programs of President Franklin D. Roosevelt's New Deal to be implemented, it simultaneously helped create work for those left jobless by the Great Depression and helped save eroding natural resources.

ALSO KNOWN AS: Emergency Conservation Work; Executive Order 6101; CCC
LOCALE: Washington, D.C.
CATEGORIES: Organizations and institutions; natural resources; government and politics

KEY FIGURES

Franklin D. Roosevelt (1882-1945), president of the United States, 1933-1945
Robert Fechner (1876-1939), American labor leader who served as the first director of the Civilian Conservation Corps, 1933-1939
James J. McEntee (fl. mid-twentieth century), second director of the Civilian Conservation Corps, 1939-1942

SUMMARY OF EVENT

On March 29, 1933, the U.S. Congress authorized Public Act No. 5, which was known as the Reforestation Relief Act. This act gave the president the authority to establish a chain of forest camps in which unemployed young men could be put to work protecting and improving millions of acres of forest land. President Franklin D. Roosevelt signed the bill into law on March 31, 1933. Less than a week later, on April 5, 1933, Roosevelt, by Executive Order 6101, established the Emergency Conservation Work (ECW), making this plan a reality. On June 28, 1937, Congress officially changed the name of the agency from the ECW to the Civilian Conservation Corps (CCC), the name by which it is best known to history.

Roosevelt has been called the father of the CCC because of his vast experience in conservation. As a young legislator in New York, he was made chairman of the Committee on Forests, Fish, and Game. As chairman, he invited Gifford Pinchot, chief forester of the United States, and other notable conservationists to the state capitol at Albany to present lectures on forestry to the legislature. Roosevelt helped pass legislation that provided the first practical government-supervised forestry in the eastern United States.

As governor of New York, Roosevelt continued to support reforestation programs. Land was purchased for reforestation and paid for by individual counties and the state. More than $20 million was appropriated in 1931 for the growing of trees. More than one million trees were planted, and more than ten thousand unemployed people were put to work in the last year of Roosevelt's governorship.

In March, 1933, when Roosevelt became president, the United States was in the middle of the Great Depression, and more than thirteen million Americans were unemployed. Almost everyone was affected by the devastated economy. Several million people were living as nomads, drifting around the country looking for work. Many people left their homes and moved in with relatives to help cut costs. Others simply stayed home, tired of looking for nonexistent jobs. Five million of those looking for work were between the ages of eighteen and twenty-five, with no opportunity to get a start in life. Many of these young people left home looking for any kind of work but ended up in jail, municipal shelters, soup lines, and worse. A perfectly capable workforce was wasting away. The country was ready for a conservation program similar to the one Roosevelt had started in New York.

At the 1932 Democratic National Convention, Roosevelt had pointed out that many abandoned farms and cutover forests were growing worthless brush. He also stated that every European nation had a definite land policy and that the United States had none, an omission that could result in soil erosion and timber famine. In his candidacy acceptance speech, Roosevelt said, "Let us use common sense and business sense, and, just as one example, we know that every hopeful and immediate means of relief, both for the unemployed and for agriculture, will come from a wide plan of the converting of many millions of acres of marginal and unused land into timber land through reforestation." Much of the nation's timber had been squandered. Only 100 million acres out of more than 800 million acres were left. Soil erosion, wind, and water was carrying away six billion tons of soil each year. Something had to be done.

On March 4, 1933, Roosevelt took the oath of office as the thirty-second president of the United States. On March 9, he called a meeting of the secretaries of war, agriculture, and the interior, the judge advocate general of

More than eighteen hundred recruits line up for their noon meal at the CCC camp in Fort Slocum, New York, in April, 1933. (AP/Wide World Photos)

the U.S. Army, and the solicitor of the Department of the Interior to hear his conservation plan. They formulated a plan that same day, and it was introduced to Congress on March 13. This original proposal was withdrawn because of problems, and a revised plan was resubmitted on March 21, 1933. The new plan had three major provisions: Direct relief would be given to the states, a large public works program would be started, and a carefully designed soil-erosion and forestry program would be undertaken. Less than one month had passed since Roosevelt had been sworn in as president.

On April 6, 1933, Roosevelt appointed Robert Fechner, an authority on labor, as the first director of the ECW. James J. McEntee was appointed assistant director. Four departments and one independent agency were responsible for the enrollment of men, administration

of the camps, and planning and supervision of the work programs. The Departments of Labor, War, Interior, and Agriculture, as well as the Veterans Administration, were to cooperate in administering the program.

The War Department was responsible for the physical conditioning of the enrollees, as the recruits were called. It was also charged with organization, enrollment, transportation, and provision of equipment. The War Department was chosen to organize and administer the camps because it had a standing force that could provide the camp leadership needed to supervise men in groups (or companies) of two hundred men each. The War Department also provided the enrollees with food, clothing, housing, and medical care and educational, religious, and recreational facilities. The chief of finance of the army was given the chief fiscal responsibility to see that everyone was paid.

The Department of Labor was responsible for the selection of enrollees. This department delegated this authority to directors in each state. Names of qualified persons who wished to enroll were provided from town, county, and political subdivisions to the state coordinator. These state and local units were usually welfare agencies who knew which people were qualified for enlistment. The selection of enrollees was transferred to the office of the director in May, 1939.

The Department of the Interior was responsible for the planning and supervision of work projects. The National Park Service, General Land Office, Bureau of Reclamation, Office of Indian Affairs, and Grazing Service were major subdivisions of the department that participated in the program. The Office of Indian Affairs was in charge of selecting Indian enrollees and personnel who worked on reservations. The National Park Service administered the enrollment in Hawaii and the Virgin Islands.

Under the Department of Agriculture, the U.S. Forest Service and the Bureaus of Animal Industry, Biological Survey, and Agricultural Engineering provided technical and supervisory personnel for work projects. The Forest Service also provided full administration over enrollees in Alaska and Puerto Rico. The Veterans Administration selected the quota of veteran enrollees. The number of veterans was not to exceed 10 percent of the total national enrollment. The first enrollment period was to enroll no more than 250,000 men. All were between the ages of eighteen and twenty-five, and all were unemployed and unmarried. Each enrollment period was six months long, and anyone could apply to stay for more than one period. The enrollees were required to send part of their monthly cash allotment to their dependents. This afforded enrollment of those with the greatest need. Each state was assigned a quota based on its population in proportion to the total national population.

The country was divided into nine corps areas for military purposes. The CCC retained these corps areas for its own use, as each area already had training camps that would be used as conditioning camps for enrollees before they reported to work camps. Problems developed early in the selection process. Enrollees who found work were no longer eligible to participate. Some enrollees would get homesick and leave camp. Others would get married. These and other problems were solved by increasing the number of men selected. When an enrollee could not fulfill his obligation, one of the extras would take his place. The importation of large groups of men into a certain geographic location could deprive local men of local employment. Local experienced men

(LEMs) were therefore hired to advise the enrollees on the proper methods of carrying out local work projects.

On July 1, 1933, the War Department reported that mobilization was complete. More than 1,315 camps had been established. They were staffed by 3,641 regular and 1,774 reserve officers. A typical army camp staff included a company commander, an executive officer, and a medical officer. There was to be no connection with the military other than the administration of the camps. Drilling and maneuvers were not part of the daily routine. The army was simply the national agency most experienced in handling large number of enrollees. The first camps were set up as tent camps. Later, wooden barracks were constructed.

In addition to the commanding officer, each camp had a civilian superintendent and local staff supplied by the Works Progress Administration (WPA). Educational, recreational, and vocational activities were under the supervision of these men. The representatives of the Departments of the Interior and Agriculture were in charge of the men when they left camp on work details. With this foundation, the enrollees were ready to get to work.

SIGNIFICANCE

The accomplishments of the Civilian Conservation Corps were numerous. More than 150 types of work were accomplished by the enrollees. There were ten basic types of work projects. These included forest protection, forest culture, soil-erosion control, flood control, aid to wildlife, irrigation and drainage, transportation improvements, structural improvement, range development, and landscape and recreational development. The fuits of many of the projects of the 1930's are still evident in state and national parks throughout the country.

The CCC program also served the socialization needs of American youth. Men were assigned to camps in other states, so they could not go home or leave camp any time they wished. They learned to eat three healthy meals a day, and to work eight hours a day, five days a week. They got into a routine of getting up, doing a fair day's labor, coming back to the barracks, cleaning up, and going to dinner. Their evenings were devoted to recreational and educational activities. Men who had never worked in groups before learned to work in teams and interrelate with other people. They were preparing for their future.

CCC enrollees built many of the state and national parks that are visited by millions of people annually. They built fire towers, hiking trails, dining pavilions, cooking pits, culverts, and bridges. They fought forest fires and thinned woods so trees would grow better.

Many cabins that still house campers were constructed by these men. Electric and telephone lines were strung in areas needing these services. Water lines were run to camping areas in state and national parks. Emergency service was provided where needed. Flood control and cleanup work was performed by enrollees. Each company of men did the jobs specified by their camp supervisors. Many enrollees learned trades that turned into occupations they followed the rest of their lives.

The country benefited from the CCC in several ways as well. Enrollees were required to send home twenty-five dollars of their thirty-dollar monthly pay. This enabled the people at home to start recovering financially. This money was put back into the local economies. The enrollee kept five dollars per month for spending money. Local economies were aided in other ways. Lumber for the buildings constructed in the CCC camps was purchased from local lumber mills. Buildings were constructed to uniform standards, and blueprints were furnished to local contractors to supply materials. Food for the camps was also purchased locally. The enrollee could have all the food he wanted. Most of them gained weight and grew physically fit during their stay in the camps. Many opted to re-enlist when their six-month enrollment period was over.

The country was getting back into shape. The economy was recovering, and the people were getting the work and training they needed to carry on a productive life. More than three million men joined the Civilian Conservation Corps during its eight-year life. The contributions of these men stand as tributes to one of the most successful government programs ever established.

The CCC, the largest government relief program ever attempted in the United States, came to an end in 1942, after the start of World War II. Many men traded their CCC uniforms for military uniforms—the nation's youths were prepared to defend democracy.

—*Larry N. Sypolt*

Further Reading

Cohen, Stan. *The Tree Army: A Pictorial History of the Civilian Conservation Corps, 1933-1945*. Missoula, Mont.: Pictorian Histories, 1980. Heavily illustrated with pictures from around the country, brief historical references, and captions. A great reference work.

Cornebise, Alfred Emile. *The CCC Chronicles: Camp Newspapers of the Civilian Conservation Corps, 1933-1942*. Jefferson, N.C.: McFarland, 2004. Study of daily life in CCC camps and the culture of the CCC through the lens of the newspapers published by and for campers. Bibliographic references and index.

Dearborn, Ned H. *Once in a Lifetime: A Guide to the CCC Camp*. New York: Charles E. Merrill, 1936. A very good reference work on the CCC program, presented in question and answer format.

Holland, Kenneth, and Frank Ernest Hill. *Youth in the CCC*. Washington, D.C.: American Council on Education, 1942. Describes the history, programs, and activities of the CCC.

Hoyt, Ray. *We Can Take It: A Short Story of the C.C.C.* New York: American Book Company, 1935. Good background information and history of the first two years of the CCC program.

Lacy, Leslie Alexander. *The Soil Soldiers: The Civilian Conservation Corps in the Great Depression*. Radnor, Pa.: Chilton, 1976. A good descriptive history of selected CCC work programs.

Merrill, Perry H. *Roosevelt's Forest Army: A History of the Civilian Conservation Corps, 1933-1942*. Montpelier, Vt.: Perry H. Merrill, 1981. Concise history of the Civilian Conservation Corps.

Oliver, Alfred C., Jr., and Harold M. Dudley. *This New America: The Spirit of the Civilian Conservation Corps*. New York: Longmans, Green, 1937. A good reference source to the CCC written during the height of the program.

Paige, John C. *The Civilian Conservation Corps and the National Park Service, 1933-1942: An Administrative History*. Washington, D.C.: Government Printing Office, 1985. This book describes the relationship between the National Park Service and the CCC. Good illustrations of work projects.

Pfaff, Christine. *The Bureau of Reclamation and the Civilian Conservation Corps, 1933-1942*. Denver, Colo.: Dept. of the Interior, Bureau of Reclamation, 2000. Study of the history of the CCC and its relationship to the Bureau of Reclamation. Bibliographic references.

Salmond, John A. *The Civilian Conservation Corps, 1933-1942: A Case Study*. Durham, N.C.: Duke University Press, 1967. Probably the best-known work on the subject and one of the earliest histories of the CCC.

See also: Jan., 1922: Izaak Walton League Is Formed; Oct. 29, 1929-1939: Great Depression; Jan. 22, 1932: Reconstruction Finance Corporation Is Created; Nov. 8, 1932: Franklin D. Roosevelt Is Elected U.S. President; Mar. 9-June 16, 1933: The Hundred Days; June 18, 1934: Indian Reorganization Act; June 28, 1934: Taylor Grazing Act; Apr. 8, 1935: Works Progress Administration Is Established; Apr. 27, 1935: Soil Conservation Service Is Established.

1933

May 18, 1933
TENNESSEE VALLEY AUTHORITY IS CREATED

After decades of debate over government versus private ownership of electric power, the U.S. Congress created the Tennessee Valley Authority, demonstrating the critical relationship between economic and environmental decisions.

ALSO KNOWN AS: TVA

LOCALE: Tennessee River Valley system, southeastern United States

CATEGORIES: Environmental issues; natural resources; energy; government and politics

KEY FIGURES

George W. Norris (1861-1944), U.S. representative from Nebraska, 1903-1913, and senator, 1913-1943

Franklin D. Roosevelt (1882-1945), president of the United States, 1933-1945

Woodrow Wilson (1856-1924), president of the United States, 1913-1921

Herbert Hoover (1874-1964), president of the United States, 1929-1933

Arthur Ernest Morgan (1878-1975), engineer and first chairman of the TVA

David Eli Lilienthal (1899-1981), attorney and TVA board member

Harcourt A. Morgan (1867-1950), agronomist and TVA board member

SUMMARY OF EVENT

On May 18, 1933, President Franklin D. Roosevelt signed a bill creating the Tennessee Valley Authority (TVA) as the first public regional development agency in the nation. The history of the founding of the TVA is also the history of an enduring national debate over the appropriateness of publicly versus privately owned electric power generation. This controversy illustrates the critical links among economic development, environmental use, and the role of the federal government in economic and environmental decisions.

The debate originated in the nineteenth century and pitted conservationists and Progressive politicians against the electric power industry. Unregulated capitalist ventures in the 1880's and 1890's had caused widespread environmental destruction for economic gain. The conservation movement emerged, urging that natural resources be regulated by the federal government to ensure that they would be protected and carefully used. Conservation meant controlled economic development

in the first half of the twentieth century. Pioneering conservationist Gifford Pinchot first developed the concept of multiple-use management for the conservation of forest resources and then extended the idea to water resources. He argued that private power companies' exploitation of only the hydroelectric power of rivers would waste the rivers' potential for flood control and increased navigation, which could only be realized by public entities. Conservationists were also motivated by changes in technology. Steam-electric power generated by burning coal or oil had been the main source of power since the 1880's. For the first time, power transmission technology made possible the transport of electric power from remote rivers to cities. Ownership and control of electrical power generation was a critical issue because of the enormous amounts of power needed to run the production processes on which the economy depended.

Progressive politicians supported the regulation of industry for environmental and social purposes. Progressives such as Republican senator George W. Norris of Nebraska accepted the sagacity of the multipurpose use of natural resources. More important, the Progressive politicians feared that if private utilities monopolized hydroelectric resources, they would soon control all industry and, ultimately, the country. Believing that regulatory policy would not be enough, Progressives emphasized the need for competition from public power.

An important focal point for the controversy over public versus private power was the development of the federally owned Muscle Shoals site on the Tennessee River. Near Florence, Alabama, the Tennessee River falls 137 feet over thirty-seven miles. Known as Muscle Shoals, this series of rapids, pools, and rocks constituted an obstruction to navigation. Near the end of the century, the waterpower potential of the shoals was recognized. In 1906, the Muscle Shoals Hydroelectric Power Company began a ten-year attempt to secure congressional approval for a joint navigation and power project at Muscle Shoals in which the government was to bear a substantial portion of the cost. The company failed. Other private developers also tried and failed to purchase the site from the government.

In 1916, the passage of the National Defense Act mandated that Muscle Shoals was to be used by the government to produce the nitrates needed for explosives in the anticipated war effort. Muscle Shoals was chosen primarily because it was both a technically feasible and a politically desirable site. Additionally, the nitrate plants could be used in peacetime to produce the nitrates required for cheap fertilizer needed by southern farmers.

The U.S. Army Corps of Engineers constructed a steam-electric plant to provide power for the nitrate facilities because the urgency of the need for nitrates was so great that there was no time to construct a hydroelectric dam. President Woodrow Wilson ordered the dam—eventually named Wilson Dam—built in addition to the steam plants. The nitrate plants never worked, however, and the dam was not completed until 1925. For ten years, little use was made of Wilson Dam's power-producing capacity.

After World War I, President Wilson attempted to carry out the mandate of the National Defense Act of 1916 to produce peacetime nitrates for fertilizer, but his plan became enmeshed in the dispute over public versus private operation of hydroelectric plants. The electric power industry expanded rapidly in the decade after the war, and companies were eager to buy Muscle Shoals. In 1921, Henry Ford offered to purchase the site. Several other companies made bids to buy it, but their efforts

were consistently foiled by Senator Norris. In 1926, Norris proposed his first bill for the multipurpose development of the Tennessee River watershed. Congress passed the bill in 1928, but President Calvin Coolidge killed it with a pocket veto. Congress passed Norris's second bill in 1930, but President Herbert Hoover vetoed it amid charges that it was socialistic.

The Democratic Party's 1932 platform reflected the public-versus-private-power debate by advocating the conservation, development, and use of the nation's waterpower in the public interest. President Franklin D. Roosevelt took office in March, 1933, with 15 million Americans unemployed and the banks closed by executive order to prevent collapse. As governor of New York, Roosevelt had taken a strong position on the power question, attempting to increase the effectiveness of state regulation. Soon after taking office, he called Congress into special session and asked for legislation similar to Norris's to create the TVA. He signed the bill as part of his New Deal legislation to bolster economic development and appointed Arthur Ernest Morgan, a renowned engineer, as the first chairman of the TVA Board of Directors. The TVA was administered by the chairman and two directors, who answered to Congress.

The TVA was created as the first public regional development agency. It was charged with planning regional economic development while protecting natural resources in order to create wealth for the people from the resources of the valley. The act defined the TVA region as the area drained by the Tennessee River, which included parts of Alabama, Georgia, Kentucky, Mississippi, North Carolina, Tennessee, and Virginia. The agency was granted three major powers: to construct dams for flood control and hydroelectric power, to deepen the river channel to aid navigation, and to produce and distribute electricity and fertilizer.

SIGNIFICANCE

The creation of the TVA had both immediate effects and a long-term impact on the history of U.S. environmental policy. Its most important immediate effect was the agency's

President Franklin D. Roosevelt (left), Eleanor Roosevelt, and Arthur Ernest Morgan during an inspection tour of TVA projects in late 1934. (Tennessee Valley Authority)

control over the 650-mile-long Tennessee River. Dams constructed for flood control and for hydroelectric power to electrify the rural hinterlands also created large lakes for recreation that brought land developers and tourist dollars to the region.

At least three important long-term trends emanated from the creation of the TVA. The first was that, although the TVA's establishment did not stop the public-versus-private-power debate, it gave it form and served as a concrete symbol of the continuing debate. Private-power advocates lost the battle for the Tennessee Valley but won a qualified victory in the war against public power. The second trend concerned the exposure of the fundamental relationship between economic growth and environmental use. The TVA represented an organizational effort simultaneously to promote economic growth and to conserve resources. Several important legal and political conflicts have been generated by the TVA's attempts to carry out these seemingly contradictory tasks over the years.

The third important long-term impact of the TVA was the precedent the agency set for government intervention in power technology. With the government's participation in the development of hydroelectric power and its emphasis on electric power as important to national defense, the way was paved for the later federal direction of nuclear technology. The government's Manhattan Project was designed to research and develop the atomic bomb for use in World War II. Oak Ridge, Tennessee, was chosen as one of three secret sites constructed for working on the bomb, in part because of its proximity to an enormous source of electric power: the TVA. In its postwar bid to control the development of nuclear technology, the federal government again turned to the TVA. In 1946, Director David Lilienthal left the TVA to become the first chairman of the Atomic Energy Commission (AEC), the federal regulatory agency for nuclear technology. The TVA was complicit in creating the Cold War nuclear arms race, buying coalfields, increasing their strip-mining operations, and building a vast coal-fired power system to power the federal nuclear operations.

The TVA's effects have been varied, both in their consequences and in their capacity for social progress. The agency set an important precedent, however, that may benefit many future generations. The TVA was the first organization to seek the protection of public resources as defined by regional, rather than legal, boundaries, resulting in planned efforts toward coastal management, wetlands management, and the protection of the Everglades.

—*Sherry Cable and Thomas E. Shriver*

FURTHER READING

Chandler, William U. *The Myth of TVA: Conservation and Development in the Tennessee Valley, 1933-1983*. Cambridge, Mass.: Ballinger, 1984. Economic analysis of the TVA's impact in navigation, flood control, power production, agriculture, and environmental protection concludes that the TVA was a bad investment of tax dollars. The book is flawed in that it uses surrounding non-TVA areas with different economic bases as a control group.

Colignon, Richard A. *Power Plays: Critical Events in the Institutionalization of the Tennessee Valley Authority*. Albany: State University of New York Press, 1997. A study of the legal and institutional struggles that—through the precedents they set—established the insitutional power of the TVA.

Creese, Walter L. *TVA's Public Planning: The Vision, the Reality*. Knoxville: University of Tennessee Press, 1990. Well-written, lavishly illustrated book demonstrates the relationship between the physical impact of TVA on the visual environment of the region and the policy goals of the agency's leaders.

Gray, Aelred J., and David A. Johnson. *The TVA Regional Planning and Development Program: The Transformation of an Institution and Its Mission*. Burlington, Vt.: Ashgate, 2005. Study of institutional change within the TVA and its causes and effects in relation to its fundamental mission. Bibliographic references and index.

Hubbard, Preston. *Origins of the TVA: The Muscle Shoals Controversy, 1920-1932*. Nashville: Vanderbilt University Press, 1961. Documents the various attempts to deal with the Army Corps of Engineers project at Muscle Shoals. Useful for understanding the roots of TVA in the Progressive ideology of the early twentieth century.

McCraw, Thomas K. *Morgan vs. Lilienthal: The Feud Within the TVA*. Chicago: Loyola University Press, 1970. Detailed analysis of the feud between TVA Chairman Arthur E. Morgan and TVA Director David E. Lilienthal. The feud and its outcome determined the shape that the agency would take.

_____. *TVA and the Power Fight, 1933-1939*. New York: J. B. Lippincott, 1971. Good, nuanced study of the continuation of the debate over publicly versus privately owned electric power after the TVA was founded, and the role of the TVA in that debate. Particular emphasis on the lawsuits brought against the TVA.

McDonald, Michael J., and John Muldowny. *TVA and the Dispossessed*. Knoxville: University of Tennessee Press, 1982. Examines resettlement of the population in Norris after construction of Norris Dam. Good analysis of how the TVA used the power of eminent domain as a threat to force residents to sell their land.

Schlesinger, Arthur M., Jr. *The Coming of the New Deal.* Vol. 2 in *The Age of Roosevelt.* Boston: Houghton Mifflin, 1958. A classic liberal narrative. Brilliantly written and informed. Part 5 is pertinent to the origins of the TVA. Page notes serve as a bibliography. Fine index. Well worth reading in its entirety.

_____. *The Politics of Upheaval.* Vol. 3 in *The Age of Roosevelt.* Boston: Houghton Mifflin, 1960. Superb narrative. Chapter 20 deals with court challenges to

the TVA. Wonderful historical work on a dramatic subject. Page notes function as a bibliography. Excellent index.

Wilcox, Clair. *Public Policies Toward Business.* Homewood, Ill.: Richard D. Irwin, 1966. Superb for essentials on the TVA as a government authority and its effects on the business community. Clear basic presentation, objectively handled. Many page notes, excellent index.

SEE ALSO: 1910: Steinmetz Warns of Pollution in "The Future of Electricity"; Mar. 9-June 16, 1933: The Hundred Days; Mar. 11, 1936: Boulder Dam Is Completed.

June 16, 1933
BANKING ACT OF 1933 REORGANIZES THE AMERICAN BANKING SYSTEM

The Banking Act of 1933 established deposit insurance, regulated interest paid on deposits, prohibited underwriting of corporate securities by commercial banks, and restricted loans to buy securities.

ALSO KNOWN AS: Glass-Steagall Act
LOCALE: Washington, D.C.
CATEGORIES: Laws, acts, and legal history; banking and finance

KEY FIGURES
Carter Glass (1858-1946), former U.S. secretary of the treasury and member of the Senate Banking Committee
Ferdinand Pecora (1882-1971), counsel to the Senate Banking Committee and an original member of the Securities and Exchange Commission
Henry Bascom Steagall (1873-1943), U.S. congressman from Alabama, 1915-1943
Arthur Hendrick Vandenberg (1884-1951), U.S. senator from Michigan, 1928-1951
Franklin D. Roosevelt (1882-1945), president of the United States, 1933-1945

SUMMARY OF EVENT
Hundreds of American banks failed every year during the 1920's, and thousands failed in the period 1930-1933. The existing banking and financial oversight systems were clearly inadequate, and Senator Carter Glass began pushing for reform of the system in 1931. In a re-

port on the bill that became the Banking Act of 1933, the Senate Banking Committee explained that "a completely comprehensive measure for the reconstruction of our banking system" had been deferred. The purposes of the committee's emergency bill were more modest: It aimed "to correct manifest immediate abuses, and to bring our banking system into a stronger condition." The new law significantly amended the Federal Reserve Act (1913) and the National Bank Act (1864) and added the Federal Deposit Insurance Corporation (FDIC) to those agencies already regulating and monitoring the banking system.

When the stock market collapsed, share prices fell an average of one-sixth of the value they had previously held in the period 1929-1932. Generous credit to stock speculators—funneled through stockbrokers—had fueled the Wall Street boom in the late 1920's, and the crash was largely blamed on excessive loans to these stockbrokers and stock speculators. A major purpose of the Banking Act of 1933, signed into law on June 16 of that year, was to prevent the "undue diversion of funds into speculative operations." This meant that banks belonging to the Federal Reserve system (member banks) were forbidden to act as agents to brokers and dealers on behalf of nonbank lenders.

Congress was concerned that businesses engaged in agriculture, industry, and commerce would be deprived of adequate credit. The Federal Reserve Board, a presidentially appointed group that governed the Federal Reserve, was to ascertain whether bank credit was being used for speculative purposes. The board could limit the

1933

2659

amount of stock and bond collateral that could be used to secure member banks' loans, and banks whose lending policies fostered speculation would be denied the privilege of borrowing from the Federal Reserve bank. Most of the loans financing speculation in stocks and bonds had been made by banks in financial centers; there was no evidence that these banks turned down requests by businesses for short-term loans. Moreover, corporations could finance expansion through the sale of new securities. The Federal Reserve Board also set ceilings on the rates that member banks were permitted to pay on time and savings deposits. In 1935, the FDIC was given the power to set ceilings for all insured banks. Regulation Q, issued by the Federal Reserve Board, established a ceiling of 3 percent—well above what most banks paid—as of November 1, 1933.

One section of the Banking Act of 1933, often referred to as the Glass-Steagall Act (although this name was originally attached to the entire Banking Act of 1933), ordered that the practice of taking deposits be separated from investment banking activities within one year. This meant that financial institutions had to choose to be either commercial banks or investment houses; investment banks could no longer accept deposit accounts, and member banks could no longer underwrite securities issues of business corporations. Banks with national charters were, however, permitted to underwrite and deal in securities issued by all levels of government in the United States for resale to the investing public. Separation of commercial banking and investment banking was expected to contribute to the soundness of commercial banks and to increase the overall stability of the economy.

In the 1920's, commercial banks began the large-scale development of affiliates that dealt in securities. By 1930, these affiliates brought more than half of all new securities issues to market, making them a significant threat to established investment banks. Ferdinand Pecora, counsel to the Senate Banking Committee, conducted extensive hearings on abuses by the affiliates, and his investigation generated negative publicity. There is little evidence to support the idea, which prevailed in 1933, that many bank failures were the result of affiliates' activities in securities. At the time, many small-bank failures were blamed on the poor results from securities portfolios, which had been purchased on the advice of larger correspondent banks eager to promote issues held by their affiliates. As a result of this (mistaken) perception, member banks were forbidden from investing in corporate stock. They could continue to buy corporate

bonds for their investment portfolios, however, provided that those bonds were of investment (rather than speculative) quality.

Senator Glass was convinced that banks should confine their activities to short-term business loans, because most deposits held in banks had to be payable on demand. Glass believed that banks should not lock themselves into long-term loans when their deposits, the source of funding for loans, could be quickly withdrawn. In the past, banks had made riskier loans and investments so that they could offer higher interest rates to their depositors—a situation that would occur again in the 1970's and 1980's. To encourage safer portfolios, Congress resorted to regulating interest rates. For deposits payable on demand, no explicit interest payments were allowed. The ban on interest was also intended to discourage the exchange of deposits between small banks and correspondent banks; Congress wanted funds to go to local borrowers instead. Small banks, however, continued to hold deposits with correspondent banks. Rather than paying interest, the correspondent banks offered various services free of charge.

Congressman Henry Bascom Steagall spearheaded the inclusion of deposit insurance provisions of the Banking Act of 1933. For fifteen years he had battled for the reform, which he saw as a way of instilling confidence in the safety of deposits made in local banks. Senator Arthur Hendrick Vandenberg pushed for deposit insurance to take effect immediately, but President Franklin D. Roosevelt was opposed. As a compromise, a temporary plan covering the first $2,500 in insured accounts went into effect on January 1, 1934. In the meantime, infusions of capital strengthened the banks that were permitted to reopen after Roosevelt's banking holiday, which lasted from March 6 to March 13, 1933.

From 1920 through 1933, thousands of minuscule, small-town banks had failed, and so the Banking Act of 1933 raised the minimum amount of capital required to open a national bank from $25,000 to $50,000. The capital held by each branch of a national bank had to match or exceed the capital required for a one-office bank in the same location. To prevent the creation of unhealthy competition caused by bank proliferation, the Banking Act of 1935 (passed on August 23, 1935) further tightened the requirements for a bank to obtain a charter. The FDIC stood ready to deny insurance if excessive competition posed a threat.

Prior to the stock market crash of 1929, banks in the United States were undiversified institutions that did almost all their business at a single location. As a result, their fates were tied to the fortunes of local economies. To provide some banking services in places where banks had closed, states began to ease restrictions on branch banking, and a heated battle for permission to operate branches began to take place in state legislatures and in Congress. In 1927, national banks with federal charters were authorized to have branches in the same community as their head offices if branch banking was allowed by the state's law. The Banking Act of 1933 permitted branches to be developed outside the headquarter's community, so that national banks could branch just as easily as state banks. Interstate branch banking remained forbidden, however.

In 1922, the Federal Reserve banks had begun to coordinate purchases and sales of government securities (known as open-market operations). The 1933 act placed open-market operations under regulation by the Federal Reserve Board; the board could now disapprove policies that had been recommended by the Federal Open Market Committee. Further, all relationships and transactions made between the Federal Reserve banks and foreign institutions were placed under control of the Federal Reserve Board. Both measures diminished the policy-making roles previously played by the twelve Federal Reserve banks, particularly the powerful one in New York City. The 1933 act also gave the Federal Reserve system its first measure of authority over bank holding companies that owned shares in member banks. A bank holding company could avoid supervision if control over a member bank was exerted without the need to vote shares. Involvement of the Federal Reserve system with bank holding companies remained limited.

SIGNIFICANCE

Exercise of authority over banking by individual states had led to a "competition in laxity" among federal regulators. Over the years, federal authorities had eased restrictions on national banks in order to prevent them from switching to state charters and to encourage state banks to convert to national charters. Many states had weak or inadequate banking supervision, and state banks failed at a much higher rate than national banks in the period 1920-1933.

Supporters of states' rights had prevented a federal takeover of commercial banks' chartering, supervision, and regulation. After the Banking Act of 1933, however, states had to share jurisdiction with the FDIC for nonmember banks covered by that agency's insurance. States retained the power to decide their own policies on branch banking. Some persisted in prohibiting all

branches, but most broadened the territory in which branching was authorized. No state allowed the extension of branches across state lines.

Deposit insurance, which was fiercely opposed by some bankers in 1933, became permanent in the Banking Act of 1935. Advocates hoped that, as deposits increased, deposit insurance would stimulate bank lending to the private sector. Bank deposits increased by more than 46 percent from 1934 through 1939, surpassing the record 1930 total by more than $2.6 billion. Total loans, however, failed to significantly increase, reflecting the weak recovery of businesses' investment spending and the timidity of bank lending officers.

After the FDIC was organized in September, 1933, all member banks were required to join, and solvent nonmember banks were also eligible. Banks paid an initial premium of .25 percent of insurable deposits. By the beginning of 1934, 87 percent of all commercial banks had joined the FDIC, and more than 96 percent of all deposits were covered. By the end of that year, 93 percent of commercial banks had joined, and 98 percent of deposits were covered. All but about 1 percent of applicant banks qualified for deposit insurance. To remain insured, nonmember banks were expected to become member banks by mid-1936. This deadline was first extended and then abandoned in 1939. A majority of American banks continued to be nonmembers, largely because state charters had lower minimum capital and lower reserve requirements than did the Federal Reserve Board.

The FDIC later proved successful in one of its goals: preventing a new wave of bank failures triggered by depositors' fears. Even as hundreds of banks were forced to close in the 1980's, depositors did not panic and rush to remove their funds. Ceilings on interest rates did not hamper the gathering of deposits by banks until the 1950's, when competition with investment outlets that offered returns higher than those permitted under Regulation Q caused some hardships for banks. Interest rate regulations for time and savings deposits were eliminated in 1986.

Banks had begun to separate their commercial and investment banking programs before the Banking Act of 1933 required that they do so. The two leading American banks, Chase National Bank and National City Bank, announced plans to eliminate their affiliates in March, 1933. The Morgan investment banking business, sharply reduced by the Depression, continued under the leadership of several partners who left to form Morgan Stanley. The historic name J. P. Morgan & Company now belonged to a commercial bank that became Morgan Guaranty Trust Company in 1959. Other large investment banks chose to eliminate their deposit-taking activities.

The 1933 act began the process of diminishing the autonomy of the twelve Federal Reserve banks and centralizing power in the Federal Reserve Board in Washington, and the Banking Act of 1935 completed that shift. In many significant ways, however, the American banking system was unchanged by New Deal legislation. Several major problems were left unresolved, including those posed by the dual banking system (of state and national banks), the division of responsibilities among federal agencies, and banks' limited ability to branch (and thus to diversify their lending and deposit bases). The 1933 act also created some problems by failing to make deposit insurance premiums related to risk and by banning interest on demand deposits, which made it more difficult for banks to get those deposits.

—*Benjamin J. Klebaner*

FURTHER READING

Benston, George J. *The Separation of Commercial and Investment Banking: The Glass-Steagall Act Revisited and Reconsidered.* New York: Oxford University Press, 1990. A well-argued case for the repeal of separation of the two types of banking.

Burns, Helen M. *The American Banking Community and New Deal Banking Reforms, 1933-1935.* Westport, Conn.: Greenwood Press, 1974. Useful background material and a detailed exposition of the attitudes of bankers regarding proposals that led to the banking acts of 1933 and 1935.

Chandler, Lester Vernon. *America's Greatest Depression, 1929-1941.* New York: Harper & Row, 1970. Provides the economic setting of the era.

_____. *American Monetary Policy, 1928-1941.* New York: Harper & Row, 1971. A leading economic historian discusses banking issues as well as central bank policy.

Friedman, Milton, and Anna Jacobson Schwartz. *A Monetary History of the United States, 1867-1960.* Princeton, N.J.: Princeton University Press, 1963. Masterful and comprehensive. Covers the banking collapse and legislation of the 1930's in great detail, from a monetarist perspective.

Ginzberg, Eli. *New Deal Days, 1933-1934.* New Brunswick, N.J.: Transaction Publishers, 1997. A lighter, less scholarly treatment of early New Deal legislation.

Kennedy, Susan Estabrook. *The Banking Crisis of 1933.* Lexington: The University Press of Kentucky, 1973. Carefully researched, authoritative treatment of events of the period after 1929 and measures to deal with the banking crisis.

Klebaner, Benjamin J. "Banking Reform in the New Deal Era." *Quarterly Review (Banca Nazionale de Lavoro)* 178 (September, 1991): 319-341. An analysis of the limited changes made from 1933 through 1939 in commercial and central banking.

Krooss, Herman Edward, comp. *Documentary History of Banking and Currency in the United States.* 4 vols. New York: Chelsea House Publishers, 1969. Volume 4 contains the text of the Banking Act of 1933 and useful commentary by an eminent financial historian.

Studenski, Paul, and Herman Edward Krooss. *Financial History of the United States.* 2d ed. New York: McGraw-Hill, 1963. Excellent, concise treatment of developments since 1789 by two leading experts.

Westerfield, Ray B. *Money, Credit, and Banking.* New York: Ronald Press, 1938. The most comprehensive treatise of the period. Well written. A less-detailed second edition appeared in 1947.

Wicker, Elmus. *The Bank Panics of the Great Depression.* New York: Cambridge University Press, 1996. The first analysis of five major banking panics that occurred during the Great Depression. A thorough discussion.

SEE ALSO: Oct.-Nov., 1907: Panic of 1907; Dec. 23, 1913: Federal Reserve Act; Feb. 25, 1927: McFadden Act Regulates Branch Banking; Oct. 29, 1929-1939: Great Depression; Dec. 11, 1930: Bank of United States Fails; May 8, 1931: Credit-Anstalt Bank of Austria Fails; Jan. 22, 1932: Reconstruction Finance Corporation Is Created; Aug. 23, 1935: Banking Act of 1935 Centralizes U.S. Monetary Control.

June 16, 1933
ROOSEVELT SIGNS THE NATIONAL INDUSTRIAL RECOVERY ACT

The National Industrial Recovery Act was an attempt to help businesses recover from the Great Depression. It temporarily replaced the U.S. market system with a system of planning boards under which labor and management would decide on wages, prices, and output levels.

LOCALE: Washington, D.C.
CATEGORIES: Laws, acts, and legal history; business and labor; trade and commerce; organizations and institutions

KEY FIGURES

Franklin D. Roosevelt (1882-1945), president of the United States, 1933-1945
Hugh S. Johnson (1882-1942), first head of the National Recovery Administration, 1933-1934
Rexford Guy Tugwell (1891-1979), American economist and Roosevelt adviser
Robert F. Wagner (1877-1953), U.S. senator from New York, 1927-1949
William E. Borah (1865-1940), U.S. senator from Idaho, 1907-1940
Clarence Darrow (1857-1938), American attorney and head of the National Recovery Review Board
Harold Ickes (1874-1952), U.S. secretary of the interior, 1933-1946

SUMMARY OF EVENT

The National Industrial Recovery Act was passed by Congress on June 16, 1933, in an attempt to bring relief from the Great Depression by overhauling the way in which American industry was organized. The experiences of the War Industries Board during World War I had convinced many in Washington that it was possible greatly to expand production if the competitive system were replaced with a system of industrial cooperation, guided by government. By the spring of 1933, the severity of the Depression was such that even the U.S. Chamber of Commerce was urging the new administration of Franklin D. Roosevelt to expand government's role in the economy. Rexford Guy Tugwell, an economist at Columbia University and a member of Roosevelt's Brain Trust (a distinguished group of presidential advisers), had sketched out a plan for peacetime governmental direction of production through the use of industry codes in his book *The Industrial Discipline and the Governmental Arts*, published in early 1933.

The National Industrial Recovery Act (NIRA) as sent by President Roosevelt to Congress on May 15, 1933, was divided into two parts. Title I closely followed Tugwell's recommendations. It authorized a suspension of antitrust laws to allow management and labor in each industry to write binding codes specifying standards of fair competition. The National Recovery Administration (NRA) was established to administer the codes. Section 7a of Title I was aimed at securing the rights of labor by guaranteeing the right to collective bargaining and by including minimum wage and maximum hour stipulations. Title II of the bill established the Public Works Administration and appropriated $3.3 billion for carrying out public works.

The bill was passed quickly by the House of Representatives with little dissent, but it ran into trouble in the Senate. Many senators feared that suspending antitrust laws would give industry free rein to fix prices and restrict output. A group led by Senator William E. Borah of Idaho attempted to amend the bill to preclude price fixing, but the bill's Senate sponsor, Robert F. Wagner of New York, arguing that the drafters of the industry codes should be given maximum flexibility, was able to defeat the amendment. The Senate finally passed the bill on June 13, 1933, by a vote of forty-six to thirty-nine. Roosevelt signed the bill on June 16.

Roosevelt chose Hugh S. Johnson to head the National Recovery Administration and decided to place the Public Works Administration under the control of Secretary of the Interior Harold Ickes. Johnson had had considerable relevant administrative experience serving as an aide to Bernard Baruch on the War Industries Board during World War I. Although Johnson appeared to have considerable authority to impose codes of fair practice on industry, he chose instead to attempt to obtain voluntary cooperation. He hoped to establish a system of industrial self-government not dissimilar to the European doctrine of syndicalism, although Johnson saw himself as building on the industry trade associations that had arisen and grown during the 1920's. Johnson's reliance on voluntary cooperation was reinforced by doubts about the constitutionality of the NIRA and fear that disgruntled industrialists might bring lawsuits against it.

The process of writing codes took place largely in offices at the Department of Commerce, with NRA administrators mediating between delegations of owners and workers from each industry. The reliance on voluntary

1933

cooperation resulted in few codes being drawn up during the early months. In July, Johnson persuaded Roosevelt to agree to a stopgap proposal under which essentially every business in the country would adopt NRA standards on minimum wages and maximum hours immediately. Businesses in compliance with what was called the President's Reemployment Agreement would be allowed to display a sign featuring the NRA's Blue Eagle and the motto We Do Our Part. Gradually, NRA administrators began to hammer out the industry codes. By June, 1934, codes covering 450 industries with twenty-three million workers had been drawn up.

The industry codes all included provisions establishing minimum wages and maximum hours and guaranteeing the collective bargaining rights of workers. Employment of children under the age of sixteen was also generally prohibited. Most codes specified minimum prices and otherwise attempted to restrict competition. Examples of restrictions on competition included production quotas, under which individual companies would be assigned a specified share of total industry output, which would itself be limited; restrictions on the installation of new machinery; and restrictions on the hours during which existing machinery could be operated.

Supporters of the NIRA in Congress and in the Roose-

velt administration had always been ambivalent concerning the wisdom or necessity of allowing business to restrict output and fix prices. The ambivalence is evident in a parenthetical phrase included in the following passage from section 1, Title I of the act, which states that the purpose of the legislation is "to promote the fullest possible utilization of the present productive capacity of industries, [and] to avoid undue restriction of production (except as may be temporarily required)." In practice, it became clear during the negotiations for drawing up the codes that industry saw output restrictions and price fixing as a quid pro quo for agreeing to the restrictions on wages and hours and guarantees of collective bargaining.

Support for the NRA began to wane as it became clear to what extent the industry codes allowed the code authorities to replace determination of wages, prices, and output through the market with determination by administrative fiat. Support was also undermined by the mercurial and erratic behavior of Johnson as administrator. Responding to criticism, Roosevelt set up the National Recovery Review Board, chaired by attorney Clarence Darrow, to review the industry codes. Johnson was finally obliged to resign in late September, 1934. He was replaced as the administrative authority by a five-person National Industrial Recovery Board (NIRB). The NIRB, particularly under the influence of Leon Henderson, the NRA's chief economist, attempted to scale back the regulation of smaller industries and to modify the price fixing and output-restricting provisions in existing codes.

The original act was set to expire in June, 1935. In February, Roosevelt formally asked for a two-year extension. Privately, however, Roosevelt appeared to have been ready to abandon the NIRA as having done little to help economic recovery. Many in Congress were also skeptical. In the end, congressional consideration of an extension of the NIRA was rendered moot when the Supreme Court ruled in *Schechter Poultry Corporation v. United States* (1935) that the NIRA was unconstitutional. The Court was unanimous in ruling that the act was an unconstitutional delegation of legislative authority to the executive branch and that the commerce clause of the Constitution did not allow the federal

A 1934 political cartoon satirizes the proliferation of New Deal legislation. (Library of Congress)

government to control the details of the operations of businesses that had only a slight involvement in interstate commerce.

SIGNIFICANCE

Following the Supreme Court decision, the vast apparatus of industrial codes and industrial authorities that had been created under the authority of the National Industrial Recovery Act was rapidly dismantled. Congress preserved the labor legislation embodied in the NIRA by passing the National Labor Relations Act (NLRA, popularly known as the Wagner Act), which actually went beyond section 7a of the NIRA in attempting to ensure fair labor practices. The NLRA created the National Labor Relations Board (NLRB) to police labor relations.

In the years since the demise of the NIRA, the law's impact has been debated by economists and historians. Economists have generally viewed the NIRA as having retarded recovery from the Great Depression. Economists have tended to be critical of the industry codes for artificially raising wages and prices and authorizing—in fact, often promoting—output restrictions. Some historians have been kinder to the NIRA, which they are inclined to view favorably in light of the social consequences of the labor law reforms contained in the act. Arthur Schlesinger, for example, although conceding that the NIRA contributed little economically to the recovery, has argued that legislative sanction for maximum hours, minimum wages, and collective bargaining and against child labor would have been difficult to obtain any other way.

A careful analysis of the economic impact of the act has been carried out by Michael M. Weinstein, who argues that the codes had a substantial effect on wages and prices. The NIRA's impact on wages resulted, first, from the enactment of minimum wage regulations that raised the wages of workers who previously had been earning below the minimum and, second, from increases in the wages of those who had been earning more than the minimum in order to restore previous wage differentials. Weinstein estimates that in the absence of the NIRA, average hourly earnings in manufacturing in May, 1935, would have been less than $.35 per hour, rather than almost $.60 per hour. The act resulted in higher prices as a result of its effect on wage costs and its encouragement of collusive behavior and price fixing. Weinstein estimates that in the absence of the NIRA, the price level in May, 1935, would have been more than 20 percent lower than it actually was.

Higher prices reduced the purchasing power of the ex-

isting stocks of money and wealth. This resulted in lower levels of consumption than would otherwise have occurred. The lower real value of the money stock also resulted in higher interest rates than would otherwise have existed. These higher interest rates, in turn, retarded borrowing by businesses to finance new machinery and equipment and borrowing by households to finance houses and, to a lesser extent, automobiles, furniture, and other consumer durables.

In fact, industrial production had increased, on a seasonally adjusted basis, by more than 50 percent between March and July, 1933, before the NRA began operations. During the operating life of the NRA, industrial production actually declined slightly. Perhaps most damning was the fact that after the Supreme Court ruled in May, 1935, that the NIRA was unconstitutional, industrial production during the rest of 1935 increased by almost 15 percent.

Investment spending performed somewhat better during the NRA period. Spending by businesses on new machinery and equipment and new factories and office buildings rose more than 40 percent between the depressed second quarter of 1933 and the second quarter of 1935. This increase, however, still left business investment spending more than 60 percent below its level in 1929 and further still below the level necessary if the economy was to return to full employment. Similarly, spending by consumers on new houses more than doubled during the time of the NRA, but residential construction remained more than 70 percent below its peak level of the late 1920's.

Peter Temin has provided an interesting argument that reinforces the view that the NRA retarded recovery from the Great Depression. Temin notes that there are a number of parallels between the course of the early years of the Depression in the United States and in Germany. After 1933, however, the paths of the two countries diverged economically. Germany experienced very rapid employment gains, whereas employment recovered only slowly in the United States. Temin argues that the recovery in Germany was spurred, in part, by the determination of the Nazis, who came to power in January, 1933, to hold down the growth of wages. In the United States, in contrast, the NRA acted to keep wages far above market-clearing levels. Although there are many striking contrasts between U.S. and German economic policy in the post-1933 period, Temin believes that differences in wage policies are central to understanding the differing pace of employment recovery in the two countries. The NRA effectively precluded the possibility that the large numbers of unemployed workers in the United States would be able to find jobs by competing on the basis of wage rates.

　　　　　　　　　　　　　　—*Anthony Patrick O'Brien*

FURTHER READING

Fine, Sidney. *The Automobile Under the Blue Eagle: Labor, Management and the Automobile Manufacturing Code*. Ann Arbor: University of Michigan Press, 1963. Detailed case study. Emphasizes labor aspects of the NIRA; also deals with Henry Ford's resistance to the NIRA.

Hawley, Ellis W. *The New Deal and the Problem of Monopoly*. Princeton, N.J.: Princeton University Press, 1966. Puts the NRA in a broader context of New Deal concern with economic planning and the revival of antitrust after *Schechter Poultry Corporation v. United States*.

Johnson, Hugh S. *The Blue Eagle from Egg to Earth*. Garden City, N.Y.: Doubleday Doran, 1935. A colorful, opinionated account of the top NRA administrator's life and the NRA experience, which he regarded as "a holy thing."

Ohl, John Kennedy. *Hugh S. Johnson and the New Deal*. De Kalb: Northern Illinois University Press, 1985. Lively, objective, scholarly account of Johnson's life and of the achievements and problems of the NRA.

Roos, Charles F. *NRA Economic Planning*. Bloomington, Ind.: Principia Press, 1937. An economist who worked in the NRA tries to assess its relevance to the issue of economic planning. Long, scholarly, and analytic.

Rosenof, Theodore. *Economics in the Long Run: New Deal Theorists and Their Legacies, 1933-1993*. Chapel Hill: University of North Carolina Press, 1997. Examination of the New Deal and its theorists from the perspective of their impact on later years. Contains an extensive bibliography and index.

Schlesinger, Arthur M., Jr. *The Coming of the New Deal*. Vol. 2 in *The Age of Roosevelt*. Boston: Houghton Mifflin, 1958. Chapters 6-10 provide a sympathetic treatment of the formulation and administration of the NRA by one of the best-known biographers of Roosevelt.

Storrs, Ladon R. Y. *Civilizing Capitalism: The National Consumers' League, Women's Activism, and Labor Standards in the New Deal Era*. Chapel Hill: University of North Carolina Press, 2000. Examination of the interrelationship between New Deal programs and women activists fighting for social justice and consumer rights. Includes the chapter "The Acid Test of the New Deal: The National Recovery Administration, 1933-1935."

Temin, Peter. *Lessons from the Great Depression*. Cambridge, Mass.: MIT Press, 1989. Chapter 3 presents Temin's argument that the high wages resulting from the NRA retarded economic recovery in the United States. Contains references to fairly advanced economic theory, but the basic argument is easily understood.

Tugwell, Rexford G. *The Industrial Discipline and the Governmental Arts*. New York: Columbia University Press, 1933. Contains Tugwell's rationale for the sort of system embodied in the NRA codes. Reveals the extent to which confidence in the free market system had declined by 1933.

Weinstein, Michael M. "Some Macroeconomic Impacts of the National Industrial Recovery Act." In *The Great Depression Revisited*, edited by Karl Brunner. Boston: Martinus Nijhoff, 1981. A brief analysis of the economic impact of the NIRA. Relatively nontechnical, but some knowledge of elementary economics is presumed.

SEE ALSO: Mar. 23, 1932: Norris-La Guardia Act Strengthens Labor Organizations; Mar. 9-June 16, 1933: The Hundred Days; Apr. 8, 1935: Works Progress Administration Is Established; May 27, 1935: Black Monday; July 5, 1935: Wagner Act; Feb. 5-July 22, 1937: Supreme Court-Packing Fight; June 25, 1938: Fair Labor Standards Act; June 14, 1940: United States Begins Building a Two-Ocean Navy.

July 6, 1933
FIRST MAJOR LEAGUE BASEBALL ALL-STAR GAME

The template for all-star games in every sport was set when stars from baseball's American and National Leagues met in baseball's first All-Star Game. The game's popularity immediately made it one of the premier events in sports.

LOCALE: Comiskey Park, Chicago, Illinois
CATEGORY: Sports

KEY FIGURES

Arch Ward (1896-1955), sports editor for the *Chicago Tribune*, 1930-1955
Will Harridge (1883-1971), president of the American League, 1931-1958
John Heydler (1869-1956), president of the National League, 1918-1934
Bertie McCormick (1880-1955), publisher of the *Chicago Tribune*
Babe Ruth (1895-1948), star outfielder for the New York Yankees, 1920-1934
Lefty Gomez (1908-1989), American League pitcher, 1930-1943
Bill Hallahan (1902-1981), National League pitcher, 1925-1938
William L. Veeck (1878-1933), president of the Chicago Cubs, 1919-1933
Sam Breadon (1876-1949), owner of the St. Louis Cardinals, 1920-1947

SUMMARY OF EVENT

On Thursday, July 6, 1933, more than forty-nine thousand enthusiastic spectators jammed into Chicago's Comiskey Park to watch top players from both the American and National Leagues compete in the first ever All-Star Game. The American League emerged victorious, 4-2. Arch Ward, sports editor of the *Chicago Tribune*, had conceived of the game as the once-in-a-lifetime battle between baseball's best players. A native of Illinois's Kankakee County, Ward had been publicity director for legendary Notre Dame football coach Knute Rockne and sports editor of the *Rockford Star* before coming to the *Tribune* in 1925.

In 1933, Depression-ridden Chicago was playing host to the World's Fair, the theme of which was "Century of Progress." Scholars disagree about the nature of Ward's involvement in the fair: Some say that fair officials asked local sports editors to help them develop a grand sporting event to focus attention on the city, while others argue

that Chicago mayor Ed Kelly asked *Tribune* publisher Bertie McCormick to help develop a major sporting event. Either way, Ward was soon involved in the process. Ward, who considered himself more of an idea man and promoter than a writer, proposed an exhibition baseball game between the best players from the American and National Leagues. The game's profits would go to the Association of Professional Baseball Players of America, and fans from all over the United States would select the teams' players. McCormick had doubts about whether the game would be popular, but he agreed to underwrite its costs.

The office of the American League's president, Will Harridge, was located in Chicago at the time, and on April 20, 1933, Ward walked over to see him. A negative reaction from Harridge would have almost certainly prevented the game from taking place, but Harridge enthusiastically embraced the idea. William E. Veeck, president of the National League's Chicago Cubs, was equally supportive. Others were not, however: Three National League teams—the New York Giants, the Boston Braves, and the St. Louis Cardinals—vetoed the idea. The Giants and Braves pointed out that they were scheduled for a doubleheader in Boston on July 5, and that it was impossible for players from these two teams to get to Chicago in time for the game.

Fortunately for Ward, John Heydler, the president of the National League, supported the idea of the All-Star Game, and he agreed to postpone the doubleheader. Sam Breadon, owner of the Cardinals, had other concerns: He was afraid that the game would set a precedent and that future contests would be forced to give the proceeds to charity. Breadon only agreed to the game after Ward pointed out that the game would bring financial benefits to its host city.

To help tabulate the ballots produced by fan voting, Ward asked fifty-five sportswriters from various cities for help. The *Tribune*'s editors did not think that other newspapers would collaborate, but all fifty-five accepted. The fans' choices included Chicago White Sox outfielder "Bucketfoot" Al Simmons, who was tied for the American League's batting lead with a .368 average. Simmons polled more ballots (346,291) than any other player and was followed by Philadelphia Phillies outfielder Chuck Klein, whose banner season earned 342,283 votes, the highest number in the National League. Other outstanding players selected included New York Yankee first

ALL-STAR GAME WINNERS, 1933-1955

Major League Baseball's All-Star Game remained a popular event throughout the twentieth century. Listed below are the winners, the final scores, and the game locations for the All-Star Games played from 1933 through 1955.

Year	Winning League	Score	Venue
1933	American	4-2	Comiskey Park (home of the Chicago White Sox)
1934	American	9-7	Polo Grounds (home of the New York Giants)
1935	American	4-1	Municipal Stadium (home of the Cleveland Indians)
1936	National	4-3	Braves Field (home of the Boston Braves)
1937	American	8-3	Griffith Stadium (home of the Washington Senators)
1938	National	4-1	Crosley Field (home of the Cincinnati Reds)
1939	American	3-1	Yankee Stadium (home of the New York Yankees)
1940	National	4-0	Sportsman's Park (home of the St. Louis Cardinals)
1941	American	7-5	Briggs Stadium (home of the Detroit Tigers)
1942	American	3-1	Polo Grounds (home of the New York Giants)
1943	American	5-3	Shibe Park (home of the Philadelphia Athletics)
1944	National	7-1	Forbes Field (home of the Pittsburgh Pirates)
1945	Not held		
1946	American	12-0	Fenway Park (home of the Boston Red Sox)
1947	American	2-1	Wrigley Field (home of the Chicago Cubs)
1948	American	5-2	Sportsman's Park (home of the St. Louis Browns)
1949	American	11-7	Ebbets Field (home of the Brooklyn Dodgers)
1950	National	4-3	Comiskey Park (home of the Chicago White Sox)
1951	National	8-3	Briggs Stadium (home of the Detroit Tigers)
1952	National	3-2	Shibe Park (home of the Philadelphia Phillies)
1953	National	5-1	Crosley Field (home of the Cincinnati Reds)
1954	American	11-9	Municipal Stadium (home of the Cleveland Indians)
1955	National	6-5	County Stadium (home of the Milwaukee Braves)

baseman Lou Gehrig, New York Giants players Bill Terry and Carl Hubbell, and Detroit Tiger second baseman Charlie Gehringer. Fans also elected the thirty-eight-year-old Babe Ruth, the oldest player on the field, even though he was heavier, slower, and clearly nearing the end of his legendary career as a right fielder in the American League.

Ward chose the game's managers. For the National League he selected famed New York Giants skipper John McGraw, who had retired the previous year but returned for this game. The Philadelphia A's Connie Mack, nicknamed the "Tall Tactician," was tapped to lead the American League. To ensure fairness, the leagues agreed to use the American League's ball, which was considered livelier, for the first four and one-half innings. The less lively National League ball would then be used to finish the contest. The game's starting pitchers were Lefty Gomez (for the American League) and Bill Hallahan (for the National League).

Some had feared that the game would not attract fans, but Chicago's Comiskey Park was filled to capacity on July 6; even the 2,250 bleacher seats that had been added a few days before were filled. The game got under way at 1:15 P.M. Because Comiskey Park was the home of the American League's Chicago White Sox, the American League was considered the home team, and so the National League batted first. Gomez retired St. Louis Cardinal third baseman Pepper Martin, the first batter, on a ground ball. With the help of Hallahan's characteristic wildness, the American League scored the first run in the second inning. Two walks put runners on first and second base, and pitcher Gomez—usually a feeble hitter—plated the first run with a single.

Babe Ruth came to bat in the third inning. With Gehringer on first base, Ruth belted a home run into the right-field seats, and the delighted crowd roared as "the Babe" rounded the bases. The first home run in All-Star history gave the American League a seemingly insurmountable three-run lead. Gomez blanked the National League's players for the first three innings, and the Washington Senators's star hurler Alvin Crowder did the same in the fourth and fifth innings. In the sixth inning, however, the National League showed signs of life. Chicago Cubs pitcher Lon Warneke got a triple on a fly ball down the right-field line that a younger and quicker Ruth might have held to a single. Warneke scored and was followed by Frankie "Fordham Flash" Frisch, who hit the National League's first home run by smacking a shot into the right-field seats. The American League's lead narrowed to 3-2.

In the bottom of the sixth inning, the American League scored another run. The New York Giants' masterful screwball pitcher Carl Hubbell completely dominated during the seventh and eighth innings, although the National League came close to tying the game in the top of the eighth when Cincinnati Reds outfielder Chick Hafey hit a long fly ball to right field with a runner on first. Ruth caught the ball with his back to the wall, although in a smaller ballpark Hafey's ball would almost certainly have been a home run. The ninth inning was a quiet one, and the game ended with a 4-2 victory for the American League and more than forty-six thousand dollars raised for the Association of Professional Baseball Players of America. The game's popularity led Baseball Commissioner Judge Kenesaw Mountain Landis to declare the game an annual event.

SIGNIFICANCE

The first baseball All-Star Game cemented the idea of a showcase exhibition contest among a sport's most prominent players. Most other sports—including football, basketball, and hockey—eventually followed suit, although both the complexity of scheduling such a game and the threat of injury remained controversial issues. However, sports fans continued to show support for such a contest, and the leagues used the games as venues for promoting their best athletes. Some players saw the games as barometers of their skill and popularity, particularly as free agents became more common; players could use their success in an All-Star Game as a tool in contract negotiations.

—Russell Roberts

FURTHER READING

The Baseball Chronicle: Year-by-Year History of Major League Baseball. Lincolnwood, Ill.: Publications International, 2003. Illustrated history covers Major League Baseball from the nineteenth century through 2002. Includes tidbits about players who appeared in All-Star Games.

The Baseball Encyclopedia: The Complete and Definitive Record of Major League Baseball. 10th ed. New York: Macmillan, 1996. An encyclopedic reference of baseball player records, nicknames, and first-person accounts, and highlights of All-Star Games through 1992.

Olson, Drew. "Ward's Simple Idea a Classic Success: All-Star Game a Big Hit from the Start." *Milwaukee Journal Sentinel*, June 19, 2002.

Vincent, David, Lyle Spatz, and David W. Smith. *The Midsummer Classic.* Lincoln: University of Nebraska Press, 2001. Exhaustively researched accounts of every baseball All-Star Game from the first in 1933 to 2000. Includes play-by-play accounts by inning of the games, plus player rosters, career statistics for all players, and career and game statistical rankings.

SEE ALSO: Jan. 1, 1902: First Rose Bowl Game; Oct. 1-13, 1903: Baseball Holds Its First World Series; Jan. 12, 1906: American College Football Allows the Forward Pass; Oct. 1-9, 1919: Black Sox Scandal; Jan. 3, 1920: New York Yankees Acquire Babe Ruth; Aug. 20-Sept. 17, 1920: Formation of the American Professional Football Association; June 12, 1939: Dedication of the Baseball Hall of Fame.

August 2, 1933
SOVIETS OPEN THE WHITE SEA-BALTIC CANAL

By using prisoner labor, Soviet political police built the White Sea-Baltic Canal in less than two years. The canal's rapid construction came at the cost of at least twenty-five thousand lives.

LOCALE: Karelia, Russia
CATEGORIES: Engineering; government and politics; transportation

KEY FIGURES

Joseph Stalin (Joseph Vissarionovich Dzhugashvili; 1878-1953), general secretary of the Communist Party in Russia and dictator in the Soviet Union, 1929-1953

Genrikh Grigoryevich Yagoda (1891-1938), deputy head of the Soviet political police

Maxim Gorky (Alexsey Maksimovich Peshkov; 1868-1936), Russian writer

Matvei Davidovich Berman (1898-1939), head of the Gulag

Lazar Iosifovich Kogan (1899-1939), head of the White Sea-Baltic Canal construction project

Naftaly Aronovich Frenkel (1883-1960), deputy head of the White Sea-Baltic Canal construction project

SUMMARY OF EVENT

On August 2, 1933, the Council of People's Commissars of the Soviet Union issued a decree proclaiming the opening of a canal connecting the White Sea with the Baltic Sea. The canal, which had been built in just twenty months by tens of thousands of prison-camp inmates working under the direction of the Soviet political police (OGPU), was to be named in honor of Joseph Stalin, general secretary of the Communist Party of the Soviet Union (CPSU). The decree celebrated the new canal as a triumph of Soviet engineering and an enlightened penal administration, and the canal was hailed as a key to the future economic and cultural value of the entire Soviet north. In reality, the decree vastly overstated the economic value of the White Sea-Baltic Canal and concealed the brutality with which it had been constructed.

The idea of building a canal across the desolate, thinly populated area known as Karelia first arose in the eighteenth century. Only five hundred miles separated the new city of St. Petersburg (renamed Leningrad in 1924) and Arkhangel'sk, Russia's principal port on the White Sea, but there was no direct water route between the two cities. Ships had to sail around Scandinavia using the Arctic Ocean, the North Sea, and the Baltic Sea, a distance of more than 3,500 miles. Czarist-era governments, however, repeatedly concluded that the estimated expenses of building a canal far outweighed any foreseeable economic or strategic benefits.

Stalin was determined to prove that the Soviet Union's communist system could succeed where its prerevolutionary, capitalist predecessors had failed. He believed that the answer to the problem of cost was to use political prisoners and ordinary criminals as unpaid laborers. Many of the OGPU's concentration camps were located in Karelia and on the Solovetskiye Ostrova (the Solovetski Islands) in the White Sea. Since the mid 1920's, Solovetski prisoners had been working in an OGPU logging enterprise operated by Naftaly Aronovich Frenkel, a former inmate who had been recruited into the Solovetsky prison-camp administration. At Stalin's insistence, the OGPU was commissioned to build the White Sea-Baltic Canal in just twenty months. The organization lacked modern construction equipment, and their labor consisted of tens of thousands of prisoners instead of skilled workers. OGPU deputy chairman Genrikh Grigoryevich Yagoda had overall responsibility for the project. In late 1930 or early 1931, the OGPU created the chief administration of camps (Glavnoe Upravlenie Lagerei in Russian, or Gulag for short) to coordinate the supply of labor for this and the other large-scale projects that it would eventually undertake.

Survey work on the canal route began in February, 1931, and actual digging began in September. The proposed route would make use of Leningrad's Neva River and two deep lakes, Ladoga and Onega, but 141 miles would still need to be excavated between the two lakes and between Lake Onega and the White Sea. Plans called for the construction of nineteen locks, but Stalin's timetable and the lack of up-to-date equipment and materials obliged the project's administrators to resort to cutting corners wherever possible. The locks and dikes were constructed out of logs, rocks, and earth rather than metal and cement. Moreover, canal engineers decided to excavate the canal to a depth of only twelve to fifteen feet, which would be much too shallow for most oceangoing vessels and would undermine the reasons for building the canal in the first place.

According to documents found in Soviet archives after the collapse of the Soviet Union, about 170,000 prisoners worked on building the canal. They were forced to work year round in a harsh environment close to the Arctic Circle, and they had to fulfill high work quotas using primitive, homemade tools. Prisoners had to build their own barracks. It is difficult to determine how many of them died building the White Sea-Baltic Canal, but the memoirs of survivors indicate that the death rate was high. Fragmentary archival evidence suggests that more than twenty-five thousand people perished; the actual number was probably much higher.

On May 1, 1933, Yagoda notified Stalin that construction of the canal had been completed on schedule, and Stalin himself sailed through the canal in late July on an inspection tour. The Soviet government bestowed its highest award, the Order of Lenin, on eight of the men who had overseen the project, including Yagoda; Matvei Davidovich Berman, head of the Gulag; Lazar Iosifovich Kogan, who had headed the construction project; and Frenkel, who had taken over daily operations in November, 1931.

On August 17, a group of 120 Soviet writers, led by Maxim Gorky, sailed through the canal. In February of 1934, thirty-six of them published an official history, edited by Gorky, of the building of the White Sea-Baltic Canal. This volume praised not only the project's managers for their achievement but also presented the project as a successful penal experiment in rehabilitating enemies of socialism and ordinary criminals, and it concealed the degree to which human suffering and death had occurred. By the end of the 1930's, Yagoda, Berman, and Kogan—though not Frenkel—had all been executed in Stalin's purges. All copies of the official history were withdrawn from public libraries and destroyed.

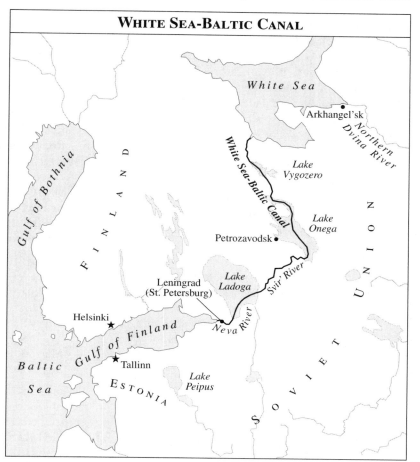

SIGNIFICANCE

The construction of the White Sea-Baltic Canal was the first major industrial project undertaken by the Soviet political police. Its organizers pioneered the use of forced labor by massive numbers of Gulag prisoners as a substitute for scarce financial resources, advanced technology, and skilled labor. Their example would be followed in subsequent mammoth construction and mining projects located in remote and inhospitable regions of the Soviet Union up to Stalin's death in 1953.

The completed White Sea-Baltic Canal typified the achievements and shortcomings of Stalinist methods for transforming Russia into a modern industrial country. It was a remarkable achievement given the primitive technology employed in its construction, but its usefulness was limited. Stalin, Yagoda, and the police officials who oversaw the project were completely indifferent to its human costs. It was built more for prestige and propaganda and to prove Stalin's belief in the efficacy of slave labor than as part of a carefully developed plan.

—*Richard D. King*

FURTHER READING

Applebaum, Anne. *Gulag: A History*. New York: Doubleday, 2003. Winner of the Pulitzer Prize for history; argues that Stalin considered slave labor to be indispensable to Soviet industrialization.

Baron, Nick. "Conflict and Complicity: The Expansion of the Karelain Gulag, 1923-1933." *Cahiers du monde russe* 42 (April-December, 2001): 615-48. Using local archives, this article provides estimates of the number of inmates who were employed and who died on the building of the White Sea-Baltic Canal.

Gorky, Maxim, L. Auerbach, and S. G. Firin, eds. *Belomor: An Account of the Construction of the New Canal Between the White Sea and the Baltic Sea.* Edited and translated by Amabel Williams-Ellis. 1935. Reprint. Westport, Conn.: Hyperion Press, 1977. An abridged and greatly altered English translation of the Russian, which was an official history prepared by a team of thirty-six writers headed by Maxim Gorky.

Khlevniuk, Oleg V. *The History of the Gulag: From Collectivization to the Great Terror.* Translated by Vadim A. Staklo. New Haven, Conn.: Yale University Press, 2004. Argues that the vast expansion of the Gulag and the Great Terror were planned by the Stalinist leadership and that the need for labor with special skills influenced the pattern of arrests.

Service, Robert. *Stalin: A Biography.* Cambridge, Mass.: Harvard University Press, 2005. An assessment of Stalin's life and rule that emphasizes the complexity of his character and his fascination with ideas.

Solzhenitsyn, Aleksandr I. *The Gulag Archipelago, 1918-1956: An Experiment in Literary Investigation.* Translated by Thomas P. Whitney. 4 vols. New York: Harper & Row, 1975. Second volume of Solzhenitsyn's trilogy contains a sarcastic critique of the official history edited by Gorky. Utilizes recollections from surviving inmates.

Tolczyk, Dariusz. *See No Evil: Literary Cover-ups and Discoveries of the Soviet Camp Experience.* New Haven, Conn.: Yale University Press, 1999. Critiques representations of Soviet concentration camps in official Soviet literature, including the official history of the construction of the White Sea-Baltic Canal.

SEE ALSO: 1924: Soviets Establish a Society for the Protection of Nature; May 18, 1928: Shakhty Case Debuts Show Trials in Moscow; Oct. 1, 1928: Stalin Introduces Central Planning; Nov. 16, 1933: United States Recognizes Russia's Bolshevik Regime; Dec., 1934: Stalin Begins the Purge Trials; Nov. 30, 1939-Mar. 12, 1940: Russo-Finnish War; Apr.-May, 1940: Soviets Massacre Polish Prisoners of War.

August 11-13, 1933
IRAQI ARMY SLAUGHTERS ASSYRIAN CHRISTIANS

A long history of tense Iraqi nationalism climaxed when the members of an Assyro-Chaldean Christian community were slaughtered and their homes were looted and burned by Iraqi troops and mostly Kurdish and Arab tribesmen.

ALSO KNOWN AS: Simmele Massacre
LOCALE: Simmele, Mosul, Iraq
CATEGORIES: Atrocities and war crimes; wars, uprisings, and civil unrest

KEY FIGURES

Bakr Sidqi (1885-1937), prominent Iraqi officer of Kurdish origin commanding the northern Iraq district where the Assyrians had settled

Mar Eshai Shimun XXIII (1908-1975), patriarch of the Nestorian Christian Assyrian community during the Simmele Massacre

SUMMARY OF EVENT

After the Assyrians sided with the British and against their Turkish overlords in World War I, the British forces (the dominant power in Iraq between 1920 and 1932) had several thousand Assyrians resettled as refugees from the Hakkâri Mountains in Anatolia, which had been part of the Ottoman Empire. The Assyrians had been in the Ottoman Empire for centuries, and they had enjoyed a special status as a *millet* (a term essentially equivalent to "nation"). After the empire's dissolution at the end of World War I, the Assyrians became a homeless minority, and they were eventually resettled by their British patrons in several villages near the northern Iraqi town of Mosul. These villages included Dahuk, Zakhu, and Simmele.

However, the Assyrian Christian refugees, who had arbitrarily been planted among the area's native Muslim Kurds, came to be viewed as British protégés or clients. Indeed, the Assyrian intrusion had been sponsored by the British, and many of the officers among the British-sponsored Iraq enlistees were Assyrian militiamen doing guard duty at Britain's two Royal Air Force bases, which Britain retained after Iraq was given formal independence in 1932. These troops had even been used to put down Arab Shiite and Kurdish revolts against the British authorities in the 1920's. However, Iraq's position on the strategically important route to India and its large oil reserves (which were exploited by the British-controlled Iraq Petroleum Company) meant that the British government had a vested interest in remaining in the country.

The twenty-five-year-old Assyrian patriarch Mar Eshai Shimun XXIII was obstinate and not given to compromise, and this further complicated the situation. Indeed, Mar had long been agitating with Iraq's central government and the League of Nations (of which Iraq had become a member when it achieved independence) to agree to Assyrian administrative autonomy in a compact national enclave in the northern region. The Assyrians' wish was motivated by a fear of being overpowered by other ethnic groups after independence and by the relative loosening of British control (and therefore protection of the Assyrians). Their desire, however, was perceived by the Iraqi government and many of its citizens as an uninvited intrusion into Iraqi sovereignty and an attempt to prevent national unity. The Assyrians became the targets of deep resentment, especially by the Kurds, who saw the Assyrians as intruders in Kurdish territory.

On August 4, 1933, a number of violent clashes began to erupt in this tense environment. They were largely confined to conflicts between Assyrian Christians on one hand and Muslim villagers and tribesmen—mostly Kurds—on the other. In the latter part of July, 1933, armed bands of Assyrians had crossed the Tigris River into Syrian territory, where they sought permission to establish a sanctuary. French authorities in Syria would not approve such a settlement, however, and they eventually forced the Assyrians to choose between being disarmed and interned or returning to Iraq.

During the Assyrians' return to northern Iraq, Kurdish forces under the general command of Colonel Bakr Sidqi confronted these armed Assyrian militiamen and tried to disarm them. The most intense clash occurred in Simmele from August 11 through August 13, 1933. Other confrontations occurred in neighboring villages. While the well-armed Iraqi soldiers did most of the killing, the Kurdish tribesmen did most of the arson and the looting of Assyrian property in Simmele and other towns, including Dahuk, Amadiyah, and Shaikhan. Apparently, Sidqi had obtained permission from higher authorities to retaliate with an iron fist, a move supported by much of Iraqi public opinion. Indeed, the Assyrians were represented in the Iraqi press as a threat to Iraq's national integrity and as pawns in a strategic part of the country. Following the Simmele event, Sidqi was pro-

moted to the rank of brigadier general, and he became a national hero. The army was soon engaged in a "pacification" program involving restless minorities.

In fact, however, even close witnesses and experts disagreed on who fired the first shot and on the extent of casualties—which ranged from a few hundred to three thousand—and of property damage. Britain did not want to jeopardize its position in the newly independent Iraq, and so after the incident it obtained a generous whitewash for Baghdad at the League of Nations. The League had been briefed by Mar, who had stressed his people's mistreatment, but Britain's imperialist desire to secure Iraq's cooperation proved more important than loyalty to the Assyrians.

SIGNIFICANCE

The Simmele Massacre proved a dismal beginning to Iraq's independent existence and did not bode well for future relations between Iraq's Muslim majority and its non-Muslim—mostly Christian and Jewish—minorities. Unfortunately, distrust between the central government in Baghdad and the minorities would continue well into the future. The Assyrians' connection with the British made them particularly vulnerable as both anti-imperialist and nationalist sentiments grew among Iraqis.

The Assyrian National Pact of 1932 (created under Mar's leadership) had defined the Assyrian minority as a separate nation and culture, but the Iraqi government came to consider them a threat to national integrity. As a result, Mar was stripped of his Iraqi citizenship and exiled to Cyprus, which at the time was a British colony. He later became a U.S. citizen.

Crucially, the slaughter of Assyrian Christians also marked the emergence of the Iraqi army onto the national scene, and the event helped the army claim a larger share of public funds and add recruits to its ranks. By 1936, Sidqi was staging his own coup d'état, although this upheaval would prove to be merely the first in a series of subsequent intrusions by the military into Iraqi political life. In turn, Sidqi's assassination by ambitious army officers in 1937 was the first of many power struggles within the army.

—Peter B. Heller

FURTHER READING

Husry, Khaldun S. "The Assyrian Affair of 1933." *International Journal of Middle East Studies* 5 (1974): 161-176, 344-360. With its something of a nationalist, pro-Iraqi bias, this work contrasts with Stephen Longrigg's and Ronald Stafford's pro-Assyrian account of the 1933 event.

Longrigg, Sir Stephen. *Iraq, 1900-1950*. London: Oxford University Press, 1953. A renowned British historian expresses sympathy for the Assyrians' plight despite what he considers to be the intemperate attitude of Mar Eshai Shimun XXIII.

Mansoor, Menahem, ed. *1900-1941*. Vol. 1 in *Political and Diplomatic History of the Arab World, 1900-1967*. 16 vols. Washington, D.C.: NCR/Microcard Editions, 1972-1977. Includes a day-to-day report of the Assyrian disturbances in July and August of 1933.

Marr, Phebe. *The Modern History of Iraq*. Boulder, Colo.: Westview Press, 2004. Provides cogent analysis of several consequences of the 1933 massacre.

Stafford, Ronald S. *The Tragedy of the Assyrians*. 1935. Reprint. New York: Columbia University Press, 2004. A senior British official in Iraq strives to provide an objective account of the Assyrian tragedy of 1933, explaining that the underlying problem was that, after alienating the Turks by mandating their departure from their ancestral homes, the Assyrians were not welcome by any other country.

Tarbush, Mohammad A. *The Role of the Military in Politics: A Case Study of Iraq to 1941*. London: Kegan Paul, 1982. A well-documented work that presents the Assyrian massacre as an important stepping-stone for the Iraqi army as it strove to become an important political power center in Iraq.

Tripp, Charles. *A History of Iraq*. 2d ed. Cambridge, England: Cambridge University Press, 2000. Explains the ambivalence of the Assyrians' position in Iraq given their status as a minority religion, the reputation as uninvited intruders under British protection, and their subservience to the former imperial power as it continued to maintain a military presence in "independent" Iraq.

SEE ALSO: Dec. 30, 1906: Muslim League Protests Government Abuses of Minority Rights in India; Apr. 26, 1920: Great Britain and France Sign the San Remo Agreement; May-Nov., 1920: Great Iraqi Revolt; July 18, 1926: Treaty of Ankara; Sept. 17, 1928: Oil Companies Cooperate in a Cartel Covering the Middle East; Mar. 3, 1938: Rise of Commercial Oil Industry in Saudi Arabia.

September, 1933
MARSHALL WRITES *THE PEOPLE'S FORESTS*

In The People's Forests, *Robert Marshall advocated the preservation of untouched wilderness areas in the national forests.*

LOCALE: United States
CATEGORIES: Environmental issues; publishing and journalism

KEY FIGURES
Robert Marshall (1901-1939), American conservationist, bureaucrat, and hiker who fought to preserve wilderness lands within national forests
Gifford Pinchot (1865-1946), first chief of the U.S. Forest Service
Ferdinand A. Silcox (1882-1939), chief of the U.S. Forest Service who supported Marshall's fight for wilderness preservation

SUMMARY OF EVENT
In *The People's Forests* (1933), Robert Marshall decried the devastation of American forests by private owners and called for increased federal regulation and public ownership of these lands. The book followed Marshall's 1930 pamphlet *The Social Management of American Forests* and the U.S. Forest Service's *National Plan for American Forestry* (1933), for which Marshall wrote the chapter on recreation (one of the most articulate and widely read treatises on the topic). Marshall's work as a conservationist and writer ultimately led to the passage of important regulations protecting wilderness areas in the United States, including the Forest Service's 1939 U-Regulations and the Wilderness Act of 1964.

The People's Forests demonstrated Marshall's interest in conservation as well as his gift for writing. The book is clear and straightforward, and at times both eccentric and passionate. Marshall began his book by harking back to the Pilgrims' first encounter with the New World, when half of what is now the continental United States was forest land. He created beautiful images of million-acre stands of tall trees with no unnatural sounds or sights, and he described how the wild animals and the Native Americans benefited from the trees without harming them. In harsh language, he showed how settlers destroyed the land and narrowed the forests for the next three hundred years.

Carefully and thoroughly, Marshall explained the state of the forests and the timber industry as it existed in the 1930's. With statistics and tables, he showed how much lumber was produced over the years from 1809 to 1932, how the lumber was used, and how many acres of forest had disappeared. He persuasively argued that the nation's forests had been dealt great harm under the private ownership of timber companies. (Modern readers who study the statistics will find interesting gems: For example, the third-highest volume of wood used in the 1930's was for railroad ties, and the sixth-greatest use was for barrel staves. The automobile industry was also a great consumer of wood.)

Marshall conceded the importance of forests as a source of raw material but asserted they also were important for soil and water conservation and for recreation. Recreation, however, was Marshall's chief concern. He believed that walking through the woods was important to human happiness, and that this preservation became more important as the world became more mechanized:

Finally, there are those whose chief purpose in visiting the forests is simply an escape from civilization. These people want to rest from the endless chain of mechanization and artificiality which bounds their lives. In the forest they temporarily abandon a routine to which they cannot become wholly reconciled, and return to that nature in which hundreds of generations of their ancestors were reared.

Marshall acknowledged that few people would ever take advantage of the chance to spend significant amounts of time in the forest. Still, he believed that their right to do so was important and that a democracy should protect the rights of such minorities. His cause, he said, was important enough that the government should take control of the forests from their owners, either by purchase or by foreclosure. Without this control, there would not be any wilderness left, since the private owners had shown themselves incapable of taking care of their land. If the government operated forest land, Marshall believed, the timber industry could still thrive; with proper management and replanting, the forests could be replenished. In addition, large tracts of land could be set aside for recreational use, with restrictions on cutting, the building of roads, and other intrusions.

Marshall proposed several types of recreational forest land that people could enjoy: "superlative areas" such as the Grand Canyon or Yosemite, of such profound beauty that they should be protected and carefully developed for everyone; "primeval tracts" of at least one thousand acres of virgin timber; "wilderness areas"; "roadside areas"; "campsite areas"; and "residence areas," which could contain homes, hotels, and resorts. His chief concern was with the wilderness areas, and it was to those areas that he devoted much of his professional and personal life.

Marshall defined "wilderness" as an area with no residents, no roads or means for motorized or mechanical travel, no power lines, and no hotels, restaurants, or souvenir stands. The idea was that travelers in the wilderness should be self-sufficient, just as travelers had been for centuries. Simple shelters and trails would be permitted, because they had been available to early travelers. Marshall thought such an area should be large enough for visitors to spend at least a week actively hiking without recrossing their tracks. Since he often hiked twenty or thirty miles a day, wearing common tennis shoes and carrying heavy, old-fashioned equipment, the wilderness areas would need to be sizable.

Large virgin forests could no longer be found in the continental United States, although such areas did exist in northern Canada and in Alaska, which was not yet a state. Since Marshall was concerned mainly with getting away from modern conveyances and conveniences, he was willing to accept land that had been logged and retimbered for his wilderness areas. Primeval areas gave him access to primitive plants, while wilderness areas gave him access to primitive transportation. Marshall estimated that it would take 55 million acres of forest land to supply the recreational needs of the nation—approximately 11 percent of the 506 million acres of commercial timber land of the time. He proposed that 20 million acres be set aside as wilderness areas, in tracts ranging from 200,000 acres to a million acres or more. As he said, "This seems like a very conservative area to devote to the purpose of assuring tens of millions of our citizens a fitting environment for the finest moments of their lives."

1933

SIGNIFICANCE

The publication of *The People's Forests* came at a time when American forests seemed to be in real danger of disappearing. Although national "forest reserves" had been established as early as 1871 and Yosemite had been designated a national park in 1890, federal agencies did not necessarily consider that national lands should be protected from use or even from overuse. Gifford Pinchot saw a need in the early part of the twentieth century for a national agency to regulate federal forest lands, and he became the first chief of the U.S. Forest Service. Yet even Pinchot believed that scenic areas should not be preserved if a "better"—that is, more utilitarian—use could be found for them. National forest lands were being leased to private timber companies and cleared, and there was little interest in acquiring and protecting more acreage.

Even more alarming was the rate at which privately owned forest land was being cleared. Private companies were not farsighted, and they cleared their land without adequately replanting. The total area covered by forest was rapidly shrinking, and the land might never recover if more careful reforesting plans were not put into effect. Forest tracts of hundreds of thousands of acres were rapidly disappearing. There were, however, a few men who actively worked for wilderness conservation in the early part of the century and who won a place for conservation in national policy. Some of these men, such as John Muir and Aldo Leopold, were well known during their lifetimes and on to the end of the twentieth century. Marshall was a quieter figure who devoted a short life to public service and to solitary travel. He never achieved great fame, but his work had important and lasting effects.

As a bureaucrat and a well-educated conservationist, Marshall wrote government reports and scientific articles outlining his plans for national wilderness areas. With *The People's Forests*, he brought his case to the citizens, the common people who would most benefit from his plans. He gave them enough statistical information to understand what was happening to the forests and presented it in a clear, easy-to-read, and passionate style. He urged them to consider the effects of increased mechanization on their lives and to find peace by spending time in the forest.

The result was not a great public outcry. There were no public demonstrations, no boycotts, no letter-writing campaigns. Yet the stage was set for Marshall to use the powers of bureaucracy. In 1933, he was director of forestry for the Bureau of Indian Affairs, and he encouraged Native Americans to manage the natural resources on reservation lands wisely. He also worked to limit public roads on reservations so that reservation residents would be able to limit their contact with outsiders.

In 1935, dissatisfied with the support he received from other bureaucrats, Marshall joined Leopold and others to form the Wilderness Society. Marshall put up part of his own family fortune to support the group's lobbying and educational efforts. In 1937, Marshall became chief of the new Division of Recreation and Lands in the Forest Service. He was sure his stance on preserving forests was right, and he was encouraged by public response to the Wilderness Society and to *The People's Forests*. As chief, he worked hard to protect large wilderness areas within national forests and to keep them from being leased to timber companies or overdeveloped. He never forgot that the forests belonged to the people, however; in overseeing recreational developments in the national forests, he tried to make sure that provisions were made for visitors from all income groups.

Shortly before his sudden death in 1939, Marshall pushed for the adoption of a new set of Forest Service rules called the U-Regulations. Supported by the chief of the Forest Service, Ferdinand A. Silcox, these regulations established three categories of primitive areas within the national forest: U-1 Wilderness areas of more than 100,000 acres, which could have grazing and emergency access but no roads, timber harvesting, or motorized transportation; U-2 Wild areas of 5,000 to 100,000 acres, managed as wilderness; and U-3 Recreation areas, in which some timber cutting would be permitted away from scenic views. These new rules were stronger than the regulations they replaced and should have protected the people's forests.

Unfortunately, after Marshall died there was no one in the Forest Service to take up his fight; Silcox died during the same year. Soon afterward, World War II demanded the government's attention, and conservation was largely forgotten. Private groups such as the Wilderness Society and the Sierra Club were disappointed as the U-Regulations were poorly enforced during the next two decades. Not until the late 1950's did the government again show a strong interest in conservation. This renewed call, which echoed the language and arguments Marshall had set down in *The People's Forests*, led eventually to the passage of the Wilderness Act of 1964.

—*Cynthia A. Bily*

FURTHER READING

Allin, Craig W. *The Politics of Wilderness Preservation.* Westport, Conn.: Greenwood Press, 1982. A political scientist's view of American wilderness policy throughout the nation's history. According to the author, when the nation was new, government policy was directed toward conquering and exploiting the wilderness; more recent public policy seeks to protect it. How this change has come about, shaped by tension between economic and social needs, is the subject of this rather scholarly work.

Fox, Stephen. *John Muir and His Legacy: The American Conservation Movement.* Boston: Little, Brown,

1981. An important and insightful biography of the famous naturalist John Muir. This book looks beyond Muir's life to the 1980's, providing a history of the conservation movement and its most colorful characters, including Robert Marshall.

Frome, Michael. *Battle for the Wilderness*. New York: Praeger, 1974. Part 1 traces the importance of the wilderness to American artists and authors, including Henry David Thoreau, John Muir, and Robert Marshall. Part 2 gives the history of the American conservation movement and calls on the reader to support conservation philosophy and policy.

_____. *The Forest Service*. 2d ed. Boulder, Colo.: Westview Press, 1984. Frome, a journalist, has more than twenty-five years of experience with the Forest Service and its leaders. He formed clear opinions about the agency's strengths and weaknesses through this contact and through extensive research into the earlier history of the agency, and he gives a balanced view of them in this book.

Hays, Samuel P. *Conservation and the Gospel of Efficiency*. 1959. Reprint. Pittsburgh: University of Pittsburgh Press, 1999. A seminal work on the early history of conservation. Argues that the movement began as a search for greater efficiency in resource management, not as a democratic crusade against supposed business rapacity.

Merchant, Carolyn. *The Columbia Guide to American Environmental History*. New York: Columbia University Press, 2002. Discusses how humans and environment have interacted throughout American history, including human impacts on animal species.

Includes an environmental history time line and an extensive guide to resources.

Nash, Roderick Frazier. *Wilderness and the American Mind*. 4th ed. New Haven, Conn.: Yale University Press, 2001. An exploration of the physiological and psychological significance of wilderness, especially for Americans of European descent. The book looks backward to prehistoric humans, treats notions of the wilderness in classical and medieval Europe, and focuses on American efforts to define, explore, and conquer the wilderness up to the end of the twentieth century.

Wellman, J. Douglas. *Wildland Recreation Policy: An Introduction*. New York: John Wiley & Sons, 1987. Recounts the history of national parks and wilderness areas and analyzes their management. Instead of attempting to cover every regulation and agency, the author focuses on the careers and thoughts of key people, including Robert Marshall.

SEE ALSO: May, 1903: Roosevelt and Muir Visit Yosemite; Jan. 3, 1905: Pinchot Becomes Head of the U.S. Forest Service; Jan. 5, 1905: National Audubon Society Is Established; Feb. 1, 1919: Lenin Approves the First Soviet Nature Preserve; Jan., 1922: Izaak Walton League Is Formed; 1924: Soviets Establish a Society for the Protection of Nature; June 3, 1924: Gila Wilderness Area Is Designated; May, 1927: Indiana Dunes Are Preserved as a State Park; May 30, 1930: Canadian National Parks Act; Oct. 19, 1934: Marshall and Leopold Form the Wilderness Society; 1938: John Muir Trail Is Completed.

1933

September 8, 1933
WORK BEGINS ON THE GRAND COULEE DAM

The Grand Coulee Dam was designed to pump water from the Columbia River, convey it more than one hundred miles to the south, and use the water to irrigate more than one million acres of arid land while simultaneously generating electricity.

LOCALE: Eastern Washington State
CATEGORIES: Engineering; environmental issues; natural resources; energy

KEY FIGURES
James O'Sullivan (1876-1949), teacher, lawyer, self-taught engineer, and tireless proponent of the Grand Coulee Dam
Rufus Woods (1878-1950), editor and publisher of several newspapers and an enthusiastic advocate of the dam

SUMMARY OF EVENT

The biggest, most powerful hydroelectric dam in North America was built as an irrigation project. Its construction marked the end of a battle of conflicting interests that had waxed and waned over thirty years. Originally, the plan had been to use the channel—the Grand Coulee—cut by the Columbia River during the Ice Age to distribute some of its waters to the arid land of southeastern Washington. (Steep, dry gulches in the American West are often called "arroyos" in areas historically influenced by the Spanish; in more French-influenced regions, such gulches are often referred to as "coulees.") This particular dry gulch, among the largest known, was a very straight valley that extended fifty miles to the south and was one thousand feet deep and two miles wide. The Grand Coulee, however, was six hundred feet above the floor of the Columbia River.

Clearly, the river had cut a channel far above its present course. Glacial forces had deposited a huge pile of ice and debris to form a natural dam where the Grand Coulee Dam was constructed, and this natural dam—which was much larger than the present dam—impounded a lake that stretched into Canada. Initially, the pile of ice and debris was higher than the bedrock wall at Grand Coulee, so when the lake was full, the glacial Columbia River would overflow through this valley. Its flow eroded the valley floor and produced magnificent waterfalls through the hard basalt. At the same time, rain and snow fell on the ice and debris of the dam. Although this precipitation had much less erosive power than did the Co-

lumbia River, it was only working on ice and unconsolidated soils, and it was eventually able to erode the dam to the level of the lake. When the dam failed, all the water stored behind it rushed through, causing a catastrophic flood. The Grand Coulee was left high and dry by the river, which now could return to its earlier course.

Thousands of years later, in 1918, engineers proposed the return of some of the Columbia River's water to the abandoned channel. The goal was to irrigate the Columbia basin, an area of nearly one million acres that had been inhabited, cleared, and farmed by homesteaders who settled there in the 1890's. Mountains to the west of the basin caused the moist air coming in from the Pacific Ocean to rise and cool, wringing out its moisture on the western slopes and creating a rain shadow to the east where these settlers were trying to eke out a living. As farmers began to understand that the average natural precipitation would not be adequate for agriculture, they either left the region or tried to develop irrigation.

If this situation had occurred in a modern, environmentally aware society, relocation subsidies for the residents of the basin might have been provided. The Columbia basin itself might have been seen as a vast wilderness area, and adequate funding might have restored it to its original pristine condition. Wilderness, however, was not seen as valuable at that time. Instead, growth and development were paramount. The U.S. Reclamation Service had been formed in 1902 in order to convert much of the arid and semiarid land of the American West into productive acreage.

Water for irrigation was generally sought at elevations that were higher than the land to be irrigated, and aqueducts, tunnels, and canals were used to transport and distribute the water. Such plans for the Columbia basin generally had the Pend Oreille Lake or Pend Oreille River, a tributary of the Columbia River in Idaho, as their water source. The idea of letting power from a dam pump water up to a natural distribution channel was new and widely derided.

Much of the opposition to the dam, and support for the gravity plan, came from private electric-power companies in Washington. These companies knew how much power could be generated from this river, and they were not eager to have competition from an irrigation project. Furthermore, excess water from the gravity system would have ended up in the Columbia River, where it could supply additional generating capacity for the private power companies during the winter, when flow was diminished.

Other opposition came from the East, where people still considered Washington State to be wilderness area with little need for electricity. Many people were concerned that government ownership of power production was a step toward socialism, and some argued that the federal government should not get involved in local politics. James O'Sullivan, a lawyer and schoolteacher, and Rufus Woods, the editor and publisher of the Wenatchee *World*, led the fight for the high dam for thirty years. In the end, they triumphed, and construction began. As World War II developed, it became clear that the need for greater generating capacity was of much greater strategic importance than additional agricultural acreage, and so resources were allocated to the dam and its power generators and were withheld from the irrigation part of the project. The dam began producing electricity in 1941, but it would be another eleven years before it began to irrigate the Columbia basin.

SIGNIFICANCE

The Grand Coulee Dam is 4,173 feet long and 500 feet thick at its base, and it stands 550 feet above bedrock. It contains 10,230,776 cubic yards of concrete and weighs twenty-two million tons. It impounds the Franklin Delano Roosevelt Lake, which stretches 150 miles from the Grand Coulee to Canada. At the time construction began it was the largest dam in the world, and it has remained the largest concrete structure in the United States.

More than any other dam, the Grand Coulee Dam symbolized man's attempt to subordinate nature. Often called the "eighth wonder of the world," the dam drew huge crowds of tourists who marveled at its engineering, and Woody Guthrie wrote a folk song about it. Power generated by the dam was used to create aluminum used

1933

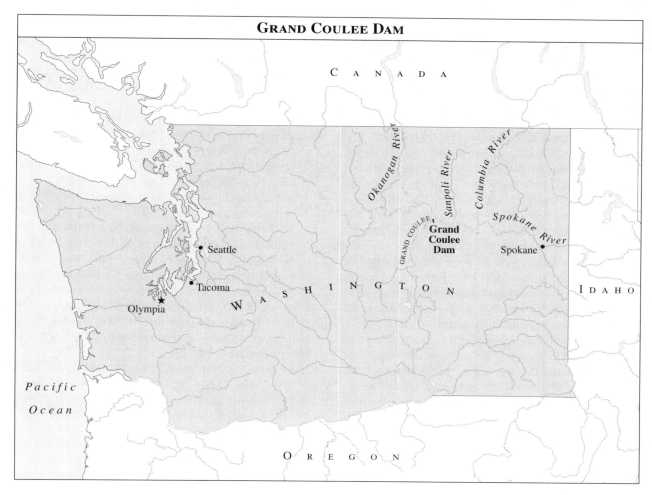

GRAND COULEE DAM

in aircraft in World War II and permitted the expansion of industry into the American Northwest. Many saw the dam as the key to progress and prosperity, and soon dams were being built all over the country. Thirteen were built on the Columbia River alone.

The original Grand Coulee Dam could generate about 2,000 megawatts of electricity. Additional power-generation capability was subsequently added, so that by 1991 it had a rated capacity of 9,070 megawatts and a planned capacity of 10,830 megawatts. It housed one of the largest hydroelectric plants in the world. Other large dams include the Guri Dam in Venezuela, which has a rated and planned capacity of 10,300 megawatts, and the Itaipu Dam in Brazil and Paraguay, which has a rated capacity of 7,400 megawatts and a planned capacity of 13,320 megawatts.

If the dam operates nonstop for one year, it produces about 80 billion kilowatt-hours, or about 0.25 quads (quadrillion BTU) of power. In 1990, all 112 nuclear power plants operating in the United States together produced 577 billion kilowatt-hours of power. Roughly speaking, then, the Grand Coulee Dam could generate as much electricity as 15 nuclear reactors. It would take 30 million tons of coal, or 20 million tons of oil, to produce this much energy each year, and burning this much oil would add 6.25 million tons of carbon to the atmosphere in the form of carbon dioxide every year.

The dam's most direct cost was the loss of a wild and scenic stretch of the Columbia River. Had the Grand Coulee Dam been the last dam created on the Columbia, the loss of this stretch might have been less significant, but the Grand Coulee Dam's success encouraged the construction of other dams. In the United States alone, some 75,000 dams have been constructed, each of which wiped out a stretch of wild river. Unfortunately, often the most scenic, beautiful spots are those most desirable for dam construction. As the supply of wild and scenic rivers diminished, the value of those remaining increased. By some estimates, only 9 percent of river miles in the lower forty-eight states remain undeveloped.

The irrigation of the Columbia basin also had significant impact. Historically, the dry climate and basalt flows made water too scarce for many plants to grow. However, the soil in this region is very fertile, and the arid climate permits an exceptional growing season, with many clear, sunny days. Once the Grand Coulee Dam delivered water, orchards and fields in the half million acres irrigated by the dam became some of the most productive in the country. Such agricultural accomplishments came at a cost, however. Orchards and hop yards

in the East suffered with the new competition. Furthermore, the long-term effects of irrigation on the environment in the Columbia basin are not yet known: Evaporation from the huge lake and the diversion of six billion gallons of water per day during the growing season may be causing subtle changes in the Columbia River.

—*Otto H. Muller*

FURTHER READING

Borah, Leo A. "From Sagebrush to Roses on the Columbia." *National Geographic* 102 (November, 1952): 571-611. Written shortly after the arrival of the first irrigation waters from the Grand Coulee Dam, this article celebrates the transformation of "desolate and useless" land into fertile farms. The bias is strongly in favor of development, as environmental concerns were uncommon in the early 1950's.

Boyer, David S. "Powerhouse of the Northwest." *National Geographic* 146 (December, 1974): 820-847. This beautifully illustrated article about life along the Columbia River gives a picture of the costs and benefits of the dams and the changes they have produced. Includes several personal viewpoints that tend to point out the human and environmental costs. It is written with a bias in favor of environmentalism and against development.

Merchant, Carolyn. *The Columbia Guide to American Environmental History*. New York: Columbia University Press, 2002. Discusses how humans and environment have interacted throughout American history, including human impacts on animal species. Includes an environmental history time line and an extensive guide to resources.

Moss, Frank E. *The Water Crisis*. New York: Praeger, 1967. A good general background to water resource development throughout the country. Written from the perspective of a U.S. senator who was very active in water legislation, it begins by deploring the squandering of many of the nation's resources, and argues that if proper planning had occurred, much larger dams could have been constructed, and there would have been less waste.

Nash, Roderick Frazier. *Wilderness and the American Mind*. 4th ed. New Haven, Conn.: Yale University Press, 2001. Intellectual history of Americans' relationship with the wilderness, beginning with the earliest days of European contact. Includes bibliography and index.

Sundborg, George. *Hail Columbia*. New York: Macmillan, 1954. This thorough book develops the story of the Grand Coulee Dam as it follows the life of James O'Sullivan, who is probably the individual most responsible for its creation. Tiny details, such as the age and type of car he drove, add color to an elaborate account of this man's commitment to the idea of a high dam on the Columbia. Permits the reader to appreciate the glacial pace at which support for the dam actually progressed.

U.S. Department of the Interior. *The Columbia River.* Washington, D.C.: Government Printing Office, 1947. This comprehensive report details the development of the water resources of the Columbia River.

The weather, soil, and wildlife in each of the seven subdivisions of the drainage basin are described, and the past, present, and future development activity is outlined. Prospective sites for power dams are listed. Seven large maps, dozens of page-sized maps, and illustrations.

SEE ALSO: June 17, 1902: Reclamation Act Promotes Western Agriculture; Dec. 19, 1913: U.S. Congress Approves a Dam in Hetch Hetchy Valley; 1923: Federal Power Commission Disallows Kings River Dams; Mar. 11, 1936: Boulder Dam Is Completed.

Fall, 1933-October 20, 1949
LEWIS CONVENES THE INKLINGS

C. S. Lewis united a group of Oxford professors and friends who came to call themselves the Inklings. The group met once a week to read from new works and discuss topics of interest. Some of the most famous works of modern fantasy, particularly The Lord of the Rings *(1955), might never have emerged without these meetings.*

LOCALE: Oxford, England
CATEGORY: Literature

KEY FIGURES
C. S. Lewis (1898-1963), author and professor of English at Oxford and Cambridge Universities
J. R. R. Tolkien (1892-1973), author and professor of Anglo-Saxon at Oxford University
Charles Williams (1886-1945), author, editor at Oxford University Press, and lecturer in English at Oxford University
Warren Lewis (1895-1973), author, army major, and brother of C. S. Lewis
Owen Barfield (1898-1997), author, anthroposophist, and solicitor
Hugo Dyson (1896-1975), professor of English at Reading and Oxford Universities
Christopher Tolkien (b. 1924), son of J. R. R. Tolkien and editor of his father's voluminous papers

SUMMARY OF EVENT
In hindsight, the formation of the Inklings seems almost predestined, for such groups were common in the Oxbridge (a synthesis of "Oxford" and "Cambridge" connoting British academic circles) life of the time, and

both of the founding members, C. S. Lewis and J. R. R. Tolkien, had belonged to similar groups. At University College, Oxford, were the Martlets, an informal literary society at which Lewis read papers, and during the 1920's Lewis attended meetings of philosophy dons (instructors) called the Wee Teas. At King Edward's School in Birmingham, Tolkien belonged to a small group of informal friends who called themselves the Tea Club and Barrovian Society, and this group had a meeting that Tolkien called the Council of London.

Tolkien and Lewis first became acquainted during Tolkien's attempts to reform the English syllabus at Oxford as a member of a group called the Cave or the Junto. Lewis eventually joined Tolkien's cause, and the two soon got into the habit of meeting every Monday morning for an hour or so over beer. Lewis had earlier instituted what he called evenings of "Beer and Beowulf" for his pupils. This later metamorphosed into the Coalbiters, a group of dons who read old Norse sagas under the direction of Tolkien and others. So, when like-minded friends took the name "Inklings" from a group that an undergraduate, Edward Tangye Lean, had formed and began meeting in Lewis's rooms in Magdalen College on Thursday nights, they were taking another step in the evolution of such groups.

Lewis loved to hear, read, and comment on his friends' work, and he loved to get feedback on his own work. Owen Barfield, whom Lewis met as an undergraduate, had read and commented on Lewis's *Dymer* (1926), a book of poetry. In 1929, Tolkien had offered his poem about Beren and Luthien to Lewis, who responded with a mock-critical analysis, and just before the Inklings began meeting, Lewis read an early version of Tolkien's *The Hobbit* (1937). From the beginning, then, the Inklings shared scholarly and imaginative works with sympathetic friends.

Lewis and Tolkien had similar tastes in literature, but Lewis had read far more widely in postmedieval literature. Little is known about the Inklings' early meetings or their subsequent weekly meetings at the Oxford pub the Eagle and the Child (affectionately called the Bird and the Baby), because after Lewis's brother Warren returned home from China, Lewis stopped corresponding with him, and Warren did not keep a diary covering those years. However, when Warren Lewis returned to the army at the beginning of World War II, C. S. Lewis began writing to him again, and these letters, along with Warren's resumed diary, provide the best evidence about the Inklings' meetings.

The Lewis brothers and Tolkien formed the group's cornerstones. Owen Barfield and Hugo Dyson also became famous members, but their attendance was sporadic until Dyson was hired at Oxford in 1945. Less famous members of the group included Dr. Robert "Humphrey" Havard, physician to the Lewises and the Tolkien family; Adam Fox, dean of divinity and professor of poetry at Oxford; Lord David Cecil, critic and Oxford English don; and Neville Coghill, Oxford English don. Later additions included author John Wain, a pupil of Lewis, and Tolkien's son Christopher joined after he returned from World War II. By far the most important addition, however, was Charles Williams, whose novel *The Place of the Lion* (1931) earned Lewis's immediate admiration. Williams was a regular member of the Inklings from 1939 (when his employer, Oxford University Press, had to move to Oxford from London because of the war) until his death in 1945. Other members came and went; the chief requirement for permanent membership was C. S. Lewis's approval.

Admirers of these authors' literary works might wish to have attended one of these sessions, when Tolkien read from the "new Hobbit" (as they called *The Lord of the Rings*) or when Lewis read from *Perelandra* (1943), which Tolkien admired immensely. However, friction certainly existed among group members. Williams was the first major figure to come between Tolkien and Lewis, and while Lewis was a Williams fan, Tolkien was not. Dyson disliked hobbits, and he once vetoed a proposed reading from *The Lord of the Rings*. (He also threatened to leave the group if any more Roman Catholics were admitted.)

The Inklings lost much of their momentum when Williams died, and by the late 1940's the group was largely sustained by the prospect of another ham supper (one of Lewis's fans in the United States sent food parcels to England, where strict rationing was still in effect in the postwar period). The Thursday meetings petered out in late 1949, but reading of *The Lord of the Rings* had ceased by 1947, and none of Lewis's Narnia stories (published as *Chronicles of Narnia* from 1950 through 1956) were read to the group. The last ham supper was held on October 20, 1949.

SIGNIFICANCE

When the works of the main Inkling authors began to grow immensely popular and reminiscences about the group became more widely known, researchers quickly undertook studies that tried to gauge the group's influence on the works. Most of these studies were dismissed by those who knew the group best, however. Upon reading one such study by Charles Moorman in 1967, Warren Lewis wrote, "I smiled at the thought of Tollers [Tolkien] being under the influence of Moorman's group mind." Lewis realized that Tolkien, the most obdurate of the group, resisted most attempts to change his subject matter or style.

It was C. S. Lewis who was the most open to influence, whether it was by Tolkien's use of language (many of Tolkien's invented words turn up in Lewis's works) or by Williams's view of the penetration of the supernatural into the real world. Disagreements among group members certainly existed; Tolkien, for example, disliked Lewis's famous book *The Screwtape Letters* (1942). Lewis was quite stubborn in his own way, however, and the group's disapprobation may not have reached him.

C. S. Lewis was a bit disingenuous when he claimed the Inklings were "only a circle of Christian friends by a good fire." Although some of the group's members produced works that had nothing to do with religion or quasi-allegorical subjects, including Warren Lewis's excellent books on France at the time of Louis XIV, other examples of Inklings' works were clearly related. It has been convincingly suggested, for example, that Tolkien's semiautobiographical allegory "Leaf by Niggle" (1945) was influenced by Williams's fiction. Whatever the extent of their influence on one another, the Inlings' encouragement of one another's work was crucial. C. S. Lewis once wondered whether *The Lord of the Rings* would be popular outside the warmth of the fire of their little group, but the enthusiastic reception it received from Warren Lewis and Dr. Havard, both intelligent yet unscholarly readers, convinced Lewis that their appreciation would be echoed by millions of other readers.

— *William Laskowski*

FURTHER READING

Carpenter, Humphrey. *The Inklings: C. S. Lewis, J. R. R. Tolkien, Charles Williams, and Their Friends*. Boston: Houghton Mifflin, 1979. Volume by a biographer of Tolkien includes not only some valuable insights on the Inklings but also some of the most level-headed consideration of Lewis available in print.

Duriez, Colin. *Tolkien and C. S. Lewis: The Gift of Friendship*. Mahwah, N.J.: Hidden Spring, 2003. Presents often pedestrian and partisan analysis (Lewis did have a major problem with women), but benefits from the use of a great deal of new material on Tolkien and Lewis.

Duriez, Colin, and David Porter. *The Inklings Handbook: The Lives, Thought, and Writings of C. S. Lewis, J. R. R. Tolkien, Charles Williams, Owen Barfield, and Their Friends*. St. Louis, Mo.: Chalice Press, 2001. Handy compendium of data, although the arguments presented are sometimes rather obvious. Somewhat misleading at times; for example, Warren Lewis's alcoholism is mentioned, but not in the essay on him.

Lewis, C. S. *Books, Broadcasts, and War, 1931-1949*. Vol. 2 in *Collected Letters*, edited by Walter Hooper. New York: HarperSanFrancisco, 2004. A valuable primary source on Inkling meetings, this edition of Lewis's letters is by far the most comprehensive and gives much of the flavor of the man. Includes useful notes and biographical appendixes.

_____, ed. *Essays Presented to Charles Williams*. Oxford, England: Oxford University Press, 1947. The most tangible production of the Inklings as Inklings (with one essay by the quasi Inkling Dorothy Sayers). Includes extremely important essays by Lewis and Tolkien on writing stories.

Lewis, Warren. *Brothers and Friends: The Diaries of Major Warren Hamilton Lewis*. Edited by Clyde Kilby and Marjorie Mead. San Francisco: Harper & Row, 1982. A valuable primary source, especially about the Inkling meetings during the 1940's. Warren Lewis is an interesting author in his own right.

SEE ALSO: 1905: Baker Establishes the 47 Workshop at Harvard; Fall, 1905: Stein Holds Her First Paris Salons; Sept. 30, 1925: Chesterton Critiques Modernism and Defends Christianity; Winter, 1932: Huxley's *Brave New World* Forecasts Technological Totalitarianism; Sept., 1937: Tolkien Redefines Fantasy Literature; 1938-1950: Golden Age of American Science Fiction.

1933

October 18, 1933
ROOSEVELT CREATES THE COMMODITY CREDIT CORPORATION

Established as a supplement to the crop reduction program of the Agricultural Adjustment Act of 1933, the Commodity Credit Corporation became the major instrument for implementing government farm price supports.

LOCALE: Washington, D.C.
CATEGORIES: Agriculture; government and politics; trade and commerce

KEY FIGURES

Franklin D. Roosevelt (1882-1945), president of the United States, 1933-1945
Charles W. Macune (1851-1940), leader whose subtreasury plan foreshadowed the Commodity Credit Corporation
Herbert Hoover (1874-1964), president of the United States, 1929-1933

Lynn P. Talley (1881-1942), Texas banker, president of the Commodity Credit Corporation from 1933 to 1940
Henry A. Wallace (1888-1965), U.S. secretary of agriculture, 1933-1940
Jesse H. Jones (1874-1956), chairman of the Reconstruction Finance Corporation, 1933-1945
Harry S. Truman (1884-1972), president of the United States, 1945-1953

SUMMARY OF EVENT

The agricultural sector of the U.S. economy began a decline in the early 1920's, and the general slump in the economy following the stock market crash in the fall of 1929 aggravated the situation. The crux of the farm problem was overproduction. Crops that exceeded domestic demand pushed prices down to the low levels

prevailing in world markets. The solution adopted by
President Franklin D. Roosevelt and incorporated in
the Agricultural Adjustment Act of 1933 was the Voluntary Domestic Allotment Plan. The idea was to reduce production so that prices would rise to parity, a
level at which each commodity would have the same
purchasing power as it had during the period from 1909
to 1914. The mechanism for achieving that goal was to
pay farmers who agreed to limit the number of acres they
cultivated. The program covered seven basic commodities: wheat, cotton, corn, hogs, rice, tobacco, and milk.
Later additions to the list included rye, flax, barley, grain
sorghum, cattle, sheep, peanuts, sugar beets, sugar cane,
and potatoes.

Farmers had long complained about short-term fluctuations in prices. Most farmers had to sell their crops at
or soon after harvest, when prices were artificially depressed by the influx into the market. At the same time,
the Roosevelt administration was under heavy pressure
to do something to give an immediate boost to agricultural prices and put cash into farmers' hands. In response,
Roosevelt's Executive Order 6340 of October 18, 1933,
established the Commodity Credit Corporation. The
agency had $3 million that could be used to make low-
interest loans available to farmers so that they could hold
their crops off the market. The loans, however, were to be
limited to those who signed the Agricultural Adjustment
Administration (AAA) acreage limitation contracts.
These were nonrecourse loans, meaning that if the market price rose above the loan level, the grower could repay the loan and sell the crop. If the price fell below the
loan level, the grower could have the loan canceled without liability; the Commodity Credit Corporation would
take over the crop and thus bear the loss.

The roots of the Commodity Credit Corporation lay in
the farm protest movements of the late nineteenth century. Many of the protesters blamed the decline in farm
prices, which began in the 1870's, on an insufficient supply of money. Failure of the money supply to expand to
meet the needs of a growing economy was in turn blamed
on the gold standard. A popular solution recommended
that the money supply—and thus farm prices—be inflated by the issue of paper money. The most ambitious
of those proposals was the "subtreasury" plan advanced
in the late 1880's and early 1890's by Texas farm protest leader Charles W. Macune. Macune proposed that
every county in which a minimum of $500,000 worth
of agricultural produce was sold a year should have a
subtreasury office along with crop storage facilities.
Farmers who brought in their crop for storage would be

advanced 80 percent of the local price in paper money at
an interest charge of 1 percent a year, on the condition
that the produce be redeemed or sold at auction within
one year. Support for the plan faded even among farmers because of the appeal of William Jennings Bryan's
call for free silver as the solution to the money-supply
problem.

The more direct antecedents of the Commodity Credit
Corporation lay in the agricultural programs introduced
by President Herbert Hoover. The major thrust of Hoover's solution to the farm problem, incorporated in the
Agricultural Marketing Act of 1929 and administered by
the Federal Farm Board, was government assistance to
promote better-organized and more orderly marketing of
agricultural products through larger and stronger cooperative marketing associations. The cooperative marketing associations set up under the new law, such as the
Farmers National Grain Corporation and the National
Wool Marketing Corporation, included programs in
which farmers could receive an advance on delivery of
their crop for later resale. A tool meant to iron out short-
term fluctuations in price, the legislation provided for the
establishment of "stabilization corporations" that would
purchase farm products at harvest time and would resell
them when prices rose. When prices for cotton, corn, and
wheat fell sharply after the stock market crash, the stabilization corporations made large-scale purchases in a fu-
tile bid to sustain prices. The resulting losses exhausted
most of the $500 million revolving fund allotted to the
Federal Farm Board and forced suspension of stabilization corporation purchases.

SIGNIFICANCE

The Commodity Credit Corporation was a continuation
of the Federal Farm Board's stabilization corporations,
but with more generous funding. Its $3 million in start-
up capital was supplied by the secretary of agriculture
and governor of the Farm Credit Administration from
funds provided by the National Industrial Recovery Act
(1933). During its early years, however, most funding
came as loans from the Reconstruction Finance Corporation (RFC). Although technically a corporation organized under the laws of Delaware, the Commodity
Credit Corporation was largely administered as an RFC
subsidiary. Lynn P. Talley, a Texas banker who was a
longtime friend of Jesse H. Jones, chairman of the RFC,
was made president of the new agency and retained
that position until health problems forced his retirement
in early 1940. Under Roosevelt's 1939 reorganization
of the executive branch, the Commodity Credit Corpo-

ration became a part of the Department of Agriculture and was wholly responsible to the secretary of agriculture. Although Congress placed the Commodity Credit Corporation on a statutory basis in January, 1935, the agency continued to depend on periodic renewals of its authorization until June, 1948, when Congress gave it permanent status.

Although the Commodity Credit Corporation had authority to make loans directly to farmers, few were made in that fashion. The agency's managers preferred to encourage private banks to extend loans by guaranteeing that the Commodity Credit Corporation would, on demand, buy all such loans. Even this guarantee failed to overcome private bankers' nervousness about the soundness of farm loans, however, and as a result, most of the loans were made by the Commodity Credit Corporation itself, with private lending agencies acting only as brokers. Thanks to the strength of the farm bloc in Congress, the agency had even larger amounts of money to lend, and its capital was raised to $100 million in 1938. More important, lawmakers repeatedly increased its authority to borrow on the credit of the United States: Farmers could borow $900 million in 1939, $1.4 billion in 1940, $2.65 billion in 1941, and $10 billion by 1954. The Agricultural Adjustment Act of 1938 shifted the major thrust of the Commodity Credit Corporation from ironing out short-term fluctuations in supplies and prices to a new goal of maintaining farm prices above their free-market levels. The agency's mission thus became one of subsidization rather than stabilization.

The Commodity Credit Corporation's first major loan undertaking, the corn program of 1933-1934, proved successful because of a drought that caused a sharp reduction in the size of the 1934 corn crop and therefore increased the price per bushel. Most of the loans were repaid, and the Commodity Credit Corporation even made a profit on the operation. This success inspired Secretary of Agriculture Henry A. Wallace to urge a permanent commodity-loan program for maintaining an ever-normal granary—that is, stabilization of supplies and prices through loans that allowed farmers to withhold part of their crops from the market in years of high output and release them in years of short production.

The ever-normal granary idea was a handy rationale for permanent establishment of the Commodity Credit Corporation. The decisive factor in its transformation into the major instrument for long-term farm price maintenance was the failure of the production-limitation program of the Agricultural Adjustment Act of 1933 and its successor, the Soil Conservation and Domestic Allot-

ment Act of 1936. This failure was partly the result of the lack of voluntary cooperation from farmers and partly the result of contract violations by cooperating farmers. The major difficulty faced by the corporation was that advances in technology were rapidly increasing output per acre.

When the Agricultural Adjustment Act of 1938 was written, Farm Belt lobbyists managed to include directing the Commodity Credit Corporation to make mandatory nonrecourse loans on a number of crops whenever their prices fell too low or their production rose too high. Such loans were available only to those who cooperated with the legislation's acreage limitation program, in which the major crops were cotton, corn, and wheat. As of 1940, however, the Commodity Credit Corporation was making loans on butter, dates, figs, hops, mohair, peanuts, pecans, prunes, raisins, rye, tobacco, turpentine and rosin, and wool. Congress also repeatedly raised the loan rate and offered higher guaranteed prices.

Given the continued failure of meaningful production limitations, the net effect was to give farmers a virtually blank check from the treasury, and the Commodity Credit Corporation accumulated increasingly large collections of stocks and commodities as more and more farmers defaulted on their loans. The carryover of cotton, for example, reached an all-time high of 13.3 million bales in 1939, more than a full year's supply for both domestic use and export. The carryover of corn rose to a record level of 687 million bushels in 1940, more than double the carryover of the early 1930's. Only World War II prevented what appeared to be the impending collapse of the farm-price support system.

As the price of allowing the imposition of wartime price ceilings on farm products, the farm bloc in Congress wrote into the Stabilization Act (or Anti-inflation Act) of October, 1942, a provision requiring the Commodity Credit Corporation to provide loans at 90 percent of parity for two years after the official end of hostilities for a broad range of crops, including cotton, corn, wheat, rice, tobacco, peanuts, hogs, chicken, eggs, milk, butterfat, and potatoes. This provision did not raise major difficulties because the exceptional need for foodstuffs abroad absorbed nearly all available production during 1946 and 1947. The Agricultural Act of 1948 continued the loan program of the Commodity Credit Corporation at 90 percent of parity until June 30, 1950, when a flexible system was supposed to support prices at a level ranging between 60 and 90 percent of parity, depending on production totals. The move to avoid the rigidities of the parity formula, however, was undone by the surprise victory of Democratic Party presidential nominee Harry S. Truman in the 1948 election, a victory that owed much to farmer discontent over falling prices.

The Agricultural Act of 1949 was largely a victory for those who favored high price supports. Commodity Credit Corporation loans remained the major instrument for implementing the price-support program, and its loan rate became farmers' minimum-price guarantee.

High price supports, coupled with rapid growth in agricultural productivity because of the continuing revolution in technology, brought larger and more burdensome surpluses that were only temporarily alleviated by the Korean War (1950-1953). The Agricultural Act of 1954 represented a victory for more flexible and market-oriented price supports, but it did not change the system's basic structure. As output continued to grow, so did the stock of farm commodities in government hands. Farmers' resistance blocked a bid by the administrations of John F. Kennedy and Lyndon B. Johnson to impose mandatory production controls. By the 1960's, however, even farm bloc lobbyists recognized that high price supports were having a damaging influence on U.S. farm exports. The Food and Agricultural Act of 1965 introduced a new gimmick that became a standard part of the farm program: the "two-price" plan. To make American products competitive in the international market, domestic price supports were reduced to the world-market level through Commodity Credit Corporation loans. Producers were then paid a deficiency payment that amounted to the difference between the loan rate and the official target (or ought-to-be) price.

Most agricultural economists agreed that this approach had major flaws. It saddled the federal government with a multibillion-dollar commitment whose costs were unpredictable and encouraged chronic overproduction. Because of the alarmingly high levels to which Commodity Credit Corporation inventories and loans had risen by 1983, Ronald Reagan's presidential administration introduced the payment-in-kind (or PIK) program, whereby farmers were paid to take land out of production in return for a payment of government-owned stocks rather than cash. The 1983 PIK program temporarily relieved the carryover problem, but falling export demand in the years that followed produced a major crisis, and farm subsidy costs skyrocketed to an estimated $26 billion in 1986 alone. Because farming interests remained sources of political power, the demand for subsidies remained high, and Congress usually responded to pressures from the farming industry. Subsidies distorted the marketplace, and this put pressure on the federal budget. These problems persisted into the early 2000's, as Congress made historic increases in farm subsidy levels that largely benefited the wealthiest farmers and agribusinesses.

—John Braeman

FURTHER READING

Benedict, Murray. *Can We Solve the Farm Problem? An Analysis of Federal Aid to Agriculture.* New York: Twentieth Century Fund, 1955. Analytic and evaluative. Chapter 10 has an excellent summary of Commodity Credit Corporation activities from 1933 up to the early 1950's.

_____. *Farm Policies of the United States, 1790-1950: A Study of Their Origins and Development.* New York: Twentieth Century Fund, 1953. An indispensable, comprehensive, and detailed history both of the demands of farmers and farm organizations and of government policies regarding agriculture.

Cochrane, Willard W., and C. Ford Runge. *Reforming Farm Policy: Toward a National Agenda.* Ames: Iowa State University Press, 1992. An illuminating critical analysis of the shortcomings of contemporary U.S. government farm programs by two leading agricultural economists. Offers recommendations for reform.

Cochrane, Willard W., and Mary E. Ryan. *American Farm Policy, 1948-1978.* Minneapolis: University of Minnesota Press, 1976. A history of the U.S. government's farm policies.

Gup, Benton E., ed. *Too Big to Fail: Policies and Practices in Government Bailouts.* Westport, Conn.: Praeger, 2004. Collection of essays includes discussion of the farming industries.

Hamilton, David E. *From New Day to New Deal: American Farm Policy from Hoover to Roosevelt, 1928-1933.* Chapel Hill: University of North Carolina Press, 1991. An important revisionist account that emphasizes, in contrast with most treatments of the New Deal, the large degree of continuity between the farm programs of the Herbert Hoover and Franklin D. Roosevelt administrations.

Hansen, John M. *Gaining Access: Congress and the Farm Lobby, 1919-1981.* Chicago: University of Chicago Press, 1991. An illuminating analysis of the politics of congressional farm policy making that documents the farm lobby's continuing success in gaining lavish subsidies for farmers despite their dwindling numbers.

Himmelberg, Robert F. *The Great Depression and the New Deal*. Westport, Conn.: Greenwood Press, 2000. Discusses the causes of the Depression and the actions taken in the United States to alleviate its effects. Features chronology, glossary, and index.

Olson, James S. *Saving Capitalism: The Reconstruction Finance Corporation in the New Deal, 1933-1940*. Princeton, N.J.: Princeton University Press, 1988. A thorough examination of the role of the Reconstruction Finance Corporation in the New Deal that includes coverage of the activities of the Commodity Credit Corporation during the years when it was virtually an RFC subsidiary.

Saloutos, Theodore. *The American Farmer and the New Deal*. Ames: Iowa State University Press, 1982. The most comprehensive treatment of New Deal agricultural programs.

SEE ALSO: June 17, 1902: Reclamation Act Promotes Western Agriculture; 1904: Canadian Cultivation of Marquis Wheat; June 15, 1929: Agricultural Marketing Act; Oct. 29, 1929-1939: Great Depression; Nov. 8, 1932: Franklin D. Roosevelt Is Elected U.S. President; 1934-1939: Dust Bowl Devastates the Great Plains; May 16, 1939: First U.S. Food Stamp Program Begins.

November-December, 1933
FERMI PROPOSES THE NEUTRINO THEORY OF BETA DECAY

Enrico Fermi used quantum mechanics to derive a theory of radioactive beta decay involving the neutrino and a new weak force of nuclear interactions, which led to many new elementary particle discoveries.

LOCALE: Rome, Italy
CATEGORIES: Science and technology; physics

KEY FIGURES

Enrico Fermi (1901-1954), Italian American nuclear physicist

Wolfgang Pauli (1900-1958), Austrian American theoretical physicist

Paul Adrien Maurice Dirac (1902-1984), British American theoretical physicist

Antoine-Henri Becquerel (1852-1908), French physicist

Hideki Yukawa (1907-1981), Japanese theoretical physicist

SUMMARY OF EVENT

Enrico Fermi's theory of beta decay solved one of the most puzzling problems of radioactivity and provided strong evidence for the existence of the neutrino and of a new type of weak force in nuclear interactions. Radioactivity was discovered by Antoine-Henri Becquerel in 1896 in the form of spontaneous and continuous radiation from various compounds of uranium that could penetrate layers of black paper to expose a photographic plate. Additional radioactive elements were discovered by Marie Curie and others in the next few years, and Ernest Rutherford demonstrated more than one type of

radiation from these materials in 1898 at the Cavendish Laboratory in Cambridge. He showed that one component could be absorbed by a single piece of paper, whereas another component was about one hundred times more penetrating. He called the short-range radiation alpha rays and the penetrating radiation beta rays.

By the end of 1899, Becquerel and several other researchers had shown that beta rays are deflected by a magnetic field in the same direction as cathode rays (electrons) and thus consist of negatively charged particles. In 1900, Paul Villard in France discovered an even more penetrating radiation that was not deflected by a magnetic field. These rays were eventually called gamma rays and were shown to be electromagnetic waves like X rays but with higher frequencies. Meanwhile, Becquerel showed that the deflection of beta particles was consistent with the behavior of electrons, with some of them ejected at speeds of up to about half the speed of light.

By 1903, Rutherford succeeded in observing a much smaller magnetic deflection of alpha rays in the direction of positively charged particles, and by 1909 he had identified them as positive helium ions (helium atoms that have lost their two electrons). Other differences between alpha and beta particles soon became evident. The deflection of alpha particles was found to be well collimated, whereas beta particle deflections formed a diffuse and extended image on a photographic plate. Thus alpha decay seemed to produce particles of a single velocity compared with beta particles with a variety of energies.

By the end of 1903 at McGill University in Montreal,

Rutherford and Frederick Soddy proposed that alpha and beta decay result from a transmutation of the atoms of one element into another. Eventually, it was shown that alpha decay produces a new element with atomic number (of nuclear protons) reduced by two and atomic mass number (protons and neutrons) reduced by four, corresponding to the charge and mass of the helium nucleus. Beta decay increases the atomic number by one with no change in atomic mass number.

The spontaneous energy associated with radioactive decay was at first a mystery that seemed to contradict the law of conservation of energy. This mystery was partially resolved with Albert Einstein's theory of relativity in 1905, which showed the equivalence of mass and energy and could account for radioactive energy from the decrease in mass between the parent and product nuclei. The energy of alpha particles was found to agree closely with this change in mass, but beta particles did not fit as well. By 1914, James Chadwick confirmed the continuous distribution of beta particle energies, in addition to some definite energies associated with so-called conversion electrons ejected from their orbits around the nucleus by gamma rays. The continuous beta energy spectrum was found to vary from small energies up to a maximum value that corresponded to the decrease in mass in the nuclear transmutation.

For several years, the problem of the continuous distribution of energies among beta particles perplexed physicists. Calorimeter measurements by Lise Meitner and others showed that the average energy of beta decay was only about one-third the value expected from the difference in masses of the parent and product nuclei. In his Faraday lecture of 1931, Niels Bohr suggested that energy conservation might not apply to beta decay. Additional problems arose with the quantum concept of particle spin, indicating that angular momentum might not be conserved in the beta decay of an electron with spin.

One way to save the conservation principles was suggested by Wolfgang Pauli at a meeting of the American Physical Society in Pasadena, California, in June, 1931. He suggested that the beta decay electrons might be accompanied by light neutral particles too penetrating to be observed or have any effect on a calorimeter experiment. The beta particle and the neutral particle would share the available energy so that their sum would be equal to the mass-energy difference between parent and product nuclei. Such a particle would have zero or near-zero rest mass, given that some beta electrons were at or near the maximum possible energy. It would be neutral to conserve charge and have spin equal to the electron spin but

possibly in the opposite direction to conserve angular momentum.

In Rome, Pauli's light neutral particle was called the neutrino (Italian diminutive form of the word "neutron") to distinguish it from the neutron, which was discovered by Chadwick in 1932 and shown to have a mass slightly greater than the proton. Pauli's neutrino hypothesis was first published in a report on discussions at the Solvay Conference on physics held in Brussels in October of 1933. After returning from the conference, Fermi began to develop a quantitative theory for the role of the neutrino in beta decay from the equations of quantum mechanics. He followed the same approach that Paul Adrien Maurice Dirac used in his 1928 relativistic quantum theory of photon emission and pair creation (particle and antiparticle). He postulated the simultaneous creation of an electron and an antineutrino (same as a neutrino except for spin) when a nuclear neutron converts into a proton during beta decay. In doing this, Fermi introduced a new

Enrico Fermi. (The Nobel Foundation)

weak force of much shorter range than the familiar gravitational and electromagnetic forces. The equation he derived for the probability of beta emission contained a coupling constant for the weak interaction that was determined from beta decay data to be 100 billion times smaller than the corresponding coupling constant in Dirac's theory of electromagnetic interactions. The weakness of this interaction is one factor in the relatively long half-life for beta decay.

Fermi sent his findings to the British journal *Nature* at the end of 1933, but it was promptly rejected. It was then accepted for publication in the German journal *Zeitschrift für Physik* in January, 1934. Fermi's theory successfully explained the exact form of the beta decay energy spectrum, the decay half-life, and its relation to beta particle energies, and other characteristics of beta decay. After the 1934 discovery of artificial radioactivity with positron (positive electrons) emission, physicists realized that Fermi's theory also fit this positive beta decay in which nuclear protons convert to neutrons by the emission of a positron and neutrino. The discovery of electron capture in 1937, in which a nuclear proton converts to a neutron by capturing one of its atomic electrons, could also be explained with Fermi's theory by assuming the emission of a neutrino. The beta decay theory was Fermi's theoretical masterpiece and the foundation for many new discoveries.

SIGNIFICANCE

Fermi's beta decay theory led to the development of new concepts of nuclear interactions and the discovery of new elementary particles. In 1935, Hideki Yukawa used the theories of Fermi and Dirac (for weak and electromagnetic interactions) as models for his theory of the strong nuclear force that holds protons and neutrons together in the nucleus. His theory included the prediction of the meson as the field quantum to transmit the strong interaction, and he also proposed a field quantum to mediate weak interactions in beta decay instead of the direct coupling used by Fermi. Yukawa showed that the meson would have mass equal to about two hundred electron masses; his theory implied a much larger mass for the field quantum to transmit weak interactions, now called the W-particle because of its much shorter range.

In 1937, a 207-electron-mass particle was discovered in cosmic rays, but Fermi and his associates showed that this so-called muon interacted with matter by a weak force. A 273-electron-mass particle, now called the pion, was discovered in 1947. It interacted by a strong force and matched the properties of Yukawa's meson. The

neutrino was more difficult to detect because it passed readily through matter. In 1956, C. L. Cowan and Frederick Reinries confirmed the effects of neutrinos near a nuclear reactor, where enough were produced for a few to interact with protons to yield nearly simultaneous neutrons and positrons, easily detected in this so-called reversed beta decay. By 1961, experiments revealed a difference between the electron neutrino of ordinary beta decay and the muon neutrino produced when pions decay into muons. Theories predicting a large production of neutrinos when stars explode were confirmed by the supernova of February, 1987, when about ten neutrino events were recorded in a Japanese detector.

The most important result of Fermi's beta decay theory was the development of a unified electroweak theory in 1967 by Steven Weinberg and independently by Abdus Salam. These researchers showed that the electromagnetic and weak interactions are different aspects of a single electroweak force requiring three new massive field quanta. The electroweak theory was dramatically confirmed in 1983 when a 135-member team led by Carlo Rubbia used proton collisions in a giant accelerator in Geneva to produce positive and negative W-particles with mass about eighty-five times the proton mass and neutral Z-particles with about ninety-seven proton masses, in exact agreement with the Weinberg-Salam theory.

—*Joseph L. Spradley*

FURTHER READING

Beyer, Robert T., ed. *Foundations of Nuclear Physics.* New York: Dover, 1949. This volume contains facsimile copies of a dozen foundational articles, including Fermi's original 1934 beta decay article in German, the 1932 article by Chadwick on the existence and mass of the neutron, and Yukawa's 1935 article on the meson theory of the strong nuclear force and beta decay. The second half of the book is a 120-page bibliography of the most important early articles on nuclear physics.

Cropper, William H. *Great Physicists: The Life and Times of Leading Physicists from Galileo to Hawking.* New York: Oxford University Press, 2001. Presents portraits of the lives and accomplishments of important physicists and shows how they influenced one another with their work, including Fermi, Pauli, and others. Includes glossary and index.

Eisberg, Robert, and Robert Resnick, ed. *Quantum Physics of Atoms, Molecules, Solids, Nuclei, and Particles.* 2d ed. New York: John Wiley & Sons, 1985. An intermediate-level college physics textbook with good sections on beta decay, Fermi's theory of weak interactions, and the electroweak theory. Theoretical results are discussed with equations, graphs, and diagrams, but without lengthy mathematical derivations.

Evans, Robley D. *The Atomic Nucleus.* New York: McGraw-Hill, 1955. A classic graduate-level textbook on nuclear physics with excellent historical documentation, with more than thirty pages of bibliography. A chapter on beta-ray spectra gives a good outline of experimental data and a twenty-page sketch of the mathematical details of Fermi's beta decay theory.

Glasstone, Samuel. *Sourcebook on Atomic Energy.* 3d ed. Princeton, N.J.: D. Van Nostrand, 1967. A well-organized introduction to atomic and nuclear physics with good historical detail. Chapters on radioactivity, nuclear radiations, and elementary particles provide good background on the discovery of beta decay, Fermi's theory, and the neutrino.

Piel, Gerard. *The Age of Science: What Scientists Learned in the Twentieth Century.* New York: Basic Books, 2001. An overview of the scientific achievements of the twentieth century. Includes many illustrations and index.

Polkinghorne, John. *Quantum Theory: A Very Short Introduction.* New York: Oxford University Press, 2002. Aims to make quantum theory accessible to the general reader. Among the concepts discussed are uncertainty, probabilistic physics, and the exclusion principle. Includes mathematical appendix and index.

Segrè, Emilio. *From X-Rays to Quarks: Modern Physicists and Their Discoveries.* San Francisco: W. H. Freeman, 1980. A very readable historical account of modern physics and of the personalities involved in it. A chapter on radioactivity and a brief treatment of Fermi's beta decay theory provide personal details by an early associate of Fermi. Many interesting historical photographs and diagrams are included.

Strachan, Charles. *The Theory of Beta-Decay.* Elmsford, New York: Pergamon Press, 1969. An introduction to the theory of beta decay, the neutrino, and weak interactions is given in part 1. In part 2, several original articles are reprinted, including an English translation of Fermi's 1934 article on beta decay.

SEE ALSO: Early 20th cent.: Elster and Geitel Study Radioactivity; Dec. 10, 1903: Becquerel Wins the Nobel Prize for Discovering Natural Radioactivity; 1905-1907: Boltwood Uses Radioactivity to Determine Ages of Rocks; Feb. 11, 1908: Geiger and Rutherford Develop a Radiation Counter; 1914: Rutherford Discovers the Proton; 1933-1934: First Artificial Radioactive Element Is Developed; Jan.-Sept., 1937: Segrè Identifies the First Artificial Element; Dec., 1938: Hahn Splits the Uranium Atom.

November 16, 1933
UNITED STATES RECOGNIZES RUSSIA'S BOLSHEVIK REGIME

The United States and the Soviet Union established formal diplomatic relations in November of 1933, ending sixteen years of disagreement regarding the legitimacy of the Communist government in Moscow.

LOCALE: Washington, D.C.; Moscow, Soviet Union (now Russia)

CATEGORIES: Diplomacy and international relations; government and politics; trade and commerce

KEY FIGURES

Franklin D. Roosevelt (1882-1945), president of the United States, 1933-1945

Maksim Maksimovich Litvinov (Meier Moiseevich Wallach; 1876-1951), Soviet minister of foreign affairs

Cordell Hull (1871-1955), U.S. secretary of state, 1933-1944

Joseph Stalin (Joseph Vissarionovich Dzhugashvili; 1878-1953), general secretary of the Communist Party and premier of the Soviet Union, 1929-1953

William Bullitt (1891-1967), adviser to Cordell Hull and first U.S. ambassador to the Soviet Union, 1933-1936

Alexander Troyanovsky (1882-1955), first Soviet ambassador to the United States, 1935-1939

SUMMARY OF EVENT

Prior to 1933, the U.S. government refused to recognize the legitimacy of the government of the Soviet Union because the Bolsheviks (later renamed Communists) had seized power through force rather than through democratic means. During the Russian Civil War (1918-1921), the United States even sent troops to Russia to assist opponents of the Bolshevik regime. Americans also opposed the Soviets' support of communist propaganda in other nations (especially in democratic states) and their refusal to repay debts owed by previous Russian governments. Moscow's hostility toward the League of Nations during the 1920's further complicated the Soviet Union's reputation in world affairs.

Nevertheless, during the 1920's American businesses—including prominent companies such as American Locomotive, Du Pont, General Electric, Radio Corporation of America, and Standard Oil—signed trade agreements with Soviet agencies that promised assistance in developing the nation's economy. In 1929, Ford Motor Company signed a contract to build a plant in Russia that would produce one hundred thousand vehicles annually. Many Americans traveled to the Soviet Union to help design and build industrial facilities and to participate in other economic projects. Many Americans also provided major assistance during the massive famine that took place in the Soviet Union in the period 1921-1923. Relief agencies in the United States and other Western states helped ameliorate widespread hardship by providing food and medicines.

By the early 1930's, Washington had begun to reconsider its policy toward the Soviet Union. Several major governments already had given diplomatic recognition to the Soviet Union: Germany (1922), Great Britain, Italy, and France (1924). The United States was one of the last major world powers to withhold this acknowledgment. Furthermore, the Great Depression was having an adverse effect on American farmers, who needed to find markets for their surplus grain. The possibility of selling grain to Russia through government-sponsored arrangements was extremely appealing. Similarly, manufacturers hoped to increase sales of industrial products by opening their market to the Soviet Union. The Communist Party's ability to maintain power for more than a decade had proved that the regime would not disappear, and this reality had to taken into consideration by those dealing with Russia's role in the international diplomatic scene.

By the early 1930's, the development of other issues had raised concerns in both Washington and Moscow. The rise of Adolf Hitler and the Nazi Party in Germany and the growing power of militaristic Japan and its invasion of Manchuria in 1 931 were sources of concern to both the United States and the Soviet Union. Americans were particularly aware that their interests and territorial possessions in the western Pacific could be threatened by increased Japanese influence and expansion in the region.

The 1932 election of Franklin D. Roosevelt as presi-

dent was the deciding factor in the creation of the opportunity for a change in U.S. policy. The new president and his congressional majority took massive steps to promote economic recovery—the New Deal—and simultaneously modified several other well-established policies. Among other changes, Roosevelt's administration ended Prohibition (overriding the Eighteenth Amendment) and expressed a willingness to open negotiations with Moscow. At the same time, the Soviet Union had reached a point that made a diplomatic opening possible. Joseph Stalin's government had enunciated a more cooperative policy toward the Western democracies and the League of Nations, and it had participated in economic and disarmament conferences in the early 1930's. Furthermore, as it confronted Japan's conquest of Manchuria along the Soviet frontier, the Soviet Union saw the United States as a potential ally who could help counter further Japanese expansion. Maksim Maksimovich Litvinov, who favored better relations with the West, became foreign minister in 1930, and he used his position to help mend U.S.-Soviet relations.

During the first half of 1933, Roosevelt solicited detailed studies and other relevant information to help him decide whether to approach the Russians for a possible rapprochement. Secretary of State Cordell Hull submitted a lengthy report to the president in September outlining reasons to contact the Soviet government with a goal of opening diplomatic relations and resolving other points of dispute. Many others encouraged a review of the existing policy. Roosevelt agreed with their views, and in mid-October he wrote to the Russian authorities with an American proposal to open high-level negotiations on issues of interest to both states. The Soviets replied positively, and formal talks began in Washington on November 9. Foreign Minister Litvinov headed the Soviet delegation, and Hull led the Americans.

The talks made quick progress and the agreements, signed on November 16, 1933, dealt with most of the major issues. Roosevelt personally took part in several of the negotiations with Litvinov. These agreements covered a variety of important topics: financial arrangements (which focused on increasing U.S. trade credits to the Soviet Union), the establishment of formal diplomatic relations between the two states, the outline of procedures for protection of legal rights and religious freedoms of American citizens in the Soviet Union, and the ban of hostile communist propaganda and other disruptive activity directed toward the United States.

The agreements and public statements never used the word "recognition," referring instead to the creation of "normal diplomatic relations." On November 17, 1933, the United States announced that William Bullitt would be the new American ambassador to the Soviet Union, and on November 20, the Soviet government named Alexander Troyanovsky as its ambassador to the United States. Both governments agreed to meet to deal with unresolved issues, and in January of 1937, they reached a compromise settlement on claims of American property seized by the Communists. Later negotiations led to a trade agreement in July of 1935, followed by one in August of 1937.

SIGNIFICANCE

Moscow's foreign policy during the 1930's illustrated a willingness to take a more cooperative position in world affairs. The Soviet Union's entry into the League of Nations in 1934 was an important step in this regard, as were the diplomatic and military agreements that the Soviet Union signed with several European nations during the decade.

The 1933 Soviet-American agreement had an uneven impact, and it failed to fill its American supporters' high hopes. Increased Soviet-American trade did not reach predicted levels. Promises regarding religious freedom and legal rights of U.S. citizens in the Soviet Union meant relatively little. Communist propaganda and revolutionary activities, emanating from Moscow and the Comintern (Communist International), continued in the United States throughout the decade. Hull later wrote that the results fell far short of creating meaningful trust and cooperation, and by 1935 the relationship had deteriorated. Soviet leaders believed that the Soviet Union could benefit from the agreement without conceding any of its fundamental interests on major issues.

Behind occasional improvement in Soviet international behavior during the 1930's remains the reality that the Soviet Union was a one-party dictatorship under the firm hand of Stalin and the Communist Party. No complete accommodation, cooperation, or trust could exist in the relationship between the Soviets and Americans, who represented diametrically opposed value systems and political institutions. Only during World War II, when both countries faced Germany as a common enemy, was a revitalized—but temporary—bond of cooperation created. Nonetheless, even during times of confrontation, the diplomatic understanding that began in 1933 provided the formal government-to-government contacts needed for important dialogue on many future issues.

—*Taylor Stults*

FURTHER READING

Bennett, Edward M. *Recognition of Russia: An American Foreign Policy Dilemma*. Waltham, Mass.: Blaisdell, 1970. Discusses the political and legal aspects of the U.S. government's decision.

Bishop, Donald G. *The Roosevelt-Litvinov Agreements: The American View*. Syracuse, N.Y.: Syracuse University Press, 1965. Explanation of the issues negotiated.

Farnsworth, Beatrice. *William C. Bullitt and the Soviet Union*. Bloomington: Indiana University Press, 1967. Bullitt, the first ambassador to the Soviet Union, also participated in prior negotiations between the Russians and the Americans.

Gambone, Michael D. *Documents of American Diplomacy from the American Revolution to the Present*. Westport, Conn.: Greenwood Press, 2002. A good source for the correspondence between Roosevelt and Litvinov that restored diplomatic relations.

Glantz, Mary E. *FDR and the Soviet Union: The President's Battles over Foreign Policy*. Lawrence: University Press of Kansas, 2005. Discusses changing U.S. policy toward the Soviet Union in 1933.

Hull, Cordell. *The Memoirs of Cordell Hull*. New York: Macmillan, 1948. Personal recollections of the U.S. secretary of state on American-Russian relations.

Morris, M. Wayne. *Stalin's Famine and Roosevelt's Recognition of Russia*. Lanham, Md.: University Press of America, 1994. Analysis of the economic factors behind U.S. recognition of the Soviet Union.

Richman, John. *The United States and the Soviet Union: The Decision to Recognize*. Raleigh, N.C.: Camberleigh & Hall, 1980. Valuable source with details not found in other accounts.

Sibley, Katherine A. S. *Loans and Legitimacy: The Evolution of Soviet-American Relations, 1919-1933*. Lexington: University Press of Kentucky, 1996. Traces the impact of economic ties on decisions in Washington and Moscow.

Wilson, Joan H. *Ideology and Economics: U.S. Relations with the Soviet Union, 1917-1933*. Columbia: University of Missouri Press, 1974. Assesses advocates and opponents of American recognition in the debate over potential benefits.

SEE ALSO: Nov. 6-7, 1917: Bolsheviks Mount the October Revolution; Mar. 2-6, 1919: Lenin Establishes the Comintern; Nov. 8, 1932: Franklin D. Roosevelt Is Elected U.S. President; Dec., 1934: Stalin Begins the Purge Trials; Nov. 25, 1936: Germany and Japan Sign the Anti-Comintern Pact; Aug. 23-24, 1939: Nazi-Soviet Pact; May, 1940: Roosevelt Uses Business Leaders for World War II Planning.

December 8, 1933
CANONIZATION OF BERNADETTE SOUBIROUS

The Roman Catholic Church canonized Marie-Bernade Soubirous in recognition of her devout faith and humility after she had visions of the Virgin Mary in 1858. Bernadette was designated the patron saint of those afflicted with illness, and Christians from all over the world continued to pray to her and to make the pilgrimage to Lourdes, France.

LOCALE: Vatican City; Lourdes, France
CATEGORY: Religion, theology, and ethics

KEY FIGURES
Bernadette of Lourdes (Marie-Bernarde Soubirous; 1844-1879), French nun who saw visions of the Virgin Mary
Pius XI (Ambrogio Damiano Achille Ratti; 1857-1939), Roman Catholic pope, 1922-1939
Pius X (Giuseppe Melchiorre Sarto; 1835-1914), Roman Catholic pope, 1903-1914

SUMMARY OF EVENT
Born in Lourdes, France, on January 7, 1844, Marie-Bernarde Soubirous (more commonly known as Bernadette) was the eldest child of Francis and Louise Soubirous. Her childhood was beset with poverty and illness. On February 11, 1858, while gathering wood with one of her siblings and a neighborhood friend, fourteen-year-old Bernadette witnessed her first apparition of the Virgin Mary in the Grotto of Massabielle, situated near the Gave River. The figure in the vision, whom Bernadette called "the lady," continued to appear to Bernadette in seventeen similar apparitions at the cave. Bernadette described the lady as a young woman wearing a white robe and veil with a blue sash. The vision's feet were decorated with golden roses, and she held a rosary in her right hand.

Although all of the apparitions were important, three of Bernadette's encounters with the lady had especially significant impacts on history. On February 26, 1858, at the apparition's urging, Bernadette discovered a small stream of water in the cave that eventually grew to a significant size and flowed into the Gave River. On March 2, the lady told Bernadette to ask the local clergy to have a chapel built on the site. Finally, on March 25, the spirit revealed herself to be the embodiment of the Immaculate Conception. Bernadette's visions of the Virgin Mary were viewed by many as miraculous, and as word spread, pilgrims began to descend on Lourdes to witness the phenomenon themselves.

Both ecclesiastical and government officials questioned the authenticity of Bernadette's claims and tried to restrict access to the site, but public outcry forced them to keep the grotto open. Amid staunch skepticism, Bernadette retold her story often, and she never changed any of the details of her experiences, never wavered under the pressure of those who doubted her truthfulness, and never accepted any gifts. Instead, she took refuge from all of the public attention at a local school run by the Sisters of Notre Dame in Nevers. Then, in September of 1878, she took her vows and became Sister Marie-Bernard. She remained at the convent, where she suffered from numerous health problems, until her death on April 16, 1879.

In 1908, Bishop Gauthey of Nevers formally began the process of canonizing Bernadette by initiating a series of 132 sessions in which church officials interviewed Bernadette's family members, friends, and clergy about her life and character. On September 22, 1909, Bernadette's remains were exhumed from their resting place near St. Joseph's Chapel in Nevers. To everyone's surprise, the exhumed body was intact and practically undamaged after being interred for thirty years, and many considered the body's preservation to be a miracle. On August 13, 1913, Pope Pius X bestowed the title of venerable on Bernadette, indicating that she had completed the first stage of canonization. In accordance with the Church's canonization guidelines, Bernadette's body was exhumed two more times for identification purposes. The second exhumation occurred on April 3, 1919, and the third on April 18, 1925. Both exhumations revealed that her body remained almost entirely intact.

On May 2, 1925, the Church certified that two miracles had been performed in Bernadette's name. The first involved Henri Boisselet, who was cured of tubercular peritonitis after a novena to Bernadette was started. The second involved Sister Marie-Melanie Meyer, who was cured of a gastric ulcer after making a pilgrimage to Bernadette's tomb. Following the Church's authentication of these miracles, Pope Pius XI presided over Bernadette's beatification ceremony on June 14, 1925, in which she was declared blessed and was given a feast day of April 16. Her body was permanently laid to rest in a crystal coffin at the chapel of Saint Gildard, in Nevers, on August 3, 1926. Following the beatification ceremony, the church was required to verify two additional miracles performed in the candidate's name. Both of these miracles occurred within three years of Bernadette's beatification and involved the miraculous healings of Archbishop Lemaître Carthage, who suffered from a chronic amoebic infection, and of Sister Marie de Saint-Fidele, who suffered from Pott's disease. Once these miracles were certified, the Church published the *decree de tuto*, the last step in the canonization process, on July 2, 1933. Finally, on December 8, 1933, on the Feast Day of the Immaculate Conception, the Pius XI canonized Bernadette in a special ceremony in St. Peter's Basilica in the Vatican. Bernadette was made a saint as much for her honesty and humility as for her visions of the Virgin Mary, and she became known as the patron saint of those suffering from illness.

SIGNIFICANCE

The historical significance of Bernadette's visions of the Virgin Mary at Lourdes and her subsequent canonization as Saint Bernadette is enormous. Immediately following Bernadette's first apparition, people began to travel to Lourdes to witness the miracle at the grotto, and in 1876, a shrine was built above the grotto to accommodate all of the visitors. By the late nineteenth century, reports of miraculous healings at the grotto's springs began being reported. In response, people from all over the world—many of them ill and in search of a cure—descended on Lourdes.

In 1943, Bernadette's story was popularized for millions by the film *The Song of Bernadette*, which was based on the book *Das Lied von Bernadette* (1941; *The Song of Bernadette*, 1942) by Franz Werfel. Jennifer Jones won an Academy Award in the title role.

In 1958, a church capable of holding twenty thousand people was built at the site. Lourdes remained one of the most visited destinations for religious pilgrimage: At the beginning of the twenty-first century, an estimated six million people visited the grotto at Massabielle each year. Many of these visitors came to drink or bathe in the spring water discovered by Saint Bernadette in hope of being cured of their ailments. The spring produces approximately twenty-seven thousand gallons of water per week.

On November 9, 2005, the Medical Bureau of the Sanctuary of Our Lady of Lourdes verified the sixty-seventh miraculous cure at the Grotto. It involved the immediate healing of Anna Santaniello, who suffered from Bouillard's disease until she was instantly cured after bathing in the spring water at Lourdes in August of 1952.

Saint Bernadette's body, which remained uncorrupted, continued to be on view for visitors at the chapel of Saint Gildard in Nevers. For Catholics and other believers worldwide, her corpse's preservation was yet another example of Bernadette's miraculous healing powers.

—Bernadette Zbicki Heiney

FURTHER READING

Carroll, Michael P. "The Virgin Mary at LaSalette and Lourdes: Whom Did the Children See?" *Journal for the Scientific Study of Religion* 24 (1985): 56-74. Explores why apparitions of the Virgin Mary appear to certain people and not to others. Also examines the theory that these visions might be modeled after a parental figure.

Heffernan, Anna Eileen, and Mary Elizabeth Tebo. *Saint Bernadette Soubirous*. Boston: Pauline Books & Media, 1999. Written for a young-adult audience, this book provides readers with a short biography of Bernadette of Lourdes as well as a description of the shrine at Lourdes at the end of the twentieth century.

Laurentin, René. *Bernadette Speaks: A Life of Saint Bernadette Soubirous in Her Own Words*. Boston: Pauline Books & Media, 2000. A fact-based account of the life of Bernadette of Lourdes.

Taylor, Thérèse. "So Many Extraordinary Things to Tell: Letters from Lourdes, 1858." *Journal of Ecclesiastical History* 46 (July, 1995): 457-482. Explores Bernadette's visions by examining letters written by Adelaide Monlaur, an eyewitness to the events at Lourdes. Describes how the visions led to the establishment of Lourdes as a world-renowned religious shrine.

Trochu, Francis. *Saint Bernadette Soubirous, 1844-1879*. Rockford, Ill.: Tan Books, 1985. Comprehensive biography traces the saint's life from her childhood in Lourdes to her death as a nun at the convent in Nevers.

Werfel, Franz. *The Song of Bernadette*. 1942. Reprint. New York: St. Martin's Press, 1998. Based on fact, this novel tells the story of the saint's life.

SEE ALSO: May 13-Oct. 17, 1917: Marian Apparitions in Fátima, Portugal; May 16, 1920: Canonization of Joan of Arc; May 17, 1925: Thérèse of Lisieux Is Canonized; Oct. 5, 1938: Death of Maria Faustina Kowalska.

December 17, 1933
END OF THE THIRTEENTH DALAI LAMA'S RULE

During the tumultuous rule of Thubten Gyatso, the Thirteenth Dalai Lama, Tibet faced threats from China, British India, and Russia. Thubten instituted important cultural changes in Tibet and gave Tibetans pride in their heritage, and he was widely considered the greatest and most powerful leader of Tibet since the Fifth Dalai Lama.

ALSO KNOWN AS: Thubten Gyatso
LOCALE: Lhasa, Tibet
CATEGORIES: Religion, theology, and ethics; government and politics; social issues and reform

KEY FIGURE
Thubten Gyatso (1876-1933), Thirteenth Dalai Lama

SUMMARY OF EVENT

Independent Tibet was governed by a theocracy headed by the spiritual leader of Tibetan Buddhism, the nation's predominant religion. This leader is called the Dalai Lama, which is roughly translated as "ocean of wisdom." The first Dalai Lama was born to a herdsman in the western reaches of Tibet in 1391. He founded great monasteries of Drepung and Tashi Lhunpo, and it was believed that his spirit found its home in the body of another priest upon his death.

Reincarnation is a fundamental aspect of Tibetan Buddhism. Under this view, death is almost never final, and the spirit of a living thing can be incarnated or reborn into the body of another creature, even if that creature belongs to a separate species. The Dalai Lama is said to be the reincarnation of the bodhisattva Avalokitesvara. A bodhisattva is an individual who has achieved enlightenment through hard training and a well-lived life. The usual reward for this achievement is entering Nirvana, the realm of enlightenment and total, absolute, infinite peace. Some individuals—including the Dalai Lamas—achieve enlightenment but decide to delay entering Nirvana until they have helped all other living things to achieve enlightenment. Calling the Dalai Lamas an incarnation of Avalokitesvara is a recognition of the belief that the Dalai Lamas are reincarnations of previous leaders who are no longer bound to the cycle of karma (which compels beings' return to Earth) but who have decided to return to the world to help all beings achieve enlightenment.

The Thirteenth Dalai Lama, Thubten Gyatso, was born in 1876 in Thakpo Langdun in south Tibet to Kunga

Rinchen and Lobsang Dolma, a herdsman and his wife. His status as the reincarnation of the Twelfth Dalai Lama was recognized in 1878, and he was enthroned in 1879 at the Potala Palace in Lhasa, Tibet's capital. Upon reaching maturity, he was granted the political power of a Dalai Lama, although the political situation he inherited was a complicated one. Under the four Dalai Lamas who preceded him, monasteries had amassed too much power, and political corruption was rampant. As a result, the rulers had not possessed much power over Tibet or its people.

An important example of monasterial power in Tibet was the Great Prayer Festival, the Monlam Chenmo. Tibetans came from all over the country to see the festival, and they packed Lhasa. Tradition held that control of the city was given to one of the more prominent monasteries during the festival; this responsibility largely consisted of ensuring security and leading ceremonies and rituals. However, prior to the Thirteenth Dalai Lama's ascendance, the monastery controlling the festival had begun to levy heavy taxes and fines on Lhasa's lay population. As a result, during the festival most of the city's residents fled to the country in order to avoid being virtually robbed of all their possessions. A story recounts an exchange in which the Thirteenth Dalai Lama summoned the monks in charge of the festival and required them to divulge the name of the person who had ordered the taxes. They replied that the Great Fifth Dalai Lama had given them their authority. Thubten's response was to ask to whom the monks thought they were talking, a reminder that Thubten himself was the reincarnation of all the Dalai Lamas before him.

The period in which the Thirteenth Dalai Lama rose to power was sometimes called the time of "the Great Game," as the struggle to control Tibet came to be known. The British were suspicious of Tibet's relationship with Russia, and they invaded Tibet in 1904, which forced the Thirteenth Dalai Lama to flee to Mongolia and then to China. The Chinese were afraid of British power in the region, and so they invaded Tibet. Upon learning that General Chao Er-feng of China had reached Lhasa in 1909, the Thirteenth Dalai Lama and some of his political leaders ran from Lhasa to India. After the Manchu Dynasty was overthrown in the Chinese Revolution of 1911, Tibet forced the remaining Chinese out of their nation, and the Thirteenth Dalai Lama returned to his homeland and gained considerable political power, the likes of which had not been seen since the Great Fifth Dalai Lama.

The British wanted to use Tibet as a buffer state between their territories in India and China, and in 1913 they organized the Simla Conference, the goal of which was to formalize Tibetan independence. However, this convention failed to secure China's recognition of Tibet. A secret agreement in 1914 between India and Tibet established the McMahon line, the official boundary between Tibet and India, but China refused to recognize this border, and the agreement's effectiveness was doomed. However, this did not prevent the institution of regulated trade between Tibet and the British.

In 1920, Sir Charles Bell of England visited Tibet and received permission for explorers from England to pass through Tibet on the way to Mount Everest. Tibet revoked these permissions from 1924 to 1933, however, after an adventurer exploited lamas and sold their photographs. Nonetheless, Bell enjoyed a friendship with the Thirteenth Dalai Lama and ultimately produced a biography on him.

Many of the reforms credited to the Thirteenth Dalai Lama were technological. While in exile in British India, the Thirteenth Dalai Lama became extremely interested in technology, and he tried to bring a basic degree of modernization to Tibet. From India he brought Tibet's first telephone, set up the first Tibetan postal office in 1913, and sent four young Tibetans to Great Britain in order to learn about modern engineering.

The Thirteenth Dalai Lama's rule also oversaw many cultural changes. He founded the first English school in Tibet in 1923 at Gyaltse and designed the Tibetan flag, which is still in use by the Tibetan government in exile today. On January 8, 1913, the Thirteenth Dalai Lama publicly expounded the five points of Tibetan independence, and he personally composed Tibet's national anthem. He also increased Tibet's military power: In 1914, he instituted special training for the Tibetan army. Two years later, he oversaw the establishment of the Tibetan Medical Institute, and in 1923 he set up a security headquarters in Lhasa in order to protect the Tibetans from invasions of their capital city. Thubten died on December 17, 1933, at the age of fifty-eight.

SIGNIFICANCE

Thubten Gyatso was responsible for various cultural, economic, and political changes that did much to improve the Tibetan way of life. During his tenure, diplomatic relations between Tibet and Great Britain matured, but the threat of external dominance persisted. Just be-

---

THUBTEN GYATSO'S PREDICTION

Shortly before his death in 1933, Thubten Gyatso predicted that Tibet would soon face considerable challenges:

Very soon in this land (with a harmonious blend of religion and politics) deceptive acts may occur from without and within. At that time, if we do not dare to protect our territory, our spiritual personalities including the Victorious Father and Son (Dalai Lama and Panchen Lama) may be exterminated without trace, the property and authority of our Lakangs (residences of reincarnated lamas) and monks may be taken away. Moreover, our political system, developed by the Three Great Dharma Kings (Tri Songtsen Gampo, Tri Songdetsen and Tri Ralpachen) will vanish without anything remaining. The property of all people, high and low, will be seized and the people forced to become slaves. All living beings will have to endure endless days of suffering and will be stricken with fear. Such a time will come.

---

fore his death in 1933, the Thirteenth Dalai Lama issued a statement in which he predicted difficult times for Tibet, and he could not have been more correct. In 1950, the Chinese army defeated the Tibetan military and invaded. The Tibetan government, led by Thubten Gyatso's successor, the Fourteenth Dalai Lama, began to operate in exile in 1959 in Dharamsala, India. After this date, China claimed Tibet as part of its territory, while the exiled Tibetan government maintained that China was violating Tibetan sovereignty.

—*John F. Gamber, Jr.*

FURTHER READING

Bell, Charles. *Portrait of a Dalai Lama: The Life and Times of the Great Thirteenth.* 1946. Reprint. Boston: Wisdom, 1987. Biography of the Thirteenth Dalai Lama by a British man who befriended him.

Goldstein, Melvyn C. *The Snow Lion and the Dragon: China, Tibet, and the Dalai Lama.* Berkeley: University of California, 1997. Presents possible means for achieving an independent Tibet in light of the country's historical development.

Gould, Basil. "Tibet and Her Neighbors." *International Affairs* 26, no. 1 (January, 1950): 71-76. Sentimental article about the Tibetan people on the eve of the Chinese occupation.

Gupta, Karunakar. "The McMahon Line, 1911-45: The British Legacy." *China Quarterly* 47 (July-September, 1971): 521-545. Article detailing the debate over the McMahon line, which was to divide India and Tibet.

Hansen, Peter H. "The Dancing Lamas of Everest: Cinema, Orientalism, and Anglo-Tibetan Relations in the 1920's." *The American Historical Review* 101, no. 3 (June, 1996): 712-747. Reexamines the diplomatic relationship between Tibet and England by adding the realm of cultural representation to traditional politics.

SEE ALSO: 1901-1911: China Allows Some Western Reforms; Sept. 7, 1904: Lhasa Convention Is Signed in Tibet; May 4, 1919: May Fourth Movement; 1926-1949: Chinese Civil War; July 7, 1937: China Declares War on Japan.

1934
BENEDICT PUBLISHES *PATTERNS OF CULTURE*

Ruth Benedict's Patterns of Culture *contributed to new directions in anthropological theory, methodology, and philosophy.*

LOCALE: New York, New York
CATEGORIES: Anthropology; publishing and journalism

KEY FIGURES
Ruth Benedict (1887-1948), American anthropologist
Franz Boas (1858-1942), American anthropologist

SUMMARY OF EVENT
The field of anthropology began to develop new concerns and methods in the beginning of the twentieth century. Having its origins in the nineteenth century, it focused originally on the concerns of that period: classification and development of human races, languages, and societies. Charles Darwin's *On the Origin of Species by Means of Natural Selection: Or, The Preservation of Favoured Races in the Struggle for Life* (1859), with the general concept of evolution, strongly influenced the thinking of the time, so that by the end of the nineteenth century, studies classified societies on a hierarchical scale to determine the phases, stages, and states through which all human groups passed. Karl Marx and Friedrich Engels added to this evolutionary perspective by stressing the causes of human evolution and argued that the mode of production is the prime force on which political, judicial, and ideological superstructures are based. The evolutionary perspective, however, assumed that there is a universal "human nature" and did not consider the different meanings and functions similar traits can have when in different contexts.

It was in this era that Franz Boas, a German-born American and the father of American anthropology, joined the staff of the American Museum of Natural History and Columbia University. He scorned the sweeping generalizations of many evolutionists because they were selective in the facts they used and their ideas did not account for the more sophisticated observations of cultural variability. Boas emphasized fieldwork and firsthand observation. He founded the culture history school, the name of which is misleading, given that Boas tended to favor the functionalist approach, which considered societies as likened to organisms where the parts are interdependent. Boas argued that cultures should be considered as a whole. He emphasized the importance of life histories and drew attention to the relationship between culture and personality.

Boas inspired a number of students who became prominent anthropologists, one of whom was Ruth Benedict. Benedict's humanistic ideas led her not only to challenge the rigid scientific methodology that some considered to be essential in anthropological research but also to argue that anthropology belonged with the humanities and not the social sciences. She discovered anthropology after the age of thirty, and she believed that the discipline enabled her to contrast different peoples and different historical periods. She was a student at the New School for Social Research, where she was greatly influenced by Boas. She was also influenced by Robert Lowie and was directed in her fieldwork among the Serrano Indians by Alfred Kroeber.

Benedict completed her doctoral dissertation in 1923 and was appointed an assistant to Boas. In 1927, she studied the Pima Indians and was struck by the contrast between them and the Pueblo Indians. The Pueblo emphasized harmony, whereas the Pima emphasized extremism. During this time, Benedict began to view culture as a total configuration, not merely a matrix in which personalities develop; she saw culture as being like a personality on a large scale. She presented this view of culture, which developed into the theoretical framework for her book *Patterns of Culture*, at the Twenty-third Con-

1934

gress of Americanists in 1928. She did not publish her book until 1934, however.

After Boas's retirement, Benedict became chair of the anthropology department at Columbia University. She also served as editor of the *Journal of American Folklore*, directed field trips, and wrote poetry. World War II opened up new avenues, and Benedict received a research posting in Washington, D.C., where she applied anthropological thought to contemporary societies. After returning to Columbia University in 1946, she published *The Chrysanthemum and the Sword: Patterns of Japanese Culture*, a book that some consider to be her masterpiece.

Patterns of Culture, however, remained Benedict's most popular work, and its publication was the central event in her life. The work was not only a culmination of her questioning in the 1920's but also the fulfillment of a sense of social responsibility and a desire to lead society to new values and goals. It was a course given at Columbia University by Kroeber, however, that triggered the

Ruth Benedict. (Library of Congress)

effort. At the insistence of Boas, Kroeber acquiesced to give a series of lectures on the cultures of Highland South America. Benedict thought that Kroeber's lectures and contributions were dry, and out of exasperation she made the impulsive decision to write her own book, which became *Patterns of Culture*. In *Patterns of Culture*, Benedict argued that every culture is an integrated whole, a "personality writ large." As her friend Margaret Mead later explained, Benedict showed that "each historical culture represents a many-generational process of paring, sifting, adapting, and elaborating on an available 'areal forma,' and that each culture, in turn, shapes the choices of those born and living within it." Benedict recognized that hereditary factors contribute to differences in behavior and also that those who do not conform to the culture within which they live have difficulties.

To support her argument, Benedict analyzed and compared the cultures of three peoples: the Kwakiutl of western Canada, the Zuni of the southwestern United States, and the Dobuans of Melanesia. She chose them because she considered the data available on each culture viable. She had studied the Zuni, was familiar with the literature concerning them, and could also draw on Ruth Bunzel's field materials. Boas had studied and written extensively on the Kwakiutl, and she had full access to his published and unpublished materials, as well as spending many hours discussing the Kwakiutl with him. Benedict had a high regard for Reo Fortune's work on the Dobuans and got permission from him to use his material.

Building on her earlier work, she used Friedrich Nietzsche's terms "Apollonian" and "Dionysian" as classification terms but used the psychological term "paranoid" for her third category. Also, she had become acquainted with Gestalt psychology, an approach that agreed with her insights, so she used the Gestalt framework in her analysis. She compared the three cultures. The Kwakiutl were "Dionysian" because, as she viewed them, they were egocentric, individualistic, and ecstatic in their rituals. Located on a narrow strip of the Alaskan coast, the Kwakiutl were wealthy, living off the products of the sea. Technologically, they were superior; they worked wood without metal tools, built houses and ceremonial halls, and raised great totem poles. In spite of this wealth, however, they were Dionysian in their ecstatic dancing. Often, a dance leader foamed at the mouth, seemed mad, and sometimes even threw himself on burning coals. Wealth was for display, not use. The Kwakiutl would lend out etched sheets of copper, blankets, and canoes with obligatory interest, which often began with the children. The potlatch was a ritual competition in which gifts

THE DIVERSITY OF CULTURES

Ruth Benedict begins the third chapter of Patterns of Culture *with a discussion of the diversity of cultures around the world, using as an example the variety of reactions to the taking of a life:*

The diversity of cultures can be endlessly documented. A field of human behaviour may be ignored in some societies until it barely exists; it may even be in some cases unimagined. Or it may almost monopolize the whole organized behaviour of the society, and the most alien situations be manipulated only in its terms. Traits having no intrinsic relation one with the other, and historically independent, merge and become inextricable, providing the occasion for behaviour that has no counterpart in regions that do not make these identifications. It is a corollary of this that standards, no matter in what aspect of behaviour, range in different cultures from the positive to the negative pole. We might suppose that in the matter of taking a life all peoples would agree in condemnation. On the contrary, in a matter of homicide, it may be held that one is blameless if diplomatic relations have been severed between neighbouring countries, or that one kills by custom his first two children, or that a husband has right of life and death over his wife, or that it is the duty of the child to kill his parents before they are old. It may be that those are killed who steal a fowl, or who cut their upper teeth first, or who are born on a Wednesday. Among some peoples a person suffers torments at having caused an accidental death; among others it is a matter of no consequence. Suicide also may be a light matter, the recourse of anyone who has suffered some slight rebuff, an act that occurs constantly in a tribe. It may be the highest and noblest act a wise man can perform. The very tale of it, on the other hand, may be a matter for incredulous mirth, and the act itself impossible to conceive as a human possibility. Or it may be a crime punishable by law, or regarded as a sin against the gods.

Source: Ruth Benedict, *Patterns of Culture* (Boston: Houghton Mifflin, 1934).

were heaped on a rival who could not repay or a contest of wild destruction during the recitation of hymns of self-glorification. If the guest could not destroy an equal amount, he was shamed. The same contest was performed at a wedding, where the bridegroom's party might try to overpower the father of the bride with heaps of gifts. During other forms of revenge, innocent parties were killed to avenge natural deaths. A boy struck by his father was shamed into committing suicide; similarly, a wife heaped with accusations of adultery was sent home to take her own life eventually. The ideal character among the Kwakiutl was to strive constantly to escape limitations, to achieve excesses, and to break into the order of experience. Thus they valued drugs and alcohol, fasted, and used self-torture and frenzy.

The Zunis were "Apollonian" because they were restrained—they did not condone excessive or disruptive psychological states. They preferred a noncompetitive, gentle, peace-loving, and middle-of-the-road existence.

In fact, it was forbidden for a serving priest even to feel anger. They emphasized the ceremony, the perfection of ritual, and had hierarchies of kachinas, or masked gods, some of which were impersonated in dances. Marriage was a personal affair with little ceremony attached to it, and divorce was easy. The society was matrilineal, and when a wife became tired of her husband, she merely laid his belongings on the doorstep and he went home to his mother. Dreams and hallucinatory experiences were avoided, but prayers lasting an hour long were repeated without mistakes. Aggressive, ambitious individuals were frowned upon and suspected of sorcery. The ideal person was easygoing and socially poised and made others feel comfortable.

The Dobuans, were considered paranoid because they emphasized magic, and everyone feared and hated everyone else. The Dobuans were of Melanesia and part of the kula ring studied by Bronisław Malinowski. Unlike Malinowski's Trobrianders, the Dobuans displayed antagonisms and hostility. They used charms to defend their yam crops against competitors. If there was a problem, it was ascribed to evil magic. They saw life as dominated by treacherous rivalry; adultery was common and violent jealous outbursts were frequent. Dobuans used incantations to cause disease in those they disliked, and all had antidotal spells. They used charms to protect themselves and their property as well as to infect trespassers and thieves. Death was always attributed to magic, with women being particularly suspect. Often on the death of a spouse, the survivor was suspected of magical murder. The Dobuans disapproved of laughter and believed that laughter during gardening prevented yams from growing. The ideal person cheated, stole, charmed, and poisoned his way to eminence.

SIGNIFICANCE

When *Patterns of Culture* was published, it initially received acclaim. *The New York Times* said it was "expertly conceived and brilliantly developed." Kroeber, in the *American Anthropologist*, called it "an important

1934

contribution" but also noted that Benedict's configuration approach should be further developed to give anthropology "new stimuli and insights." In spite of the initial favorable reaction and the book's popularity among nonanthropologists, the approach was eventually abandoned because it was considered impressionistic, reductionist, and not susceptible to replication. It explained behavior by focusing on cultural patterns and did not account for the variation within particular groups. Also, some of the data came to be challenged by other studies.

In spite of these limitations, however, *Patterns of Culture* made a significant impact at a crucial time, influencing both anthropologists and nonanthropologists. It raised philosophical and theoretical issues while building on and developing existing concepts. Some of the criticisms were exactly what Benedict had argued against. For twenty years, many had tried to discredit subjectivity in anthropology. Benedict, with her humanistic orientation, reintroduced subjectivity into analysis, but it was subjectivity based on verifiable facts. This marked a clear split between what Kroeber termed "scientific" anthropology and "historical" anthropology. A debate within the discipline of anthropology concerning the merits and validity of each approach followed. Benedict defined anthropology as a discipline that studies differences between cultural traditions, so that the concern is what particular cultures do to people. She presented "culture" as an integrated whole made by humans, which means that every culture is integrated and implies that a culture is more than the sum of its parts.

By studying whole cultures and seeing culture as a total configuration, Benedict adopted Boas's emphasis on the collection of information and took it further by integrating data around a concept; in her case, it was the cultural configuration. This gave impetus to cultural relativism, which argued that whole cultures should be studied rather than cultural traits or culture as a general concept. Benedict also brought forth the issue of the relationship between the individual and society. She showed that culture provides a stimulus for certain behavioral patterns and that individuals influence their culture—that is, influence flows both ways. People who do not fit into a society thus do not necessarily have to blame themselves. In fact, Benedict showed that even though some cultures evaluate certain behaviors as abnormal, other cultures provide environments where people practicing those behaviors function well. These revelations gave impetus to the culture and personality focus in anthropology.

For nonanthropologists as well as anthropologists, Benedict set forth a concept of culture and showed the importance it has in everyday life, even in modern society. She challenged the biological deterministic position that dominated the thinking of the time and replaced biology with culture as a prime determinant in human behavior. She also communicated the concept of cultural relativity to the public, leading people to be more open to evaluating others on their own terms rather than from outsiders' ethnocentric bias. This formed the basis for reevaluation of cultural practices, such as sex roles. One ramification was that women did not have to be seen as innately weaker or inferior, given that in other cultures they hold a dominant position.

Patterns of Culture has remained a popular book, and much of the philosophy and many of the concepts it sets forth are as relevant in the twenty-first century as they were at the time it was initially published. The appearance of this book was an important step toward an understanding of human behavior that is part of the foundation of human knowledge.

—*Arthur W. Helweg*

FURTHER READING

Benedict, Ruth. *Patterns of Culture*. 1934. Reprint. New York: Mariner Books, 1989. Classic work sets forth Benedict's philosophical and theoretical views concerning the analysis of human behavior.

Bohannan, Paul, and Mark Glazer, eds. *High Points in Anthropology*. 2d ed. New York: McGraw-Hill, 1988. Briefly describes some of Benedict's contributions to anthropology as well as criticisms of her ideas. Includes Benedict's original writings to allow readers to judge the ideas as they appeared in the primary sources.

Caffrey, Margaret M. *Ruth Benedict: Stranger in This Land*. Austin: University of Texas Press, 1989. Highly acclaimed, well-researched, and insightful portrayal of Benedict and her works. Includes selected bibliography and index.

Harris, Marvin. *The Rise of Anthropological Theory: A History of Theories of Culture*. Updated ed. Lanham, Md.: AltaMira Press, 2000. Presents analysis of anthropological theories from the cultural materialist perspective.

Hays, H. R. *From Ape to Angel: An Informal History of Social Anthropology*. 1958. Reprint. Westport, Conn.: Greenwood Press, 1979. An account of the development of anthropology from a literary perspective.

Honigmann, John J. *The Development of Anthropological Ideas*. Homewood, Ill.: Dorsey Press, 1976. Addresses the development of anthropology from the cultural perspective of the American school.

Mead, Margaret. *Ruth Benedict: A Humanist in Anthropology.* 30th anniversary ed. New York: Columbia University Press, 2005. A portrayal of Benedict by a close friend and scholar who had access to much of her correspondence.

Modell, Judith Schachter. *Ruth Benedict: Patterns of a Life.* Philadelphia: University of Pennsylvania Press, 1983. Insightful biography offers analysis of Benedict's life and work.

Young, Virginia Heyer. *Ruth Benedict: Beyond Relativity, Beyond Pattern.* Lincoln: University of Nebraska Press, 2005. Biography by one of Benedict's last graduate students draws on the anthropologist's unpublished and lesser-known works as well as her personal correspondence and other materials to illuminate the final years of her life.

SEE ALSO: 1911: Boas Publishes *The Mind of Primitive Man*; Sept. 30, 1925: Chesterton Critiques Modernism and Defends Christianity; Aug., 1928: Mead Publishes *Coming of Age in Samoa.*

1934
DISCOVERY OF THE CHERENKOV EFFECT

Pavel Alekseyevich Cherenkov undertook a detailed study of the properties of the faint blue light emitted by charged particles moving through a material faster than the speed of light in that material.

LOCALE: Soviet Academy of Science, Moscow, Soviet Union (now Russia)

CATEGORIES: Science and technology; physics

KEY FIGURES
Pavel Alekseyevich Cherenkov (1904-1990), Soviet physicist
Ilya Mikhailovich Frank (1908-1990), Soviet physicist
Igor Yevgenyevich Tamm (1895-1971), Soviet physicist
Emilio Gino Segrè (1905-1989), Italian physicist

SUMMARY OF EVENT

In the early twentieth century, many scientists noticed that transparent materials placed near intense radioactive sources emitted a very faint blue light. Pierre Curie, co-discoverer of the radioactive element radium, was said to have fascinated dinner guests by producing from his pocket a tube of radium salt that illuminated the dinner table with a mysterious blue glow visible in the fading evening light. At the time, however, scientists were interested in the isolation and identification of new chemical elements, and little or no effort went to understanding the origin of the bluish glow. The first systematic attempt to understand this emission of blue light was made by Lucien Mallet from 1926 to 1929. He found that the light emitted from a wide variety of different transparent materials placed next to radioactive sources always had the same bluish-white color and that its spectrum was continuous. This later observation was very important because it distinguished this light from the fluorescent light emission, which occurred in narrow, discrete color bands, also observed when materials were bombarded with the rays from radioactive sources. Mallet, however, completed his work without attempting to offer any explanation for the mechanism that produced the light.

In 1934, Pavel Alekseyevich Cherenkov was working at the Institute of Physics of the Soviet Academy of Science in Moscow, where he undertook an exhaustive series of experiments to characterize the properties of the blue emission. He had been studying the problem of fluorescent emission from materials exposed to radiation. Apparently unaware of Mallet's earlier efforts, Cherenkov noticed the very weak emission of visible light from liquids exposed to gamma rays, high-energy light invisible to the human eye. In his first experiment to determine the nature of this emission, Cherenkov inserted a vial containing about 100 milligrams of radium into a wooden block. The wood absorbed all the radiation from the decaying radium except the gamma rays. A container of liquid was then placed above the radioactive source and an optical microscope system was used to observe the intensity and color of the light emitted by the liquid. Sixteen different pure liquids including distilled water, paraffin, and various alcohols were examined. After studying the liquids, Cherenkov concluded that the intensity of the emission varied little when one liquid was substituted for another, that the emission was mainly in the blue and violet regions of the color spectrum, and that the color of the emission did not change significantly when a different liquid was substituted. These properties of the emission were quite different from what would be expected from the fluorescence emission process. In addition, when Cherenkov added compounds such as potassium iodide or silver nitrate (known to inhibit the fluorescence process) into the liquids, the intensity of the emitted light did not decrease.

By the early 1930's, the mechanism for the fluorescent emission from materials bombarded with the rays from radioactive sources was well understood. Soviet scientists, who were the first to become aware of Cherenkov's observations, took up the challenge of attempting to explain the mechanism for this new emission process. In 1934, Sergei Ivanovich Vavilov proposed the emission might be caused by the energy lost as electrons produced by the passage of the gamma rays through the liquid slowed down, a process known as bremsstrahlung. Cherenkov undertook a second series of experiments in 1936 to understand better the mechanism of the emission process. He investigated the influence of a magnetic field on the emitted light and concluded that the emission must be from electrons produced in the liquid by the gamma rays, not directly from the gamma rays themselves, but that the process was inconsistent with bremsstrahlung.

In 1937, two other Soviet physicists, Ilya Mikhailovich Frank and Igor Yevgenyevich Tamm, developed a theory to explain the emission process. Frank and Tamm recognized that the speed of light in solids, liquids, and gases is slower than in a vacuum. According to Albert Einstein's theory of special relativity, no particle can travel faster than the speed of light in a vacuum, but it is possible for a particle to travel faster than the speed of light in the medium through which it is moving.

After applying their knowledge about electricity and magnetism, Frank and Tamm concluded that when a charged particle travels faster than the speed of light in the medium through which it is moving, it will give off light directed in a cone oriented along its direction of motion. This emission is analogous to the bow wave produced by a boat moving through water or the sonic boom produced by an airplane moving through air faster than the speed of sound in the medium. The theory predicted that the angle of the cone of emitted light would depend on the speed of the charged particle as well as the properties of the medium. Their theory also predicted the distribution of colors to be expected in the emitted light.

Cherenkov and two American physicists, George B. Collins and Victor G. Reiling, undertook a series of experiments to test the new theory. Cherenkov succeeded in photographing the emission in 1937 and showed that it had a shape crudely consistent with the cone predicted by the theory. In 1938, Cherenkov improved his apparatus and was able to verify that the angle the cone of emitted light made with the path of the particle varied in a manner

Pavel Alekseyevich Cherenkov. (The Nobel Foundation)

consistent with the theory of Frank and Tamm. In addition, Cherenkov confirmed that the intensity of the emitted light and its color distribution were consistent with the theory. Independently, in 1938, Collins and Reiling published results on the intensity and angle of the emitted light, generally referred to as the Cherenkov effect. Their observations were also consistent with Frank and Tamm's theory.

These early experiments all involved the examination of the Cherenkov radiation from an intense beam of particles. The emission from a single particle, however, was so faint that it could not be seen using the tools available in the 1930's. The development of the photomultiplier tube, an extremely sensitive light detector, provided the hope that the Cherenkov radiation from a single particle passing through a liquid or solid could be detected. After several unsuccessful attempts by a number of researchers, in 1951 John V. Jelley succeeded in detecting the Cherenkov emission from a single, fast-moving charged particle passing through distilled water. Almost immediately, other scientists succeeded in using Cherenkov radiation for the direct measurement of particle velocities. By the mid-1950's, Cherenkov detectors were being employed by particle physicists worldwide to detect unusual atomic particles at accelerators and in the cosmic rays. For their efforts in characterizing the properties of the radiation and developing a theory to explain its emission mechanism Cherenkov, Frank, and Tamm were jointly awarded the 1958 Nobel Prize in Physics.

SIGNIFICANCE

Although initially regarded as little more than a scientific curiosity, the distinctive Cherenkov effect has found widespread applications in the fields of particle physics, astronomy, and chemistry. In 1955, Emilio Gino Segrè and his colleagues set up an apparatus at the Bevatron particle accelerator in Berkeley, California, to search for the antiproton. They expected only a few antiprotons in a background of many other particles called pions, and their experiment was set up to allow the pions to move more rapidly than the antiprotons. To facilitate this movement, they built a Cherenkov detector filled with a particular organic liquid in which the speed of light was faster than the expected antiproton speed but slower than the pion speed. This detector provided a signal when a pion went through, but no signal was given when the antiproton passed. They also used a second detector sensitive to both types of particles, and by comparing the two outputs, they were able to identify the antiprotons. On September 21, 1955, Segrè and his colleagues obtained their first evidence for the antiproton using detectors based on Cherenkov radiation.

Cherenkov detectors have been employed in the investigation of the stability of the proton. Although the proton was once believed to be a stable particle, certain theories predict that eventually the proton will decay. Its lifetime must be very long; therefore, to see a decay, scientists would have to watch a single proton for billions and billions of years or watch a large number of protons for a shorter time. Cherenkov radiation provides the tool to undertake such an experiment. Physicists from the University of California at Irvine, the University of Michigan, and the Brookhaven National Laboratory costructed a huge pool of eight thousand tons of pure water at a Morton Thiokol salt mine in Ohio. If any single proton in one of the water molecules were to decay, the resulting fragments traveling through the water would produce a pulse of Cherenkov light to be detected by one or more of the 2,048 individual Cherenkov detectors surrounding the pool.

Another large, water-filled Cherenkov detector, the Kamiokande II, operated by Japanese physicists at a site 300 kilometers west of Tokyo (originally designed to search for proton decays) has been upgraded to allow detection of neutrinos from space. This detector has provided confirmation of the unexpectedly low neutrino flux from the Sun, which has puzzled astronomers since it was reported by Raymond Davis, Jr., in 1967 using another type of neutrino detector. The Kamiokande II also detected the neutrino burst from the 1987 supernova, confirming models of the duration and intensity of neutrino emission in supernovas.

Cherenkov detectors are also employed by radiochemists to identify and count decaying nuclei. Because Cherenkov radiation occurs only if the charged particle is traveling faster than the speed of light in the detection material, Cherenkov detectors can be used to count rare decays in which a high energy, or fast-moving, particle is emitted in a background of many more low-energy events below the detection threshold. Cherenkov detectors have been used to determine the amount and type of radioactive material present in plant and animal tissue, environmental materials, nuclear reactor effluents, and biomedical fluids.

Astronomers have used Cherenkov detectors to understand the properties of the cosmic rays. In 1956, Frank McDonald of the University of Iowa combined Cherenkov detectors with scintillation counters to obtain the charge and energy of individual cosmic rays. Early balloon-borne experiments using this combination of detectors were able to determine the relative proportions of each element in the cosmic rays. Cosmic ray analysis advanced further when similar paired detectors measuring 6 square meters flew in the third High Energy Astronomical Observatory satellite launched by the National Aeronautics and Space Administration (NASA) in 1979. The blue glow of Cherenkov radiation emitted from the water pools surrounding many nuclear reactors is also a familiar sight to reactor workers and members of the public who have been permitted to tour nuclear reactor sites.

—*George J. Flynn*

FURTHER READING

Close, Frank, Michael Marten, and Christine Sutton. *The Particle Explosion*. New York: Oxford University Press, 1987. This well-illustrated book makes extensive use of color photographs in explaining the world of subatomic particles to general audiences. It describes how Cherenkov detectors were used in Segrè's discovery of the antiproton, the search for

1934

proton decay, neutrino experiments, and efforts to reveal other elusive subatomic particles.

Collins, George B., and Victor G. Reiling. "Cherenkov Radiation." *Physical Review* 54 (October 1, 1938): 499-503. This article reviews the discovery of Cherenkov radiation, describes the theory of its emission, and reports the authors' results in determining the color spectrum of the emitted light. Although a technical article, it should be understandable to students in a high school-level physical science course.

Cropper, William H. *Great Physicists: The Life and Times of Leading Physicists from Galileo to Hawking*. New York: Oxford University Press, 2001. Presents portraits of the lives and accomplishments of important physicists and shows how they influenced one another with their work. Includes glossary and index.

Jelley, John V. *Cherenkov Radiation and Its Applications*. Elmsford, N.Y.: Pergamon Press, 1958. This book is the definitive scientific description of Cherenkov radiation. Although intended for specialists, the first chapter, which presents an extensive historical account of Cherenkov's contribution and the observations of this phenomenon that predate his work, is appropriate for general audiences. The extensive citations and reference list will assist readers interested in locating original papers on the topic.

Jordan, W. H. "Radiation from a Reactor." *Scientific American* (October, 1951): 54-55. Provides a nonmathematical description of how Cherenkov light is emitted and describes the early experiments in the United States to follow up on Cherenkov's discovery. The blue glow of Cherenkov radiation surrounding an operating nuclear reactor is shown on the cover.

Koshiba, Masa-Toshi. "Observational Neutrino Astrophysics." *Physics Today* 40 (December, 1987): 38-42. This well-illustrated, nontechnical article describes the construction, operation, and results from the Japanese Kamiokande II proton decay and neutrino detector. How Cherenkov radiation from these particles is produced and detected is described, and the results for solar neutrino observations and the 1987 supernova are discussed.

Piel, Gerard. *The Age of Science: What Scientists Learned in the Twentieth Century*. New York: Basic Books, 2001. An overview of the scientific achievements of the twentieth century. Includes many illustrations and index.

Ross, H. H., and G. T. Rasmussen. "Modern Techniques and Applications in Cherenkov Counting." In *Liquid Scintillation Counting: Recent Developments*, edited by Philip E. Stantey and Bruce A. Scoggins. New York: Academic Press, 1974. Although written for specialists, this chapter provides a clear description of many of the applications of Cherenkov detectors to problems in chemistry, biology, and environmental science. The authors explain how the unique characteristics of Cherenkov detectors make them the instrument of choice for particular scientific experiments.

Segrè, Emilio. *From X-Rays to Quarks: Modern Physicists and Their Discoveries*. San Francisco: W. H. Freeman, 1980. Segrè was one of the few physicists who both participated directly in nuclear physics (for which he received a Nobel Prize) and wrote a number of popular accounts on the history of physics. The earlier sections of this volume cover the discoveries and theories of those who produced a coherent picture of the atom.

SEE ALSO: Early 20th cent.: Elster and Geitel Study Radioactivity; Dec. 10, 1903: Becquerel Wins the Nobel Prize for Discovering Natural Radioactivity; Fall, 1905: Einstein States His Theory of Special Relativity; Dec. 10, 1906: Thomson Wins the Nobel Prize for Discovering the Electron; 1914: Rutherford Discovers the Proton; 1923: De Broglie Explains the Wave-Particle Duality of Light; 1923: Discovery of the Compton Effect; Feb.-Mar., 1927: Heisenberg Articulates the Uncertainty Principle; Nov., 1934: Yukawa Proposes the Existence of Mesons.

1934

LUBITSCH'S *THE MERRY WIDOW* OPENS NEW VISTAS FOR FILM MUSICALS

Ernst Lubitsch brought visual and verbal wit, European sophistication, dance, and song together into a fully integrated musical myth that popularized cinematic operetta.

LOCALE: Metro-Goldwyn-Mayer studios, Culver City, California

CATEGORY: Motion pictures

KEY FIGURES

Ernst Lubitsch (1892-1947), German actor and motion-picture director

Jeanette MacDonald (1903-1965), onetime Broadway chorus girl who played Sonia, the title character in *The Merry Widow*

Maurice Chevalier (1888-1972), former French cabaret singer turned international film star who played Captain Danilo in *The Merry Widow*

Edward Everett Horton (1886-1970), comedian who played fussy, blundering Ambassador Popoff

SUMMARY OF EVENT

Early film musical directors were troubled by the role of song and dance: They wondered how to explain a performer's decision to stop the action, turn to the audience, and begin to sing within the context of a story. Efforts to justify production numbers explain why many early musicals were set in theaters or nightclubs, where music was the logical outgrowth of the setting. On stage, operetta came closer than any other form to fully integrating music, dance, plot, and character development into a coherent whole. That integration was most successful in Jerome Kern's *Show Boat*, which opened on Broadway in 1927.

In Germany, Ernst Lubitsch, once a comic and a student of famed director Max Reinhardt, had become a director himself. His first success in this area was *Schuhpalast Pinkus* (*Shoe Salon Pinkus*), a silent musical released in 1916. (Silent films were not, to their audiences, silent; they were always accompanied by music, and in urban centers, the films might be accompanied by full orchestras.) After Lubitsch's arrival in the United States, he made *Rosita* (1923), which featured Mary Pickford as a street singer; *So This Is Paris* (1926), with an extravagant production number; *The Student Prince* (1927), which drew from the Sigmund Romberg oper-

etta; and *Love Parade* (1929), with Jeanette MacDonald and Maurice Chevalier.

The Merry Widow had been filmed before. In fact, Lubitsch's film was overshadowed, at the time, by the 1925 silent version, which starred screen idol John Gilbert and popular actress Mae Murray; the director of the earlier version was Erich von Stroheim. Lubitsch, however, brought a new perspective to the film, as well as new and witty songs by Richard Rodgers and Lorenz Hart and by Gus Kahn. The major characters, Sonia and Danilo, are treated both tenderly and poignantly. Comedy derives partly from his vanity and her pride but primarily from the pair's struggles to resist the social order and the necessary cycles of marriage—and, by implication, reproduction—to which they must ultimately yield.

The film is based on an operetta by Franz Lehár that was first staged in Vienna in 1905. The plot is simple. Sonia, wealthy and widowed, is lonely and bored. Captain Danilo, a happy womanizer, is eager to meet the heavily veiled widow, but he has been spoiled by the bored women of Maxim's bordello in Paris, the equally bored peasant women of Marshovia, and the even more bored Queen Dolores (first played by the famous actress Una Merkel) of that country. When he meets Sonia, his remarks are directly sexual. She is attracted, but her pride causes her to rebuff him. She flees to Paris. Danilo's government sends him after her to marry her and keep her wealth in the country. He wins her at an embassy party, but she learns he is courting her under orders. Now truly in love, Danilo refuses to defend himself. He is arrested and returned to Marshovia to be tried for treason. She appears at his trial and visits him in jail. There, the king and ambassador lock them in until they agree to be married by a priest the king has conveniently provided.

Lubitsch added contrast to the story. Chevalier's untrained, French-cabaret voice represents the forces of passion and freedom; MacDonald's trained, operatic soprano is the voice of love and marriage. At Maxim's, where Sonia follows Danilo, the audience first sees a cancan, an exhibitionist dance in which women display themselves to male viewers. That dance gives way to an awkward hopping dance that Chevalier performs with a crowd of women, not with a single partner. The scene switches to the embassy, where a disciplined folk dance balances the cancan of the earlier scene. Then the waltz

THE HAYS CODE

In 1930, Will Hays devised the "Code to Govern the Making of Talking, Synchronized and Silent Motion Pictures. Formulated and Formally Adopted by the Association of Motion Picture Producers, Inc. and The Motion Picture Producers and Distributors of America, Inc. in March 1930." Known as the Production Code or simply the Hays Code, it was used by the film industry as an instrument to regulate material depicted in motion pictures, such as the sexual subject matter of Lubitsch's films. Among its provisions were the following:

GENERAL PRINCIPLES

1. No picture shall be produced that will lower the moral standards of those who see it. Hence the sympathy of the audience should never be thrown to the side of crime, wrongdoing, evil or sin.
2. Correct standards of life, subject only to the requirements of drama and entertainment, shall be presented.
3. Law, natural or human, shall not be ridiculed, nor shall sympathy be created for its violation.

PARTICULAR APPLICATIONS

I. Crimes Against the Law

These shall never be presented in such a way as to throw sympathy with the crime as against law and justice or to inspire others with a desire for imitation. . . . The technique of murder must be presented in a way that will not inspire imitation. . . . Methods of Crime should not be explicitly presented. . . . Illegal drug traffic must never be presented. . . . The use of liquor in American life, when not required by the plot or for proper characterization, will not be shown.

II. Sex

The sanctity of the institution of marriage and the home shall be upheld. Pictures shall not infer that low forms of sex relationship are the accepted or common thing. . . . In general passion should so be treated that these scenes do not stimulate the lower and baser element. . . . Seduction or Rape . . . should never be more than suggested, and only when essential for the plot, and even then never shown by explicit method. . . . Sex perversion or any inference to it is forbidden. . . . Miscegenation (sex relationships between the white and black races) is forbidden. . . .

III. Vulgarity

The treatment of low, disgusting, unpleasant, though not necessarily evil, subjects should always be subject to the dictates of good taste and a regard for the sensibilities of the audience.

IV. Obscenity

Obscenity in word, gesture, reference, song, joke, or by suggestion (even when likely to be understood only by part of the audience) is forbidden.

V. Profanity

Pointed profanity (this includes the words, God, Lord, Jesus, Christ—unless used reverently—Hell, S.O.B., damn, Gawd), or every other profane or vulgar expression however used, is forbidden. . . .

begins. In contrast to Danilo's hopping dance at the club, the circles of the waltz are disciplined. They represent the eternal cycles of mating, childbirth, and death, a notion given particular poignancy by a single shot of viewers—older people, whose time of youth and joy is ended—on a balcony. They are observers, as Sonia and Danilo must someday be. Below, the lovers dance alone, merge into the crowd, dance alone, and are surrounded by dancers again, in a scene that symbolizes the difficulty they are having accepting their destiny. When Sonia rejects Danilo, however, and he is arrested, she begins a hysterical parody of the waltz; in its disorder, it is comparable to Danilo's earlier hopping dance.

Both visual and verbal wit suggest that social order is necessary but not flawless. Much of the film's considerable comedy comes at the government's expense. In the opening credits, a magnifying glass appears over a map of central Europe so that the audience can find tiny Marshovia. The Marshovian government, however, takes itself very seriously. King Achmed communicates clichés and trivia to Ambassador Popoff in an elaborate secret code. He tolerates his queen's adultery because he possesses a politician's desire to avoid scandal. Yet livestock must be removed from a Marshovian courtroom before Danilo can be tried for treason; significantly, a goat is led out as Danilo enters.

Set design and costume are important to the film's mythic dimension. Exterior shots of Sonia's castle are unrealistically presented in ways that suggest German expressionist theater. Hers is a fairy-tale castle in which a widow is imprisoned by convention. As the film develops, black comes to represent confinement, and white is a symbol of freedom: Alone in her castle, Sonia wears a widow's mourning clothes, and the audience sees a closet of mourning gowns, mourning veils, and mourning corsets; even her dog is black. When she resolves to leave for Paris, everything (even the dog) turns white. In the cancan at Maxim's, the girls' costumes are white edged in black; at the embassy the waltzers at first wear black and white.

SIGNIFICANCE

Lubitsch popularized operetta on film, but for Lubitsch himself, *The Merry Widow* was an ending, not a beginning. He made more than forty films in Hollywood, but no other musicals. His later credits include *Ninotchka* (1939), with Greta Garbo; *The Shop Around the Corner* (1940), with Margaret Sullavan and James Stewart; *To Be or Not to Be* (1942), with Carole Lombard and Jack Benny; *Heaven Can Wait* (1943), with Gene Tierney; and *Cluny Brown* (1946), with Charles Boyer and Jennifer Jones. The film also was an ending for Chevalier. After appearing in *Folies Bergère* (1935), he returned to Europe and made no more Hollywood films until *Gigi* (1958).

The "Lubitsch touch," as the director's influence came to be known, was affected by increasing censorship. Following a decade of Hollywood scandals, the institution of the Catholic Church's League of Decency in 1933 caused Hollywood to enforce the production rules known as the Hays Code, which prohibited the type of wit that had informed *The Merry Widow*. Danilo's casual promiscuity would become unacceptable; clearly, in the film, when he marries Sonia, he gives up a life that has given him great pleasure. This is sacrifice, not repentance. The obvious sexual reference of the trial scene—when the entrance of Danilo, now romantically in love, is associated with the exit of the goat, a traditional symbol of lechery—would also be unacceptable, as would the blatant sexuality of the queen and the obvious prostitutes at Maxim's. Specific kinds of stage business would not be seen again for two decades. For example, there is considerable symbolic byplay involving a comparison of swords and swordbelts in the scene in which the king learns of his wife's adultery with Danilo. When Danilo thinks the king is gone, he suggestively sheaths his sword before entering the queen's bedroom. The king, however, returns after forgetting his sword and belt. He accidentally picks up the now-abandoned sword and belt of

Ernst Lubitsch with star Jeanette MacDonald and other cast members of The Merry Widow. *(Hulton Archive/Getty Images)*

Danilo, which obviously belong to a younger, trimmer, and—by implication—more virile man. This broadly sexual use of visual humor would go underground until such films as the Beatles' *A Hard Day's Night* (1964) and *Help!* (1965), which were released after censorship had ended.

It is possible, too, that with Adolf Hitler and Benito Mussolini on the march in Europe, neither the public nor studio heads, many of them Jewish, were as amused as they had once been by the self-important doings of heads of small European nations. Certainly, Lubitsch was harshly criticized for his treatment of European politics in his later *To Be or Not to Be*. *The Merry Widow*, however, heavily depends on such topical humor. For example, when Sonia leaves Marshovia, the threat to the economy is so great that the king hears of impending revolution. The shepherds, he is told, are threatening to organize into a Black Sheep movement. The king is later relieved to hear that the leaders are merely "Left Bank intellectual" shepherds and, consequently, not a force to be feared. Such humor savors more of the Weimar Republic than of the United States of the 1930's and 1940's.

Lubitsch's use of operetta was influential, although it was changed in ways that offered revealing insights into popular culture in the 1930's. With the Depression's heightening impact and the increasing threat of war in Europe, the public demanded simpler emotions and more stereotyped characters than were to be found in Lubitsch musicals. Audiences clearly rejected Lubitsch's characters' complex ambivalence about their proper roles. Chevalier's European sophistication was thus replaced by Nelson Eddy's boyish earnestness. Eddy and Jeanette MacDonald were rivaled only by Ginger Rogers and Fred Astaire as the most popular couple in film history.

Eddy had a trained operatic voice and had sung with the Philadelphia Civic Opera. Without acting ability, he simply portrayed manly courage, protectiveness toward women, and American virtue. Even in films such as the disastrous *I Married an Angel* (1942), which concluded the Eddy-MacDonald series and in which Eddy is described as a womanizer, he obviously viewed women with great alarm. Unlike Chevalier's Danilo, Eddy greeted his rescue by a virtuous woman with absolute relief. MacDonald played innocent girls, not experienced women, until, in *I Married an Angel*, the camera shows her forty-one years in her chin line and eyes—even as she simpers like a teenager in a film caught between pure sentimentalism and self-parody. The MacDonald-Eddy partnership began in 1935 with *Naughty Marietta* and continued through *Rose Marie* (1940), *Bitter Sweet*

(1940), and *The Chocolate Soldier* (1942), among others. In these films, worldliness and social satire were replaced with sentimentality.

Lubitsch's synthesis of fairy-tale musical and myth would not reappear for a long time. A number of films in the folk-musical tradition subordinated romance and melodrama to mythic structure; these began with King Vidor's *Hallelujah* (1929) and continued through the filmings of *Show Boat* (1936 and 1951), *The Wizard of Oz* (1939), and such later musicals as *Carousel* (1956) and *Oklahoma!* (1955). Audiences were not prepared to accept the more sophisticated Lubitsch myths until after World War II, when Lubitsch's aware, experienced, and commitment-phobic couple appeared in *South Pacific* (1958). A similar story is told in *Gigi*, in which Chevalier also reappears, and Lubitsch's mythic kingdom is alive, but sentimentalized, in the 1967 *Camelot*. These films shared something of Lubitsch's archetypes, but audiences never again saw his ideas portrayed with such dazzling effect and such wit as in *The Merry Widow*.

—*Betty Richardson*

FURTHER READING

Altman, Rick. *The American Musical*. Bloomington: Indiana University Press, 1989. The reader put off by academic jargon should avoid the theoretical chapters here, but the chapter "The Fairy Tale Musical" contains an excellent analysis of Lubitsch, and "The Folk Musical" introduces the use of mythic elements.

Eisner, Lotte H. "Lubitsch and the Costume Film." In *The Haunted Screen: Expressionism in the German Cinema and the Influence of Max Reinhardt*. London: Thames and Hudson, 1969. Eisner is annoyingly condescending to Lubitsch as a lower-middle-class Jew, but Eisner's work, first published in France in 1952, recognizes expressionistic and mythic elements overlooked by most critics.

Kislan, Richard. *The Musical: A Look at the American Musical Theater*. Rev. ed. New York: Applause Books, 1995. Textbook for a general course in musical theater includes a brief but thorough history and a study of the various crafts and artists in the musical theater. Includes excellent photographs.

Knapp, Raymond. *The American Musical and the Formation of National Identity*. Princeton, N.J.: Princeton University Press, 2004. History of the genre focuses on how themes in American musical theater productions relate to how Americans view themselves. Includes useful appendixes, notes, bibliography, and index.

Manvell, Roger, and Heinrich Fraenkel. *The German Cinema*. New York: Praeger, 1972. The first two chapters provide a solid overview of the German film from 1895 to the 1920's, when Lubitsch was learning acting and directing. The authors emphasize spectacular films, such as Lubitsch's *Madame Dubarry* (1929), and the influence on Lubitsch's later, more intimate work of such directors as Mauritz Stiller.

Poague, Leland. *The Cinema of Ernst Lubitsch*. South Brunswick, N.J.: A. S. Barnes, 1978. Deals somewhat superficially with Lubitsch's American work but provides good synopses of these films, although Poague's conclusions about Lubitsch's dawning self-awareness are dubious. Contains a valuable filmography of Lubitsch's American films and a useful, if brief, bibliographical note.

Pratt, George C. "Foreign Invasion (II) Ernst Lubitsch." In *Spellbound in Darkness: A History of the Silent Film*. Rev. ed. Greenwich, Conn.: New York Graphic Society, 1973. Less a history than a filmography, but contains valuable extracts from hard-to-find feature articles and reviews, the latter only concerning Lubitsch's American silents. Only one illustration.

Sennett, Ted. "The First Sounds of Music." In *Hollywood Musicals*. New York: Harry N. Abrams, 1985. This lavishly illustrated coffee-table volume contains an intelligent, if superficial, overview of Lubitsch's work and a brief bibliography.

Weinberg, Herman G. *The Lubitsch Touch: A Critical Study*. 3d ed. New York: Dover, 1977. Otherwise excellent book on Lubitsch's total career is marred by the author's coy prose style, by some thirty-five pages of tributes from contemporaries given without the documentation that would allow readers to consult the sources, and by a bibliography arranged, inexplicably, in chronological rather than alphabetical order.

SEE ALSO: Dec. 27, 1927: *Show Boat* Is the First American Musical to Emphasize Plot; 1929: *Hallelujah* Is the First Important Black Musical Film; 1930's: Hollywood Enters Its Golden Age; 1930's-1940's: Studio System Dominates Hollywood Filmmaking; 1933: *Forty-Second Street* Defines 1930's Film Musicals; Sept. 6, 1935: *Top Hat* Establishes the Astaire-Rogers Dance Team; Aug. 17, 1939: *The Wizard of Oz* Premieres.

1934
SOVIET UNION BANS ABSTRACT ART

Initial hopes for a true revolution in art in the new Soviet Union were dashed when the leaders of the Communist Party centralized control of artistic production and outlawed all forms of art except Socialist Realism.

LOCALE: Moscow, Soviet Union (now Russia)
CATEGORIES: Arts; government and politics; civil rights and liberties

KEY FIGURES
Vladimir Ilich Lenin (Vladimir Ilich Ulyanov; 1870-1924), chairman of the Council of the People's Commissars of the Soviet Union, 1917-1924
Joseph Stalin (Joseph Vissarionovich Dzhugashvili; 1878-1953), general secretary of the Central Committee of the Communist Party of the Soviet Union, 1922-1953
Vladimir Tatlin (1885-1953), Soviet sculptor
Kazimir Malevich (1878-1935), Soviet abstract artist
Anatoly Lunacharsky (1875-1933), first commissar of education in the Soviet Union

Wassily Kandinsky (1866-1944), Soviet artist, theoretician, and museum director
Marc Chagall (1887-1985), Soviet abstract artist

SUMMARY OF EVENT
When, in 1934, the First Congress of the Soviet Writers' Union decreed that Socialist Realism was to be the only acceptable form of artistic expression in the Soviet Union, the final nail was driven into the coffin of Soviet abstract art. The pronouncement was not unexpected, for abstract artists who had been heartened by the promises of new freedom under the Communists had already seen their early hopes dashed by a series of actions—beginning in 1922—that had made it increasingly difficult for them to survive and practice their art in the Soviet Union. Nevertheless, the declaration was a particularly insidious blow to men such as Vladimir Tatlin, Kazimir Malevich, and Wassily Kandinsky, whose rise to prominence in the decades before the 1934 congress had signaled a true revolution in Russian art. Under their leadership, men and women in what was now the Soviet Union

had become part of the larger European artistic community and were advancing the boundaries of artistic expression in a country that had had a history of imposing on its artists long before the Communists had come to power.

During the latter half of the nineteenth century, a group of artists who came to be known as the Wanderers rebelled against the classical style being taught in Russian academies; rejecting both classicism and the new notion of art for art's sake, the Wanderers focused on the folk aspects of Russian life and embedded in their realist works a sense of social consciousness. At almost the same time, a different group of young Russian artists were discovering the new theories emerging in other European countries. Reacting against both the academies and the Wanderers, these artists brought various forms of abstractionism into the Russian salons and museums. This group reached its zenith in the years immediately before the 1917 revolution swept the Communists into power. Experimentation became the byword for these

artists; Impressionism, cubism, Imagism, Futurism, and Russia's own contributions to the movement—constructivism, under the leadership of Vladimir Tatlin, and Suprematism, inspired by Kazimir Malevich—gained strong footholds in artistic circles.

It was inevitable that these two major forms of artistic expression would come into conflict. There was already bad blood between champions of realist art and the abstractionists before the 1917 revolution. The Wanderers, whose popularity waned in the early years of the twentieth century, stressed the importance of content in their works. The various practitioners of abstract art, on the other hand, were interested in the technical possibilities of the various media. For example, constructivist sculptors combined various materials—steel, concrete, wrought iron, even paper—to suggest the variety of human experience that formed the impetus for artistic creation. More attention was paid to form than to substance; meaning was subordinated to the aesthetic experience. In the opinion of more conservative artists, art critics, and (most important) influential Communist leaders, such art had no social conscience.

The 1917 revolution promised to free art from its capitalist bonds. Communist leaders announced that all forms of artistic expression were to be supported under the new government. Initially, steps were taken to see that this happened. Although he was essentially conservative in his tastes in art, Bolshevik leader Vladimir Ilich Lenin made no overt attempts to control the production of art in the new Soviet Union. On the contrary, Lenin's close associate Anatoly Lunacharsky, the first Soviet commissar of education, appointed important abstract artists to positions of prominence: Kandinsky was named director of the Museum of Pictorial Culture in Moscow, and Malevich and noted painter Marc Chagall were given positions as professors of art.

The euphoria was short-lived, however. By 1921, Kandinsky had resigned his position and had emigrated, expressing frustration at what he saw as meddling by government

Wassily Kandinsky. (The Granger Collection, New York)

officials in the handling of commissions and direction of artists' work. Chagall and others were to follow him into self-imposed exile within a few years. By 1922, the proponents of realism had won the sympathy of various influential groups within the Communist hierarchy, especially members of the Soviet military; with their help, realism began to reclaim the position of prominence it had held in the last decades of the nineteenth century. From 1922 forward, the various organizations that had sprung up immediately after the revolution to support a multiplicity of artistic viewpoints found themselves increasingly regulated by the central government.

The death of Lenin and the ascension of Joseph Stalin as the new ruler of the Soviet state signaled the death knell for Soviet abstract art. The last vestiges of real freedom were swept away in 1928, when the government ordered that all artists' organizations be consolidated under a single agency run from Moscow. Few artists held out any hope that this "oversight" agency would permit the freedoms that had become commonplace in the smaller, more specialized groups founded by the artists themselves. Their fears were confirmed in a mandate of the Central Committee of the Communist Party, issued on April 23, 1932. Titled the "Decree on the Reconstruction of Literary and Artistic Organizations," the proclamation dissolved all other organizations previously set up for supporting the arts and centralized commissions, sales, and exhibitions under the control of the party. In effect, this meant that artists already subjected to regulation in housing, studio space, and supplies would be solely dependent on the government for their livelihood.

By this time, it was apparent that the government was interested in supporting only those artists whose work could be readily understood by the masses—in effect, realist art with a strong socialist message. Socialist Realism, the new, official art form—named by Stalin himself—was decreed by the Congress of the Soviet Writers' Union in 1934. The decree effectively banned all forms of abstractionism in the arts. Painters, sculptors, writers, and architects found that they would have to conform to the dictates of party censors or suffer serious consequences for their transgressions.

SIGNIFICANCE

The ramifications of the 1934 decree were both immediate and long-lasting. During the next several decades, an elaborate apparatus was constructed to control the production of Soviet art, and bureaucrats whose primary interest lay in promoting party ideals sat in judgment of artists' creations. As historian Joel Carmichael has

observed, the "indispensable component" of the new artistic program "had to be an absolutely unswerving obedience to the Party"; the result was a "totalitarian homogenizing of culture." The demands that all forms of art have a strong propagandistic quality that could be easily understood by the masses and by party censors led to uniformity in production. Painting, sculpture, literature, and even architecture became forums for celebrating the worker and the Soviet hero. More often than not, this meant a glorification of the revolutionary leaders, specifically Stalin during his reign and Lenin after Stalin died and was denounced by Nikita S. Khrushchev.

Artists were forced to conform or suffer the consequences. Several of the most prominent abstractionists had already emigrated before Stalin imposed the monolithic principles of Socialist Realism on the entire creative community. Those who stayed behind either returned to producing works according to the Communist plan or found themselves without supplies for either working or living. Experimentation ceased, and the principles of realism expounded by the Wanderers more than half a century earlier were eagerly embraced by party officials and reluctantly adopted by those who wished to earn their livelihood as painters, sculptors, or artists in any other medium.

At the same time, contact with the West was discouraged, ostensibly to prohibit decadent influences from cheapening Soviet art. Museum collections were purged of offensive works, and books about abstract art were banned from libraries and art academies. Aspiring artists in the Soviet Union were taught that the function of their work was to serve as a means of conveying a socialist message, and that its ideological content was the primary—in some cases the sole—criterion for judging excellence. With no models to guide them in any direction other than that charted by Socialist Realism, the burgeoning artists of the decades between 1930 and 1970 either passively accepted their role as soldiers in the war against capitalism or groped along blindly to fashion works that challenged the bounds of realism or that ignored the demands of the dominant ideology. Striking out in any direction except that charted by the party, however, often proved dangerous. Artists who did so had their works confiscated and destroyed, and they were usually blacklisted by government officials who controlled the assignment of commissions; such commissions represented the only guaranteed source of income for Soviet artists, whose works could not be sent abroad without party approval.

Making matters even worse was the fact that there

1934

were no published guidelines for what constituted acceptable art. Only after a work was completed could the artist gain a review by party officials, who would then pass judgment on the work's adherence to Socialist Realist principles. What could be considered ideologically sound by one group of bureaucrats might be dismissed as wrongheaded and corrupt by another. As the years passed, artists became more and more conservative in their productions. Any strains of genuine creativity that may have existed in the young men and women who followed in the footsteps of Kandinsky, Malevich, and Tatlin during the reigns of Stalin and his successors were effectively stifled, as art became a tool of the party in its battle to liberate the masses from bourgeois domination.

— *Laurence W. Mazzeno*

FURTHER READING

Bendavid-Val, Leah. *Propaganda and Dreams: Photographing the 1930's in the U.S.S.R. and the U.S.* New York: Edition Stemmle, 1999. Comparison of Soviet Socialist Realist photography of the 1930's and American photography during the Great Depression. Published in conjunction with an exhibition of photographs held at the Corcoran Gallery in 1999. Bibliographic references.

Billington, James H. *The Icon and the Axe: An Interpretive History of Russian Culture.* New York: Alfred A. Knopf, 1966. Thoughtful and thoroughly researched examination of the roots of Russian culture, its development under the various czars, and its demise under the Communists. Explains how Socialist Realism is linked to earlier forms of Soviet artistic and architectural styles.

Bown, Matthew Cullerne. *Socialist Realist Painting.* New Haven, Conn.: Yale University Press, 1998. Lenghty treatise on Soviet Socialist Realism from 1917 through 1991. Many illustrations, some in color, bibliographic references, and index.

Carmichael, Joel. *A Cultural History of Russia.* New York: Weybright and Talley, 1968. Examines the culture of Russia from the founding of the nation to the twentieth century. Provides insight into the ways all forms of artistic expression suffered under the control of the Communists, who insisted that art serve the aims of the revolution.

Douglas, Charlotte. *Swans of Other Worlds: Kazimir Malevich and the Origins of Abstraction in Russia.* Ann Arbor: University of Michigan Research Press, 1976. Analysis of the rise of abstract art in Russia and the initial reaction of Soviet revolutionaries to non-representational works. Outlines the principles on which such art was based. A useful summary of the movement against which Stalin reacted in demanding a return to realism in all the arts.

James, C. Vaughn. *Soviet Socialist Realism: Origins and Theory.* New York: St. Martin's Press, 1973. Outlines the principles on which Socialist Realism was founded. Describes the ways art in the Soviet Union was intended to serve both the people and the party. Traces the origins of the movement to Leninist ideology. Contains useful appendixes by Lenin and the Communist Central Committee on reforms in the arts necessary to make them compatible with socialist aims.

Medvedev, Roy A. *Let History Judge: The Origins and Consequences of Stalinism.* New York: Alfred A. Knopf, 1972. Study of Communism under the brutal reign of Stalin by a prominent Soviet historian; shows how Stalin's oppressive policies stifled all forms of creativity. Includes a lengthy chapter on the impact of these policies on the arts and sciences; notes how artists were driven to become puppets of the Communist hierarchy or suffer economic and physical hardships.

Salisbury, Harrison E., ed. *The Soviet Union: The Fifty Years.* New York: Harcourt, Brace & World, 1967. Collection of essays reviewing the impact of Communist policies on the Soviet Union. Includes a chapter on the arts, focusing on the deadening influence of official policies that stifled creativity and drove artists into exile or underground.

Valkenier, Elizabeth. *Russian Realist Art: The State and Society.* New York: Columbia University Press, 1989. Studies the influence of the realist tradition in nineteenth century Russia and in the Soviet Union during the twentieth century. Explores the rise of the Wanderers, whose folk style formed the basis of Socialist Realism. Examines the reaction of the abstract schools of art to the Wanderers, the abstractionists' ascendancy during the early decades of the twentieth century, and their demise under Communist oppression.

SEE ALSO: Dec. 17, 1915: Malevich Introduces Suprematism; 1929-1930: *The Bedbug* and *The Bathhouse* Exemplify Revolutionary Theater; Apr. 23, 1932: Stalin Restricts Soviet Composers; Apr. 23, 1932-Aug., 1934: Socialist Realism Is Mandated in Soviet Literature; Feb., 1934: Rivera's Rockefeller Center Mural Is Destroyed; Jan. 28, 1936: Soviets Condemn Shostakovich's *Lady Macbeth of the Mtsensk District.*

1934
SQUIER FOUNDS MUZAK

The Muzak company, founded by George O. Squier, became the leading provider of recorded music designed to increase employee production.

LOCALE: Cleveland, Ohio
CATEGORIES: Communications and media; marketing and advertising; music

KEY FIGURES
George O. Squier (1865-1934), inventor of Muzak
William Benton (1900-1973), owner of Muzak, 1939-1957
Harry E. Houghton (fl. mid-twentieth century), advertising and marketing expert for Muzak

SUMMARY OF EVENT

George O. Squier, a military general, had a job that required him to determine if an invention had any military use. An inventor himself, he developed a method to send many messages through power lines at the same time and invented the photochronograph, which allowed calculation of the velocity of an object. In 1908, while on military duty, he flew a plane made by the Wright brothers. In 1922, Squier brought his invention for signal transmission to the North American Company. A holding company for public utilities, North American Company had financed Thomas Edison's lightbulb and later went on to form General Electric. When the North American Company purchased Squier's invention, it formed Wired Radio, Inc. Wired Radio wanted to compete with wireless radio, which was steadily growing in popularity.

The North American Company also purchased a music publishing company that became Associated Music Publishers, Inc. With these two companies, the North American Company was in a position to send music, commercials, announcements, and news to individual homes. Squier hoped that his invention would allow the general public to receive all these media in their homes.

Wired Radio, Inc., changed its name in 1934, when Squier decided to combine the word "music" with "Kodak," the name of an already popular company, to get Muzak. That same year, Muzak started sending transmissions to individual homes in Cleveland. These transmissions combined music with commercials and announcements. Muzak also got involved in "functional music," which was broadcast in hotels and restaurants. The functional music did not contain commercials or announcements and was meant to be unobtrusive to cus-

tomers. It also provided privacy for restaurant clients by masking their conversations. At the same time, Muzak also switched transmission of its programs from electric power lines to telephone lines, which made transmission easier and less expensive.

In 1936, Muzak started its commercial services in New York. Many clubs, restaurants, and hotels subscribed to it, but individual subscriptions to Muzak were very expensive, and so the number of clients was limited. In 1938, the North American Company sold Muzak and Associated Music Publishers to Warner Bros. By 1939, Muzak had only 30 individual homes but more than 360 restaurants as clients, and it soon introduced a program for apartment complexes. This program was relatively inexpensive and included four New York radio stations in addition to Muzak. Wireless radio reception was still not very clear, and Muzak's reception was a substantial improvement. By 1945, 60 apartment houses in New York were wired with this program.

Since Muzak had grown in popularity in New York, the company decided to franchise. The first franchises were located in Buffalo, Detroit, Los Angeles, Boston, Washington, and Philadelphia. All the franchises were obligated to play only Muzak productions and were not allowed to alter them in any way. After a year of ownership, Warner Bros. sold both Muzak and Associated Music Publishers to a group of businessmen. Out of this group, William Benton owned the largest percentage of the companies. When Benton took over, Muzak had just begun to make a profit. By 1942, Benton was the sole owner of Muzak. In that year, Muzak went from a 17.5-hour programming day to producing broadcasts all day, every day.

Benton was interested in producing an information service for the government. Muzak could be transmitted even while the country was at war or being raided, when wireless radio stations would no longer be able to transmit communications. In case of such an emergency, Muzak purchased gasoline-operated generators for its offices in New York so that broadcasting could continue during a power failure. Muzak would be able to warn its clients of coming attacks and be able to advise them on what to do afterward. This service was never used, however.

Muzak spent a large portion of its profits on research and on producing functional music. The armed services reported less tardiness, better morale, and more work accomplished in barracks where soldiers listened to Muzak. Factory experiments showed that the introduction of Muzak was followed by lower turnover rates, increased efficiency, and decreased sick days reported. The effects of Muzak were not limited to humans. One farm that received Muzak reported increases in milk production from cows and egg production from chickens. This experiment increased the credibility of the effect of Muzak. Since animals could not have been affected by a self-fulfilling prophecy, the results were unquestionable. In other words, farmers could not have informed cows that the music would increase the amount of milk they produced, thus leading them to produce more because that was expected.

Factories reported increases in production ranging from 2 to 11 percent. Workers remarked that Muzak was soothing, and many thought that relationships with managers improved. Muzak was programmed to counteract the lows that workers experience at midmorning and midafternoon by manipulating the tempo and type of music. This increased production, and the general calmness of the music contributed to maintaining even tempers in the workplace.

After World War II ended, Muzak had three major concerns. The first and most important was a dispute with the American Society of Composers, Authors, and Publishers (ASCAP). When Muzak had been short of funds, it had stopped paying ASCAP for the use of its copyrighted materials; as a result, Muzak had to pay the ASCAP royalties. The second problem, which had not plagued Muzak prior to the war, was competition. Muzak's solution to this problem was to hire an advertising and marketing expert, Harry E. Houghton. Houghton helped end the dispute with ASCAP and a dispute with the American Federation of Musicians, the third difficulty faced by Muzak. The disagreement had kept Muzak out of the Chicago area, but shortly after Muzak hired Houghton, the company entered the Chicago market.

During Benton's ownership, Muzak gained several large companies as subscribers, including Sears, Ford, Chrysler, General Motors, General Electric, and Dow Chemical. Most of these companies continued their membership through the 1980's. Benton sold Muzak in 1957 to the Wrather Corporation. It was during the period when the Wrather Corporation owned Muzak that the programming became solely functional.

In 1972, Muzak was sold again and became part of the TelePrompTer Corporation. Muzak continued to grow and was purchased by Westinghouse in 1981. With the acquisition of Muzak, Westinghouse became the largest telecommunications and cable operation in the world. Muzak was part of Westinghouse's Radio Group W Broadcasting Network and continued research on functional music. Muzak changed hands several more times and in 1992 was bought by New-York based Centre Partners. In 1996, it formed an alliance with EchoStar Communications. Under the name DISH Network for Business, Muzak began to provide direct-broadcast satellite services in both audio and video formats.

SIGNIFICANCE

Muzak conducted many experiments in order to substantiate its claims of increased worker productivity. Several grocery stores wired with Muzak reported increases in sales of up to 40 percent. Muzak apparently made shoppers feel more comfortable and more relaxed, which ultimately caused them to purchase more items. These results were enough proof to persuade many grocery stores to subscribe to Muzak. In the early 1990's, Muzak started creating programs for specific stores based on location and clientele.

Once a company started subscribing to Muzak, the likelihood of its discontinuing the service was small. Workers became accustomed to Muzak and found that the silence left in its absence became unbearable. Although most people agree that Muzak is relatively benign, it is still perceived as a form of influencing people. Many arguments have been made that regardless of its effects, something that affects people without their knowledge should be illegal. Because Muzak is difficult to avoid, almost all people are involuntarily affected by it.

One debate over the use of Muzak occurred in Washington, D.C. Although Capital Transit was a privately owned company, the District of Columbia had given it a monopoly on public transportation. The agreement stated that no other companies would be allowed to operate buses in the District of Columbia unless Capital Transit could no longer accommodate all the passengers. This agreement was signed in 1925. In March, 1948, Capital Transit began to install radios on its buses. Passengers complained that they were being subjected to listening against their will. Given that Capital Transit had a monopoly, the passengers did not have the choice to use a different company. The original complaint was aimed at commercials, because passengers were obligated to listen to spots promoting various companies' products. They claimed that this was unconstitutional and took Capital Transit to court.

The case began on March 3, 1952, and revolved around whether it was constitutional for a public transportation company to play a radio station on its vehicles. The programs played included Muzak and many other stations. The U.S. District Court found radio programming on buses to be acceptable. The passengers objected and took the case to the U.S. Court of Appeals. Although the Court of Appeals reversed a portion of the earlier verdict, the passengers still were not satisfied. Up until that point, the music portion of the programming had not been questioned. The passengers decided that the music portion should be included in the case, and when the case went to the U.S. Supreme Court, all the program content was included.

The Supreme Court decided that the case would be limited to concerns for passengers' safety and comfort. Many reports were submitted to the Court that stated that buses with the programming did not have any more accidents than buses without it. A report on public opinion of the programming stated that more than 90 percent of individuals surveyed were not opposed to the programming. Only 3 percent reported that they were strongly opposed to the programming. Justice Harold H. Burton believed strongly that the rights of the passengers were not being violated. Only Justice William O. Douglas thought that forcing people to listen against their will was unconstitutional regardless of whether the majority was pleased. Douglas stated that if a person can be forced to listen to something beneficial, there is only a small step to forcing him or her to listen to something detrimental. Despite Douglas's objections, the Supreme Court ruled in *Public Utilities Commission v. Pollak* (1952) that public transportation companies could play radio programs in their vehicles.

The Muzak company was questioned about the ethical aspect of manipulating listeners, but the company was largely able to avoid lawsuits on this matter. Because the effects of Muzak are beneficial for the employer, because most employees enjoy Muzak, and because most listeners are unaware of the effects that Muzak has on them, the product has not generated much controversy.

Muzak put time and effort into making its music functional. Because transmitting to individual homes proved to be too costly, Muzak aimed its efforts at factories, offices, shopping centers, and grocery stores. Muzak stopped using commercials, announcements, and vocal music, and instead concentrated on becoming almost unnoticeable, striving to avoid interrupting the work environment. Content was strictly edited; no jazz or blues music was included, nor was any music that might entice someone to sing or clap along, as this would distract

workers and counteract Muzak's goal of increasing work productivity. Despite a number of changes over the years of Muzak's operation, functional music remained its most important product.

—*Dan Kennedy*

FURTHER READING

Barnes, Stephen H. *Muzak: The Hidden Messages in Music: A Social Psychology of Culture*. Lewiston, N.Y.: Mellen Press, 1988. Discusses the beginning of Muzak and its history. Includes many portraits of leaders of Muzak. Addresses the effects of music on subjects and the subconscious. Describes the influencing part of music and its potential use as a control by government.

Hoffman, Thomas. "Muzak Offers New Tune for Data Flow: Retailers Are Increasingly Using Satellite Data Transmission to Distribute Corporate Information." *Computerworld* 26 (September 14, 1992): 72. Discusses transmitting music along with many other possibilities, including e-mail, credit card processing, and teleconferencing. Describes Muzak's relationship with other companies and the ability of Muzak's satellites to send more than music.

Katz, Mark. *Capturing Sound: How Technology Has Changed Music*. Berkeley: University of California Press, 2004. A well-written and accessible analysis of the history of recorded music; a good introduction to the field. Includes CD.

Lanza, Joseph. *Elevator Music: A Surreal History of Muzak, Easy Listening, and Other Moodsong*. London: Picador, 1995. Rejects the standard scholarly approach to musical analysis; argues that Muzak has been unfairly maligned and chronicles its history.

McDermott, Jeanne. "Muzak Is the Music We Hear but Don't Listen To." *Smithsonian* 20 (January, 1990): 70-78. Discusses Muzak's intent not to disturb people by playing music that might entice them to hum, clap, or dance. Describes how Muzak edits material.

Sutherland, Alastair. "Sorry, No Kazoo Players Required." *Canadian Composer* 1 (Summer, 1990): 4. Discusses Muzak's tough restrictions and requirements of pieces that it plays.

Yang, Dori Jones. "Hear the Muzak, Buy the Ketchup: The Elevator-Music Folks' New Push—Customized In-Store Ads." *BusinessWeek*, June 28, 1993, 70-71. Discusses Muzak's influence on customers in supermarkets. Describes Muzak as an advertising strategy and describes the different choices of music for different stores, depending on location and clientele.

1934

SEE ALSO: Dec. 24, 1906: Fessenden Pioneers Radio Broadcasting; Feb. 13, 1914: ASCAP Forms to Protect Writers and Publishers of Music; Aug. 20-Nov. 2, 1920: Radio Broadcasting Begins; 1923: A. C. Nielsen Company Pioneers in Marketing and Media Research; Nov. 28, 1925: WSM Launches *The Grand Ole Opry*; Sept. 9, 1926: National Broadcasting Company Is Founded; 1930's: Americans Embrace Radio Entertainment; Nov. 5, 1935: Armstrong Demonstrates FM Radio Broadcasting.

1934
TOYNBEE'S METAHISTORICAL APPROACH SPARKS DEBATE

When the famous British historian Arnold J. Toynbee issued the first three volumes of his multivolume classic A Study of History, *his metahistorical approach was challenged and championed by other historians, social scientists, and politicians around the world.*

ALSO KNOWN AS: *A Study of History*
LOCALE: London, England
CATEGORIES: Historiography; sociology; publishing and journalism

KEY FIGURES
Arnold Joseph Toynbee (1889-1975), British historian
Oswald Spengler (1880-1936), German historian and philosopher
Karl Marx (1818-1883), German economist and philosopher
William H. McNeill (b. 1917), Canadian historian

SUMMARY OF EVENT
In 1934, Oxford University Press published the first three volumes of the historian Arnold J. Toynbee's monumental work *A Study of History* (1934-1961; 12 volumes). Volumes 4, 5, and 6 followed in 1939, and volumes 7, 8, 9, and 10 were released in 1954. In 1959, a historical atlas and gazetteer was added as volume 11, and finally, in 1961, Toynbee published his response to criticisms of his work in volume 12, titled *Reconsiderations*. D. C. Somervell, a British schoolmaster, published an abridgment of volumes 1-6 of *A Study of History* in 1946, and a second, of volumes 7-10, in 1957. The Somervell condensation of the twentieth century's most massive single-authored historical work made it accessible to a far larger audience. Toynbee sought to glean meaning from the entire course of human history, and the monumental work of erudition and speculation he produced was vigorously attacked by professional historians and widely read (especially in the Somerville abridgment and in the decades immediately after World War II). Arguably, Toynbee proposed a view of human history that was more expansive than that of any previous historian.

Toynbee began his inquiry by identifying the basic intelligible unit of historical study: those societies he called "civilizations," which he distinguished from "primitive" societies. He identified twenty-one different civilizations (although later he would expand the number to twenty-six). In his first six volumes, Toynbee's basic questions focused on the geneses of civilizations from primitive societies; the growth, breakdown, and disinte-

Arnold Joseph Toynbee. (Hulton Archive/Getty Images)

gration of civilizations; and the emergence of what he called "universal states" out of civilizations' disintegration. In short, Toynbee sought to compare the historical development of all human civilizations in an effort to fathom the deeper meanings of the human past. It was an effort similar to that of German cultural historian Oswald Spengler in his *Die Untergang des Abendlandes* (1918-1922; *The Decline of the West*, 1926-1928). After reading Spengler's work in 1920, Toynbee had determined to pursue his own inquiry into the comparative history of civilizations so provocatively anatomized in *The Decline of the West*.

Toynbee argued that civilizations emerge out of a process he termed "challenge and response." The challenge a particular primitive society might face could be environmental or social, but a successful response to challenge, mediated by the leadership roles played by creative individuals, put that society on the path toward civilization. Interestingly, although Toynbee's most basic concept was "civilization," he never clearly defined this idea in the twelve volumes of *A Study of History*. Civilizations were inadequate units of studying the historical development of humankind, Toynbee ultimately determined, and several volumes of his work are devoted to the search for the best unit for this type of study. If any one civilization was a model or paradigm of what a civilized society should be, from Toynbee's point of view, it was the Hellenic civilization of ancient Greece and Rome. (Toynbee had become intimately familiar with these cultures during his training as a classical scholar at Oxford University.)

If the leadership of creative individuals guides a civilization's growth, the breakdown of a civilization occurs, Toynbee argued in volume 4, when this creative minority loses its élan and the majority no longer follows it. The minority rest on their laurels, so to speak, and are therefore unprepared for further challenges. Disintegration ensues, as Toynbee showed in the next two volumes, and this disintegration of a civilization takes a specific form: A "dominant minority" emerges, which is the formerly creative minority, and it is joined by both an "internal proletariat," the mass of people who no longer follow the minority and may rebel against it, and an "external proletariat," which lives outside the civilization's boundaries and may launch attacks against it.

Although the internal proletariat may react with violence against the dominant minority, creative leaders within it may also produce a "higher religion." (The intellectual inspiration behind Toynbee's discussion of internal and external proletariats was the work of Karl

Marx, but Toynbee transformed Marx's key ideas into political and religious categories.) As a civilization disintegrates, the dominant minority regroups and creates what Toynbee calls a "universal state." These universal states have two functions: They bring unity to the areas over which they rule, and they can act as a chrysalis out of which a higher religion will emerge. The archetype for such a universal state was the Roman Empire and the development of Christianity within it.

Toynbee had developed these arguments in the first six volumes of *A Study of History* (1934-1939). However, the combined impress of World War II and Toynbee's personal and spiritual development led Toynbee to shift his emphasis in volumes 7-10. In the earlier volumes, he had seen the higher religions essentially as by-products of ongoing civilizational development, but he now argued that the deeper meaning of civilizational development was to produce the "higher" religions, such as Christianity, Hinduism, Buddhism, and Islam. Their emergence was the ultimate product and final meaning of the story of humankind's development. These universal religions now became a third kind of society in human history, in addition to primitive and civilized societies. During the last several decades of his life, Toynbee became increasingly convinced that the future hope of humanity lay in the values of expressed by these higher religions, especially love, compassion, and selflessness.

SIGNIFICANCE

Among the community of professional historians, Toynbee's *A Study of History* met with widespread criticism. For many, his work smacked more of the speculative philosophy of history that dated to Augustine than of the sober empirical approach to the past favored by academic historians. On the other hand, within the broader literate public, Toynbee's work, especially in Somervell's excellent abridgment, was widely read. During the last decades of his life, Toynbee became a public intellectual whose pronouncements on world affairs were listened to around the world. In fact, his willingness to offer his interpretation of current events and to make pronouncements on the current and future condition of humankind was a second reason for the severely critical response Toynbee's work received. Many historians disliked the idea of a pundit and prophet who made metahistorical speculations.

Toynbee himself, of course, always saw himself as a historian, and he took enormous care to respond to all the criticisms of his work in what constituted the twelfth volume of *A Study of History*. Although the popularity of

1934

Toynbee's monumental volumes lessened, his belief in the unity behind humankind's history and his conviction that this unity can be made understandable inspired later academic historians led by important figures such as William H. McNeill. Toynbee's lifelong intellectual and spiritual endeavor to understand the modern world and to critically probe the human condition made significant contributions to the twentieth century's intellectual history.

—*Michael W. Messmer*

FURTHER READING

McIntire, C. M., and Marvin Perry, eds. *Toynbee: Reappraisals*. Toronto: University of Toronto Press, 1989. Interesting compilation of essays examining Toynbee's work from multiple perspectives.

McNeill, William. *Arnold J. Toynbee: A Life*. New York: Oxford University Press, 1989. Excellent biography of Toynbee by a renowned world historian who knew and was inspired by Toynbee.

Navari, Cornelia. "Arnold Toynbee (1889-1975): Prophecy and Civilization." *Review of International Studies* 26 (2000): 289-301. An article situating Toynbee's theory of international relations and his concern with the future of Western civilization in his grand narrative of universal historical process.

Perry, Marvin. *Arnold Toynbee and the Western Tradition*. New York: Peter Lang, 1996. Sees Toynbee's historical vision as a response to the intellectual and political crises of the twentieth century and a call for critical reflection on the Enlightenment tradition and the human condition.

Toynbee, Arnold J. *A Study of History*. 2 vols. Abridged by D. C. Somervell. Oxford, England: Oxford University Press, 1957. Somervell's excellent condensation of *A Study of History* received the imprimatur of Toynbee himself and made the basic arguments of his massive work accessible to a wide reading public.

SEE ALSO: 1907: Meinecke Advances the Analytic Method in History; Summer, 1918: Rise of Cultural Relativism Revises Historiography; 1923-1939: *Cambridge Ancient History* Appears; Sept. 30, 1925: Chesterton Critiques Modernism and Defends Christianity; 1932: Gilson's *Spirit of Medieval Philosophy* Reassesses Christian Thought.

1934
ZWICKY AND BAADE PROPOSE A THEORY OF NEUTRON STARS

Fritz Zwicky and Walter Baade proposed that a neutron star forms during the explosion of a supernova.

LOCALE: Mount Wilson Observatory, California
CATEGORIES: Science and technology; astronomy

KEY FIGURES
Walter Baade (1893-1960), German American astronomer
Fritz Zwicky (1898-1974), Swiss astronomer
Lev Davidovich Landau (1908-1968), Soviet physicist

SUMMARY OF EVENT

The Greek philosopher Aristotle taught that the stars, the Sun, and the planets were located on crystal spheres that moved around the stationary Earth. On rare occasions, a new star would appear in the sphere, shining so brightly that it was visible during the day, and finally growing dim over several months. These were called "novas" (or "novae") from the Latin word for "new," because they seemed to be new stars. (Centuries later, research would reveal how wrong that name is.)

In the past two thousand years, only seven bright novas remained visible in the northern sky for at least six months each. In 185 C.E., for example, the Chinese recorded the appearance of a "guest star" that lasted for twenty months. Another such star in 393 C.E. lasted for eight months. The nova of 1006 was visible for several years and was recorded by the Chinese, Japanese, Europeans, and Arabs. The nova in 1054 lasted twenty-two months and was noted by the Chinese and Japanese; there is evidence from several petroglyphs in the American Southwest that Native Americans also observed the event.

A nova that appeared in 1572 was observed by the last great astronomer before the age of telescopes, Tycho Brahe. It was Brahe who gave novas their name. Because of his study of that nova, known as Brahe's star, and his subsequent book titled *De Nova Stella*, Brahe's reputation was made. The German astronomer Johannes Kepler, who was Brahe's assistant in later years, studied the 1604 nova, Kepler's star. After Brahe's death in 1601, Kepler used the astronomer's data to explain the motion of the planets. The appearance of the nova drove

NEUTRON STAR

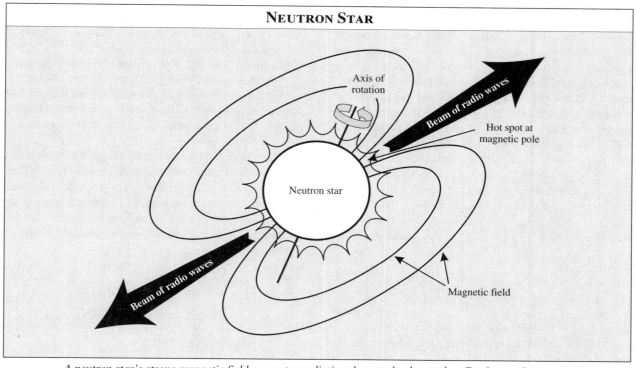

A neutron star's strong magnetic field generates radiation that can be detected on Earth as radio waves.

Kepler to greater efforts that resulted in three laws of planetary motion.

Over the centuries, advances in telescopes and other astronomical instruments led to a better understanding of novas. Studies suggested that novas were not a simple class of stars. Some were bright and rare, whereas others were much fainter and more common. Fritz Zwicky and Walter Baade recognized in 1934 that a division was necessary and renamed the brighter novas "supernovas."

Stars are "born" from collapsing clouds of gas and dust. As they become older, the interior pressure and temperature increases, producing chemical reactions in which hydrogen fuses into helium. Energy is released from this reaction in the form of light and other electromagnetic radiation. The length of a star's life cycle is determined by its mass. Low-mass stars such as the Sun fuse the hydrogen slowly and have lifetimes of tens of billions of years. The most massive stars have lifetimes of tens of millions of years. As the star "dies," it can do so in one of several ways. The low-mass star depletes its hydrogen supply, grows in size to become a "red giant," and then collapses to a "white dwarf" phase. It shines by its stored heat until eventually it cools and reaches the "black dwarf" stage. A star the size of the Sun will shrink to the size of Earth.

A binary star system is a pair of stars that orbit a common center of gravity. A binary star system whose stars are near the end of their life cycles is the common source of nova explosions. Material from one of the stars is pulled onto the surface of the other star. When enough of it accumulates, it will fuse to helium and produce the brightening that can be seen as a nova. That is why the word "nova" is not really correct—a nova is not a new star, but rather the death of a star in a binary system.

A supernova, however, is the very rapid explosion of a very massive star near the end of its life cycle. This is evident because in the constellation Taurus, the location of the 1054 nova, lies a gaseous mass known as the Crab nebula. This gas cloud is expanding outward. Calculations of the velocity of the cloud's gas show that, after the explosion, it started its outward journey in 1054.

When a massive star depletes its supply of hydrogen, it collapses and its internal heat and pressure increase until helium is converted to carbon. Elements with increasingly higher atomic numbers are formed as the collapse continues. Once the core becomes the element iron, the process cannot continue until more energy is added. At this point, the collapse continues because of gravity; in the last stages, the star's outer layers hit the core and

1934

bounce. The star explodes, sending a large part of its mass into space. The remainder of the supernova collapses to become a neutron star or a black hole, depending on its mass.

Zwicky and Baade, and independently Lev Davidovich Landau, postulated that, after this explosion, the pressure of the star's collapse overcomes the atoms' electrical forces and fuses protons and electrons into neutrons. This explanation was not verified experimentally until Jocelyn Bell, a graduate student at Cambridge, discovered the first pulsar in 1967. A pulsar is a neutron star that spins very rapidly, emitting radio waves from its rotating magnetic field. First thought to be signs of extraterrestrial intelligence, these pulsars were the first observational evidence of Baade and Zwicky's theory.

SIGNIFICANCE

For thousands of years, people have tried to figure out how the planets came into being. The discovery and understanding of neutron stars and supernovas have helped scientists to solve the puzzle. The "big bang theory" suggests that the universe began about fifteen billion years ago. At that time, all the energy and matter in the universe were contained within a small sphere that exploded. As the universe—the pieces of matter sent flying by the explosion—cooled and expanded, hydrogen and helium began to form. Eventually, clouds of hydrogen and helium collapsed to form stars, and these formed into galaxies.

As these stars aged, the more massive ones exploded as supernovas. The blast spewed into the surrounding space all the chemical elements contained in the star, enriching the interstellar medium with essential ingredients. After enough stars had become supernovas, planets could begin to form. So, too, could the next generation of stars, which would benefit from the enriched gas and dust clouds of the planets. Before this time, planets could not exist. Life as it is now known could not exist because the essential elements on which life depends—carbon, nitrogen, and others—did not exist.

—*Stephen J. Shulik*

FURTHER READING

Bethe, Hans, and Gerry Brown. "How a Supernova Explodes." *Scientific American* 252 (May, 1985): 60-68. Bethe was the first person to show how stars convert mass into energy. Discusses the mechanics of the massive star's implosion and resulting explosion. Also explores the star's preexplosion history. Rich with figures and diagrams. Intended for informed readers.

Charles, Philip, and J. Leonard Culhane. "X-Rays from Supernova Remnants." *Scientific American* 233 (December, 1975): 36-46. Points out that when a supernova occurs, huge amounts of energy in the form of electromagnetic radiation are sent into space. X rays produced by the explosion are analyzed for information about the explosion.

Herbst, William, and George Assousa. "Supernovas and Star Formation." *Scientific American* 241 (August, 1979): 138-145. Shows how theory and observations support the idea that supernovas trigger the formation of other stars. Also discusses the formation of the spiral structure of some galaxies.

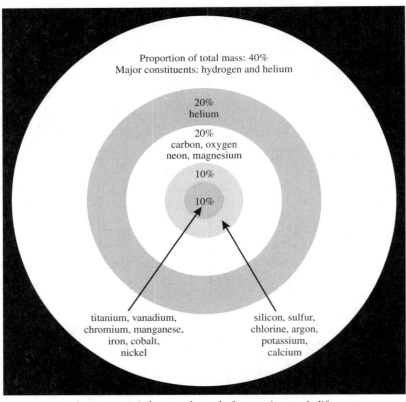

A supernova is born at the end of a massive star's life.

Kirshner, Robert. "Supernovas in Other Galaxies." *Scientific American* 235 (December, 1976): 89-101. Points out that, because supernovas are rare phenomena in Earth's galaxy, scientists must look to other galaxies such as the Andromeda galaxy to find examples to study. This reveals a difference in supernovas that leads to the classifications of Type I and Type II supernova explosions.

Mitton, Simon. *The Crab Nebula.* New York: Charles Scribner's Sons, 1978. An in-depth study of the 1054 supernova in the constellation Taurus. Covers the historical records of the Asian and American Indian observers, the telescopic observations of the Crab nebula, the formation of a neutron star, and how pulsars pulse.

Motz, Lloyd, and Jefferson Hane Weaver. *The Story of Astronomy.* New York: Plenum, 1995. Presents the history of astronomy from ancient times to the end of the twentieth century. Chapters 16 and 17 include discussion of supernovas and galactic research in general. Features bibliography and index.

Schramm, David, and Robert Clayton. "Did a Supernova Trigger the Formation of the Solar System?" *Scientific American* 239 (October, 1978): 124-139. Explores the implications of small amounts of decay product from short-lived radioactive isotopes found in primitive meteorites. Concludes that the original isotopes were formed in a nearby supernova explosion that triggered the formation of the solar system.

Seward, Frederick, Paul Gorenstein, and Wallace Tucker. "Young Supernova Remnants." *Scientific American* 253 (August, 1985): 88-96. Reports on the X-ray data obtained from the Einstein X-Ray Observatory and its relationship to supernova remnants.

Shows that the X-ray spectrums for Type I and Type II supernovas are different.

Silk, Joseph. *The Big Bang.* 3d ed. New York: W. H. Freeman, 2000. Presents a sweeping account of the formation and evolution of the universe. Recounts the history of astronomical speculation about the universe and examines evidence for the big bang theory. Includes glossary and index.

_____. *On the Shores of the Unknown: A Short History of the Universe.* New York: Cambridge University Press, 2005. A history of the universe and the development of humankind's knowledge about it. Accessible to lay readers. Includes illustrations and index.

Stephenson, F. Richard, and David Clark. "Historical Supernovas." *Scientific American* 234 (June, 1976): 100-107. Reports on seven supernovas of the last two millennia and the search for their remnants. Also discusses the recorded observations of various cultures.

Wheeler, J. Craig, and Robert Harkness. "Helium-Rich Supernova." *Scientific American* 259 (November, 1988): 50-58. Reveals that there is a Type Ib subcategory supernova, similar to a nova explosion because it occurs in a binary star system. A massive companion star expands and drives matter into the other star, ripping that star's outer layer away and exposing the core, which subsequently collapses and explodes.

SEE ALSO: Aug. 7 and 12, 1912: Hess Discovers Cosmic Rays; Dec., 1913: Russell Announces His Theory of Stellar Evolution; 1916: Schwarzschild Solves the Equations of General Relativity; 1924: Hubble Determines the Distance to the Andromeda Nebula; 1931-1935: Chandrasekhar Calculates the Upper Limit of a White Dwarf Star's Mass; Feb. 15, 1939: Oppenheimer Calculates the Nature of Black Holes.

1934

1934-1935
HITCHCOCK BECOMES SYNONYMOUS WITH SUSPENSE

With The Man Who Knew Too Much *and* The Thirty-Nine Steps, *Hitchcock revitalized a sagging career, creating a mixture of themes and cinematic techniques that would make his name synonymous with suspense.*

LOCALE: Great Britain
CATEGORIES: Motion pictures; entertainment

KEY FIGURES

Alfred Hitchcock (1899-1980), British film director who established his reputation with thrillers

Michael Balcon (1896-1977), British film producer who helped Hitchcock to reemerge as an important filmmaker

Robert Donat (1905-1958), lead actor in *The Thirty-Nine Steps* and the first truly Hitchcockian hero

Madeleine Carroll (1906-1987), actor whose portrayal of Pamela in *The Thirty-Nine Steps* created the prototype of the Hitchcock blond

Peter Lorre (1904-1964), actor who was able to make evil somewhat sympathetic in *The Man Who Knew Too Much*

SUMMARY OF EVENT

By 1933, Alfred Hitchcock was stymied; his career appeared to be going nowhere. In 1926, he had made *The Lodger*, a melodramatic thriller involving a Jack-the-Ripper motif that had won stunning praise and instantly placed him among Great Britain's top directors. *The Lodger* had been his third film, but since then he had directed thirteen more, none of which matched *The Lodger*'s popularity. Although some of his pictures had been well received, most met with indifference, and his last few films had been outright flops. He had tried other thrillers, romance, comedy, filmed plays, and even musicals, but nothing seemed to work. At this point, as he seriously questioned whether he had any future in the film industry, Hitchcock was approached by an old colleague, Michael Balcon. Balcon, who had produced some of Hitchcock's early pictures, including *The Lodger*, was now in charge of production for the Gaumont-British Studio, and he wanted Hitchcock for his film company. Some of Hitchcock's problems in the past had stemmed from his working for studios that gave him little control over which films he was to direct. Balcon offered Hitchcock freedom of choice and personal moral support. Agreeing to join Balcon, Hitchcock decided to return to the genre that he preferred and that had given him his first success—the thriller.

The Man Who Knew Too Much, released in 1934, was a tale of murder, kidnapping, and attempted assassination centering on an English family caught in a web of international intrigue. While vacationing in Switzerland, Bob and Jill Lawrence (Leslie Banks and Edna Best) inadvertently stumble on a plot to slay a leading European statesman in London. Their young daughter Betty (Nova Pilbeam) is then abducted by the conspirators. Bob and Jill return to England and, through a series of adventures, foil the assassination and rescue Betty. *The Man Who Knew Too Much* reawakened interest in Hitchcock and captured public and critical acclaim, but *The Thirty-Nine Steps*, released in 1935, would be an even greater triumph.

The Thirty-Nine Steps deals with espionage. Richard Hannay (Robert Donat), a Canadian visiting London, meets a mysterious woman who tells him that she is trying to stop a group of spies from smuggling an important military secret out of the country. She is murdered in Hannay's apartment; Hannay is suspected and flees from the police. He soon discovers that the foreign agents are trying to kill him in order to prevent him from revealing their plans, and he is pursued from London to the Scottish Highlands, across fog-swept moors, and back to London. In the process, he becomes romantically involved with Pamela (Madeleine Carroll), a young woman who at first believes he is a killer and who then becomes convinced of his innocence. Together, Hannay and Pamela save the secret, help break up the spy ring, clear Hannay's name, and go off to live happily ever after.

SIGNIFICANCE

The Man Who Knew Too Much and *The Thirty-Nine Steps* reestablished Alfred Hitchcock as Great Britain's premier director, setting him on a path that would lead to Hollywood and greater fame. The two films represent the mature realization of several of Hitchcock's trademark techniques and approaches. He had always favored spectacular scenes, an expressionist mood, and editing that kept viewers off balance and the pace moving. Both films skillfully mix these elements. *The Man Who Knew Too Much* features several exciting moments, including three scenes that have become part of Hitchcockian lore: the assassination attempt during a symphony in the vast Albert Hall, a shootout with besieged conspirators that seems to engage half of London's police force, and a desperate moment at the picture's conclusion, when one of the assassins stalks Betty across a high roof in an attempt to kill her before she can be saved. Although *The Thirty-Nine Steps* does not offer as many memorable scenes, it does have a striking conclusion in London's Palladium; it is also a faster-paced film, with almost nonstop action. Both films are darkly expressionistic, and both are filled with sudden, jarring changes of mood.

Although sound was still a primitive art in the industry, Hitchcock was among the first to experiment with the different ways it could be used to enhance films. He made great strides in this area in these two pictures. The films' use of dialogue is more extensive and more assured than in Hitchcock's previous talkies. In *The Man Who Knew Too Much*, Hitchcock employed sound to accompany the assassination; the attempt is made in the midst of a symphonic performance, at the precise instant when the drums beat and the cymbals clash. The music becomes an integral part of the plot, heightening the anxiety for the viewer. In *The Thirty-Nine Steps*, when a maid finds the murdered woman in Hannay's apartment, she opens her mouth to scream, but what the audience hears is the whistle of the train on which Hannay is fleeing London. Sudden and unsettling, the segue became one of the historic cinematic moments. With it, Hitchcock broke with the convention of early sound films that required the camera and the soundtrack to stay in sync, and in doing so he enlarged the possibilities for the use of sound in films.

Hitchcock liked to utilize humor to relieve tension, and he also liked to follow comic incidents with the return of menace, allowing the humor to make the shift to danger all the more potent. *The Man Who Knew Too Much* was, to that point, his most extensive melding of the comical into the thriller, but the film's humor is largely limited to witty dialogue. In contrast, humor permeates *The Thirty-Nine Steps*. The banter is even sharper than that of *The Man Who Knew Too Much*, and the film is replete with laughable situations that temporarily mask Hannay's peril. Hannay is sitting in a railway car, expecting to be caught, and he finds himself having to listen to a lingerie salesman display his wares and make risqué jokes. Running from the police, Hannay stumbles into a political meeting, is mistaken for a speaker, and gives an

absurd oration. Pamela and Hannay are handcuffed together and awkwardly try to eat and sleep together. These are diverting, antic scenes; however, they soon give way to renewed suspense. In *The Thirty-Nine Steps* (and in other films) Hitchcock never allows his viewers to relax fully.

These two films also introduced new elements that would be crucial in the evolution of Hitchcock's work. *The Man Who Knew Too Much* was his first foray into espionage. By 1934, fascism was entrenched in Italy, Adolf Hitler had taken power in Germany, and the English were beginning to feel the onset of war jitters. Fear was in the air, and Hitchcock's ability to tap this appre-

Alfred Hitchcock. (Hulton Archive/Getty Images)

1934

hension helped to ensure the success of *The Man Who Knew Too Much* and *The Thirty-Nine Steps*. After 1934, a significant proportion of Hitchcock's work would revolve around international intrigue. The world would be plagued by tension and conflict for the rest of his life; the espionage film would become a special type of thriller, and Hitchcock was one of its most skilled practitioners. Part of the reason was financial—spies could be big successes in the box office, as Hitchcock discovered with *The Man Who Knew Too Much*—yet he also found he enjoyed fashioning stories around the shadowy life of the secret agent.

The archetypal Hitchcock hero, heroine, and villain were first seen in these films. *The Man Who Knew Too Much* provides the villain in the leader of the conspirators, played by Peter Lorre. Dangerous, yet perversely appealing, a terrorist at once droll, sophisticated, and menacing, Lorre is the most dynamic character in the film; his character was the first of a number of similarly fascinating evil figures who would energize many of Hitchcock's future films. After *The Thirty-Nine Steps*, moreover, Hitchcock's male and female protagonists would be made to resemble Hannay and Pamela. His previous heroes and heroines, including the Lawrences in *The Man Who Knew Too Much*, tended to be one-dimensional; their characters were secondary to plot and to Hitchcock's special cinematic techniques. In *The Thirty-Nine Steps*, both primary roles are multifaceted and central to the story's development, and they are played by actors of major talent and star presence. Hannay, as envisioned by Hitchcock and realized by Robert Donat, is a witty and courageous man of action and charm. Similar characters would reappear in Hitchcock films over the years in roles played by Michael Redgrave, James Stewart, Paul Newman, and Cary Grant. Madeleine Carroll is the original "Hitchcock blond"; strong blond women, seemingly icy but actually passionate, would become a Hitchcock hallmark. While he had featured blond women in films before *The Thirty-Nine Steps*, Madeleine Carroll's Pamela was the first personification of his ideal heroine. Later Hitchcock stars such as Grace Kelly, Eva Marie Saint, and Tippi Hedren were cast in her lineage.

The Thirty-Nine Steps presents one of Hitchcock's favorite thriller structures: An honest man, made to look guilty by circumstances, is chased over long and picturesque distances while trying to establish his innocence. It also contributes the legendary Hitchcock device, the "MacGuffin." The MacGuffin is a secret that inaugurates the action, a secret apparently so crucial that everyone wants to control it, although it ultimately turns out to be

rather inconsequential. In *The Thirty-Nine Steps*, the MacGuffin is a military secret, a type of aircraft engine design. The viewer never really learns much about it, and, indeed, the secret is soon lost sight of in the plot. The film is not about the engine design; it is about Hannay's attempt to prove his innocence and his growing relationship with Pamela. The MacGuffin could have been anything; its only real importance is to get events started. After *The Thirty-Nine Steps*, Hitchcock incorporated the MacGuffin into his repertoire, and a favorite game for Hitchcock buffs would be to look for the MacGuffins in his pictures.

Of the two films that restored Hitchcock's reputation, *The Thirty-Nine Steps* is the more significant. Audiences at the time felt this was so, as did critics. Hitchcock himself believed it a richer, more professional accomplishment, and cinema scholars have agreed. They see it as a compendium of his best early work and the first clear indication of the Hitchcock that was to come. Nevertheless, *The Man Who Knew Too Much* is not without its importance. The film did begin Hitchcock's relationship with the spy thriller and was quite popular, and its success was the turning point of Hitchcock's career. After that film, there was no doubt of Hitchcock's ability as a director.

Hitchcock crafted two more espionage thrillers for Michael Balcon: *Secret Agent* (1936) and *Sabotage* (1936). While neither was as admired as *The Man Who Knew Too Much* or *The Thirty-Nine Steps*, both added to his indisputable standing as Great Britain's finest director. The fruitful collaboration with Balcon, however, did not last. Gaumont-British, destroyed by executive wrangling, gave up film production. Hitchcock made two films for Gainsborough Studios: *Young and Innocent* (1937), a lighthearted thriller, and *The Lady Vanishes* (1938), a spy film that many consider one of his best. He then decided to quit Great Britain for the United States. Ever since making *The Man Who Knew Too Much* and *The Thirty-Nine Steps*, he had received approaches from Hollywood. After much hesitation, he finally chose to accept an offer from David O. Selznick. The working relationship with Michael Balcon was gone, and there would be more money, better production facilities, and perhaps more artistic challenges in the United States. Before he left, he directed one last film, *Jamaica Inn* (1939), a pirate melodrama, for actor and producer Charles Laughton. Although the film earned money, it was a critical failure and confirmed evidence that his strength lay in thrillers.

Hitchcock went to the United States in 1939; he

would die there in 1980. The forty-one years in Hollywood would make him perhaps the best-known filmmaker in the world. Building on his experience in Great Britain, he would create a remarkable number of varied landmark thrillers, including *Rear Window* (1954), *Vertigo* (1958), *North by Northwest* (1959), *Psycho* (1960), and *The Birds* (1963). He would influence generations of filmmakers, especially in the suspense genre. His films continue to be watched, and universities and film schools produce studies in ever-increasing numbers that interpret his pictures in minute detail. If Hitchcock had not made *The Man Who Knew Too Much* and *The Thirty-Nine Steps*, none of this might have happened.

—*Clarke Wilhelm*

FURTHER READING

Chandler, Charlotte. *It's Only a Movie: Alfred Hitchcock—A Personal Biography*. New York: Simon & Schuster, 2005. Chandler's treatment is less than scholarly, but her book includes a number of rare, entertaining, and revealing insights about Hitchcock, most of which were provided by his family.

Durgnat, Raymond. *The Strange Case of Alfred Hitchcock*. Cambridge, Mass.: MIT Press, 1974. Especially helpful in illuminating Hitchcock's work in the 1920's and 1930's. Quite intellectual in its approach, but written clearly enough for the general reader. Bibliography, filmography, and index.

Harris, Robert A., and Michael S. Lasky. *The Complete Films of Alfred Hitchcock*. Rev. ed. Sacramento, Calif.: Citadel Press, 2002. A fully illustrated analysis of all Hitchcock's work, picture by picture. Despite its slick appearance, this is a serious, well-written overview of the films.

Spoto, Donald. *The Art of Alfred Hitchcock*. 1976. Rev. ed. New York: Doubleday, 1992. This massive book looks at each film separately. Spoto's style is accessible, and his insights are rewarding. A necessary source. Index and filmography.

Truffaut, François. *Hitchcock*. 1967. Rev. ed. New York: Simon & Schuster, 1984. A series of interviews of Hitchcock by Truffaut, the noted French director, in which Hitchcock tells his own story. Illustrations, extended filmography, short bibliography, index.

Taylor, John Russell. *Hitch: The Life and Times of Alfred Hitchcock*. New York: Pantheon Books, 1978. Perhaps the best biography of Hitchcock; easy to read and comprehensive. Index.

SEE ALSO: 1925-1927: Gance's *Napoléon* Revolutionizes Filmmaking Techniques; 1927: Kuleshov and Pudovkin Introduce Montage to Filmmaking; 1927: Lang Expands the Limits of Filmmaking with *Metropolis*; May 16, 1929: First Academy Awards Honor Film Achievement; 1930's: Hollywood Enters Its Golden Age; 1930's-1940's: Studio System Dominates Hollywood Filmmaking; 1931-1932: Gangster Films Become Popular; 1934-1938: Production Code Gives Birth to Screwball Comedy; 1937-1939: Renoir's Films Explore Social and Political Themes.

1934

1934-1938
PRODUCTION CODE GIVES BIRTH TO SCREWBALL COMEDY

Romantic Hollywood comedies featuring bickering lovers flourished with the release of such films as It Happened One Night *and* Bringing Up Baby. *Filmmakers had to be creative in their presentation of sexual themes, which were heavily regulated.*

LOCALE: United States
CATEGORIES: Motion pictures; entertainment

KEY FIGURES
Frank Capra (1897-1991), American film director
Claudette Colbert (1903-1996), American film actor
Clark Gable (1901-1960), American film actor
Howard Hawks (1896-1977), American film director
Cary Grant (1904-1986), American film actor
Katharine Hepburn (1907-2003), American film actor
Carole Lombard (1908-1942), American film actor
Walter Connolly (1887-1940), American film actor

SUMMARY OF EVENT

When films learned to talk, they also learned to be naughty. Many American films of the early 1930's, especially those starring Mae West and Jean Harlow and the sophisticated comedies directed by Ernst Lubitsch, featured strong sexual innuendoes. Fear of government censorship led in 1934 to the implementation of a production code that severely restricted the amount of sex and violence in American films. One of the sillier results of the code, ferociously enforced by Joseph L. Breen of the Motion Picture Producers and Distributors of America, was that two people of the opposite sex could not appear on a bed together unless one had at least one foot on the floor. The production code remained in effect, with only slight modifications, until 1966. The screwball comedy evolved in part as a response to the limitations of the code. The inability of filmmakers to spell out the sexual attraction of their films' protagonists resulted in the production of films in which the romantic leads battled both verbally and physically for much of the running time.

Quarreling lovers on the stage go back at least as far as William Shakespeare's *The Taming of the Shrew* (1593-1594). By the 1930's, they had become prominent in such Noël Coward plays as *Private Lives* (1930). One of the main precursors of the screwball comedy is Lubitsch's Americanized 1933 version of Coward's *Design for Living*, in which two young Americans in Paris, Tommy Chambers (Fredric March) and George Curtis (Gary Cooper), fall in love with the same woman, Gilda Farrell (Miriam Hopkins). Despite discreet fadeouts, Lubitsch clearly implies that Gilda has sex with both George and Tommy. After the implementation of the production code, sexual innuendo became more subtle and was often hidden behind a veil of slapstick.

Most experts consider *It Happened One Night* (1934) to be the first screwball comedy. Directed by Frank Capra and written by Robert Riskin (based on two short stories by Samuel Hopkins Adams), *It Happened One Night* presents the efforts of spoiled heiress Ellie Andrews (Claudette Colbert) to escape her father, Alexander Andrews (Walter Connolly), and marry playboy King Westley (Jameson Thomas). On a bus from Florida to New York, Ellie meets newspaper reporter Peter Warne (Clark Gable), who eventually offers to help her in exchange for her story. After numerous adventures, she finds herself in the middle of an elaborate wedding ceremony only to forsake Westley for Peter.

Although the film's studio, Columbia, had no such expectations, *It Happened One Night* was an enormous success and had a tremendous influence on Hollywood. According to legend, the film popularized bus travel, saving the Greyhound Bus Company from bankruptcy, and a scene in which Gable undressed to reveal he wore no undershirt drastically affected the sales of men's underwear. The film won Academy Awards for best picture, best actor, best actress, best director, and best adapted screenplay.

It Happened One Night introduced several plot features that would become familiar as the screwball genre flourished through the early 1940's. The most significant element was the constant bickering that occurred between the film's protagonists. When Ellie and Peter meet, they argue over the last remaining bus seat, and Peter forces Ellie, who is used to sharing nothing, to give him enough room to sit. Throughout the trip, they argue over money, food, and sleeping arrangements. When they are compelled to share a motor-camp cabin after roads are flooded, Peter erects a blanket between their beds to ensure, he says, his privacy. Peter calls the blanket, suspended on a rope, "the walls of Jericho." The blanket represents the sexual tension between Peter and Ellie. Ellie is drawn to a man who stands up to her peevishness, and Peter is drawn to her spunk. The film ends with Capra's camera outside another motel cabin, and a trumpet is heard inside as the walls of Jericho come down at last.

In most screwball comedies, the protagonists battle on almost equal terms. Ellie's audacity allows her to escape her father's yacht by jumping into water fully clothed. When detectives confront them at the first motor camp, Peter begins a mock argument to divert suspicion, and Ellie is quick-witted enough to assume immediately the persona of a crying southern belle. In the film's most famous sequence, Peter attempts to show Ellie his foolproof hitchhiking techniques and fails miserably; Ellie then raises her skirt to stop the next passing car, proving to Peter that she has resources he does not have.

SIGNIFICANCE

It Happened One Night conveyed a notably sympathetic attitude toward the rich that was evident in many screwball comedies. Ellie is condemned more for being spoiled than for being privileged, and her father, far from being a capitalist ogre, immediately perceives that the earthy Peter will make a much better son-in-law than the oily Westley. This attitude was taken to further extremes in Gregory La Cava's *My Man Godfrey* (1936) and Mitchell Leisen's *Easy Living* (1937). In the former, a homeless man turned butler (William Powell) is really a Boston Brahmin who has chosen poverty after an unhappy love affair. When the family employing him faces financial disaster, Godfrey uses his understanding of the stock market to rescue them, essentially rewarding them for their selfishness, eccentricity, and incompetence. *Easy Living*, written by Preston Sturges, pokes fun at the pompous banker J. B. Ball (Edward Arnold) by having his servants and secretary make sneering remarks, but the film ends with another narrow escape from ruin, thereby justifying Ball's way of life.

It Happened One Night initiated the tradition of spoiled heiresses and cynical reporters at the center of screwball comedies, including Carole Lombard's ex-

MEMORABLE SCREWBALL COMEDIES

The films listed below are acknowledged to be among the very best in screwball comedy.

Year	Film	Director
1934	*It Happened One Night*	Frank Capra
1934	*Twentieth Century*	Howard Hawks
1936	*My Man Godfrey*	Gregory La Cava
1937	*The Awful Truth*	Leo McCarey
1937	*Nothing Sacred*	William A. Wellman
1938	*Bringing Up Baby*	Howard Hawks
1938	*Holiday*	George Cukor
1940	*His Girl Friday*	Howard Hawks
1940	*The Philadelphia Story*	George Cukor
1941	*The Lady Eve*	Preston Sturges
1941	*Mr. and Mrs. Smith*	Alfred Hitchcock
1942	*The Palm Beach Story*	Preston Sturges
1942	*To Be or Not to Be*	Ernst Lubitsch
1944	*Arsenic and Old Lace*	Frank Capra

ceedingly empty-headed rich girl in *My Man Godfrey* and Fredric March's tough newspaperman in William Wellman's *Nothing Sacred* (1937). March's character falls in love with a young woman (Lombard again) who is supposedly dying of radium poisoning. Hostilities between heiresses and reporters that dissolve into romance appear in several screwball comedies, most notably with Myrna Loy and William Powell in Jack Conway's *Libeled Lady* (1936) and Barbara Stanwyck and Henry Fonda in Leigh Jason's *The Mad Miss Manton* (1938).

The most important influence of *It Happened One Night* is the tradition of bickering it engendered. Among the many variations on the Ellie-Peter model are the married couple (Irene Dunne and Cary Grant) who cannot stop their altercations even after divorcing in Leo McCarey's *The Awful Truth* (1937) and the multiple battling couples of *Libeled Lady:* Jean Harlow and Spencer Tracy, Loy and Powell, and Harlow and Powell.

Before the genre reached its apex with *Bringing Up Baby* (1938), several more essential screwball elements had to be introduced, the most significant of which was slapstick. Because the production code prohibited suggestive physical contact between the battling lovers, pratfalls were substituted as a means of releasing pent-up sexual energy. In William A. Seiter's *The Moon's Our Home* (1936), an heiress (Margaret Sullavan) and an explorer (Henry Fonda) take spills off a sled, a sleigh, and skis. They are thrown from their sleigh when their horse,

a mare, takes off in romantic pursuit of another horse. In *Nothing Sacred*, Lombard and March knock each other out, and in Alfred Santell's *Breakfast for Two* (1937), an heiress (Barbara Stanwyck) conceals a doorknob in a boxing glove to give a black eye to a playboy (Herbert Marshall).

Many screwball comedies offered satirical elements: *My Man Godfrey* made fun of the trivialities of the Park Avenue rich, *Nothing Sacred* punctured the excesses of the sensationalist press, and *The Moon's Our Home* attacked the inflated egos of celebrities. The most penetrating satire came in Richard Boleslawski's *Theodora Goes Wild* (1936), which is based on a story by Mary McCarthy. In the film, a young woman (Irene Dunne) writes a best seller whose sexual suggestiveness is condemned by her puritanical hometown. The film constantly ridicules the smug hypocrisy of small-town America, especially when Theodora delights in making the community think she has given birth to an illegitimate child.

Bringing Up Baby, although it lacks a satiric edge, is the culmination of these screwball elements. Directed by Howard Hawks and written by Dudley Nichols and Hagar Wilde, it presents the dizziest of dizzy heiresses, Susan Vance (Katharine Hepburn), who hopes for a million-dollar bequest from her Aunt Elizabeth (May Robson). Paleontologist David Huxley (Cary Grant) wants the same million for his museum. Susan soon falls in love with David and wants him to get the money, but all of her assistance leads to disaster. Susan's brother has sent a domesticated leopard from South America as a present for Aunt Elizabeth. Susan tricks David into helping her take the leopard, called Baby, to her aunt's Connecticut farm so that he will miss his wedding to the stuffy Alice Swallow (Virginia Walker). Aunt Elizabeth's fox terrier steals and buries the bone David has just received to complete the dinosaur skeleton he has been working on for years, Baby escapes, Susan releases a dangerous leopard she thinks is Baby from a circus van, and all the protagonists end up in jail suspected of a variety of offenses.

Aunt Elizabeth becomes convinced of David's instability and gives her money to Susan. Alice is also shocked by his behavior and decides not to marry him. *Bringing Up Baby* ends with Susan giving the million to David, who has spent the entire film resisting her aggressive advances. As Susan climbs onto his dinosaur skeleton to express her love, causing the skeleton to collapse, David finally accepts the inevitable.

The collapsing dinosaur is a fitting conclusion to a film filled with slapstick. David and Susan are constantly

1934

Cary Grant and Katharine Hepburn in a scene from the 1938 film Bringing Up Baby. *(AP/Wide World Photos)*

falling down. Aunt Elizabeth's explorer friend, Major Horace Applegate (Charles Ruggles), and her drunken servant Gogarty (Barry Fitzgerald) chase and are chased by the leopards. Viewers and reviewers of 1938 apparently felt that the physical humor was excessive; the film was a commercial and critical flop. However, audiences and film historians in the years since have embraced the silliness, which includes Grant's dressing up in a woman's fluffy dressing gown, as essential to the genre. The romance at the center of the film is notable for the extroverted antics of Susan, who is willing to try anything that might lead to fun. David, stiff and humorless at the beginning of the film, learns from Susan to accept the unpredictability of life and becomes more human.

Physicality was important in *Bringing Up Baby* and other screwball comedies, and the preeminent performers of the genre were Grant, who displayed his debonair athleticism also in *The Awful Truth* and in Norman Z. McLeod's *Topper* (1937), and Lombard, who showcased her combination of beauty, vulnerability, physical vitality, and buffoonery in Howard Hawks's *Twentieth Century* (1934), *My Man Godfrey*, Wesley Ruggles's *True Confession* (1937), and *Nothing Sacred*.

As important as the stars of screwball comedies were the contributions of the supporting performers. More notable character actors appeared in Hollywood films during the 1930's and early 1940's than at any other time,

and many received their best parts in screwball comedies. In addition to Robson, Ruggles, and Fitzgerald, *Bringing Up Baby* offered Walter Catlett as a hot-tempered, easily confused sheriff and Fritz Feld as a stodgy psychiatrist. The most significant supporting performer in these films may be Walter Connolly, who played the father in *It Happened One Night*, the assistant constantly being fired by theatrical producer John Barrymore in *Twentieth Century*, Myrna Loy's fishing-obsessed father in *Libeled Lady*, and the easily angered editor in *Nothing Sacred*.

Other notable supporting performers in screwball comedies included Luis Alberni and Franklin Pangborn (*Easy Living*); Mischa Auer, Alice Brady, Eugene Pallette, and Gail Patrick (*My Man Godfrey*); Eric Blore and Donald Meek (*Breakfast for Two*); Charles Butterworth and Margaret Hamilton (*The Moon's Our Home*); Spring Byington (*Theodora Goes Wild*); Roscoe Karns (*It Happened One Night* and *Twentieth Century*); Edgar Kennedy and Una Merkel (*True Confession*); and Maxie Rosenbloom and Charles Winninger (*Nothing Sacred*).

Bringing Up Baby is especially praiseworthy for the speed and surety of its comic timing. Screwball comedies are generally fast-paced, but those directed by Hawks are the fastest of all. The director made films in this genre longer than anyone, continuing into the 1940's with *His Girl Friday* (1940), with Grant and Rosalind Russell; *Ball of Fire* (1942), with Stanwyck and Cooper; *I Was a Male War Bride* (1949), with Grant and Ann Sheridan; and *Monkey Business* (1952), with Grant and Ginger Rogers.

Other important screwball comedies made after *Bringing Up Baby* included Leisen's *Midnight* (1939), with Colbert and Don Ameche; Garson Kanin's *My Favorite Wife* (1940), with Dunne and Grant; Alfred Hitchcock's *Mr. and Mrs. Smith* (1941), with Lombard and Robert Montgomery; Preston Sturges's *The Lady Eve* (1941), with Stanwyck and Fonda, and *The Palm Beach Story* (1942), with Colbert and Joel McCrea; Billy Wilder's *The Major and the Minor* (1942), with Rogers and Ray Milland; and George Stevens's *The More the Merrier* (1943), with McCrea and Jean Arthur. The last of these is perhaps the most romantic screwball comedy, as the sexual longing of the protagonists is made as explicit as the production code allowed.

Screwball elements continued to appear in varying degrees after the genre's heyday, resurfacing, for example, in Wilder's *Some Like It Hot* (1959). In 1972, Peter Bogdanovich attempted a contemporary version of *Bringing Up Baby* with his *What's Up, Doc?* with Barbra Streisand and Ryan O'Neal. Although the film was a popular success, most reviewers condemned it as heavy-handed, cartoonish, and mean-spirited. Many critics have claimed that the classic screwball comedy is extinct, largely because attaining the appropriate combination of versatile performers, sophisticated writing, and perfect timing is so difficult. Of recent works, perhaps Sydney Pollack's *Tootsie* (1982), with Dustin Hoffman and Jessica Lange, comes closest to the classic formula.

—*Michael Adams*

FURTHER READING

Byrge, Duane, and Robert Milton Miller. *The Screwball Comedy Films: A History and Filmography, 1934-1942*. Jefferson, N.C.: McFarland, 2005. An informative, informed, and relatively complete survey of the genre.

Cavell, Stanley. *Pursuits of Happiness: The Hollywood Comedy of Remarriage*. Cambridge, Mass.: Harvard University Press, 1981. Examines seven comedies of the 1930's and 1940's, including *It Happened One Night*, *Bringing Up Baby*, and *The Awful Truth*, to show how they create a comic genre of remarriage. Shows how the genre grows out of Shakespearean comedy. Photographs and index.

Everson, William K. "Screwball Comedy: A Reappraisal." *Films in Review* 34 (December, 1983): 578-584. Thought-provoking but unconvincing argument that screwball comedies are period pieces of little interest to modern audiences.

Gehring, Wes D. *Romantic Versus Screwball Comedy: Charting the Difference*. Lanham, Md.: Scarecrow Press, 2002. Discusses the differences between the two genres and places them in their social and political contexts. Includes sixteen photo stills.

Harvey, James. *Romantic Comedy in Hollywood from Lubitsch to Sturges*. New York: Alfred A. Knopf, 1987. Analyzes comic style of the 1930's and 1940's, with particular attention to the films of Lubitsch and Sturges. Also discusses such directors as Capra and Hawks and such performers as Colbert, Grant, and Lombard. Includes photographs, index, and an interview with Dunne.

Kendall, Elizabeth. *The Runaway Bride: Hollywood Romantic Comedy of the 1930's*. New York: Alfred A. Knopf, 1990. Traces the device of the runaway bride and its variations through several films of the 1930's and early 1940's, including *It Happened One Night*, *My Man Godfrey*, and *The Awful Truth*. Provides considerable background about the stars and directors. Excellent study includes photographs, bibliography, and index.

Sarris, Andrew. "The Sex Comedy Without Sex." *American Film* 3 (March, 1978): 8-15. Discusses the difficulty of defining the genre and of determining what films are truly "screwball." Argues that female comedians are the most crucial ingredient. Excellent brief introduction to the genre.

Sikov, Ed. *Screwball: Hollywood's Madcap Romantic Comedies*. New York: Crown, 1989. The most thorough examination of the genre. Analyzes the major examples and divides screwball comedies into clearly defined categories. Extensively and beautifully illustrated. With excellent filmography and bibliography. Index.

Weales, Gerald. *Canned Goods as Caviar: American Film Comedy of the 1930s*. Chicago: University of Chicago Press, 1985. Attempts to place twelve 1930's comedies in the context of the social and political life of the decade. Analyzes *Bringing Up Baby*, *My Man Godfrey*, *Libeled Lady*, and *Nothing Sacred*. Photographs and index.

SEE ALSO: Aug., 1912: Sennett Defines Slapstick Comedy; 1923: *The Ten Commandments* Advances American Film Spectacle; June 26, 1925: Chaplin Produces His Masterpiece *The Gold Rush*; May 16, 1929: First Academy Awards Honor Film Achievement; 1930's: Hollywood Enters Its Golden Age; 1930's-1940's: Studio System Dominates Hollywood Filmmaking; 1931-1932: Gangster Films Become Popular; 1934: Lubitsch's *The Merry Widow* Opens New Vistas for Film Musicals; Dec. 15, 1939: *Gone with the Wind* Premieres.

1934

1934-1939
DUST BOWL DEVASTATES THE GREAT PLAINS

A massive drought ruined farms on a large scale throughout the plains states. Coming in the midst of the Great Depression, the so-called Dust Bowl exacerbated an already desperate situation, driving hundreds of thousands of people out of the Great Plains and prompting them to migrate westward to California.

LOCALE: American Great Plains
CATEGORIES: Economics; environmental issues; agriculture; disasters

KEY FIGURES
Robert Geiger (fl. early twentieth century), reporter who coined the term "Dust Bowl"
Franklin D. Roosevelt (1882-1945), president of the United States, 1933-1945
Hugh Hammond Bennett (1881-1960), chief of the Soil Conservation Service
Ferdinand A. Silcox (1882-1939), chief forester of the United States
Chester C. Davis (1887-1975), director of the Agricultural Adjustment Administration
Dorothea Lange (1895-1965), American photographer

SUMMARY OF EVENT
Farmers all across the Great Plains apprehensively watched the skies during the spring of 1934. Day after day, the weather offered no relief. Instead, there was intense sun, wind, drought, more sun, and then gales. Massive clouds of dust blotted out sunlight over western Kansas. At first, the wind raced along the surface, tearing at the stunted wheat and kicking up the topsoil. Then the dust thickened into low, heavy, dirt-laden clouds. From a distance, the storm had the appearance of a cumulus cloud, but it was black, not white; and it seemed to eat its way along with a rolling, churning motion.

As the storm swept toward Oklahoma and Texas, the black clouds engulfed the landscape. Birds and jackrabbits fled before it, and people scurried to safety. For those engulfed in the storm, there was an eerie sensation of silence and darkness. There was little or no visibility, and wind velocity hit forty to fifty miles per hour. That spring was exceedingly hot, with the temperature often above one hundred degrees. On May 10, the wind returned. Unlike the previous storm, these winds whipped up a formless, light brown fog that spread over an area nine hundred miles long. During the next day, an esti-

mated twelve million tons of soil fell on Chicago, and dust darkened the skies over Cleveland. On May 12, dust hung like a pall over the entire eastern seaboard. These two storms alone blew 650 million tons of topsoil off the plains.

The Dust Bowl was an elusive and constantly moving phenomenon. The entire decade of the 1930's was unusually hot and dry. In 1930, there was a drought in the eastern half of the nation. In 1931, the drought shifted to the northern plains of Montana and the Dakotas, and local level dust storms throughout the plains became more common. The storm that first brought the Dust Bowl to national attention, however, and gave it its name, was the one in May, 1934, which originated mostly on the northern plains and drew the dust high into the atmosphere, allowing the jet stream to deposit it over much of the eastern United States and even into the Atlantic Ocean. After that, the worst storms shifted to the southern plains and were typically more localized in extent. By many statistical measures, 1937 was the peak year for dust storm occurrence and severity, but in popular memory, the worst of the Dust Bowl over the largest area was probably in the early spring of 1934, including the famous "Black Sunday" storm of April 14.

The heart of the Dust Bowl is usually considered to be an area of 300,000 square miles in western Kansas, Oklahoma, and Texas and eastern Colorado and New Mexico, although conditions in the northern plains were, at times, equally deserving of the name Dust Bowl. In the hardest-hit areas, agriculture virtually ceased. With successive storms, the wind and the flying dust cut off the wheat stalks at ground level and tore out the roots. Blowing dirt shifted from one field to another, burying crops not yet carried away from the wind. Cattle tried to eat the dust-laden grass and filled their stomachs with fatal mud balls.

The dust banked against houses and farm buildings like snow, burying fences up to the post tops. Dirt penetrated into automobile engines and clogged the vital parts. Housewives fought vainly to keep it out of their homes, but it seeped in through cracks and crevices, through wet blankets hung over windows, through oiled cloth and tape, covering everything with grit. Hospitals reported hundreds of patients suffering from "dust pneumonia." The black blizzards struck so suddenly that people became lost and disoriented and occasionally suffocated, some literally within yards of shelter. As a result, more than 350,000 people fled the Great Plains in the

THE DUST BOWL

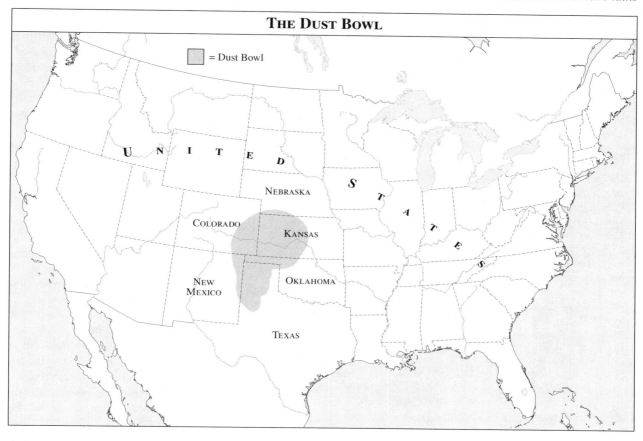

□ = Dust Bowl

1930's. These "Okies" loaded their meager household goods on flivvers and struck out along Route 66 for California.

Wind and drought alone did not create the Dust Bowl. Nature's delicate balance of wind, rain, and grass had been disturbed by human settlement. Fifty years earlier, a strong protective carpet of grass had covered the Great Plains. The grass held moisture in the soil and kept the soil from blowing away. In dry years, the wind blew out huge craters, later mistakenly called "buffalo wallows"; but as long as the turf remained, the land could recover. After the Civil War, farmers began staking out homesteads in regions once considered too arid for use as anything but range land. Wherever they went, they plowed under the grass. During World War I, the demand for wheat, along with the invention of the tractor, led them to plow larger areas of the virgin grassland. Between 1914 and 1917 the area of wheat planted increased to twenty-seven million acres; more than 40 percent of this land was being plowed for the first time. After the war, the plowing continued. Larger tractors and combines, new machines that could harvest and thresh grain in one operation, inaugurated the age of the wheat kings. By 1930, there were almost three times as many acres in wheat production as ten years earlier, and the tractors were still tearing open the turf. The plow exposed the land to rain, wind, and sun. By 1932, the earth on the plains was ready to blow.

SIGNIFICANCE

The Dust Bowl speeded the development of long-range federal programs in the new field of soil conservation. A veteran conservationist, President Franklin D. Roosevelt in late 1933 created the Soil Erosion Service, later the Soil Conservation Service (SCS), with Hugh Hammond Bennett as its head. The SCS's task was to supply technical assistance and leadership, while local soil-conservation districts carried out Bennett's program of strip cropping, contour plowing, stubble-mulch farming, and terracing. In 1934, the Forest Service, under Ferdinand A. Silcox, started planting a shelter belt of trees within a zone one hundred miles wide from Canada to the Texas

THE DUST BOWL EXPLAINED

In 2004, scientists at the National Aeronautics and Space Administration determined the causes of the Dust Bowl disaster.

NASA scientists have an explanation for one of the worst climatic events in the history of the United States, the "Dust Bowl" drought, which devastated the Great Plains and all but dried up an already depressed American economy in the 1930's.

Siegfried Schubert of NASA's Goddard Space Flight Center, Greenbelt, Md., and colleagues used a computer model developed with modern-era satellite data to look at the climate over the past 100 years. The study found cooler than normal tropical Pacific Ocean surface temperatures combined with warmer tropical Atlantic Ocean temperatures to create conditions in the atmosphere that turned America's breadbasket into a dust bowl from 1931 to 1939. The team's data is in this week's [March 19, 2004] *Science* magazine.

These changes in sea surface temperatures created shifts in the large-scale weather patterns and low level winds that reduced the normal supply of moisture from the Gulf of Mexico and inhibited rainfall throughout the Great Plains.

"The 1930s drought was the major climatic event in the nation's history," Schubert said. "Just beginning to understand what occurred is really critical to understanding future droughts and the links to global climate change issues we're experiencing today." . . .

The researchers used NASA's Seasonal-to-Interannual Prediction Project (NSIPP) atmospheric general circulation model and agency computational facilities to conduct the research. The NSIPP model was developed using NASA satellite observations, including: Clouds and the Earth's Radiant Energy System radiation measurements; and the Global Precipitation Climatology Project precipitation data.

The model showed cooler than normal tropical Pacific Ocean temperatures and warmer than normal tropical Atlantic Ocean temperatures contributed to a weakened low-level jet stream and changed its course. The jet stream, a ribbon of fast moving air near the Earth's surface, normally flows westward over the Gulf of Mexico and then turns northward pulling up moisture and dumping rain onto the Great Plains. As the low level jet stream weakened, it traveled farther south than normal. The Great Plains dried up and dust storms formed.

Source: "NASA Explains 'Dust Bowl' Drought." National Aeronautics and Space Administration, March 18, 2004.

Panhandle. Ten years later, more than two hundred million trees were serving as windbreaks and helping to conserve moisture. In 1936, the Agricultural Adjustment Administration (AAA), directed by Chester C. Davis, adopted soil conservation as a subterfuge to get around an unfavorable Supreme Court decision. On the Great Plains, however, soil conservation was a legitimate part of the AAA program. Farmers received government checks for both acreage reductions and wind control practices.

After 1936, the New Deal added little to its conservation program. Roosevelt did appoint two special committees, one to study Dust Bowl conditions and the other to recommend specific legislation. Congress passed a water-storage bill along the lines that the latter committee had suggested, but it did little else. In documenting the extent of the Dust Bowl and providing information and arguments to support their own programs, however, federal agencies created a wealth of documentary information on the Dust Bowl, including human responses to it, as recorded in the photographs of Dorothea Lange.

There has continued to be a lively debate over who or what—government programs, conservation practices of individual farmers, or Mother Nature—should receive most of the credit for bringing the Dust Bowl to an end, with the majority of scholars placing the greatest responsibility with nature. In any case, by 1938, the scale of wind erosion had dropped dramatically, and by 1941, temperature and rainfall levels had returned to near or above normal and the Dust Bowl had effectively disappeared. More to the point is the question of its possible recurrence. In the 1970's, Great Plains farmers were once again plowing "fence row to fence row" for export, grasslands were plowed up for irrigation farming, and the shelter belt had mostly been destroyed or allowed to deteriorate. Whether the government and the people of the plains learned the appropriate lessons from the terrible experience of the Dust Bowl remains an open question.

—Donald Holley and Kent Blaser

FURTHER READING

Bonnifield, Mathew Paul. *The Dust Bowl: Men, Dirt, and Depression.* Albuquerque: University of New Mexico Press, 1979. Emphasizes the roles of nature and government policy in creating the Dust Bowl, and the efficacy of grass-roots human responses in alleviating the problem.

Clements, Frederic, and Ralph Chaney. *Environment*

and Life in the Great Plains. Washington, D.C.: Carnegie Institution, 1937. Written during the Dust Bowl crisis, this brief work contains Clements's ideas for land management and agricultural practices based on ecological principles.

Cunfer, Geoff. *On the Great Plains: Agriculture and Environment*. College Station: Texas A&M University Press, 2005. Study of the agricultural and environmental history of the area at the center of the Dust Bowl. Includes a chapter on the drought and its impact. Bibliographic references and index.

Egan, Timothy. *The Worst Hard Time: The Untold Story of Those Who Survived the Great American Dust Bowl*. Boston: Houghton Mifflin, 2006. Comprehensive history and analysis of the causes and effects of the Dust Bowl, beginning with agricultural developments in the first years of the twentieth century. Map, bibliographic references, and index.

Gregory, James N. *American Exodus: The Dust Bowl Migration and Okie Culture in California*. New York: Oxford University Press, 1989. Historical study of the migrants from Oklahoma and other southern Great Plains states who settled in California in the 1930's. Excellent social history, with emphasis on the continuity in culture and traditions among the Oklahoma migrants as they became part of California's complex social and ethnic mix.

Hurt, R. Douglas. "Agricultural Technology in the Dust Bowl, 1932-1940." In *The Great Plains: Environment and Culture*, edited by Brian W. Blouet and Frederick C. Luebke. Lincoln: University of Nebraska Press, 1977. Succinct summary of the changes in agricultural techniques and technology in response to the drought of the 1930's, with emphasis on the work of the Soil Conservation Service.

_____. *The Dust Bowl: An Agricultural and Social History*. Chicago: Nelson Hall, 1981. A broad historical survey of the Great Plains region during the 1930's. Contains much useful information on economic conditions, agricultural practices and technology, and the human responses to the crises of the era.

Lange, Dorothea, and Paul Taylor. *An American Exodus: A Record of Human Erosion*. New York: Reynal & Hitchcock, 1939. Lange's stunning photographs of the Dust Bowl and migration to California provide some of the most famous images available of those events.

Lowitt, Richard. *The New Deal and the West*. Bloomington: Indiana University Press, 1984. A well-written synthesis that presents the national, political, and economic background for New Deal programs that had an impact in the Great Plains. Also discusses the impact of national policies in the context of regional, state, and local political and economic conditions.

Sears, Paul. *Deserts on the March*. Norman: University of Oklahoma Press, 1935. A contemporary assessment by a pioneering popular writer in the field of ecology who attempted to explain the Dust Bowl as an example of a long-term worldwide trend. Controversial and stimulating.

Svobida, Lawrence. *An Empire of Dust*. 1940. Reprint. *Farming the Dust Bowl: A First-Hand Account from Kansas*. Lawrence: University Press of Kansas, 1986. A classic account of the Dust Bowl, written by a Kansas farmer who battled the Dust Bowl conditions for almost a decade.

Watkins, T. H. *The Great Depression: America in the 1930's*. Boston: Little, Brown, 1993. Readable, informed general history of the decade; includes a brief but insightful section on the Dust Bowl. Companion volume to a public television program.

Worcester, Donald. *Dust Bowl: The Southern Great Plains in the 1930's*. New York: Oxford University Press, 1979. Well-researched, thought-provoking analysis of the economic and cultural causes of the Dust Bowl, the strengths and weaknesses of the government and private-sector responses to the crisis, and long-term consequences of the experience.

_____. *Nature's Economy: A History of Ecological Ideas*. Cambridge, England: Cambridge University Press, 1985. A survey of the evolution of ecological thought from the 1700's to the 1970's. The arrival of agriculture on the Great Plains and the development of the Dust Bowl are important episodes in the emergence of ecological theory in the twentieth century. Glossary is helpful for introductory students.

SEE ALSO: Oct. 29, 1929-1939: Great Depression; 1930's: Guthrie's Populist Songs Reflect the Depression-Era United States; Apr. 27, 1935: Soil Conservation Service Is Established; Apr., 1939: *The Grapes of Wrath* Portrays Depression-Era America.

1934

1934-1945
RADAR IS DEVELOPED

The development of radar, which made the identification of distant objects possible, revolutionized both wartime and peacetime industries.

LOCALE: United States; Europe
CATEGORIES: Science and technology; military history; inventions

KEY FIGURES

Christian Hülsmeyer (1881-1957), German engineer acknowledged as inventor of the world's first practical radar system

Robert M. Page (1903-1992), American physicist who developed a practical technology for pulse radar

Leo C. Young (b. 1926), American physicist and colleague of Page

Robert Alexander Watson-Watt (1892-1973), Scottish physicist who initiated development of radar in Britain

Henry Thomas Tizard (1885-1959), British scientist who led a delegation to the United States for cooperative development of radar

SUMMARY OF EVENT

"Radar" is an acronym for "radio detection and ranging." The principle of radar involves the transmission of high-frequency pulses of electromagnetic energy through a directional antenna. The pulses are reflected by objects that intercept them. Radar receivers pick up the reflections, process them electronically, and convert them into dots of light (blips) on the face of a fluorescent screen that forms part of a cathode-ray tube. In this way, the receivers determine with instant precision the direction, distance, velocity, altitude, and even form of the targeted object, such as an airplane, ship, submarine, iceberg, body in space, thunderstorm, or landmass.

Radar came into widespread use during World War II and has been credited with changing the course of history, and certainly that of North American history. During the 1930's, radar development was pioneered independently and simultaneously in

Britain, France, Germany, and the United States. While several proposals to build radar-type detection devices had been made since the late nineteenth century—including a demonstration by Germany's Christian Hülsmeyer in 1904—it was not until the 1930's that the study of radio-echo signals from moving objects was considered important. Early in 1934, Robert M. Page, an American physicist pursuing the theory of his colleague Leo C. Young at the U.S. Naval Research Laboratory, worked out a practical technology for pulse radar. This development marked the beginning of an effective radar program in the United States.

By this time, Britain was becoming increasingly apprehensive of Adolf Hitler's rearming of Nazi Germany. Responding to rumors about a German "death ray" initiated by a speech by the Nazi leader, Scottish physicist Robert Alexander Watson-Watt wrote a report in which he demolished the death-ray fiction but observed that the echoes of shortwave pulses could be used to locate approaching aircraft and the like. To boost the British effort, a special committee headed by scientist Henry Thomas Tizard was formed to give top priority to the systematic research and development of British radar. By 1935, Watson-Watt had completed a practical radar system that was to contribute to the successful outcome of

Three U.S. soldiers sit in place at a radar installation used in Casablanca, French Morocco, during World War II. (NARA)

the Battle of Britain five years later. Simultaneously, the French were placing their own version of radar on the luxury liner *Normandie* to assist in the detection of icebergs on crossings of the North Atlantic.

Thus, by the beginning of World War II, several nations benefited from functioning radar systems. These systems were based on fundamentally different designs. The further diversification of radar designs and their applications by the Allies and Germany would improve the technology considerably by the end of the war. The British won the Battle of Britain by using radar to help intercept approaching aircraft. When Germany switched to night bombing in 1941, British ground and airborne radar enabled British fighters to zero in on the attackers. The German threat of invasion was thus foiled, and Britain in turn became the strategic staging area from which the Allied forces launched their landing in Nazi-held "fortress Europe" in 1944.

SIGNIFICANCE

In some respects, radar was a typical product of mid-twentieth century scientific technology. It was made possible by an earlier effort, a research project committed solely to an understanding of pertinent scientific phenomena. Two names stand out in this connection: James Clerk Maxwell in Britain, whose mathematical predictions in 1864 regarding the nature of light and electromagnetic phenomena indicated that the latter, like the former, could be reflected, and Heinrich Hertz, a German physicist who in 1887 demonstrated that Maxwell was right. Hertz's efforts were based on the sophisticated understanding of electronics that had formed over three decades of experiments with radio communications. So many individuals were involved in this development that it can be said that radar—like most scientific breakthroughs—evolved rather than was invented.

The fact that radar did not have any single inventor was also a result of its complexity, its design variations, and the number of different components used in radar systems. Moreover, the national emergency of war mandated a total mobilization of resources on the parts of all involved. Accordingly, for perhaps the first time in history, scientists, policy makers, military personnel, and others on both sides of the Atlantic became completely devoted to research and development on a single project. In tribute, former World War II German navy head Admiral Karl Doenitz said in 1945, "The one single weapon which defeated the [German] submarine and the Third Reich was the long-range airplane with radar." In subsequent years, scientists were to focus on technologies that enabled aircraft to avoid radar detection, radar contact with planets and other celestial bodies (radio astronomy), and the use of radar to improve the safety of air travel.

—*Peter B. Heller*

FURTHER READING

Bowen, E. G. *Radar Days*. Bristol, England: Adam Hilger, 1987. Describes how airborne radar helped to defeat Hitler and the bombers of the Luftwaffe. Early accounts of English radar usually were written from the viewpoint of someone in the higher echelons of government or as seen by the management, but this work was written from the point of view of those who performed laboratory studies, which were followed by flight trials in which the lone experimenter tried to simulate the problems likely to be met in upcoming battles.

Brown, L. *A Radar History of World War II: Technical and Military Imperatives*. Boca Raton, Fla.: Taylor & Francis, 1999. Comprehensive volume discusses radar programs in every nation that participated in World War II.

Buderi, Robert. *The Invention That Changed the World: How a Small Group of Radar Pioneers Won the Second World War and Launched a Technical Revolution*. Carmichael, Calif.: Touchstone Books, 1998. Provides a clear and logical explanation of the technology behind radar and its development. Includes several short biographies of the individuals involved.

Burns, Russell W., ed. *Radar Development to 1945*. London: Peregrinus, 1988. Illustrated, blow-by-blow account of the development of radar in various countries. Among those writing the history of American radar is one of its principal developers, Dr. Robert M. Page, the retired head of the U.S. Naval Research Laboratory.

Clark, Ronald W. *Tizard*. Cambridge, Mass.: MIT Press, 1965. In 1940, the Tizard mission was sent to the United States to disclose English secret technical advances, including radar, in return for U.S. help on technical and production matters. No comprehensive account of the Tizard mission has ever been written, but this book is a step in that direction.

De Arcangelis, Mario. *Electronic Warfare: From the Battle of Tsushima to the Falklands and Lebanon Conflicts*. Poole, England: Blandford Press, 1985. Fascinating, clearly written account of important military operations involving radar and other technologies.

Fisher, David E. *A Race on the Edge of Time: Radar, the Decisive Weapon of World War II*. New York: McGraw-Hill, 1988. Competent account of radar's

1934

use during the war. Based on interviews with those involved.

Pritchard, David. *The Radar War: Germany's Pioneering Achievement, 1904-1945.* Wellingborough, England: P. Stephens, 1989. Traces the development of German radar from Hülsmeyer's demonstration to the end of the war. Includes photographs of individuals and equipment.

Rowe, Albert P. *One Story of Radar.* Cambridge, England: Cambridge University Press, 1948. The period at St. Athan will be remembered for the start of mass production of airborne radar and for fitting these sets to aircraft at an unprecedented rate. As that work drew to a close, another move was contemplated. The decision of where to relocate was decided by events at Dundee, where things had reached crisis point. The fiction that Dundee was a good place for radar research could no longer be maintained and another move had to be made.

Skolnik, Merrill I. *Introduction to Radar Systems.* 2d ed. New York: McGraw-Hill, 1980. Includes a few pages devoted to radar development prior to World War II. Surveys the efforts of both Allied and Axis powers.

Watson-Watt, Robert A. *The Pulse of Radar: The Autobiography of Sir Robert Watson-Watt.* New York: Dial Press, 1959. Account by the gifted Scottish pioneer of radar, including a perceptive chapter on why the Americans ignored radar warnings of the impending Japanese attack at Pearl Harbor on December 7, 1941.

SEE ALSO: Dec. 12, 1901: First Transatlantic Telegraphic Radio Transmission; Mar. and June, 1902: Kennelly and Heaviside Theorize Existence of the Ionosphere; Nov. 16, 1904: Fleming Patents the First Vacuum Tube; 1919: Principles of Shortwave Radio Communication Are Discovered; Jan. 1, 1925: Bell Labs Is Formed; June-Sept., 1937: Reber Builds the First Intentional Radio Telescope; Aug., 1939: United States Begins Mobilization for World War II; July 10-Oct. 31, 1940: Battle of Britain.

February, 1934
RIVERA'S ROCKEFELLER CENTER MURAL IS DESTROYED

When Diego Rivera included an image of Soviet leader Vladimir Ilich Lenin in a mural for the newly constructed RCA Building, controversy arose and the painting was destroyed.

LOCALE: New York, New York
CATEGORY: Arts

KEY FIGURES
Diego Rivera (1886-1957), painter and muralist who vibrantly depicted Mexican folk and American working classes
Nelson A. Rockefeller (1908-1979), millionaire philanthropist and art collector who commissioned and later dismissed Rivera
José Clemente Orozco (1883-1949), renowned Mexican muralist
David Alfaro Siqueiros (1896-1974), renowned Mexican muralist
Frida Kahlo (1907-1954), respected Mexican painter and Rivera's second wife

SUMMARY OF EVENT
Mexican painter and muralist Diego Rivera managed to earn commissions from mainstream government and corporate leaders while simultaneously portraying the struggles and epics of the laboring classes. His murals, which frequently embellished the walls of public buildings, drew attention to native farmers, peasants, and urban dwellers. In the United States, he often focused on those who worked on assembly lines and thereby fueled industrial processes.

Rivera's subject matter evolved from his political beliefs. An activist who was kicked out of but later reinstated in the Mexican Communist Party, his artistic interpretations of doctrine were direct and uncomplicated. Rivera's murals also displayed an understanding of higher mechanics and of the ways in which various physical and human elements interacted. From a political perspective, his work could move the masses; from a technical perspective, it appealed to the cognoscenti.

The collision between subject matter and patronage had surfaced before Rivera was commissioned to do a mural at the RCA Building at Rockefeller Center in New York City, but to a different degree. In the United States, the conflict proved to be more acute than in Mexico, where the Revolution of 1910 had empowered the country's vast citizenry and diminished the European, particularly Spanish, influences of the reigning elite. Rivera's

American debut took place in San Francisco in 1930. His murals soon graced the walls of the local stock exchange and the California School of Fine Arts. Although some condemned the painter for being a Communist, his San Francisco tenure proved personally enjoyable, and it ended without incident.

Rivera's next major assignment foreshadowed the events that would transpire in New York City. The Detroit Art Commission, under the chairmanship of automobile mogul Edsel Ford, gave the artist complete freedom to decorate the courtyard of the Detroit Institute of Arts. The resulting epic consisted of twenty-seven panels, the artist's self-described vision depicting "in color and form the story of each industry and its division of labor." Given the sheer number of political statements that could be interpreted in such a massive work, controversy was hardly surprising. Father Charles Coughlin, a conservative, virulently jingoistic, Detroit-based priest then at the height of his national influence, proved to be one of the most threatening critics. Rivera's creation provoked extreme reactions on all fronts, drawing support as well as criticism. A disparate group of workers coalesced solely for the purpose of protecting the murals, and they threatened the use of force.

Nelson A. Rockefeller was a Diego Rivera supporter, and his wife, Mary Todhunter Clark Rockefeller, had several of the artist's works in her collection. After expressing a desire to see the Detroit murals, the millionaire philanthropist soon followed up with a letter describing another project: decoration of the new RCA Building in Manhattan. The project's parameters appeared to be circumscribed from the start. Rockefeller's contractors sent proposals to three chosen artists—Pablo Picasso, Henri Matisse, and Rivera—inviting them to participate in a "contest." Instructions were clear, down to the size of the figures, color scheme (black and white), and varnishing requirements. All three painters, well respected enough by this time to demand artistic freedom, rejected the offer. Rockefeller personally set out to persuade Rivera. After some of the rules were softened, including allowing

Diego Rivera in May, 1933, working on the Rockefeller Center mural that was later destroyed. (AP/Wide World Photos)

the use of color, the muralist acceded.

Rivera submitted a sketch addressing the predesignated theme, "Man at the Crossroads Looking with Hope and High Vision to the Choosing of a New and Better Future." The design concept, which extolled workers and shunned some of the more egregious facets of industrial society, won Nelson Rockefeller's approval. Work commenced in March, 1933. The technical aspects of Rivera's mural painting were labor-intensive. A cadre of assistants applied three surface coatings to ensure stability and enhance color, ground the paints, and transferred the lines of the artist's sketches to the wall. Rivera then proceeded with his brushwork.

As the painting neared completion in late April, a *New York World-Telegram* reporter, Joseph Lilly, visited the

RCA Building for a preview. The resulting article, headlined "Rivera Paints Scenes of Communist Activity and John D. [Rockefeller], Jr., Foots Bill," highlighted many themes that were not new to those familiar with the artist's work. Representations of toxic materials and poisonous gases, for example, had appeared in the Detroit murals. One element was to make its debut: the figure of Russian revolutionary leader Vladimir Ilich Lenin.

Nelson Rockefeller viewed the mural after reading the article. Claiming to find the work "thrilling," he nevertheless wrote Rivera a letter requesting that another figure be substituted for Lenin. Rivera sought the counsel of his friends and assistants before telling Rockefeller that Lenin would remain. In an attempt to compromise, Rivera suggested that some additional elements, such as the figure of a great American, could be used for balance.

Several days later, Rockefeller's contractors and a band of security guards escorted Rivera off the scaffold, paid his full $21,000 commission, and placed canvas over the mural. Workers protested by picketing, and intellectuals, artists, and businesspeople mounted strong pro- and anti-Rivera campaigns. After he paid his expenses and reimbursed his assistants, Rivera retained almost $7,000 from the RCA job. He used his "Rockefeller money" to paint murals in two American Communist institutions, the New Workers' School and Trotskyite headquarters. The New York frescoes were to be Rivera's last permanent works in the United States, since all the commissions planned in the United States were canceled or never materialized. Rivera did, however, continue to exhibit and paint on movable panels. In February, 1934, after returning to Mexico, Rivera learned that his previously covered RCA mural had been removed. He gained a commission from the Mexican government and reconstructed the work, with several changes. As Rivera himself described it, a scene of nightclub carousing now included John D. Rockefeller, Jr., "his head but a short distance away from . . . venereal disease germs."

SIGNIFICANCE

Although Rivera received no more large American commissions after the Rockefeller incident, other offers came from around the world. Nevertheless, the artist soon turned to easel painting and to the interests of private collectors who would use his work to decorate their homes, galleries, and offices. Mural painting, however, had not yet reached its pinnacle in either the United States or Mexico. Rivera surely contributed to the explosion that followed, but he left the genre before it could be considered common.

Sometimes an extraordinary event can push politics or culture in a certain direction. The RCA mural may have had such an effect. Left-wing politics, wrought out of the Great Depression and Soviet influence, brought about two related art forms, social realism and Socialist Realism. Both elevated the ordinary person, celebrated daily existence, and called attention to widespread social and economic inequities. Socialist Realism suggested a political, clearly Marxist answer to working-class dilemmas, and it was the more blatantly propagandistic of the two schools. In the Soviet Union, Joseph Stalin mandated Socialist Realism as the cultural medium. Artists who did not pursue it were denied commissions, banished, or even killed.

Some historians pointed out that the RCA murals represented a leap for Rivera from social realism to Socialist Realism. Meanwhile, in the United States, critics wondered whether President Franklin D. Roosevelt was leading the country toward socialism. If that were the case, however, the course was temporary and motivated by economics. Roosevelt's first term, which began in 1933, saw a flurry of progressive legislation aimed at reducing widespread unemployment. One of these programs was the Works Progress Administration (WPA), initiated in 1935. Part of that program engaged artists and writers in the celebration and documentation of American cultural heritage. WPA commissions soon enlivened post office walls, government buildings, and many other public venues. Rivera's influence radiated from these brightly colored murals, which were often rendered in social realist style, were filled with historical references, and illustrated themes inspired by the working class.

It is impossible to address the work of Diego Rivera without mentioning two of his contemporaries, José Clemente Orozco and David Alfaro Siqueiros. The *tres grandes*, or big three, differed in techniques and in their personal and artistic responses to political events, yet they collectively elevated their chosen genre. According to one expert, Mexican mural commissions reached their peak in the late 1950's, although in the decade that followed a whole new generation of Mexican artists concerned with social values drew their inspiration from the great muralists. Siqueiros was particularly influential in helping to organize the Syndicate of Revolutionary Painters, Sculptors, and Engravers, a sort of postrevolutionary union that was ultimately responsible for instituting mural painting as a national art form in Mexico. The *tres grandes* experienced the United States in similar ways. All worked there during the Depression, and after the Rockefeller Center incident, they were never again to receive large, permanent commissions.

Rivera possibly held more of a universal appeal than did either Siqueiros or Orozco. Unlike his respected colleagues, he benefited from a solid general education and from formal artistic training in Europe. Rivera first studied in Spain, then moved to Paris, where he was mentored by Picasso and was captured on Amedeo Modigliani's canvas. His use of color is said to have been derived from classical Italian frescoes, and for a while he dabbled in cubism. Europe during Rivera's stay (1907-1921) also blazed with differing political philosophies, including nationalism and Marxism. As a result, the artist gained a sense of history and learned how to incorporate his ideas into unique and timely contexts. On his Detroit commission, he conducted interviews, and he sent his assistants to research American historical figures for the RCA mural. Later, in the midst of the 1936 controversy concerning his Communist credentials, Rivera was invited by fascist leader Benito Mussolini to paint in Italy.

The muralist exuded a personal charm that drew fledgling artists to him. His wife, the painter Frida Kahlo, respected for her sensitive portrayal of women's emotional needs and feelings, declared at the age of thirteen that she wanted to have a child by Rivera. In a different way, his assistants formed a cadre of steadfast supporters. There is evidence, for example, that Rivera might have acceded to Rockefeller's demands if these young men and women had not threatened to strike over such terms. In addition to his own enduring artistic legacy, the Rivera influence survived through the work of assistants Lucienne Bloch, John Hastings, and, most notably, social realist painter Ben Shahn.

Decades after his death, Rivera's influence endures. During the early 1990's, the Mexican and U.S. governments promoted a traveling art exhibit of Rivera's work that was so large that, with some extra borrowing or by digging into permanent collections, museums could focus on any number of styles, historic eras, or themes. In this way, the ever-buoyant Diego Rivera was introduced to a new generation. (Frida Kahlo also enjoyed a revival during the early 1990's, particularly attracting the attention of young women who could relate to her style and empathize with her spirit.)

—*Lynn Kronzek*

FURTHER READING

Chavez, Augustin Velazquez. *Contemporary Mexican Artists.* New York: Covici-Friede, 1937. Thumbnail sketches, typically two pages in length, and four black-and-white plates are used to present each of the twenty-five artists included here. A short introductory section lends unity to the book.

Goldman, Shifra M. *Contemporary Mexican Painting in a Time of Change.* Austin: University of Texas Press, 1977. Although most of this book focuses on a later generation, this work portrays Rivera and other muralists as wellsprings of modern Mexican art. Goldman demonstrates the interrelationships among various painters, how they inspired each other and split to create new schools or perspectives. The historical and political nature of art is an important theme.

Helm, MacKinley. *Modern Mexican Painters.* New York: Dover, 1974. A chapter on Rivera lends insight into the artist's technique and evolution over the years. It is evident that Helm, a collector with informed opinions, came to know the muralist through both personal interviews and exhibitions. Their conversations periodically surface on these pages. A good discussion of the differences between Rivera the person and Rivera the artist.

McMeekin, Dorothy. *Diego Rivera: Science and Creativity in the Detroit Murals.* Lansing: Michigan State University Press, 1985. A massive mural project—twenty-seven frescoes in the courtyard of the Detroit Institute of Arts—is used to illustrate Rivera's comprehension of biology, geology, and technology. The broader political feelings are apparent, too, thus providing a good basis of comparison with the Rockefeller Center work.

Marnham, Patrick. *Dreaming with His Eyes Open: A Life of Diego Rivera.* Berkeley: University of California Press, 2000. Thoroughly researched biography strikes a perfect balance between providing enough historical context to orient the reader well and providing so much that the book's subject is obscured.

Museum of Modern Art (New York). *Diego Rivera.* New York: Arno Press, 1931. Published to celebrate Rivera's one-person show at the museum, this catalog contains more than one hundred black-and-white plates. A short bibliography and a time line offer an excellent perspective on early, enduring influences including the artist's nurturing and liberal family; impressive general education; and encouragement, from the age of three, to pursue creative avenues.

Rivera, Diego, with Gladys March. *My Art, My Life: An Autobiography.* New York: Citadel Press, 1960. Rivera writes in an informal voice, divulging details and presenting his side of an often controversial life story. The appendix features "statements" from each of the four women whom he lived with or married.

1934

Rochfort, Desmond. *Mexican Muralists: Orozco, Rivera, Siqueiros.* San Francisco: Chronicle Books, 1998. Lavishly illustrated. A good place to begin for readers interested in comparing these three giants' works.

Wolfe, Bertram D. *The Fabulous Life of Diego Rivera.* New York: Stein & Day, 1963. Perhaps the most comprehensive basic biography of Rivera, this book includes a chapter on "The Battle of Rockefeller Center." The author was an adviser to the artist during the

episode, and he uses correspondence, business documents, and contemporary accounts to describe it.

SEE ALSO: Feb. 17-Mar. 15, 1913: Armory Show; Mar. 31, 1924: Formation of the Blue Four Advances Abstract Painting; Nov. 8, 1929: New York's Museum of Modern Art Opens to the Public; Nov. 17, 1931: Whitney Museum of American Art Opens in New York; Nov. 1, 1939: Rockefeller Center Is Completed.

February 6, 1934
STAVISKY RIOTS

The public violence known as the Stavisky riots helped polarize political life in the Third French Republic and weakened the centrist parties' capacity to resist the growth of Fascism at home and abroad.

LOCALE: France
CATEGORIES: Government and politics; wars, uprisings, and civil unrest

KEY FIGURES
Édouard Daladier (1884-1970), Radical Party leader and premier of France, January-October, 1933, and January 28-February 7, 1934
Serge Alexandre Stavisky (1886-1934), petty criminal turned international swindler who occasioned a major political scandal in France
Jean Chiappe (1878-1940), prefect of Paris police, 1928-1934
Camille Chautemps (1885-1963), Radical Party leader and premier of France, November, 1933-January 27, 1934
Léon Blum (1872-1950), Socialist Party leader and statesman

SUMMARY OF EVENT
The French governmental crisis of 1934 began in late 1933, when newspapers noted that Serge Alexandre Stavisky, a member of the underworld, had been accused of defrauding hundreds of investors using municipal bonds in the city of Bayonne. Stavisky had been a police informer, a cabaret backer, a theater promoter, and a peddler of political influence. Called "King of the Crooks," he was actually a petty gangster. The legal protection he had received from both judges and police was not uncommon in the Third Republic, where officials frequently protected men of Stavisky's caliber in return for information. He had also made major contributions to the dominant Radical Party (officially called the Parti Républicain Radical et Radical-Socialiste, or Radical Socialist and Radical Republican Party).

Further revelations that Stavisky had been protected by Radical Party politicians created a scandal that was trumpeted by right-wing critics. Long active as a financial swindler, Stavisky had been indicted for fraud in 1927, but nineteen attempts to try him had mysteriously failed. He fled the warrant issued for his arrest in 1933, and was found shot to death in January, 1934. Many French people doubted the police reports of suicide and asked two questions: Who had protected Stavisky? Who had killed him? The political scandal forced the Radical premier, Camille Chautemps, to resign in January, 1934, after reports revealed that he had indirectly supported Stavisky.

France's problems helped to turn the scandal into a crisis. The French normally suspected public officials of incompetence or dishonesty. The right-wing press normally ranted about conspiracies to destroy France. It took the economic and political failures of the Republic to convert myths and half-truths into politically potent beliefs. Adolf Hitler's Germany was challenging French dominance in Europe, which had been gained at a terrible price in World War I, and the Great Depression overwhelmed the Third Republic's politicians. Foreign threats and economic insecurity created an atmosphere in which radical propagandists could use the Stavisky scandal as an excuse to challenge republicanism. France's woes made the rightist version of the Stavisky affair credible.

Numerous political organizations wanted to destroy the Third Republic and replace it with a republican or monarchical authoritarian regime. Foremost among these groups was Action Française, a rightist and monarchist movement whose daily newspaper, *L'Action française*, had exposed the Stavisky affair. Action Française also encompassed a violent youth movement, the Camelots du Roi. Other rightist organizations made Action Française seem moderate by comparison: There was the semifascist Croix de Feu, whose tendencies were exceeded only by the openly Fascist Francistes. Politically embittered veterans had formed leagues, some of which sought an "honest and authoritarian" regime. Rightists led the opposition in 1934, and the Communists played only a minor role.

Right-wing papers inflamed the public's suspicions. Perhaps the police, who were embroiled in politics, had Stavisky killed to protect unknown politicians. Perhaps Germans, Jews, Communists, or all three groups, had planned the entire affair. These opinions, and the government's silence, caused riots in January, in which the Camelots du Roi and similar young toughs gleefully participated.

Édouard Daladier, a relatively unknown moderate Radical politician, finally promised to investigate the case and restore order. His initial moves, aimed at forming a coalition government, provided the pretext for the February 6 riots. Unable to gather sufficient support from the rightist deputies, who often supported Action Française, Daladier turned to the Left, appointing a Socialist, Eugène Frot, to be minister of the interior. In a further bid for support, he dismissed the head of the Paris police, Jean Chiappe, a tough Corsican with a reputation for meting out harsh treatment to leftist demonstrators while treating rightist demonstrators with relative care. Chiappe refused to accept his dismissal gracefully, and *L'Action française* declared him a martyr to the "rotten" Republic.

Right-wing leaders were willing to take the Stavisky and Chiappe affairs to the people, but they did not predict their followers' enthusiasm. On February 6, an unplanned demonstration began while the new government presented itself to the Chamber of Deputies. People had filled the vast Place de la Concorde by 6:30 P.M. The crowd unsuccessfully charged police stationed on the Pont de la Concorde, a bridge that led to the deputies' meeting place at the Palais Bourbon. The police, disgruntled after Chiappe's dismissal, offered only halfhearted resistance until the mob began to use lead pipes, paving bricks, and even razors fixed on poles to cripple the horses of the mounted police. The struggle raged until midnight, and both sides suffered heavy losses. Thirteen rioters and one police officer were killed, and hundreds were injured.

SIGNIFICANCE

The events of February 6 had a major influence on later French politics. Daladier's resignation on February 7 was a clear victory for the rioters. The right-wing factions were excited by the republic's weakness, and Fascists argued that a more systematic attack on the government could end the Republic. In the short run, Action Française, whose Camelots du Roi had supplied the most committed members of the mob, gathered support from those who blamed the republic and its police for the rioting. In the long run the crisis damaged Action Française. Its Fascist competitors emphasized that inept Action Française leadership had caused the February riots to fall short of their professed goal of a new authoritarian regime.

This failure pointed to larger shortcomings within Action Française, whose leaders could neither comprehend nor exploit the revolutionary possibilities in France before, during, and after the 1934 crisis. They needed to be mindful of their aristocratic and bourgeois allies, who could not formally approve of any serious disruption of public order. Action Française's failure to seize the opportunity for a coup drove rightist youth into more activist organizations. After 1934, Action Française declined as more radical rightist movements prospered, and this shift helped to undermine French unity at a time when it was sorely needed.

The Left, frightened by the events of February 6, became less revolutionary. Although its massive antifascist demonstration on February 12 alarmed some legislators, it had actually been intended as a show of leftist loyalty to the republic. Communist workers eventually forced their leadership to support the existing regime. Leftist fear of a Fascist coup helped create the Popular Front coalition of Radicals, Socialists, and Communists in 1936, led by Socialist leader Léon Blum, who had also supported the government during the riots. Workers, realizing that the likely alternatives to a bourgeois republic would probably not have their best interests at heart, intensified their plans to defend themselves if the next crisis became a coup. The riots, then, had the longer term result of strengthening both the Left and the Right and helping to shatter the coalition of centrist parties that had long stabilized the Republic.

Officially, Stavisky's death remained a suicide, but a new sense of mystery was added when a judge who supposedly possessed papers relevant to the case died under strange circumstances. The police were again accused of political murder, and even the relatively limited corruption revealed by commissions investigating the Stavisky case discredited some Republican politicians and led to charges that others were hiding evidence. The Stavisky affair remained as both a symbolic cause and effect of France's political sickness in the 1930's.

—*Charles H. O'Brien*

FURTHER READING

Agulhon, Maurice. *The French Republic 1879-1992.* Oxford: Blackwell, 1993. The first half of this prize-winning book offers a vivid, lucid, and comprehensive survey of the history of the Third Republic.

Colton, Joel. *Léon Blum, Humanist in Politics.* New York: Alfred A. Knopf, 1966. This biography of the great Socialist Party leader of the 1930's includes a discussion of the Left's reaction to the 1934 crisis.

Eley, Geoff. *Forging Democracy: The History of the Left in Europe, 1850-2000.* Oxford, England: Oxford University Press, 2002. A sympathetic history of the European Left, arguing that radical movements played the central role in the creation and evolution of democracy in Europe.

Horn, Gerd-Rainer. *European Socialists Respond to Fascism: Ideology, Activism, and Contingency in the 1930s.* New York: Oxford University Press, 1996. Study of developments in Europe in the years 1933-1936 provides background for the move toward nationalization in France.

Lamour, Peter J. *The French Radical Party in the 1930's.*

Stanford, Calif.: Stanford University Press, 1964. Offers an entire chapter analyzing the impact of the 1934 crisis on the Radical Party.

Soucy, Robert. *French Fascism: The Second Wave, 1933-1939.* New Haven, Conn.: Yale University Press, 1995. The author exposes the conservative, traditionalist essence of French fascism.

Weber, Eugen. *Action Française: Royalism and Reaction in Twentieth Century France.* Stanford, Calif.: Stanford University Press, 1962. An exhaustive, well-written, and fair-minded study, based almost entirely on original sources.

_____. *The Hollow Years: France in the 1930's.* New York: W. W. Norton, 1994. A lively, masterfully detailed picture of the riots and their social context.

Werth, Alexander. *The Twilight of France, 1933-1940.* New York: Harper & Row, 1942. Places the 1934 crisis within the general framework of France's decline.

SEE ALSO: Apr. 18, 1904: *L'Humanité* Gives Voice to French Socialist Politics; Sept. 5-8, 1915, and Apr. 24-30, 1916: Zimmerwald and Kienthal Conferences; Jan. 11, 1923-Aug. 16, 1924: France Occupies the Ruhr; 1936-1946: France Nationalizes Its Banking and Industrial Sectors; Mar. 7, 1936: German Troops March into the Rhineland; May 10-June 22, 1940: Collapse of France.

March 16, 1934

MIGRATORY BIRD HUNTING AND CONSERVATION STAMP ACT

While legislation had been passed five years earlier to protect waterfowl populations in the United States, it had lacked any funding mechanism. Enactment of the Migratory Bird Hunting and Conservation Stamp Act provided the nation's first regular federal funding for waterfowl management, thereby enabling such management to be accomplished rather than merely recommended.

ALSO KNOWN AS: Duck Stamp Act
LOCALE: Washington, D.C.
CATEGORIES: Environmental issues; laws, acts, and legal history

KEY FIGURES

Aldo Leopold (1887-1948), American conservation philosopher and wildlife biologist
Thomas Beck (fl. early twentieth century), American magazine editor

Jay Darling (1876-1962), American artist, cartoonist, and director of the U.S. Bureau of Biological Survey
Franklin D. Roosevelt (1882-1945), president of the United States, 1933-1945
Peter Norbeck (1870-1936), U.S. senator from South Dakota, 1921-1936
George A. Lawyer (fl. early twentieth century), chief U.S. game warden
Frederic Collin Walcott (1869-1949), U.S. senator from Connecticut, 1929-1934
August H. Andresen (1890-1958), U.S. representative from Minnesota, 1925-1932, 1935-1958

SUMMARY OF EVENT

On March 16, 1934, the U.S. Congress enacted the Migratory Bird Hunting and Conservation Stamp Act (also known as the Duck Stamp Act) to provide critical funds for wetlands and waterfowl conservation programs. Until this act was passed, no stable funding source was available for such conservation work. As has been the case with many conservation programs, a long, twisting journey was taken over many years to enact this far-reaching legislation.

Waterfowl populations declined sharply in the early 1900's. Extensive habitat loss caused by the long drought of the 1930's, overharvest by market hunting, and the Great Depression created both ecological and financial crises for resource management programs. Water from prairie potholes, ponds, and marshes had disappeared, and with it the nesting and rearing habitat for waterfowl. Dust storms raged, and the Dust Bowl created a biological crisis. Waterfowl numbers in North America reached their lowest point in history. Many conservationists predicted the extinction of ducks and geese in the United States.

In January, 1934, President Franklin D. Roosevelt appointed a special waterfowl committee of Jay Darling, Thomas Beck, and Aldo Leopold to determine the needs of waterfowl management and outline a plan for saving this disappearing resource. The committee estimated that $50 million was needed for the purchase and restoration of wetlands for wildlife, with special emphasis on migratory waterfowl. Finding such an immense sum during the Depression was improbable. Indeed, Congress had already passed legislation in 1929 to buy land for waterfowl refuges, but had yet to provide any stable funding

sources for such land purchases. Without funds to implement the 1929 legislation and the recommendations of Roosevelt's blue-ribbon committee, programs to protect waterfowl would exist only on paper. Darling—who was the new director of the Bureau of Biological Survey (later known as the U.S. Fish and Wildlife Service)— came up with a potential solution to this problem: He revived the idea of requiring a federal stamp on duck-hunting licenses and stipulating that revenue from its sale be used to restore lost waterfowl habitat.

The idea of issuing a federal waterfowl stamp to provide funds for the acquisition of public hunting grounds had first been proposed by George A. Lawyer, chief U.S. game warden, shortly after the end of World War I. Such a bill was debated several times in Congress but failed to pass four times between 1921 and 1926. Dr. William T. Hornaday led the formidable opposition against the Game Refuge-Public Shooting Grounds Bill. Hornaday believed that liberal bag limits and the use of semiautomatic shotguns was causing the slaughter of too many ducks and geese, and he argued that the creation of game refuges was simply a method of concentrating waterfowl for more killing by hunters. He called supporters of this bill "game hogs" and "butchers."

Senator Peter Norbeck had reintroduced the Game Refuge-Public Shooting Grounds Bill in the opening days of the Seventieth Congress (1927-1928). After bitter debate, the federal licensing and public hunting-grounds features were removed from it, and the Norbeck bill passed the Senate. Congressman August H. Andresen of Minnesota authored a new bill identical to the amended Norbeck bill on January 23, 1929. Without provision for congressional moneys, this bill quickly passed the House. After eight years of disagreement and acrimonious charges, on February 8, 1929, the Norbeck-Andresen Act established a feasible waterfowl refuge law.

The idea of a federal hunting license for waterfowl had seemed defeated with the passage of the final version of the Norbeck-Andresen Act, but in the wake of the onset of the Great Depression and the Dust Bowl, it acquired new life and new urgency. In early 1927, drought, drainage of wetlands, and expanding hunting and poaching pressure had

The first Duck Stamp, featuring art by Jay Darling. (U.S. Fish and Wildlife Service)

1934

2743

caused waterfowl numbers to decline sharply. In the fall of 1929, drought-stricken populations of waterfowl had begun to plummet sharply. On December 31, 1929, the bag limit had been reduced from twenty-five to fifteen ducks a day, but the waterfowl crash had continued.

Frederic Collin Walcott, a Connecticut senator and an avid duck hunter, viewed the waterfowl crash with alarm. His great desire for wildlife conservation led him to establish the Senate Special Committee on the Conservation of Wildlife Resources. As its first chairman, he proposed a greatly intensified waterfowl management program in 1931. The funding of this management effort revived the American Game Association's idea of a federal hunting stamp. On April 4, 1932, more than one hundred witnesses were heard by Walcott's committee. Most of the witnesses favored the hunting stamp proposal.

By 1934, then, the way had been largely prepared for the recommendation of Darling's committee, which seemed to confirm what Walcott's committee had already decided. Darling lobbied Congress for a duck stamp, and progress toward its enactment was rapid: The Migratory Bird Hunting and Conservation Stamp Act became law on March 16, 1934. The law required all waterfowl hunters sixteen years of age and older to buy federal duck stamps, sign them, and paste them to the back of their state-issued hunting licenses. Sold at local U.S. Post Offices, the stamps were required only for hunting ducks and geese, not for hunting any other migratory game birds. Darling, an astute political cartoonist and an outstanding artist, designed the first duck stamp in 1934; it sold for one dollar. All funds from the sale of this stamp were to be used for waterfowl management and the acquisition of wetland habitats essential for restoring waterfowl numbers. The act was the first major federal statute to establish a special fund to be used exclusively for wildlife conservation purposes.

SIGNIFICANCE

Before the crash of waterfowl populations in the 1920's, the U.S. government had set aside about 744,000 acres of habitat for all wildlife. By 1942, almost 3 million acres had been set aside for the preservation of waterfowl alone. Much of the money for this land acquisition came from the Migratory Bird Hunting and Conservation Stamp Act of 1934. Duck stamp receipts are available for use without congressional appropriation. In the first fifty years of the program's existence, more than eighty-eight million duck stamps provided more than $300 million for waterfowl conservation.

On August 12, 1949, in response to fiscal crises, the price of the duck stamp was doubled from one dollar to two dollars. The 1949 amendment to the Migratory Bird Hunting and Conservation Stamp Act also authorized the secretary of the interior to set aside wildlife management areas on up to 25 percent of any land acquired with duck stamp revenues. Hunting of resident and migratory game birds was to be allowed on these lands. In 1958, another amendment to the act increased hunter access to 40 percent of lands acquired with duck stamp moneys. The issue of whether to allow sport hunting on lands acquired with duck stamp revenues in the National Wildlife Refuge System remains controversial.

Inadequate funding for acquisition of lands for wildlife, especially waterfowl, is a continuing problem for wildlife conservationists. For example, the price of a duck stamp increased nearly 750 percent between 1934 and 1986. In the same interval of time, however, the price of farmland rose 2,600 percent. Thus revenues generated by duck stamps alone cannot buy and maintain all the needed remaining wetlands of the United States.

In the United States, about 5.2 million acres of waterfowl habitat have been preserved since the 1930's through the duck stamp program. Because of the success of the U.S. government in raising moneys through the sale of duck stamps for waterfowl conservation, many states in the United States also issue hunting stamps to fund their conservation needs. Stamps for upland game birds, trout, turkeys, and nongame animals raise several million dollars each year for important conservation activities. Such programs are thus legacies of a time when it seemed that waterfowl, one of the nation's priceless resources, might disappear forever from North America.

—*David L. Chesemore*

FURTHER READING

Day, Albert M. *North American Waterfowl*. Harrisburg, Pa.: Stackpole, 1959. Provides an excellent overview of the historical progress of waterfowl management in North America through the 1950's.

Farley, John L. *Duck Stamps and Wildlife Refuges*. Washington, D.C.: U.S. Department of the Interior. Fish and Wildlife Service, 1959. Circular no. 37. A capsule summary of the history of the enactment of the Duck Stamp Act and how it has benefited waterfowl conservation.

Gilmore, Jene C. *Art for Conservation: The Federal Duck Stamps*. Barre, Mass.: Barre, 1971. Each duck stamp from 1934 through 1971 is portrayed in black and white. Additional information on number of stamps sold, a brief biography of the artist who produced the stamp, and information on the stamps' production is given clearly and concisely in this book.

Linduska, Joseph P. *Waterfowl Tomorrow*. Washington, D.C.: Government Printing Office, 1964. An updated version of Day's book on waterfowl history, this is a good first book from which to learn the history of waterfowl management.

McBride, David P. *The Federal Duck Stamps: A Complete Guide*. Piscataway, N.J.: Winchester Press, 1984. The best book on duck stamps. Details the enactment of the Duck Stamp Act and includes black-and-white reproductions of the stamps from 1934 through 1984. Eleven appendixes and a bibliography add considerable information about duck stamps.

Reiger, John F. *American Sportsmen and the Origins of*

Conservation. 3d rev. and expanded ed. Corvallis: Oregon State University Press, 2001. Study emphasizing the connection between sport and conservation in American history. Largely a prehistory of the Duck Stamp Act, but includes an epilogue on Aldo Leopold and his place in the history of conservation and sport. Bibliographic references and index.

Trefethen, James B. *Crusade for Wildlife: Highlights in Conservation Progress*. Harrisburg, Pa.: Stackpole, 1961. One of the best books on the history of wildlife conservation in the United States. Written in a readable style that makes historical facts come alive.

SEE ALSO: Mar. 14, 1903: First U.S. National Wildlife Refuge Is Established; Nov. 19, 1929: Serengeti Game Reserve Is Created.

March 24, 1934
PHILIPPINE INDEPENDENCE ACT

In the Philippine Independence Act, the United States promised independence to the Philippines by 1944, and in doing so it paved the way for expansion of U.S. economic interests in the islands.

ALSO KNOWN AS: Tydings-McDuffie Act
LOCALE: Washington, D.C.
CATEGORIES: Laws, acts, and legal history; independence movements; colonialism and occupation

KEY FIGURES

Harry B. Hawes (1869-1947), former senator from Missouri

John McDuffie (1883-1950), representative from Alabama

Sergio Osmeña (1878-1961), vice president of the Philippines

Manuel Quezón (1878-1944), president of the Philippines

Franklin D. Roosevelt (1882-1945), president of the United States, 1933-1945

Millard Tydings (1890-1961), senator from Maryland

SUMMARY OF EVENT

On March 24, 1934, President Franklin D. Roosevelt signed the Philippine Independence Act, popularly known as the Tydings-McDuffie Act. The law promised independence to the Philippine islands by 1944, follow-

ing a ten-year transition period of "commonwealth status." During that time, the islands were to be governed by their own national legislature and executive branches; policy-making power, however, would continue to remain in the United States. This commonwealth system was in place when the Philippines were invaded and occupied by the Japanese in 1942, an event that delayed Philippine independence for two years (until 1946).

Initial support for the Philippine legislation came from particular special interest groups both in the United States and in the Philippines. Striving for their own nationhood, many native Filipino lobbying groups pushed hard for the act's passage. A more economically based pressure came from American beet-sugar producers, who sought to eliminate competition from island goods, and from trade-union leaders, who wanted to prevent the influx of Filipino workers into the Hawaiian islands and the U.S. mainland. These groups had earlier lent similar support to the legislative predecessor of the Philippine Independence Act, the Hare-Hawes-Cutting Act of 1933. The earlier act's attempt to curb competitive imports from the Philippines was rejected by the U.S. Senate in a close vote.

After the defeat of the Hare-Hawes-Cutting legislation, a new contingent of Filipino supporters of independence traveled to Washington, D.C., where they were joined by those groups of politically influential Americans who supported Philippine autonomy. Sergio Osmeña led the Philippine delegation, but his call for immediate independence was too drastic for many in the American group. He was subsequently recalled to Manila. His replacement, Manuel Quezón, took a less politically offensive position, emphasizing a gradualist approach to independence for the islands. He was thus able to enlist the support of additional American politicians who favored a more moderate approach to Philippine independence. The resulting coalition influenced the passage of the Philippine Independence Act.

Following enactment of the Philippine Independence Act's legislation, the Filipino delegation returned home to draft a constitution and to elect officials who would oversee the gradual transition to Philippine autonomy. Quezón and Osmeña were elected president and vice president, respectively, of the new commonwealth. Although steps were taken to create a Filipino-based political structure, most of the political decision-making authority still rested with the United States. Filipinos did, however, retain limited control over internal political affairs, but all foreign policy, defense, and monetary matters were defined and implemented in Washington. This political arrangement clearly benefited the United States at the expense of the Filipinos: The commonwealth was prohibited from legislating most of its own economic policies, and In particular, legislation was passed that imposed duties on Philippine exports to the United States.

SIGNIFICANCE

The Philippine Independence Act ensured that, under the new commonwealth system, the cliental politics and economics of the old colonial structure were perfected. Increasingly, the Philippine presidency came to resemble the office of an American state governor: Quezón was accorded certain discretionary powers, but only where American interests were not affected. Quezón could organize an army, but he could not deploy it without President Roosevelt's consent. Travel to foreign lands and discussion of trade agreements with foreign officials could take place, but Quezón was powerless to conclude any formal agreement. The enactment of any official Philippine trade agreements remained under the authority of the U.S. high commissioner of the Philippines. This position, strengthened by the provisions of the Philippine Independence Act, protected the interests of the United States in all foreign relations and established official relationships between the Philippines and all other nations.

Looking after American interests abroad required the centralization of political authority in Manila. As a re-

sult, domestic policies were often delegated from the top level of Philippine government. It was under such an arrangement that President Quezón increasingly took advantage of his position. As long as his policy initiatives did not conflict with American interests, he wielded immense power, especially toward those who opposed his policies. Quezón often crushed his opposition with American blessings, and the elimination of domestic competition greatly increased Quezón's confidence. He began to challenge some of the policies of American commonwealth administrators and even, at times, those of the high commissioner. Chastised at this level, he boldly began to take his conflicts to the American president. Although he was successful in protesting the directives of the high commissioner on some occasions, his appeals to President Roosevelt most often produced results that reinforced American hegemony in the Philippines.

Under the structure authorized by the Philippine Independence Act, the goal of true Philippine independence was increasingly circumvented, and American sovereignty over the Philippines continued in the name of independence. American suzerainty was magnified by a commonwealth political system that furthered American economic interests at the expense of the islands' position as a competitor in the world market, and in the end, the Philippines became increasingly dependent on American economic interests. Commonwealth status destroyed what the Philippines needed in order to compete economically on a global scale: revenue from the export of duty-free goods to the United States. Without trade revenues, the Philippines became increasingly dependent on the United States for loans and investments, which were always made, of course, with the understanding that U.S. interests came first. As the Philippine treasury emptied, the commonwealth thus became more indebted to the United States. The implementation of the Philippine Independence Act both initiated and reinforced this condition.

The new relationship between the Philippines and the United States established by the Philippine Independence Act produced a paradox: The closer the Philippines came to political independence, the more economically dependent on the United States it became. In the end, the Philippine Independence Act reinforced the idea that the only kind of independence that would be granted to the Filipinos was the kind that the United States could not grant, at least under the conditions of the day. Ultimately, after intense cooperation during the ravages of World War II, Filipinos were granted independence in

1946, when they were saddled with the task of fashioning a truly national political life and an independent foreign policy.

—Thomas J. Edward Walker,
Cynthia Gwynne Yaudes, and Ruby L. Stoner

FURTHER READING

Constantino, Renato. *A History of the Philippines*. New York: Monthly Review Press, 1975. A clearly written historical analysis of the Filipino struggle against imperialism. Provides a regional examination of Philippine political, economic, sociocultural, and religious colonization; also includes an intellectual examination of the decolonization process. Excellent non-Western documentation.

Delmendo, Sharon. *The Star-Entangled Banner: One Hundred Years of America in the Philippines*. New Brunswick, N.J.: Rutgers University Press, 2004. History of the troubled relationship between the United States and the Philippines in the twentieth century. Examines several issues, including the long-term effects of American imperialism. Includes illustrations, bibliography, and index.

Feuer, A. B. *America at War: The Philippines, 1898-1913*. New York: Praeger, 2002. Employs previously unpublished letters, diaries, and photographs to present a look at the Philippine-American War from the point of view of American soldiers, sailors, and marines who participated.

Gallego, Manuel. *The Price of Philippine Independence Under the Tydings-McDuffie Act: An Anti-view of the So-Called Independence Law*. Manila: Barristers Book Company, 1939. A Philippine account of the implementation of the act and the evolution of the commonwealth period; provides personal narratives documenting political, economic, and social oppression.

Grunder, Garel A., and William E. Lively. *The Philippines and the United States*. Norman: University of Oklahoma Press, 1951. An overview of the origin and evolution of U.S. policy toward the Philippine islands during the first half of the twentieth century. Explains how such policy affected American Filipino economic relations, examines the evolution of Filipino political institutions, and defines the structure of the independence of the Philippine nation.

Hayden, John Ralston. *The Philippines: A Study in National Development*. New York: Macmillan, 1942. A somewhat patronizing account of the Philippine interaction with the United States during the first four decades of the twentieth century. Through primary source materials, provides a positive opinion of U.S. contributions to the development of an independent nation.

Karnow, Stanley. *In Our Image: America's Empire in the Philippines*. New York: Random House, 1989. Journalistic account of the American imperial experience in the Philippines. Suggests that the U.S. attempts to remake the Philippines in its own image through the establishment of political, educational, and sociocultural institutions barely affected traditional Filipino values yet such activity resulted in a unique relationship between the two countries. Indexed with bibliography.

Paredes, Ruby R., ed. *Philippine Colonial Democracy*. New Haven, Conn.: Yale University Press, 1988. Analyzes the patron-client relationship between the United States and the Philippines. Suggests that the interaction was mutually corruptive for both nations: devastating to the evolution of Philippine democracy and detrimental to U.S. foreign policy. Indexed.

SEE ALSO: May 27, 1901: Insular Cases; 1902: Philippines Ends Its Uprising Against the United States; May 22, 1903: Platt Amendment; Mar. 2, 1917: Jones Act of 1917.

1934

May 23, 1934
POLICE APPREHEND BONNIE AND CLYDE

Clyde Barrow and Bonnie Parker carried out one of the most celebrated crime sprees of the Great Depression era before meeting their violent end in a controversial police ambush.

LOCALE: Gibsland, Louisiana
CATEGORY: Crime and scandal

KEY FIGURES

Clyde Barrow (1909-1934), serial armed robber and murderer
Bonnie Parker (1910-1934), serial armed robber and accomplice of Clyde Barrow
Frank Hamer (1884-1955), Texas Ranger who led the party that killed Barrow and Parker
Marhall Lee Simmons (1873-1957), manager of the Texas prison system
Henry Methvin (1912-1948), police informant and Barrow and Parker's accomplice

SUMMARY OF EVENT

The exploits of Clyde Barrow and Bonnie Parker, commonly known as Bonnie and Clyde, inspired one of the most popular criminal legends to emerge from the era of the Great Depression. From 1932 until 1934, Parker and Barrow embarked on a crime spree that extended from Texas into several southern and midwestern states. Their crimes were small but occasionally violent and generally focused on holdups of small businesses and banks. By 1934, Barrow, Parker, and a rotating gang of accomplices had been implicated in more than a dozen murders, including the killing of several law-enforcement officers, and they were among the most wanted criminals in the United States.

Their criminal activities also made Parker and Barrow minor celebrities. Widespread economic privation and a sensationalist press helped construct a popular image of the bandit as a romantic antihero during the Great Depression, and many of the era's criminals, including Barrow and Parker, cultivated this image. The pair would often leave their kidnapped robbery victims unharmed and even gave them enough money to return home. Parker, an amateur poet, sent letters and verse to newspapers and left her work behind for authorities. Barrow, whose experiences with high-speed chases had made him a skilled driver, allegedly wrote automobile magnate Henry Ford a letter in which he praised the performance of a stolen Ford sedan.

By late 1933, the pair were living a life much less romantic than their popular image. A police raid on their safehouse in Joplin, Missouri, forced them to leave most of their possessions, and they had begun using a series of increasingly remote hideouts. Further encounters with the police led to more shootouts, resulting in the death of Barrow's brother, Buck Barrow. In early 1934, the Barrow gang freed several inmates at the Eastham Prison Farm, the brutal prison where Barrow allegedly committed his first murder in 1931. The bold act and ensuing publicity enraged Texas officials, who hired former Texas Ranger Frank Hamer to track down Parker and Barrow. Hamer, who had killed dozens of criminals in shootouts, began tracking the Barrow gang in February, 1934. He found an unlikely source of assistance in former accomplice Henry Methvin, whom the gang had freed from Eastham in the raid. In exchange for immunity from pending charges in Texas and Louisiana, Methvin informed authorities about a planned meeting between Barrow and Methvin that was to take place on May 23 at Methvin's parents' house outside Gibsland, Louisiana, approximately 50 miles from the Texas border.

Hamer assembled a posse composed of four officers from Texas and two from Louisiana and made plans to wait for Parker and Barrow along State Highway 154, the most likely route to their meeting place. The officers were hidden and heavily armed behind natural barricades when they deployed along the roadside just after dusk on the evening of May 21, the designated time of the meeting. Parker and Barrow did not show that evening, and the pair waited through the next day and into the morning of May 23 before the Ford sedan driven by Barrow and occupied by Parker came into view. The posse remained hidden as Barrow stopped to talk with Methvin's father, who had been enlisted as a decoy and had parked his truck in the road to force the couple's vehicle into the lane closest to the officers' hiding place.

What happened immediately afterward is the source of controversy. As Methvin's father dove for cover, the assembled officers opened fire, striking the sedan and its occupants with approximately 130 rounds of ammunition. Barrow, struck in the head with the first bullet fired, died instantly, but participants claimed that they could hear Parker screaming in agony as she was hit by multiple gunshots. Authorities did little to secure the scene of the ambush, which was soon inundated with reporters, souvenir seekers, and onlookers. Bystanders reportedly removed locks of hair from Parker's corpse, and Hamer and other members of the posse took weapons from the car as souvenirs. American newspapers, capitalizing on the sensational nature of the deaths, published front-page stories of the ambush of along with photographs of the bullet-riddled automobile. Popular media trumpeted the killing of the famous duo as a victory for law enforcement and evidence of the devastating and inevitable consequences of a life of crime. Yet the romantic legend of Parker and Barrow survived, spawning a multitude of books, articles, feature films, and other popular culture references.

Many questioned the ambush's propriety, particularly the killing of Bonnie Parker, who was not wanted for a capital crime. Some evidence indicates that the head of the Texas prison system, Marshall Lee Simmons, may have issued a direct order to Hamer to kill both Parker and Barrow. All accounts of the incident suggest that the couple was completely taken by surprise: Barrow was driving without shoes, and Parker was reportedly eating a sandwich as they approached the point of ambush. Although Barrow had killed numerous policemen in shootouts and the sedan he was driving contained numerous weapons, there is no evidence that either he or Parker attempted to use force or that they were even aware of the presence of the posse. Although the posse possessed high-powered weaponry capable of disabling the sedan's tires and engine and thus removing the only available escape option, accounts indicate that the first shot fired hit Barrow in the head at close range. The well-documented frustration expressed by authorities and Hamer's violent reputation prompted further speculation that the killing of the infamous couple was unjustified and premeditated.

Bonnie Parker and Clyde Barrow. (Library of Congress)

1934

SIGNIFICANCE

Many scholars suggested that Americans traumatized by the Great Depression seized on the true-crime gangster stories of the era as a means of assuaging frustration and escaping the reality of daily life by living vicariously through the exploits of high-profile outlaws, whom the media often portrayed as morally ambiguous figures op-

posing a broken, corrupt, and oppressive system and capable of random acts of compassion toward ordinary citizens. The crimes and violent deaths of Clyde Barrow and Bonnie Parker occurred during the final wave of the "public enemy" era and paralleled the careers of other famous criminal gang leaders such as John Dillinger and Arizona Donnie "Ma" Barker. Yet the story of Bonnie and Clyde proved one of the most popular and durable criminal legends of the twentieth century, and it periodically resurfaced in motion pictures such as *The Bonnie Parker Story* (1958), *Bonnie and Clyde* (1967), and *Natural Born Killers* (1994); popular songs such as the 1968 Merle Haggard hit "The Legend of Bonnie and Clyde;" and numerous biographies and other literary treatments. At the end of the twentieth century, the legend had gained a measure of popularity in American hip-hop; several musical recordings contained references to Parker and Barrow.

When the U.S. government consolidated federal law-enforcement agencies into the Federal Bureau of Investigation (FBI) in 1935, the federal government took a more active role in combating organized crime and in inspiring the federalization of a number of crimes whose enforcement had been the states' responsibility. The government's efforts to prevent interstate criminal activity continued to grow throughout the twentieth century as organized crime and gang violence remained sources of media attention and public concern.

—*Michael H. Burchett*

FURTHER READING

Barrow, Blanche, and John Neal Tebo Phillips . *My Life with Bonnie and Clyde.* Norman: University of Oklahoma Press, 2004. Memoir written in prison by Barrow's sister-in-law. Edited by noted researcher of Parker and Barrows. Includes accounts of Blanche Barrow's experiences with the Barrow gang and previously unpublished photographs from author's personal collection.

Bruns, Roger. *The Bandit Kings: From Jesse James to Pretty Boy Floyd.* New York: Crown, 1995. Examination of the outlaw as folk hero discusses prominent American criminals from 1850 through 1940.

Knight, James, and Jonathan Davis. *Bonnie and Clyde: A Twenty-First Century Update.* Austin, Tex.: Eakin Press, 2003. Detailed biography of Parker and Barrow contains previously unpublished information and photographs as well as refutations of previously unchallenged theories and allegations.

Phillips, John Neal. "The Raid on Eastham." *American History* 35, no. 4 (October, 2000): 54. Narrative account of the prison break that led to the ambush of Parker and Barrow; the author alleges that Marshall Lee Simmons ordered Frank Hamer to kill the couple.

Prassel, Frank Richard. *The Great American Outlaw: A Legacy of Fact and Fiction.* Norman: University of Oklahoma Press, 1993. Scholarly discussion of the outlaw in American popular culture.

SEE ALSO: Jan. 16, 1920-Dec. 5, 1933: Prohibition; Dec. 10, 1924: Hoover Becomes the Director of the U.S. Bureau of Investigation; Oct. 24-29, 1929: U.S. Stock Market Crashes; Oct. 29, 1929-1939: Great Depression; 1930's: Guthrie's Populist Songs Reflect the Depression-Era United States; 1931-1932: Gangster Films Become Popular; Mar. 9-June 16, 1933: The Hundred Days; 1934-1939: Dust Bowl Devastates the Great Plains.

June 6, 1934
SECURITIES AND EXCHANGE COMMISSION IS ESTABLISHED

The Securities Exchange Act of 1934 created a quasi-judicial administrative body, the Securities and Exchange Commission, with broad powers to regulate the securities markets and protect the public interest.

LOCALE: Washington, D.C.
CATEGORIES: Laws, acts, and legal history; banking and finance; business and labor

KEY FIGURES

Franklin D. Roosevelt (1882-1945), president of the United States, 1933-1945
Ferdinand Pecora (1882-1971), legal counsel to the U.S. Senate Banking and Currency Committee
Sam Rayburn (1882-1961), U.S. congressman from Texas
Duncan U. Fletcher (1859-1936), U.S. senator from Florida
Richard Whitney (1888-1974), president of the New York Stock Exchange

SUMMARY OF EVENT

The Securities Exchange Act of 1934 solidified the expanding role of the federal government in protecting the investing public. Passed in the aftermath of the greatest stock market collapse in history, this legislation established a new administrative agency with broad powers to ensure that many of the financial abuses and deceptive practices of the past would not recur.

Historically, as economic activity increases in volume, complexity, and sophistication, the corporation emerges as the dominant form of business organization. Corporate entities thrive because of the continued and expanding capital investment of people willing to accept the risks and rewards of ownership but unwilling or unable to participate in actual management of the business operation. Through the issuance of securities by corporations, ownership can be spread over a broad base of individuals, thus maximizing the potential for invested resources.

In order to facilitate this capital exchange process, organized marketplaces have developed throughout the world. These capital markets provide the mechanism for the corporate distribution of debt and equity securities as well as the subsequent transfer of these securities between individuals.

Because of the inherent separation of corporate management from ownership, current and potential investors operate under a distinct informational disadvantage. Capital contributors are at the mercy of claims made by "insiders." Exploitation of unwary investors inevitably occurs, and securities markets merely serve to provide an organized forum within which to execute such schemes on a broad scale.

Government, concerned with ensuring an adequate supply of available capital in order to sustain economic growth, has a natural interest in protecting investors and maintaining public confidence in these securities markets. In the United States, attempts at regulation of securities were first made at the state level. In response to widespread fraudulent activities of stock promoters, Kansas enacted a statute in 1911 to protect the public interest. In the first year following enactment of this law, approximately fifteen hundred applications to sell securities in Kansas were filed. Only 14 percent were accepted; the rest were judged to be fraudulent (75 percent) or too highly speculative (11 percent).

Other legislatures followed Kansas's lead, and by 1913, twenty-two other states had passed laws similar in intent but widely varying in approach. These state securities laws are often called blue-sky laws, because the speculative schemes they attempted to foil often involved little more than selling "pieces of the sky," or worthless securities.

For various reasons, the individual state attempts to regulate securities markets were not very effective. Perhaps the greatest problem arose from the tactic of "interstate escape." Individuals or companies could continue deceptive and fraudulent practices merely by moving across state lines (physically or through the mails) to other jurisdictions where regulations were inadequate, poorly enforced, or perhaps even nonexistent. To limit such evasion, some form of federal intervention was needed.

During the 1920's, a veritable explosion took place in securities market activity. Small investors entered the market in numbers larger than ever before. National brokerage firms doubled the number of their branch offices and reported phenomenal increases in business. Despite the vigorous trading and investing activity that was oc-

curring, the strength of the market was quickly eroding as a result of a number of prevailing traditions.

First, stock price manipulation was common. This was often executed by means of a manipulation pool, in which a syndicate of corporate officials and market operators join forces and, through a succession of equally matched buying and selling orders ("wash sales") among themselves, create the false impression of feverish activity, thus driving up the price of the stock. At the height of this artificial activity, the stock is sold, huge profits are reaped by the syndicate, and the stock price subsequently plummets. As an example of the success of this gambit, a pool formed in March, 1929, to trade in Radio Corporation of America (RCA) stock operated for only a seven-day period and netted a profit of almost $5 million.

The excessive use of credit to finance speculative stock transactions (that is, buying stocks "on margin") was another tradition that undermined the stability of the market. An investment as small as one hundred dollars could purchase one thousand dollars in securities (with a 10 percent margin), and there were no limits to the level of credit a broker could extend to a customer. This practice effectively lured potential capital away from productive economic investment and toward mere market speculation.

A third practice that hindered the efficient operation of the securities market relates to the misuse of corporate information by insiders. Corporate officials could withhold information, either positive or negative. By timing the release of information until after they had already positioned themselves in the market, they could benefit from price fluctuations when the news finally became public.

The weight of these traditions finally culminated in the stock market crash of October, 1929, which was a financial earthquake of dramatic proportions. The aggregate value of all stocks listed on the New York Stock Exchange (the largest capital market in the United States, handling 90 percent of all stock transactions on a dollar basis) declined from $89 billion before the crash to only $15 billion by 1932. The economic depression that rapidly deepened following the crash was the worst economic crisis in U.S. history.

In March, 1932, the Senate Banking and Currency Committee was empowered to investigate the securities industry. This inquiry was continued and greatly expanded in scope after the election of Franklin D. Roosevelt as president in November, 1932. Roosevelt had been on record since his tenure as governor of New York as being highly critical of various stock market activities.

1934

The 1932 Democratic national platform on which he ran explicitly called for federal supervision of securities transactions.

Ferdinand Pecora served as legal counsel to this committee during its extensive investigations in 1933 and 1934. He compiled an impressive body of evidence concerning financial corruption and malpractice. Pecora personally elicited much of the damaging evidence from the most prestigious financial leaders of the time and was invaluable in documenting the need for securities regulation. For example, his investigation disclosed that of the $50 billion of new securities issued during the decade after World War I, half had proved to be worthless.

With the passage of the Securities Act in 1933 (signed into law on May 5, 1933, soon after Roosevelt's inauguration), the federal government finally entered the arena of securities regulation. This bill was championed in Congress by Representative Sam Rayburn of Texas and Senator Duncan U. Fletcher of Florida. The 1933 act is primarily a disclosure statute, concerned only with the initial distribution of a security. Although it was an important first step and forerunner to more ambitious efforts in securities regulation, this legislation failed to address adequately many of the practices in the capital market that contributed to the 1929 collapse.

Fletcher and Rayburn once again introduced bills in Congress, based in large part on drafts written by investigator Pecora. At the time, there was significant and widespread opposition to stock market regulation. Government interference, it was argued, would likely upset the delicate workings of Wall Street. Richard Whitney, president of the New York Stock Exchange (NYSE), was at the vanguard of this resistance. Whitney organized a well-financed protest campaign and mobilized forces to defeat the proposed legislation. Overt threats were even made to relocate the NYSE to Montreal, Canada, which offered a less obtrusive regulatory environment. Intense lobbying efforts did result in some modifications of the original bills, but finally, on June 6, 1934, Roosevelt signed the Securities Exchange Act.

SIGNIFICANCE

The major provisions of the Securities Exchange Act deal with three broad areas of regulation in an attempt to prevent the abuses previously cited and thereby protect the public interest: full and fair disclosure, supervision of capital market practices, and administration of credit requirements. This act requires that all national securities exchanges register with and be subject to the regulations of the Securities and Exchange Commission (SEC), an administrative agency with quasi-judicial powers that was created by this legislation. The immediate result was the closing of nine stock exchanges that could not meet the new requirements, including a one-man exchange operating out of an Indiana poolroom.

All corporations with securities listed on a national exchange must file detailed registration statements with the SEC and are required to disclose financial information on a periodic basis in a form that meets certain standards. The SEC retains discretionary power over the form and detail of such disclosures. The SEC also requires periodic audits of these firms by independent accountants.

This last requirement has had a dramatic impact on the growth and development of the accounting profession. Certified public accountants were effectively granted a franchise to audit corporations with publicly traded securities. There was a substantial cost involved in terms of increased risk exposure. By expressing an opinion on the veracity of financial statements filed with the SEC, the auditor becomes legally liable to third parties (including investors) who may subsequently be harmed by reliance on that information.

In the area of actual market practices, the SEC had immediate and far-reaching impact. Because of the relative informational advantage that market participants have over the public, the SEC now closely scrutinizes their activities. Exchanges, brokers, and dealers must all register with the SEC and file periodic disclosure reports. Corporate insiders are subject to especially strict rules designed to prevent unfair profit-taking. Certain stock market manipulation schemes (for example, wash sales) are prohibited. In fact, any fraudulent, manipulative, or deceptive securities dealings, whether specified by the act or not, are prohibited for all market participants. The penalties for infraction include fines, imprisonment, or both.

Finally, in the area of credit, the 1934 act authorizes the Federal Reserve system to administer the extension of margin credit in securities trading, with the SEC as ultimate enforcer. This important component of government economic and monetary policy was no longer to be left in the hands of individual brokers.

The first Securities and Exchange Commission was composed of a presidentially appointed five-member bipartisan panel that included Ferdinand Pecora. Ironically, Pecora was passed over as chairman in favor of Joseph P. Kennedy, who the year before had participated in a pool syndicate operation.

Since its inception, the SEC has progressed through a

number of different phases. The first decade of operation was an innovative period in which the permanent machinery and procedures necessary to carry out the functions and responsibilities of the SEC were established. This period was also marked by a concerted effort on the part of the early commissioners to promote the agency to both the public and the business community as a powerful partner in the quest for honest financial activity, not as a mere enforcement arm of the government.

It was during this early period that a philosophy of operation began to evolve. Rather than merely coercing compliance through enforcement actions, the SEC often adopted the policy of encouraging self-regulation within a framework of governmental constraints. By inspiring confidence in the laws that it administered, the SEC hoped to foster a heightened sense of social responsibility and ethics among the private sector, leading to development of self-monitoring systems. This pragmatic approach was perhaps most evident in the area of establishing accounting and reporting standards. Although the SEC had been empowered to develop and maintain standards and principles of accounting practice, it generally deferred to the accounting profession. Such concession did not occur automatically. The SEC first had to satisfy itself that the private sector's system of establishing accounting and auditing standards had progressed to an acceptable level.

The next twenty-year period was characterized by very little significant legislation or innovation. Investor confidence in the capital markets was generally high, and the SEC routinely carried on the mission that had been developed. Revitalization of the SEC came in the early 1960's, after a rash of litigation related to the civil and criminal liability issues involved in inaccurate financial disclosures. Various amendments to legislation administered by the SEC followed. In the 1970's, major legislation was passed to combat corporate bribery and other illegal business practices.

During the 1980's, the SEC was guided by a doctrine of facilitation. Major efforts to expand full and fair disclosure and to streamline and standardize reporting requirements demonstrated the SEC's commitment to improving the efficiency of the flow of information and ultimately the flow of capital investment in the economy. Continuation of this tradition will likely ensure that the SEC remains a potent regulatory force in the mission of protecting the public interest.

In 2002, after a raft of high-profile bankruptcies involving corporate fraud, Congress passed the Sarbanes-Oxley Act, which represented the most comprehensive reform of corporate business practice since passage of the Securities Exchange Act in 1934.

—Jon R. Carpenter

FURTHER READING

Chatov, Robert. *Corporate Financial Reporting*. New York: Free Press, 1975. Readable scholarly study of the broad regulatory process and the various social and political controls used in public policy formation and implementation. The SEC serves as the focal point for this detailed analysis of independent regulatory agency behavior.

De Bedts, Ralph F. *The New Deal's SEC*. New York: Columbia University Press, 1964. Provides an interesting historical perspective on the origins of the SEC and a description of its early, formative years of operation. Offers in-depth coverage not normally found in writings on New Deal reforms. Relaxed narrative form.

Ginzberg, Eli. *New Deal Days, 1933-1934*. New Brunswick, N.J.: Transaction, 1997. Relatively light treatment of early New Deal legislation for nonspecialist readers.

Hughes, Jonathan, and Louis P. Cain. *American Economic History*. 6th ed. Boston: Addison-Wesley, 2002. Comprehensive volume on the economic history of the United States includes discussion of securities legislation.

Kindleberger, Charles P. *Manias, Panics, and Crashes: A History of Financial Crises*. 4th ed. New York: John Wiley & Sons, 2000. General survey of financial speculation and monetary crises from the eighteenth century to the late twentieth century.

Pointer, Larry Gene, and Richard G. Schroeder. *An Introduction to the Securities and Exchange Commission*. Plano, Tex.: Business Publications, 1986. Designed as a supplemental text for undergraduate accounting students, this booklet is nontechnical and serves as a good, brief overview of the SEC for the general reader. Provides some historical perspective but focuses on the SEC's structure and operation.

Rappaport, Louis H. *SEC Accounting Practice and Procedure*. 3d ed. New York: Ronald Press, 1972. Exhaustive reference work and guide to the broad range of financial reporting requirements of the SEC. Often very technical in presentation, a natural outcome of the inherent complexity of the subject matter. Provides numerous illustrative examples.

Tyler, Poyntz, ed. *Securities, Exchanges, and the SEC*. New York: H. W. Wilson, 1965. Provides the general

1934

reader with background information essential to an understanding and appreciation of more complex writings in the area of investing, capital markets, and regulation. Contains reprints of short articles, excerpts from books, and other documents. An interesting and very readable compendium.

SEE ALSO: Oct.-Nov., 1907: Panic of 1907; Aug. 5, 1909: Tariff Act of 1909 Limits Corporate Privacy;

Dec. 23, 1913: Federal Reserve Act; 1915: Merrill Lynch & Company Is Founded; 1919-1920: Ponzi Cheats Thousands in an Investment Scheme; Oct. 24-29, 1929: U.S. Stock Market Crashes; Dec. 11, 1930: Bank of United States Fails; 1932: Berle and Means Discuss Corporate Control; June 16, 1933: Banking Act of 1933 Reorganizes the American Banking System.

June 10, 1934
FEDERAL COMMUNICATIONS COMMISSION IS ESTABLISHED BY CONGRESS

Congress created the Federal Communications Commission in response to President Franklin D. Roosevelt's desire to consolidate regulatory powers over communications. The organization became an important testing ground for ideas about the First Amendment and the role of advertising in American culture.

ALSO KNOWN AS: Communications Act of 1934
LOCALE: Washington, D.C.
CATEGORIES: Communications and media; laws, acts, and legal history; radio and television

KEY FIGURES
Franklin D. Roosevelt (1882-1945), president of the United States, 1933-1945
Daniel C. Roper (1867-1943), U.S. secretary of commerce
Frank McManamy (1870-1944), chairman of the legislative committee of the Interstate Commerce Commission
Eugene O. Sykes (1876-1945), chairman of the Federal Radio Commission
Lionel Van Deerlin (b. 1914), chairman of the House Subcommittee on Communications

SUMMARY OF EVENT
The Radio Act of 1927 created the Federal Radio Commission (FRC), which sought to ensure that radio broadcasting served the public interest. The FRC had the central authority to grant licenses to radio stations, however, and it soon faced a regulatory nightmare. Radio broadcasters with long histories enjoyed a favored status that they vigorously fought to retain, many radio stations were broadcasting on frequencies reserved for Canada, and several unregulated amateurs had ventured into ra-

dio broadcasting. To add to these problems, the FRC had been created on a temporary basis; its authority was assured for only one year. As a result, its life had to be extended annually through a congressional renewal process that was used to impose restrictions on the FRC. For example, the Davis Amendment to the 1928 congressional renewal of the Radio Act severely restricted the FRC by requiring it to divide licenses and broadcast frequencies equally across five geographic zones.

Although such congressional mandates elicited protests from President Herbert Hoover, the regulation of broadcasting remained in this unsatisfactory state until 1933, when President Franklin D. Roosevelt directed Daniel C. Roper, the U.S. secretary of commerce, to study radio broadcasting. In January, 1934, a committee chaired by Roper recommended that the communications-oriented regulatory activities of the FRC (which centered on radio frequencies), the Interstate Commerce Commission (focused on the telephone, telegraph, and cable), the postmaster general, and the president be consolidated into a single regulatory body. Extensive congressional hearings followed. Witnesses offered testimony, including Frank McManamy, chairman of the legislative committee of the Interstate Commerce Commission, and Eugene O. Sykes, chairman of the Federal Radio Commission. As a result of the hearings, Congress enacted the Communications Act of 1934, which established the Federal Communications Commission (FCC).

Congress directed the FCC to uphold the "public interest, convenience, and necessity" in regard to broadcasting, the same mandate that it had imposed on the FRC. This mandate had the potential to curb the broadcasters' rights to free speech rights, which had been guaranteed by the First Amendment to the U.S. Constitution.

For example, a central theme of the Communications Act was that the airwaves should serve the needs and interests of the public, and so broadcast licensees were expected to be "socially responsible." This idea found expression in many FCC policies relating to broadcast-media content, including the fairness doctrine, which stipulated that opportunities should be provided for expression of opposing viewpoints about any topic of public importance, and FCC policy statements on scheduling television programs for children. Such policies were applied only to the broadcast-media context and would be construed as illegal censorship in a print-media context. Court rulings reconciled this apparent anomaly by perpetuating the view that government supervision of broadcast content is more acceptable than review of print outlets. This interpretation underscored complaints that the broadcast media enjoyed less First Amendment protection than did the print media.

A basic justification for the "socially responsible" orientation of broadcast regulations enforced by the FCC was that the right of the public to receive useful and unbiased information should outweigh the First Amendment rights of broadcast licensees to be free of government control. According to this view, the broadcasting media are "scarce" because of the finite range of airwave frequencies available for licensing. In addition, the ability to reach mass audiences bestows broadcast licensees with substantial power to influence public opinion. Under these circumstances, Congress decided that it was appropriate to allow some form of government control to ensure that broadcasts served the public interest.

SIGNIFICANCE

The FCC consisted of seven commissioners and several professional or middle-level staff personnel. Over the years, both these groups substantially influenced the direction and thrust of FCC policies. Analysis has suggested that the education and occupational background of FRC and FCC commissioners were key variables that affected decisions in these administrative agencies. In contrast to the commissioners, who directly administer broadcast policy, FCC staff members influence policy matters indirectly by controlling the content and flow of information provided to commissioners before they make their decisions.

Broadcast regulation is an intensely political enterprise, and studies found that the political orientation of FCC commissioners strongly affected FCC regulation activities. For example, the speeches of Commissioner

Newton Minow in the early 1960's reflected the political stance of John F. Kennedy's presidential administration toward enforcing stricter regulation of broadcast programming. In the 1980's, under the leadership of Mark Fowler, the FCC reflected a deep commitment to follow President Ronald Reagan's political philosophy that government should make regulations less intrusive. The FCC's policies and actions changed over time to accommodate the philosophies of elected officials. Because commissioners were appointed and because the Communications Act of 1934 required that no more than four commissioners share a party affiliation, virtually every president tried to select commissioners who agreed with the administration's philosophy and policy objectives, regardless of party identification.

Politically driven changes in FCC policy were instrumental in the evolution of a new form of commercial communication labeled "program-length commercials" or PLCs (also called infomercials). PLCs are commercials that usually resemble regular television talk show or documentary programs in both content and length. In the early 1970's, the FCC expressed concern over broadcast of PLCs because they had the potential to subordinate public-interest programming to commercial programming. The commission launched two policy initiatives to outlaw PLCs. First, widespread concern over television advertising directed toward children led the FCC to stress the need for distinguishing between program content and advertising material. The FCC expressed concern over children's shows that focused on particular toys, which were sometimes characters in animated shows. Second, the commission adopted a limit of sixteen minutes of commercial matter per broadcast hour. The FCC reversed this policy in 1984 by eliminating quantitative advertising guidelines for television broadcasting on the grounds that marketplace forces were adequate to regulate the level of advertising. Then, as part of the broadcast deregulation effort launched by the Reagan administration, the FCC rescinded its earlier policy banning PLCs. By underscoring the acceptability of PLCs, these developments also enhanced their popularity. As a result, PLC programming registered impressive growth in the late 1980's and early 1990's. The infomercial industry, which barely existed in the early 1980's, became an industry that generated billions of dollars in sales.

Broadcast regulation in the United States is dynamic and complex, and the FCC is only one of several organizations involved in such regulation. Other key participants include industry groups such as the National Asso-

1934

ciation of Broadcasters (NAB), various citizens' groups, the courts, Congress, and the White House. It is important to understand how the FCC is influenced by each of these participants. The NAB commanded substantial lobbying power until the mid-1960's, and other organizations, such as the Association of Maximum Service Telecasters, Clear Channel Broadcasting Service, and the Daytime Broadcasters Association emerged as specialist lobbying groups. The broadcast industry influenced FCC policies through successful congressional lobbying efforts. This industry's substantial political clout in Congress stems from its control over electronic media exposure, an important resource for politicians.

Citizens' groups also have influenced FCC activities. In 1966, a landmark decision by the U.S. Court of Appeals for the District of Columbia recognized the right of responsible civic groups to object to license renewal applications that were under FCC consideration. In the case *Community of the United Church of Christ v. FCC*, the Office of Communication of the United Church of Christ was allowed to challenge the license renewal of WLBT-TV in Jackson, Mississippi, because this broadcaster discriminated against African American audiences. Groups such as the National Citizens Committee for Broadcasting and Action for Children's Television sought to influence the FCC on policy matters relating to the content of broadcast material. During the 1960's, several citizens' groups settled differences with specific broadcasters through petitions to the FCC that requested denial of license renewal for these broadcasters. In the 1970's, the first African American commissioner was appointed to the FCC at the urging of such groups, which also actively participated in congressional hearings to urge funding support for consumer group activities.

The continual threat of judicial review tended to have an impact on policies of the FCC even when these policies were not formally adjudicated. The Communications Act stipulated that appeals concerning FCC decisions on broadcasting licensing should be filed with the U.S. Court of Appeals for the District of Columbia Circuit and that the decisions of that court are final, except for review by the U.S. Supreme Court. Congress also exercised substantial control over federal administrative agencies such as the FCC, and the FCC was often targeted for special congressional investigations. Investigations supervised by Congressman Oren Harris, Democrat from Arkansas, in the early 1960's provided insights into "payola" problems prevalent in the recording and broadcast industries and led to revisions in the Communications Act.

Several powerful standing committees in Congress continuously reviewed FCC performance and the adequacy of the broadcasting regulatory framework. These committees held general oversight hearings and other hearings designed to evaluate any relevant legislation. A 1981 decision by Congress to change the FCC's status from a permanently authorized agency to one requiring congressional reauthorization every two years underscored the power of the standing committees, which ultimately had the authority to approve such reauthorization. Finally, Congress and the White House both influenced the FCC through the nomination and confirmation process for commissioners. The White House Office of Management and Budget exercised authority through reviewing and revising the annual FCC budget.

In 1976, Congressman Lionel Van Deerlin, a Democrat from California, proposed a major revision to the Communications Act. The motivation for the proposal was that the law had become antiquated: New technologies such as cable television had transformed broadcasting. In 1978, Van Deerlin introduced a bill that proposed abolition of the FCC and replacement with a Communications Regulatory Commission. This proposal was abandoned in 1979, but in retrospect, the proposal was beneficial to the FCC because it pushed the agency toward major deregulation decisions on the radio and cable television industries.

—*Siva Balasubramanian*

FURTHER READING

Head, Sydney W., et al. *Broadcasting in America: A Survey of Electronic Media.* 9th ed. Boston: Houghton Mifflin, 2000. The standard introduction to the institutions of radio and television in the United States. Begins with an analysis of the invention of wireless radio broadcasting.

Krasnow, Erwin G., Lawrence D. Longley, and Herbert A. Terry. *The Politics of Broadcast Regulation.* New York: St. Martin's Press, 1982. Authoritative account of the laws and policies that govern broadcasting in the United States. Traces the history of both the FRC and the FCC and offers insights into the political factors that shaped their creation and growth. Offers forceful, thought-provoking, and well-researched arguments and perspectives. Presents five case studies on diverse topics, including ultrahigh frequency television, commercials, and congressional efforts to rewrite the Communications Act during the 1970's.

Lichty, Lawrence. "The Impact of FRC and FCC Commissioners' Backgrounds on the Regulation of Broadcasting." *Journal of Broadcasting* 6 (Spring, 1962): 97-110. Suggests that factors such as the education, occupational history, and personal experience of commissioners affect policies.

Robinson, Glen O. "The Federal Communications Commission: An Essay on Regulatory Watchdogs." *Virginia Law Review* 64 (March, 1978): 169-262. A former FCC commissioner offers some rare and useful perspectives on the FCC.

Sterling, Christopher H., and John Michael Kittross. *Stay Tuned: A History of American Broadcasting.* 3d ed. Mahwah, N.J.: Lawrence Erlbaum, 2001. The standard one-volume history of radio and television in the United States. A good place to begin.

U.S. Congress. House. Committee on Interstate and Foreign Commerce. *Federal Communications Commission: Hearings Before the Committee on Interstate and Foreign Commerce, House of Representatives, Seventy-third Congress, Second Session on H.R. 8301, a Bill to Provide for the Regulation of Interstate and Foreign Communication by Wire or Radio, and for Other Purposes.* 73d Congress, 2d session, 1934. Contains verbatim transcripts of hearings on the Communications Act.

Williams, Wenmouth, Jr. "Impact of Commissioner Background on FCC Decisions: 1962-1975." *Journal of Broadcasting* 20 (Spring, 1976): 244-256. Extends Lichty's work on how the backgrounds of FCC commissioners have influenced FCC policy.

SEE ALSO: Dec. 12, 1901: First Transatlantic Telegraphic Radio Transmission; Dec. 24, 1906: Fessenden Pioneers Radio Broadcasting; Oct. 21, 1915: First Demonstration of Transatlantic Radiotelephony; Aug. 20-Nov. 2, 1920: Radio Broadcasting Begins; Sept. 9, 1926: National Broadcasting Company Is Founded; 1930's: Americans Embrace Radio Entertainment; Nov. 5, 1935: Armstrong Demonstrates FM Radio Broadcasting; Oct. 30, 1938: Welles Broadcasts *The War of the Worlds*; Apr. 30, 1939: American Television Debuts at the World's Fair; Sept. 1, 1940: First Color Television Broadcast.

June 18, 1934
INDIAN REORGANIZATION ACT

Passage of the Indian Reorganization Act by the U.S. Congress permitted Native American groups to form self-governing bodies, ending decades of forced assimilation.

LOCALE: Washington, D.C.

CATEGORIES: Laws, acts, and legal history; indigenous peoples' rights; social issues and reform

KEY FIGURES

John Collier (1884-1968), commissioner of Indian affairs, 1933-1945

Charles J. Rhoads (1872-1956), commissioner of Indian affairs, 1929-1933

Felix Cohen (1907-1953), expert in Native American law who helped draft the original Wheeler-Howard bill

William F. Zimmerman, Jr. (1890-1967), assistant commissioner of Indian affairs who worked with Collier

Franklin D. Roosevelt (1882-1945), president of the United States, 1933-1945

Harold Ickes (1874-1952), U.S. secretary of the interior, 1933-1946

Edgar Howard (1858-1951), U.S. congressman who cosponsored the Indian Reorganization Act

Burton Kendall Wheeler (1882-1975), U.S. senator who cosponsored the Indian Reorganization Act

SUMMARY OF EVENT

From earliest colonial times, the U.S. government sought to assimilate Native Americans into mainstream American culture. Whether government policy called for abrupt, forced acculturation or advocated gradual change, politicians generally believed that ultimately American Indians must adopt the lifestyle of the whites or perish. The Indian Reorganization Act of 1934 was the first legislation designed to preserve, not to destroy, Native American cultures and to give back some of what had been taken away during the settlement of the United States, including Indian lands.

The greatest loss of Indian lands after the assigning of reservation territories to the various surviving tribes occurred as a result of the Indian General Allotment Act (also known as the Dawes Act) of 1887. The goal of this legislation was to destroy tribal structure and the communal lifestyle of Native Americans by encouraging tribal Indians to become individual farmers. Tribal structure and authority were bypassed as allotments of acreage were made to individuals. A patent in fee, or negotiable title, was issued on this land, which was held in trust by the federal government for twenty-five years and could not be sold until that period expired. Any surplus lands remaining after allotments had been made for a particular reservation were then auctioned off, which often created a massive land grab by eager white settlers. The funds from the sale of these surplus lands were held in a trust fund for the tribes by the federal government. However, when few Native Americans attempted to farm their allotments, the lands were leased to non-Indians and the meager fees were given to the allottees as rental income.

This system proved too slow in breaking up the reservations, and so the Burke Act was passed in 1906. It permitted the secretary of the interior, through a declaration of competence, to release a particular allottee from the twenty-five-year restriction of federal supervision. By the 1930's, ninety million acres of reservation lands had been lost through legal means. Unscrupulous, land-hungry settlers often cheated Native Americans out of their allotments, leaving them destitute and no more acculturated than they had been before implementation of the Indian General Allotment Act.

Although Native Americans had always had a few champions, it was not until the Bursum Bill of 1922 was introduced that the Indian reform movement gathered appreciable force and Indian affairs garnered sustained interest. This bill was designed to permit non-Indians to gain title to lands within the Pueblo Indian land grants. It was defeated by protest of the Pueblo people and their many supporters.

One of the champions of Indian rights was John Collier, who would be appointed commissioner of Indian affairs eleven years later by President Franklin D. Roosevelt and would be instrumental in the passage of the Indian Reorganization Act. In the meantime, as executive secretary of the Indian Defense Association, he tirelessly questioned and protested government policy regarding Native Americans and made the case for desperately needed reforms.

In 1923, Herbert Work became secretary of the interior. Work commissioned several examinations of the Indian Service, including the Meriam Report of 1928, which served as the blueprint for reforms sought through the Indian Reorganization Act. Unfortunately, reforms were not attempted until the next administration, in which Ray Lyman Wilbur was appointed secretary of the

interior, Charles J. Rhoads was commissioner of Indian affairs, and J. Henry Scattergood was assistant commissioner. Although Wilbur wanted to move quickly on the issue of assimilation, Rhoads and Scattergood were cautious. Rhoads's only direct victory was the Leavitt Act of 1932, which concerned the issue of reimbursable debts, in which Native American tribes would be relieved from millions of dollars in liens placed on their lands for projects that they had not requested and that gave them little benefit.

Another reform targeted by the Meriam Report was the incorporation of tribes for the purpose of self-government and the management of tribal resources, an issue that was basic to the Indian Reorganization Act. The report suggested a special claims commission to hear the claims of individual Indian tribes against the United States. Education and health care were examined and targeted for reforms of often dismal conditions. State employees and agents were permitted to enter reservations to inspect health and educational conditions, and they found a higher death rate among Native Americans than in the general population, mainly from diseases such as tuberculosis. Sanitation and quarantine regulations were enforced by the state employees, and efforts were made to improve conditions by teaching personal hygiene and disease prevention. Compulsory school attendance was enforced for Native American children, and some attempt was made to improve the boarding schools. Although the Rhoads administration of the Bureau of Indian Affairs (BIA) improved some conditions, much more was needed.

John Collier was appointed commissioner of Indian affairs in 1933. He set about designing legislation to redress problems made clear by the Meriam Report. Collier's team included assistant commissioner William F. Zimmerman, Jr., and Felix Cohen. The latter became an expert on Indian law and helped to draft the Wheeler-Howard bill, which evolved into the Indian Reorganization Act.

While the act was being assembled, Collier's administration moved ahead with some reforms. Where possible, Native American children were transferred from boarding schools to community-based day schools. The boarding schools that remained in use were developed as special facilities for certain children with needs best met by these institutions. A statement was issued to the effect that BIA employees would no longer interfere with Native American culture, religion, and languages. The bureau itself sought to employ Native Americans in increasing numbers.

President Roosevelt's New Deal reforms were extended to Native Americans through a specially organized branch of the Civilian Conservation Corps (CCC) called Emergency Conservation Work (ECW). This program provided work for Native Americans on the reservations in conservation and improvement projects similar to that offered to other Americans through the CCC. This wage labor caused a temporary increase in income for many Native Americans, but it worried Collier, who wondered what would take its place when the relief projects ended.

In 1934, Congress passed the Indian Reorganization Act, which officially stated the changes that studies such as the Meriam Report had recommended. Congresses were held to permit Native Americans to discuss the act and to vote whether to accept it for their individual tribes.

The Indian Reorganization Act allowed tribes to incorporate and form governing bodies in a democratic fashion. These governing bodies were designed to resemble boards of directors and had an elected chairperson. Individual Native Americans acted as "shareholders" who had the right to vote.

Furthermore, the act officially ended the allotment process and sought to restore lands lost in the past, or at least to replace them with other lands purchased for the tribes. Native American culture and religions were encouraged, often to the dismay and the protest of Christian missionaries. The boarding school system was further improved, and more community-based day schools were established. A revolving credit system was established based on the principle of a credit union, whereby Indians could borrow funds to improve their lands or establish businesses. Native American arts and crafts were encouraged as a form of industry and a source of ethnic pride.

Critics argued that the act was not properly implemented, and they were especially critical of the fact that Native Americans were not fully cognizant of the reorganization process and that the new forms of self-government were alien to the cultural practices of many groups. BIA personnel were not adequately prepared for changes in policy, and the new policy often conflicted with past goals and with personal philosophies concerning American Indians. Many people concerned about American Indians were not sure that the act provided the best means for improving their conditions. Under the terms of the Indian Reorganization Act, however, Native Americans could retain their lands and their culture and still find ways to survive in the modern world.

SIGNIFICANCE

The Indian Reorganization Act was the first responsible effort to deal with the problems of a people who the federal government had for years assumed would "vanish" either by assimilation or by extinction. Although BIA personnel sometimes failed to implement its good designs, the act was the first major reform that attempted to give Native Americans a choice in determining their own lives. As politicians prepared to implement the Indian Reorganization Act, they followed a unique procedure: Indians themselves were asked to express their opinions on the legislation affecting them and to vote on whether such legislation should be accepted by their tribes. By giving Native Americans a choice, the act implicitly validated them as a people, something that had never before been done by the federal government.

The government also reversed its policy by encouraging Native American cultures, languages, and religious practices. Not all Indians, and certainly not all non-Indians, welcomed this change. Some feared that acculturated Indians would be forced back onto the reservations and into an outdated lifestyle, but this did not occur. Other people were alarmed and offended that the federal government would officially sponsor—and use public funds to support—cultures whose beliefs and practices deviated from those of mainstream American culture. These people were deeply suspicious of the communal lifestyles that many tribes maintained. Others who rejected the Indian Reorganization Act sought to acquire use of—or title to—Indian lands for themselves or for corporations. The act curtailed the number of these opportunities and made them less profitable. The demand for such lands, however, was not great at this time, as the United States was suffering through the Great Depression.

The timing for the Indian Reorganization Act was especially good. Assimilated Indians had suffered more during the Depression than had reservation Indians engaged in subsistence farming. Because there was little demand for land, it was a good time to give back the lands lost through allotment. More than two million acres were purchased and returned to Native American title, including some purchases made for "landless" tribes.

The act's reformation of the boarding school system radically improved a system that had not provided adequate food or clothing for its charges and had often exploited their labor. Where possible, community-based day schools were established. Indian children were also encouraged to attend public schools where feasible. Educational goals were shifted from irrelevant, elitist train-

1934

ing to more practical, agrarian-based learning and technical and professional training. Many graduates chose to return to the reservations and contribute their skills to improving their communities.

One tragic incident involved the BIA's attempt to improve reservation land resources of soil, water, and vegetation. The livestock population had exceeded the carrying capacity of the arid lands on the Navajo reservation. When the Navajo resisted Collier's plan to reduce the livestock, it was forced on them. Navajos had to watch helplessly as their animals were sold off or slaughtered. Although the reduction plan allegedly resulted in improved livestock and vegetation, bitter feelings remained among the Navajo, who had voted to reject the Indian Reorganization Act.

—Patricia Alkema

FURTHER READING

Dippie, Brian W. *The Vanishing American*. Middletown, Conn.: Wesleyan University Press, 1982. A comprehensive and sympathetic study of Native American relations with the federal government. Good coverage of the climate of reform leading up to passage of the Indian Reorganization Act. Extensive notes and a good index.

Donns, James F. *The Navajo*. New York: Holt, Rinehart and Winston, 1972. Specific ethnographic study of the Navajo people serves as a useful introduction to the culture and lifestyle of the largest Native American group. Explains the relationship of livestock to Navajo livelihood and culture, a relationship that was disrupted by Collier's plan to reduce the livestock population.

Fey, Harold E., and D'Arcy McNickle. *Indians and Other Americans: Two Ways of Life Meet*. Rev. ed. New York: Harper & Row, 1970. Good account of the Collier years. McNickle, a Montana Blackfoot, was a BIA employee during this era.

Hoxie, Frederick, ed. *Indians in American History: An Introduction*. 2d ed. Arlington Heights, Ill.: Harlan Davidson, 1998. Collection of chronologically arranged essays by authors who speak from a variety of disciplines and perspectives provides an introduction to the Indian side of U.S. history. Draws attention to the depth and complexity of the American Indian experience. Includes list of suggestions for further reading following each chapter, illustrations, and index.

Kelly, Lawrence C. "The Indian Reorganization Act: The Dream and the Reality." *Pacific Historical Review* 44 (August, 1975): 291-312. Balanced look at what the act failed to achieve in contrast to the claims of some proponents. Discusses Collier's strong points and shortcomings as American Indian commissioner during the New Deal era.

Kelly, William H., ed. *Indian Affairs and the Indian Reorganization Act: The Twenty Year Record*. Tucson: University of Arizona Press, 1954. A collection of scholarly essays on this subject.

Parman, Donald L. *The Navajos and the New Deal*. New Haven, Conn.: Yale University Press, 1976. A study of the troubled relations between the American Indian policy reformers in the Roosevelt administration and the nation's largest tribe.

Philp, Kenneth R. *John Collier's Crusade for Indian Reform, 1920-1954*. Tucson: University of Arizona Press, 1977. A detailed, objective account of Collier's achievements and shortcomings as a policy critic, activist, reformer, and administrator.

Taylor, Graham D. *The New Deal and American Indian Tribalism: The Administration of the Indian Reorganization Act, 1934-1945*. Lincoln: University of Nebraska Press, 1980. Argues that the act, although enlightened compared to previous policies, was weakened by its emphasis on tribal reorganization and its mistaken assumptions about contemporary American Indian societies.

Tyler, S. Lyman. *A History of Indian Policy*. Washington, D.C.: U.S. Department of the Interior, Bureau of Indian Affairs, 1973. An extremely well-organized and detailed historical account of U.S. government policy toward Native Americans. Covers criticism and accomplishments of government programs. A useful guide to the philosophy and expedients behind historical government policy. Highly recommended for the serious student. Includes tables and charts, foldout maps, and black-and-white photographs. Extensive bibliography.

Wilkins, David E., and K. Tsianina Lomawaima. *Uneven Ground: American Indian Sovereignty and Federal Law*. Norman: University of Oklahoma Press, 2002. Reviews the often inconsistent federal legal precedents related to issues concerning Native Americans.

SEE ALSO: Jan. 5, 1903: *Lone Wolf v. Hitchcock*; Oct. 12, 1912: First Conference of the Society of American Indians; June 2, 1924: Indian Citizenship Act.

June 26, 1934
FEDERAL CREDIT UNION ACT

By establishing a federal credit union system, the Federal Credit Union Act of 1934 legitimated the developing credit union movement in the United States. It encouraged savings and made credit more available to people of limited means, providing American consumers with greater spending power.

LOCALE: Washington, D.C.
CATEGORIES: Banking and finance; laws, acts, and legal history

KEY FIGURES

Alphonse Desjardins (1854-1920), Canadian journalist
Edward A. Filene (1860-1937), Boston merchant, philanthropist, and founder of the Credit Union National Extension Bureau
Roy F. Bergengren (1879-1955), first manager of the Credit Union National Association
Hermann Schulze-Delitzsch (1808-1883), German urban cooperative credit founder
Friedrich Wilhelm Raiffeisen (1818-1888), German rural cooperative credit founder
Arthur Capper (1865-1951), U.S. senator from Kansas, 1919-1948

SUMMARY OF EVENT

A federal credit union is a nonprofit, member-owned co-operative. The union encourages its members to put money into savings, and it uses these accumulated savings to make loans to individual members. It also educates members on how to manage their finances. The U.S. government, through the National Credit Union Administration (NCUA), charters credit unions as corporations, as well as supervising and insuring them.

In order to generate and maintain a feeling of mutual responsibility, members of a federal credit union generally have a common bond of employment, association, or residence. The members, with one vote each, elect a volunteer board of directors from the membership at an annual meeting. The board has the authority to determine the maximum limits on loans and the interest rates to be charged. Interest rates tend to be favorable in comparison to those offered by other lenders because of the lower labor costs in volunteer organizations, lower losses on defaulted loans, and lower marketing costs. In addition to an unpaid board of directors, credit unions have officers who are generally unpaid or receive nominal salaries. The ratio of delinquent to outstanding loans is generally far lower than that of federally insured commercial banks. Personal contact and personal credit judgments play a large role in keeping this ratio low. Two major marketing advantages are the bond of clients to the credit union through membership and the close proximity of clients, with the credit union often located at an employee's place of work.

Loans can be designed to meet the needs of individual members. Federal credit unions must comply with all federal consumer protection laws, such as the Truth in Lending Act (1980) and the Equal Credit Opportunity Act (1975). Deposits by members take the form of purchases of shares in the credit union and are frequently made through payroll deductions. Profits from lending money and other sources may be distributed to the members as dividends.

The development of credit unions resulted from the needs of lower income groups. Prior to the existence of credit unions, there were a limited number of outlets for small savings or loans. In 1844, the first credit union was organized in Belgium. Around the same time in Germany, Hermann Schulze-Delitzsch organized cooperative credit societies and developed the principle that the funds to be loaned to members would come from the savings of members. By 1880, about three thousand cooperative credit societies had been organized in Germany. Friedrich Wilhelm Raiffeisen also organized cooperative credit societies in Germany but put greater emphasis on unselfish service to the organization. By 1920, his model for the earliest credit unions was being used in most countries in the world.

The credit union movement spread to the North American continent with the help of Alphonse Desjardins, a Québécois legislative journalist who was studying economic conditions in Europe in the late 1890's. In 1900, Desjardins used ideas from the Schulze-Delitzsch and Raiffeisen financial cooperatives to establish the first cooperative bank, La Caisse Populaire (the people's bank), in the city of Levis in the province of Quebec, Canada. Edward A. Filene, a wealthy Boston merchant and philanthropist, was influential in bringing credit unions to the United States. His interest in the subject resulted from extensive travel throughout the world. He convinced Pierre Jay, commissioner of banking for Massachusetts, to work toward establishing a cooperative credit society in that state.

Jay asked Desjardins to assist in passing a credit union

act in Massachusetts. The Massachusetts Credit Union Act, the first complete credit union act in the United States, was enacted in 1909. In the same year, in Manchester, New Hampshire, Desjardins helped organize the first legally chartered cooperative credit society in the United States. Growth in the credit-union movement was slow during the decade after passage of the Massachusetts act. By 1919, however, Filene believed that there was a sufficient number of credit unions to justify an organized move toward national legislation. He organized the National Committee on People's Banks to spearhead this task. The development of credit unions was aided by favorable conditions during the 1920's. General prosperity and development of new consumer goods resulted in higher savings by workers and greater demand for consumer credit.

Three factors were necessary to expand the movement: legislation allowing the chartering (incorporation) of credit unions, education of the general public regarding the movement, and voluntary associations of credit unions at the state level to further expand the movement. To facilitate each of these, Filene created and financed the Credit Union National Extension Bureau (which became the Credit Union National Association in 1934). He hired Roy F. Bergengren as manager and Thomas W. Doig as assistant manager. Bergengren had started as the managing director of the Massachusetts Credit Union Association in 1920. He used the extension bureau to promote enabling legislation authorizing credit unions and helped organize individual credit unions.

The Great Depression had a favorable impact on the movement. In 1932, Congress authorized credit unions in the District of Columbia and allowed them to borrow from the Reconstruction Finance Corporation. By 1934, thirty-eight states had enacted credit union laws and more than twenty-four hundred credit unions were in operation.

Bergengren became increasingly convinced that national legislation was necessary. He argued that a federal law would permit the organization of credit unions in states that had refused to pass such legislation; that there was some possibility that other states might repeal their credit union laws, as West Virginia had done in 1931; that a federal statute would be useful as a basis of organization in those states that had weak or defective laws; and that federal legislation should be complete before credit unions formed a national association.

The culmination of the legislative efforts of the Credit Union National Extension Bureau came on June 26, 1934, when the U.S. Congress enacted the Federal Credit Union Act. The act provided for the chartering, supervision, and examination of federal credit unions by the U.S. government. The writers of the act tried to incorporate the best ideas from state laws.

In the same year, Congress chose the Farm Credit Administration (FCA) to supervise credit unions because of its expertise in examining other types of financial cooperatives chartered by the U.S. government. Claude R. Orchard was appointed the first director of the Credit Union Section, FCA. More than eighty-seven hundred federal credit unions were chartered during the nineteen years he served as director. Also in 1934, Bergengren and Filene held a national meeting of credit union delegates that led to the development of the Credit Union National Association (CUNA).

SIGNIFICANCE

The most important result of the Federal Credit Union Act of 1934 was the confidence it inspired in the American public regarding credit unions. Involvement by the federal government played a major role in the growth of credit unions, from almost 2,500 credit unions when the act was passed to 3,372 by the end of 1935. In 1937, Congress passed legislation prohibiting the taxation of federal credit unions except on the basis of real or personal property. This legislation further supported growth in the number of entities, which approached 8,000 by 1939.

Individual credit unions also grew at an impressive rate. By March, 1936, Armour and Company employee credit unions had more than twenty-two thousand members, had $1.25 million in assets, and had made loans up to that date of almost $7 million. There were twenty-four credit unions among Sears, Roebuck and Company employees, with almost eight thousand members, and credit unions associated with the United States Steel Corporation had almost twenty-three thousand members. A credit union served employees of the U.S. Senate. Another credit union at the Twentieth Century-Fox film studio had more than one thousand members.

Many employers considered a credit union to be an important fringe benefit, with the advantage of involving no necessary cost to them. Space for the credit union's offices often was provided on the premises, perhaps at reduced cost. Payroll withholding both for regular savings and for installment collection of loans was another service commonly provided by employers.

In 1935, CUNA's national board of directors agreed to establish the CUNA Mutual Insurance Society. The society provided only borrowers' protection insurance to credit unions at first, adding life insurance for officers and families associated with CUNA in August, 1936. At the same time, the society considered writing automobile insurance but took no action. By the end of 1936, 437 credit unions in thirty states were members of the society. A total of twenty-three thousand loans were insured, with a total coverage of $2,425,000. The reserves of the society for payment of claims amounted to $11,000.

In later years, new legislation designed to modernize credit unions, combined with favorable regulatory changes, made credit unions more competitive with banks and savings and loans. The industry was permitted to use a greater variety of sources for both assets and liabilities, and a greater range of financial activities was allowed. The interest rates that credit unions could pay on savings and charge for loans were relatively free from government control. Finally, credit unions still enjoyed the political and economic benefits of being nonprofit organizations. The benefits of credit union membership combined with the decline in reputation of savings and loans in the late twentieth century to ensure that credit unions remained an attractive, and in some cases a vital, option for financial services.

—*Richard Goedde*

FURTHER READING

Bergengren, Roy F. "Achievement: United States." In *Credit Union: North America*. New York: Southern, 1940. Gives a detailed summary of the growth of credit unions by state.

_____. *Crusade: The Fight for Economic Democracy in North America, 1921-1945*. New York: Exposition Press, 1952. A detailed history of the credit union movement, written by the man who had the greatest influence in passage of the Federal Credit Union Act and growth of credit unions. Reads like an autobiography in parts. Includes a six-page photograph section of early crusaders and administrators in the movement.

_____. *CUNA Emerges*. Madison, Wis.: Credit Union National Association, 1935. Summarizes the functions and operations of credit unions one year after passage of the Federal Credit Union Act of 1934. Discusses the organization of CUNA. The final chapter offers an interesting, almost philosophical, explanation of how credit unions can lead to a better society.

Croteau, John T. *The Economics of the Credit Union*. Detroit: Wayne State University Press, 1963. Credit unions have many unique economic characteristics because they do not maximize profits as their sole goal. After analyzing data from credit union questionnaires, the author recommends ways to improve financial efficiency in large credit unions. Topics include reserves, liquidity, growth, and investment yields. Written to be comprehensible by noneconomists.

_____. *The Federal Credit Union: Policy and Practice*. New York: Harper & Brothers, 1956. An analytic study of the growth, policies, and practices of credit unions on a national scale from 1934 to 1954. Provides statistics on assets and liabilities, operating costs, earnings, and dividends. Includes an interesting chapter on structural change and suggested improvement.

Emmons, William R. *Bank Competition and Concentrations: The Impact of Credit Unions*. Ann Arbor: Institute for Social Research, University of Michigan, 2000. Discusses the effects on the U.S. banking and finance sector of direct competition between for-profit instutions (banks) and not-for-profit institutions (credit unions).

Isbister, John. *Thin Cats: The Community Development Credit Union Movement in the United States*. Davis: University of California, Center for Cooperatives, 1994. A history of the community development and credit union movements and their intersections in helping communities to grow and flourish in the United States. Bibliographic references.

Moody, J. Carroll, and Gilbert C. Fite. *The Credit Union Movement: Origins and Development, 1850-1970*. Lincoln: University of Nebraska Press, 1971. Traces and analyzes the history of credit unionism as a national social movement, with a focus on the founders and leaders. Detailed and comprehensive. Source of many of the statistics in this article.

Pugh, Olin S., and F. Jerry Ingram. *Credit Unions: A Movement Becomes an Industry*. Reston, Va.: Reston Publishing Company, 1984. A comprehensive look at the growth of the credit union movement. Describes the structure of the industry, regulations, financial management, and role in the financial marketplace. Also discusses the future of the industry from an early 1980's perspective, including likely effects of legislation of that era.

U.S. Department of the Treasury. *Credit Unions*. Washington, D.C.: Author, 1997. Overview of all federal legislation through 1997 relating to credit unions and to deposit insurance covering credit unions. Bibliographic references.

U.S. National Credit Union Administration. *Development of Federal Credit Unions*. Washington, D.C.: Author, 1972. Focuses on the role of the U.S. government in the credit union movement. Explains the ben-

1934

efits of federal government participation in the movement. Also describes the Credit Union National Association, Inc. (CUNA) and organizations associated with it.

SEE ALSO: Apr. 5, 1910: First Morris Plan Bank Opens; Oct. 29, 1929-1939: Great Depression; Jan. 22, 1932: Reconstruction Finance Corporation Is Created; Feb. 10, 1938: Fannie Mae Promotes Home Ownership.

June 28, 1934
TAYLOR GRAZING ACT

The Taylor Grazing Act brought belated federal control of grazing to the public domain rangelands of the West and marked the end of the homestead movement and the closing of the public domain.

LOCALE: Washington, D.C.

CATEGORIES: Expansion and land acquisition; laws, acts, and legal history; natural resources

KEY FIGURES

Edward T. Taylor (1858-1941), U.S. congressman from western Colorado

Farrington Carpenter (1886-1980), attorney and northwestern Colorado rancher

Harold Ickes (1874-1952), U.S. secretary of the interior, 1933-1946

Franklin D. Roosevelt (1882-1945), president of the United States, 1933-1945

Theodore Roosevelt (1858-1919), president of the United States, 1901-1909

SUMMARY OF EVENT

Until the forest reserves were established in the 1890's, the U.S. Congress envisioned an American West of cultivated, 160-acre homesteads. However, the Homestead Act (1862) failed to recognize the arid nature of much of the country's unoccupied land. In response, the livestock industry saw opportunity and profit in the uncultivated rangelands that had been vacated by the relocation of Native Americans and the demise of the bison. Increases in U.S. population and development of the country's railroads made commercial livestock production lucrative, and foreign capital sought profit in the new trade. The U.S. Department of Agriculture estimated that the cattle population increased from about 8 million to more than 21 million from 1870 through 1886 in the seventeen western states. The boom was followed by a bust of dramatic proportions. Many cattle, weakened by a lack of forage from overgrazing, died in the severe winters of 1885-1886 and 1886-1887. Livestock mortality was estimated at 40 to 60 percent, and some areas reported death rates of 85 percent.

As homesteaders pushed West, conflicts with ranchers followed. There was no provision for acquiring grazing land under the public-land laws, and in many cases, ranchers used fraud to gain title to large areas of public land. This fraud, coupled with their foreign financing, made them easy political targets, and they were considered land barons and monopolists.

In the 1880's, Congress ignored the recommendations made by the first Public Lands Commission to sell grazing lands in 2,560-acre parcels. Ranchers illegally fenced public lands and limited access to water resources to protect their range rights. In 1885, Congress declared public domain fencing illegal, but the practice prevailed. In 1901, the federal government prosecuted 161 cases of illegal fencing and estimated that about 2.5 million acres had been illegally enclosed. These rancher-homesteader conflicts were often apparent in state and local politics. Community boosters encouraged farming and settlement. States and railroads encouraged immigration for farming and opposed early bills that would have allowed ranchers to fence or lease public domain rangeland. Many ranchers feared any government regulation. The results were political stalemate and continued damage to the rangeland ecosystem.

By 1890, the effects of overgrazing were becoming obvious. Western soil and water resources were severely depleted, and a group of cattle and sheep ranchers began to form a consensus about the lease of public rangelands. The states of Texas and Wyoming, the Northern Pacific Railroad Company, and the federally managed Indian reservations reported success in reducing overgrazing through leasing as early as 1883. Rangeland leasing bills were introduced in Congress in 1901 and 1902, but they failed in the face of opposition from western governors and homestead interests.

Despite political risk, President Theodore Roosevelt began to support rangeland leasing proposals after the 1904 election. However, many people believed that Roosevelt was siding with monopolistic, big business interest groups at the expense of farmers, and his support of the leasing proposal was particularly opposed by irrigation and reclamation interests. Still, a provision for leasing public rangelands under the Department of Agriculture was included in the 1907 Agriculture Appropriations Bill and was at least partially responsible for the first major defeat of Roosevelt's conservation program. The defeat precluded serious consideration of additional leasing bills until the 1920's.

From 1909 through 1915, Congress passed a series of enlarged homestead acts that established 320-acre homesteads. Millions of acres of rangeland were plowed and sown to grain, which had disastrous consequences for the soil. Declining prices and severe drought ended the boom after World War I. In 1916, in spite of the opposition of ranchers, Congress passed a law to allow individuals to obtain 640 acres of public land that was valuable chiefly for grazing and cultivating forage crops. In the law's first year, about sixty thousand applications were filed for some 20 million acres under the Stock-Raising Homestead Act (1916). Unfortunately, it was only through firsthand experience that many applicants learned that the twenty to thirty cattle that could be supported on 640 acres of good rangeland were too few to support a family.

With the support of the livestock industry, the U.S. Forest Service had made significant progress in controlling livestock grazing in the national forests. By establishing allotments, carrying capacities, and grazing fees, the Forest Service had brought a semblance of order to a disorderly field. In 1919, ranchers in northeastern California petitioned the government to move 400,000 acres of public domain rangeland into the Modoc National Forest.

During the early 1920's, many ranchers supported proposals to have the Department of Agriculture administer a leasing program, but a proposal to increase grazing fees on the national forests rapidly ended their support. In 1925, a Senate committee introduced a bill that called for reform of Forest Service's rules about grazing and leasing of the public domain. The administration and the ranchers eventually reached a compromise, and it appeared that a leasing bill would pass, but the ranchers' rhetoric inflamed the conservationists. The American Forestry Association and the Society of American Foresters rallied opposition to the bill, and it failed. In 1928, Congress authorized an experimental cooperative grazing program in southeastern Montana. The Mizpah-Pumpkin Creek Grazing District combined lands from the public domain, the Northern Pacific Railroad, the state of Montana, and private lands and leased them to a grazing association.

In 1931, members of Congress from Utah and Idaho introduced a general public domain leasing bill after consulting with the Departments of Agriculture and the Interior and gathering support from the White House. In 1933, Congressman Edward T. Taylor reintroduced a modified version of this bill and shepherded it through the opposition's objections, which were largely centered on contentions that the new bill unfairly favored large interest groups. Taylor also found a way to skirt the growing feud between the Departments of Agriculture and the Interior over which department would administer the public domain program. When the bill initially failed, Secretary of the Interior Harold Ickes threatened to withdraw the lands. President Franklin D. Roosevelt's active support of the Taylor bill also improved its chances for passage. The Taylor Grazing Act passed the House of Representatives on April 11, 1934, and a slightly different version passed the Senate on June 12, 1934. Roosevelt signed the conference committee version on June 28, 1934.

SIGNIFICANCE

The Taylor Grazing Act of 1934 marked the end of fifty years of political struggle over control of the unallocated public lands in the western United States. The act gave the secretary of the interior broad powers to control livestock grazing by establishing grazing districts and regulating the use of the public domain pending its final disposal by Congress. It also ended free access to the public range and began the process of controlling livestock grazing, firmly established local control over allocation of public rangelands, and effectively ended large-scale public-land disposals. The first grazing district was established in Wyoming in 1935, and others followed in Arizona, California, Colorado, Idaho, Montana, Nevada, New Mexico, Oregon, and Utah. Ranchers recommended fifty districts covering 142 million acres. Since this area was larger than the one provided by the original act, in 1936 the act was amended to allow the larger area.

The effort to implement the Taylor Act was one of the most ambitious land-management actions undertaken by the federal government. Allocation of grazing privileges and fees, fencing, water development, erosion, and fire control were initiated, and in the act's first year, the Civilian Conservation Corps (CCC) operated sixty camps with twelve thousand men to aid the program. In many areas, recovery from decades of abusive grazing was a stubborn problem. By the mid-1960's, experts estimated that production in three-fourths of western ranges was at less than half of its potential.

In some areas, large reductions in livestock use were required to bring grazing into balance with carrying capacity. Organized local opposition to the reductions was often strong. To restore productivity, managers undertook forage improvement projects that often relied on clearing sagebrush and woodlands and reseeding with improved forage grasses. As the environmental movement gained strength in the 1960's and 1970's, range managers were often criticized for concentrating on livestock production at the expense of wildlife habitat. Protection and recovery of degraded riparian areas became a particular concern in the 1980's.

When the Taylor Act passed, Farrington Carpenter, a Colorado rancher and lawyer, was selected to head its implementation. By the end of 1935, the Division of Grazing employed fewer than thirty people and administered 258 million acres of rangeland. Carpenter relied on local advisory committees authorized by the act. These committees allocated each district's forage based on a complex system of historical use and adjacent private land or water to establish "preference," which in many cases exceeded the available forage. In 1944, the Grazing Service was administering more than twenty-two thousand licenses and permits and approximately 3.8 million animal units of forage. (An animal unit is the amount of forage necessary to feed a 1,000-pound animal for twelve months.) In 1992, the Bureau of Land Management reported about 1.1 million animal units of preference and about 833,000 animal units of actual use.

By the end of the second year, the ranchers had elected 523 district advisers. The advisory boards' role was clearly defined in a 1939 amendment to the Taylor Act: Boards were to consist of at least five but no more than twelve members to be appointed by the secretary of the interior following election and recommendation of the boards. The secretary of the interior was also allowed to add one member to represent wildlife interests. District advisory committees later elected state and national advisory committees.

The 1930's were a period of intense rivalry between the Department of Agriculture and the Department of the Interior. In his bid for control of the program, Secretary Ickes had promised that the Interior Department could manage public lands for $150,000 per year, and he also promised a grazing fee based on that low administrative cost. By giving the ranchers a largely autonomous program, Ickes thwarted the efforts of the Department of Agriculture and the Forest Service to gain control of the lands as the original bill was amended.

The Taylor program ensured continuing support from the Department of the Interior by relying on local advisory committees. In addition, however, more general forms of local assistance and cooperation were necessary. In some respects, this form of home rule seemed an ideal mechanism for undertaking a large-scale land-management program at a minimal cost. Advisory board members were commended as outstanding examples of citizen participation in government. In contrast, conservation groups often lacked organized, effective representation in the rural West. Amenity interests were not well protected by the ranchers, and after the growth of the environmental movement in the 1960's and 1970's, their absence in the decision-making process became a source of continuing conflict.

Although Taylor initiated the act that effectively ended public-land disposal, he was, like many rural westerners, opposed to a continual federal presence in the region. He generally supported decreasing the restrictions on homesteaders and was one of the authors of the 1916 Stock-Raising Homestead Act. Like many westerners, he viewed the Taylor Act as a temporary measure to stabilize the livestock industry. The clause that referred to the land's final disposition would cause considerable consternation and political upheaval before it was finally resolved in the Federal Land Policy and Management Act of 1976.

—*Donald W. Floyd*

FURTHER READING

Barnes, Will C. *The Story of the Range*. Washington, D.C.: Government Printing Office, 1926. Detailed historical account of the early livestock industry in the American West.

Clarke, Jeanne Nienaber, and Daniel C. McCool. *Staking Out the Terrain: Power and Performance Among Natural Resource Agencies*. 2d ed. Albany: State University of New York Press, 1996. A well-developed assessment of the rise and fall of natural resource bureaucracies in the United States. Includes illustrations, tables, bibliography, and index.

Donahue, Debra L. *The Western Range Revisited: Removing Livestock from Public Lands to Conserve Native Biodiversity*. Norman: University of Oklahoma Press, 1999. A controversial volume that does much to advance the debate over grazing's costs and benefits.

Foss, Phillip O. *Politics and Grass*. Seattle: University of Washington Press, 1960. A detailed analysis of the influence of grazing advisory boards and the capture of the Grazing Service and BLM by the livestock industry.

Hays, Samuel P. *Conservation and the Gospel of Efficiency.* Cambridge, Mass.: Harvard University Press, 1959. An authoritative history of the conservation movement in the Theodore Roosevelt administration.

Muhn, James, and Hanson R. Stuart. *Opportunity and Challenge: The Story of the BLM.* Washington, D.C.: U.S. Department of the Interior. Bureau of Land Management, 1988. A reasonably detailed, in-house chronology of the BLM and its predecessor organizations.

Peffer, E. Louise. *The Closing of the Public Domain.* Stanford, Calif.: Stanford University Press, 1951. The principal and authoritative history of the public domain in the first half of the twentieth century.

U.S. Department of the Interior. Bureau of Land Management. *Fifty Years of Public Land Management: 1934-1984.* Washington, D.C.: Author, 1984. An in-house BLM pamphlet that celebrates the fiftieth anniversary of the Taylor Grazing Act.

SEE ALSO: June 17, 1902: Reclamation Act Promotes Western Agriculture; Sept. 8, 1933: Work Begins on the Grand Coulee Dam; 1934-1939: Dust Bowl Devastates the Great Plains; Apr. 27, 1935: Soil Conservation Service Is Established.

June 30-July 2, 1934
GREAT BLOOD PURGE

The Great Blood Purge eliminated the Sturm Abteilung's leadership and gained support for Adolf Hitler's radical restructuring of German society among German military leaders and industrialists.

ALSO KNOWN AS: Night of the Long Knives (Nacht der langen Messer); Reichsmordwoche; Operation Hummingbird; Röhm Purge; Blood Purge
LOCALE: Berlin, Munich, Bad Wiessee, and other locations in Germany
CATEGORIES: Terrorism; atrocities and war crimes; government and politics

KEY FIGURES
Adolf Hitler (1889-1945), chancellor of Germany, 1933-1945
Ernst Röhm (1887-1934), chief of staff of the paramilitary Sturm Abteilung
Hermann Göring (1893-1946), prime minister of Prussia and president of the German parliament
Heinrich Himmler (1900-1945), commander of the Schutzstaffel (SS), Hitler's elite guard
Paul von Hindenburg (1847-1934), president of the Weimar Republic, 1925-1934
Werner von Blomberg (1878-1946), German minister of war, 1935-1938
Franz Pfeffer von Salomon (1888-1968), leader of the Sturm Abteilung, 1926-1930

SUMMARY OF EVENT
From June 30 through July 2, 1933, members of the SS summarily executed several hundred Germans on direct orders from Chancellor Adolf Hitler. Hitler targeted the top leadership of the Sturm Abteilung, or SA (also known as the Brownshirts), including the SA chief of staff, his old friend Ernst Röhm. These murders, which were often called the Röhm Purge or the Night of the Long Knives, resulted from a series of intrigues among top leaders of the Nazi Party, members of the German general staff, and non-Nazi members of the German government.

The origins of the purge dated to the beginnings of Hitler's movement. Röhm, a World War I hero and career army officer, joined the fledgling Nazi Party in 1919, shortly after Hitler's own entry. Röhm became a valuable liaison between Hitler and the German general staff during the years before Hitler's first attempt to seize political power in Germany in 1923. During the eleven months of Hitler's imprisonment after the failed Beer Hall Putsch in 1923, Röhm, with Hitler's authorization, managed to reorganize the SA under another name and keep its members together, despite a government ban on the Nazi Party and its affiliated organizations.

Hitler had authorized the formation of the SA as the paramilitary arm of the Nazi Party in 1922. Its members had protected party meetings and rallies from being broken up by organizations affiliated with rival political parties, particularly those with Marxist orientations. Members of the SA had also broken up the rallies of other parties in bloody confrontations on the streets of many German cities.

By the time the German government released Hitler from prison in December, 1924, Röhm had built the SA into an organization with thirty thousand members. Röhm wanted to maintain the SA as an autonomous organization under his own direct command, and when Hitler

THE FÜHRER MAKES A SURPRISE VISIT

Nazi theorist and early party leader Alfred Rosenberg recalled in his memoirs Hitler's surprise visit to Ernst Röhm on June 30, 1934:

With an SS escort detachment the Führer drove to Weissee and knocked softly on Röhm's door: "Message from Munich," he said with disguised voice. "Well come in," Röhm called to the supposed messenger, "the door is open." Hitler tore open the door, fell on Röhm as he lay in bed, seized him by the throat and screamed, "You are under arrest, you swine." Then he turned the traitor over to the SS. At first Röhm refused to get dressed. The SS then threw his clothes in the Chief of Staff's face until he bestirred himself to put them on. In the room next door, they found young men engaged in homosexual activity. "And these are the kind who want to be leaders in Germany," the Führer said trembling.

Source: Quoted in Jackson J. Spielvogel, *Hitler and Nazi Germany: A History* (Upper Saddle River, N.J.: Prentice Hall, 2001).

insisted that the SA be subordinated to the party leadership rather than to Röhm, Röhm resigned from both the party and the SA. During the next five years, Röhm tried several jobs with little success. In 1928, he accepted a position as an instructor with the Bolivian army.

In 1930, Franz Pfeffer von Salomon, Röhm's successor as chief of staff of the SA, resigned his post after a dispute with Hitler. Röhm returned to Germany the next year to resume his command of the SA on Hitler's personal invitation. During the next two politically turbulent years, Röhm built the SA into a private army almost a million strong (the German army, by comparison, had slightly more than one hundred thousand officers and enlisted men). The members of the organization came largely from the ranks of the unemployed, were mostly young (under twenty-five), and espoused radical solutions to Germany's social and economic problems. Röhm himself began to envision the SA as becoming a people's militia that would absorb the regular army once the Nazis came to power.

During the period 1931-1933, Hitler came under increasing criticism from conservative circles in German society because of Röhm's open homosexuality and his appointment of other homosexuals to high posts in the SA. Röhm and his friends gained reputations as being corrupt and engaged in criminal activities as well as being morally dissolute. Despite this criticism, Hitler refused to replace Röhm. He argued that only Röhm could control the radicalism of the SA members and turn it to the advantage of the Nazi struggle for political power. After the parliamentary elections of March, 1933, how-

ever, Hitler's attitude toward his old comrade began to change.

The March elections gave the Nazis and their coalition partners a slight majority in the German parliament. The parliament immediately passed the Enabling Act, which gave Hitler dictatorial powers to solve the problems created by the Great Depression in Germany. Rank-and-file members of the SA became uncontrollable after Hitler's success, and many began to launch physical attacks against Germans they considered inimical to the creation of an egalitarian society. Wealthy and prominent Jews became favorite targets of SA violence. The SA membership and leadership talked openly of an imminent "second revolution" during which they would replace the old institutions of Germany with new institutions.

As his men and officers became more impatient with Hitler's failure to elevate them to top positions in Germany and institute the "second revolution," Röhm began to openly criticize the Nazi Party's leaders. He also began to criticize Hitler in private, although his basic sense of loyalty remained. Still, SA violence, Röhm's homosexuality, and his criticism of members of the party's top hierarchy had won him the enmity of several Nazi officials by early 1934. Hermann Göring, prime minister of Prussia and the most powerful Nazi after Hitler, joined forces with Wilhelm Frick, minister of the interior. These two men began conspiring to oust Röhm from the leadership of the SA. Göring and Frick gained an important ally when Heinrich Himmler, commander of the SS, joined the anti-Röhm coalition. Despite the mounting criticism of Röhm, Hitler refused to dismiss the man who had been instrumental in the Nazi electoral successes of 1930-1933.

In April, 1934, Hitler met with leaders of Germany's general staff. He needed the support of the army if his plans for a rejuvenated Germany were to succeed. The representatives of the general staff demanded that in return for their support Hitler initiate a massive expansion of the German armed forces and greatly diminish the size and power of the SA. The army leadership feared that Röhm's plan to absorb the regular army into the SA might actually be realized. Then, on June 17, 1933, Hitler's vice chancellor, Franz von Papen (a member of the conservative establishment of Germany who was never a Nazi Party member), delivered a speech at Marburg criticizing Röhm and the SA leadership. Hitler interpreted Papen's speech as the official position of German conservatives, and President Paul von Hindenburg of Germany confirmed the conservatives' determination to be rid of Röhm in a meeting with Hitler on June 21. Hindenburg and Minister of War Werner von Blomberg warned that unless Hitler dismissed Röhm and curbed the SA, they were prepared to declare martial law. Even in the face of mounting pressure from his own party leadership and the conservative circles whose support he needed, Hitler continued to vacillate about replacing Röhm. In reaction to the growing criticism of Röhm and the SA, Hitler ordered the entire membership of the SA to go on leave effective July 1. He also scheduled a meeting with Röhm for 11:00 A.M. on June 30.

Göring finally pushed Hitler into action. Göring and Himmler met with Hitler shortly after 1:00 A.M. on June 30 and gave him details of a supposed plot by Röhm and his SA officers to arrest Hitler and take control of the government. Accepting the accusations without investigation, Hitler ordered Himmler's SS to arrest and execute the SA officers supposedly involved in the plot. Hitler personally led a detachment of SS troops in the predawn hours to arrest Röhm. Over the next three days, SS troops executed many SA officers, including Röhm, in several German cities.

Significance

Röhm and his SA leaders were not the only victims of the purge. As early as June 24, Göring and his coconspirators began drawing up lists of Germans to be eliminated. Included on the list were their own personal enemies and people they felt were dangerous to Nazi aspirations. Hitler added other names to the list on July 1 and 2. Included among the non-SA victims of the purge were individuals who had opposed Hitler during the preceding years, including Kurt von Schleicher (Hitler's immediate predecessor as German chancellor) and his wife, and Gregor Strasser, who had once challenged Hitler for leadership of the National Socialist German Workers' Party (the Nazi Party).

Hitler announced to the German parliament on July 13 that the SS had executed seventy-seven people during the purge, all of whom were involved in a plot to overthrow his government. The parliament immediately passed a law legalizing everything Hitler had done to protect Germany, and President Hindenburg sent him a congratulatory message. The purge won Hitler the support of the army and eliminated the primary target of domestic criticism of the Nazi party. Historians of the period put the purge's death toll much higher; estimates range from 150 to more than 1,000. Although Hitler con-

solidated his position in Germany, the brutality and lawlessness of the purges revealed the true face of Nazism for the first time.

—*Paul Madden*

Further Reading

Bornstein, Joseph. *The Politics of Murder*. Toronto: George J. McLeod, 1950. Surveys political murders in the twentieth century, including the Röhm purge.

Burleigh, Michael. *The Third Reich: A New History*. New York: Hill & Wang, 2000. Less accessible than the Evans volume cited below. Includes an interesting and thorough analysis of the role of the purge in Nazism.

Evans, Richard J. *The Coming of the Third Reich*. New York: Penguin Books, 2004. A work of impressive and engaging scholarship on the events that led to the purge.

Gallo, Max. *The Night of the Long Knives*. Translated by Lily Emmet. Toronto: Harper & Row, 1972. The most complete account of the Röhm purge in English.

Kershaw, Ian. *Hitler, 1889-1945: Hubris*. New York: W. W. Norton, 1999. The Rhineland rearmament is viewed as the triumphant capstone of Hitler's early political career and the springboard for his more aggressive global initiatives.

Smelser, Ronald, and Rainer Zitelmann, eds. *The Nazi Elite*. Translated by Mary Fischer. New York: New York University Press, 1989. Biographical sketches of twenty-two leading Nazis, including Ernst Röhm. Concise account of Röhm's life and the events of the purge.

Spielvogel, Jackson J. *Hitler and Nazi Germany: A History*. Englewood Cliffs, N.J.: Prentice Hall, 1988. Introductory college text includes a brief account of the Röhm purge.

Tolstoy, Nikolai. *Night of the Long Knives*. New York: Ballantine, 1972. Concise account of the purge, accessible to most readers. Replete with a number of rare photographs.

See also: Nov. 8, 1923: Beer Hall Putsch; Jan. 30, 1933: Hitler Comes to Power in Germany; Feb. 27, 1933: Reichstag Fire; Mar., 1933: Nazi Concentration Camps Begin Operating; Mar. 23, 1933: Enabling Act of 1933; Mar. 7, 1936: German Troops March into the Rhineland; Feb. 12-Apr. 10, 1938: The Anschluss; Sept. 29-30, 1938: Munich Conference; Nov. 9-10, 1938: Kristallnacht; 1939-1945: Nazi Extermination of the Jews; Aug. 23-24, 1939: Nazi-Soviet Pact.

1934

September 1, 1934
MILLER'S *TROPIC OF CANCER* STIRS CONTROVERSY

Henry Miller's autobiographical novel Tropic of Cancer, *which was based on his first two years as an expatriate in Paris, created a sensation and began a new phase in American literature.*

LOCALE: Paris, France
CATEGORY: Literature

KEY FIGURES

Henry Miller (1891-1980), American writer who used his life as the basis for his art

Anaïs Nin (1903-1977), Paris-born writer who befriended Miller during his stay in Paris and who was instrumental in getting *Tropic of Cancer* published

Jack Kahane (1887-1939), English expatriate who owned the Obelisk Press in Paris and who first published *Tropic of Cancer*

Michael Fraenkel (1896-1957), writer who let Miller share his Paris apartment in 1931 and who encouraged Miller in the writing of *Tropic of Cancer*

June Edith Smith (b. 1902), dancer and actress whom Miller married in 1924

SUMMARY OF EVENT

It is now the fall of my second year in Paris. I was sent here for a reason I have not yet been able to fathom.

I have no money, no resources, no hopes. I am the happiest man alive.

Thus begins *Tropic of Cancer*, Henry Miller's opus of self-liberation and rebirth. *Tropic of Cancer* records Miller's unflinching look at himself as he struggled to survive amid the bohemian milieu of Paris in the early 1930's. It is the record of an odyssey of the spirit in which Miller experiences the hard, essential truth of what it means to be truly alive and open to the moment as it unfolds. By transforming the chaos of his struggle into art, he fashioned a document that captures the turbulent spontaneity of existence.

Henry Miller was born the son of lower-middle-class parents in the Yorkville section of New York City on December 26, 1891. In 1892, Miller's family moved to Brooklyn, where Miller learned to play the piano and developed a love for the romantic adventure stories of Knut Hamsun and the poetry of Walt Whitman. In 1909,

Miller attended the City College of New York, but he left after two months. He spent the next several years traveling through the Southwest and working odd jobs. When he returned to New York City, he assisted his father in the family tailor shop. In 1917, he married Beatrice Wickens, a piano teacher, and they had a daughter, Barbara. In 1920, after a succession of dreary jobs, he was hired as employment manager for the Western Union Telegraph Company in Manhattan. In 1924, Miller divorced his wife and married a Broadway taxi dancer, June Edith Smith, whom he had met during his late-night wanderings in the city. Their relationship was tumultuous, and Smith's promiscuity was destructive for Miller. Smith, however, encouraged Miller's aspirations to become a writer, and with her support, Miller quit his job to write full time.

His early efforts met with little success, and in 1928, Miller and Smith left for Europe for a brief stay. Running low on funds, they returned to the United States after eight months. In 1930, with Smith's urging and promises of financial support, he returned alone and settled in Paris. Now that they were separated, their marriage fell apart under the weight of Smith's emotional instability, and four years later, Smith obtained a Mexican divorce. In Paris, Miller was free from the demands of American society, but he also faced new problems. Miller was in a strange country where he had no friends, little money, and no prospects. He did not even speak the language. After arriving in Paris in 1930, Miller moved to a cheap hotel on the rue Bonaparte. From there, he began wandering the streets of Paris, taking notes and keeping a daily record of his life, including the things he saw and the people he met. He would relate these adventures in long letters to his friends in the United States, and many of these letters were later included in *Tropic of Cancer*. His adventures with prostitutes and the characters he met on the street and in cafés became the fabric of his book.

When Miller's money ran out, he was forced to panhandle and find lodging wherever he could. He had, in reality, become homeless, and he was dependent on fate and others' charity. He did not become dejected, however. Instead, by using these deprivations and desperate situations as the raw material for his letters, he turned his destitution into a testament to the human spirit.

Miller met a number of writers, artists, and intellectuals in Paris who befriended him. After months of living hand to mouth, he landed a job as a proofreader for the

Paris edition of the *Chicago Tribune*. While there, he met Michael Fraenkel, a writer and occasional publisher who let Miller move in with him. While living with Fraenkel, Miller began to work on *Tropic of Cancer*. Fraenkel, a man given to abstract debates about death, is portrayed in the novel as Boris, a character frozen by philosophical introspection. Miller, on the other hand, is the hero who opens himself to the richness and sensuality of life in Paris.

Although he was still very much in love with Smith, who was back in New York, Miller met and began an intimate relationship with the French writer Anaïs Nin. When they met, they were immediately drawn to one another, and although Nin lived outside Paris with her husband, Miller frequently visited her. During 1931 and 1932, they exchanged a voluminous correspondence. At one point, when Miller was depressed over his estrangement from Smith, Nin arranged for him to teach English at a preparatory school in Dijon. The position paid little, and Dijon was a depressingly provincial town that added to Miller's sense of isolation. He left after two months. Back in Paris in the summer of 1932, he completed work on the manuscript of *Tropic of Cancer*.

An American literary agent in Paris read *Tropic of Cancer*, liked it, and gave it to English expatriate Jack Kahane, who owned the Obelisk Press. Kahane read the novel and was so impressed that he offered Miller a contract. The raw, uninhibited style Miller used in the *Tropic of Cancer* contained obscene language and graphic accounts of sex. Although the Obelisk Press had a reputation for publishing risqué novels, Kahane stalled publication because of fears of French censorship laws. Kahane persuaded Miller to write another, more "serious" book, one that would give his work an air of respectability. Although Miller attempted a scholarly study of D. H. Lawrence, he failed to produce a publishable book. Finally, after nearly two years of delays, Anaïs Nin came to the rescue with six hundred dollars to underwrite the publication of *Tropic of Cancer* with the Obelisk Press. Miller's turbu-

lent and euphoric autobiographical novel went to press on September 1, 1934.

SIGNIFICANCE

Miller began receiving praise for *Tropic of Cancer* soon after its publication. Among the writers and artists who applauded the novel were Ezra Pound, T. S. Eliot, Marcel Duchamp, and Blaise Cendrars. As his reputation grew, Miller became the subject of a great deal of interest. Other publishers, such as Alfred A. Knopf in New York and Faber & Faber in London, expressed interest in Miller's work but did not make definite offers. After completing *Tropic of Cancer*, Miller had begun his second autobiographical novel, *Tropic of Capricorn* (1939), which was about his life in New York City and his exploration of sexuality during a period of personal frustration

---

MILLER'S PHILOSOPHICAL REFLECTIONS

Although the novel's sexually explicit passages garnered the most attention, Tropic of Cancer *also gives some fascinating insights into Miller's ego and worldview, as this excerpt shows.*

There are days, nevertheless, when the sun is out and I get off the beaten path and think about her hungrily. Now and then, despite my grim satisfaction, I get to thinking about another way of life, get to wondering if it would make a difference having a young, restless creature by my side. The trouble is I can hardly remember what she looks like, nor even how it feels to have my arms around her. Everything that belongs to the past seems to have fallen into the sea; I have memories, but the images have lost their vividness, they seem dead and desultory, like time-bitten mummies stuck in a quagmire. If I try to recall my life in New York I get a few splintered fragments, nightmarish and covered with verdigris. It seems as if my own proper existence had come to an end somewhere, just where exactly I can't make out. I'm not an American any more, nor a New Yorker, and even less a European, or a Parisian. I haven't any allegiance, any responsibilities, any hatreds, any worries, any prejudices, any passion. I'm neither for nor against. I'm neutral.

When we walk home of a night, the three of us, it often happens after the first spasms of disgust that we get to talking about the condition of things with the enthusiasm which only those who bear no active part in life can muster. What seems strange to me sometimes, when I crawl into bed, is that all this enthusiasm is engendered just to kill time, just to annihilate the three-quarters of an hour which it requires to walk from the office to Montparnasse. We might have the most brilliant, the most feasible ideas for the amelioration of this or that, but there is no vehicle to hitch them to. And what is more strange is that the absence of any relationship between ideas and living causes us no anguish, no discomfort. We have become so adjusted that, if tomorrow we were ordered to walk on our hands, we would do so without the slightest protest. Provided, of course, that the paper came out as usual.

Source: Henry Miller, *Tropic of Cancer* (Paris: Obelisk Press, 1934).

and upheaval. In 1939, that work also was published by the Obelisk Press.

Another work that Miller had begun writing in 1933 was a surrealistic self-portrait filled with fragments of letters, dreams, and reminiscences. Finally given the title *Black Spring*, it was published in Paris in 1936. Meanwhile, Miller's life had begun to settle somewhat. While in Paris, he wrote steadily and worked on various publishing projects, but with the outbreak of war in Europe and the threat of invasion by the Germans, Miller decided to leave his Paris home for good. After nearly ten years, his time in France was drawing to an end. In 1939, he sailed for Greece at the urging of his friend Lawrence Durrell. After arriving in Corfu, he stayed with the Durrells and then traveled around Greece. His adventures were later published as *The Colossus of Maroussi: Or, The Spirit of Greece* (1941), a kind of spiritual travelogue praised as one of his best books.

In 1940, Miller left Greece for New York. Although his books had continued to sell briskly in Paris, he was unable to obtain royalties owed him, and when he arrived back in the United States he was almost as broke as when he had left ten years earlier. Miller eventually moved to California and settled in Big Sur, where he became the focal point in a growing artists' colony. There he worked on *The Rosy Crucifixion*: *Sexus* (1949, 2 volumes), *Plexus* (1953, 2 volumes), and *Nexus* (1960), the story of his ill-fated relationship with June Smith.

All through the 1930's, *Tropic of Cancer* continued to sell in Paris, although it was not until the German occupation of the 1940's that sales dramatically increased. By the war's end, Miller's accumulated royalties from French sales of *Tropic of Cancer* totaled some forty thousand dollars. By 1947, he was owed ten times that amount. Because of postwar restrictions and rapid devaluation of the franc, however, he was unable to collect his earnings. Meanwhile, Miller's Paris publisher faced other problems. In 1946, French authorities brought charges against the owners of the Obelisk Press and managed to convict them of distributing pornographic materials. Fortunately, several famous and influential French writers, including Albert Camus, Paul Éluard, and Jean-Paul Sartre, came to the book's defense, and the verdict was overturned. Meanwhile, *Tropic of Cancer* had still not been published in the United States.

For years, *Tropic of Cancer* and *The Rosy Crucifixion* were deemed obscene and were banned from publication in the United States. In 1961, however, Grove Press brought out an American edition of *Tropic of Cancer*. Sales of the book were phenomenal, and Miller became an overnight celebrity. The publication was met with controversy, however, and numerous attempts were made to have the book banned. Finally, in 1963, a U.S. Supreme Court decision ended censorship of Miller's books.

In spite of—or perhaps because of—such controversy, *Tropic of Cancer*'s effect on American literature was significant. The unrestrained language and lack of literary pretenses in Miller's autobiographical novel influenced such writers as William S. Burroughs, Jack Kerouac, and Norman Mailer. Miller's work explored the meaning of what it was to be alive in a civilization that was being torn apart by forces it had unleashed on itself, one in which dehumanizing technology, the forced conformity of the masses, poverty, and war all threatened to destroy the individual's spirit and imagination. *Tropic of Cancer* recorded Miller's fight to save his own soul, and it is a work that reverberates with a desperate energy and a liberating vision.

—*Francis Poole*

FURTHER READING
Brassaï. *Henry Miller, Happy Rock*. Translated by Jane Marie Todd. Chicago: University of Chicago Press, 2002. Rerelease of Brassaï's reflections on his friendship with Miller. Includes valuable advice for young writers.
Dearborn, Mary V. *The Happiest Man Alive: A Biography of Henry Miller*. New York: Simon & Schuster, 1991. A valuable biography that raises questions about the lack of serious academic criticism of Miller's work. Successfully depicts the man and all of his contradictions. Includes numerous photographs and detailed notes.
Decker, James M. *Henry Miller and Narrative Form: Constructing the Self, Rejecting Modernity*. New York: Routledge, 2005. Studies Miller's frequent transitions between realism and an interest in the fantastic. Analyzes the influences of James Joyce, Walt Whitman, and Friedrich Nietzsche, among others.
Durrell, Lawrence. *Durrell-Miller Letters, 1935-80*. Edited by Ian S. MacNiven. London: Faber & Faber, 1988. A collection of letters that nearly doubles the published correspondence between the two writers. The letters illustrate and confirm the affection between them and the vitality of their relationship.
Gordon, William A. *The Mind and Art of Henry Miller*. Baton Rouge: Louisiana State University Press, 1967. The first serious, full-length study of Henry Miller as an artist. Insightful and objective. Examines Miller's

principal themes and studies his growth toward self-liberation through his writing.

Lewis, Leon. *Henry Miller: The Major Writings*. New York: Schocken Books, 1986. An examination of Miller scholarship and a perceptive discussion of Miller's life and major works. Offers insight into reasons for Miller's enduring popularity.

Miller, Henry. *Letters to Emil*. Edited by George Wickes. New York: New Directions, 1989. A collection of several dozen letters from Henry Miller to Emil Schnellock, written when Miller was in Paris. The letters offer a unique record of Miller's literary apprenticeship.

Winslow, Kathryn. *Henry Miller: Full of Life*. Los Angeles: J. P. Tarcher, 1986. A memoir by a longtime friend of Miller who met the novelist in 1944, after he had moved to Big Sur.

SEE ALSO: Fall, 1905: Stein Holds Her First Paris Salons; 1913-1927: Proust Publishes *Remembrance of Things Past*; 1915: *The Metamorphosis* Anticipates Modern Feelings of Alienation; 1920-1924: Melville Is Rediscovered as a Major American Novelist; 1922: Eliot Publishes *The Waste Land*; Feb. 2, 1922: Joyce's *Ulysses* Redefines Modern Fiction; 1924: Mann's *The Magic Mountain* Reflects European Crisis; Apr. 10, 1925: Fitzgerald Captures the Roaring Twenties in *The Great Gatsby*; 1935: Penguin Develops a Line of Paperback Books.

Fall, 1934-May 6, 1953
GIBBON DEVELOPS THE HEART-LUNG MACHINE

John H. Gibbon, Jr., developed and tested, in animals and then humans, the first artificial device to oxygenate and circulate blood during surgery. The machine made open-heart surgery possible.

ALSO KNOWN AS: Pump-oxygenator
LOCALE: United States
CATEGORIES: Health and medicine; inventions

KEY FIGURES

John H. Gibbon, Jr. (1903-1973), American cardiovascular surgeon

Mary Hopkinson Gibbon (fl. mid-twentieth century), American research technician

Thomas J. Watson, Sr. (1874-1956), founder and head of IBM

T. L. Stokes (fl. mid-twentieth century), researcher in Gibbon's laboratory

J. B. Flick (fl. mid-twentieth century), researcher in Gibbon's laboratory

Bernard J. Miller (fl. mid-twentieth century), American cardiovascular surgeon and research associate

Cecelia Bavolek (fl. mid-twentieth century), first human to undergo successful open-heart surgery using the heart-lung machine

SUMMARY OF EVENT

In the first half of the twentieth century, cardiovascular medicine had many triumphs. Effective anesthesia, antiseptic conditions, and antibiotics made surgery of all kinds safer; blood typing, anticlotting agents, and blood preservatives made blood transfusion practical; cardiac catheterization (feeding a tube into the heart), electrocardiography (noninvasive measurement of the electrical changes in the heart caused by its beating), and fluoroscopy (visualizing living tissues with an X-ray machine) made the nonsurgical diagnosis of cardiovascular problems possible. These advances were put to use solving problems of disease, injury, and birth defects in blood vessels and around the heart.

Before the 1950's, however, there was no safe way to treat damage or defects within the heart. To make such a correction, the vital organ's function must be interrupted, and the body's tissues must be kept alive artificially during that interruption. Some surgeons practiced so-called blind surgery, inserting a finger into the heart through a small incision to attempt to make corrections without observing what they were doing; others attempted to reduce the body's need for circulation by slowly chilling the patient until the heart stopped. Still other surgeons used "cross-circulation," a procedure in which the patient's circulatory system was temporarily connected to a donor's system. All these approaches carried profound risks of hemorrhage, tissue damage, and death.

Not until the successful development of the pump-oxygenator, or heart-lung machine, did heart surgery as it is known today become possible. The heart-lung machine uses mechanical devices to oxygenate and circulate the blood during heart surgery. It was developed over a period of more than twenty years through the persistence of John H. Gibbon, Jr., who, on May 6, 1953, first used it successfully in a human being.

Ironically, Gibbon's first interest in such a machine arose from his concern for a patient with an obstruction of lung circulation rather than a heart defect. In February of 1931, Gibbon witnessed the death of a young woman whose lung circulation was blocked by a blood clot. Because her blood could not pass through her lungs, she slowly lost consciousness from lack of oxygen. As he monitored her pulse and breathing, Gibbon thought about ways of circumventing the obstructed lungs and straining heart and providing the required oxygen to the rest of her body. Because surgery to remove such a blood clot in the pulmonary artery was often fatal, her surgeons operated only as a last resort. Their reluctance proved appropriate: Although the surgery took only 6.5 minutes, the young woman never regained consciousness.

This experience prompted Gibbon to pursue what few people then considered a practical line of research. At the time, researchers were still experimenting with separate devices for pumping blood during transfusion or for oxygenating blood during isolated perfused-organ experiments. Gibbon, however, sought to create a device capable of doing both at once, circulating blood around the heart and oxygenating it. If such a device could be created, it would permit the treatment of not only pulmonary obstruction but also abnormalities of the heart.

Gibbon began the project in earnest in the fall of 1934, when he returned to the laboratory of Edward D. Churchill at Massachusetts General Hospital for his second surgical research fellowship. He was assisted by his wife, Mary Hopkinson Gibbon. Together, they developed an experimental surgical preparation in cats to remove blood from a vein, supply it with oxygen, and return it to an artery using tubes inserted into the blood vessels. Their objectives were to assemble a device that would keep the blood moving, spread it over a very thin layer to pick up oxygen efficiently and remove carbon dioxide, and avoid both clotting and damaging blood cells.

The Gibbons' initial attempts included using a vertical revolving cylinder for gas exchange. This device applied centrifugal force to spread the blood over a very thin layer in an oxygen-filled chamber. A piston-type pump was used for blood circulation. Ultimately, they modified this arrangement to use a gentler roller pump that had no valve surfaces. This reduced the damage to blood cells, as well as the surface area available for clot formation. They reported in 1937 that heart and lung function could be artificially maintained for fifty min-

utes, and the animal's normal heart function could be restored for a period of several hours. After their return to the University of Pennsylvania School of Medicine in 1935, they repeated their experiments under sterile conditions and reported in 1939 that prolonged survival after heart-lung bypass was possible in animals.

World War II interrupted the progress of Gibbon's work, but he resumed his research at Jefferson Medical College in 1944. Shortly thereafter, he attracted the interest of Thomas J. Watson, Sr., chairman of the board of International Business Machines (IBM), who provided the services of IBM's experimental physics laboratory and model machine shop, as well as the assistance of engineers Al Malmrose, Don Rex, Leo Farr, and John Enstrom. IBM constructed and modified two experimental machines during the next seven years, and these engineers contributed significantly to the evolution of a machine that would be practical in humans.

The most critical problem presented by the ambition to take over heart-lung function in humans mechanically was that of achieving the efficiency of gas exchange required to oxygenate such a large flow of blood. This problem was addressed by T. L. Stokes and J. B. Flick,

John H. Gibbon, Jr. (National Library of Medicine)

who, while working in Gibbon's laboratory, observed that turbulence in the blood greatly enhanced gas exchange in the oxygenator. They demonstrated and reported in 1950 that lining the oxygenation cylinder with a wire screen could produce turbulence and the desired oxygenation effect without creating a foam from broken blood cells.

Bernard J. Miller joined Gibbon's group in January of 1950 and contributed to the final stages in developing the second IBM machine, which was completed in 1951. After testing a series of materials to improve the oxygenation surface, they settled on multiple stainless-steel wire mesh screens suspended in parallel within an oxygen-filled plastic chamber. The screens were coated with a protein solution to permit a complete film to spread over them. The electronic circuit developed to control blood flow through the system was improved, and a filter was incorporated into the circuit to prevent air bubbles or incipient blood clots from reentering the body. Safety systems to maintain power and prevent combustible gases (then used as anesthetics) from entering the system were incorporated into the device, and blood pressure, flow, and hydrogen-ion concentration were continuously monitored in the circuit. By 1952, the survival rate for animals maintained by this device was 90 percent.

Gibbon's first attempt to use the pump-oxygenator in a human was in a fifteen-month-old baby. This attempt failed, not because of a malfunction or a surgical mistake but because of misdiagnosis. The child died following surgery because the real problem was not corrected by the surgery. On May 6, 1953, the heart-lung machine was first used successfully on a human being, Cecelia Bavolek.

In the six months before surgery, Bavolek was hospitalized three times for symptoms of heart failure when she could not engage in normal activity. With her circulation connected to the heart-lung machine for forty-five minutes, the surgical team headed by Gibbon was able to observe directly and to close an opening between her atria, thereby establishing normal heart function. Two months later, an examination of the defect revealed that it was fully closed, and Bavolek resumed a normal life. Although Gibbon reflected some years later that he may have opened a Pandora's box, the age of open-heart surgery had begun.

SIGNIFICANCE

John Gibbon devoted most of his career to developing the pump-oxygenator, or heart-lung machine. His success depended on a network of critical discoveries made by many others before him, and it combined with concurrent discoveries to make possible future advances, some of which could not even be anticipated by cardiovascular scientists of the time. Heart-lung bypass alone could not make open-heart surgery a truly practical technique. Therefore, once it was possible to keep they body's tissues alive by diverting blood around the heart and oxygenating it, other questions already under investigation became even more critical. Scientists had yet to determine how to stop and restart the heart, how to evaluate and prevent or correct erratic heartbeats, how to prolong the survival of bloodless organs, how to measure oxygen and carbon dioxide levels in the blood, and how to prolong anesthesia safely during complicated surgery. Thus, following the first successful use of the heart-lung machine, surgeons and engineers continued to refine the methods of open-heart surgery. Many scientists, including those working with Owen Wangenstein at the University of Minnesota and John Webster Kirklin at the Mayo Clinic, employed and improved the technique so consistently in the late 1950's that by 1960 it was a standard operative procedure.

The immediate result of Gibbon's invention and its subsequent refinements was the development of reliable surgical techniques to correct congenital heart defects. For example, a hole in the wall between two of the heart's chambers, such as an atrial septal defect or a ventricular septal defect, could be exposed now to plain view and sewn closed, because blood was diverted around the heart. Valvular stenosis, a stiffening or narrowing of the heart valves, could be relieved with far less risk of permanent damage to the valve because surgeons could now judge the appropriate type and size of correction necessary. Transposed great arteries (that is, misdirected major arteries) could be severed now and rejoined to their appropriate connections with the aid of heart-lung bypass.

Furthermore, the heart-lung apparatus set the stage for the advent of "replacement-parts" solutions for many types of cardiovascular problems. In 1960, Albert Starr and M. L. Edwards first successfully accomplished cardiac valve replacement by placing an artificial ball valve between the left atrium and ventricle. In 1967, R. G. Favaloro performed the first coronary bypass surgery, grafting sections of a leg vein into the heart's circulation to divert blood around clogged coronary arteries. Likewise, the first successful heart transplant (Christiaan Barnard, 1967) and the controversial Jarvik-7 artificial heart (William DeVries, 1982) required the ability to stop the heart and keep the body's tissues alive during time-

1934

consuming and delicate surgical procedures. While cardiovascular science awaits the developments that will permit the prevention or true cure of the conditions that compromise cardiac functions, these corrective surgical measures, which make use of the heart-lung apparatus, continue to contribute to prolonging life.

—*Laura Gray Malloy*

FURTHER READING

Comroe, Jr. Julius H. "The Heart and Lungs." In *Advances in American Medicine: Essays at the Bicentennial*, edited by John Z. Bowers and Elizabeth F. Purcell. Vol. 2. New York: Joshua Macy, Jr. Foundation, 1976. An excellently written history of American contributions to the knowledge of cardiovascular and pulmonary function. Puts the significance of Gibbon's success into context by examining the many scientific discoveries on which it built (including contributions from two important but often uncredited female scientists, Maude Abbott and Helen Taussig) and the many important developments to which it led.

_____. *The Retrospectroscope: Insights into Medical Discovery*. Menlo Park, Calif.: Von Gehr Press, 1977. Comroe uses a historical perspective to make an insightful and readable examination of the conditions in which important medical discoveries have been made. This work is invaluable to anyone interested in studying the process of science. Included are several references to John and Mary Gibbon, who worked at the University of Pennsylvania when Comroe was an instructor there in pharmacology.

Davis, Goode Edwards, Jr., Edwards Park, and Editors of U.S. News Books. *The Heart: The Living Pump*. Washington, D.C.: U.S. News Books, 1981. A beautifully illustrated and photographed volume for the general public. Historical, experimental, and clinical aspects of the heart's function are presented simply and accurately. Treatment and prevention of cardiovascular disease are given ample consideration, as are experimental and clinical techniques. Gibbon's work is put in perspective with other surgical research of the time. Glossary. Excellent for high school or college students.

Fenster, Julie M. "Long Way to Bypass: John H. Gibbon Jr., the Heart-Lung Machine." In *Mavericks, Miracles, and Medicine: The Pioneers Who Risked Their Lives to Bring Medicine into the Modern Age*. New York: Carroll & Graf, 2003. Profile of Gibbon in a companion volume to a documentary series produced on the History Channel detailing advances in medical science. The volume also discusses blood transfusion, kidney transplantation, and the cardiac pacemaker, among many such advances. Bibliographic references and index.

Gibbon, John H., Jr. "The Development of the Heart-Lung Apparatus." *The Review of Surgery* 27 (1970): 231-244. John Gibbon's very readable personal account of his experiences through a career devoted to the development of the heart-lung machine, with a consideration of the problems to be solved in the project and its impact on his life. Includes photographs of the original device and experimental surgery in progress.

Miller, Bernard J. "The Development of Heart-Lung Machines." *Surgery, Gynecology, and Obstetrics* 154 (1982): 403-414. Miller's account of the evolution of heart-lung apparatus from before Gibbon's era through stages following the first successful use of the apparatus. It is technically complete, especially with respect to modifications made during the stages of development from 1950 to 1954, when Miller was a research associate at Jefferson Medical College.

Moore, Francis D. "Surgery." In *Advances in American Medicine: Essays at the Bicentennial*, edited by John Z. Bowers and Elizabeth F. Purcell. Vol. 2. New York: Joshua Macy, Jr. Foundation, 1976. An accessible review of the history of American surgery from colonial times to the present. Moore asserts that two features unique to American surgery after World War II contributed to developments such as Gibbon's: government support and the availability of animals as experimental models. Includes a photograph of John and Mary Gibbon inspecting the heart-lung machine.

SEE ALSO: 1905: Einthoven Begins Clinical Studies with Electrocardiography; Sept., 1915-Feb., 1916: McLean Discovers the Natural Anticoagulant Heparin.

October 16, 1934-October 18, 1935
MAO'S LONG MARCH

Facing a Nationalist assault on the Communist stronghold in southern China's Jiangxi Province, Mao Zedong joined the Communist retreat toward a sanctuary at Yan'an in the remote northern Ningxia Huizu Province. On a trek that covered about five thousand miles, Mao engineered his rise to supremacy of the Chinese Communist Party and turned the event into a core myth of Communist triumph.

LOCALE: China

CATEGORIES: Wars, uprisings, and civil unrest; military history; government and politics

KEY FIGURES

Mao Zedong (Mao Tse-tung; 1893-1976), chairman of the Chinese Communist Party, 1935-1976

Chiang Kai-shek (1887-1975), leader of the Kuomintang or Nationalist Party

Zhang Guotao (Chang Kuo-t'ao; 1897-1979), Communist general and rival of Mao Zedong

Zhou Enlai (Chou En-lai; 1898-1976), Communist leader

Zhu De (Chu Teh; 1886-1976), commander of the Communist army who helped establish the Chinese soviets

SUMMARY OF EVENT

The Chinese Communist Party formed an alliance with the Nationalist Party (the Kuomintang) in 1923 in order to unify China by defeating independent warlords, but this alliance broke apart in the period 1926-1927. When Chiang Kai-shek, leader of the Kuomintang after 1925, launched a devastating attack on the Communists and purged his new government of all Communists on October 10, 1927, the Communists retreated into remote rural sanctuaries throughout China. One of the Communists' most important southern strongholds, ruled through terror by Mao Zedong and Zhu De, was the Jiangxi Soviet state, which they proclaimed on November 7, 1931.

Even though he faced challenges from independent warlords and Japanese aggression, in late 1933 Chiang Kai-shek moved to destroy the Jiangxi stronghold. Turning for advice to a German World War I general, Hans von Seeckt, Chiang Kai-shek trapped the Communists inside a series of blockhouses, where he hoped hunger would eventually force them to surrender. When the key Communist leaders—Red Army commander Zhu De, party officials Bo Gu and Zhou Enlai, and Joseph Stalin's

German envoy Otto Braun (who was married to a Chinese woman)—met in August, 1934, they decided to evacuate Jiangxi and move their forces to a sanctuary in northern China, which was closer to the border with the Soviet Union. Mao Zedong, president of the Jiangxi Soviet, made sure he joined the breakout against the wishes of his rivals.

After killing thousands of Chinese deemed unworthy in Jiangxi, Zhou Enlai coordinated the breakout of the Communist forces. The Communists chose a path through the southwest, which was guarded only by unreliable allied warlord troops from Guangxi Zhuangzu and Guangdong. Two days into the event, on October 18, 1934, Mao Zedong traveled across Yudu bridge and out of Jiangxi.

The Communists moved with relative ease through the four Kuomintang lines, and they crossed the Xiang River into the Guangxi Zhuangzu region in December, 1934. They took the town of Zunyi on January 7, 1935, after crossing the Wu River in Guizhou Province with their remaining forty thousand troops. Traditionally, the success of the Communist breakout was blamed on poor performance of the Kuomintang and warlord troops, but more recent historical evidence suggests that Chiang Kai-shek may have been willing to allow an escape by reduced Communist forces. He wanted to please Joseph Stalin, leader of the Soviet Union, which China hoped would be its ally against Japan. Matters were made even more complicated by the fact that Chiang's son Jiang Jingguo was essentially a hostage in Moscow, where the young man had gone to study in 1925. Additionally, Chiang confided to his secretary that by pursuing the Communists into provinces still held by semi-independent warlords, the Kuomintang would establish its power there.

At a high-level Communist Party meeting in Zunyi from January 15 to 18, Mao cemented his position by becoming a member of the Secretariat of the Communist Party's Politburo and by blaming others, including Otto Braun, for the Jiangxi defeat that made the Long March necessary. Contrary to later claims, Mao was not made chairman of the party until later. He did, however, become military adviser to Zhou Enlai at this time. After the Zunyi Conference, the Communists decided to move north into Sichuan, where they planned to double their strength by joining an army—led by the ruthless Zhang Guotao—already stationed in the region.

MAO'S LONG MARCH

⟵ = Route of Long March

out the Long March, Mao and his leadership circle were carried on chairs by porters, although Communist legend states that this happened only when Mao was ill with malaria.

The Long Marchers finally reached the Sichuan town of Mougong on June 12, 1935, after crossing the inhospitable passes across the Snow Mountains (the altitude of which exceeded 10,000 feet). On this part of the journey, Mao abandoned his sedan chair and walked with his men. By the time Mao was joined by a furious Zhang Guotao and his eighty thousand troops on June 25, his suffering troops numbered only about ten thousand.

Mao was in control of the party's leadership, and to ensure that his troops would reach the sanctuary first, Mao proposed a two-pronged approach into Shaanxi Province. His forces would go directly northeast through the Banyou marshes, while Zhang's troops were to take a more northwesterly route. The two Communist columns departed in early Au-

Fearing that a successful linkup could result in a loss of his power, Mao made sure the forces could not meet. With Zhou Enlai's approval, Mao ordered his troops southward, where they attacked a Nationalist force in the Battle of Tucheng on January 28. The Communists lost four thousand soldiers, and Mao used the defeat to argue against a breakthrough to Sichuan. Instead, he led the Long Marchers back into Guizhou and then back into Zunyi on February 27. In Zunyi, Mao was appointed commander of the general front after the Communists repelled a Kuomintang attack. Communist anger grew when Mao refused to go north, and he was finally forced to move west into Yunnan and Sichuan.

On May 29, 1935, Mao's forces reached the hundred-yard-long Luding (or Dadu) Bridge, which spanned the raging Datong River. Communist mythology describes the events there as a fierce battle in which the Communists heroically captured the bridge. Later historical research, however, revealed that there was no real battle; Chiang Kai-shek wanted the Communists to go north. Mao turned the May 31 crossing into a legend in order to build his status. Similarly, during this time and through-

gust. Bogged down in the dangerous marshes, Mao feared that Zhang would overtake him, and in the name of the party Mao ordered Zhang to go through the marshes as well. Even though he objected, Zhang obeyed, and after realizing that he could not cross the marshes that late in the year, Zhang issued a September 3 order for all Communist troops to rest for the winter.

Mao and his allies refused this military order, denounced Zhang, and took their most loyal troops away to the north. The group stopped in surprisingly hospitable Muslim minority territory in south Gansu Province, where a rash of desertions caused Mao to release an October 2 order promising harsh punishments for stragglers. Many soldiers were executed under the order. On October 18, 1935, Mao and a mere four thousand Communists reached Communist-controlled territory in Ningxia Huizu Province; they entered the city of Wuqizhen on October 20.

In Moscow, Mao's envoy Chen Yun gave a glowing report of Mao's leadership on the Long March, and this account earned Mao an admiring article in the Soviet *Pravda* newspaper in late October. By December, 1935,

Mao had ended his Long March in Yan'an and was busy ensuring that his version of the event was enshrined in history. In the spring of 1936, Zhang Guotao's army arrived; over the course of the winter, the army had lost half its men.

SIGNIFICANCE

The Long March provided Mao Zedong with an extraordinary chance to take hold of the Chinese Communist Party, and he ruthlessly exploited this opportunity. By brilliantly outmaneuvering his Communist adversaries (at staggering human costs to his fellow Communists), Mao rose to a near-mythical status without any real challenges. He consistently used propaganda to emphasize the Long March's importance, and in the process he built a solid foundation for his rule.

If, as history suggests, Chiang Kai-shek's political and personal interests led him to allow a small band of Communists to escape from Jiangxi into Yan'an, his move backfired. The Communists were quick to spread their version of a heroic Long March to receptive Chinese and other sympathizers from around the world. Within a few years, Mao's account of the Long March gathered support from Chinese and international supporters such as American journalist Edgar Snow, whose interviews with Mao fascinated an international audience.

The Long March allowed Mao's Communists to build a secure base of power that provided crucial support during Japan's 1937-1945 war on China and launched the 1946-1949 conquest of mainland China during the final phase of China's civil war. The Communist myths and memoirs of the Long March became an accepted part Chinese history, and historians whose research contradicted Mao's long-accepted version of the event faced a challenging battle.

—*R. C. Lutz*

FURTHER READING

Chang, Jung, and Jon Halliday. *Mao: The Unknown Story*. New York: Alfred A. Knopf, 2005. Controversial but based on fresh eyewitness accounts. Questions conventional wisdom built on Communist propaganda and highlights Mao's ambitions, which caused a great deal of suffering for his followers and for his Communist rivals. Illustrated with maps, notes, bibliography, and index.

Salisbury, Harrison E. *The Long March: The Untold Story*. New York: Harper & Row, 1985. Descrip-

---

MAO DRAWS CLASS DISTINCTIONS

In October, 1933, Mao Zedong outlined the following distinctions in an attempt to clarify some of the confusion resulting from his land-reform campaigns.

1. THE LANDLORD

A landlord is a person who owns land, does not engage in labour himself, or does so only to a very small extent, and lives by exploiting the peasants. The collection of land rent is his main form of exploitation; in addition, he may lend money, hire labour, or engage in industry or commerce. But his exaction of land rent from the peasants is his principal form of exploitation. . . .

Warlords, officials, local tyrants and evil gentry are political representatives and exceptionally ruthless members of the landlord class. Minor local tyrants and evil gentry are also very often to be found among the rich peasants.

2. THE RICH PEASANT

The rich peasant as a rule owns land. But some rich peasants own only part of their land and rent the remainder. Others have no land of their own at all and rent all their land. The rich peasant . . . always relies on exploitation for part or even the major part of his income. . . . Rich peasants regularly practice exploitation and many derive most of their income from this source.

3. THE MIDDLE PEASANT

Many middle peasants own land. Some own only part of their land and rent the rest. Others own no land of their own at all and rent all their land. All of them have a fair number of farm implements. A middle peasant derives his income wholly or mainly from his own labour. As a rule he does not exploit others and in many cases he himself is exploited by others, having to pay a small amount in land rent and in interest on loans. But generally he does not sell his labour power. Some middle peasants (the well-to-do middle peasants) do practice exploitation to a small extent, but this is not their regular or their main source of income.

4. THE POOR PEASANT

. . . In general, a middle peasant does not need to sell his labour power, while the poor peasant has to sell part of his labour power. This is the principal criterion for distinguishing between a middle and a poor peasant.

5. THE WORKER

The worker (including the farm labourer) as a rule owns no land or farm implements, though some do own a very small amount of land and very few farm implements. Workers make their living wholly or mainly by selling their labour power.

Source: Mao Zedong, "How to Differentiate the Classes in the Rural Areas," in *Selected Works of Mao Tse-tung*, vol. 1 (Beijing: Foreign Languages Press, 1967).

1934

tion of the event by a journalist who later traveled Mao's route by himself. Endorses the Communist version of events.

Snow, Edgar. *Red Star Rising over China*. Rev. ed. New York: Grove Press, 1968. Originally published in 1937 and based on the author's interviews with Mao after the event. Decisively pro-Communist, this account had considerable influence on America's view of events. Uses Wade-Giles romanizations.

Spence, Jonathan. *The Search for Modern China*. Rev. ed. New York: W. W. Norton, 2001. Gives a succinct and balanced account of the event based on the conventional historical belief biased in Mao's favor.

Maps, illustrations, notes, glossary, bibliography, and index. Uses Pinyin romanizations.

Young, Helen Praeger. *Choosing Revolution: Chinese Women Soldiers on the Long March*. Urbana: University of Illinois Press, 2001. Detailed account of women's experience of the Long March through analysis of twenty-two interviews with survivors, including four in-depth case studies. Illustrated, bibliography, index. Uses Pinyin romanizations.

SEE ALSO: May 4, 1919: May Fourth Movement; 1926-1949: Chinese Civil War; July 7, 1937: China Declares War on Japan; Aug., 1940: Japan Announces the Greater East Asia Coprosperity Sphere.

October 19, 1934
MARSHALL AND LEOPOLD FORM THE WILDERNESS SOCIETY

The Wilderness Society became the leading critic of development and the destruction of the environment that attended that concept.

LOCALE: United States
CATEGORIES: Environmental issues; organizations and institutions

KEY FIGURES

Robert Marshall (1901-1939), first president of the Wilderness Society

Aldo Leopold (1887-1948), American wildlife biologist, ecologist, and author

Robert Sterling Yard (1861-1945), second president of the Wilderness Society and editor of its journal, *The Living Wilderness*

Harold Ickes (1874-1952), U.S. secretary of the interior, 1933-1946

John Collier (1884-1968), American social reformer and commissioner for the Bureau of Indian Affairs, 1933-1945

SUMMARY OF EVENT

On October 19, 1934, Robert Marshall gave the keynote speech at the American Forestry Association Conference in Knoxville, Tennessee. That afternoon, he and four friends—Benton McKaye, a naturalist and city planner; Harold C. Anderson, an accountant, avid hiker, and developer of the Appalachian Trail; Harvey Broome, a Knoxville attorney; and Bernard Frank, associate forester with the Tennessee Valley Authority—had taken a trip into the mountains north of Knoxville. On the drive,

Marshall, who was director of forestry in the Bureau of Indian Affairs of the Department of the Interior, talked about organizing a national group interested in promoting the preservation of wilderness areas in the United States. No such group existed, he explained, because nationwide organizations such as the Audubon Society and the Izaak Walton League focused most of their attention on saving wildlife rather than on wilderness in general. The Sierra Club focused on such a program, but that group, founded by the famous naturalist John Muir, had offices only in California. After Marshall's talk, the other passengers in the car began creating a plan to organize the Wilderness Society.

Marshall had become interested in conservation as a teenager. Born to a wealthy family in New York City, he had spent many of his childhood summers at the family's summer home in New York's Adirondack Mountains. He studied forestry in college and received a master's degree in forestry from Harvard University before going to The Johns Hopkins University, where he earned a doctorate in plant pathology. Before he joined the Department of the Interior, Marshall spent five years in Alaska, where he helped identify hundreds of Arctic plants and assembled a lengthy catalog of species.

In the Arctic, Marshall became a wilderness preservation advocate. Cities and industrial civilization, he believed, destroy the human connection with nature. Wilderness not only satisfies the human need for freedom and adventure but also makes people more self-sufficient, improves their health, and liberates them from the tension and pressure of civilization.

Marshall saw wildness as comparable to works of art and music in its importance to the human spirit. It presents opportunities for contemplation and meditation. All human senses are aroused by the sights and sounds of wild places, and the beauty of the wilderness cannot be matched by any synthetic objects. For these reasons, Marshall believed wilderness had to be preserved.

Secretary of the Interior Harold Ickes, a supporter of conservation, brought Marshall into his department because of Marshall's reputation as a defender of wilderness. The Bureau of Indian Affairs controlled vast tracts of forest in the American West, and in the 1920's agency leaders had advocated economic development on these lands. Roads and hotels would bring tourists into the forests and increase Native American prosperity. Marshall argued that the so-called benefits of civilization would never compensate for the loss of true wilderness. Wilderness was as important a resource as coal, oil, or lumber, and all of these resources needed to be preserved. On this point, Marshall won the support of Indian Affairs Commissioner John Collier, who set up sixteen wilderness areas on reservations. That meant that no development would be allowed. The principle of no development became a key part of the Wilderness Society's creed.

Shortly after the October 19 car trip, the organizers sent out an invitation to people believed to be interested in a movement to preserve the American wilderness. The letter stated that wild places had to be kept "sound-proof and sight-proof from mechanized life." The recipients included Ernest Oberholtzer, a naturalist and leading defender of maintaining the Quetico-Superior region of Minnesota as a wilderness area; Robert Sterling Yard, a retired Park Service employee and critic of the government's conservation policies; and Aldo Leopold, who had written essays on wildlife preservation and the ethics of conservation. John Collier and John C. Merrian, president of the Carnegie Institute in Washington, declined to participate.

Leopold was a former National Park Service ranger, a manager of national forests in Arizona and New Mexico, and a professor of wildlife management at the University of Wisconsin after 1933. His stature among naturalists and preservationists led Marshall to suggest that he be offered the Wilderness Society's first presidency. Leopold initially agreed to serve, but he raised several questions concerning the group's goals, membership, and agenda. Marshall envisioned a small, tightly organized group of "thoroughly earnest" wilderness lovers who appreciated the beauty and purity of the outdoors. In contrast, Leopold, who was a scientist as well as a wil-

derness advocate, believed that the group should be open to like-minded explorers who searched for a place to study animals, plants, and their relationship with the environment. When the Wilderness Society held its first conference in Washington, D.C., in January, 1935, the Wisconsin professor did not attend. Yard and other members chose Marshall as the group's first president.

Marshall accepted the position, but his job with the government created a conflict of interest, and within a few months he had stepped down from the presidency. He could not promote wilderness and cooperate with the Bureau of Land Management at the same time because the bureau leased millions of acres of grasslands to western cattle ranchers. Secretary Ickes told Marshall that he could not hold both jobs, and so Marshall turned leadership of the society over to Robert Sterling Yard, the seventy-four-year-old former Park Service publicity director. Yard had quit that job after criticizing the agency for building too many roads and making parks too accessible to the public.

During its early years as a two-man organization, the Wilderness Society pushed for reversal of President Franklin D. Roosevelt's conservation priorities. Roosevelt considered himself a conservationist, but his priorities differed greatly from the society's. During the Great Depression of the 1930's, Roosevelt and his advisers stressed recreation, forestry and lumber milling, range management, soil and water conservation, land reclamation, and wilderness in their conservation agenda. The founders of the Wilderness Society agreed that these priorities needed to be reversed.

In its first statement, the society called for maintaining primitive areas in the United States. The statement asserted that, since many of the most beautiful areas in the country had already been opened to automobile traffic, all future road construction should be halted (though exceptions could made for unusually compelling cases).

By the end of its first year, the society had 576 members and was slowly growing. The pace of growth did not dishearten Marshall and Yard; both men believed that a small, well-organized group of wilderness lovers would have more impact on Interior Department policy than would a large group of sports lovers, tourists, and fishermen. Wilderness had spiritual as well as recreational or economic importance, they agreed, and only those people concerned about preserving the most obscure plants and animals in the country would have the proper understanding of the society's ethic. For these two men, preservation was important not only for human health but also for even deeper and more spiritual reasons. Main-

1934

taining undisturbed tracts of wilderness demonstrated a human commitment to living as part of the natural world rather than as destroyer and master of living things. The human being, in Aldo Leopold's view, must learn to think "like a mountain" and must give up the drive to conquer everything. Mountains prosper because of the great abundance of life that they support. Respect for all life was the key to survival for all things, living or nonliving. The Wilderness Society sought to impart these values.

Marshall contributed most of the money, and Yard wrote the society's newsletter and edited its magazine, *The Living Wilderness*. Yard did not want people in the group unless they were absolute purists on wilderness preservation. Aldo Leopold contributed an essay to the first issue of *The Living Wilderness* in which he summarized the society's view of the human place in nature. Humankind, he said, had become far too arrogant toward the natural world and had to relearn its place in the biosphere. People needed to treat nature with "an intelligent humility," and that meant leaving much of nature alone; no development or improvement was needed. Civilization was corrupt; nature was pure and free.

Yard promoted the society's cause before Congress, the National Park Service, and the Forest Service (he received a salary from Marshall). In his view, and in Marshall's, the Park Service had already gone too far in prioritizing accessibility over preservation. In the 1920's, the Park Service had built roads, tunnels, and tourist facilities in an effort to encourage more people to use the parks, and these actions had thoroughly upset wilderness supporters. In the mid-1930's, three projects especially troubled the preservationists: the Skyline Drive being built through Shenandoah National Park in Virginia, the proposed Ridgeline Highway cutting through the Great Smoky Mountains National Park, and the proposed 450-mile National Parkway along the Blue Ridge Mountains from Shenandoah to the Smokies. Park and Marshall set out to fight these projects' completion, but when their opposition met with little success, they turned away from the Park Service and decided to push for wilderness protection in the Forest Service. They reasoned that the national forests were more geared toward preservation, since they contained more than 188 million acres of land, while the national parks contained only 16 million acres.

Late in 1937, Marshall became the director of the Division of Recreation and Lands in the U.S. Forest Service. The agency had maintained primitive areas since 1929 but had no specific ban on road building or other improvements. The new director quickly set about issuing regulations restricting all development on Forest Service land. Unfortunately for wilderness advocates, Marshall died of heart failure early in 1939 while on a train trip to New York City. During his brief tenure with the Forest Service, however, he had set aside more than 14 million acres of land as pure wilderness.

Aldo Leopold became the intellectual leader of the Wilderness Society after Marshall's death. Leopold served as Yard's principal adviser and his link to other conservation groups around the country. He continued to write for *The Living Wilderness* and to expand his philosophy. In 1941, when the *Saturday Evening Post* accused Marshall of having been a member of the American Communist Party, Leopold came to his defense. The *Post* also informed its readers that Marshall's brother George, who was a member of the board of the Wilderness Society, maintained his membership in the party. Leopold publicly supported the Marshall brothers and maintained that, as long as George did his job, political labels were not important.

SIGNIFICANCE

The Wilderness Society became the nation's strongest supporter of untouched wilderness areas. While other conservation groups, such as the National Wildlife Society and the American Forestry Association, tried to make accommodations with hunters, developers, and tourists, the Wilderness Society tried to remain faithful to the ethic established by Marshall and elaborated by Leopold. As Leopold wrote in an article titled "The Conservation Ethic," human beings would have to totally transform their attitudes toward private property and nature if the earth were to survive. Land and the natural environment could no longer be treated like slaves to humankind. Human beings would have to learn that destruction and abuse were wrong, whether they were directed at human beings or at the land and nature.

According to its critics, the Wilderness Society advocated an antidevelopment agenda. The society's publications, indeed, argued that development led to "the enslavement of the earth," and that human beings needed to stop themselves from destroying the environment. Instead, the society argued, people needed to recognize their part in a community of plants and animals that needed to be treated with love and respect. It was imperative that some wild places be kept free from human access and economic development.

—Leslie V. Tischauser

Further Reading

Glover, James M. *A Wilderness Original: The Life of Bob Marshall*. Seattle: Mountaineers, 1986. Tells the life story of the founder of the Wilderness Society. Based on original research and on interviews with friends and relatives. Includes a balanced account of the founding of the Wilderness Society. Extensive bibliography and index.

Hays, Samuel P. *Conservation and the Gospel of Efficiency*. 1959. Reprint. Pittsburgh: University of Pittsburgh Press, 1999. A seminal work on the early history of conservation. Argues that the movement began as a search for greater efficiency in resource management, not as a democratic crusade against supposed business rapacity.

Meine, Curt. *Aldo Leopold: His Life and Work*. Madison: University of Wisconsin Press, 1988. The most detailed biography of the great conservationist. Based on extensive research in Leopold's vast collection of papers, it includes useful information about the aims and goals of the Wilderness Society. Detailed bibliography and useful index.

Merchant, Carolyn. *The Columbia Guide to American Environmental History*. New York: Columbia University Press, 2002. Discusses how humans and the environment have interacted throughout American history, including human impacts on animal species. Includes an environmental history time line and an extensive guide to resources.

Nash, Roderick Frazier. *The Rights of Nature: A History of Environmental Ethics*. Madison: University of Wisconsin Press, 1989. Nash is the foremost authority on the history of conservation movements in the United States. This book conveys the spirit of the movement, discusses its successes and failures, and describes the major difficulties involved in challenging the basic values of modern society: production and consumption. Both do harm and destroy much of the natural environment. The Wilderness Society was among the first groups to challenge these values. Nash includes a lengthy bibliography.

_____. *Wilderness and the American Mind*. 4th ed. New Haven, Conn.: Yale University Press, 2001. Nash's first history of the environmental movement and its challenge to modern ways of life. Includes much useful information about the founding of the Wilderness Society and especially about the role of Robert Marshall.

_____, ed. *The American Environment: Readings in the History of Conservation*. Reading, Mass.: Addison-Wesley, 1968. Collection of essays includes Robert Marshall's "Wilderness," written in 1930 and one of the few essays he ever published, and Aldo Leopold's "An Ethic for Man-Land Relations."

See also: May, 1903: Roosevelt and Muir Visit Yosemite; Jan. 3, 1905: Pinchot Becomes Head of the U.S. Forest Service; Jan. 5, 1905: National Audubon Society Is Established; Feb. 1, 1919: Lenin Approves the First Soviet Nature Preserve; Jan., 1922: Izaak Walton League Is Formed; 1924: Soviets Establish a Society for the Protection of Nature; June 3, 1924: Gila Wilderness Area Is Designated; May 30, 1930: Canadian National Parks Act; Sept., 1933: Marshall Writes *The People's Forests*; Jan., 1937-Feb., 1940: Adams Lobbies Congress to Preserve Kings Canyon; 1938: John Muir Trail Is Completed.

1934

November, 1934
YUKAWA PROPOSES THE EXISTENCE OF MESONS

Hideki Yukawa first postulated the existence of mesons, which later became known as pi-mesons or pions, as fundamental carriers of the nuclear force. His prediction of the particles' existence was confirmed in 1948, when they were discovered by Cecil Frank Powell. Moreover, although the particles later proved not to be fundamental, they were still intimately connected with the nuclear force, largely confirming Yukawa's other prediction.

LOCALE: Osaka, Japan
CATEGORIES: Physics; science and technology

KEY FIGURES
Hideki Yukawa (1907-1981), Japanese physicist
Cecil Frank Powell (1903-1969), British physicist
Erwin Schrödinger (1887-1961), Austrian physicist and philosopher
Werner Heisenberg (1901-1976), German physicist

SUMMARY OF EVENT
The existence of positively charged nuclear states was experimentally confirmed by physicists working between 1910 and 1920. They found that atomic nuclei contained several positive charges, which seemed to indicate that the centers of atoms should fly apart as a result of electromagnetic coulomb repulsion. The unexplained failure of atomic nuclei to explode became a foremost concern of theoretical physicists.

In 1932, three new particles—the neutron, the positron, and deuteron (a heavy nuclear isotope of hydrogen)—were discovered, adding confusion to some fledgling nuclear models that were emerging. In the same year, nuclei were broken apart by particle accelerators. Prior to 1932, only the proton, the electron, and the massless photon were known to inhabit the realm of elementary particle physics. Most working physicists were trying to model nuclear structure with some combination of protons, electrons, and the newly discovered neutrons, which caused considerable confusion.

At the age of twenty-two, Hideki Yukawa set two goals for himself: to investigate the quantum mechanics of the atomic nucleus and to develop relativistic quantum mechanics. Quantum mechanics had been developed by Werner Heisenberg, Max Born, and Erwin Schrödinger in the 1920's, and the wave descriptions that Schrödinger in particular had developed were appealing to Yukawa.

By 1932, Yukawa had arrived at the notion that the nuclear force (that is, the force holding nuclei together despite their electromagnetic repulsion) was a primary force and not derivable from electromagnetism or gravity. This was a break with most thinking in theoretical physics, which was attempting to explain nuclear structure as some combination of positive charges (protons) and negative charges (electrons). Unfortunately, there were a considerable number of problems associated with Yukawa's theory. First, electrons and protons each have a "spin" of $\frac{1}{2}$, as does the neutron. If one takes as an example the deuteron, the simplest compound nucleus in nature, one finds that it has a charge of +1 and a spin of 1. If it were composed of two protons and one electron, it would have a charge of +1, but its spin would be either $\frac{1}{2}$ or $\frac{3}{2}$, because spins, like charges, are arithmetically additive.

In October, 1934, Yukawa became convinced that a meson was responsible for nuclear forces. Mesons ("middle ones") originally were defined as being midsized or middleweights, as compared with lightweight leptons ("light ones") or heavyweight baryons ("massive ones"). Yukawa realized that the small range of nuclear forces required a force carrier of a particular mass. Nuclear forces, as was known at the time, had a range of the order of only 0.02 trillionth of a centimeter, or 2×10^{-15} meters. Yukawa saw that there was an inverse relationship between mass and distance or range. A small-mass particle such as the electron acted over distances hundreds of times greater than the diameter of the nucleus. Protons and neutrons, being relatively massive, acted over distances of the order of $\frac{1}{10}$ that diameter.

In November, 1934, Yukawa presented his initial paper on the existence of such mesons to the Osaka branch of the Physico-Mathematical Society of Japan. Yukawa's paper, which later earned him the Nobel Prize in Physics, postulated the existence of what were to become known as pi-mesons, or pions. He concluded that their masses should be about two hundred times that of the electron, or about $\frac{1}{10}$ that of the proton or neutron. In fact, when pions were discovered experimentally after World War II, their masses were found to be about 270 times that of the electron, or $\frac{1}{7}$ that of the proton: The uncharged pion, called the pi-naught, has a mass 264 times that of the electron, whereas the charged pions—pi-plus and pi-minus—each have a mass about 271 times that of the electron. Yukawa wrote his paper in English, and it was published in the February, 1935, *Proceedings of the Physico-Mathematical Society of Japan.*

Yukawa viewed the nuclear force as a quantum effect whereby a sizable quantum of energy was exchanged between the proton and the neutron in the nucleus. His original paper called for only two such quanta, the pi-plus and the pi-minus. He did not predict the existence of the pi-naught. These pions, or nuclear quanta, have 0 spin and thus contribute nothing to the nuclear spin states of the particles they compose. This 0 spin feature makes them "bosons," obeying Bose-Einstein statistics, which in turn allows two or more to exist in the same quantum states within a specific nucleus.

In 1937, two American physicists, Seth Neddermeyer and Carl David Anderson, discovered what they thought was Yukawa's meson family in cosmic rays. Ten years later, it was generally agreed that their particle, now named the muon, or mu-meson, was not the carrier of the strong nuclear interaction, even though it had almost exactly the mass and charge states predicted by Yukawa.

In 1948, Cecil Frank Powell and his coworkers at Bristol, England, found pi-plus and pi-minus meson tracks in photographic emulsions left for several months on mountain tops. Only the year before, in 1947, the American physicist J. Robert Oppenheimer had suggested in a cogent theoretical argument that the uncharged pion not predicted by Yukawa might also exist. It was found experimentally in 1950 at both Berkeley and Stanford in California.

With Powell's discovery confirming his prediction, Yukawa had fulfilled his first research objective in bringing quantum theory into nuclear physics to explain nuclear structure. That he had done so in such a spectacular way earned for him the 1949 Nobel Prize in Physics and elevated the reputation of Japanese physics in the worldwide scientific community. Powell himself won the award in 1950 for developing the photographic emulsion technique of detecting subatomic particles. Yukawa was able to enter the scientific elite by predicting theoretically the existence of a clearly detectable family of subatomic particles whose mass, spin, and charge he was able to describe. Seldom if ever has such a clear, incisive, and elegant prediction been verified in physics. Pions proved to be universal carriers of nuclear force at low energies (or residual strong force) and largely responsible for holding nuclei together.

SIGNIFICANCE

Yukawa's paper did not catch the attention of the physics community until the discovery of muons two years later. Yukawa wrote a letter to *Nature*, a prestigious science journal in England, stating that this discovery might be the particles that he had predicted. The editors rejected his paper and claim, but he published a note in a Japanese journal that established precedence for his claim. The discovery of muons at several places throughout the world in the next few years motivated physicists to look for explanations of what they might be, and Yukawa's mesons seemed close enough to focus the attention of many theorists.

Yukawa's paper clearly delineated nuclear forces from the electromagnetic and gravitational forces of nature and laid the theoretical groundwork for accounting for the behavior of protons in the nucleus by recourse to a separate fundamental force. Later physicists would complicate Yukawa's model, especially once it came to be believed that pions are not themselves fundamental particles but are made up of such particles, known as quarks. A model then developed in which "strong nuclear force" referred to a force—carried by particles called gluons—that holds quarks together, while the force holding protons and neutrons together came to be seen as a side effect of strong force, known as simply "nuclear force," or sometimes "strong residual force." However, even within this more complicated model, it was still believed that pions were largely responsible for binding protons and neutrons together, making Yukawa's prediction all the more impressive.

Physicists now recognize hundreds of mesons, of which Yukawa's pions were the first predicted types. Newer and higher-energy particle accelerators have caused the number of known mesons to rise almost exponentially every decade since Yukawa proposed them. More than two hundred mesons are firmly established, and more have given experimental hints of existing. Most experimental physicists expect that many more mesons will be discovered in the future as newer and more energetic particle accelerators are built. Many of the newer mesons are very heavy, much heavier than protons and neutrons; therefore, the word "meson" has lost its middle-weight meaning and now designates any integral spin particle that undergoes the strong nuclear interaction, as defined by Yukawa in 1935. Modern elementary physics owes its existence to Yukawa's efforts in predicting pions.

—*John P. Kenny*

FURTHER READING

Böhm, Manfred, Ansgar Denner, and Hans Joos. *Gauge Theories of the Strong and Electroweak Interaction.* Stuttgart: Teubner, 2001. Details the place of pions within the complex set of subatomic interactions carrying the fundamental forces of nature. Bibliographic references and index.

1934

Brown, Laurie M. "Hideki Yukawa and the Meson Theory." *Physics Today* 39 (December, 1986): 55-62. This brief article describes how Yukawa's ideas contrasted with and were received by physicists of the time.

Fuchs, Walter R. *Physics for the Modern Mind.* Translated by M. Wilson and M. Wheaton. New York: Macmillan. 1967. Chapter 7 is devoted to elementary particles but gives a series of models of how Yukawa's meson exchange works between protons and neutrons in nuclei by considering pions as balls in a ballgame. Excellent descriptions and graphics for precollege-age students.

Nobel Foundation. *Physics.* Vol. 3. New York: Elsevier, 1964. Contains Yukawa's brief Nobel acceptance speech and a good motivation essay on his work. The Yukawa article is followed by one on Powell, the experimental discoverer of the pions; it sheds considerable perspective on Yukawa's insights.

Stuewer, Roger E., ed. *Nuclear Physics in Retrospect.* Minneapolis: University of Minnesota Press, 1979. A good reference for physics students and those interested in majoring in physics in college. Gives a good view of Yukawa's contribution as seen by a fellow nuclear theorist.

Weinberg, Steven. *The Discovery of Subatomic Particles.* Rev. ed. New York: Cambridge University Press, 2003. Discusses the discovery and importance of pions alongside muons and W and Z particles (the carriers of weak nuclear force). Bibliographic references and index.

Yukawa, Hideki. *Tabibito (The Traveler).* Translated by L. Brown and R. Yoshida. Singapore: World Scientific, 1982. This book is a personal testament of Yukawa from his early childhood until he published his mesonic theory of nuclear forces in 1935. Includes an excellent description of how working Japanese academic scientists lived and worked before World War II.

SEE ALSO: Dec. 10, 1901: Röntgen Wins the Nobel Prize for the Discovery of X Rays; 1902: Zsigmondy Invents the Ultramicroscope; Mar., 1905: Einstein Describes the Photoelectric Effect; Dec. 10, 1906: Thomson Wins the Nobel Prize for Discovering the Electron; 1912-1913: Bohr Uses Quantum Theory to Identify Atomic Structure; Aug. 7 and 12, 1912: Hess Discovers Cosmic Rays; Nov.-Dec., 1933: Fermi Proposes the Neutrino Theory of Beta Decay.

December, 1934
STALIN BEGINS THE PURGE TRIALS

Soviet leader Joseph Stalin undertook a brutal campaign of terror against those he believed to be his political enemies in the Communist Party.

ALSO KNOWN AS: Great Purge
LOCALE: Soviet Union
CATEGORIES: Atrocities and war crimes; government and politics

KEY FIGURES
Joseph Stalin (Joseph Vissarionovich Dzhugashvili; 1878-1953), general secretary of the Central Committee of the Communist Party of the Soviet Union, 1922-1953
Sergey Mironovich Kirov (1886-1934), secretary of the Communist Party in Leningrad, 1926-1934
Leon Trotsky (Lev Davidovich Bronstein; 1879-1940), Russian revolutionary leader and Soviet politician
Nikolay Ivanovich Yezhov (1895-1940), head of the NKVD (Soviet secret police) during the most intense period of the purge

Lev Borisovich Kamenev (Lev Borisovich Rosenfeld; 1883-1936), Soviet politician and former chairman of the Moscow Soviet, 1918-1925, and of the Politburo, 1923-1924
Grigory Yevseyevich Zinovyev (Ovsel Gershon Aronov Radomyslsky; 1883-1936), Soviet politician and former head of the Comintern, 1919

SUMMARY OF EVENT
The murder of Sergey Mironovich Kirov, the Communist Party leader in Leningrad and a member of the Soviet Politburo (policy-making committee), gave Joseph Stalin an excuse to begin a reign of terror similar to those carried out by earlier Russian leaders Ivan the Terrible and Peter the Great. Scholars have engaged in debate for some time concerning what motivated Stalin to embark on such a destructive course. Some have argued that he was disappointed by the failure of his First Five-Year Plan (1928-1933) to achieve all the goals he had set, whereas others have suggested that his intent was to cen-

tralize power in his own hands at the expense of the Communist Party. More than a few have contended that the purging stands as proof of Stalin's unstable and unbalanced state of mind.

Although the Great Purge began in December, 1934, there were harbingers of what was to come during the period from 1927 (when Stalin consolidated his power) to 1934. On several occasions, the party, at Stalin's urging, had removed hundreds of local Communist leaders from their posts. They were charged with falling under capitalist influence or not pushing hard enough to fulfill Stalin's drive to collectivize the countryside. The areas most affected were Odessa, Kiev, and the Urals. These "preliminary purges," widespread as they were, paled by comparison to what occurred after the murder of Kirov in December, 1934.

Kirov was shot by Leonid Nikolayev, a Communist

Party member described by some at the time as disgruntled. Stalin immediately blamed the assassination on his principal political enemies, Leon Trotsky (in exile at the time), Lev Borisovich Kamenev, and Grigory Yevseyevich Zinovyev. It is now generally agreed by scholars that Stalin himself arranged the murder of Kirov, his friend and ally, to generate an excuse to eliminate his rivals.

On the day of Kirov's murder, Stalin asked the party to issue a decree eliminating civil and legal rights for all persons accused of "terroristic acts." This made it possible for the government to arrest, detain (for the purpose of gaining forced confessions), or execute anyone it wished. In January, 1935, Kamenev, Zinovyev, and two others were tried, convicted, and sentenced to prison for their alleged roles in the Kirov murder. The length of the sentences was irrelevant, as none of those arrested was

1934

Joseph Stalin (left) in 1925 with Lev Borisovich Kamenev (second from right) and Grigory Yevseyevich Zinovyev (right). (AP/Wide World Photos)

ever released. This was the beginning of what became known as the "purification" of the Communist Party. Stalin began with Kamenev and Zinovyev because he perceived them as especially treacherous. They had once worked closely with him in the 1920's but then had turned against him and given their loyalty to Trotsky. After the January convictions, hundreds, perhaps thousands, of party members came under suspicion. Many were shot, detained, or sent to distant regions of the Soviet Union. Although some in the Politburo were uneasy with this development, Stalin insisted that it was necessary to protect the country from those who wished to "wreck" his great drive for full communization.

The first victims when Stalin began purging the party were those considered to be "Old Bolsheviks," party members who had been associated with Vladimir Ilich Lenin and Trotsky during the 1917 revolution and in the formative days of the Soviet state. Many had been supporters of Lenin's moderate New Economic Policy begun in 1921. The greatest number of those purged in 1935 were individuals who, after Lenin's death in 1924, had supported Trotsky's claim to succeed Lenin as head of the party and the state. Between 1924 and 1927, Trotsky and Stalin competed for control. Stalin was ultimately successful, and Trotsky went into exile for the remainder of his life. Stalin continued to insist, however, that Trotsky's followers ("Trotskyites"), guided by their leader from abroad, were working to remove him from power. Having been established as his enemies, they became convenient scapegoats to explain every failure that Stalin experienced. He could simply say that the Trotskyites had wrecked his plans.

In 1936, Stalin intensified the purging. Public trials ("show trials") were held in which those accused were expected to confess their misdeeds and to implicate others involved in plots against Stalin. Kamenev and Zinovyev, already in prison, were among sixteen Old Bolsheviks put on public trial in August, 1936. All were charged with conducting a terrorist campaign at Trotsky's bidding, and all were sentenced to death. From that point, the purging began to mushroom. After a second round of show trials in January, 1937, there was no way to brake the terror that Stalin had instigated in 1935. No one except Stalin was insulated from the possibility of being charged as a Trotskyite.

For the first eighteen months after Stalin started the purges, the country at large remained relatively unaffected. That changed in 1937. Nikolay Ivanovich Yezhov, the new chief of the NKVD (secret police), understood that Stalin expected him to dispatch all of the Soviet leader's political opponents as quickly as possible. With Yezhov in charge, the purging became much better organized. The NKVD began to arrest people by the thousands, usually in the predawn hours. Anyone accused of disloyalty to Stalin was presumed to be guilty of "wrecking." Desperate to prove their loyalty to the regime, officials and ordinary citizens began to accuse others of treason. Neighbors denounced neighbors, fellow workers denounced one another, subordinates denounced their superiors, and relatives denounced relatives. In each instance, the person denounced to a local official was arrested and charged as an "enemy of the people." Falling victim to the purge was largely a matter of chance for those outside the party, but those most frequently denounced were persons of foreign birth or members of minority groups, especially Ukrainians, Jews, and Armenians. All who were accused were expected to confess (the NKVD used torture when persuasion failed) and to implicate others.

There is evidence that Stalin was aware of the effect on the country of the expanded purge, but by the middle of 1937 even he was powerless to slow it down. The general hysteria in the country made the terror an unstoppable force. Citizens throughout the Soviet Union lived in fear of a late-night or early-morning knock on the door. The terror reached its peak in 1937 and early 1938; thereafter, the NKVD no longer had sufficient resources to respond to the huge number of accusations it received. Yezhov, architect of this worst phase of the purging, was himself charged with "Trotskyite" leanings in 1938 and purged. The coming of World War II in the late summer of 1939 finally brought the purging to an end, as internal enemies were replaced by external enemies and capitalist powers became temporary allies of the Soviet Union.

SIGNIFICANCE

Stalin's purging of political opponents created great problems for the Communist Party and, ultimately, for the country at large. Those officials and party leaders who were purged had to be replaced, and the replacements were frequently ill equipped to handle their new responsibilities. The dimensions of the purging serve to illustrate this point. More than one-half of the Communist Party's Central Committee (78 of 139 members) were purged, and more than one-third of those who sat in the Politburo between 1927 and 1938 were expelled. The army and the government suffered staggering losses: Thirteen of the fifteen commanders of the Soviet Army were purged between 1935 and 1938, as were fourteen of the eighteen ministers of state. Thus, throughout the ordeal, the purgers were themselves always subject to being purged.

As the purging expanded beyond the confines of the party, the effect on the country became devastating. Business and industry came virtually to a standstill, as workers and supervisors were afraid to make an error, lest they be charged with "wrecking." In the major cities—Moscow, Leningrad, and Kiev—there was little activity, as residents tried to limit their associations. The Moscow telephone directory was not published in 1938 because most people wanted to keep their telephone numbers and street addresses secret. Artists, writers, and intellectuals dared not express themselves freely. All were expected to produce works that somehow glorified the Stalinist state and reflected negatively on what had existed before Stalin. Stalin wanted paintings of tanks and factories, not romantic sunsets or anything that might be considered bourgeois. Writers of history were to make it clear that Stalin's regime represented the culmination of all that had gone before in Russia's past.

The most important political consequence of the Great Purge was that Stalin obliterated all political debate and discussion. Members of the Politburo no longer raised questions during their meetings with Stalin. He had succeeded in creating one-person rule, or, as Nikita S. Khrushchev called it, "the cult of personality." Although World War II made Stalin a hero in the Soviet Union, the legacy of fear that he instigated was not seriously challenged until three years after his death, when Khrushchev, who had risen to prominence as Stalin's ally during the purge, addressed the Communist Party Congress. In that February, 1956, speech, Khrushchev—before an astonished group of party leaders—condemned Stalin as a murderer and Stalinism as a misguided formula for a successful Communist state.

—*Ronald K. Huch*

FURTHER READING

Conquest, Robert. *The Great Terror: A Reassessment.* New York: Oxford University Press, 1990. An expanded and revised edition of Conquest's pioneering 1968 work on the subject.

_____. *The Great Terror: Stalin's Purge of the Thirties.* Rev. ed. New York: Macmillan, 1973. This is the most popular, most readable, and perhaps most thoroughly documented account of the Great Purge. Conquest, an English political writer, provides a comprehensive discussion of all aspects of the purge. His epilogue on the "Heritage of the Terror" is especially valuable. Scholars have questioned some of Con-

quest's conclusions. Appendixes, bibliographical note, select bibliography, and index.

_____. *Stalin and the Kirov Murder.* New York: Oxford University Press, 1989. This small book investigates Stalin's probable responsibility in causing Kirov's death.

_____. *Stalin: Breaker of Nations.* New York: Penguin Books, 1991. This psychological study emphasizes Stalin's paranoia and his desire to achieve massive power.

Crowley, Joan Frances, and Dan Vaillancourt. *Lenin to Gorbachev: Three Generations of Communists.* Arlington Heights, Ill.: Harlan Davidson, 1989. A very useful introduction to Communist leaders from Karl Marx and Friedrich Engels to Gorbachev. Crowley and Vaillancourt write in a style that is clear and without jargon. The section on Stalin is excellent. Suggestions for further reading and index.

Getty, J. Arch, and Oleg V. Naumov. *The Road to Terror: Stalin and the Self-Destruction of the Bolsheviks, 1932-1939.* New Haven, Conn.: Yale University Press, 1999. This detailed account of Stalin's campaign is the first to utilize formerly secret Soviet documents. Includes appendixes.

Levytsky, Boris. *The Stalinist Terror in the Thirties: Documentation from the Soviet Press.* Stanford, Calif.: Hoover Institution Press, 1974. Includes more than two hundred biographies of purge victims, plus the later Soviet rehabilitation campaign of some of those unjustly accused and punished.

_____. *The Uses of Terror: The Soviet Secret Police, 1917-1970.* New York: Coward, McCann & Geoghegan, 1972. Broad survey of the topic includes a description and assessment of the purges of the 1930's.

Potok, Chaim. *The Gates of November: Chronicles of the Slepak Family.* New York: Alfred A. Knopf, 1996. Biography of a family who survived Stalin's purge.

Radzinsky, Edvard. *Stalin: The First In-Depth Biography Based on Explosive Documents from Russia's Secret Archives.* New York: Doubleday, 1996. Provides more details on specific cases and Stalin's role during the purges, based on previously classified files.

Thurston, Robert W. *Life and Terror in Stalin's Russia: 1934-1941.* New Haven, Conn.: Yale University Press, 1996. A controversial account of Stalin's purges, proposing an alternative interpretation of the terror campaign. Illustrated, includes maps.

Volkogonov, Dmitri. *Stalin: Triumph and Tragedy.* New

1934

York: Grove Weidenfeld, 1991. This substantial biography by a noted Russian historian provides a post-
Communist perspective of Stalin.

Von Laue, Theodore. *Why Lenin? Why Stalin?* 2d ed.
Philadelphia: J. B. Lippincott, 1971. This may be the
single best essay written about the formative years
of the Communist Revolution. Von Laue's grasp of
Russian history and its application to early twentieth
century events is impressive. Highly recommended
for all readers. Suggestions for further reading and
index.

SEE ALSO: 1917-1924: Russian Communists Inaugurate
the Red Terror; Mar. 2-6, 1919: Lenin Establishes the
Comintern; May 18, 1928: Shakhty Case Debuts
Show Trials in Moscow; Oct. 1, 1928: Stalin Introduces Central Planning; Dec., 1932-Spring, 1934:
Great Famine Strikes the Soviet Union; Aug. 2, 1933:
Soviets Open the White Sea-Baltic Canal; Nov. 16,
1933: United States Recognizes Russia's Bolshevik
Regime; Summer, 1939: Stalin Suppresses the Russian Orthodox Church; Dec., 1940: Koestler Examines the Dark Side of Communism.

December 1, 1934
GOODMAN BEGINS HIS *LET'S DANCE* BROADCASTS

Benny Goodman's Let's Dance *broadcasts on network
radio led to the launching of the "swing era," in which
big band music achieved huge popularity.*

LOCALE: New York, New York
CATEGORIES: Music; radio and television;
entertainment

KEY FIGURES
Benny Goodman (1909-1986), virtuoso clarinetist and
bandleader who helped establish swing music as the
dominant popular style of 1935-1945
Fletcher "Smack" Henderson (1897-1952), pioneering
black orchestrator and bandleader
John Hammond (1910-1987), scion of a wealthy
family who recorded some of the most important
American musicians
Gene Krupa (1909-1973), drummer whose drive and
showmanship contributed to the popularity of the
Goodman band
Teddy Wilson (1912-1986), African American pianist
who joined Goodman's trio and became part of the
first famous integrated group in American music
Lionel Hampton (1908-2002), vibraphonist and
drummer who helped turn Goodman's trio into an
influential jazz quartet

SUMMARY OF EVENT
Benny Goodman's prodigious talent as a clarinetist freed
him from an early life of poverty in a Jewish ghetto in
Chicago; by the age of thirteen, he was a member of the
American Musicians Union, and he became a full-time
professional within the following year. He quickly combined his traditional European classical training with an

interest in the New Orleans-style jazz that was flourish-
ing in Chicago and paid special attention to important
players such as Jimmy Noone, Albert Nicholas, Johnny
Dodds, and Barney Bigard. Goodman played with various dance bands, and at the age of sixteen he joined
drummer Ben Pollack's Chicago-based band, which was
working in California at the time.

In 1926, Goodman made his first recordings with Pollack, and he had recorded under his own name by 1928.
He played with most of the promising white jazz players
in Chicago, including Dave Tough, Bud Freeman, Gene
Krupa, and the visiting Bix Beiderbecke, before moving
with Pollack to New York, where he continued to record
and broaden his experience. As economic times became
increasingly difficult, the talented Goodman found work
in a variety of dance bands and as a freelance musician
playing in theater-pit bands, film sound-track studios,
and radio-studio orchestras. His first love was jazz, and
in 1934 he decided to form a big band that would satisfy
both his taste in music and his need for stable employment.

On a shoestring budget, Goodman assembled a band,
and with the encouragement of his future brother-in-law
John Hammond, he landed an engagement at the new
Billy Rose Music Hall. After four months, the management changed and the band was fired. During this period,
Goodman struggled to give his undistinguished band a
musical identity. Plans to take an all-star, racially mixed
band to England fell through, and Goodman hung all his
hopes on being hired for an exciting new radio program
sponsored by the National Biscuit Company (later
Nabisco) to advertise its new product, Ritz crackers. The
program, called *Let's Dance*, was to feature a "sweet"

band, a Latin band, and a "hot" or jazz band in a three-hour program broadcast on Saturday nights to fifty-three stations nationwide on the National Broadcasting Company (NBC) network. Goodman narrowly won the audition in the hot band category, in which he played a brassy and rhythmic jazz-oriented dance music that became known as swing.

On December 1, 1934, the Benny Goodman Band made its first broadcast in the *Let's Dance* series before a large studio audience. Goodman's contract provided for generous salaries and the purchase of the musical arrangements necessary to supply a band of fourteen musicians with fresh material for each program. These written arrangements were essential to the establishment of the band's identifying and distinctive sound, and Goodman, who was not an arranger, set about commissioning writers who could work to his specifications. Goodman's ideal was to assemble a band that featured ample room for improvised solos, a disciplined yet swinging ensemble, and an inspiring rhythm section. As his career progressed, Goodman made frequent personnel changes in an attempt to find better musicians, and this contributed to his reputation as a difficult employer. The most significant of the early additions were the flamboyant drummer Gene Krupa and the gifted trumpet player Bunny Berigan, who would both become famous musicians in their own right.

Benny Goodman plays the clarinet with his orchestra at the Roseland Ballroom in New York City in 1938. (AP/Wide World Photos)

1934

Goodman had long been an admirer of Fletcher "Smack" Henderson's orchestra, an aggregation of African American musicians that had been well known among other musicians since the mid-1920's. Henderson and his collaborators are usually credited with perfecting the basic formulas used by most large jazz-oriented bands in their written orchestrations. Unfortunately, Henderson's abilities as a leader did not match his musical talent; by 1934 his influential band was disintegrating and the Depression was exacerbating his financial problems. John Hammond, a member of the Vanderbilt family and one of the most important nonmusicians in American musical history, was a lifelong supporter and promoter of African American artists. Hammond encouraged Goodman to buy some of Henderson's arrangements for his own band. In effect, this meant adopting the Henderson sound.

Henderson's influence strengthened when he agreed to write orchestrations especially for Goodman, whose well-trained band executed them with a flawless rhythmic drive seldom heard in white bands of the day. Although Goodman continued to use a number of talented arrangers, the bulk of his band's repertoire (including important pieces such as "King Porter Stomp" and "Down South Camp Meetin'") and much of its fundamental style originated with Fletcher Henderson. Goodman put his own stamp on the band through his insistence on excellence and his meticulous attention to nuance and musical detail. His virtuoso clarinet playing became a trademark that appealed to a wide audience while remaining true to its jazz roots.

The national exposure afforded by the *Let's Dance* broadcasts started Goodman on the road to stardom if not immediate popular success. However, when the *Let's Dance* series was canceled after twenty-six broadcasts as a result of the sponsor's labor troubles, Goodman found himself out of work. Hired to replace Guy Lombardo and his orchestra at New York's prestigious Hotel Roosevelt, Goodman's band was abruptly fired as too loud and jazzy. In a desperate attempt to save the band, Goodman embarked on a long cross-country tour. Audiences ranged from mildly enthusiastic to indifferent, and the dispirited Goodman expected that he would be forced to disband in California. When the band appeared at the Palomar Ballroom in Los Angeles, however, it was greeted by excited crowds of mainly young people who came not only to dance but also to listen. The way had been prepared by the *Let's Dance* live broadcasts, the local disc jockeys who often featured Goodman's recorded music, and the increased availability and sales of the records Goodman had made during and after the period of his network broadcasts. Crowds grew in size and enthusiasm, and the Palomar engagement was extended from one month to two. Public taste was shifting and Goodman, soon to be dubbed the "King of Swing" by a press agent, had caught the crest of the wave.

SIGNIFICANCE

After his triumph at the Palomar, Goodman's next major appearance was at Chicago's Congress Hotel, where an engagement of one month was extended to six. During this period, the popular press joined jazz journalists in paying increasing attention to Goodman's music. Goodman's success allowed him, with the encouragement of some Chicago socialites, to confront the de facto racial segregation that existed in American entertainment. At a specially arranged benefit performance, both Goodman and Krupa played on stage with a group of black musicians in what Goodman believed was the first integrated performance before a paying audience in the United States.

Jazz is essentially the product of African American culture, and most white jazz musicians had taken outstanding black musicians as their models. Interracial performances were common at informal jam sessions and had occurred from time to time in public, but they seldom took place at important venues. Goodman himself was one of many who had played with racially mixed groups on recordings, where color could be ignored, but those who controlled the music industry were convinced that the public would not accept black and white musicians who openly performed together as equals. Despite his own concern about the financial and other consequences,

Goodman decided to use his growing popularity to publicly challenge prevailing racism.

Goodman already had made several popular trio recordings with Gene Krupa and the impressive young black pianist Teddy Wilson. With the urging of John Hammond and others, he introduced his trio as part of a special concert. When the feared adverse reaction did not materialize, Goodman made trio appearances a part of his regular band performances, but he did not yet dare to actually integrate his band. Instead, he presented the trio as a unit by itself. Despite the tentative nature of Goodman's initial actions, he showed considerable courage in breaking the color barrier, and his success was well publicized. When Goodman expanded his trio to a quartet in 1936, he hired another black musician, vibraphonist Lionel Hampton. Wilson and Hampton's association with Goodman made both famous, and Hampton credited Goodman's example with opening up opportunities for African Americans not only in music but also eventually in baseball and other fields. Although notoriously parsimonious, Goodman accepted the financial and social problems that threatened integrated groups. He wanted the best musicians he could find and continued to employ African Americans throughout the rest of his career.

Goodman's small groups also had an influence on American culture. He often set up his trio or quartet on the dance floor so that audiences were enticed to pay close attention to these exciting ensembles. This chamber music approach introduced a broad audience to the conventions and delights of superior small-group jazz performance and presented jazz as both an accompaniment to dancing and socializing and as music worthy of serious attention. Goodman's example was copied frequently by other big band leaders, including his rival clarinetist Artie Shaw, who formed a small group called the Gramercy Five. Some critics who found Goodman's big band performances artistically uneven point to his trio, quartet, and sextet recordings as examples of his highest musical achievements.

As Goodman's fame and success increased, the jazz that his band and others like it played became the popular music of the day. For about a decade, commercial success accompanied a significant elevation in the public's musical taste. Not only leaders but also sidemen such as Goodman's outstanding trumpet soloist Harry James became celebrities on a par with the most famous film stars. Goodman's band itself appeared in a number of Hollywood films, as did other swing bands such as those of Duke Ellington, Tommy Dorsey, and Glenn Miller.

Goodman's success in presenting jazz as a respectable music purely for listening was demonstrated triumphantly in 1938 by his historic concert at Carnegie Hall, a hallowed venue previously reserved largely for classical music. The absentminded Goodman discovered twelve years later that he had recordings of the concert, and these records went on to sell more than one million copies and became some of the most popular jazz recordings of all time. As Goodman sought to make jazz more respected, his classical music performances enhanced his own credibility as well as that of other jazz musicians. Many who had disparaged jazz and its players came to see that the boundaries between genres were fundamentally artificial as Goodman commissioned and performed music by such composers as Béla Bartók, Aaron Copland, and Paul Hindemith.

During the height of swing music's popularity in the late 1930's and early 1940's, there were at least fifty dance bands with national reputations and significant followings and hundreds of lesser-known and local professional orchestras. Dance styles such as the jitterbug were based on swing music, fan clubs boosted individual bands, and thousands of high school and college students, especially young women, flocked to performances, where they often mobbed the bandstands and drowned out the music in their enthusiasm (this occurred in 1937 at Goodman's legendary Paramount Theater appearances in New York City). Radio broadcasts, record sales, public dances and performances, and extensive media coverage all confirmed that swing was the period's dominant form of American musical entertainment, and Goodman had played a central role in its development.

—Douglas Rollins

FURTHER READING

Baron, Stanley. "Introduction." In *Benny, King of Swing: A Pictorial Biography Based on Benny Goodman's Personal Archives*, by Benny Goodman. New York: William Morrow, 1979. The handsome coffee-table book has more than two hundred photographs and Baron's long introduction, replete with interesting anecdotes and biographical details but little musical commentary. No index.

Collier, James Lincoln. *Benny Goodman and the Swing Era*. New York: Oxford University Press, 1989. A comprehensive and detailed study of Goodman, his many sidemen, and their music within the musical, social, and historical context of the swing period. Its scholarly method and personal opinion make this a lively if at times quirky approach to the subject. An attempt is made to debunk many popular myths. Photographs, a selected discography, and index.

Connor, D. Russell, and Warren W. Hicks. *BG on the Record: A Bio-Discography of Benny Goodman*. New Rochelle, N.Y.: Arlington House, 1969. A standard and highly detailed reference for the study of most of Goodman's recordings, including dates, locations, and personnel. Biographical details and anecdotes place the recordings in context. Photographs and a variety of indexes, including song titles, artists, and arrangers.

Douglas, George H. *The Early Days of Radio Broadcasting*. 1987. Reprint. Jefferson, N.C.: McFarland, 2001. Provides excellent coverage of the start of networking and the rise of announcers, news, and sportscasting. An admiring and sympathetic—although not uncritical—view of the subjects. Includes photographs, bibliography, and index.

Douglas, Susan J. *Listening In: Radio and the American Imagination*. New York: Crown, 1999. Focuses on the effects of radio listening on Americans' social, political, and economic attitudes and beliefs. Covers the period from radio's golden age in the 1930's to the end of the twentieth century.

Goodman, Benny, and Irving Kolodin. *The Kingdom of Swing*. New York: Frederick Ungar, 1939. Goodman's autobiography, written near the height of his success. Highly readable. A few photographs, no index.

Hammond, John, with Irving Townsend. *John Hammond on Record: An Autobiography*. New York: Penguin Books, 1981. By the man who discovered and first recorded performers ranging from Billie Holiday and Count Basie to Bob Dylan and Bruce Springsteen. Hammond, associated with Goodman through common interests and family ties (Goodman married his sister several years after the men had first met), provides an insider's view of Goodman's career. Photographs, a selective discography, and index.

Schuller, Gunther. "The 'King' of Swing: Benny Goodman." In *The Swing Era: The Development of Jazz, 1930-1945*. New York: Oxford University Press, 1989. A valuable and at times technical evaluation of Goodman's musical achievements by one of the foremost experts in the field. Transcribed musical illustrations, a selected discography, glossaries, and indexes.

Southern, Eileen. *The Music of Black Americans: A History*. 3d ed. New York: W. W. Norton, 1997. Excel-

1934

lent scholarly account of the subject provides both background and important detail. Includes critical bibliography and discography as well as numerous selections from scores and an extensive index.

SEE ALSO: 1910's: Handy Ushers in the Commercial Blues Era; 1920's: Harlem Renaissance; Jan. 16, 1920: Formation of Les Six; Feb. 12, 1924: Gersh-

win's *Rhapsody in Blue* Premieres in New York; Nov., 1925: Armstrong Records with the Hot Five; 1929: *Hallelujah* Is the First Important Black Musical Film; 1930's: Americans Embrace Radio Entertainment; 1933: Billie Holiday Begins Her Recording Career; Sept. 6, 1935: *Top Hat* Establishes the Astaire-Rogers Dance Team.

December 6, 1934
BALANCHINE'S *SERENADE* INAUGURATES AMERICAN BALLET

George Balanchine's Serenade *presaged a new era for ballet in the United States.*

LOCALE: Avery Memorial Theater, Hartford, Connecticut
CATEGORY: Dance

KEY FIGURES
George Balanchine (1904-1983), Russian American choreographer
Lincoln Kirstein (1907-1996), American impresario
Edward Warburg (1908-1992), American patron of the arts

SUMMARY OF EVENT
Born Georgi Melitonovich Balanchivadze in St. Petersburg, Russia, George Balanchine was enrolled in the Imperial Ballet School in that city at age ten and danced in productions at the Mariinsky Theatre. After becoming known for his experimental choreography, he formed a small troupe of dancers to tour Germany in 1924, with the full intention of never returning to the revolutionary turmoil in Soviet Russia. He joined Sergei Diaghilev's Ballets Russes the next year and remained the company's chief choreographer until the company disbanded after Diaghilev's death four years later. For the next three years, Balanchine worked in London, Paris, Monte Carlo, and Copenhagen for various theaters, but the insecurity of this peripatetic life did not appeal to him. When Lincoln Kirstein appeared on the scene in 1933 and offered him the directorship of a company that was yet to come into existence, Balanchine took a gamble and moved to the United States, a country that had fascinated him for much of his life. This decision was to change the shape of American ballet.

Balanchine was not the first Russian dancer to seek his fortune in the United States. Anna Pavlova had toured the country from coast to coast beginning in 1910, and

several of her partners had settled in the United States to teach. Vaslav Nijinsky led Diaghilev's Ballets Russes for a series of American appearances in 1916. Other of Diaghilev's chief choreographers and dancers, most notably Michel Fokine and Adolf Bolm, had come to the United States to teach and perform. By the time Balanchine arrived on October 17, 1933, well-established pockets existed across the country where young dancers could receive adequate training in ballet. Balanchine, however, recognized the need for an academy with unified standards where talented dancers could be molded to suit his stylistic needs. The first auditions for the School of American Ballet were held on January 1, 1934, and a first performance was scheduled for June of that year.

Balanchine chose as music for the ballet a piece that he had loved ever since he was a child, Peter Ilich Tchaikovsky's Serenade in C for String Orchestra (1880). The composer was one with whom Balanchine felt a close spiritual affiliation all his life. More practical considerations were involved as well; for example, the piece required only a small orchestra, which was all the company could afford. For the premiere, Balanchine utilized the first three movements of the Tchaikovsky work; in 1940, he added the final section (which he interposed before the third movement).

Working in a style that anticipated modern dancer Merce Cunningham's "chance" choreography, in which a flip of a coin may determine dance sequences, Balanchine choreographed *Serenade* with whichever dancers happened to show up each day for rehearsal. For example, the beginning section of *Serenade* has a corps de ballet of seventeen female dancers—because that was how many were enrolled in the class. Not until Charles Laskey joined the rehearsals was a male dancer introduced into the second section. A dancer entered late one day and walked through the lines to search out her place;

Balanchine mischievously retained the sequence, a pointed lesson to remind others to come on time. Another dancer slipped, fell, and began to cry, and Balanchine told her to repeat the incident thereafter at the exact same spot in the piece. The ballet, then, became a living witness to the company's transition from amateur to professional, a veritable history of individual growth.

Serenade begins with daring simplicity: Seventeen girls pose with right arms lifted in salute. They perform standard *ports de bras* exercises with arms moving slowly along circular paths, movements drawn from the five classic positions of ballet. Then, with deliberate abruptness, the dancers face forward, toward the audience. Suddenly, their legs rotate outward so that they stand resolutely with heels touching. The underlying message is obvious: They acknowledge the three-hundred-year-old tradition of classic ballet and yet announce that they are fully prepared to face whatever the future may bring. They are ready to dance. Extravagantly full-blown movements follow, with great arm sweeps, full backbends, and the fleet footwork that was to become a Balanchine signature.

The ballet's most gripping sequence is its conclusion, a dreamlike scene in which a man walks slowly across the stage followed by a darkly dressed woman, who covers his eyes with one hand and holds her other hand over his heart. The man's eyes open, and he beholds a woman at his feet. The three begin to dance, but they are interrupted by streams of dancers who throw themselves into the man's arms. He attempts to express his love for the woman, but when he places his hand over his heart to pledge his devotion, the dark shadow behind him again covers his eyes and places her chill hand over his heart. He walks away, and the distraught woman is borne offstage by a solemn procession of dancers.

The final scene is noteworthy for its psychological ambiguity: Strong emotions appear to underlie the dancers' relationships, yet the ballet's creator denied any attempt to portray a story. Balanchine prided himself on his innovative "plotless" ballets, which discarded the dramatic story line and lush scenery characteristic of many Diaghilev ballets. When a puzzled dowager once demanded to know what one particular ballet was about, he is alleged to have replied pertly, "About twenty minutes." *Serenade* evidently held a special meaning for him, however; one night he confessed to a friend that the final scene was "like fate. . . . Each man going through the world with his destiny on his back. He meets a woman—he cares for her—but his destiny has other plans."

The Hartford premiere was adjudged a glamorous event by its fashionable audience, which included George Gershwin and Salvador Dalí. The American Ballet made its New York City debut with *Serenade* on March 1, 1935, and Balanchine was to retain his ties with the city, except for a brief period, from then on. Neither the puzzled critic for the *New York Post* nor John Martin of *The New York Times* was particularly impressed with *Serenade*, however. Martin even had the effrontery to suggest that Balanchine ought to be sent back to Paris, where his avant-garde "Riviera esthetics" really belonged, so that he could be replaced by an American-born director.

Kirstein, however, praised *Serenade*'s "cool frankness, a candor that seemed at once lyric and natively athletic; a straightforward yet passionate clarity and freshness suitable to the foundation of a non-European academy." He was echoed by the critic of the *Dancing Times* in London, who commented that "*Serenade*, which opened the bill, contains some of Balanchine's most unusual groupings, breathtaking in the sheer beauty of their arrangement. The 'Elegy,' which forms the closing movement of this ballet, is a little masterpiece of choreographic design."

SIGNIFICANCE

The company's size grew from the original twenty-eight dancers who performed in Hartford that December to forty-five within the next nine months. The season, boasted company supporter Edward Warburg, proved that a first-rate company of American-born dancers could be put together, and that these dancers could even be comparable on a technical level with European imports. Martin of *The New York Times* had "nothing but praise" for these "hard-working youngsters," who conveyed "the dignity and purity of the classic style at its best." The writer for the *Dancing Times* agreed that inexperienced dancers had been magically transformed into skilled dancers, but pointed out that their artistic maturity still lagged behind.

The company not only proved that Americans could dance well but also raised hopes of establishing an American tradition of ballet that would equal the Russian tradition. Martin had originally welcomed the company in "An Open Letter of Greeting," in which he complimented the organizers for their "sincere and almost passionate purpose to create an American ballet." He expressed reservations about the choice of a Russian choreographer—one who would take many years to acquire "a feeling of America, its life and background" and

1934

who would "inevitably put the stamp of Europe upon his pupils and dancers in these sensitive and formative years." The directors of the American Ballet, however, remained adamant in their conviction that their work would one day come to be seen as the building of an American tradition in classical dance. In their brave aspirations and high expectations, they could cite the successes of the early modern dancers of the time such as Martha Graham, Doris Humphrey, Charles Weidman, and Helen Tamiris, who were founders of an American dance form of great originality. After the company moved to New York, the American Ballet joined with the Metropolitan Opera ballet for the 1935 to 1938 seasons; in 1946, Balanchine and Kirstein founded the Ballet Society, and in 1948 they were invited to join the New York City Center with the company that became known as the New York City Ballet. *Serenade* became the company's signature piece.

The New York City Ballet style associated with Balanchine became an international standard by the end of the twentieth century, and plotless ballets, once dismissed as mere avant-garde experiments, became the norm. The cool neoclassicism of the so-called Balanchine ballerina was soon imitated everywhere. The choreographer acknowledged that women had primacy in his ballets—"Ballet is woman," he was fond of saying. His women all looked alike, even down to their diamond stud earrings; he declared that they must have "skin the color of a peeled apple," and he chose dancers with coltishly long legs, long necks, small heads, long hair, and prepubescent, even anorexic, physiques. Balanchine's vision came to dominate the ballet world, with the unfortunate consequence that, even years after his death, many talented dancers, including African American women and women with bustlines, could find only limited performance opportunities in ballet.

In the end, Kirstein and Warburg's faith in Balanchine was confirmed, and John Martin confessed error. At the moment of *Serenade*'s premiere, Kirstein was beside himself with impatience to get the company moving, for he had set a deadline to deliver "an American ballet," free of alien influences and danced by American youths, within a few years after Balanchine's arrival. It was going to take longer than that, but their vision eventually made debtors of everyone in the ballet world.

—*Maureen Needham Costonis*

FURTHER READING

Balanchine, George, and Francis Mason. *Balanchine's Complete Stories of the Great Ballets*. Rev. ed. Garden City, N.Y.: Doubleday, 1977. Useful reference source. Chapter on *Serenade* describes the ballet's action, with a rare commentary by Balanchine on his own work in which he rejects the notion of "storytelling." Includes descriptions of other Balanchine works and index.

Barnes, Clive. "*Serenade*." In *Dance and Dancers*. London: Hansom Books, 1976. A description of *Serenade* in honor of the ballet's performance by the Royal Ballet in 1964. Most writers focus on the ballet's historical importance as the first Balanchine ballet in the United States, so Barnes's reactions to the Royal Ballet version, although more journalistic than scholarly, are refreshing. Includes photographs.

Buckle, Richard, with John Taras. *George Balanchine: Ballet Master*. New York: Random House, 1988. One of the most comprehensive biographies of Balanchine available includes previously unpublished information about his early life in Russia. Unfortunately, the author's effusive praise does a disservice to a subject known for excessive modesty. Features limited bibliography, source notes, photographs, and index.

Garafola, Lynn. *Legacies of Twentieth-Century Dance*. Middletown, Conn.: Wesleyan University Press, 2005. A selection of essays and reviews by one of the most influential scholars of the history of dance. Covers the transformation of dance, especially ballet, since the early twentieth century. Includes many photographs.

Kirstein, Lincoln. *The New York City Ballet*. New York: Alfred A. Knopf, 1973. Blends Kirstein's intensely personal diary jottings with his later recollections. Provides invaluable insights into the founding of the American Ballet. Profusely illustrated with exquisite photographs. Includes appendix containing a list of premiere performances produced by all the Balanchine companies and index.

Teachout, Terry. *All in the Dances: A Brief Life of George Balanchine*. Orlando, Fla.: Harcourt, 2004. Biography by a literary critic emphasizes Balanchine's personal life while moving through a chronological discussion of the ballets. Includes photographs.

Volkov, Solomon. *Balanchine's Tchaikovsky: Interviews with George Balanchine*. Translated by Antonia W. Bovis. New York: Simon & Schuster, 1985. Although normally shy in talking about his sources of creative inspiration or working methods, Balanchine opened up to Volkov, a fellow Russian émigré. The author, a trained musicologist, succeeds in making this provocative book much more than a series of formulaic questions and answers. Sheds indirect light on Balanchine's emotional life. Includes parallel chronologies of events in Tchaikovsky's and Balanchine's lives and index.

SEE ALSO: May 19, 1909: Diaghilev's Ballets Russes Astounds Paris; June 2, 1909: Fokine's *Les Sylphides*

Introduces Abstract Ballet; June 25, 1910: *The Firebird* Premieres in Paris; May 29, 1912: *L'Après-midi d'un faune* Scandalizes Parisian Audiences; May 29, 1913: *The Rite of Spring* Stuns Audiences; Jan. 26, 1936: Tudor's *Jardin aux lilas* Premieres in London; Apr. 5, 1938: Ballet Russe de Monte Carlo Debuts.

December 29, 1934
JAPAN RENOUNCES DISARMAMENT TREATIES

The renunciation of the Washington and London naval treaties was a significant step in Japan's move toward militarism in the early 1930's.

LOCALE: Tokyo, Japan; London, England; Geneva, Switzerland
CATEGORY: Diplomacy and international relations

KEY FIGURES

Shidehara Kijūrō (1872-1951), ambassador to the United States, 1919-1922, and Japanese foreign minister, 1924-1927, 1929-1931

Katō Tomosaburō (1861-1923), Japanese navy minister, 1915-1923

Katō Hiroharu (1870-1939), senior naval expert, Washington conference delegation, 1921-1922, and chief of the navy general staff, 1930

Hirota Kōki (1878-1948), Japanese foreign minister, 1933-1936

Ōsumi Mineo (1876-1941), Japanese naval minister, 1934-1936

Okada Keisuke (1868-1952), Japanese prime minister, July, 1934-March, 1936

Hamaguchi Osachi (1870-1931), Japanese prime minister, July, 1929-April, 1931

SUMMARY OF EVENT

On December 29, 1934, the Japanese government formally renounced the Washington Naval Treaty of 1922. This action, which occurred after the Japanese occupation of Manchuria in 1931 and the international reaction condemning it, was a further step along the road to Japan's participation in World War II.

The Washington Naval Treaty had been an attempt to deal with the growing tensions between Japan and the Western powers—especially the United States and Great Britain—in the years following World War I. Although Japan had fought on the winning side in the war and was a

participant in the 1919 Paris Peace Conference that concluded it, Japan disagreed with the Western powers on several key issues. Most notable among these was Japan's territorial claim resulting from the war and its plans for naval expansion in the Pacific. In response to these matters, an international conference was held in Washington from November of 1921 to February of 1922. Three treaties with major implications for Japan's future resulted from this conference. The first, the Four-Power Treaty (involving the United States, Great Britain, France and Japan) committed the participants to maintenance of the status quo in the Pacific. The second treaty, the Nine-Power Treaty (including these same four countries and Belgium, Italy, Portugal, the Netherlands, and China) affirmed China's territorial integrity and created an open-door policy for foreign trade and investment there. The third treaty, the Washington Treaty, dealt with placing limits on naval expansion. It was also known as the Five-Power Treaty and was signed by the United States, Great Britain, France, Japan, and Italy.

In particular, the negotiation of the naval treaty caused a considerable amount of controversy. The process focused on the establishment of ratios for the relative size of each country's navy: The United States and Great Britain favored a ratio of 10:10:6 for the number of battleships held by their countries and by Japan, but the Japanese representatives were divided on this question. Navy minister Admiral Katō Tomosaburō and ambassador to the United States Shidehara Kijūrō indicated willingness to accept the formula if compromises could be reached on other issues, whereas senior naval adviser Rear Admiral Katō Hiroharu supported a ratio of 10:10:7. In the end, Katō Tomosaburō and Shidehara prevailed, and the 10:10:6 ratio was accepted. Attempts to expand the treaty to include smaller ships failed, and the treaty, with only the larger ships included, was signed on February 6, 1922. Formal ratification by the Japanese assembly occurred on August 5. Although in the 1930's, Japanese militarists viewed the treaty as a sign of weakness, the Washington treaty came to stand as one of the key events of what is often called "Shidehara diplomacy," named for the aforementioned Japanese diplomat whose efforts to maintain positive relations with the West dominated Japanese foreign policy during this period.

After the three 1922 treaties were signed, future meetings to update and possibly expand the agreements were scheduled for Geneva in 1927 and London in 1930. At the Geneva meeting, Japanese negotiators again put forward the 10:10:7 ratio, this time in connection with the discussion of limitations on smaller naval vessels. When negotiations on this issue failed, the matter was held over until the London meeting. When that latter meeting convened, on January 21, 1930, the lines between Japan and the two Western powers seemed more firmly drawn. After considerable discussion, an agreement was reached on April 22 that partially met the Japanese demands, although the 10:10:6 formula remained in place for ships of the larger cruiser class. Although it was formally ratified in the Japanese diet on October 2, the agreement was met with an outpouring of dissent. Key government and military officials resigned, including Admiral Katō Hiroharu, who had become chief of the navy general staff. Furthermore, the treaty was almost certainly a factor that led to the assassination attempt on Prime Minister Hamaguchi Osachi in November. (Hamaguchi died from injuries related to the attempt in April of 1931.)

In the years that followed, Japan slipped under the control of the militarists, and relationships with the Western powers became increasingly tense. In September of 1931, the Japanese military—acting totally outside of the control of the civil government in Tokyo— moved to occupy Manchuria. In response to this action, the U.S. government formally proclaimed the Stimson Doctrine (named for U.S. secretary of state Henry L. Stimson), which refused to recognize Japan's right to its newly gained territory, in January of 1931. In May of 1932, right-wing extremists staged an armed rebellion in an attempt to overthrow the civil government. The rebellion was successfully put down, but the military's power grew as a result.

The following year, in February of 1933, Japan officially withdrew from the League of Nations in response to the release of the League's Lytton Commission report, which condemned Japanese aggression in Manchuria and refused to recognize its newly established puppet state of Manchukuo. As a result of these events, strong sentiments were taking shape within Japan to formally renounce the Washington and London treaties and move toward full parity in naval power with the United States and Great Britain.

The movement to end the naval treaties reached a crescendo in July of 1934, when the naval minister, Admiral Ōsumi Mineo, threatened to resign from the government of Prime Minister Okada Keisuke if the treaties were not formally ended. A number of efforts were made to moderate the crisis. The Japanese foreign minister, Hirota Kōki, set forth a plan to move toward parity with the United States and Britain in stages. By September, however, efforts to gain United States and British support for this plan had failed. Following a period of further debate, the Okada government formally renounced the treaties on December 29.

SIGNIFICANCE

In the aftermath of these events, one more effort was made to settle the differences. A meeting of representatives from Japan, Britain, the United States, France, and Italy took place in London in 1935. When the Japanese again argued for full parity with the United States and Britain, the proposal was again rejected by the Western powers, and the Japanese left the conference. From that point, events continued their downward spiral to the eventual onset of the war in the Pacific.

The Japanese renunciation of the 1922 Washington and London naval treaties was as a significant event in Japan's movement toward militarism, both at home and abroad. It demonstrated both the military's growing power of over Japan's civil governments as well the rejection of the pattern of Shidehara diplomacy and international cooperation that had characterized Japanese foreign policy during the previous decade. These trends would lead the nation into World War II.

—Scott Wright

FURTHER READING

Barnhart, Michael A. *Japan and the World Since 1868.* London: Edward Arnold, 1995. Offers a brief overview of the topic viewed within the larger context of Japan's foreign policy since the Meiji Restoration.

Dingman, Roger. *Power in the Pacific: The Origins of Naval Arms Limitation, 1914-1922.* Chicago: University of Chicago Press, 1976. In-depth background on the Washington conference.

LaFeber, Walter. *The Clash: U.S.-Japanese Relations Throughout History.* New York: W. W. Norton, 1997. Contains background on the Washington and London conferences viewed from the perspective of U.S.-Japanese relations.

Morley, James William, ed. *Japan's Foreign Policy, 1868-1941.* New York: Columbia University Press, 1974. Contains a broad overview of the Washington treaty system as well as individual essays on Japan's long-term relations with Britain (by Ian Nish) and on the United States (by Akira Iriye).

Nish, Ian. *Japanese Foreign Policy, 1869-1942.* London: Routledge & Kegan Paul, 1977. Provides a broad view of the topic with particular emphasis on the personalities and policies of the various Japanese foreign ministers involved.

O'Connor, Raymond G. *Perilous Equilibrium: The*

United States and the London Conference of 1930. Lawrence: University of Kansas Press, 1962. In-depth background on the first London conference.

Pelz, Stephen E. *Race to Pearl Harbor: The Failure of the Second London Naval Conference and the Onset of World War II.* Cambridge, Mass.: Harvard University Press, 1974. Offers a good overview of the topic and on the events leading from it to the beginning of World War II.

SEE ALSO: Feb. 24, 1933: Japan Withdraws from the League of Nations; Nov. 25, 1936: Germany and Japan Sign the Anti-Comintern Pact; Aug., 1940: Japan Announces the Greater East Asia Coprosperity Sphere; Sept., 1940: Japan Occupies Indochinese Ports.

1935

CHAPMAN DETERMINES THE LUNAR ATMOSPHERIC TIDE AT MODERATE LATITUDES

Sydney Chapman's determination of the lunar atmospheric tide (the effect of the Moon's gravitation on Earth's atmosphere) helped later scientists in their study of heat and radio physics.

LOCALE: Imperial College, London, England
CATEGORIES: Science and technology; earth science; physics

KEY FIGURES

Sydney Chapman (1888-1970), English mathematician and geophysicist

Julius Bartels (1899-1964), German geophysicist

Pierre-Simon Laplace (1749-1827), French astronomer and mathematician

James Clerk Maxwell (1831-1879), Scottish physicist

SUMMARY OF EVENT

In 1951, Sydney Chapman, an applied mathematician and geophysicist who had been a professor in Manchester, London, and Oxford, was named the advisory scientific director and professor of geophysics at the University of Alaska. Four years later, he became the senior research fellow at the National Center for Atmospheric Research in Boulder, Colorado. His colleagues recognized that Chapman was a prolific producer and contributor to a greater understanding of the atmosphere: His work in the determination of the lunar air tide led to several (but by no means most) of the more than three hundred scientific papers he either authored or coauthored in

such areas as Earth's magnetism; theory of nonuniform gases; solar plasma, geomagnetism, and aurora; and composition of the ionosphere. During the period 1912-1917, he also modified the accurate kinetic theory of gases that James Clerk Maxwell had proposed in 1867, and in the process Chapman discovered gaseous thermal diffusion and confirmed it through experiments. He also demonstrated the power of thermal diffusion in highly ionized gases such as those in a solar corona.

Atmospheric tide, or atmospheric oscillation, is an atmospheric motion of the scale of Earth in which vertical accelerations are neglected. Atmospheric tides are produced by both the Sun and the Moon. They may be thermal, if the variation in atmospheric pressure is caused by the diurnal differential heating of the atmosphere by the Sun, or they may be gravitational, if the variation is caused by the attraction of the Sun or Moon. The semidiurnal lunar atmospheric tide is gravitational. On the other hand, atmospheric tides produced by solar twenty-four-, twelve-, eight-, and six-hour pressure fluctuations act on Earth's atmosphere by means of its gravitational field and also by emitting electromagnetic radiation and particles toward it. The amplitude of the lunar atmospheric tide is so small that it is detected only by careful statistical analysis of a long record, such as that conducted by Chapman in 1918 and 1935.

The lunar tide is the rise and fall of the oceanic surface twice each lunar day as a result of Earth's rotation in a nonuniform external gravitational field. The atmosphere

Sydney Chapman. (National Science Foundation)

is subject to the same tide-producing gravitational forces as the oceans; this periodic change in atmospheric pressure is called the "equilibrium atmospheric" tide. At the equator, the calculated equilibrium tide-pressure variation at ground level is 0.022 millimeters of mercury (mmHg). Lunar twelve-hour fluctuations in pressure have been observed on the ground and are believed to be of purely gravitational origin; however, it is customary to refer to those periodic pressure fluctuations as atmospheric tides.

The dynamical theory of atmospheric tides goes back to 1778, when Marquis Pierre-Simon Laplace first published his conclusions on the theory. According to Laplace, the barometric amplitudes in equatorial regions, as a result of the gravitational action of the Sun and Moon, should be about 0.0109 millimeter and 0.025 millimeter, respectively, and decrease rapidly with the increase of latitude. In 1842, at an observatory on the British island of Saint Helena in the South Atlantic Ocean, the lunar semidiurnal pressure oscillation was determined to have a mean of about 0.055 millimeter, an

amount that exceeded the calculated equilibrium tide of 0.022 millimeter by a factor of 2.5.

In 1918, Chapman had become the first to determine the lunar atmospheric tide from barometric readings taken at a moderate latitude at the Royal Greenwich Observatory in England. His conclusions were based on meteorological records of the barometer, wind, and temperature, which had been collected by the Greenwich Observatory during the period from 1854 to 1917. He also analyzed the magnetic data to determine the lunisolar daily variations of the magnetic field. ("Lunisolar" is a term used to describe the mutual relationship, or combined attraction, of the Moon and Sun.) Solar and lunisolar daily magnetic variations are caused by electric currents in the ionosphere, which are induced motions produced thermally and tidally. This relationship between the ionosphere and air tides led to Chapman's later formulation of an idealized ionized layer.

In these and later calculations, Chapman used the mathematical theory of statistics, which was emerging as a major scientific tool. (Statistics is a branch of mathematics dealing with the collection, analysis, interpretation, and presentation of masses of numerical data.) He saw that statistics could be used to improve the quality of inferences in important sections of his study of atmospheric lunar tides. The rigorous statistical procedures allowed him to make clearer determinations and to elucidate features of tides in Earth's atmosphere that are caused by the Moon's gravitational attraction. Of specific importance were significant figures, which are the figures of a number that begin with the first figure to the left that is not a zero and end with the last figure on the right that is not a zero, or is considered to be exact. Mathematical numbers are known to any accuracy required and carry any number of significant figures. The mean of more than ten and less than one thousand numbers may contain one or more significant figures.

Using this basis gave Chapman an advantage in finding the lunar tide from barometric readings in high latitudes. He followed his achievement with similar readings at more than fifty stations of the amplitude (in millimeters) during phases of the lunar semidiurnal mean atmospheric tide for the four equinoctial months (March, June, September, and December), and he presented his conclusions in 1935. Chapman found that the fundamental period of the free oscillation of the atmosphere as a whole is about twelve mean solar hours. Mean amplitudes and phases of the lunar semidiurnal atmospheric tide for the four equinoctial months had a mean of approximately 0.03 millimeter at 30 degrees south latitude, 0.038 millimeter at 20 degrees, 0.045 millimeter at 10 degrees, and 0.060 millimeter at the equator. At 10 degrees north, the barometric pressure was about 0.052 millimeter; it was 0.028 millimeter at 20 degrees, 0.022 millimeter at 30 degrees, 0.018 millimeter at 40 degrees, and 0.013 millimeter at 50 degrees.

This work aroused Chapman's interest in geomagnetism and its connection with solar phenomena and led to his theoretical researches in these fields. He became best known for his research in geomagnetism and his pioneering work on both the photochemistry of the upper atmosphere and on nocturnal emission of light by atoms of oxygen and sodium. In 1940, he coauthored, with Julius Bartels, a two-volume work on geomagnetism. This complete work was an excellent contribution to the understanding of the external field of a uniformly magnetized sphere, the magnetic field at Earth's surface, electric currents in and beyond the ionosphere, local and world indices of geomagnetic disturbance, sunspots and magnetism, and the twenty-seven-day recurrence in geomagnetic disturbance. As part of his study of the lunar tide, he investigated why Earth's magnetic field varies with periods equal to the lunar day (27.3 days) and its submultiples. He showed that this was the result of a tidal movement in Earth's atmosphere caused by the Moon.

SIGNIFICANCE

Chapman's contributions had major impacts in the extension of knowledge about the lunar tide and Earth's atmosphere. His analysis of many years of barometer, wind, and temperature recordings, along with his magnetic data, was facilitated by expert use of statistical analysis, which at the time of his study was a new mathematical theory. The use of physical observations and an innovative mathematical theory were truly pioneering. As a consequence of his work in the atmosphere and magnetic field, Chapman developed a deep interest in geomagnetism and its connection with solar phenomena. These interests led to several major publications: *The Earth's Magnetism* (1936; 2d ed. 1951); *The Mathematical Theory of Non-uniform Gases*, with T. G. Cowling (1939; 3d ed. 1970); *Geomagnetism*, with Julius Bartels (1940); *IGY: Year of Discovery* (1959); *Solar Plasma, Geomagnetism, and Aurora* (1964); *Atmospheric Tides: Thermal and Gravitational*, with Richard S. Lindzen (1970); and *Solar-Terrestrial Physics*, with Syun-Ichi Akasofu (1972).

Chapman's research and studies of the atmospheres of Earth and the Sun produced a photochemical theory of atmospheric ozone and inferred that the oxygen in the upper atmosphere (which begins 100 kilometers above ground level) would be largely dissociated. This conclusion was confirmed later by rocket-borne mass spectrometers. Another of his inferences was that airglow, or the self-luminescence of the atmosphere at night, was energized mainly by the oxygen dissociation energy stored in the atmosphere during the sunlight hours. His work in this area led later to his 1953-1959 presidency of the central organizing committee for the International Geophysical Year, for which he led the planning of the auroral program.

Solar and lunisolar magnetic variations are caused by electric currents in the ionosphere, and Chapman's research efforts in this area led the formulation of an ideally ionized layer—the Chapman ionized layer—which was used much later by radio physicists in studies of radio propagation and other research. His work in thermal diffusion—heat transfer between two parts of a solid, liquid, or gas at different temperatures—in the absence of convection was important for separating isotopes for atomic fission. Chapman made major contributions to the history of science, and his creative genius was recognized by his peers by the many awards he received.

—*Earl G. Hoover*

FURTHER READING

Aguado, Edward, and James E. Burt. *Understanding Weather and Climate.* 3d ed. Upper Saddle River, N.J.: Prentice Hall, 2003. Meteorology textbook aimed at both science majors and non-science majors focuses on the processes that produce weather and climate. Includes many illustrations and other learning aids.

Chapman, Sydney. *IGY: Year of Discovery; the Story of the International Geophysical Year.* Ann Arbor: University of Michigan Press, 1959. A popular account of the events that took place during the International Geophysical Year of 1957 to 1958; taken from four lectures Chapman gave at the University of Michigan in October, 1958. A good reference for the general public, as well as high school and college students.

Clancy, Edward P. *The Tides: Pulse of the Earth.* Garden City, N.Y.: Doubleday, 1968. Primarily about ocean tides, but refutes Chapman's resonance theory of solar semidiurnal oscillation in the chapter on tides in the atmosphere. Suggests that the diurnal oscillation is the extraordinary phenomenon. Well written and a good general reference.

Fleagle, Robert C., and Joost A. Businger. *An Introduction to Atmospheric Physics.* New York: Academic Press, 1963. A college-level text that presents a good

1935

understanding of the relationship of matter as expressed in the principles of physics. Some of the areas covered include gravitational effect, properties of atmospheric gases, properties and behavior of cloud particles, and solar and terrestrial radiation. Numerous mathematical formulas and graphs and a good bibliography.

Hanle, Paul A., and Von Del Chamberlain, eds. *Space Science Comes of Age: Perspectives in the History of the Space Sciences*. Washington, D.C.: Smithsonian Institution Press, 1981. A compilation of essays from a symposium held at the National Air and Space Museum. A good reference for the general public on the early contributions to the field. Contains little mathematics or physics.

Lutgens, Frederick K., and Edward J. Tarbuck. *The Atmosphere: An Introduction to Meteorology*. 9th ed. Upper Saddle River, N.J.: Prentice Hall, 2003. Introduction to meteorology for college students is accessible to advanced upper-level high school students as well. Well illustrated. Includes glossary and index.

Wylie, Francis E. *Tides and the Pull of the Moon*. Brattleboro, Vt.: Stephen Greene Press, 1979. An easy-to-read book written for the general public. Covers the lore and legends of tides and the Moon in history, astrology, and astronomy. Explains how gravitational attraction of the Moon and Sun causes tides. A few black-and-white photographs and reference notes after each chapter help explain the text.

SEE ALSO: Mar. and June, 1902: Kennelly and Heaviside Theorize Existence of the Ionosphere; June 26, 1908: Hale Discovers Strong Magnetic Fields in Sunspots; Aug. 7 and 12, 1912: Hess Discovers Cosmic Rays; Jan. 17, 1913: Fabry Quantifies Ozone in the Upper Atmosphere; 1919-1921: Bjerknes Discovers Fronts in Atmospheric Circulation; 1920-1930: Millikan Investigates Cosmic Rays; 1930-1932: Jansky's Experiments Lead to Radio Astronomy; May 27, 1931: Piccard Travels to the Stratosphere by Balloon; June-Sept., 1937: Reber Builds the First Intentional Radio Telescope.

1935
PENGUIN DEVELOPS A LINE OF PAPERBACK BOOKS

The public's acceptance of paperback books that began with Penguin Books Limited's introduction of a series of ten reprinted titles established a new market for publishing.

LOCALE: London, England
CATEGORIES: Publishing and journalism; literature; trade and commerce

KEY FIGURES
Allen Lane (1902-1970), founder and managing director of Penguin Books Limited, 1935-1970
Sir William Emrys Williams (1896-1977), author, literary critic, and chief editor and director of Penguin Books Limited, 1935-1965

SUMMARY OF EVENT
The first ten titles of Penguin paperback books reached the booksellers of England in 1935. The softcover editions were reprints of works already available in hardback, and Penguin's approach mystified skeptics. The initial selection consisted of books that had already done well in hardcover sales, including works by Agatha Christie, Dorothy L. Sayers, and Beverly Nichols. High-

lights of the series included Ernest Hemingway's *A Farewell to Arms* (1929) and Andre Maurois's *Ariel: Ou, La Vie de Shelley* (1923; *Ariel: Or, The Life of Shelley*, 1924).

The books went on sale for sixpence, one-fifteenth of the price of a hardback novel. Allen Lane, who had started Penguin after a short career with publisher Bodley Head, saw his mission as providing mass access to affordable books of good taste. He was determined to offer nothing that was trite, salacious, or sadistic. For one of these books to break even at the low price, fifteen to twenty thousand copies—a huge number at the time—of each book had to be sold. Critics were puzzled. They thought that people who already bought books would spurn the softcovers, which would quickly perish, and people who were accustomed to using public libraries would not start buying their own copies. Moreover, the existing hardback market would be undercut by the success of paperbacks; surely, critics argued, publishers would not grant reprint rights. Advance orders of seven thousand per volume did not dispel the doubts.

The first ten Penguin releases were an instant success, and over a period of eighteen months other titles were added. A total of nearly one hundred titles consisted primarily of fiction but also included some biography and travel. The first Penguins were given a distinctive look: Each had the Penguin emblem and bands of white and color—orange for general fiction, green for detective novels, and blue for biographies. The covers were plain but instantly recognizable. Lane eschewed using pictorial covers as an allure. The interior of each book was, however, carefully planned by the Penguin typographical department, which worked in the company's makeshift headquarters in an old church crypt in North London. Outside commercial printers were in charge of production.

Marketing the books to booksellers was a challenge, as it took twelve softcover sales to make the same profit as one hardback sale. Booksellers could not devote that much extra shelf space, and so they had to depend on rapid turnaround. Many booksellers believed that people who loved books would not buy the Penguin editions, especially because the first issues (unlike later ones) were flimsy, would not stay straight on a shelf, and were easily marred.

The booksellers were soon convinced, however, by Penguin's early success. Other outlets, such as department stores and chain stores, also sold Penguins. Lane devoted his personal attention to both large and small sellers. Because the first Penguin paperbacks were reprints, relations with other publishing houses were crucial. Hardback publishers feared that softcover sales would erode hardback sales, but it soon became apparent that the paperbacks created a new market, and before long every major publisher in Great Britain had granted reprint rights for one of its works to Penguin. Publishers were quickly won over, as were authors. The extra sales from paperback editions gave authors exposure to a wider market, and the attention increased the prospects of selling future works. If hardback sales were dropping and further printings could not be justified, a Penguin edition offered hope of a second lease on life. The success of the original ten Penguin books disproved the skeptics and began a project of bringing good books to the masses at low prices. In eighteen months, the gathering successes of a hundred reprint titles whose sales did not damage existing

trade in hardbacks had established a whole new market of readers.

SIGNIFICANCE

The significance of the first Penguins was not immediately evident. Cheap reprints were not without precedent: Several series of reading matter for travelers had been offered at railway stations beginning in the nineteenth century. These books were usually fiction of nonenduring interest. Modestly priced hardback reprints of major works had also been offered as parts of various series, including the Everyman's Library, which began in London in 1906.

Allen Lane's initial vision was based on his understanding that there might be a market for softcover books

---

PENGUIN'S FIRST PAPERBACK TITLES

Penguin published the following twenty-six paperback titles, in the order shown, in 1935. The works included mysteries such as The Unpleasantness at the Bellona Club, *by Dorothy Sayers, and* The Mysterious Affair at Styles, *by Agatha Christie, as well as collections of stories such as* Naval Occasions, *by Bartimeus.*

- *Ariel*, by André Maurois
- *A Farewell to Arms*, by Ernest Hemingway
- *Poets Pub*, by Eric Linklater
- *Madame Claire*, by Susan Ertz
- *The Unpleasantness at the Bellona Club*, by Dorothy Sayers
- *The Mysterious Affair at Styles*, by Agatha Christie
- *Twenty-Five*, by Beverley Nichols
- *William*, by E. H. Young
- *Gone to Earth*, by Mary Webb
- *Carnival*, by Compton Mackenzie
- *South Wind*, by Norman Douglas
- *The Purple Land*, by W. H. Hudson
- *Patrol*, by Phillip MacDonald
- *The Thin Man*, by Dashiell Hammett
- *Four Frightened People*, by E. Arnat Robertson
- *The Edwardians*, by Vita Sackville-West
- *The Informer*, by Liam O'Flaherty
- *Debonair*, by G. B. Stern
- *The Strange Case of Miss Annie Spragg*, by Louis Bromfield
- *Erewhon*, by Samuel Butler
- *Our Mr. Wrenn*, by Sinclair Lewis
- *Dr. Serocold*, by Helen Ashton
- *Esther Waters*, by George Moore
- *Hangman's House*, by Donn Byrne
- *Naval Occasions*, by Bartimeus
- *Odd Craft*, by W. W. Jacobs

1935

for serious readers who liked to read but were not concerned with collecting books. The railway-stall works, in comparison, were essentially an appendage to the magazine market. Eighteen months after the first Penguin titles were released, Lane clarified Penguin's niche: The group would focus on inexpensive editions of nonfiction works. Publication of these books reflected an idea more akin to the Everyman concept and established the position of Penguin as a popular educator. Penguin offered not only good fiction but also a range of nonfiction written by experts for nonspecialists.

In 1937, when a hundred novels already had been issued as Penguin reprints, the publisher made its educational purpose explicit by publishing its first nonfiction titles, called Pelicans. The first title was *The Intelligent Woman's Guide to Socialism and Capitalism* (1928), by George Bernard Shaw, who added some new material for the reprint. Other early Pelicans were works by Julian Huxley, Roger Fry, Arnold Bennett, and Sigmund Freud. These works, like the novels, cost sixpence, and all were unabridged.

In the same year, the Penguin company made the natural extension of commissioning its own works. Against a background of crisis in Europe, the new works, called Penguin Specials, focused on current affairs. These included *Searchlight on Spain* (1938), by the Duchess of Atholl; *The Jewish Problem* (1938), by Louis Golding; *Europe and the Czechs* (1938), by Sheila Grant Duff; and *Mussolini's Roman Empire* (1938), by G. T. Garratt. These works helped Penguin transition from being solely a reprint house to being a publisher of new works. Remarkably, this was achieved without any competitive response from other publishers, whose own sales had so far not been affected by the arrival of Penguin. The publishing of new works put Penguin in direct competition with other houses, but the others did not respond by issuing their own softcover series or by becoming alarmed about losing authors to Penguin.

The Penguin Specials had an enormous impact. Some of these books sold a quarter of a million copies, and the unprecedented achievement of selling a large volume of serious books gave a mass of people a deep understanding of the questions of the day. In an era of immense turmoil, when fascist, communist, and democratic philosophies actively challenged each other, Penguin books were vitally important resources for promoting and informing widespread discussion. The Penguin Specials' success permitted Penguin to continue its mission during World War II. Paper was rationed on the basis of sales in the years prior to the war, so Penguin was allowed a far greater ration than it would have had without them.

During the war, Penguin introduced several other series, largely fulfilling its mission to publish more works of literature than any other company. King Penguins were a series of illustrated books. Puffin Picture Books were produced especially for children, and their treatments of various subjects found approval with educators. Penguin Modern Painters, a series edited by Sir Kenneth Clark, was also issued during the war. The series of Penguin Classics, with translations of Homer and other illustrious ancient writers, cemented Penguin's reputation as the publisher most concerned with educating the public. No other company had a comparable range of subjects in print.

Booksellers who were originally doubtful about the desirability of stocking paperbacks were soon persuaded. Company salespeople from Penguin maintained regular contact through personal visits, sometimes taking orders at the shops, and developed a sensitive awareness of the kinds of works that sold well in different districts. Every month, Penguin prepared a list of books in production, and this list was sent out each month with an order form. The full catalogue was sent with it, and an in-house magazine was occasionally issued.

From the start, the company was run on modest means. Unlike most other publishers, Penguin put out virtually no advertisements in the press for its books; such advertisements were simply too expensive. The press was important to the company, however, in that it often reviewed Penguin's publications. Meanwhile, Penguin pioneered its own kind of promotional initiative, called the Penguin Exhibitions. The first exhibitions were parts of other events, such as conferences of educators, but they became events in their own right. Other publishers were welcome to exhibit at these events, which were held in several British cities.

Penguin's mission to publish only books of merit and good taste was safeguarded by the long-serving editor Sir William Emrys Williams. Williams was a literary scholar and a good complement to founder Allen Lane, who was passionately interested in publishing but was not a reader. As chief editor and director, Williams brought distinguished people to the company as series editors and advisers in specific fields. Penguin was careful to place a higher priority on taste than on popular appeal, and this tendency was evidenced in the widespread adoption of Penguins in adult education courses.

Penguins changed both the publishing industry and the reading habits of entire sections of the population, but their competitors were slow to respond. In Great Britain, it was not until the late 1950's that other companies, such as Hutchinson and Methuen, started series of books with features similar to Penguin's. In the 1960's, the Open University began producing all of its printed curriculum materials in paperback. Gradually, publishers in many countries began to routinely issue softcover editions of academic books, and they sometimes did so at the same time as the hardback edition was released.

—*Richard Barrett*

FURTHER READING

Baines, Phil. *Penguin by Design.* New York: Allen Lane, 2005. A retrospective look at Penguin's covers and the general development of the British publishing industry. Heavily illustrated.

Barnes, James. "British and American Booktrade, 1819-1939." In *Economics of the British Booktrade 1605-1939*, edited by Robin Myers and Michael Harris. Alexandria, Va.: Chadwyck-Healey, 1985. A study in economic history. The author charts changes and trends in the book trade, with particular reference to mass markets. Includes American developments such as the dime novels and the impact of Book-of-the-Month Club and the Literary Guild.

Hoggart, Richard. *An English Temper: Essays on Education, Culture, and Communications.* New York: Oxford University Press, 1982. Written by a distinguished scholar of literacy who worked in adult education, this volume includes "Allen Lane and Penguin," which explains the educational significance of the Penguin nonfiction books in offering to the layperson specialized subject matter that is readable but not pedantic.

Lupoff, Richard A. *The Great American Paperback: An Illustrated Tribute to the Legends of the Book.* Portland, Oreg.: Collectors Press, 2001. A more general history of paperback books that focuses more on their seamy side. Valuable for understanding the degree to which Penguin broadened the notion of the paperback book and its readership.

Schmoller, H. "The Paperback Revolution." In *Essays in the History of Publishing in Celebration of the 250th Anniversary of the House of Longman, 1724-1974*, edited by Asa Briggs. London: Longmans, 1974. A short account of paperbacks in the publishing industry.

Williams, William E. *Allen Lane: A Personal Portrait.* London: Bodley Head, 1973. A work by a literary critic who worked for many years in association with the Penguin company as editor and adviser. Offers insights from a personal acquaintance of Penguin founder Sir Allen Lane.

_____. *The Penguin Story.* Harmondsworth, Middlesex, England: Penguin Books, 1956. An anniversary book for Penguin's twenty-first year. A well-written but terse account of the success of Penguin not only in fiction but in specialized nonfiction in various fields of knowledge. Much of the information is incorporated in Williams's 1973 book cited above.

SEE ALSO: Feb., 1922: *Reader's Digest* Is Founded; Feb. 21, 1925: Ross Founds *The New Yorker*; 1926-1927: Mail-Order Clubs Revolutionize Book Sales; Nov. 23, 1936: Luce Launches *Life* Magazine.

1935

1935-1936
TURING INVENTS THE UNIVERSAL TURING MACHINE

Alan Mathison Turing invented a precise concept of an abstract computing machine, providing a basis for both the theory of computation and the development of digital computers.

LOCALE: Cambridge, England

CATEGORIES: Computers and computer science; mathematics; science and technology

KEY FIGURES

Alan Mathison Turing (1912-1954), English mathematician, logician, and cryptanalyst

Alonzo Church (1903-1995), American logician and philosopher

David Hilbert (1862-1943), German mathematician

Kurt Gödel (1906-1978), German logician

John von Neumann (1903-1957), Hungarian American mathematician and physicist

SUMMARY OF EVENT

In 1931, Kurt Gödel proved that arithmetic (and mathematics) is either inconsistent or incomplete, meaning that any consistent axiom system for arithmetic must fail to include some true arithmetical statements. This result answered the first two of the three questions that David Hilbert had posed three years earlier: Is mathematics complete? Is it consistent? Is it decidable? The last question asks if there is a definite procedure (algorithm) that is guaranteed to produce a correct answer as to whether an arbitrary mathematical sentence is true. After Gödel's proof, there was much speculation that mathematics must be undecidable. In the late spring of 1935, shortly after having been made a fellow at King's College, Cambridge, Alan Mathison Turing set out to prove it. To do so, Turing needed a precise concept of "definite procedure," which led him to invent what are now called Turing machines.

A Turing machine is an abstract machine rather than a physical one: It is used to define or describe algorithms precisely, not to execute them. Any Turing machine has three components: a control unit, which takes any of a finite number of states; a two-way infinite tape, which is divided into squares capable of holding any one of a finite number of symbols; and a read-write head, which writes a symbol, moves left or right over the tape, and reads the new square. The behavior of such a machine on the next step is fully determined by its current state and the symbol being read. Specific Turing machines are described with tables of quintuples, such as $<Q0, A, B, R, Q1>$, which means: If the machine is in state Q0 and reading the symbol A, then write the symbol B (replacing the symbol A), move right on the square on the tape, and go into state Q1. It can be stipulated that a Turing machine will halt when it enters a state for which no quintuple exists.

As a simple example, the following represents a machine that determines the parity of a string of zeroes and ones, when the read-write head starts at the rightmost digit (that is, the machine will report "1" if the string has an odd number of ones; otherwise, it reports "0"):

$$<Q0, 0, 0, L, Q0>$$
$$<Q0, 1, 1, L, Q1>$$
$$<Q1, 0, 0, L, Q1>$$
$$<Q1, 1, 1, L, Q0>$$
$$<Q0, b, 0, L, Q2>$$
$$<Q1, b, 1, L, Q2>$$

In this machine, state Q0 signifies that the string has even parity so far, and Q1 signifies odd parity. The first tuple scans a zero in the even-parity state; the read-write head moves left, and the machine stays in even parity. The next tuple scans a one and so changes the state from even to odd parity. The next two tuples are similar but describe the machine's behavior when in the odd-parity state. The final two states recognize the end of the string (b stands for the blank symbol), write the answer (at the head of the input string), and stop (by entering the undefined state Q2).

One of the remarkable things about Turing machines is that they are universal; that is, they are capable of performing the computations done by any other Turing machine. This is achieved through the encoding of that other machine's table of quintuples in a numerical string (called the Gödel number of the machine); then, this number can be written on the universal machine's input tape. The universal machine simulates the target machine by examining and interpreting the appropriate quintuple on the tape. This encoding of the target machine is analogous to software programs on modern digital computers.

With this basis, Hilbert's third question can be answered by the proof that mathematics is undecidable. For any Turing machine, the question can be asked whether, when given a certain input, the machine will halt. One also can ask the broader question of whether there is a Turing machine-named halter that, when given the Gödel number for a target machine and that machine's input, can decide in a finite number of steps whether the target machine would stop with that input. (This is called the halting problem.) If one assumes that halter exists, one can ask the self-referential question: What happens if halter encounters the Gödel number for itself? Turing proved that in such a case, halter will halt if and only if it does not halt; in other words, whichever way one turns, there is a contradiction, so halter cannot exist. Turing also demonstrated that there are mathematical statements for which any decision procedure would presuppose the existence of halter; thus he established the existence of undecidable mathematical statements.

Turing presented these results in a paper titled "On Computable Numbers, with an Application to the *Entscheidungsproblem*" in 1936. Shortly before, however, Alonzo Church had published his proof of the undecidability of mathematics using a different formulation called the lambda calculus. Because the two methods of proof were substantially different, Turing's paper was accepted for publication. First, however, Turing was obliged to show in an appendix that Turing computability and Church's definition of effective calculability were equivalent. Both papers argued for the Church-Turing thesis (sometimes called Church's thesis), which asserts that their equivalent concepts of computability precisely capture the intuitive concept of an effective procedure or definite algorithm. Given that this intuitive concept cannot itself be exactly specified, the thesis is unprovable. Nevertheless, it is a remarkable fact that every adequate substitute for "effective procedure" has been proved to be equivalent, including the contemporaneous formulations by Emil Post and by Stephen Kleene (the latter using general recursive functions).

Furthermore, every coherent extension of the concept of Turing machines has been shown to possess exactly the same computational power as Turing machines themselves, as long as they adhere to the same standard of definiteness—for instance, not allowing randomized state changes. (Note that "power" here refers to the range of functions that can be computed and not to the informal notion of the speed of computation.) For example, adding multiple tapes or multiple read-write heads per tape in no way increases the set of functions that a Turing machine can compute, although some computations will become faster. Von Neumann machines—everyday office computers and personal computers—are likewise no more powerful than Turing machines (for that reason

they sometimes are mistakenly called Turing machines).

Of course, some machines—such as finite automata—are not as powerful as Turing machines. The convergence of all sufficiently general kinds of machines on the class identified by Church and Turing seems explainable only if one assumes the truth of the Church-Turing thesis.

SIGNIFICANCE

The invention of the Turing machine provided a precise concept of computation, which helped to pave the way for the introduction of practical computing machinery. While the Turing machine as such would make an impractical computing device (given that storing everything on tape would be impossibly slow), it anticipated much of the function required for practical computers. During and immediately after World War II, various engineering efforts produced the first working electronic digital computers. Especially noteworthy are the Electronic Numerical Integrator and Calculator (ENIAC), developed from 1943 to 1946 at the University of Pennsylvania, and the Automatic Computing Engine (ACE) at England's National Physical Laboratory, designed by Turing in 1945. The ENIAC led to a more general computer design by John von Neumann that has had a pervasive effect in the computer industry; most modern computers are classified now as von Neumann machines.

Beyond providing a model for practical computation, the concept of Turing computability has supported the development of much of the theory of computer science. In addition to its bearing on the nature of unsolvable problems, Turing computability has been instrumental in the study of the degrees of solvability of problems—more accurately, the computational complexity of problems—a major research area in theoretical computer science. Computational complexity is measured by the amount of time (number of steps) required by an optimal Turing machine to solve a problem. The complexity of a problem is expressed as a function of its size; thus the size of the problem to search sequentially a list of N items to find a specific item is merely N; the time it takes, on average, is directly proportional to $N/2$. Two classes of complexity are of special interest: polynomial time problems and exponential time problems. Polynomial time problems require a polynomial function of the problem size to complete—such as $N/2$, N, N^2, and so on. Exponential time problems require 2 to the Nth power, or 2 to the N^2 power, and so on, to complete. Exponential problems always grow faster than polynomial problems in the computation time required, and so they are often called intractable. An important set of problems, called *NP* problems, are defined in terms of a special class of Turing machine. It is an unproved, but widely believed, thesis that many *NP* problems are necessarily exponential.

Given that Gödel, Turing, and others collectively proved that mathematics cannot be completely mechanized, it might be thought that Turing should have been pessimistic about the prospects for artificial intelligence—that is, the attempt to mechanize intelligence. In fact, however, Turing believed that whatever limits apply to machines in this regard apply equally to humans—that neither humans nor machines can have access to all mathematical truths or to an infallible decision procedure. Turing, in his 1950 paper "Computing Machinery and Intelligence," created the well-known Turing test for intelligence, which has provided the main backdrop for philosophical inquiries in artificial intelligence since that time. In recognition of Turing's achievements, the Association for Computing Machinery named its most prestigious annual research prize the ACM Turing Award.

—*Kevin B. Korb*

FURTHER READING

Ceruzzi, Paul E. *A History of Modern Computing.* 2d ed. Cambridge, Mass.: MIT Press, 2003. A straightforward, comprehensive history of computing. Places the technology in its appropriate social context.

Davis, Martin, ed. *The Undecidable.* New York: Raven, 1965. A collection of many of the seminal articles in the development of computation theory and logic. Includes original papers alluded to above by Church, Gödel, Kleene, and Post. These papers are accessible to those already acquainted with formal logic. Reprints the original paper by Turing, "On Computable Numbers, with an Application to the Entscheidungsproblem." *Proceedings of the London Mathematical Society* 42 (January, 1937): 230-265.

Dewdney, A. K. *The Turing Omnibus.* New York: Owl Books, 1993. Collection of short and engaging tutorials on sixty-one different topics in computer science by the "Mathematical Recreations" columnist for *Scientific American.* Chapter titled "The Halting Problem" presents an informative discussion of that issue.

Garey, Michael R., and David S. Johnson. *Computers and Intractability: A Guide to the Theory of NP-Completeness.* San Francisco: W. H. Freeman, 1979. A standard, introductory college text on computational complexity. Provides a very accessible survey for those with some college-level mathematics or logic. Contains an exhaustive list of NP-complete problems known as of 1979.

Hodges, Andrew. *Alan Turing: The Enigma.* New York: Simon & Schuster, 1983. A thorough, enjoyable biography of Turing. Includes a lengthy, fascinating account of Turing's successful cracking of Nazi Germany's encryption devices. Also provides background material to Turing's foundational work on artificial intelligence in the late 1940's.

Hofstadter, Douglas R. *Gödel, Escher, Bach: An Eternal Golden Braid.* New York: Basic Books, 1999. The concepts of self-reference, recursion, and infinite regress are woven into an absorbing tapestry. Explicates Gödel's incompleteness theorem, drawing analogies with M. C. Escher's reflexive drawings and the musical edifices of Bach. Nontechnical but lengthy.

Minksky, Marvin. *Computation: Finite and Infinite Machines.* Englewood Cliffs, N.J.: Prentice-Hall, 1967. An especially clear introduction to automata and computation theory, used as a freshman college textbook. Presupposes no college-level mathematics, but it does introduce and use formal notation. Minsky is a leading figure in artificial intelligence.

Turing, Alan. "Computing Machinery and Intelligence." *Mind* 59 (October, 1950): 433-460. An exploration of the concepts of human and machine intelligence. Introduces the famous Turing Test for intelligence. Reprinted frequently; for example, in Alan Ross Anderson, ed. *Minds and Machines.* Englewood Cliffs, N.J.: Prentice-Hall, 1964.

SEE ALSO: 1904-1907: Brouwer Develops Intuitionist Foundations of Mathematics; 1906: Markov Discovers the Theory of Linked Probabilities; 1910-1913: *Principia Mathematica* Defines the Logistic Movement; 1918: Noether Shows the Equivalence of Symmetry and Conservation; Feb., 1924: IBM Changes Its Name and Product Line; 1928: Bush Builds the First Differential Analyzer; July, 1929-July, 1931: Gödel Proves Incompleteness-Inconsistency for Formal Systems; 1939: Bourbaki Group Publishes *Éléments de mathématique.*

January, 1935
RICHTER DEVELOPS A SCALE FOR MEASURING EARTHQUAKE STRENGTH

Charles Francis Richter devised a scale for measuring the strength of earthquakes based on their seismograph recordings.

LOCALE: Pasadena, California

CATEGORIES: Science and technology; earth science; geology

KEY FIGURES

Charles Francis Richter (1900-1985), American seismologist

Beno Gutenberg (1889-1960), German American seismologist

Kiyoo Wadati (1902-1995), Japanese seismologist

Giuseppe Mercalli (1850-1914), Italian physicist, volcanologist, and meteorologist

Michele Stefano de Rossi (1834-1898), Italian geologist and archaeologist

François-Alphonse Forel (1841-1912), Swiss geologist and geographer

SUMMARY OF EVENT

Earthquakes range in strength from barely detectable tremors to catastrophes that devastate large regions and cause the loss of hundreds of thousands of lives. The human impact of earthquakes is not an accurate measure of their power; minor earthquakes in heavily populated regions may cause great destruction, whereas powerful earthquakes in remote areas may go unnoticed. To study earthquakes, it is essential to have an accurate means of measuring their power.

The first attempts to measure the power of earthquakes involved the development of intensity scales that relied on damage effects and the reports of witnesses as measures of the force of vibration. The first such scale was devised by Michele Stefano de Rossi and François-Alphonse Forel in 1883. It ranked earthquakes on a scale of 1 to 10. The de Rossi-Forel scale proved to have two serious limitations: Its level 10 encompassed a great range of effects, and its description of effects on human-made and natural objects was so specifically European that the scale was difficult to apply elsewhere. To remedy these problems, Giuseppe Mercalli published a revised intensity scale in 1902. The Mercalli scale, as it came to be called, added two levels to the high end of the de Rossi-Forel scale, making its highest level 12. It also was rewritten to make it more globally applicable. With later modifications by Charles Francis Richter, the Mercalli scale is still in use.

Intensity measurements, even though they are somewhat subjective, are very useful in mapping the extent of earthquake effects. Nevertheless, intensity measurements are still not ideal measuring techniques. Intensity varies from place to place and is strongly influenced by local geologic factors, and different observers frequently report different intensities. There is a need for an objective method of describing the strength of earthquakes with a single measurement.

Richter devised an objective technique for determining the power of earthquakes in the early 1930's at the California Institute of Technology in Pasadena, California. The eventual usefulness of what became known as the Richter scale was completely unforeseen at first. In 1931, the California Institute of Technology was preparing to issue a catalog of all earthquakes detected by its seismographs in the preceding three years. Several hundred earthquakes were listed, most of which had not been felt by humans, only detected by instruments. Richter was concerned about possible misinterpretations of the listings. With no indication of the strength of the earthquakes, the public might overestimate the risk of earthquakes in areas where seismographs were numerous and underestimate the risk in areas where seismographs were few. To remedy the lack of a measuring method, Richter devised the scale that now bears his name.

Richter defined the magnitude of an earthquake as the logarithm of the height of its seismograph trace in microns (thousandths of a millimeter), as recorded on a standard instrument. Thus an earthquake that produces a trace one millimeter (1,000 microns) high would be magnitude 3, one that produces a trace 1 centimeter high (10,000 microns) would be magnitude 4, and so on. These measurements were defined for a standard seismograph magnifying ground motion twenty-eight hundred times and located 100 kilometers (about 62 miles) from the earthquake. The magnification of the instrument means that the actual ground motion caused by a magnitude 3 earthquake 100 kilometers away is not 1 millimeter but only 1/2,800 millimeter, or only about three thousand times the diameter of an atom. By comparing records for earthquakes recorded on different devices at different distances, Richter was able to create conversion tables for measuring magnitudes for any instrument at any distance. He also set up the scale so that any event likely to be felt by humans would have a positive magnitude, because scales with zero and negative numbers tend to be confusing to most people.

Richter had hoped to create a rough means of separating small, medium, and large earthquakes, but he found that his scale was capable of making much finer distinctions. Most magnitude estimates made with a variety of instruments at various distances from earthquakes agreed to within a few tenths of a magnitude. Richter formally published a description of his scale in January, 1935, in the *Bulletin of the Seismological Society of America*. Other systems of estimating magnitude had been attempted, notably that of pioneering Japanese seismologist Kiyoo Wadati, published in 1931, but Richter's system proved to be the most workable scale yet devised and rapidly became the standard.

Over the next few years, the scale was refined. One critical refinement was in the way seismic recordings were converted into magnitude. Earthquakes produce many types of seismic waves, but it was not known which type should be the standard for magnitude. So-called surface waves travel along the surface of the earth. It is these waves that produce most of the damage in large earthquakes; therefore, it seems logical to let these waves be the standard. On the other hand, earthquakes deep within the earth produce few surface waves. Magnitudes based on surface waves would be too small for these earthquakes. Deep earthquakes produce mostly waves that travel through the solid body of the earth, or so-called body waves. Actually, two scales are needed: one based on surface waves and one on body waves. Richter and his colleague Beno Gutenberg developed scales for the two different types of waves that are still in use. Magnitudes estimated from surface waves are symbolized by a capital *M*, and those based on body waves are denoted by lowercase *m*.

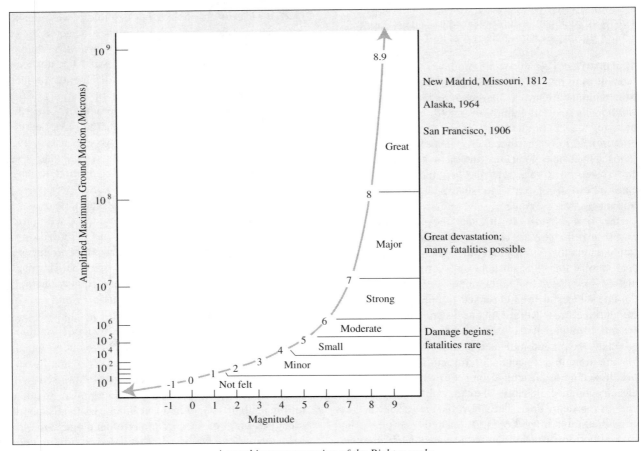

A graphic representation of the Richter scale.

From a knowledge of movements of the earth associated with seismic waves, Richter and Gutenberg succeeded in relating the energy output of an earthquake with its magnitude. Each increase of one Richter magnitude corresponds to about a thirtyfold increase in energy. A magnitude 6 earthquake releases about as much energy as a one-megaton nuclear explosion; a magnitude 0 earthquake releases about as much energy as a small car dropped off a two-story building.

An additional refinement to the Richter scale was developed in the 1970's. Extremely large earthquakes release their energy over time spans as long as several minutes and over a fault break of hundreds of kilometers. The highest seismograph trace for the earthquake, however, measures the energy received at only one instant. It is also possible to estimate energy released from the length of the fault rupture and the amount of fault displacement, and by this measure, conventional magnitudes for the largest earthquakes are too small. A magnitude corrected for the long duration and great spatial extent of the largest earthquakes is called a seismic-moment magnitude. Japanese seismologist Hiroo Kanamori devised a seismic-moment magnitude scale during the 1970's; on this scale, unlike the conventional Richter scale, some of the greatest earthquakes exceed magnitude 9.

SIGNIFICANCE

The Richter scale is a good example of an accidental scientific discovery. Richter's original intent had been to develop a scale for very rough measurements, but the scale proved to be useful on a completely unforeseen scale. Richter scrupulously avoided using the term "Richter scale" in his writings and went to some length to give credit to other researchers who also had similar ideas. The Richter scale has now become firmly established in popular and professional usage.

The Richter scale had been in use among scientists for about fifteen years before Richter scale readings began to be widely quoted by the press in the 1950's. Just as scientists had, the press found the scale a useful tool for defining the strength of earthquakes. Initially, there was much confusion among laypersons over the difference between magnitude and intensity. Also, the logarithmic nature of the scale, clear enough to scientists, was widely misunderstood. It was not until about 1970 that the press generally stopped describing the Richter scale as running from 1 to 10.

Charles Francis Richter studies earthquake tremors in his laboratory in Pasadena, California, in 1963. (AP/Wide World Photos)

The scientific utility of the Richter scale stems from its logarithmic nature. Wave phenomena occur over a great range of intensities and are best described by logarithmic scales; other examples include the speed and shutter settings on cameras (each step doubles or halves the original amount of light) and the decibel scale for sound. Virtually all the important physical quantities associated with waves are proportional to the amplitude of the wave raised to some power; such relationships are very simple to express in logarithmic terms. Because the magnitude of an earthquake is defined as the logarithm of its ground motion, many of the physical dimensions of earthquakes, such as their energy release, are directly and simply related to magnitude. Also, it is simple to develop equations to relate ground motion, magnitude, and distance from an earthquake.

The Richter scale made it possible for scientists to

compare the energy outputs of earthquakes in a quantitative way and to derive new understandings of earthquake phenomena. For example, most of the energy released by earthquakes is released by the few most powerful ones. Also, earthquakes are more powerful in some geologic settings than in others. The greatest earthquakes (above magnitude 6.5) are associated with faults on or bordering the continents, whereas earthquakes along the midocean ridges rarely exceed magnitude 6.5. Deep earthquakes are rarely as strong as magnitude 7. These differences provide scientists with important insights into the forces at work in the earth.

—Steven I. Dutch

FURTHER READING

Bolt, Bruce A. *Earthquakes*. 5th ed. San Francisco: W. H. Freeman, 2003. Presents a generally nontechnical account of earthquakes, their effects, and methods of studying them. Includes a good description of magnitude and intensity.

Boore, David M. "Motion of the Ground in Earthquakes." *Scientific American* 237 (December, 1977): 68-87. Describes the types of waves generated by earthquakes and the instrumental techniques used in measuring them. Includes a description of the seismic-moment magnitude scale.

Gutenberg, Beno, and Charles F. Richter. *Seismicity of the Earth*. 2d ed. New York: Hafner, 1965. A pioneering study of earthquake locations and magnitudes around the world. Includes extensive tables of large earthquakes.

Hough, Susan Elizabeth. *Earthshaking Science: What We Know (and Don't Know) About Earthquakes*. Princeton, N.J.: Princeton University Press, 2002. Presents information on earthquake science for lay readers, including discussion of earthquake measurement and the Richter scale.

Press, Frank. "Earthquake Prediction." *Scientific American* 232 (May, 1975): 14-20. Interesting summary of research efforts and seismic clues used in attempts to predict earthquakes. Somewhat dated, in that short-term prediction of earthquakes has turned out to be much more difficult than was believed in the mid-1970's.

Richter, Charles F. *Elementary Seismology*. San Francisco: W. H. Freeman, 1958. College-level textbook on seismology is dated but valuable for Richter's personal description of the origin of the Richter scale.

U.S. Geological Survey. *Earthquakes and Volcanoes* 21 (January/February, 1989). Special issue devoted to the measurement of earthquakes and an excellent short survey of seismology. Includes maps of seismic activity, locations of seismographs, and explanations of how seismographs work.

Wesson, Robert L. "Predicting the Next Great Earthquake in California." *Scientific American* 252 (February, 1985): 35-43. Presents a summary of modern field and theoretical techniques used in estimating earthquake risk and predicting earthquake magnitudes. Of particular interest is the fact that the article accurately predicts the location and approximate magnitude of the 1989 Loma Prieta earthquake.

SEE ALSO: 1906-1910: Oldham and Mohorovičić Determine the Earth's Interior Structure; Apr. 18, 1906: San Francisco Earthquake; Dec. 28, 1908: Earthquake and Tsunami Devastate Sicily; 1913: Gutenberg Discovers Earth's Mantle-Outer Core Boundary; Sept. 1, 1923: Earthquake Rocks Japan; 1936: Lehmann Discovers the Earth's Inner Core.

January, 1935
SCHIAPARELLI'S BOUTIQUE MINGLES ART AND FASHION

Elsa Schiaparelli collaborated with Surrealist artists to create a reputation for outrageous fashion designs while developing new and successful means of marketing her creations.

LOCALE: Paris, France
CATEGORIES: Fashion and design; arts

KEY FIGURES
Elsa Schiaparelli (1890-1973), French fashion designer who linked high society, the fine arts, and haute couture
Salvador Dalí (1904-1989), Surrealist painter who collaborated with Schiaparelli on designs for clothing and furniture
Jean Cocteau (1889-1963), poet, essayist, and film writer whose drawings were adapted by Schiaparelli for clothing
Jean-Michel Franck (1893-1941), interior designer responsible for the Schiaparelli boutique and home
Léonor Fini (1908-1996), Surrealist painter, sculptor, and designer who worked closely with Schiaparelli

SUMMARY OF EVENT
In January, 1935, Elsa Schiaparelli moved her couture house into new quarters at 21, place Vendôme in Paris. Although she had been showing her designs since 1926, she had presented major collections for only six years. Beginning with sportswear and her signature knits—her trompe l'oeil sweaters were the first of her creations to make fashion news—she expanded to designing day wear and, in 1930, to evening wear. She defined the feminine silhouette of the 1930's, with its broad and squared shoulders, and she repeatedly shocked the establishment with new fabrics, refined shapes, and unusual buttons and accessories. In six years, she gained significant recognition. Recognition translated into financial success, and her new house, at the center of one of the most exclusive districts in Paris, symbolized that success.

The move, however, meant more than a larger space. In addition to her studio, workrooms, and sales salons, Schiaparelli dedicated three rooms with windows fronting on the square to the display and sale of separates, perfumes, and accessories—the daring hats, scarves, gloves, and jewelry on which her reputation was in part based and which had become known as "Schiaparelli-isms." Unlike the designs offered in the salons upstairs, which were custom-made for individual clients, these separates could be purchased "ready to wear." Schiaparelli's boutique combined high-fashion appeal with remarkable business acumen and the outrageousness of the avant-garde. It took a person of Schiaparelli's background to hit upon the idea.

Unlike the Parisian designers with whom she competed, Schiaparelli was born to the class that made up her clientele. Her family combined Italian aristocracy and intelligentsia; a brief marriage had given her the title of countess. She had lived in Rome, London, New York, and Paris, and she spoke four languages, three of them fluently. Her society connections, especially those with Americans in Paris, were useful and helped to provide her with financing, expertise, and notoriety, as well as with clients. Her connections with the cultural elite were essential for her sense of design, and her collaboration with the Surrealist avant-garde resulted in the creations for which she became best known.

The boutique itself was an act of collaboration: The idea was pure Schiaparelli, but the interior was designed by Jean-Michel Franck to resemble a great gilded cage. Schiaparelli's longtime American associate Bettina Jones broke new ground in creating the striking window displays. Spanish expatriate Salvador Dalí designed a couch in the form of enormous Surrealist lips, which Schiaparelli had made in shocking pink—her signature color, which she developed and introduced in 1936. Her perfume bottles were designed by Léonor Fini, an artist known for Surrealist erotica.

Throughout the mid-1930's, the cross-fertilization between Schiaparelli's designs and the work of artists stamped Schiaparelli's most characteristic designs. To her, fashion design was an art, and as such, it had to be daring and shocking. Surrealism gave her the images and techniques to fulfill her vision. This art form sought to deconstruct the world of experience by means of metamorphosis, fragmentation, and dislocation; the designs Schiaparelli and her Surrealist friends created from 1935 through 1939 achieved those ends. In 1937, Schiaparelli applied to an evening coat a Jean Cocteau drawing of a vase of flowers that is transformed, by the addition of eyes, into a picture of two lovers kissing. In the same year, Schiaparelli produced a jacket animated by Cocteau's drawing of a female figure whose hair cascades down the jacket's sleeves and whose hands clasp the wearer's waist.

Schiaparelli worked with many artists, but Dalí was

1935

Elsa Schiaparelli. (AP/Wide World Photos)

her most frequent collaborator, and it was with him that she created her most notorious works. To celebrate the boutique, Dalí presented her with a life-sized model of a bear into whose body he had constructed drawers reminiscent of his *Venus de Milo with Drawers* (1936). Under this influence, Schiaparelli in 1936 created her "desk suit," on which real and false pockets are treated as drawers, with drawer pulls substituting for buttons. In the following year, she showed several Dalí-inspired designs: a dress made of fabric painted by Dalí with a depiction of a large, cooked lobster across the center of the skirt (a garment chosen by Wallis Warfield Simpson as part of her trousseau when she married the duke of Windsor). The evening gown known as the "tear dress" had both painted tears and actual rends in the fabric, causing the viewer to question the function of clothing and the gap between the wealth of couture and the poverty of rags.

It was in the creation of hats, the perfect Freudian ve-

hicle for social and sexual displacement, that Dalí and Schiaparelli were at their most outrageous. Schiaparelli designed a hat that was also a shoe; in one version, the fetishized high heel was shocking pink. Another hat, which, like the lobster dress, alluded to the woman wearer as comestible object, was in the shape of the lamb chop, complete with white patent-leather frill to mimic paper trim at the bone end. Only Schiaparelli was audacious enough to wear this version.

Beyond such examples of specific influence, many of Schiaparelli's creations bore the imprint of Surrealism. The early trompe l'oeil sweaters presented one thing as something else. Schiaparelli's buttons were often adapted from unusual objects, including fruit forms, kitchen utensils, and insects. She designed a line of gloves that mimicked the hands they were meant to cover, and she was the first designer to engage artists to paint designs—including musical notes, circus performers, and poodles—which she then had translated to fabrics.

SIGNIFICANCE

Schiaparelli successfully marketed her designs to shoppers at her boutique and to clients for whom she did custom work, and she continued to affect the shape of fashion. Paris in the 1930's placed great emphasis on youth, style, and bravura: Gaiety in the face of an absurd and darkening world was the order of the day. Furthermore, the economics of fashion were changing. Style was no longer only for the upper classes. More women worked and had wages to spend, fashion publications were growing in circulation and influence, skilled copyists were imitating couture designs before models left the runway, and American designers were pioneering moderately priced, ready-to-wear clothing. These trends were captured in Schiaparelli-isms and in the boutique that sold them.

Schiaparelli altered the relationship between social class and fashion in two ways. As the first of the socialite designers—women of high station who turned to fashion design and merchandizing as genteel employment and diversion—Schiaparelli capitalized on the panache of her own breeding, and she also employed a number of wealthy or titled women as models and associates. She and her aristocratic models could not only display designs within the salon but could also wear such designs at social events. Second, Schiaparelli pioneered the notion of offering items of high fashion to buyers who had neither the courage nor the money for couturier designs. The boutique became a tourist attraction, and Schiaparelli-isms were carried home by many upper-middle-class travelers as souvenirs of Paris.

Of course, Schiaparelli's designs had a major impact on the fashion industry. Her early collections emphasized coordinated separates, and this economical, logical tactic set the precedent for women's clothing. She also pioneered the use of many synthetic fabrics and of the zipper for closures. Her suited silhouette of the 1930's, popularized by film stars such as Joan Crawford, became the uniform for career women of the prewar period. Schiaparelli's exploitation of fantasy and the absurd was adapted by Parisian designers Yves Saint-Laurent and Jean-Paul Gauthier and by the punk designers of the 1970's in Great Britain.

One of Schiaparelli's most formidable business skills was her ability to identify talent in young people and her willingness to let such talent loose. It is no surprise, therefore, that several of her associates went on to have spectacular careers. For example, both Hubert de Givenchy and Pierre Cardin were her apprentices after World War II. She also recognized early the talents of a young jewelry designer, Jean Schlumberger, who worked with her from 1937 to 1939.

Schiaparelli was one of very few designers who was able to maintain close collaborations with avant-garde artists, but the links she forged between fashion and art would continue to hold. Through her work, Surrealism came to be recognized by a broader public, and publishers of fashion magazines came to realize the movement's potential. Surrealism's stress on the eroticism of the female form, the potential of the fragmented, fetishized image, the linking of fashion with the subconscious and the absurd—all aspects explored in the illustrations of Schiaparelli's designs by such artists as Léonor Fini, Man Ray, Cecil Beaton, and others—became standard elements in fashion layouts. Even after Schiaparelli had largely retired from designing, the relationship between Surrealism and commercial fashion continued: Dalí, for example, continued to design for fashion publications long after World War II.

It is probably in the field of fashion merchandizing, however, that Schiaparelli and her boutique—which was the first of its kind—had the greatest influence. Other designers had brought out perfumes linked to their design houses, but Schiaparelli added designer cosmetics and beauty supplies. She made her scarves such fashion accents that they were in much greater demand than the clothes they accessorized, and then she broke major ground by combining these cosmetics and accessories with a truly ready-to-wear line that could be sold directly to customers. While Schiaparelli's one-of-a-kind couture creations made her reputation, it was the boutique, and especially the perfume business, that made her fortune.

After Schiaparelli began the practice, most designers exploited licensing's financial potential, and most operated boutiques. In fact, while designers came to base their reputations on couture designs shown in fall and spring exhibitions, such designs are so labor-intensive and costly to produce that designers' profits depend on the proceeds from the sale of diverse items, many of which (such as bed sheets) are only indirectly related to fashion.

—Jean Owens Schaefer

FURTHER READING

Blum, Dilys E. *Shocking! The Art and Fashion of Elsa Schiaparelli.* New Haven, Conn.: Yale University Press, 2003. Richly illustrated volume that emphasizes the relationship between Schiaparelli's designs and architecture.

De Marly, Diana. *The History of Haute Couture, 1850-1950.* London: B. T. Batsford, 1980. A history of the beginnings of haute couture, with emphasis on the late nineteenth and early twentieth centuries. Interesting chapters on the organization and financial aspects of the couture industry and on clients and their wardrobe requirements. Schiaparelli is discussed primarily in chapter 9. Black-and-white illustrations; brief bibliography.

Hall, Carolyn. *The Thirties in "Vogue."* New York: Harmony Books, 1985. A montage of images and ideas covered in *Vogue* magazine during the decade. Divided into broad groupings—the social scene, arts and entertainment, and travel and leisure. Important for the flavor of the times and for photographs of celebrities in couture creations, including those by Schiaparelli. A brief section on the magazine's coverage of and links with Surrealism.

Martin, Richard. *Fashion and Surrealism.* New York: Rizzoli, 1987. A richly illustrated overview of the interactions between clothing design and Surrealist art. Discussion of Schiaparelli is scattered throughout; a chapter is dedicated to her collaborations with Dalí. Of particular interest are many illustrations of otherwise seldom shown Surrealist pieces. Gives attention to contemporary Surrealist designs.

Mulvagh, Jane. *"Vogue" History of Twentieth Century Fashion.* London: Viking, 1988. A chronological discussion of fashions featured in *Vogue.* The period is

1935

divided into segments of six to nine years; the sections dealing with each segment are introduced with brief essays. Useful because so many other works are cavalier about the specific dates of fashion events. Copiously illustrated, but in small black-and-white reprints from the magazine.

Schiaparelli, Elsa. *Shocking Life*. New York: E. P. Dutton, 1954. Schiaparelli's autobiography. A good source for information about her cultural background, the network within which she operated in the 1930's, her career, and her travels. Considerably less revealing of her inner and personal life.

Steele, Valerie. *Women of Fashion: Twentieth Century Designers*. New York: Rizzoli, 1991. A history of women in fashion, written from a contemporary feminist perspective and highlighting the major role played by female designers in the period between the

two world wars. Attention is also given to an international range of contemporary women designers. Moving postscript about acquired immune deficiency syndrome (AIDS). Extensive notes and bibliography. Many illustrations, some in color.

White, Palmer. *Elsa Schiaparelli, Empress of Paris Fashion*. London: Aurum Press, 1996. One of the best biographies of the designer available, based largely on her autobiography but in many ways more complete than that work and more informative about her personality. Lavishly illustrated, with fine color depictions of Schiaparelli designs.

SEE ALSO: Spring, 1910: Poiret's Hobble Skirt Becomes the Rage; 1920's: Chanel Defines Modern Women's Fashion; 1920's: Jantzen Popularizes the One-Piece Bathing Suit.

February, 1935-October 27, 1938
CAROTHERS INVENTS NYLON

By applying his insights to the synthesis of new high molecular weight substances, including nylon, Wallace Hume Carothers developed the theory of condensation polymers and created a substance that would come to be used every day by millions of people around the world.

LOCALE: Wilmington, Delaware

CATEGORIES: Chemistry; inventions; science and technology

KEY FIGURES

Wallace Hume Carothers (1896-1937), American organic chemist who did the research in polymer chemistry that led to the development of nylon

Charles M. A. Stine (1882-1954), American chemist and director of chemical research at the Du Pont Corporation

Elmer K. Bolton (1886-1968), American industrial chemist who directed the development of nylon into a commercial textile fiber

SUMMARY OF EVENT

Although the Du Pont Corporation's industrial research laboratory was only one of many, its most famous invention—nylon—became the model for scientifically based industrial research in the chemical industry. Nylon, however, was not the first commercially important poly-

meric material. From the late nineteenth century, several cellulose derivatives appeared, including celluloid and rayon. In the 1890's, people began to use the word "plastic" to describe this class of materials. The first important purely synthetic polymer was Bakelite. Invented in 1907 by Leo Hendrik Baekeland, Bakelite was a phenol-formaldehyde moldable plastic and a major commercial success. Its success encouraged American industry to search for more special-purpose plastics.

During World War I, Du Pont tried to diversify; the company was concerned that after the war it would not be able to expand, since explosives had been its primary product. It hired organic chemists and built a research laboratory in the hope of mastering organic chemical reactions and producing synthetic dyestuffs. By 1921, Du Pont had put $20 million into the venture but lacked both the theoretical understanding and knowledge about how to succeed in organic synthesis. Instead, the company bought what it needed to diversify from outside, becoming a producer of rayon, cellophane, and other products.

In this context of dependency on outside inventions, Charles M. A. Stine, Du Pont's director of chemical research, proposed that Du Pont move into fundamental research by hiring first-rate academic scientists and giving them freedom to work on important problems in organic chemistry. He convinced company executives that a program to explore the fundamental science underlying Du

Pont's technology would ultimately result in discoveries of value to the company. In 1927, Du Pont gave him a new laboratory for research. Stine had given a new role to the industrial research laboratory; it was not to be affiliated with manufacturing departments but was to generate new knowledge. Stine visited universities in search of brilliant young scientists who had not yet established their reputations, and he hired Wallace Hume Carothers.

Stine suggested that Carothers do fundamental research in polymer chemistry, a field that had been a mystery to chemists. Polymeric materials were the result of ingenious laboratory practice, and this practice ran far ahead of theory and understanding. German chemists debated whether polymers were mysterious aggregates of smaller units held together by some unknown special force or genuine molecules held together by ordinary chemical bonds. Chemist Hermann Staudinger, who won the Nobel Prize in Chemistry in 1953, asserted that they were large molecules with endlessly repeating units. Carothers shared this molecular view, and he devised a scheme to prove it by synthesizing very large molecules through simple reactions that would leave no doubt about their structure. Carothers clarified the nature of polymers, distinguished between addition and condensation types, and lay the basis for much of modern polymer science in terms of its methods, vocabulary, and understanding. His syntheses of polymers revealed that they were giant but ordinary molecules.

In April of 1930, Carothers's group produced two major innovations: neoprene synthetic rubber and the first laboratory-synthesized fiber. However, neither discovery was Du Pont's initial intention. Neoprene appeared unexpectedly when, during a project to study short polymers of acetylene, the substance began to polymerize spontaneously. Carothers studied its chemistry and developed the process into the first successful synthetic rubber made in the United States. The other discovery was an unexpected outcome of the group's project to synthesize polyesters by the reaction of acids and alcohols, both of which had two functional groups in their molecules, which allowed the newly formed ester to continue to react indefinitely and thus form a substance with a high molecular weight. These polyesters' molecular weight was limited to about 5,000.

Carothers realized that the reaction also

produced water, which was decomposing polyesters back into acid and alcohol. Carothers and his associate Julian Hill devised an apparatus to remove water as it formed. The result was a polyester with a molecular weight of more than 12,000, far higher than any previous polymer. Hill, while removing a sample from the apparatus, found that he could draw it out into filaments that, when cooled, could be stretched to form very strong fibers. This procedure, called "cold-drawing," oriented the molecules from a random arrangement into a long, linear one of great strength. The polyester fiber, however, was unsuitable for textiles because of its low melting point.

In June, 1930, Du Pont promoted Stine; his replacement as research director was Elmer K. Bolton. Both were organic chemists, but Bolton was a far more traditional industrial chemist. He had opposed Stine's 1927 fundamental research program; now he was in charge of it. Bolton wanted fundamental research to be more closely controlled, relating it to projects that would pay off and not allowing the research group freedom to pursue purely theoretical questions. Despite their differ-

Wallace Hume Carothers. (Courtesy, Hagley Museum and Library)

ences, Carothers and Bolton shared an interest in fiber research. Carothers began to work on the synthesis of polyamides from acids and amines, reasoning that since simple amides had higher melting points than simple esters, the same would hold for their polymers. The polyamide research, however, was unsuccessful and by the end of 1933, all fiber work had ceased. In 1934, Bolton pressured Carothers to resume polyamide research. Carothers began trying different approaches to synthesis. On May 24, 1934, his assistant Donald Coffman drew a strong fiber from a new polyamide. This was the first nylon fiber, although not the one commercialized by Du Pont. The nylon fiber was high melting and tough, and it seemed a practical synthetic fiber might be feasible.

By the summer of 1934, the fiber project was the heart of the research group's activity. It prepared polyamides from many combinations of acids and amines. The one that had the best fiber properties was nylon 5-10 (the numbers referred to the number of carbon atoms in the amine and acid chains). Still, it was the nylon 6-6, prepared on February 28, 1935, that became Du Pont's nylon. Nylon 5-10 had some advantages, but Bolton realized that its components would be unsuitable for commercial production, whereas those of nylon 6-6 could be obtained from chemicals in coal. Bolton pursued nylon's practical development, a process that lasted nearly four years. In April, 1937, Du Pont filed a patent for synthetic fibers, which included a statement by Carothers that there was no previous work on polyamides, and that this was a major breakthrough. After Carothers's death on April 29, 1937, the patent was issued posthumously and assigned to Du Pont.

Carothers was responsible for the discovery of the laboratory process for nylon, but Bolton was responsible for the commercial process. Du Pont wisely decided not to pursue the full range of possibilities, confining its efforts to the silk hosiery market. The company knew that about $70 million was spent on silk hosiery each year. By focusing on this use of nylon, Du Pont would find it easier to overcome the considerable obstacles involved in commercializing the fiber. The practical development was as exceptional as the laboratory discovery, and it took several years for Du Pont's skilled and ingenious chemists and engineers to bring nylon into the marketplace. The first test of a yarn knitted into stockings came in February, 1937. It was not satisfactory, and it took until the end of 1937 to obtain high-quality nylon hosiery. Du Pont made the first public announcement of nylon on October 27, 1938.

SIGNIFICANCE

Nylon, a generic term for polyamides, became an important component of several commercial products. In addition to nylon 6-6, other kinds of nylons found widespread use as both a fiber and as a moldable plastic. Since it resisted abrasion and crushing, was nonabsorbent, stronger than steel on a weight-for-weight basis, and almost nonflammable, it embraced an astonishing range of uses: laces, screens, surgical sutures, paint, toothbrushes, violin strings, coatings for electrical wires, lingerie, evening gowns, leotards, athletic equipment and clothing, outdoor furniture, shower curtains, handbags, sails, luggage, fish nets, carpets, slip covers, subway and bus seats, and in space as the safety nets on the space shuttle.

The day after Du Pont's announcement in 1938, *The New York Times* ran articles on nylon, headlining one "New Hosiery Strong as Steel." Another article focused on nylon's indestructibility, stressing that it was made from simple substances in coal, air, and water. A well-orchestrated publicity campaign kept the public aware of nylon until May, 1940, when the first nationwide sales took place. During the eighteen-month period between Du Pont's announcement and nylon's sale, sample nylon stockings became available, and rave notices appeared. Du Pont called its exhibit at the New York World's Fair "The Wonder World of Chemistry," and the display celebrated its acetate, cellophane, and neoprene products and, above all, nylon. Visitors to the exhibit also saw a machine that rolled out sheer nylon stockings.

Newspapers reported that four million pairs of nylon hosiery were sold, and the supply was exhausted in one day. Before year's end, 60 million pairs had been sold. Nylon heralded a future of synthetic polymers that would become standard in clothing, building materials, and furnishings. The American military began to use nylon when the United States entered World War II, and Du Pont tripled its production during the war. Nylon served as a replacement for the silk of parachutes, as mosquito screens in tropical hospitals, as rope for towing gliders and mooring ships, and as surgical sutures and filters for blood plasma. In its moldable plastic form, nylon was made into gears, valves, bearings, and propellers for outboard motors. On the home front, nylon became a black-market item in great demand.

After the war, it took more than two years to retool manufacturing processes so that nylon stockings could be made. When the hosiery reappeared, demand again outstripped supply, and there were near riots in some stores. Nylon became the biggest moneymaker in Du Pont's history, and its striking success led the company to create new uses for the material and to create new forms of nylon hosiery. By the mid-1950's, Du Pont had produced more new textile fibers, notably Orlon, a polyacrylic, and Dacron, a polyester. These new materials and nylon's spectacular growth helped Du Pont effect a revolution in manufacturing that propelled its earnings.

The invention of nylon stimulated notable advances in the chemistry and technology of polymers. Some historians of technology have even dubbed the postwar period the "age of plastics" in recognition of the importance of the giant molecules made by ingenious chemists and engineers. The increasing use of synthetics has also been regarded as a measure of a country's prosperity, although such success comes at a cost. Several environmental problems have been found to be related to synthetic materials: Some plastics are not biodegradable, and sustainability has been threatened by the utilization of valuable, vanishing natural resources such as petroleum, which contains the essential chemicals needed to make polymers.

—*Albert B. Costa*

FURTHER READING

Adams, Roger. "Wallace Hume Carothers." *Biographical Memoirs of the National Academy of Sciences* 20 (1939): 291-309. This official biography of the National Academy of Sciences was written by Carothers's doctorate professor. It includes a bibliography of his articles and a listing of his patents.

Brun, Roger. "Of Miracles and Molecules." *American History Illustrated* 23 (December, 1988): 24-29, 48. This is an outstanding and well-written article on the social impact of nylon, from its introduction as hosiery to its many uses over five decades to its association with both glamor and toughness.

Dickerson, Kitty G. *Textiles and Apparel in the International Economy.* New York: Macmillan, 1991. An excellent overview of the global textile industry.

Fenichell, Stephen. *Plastic: The Making of a Synthetic Century.* New York: Collins, 1996. Traces the history of plastics and discusses their sociological importance as they revolutionized many fields, from fashion to medicine.

Garrett, Alfred. *The Flash of Genius.* Princeton, N.J.: D. Van Nostrand, 1963. Chapter 13 provides a narrative of the discovery of nylon. The use of nontechnical language enables those not trained as chemical scientists to appreciate the discovery and to become acquainted with Carothers's work.

Hounshell, David A., and John Kenly Smith, Jr. "The Nylon Drama." *American Heritage of Invention and Technology* 4 (Fall, 1988): 40-55. Two American historians explore how Du Pont took Carothers's discoveries on synthetic fibers and translated them into a commercial textile fiber. This is the best account available on the difficult technological development that made nylon possible.

Joseph, Marjory L., Peyton B. Hudson, Anne Calvert Clapp, and Darlene Kness. *Joseph's Introductory Textile Science.* 6th ed. Fort Worth, Tex.: Harcourt Brace Jovanovich, 1992. The authors relate fiber properties to end-use performance. The section on the modification of nylon is easy to understand.

Kadolph, Sara J., Anna Langford, Norma Hollen, and Jane Saddler. *Textiles.* 7th ed. New York: Macmillan, 1993. Chapter 8 offers a basic understanding of how nylon is made. Properties and end uses of nylon are provided in an easy-to-read manner. Chapters 6 and 7 provide excellent background material on synthetic fibers.

Marvel, Carl S. "The Development of Polymer Chemistry in America: The Early Days." *Journal of Chemical Education* 58 (July, 1981): 535-539. A good description by a leading American organic chemist of Carothers's contribution and the contributions of his contemporaries to the theory and practice of polymerization.

Mossman, Susan, ed. *Early Plastics: Perspectives 1850-1950.* New York: Continuum, 2000. A collection of essays by historians of art and technology on all aspects of the social history of the first century of plastic. Includes twenty color plates.

Smith, John K., and David A. Hounshell. "Wallace H. Carothers and Fundamental Research at Du Pont." *Science* 229 (August 2, 1985): 436-442. The authors contribute an excellent article on Carothers and his work at Du Pont. They provide a coherent narrative as well as insight into his brilliance as a theoretical chemist who could also lead a research group into unchartered territory and make important laboratory discoveries.

Tortora, Phyllis. *Understanding Textiles.* 4th ed. New York: Macmillan, 1992. The types of nylon, along with consumer considerations, are discussed.

SEE ALSO: 1901: Creation of the First Synthetic Vat Dye; 1901-1904: Kipping Discovers Silicones; 1904-1912: Brandenberger Invents Cellophane; 1905-1907: Baekeland Invents Bakelite; Dec., 1930: Du Pont Introduces Freon.

1935

February 12, 1935
EXHIBITION OF AMERICAN ABSTRACT PAINTING OPENS IN NEW YORK

The Whitney Museum of American Art mounted the first comprehensive exhibition of American abstract painting, opening the way for many changes in the American art world.

ALSO KNOWN AS: Abstract Painting in America
LOCALE: New York, New York
CATEGORIES: Arts; organizations and institutions

KEY FIGURES

Stuart Davis (1894-1964), leading American abstract painter who exhibited in *Abstract Painting in America*, wrote the essay for the exhibition catalog, and drew the catalog's cover illustration

Hermon More (1887-1968), chief curator at the Whitney Museum

Juliana Rieser Force (1876-1948), director of the Whitney Museum of American Art

Lloyd Goodrich (1897-1987), curator at the Whitney Museum of American Art

David Smith (1906-1965), young sculptor who wrote to the museum on behalf of several artists demanding inclusion in the 1935 exhibition

Byron Browne (1907-1961), abstract painter who participated in the exhibition and helped to found the influential American Abstract Artists group

Arshile Gorky (c. 1905-1948), leading abstractionist who exhibited in the 1935 show

Alfred Stieglitz (1864-1946), renowned photographer and art dealer who promoted modern art in the United States

SUMMARY OF EVENT

In February, 1935, the Whitney Museum of American Art mounted an exhibition titled *Abstract Painting in America* that traced the development of an abstract style of painting in the United States during the early part of the twentieth century. The show also examined the extent of American artists' commitment to abstraction. Although the exhibit fell short of some expectations, it was a serious attempt to address artistic modernism in the United States.

American abstract art during this period was closely tied to European models and employed a broad range of artistic expression. Whether avant-garde American artists employed a cubist breakup of space, the geometry of nonobjective form, or merely stylized form, "abstrac-

tion" was the rubric under which all of their work was grouped. Some of these artists were committed to an agenda of abstraction, whereas others only dabbled in an abstract stylization of form. Many of those represented in the Whitney's exhibit had already abandoned abstraction by the time of the show, and it was generally thought that the American abstract movement had ended. Nevertheless, the exhibition was the first attempt by a major museum to deal with the issue of abstraction in American art, and it was an important historical event that was crucially tied to the art production of the time and to the political and social matrix in which such art was made.

The issue of abstraction in American art had been blurred during the 1930's. An ideological schism erupted between figurative and abstract painters, between social realist and "American scene" artists on one side and their abstract counterparts on the other. American scene painters such as Thomas Hart Benton and Grant Wood received support from galleries and museums, while the abstract artists were considered outsiders and often felt disfranchised. Yet American abstractionists continued their engagement with the abstract, and some formed a coalition with European abstract and nonobjective artists called the Abstraction-Création group.

This debate over figurative and abstract art was a major concern for artists, and the Whitney responded by holding a symposium on April 10, 1933, to discuss the issue. Led by Cooke Glassgold, the panel included Whitney curator Lloyd Goodrich, art critic and artist Walter Pach (who had been one of the organizers of the 1913 Armory Show), and artists Leo Katz and Morris Davidson. The panel discussed the topic "The Problem of Subject Matter and Abstract Esthetics in Painting." The Whitney curators were more comfortable with figuration, and Goodrich spoke on behalf of that style of imagery. The young Arshile Gorky spoke up and challenged their view, calling for recognition of abstract art as a valid means of expression, one that could be judged and evaluated by the same criteria employed for more traditional work. Gorky's work was represented by four paintings in the 1935 show; in 1937, Goodrich would reconsider his position, and the Whitney would purchase a painting by Gorky for its permanent collection. The sale was the artist's first to a major public collection.

By 1935, with all the interest and discussion sur-

Stuart Davis's 1932 painting Landscape with Garage Lights. *Davis was the leading American abstract painter featured at the* Abstract Painting in America *exhibition.* (AP/Wide World Photos)

rounding abstraction in the United States, the Whitney decided to mount an exhibition. The museum's curator, Hermon More, his assistant Karl Free, and museum director Juliana Rieser Force proceeded to make plans for a comprehensive show. More was well regarded for his installation techniques, and his judgment of American art was sound. He asked Stuart Davis, a leading American abstract painter and the editor of *Art Front* magazine, to write the introductory essay for the exhibit's catalog, and a drawing of Davis's was used for the catalog's cover illustration. Ironically, the drawing chosen for the cover was an ordinary line drawing, a representational still life, rather than an abstraction. Davis's abstract work was well represented in the show, however, by five oil paintings and one gouache (a kind of watercolor painting), including two paintings from his seminal *Eggbeater* series. Yet the cover illustration and the accompanying essay

had further resonance for the exhibition. In his essay, Davis stated that the greatest period of abstract art had occurred from 1915 through 1927. The outlook of the museum's curators and its spokesman artist, therefore, was that abstraction for the most part was over, and that the Whitney's exhibition was an overview of a movement that was now part of the past.

While Davis seemed to think that the abstract movement had waned, he did present an eloquent summary of the abstract artist's objectives. He wrote that "the generative idea of abstract art is alive. It changes, moves and grows like any other living organism." Davis continued by explaining that "art is not and never was a mirror reflection of nature. All efforts at imitation of nature are foredoomed to failure. Art is an understanding and interpretation of nature in various media." While key figures of abstraction were represented in the Whitney's show,

1935

many of the artists included were mere stylists; some, too, had by then abandoned abstraction altogether.

The Whitney may have mounted a less-than-inspired show, but the fact that the exhibition took place at all was important. The Museum of Modern Art, New York's other leading venue for the exhibition of modern works, was entrenched in European modernism and was virtually closed to American artists. Countering the Museum of Modern Art's disregard for American modernism, the Whitney championed neglected American talent.

When American abstract artists heard of the upcoming exhibition, they were heartened that the museum was going to address the issue of abstraction; many hoped that the show would somehow validate their position and promote their ideas and their careers. This was an invitational exhibition, but many lesser-known artists openly solicited the museum for inclusion. One such artist was the young sculptor David Smith, who, together with a group of artist friends—including Willem de Kooning, Arshile Gorky, John Graham, Edgar Levy, and Mischa Resnikoff—drafted a letter to the museum stating that they had formed an alliance and would exhibit in the show only if they all were accepted. Only three were invited to participate, however, and the group disbanded.

A number of galleries were asked to contribute work to the show, including that of Alfred Stieglitz, who secured the work of Arthur Dove, Marsden Hartley, John Marin, Georgia O'Keeffe, and Stanton Macdonald-Wright, members of his illustrious gallery. Edith Halpert's Downtown Gallery supplied the works of several of the precisionist painters, including George Ault, Preston Dickinson, and, most notably, Stuart Davis. Work by Gorky was secured through the J. B. Neumann Gallery, which handled the work of many leading European painters. All the artists, collectors, and dealers concerned cooperated with the museum in the venture, and *Abstract Painting in America* opened on February 12, 1935.

SIGNIFICANCE

Abstract Painting in America baffled most New York critics; even abstract stylization was too much for many of them to comprehend and appreciate. The only critics who offered favorable reviews of the show were Forbes Watson and Henry McBride. The Whitney's next exhibition was *American Genre: The Social Scene in Paintings and Prints*, which was certainly a retrenchment to safer ground.

The following year, however, the Museum of Modern Art mounted an abstract exhibit assembled by Alfred H. Barr, Jr. Barr's impressive *Cubism and Abstract Art* show traced the genesis of abstraction from its post-Impressionist roots through neoplasticism and beyond. The only American artist included was Alexander Calder, and the show's Eurocentric emphasis gave a stamp of approval to artists across the Atlantic. Barr had said that he felt that abstraction was a European feature, not an American one, and that Americans were not, by nature, abstract. A decade later, he would change his mind, but in the mid-1930's the Modern's edicts were law. In December, 1935, Barr mounted another important show, *Fantastic Art, Dada, and Surrealism*, which dealt another blow to the Americans by exhibiting yet more examples of important art from abroad.

Although the Whitney's show had not done much to further the cause of American abstraction, at least it had addressed the issue. Artists in the United States knew that galleries, museums, and critics remained hostile to abstraction, but a new idea emerged: American abstractionists would form an exhibition group to popularize abstract art, and they would hold group exhibitions promoting abstraction. At Ibram Lassaw's studio, a band of artists, including Burgoyne Diller, Gertrude Greene, Harry Holtzman, and Byron Browne, met to discuss exhibitions and the creation of a school for modern art. While the school idea was abandoned, the idea of an exhibition group took root. Browne took a major role in the group, which in 1936 formed the American Abstract Artists.

Browne was one of the younger artists included in the Whitney exhibition, and as a founding member of the American Abstract Artists, he helped to mount the group's first annual exhibition on April 3, 1937, at the Squibb Building Gallery on New York's Fifth Avenue. The exhibit was the largest abstract show held outside a museum venue. Large numbers of visitors filled the gallery, and New York's art critics did review the show, although their opinions were mixed. The artists involved wanted to make a strong statement about abstract art, and Václav Vytlacil compiled a portfolio of affordable lithographs of the exhibitors' work to help acquaint the public with the new work. At the lively opening, Gorky carried around a large reproduction of a painting by the nineteenth century French classicist Jean-Auguste-Dominique Ingres and pointed out the painting's abstract qualities. This group established the viability of abstraction in the United States, providing a forum for young abstract artists to discuss their ideas and to display their work. Many of the group's members would later go on to establish the New York school of abstract expressionism.

—Nancy Malloy

Further Reading

Berman, Avis. *Rebels on Eighth Street: Juliana Force and the Whitney Museum of American Art.* New York: Atheneum, 1990. An excellent history of the founding of the Whitney and of the leading artists and other figures involved in its development. An engrossing look at a pivotal period in American art.

Chipp, Herschel B. *Theories of Modern Art.* Berkeley: University of California Press, 1968. An anthology of writings by various critics, historians, and artists. Includes "The Artist Today," written by Stuart Davis in 1935, and "Is There an American Art," dated 1930, which first appeared in *Creative Art* magazine as a reply to critic Henry McBride.

Harrison, Charles, and Paul Wood, eds. *Art in Theory, 1900-2000: An Anthology of Changing Ideas.* 2d ed. Malden, Mass.: Blackwell, 2002. Excellent reference guide. Although not illustrated, includes a variety of materials, including academic essays, excerpts from artists' diaries and letters, and thorough philosophical, political, and artistic analyses of specific movements, including American abstract painting.

Lane, John R., and Susan C. Larsen, eds. *Abstract Painting and Sculpture in America, 1927-1944.* New York: Harry N. Abrams, 1983. A thorough examination of abstract painting in America during an important period.

Rose, Barbara. *American Art Since 1900.* Rev. ed. New York: Praeger, 1975. A good survey of the development of modern art in twentieth century America.

Schapiro, Meyer. "Nature of Abstract Art." In *Modern Art, Nineteenth and Twentieth Centuries.* New York: George Braziller, 1982. A seminal essay that shows the political matrix involved in abstract painting during this period of early modernism.

Tuchman, Maurice, ed. *The Spiritual in Art: Abstract Painting, 1890-1985.* New York, Abbeville Press, 1999. An interesting analysis of the relationship between modern art and the occult. Produced in conjunction with a show at the Los Angeles County Museum of Art, this catalog comprises a series of essays by noted academics.

See also: Sept., 1911: Der Blaue Reiter Abandons Representation in Art; Dec. 17, 1915: Malevich Introduces Suprematism; 1917: *De Stijl* Advocates Mondrian's Neoplasticism; Mar. 31, 1924: Formation of the Blue Four Advances Abstract Painting; 1925: New Objectivity Movement Is Introduced; Nov. 8, 1929: New York's Museum of Modern Art Opens to the Public; Nov. 17, 1931: Whitney Museum of American Art Opens in New York; 1934: Soviet Union Bans Abstract Art; July 19-Nov. 30, 1937: Nazi Germany Hosts the *Degenerate Art Exhibition*; 1940-1941: Moore's Subway Sketches Record War Images.

February 19, 1935
Odets's *Awake and Sing!* Becomes a Model for Protest Drama

With its depiction of the social and economic consequences of the Great Depression for three generations of a working-class Jewish American family in the Bronx, Clifford Odets's play Awake and Sing! *influenced the nature of protest drama.*

Locale: New York, New York
Categories: Theater; social issues and reform

Key Figures
Clifford Odets (1906-1963), American playwright
Lee Strasberg (1901-1982), American theater director
Stella Adler (1902-1992), American actor

Summary of Event
Awake and Sing! is largely a product of Clifford Odets's success after *Waiting for Lefty* (pr., pb. 1935) catapulted him to instant prominence in 1935 by winning the New Masses/New Theatre Award and galvanizing audiences during its first performance at the Civic Repertory Theatre in Lower Manhattan. *Waiting for Lefty*, about a strike of taxicab drivers, was written in three days and could not have been more appropriate to its times.

Odets, a member of the Group Theatre, had acted in a few of that company's plays and was an indifferent actor. He lived with members of the Group Theatre during summers in the countryside outside New York City and during winters in the sprawling tenement apartment they rented collectively on New York's West Fifty-seventh Street. In 1933, he wrote *I've Got the Blues*, which later that year was retitled *Awake and Sing!* The play was optioned to Frank Merlin, who shortly afterward went bankrupt. Odets then read his script to members of the

1935

Group Theatre in the hope that they would produce it.

The play focuses on the social adjustments faced by the members of a three-generation working-class Jewish American family in the Bronx as the Great Depression gradually robs them of their livelihoods and security. Lee Strasberg, the most dyspeptic of the Group Theatre's three directors, disliked the play, and his disapproval scuttled its chances of being staged, even though its second act was given a reading by the group during the summer of 1933 in Warrensburg, New York. Strasberg had reservations about *Waiting for Lefty* as well.

Awake and Sing! was resurrected in 1935 because *Waiting for Lefty* had left the public clamoring for more Odets. Under pressure to capitalize on the enthusiastic recognition *Waiting for Lefty* had brought him, Odets quickly polished the earlier play, which opened on February 19, 1935, at New York City's Belasco Theatre to favorable reviews.

Like most plays written with the Group Theatre in mind, *Awake and Sing!* has a cast of seven characters of relatively equal importance. An eighth character, Schlosser, is minor, but he advances some of the business of the narrative and carries part of its philosophical burden. Odets's manuscript of *I've Got the Blues* shows that

Clifford Odets. (Hulton Archive/Getty Images)

he had Stella Adler in mind for the role of Bessie Berger when he originally conceived of the play; he often referred to Bessie as "Stella" in the typescript that is now housed in the Library of Congress.

Bessie, the mother of the family, belongs to the middle generation. Her father, Jacob, lives with the family in their respectable Bronx apartment. Bessie's husband, Myron, once had potential; Bessie worked in a stocking factory for two years so that he could attend law school, which he did not complete. Myron has eked out an existence for his family, but his idealism is now badly tarnished and emerges only vestigially when, after Myron spends fifty cents for an Irish Sweepstakes ticket, he tells his skeptical brother-in-law, Morty, that the contest cannot be rigged because the government would not allow it.

The children in the family, Ralph and Hennie, are both grown; Ralph is in love with Blanche, whose name heavy-handedly suggests her purity. The two cannot realistically consider marriage, however, because Ralph does not earn a decent living; the future holds little hope for him. Ralph's sister Hennie, pregnant and unmarried, has no more hope for her future than her brother has for his.

The only people Odets brings onto the stage who have some sort of security are Moe Axelrod, the Berger's boarder, who makes no secret of his attraction to Hennie, and Uncle Morty, Bessie's cigar-chomping brother, who, although he has money, shares little of it with his aged father, Jacob. Moe Axelrod has been injured in the war and has the security of a government pension. Uncle Morty represents the dirty, self-centered capitalist indifferent to anyone's problems except his own.

Bessie lives daily in a hell of insecurity. She recounts to her family how a respectable old lady on the next block has been evicted because she lacks the money to keep her house; the woman is out on the street over on Dawson Avenue, surrounded by her belongings. The old woman's plight embodies Bessie's worst nightmare. Bessie's urgent need is to keep her family intact. She is the caregiver and the manager in a family whose father, the natural provider, has been worn down by a socioeconomic system that, in Odets's eyes, is destroying the working class. Myron, robbed of his maleness by society (and by a very domineering wife), has been neutered emotionally.

When Hennie turns up pregnant, Bessie has to find a husband for her. To do otherwise would be to jeopardize the family's respectability in the neighborhood, the limit of Bessie's encapsulated world. In order to protect this precious image, which could, in her eyes, easily be shattered, Bessie has no qualms about marrying Hennie off to Sam Feinschreiber, a hapless immigrant who is duped into thinking that Hennie's baby is his.

Both the representatives of the younger generation escape by the play's end, but the escape is not a happy one. Hennie runs off with Moe Axelrod, leaving her husband and child behind. Distant places have been calling. Odets uses the leitmotif of the evening mail plane that flies over the Berger house in the same way that earlier generations of writers used train whistles to suggest escape to some land of heart's desire.

Ralph is given his chance when Jacob, who has made Ralph the beneficiary of his small insurance policy, throws himself from the roof. Because Ralph and Hennie have been robbed of their hope, the escape Odets offers them does not involve their doing anything productive to overcome their problems. The point of the play clearly is that the accommodation each of them finds offers no realistic hope for the future, either theirs or society's.

SIGNIFICANCE

Awake and Sing! presents a stinging critique of the capitalist society that, Odets suggests, robs people of their dignity, their hope, and their potential. One cannot really call the play "angry"; the hopeless characters are too demoralized to be angry in the way that Odets's taxicab drivers are. Instead, the play touched the inner beings, the social consciences, of large audiences—the affluent audiences that sat in the expensive seats as well as the audiences that squeezed into the dollar seats in the balcony on matinee days.

In writing the play, Odets benefited from the new freedom of language that the 1920's—especially the work of Eugene O'Neill—had brought to American drama. Odets wrote in the vernacular of common people, a vernacular he had learned growing up in a Jewish American family in Philadelphia and New York. The language of *Awake and Sing!* is both lyrical and authentic. It employs the accents, the clichés, and the wisecracks that working-class people use naturally in their daily speech.

Awake and Sing! also pointed the way to a drama of the people. Odets's heroes are antiheroes. If their tragedy comes about because of a fall, they do not have far to fall. They are not Oedipuses or Lears or Macbeths. They are, rather, the people next door or around the corner. Their kinship is more to Everyman or to Geoffrey Chaucer's Wife of Bath than to the classical heroes of ancient Greek or Elizabethan tragedy.

Playwrights associated with the Group Theatre— Paul and Claire Sifton, Paul Green, Sidney Kingsley,

Maxwell Anderson, John Howard Lawson—wrote generally about the proletariat, about common people, rather than about the famous or highly placed. Odets and his compatriots during the 1930's opened new worlds for such later playwrights as Tennessee Williams, Arthur Miller, and William Inge, all of whom drew sustenance from the drama that immediately preceded their emergence as playwrights.

The trend of writing about common people continued in the work of such later playwrights as Lanford Wilson, August Wilson, Tom Stoppard, Edward Albee, and Samuel Beckett. Eugene O'Neill had made strides in this direction during the 1920's with such plays as *Anna Christie* (pr. 1921), *The Hairy Ape* (pr., pb. 1922), and *Desire Under the Elms* (pr. 1924). Writers such as Odets benefited greatly from O'Neill's daring ventures and built on them in ways that moved American theater forward into unexplored dramatic territory.

An earlier generation in Europe—Gerhart Hauptmann, Anton Chekhov, Maxim Gorky, Henrik Ibsen— had already used drama as a vehicle for advancing proletarian ideas. Those who wrote for the Group Theatre eagerly plugged into the currents these dramatic pioneers had sparked. They made their own advances, which in turn led to a burgeoning of plays about common people in the 1940's and after.

Awake and Sing! is a prime example of a play that departs from a blind acceptance of the star system. The counterbalancing of seven significant characters in the play replicates the actual dynamics of the informal human relationships that characterize family existence and interaction. The star system makes protagonists of Shakespearean proportions obligatory; the Group Theatre approach, however, reduces those proportions to dimensions common people understand.

In many respects, *Awake and Sing!* was a key element in the advance toward much of the drama in vogue in the late twentieth century. Although its impact is essentially socialistic, *Awake and Sing!* is also a significantly democratic play in that it takes seriously the lives of people who, in cultures that are less egalitarian, probably would evoke little interest or attention.

—*R. Baird Shuman*

FURTHER READING

Bentley, Eric, ed. *Thirty Years of Treason: Excerpts from the Hearings Before the House Committee on Un-American Activities.* 1971. Reprint. New York: Nation Books, 2002. It is difficult to understand Odets fully without understanding his reaction to being

1935

summoned before the House Committee on Un-American Activities, when his national loyalty and that of many others working in theater and film was questioned. Indispensable resource for readers interested in the political ramifications of Odets's work.

Brenman-Gibson, Margaret. *Clifford Odets: An American Playwright—The Years from 1906 to 1940.* 1981. Reprint. New York: Applause Books, 2002. Well-documented, comprehensive biography is a monument in its field. Covers Odets's early life in greater detail than any previous biography. Presents a brilliant and original psychoanalytic interpretation of *Awake and Sing!*

Cantor, Harold. *Clifford Odets: Playwright Poet.* 2d ed. Metuchen, N.J.: Scarecrow Press, 2000. Reviews Odets's use of language, especially of dialects, through close readings of eleven plays. This approach is particularly relevant to *Awake and Sing!* as the play's lyricism and authenticity have been widely acknowledged.

Clurman, Harold. *The Fervent Years: The Story of the Group Theatre and the Thirties.* 1945. Reprint. New York: Da Capo Press, 1983. Quintessential history of the Group Theatre, out of which much of Odets's work grew. Goes into great detail about the genesis of *Awake and Sing!*

Cooperman, Robert. *Clifford Odets: An Annotated Bibliography, 1935-1989.* Metuchen, N.J.: Scarecrow Press, 1990. Begins with a thoughtfully conceived and well-presented bibliographical essay. Part 2 provides a comprehensive list of Odets's writings, and part 3 contains an extensive bibliography of writings about Odets.

Griffin, Robert J. "On the Lovesongs of Clifford Odets." In *The Thirties: Fiction, Poetry, Drama,* edited by Warren G. French. Deland, Fla.: Everett/Edwards, 1967. Focuses on Odets's two most notable family plays, *Awake and Sing!* and *Paradise Lost* (pr. 1935). Valuable for comments on Odets's language and on his social outlook as reflected in these plays.

Herr, Christopher J. *Clifford Odets and American Political Theatre.* Westport, Conn.: Praeger, 2003. Places Odets's works in the context of the time of social, political, and economic change in which they were written. Includes chronology, selected bibliography, and index.

Miller, Gabriel, ed. *Critical Essays on Clifford Odets.* Boston: G. K. Hall, 1991. Presents essays on Odets by such critics as Joseph Wood Krutch, Brooks Atkinson, and John Mason Brown. Also includes interviews with Odets conducted by Michael Mendelsohn, Arthur Wagner, and Armand Aulicino. Includes three entries specifically on *Awake and Sing!*

Weales, Gerald. *Clifford Odets: Playwright.* Reprint. New York: Methuen, 1985. Excellent brief critical biography provides valuable insights into each of Odets's major plays, including *Awake and Sing!* Relates Odets's work to the sociopolitical currents of the period in which he was most productive.

SEE ALSO: 1905: Baker Establishes the 47 Workshop at Harvard; Jan. 21, 1908: *The Ghost Sonata* Influences Modern Theater and Drama; May 10, 1921: Pirandello's *Six Characters in Search of an Author* Premieres; 1929-1930: *The Bedbug* and *The Bathhouse* Exemplify Revolutionary Theater; 1931-1941: The Group Theatre Flourishes; Jan. 2, 1933: Coward's *Design for Living* Epitomizes the 1930's; Aug. 29, 1935-June 30, 1939: Federal Theatre Project Promotes Live Theater.

February 27, 1935
Temple Receives a Special Academy Award

Shirley Temple, America's cinema sweetheart and the top box-office draw from 1935 to 1938, received a special miniature Academy Award for her outstanding contribution to the film industry.

Locale: Los Angeles, California
Category: Motion pictures

Key Figures
Shirley Temple (b. 1928), American child film star
Damon Runyon (1884-1946), American author
Adolphe Menjou (1890-1963), American actor
Darryl F. Zanuck (1902-1979), American film
   producer

Summary of Event

Following the stock market crash of 1929, Shirley Temple, a cheery child screen star of the 1930's, quickly rose to fame by capturing the hearts of the moviegoing audience and freeing them momentarily from the worries of joblessness, homelessness, breadlines, bank failures, and other monetary disasters. For her popularity and skill in dance, voice, and acting, she was awarded a special child-size Oscar—the slender gold statuette coveted by film professionals since it was first awarded in 1929—at the 1935 Academy Awards presentation banquet. The event, as usual, was attended by the elite of Hollywood society and agency professionals and announced by searchlights, press releases, film magazine interviews, and nationwide radio coverage.

Temple, the youngest star to receive an Oscar, earned the admiration of the Academy of Motion Picture Arts and Sciences chiefly for *Little Miss Marker* (1934), a black-and-white film adapted from a Damon Runyon story and starring Adolphe Menjou, Dorothy Dell, Charles Bickford, and Lynne Overman in addition to Temple. The plot, about a seedy racetrack gambler who adopts a small girl who eventually rescues him from his adversaries, features the predictable Runyon components—cynical underworld figures and appealingly helpless ingenues who employ their charms to soften hardened hearts and bring about a quick rescue. The story concludes with a satisfying reward for good and an appropriate penalty for evil. *Variety* lauded the film for its blend of melodrama and compassion.

Shirley Temple's unprecedented success sprang from a pairing of genes and luck, with a little family push thrown in for good measure. Born in Santa Monica, Cali-

fornia, the third child and first daughter of Francis George Temple, a bank officer, and Gertrude Krieger Temple, Shirley, a sunny, smooth-limbed blond, enhanced her natural appeal by studying tap dance beginning when she was three years old. Scouted in her kindergarten classroom by an agent from Educational Studios and accompanied on location by her famous stage mother, Shirley began her screen appearances in the "Baby Burlesk" series before advancing to major roles. At the age of five, she bested two hundred candidates for her first cinema part in *Stand Up and Cheer* (1934). Success brought a contract for $1,250 a week, a phenomenal salary for Depression times.

Temple's image—the stereotypical lighthearted, dimple-cheeked minx—evolved from good grooming in little-girl fashions, including patent leather Mary Janes and anklet socks, starchy sailor suit, immaculate gloves, and saucy, cylindrical curls highlighted with a bow to match her outfit. A disarmingly bright, poised, mischievous moppet, Temple delighted fans with her self-confident, insouciant air. Hordes of worshipers and Temple look-alikes followed her wherever she appeared, at airports, the circus, the beach, and visits to department store Santa Clauses. Notables such as Albert Einstein, J. Edgar Hoover, and President Franklin D. Roosevelt counted her among their personal favorites, and fans the world over recognized her at once by her characteristically bumptious posturing and mugging and Kewpie-doll smile.

The epitome of little-girl sweetness, Temple parlayed her charms into success by maximizing talent, concentration, and hard work. She could mimic her contemporaries, including Fred Astaire and Ginger Rogers, and match the complicated dance routines of veteran hoofer Bill "Bojangles" Robinson. She balanced a variety of male costars, from Randolph Scott, Joseph Cotten, Cary Grant, and Buddy Ebsen to Ronald Reagan. Even though the plots of her films provided meager challenges to a thinking audience, much to the filmmakers' benefit, the public's rush to see Temple singing, dancing, and mugging in her costume-rich scenarios kept theater lines long.

Eager to make the most of their pint-sized box-office wonder during a period when money for film tickets was growing scarce, the studios moved swiftly to exploit every moment of her childhood. Two subsequent 1934 films, *Now and Forever*, a Paramount production starring Gary Cooper and Carole Lombard, and *Stand Up and Cheer*, with James Dunn, Nigel Bruce, and Stepin Fetchit, influenced her Academy Award nomination. The former, a likable mix of thrills and comedy, as was *Little Miss Marker*, depicts the power of a small child to transform her father, a jewel thief, and his hard-boiled mistress. *Now and Forever* received high marks from both the *New York Post* and *Variety*. In contrast, *Stand Up and Cheer*, a Fox production about a child performer who helps the fictional U.S. secretary of amusement to boost the country's Depression-racked spirits, received less favorable press because of its contrived plot. The film redeemed itself primarily through audience reaction to the engagingly talented, cherubic six-year-old star.

SIGNIFICANCE

The Shirley Temple phenomenon peaked in 1939, when the child lost her rounded cuteness and entered adolescence. Up until that point, she had been a major moneymaker for the studios. In her biography, she noted bitterly the commercialism of her success and how she was marketed like a grocery-store commodity. Signed by Darryl F. Zanuck to a Twentieth Century-Fox contract and insured by Lloyd's of London, Temple lived in a special on-site four-room cottage, complete with rabbit hutch, picket fence, and rope swing. To restrict the public's access to her, she was tutored privately. In the 1940's, returned to a semblance of normalcy, she at-

Shirley Temple in costume for her 1935 film The Little Colonel. *(AP/Wide World Photos)*

tended the Westlake School for Girls, from which she graduated at the age of seventeen. She contributed greatly in her childhood to film history, with forty film and fifty television productions, including hits such as *Baby Take a Bow* (1934), *Bright Eyes* (1934), *Curly Top* (1935), *The Little Colonel* (1935), *Poor Little Rich Girl* (1936), *Wee Willie Winkie* (1937), *Heidi* (1937), *Rebecca of Sunnybrook Farm* (1938), *The Little Princess* (1939), and *The Blue Bird* (1940).

In her teens, Temple, taller but still unmistakably dimpled and winsome, continued to please faithful fans. Her teen and postteen roles in *Since You Went Away* (1944), *Kiss and Tell* (1945), *The Bachelor and the Bobby-Soxer* (1947), *That Hagen Girl* (1947), *Fort Apache* (1948), and *A Kiss for Corliss* (1949) received less adulation, primar-

ily because they could not play on the cuteness of childhood. About the time that Temple met John Agar, a soldier turned actor whom she married to relieve the loneliness and isolation engendered by too much fame, the studio, searching for a replacement child star, considered Sybil Jason, Gigi Perreau, and others. Among the most successful post-Temple child stars were Margaret O'Brien, who premiered at the age of four in *Babes in Arms* (1939) and won an honorary Oscar in 1944, and Natalie Wood, who debuted at the age of eight in *Tomorrow Is Forever* (1946). Never as appealing as Shirley Temple, Wood earned lasting fame in the Christmas classic *Miracle on 34th Street* (1947), then grew more voluptuous and appealing to cinema audiences. Her later successes included *Splendor in the Grass* (1961) and *West Side Story* (1961).

Some male child stars met with equally long-lived popularity. Jackie Cooper scored with *The Champ* (1931) and *Skippy* (1931), for which he was nominated for an Academy Award for best actor. A stream of other cute-child scenarios brought him work in *Sooky* (1931), *Young Donovan's Kid* (1931), and *Divorce in the Family* (1932). Along with a coterie of children who composed the *Our Gang* cast, he made a notable effort that resulted in years of reruns. Through her success, Temple certainly influenced the trend toward child-oriented films.

An extended film career is not a part of the Shirley Temple legend. After her divorce from Agar, Temple, already the mother of a daughter, suffered intense depression. Following a relaxing vacation in Hawaii, she met businessman Charles Alden Black, son of a wealthy family, whose emotional maturity provided the stability she needed at the nadir of her young womanhood. They married, had a son and a second daughter, and settled south of San Francisco. Shirley Temple Black involved herself in volunteer work for the National Wildlife Federation and the National Multiple Sclerosis Society. At one point, she served as a receptionist in a children's orthopedics hospital.

From local activism, she moved into politics. To maintain a dignified professional image, she was forced to transcend the public's image of a dimpled darling in frills and tap shoes. In 1967, she failed to unseat Pete McCloskey in a bid for a seat in the U.S. House of Representatives, but from 1974 to 1976 she served as the U.S. ambassador to Ghana. Her return to the public eye brought new audiences of children to her old films, which had fallen into neglect. Hollywood, capitalizing on her late-in-life achievements, returned the spotlight to her. Honored at the fifty-seventh annual Academy Awards presentation ceremony on March 25, 1985, Shirley Temple Black received a full-sized Oscar to replace the miniature version she accepted in 1935. To recapture the mystique of the toddler star, organizers of the ceremony ran clips of her greatest films. Three years later, the documentary *Going Hollywood: The War Years* received archival footage from her canon in a montage of films from the World War II era.

Recovered from breast cancer in 1989, Shirley Temple Black was named ambassador to Czechoslovakia (now the Czech Republic and Slovakia). She took an immersion language course to expedite her pursuit of negotiations with President Gustav Husák, to whom she presented her credentials in his native tongue. She took particular pride in the nation's bloodless overthrow of an oppressive communist regime. As an outspoken supporter of the human rights that communism had violated, she remained difficult to typify as liberal or conservative, Democrat or Republican, but periodically she was considered as a vice presidential candidate or a cabinet post nominee.

Looking back on her many honors, appointments, and opportunities, Shirley Temple Black acknowledged that her film career, although it had little connection with her adult interests and capabilities, provided the requisite name recognition to people in power such as President George Bush, who nominated her for the ambassadorship to Czechoslovakia. Her prior fame opened possibilities for her to become involved with research programs on acquired immune deficiency syndrome (AIDS), assistance for homeless and disabled people, and the campaign to ratify the Equal Rights Amendment. In her 1988 autobiography, *Child Star*, she unleashed adult vengeance on Hollywood's corrupt star system, which exploited her in childhood, menaced her innocence, and enriched a cadre of opportunists, many of whom borrowed money for private use that they never repaid.

—Mary Ellen Snodgrass

FURTHER READING

Bell, Joseph N. "Shirley Temple: Her Movies, Her Life." *Good Housekeeping*, February, 1981, 114-115, 185-190. Brief biographical article features photographs of Temple's film career, including shots of her with costars Buddy Ebsen, Charles Farrell, James Dunn, and Bill "Bojangles" Robinson. Chronology covers Temple's bout with breast cancer, her role as first U.S. chief of protocol, and her service as a U.S. ambassador.

Hammontree, Patsy Guy. *Shirley Temple Black: A Bio-Bibliography*. Westport, Conn.: Greenwood Press, 1998. Thorough discussion of Shirley Temple Black's careers, from child star to diplomat. Includes chronology, filmography, bibliography, and index.

Osborne, Robert. *Seventy-Five Years of the Oscar: The Official History of the Academy Awards*. New York: Abbeville Press, 2003. Overview of the Academy Awards demands respect from historians, researchers, and serious cinema fans. Presents a thorough listing of Academy Award winners from the inception of the Oscar to 2003. Features full-color cinematic stills as well as reproductions of dust jackets from adapted novels and plays.

Temple Black, Shirley. *Child Star: An Autobiography*.

1935

New York: McGraw-Hill, 1988. Autobiography describes Temple's family life, early training in dance and music, introduction into filmdom from kindergarten, starring film roles, and adolescent screen roles, along with critical opinions of her cinematic talents. Details her eclipse in adolescence and failed marriage to John Agar. A worthy study for the cinema buff or student of Hollywood history.

Windeler, Robert. *The Films of Shirley Temple*. Secaucus, N.J.: Citadel Press, 1978. Critique of Temple's screen career focuses on information pertinent to cin-

ema history and critical commentary on the child film genre. Useful source for detailed history.

Yorkshire, Heidi. "Shirley Temple Black Sets the Record Straight." *McCall's*, March, 1989, 88-92. Describes Temple's adult career and her decision to write her autobiography *Child Star*.

SEE ALSO: 1930's: Hollywood Enters Its Golden Age; 1930's-1940's: Studio System Dominates Hollywood Filmmaking; 1933: *Forty-Second Street* Defines 1930's Film Musicals; Aug. 17, 1939: *The Wizard of Oz* Premieres.

April 8, 1935

WORKS PROGRESS ADMINISTRATION IS ESTABLISHED

The Works Progress Administration was responsible for a nationwide program of public works to alleviate unemployment. At its height, the WPA employed four million people. It funded both vital infrastructural projects, such as bridges and highways, and the creation of many works of art and literature, becoming a showcase for President Roosevelt's New Deal.

ALSO KNOWN AS: Emergency Relief Appropriation Act
LOCALE: Washington, D.C.
CATEGORIES: Government and politics; laws, acts, and legal history; business and labor; organizations and institutions

KEY FIGURES

Harry Hopkins (1890-1946), director of the Works Progress Administration
Holger Cahill (1887-1960), head of the Federal Art Project
Henry G. Alsberg (1881-1970), director of the Federal Writers' Project
Hallie Flanagan (1890-1969), director of the Federal Theatre Project
Harold Ickes (1874-1952), U.S. secretary of the interior, 1933-1946, and head of the Public Works Administration under the National Industrial Recovery Act
Franklin D. Roosevelt (1882-1945), president of the United States, 1933-1945
George Biddle (1885-1973), American artist
Frank Comerford Walker (1886-1959), head of the Application and Information Division of the Federal Relief Program

Aubrey Willis Williams (1890-1965), director of the National Youth Administration
Edward Bruce (1879-1943), American lawyer, businessman, and painter

SUMMARY OF EVENT

The history of the New Deal's relief policy is essentially one of hopeful experimentation. President Franklin D. Roosevelt was reluctant to engage in a full-scale program of deficit spending implicit in direct relief and public works, yet he was deeply committed to relieving the nation's unemployment. The National Industrial Recovery Act (NIRA), passed in June, 1933, provided for the creation of the Public Works Administration, under Secretary of the Interior Harold Ickes, for the purpose of spending some $3.3 billion to relieve unemployment. Ickes, however, approached his task with such caution that it had little effect. Also, to relieve the growing unemployment problem, Roosevelt established the Federal Emergency Relief Administration (FERA) in May, 1933, with an appropriation of $500 million to make direct grants to the states for relief services.

The director of FERA was Harry Hopkins, a former social worker. Hopkins soon realized that his agency was making little progress on the national unemployment problem. With Roosevelt's assistance, he succeeded in establishing a temporary Civil Works Administration (CWA) in October, 1933. The primary purpose of this agency was to provide employment for some four million men and women in a complete federal make-work project. Nationwide, the CWA engaged in such tasks as repairing or building in excess of 500,000 miles of roads, one thousand airports, forty thousand schools, and more than thirty-five hundred playgrounds and athletic fields. The CWA also employed fifty thousand teachers. In the winter of 1933-1934, Hopkins employed more than 3 million persons and spent $933 million. At its peak, in mid-January, 1934, the program employed 4.23 million individuals. According to historian William E. Leuchtenburg, "The CWA got the country through the winter." By March of 1934, however, the president was disturbed at the rate of expenditure; more important, he did not want the work-relief program to become a permanent form of dole to the unemployed. The CWA was terminated, and once again FERA took up primary responsibility for relief, including those projects left unfinished by the CWA.

An evaluation of the programs persuaded Roosevelt that something else was needed to combat the problem of unemployment. Neither FERA, which generally provided direct relief, nor the CWA, which had provided a disguised dole, had made much of an impact on the constantly expanding unemployment problem. Both the

president and Hopkins wanted to keep the federal government out of direct relief; instead, they wanted to concentrate on a vast public employment program that would provide honest jobs for the needy. It was this reasoning that led Roosevelt to call for a new emergency relief appropriation in January, 1935. The subsequent Emergency Relief Appropriation Act, passed April 8, 1935, provided $5 billion with few strings attached.

The appropriation of the money, however, was only one of the problems facing Roosevelt in his new work-relief program. Of immediate concern was the appointment of a director for the new program. Hopkins had much to recommend him for the task. Roosevelt sympathized with Hopkins's desire to place major emphasis on benefits for the workers. At times, however, the president seemed disturbed by the fantastic rate at which Hopkins spent federal funds. Another leading contender for the job was Ickes, who desired an expansion of his Public Works Administration. With both men campaigning for the job, and feeling unable himself to disregard

A Works Progress Administration crew rebuilds the Morris Canal in New Jersey around 1936. (Hulton Archive/Getty Images)

1935

either for fear of seeming to repudiate their past accomplishments, Roosevelt effected a compromise by creating an incredibly complex organization to spend the money and by bringing in Frank Comerford Walker, an old and tactful friend, to serve as mediator between the two men.

Despite the elaborate organization, Hopkins managed to dominate the new relief program, primarily because the president, liking his approach better than that of Ickes, provided loopholes in the rules and certain strategic assistance. Hopkins's new agency, called the Works Progress Administration (WPA), proceeded to expand into the most gigantic federal works operation ever seen in peacetime. Originally designed for the unskilled worker, the WPA was soon engaged in a variety of projects, constructing more than 600,000 miles of highways, roads, and streets, repairing and constructing more than 100,000 bridges, 100,000 public buildings, thousands of parks and airfields, and thousands of recreational facilities. In these activities, Hopkins was guided by the idea of providing legitimate employment and making sure that most of the money went into wages rather than material expenses.

The WPA also aided thousands of artists, writers, actors, and students. The Federal Theatre Project was established under the direction of Hallie Flanagan, a Guggenheim Fellow and head of Vassar College's theater. The project employed many gifted people and engaged in considerable experimentation until it was abruptly terminated by Congress in 1939. During a period of four years, live drama was brought to an audience totaling thirty million in thousands of small towns that hitherto had seen no better than small traveling tent shows. The Federal Writers' Project directed by Henry Alsberg, a former director of the Provincetown Theater, employed college professors, journalists, and other literary persons to record local and regional history. More than one thousand state and territorial guides, picture books, and other works of historical interest were written. Under the direction of Holger Cahill, the Federal Art Project provided employment for thousands of local artists whose artistic endeavors still grace hundreds of local post offices and libraries throughout the United States.

In addition to these projects, the National Youth Administration (NYA) was created to assist those young men and women of the United States unable to find jobs. Under the direction of former Alabama social worker Aubrey Williams, the NYA sought and found part-time employment for more than 600,000 college students and more than 1.5 million high school students over a five-year period.

The WPA, effective as an emergency measure, had its weaknesses. At no time did Hopkins employ more than four million people, accounting for less than half of the ten million unemployed at the time. Political problems arose because of his opposition to the use of the WPA for patronage purposes, and there was mounting concern that the jobs created by the

---

A SLAVE NARRATIVE

One of the Works Progress Administration's projects was to interview more than two thousand former slaves. This account was given by a woman known as Aunt Adeline in Fayetteville, Arkansas, in 1937.

When my mother's master come to Arkansas about 1849, looking for a country residence, he bought what was known as the old Kidd place on the Old Wire Road, which was one of the Stage Coach stops. I was about one year old when we came. We had a big house and many times passengers would stay several days and wait for the next stage to come by. It was then that I earned my first money. I must have been about six or seven years old. One of Mr. Parks' daughters was about one and a half years older than I was. We had a play house back of the fireplace chimney. We didn't have many toys; maybe a doll made of a corn cob, with a dress made from scraps and a head made from a roll of scraps. We were playing church. Miss Fannie was the preacher and I was the audience. We were singing "Jesus my all to Heaven is gone." When we were half way through with our song we discovered that the passengers from the stage coach had stopped to listen. We were so frightened at our audience that we both ran. But we were coaxed to come back for a dime and sing our song over. I remember that Miss Fannie used a big leaf for a book.

I had always been told from the time I was a small child that I was a Negro of African stock. That it was no disgrace to be a Negro and had it not been for the white folks who brought us over here from Africa as slaves, we would never have been here and would have been much better off.

We colored folks were not allowed to be taught to read or write. It was against the law. My master's folks always treated me well. I had good clothes. Sometimes I was whipped for things I should not have done just as the white children were.

Source: Works Progress Administration, *Slave Narratives: A Folk History of Slavery in the United States from Interviews with Former Slaves* (Washington, D.C.: U.S. Library of Congress, 1941).

program were in fact a dole. When Congress succeeded in gaining control of WPA appropriations, Hopkins was forced to change his approach, and the administration was restructured in 1939. It continued until 1943, when—in light of the simultaneous employment boom and conscription brought about by World War II—it was finally terminated.

SIGNIFICANCE

The WPA proved to be one of the most famous programs of the New Deal as well as one of those considered most successful. It is a mark of the ability of the program to live up to its own standards—creating real jobs rather than handouts—that the WPA is remembered more for its products than for its effects on unemployment. Many important American literary and artistic figures—including Arthur Miller and Orson Welles—produced works with WPA monies, and many of the bridges and roads created with those monies remain—with plaques attesting to the source of their funding—in the twenty-first century. Corruption was to some degree inevitable, but when the immensity of the unemployment problem posed by the Depression and the novelty of the remedy is considered, the WPA represented a gigantic effort on the part of the federal government to bring immediate succor to the country's jobless. It also proved to be a forerunner and the introductory phase of the nation's attempt to deal effectively with the ever-growing problem of unemployment and public welfare, with all the accompanying complications.

—*George Q. Flynn and Liesel Ashley Miller*

FURTHER READING

Adams, Henry H. *Harry Hopkins*. New York: G. P. Putnam's Sons, 1977. This biography of the director of the Works Progress Administration provides insight into both the private and public lives of Hopkins. Photographs, extensive bibliography, index.

Becker, Heather. *Art for the People: The Rediscovery and Preservation of Progressive- and WPA-Era Murals in the Chicago Public Schools, 1904-1943*. San Francisco: Chronicle Books, 2002. Study of populist Chicago school murals beginning thirty years before the WPA. Since it covers both WPA and pre-WPA art, the study provides a basis of comparison that allows one to determine just what the program did and did not accomplish. Bibliographic references and index.

Brinkley, Alan. *The End of Reform: New Deal Liberalism in Recession and War*. New York: Alfred A. Knopf, 1995. Brinkley sees the New Deal not merely as a reform movement, but "as part of a long process of ideological adaptation" in the United States.

Contreras, Belisario. *Tradition and Innovation in New Deal Art*. London: Associated University Presses, 1983. Discusses both the politics and aesthetics of New Deal art. Points out what was traditional and what was innovative in the art of the PWAP and the WPA/FAP. Thoroughly documented and well illustrated (black-and-white plates only).

DeNoon, Christopher. *Posters of the WPA*. Los Angeles: Wheatley Press, 1987. Identifying the period from 1935 to 1943 as one of the most innovative in the history of American graphic design, the author discusses the developments that took place as the WPA printed two million posters from thirty-five thousand designs. Illustrated with accurate color reproductions of the original posters.

Leuchtenburg, William E. *Franklin D. Roosevelt and the New Deal: 1932-1940*. New York: Harper & Row, 1963. Explores Roosevelt's role in the New Deal. Chapter 6 focuses on efforts of the Works Progress Administration to relieve unemployment.

McKinzie, Richard. *The New Deal for Artists*. Princeton, N.J.: Princeton University Press, 1973. Emphasizes the social and political forces behind the establishment of the WPA/FAP; does not focus on the evaluation or explication of the art produced under the program's auspices. A carefully documented study of the relationship between a government bureaucracy and the arts.

O'Connor, Francis, ed. *Art for the Millions*. Greenwich, Conn.: New York Graphic Society, 1973. A collection of essays written by many of the artists and administrators who were in the WPA/FAP. One of the best sources of information about the program. Also contains complete documentation: inventories of works and manuscripts, reports of expenditures, a list of community art centers, and bibliography.

Park, Marlene, and Gerald Markowitz. *Democratic Vistas: Post Offices and Public Art in the New Deal*. Philadelphia: Temple University Press, 1984. Focuses on the Treasury Department's Section of Fine Arts, which commissioned murals and sculpture for federal buildings and for eleven hundred post offices. Authors concentrate on choice of themes as well as style, while also giving helpful data on individual artists. Profusely illustrated.

Schlesinger, Arthur, Jr. *The Coming of the New Deal*. Boston: Houghton Mifflin, 1959. An essential and timeless study, this comprehensive and detailed work cannot be overlooked in any thorough examination of New Deal legislation and policies.

1935

Seaton, Elizabeth. *WPA Federal Art Project: Printmaking in California, 1935-1943.* San Francisco: Book Club of California, 2005. An example of the art projects funded by the WPA, this is a case study and collection of prints made by WPA artists in California. Bibliographic references.

White, Graham, and John Maze. *Harold Ickes of the New Deal: His Private Life and Public Career.* Cambridge, Mass.: Harvard University Press, 1985. Looks at the career of Ickes as the temperamental interior secretary and head of the Public Works Administration in the context of the New Deal.

SEE ALSO: Jan., 1922: Izaak Walton League Is Formed; Oct. 29, 1929-1939: Great Depression; Apr. 5, 1933: U.S. Civilian Conservation Corps Is Established; Feb., 1934: Rivera's Rockefeller Center Mural Is Destroyed; Aug. 29, 1935-June 30, 1939: Federal Theatre Project Promotes Live Theater.

April 15, 1935
ARBITRATION AFFIRMS NATIONAL RESPONSIBILITY FOR POLLUTION

An international jury declared that countries were responsible for their pollution and required Canada to compensate the United States for environmental damage caused by exhaust from a smelter in Trail, British Columbia.

ALSO KNOWN AS: Trail Smelter dispute; Trail Smelter arbitration
LOCALE: United States; Canada
CATEGORIES: Environmental issues; laws, acts, and legal history; diplomacy and international relations

KEY FIGURES

Richard Bedford Bennett (1870-1947), prime minister of Canada, 1930-1935
Charles Warren (1868-1954), American attorney
Oliver Wendell Holmes, Jr. (1841-1935), associate justice of the United States, 1902-1932

SUMMARY OF EVENT

On April 15, 1935, the United States and Canada signed a special agreement to resolve the Trail Smelter dispute. Canada agreed to pay the United States $350,000 in compensation for agricultural damage in northern Washington State that was caused by exhaust from a metal refinery in Trail, British Columbia. This landmark case of international environmental law articulated the idea that a country is responsible for the pollution it generates. The Trail Smelter arbitration is unique in international law because it is the only case specifically related to air pollution crossing national borders.

In the Trail Smelter arbitration, Canada and the United States also asked the international jury that refereed the dispute to decide whether Canada should repay the United States for damages that happened after the jury's award, to determine whether there was an acceptable amount of damage the smelter could cause in the future, and to decide how the smelter company should limit future damage. In another unique action in the history of resolving international disputes, the jury carried out an independent study to answer these questions. The Trail Smelter arbitration and its final decision provided guidelines for countries concerned about their responsibility for environmental pollution that affects other countries.

The problems that led to the Trail Smelter arbitration began long before 1935. Trail, British Columbia, is on the Columbia River, seven miles north of Canada's border with the United States. Metal refining, primarily of lead and zinc, had been going on in Trail since 1906. Consolidated Mining and Smelting Company of Canada owned the smelter. By the 1920's, the smelter at Trail was the largest metal-refining operation in Canada. The smelter roasted ores containing sulfides to extract and purify the metals. It also produced exhaust containing sulfur dioxide (SO_2). Prevailing winds blew this exhaust down the river valley into Stevens County, Washington, to the south.

Farmers near Trail and in Stevens County recognized that the exhaust damaged crops, livestock, and buildings as early as 1925. Daily SO_2 production sometimes exceeded seven hundred tons by 1930. Consolidated Mining and Smelting Company of Canada also recognized the damage their exhaust caused. The company made some individual settlements and obtained permission from some property owners to allow exhaust to damage their land. Eventually, the exhaust angered Stevens County commissioners enough to make the commission vote for an announcement that condemned the smelter's operation. In August, 1928, a citizen protection agency formed in Stevens County that stopped individual settlements from being made with the smelting company.

Because municipal law in the United States and Canada could not solve the ongoing problem, the U.S. government entered the dispute in 1927 and lodged an official complaint with Canada about the SO_2 exhaust. In December, 1927, the two governments agreed to refer the dispute to the International Joint Commission (IJC) for investigation. (The 1909 Boundary Waters Treaty between Canada and the United States created the International Joint Commission to referee disputes about the use and control of inland waters such as the Great Lakes on their mutual border. The IJC has six members, three from the United States and three from Canada. It has the authority to investigate and obtain precise information about any factors that might affect the existing or planned use of boundary waters.)

On August 7, 1928, the IJC began studying the Trail Smelter case to determine how much the exhaust damaged property and what compensation, if any, Canada owed the United States. On February 28, 1931, the IJC announced its unanimous decision that Canada owed the United States $350,000 for damages up to 1932. It also ruled that Consolidated Mining and Smelting Company of Canada should reduce SO_2 in the smelter's exhaust. Canada accepted the commission's report, and Consolidated Mining and Smelting Company of Canada voluntarily began reducing the SO_2 in exhaust. The United States, however, rejected the IJC decision because the United States believed the $350,000 was insufficient compensation for damages.

The United States and Canada continued to negotiate and signed an agreement in 1935 to refer their dispute to binding arbitration by an international jury. That jury had three members: Charles Warren of Massachusetts, a former U.S. attorney general, represented the United States; Robert Greenshields of Quebec represented Canada; and Jans Hostie of Belgium, the chairman, represented a neutral party to the dispute. A scientist assisted each country's representative: Reginald Dean of Missouri for the United States and Robert Swain of California for Canada.

In the 1935 agreement, Pierre Boal, the acting chargé d'affaires for the U.S. government at Ottawa, accepted the original compensation that the International Joint Commission gave the United States in 1931. Boal and Richard Bedford Bennett, the prime minister of Canada, asked the jury to find a permanent settlement to the dispute. The settlement would identify how much Canada owed the United States for environmental damage that happened after 1932. It would also issue guidelines to restrict further environmental pollution. The jury made its final decision on March 11, 1941, after several years of study. It gave the United States an additional $78,179.51

for damages that occurred between 1932 and 1937. It also imposed permanent restrictions on the smelter's SO_2 exhaust. The Trail Smelter dispute officially ended on January 24, 1950, when the United States returned $8,828.19 of unused compensation to Canada.

To meet the new exhaust limits, Consolidated Mining and Smelting Company of Canada had to remove more SO_2 from its stack than the combined exhaust of all other smelters operating in North America at the time. Over the years, SO_2 removal cost the company $20 million. SO_2 exhaust that was dispersing at a rate of 10,000 tons per month in 1930 declined to a rate of 475 tons per months by 1937. The company sold the recovered sulfur as fertilizer to help pay the costs of removing the sulfur from the exhaust.

SIGNIFICANCE

The ruling in the Trail Smelter arbitration reflected a specific incident. Its immediate effect was to solve a border dispute between the United States and Canada. The two sides agreed to accept an impartial jury's decision, and the jury established the cause and provided the solution to a clear-cut case of environmental pollution. The importance of the Trail Smelter arbitration as a precedent setter has increased with time. Its ruling became a guide for solving similar disputes on a global basis.

In international law, the principle of good neighborliness is the basis for the regulation of pollution that crosses national borders. This principle—that one must use one's own resources in a manner that will not injure another—comes from the tradition of Roman law that underlies law practice in most Western societies. The Trail Smelter dispute was the first instance in which a dispute over air or water pollution was refereed by an international jury. The jury had precedents on which to base its decision in past U.S. Supreme Court decisions.

In *State of Georgia v. Tennessee Copper Company and Ducktown Sulphur, Copper, and Iron Company* (1907), Associate Justice Oliver Wendell Holmes, Jr., stated in the Court's opinion that "the state has the last word as to whether its mountains shall be stripped of their forests and its inhabitants shall breathe pure air . . . it is a fair and reasonable demand on the part of the sovereign that the air over its territory should not be polluted." The decision in the Trail Smelter arbitration applied this idea of good neighborliness with respect to environmental pollution, ruling that "under the principles of international law . . . no state has the right to use or permit the use of its territory in such a manner as to cause injury by fumes in or to the territory of another country or to the

1935

properties or persons therein, when the case is of serious consequence and the injury is established by clear and convincing evidence."

In the Trail Smelter arbitration, studies identified the level of environmental damage by "clear and convincing evidence," and the Canadian government accepted responsibility for the damage its citizens caused. By the mid-1960's and early 1970's, air pollution crossing national borders was occurring over much of northern Europe and Scandinavia. Many scientists linked it to stream and lake acidification and forest decline. The damage, however, was not clear and convincing in many people's eyes. Identifying the polluters was difficult.

The Swedish government became very concerned with long-range air pollution and blamed SO_2 exhaust from English and German industrial complexes for the acid rain appearing in Sweden. Sweden's concern led it to organize a conference addressing this issue, and the United Nations Conference on the Human Environment took place in Stockholm in 1972. The conference provided Swedish scientists with an opportunity to present their case that acid rain was an international issue.

The U.N. Conference on the Human Environment initiated the development of international environmental law. Conference participants summarized their conclusions about international environmental issues in a series of governing principles. Principle 21 was the most appropriate for international pollution and clearly reflected the ruling in the Trail Smelter arbitration. Principle 21 stated that countries had the right to exploit their own natural resources and follow their own environmental policies, but they also had the responsibility "to ensure that activities within their jurisdiction or control do not cause damage to the environment of other states or of areas beyond the limits of national jurisdiction."

The 1972 Stockholm conference noted that humans have basic rights to freedom, equality, and adequate living conditions, including a quality environment that permits a dignified life and well-being. Development and environmental protection had to coexist. The conference report also implied that countries had a duty to avoid causing environmental damage to other countries and a duty to prevent pollution.

Modern development often produced industrial pollutants that did not respect international boundaries. The U.N. Conference on the Human Environment began an era of cooperative agreements between countries to deal with global environmental issues. Burning coal to produce energy also produced SO_2. This raised international attention because SO_2 contributed to acid rain. Industrialized nations also produced and used chlorofluorocarbons (CFCs). Chlorofluorocarbons reacted with ozone and destroyed it. CFCs may have contributed to thinning the ozone layer that protected the earth from ultraviolet radiation.

In 1985, the Vienna Ozone Layer Convention concluded that protecting the ozone layer is an urgent global responsibility. The Montreal Protocol on Substances That Deplete the Ozone Layer followed soon after. On September 16, 1987, twenty-four nations and the European Economic Community (EEC) agreed to freeze CFC consumption in 1990 at the levels that had existed in 1986. They also agreed to reduce CFCs by a formula based on a gradual reduction of global CFC emissions. Chlorofluorocarbons would be reduced 20 percent by 1994 and an additional 30 percent by 1999. The era of international cooperation to reduce global air pollution was clearly under way.

Beginning with the Trail Smelter arbitration, the world community began to recognize that the environmental consequences of pollution are global rather than local. It also recognized that individual countries are responsible for the pollution they cause. International law now requires nations to recognize this responsibility and take appropriate action. Unlike the results of the Trail Smelter arbitration, however, this responsibility is in principle only. The first tentative steps to move beyond principles and take action began with cooperative agreements such as the Montreal Protocol. The Trail Smelter arbitration, by successfully resolving an environmental dispute involving air pollution and by reducing that air pollution, remained unique in its application throughout the twentieth century.

—*Mark S. Coyne*

FURTHER READING

Boyle, Alan, and David Freestone, eds. *International Law and Sustainable Development: Past Achievements and Future Challenges.* New York: Oxford University Press, 1999. Collection of essays discusses developments in international environmental law as of the end of the twentieth century. Includes tables of cases and treaties and index.

Brunnée, Jutta. *Acid Rain and Ozone Layer Depletion: International Law and Regulation.* Dobbs Ferry, N.Y.: Transnational, 1988. Readable book places the Trail Smelter arbitration in the context of ongoing global prevention of air pollution. Chapter 2 provides a good summary of the scientific background surrounding acid rain and ozone depletion. Chapter 4 presents concise discussion of international environmental law.

Madders, Kevin. "Trail Smelter Arbitration." In *Decisions of International Courts and Tribunals and International Arbitrations*, edited by Rudolf Bernhardt. Vol. 2 in *Encyclopedia of Public International Law*. New York: North Holland, 1981. Brief legal summary of the Trail Smelter arbitration describes the case chronologically in terms accessible to lay readers.

Maine, Frank. "Address to Conference Delegates." In *Effects of Acid Precipitation on Terrestrial Ecosystems*, edited by Thomas Hutchinson and Magda Havas. New York: Plenum Press, 1980. Provides a useful summary of the issues involved in pollution across national borders. Describes the role and responsibilities of the International Joint Commission very well.

Rüster, Bernd, and Bruno Simma, eds. *International Protection of the Environment*. Vol. 15. Dobbs Ferry, N.Y.: Oceana, 1979. Collection of documents from international environmental law includes the text of the convention that initiated the original Trail Smelter arbitration, the final ruling of the arbitration tribunal, and correspondence between the United States and Canada with respect to the dispute. Excellent source for the background of the case and the reasoning behind the tribunal's final decision.

Schmandt, Jurgen, Judith Clarkson, and Hilliard Roderick, eds. *Acid Rain and Friendly Neighbors: The Policy Dispute Between Canada and the United States*. Durham, N.C.: Duke University Press, 1988. Well-documented chronological overview of atmospheric pollution negotiations between the two countries.

Social Learning Group. *Learning to Manage Global Environmental Risks*. 2 vols. Cambridge, Mass.: MIT Press, 2001. Examination of global environmental management focuses on international efforts to address climate change, acid rain, and ozone depletion.

SEE ALSO: June 27-29, 1906: International Association for the Prevention of Smoke Is Founded; 1910: Steinmetz Warns of Pollution in "The Future of Electricity"; June 7, 1924: Oil Pollution Act Sets Penalties for Polluters.

April 27, 1935
SOIL CONSERVATION SERVICE IS ESTABLISHED

The Soil Conservation Service was established to alleviate problems created by the Dust Bowl of the 1930's, in which some of the nation's most productive topsoil blew away as a result of poor land management.

LOCALE: Washington, D.C.
CATEGORIES: Environmental issues; natural resources; organizations and institutions; government and politics

KEY FIGURES
Hugh Hammond Bennett (1881-1960), soil conservationist and the first director of the Soil Conservation Service
Milburn L. Wilson (1885-1969), assistant secretary of agriculture, 1934-1937
Franklin D. Roosevelt (1882-1945), president of the United States, 1933-1945

SUMMARY OF EVENT
The Great Depression and the drought of the early 1930's alerted U.S. leaders to the need for government to take a more active role in resource management. During President Theodore Roosevelt's administration, a number of initiatives were introduced, and in 1935 Congress passed the Soil Conservation and Domestic Allotment Act, which established the Soil Conservation Service (SCS). Although the findings from field research at experimental erosion stations, the worldwide economic depression, and dust storms resulting from drought conditions were all important considerations, the legislation was largely passed as a result of efforts by Hugh Hammond Bennett, the father of modern soil conservation in the United States, who used his knowledge to garner political support for national soil-conservation programs.

Concern for soil erosion was common in the United States, especially in the South. After observing contour plowing in France, Thomas Jefferson and his brother-in-law, Thomas Mann Randolph, introduced the method in Virginia. By 1850, contour plowing was common in the South. The Southwest Soil and Water Conservation conference, held in Texas in 1929, helped to bring attention to the problem of soil erosion. Still, soil erosion did not warrant national concern until the Great Depression of

1935

the 1930's, when the connection between poor soils and poor people became apparent.

During the 1930's, millions of people were unemployed and desperate for work. The market system did not appear to be functioning, and the nation's economic woes were exacerbated by the drought. During the 1932 presidential election campaign, Franklin D. Roosevelt promised to do something about the stagnant economy and high unemployment rate by offering people a "New Deal," and after his inauguration in 1933, he initiated a large-scale government-spending program. One aspect of this initiative was the National Industrial Recovery Act (1933), a broad-based act that provided stimulus for all sectors of the economy. Although the Soil Conservation Service (SCS) was not established until 1935, its predecessor, the Soil Erosion Service, was established as a temporary agency of the U.S. Department of the Interior under the 1933 act. When the Civilian Conservation Corps (CCC) was established in 1933, several hundred CCC camps were assigned to the Soil Erosion Service, giving impetus to erosion-control efforts.

Bennett, a soil scientist for the U.S. Department of Agriculture, was employed to direct the Soil Erosion Service. He had firsthand experience with soil erosion in North Carolina; moreover, he had seen the effects of erosion while working as a surveyor and as a supervisor of surveys in the South. In 1928, he and W. R. Chapline published a paper titled "Soil Erosion: A National Menace." This U.S. Department of Agriculture publication, along with other articles that appeared in such widely read publications as *Nature*, *Geographical Review*, and *Farm Journal*, alerted politicians and the public to the severity of the nation's erosion problem.

When Bennett took control of the Soil Erosion Service in 1933, his budget was $5 million. Soil-conservation projects were strategically located in watersheds near erosion-control experiment stations so that the research findings could be readily employed, and farmers signed five-year cooperative agreements to employ the recommended conservation measures. In return, the Soil Erosion Service provided them with equipment, seeds, seedlings, lime, fertilizer, soil-conservation assistance, and labor from the CCC or the Works Progress Administration (WPA).

Many of the conservation practices promoted by the Soil Erosion Service were not new. Various methods in a conservation system, however, were designed specifically for each individual farm. For example, strip cropping under longer rotation was encouraged for hay and small grain crops. Administrators also emphasized pasture management by using fertilizers and fencing off woodland from grazing in hilly areas to reduce runoff, and many farmers were introduced to grassed outlets, grassed waterways, and grade stabilization techniques.

SIGNIFICANCE

The Soil Erosion Service was shifted from the Department of the Interior to the Department of Agriculture and was given permanent status under the Soil Conservation Act. Its name was changed to the Soil Conservation Service (SCS), and its responsibilities centered on planning and conducting a national program to conserve and develop the nation's soil and water resources. If not for the activities of the Soil Conservation Service, the physical landscape of the United States would be much less stable.

CCC workers conducted a number of demonstration projects. Seeds for nursery production of seedlings were collected for reforestation, native grasses were used to revegetate rangeland in semiarid regions, water filtration was enhanced by water-spreading systems and contour furrows, and livestock grazing was redistributed with the use of stock-watering in ponds and springs. Demonstration projects aimed at improving rangeland through range management were also implemented on Native American reservations. The demonstration projects' results were so convincing, in fact, that farmers who visited areas where these projects were being implemented also began to ask for assistance.

Realizing that the CCC and WPA workers would be available only temporarily, the assistant secretary of agriculture, Milburn L. Wilson, devised a plan for making a sustained supply of conservation expertise available to farmers. His plan called for the development of soil-conservation districts, which provided for greater local participation in the planning operations. The Standard State Conservation Districts Law was sent to state governors on February 27, 1937, by President Roosevelt. After each state passed the law, districts were organized around local watersheds or county boundaries, and supervisors were elected. Districts signed agreements with the Department of Agriculture, which provided nearly three thousand districts with trained soil conservationists, who worked directly with farmers. Through these planning districts, the SCS developed a land-classification system and associated soil management practices that did much to restore the fertility of American soils after periods of degradation.

Over the years, the responsibilities of the Soil Conservation Service grew to include a variety of tasks, and the

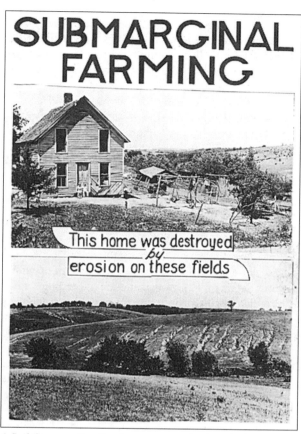

A Soil Conservation Service poster emphasizes the importance of good farming practices. (NARA)

SCS tried to promote soil conservation in a number of ways. Soil conservation was enhanced by employing conservation methods based on scientific research findings, by developing an agency of technically trained personnel to carry out soil conservation in farm communities, and by creating soil-conservation districts. Furthermore, the agency shared in the cost of establishing and implementing soil-conservation practices.

The Soil Conservation Service came to be widely recognized for its soil surveys and maps. The surveys examined the soil's physical attributes, revealing such information as soil moisture, texture, slope, erosion, and chemistry. This information was supplemented by laboratory studies and was used for selecting sites for specific land uses. Each soil survey described the key characteristics of soils in a survey area, classified and named the soil according to a nationwide system, provided information on the potential and limitations of soils for various uses, and showed the soil distribution on a detailed map. More

than one billion acres of land were mapped, and maps of millions of additional acres were added each year. The soil surveys and maps were published, and the SCS also cooperated with other agencies that prepared special reports and maps relevant to soil surveys.

More than one hundred new plants were identified by the Soil Conservation Service's Plant Materials Center. This group searched for plants that lend themselves to stabilizing waste disposal areas, extending grazing seasons, improving windbreaks and shelterbelts, and reducing air pollution, snow drift damage, and wind erosion. More than twenty-three thousand plants were examined after 1938, and more than one hundred were released for conservation purposes.

The Soil Conservation Service also became involved in a comprehensive system of land-resource conservation, and it analyzed alternate soil-conservation methods and management practices required to safeguard the soil under different cropping systems. The practices included such methods as no-till and minimum-tillage farming, contour plowing, terracing, strip cropping, stubble mulching, and the efficient use of fertilizers. On rangeland, the SCS pioneered the use of range inventory methods that incorporated ecological principles and concepts as well as practical methods for range management. Furthermore, thousands of pilot studies correlated soils with tree growth, and these analyses were made available to woodland conservationists.

Hundreds of millions of acres of land were restored or stabilized as a result of these practices, and farmers and other land users were given the latest information pertaining to crops and their use and management. Land users received assistance with wildlife conservation efforts, recreational land-use projects, and campaigns to prevent land-disturbing activities. The Food and Agriculture Act of 1962 authorized the Department of Agriculture to assist landowners with developing recreational resources. Nearly two million lakes and ponds were built on farms and ranches by the SCS, which also helped soil-conservation districts to help stabilize mine spoils and reclaim hundreds of millions of acres of land.

Watershed projects enacted in 1954 under the Watershed Protection and Flood Prevention Act established soil- and water-conservation measures on private and public land and allowed for the construction of dams and other water-control structures on upstream tributaries to ensure effective water management. This activity was administered by the Soil Conservation Service, which also administered work on watersheds that was authorized by the Flood Control Act of 1944 in eleven major

1935

watersheds covering about thirty million acres. These watershed projects helped control flooding and erosion while supplying water for irrigation, industrial, and municipal uses.

The Soil Conservation Service also became involved with some of the provisions of the Food Security Act of 1985. Under this program, SCS conservationists worked directly with farmers to determine soil erodibility as it applied to the preservation of wetlands. Some of the most erodible land was taken out of production and covered with protective vegetation, and farmers received rental payments in return. Although the effectiveness of soil-conservation efforts has been debated by some, the nation's soils are much more protected as a result of the Soil Conservation Service's work. In 1994, the Soil Conservation Service was subsumed under the National Resources Conservation Service, part of the Department of Agriculture.

—Jasper L. Harris

FURTHER READING

Bennett, Hugh H. "Soil." In *The American Environment: Readings in the History of Conservation*, edited by Roderick Nash. Reading, Mass.: Addison-Wesley, 1968. A historical perspective of the soil-erosion problem in the United States.

_____. *Soils Conservation*. New York: McGraw-Hill, 1939. A comprehensive view of soil erosion. Although not written as a history of soil conservation, Bennett's persuasive argument for soil conservation is articulated. Soils are viewed as an essential natural resource that must be protected to secure the nation's future.

Helms, Douglas. *Readings in the History of the Conservation Service*. Washington, D.C.: U.S. Department of Agriculture. Soil Conservation Service, 1992. A collection of short articles by Douglas Helms, national historian for the Soil Conservation Service. The articles focus on a general history of the Soil Conservation Service, its origin, and selected historic activities, including involvement by women and minorities.

Klee, Gary A. "Soil Resource Management." In *Conservation of Natural Resources*. Englewood Cliffs, N.J.: Prentice Hall, 1991. A brief historical view of misuse of soil that dates back to the Sumerian and Roman empires. An attempt is made to compare these ancient practices to more recent soil-conservation efforts.

Merchant, Carolyn. *The Columbia Guide to American Environmental History*. New York: Columbia University Press, 2002. Discusses how humans and environment have interacted throughout American history, including human impacts on animal species. Includes an environmental history time line and an extensive guide to resources.

Nash, Roderick Frazier. *Wilderness and the American Mind*. 4th ed. New Haven, Conn.: Yale University Press, 2001. An exploration of the physiological and psychological significance of wilderness, especially for Americans of European descent. The book looks to prehistoric humans, treats notions of the wilderness in classical and medieval Europe, and focuses on American efforts to define, explore, and conquer the wilderness up to the end of the twentieth century.

Steiner, Frederick R. *Soil Conservation in the United States: Policy and Planning*. Baltimore: The Johns Hopkins University Press, 1990. Comprehensive view of soil erosion and related legislation in the United States. Examines the activities of the Soil Conservation Service and recommends a quantitative approach to soil conservation.

SEE ALSO: Mar. 14, 1903: First U.S. National Wildlife Refuge Is Established; Jan. 3, 1905: Pinchot Becomes Head of the U.S. Forest Service; May 13-15, 1908: Conference on the Conservation of Natural Resources; Jan., 1922: Izaak Walton League Is Formed; Apr. 5, 1933: U.S. Civilian Conservation Corps Is Established; May 18, 1933: Tennessee Valley Authority Is Created; 1934-1939: Dust Bowl Devastates the Great Plains; June 28, 1934: Taylor Grazing Act; July 1, 1940: U.S. Fish and Wildlife Service Is Formed.

May 27, 1935
BLACK MONDAY

A business-oriented U.S. Supreme Court rendered a series of decisions that undermined New Deal programs.

LOCALE: Washington, D.C.
CATEGORIES: Laws, acts, and legal history; economics; government and politics

KEY FIGURES
Franklin D. Roosevelt (1882-1945), president of the United States, 1933-1945
Charles Evans Hughes (1862-1948), chief justice of the United States, 1930-1941
Louis D. Brandeis (1856-1941), associate justice of the United States, 1916-1939
Pierce Butler (1866-1939), associate justice of the United States, 1922-1939
Benjamin N. Cardozo (1870-1938), associate justice of the United States, 1932-1938
James C. McReynolds (1862-1946), associate justice of the United States, 1914-1941
Owen J. Roberts (1875-1955), associate justice of the United States, 1930-1945
Harlan Fiske Stone (1872-1946), associate justice of the United States, 1925-1941
George Sutherland (1862-1942), associate justice of the United States, 1922-1938
Willis Van Devanter (1859-1941), associate justice of the United States, 1910-1937

SUMMARY OF EVENT
In the spring of 1935, Franklin D. Roosevelt was in the last year of his first term as president of the United States. He had taken office in 1933 and had labored to end the Great Depression, which had begun with the stock market crash of October, 1929. His initiatives had resulted in an unprecedented assertion of presidential power and made inevitable a conflict with the U.S. Supreme Court. Decisions concerning the constitutionality of legislation and executive action are based on nine sitting Supreme Court justices' interpretation of the U.S. Constitution, a document written in general terms at a time when the complexities of twentieth century governing bodies could not have been imagined.

President Roosevelt received what he may not have recognized as a portent on January 7, 1935, when the Court ruled unconstitutional the provision of the National Industrial Recovery Act (NIRA) by which the president could prohibit interstate transportation of oil exceeding production quotas. By a vote of eight to one, the Court ruled that the president had usurped legislative power—a violation of the first section of Article I of the Constitution. By May, it began to be clear that the NIRA as a whole was in trouble. As often happens, the Court was considering a case that on the surface seemed to have small and merely local interest: violations of the Live Poultry Code by a Long Island firm that supplied chickens for New York-area kosher markets. The code was part of the National Recovery Administration's code-making authority, through which the Roosevelt administration was striving to pull the nation out of the Great Depression.

While the administration awaited the decision on this matter, the Court, by a five-to-four margin, on May 6 declared the Railroad Retirement Act of 1934 a violation of the Fifth Amendment property rights of the railroads, because the law required that the railroads (as well as their employees) contribute to the retirement fund. Retirement, said the Court, had nothing to do with the government's legal right to regulate interstate commerce. Because the Roosevelt administration was keenly interested in a much larger retirement program that had not yet passed the Senate—the one familiar today as Social Security—the decision on the railroad pension arrangement threatened Social Security even before it could be enacted.

Three weeks later, on Monday, May 27—a day that came to be known as Black Monday—the Court handed down a series of decisions. In the first, and crucial, decision, the Court unanimously declared that President Roosevelt had acted unconstitutionally by removing a Republican appointee, William E. Humphrey, from the Federal Trade Commission (FTC) without cause. From the president's point of view, the cause was clear enough: Humphrey had been obstructing Roosevelt's policies at the FTC. In its decision, the Court in effect reversed a 1916 decision that had justified a similar exercise of presidential power.

Next, the Court ruled unanimously that an amendment to the National Bankruptcy Act that aimed at relieving farmers who had defaulted on their mortgages was in violation of the due process clause of the Fifth Amendment. Although not, strictly speaking, a part of Roosevelt's New Deal, the act had been signed into law the year before. Here again, the Court was hedging the combined legislative power of Congress and the president and making it more difficult for the federal government to deal with the economic crisis.

Finally, in the case of *Schechter Poultry Corporation v. United States*—the "sick chicken case," as some had termed it—Chief Justice Charles Evans Hughes read a unanimous decision in favor of the former. The conviction of the Schechter brothers by a lower court for selling diseased poultry was thrown out because the Supreme Court ruled that the applicable federal code was an unconstitutional delegation of legislative power to the executive branch. This decision was significant because it voided hundreds of other NIRA codes. Again, the previously accepted power of government to regulate interstate commerce was abridged. Only activities that the Court considered as having direct effects on interstate commerce could be regulated.

SIGNIFICANCE

The Court's decisions on Black Monday dealt a devastating blow to the administration's recovery program. While opponents of the New Deal rejoiced, many industries that appeared destined to be affected by the decision in the *Schechter* case had much to worry about. The textile manufacturers of New England, for example, now were stripped of possible government protection from competing southern firms that paid significantly lower wages. More than anything else, it was that aspect of the decision abridging government's power to regulate interstate commerce that made May 27 Black Monday, for the Court's narrow interpretation of "interstate" in the interests of local industry suggested that the Court viewed most of what had commonly been regarded as interstate commerce as only indirectly interstate. If all industry was local, because it occurred in a particular locality, the government would be virtually powerless to effect economic recovery nationally.

The Court was acting sincerely as guardian of the Constitution, but its decisions were standing between the New Deal and the economic recovery that everyone wanted but that the federal government alone seemed in a position to promote. A decisive majority in Congress had been willing to accept the NIRA codes, but Hughes argued that the legislative branch had no right to abdicate or transfer to the executive the powers constitutionally vested in Congress.

Of concern also was the matter of emergency powers. The issue had come before the Court in 1934 in *Home Building and Loan Association v. Blaisdell*, when the judgment had suggested that emergencies justified enlargement of the government's ordinary constitutional powers. In the eyes of Roosevelt and his aides, the economic situation in 1935 constituted a national emergency, but the Supreme Court seemed to back away from that opinion in the Black Monday decisions. One possible explanation for this seeming inconsistency is the common background of the Court's members at the time. The Court—which consisted of Chief Justice Hughes and Associate Justices Louis D. Brandeis, Pierce Butler, Benjamin N. Cardozo, James C. McReynolds, Owen J. Roberts, Harlan Fiske Stone, George Sutherland, and Willis Van Devanter—was split then, as it has often been, between philosophical liberals and conservatives, but the fact that eight of the nine justices had backgrounds in corporate law disposed even relative liberals, such as Brandeis and Stone, to affirm the property rights of business interests. In the eyes of the administration, the Court's stalwart defense of these property rights was blocking attempts to protect the livelihoods of millions of jobless people, many of whom had already lost all the property they owned.

Far from being discouraged by the Court's most recent actions, President Roosevelt called a news conference four days later in which he attacked the Court's "horse-and-buggy definition of interstate commerce." Shortly thereafter, his administration began to redesign the National Recovery Administration programs to evade similar Supreme Court obstructions of the New Deal in the future. The Court, however, continued to strike at pillars of Roosevelt's reforms, such as the Agricultural Adjustment Act. Regarding that legislation, Associate Justice Roberts delivered the Court's majority decision in January, 1936, again employing the argument that the government was trying to regulate local enterprises that fell under the jurisdiction of the states.

The tide began to turn in 1937. Despite stern popular opposition to Roosevelt's attempt to "pack" the Court with his own appointees by raising the number of justices, the now more circumspect Court upheld the National Labor Relations Act (the Wagner Act) and the Social Security Act, two of the most vital reforms to emerge from Roosevelt's second term. In that year, the first of Roosevelt's nemeses on the Court, Van Devanter, retired. By 1941, the president had named replacements for all but one of the 1935 justices.

—*Robert P. Ellis*

FURTHER READING
Cope, Alfred Haines, and Fred Krinsky, eds. *Franklin D. Roosevelt and the Supreme Court.* Boston: D. C.

Heath, 1952. Collection of a variety of relevant writings from the 1930's, including selections from primary sources.

Cushman, Barry. *Rethinking the New Deal Court: The Structure of a Constitutional Revolution*. New York: Oxford University Press, 1998. Scholarly study focuses on the Supreme Court in the period following Roosevelt's reelection in 1936, but includes discussion of the 1935 Black Monday cases.

Davis, Kenneth S. *FDR: The New Deal Years, 1933-1937—A History*. 1986. Reprint. New York: Random House, 1995. Offers a carefully documented and evenhanded account of the series of clashes between President Roosevelt and the U.S. Supreme Court. Part of a multivolume biography.

Hendel, Samuel. *Charles Evans Hughes and the Supreme Court*. New York: King's Crown Press, 1951. Study of the man who, as chief justice, epitomized judicial opposition to New Deal innovations. Contains extended discussion of Black Monday as viewed by Supreme Court justices.

Jackson, Percival E. *Dissent in the Supreme Court: A Chronology*. Norman: University of Oklahoma Press, 1969. Discusses the dissenting opinions of Justices Hughes and Cardozo in two of the 1935 cases.

Leuchtenburg, William. *The Supreme Court Reborn: The Constitutional Revolution in the Age of Roosevelt*. New York: Oxford University Press, 1995. Focuses primarily on Supreme Court-related developments during Roosevelt's second term, but includes detailed chapters on the Black Monday railroad pension decision and the Humphrey case.

See also: May 20, 1926: Railway Labor Act Provides for Mediation of Labor Disputes; Oct. 29, 1929-1939: Great Depression; Mar. 23, 1932: Norris-La Guardia Act Strengthens Labor Organizations; Mar. 9-June 16, 1933: The Hundred Days; June 16, 1933: Roosevelt Signs the National Industrial Recovery Act; Apr. 8, 1935: Works Progress Administration Is Established; Feb. 5-July 22, 1937: Supreme Court-Packing Fight.

June 10, 1935
FORMATION OF ALCOHOLICS ANONYMOUS

Founded by two professionals who were also alcoholics, Alcoholics Anonymous began as a nonsectarian program based on mutual reinforcement and adherence to a set of twelve specified steps that led toward a healthy, alcohol-free lifestyle. The organization grew to more than three million recovering alcoholics worldwide and spawned a number of other addiction treatment groups based on the same principles.

Also known as: AA

Locale: Akron, Ohio; New York, New York

Categories: Organizations and institutions; health and medicine; social issues and reform

Key Figures

William G. Wilson (1895-1971), stockbroker and cofounder of Alcoholics Anonymous

Robert Holbrook Smith (1879-1950), physician and cofounder of Alcoholics Anonymous

William D. Silkworth (fl. early twentieth century), medical adviser and supporter of AA who was one of the first to believe that alcoholism is a disease

John D. Rockefeller, Jr. (1874-1960), American philanthropist and supporter of Alcoholics Anonymous

Summary of Event

On November 11, 1934, William G. Wilson, a failed stockbroker caught in the throes of alcoholism, checked himself into Towns Hospital in Manhattan. His few remaining associates, his wife, and even Dr. William Silkworth, the attending physician, regarded the veteran of three "cures" at this drying-out facility as a hopeless case. However, a few days before, a former colleague and fellow alcoholic had paid Wilson a visit. Rejoicing in his newfound sobriety, the friend persuaded Wilson to attend an Oxford Group meeting. Oxford Groups were an early twentieth century revival movement dedicated to moral reformation. Although nonsectarian, they were explicitly Christian, and they considered alcoholism to be a moral failing. Wilson, an agnostic with little interest in tackling any problem other than his addiction to alcohol, was a poor candidate for salvation by the Manhattan Oxford Group. What he heard there, however, persuaded him to attempt another visit to Towns Hospital. While undergo-

1935

AA'S TWELVE STEPS

Alcoholics Anonymous adopted the Twelve Steps in 1939, and they have been a crucial part of the organization ever since.

1. We admitted we were powerless over alcohol—that our lives had become unmanageable.
2. Came to believe that a Power greater than ourselves could restore us to sanity.
3. Made a decision to turn our will and our lives over to the care of God *as we understood Him.*
4. Made a searching and fearless moral inventory of ourselves.
5. Admitted to God, to ourselves, and to another human being the exact nature of our wrongs.
6. Were entirely ready to have God remove all these defects of character.
7. Humbly asked Him to remove our shortcomings.
8. Made a list of all persons we had harmed, and became willing to make amends to them all.
9. Made direct amends to such people wherever possible, except when to do so would injure them or others.
10. Continued to take personal inventory and when we were wrong promptly admitted it.
11. Sought through prayer and meditation to improve our conscious contact with God as we understood Him, praying only for knowledge of His will for us and the power to carry that out.
12. Having had a spiritual awakening as the result of these steps, we tried to carry this message to alcoholics, and to practice these principles in all our affairs.

Source: Alcoholics Anonymous World Services, *Big Book*, 4th ed. (New York: Author, 2001).

---

ing detoxification, Wilson experienced a moment of total surrender to a vague power: He felt bathed in white light and completely lost the compulsion to drink.

Bill Wilson left Towns Hospital a changed man, and he immediately set about spreading the "gospel of sobriety" to alcoholic members of the Oxford Group, inhabitants of a homeless shelter, and anyone else who would listen. With the acquiescence of his patient wife, Lois Burnham Wilson, he invited the down-and-out into their apartment and held meetings directed specifically toward alcoholics. His efforts did not meet with success, but after six months he was still sober and had recovered enough of his old dynamism that a Wall Street firm sent him to Akron, Ohio, on business.

His work in Ohio went poorly, however, and by the beginning of June of 1935, Wilson found himself in the Mayflower Hotel, his expense account depleted. For the first time since emerging from Towns Hospital, he was strongly tempted to drink. Recognizing that talking with

other alcoholics kept him sober, he called a local clergyman, who put him in touch with Robert Holbrook Smith, a physician who was also an alcoholic. Dr. Smith listened to Wilson and was inspired, although he never had a "white light" experience and never entirely lost the compulsion to drink. His more gradual recovery helped temper Wilson's enthusiasm and make the fledgling organization more receptive to tentative newcomers.

For the next several months, Wilson stayed in Smith's house, and the two men attempted to bring the message of sobriety to other alcoholics. Together, Bill Wilson and "Dr. Bob" discussed every point of strategy, ideas that were later tested among a small group of people in the early stages of recovery from active alcoholism. When Wilson returned to New York in the fall, he left behind a group of half a dozen men who were attempting to stay sober by taking one day at a time and by holding frequent meetings at which they shared their concerns.

The fact that Smith was a physician helped smooth relations between the fledgling organization and the medical community. Furthermore, the Akron Oxford Group already had a strong emphasis on recovery from alcoholism, and it was more welcoming than the New York group, which expelled Wilson in 1938. Wilson's first New York recruits came from Towns Hospital, where Dr. Silkworth had become convinced of the merits of Wilson's approach. Silkworth was willing to let Wilson work with patients and even offered Wilson a job as a lay alcoholism therapist in 1938. The offer was extremely tempting, as the Wilsons' finances were precarious, but the other members of the now-solid New York group persuaded Wilson that selling his services would undermine the organization.

At first, Alcoholics Anonymous grew slowly. When the first edition of *Alcoholics Anonymous*, the AA bible, appeared in April of 1939, membership numbered about a hundred, including a few women. By 1955, membership had increased to one hundred fifty thousand, and chapters had begun in a number of foreign countries.

Membership stood at around a million in 1976, when the third edition of *Alcoholics Anonymous* appeared, and had risen to two million by 2001.

Wilson entertained grandiose plans for spreading the message of recovery. He envisioned massive publicity campaigns, a large paid staff, and special treatment centers run according to AA principles. He approached John D. Rockefeller, Jr., who agreed that the cause was worthy and its approach was successful but believed that it could and should be self-supporting. The modest support Rockefeller provided did, however, fill a critical need from 1938 to 1945. Living within its means was a critical ingredient in AA's success. Indeed, the organization was supported by member contributions and the sale of publications, received no government grants or subsidies from religious or other charitable foundations, and refused large individual bequests. Instead, AA operated mainly with volunteer labor, and as a result it could open its doors to any suffering alcoholic with no strings attached.

AA based its program on a series of twelve steps to recovery that began with recognition of the problem and culminated in work with other alcoholics. These steps, adapted from principles employed by the Oxford Groups, included taking a moral inventory and making amends for past behavior. The Twelve Steps of AA first appeared in the 1939 edition of *Alcoholics Anonymous*, and they were soon copied by other recovery programs geared toward addressing addictions and compulsive behaviors.

The principle of anonymity was established early and served several purposes. Because of the stigma attached to alcoholism and potential legal complications, the professionals who dominated AA's early membership were anxious to avoid public identification. Wilson also knew that relapses were common and calculated that a celebrity who slipped would destroy any positive effect created by an initial recovery. AA members, therefore, identified themselves by their first names only and avoided being photographed for national publications. Wilson himself is often referred to as simply "Bill W."

From the outset, AA was an inclusive organization that welcomed alcoholics regardless of their race, gender, social class, sexual orientation, or prior criminal history. The only requirement for AA membership is a desire to stop drinking. Individual branches had considerable autonomy, and some were more restrictive than others. After some initial hostility, most medical doctors and mental health professionals came to support AA and referred patients to the organization (usually as an adjunct to treatment). Most religious groups in the United States also endorsed the program, although some found absence of sectarian dogmatism too unorthodox. On the other hand, dedicated secularists complained that mere reference to God by an organization with a prominent community role violated separation of church and state.

SIGNIFICANCE

Alcoholism is a progressive, fatal, socially devastating disease to which roughly 10 percent of people are susceptible. The foundation of Alcoholics Anonymous followed close on the heels of Prohibition, a singularly ineffective attempt to eliminate alcoholism by a constitutional amendment prohibiting the sale of alcohol in the United States. Prohibition failed to curb alcoholism, and it spawned a culture of crime that continued to plague the nation for decades. Later attempts to solve the problem of drug addiction through the criminal justice system had similarly problematic results.

In contrast, Alcoholics Anonymous's work saved the lives of many thousands of people at negligible cost. In the early years of the twenty-first century, the worldwide membership numbered somewhere between two and three million, and in the United States, the average member had been sober for four years. Although medical treatment programs became widely available, many people found AA to be the only organization that could help them achieve sobriety, and many more relied on continuing participation in AA to avoid relapse. Al-Anon, a group founded by Lois Burnham Wilson to help families of alcoholics cope with the disease's effects, provided invaluable services and support for families in crisis.

Alcoholics Anonymous faced accusations that it brainwashed its members by insisting on admissions of powerlessness, by promoting religion, or by adhering to methods that had not been rigorously tested in a controlled clinical setting. Unfortunately, AA's success rate, although probably equal to that of reputable medical programs, nonetheless remained discouragingly low. However, few people who personally experienced alcoholism or who worked in social service organizations doubted that the foundation of Alcoholics Anonymous was a major turning point in American social history.

—*Martha A. Sherwood*

FURTHER READING

Alcoholics Anonymous World Services. *Alcoholics Anonymous.* 4th ed. New York: Author, 2001. Includes unrevised text of the 1939 edition, introductions to all four editions, and forty-two personal stories of recovery spanning seventy years of AA operation. The AA bible.

1935

_____. "Early AA's Take Stock." *AA Grapevine* 60, no. 6 (November, 2003). An introduction to the work of E. M. Jellinek and his collaboration with AA in refining the concept of alcoholism as a disease.

_____, ed. *Alcoholics Anonymous Comes of Age: A Brief History of AA.* New York: Editor, 1985. Texts of talks given by Bill Wilson and other key figures at the AA General Service Conference in 1955; includes a detailed timeline.

Hartigan, Francis. *Bill W.: A Biography of Alcoholics Anonymous Cofounder Bill Wilson.* New York: St. Martin's Press, 2000. A well-researched, balanced account that presents a favorable picture of the man and organization and steers clear of the various myths surrounding AA.

SEE ALSO: Aug. 14, 1912: U.S. Public Health Service Is Established; May 14, 1913: Rockefeller Foundation Is Founded.

July, 1935
TANSLEY PROPOSES THE TERM "ECOSYSTEM"

Arthur G. Tansley coined the word "ecosystem" to emphasize the need for ecological studies to integrate the living and nonliving parts of the environment.

LOCALE: Great Britain; United States
CATEGORIES: Environmental issues; science and technology; biology

KEY FIGURES
Arthur G. Tansley (1871-1955), English plant ecologist
Frederic E. Clements (1874-1945), American ecologist
Henry Allen Gleason (1882-1975), American ecologist
Raymond L. Lindeman (1915-1942), American ecologist

SUMMARY OF EVENT
In 1935, Arthur G. Tansley, a leading English plant ecologist, wrote a paper criticizing the pioneering ecological theory of his American colleague and friend Frederic E. Clements. John Phillips, a South African plant ecologist, had carried Clements's ideas on the nature of the plant community to an extreme that Tansley found intolerable. Tansley responded with "The Use and Abuse of Vegetational Concepts and Terms," which was published in the American journal *Ecology*. In that paper, Tansley suggested the term "ecosystem" to replace Clements's "complex organism" and defined the new term to include both the living and the nonliving parts of the environment. He argued that plant interactions with the physical environment as well as interactions among plants determine community organization. He suggested that the ecosystem should be studied as the fundamental ecological unit.

Tansley was an institution in British ecological research. He did important early work on plant communities and wrote influential botanical textbooks. In 1902,

he started the first British ecology journal, the *New Phytologist*. He was instrumental in the establishment of the British Ecological Society in 1913 and served as the organization's first president. He also played an important role in nature conservation in the British Isles.

Clements was a leading American ecologist, a pioneer in the formulation of a new science. He wrote an influential ecology text, coauthored an early attempt to integrate animal and plant ecology, developed a new, mathematically based system of vegetation analysis, and developed a historically important theory on the nature of plant communities. He and his theory played important roles in early arguments for conservation of natural communities during and after the Dust Bowl tragedy of the 1930's.

According to Clements's theory, plant communities behave like complex organisms, with the different species as interdependent on one another as the organs within an organism. In addition, this organismic community has a specific and predictable developmental sequence (called ecological succession) that is analogous to embryologic development in an organism and that ends in a mature community (the climax community). Under a given set of climatic conditions, an identical climax community is reached at the end of every successional sequence. The sequence is predictable because of the intimate (organismic) interactions among community members.

Ecologists agreed that a given set of climatic conditions generally gives rise to a given type of vegetation and that a particular sequence of communities occurs in establishing this climax community. They disagreed, however, with Clements's idea of nearly complete interdependence among community members, his insistence on identical climax communities under a given set of climatic conditions, and his lack of emphasis on the role of physical factors in molding community structure.

Henry Allen Gleason suggested an alternative explanation for the phenomena of ecological succession and climax: the individualistic model. According to this theory, each individual plant responds to physical and biological factors independently, and the climax community is made up of the plants that can grow and reproduce under the physical conditions at the site. Climate is a major factor in determining which plants can grow in an area, but soils, fire, and other physical factors are also important. Interactions among the living things that occur in the area play a role in community structure, but that structure is essentially determined by each species' individual response to the physical environment. Similarly, the plants present at any given stage of succession are determined by which plants have reached the area by that stage and which plants grow best under the physical conditions present. The organization of a community is determined by individual plant characteristics, not by organismic plant interactions.

Tansley embraced many of Clements's ideas, but he held to a less literal view of the organismic community. He saw Clements's literal view as neither an accurate representation of natural communities nor a helpful framework for advancing ecological understanding. Phillips's articles triggered Tansley's direct attack on the literal organismic community; in that attack, he redirected ecological thought to the total system, in which the physical environment plays a larger role than it does in Clements's organismic community. A word was needed to designate the community, its physical environment, and all the interactions between them.

The idea was not new, and several terms were already available. In 1883, Karl August Möbius had used the term "biocoenosis" to refer to the physical and biological interactions in an oyster bed. Stephen Alfred Forbes had used "microcosm" in 1887 to describe the same set of interactions in a lake. These are often cited as the earliest expressions of the idea. Rather than use one of the older terms, however, Tansley coined his own: "ecosystem." The word and, more important, the idea it represented set the stage for elaborate studies, the results of which demonstrated the necessity of conserving entire ecosystems.

SIGNIFICANCE

Tansley's paper had little immediate impact, but the concept of the ecosystem gained acceptance over time. The ecosystem came to be viewed as an aggregation of plant, animal, and microorganismic species, each of which responds individually to its physical environment as well as to the other species sharing that environment. Community and ecosystem types are recognizable in nature (temperate deciduous forest, tropical rain forest, grassland, lake, and salt marsh, among others), but they merge gradually into one another, and a given ecosystem differs from one part of its geographic extent to another. Therefore, the community contained within the ecosystem is not a tightly integrated unit, an organism, but a group of species thrown together by their common ability to live under the available conditions. Once thrown together, the species must interact, and intimate (organismic) relationships sometimes develop between members of the community. The community's organization is based on

THE FIRST USE OF "ECOSYSTEM"

Arthur G. Tansley introduced the term "ecosystem" in this passage in a 1935 journal article:

I have already given my reasons for rejecting the terms "complex organism" and "biotic community." Clements' earlier term "biome" for the whole complex of organisms inhabiting a given region is unobjectionable, and for some purposes convenient. But the more fundamental conception is, as it seems to me, the whole *system* (in the sense of physics), including not only the organism-complex, but also the whole complex of physical factors forming what we call the environment of the biome— the habitat factors in the widest sense. Though the organisms may claim our primary interest, when we are trying to think fundamentally we cannot separate them from their special environment, with which they form one physical system.

It is the systems so formed which, from the point of view of the ecologist, are the basic units of nature on the face of the earth. Our natural human prejudices force us to consider the organisms (in the sense of the biologist) as the most important parts of these systems, but certainly the inorganic "factors" are also parts—there could be no systems without them, and there is constant interchange of the most various kinds within each system, not only between the organisms but between the organic and inorganic. These *ecosystems*, as we may call them, are of the most various kinds and sizes. They form one category of the multitudinous physical systems of the universe, which range from the universe as a whole down to the atom.

Source: Arthur G. Tansley, "The Use and Abuse of Vegetational Concepts and Terms," *Ecology* 16 (July, 1935).

the individual species' abilities to handle the physical conditions as well as these interactions.

Charles Elton, a British animal ecologist working in the general context of Tansley's earlier modification of Clements's theory of community organization, had already developed models for the transfer of energy and matter through the components of biological communities: food chains, food webs, and ecological pyramids. Elton said that plants are eaten by and are more numerous than herbivores, which are in turn more numerous than the carnivores that eat them, and so on. This reduction in numbers with each link in the food chain (or feeding level in the pyramid) restricts the number of links in the chain (or levels in the pyramid), because after a few reductions there is not enough food to support the next higher link (or level).

Elton's work inspired another British ecologist, G. Evelyn Hutchinson, who also worked within a modified Clementsian model, although he probably did not derive it from Clements directly. Hutchinson studied matter and energy flow through lake communities and introduced the idea of biogeochemical cycles in which nutrients (chemicals) move between the physical environment and the members of the community. Elton and Hutchinson, both working within modified organismic models, focused the attention of ecologists on the transfer of matter and energy from the physical environment through a series of community members back to the physical environment. These transfer events became the major topics of ecosystem ecology.

A student of Hutchinson, Raymond L. Lindeman, used Tansley's ecosystem concept and Hutchinson's methods in an analysis of the energetics of a lake ecosystem. Despite serious objection to his work by several established biologists, Lindeman's resulting paper, "The Trophic-Dynamic Aspect of Ecology," published in the journal *Ecology* in 1942, had a dramatic impact. His study served as a model and became a catalyst for similar studies of ecosystem energy relationships and helped establish the ecosystem as a fundamental ecological unit.

Lindeman's paper was highly theoretical and was not based on extensive or particularly accurate measurements of ecological parameters. The technology of the time made such measurements difficult or impossible. Beginning in the 1950's, Eugene P. Odum and Howard T. Odum, both deeply influenced by Hutchinson, pushed ecosystem ecology to its next plateau. They ran a series of ecosystem studies on abandoned farmland around the Savannah River nuclear plant in Georgia, on the Pacific island of Enewetak (a site used for nuclear testing), on

the mineral springs at Silver Springs, Florida, and at other sites. In each of these studies, they considered the energy flow and matter cycles of the entire system; they also developed new techniques for measuring such flows, most notably the use of radioactive isotopes to trace the flow of matter through a system.

In the 1960's, thirty years after Tansley's suggestion to consider entire ecosystems as units for ecological research, F. Herbert Bormann and Gene E. Likens began a series of studies in the Hubbard Brook Experimental Forest in New Hampshire. These studies evolved into a multiyear study of the entire Hubbard Brook ecosystem and involved nearly two hundred scientists. The researchers measured inputs and outputs to individual watersheds and explored the watersheds' handling of materials. They cut all vegetation from some watersheds and studied the effects. They also applied herbicides to some clear-cut watersheds and analyzed the long-term absence of plant cover. Bormann and Likens followed Tansley's advice to study entire ecosystems, and their work resulted in significantly improved understanding of ecosystem organization and function.

An even larger-scale ecosystem study was also initiated in the 1960's. The International Biological Program (IBP) was considerably more popular in Europe and Canada than it was in the United States, but even in the United States, its goals were in keeping with Tansley's suggestion. These goals included gathering sufficient data from five major ecosystems—referred to as "biomes" by the IBP—to produce computer models of the structures and functions of each. Scientists could use these models to understand the biomes in greater depth and so better direct their management. In his paper, Tansley had suggested the use of mathematical models for improved understanding of ecosystems.

The IBP did not fulfill its mission to generate functional models of biomes, but it did stimulate elaborate and cooperative studies of whole ecosystems, and so contributed to the establishment of ecosystem ecology. The Ecosystem Studies Program of the National Science Foundation followed the IBP as the organization responsible for funding large-scale ecosystem studies, and such studies increased in numbers, indicating the perceived importance of ecosystem ecology. The sequence of events that established that importance was, in a sense, initiated by Tansley's introduction of the word "ecosystem" in his criticism of Clements's "organismic community."

Once the ecosystem became established as the functional ecological unit, it became clear that conservation efforts could be successful only if they concentrated on conserving such units. Although community structure is not literally organismic, an intact ecosystem is required for continuity of many of its member species. In their day, both Clements and Tansley argued for the conservation of entire ecosystems. As researchers learned more about the structures and functions of ecosystems, their findings led to conservation efforts that attempted to save systems rather than species.

—*Carl W. Hoagstrom*

FURTHER READING

Egerton, Frank N. "The History of Ecology: Achievements and Opportunities, Part One." *Journal of the History of Biology* 16 (Summer, 1983): 259-310. An overview of the history of ecology, including ecosystem ecology. Commentaries on other sources are especially interesting. Includes extensive references.

_____. "The History of Ecology: Achievements and Opportunities, Part Two." *Journal of the History of Biology* 18 (Spring, 1985): 103-143. Continuation of the paper cited above deals with applied ecology in which ecosystem ecology has played an important role. Considers Clements's arguments for conservation during the Dust Bowl era. Includes extensive references.

Godwin, Sir Harry. "Sir Arthur Tansley: The Man and the Subject." *Journal of Ecology* 65 (1977): 1-26. Brief biography of Tansley by one of his closest colleagues. Provides insight into Tansley's personality and varied interests.

Golley, Frank Benjamin. *A History of the Ecosystem Concept in Ecology: More Than the Sum of the Parts.* New Haven, Conn.: Yale University Press, 1993. Lucid history, chronologically arranged, on the evolution of the concept of the ecosystem. Chapter 2 places Tansley's contribution in historical context. Includes extensive bibliography and index.

Hagen, Joel B. *An Entangled Bank: The Origins of Ecosystem Ecology.* New Brunswick, N.J.: Rutgers University Press, 1992. Excellent history of ecosystem ecology. Includes illustrations and index.

McIntosh, Robert P. *The Background of Ecology: Concept and Theory.* New York: Cambridge University Press, 1985. Excellent work places Tansley's contribution in context. Chapter 6 specifically covers ecosystem ecology, but related ideas are discussed throughout. Includes bibliography and index.

Pepper, David. *Modern Environmentalism: An Introduction.* New York: Routledge, 1996. Places key ideas concerning environmentalism in social and cultural context. Includes discussion of the ecosystem concept. Features figures, tables, glossary, and index.

Real, Leslie A., and James H. Brown, eds. *Foundations of Ecology: Classic Papers with Commentaries.* Chicago: University of Chicago Press, 1991. Collection of classic papers presents wide-ranging information, and commentaries provide historic perspective. Includes the paper in which Tansley coined the term "ecosystem," Lindeman's paper, and related papers by Forbes, Clements, Gleason, Eugene Odum, and Likens and Bormann.

Tobey, Ronald C. *Saving the Prairie: The Life Cycle of the Founding School of American Plant Ecology, 1895-1955.* Berkeley: University of California Press, 1981. An excellent source of information on the rise and fall of Clements's organismic community model and its impact on the drought-stimulated conservation movement. Chapter 6 outlines Tansley's criticism of Clements's ideas. Includes illustrations, bibliography, and index.

Worster, Donald. *Nature's Economy: A History of Ecological Ideas.* 2d ed. New York: Cambridge University Press, 1994. Well-written history of ecology includes ample coverage of ecosystem ecology. Provides an interesting perspective on the concept of the ecosystem and its history.

SEE ALSO: May 13-15, 1908: Conference on the Conservation of Natural Resources; 1910: *Euthenics* Calls for Pollution Control; 1910: Steinmetz Warns of Pollution in "The Future of Electricity"; Sept. 1, 1914: Last Passenger Pigeon Dies; Aug. 25, 1916: National Park Service Is Created; 1926: Vernadsky Publishes *The Biosphere*; May, 1927: Indiana Dunes Are Preserved as a State Park; Sept., 1933: Marshall Writes *The People's Forests.*

1935

July 5, 1935
WAGNER ACT

The National Labor Relations Act of 1935, also known as the Wagner Act, placed positive federal authority behind labor organizing and collective bargaining.

ALSO KNOWN AS: National Labor Relations Act
LOCALE: Washington, D.C.
CATEGORIES: Laws, acts, and legal history; business and labor; economics

KEY FIGURES
Robert F. Wagner (1877-1953), U.S. senator from New York
Franklin D. Roosevelt (1882-1945), president of the United States, 1933-1945
William Green (1873-1952), president of the American Federation of Labor
John L. Lewis (1880-1969), leader of the United Mine Workers and first president of the Congress of Industrial Organizations
Charles Evans Hughes (1862-1948), chief justice of the United States, 1930-1941

SUMMARY OF EVENT
Passage of the National Labor Relations Act on July 5, 1935, signaled the beginning of a national labor policy, a prolabor reform policy that the first administration of President Franklin D. Roosevelt, then preoccupied with the nation's economic recovery, initially had not anticipated and about which it was ill informed. Also known as the Wagner Act—for its principal author, Senator Robert F. Wagner of New York—the new law was one of the most significant pieces of labor legislation ever enacted in the United States. Moreover, unlike the Norris-La Guardia Act of 1932, which was prolabor in spirit and removed unions and their organizers from the danger of court injunctions, the Wagner Act actively placed that authority of the federal government behind economic coercions, such as strikes, believed to be essential to a vigorous and expansive labor movement. The Wagner Act also instantly provoked heated controversy both in the ranks of organized labor and in the boardrooms of many employers.

The novel presumption of the Wagner Act was that the profound labor unrest from 1933 into early 1935—much of it attended by bitter strikes, violence, critical disruptions of interstate commerce (a factor vital to federal jurisdiction), and in some quarters fears of civil war—was largely attributable to employers' general re-

fusal to recognize organized labor's conviction that collective bargaining was a prerequisite of union survival. The ability to organize unions that could bargain more equally with employers in regard to individual workers' wages, hours, and working conditions was perceived not only as a necessity but as a right. Accordingly, the act carried into public law an explicit acknowledgment that employers, especially the nation's giant corporations, enjoyed disproportionate shares of bargaining power relative to those of their employees. These imbalances were perceived to be large enough to allow employers to slash employment and wages almost at will, drastically reducing much of the nation's purchasing power and thus contributing directly to the unprecedented and persisting Depression of the 1930's. The act represented, therefore, the federal government's mandate to redress the imbalance of power.

Such were the assumptions and rationales confirmed in the act's introductory section and mortised into its substantive portions, most notably in section 7. It was this section that guaranteed workers the right to self-organization, or the forming, joining, or assisting of union organizations, as well as the right to bargain collectively through their chosen union representatives and to collaborate in their efforts to achieve collective bargaining.

The Wagner Act provided more than guarantees to labor. It further recognized the intense antiunion hostilities of corporate employers in the partially or entirely unorganized mass-production industries and consequently specified and prohibited practices that were deemed unfair to labor. Employers were prevented, for example, from interfering with, restraining, or coercing workers trying to exercise the rights extended to them by section 7. Similarly, employers could no longer with impunity interfere with the formation of unions or dominate their operations, nor could they contribute to unions' support. Hiring or tenure policies could neither encourage nor discourage workers' union membership. Workers involved in lawful strikes against employers' unfair practices, moreover, had to be reinstated when reapplying for their jobs, even when employers had replaced them, and workers who struck for higher wages or other improvements in working conditions could claim reinstatement if they had not been replaced. The Wagner Act thus sought to end employers' blacklists, "yellow-dog contracts" (under which potential employees had to renounce union membership as a condition of employment), lockouts, dual unionism, the corporate hiring of private armies or armed thugs, spying, and various other antilabor tactics.

The new quasi-legislative, quasi-judicial National Labor Relations Board (NLRB) charged with administration of the Wagner Act was resurrected from the Supreme Court's devastation of Roosevelt's early New Deal legislation. The NLRB was created under the aegis of the National Industrial Recovery Act of 1933 (NIRA), itself designed to hasten economic recovery through the formulation of industrial labor codes. The NIRA was declared unconstitutional by the Supreme Court's decision in the famed *Schechter* case two years later. The old NLRB, established specifically to ensure collective bargaining under the NIRA's section 7a, was abolished as well.

The tenacity of the chairman of the old NLRB, Senator Wagner of New York, proved the main force behind the NLRB's re-creation. A German American immigrant, Wagner had carved out a brilliant career as a labor reformer, partly during Roosevelt's incumbency as governor, in New York State's roiling politics. Wagner brought the character and experience requisite to the launching of the new NLRB to a New Deal administration less uncaring than ignorant about the labor world and more concerned, at least before 1935, with engineering recovery through business.

Formation of the NLRB embodied a dawning comprehension of the complexities of the American economy. That comprehension was based on perceptions of the growing inseparability of intrastate and interstate commerce, and it therefore incorporated Wagner's and the administration's elastic definition of what constituted interstate commerce. This implicit loose construction afforded the NLRB's three directors their jurisdiction in overseeing and enforcing workers' rights to collective bargaining and prohibiting employers' unfair labor practices. These were the battlegrounds, as it transpired, on which the effectiveness and the constitutionality of the act were to be tested.

SIGNIFICANCE

Passage of the Wagner Act coincided with the massive unemployment of the Great Depression. Union membership, which in 1920 included 12 percent of the labor force, had eroded steadily thereafter, so seriously that by the advent of the Roosevelt administration in 1933, unions could count only two million members, or 6.6 percent of the labor force. Several factors accounted for this decline. The conservative, employer-dominated governments and economy of the 1920's were character-

ized in spirit and deed by effective antilabor campaigns, sometimes masked as patriotic suppression of communism. Changes in the complexion of the industrial world also contributed. Shifting structural and technological patterns in basic industries such as railroads, steel, and coal mining, along with the spread of mass-production enterprises in the automotive, appliances, chemical, tire and rubber, oil, trucking, longshoring, meatpacking, and textile industries, led to a greater concentration of unskilled and largely nonunion workers. In addition, with 40 percent of American children completing high school by 1930, the educational level of the workforce was undergoing dramatic alteration, bringing with it predominantly urban visions of democracy and fresh perceptions of individual rights.

The traditional craft unionism that distinguished the American Federation of Labor (AFL), a federation of skilled workers' unions, seemed increasingly ill suited to the needs of the largely unskilled workers of the 1930's. In previous decades, unskilled workers had been all but precluded from joining the AFL crafts because of the nature of their occupations. AFL president William Green eventually did sanction inclusion of several industrial unions, which rapidly became the fastest growing in the AFL, but he did not aggressively recruit them. The outlook of the unskilled workers' leaders differed from that of the AFL. In opposition to the AFL's perception of government's role in the economy—basically an eschewal of any role at all—the leaders of the unskilled, in general, were far more enthusiastic than their skilled brethren in calls for governmental intervention on labor's behalf.

These were just a few of the critical differences dividing labor's house by the mid-1930's. Almost simultaneously with enactment of the Wagner Act, they grew more serious because of the emergence of the Congress of Industrial Organizations (CIO), dedicated to the recruitment of unskilled labor as well as to vigorous political activism. Subsequent antipathies between the CIO's leaders—among them the fiery United Mine Workers' chief, John L. Lewis—and the AFL's old guard, from whose camp the industrial unionists of the CIO had departed, left the labor movement as a whole without clear direction or coherent policy.

Beginning almost instantly upon its enactment and continuing through the next decade, the Wagner Act successfully promoted its major objective of relatively free collective bargaining. The proof lay in the rise of union membership. The three million unionists of 1933 swelled to more than fifteen million by 1946, more than 22 percent of the labor force. The vast majority of the labor force was composed of unskilled or semiskilled industrial workers, previously shunned by the AFL. More revealing than these overall figures, however, were union gains in manufacturing industries. Barely one-fifth of manufacturing workers were bargaining collectively in 1935, but more than two-thirds were doing so in 1946. The AFL claimed nine million members by the end of this expansion. The CIO's count came to an impressive six million members.

Behind these statistics of rising union membership lay thousands of decisions rendered by the NLRB. During the ten years following the reestablishment of the NLRB, fifty thousand union representation elections were held under its auspices and judgments were rendered on more than forty-five thousand union complaints about practices unfair to labor.

Once unions were lawfully established, labor-management disputes no longer fell under the jurisdiction of the NLRB. The Wagner Act and NLRB nevertheless contributed significantly to removing violence from, and substituting democratic procedures for, the selection of workers' union representation and thus their right to collective bargaining.

On April 12, 1937, Chief Justice Charles Evans Hughes delivered the Supreme Court's majority decision in *National Labor Relations Board v. Jones & Laughlin Steel Corp.*, in essence proclaiming the Wagner Act constitutional. The act and the NLRB, along with "little Wagner Acts" in many states, were already engulfed in controversies. The NLRB was understaffed, underfunded, and ill prepared to cope with these disputes. With only a thousand employees, even with self-imposed restrictions on its business, it handled annually roughly seven thousand representational cases and fourteen thousand complaints on practices unfair to labor, which averaged a year and a half for resolution.

Operation of the NLRB fell under different interpretations. These differences arose from confusion among employers and unionists, complicated by their traditional animosities, and differences in interpretation of the act's jurisdictions and responsibilities. There were notable lapses in the drafting of the law. It said nothing, for example, about employer (rather than employee) petitions for union elections. The act likewise had no provisions for handling the harassment of one union by another, a serious matter given the sometimes heated competition for union membership by the mutually hostile AFL and CIO. What constituted a "bargaining unit" when industries or plants were divided between craft and industrial workers was unresolved. There were problems regarding whether bargaining should be by area, company, or plant. These problems and many more were made more troublesome by immature union leadership and by inexperienced and resentful employers.

The heart of the Wagner Act's difficulties lay in its legal promotion of union activity and its prolabor bias. Official and popular sentiments soon shifted toward seeking greater balance between labor and management. Those sentiments led to amendment of the National Labor Relations Act in 1947 by the Taft-Hartley Act.

—*Clifton K. Yearley*

FURTHER READING

Babson, Steve. *The Unfinished Struggle: Turning Points in American Labor, 1877-Present.* Lanham, Md.: Rowman & Littlefield, 1999. Concise and comprehensive history of the American labor movement. Includes notes and index.

Bernstein, Irving. *The New Deal Collective Bargaining Policy.* Berkeley: University of California Press, 1950. A history of the National Labor Relations Act of 1935.

Boyer, Richard O., and Herbert M. Morais. *Labor's Untold Story.* 3d ed. New York: United Electrical, Radio & Machine Workers of America, 1975. Presents a history of labor's struggles against industrial capitalists from the point of view of labor. Focuses on key events and major personalities from the 1850's through the 1950's and examines conflicts among workers themselves. Includes bibliography and index.

Eby, Herbert O. *The Labor Relations Act in the Courts.* New York: Harper & Brothers, 1943. Provides a review of court decisions affecting the rights and responsibilities of workers and employers in the years following the enactment of the Wagner Act. Includes an excellent citation index of legal cases concerning the act as well as the full text of the act and related rules and regulations.

Galbraith, John Kenneth. *The New Industrial State.* Boston: Houghton Mifflin, 1967. Intelligent, insightful, and readable work discusses unions and related laws from the Wagner Act through the early 1960's in chapters 23 and 24. Includes index.

Hardin, Patrick, and John E. Higgins, Jr., eds. *The Developing Labor Law.* 2 vols. 4th ed. Chicago: Bureau of National Affairs, 2002. Collection provides comprehensive coverage of rights under the National Labor Relations Act. Contributions are written by members of the American Bar Association's Section on Labor and Employment Law.

Hughes, Jonathan, and Louis P. Cain. *American Economic History*. 6th ed. Boston: Addison-Wesley, 2002. Comprehensive volume on the economic history of the United States includes discussion of legislation concerning organized labor.

Mathews, Robert E., ed. *Labor Relations and the Law*. Boston: Little, Brown, 1953. Collection contains several excellent articles on various legal and historical dimensions of the relationships between organized labor and employers. Includes index and sections of several labor laws, such as the Clayton, Norris-La Guardia, and Railway Labor Acts, in appendixes.

Millis, Harry A., and Emily Clark Brown. *From the Wagner Act to Taft-Hartley: A Study of National Labor Policy and Labor Relations*. Chicago: University of Chicago Press, 1950. Provides one of the best analyses available of the events leading to the passage of the Wagner Act of 1935 and the Taft-Hartley Act of 1947. Examines in detail the acts' provisions, their implementation, and their effects on labor relations. Includes bibliography and index.

Northrup, Herbert R., and Gordon E. Bloom. *Government and Labor: The Role of Government in Union-Management Relations*. Homewood, Ill.: Richard D. Irwin, 1963. Discussion of the relations between labor and government emphasizes key questions raised by the Wagner Act and the NLRB in chapter 3. Includes notes, chapter bibliographies, and index.

Schlesinger, Arthur M., Jr. *The Coming of the New Deal*. Vol. 2 in *The Age of Roosevelt*. Boston: Houghton Mifflin, 1958. Classic scholarly work includes extensive, detailed discussion of pertinent politics and personalities associated with the Wagner Act and the NLRB. Includes bibliographic notes and index.

Wilcox, Clair. *Public Policies Toward Business*. 3d ed. Homewood, Ill.: Richard D. Irwin, 1966. Offers clear, detailed, and authoritative discussion of the relations between government and business. Chapter 32 provides excellent context for the passage of the Wagner Act and establishment of the NLRB. Includes indexes of cases, names, and subjects.

SEE ALSO: Jan. 27, 1908: U.S. Supreme Court Ruling Allows Yellow-Dog Contracts; Mar. 25, 1911: Triangle Shirtwaist Factory Fire; Oct. 15, 1914: Labor Unions Win Exemption from Antitrust Laws; Sept. 22, 1919-Jan. 8, 1920: Steelworkers Strike for Improved Working Conditions; June 16, 1933: Roosevelt Signs the National Industrial Recovery Act; Feb. 5-July 22, 1937: Supreme Court-Packing Fight; June 25, 1938: Fair Labor Standards Act.

August 14, 1935
ROOSEVELT SIGNS THE SOCIAL SECURITY ACT

Despite objections raised by those who equated it with socialism, the Social Security Act passed the U.S. Congress by an overwhelming margin, creating the first national program of economic protection for Americans during retirement, unemployment, and disability. The program achieved such great popularity that it later became known as the "third rail" of politics, meaning that any attempt to alter it would be equivalent to political suicide.

LOCALE: Washington, D.C.

CATEGORIES: Laws, acts, and legal history; economics; social issues and reform

KEY FIGURES

Frances Perkins (1880-1965), U.S. secretary of labor and chair of the Committee on Economic Security

Edwin E. Witte (1887-1960), American economist and executive director of the Committee on Economic Security

Franklin D. Roosevelt (1882-1945), president of the United States, 1933-1945

Robert F. Wagner (1877-1953), U.S. senator from New York, 1927-1949

David J. Lewis (1869-1952), U.S. representative from Maryland, 1911-1916, 1931-1938, and U.S. tarriff commissioner, 1917-1925

Francis E. Townsend (1867-1960), American lobbyist

Wilbur J. Cohen (1913-1987), staff member of the Committee on Economic Security and later a top administrator with the Social Security Board

SUMMARY OF EVENT

Although Social Security in the United States is most often associated with a program for older, retired persons, the creators of the 1935 legislation viewed old-age dependency in the larger context of major changes in the economy and in family structure. They tended to believe that if economic security could be assured to the oldest

1935

members of society, such security could also be made a reality for other citizens. The original legislation did not profess to solve deep structural problems of unemployment and poverty: It was designed to provide the first links in the safety net that would protect U.S. citizens from future economic disasters. From the beginning, social welfare programs reflected an uncertainty of purpose between adequacy—a concept that benefits should be based on the needs of the recipients—and equity—a notion that benefits should reflect contributions made by the participants.

By the 1930's, most of the nations of Western Europe had enacted some kind of social insurance legislation providing for old-age care and unemployment compensation. For a number of reasons, however, the United States had lagged behind in such efforts. It was not until the administration of President Franklin D. Roosevelt that the United States adopted an effective social security measure. The general economic depression of the decade undoubtedly contributed to the momentum needed to pass social security legislation, for during the Great Depression, many people in the United States came to see economic insecurity as a social problem, not merely a matter of individual virtue and responsibility. By 1934, considerable support had developed for utopian schemes, such as that developed by Francis E. Townsend, whose Old-Age Revolving Pension Club was lobbying for a monthly grant of two hundred dollars for every citizen over sixty years of age.

There was nothing radical about a plan for old-age

Surrounding President Franklin D. Roosevelt as he signs the Social Security Act are (from left) Representative Robert Doughton, Senator Robert Wagner, Secretary of Labor Frances Perkins, Senator Pat Harrison, and Representative David L. Lewis. (Library of Congress)

pensions. Both private pensions and veterans' benefits existed long before the New Deal. Partly because such plans had proved inadequate during the Great Depression, the Democratic platform of 1932 called for public retirement pensions and for unemployment compensation. By the 1930's, almost half the states had some kind of old-age pension, but these were generally limited in scope. Only Wisconsin had a working unemployment compensation plan. In 1932, Senator Robert F. Wagner of New York and Congressman David J. Lewis of Maryland introduced bills in Congress calling for a federal unemployment plan patterned after that of Wisconsin. The same year, Senator Clarence C. Dill of Washington and Congressman William P. Connery of Massachusetts introduced a bill providing for federal grants to those states establishing old-age pensions.

It was not until 1934 that President Roosevelt decided to take the initiative in the field of social insurance legislation. He asked Congress to delay action on the existing bills while he appointed a special committee to look into all aspects of social security, with the aim of presenting a comprehensive measure during the 1935 congressional session. In June, 1934, Roosevelt established the Committee on Economic Security, with Secretary of Labor Frances Perkins as chair and economist Edwin E. Witte as executive director. Perkins took a broad view of her job and aimed to bring U.S. social insurance up to that of advanced European countries. She soon discovered, however, that there were divergent opinions, especially on the subject of how unemployment compensation should be handled.

The debate centered on whether the compensation should be strictly a national operation. On one side of the question stood a group of Wisconsin social workers, such as Paul Rauschenbush and his wife, Elizabeth Brandeis Rauschenbush. They advocated a joint state-national plan that would allow for greater experimentation and variety. They also pointed out that a joint approach would be more likely to pass constitutional scrutiny. Others, such as Rexford Guy Tugwell, Abraham Epstein—former secretary of the American Association of Old-Age Security—and Professor Paul H. Douglas of the University of Chicago, recommended a solely national system to avoid unequal coverage and to protect the highly mobile U.S. worker. Perkins sided with the Wisconsin group, and the final recommendation of the committee followed the decentralized approach: Unemployment compensation would be financed by a federal tax on total payrolls, with 90 percent of the tax going to the states to implement the program. The report also advocated a contributory national program of old-age pensions. Roosevelt accepted the committee's report.

The Social Security bill was introduced into Congress in January, 1935, by Senator Wagner and Congressman Lewis. The air was filled with warnings that the act would destroy individual responsibility and the principles of self-help, but it was passed in the Senate by 76 votes to 6 and in the House by 371 votes to 33. On August 14, 1935, Roosevelt signed the measure.

Money to fund the old-age insurance plan was to come from a tax to be levied on employees' wages and employers' payrolls. Benefits would be payable at sixty-five years of age. The unemployment compensation provisions followed the recommendations of the Perkins Committee. In addition, the federal government would extend grants to the states for the care of those destitute elderly not covered by Social Security and provide aid on a matching basis to states for the care of dependent mothers, children, and the blind and for public health services. The Social Security Board was set up to administer the various provisions of the act.

SIGNIFICANCE

Although clearly innovative for its time, the Social Security Act was considered inadequate by many of its planners. The requirement that a worker pay one-half the cost of his or her own retirement stopped far short of most of the European plans. As Tugwell pointed out in 1934, the worker would already be paying a disproportionate share as a consumer, because the employer's payroll tax in the program would immediately be passed on in the form of higher prices. Roosevelt defended the payroll tax by pointing to the political strength it gave the program. Because workers contributed to the pension fund, they built up equity in it. The sense that workers had earned a right to future benefits would make it difficult, if not impossible, for subsequent administrations to deny coverage or to dismantle the program.

A weakness of the law was its limited scope: It omitted farmworkers and domestics from unemployment compensation and contained no health insurance provisions of any kind. The law also reflected the assumptions of its framers that men were the principal wage earners and that women were economically dependent. Nevertheless, the act represented the beginning of a growing belief that the federal government has a responsibility to ensure certain benefits to its citizens. It provided a floor of basic economic protection and a greater level of uniformity of assistance among the states.

—*George Q. Flynn and Mary Welek Atwell*

1935

FURTHER READING

Achenbaum, Andrew. *Social Security: Visions and Revisions.* New York: Cambridge University Press, 1986. An excellent general history of Social Security from the early background of the law to the 1980's. The book is especially useful as a guide to the changes in Social Security after 1935. The bibliography is very complete. Achenbaum advocates medical and other benefits for all.

Altman, Nancy J. *The Battle for Social Security: From FDR's Vision to Bush's Gamble.* Hoboken, N.J.: John Wiley & Sons, 2005. Provides the background developments leading up to passage of the Social Security Act, the history of the Social Security program, and attempts to reform the program in the late twentieth and early twenty-first centuries. Bibliographic references and index.

Berkowitz, Edward D. *America's Welfare State: From Roosevelt to Reagan.* Baltimore: The Johns Hopkins University Press, 1991. Interprets the development and history of Social Security as a series of reasonable and pragmatic responses to political and economic conditions.

Bernstein, Irving. *A Caring Society: The New Deal, the Worker, and the Great Depression.* Boston: Houghton Mifflin, 1985. An extensively researched, well-written assessment of the 1930's from labor's vantage point. Includes a comprehensive discussion of the passage of the Social Security Act. Solid documentation and full index. Crafted by a leading labor historian, this is among the best single-volume studies of the period.

Davis, Kenneth. *FDR: The New Deal Years, 1933-1937.* New York: Random House, 1979. A detailed and scholarly account of the policies and strategies of President Roosevelt, with a chapter devoted to the passage of the Social Security Act.

Douglas, Paul. *Social Security in the United States: An Analysis and Appraisal of the Federal Social Security Act.* New York: Whittlesey House, 1936. Written by one of the important participants on the Perkins Committee, the book gives a detailed account of the background and the legislative process in the passage of the act. The book reflects the period, and a complete text of the act is included in the appendix.

Haber, Carole, and Brian Gratton. *Old Age and the Search for Security: An American Social History.* Bloomington: Indiana University Press, 1993. Emphasizes the importance of Social Security in replacing intrafamilial support for the aged with an intergenerational public strategy.

Kollmann, Geoffry, and Carmen Solomon-Fears. *Social Security: Major Decisions in the House and Senate, 1935-2000.* New York: Novinka Books, 2002. Survey of all important Social Security legislation passed in the twentieth century. Bibliographic references and index.

Louchheim, Katie, ed. *The Making of the New Deal: The Insiders Speak.* Cambridge, Mass.: Harvard University Press, 1983. A collection of fascinating essays by those who participated in the making of the New Deal, with Wilbur J. Cohen and Thomas Eliot explaining their roles in the formulation of the Social Security Act.

Lubove, Roy. *The Struggle for Social Security, 1900-1935.* Cambridge, Mass.: Harvard University Press, 1968. An important work in the history of ideas, with a focus on the clash between the traditions of voluntarism and the goals of social insurance. The book is especially good in its treatment of the ideas and careers of Isaac Rubinow and Abraham Epstein.

Nelson, Daniel. *Unemployment Insurance: The American Experiment, 1915-1935.* Madison: University of Wisconsin Press, 1969. A very scholarly and well-researched study devoted to the single issue of unemployment insurance, emphasizing the importance of the British model and the passage of Wisconsin's law of 1932. The book has a great deal of interesting information about individuals such as Commons, Epstein, and Wagner. There is little information about other aspects of the Social Security Act.

Perkins, Frances. *The Roosevelt I Knew.* New York: Viking Press, 1946. A delightful personal memoir by the woman who chaired the Committee on Economic Security, including an excellent chapter on the formulation and passage of the Social Security Act.

Quadagno, Jill. *The Transformation of Old Age Security: Class and Politics in the American Welfare State.* Chicago: University of Chicago Press, 1988. An interesting study of how the elderly have coped in the United States from the nineteenth century to the 1980's. The book compares American traditions with those of Europe and espouses a sociological theory that the organization of production determines social policy. Despite much useful material, the work is marred by an excessive use of sociological generalization and terminology.

Witte, Edwin E. *The Development of the Social Security Act.* Madison: University of Wisconsin Press, 1962. An invaluable insider's account of the planning for, drafting, and adoption of the Social Security Act of

1935 by the executive director of the Committee on Economic Security.

SEE ALSO: Apr. 9, 1912: Children's Bureau Is Founded; Nov. 23, 1921-June 30, 1929: Sheppard-Towner Act;

Mar. 5, 1923: Nevada and Montana Introduce Old-Age Pensions; Oct. 29, 1929-1939: Great Depression; Nov. 8, 1932: Franklin D. Roosevelt Is Elected U.S. President; Feb. 5-July 22, 1937: Supreme Court-Packing Fight.

August 23, 1935
BANKING ACT OF 1935 CENTRALIZES U.S. MONETARY CONTROL

By centralizing monetary control, the Banking Act of 1935 assured American businesspeople of a more stable and predictable economic environment and allowed them to conduct longer-range planning.

LOCALE: Washington, D.C.
CATEGORIES: Laws, acts, and legal history; banking and finance

KEY FIGURES
Marriner Eccles (1890-1977), banker and official of the Federal Reserve system
Carter Glass (1858-1946), U.S. senator from Virginia
Benjamin Strong (1872-1928), governor of the Federal Reserve Bank of New York, 1914-1928

SUMMARY OF EVENT
The Banking Act of 1935 reorganized control of the U.S. monetary system, centralizing power in the hands of the Board of Governors of the Federal Reserve System and the Federal Open Market Committee (FOMC). Prior to the act, each of the twelve Federal Reserve banks that had been established by the Federal Reserve Act of 1913 had greater freedom to pursue policies of their own choosing. This lack of central control had the potential to create chaotic business conditions. Businesspeople could not be sure what credit policies the Federal Reserve banks would implement. As a result, entrepreneurs could not predict confidently whether their customers would face an economic upturn and easy credit in upcoming months or instead be discouraged from purchasing because of an economic downturn that might be allowed or encouraged by the local Federal Reserve bank. Furthermore, a business could unexpectedly find itself at a competitive disadvantage in relation to a rival in another city if Federal Reserve banks differed in their monetary policies. These types of uncertainties made business planning and forecasting difficult.

The Federal Reserve Act of 1913 represented a desire to put knowledge of the economy and its monetary system to work. Its passage marked the first systematic attempt to influence the U.S. economy through monetary policy (governmental control of the national money supply and credit conditions). A committee of experts with specialized knowledge not commonly held by politicians would guide monetary policy. Concern about how to balance potential control of the monetary system for political purposes against domination of it by private banking interests led to a splitting of power between private bankers and the presidentially appointed Federal Reserve Board.

The Federal Reserve Board could indirectly change interest rates charged by banks or change the amount of money available to lend, by recommending to the twelve Federal Reserve banks that they change the interest rate on loans they made to banks or by recommending purchases or sales of government bonds and bills. The Federal Reserve Board made few recommendations of either type during its first twenty years. Instead, the chief executive officers, or governors, of the twelve Federal Reserve banks took independent control of monetary policy through the Governors Conference. That group made its own policy choices, then offered them to the Federal Reserve Board for ratification. The Federal Reserve Act of 1913 did not provide for this conference; its unauthorized action was indicative of private banks' reluctance to yield to central control.

In addition, the individual Federal Reserve banks were free to ignore recommendations of the Federal Reserve Board. The Federal Reserve Bank of New York in particular acted independently. Its governor, Benjamin Strong, also acted as a powerful leader among the officials who set monetary policy for the system as a whole. Strong's death in 1928 left the system without commanding leadership. Following the 1929 stock market crash, the New York Reserve Bank favored buying government bonds from banks to provide purchasing power to the economy. It acted on this policy, but Strong's successor was unable to persuade the rest of the Federal Reserve system to follow along. The Depression might have been far less severe if he had.

1935

Between the stock market crash and the banking holiday declared by President Franklin D. Roosevelt in 1933, the Federal Reserve banks operated essentially independently, according to the beliefs of their own boards of directors. The Federal Reserve Board was weak and divided in opinion. The Open Market Investment Committee (an authorized body that replaced the Governors Conference in 1923), with one member from each Federal Reserve bank, was similarly powerless. Each bank's representative came to meetings with directions from the bank's board of directors, and those banks rarely were unified in their goals. The decentralized control in the period from 1929 to 1933 led to monetary policy that has been described as inept and as possibly worsening the Depression.

The Banking Act of 1933 set up the Federal Open Market Committee, a successor to the Open Market Investment Committee, to determine appropriate bond sales or purchases for the Federal Reserve system. The FOMC also had one member from each Federal Reserve bank. It instituted all policy actions, and the Federal Reserve Board had only the power to approve or disapprove. Federal Reserve banks remained free not to participate in any open market operations recommended by the FOMC.

System officials blamed inadequate powers, rather than misuse of powers, for their inability to stop the Depression's economic contraction and to prevent bank panics and failures. Furthermore, many system officials were willing to tolerate the bank failures, seeing them as proper punishment for poor management or excessive earlier speculation in financial markets. The failures were concentrated among smaller banks and those that were not members of the Federal Reserve system, so they were of relatively little interest to the larger banks with the most influence in the system. The larger banks, in fact, saw the failures as a way of shaking their small competitors out of the market.

In response to the behavior of the Federal Reserve system in the 1920's and early 1930's, Marriner Eccles, a banker and Treasury Department official, devised a plan to correct what he saw as flaws in the monetary control system. He and many others believed that better use of monetary policy could be a powerful tool to end the Depression. Some argued that improper use of monetary policy had exaggerated the economic downturn and that, therefore, less rather than more central control was indicated. Eccles, however, wanted to implement the powers of the Federal Reserve system more broadly and to establish conscious centralized control of the monetary system.

Eccles's proposals formed the basis for Title II of the Banking Act of 1935, which stirred strong debate in Congress. Senator Carter Glass, who had helped develop the Federal Reserve Act of 1913 and had coauthored the Glass-Steagall Act of 1932, particularly opposed changing the nature of the system. It was argued that a stronger Federal Reserve Board would become an arm of the political administration rather than provide independent judgment. These debates led to a rewording of the act to reduce control by the executive branch.

The act reorganized the central bodies of the Federal Reserve system. The Federal Reserve Board was renamed the Board of Governors of the Federal Reserve System, and the U.S. secretary of the treasury and comptroller of the currency were dropped from membership. Each of the board's seven members was to be appointed by the president, but the members' fourteen-year terms would overlap, so that no single presidential administration could appoint a majority. The FOMC was reconstituted to include all members of the Board of Governors and five presidents of Federal Reserve banks. Those five positions would be filled by the twelve Reserve bank presidents on a rotating basis. They were to give independent policy recommendations rather than being guided by their banks' boards of directors as in the past. Most important, each Federal Reserve bank was required to follow the policies recommended by the FOMC and not operate on its own.

The Board of Governors also gained the power to set reserve requirements, or the percentage of deposits that private banks in the system had to keep available to meet demands for withdrawals. The act left election of Federal Reserve bank presidents and vice presidents up to the banks' boards of directors but made those choices subject to approval by the Board of Governors. These main provisions of the Banking Act of 1935 took power from the individual Federal Reserve banks and centralized it within the Board of Governors and FOMC. Eccles, who had been made chair of the Federal Reserve Board late in November, 1934, was chosen to chair the new Board of Governors that replaced it.

SIGNIFICANCE

The most important impact of the Banking Act of 1935 was its message: In the future, there would be a centralized guiding hand behind U.S. monetary policy. Along with other New Deal reforms such as the establishment of the Federal Deposit Insurance Corporation (which the Banking Act of 1935 amended), the act helped to persuade the American business community that there would not be another Great Depression. Businesspeople could predict a more stable American economy in which the government promoted a steady course of growth, with neither excessive unemployment nor the opposite problem, high rates of inflation.

Businesspeople became relatively certain of being able to obtain bank credit for promising projects. Previously, they sometimes had faced bank loan officers who were unwilling to lend because they were uncertain about future national financial conditions and the availability of funds to their banks. Centralized and planned monetary control greatly reduced these uncertainties.

Although individual banks would still fail, depositors and borrowers could rely on the Federal Reserve system to prevent large-scale bank failures. Banks themselves could count on a steadier, more predictable monetary policy environment in which to conduct business. Centralization of power made it possible and profitable for businesses and especially financial speculators to monitor the FOMC and try to guess its policy decisions, which were kept secret for several weeks to avoid any disruptive effects on financial markets. A new job function of "Fed watcher" thus was created.

Formal centralization of control did not end debates concerning independence of the Federal Reserve system. Individual bankers still wanted influence within the system, and the Treasury Department was unwilling to relinquish control of the system completely. The Board of Governors agreed at first to cooperate with the Treasury Department by buying government bonds, as a means of keeping bond prices high to aid the financing of government operations. In 1936, the Board of Governors also exercised its new power to raise the required reserve rate. This acted to reduce the amount of money available to the financial system, more than offsetting the effects of bond purchases. The combined policy contributed to a minor recession in 1936 and 1937. Congress then proposed very specific guidelines for establishing monetary policy, leaving little room for discretion on the part of Federal Reserve system officials. The proposal was not made law, but system officials heeded the implicit warning to coordinate plans with other government agencies.

The Board of Governors and FOMC chose not to exercise their powers to any great degree during the 1930's, generally letting recovery from the Depression run its course. During World War II, the Federal Reserve banks agreed to cooperate with the Treasury Department's borrowing, buying Treasury bonds to maintain their price and keep interest rates low. As the war neared its end, however, the Treasury's desire to keep interest rates low

conflicted with the FOMC's wish to restrain the growth of the money supply as a means of preventing inflation.

The Employment Act of 1946 stated that the government had a responsibility to use all of its tools in a coordinated fashion to maximize employment, production, and purchasing power. Implicitly, the act recognized that neither fiscal policy (use of government powers to tax and spend) nor monetary policy alone was powerful enough to control the U.S. economy. The FOMC continued to buy Treasury bond issues, but Federal Reserve system officials argued more strongly against the constraint that this cooperation imposed on their decisions. In March, 1951, an agreement was reached under which the FOMC was no longer responsible for supporting the price of Treasury bonds. That left the system without a clear and specific policy objective. The public had begun to believe in the power of monetary policy, so Federal Reserve system officials wanted to state clearly how that policy would be used.

An appropriate growth rate of the money supply was chosen as one objective. The FOMC would provide enough money to finance business expansion without causing inflation. The second objective was to vary credit conditions countercyclically, reducing credit availability during business expansions and allowing easier credit during contractions, as a means of offsetting business cycles. The Board of Governors and the FOMC began to exercise their powers of central control in a manner basically independent of political or private business interests.

—A. J. Sobczak

FURTHER READING

Board of Governors of the Federal Reserve System. *The Federal Reserve System: Purposes and Functions.* Washington, D.C.: Author, 2002. An official exposition for the general public. Periodically updated.

Broaddus, Alfred. *A Primer on the Fed.* Richmond, Va.: Federal Reserve Bank of Richmond, 1988. Booklet provides useful background on the Federal Reserve system, summarizing its structure and operation. Devotes a long section to describing actions of the system in the 1970's and early 1980's and also offers case studies.

Clifford, Albert Jerome. *The Independence of the Federal Reserve System.* Philadelphia: University of Pennsylvania Press, 1965. Discusses the structural arrangement of the Federal Reserve system, including changes up to 1960. Valuable for insights into debates concerning which public or private agencies should control the U.S. monetary system.

1935

De Saint-Phalle, Thibaut. *The Federal Reserve: An Intentional Mystery*. New York: Praeger, 1985. Examines the philosophy behind the U.S. system of bank regulations, including those related to overseas bank holding companies and international lending. Includes index.

Friedman, Milton, and Anna J. Schwartz. *A Monetary History of the United States, 1867-1960*. Princeton, N.J.: Princeton University Press, 1963. Authoritative study of the operation of the U.S. monetary system by two highly respected economists. Provides a narrative discussion of the use of monetary policy, illustrated with detailed statistics. Argues for the power of monetary policy, devoting more than one hundred pages to explaining how correct use of such policy could have prevented the Great Depression or at least minimized its effects.

Hafer, R. W. *The Federal Reserve System: An Encyclopedia*. Westport, Conn.: Greenwood Press, 2005. Provides a comprehensive explanation of the structure, processes, and policies of the Federal Reserve system and describes key events in the system's history.

Moore, Carl H. *The Federal Reserve System: A History of the First Seventy-Five Years*. Jefferson, N.C.: McFarland, 1990. Highlights major events in the history of the Federal Reserve system and provides an overview of the issues the system has faced. Accessible to the general reader.

Patman, Wright. *The Federal Reserve System: A Study Prepared for the Use of the Joint Economic Committee, Congress of the United States*. Washington, D.C.: Government Printing Office, 1976. Chapter 9, "The Banking Act of 1935," gives a concise history of the political maneuvering behind passage of the act and rationales for its passage. Other chapters outline the history of the Federal Reserve system. Includes appendixes containing letters and speeches concerning aspects of the U.S. banking system.

Wells, Donald R. *The Federal Reserve System: A History*. Jefferson, N.C.: McFarland, 2004. Describes American banking practices before formation of the Federal Reserve and then presents a full history of the Federal Reserve system, including information on the system's relationship to each presidential administration and how the system has evolved over the years.

SEE ALSO: Oct.-Nov., 1907: Panic of 1907; Dec. 23, 1913: Federal Reserve Act; Sept. 26, 1914: Federal Trade Commission Is Organized; Feb. 25, 1927: McFadden Act Regulates Branch Banking; June 16, 1933: Banking Act of 1933 Reorganizes the American Banking System.

August 29, 1935-June 30, 1939
FEDERAL THEATRE PROJECT PROMOTES LIVE THEATER

From 1935 to 1939, the Federal Theatre Project brought live theater to the American general public by funding small and regional theaters all over the United States.

LOCALE: United States
CATEGORY: Theater

KEY FIGURES
Hallie Flanagan (1890-1969), American theater director
Orson Welles (1915-1985), American actor and director
John Houseman (1902-1988), American actor and director

SUMMARY OF EVENT
In May, 1935, Vassar College theater professor and director Hallie Flanagan received a call from Harry Hopkins, head of the federal Works Progress Administration (WPA), asking her to come to Washington, D.C., to discuss what to do about unemployed theater people. Out of that phone call came the Federal Theatre Project, which was designed to provide subsistence income for unemployed theater workers.

In 1935, there were fifteen million unemployed people in the United States. Six million were on relief rolls. An estimated forty thousand theater people across the country were out of work. The Federal Theatre Project's aim was to employ as many theater people then on relief rolls as possible. Approximately ten thousand people found work with the project. By the time of its demise, nearly three thousand of those workers had found employment within the private sector.

In President Franklin D. Roosevelt's famous first hundred days in office in 1933, he set up a number of agencies to alleviate the conditions under which ordinary

Americans had suffered since 1929. Businesses had gone bankrupt. Banks and savings and loans had failed, impoverishing the people whose uninsured savings were wiped out. Unemployed men sold donated apples on street corners. Many people were forced to ask for food at the back doors of those lucky enough still to have homes.

Roosevelt's Civilian Conservation Corps gave unemployed urban men work in rural areas, where they built roads, replanted deforested areas, and built picnic grounds along highways. The Public Works Administration and Works Progress Administration built post offices, schools, community swimming pools, and recreation buildings in city parks. The WPA also found work for writers, who were assigned to write books about each state. Other writers and photographers documented the plight of farmers in the southern states. Under WPA auspices, interviews were conducted with former slaves and the interview transcripts archived in Washington, D.C. Artists painted murals for local post offices and other public buildings. The Federal Theatre Project, begun under the Emergency Relief Act of April, 1935, as a measure to provide minimal wages for ten thousand unemployed theater people, was part of the same effort to combat unemployment as well as bring performance art to wider audiences.

From the time it officially came into being on August 29, 1935, the Federal Theatre Project kept thousands of future professionals in the theater. Many became famous in later years. They covered the spectrum of the arts, including among their numbers composers, set and costume designers, directors, playwrights, and actors. Among project employees were Will Geer, Canada Lee, Joseph Cotten, Virgil Thomson, Paul Bowles, Arthur Miller, Sidney Lumet, Orson Welles, John Houseman, Dan Dailey, Gene Kelly, and Burt Lancaster (as an acrobat with a Federal Theatre circus).

The Caravan Theatre, with its portable stage, presented productions in New York City parks. Multilingual productions brought theater to Spanish Harlem and presented plays in Yiddish. Admission prices ranged from nothing to a nickel to, on Broadway, one dollar. The project also produced children's theater, including puppeteers and magicians, as well as regional and community dramas.

1935

A scene from director Orson Welles's Macbeth *featuring an all-black cast, produced in New York through funding provided by the Federal Theatre Project.* (Library of Congress)

SUPPORTING THEATER IN HARD TIMES

Before the Federal Theatre Project came to an end in 1939, the project's director, Hallie Flanagan, presented a brief before the Committee on Patents of the U.S. House of Representatives on February 8, 1938. She began by stating the reasons the project was established:

Government support of the theatre brings the United States into the best historic theatre tradition and into the best contemporary theatre practice. Four centuries before Christ, Athens believed that plays were worth paying for out of public money; today France, Germany, Norway, Sweden, Denmark, Russia, Italy and practically all other civilized countries appropriate money for the theatre.

However, it was not because of historic theatre tradition, nor because of contemporary theatre practice that the Federal Theatre came into being. It came into being because in the Summer of 1935, the relief rolls of American cities showed that thousands of unemployed theatre professionals, affected not only by the economic depression but by the rapid development of the cinema and the radio, were destitute. The Federal Theatre came into being because Mr. Harry Hopkins, Administrator of the Works Progress Administration, believed not only that unemployed theatrical people could get just as hungry as unemployed accountants and engineers, but—and this was much more revolutionary—that their skills were as worthy of conservation. He believed that the talents of these professional theatre workers, together with the skills of painters, musicians and writers, made up a part of the national wealth which America could not afford to lose.

The project's national headquarters, directed by Hallie Flanagan, was located in New York City. There were five regional organizations, each with a regional director: East, Midwest, South, West, and New York City. In each region, there were various subgroups of theatrical performance. The regional organizations were either attached to already existing nonprofit theaters or, where those were lacking, set up as independent companies.

Flanagan had a plan for regional theater, to establish theaters that had the possibility of growing into social institutions in the communities where they were located. In addition to plays with nonregional content produced by these regional centers, some work based on local history and folklore was produced, such as *The Sun Rises in the West*, produced in Los Angeles, and *The Lost Colony*, produced in North Carolina.

The immediate impact of the project, in addition to removing thousands from public assistance programs, was to draw hundreds of thousands of people to performances all over the country. It is estimated that project performances drew audiences of half a million weekly and that by the project's end in 1939, thirty million people had seen its productions. Approximately 65 percent of those

people, it was estimated, had never before seen live theater.

There was trouble with Congress, the source of funding for the project, almost from the beginning; project employees were accused of "boondoggling" and of serving as fronts for New Deal and Communist Party propaganda. Attacked by the House Committee on Un-American Activities in 1938, the Federal Theatre Project came to an end on June 30, 1939, after the congressional committees in charge of appropriations decided not to continue funding.

In its brief life, the Federal Theatre Project brought free or nearly free live theater to new mass audiences and created work for thousands. Some few of them later became famous in the arts. Some production devices of its "Living Newspaper" productions were later used in professional theater. Its research division created histories of local and regional theaters. Its neighborhood ethnic productions, often performed on specially designed trucks, were the prototype for productions in the late twentieth century in New York City.

Perhaps most important, the project left a dream of the possibilities of a government-funded national theater. In television and radio in the last decades of the twentieth century, its closest counterparts may be the Public Broadcasting Service and National Public Radio.

SIGNIFICANCE

Difficulties with Congress began before the first production opened. The directors of the Living Newspaper, a subunit of the project, chose to do a piece about the Italian invasion of Ethiopia. Playwright Elmer Rice, selected by Flanagan to head New York projects, agreed with her that the productions should be fluid and timely, like a newspaper. Rice selected Morris Watson, vice president of the American Newspaper Guild, to run the Living Newspaper group, and a staff of real reporters researched the material on which the plays were based. Employing devices of agitprop (agitation propaganda) plays Flanagan had seen recently in Europe, the Living Newspaper productions were total theater, using light, music, dance, mime, posters, graphs, charts, and direct speeches to the audience. Many of the techniques became staple devices of later Broadway theater. The first production, *Ethiopia*, nevertheless was killed by congressional fiat before it could open. Elmer Rice quit in protest.

Because the subject matter of Living Newspaper plays was contemporary social and political problems, these plays always found criticism from politicians and columnists. *Triple-A Plowed Under* dealt with the plight of the farmer; *Power* with Tennessee Valley Authority attempts to control floods and harness waterpower for electricity; *One-Third of a Nation*, taking its title from Franklin D. Roosevelt's phrase "one-third of a nation ill-housed, ill-clad, ill-nourished," championed public housing for the urban poor.

Until the creation of the Federal Theatre Project, African American actors and playwrights who did not want to conform to white stereotyping of their lives had little access to theater. In New York, there were the Harlem Suitcase Theater and the Rose McClendon Players' Theater Workshop, and in Cleveland the Karamu Theater. In addition to creating its New York group, the project set up black production groups in Chicago, Birmingham, Los Angeles, Philadelphia, Seattle, and other cities and developed a repertory of fifty-five plays, nearly all original scripts.

The New York company, in particular, was highly successful. Orson Welles and John Houseman directed an all-black cast in a production of *Macbeth* set in Haiti in which the play's witches were voodoo practitioners. Productions of works by W. S. Gilbert and Arthur Sullivan by white project performers were popular, but the black group had a smash hit with an all-black cast and updated music in *The Swing Mikado*. It also produced W. E. B. Du Bois's *Haiti*, depicting the rebellion led by Toussaint Louverture. *Walk Together Chillun* dealt with the need for unity among African American factory workers.

Critics of "that man in the White House," as hard-core Republicans referred to Roosevelt, argued that the Works Progress Administration was created to buy votes by paying "boondogglers," a word coined to describe workers who allegedly did nothing. Roads, buildings, and dams provided visible evidence that somebody must be doing something; it was easier to attack the arts, which had few such tangible products. Even the Federal Theatre Project's Children's Theatre did not escape the criticism that the project was full of Communists and that its productions were Communist propaganda. The Children's Theatre performed free of charge in playgrounds, parks, and public schools and had some long-running hits, notably *The Emperor's New Clothes*. A play called *The Revolt of the Beavers*, however, in which the subjects

of an evil king throw him out so that they can remain nine years old and eat ice cream, was described by project haters as Communist allegory.

Among the project's more striking socially conscious plays were the musical *The Cradle Will Rock* and *It Can't Happen Here*. Technically, *The Cradle Will Rock* is not a Federal Theatre Project play, because Congress canceled funding for it. Unpaid theater owners padlocked their doors on opening night, and Equity actors could not appear in roles in costume. Directors Orson Welles and John Houseman led the cast and the audience that had showed up to see the show down the street to a hastily rented vacant theater, where composer Marc Blitzstein played the score on a piano and actors in street clothes stood up in the audience and sang when their cues came. The performance received great publicity and gave impetus to the Welles-Houseman Mercury Theatre, which the directors left the project to form.

It Can't Happen Here is remembered for the conditions of its staging. Novelist Sinclair Lewis, his political consciousness raised by his wife, columnist Dorothy Thompson, published a novel in 1935 that concerned the way in which a fascist pretending to be antifascist could be elected president and become a dictator. He adapted it for the stage, and on October 27, 1936, the Federal Theatre Project produced the work simultaneously in seventeen theaters across the country. Hallie Flanagan canceled productions in St. Louis and New Orleans; Louisiana politicians protested that the play was really about Governor Huey Long, and Missourians wanted script changes. Most reviews were favorable, however. The simultaneous productions reached the largest audience ever to see a play at the same time until the advent of television.

The project did not neglect the classics, performing works by William Shakespeare and the Greek playwrights, including the first performance in the United States of Euripides' *Lysistrata* as well as medieval miracle and morality plays. George Bernard Shaw let the project produce his plays for only token royalties, and T. S. Eliot's *Murder in the Cathedral* was given its premiere performance on Broadway by project actors.

Under attack from its inception by critics of Roosevelt's New Deal relief acts and by those who labeled it a hotbed of Communist propaganda, the Federal Theatre Project was weakened slowly by financial cuts and attempts at censorship. In 1938, Martin Dies's House Committee on Un-American Activities attacked the project and refused to allow Hallie Flanagan and other project officials to testify at the committee's hearings. Republican Representative J. Parnell Thomas accused the proj-

1935

ect's plays of being propaganda for Communism or the New Deal. Flanagan finally was allowed to testify before the committee in December, 1938. When she managed to refute the so-called evidence, the hearings were ended, and Flanagan was not allowed to finish her testimony.

The end of the project came in 1939, after the committees in the House and Senate that controlled appropriations for the project debated ending funding. Republican Representative Clifton Woodrum said that "every theatre critic of note has expressed his disapproval of projects of this type." The day following his statement, he received a telegram denying its truth, signed by every major critic in New York City. The House committee voted to end appropriations, but the Senate committee approved funding. A joint committee passed a compromise bill that omitted funding. On June 30, 1939, the Federal Theatre Project was killed.

Two project productions, *Pinocchio* and *Sing for Your Supper*, were still running on Broadway. As funding expired, *Pinocchio* was given a different ending. Instead of becoming a real boy at the end, Pinocchio died and was placed in a pine coffin bearing a death date of June 30, 1939. Leaving the curtain up, the stagehands struck the set; the audience then followed the cast and crew outside and down the street in a "funeral march."

Representative Woodrum, attacking *Sing for Your Supper*, said that he would eat the manuscript if there was a line in it that "contributed to the cultural or educational life of America." The next year, the closing song from the show, "Ballad for Americans," was the theme song of the Republican National Convention.

Many people involved in the Federal Theatre Project went on to professional fame. Of the rest, Hallie Flanagan wrote, "The 10,000 anonymous men and women—the et ceteras and the and-so-forths who did the work, the nobodies who were everybody, the somebodies who believed it—their dreams and deeds were not to end. They were the beginning of a people's theatre in a country whose greatest plays are still to come."

—*Katherine Lederer*

FURTHER READING

Bentley, Eric, ed. *Thirty Years of Treason: Excerpts from the Hearings Before the House Committee on Un-American Activities*. 1971. Reprint. New York: Nation Books, 2002. Collection of excerpts from transcripts of the testimony of artists, writers, and other theater people before the House Committee on Un-American Activities. Includes Flanagan's testimony.

Buttitta, Tony, and Barry B. Witham. *Uncle Sam Presents: A Memoir of the Federal Theatre, 1935-1939*. Philadelphia: University of Pennsylvania Press, 1982. Buttitta worked on the *Federal Theatre Magazine* and was press agent for some of the New York productions. Gives an eyewitness account of the project, particularly of the New York City center.

Flanagan, Hallie. *Arena*. 1940. Reprint. Pompton Plains, N.J.: Limelight, 1985. Personal history of the Federal Theatre Project by its founder and director, written immediately after the project ended. Interesting and useful source, particularly for its eyewitness accounts.

Himelstein, Morgan Yale. *Drama Was a Weapon: The Left-Wing Theatre in New York, 1929-1941*. 1963. Reprint. Westport, Conn.: Greenwood Press, 1976. Chapter 5 concerns the Federal Theatre Project. Other chapters describe various efforts in the theater conducted by the Communist Party. Includes notes, bibliography, and index.

Kazacoff, George. *Dangerous Theatre: The Federal Theatre Project as a Forum for New Plays*. New York: Peter Lang, 1989. Scholarly work focuses primarily on new plays produced by the Federal Theatre Project, including those criticized as political. Includes a useful bibliography, particularly for material in the Federal Theatre Project Collection at George Mason University in Fairfax, Virginia.

Schwartz, Bonnie Nelson. *Voices from the Federal Theatre*. Madison: University of Wisconsin Press, 2003. Created as a tie-in with a public television special on the Federal Theatre Project, brief history presents interviews with actors, directors, and others who were involved in the project.

Williams, Jay. *Stage Left*. New York: Charles Scribner's Sons, 1974. Chronicles the early years of left-wing theater in the United States, ending with a discussion of the Federal Theatre Project. Covers many of the theater groups involved in socially conscious drama. Includes index and photos.

Witham, Barry B. *The Federal Theatre Project: A Case Study*. New York: Cambridge University Press, 2003. Detailed look at the project relies on archival sources, official correspondence, and interviews. Includes production calendar, glossary of names, bibliography, and index.

August 31, 1935-November 4, 1939
NEUTRALITY ACTS

During the 1930's, strong isolationist sentiment across the United States prompted legislation to prevent the nation from becoming involved in foreign entanglements.

LOCALE: Washington, D.C.
CATEGORIES: Diplomacy and international relations; laws, acts, and legal history

KEY FIGURES

Franklin D. Roosevelt (1882-1945), president of the United States, 1933-1945
Cordell Hull (1871-1955), U.S. secretary of state
Gerald Prentice Nye (1892-1971), U.S. senator from North Dakota
William E. Borah (1865-1940), U.S. senator from Idaho
Hiram Warren Johnson (1866-1945), U.S. senator from California

SUMMARY OF EVENT

During the early 1930's, foreign policy was of secondary importance in the estimation of most people in the United States, as the nation was preoccupied in the struggle to recover from the Depression. By 1935, however, a congressional movement had been initiated to formulate legislative safeguards that would prevent the United States from becoming involved in foreign entanglements. President Franklin D. Roosevelt and Secretary of State Cordell Hull supported such safeguards, so long as the chief executive retained discretionary power in their application. Ignoring the president's wishes, Congress passed a series of neutrality acts in 1935, 1936, 1937, and 1939 that limited presidential options.

Passage of the neutrality laws stemmed, in large part, from a reevaluation of the reasons for U.S. entry into World War I. Noteworthy in this regard was Senator Gerald Prentice Nye, a North Dakota Republican, who chaired the committee investigating the munitions industry and seeking evidence of possible economic pressures leading to the nation's involvement in World War I. Supported by a vigorous peace lobby in 1934, Nye dramatically publicized the thesis that the United States had been duped into entering World War I to assist unscrupulous armaments producers and bankers, so-called merchants of death, who stood to profit financially by an Allied victory. This conclusion strengthened an existing feeling that some kind of neutrality legislation, which included

an arms embargo, was needed to prevent such a catastrophe in the future.

In March, 1935, with American public opinion staunchly against involvement in any future war, Roosevelt asked the Nye Committee to study the neutrality question and formulate appropriate legislation. Entrusted with this new task, Nye and his colleagues proposed several resolutions, one of which prohibited the export of arms and ammunition to all belligerents. Because Nye's resolutions did not give the president the authority to distinguish between aggressors and victims or to embargo the sale of arms to aggressors exclusively, Roosevelt had the Department of State draft legislation that did so. The State Department measure was lost when the Senate Foreign Relations Committee, dominated by two isolationist senators, William E. Borah of Idaho and Hiram Warren Johnson of California, produced its own bill.

The Foreign Relations Committee measure, approved by both the Senate and the House of Representatives, was to last six months. It provided for an impartial arms embargo to nations engaged in a conflict recognized by the president, prohibited U.S. ships from carrying war materiel to belligerents, and recommended that U.S. citizens be warned against traveling on belligerent ships. Roosevelt opposed the mandatory embargo and objected that the act did not apply to nonmunitions war materials. Nevertheless, he accepted the bill on August 31, fearing that failure to do so would adversely affect domestic reforms then under consideration in Congress and believing that he could persuade the legislators to revise the act by the time it expired on February 29, 1936.

Unfortunately for Roosevelt, a State Department neutrality resolution of January 3, 1936, which gave the president discretionary authority to limit the sale of raw materials to belligerents, ran into serious opposition from Nye, Borah, Johnson, and other isolationists. With the expiration date of the 1935 measure fast approaching, Congress passed a new act slightly more stringent than the first in mid-February. Extending the basic provisions of the first act, the Second Neutrality Act also required the president to extend the arms embargo to any third party that became involved in a conflict and forbade loans by U.S. citizens to belligerents. Recognizing that there was no chance for the State Department measure and wary of creating an antiadministration issue in an election year, Roosevelt signed the Second Neutrality Act on February 29, 1936.

Like its predecessor, the Second Neutrality Act carried an expiration date: May 1, 1937. When Congress began to debate a new measure in early 1937, neither the wisdom of the basic principle of keeping the United States out of war nor the implementation of this goal through an arms embargo was questioned. As the nation emerged from the Depression, however, pressure mounted for some kind of compromise that would permit business as usual with Europe, even in wartime. Bernard Mannes Baruch, a noted financier, suggested that a practical solution would be a cash-and-carry formula. He reasoned that if U.S. businesses could sell goods, with the exception of arms, on the basis of immediate delivery and payment by the buyer, the risk of U.S. involvement in war would be minimized. Both Roosevelt and the advocates of strict neutrality favored the cash-and-carry plan, the president believing it would favor Great Britain,

the European state controlling the sea. The new, permanent neutrality bill that emerged in April retained the mandatory embargo on arms, the ban on loans, and the prohibition on travel, but it gave the president discretion, until May 1, 1939, to place all belligerent trade except arms under the cash-and-carry formula. On May 1, the Third Neutrality Act, having passed both the House and the Senate, was signed by Roosevelt.

Two months later, in the first test of this act, the futility of legislating for unforeseen diplomatic contingencies was revealed. In July, 1937, without a declaration of war, Japan launched a full-scale attack against China. American adherence to the Neutrality Act would work to the advantage of the aggressor, Japan, whose powerful navy dominated the seas off the coast of China. Therefore, Roosevelt made no official recognition of the conflict, and the provisions of the Neutrality Act were not implemented in East Asia.

In the months that followed, Roosevelt had little reason to suspect that isolationism was losing strength. Public reaction to his call for collective security, given in his Chicago "Quarantine Speech" of October 5, 1937, was mixed. The Ludlow Amendment, requiring a favorable national referendum before a declaration of war, was only narrowly defeated in the House on January 10, 1938. Alarm in the United States at the ominous trend of events in Europe and the Far East must be attributed to the nation's relaxation of its policy of strict neutrality. In March, 1938, Adolf Hitler's Germany annexed Austria and began to make demands on Czechoslovakia. Meanwhile, the Japanese extended their aggression in China.

By the beginning of 1939, Roosevelt had concluded that the Neutrality Act of 1937 needed revision. On January 4, in his state of the union address, the president warned of increasing threats to peace and pointed out that U.S. neutrality laws could operate unfairly, giving aid to aggressors and denying it to victims. Although he knew that Congress would not agree to a discretionary

---

BORAH ARGUES AGAINST EUROPEAN INVOLVEMENT

The following is an excerpt from a radio address titled "Retain the Arms Embargo: It Helps Keep Us Out of War," delivered by Senator William E. Borah on September 14, 1939. Borah argued strongly against a revision of the Neutrality Act of 1937 that would end the arms embargo.

We are met on the threshold of all debate, of all consideration, of this subject of neutrality with the statement often delivered and with an air of finality that we cannot be neutral, that Europe is now so near to the United States, owing to modern inventions and the mingling of business affairs, that neutrality is impracticable if not impossible.

This seems to me a spineless doctrine. It is not the doctrine inherited from our forebears. If true, we would be the most ill-fated nation on the earth instead of being, as we had long supposed, the most favorably circumstanced of any, or all, nations. . . .

But we have no alternative, it is in effect declared, after these 150 years of self-government, we must go in some way or other into all these controversies, broils and wars of Europe. It is useless, we are told, to try to avoid this fate. . . .

Although our people have sought peace and now seek peace, still we must make war because European governments maintain an eternal saturnalia of human sacrifices. Though the law of our land banishes racial and religious persecution from our common country, still, because Europe is "near," we must join in the racial and religious conflicts and sacrifice our people over conditions which our forebears long since rejected.

Though we seek no people's territory, nevertheless, because Europe is "near," we must sacrifice the savings of our people and the sons of our mothers in this endless imperialistic strife. Though we would take no part of the loot which was divided up at the close of the World War, we are now called upon to make sure the title to a vast amount of this loot. What a fateful doctrine to propose! Let us renounce it and make the effort at least to establish freedom from the European system.

arms embargo, Roosevelt hoped it might agree to modify the law allowing for the sale of arms on a cash-and-carry basis. Although Germany and other aggressors would be eligible, the administration anticipated that Great Britain and France would benefit most, because of their control of the sea. In April, with the president's approval, Senator Key Pittman of Nevada introduced a resolution providing for the repeal of the arms embargo and the placing of all trade with belligerents on a cash-and-carry basis. Congress, under the influence of Borah, Johnson, and Nye, who were adamant in their opposition, rejected the proposal.

Attitudes in Congress toward a revision of the 1937 law changed after Germany's assault on Poland on September 1, 1939. When he learned from discussions with a number of legislators that a repeal of the arms embargo might be possible, Roosevelt called Congress into special session on September 23. Reiterating his belief that the existing law aided aggression, the president requested that the sale of all goods, including arms, be placed on a cash-and-carry basis. By shrewdly courting southern conservatives, dispensing patronage, and securing indefatigable public relations work by internationalists, the president succeeded in pushing his revision through Congress by a close vote. On November 4, 1939, Roosevelt signed the Fourth Neutrality Act, and the United States took its first step toward becoming the "arsenal of democracy," as Roosevelt would later describe it.

SIGNIFICANCE

The neutrality acts of the 1930's demonstrated the strength of isolationist sentiment among Americans that was stimulated by such factors as bitterness concerning U.S. involvement in World War I and the deprivations of the Great Depression. Despite the public's desire for isolationism, however, the acts were unsuccessful in keeping the United States out of a second world war. Because the neutrality laws made no distinction between aggressor nations and those they aggressed against, viewing both only as "belligerents," they prevented the United States from providing substantial support to Great Britain in its war with Nazi Germany until the formal American declaration of war in 1941.

—*George Q. Flynn and Bruce J. DeHart*

FURTHER READING

Cole, Wayne S. *Roosevelt and the Isolationists, 1932-1945.* Lincoln: University of Nebraska Press, 1983. Discusses the relationship between Roosevelt and the isolationists from the perspective of the latter.

Dallek, Robert. *Franklin D. Roosevelt and American Foreign Policy, 1932-1945.* 1979. Reprint. New York: Oxford University Press, 1995. Defends Roosevelt's foreign policy, showing the president as a master politician who had to consider both domestic and diplomatic objectives.

Davis, Kenneth S. *FDR: The New Deal Years, 1933-1937.* 1986. Reprint. New York: Random House, 1995. Second volume in a multivolume biography covers the period in Roosevelt's administration during which the first of the neutrality acts was passed. Includes index.

_____. *FDR: Into the Storm, 1937-1940.* New York: Random House, 1993. Third volume in a multivolume biography brings to life the people and issues involved in the passage of the neutrality acts. Includes index.

Divine, Robert A. *The Reluctant Belligerent: American Entry into World War II.* 2d ed. New York: John Wiley & Sons, 1979. A valuable source of information about the neutrality acts.

Kennedy, David M. *Freedom from Fear: The American People in Depression and War, 1929-1945.* New York: Oxford University Press, 1999. Describes how Americans responded to the deprivations of the Great Depression and the recovery period of the New Deal. Chapters 13 and 14 address the isolationist sentiments and neutrality laws of the 1930's. Includes maps and index.

Rhodes, Benjamin D. *United States Foreign Policy in the Interwar Period, 1918-1941: The Golden Age of American Diplomatic and Military Complacency.* Westport, Conn.: Praeger, 2001. In-depth examination of American diplomacy during the period covered includes discussion of the neutrality laws passed in the 1930's. Features selected bibliography and index.

SEE ALSO: July 17, 1936: Spanish Civil War Begins; Jan. 6, 1937: Embargo on Arms to Spain.

1935

September 6, 1935
TOP HAT ESTABLISHES THE ASTAIRE-ROGERS DANCE TEAM

Fred Astaire and Ginger Rogers sang and danced to Irving Berlin's music in Top Hat, *one of a series of Astaire-Rogers films that helped to popularize and define the screen musical.*

LOCALE: Los Angeles, California
CATEGORIES: Motion pictures; dance; entertainment

KEY FIGURES

Fred Astaire (1899-1987), performer who appeared with Ginger Rogers in *Top Hat* and eight other RKO musicals
Ginger Rogers (1911-1995), Astaire's dancing and acting partner
Pandro Samuel Berman (1905-1996), studio head at RKO who oversaw the development of the Astaire-Rogers series
Irving Berlin (1888-1989), American songwriter who composed five songs for the film
Mark Sandrich (1900-1945), director of *Top Hat* and four other Astaire-Rogers musicals
Hermes Pan (1910?-1990), with Astaire, dance director for the Astaire-Rogers musicals

SUMMARY OF EVENT

Fred Astaire and Ginger Rogers both made their screen debuts in the 1930's. Astaire played a small role supporting Clark Gable and Joan Crawford in *Dancing Lady* (1933) and Rogers was a wisecracking supporting player in *Young Men of Manhattan* (1930). They began to define their more familiar screen characters when paired by producer (soon to be studio head) Pandro Samuel Berman at RKO. Astaire and Rogers first appeared together in *Flying Down to Rio* (1933), although Dolores del Rio and Gene Raymond played the leads. The first true Astaire-Rogers musical was their next vehicle, *The Gay Divorcee* (1934), which had been adapted from a Cole Porter show in which Astaire had recently starred on Broadway. Although only one Porter song ("Night and Day") was kept in the film, the concluding set piece "The Continental" (by Con Conrad and Herb Magidson) won the first Academy Award ever presented for best song, and along with the Astaire and Rogers's chemistry, it helped make the film profitable.

Astaire and Rogers worked for the RKO motion-picture studio, whose initials stood for Radio-Keith-Orpheum, the names of the theater circuits (some of them former vaudeville houses) through which the studio's films were distributed. In 1933, RKO was bankrupt and under the receivership of a New York bank, and Berman, the young studio head, eagerly pursued any film property that looked financially promising. Berman also overrode Astaire's objections to being part of a film couple. Astaire had previously been teamed on Broadway with his sister Adele, who had received the greater acclaim. Now he wanted to be a solo performer, but the studio's financial straits allowed Berman to offer Astaire a rare incentive: profit points. Astaire relented, and the success of his early films with Rogers—*Roberta* (1935) followed *The Gay Divorcee*—pulled RKO out of debt. With their fourth teaming, *Top Hat* (1935), in preparation, Astaire's contract called for him to receive 10 percent of the profits above his regular salary.

Berman assigned Mark Sandrich to direct *Top Hat*, and Sandrich would go on to direct four other Astaire-Rogers films. Sandrich had an engineering background, and he took a systematic approach to filming dance musicals. He reduced a film's sequences (dialogue, action, music, dance) to a color-coded diagram that showed the order and duration of each activity in the shooting script. Sandrich understood the structural purpose of every scene, and he wanted songs that advanced the plot. For the music, Berman hired Irving Berlin. Somewhat disappointed by his previous experiences with film productions—*Puttin' on the Ritz* (1930) and *The Cocoanuts* (1929)—Berlin, a perfectionist, found a kindred spirit in the meticulous Astaire. Berlin's respect for Astaire would continue, and Berlin would later join the film *Holiday Inn* (1942) only because Astaire was part of the project. Berlin even claimed that he would rather have Astaire introduce his songs than any other performer (quite a statement, considering that Bing Crosby had performed Berlin's enormously popular "White Christmas"). The composer stayed for six weeks at a Los Angeles hotel, sometimes working for twelve hours at a stretch. "Cheek to Cheek," Berlin's longest-ever popular tune (at sixty-four bars), was written in one day; on the other hand, "The Piccolino," the big production number to conclude the film, was a throwback to the type of music Berlin had composed for Broadway revues in the 1920's and required as much work as the rest of the score.

The remainder of the creative team also worked on many of the Astaire-Rogers films. Dwight Taylor wrote the script for *Top Hat*, which emphasized romantic comedy and mistaken identity and was a virtual rewrite of

The Gay Divorcee. Allan Scott reworked the screenplay and went on to contribute to the scripts for the next four Astaire-Rogers films: *Follow the Fleet* (1936), *Swing Time* (1936), *Shall We Dance* (1937), and *Carefree* (1938). Hermes Pan is listed in the screen credits of *Top Hat* for staging the ensembles, but he was really assigned by RKO to be Fred Astaire's assistant. Pan had heard of Astaire's broken-rhythm dancing, and both he and Astaire had relocated from Broadway to Hollywood. Physically, he closely resembled Astaire, and the two would rehearse routines together and collaborate on designing choreography before Pan taught Rogers the completed steps. Astaire and Pan would collaborate throughout their long careers. As the head of the art department, Van Nest Polglase is listed in the credits for nearly all RKO motion pictures of the time, but his assistant Carroll Clark may have been more responsible for giving the musicals their sleek visual shine. Viewers of the films remember their distinctive Art Deco style nearly as much as the dance numbers.

The stars were assisted by an able group of supporting players who formed what could be called the Astaire-Rogers repertory company. The British comic actor Eric Blore, who embodied the prototypical gentleman's gentleman, played the butler Bates, Edward Everett Horton took the role of the fussy but likable theatrical producer Horace Hardwick, Helen Broderick appeared as Hardwick's sarcastic wife, and Erik Rhodes drew on his supply of accents to play Beddini (Rhodes had played a Frenchman in *The Gay Divorcee*). The studio's contract system also resulted in the casting of some performers who would later become famous, including a brief cameo by a platinum blond Lucille Ball, who plays a clerk in a flower shop.

Although Astaire would later appear with dancers who were more technically proficient than Rogers, none of these women generated the magnetism seen in the Rogers and Astaire pairing. Rogers would later win an Academy Award for her dramatic performance in RKO's *Kitty Foyle: The Natural History of a Woman* (1940), but she would always be remembered first for her work with

Astaire. As well-known actress Katharine Hepburn noted, Rogers gave Astaire sex appeal, and Astaire gave Rogers class. When *Top Hat* opened at the new Radio City Music Hall (which was partly owned by RKO) on September 6, 1935, it became an instant hit. The *New York Daily News* called it the best movie musical ever. Produced at a cost of $600,000, the film brought in more than $3 million. Only *Mutiny on the Bounty* (1935) earned more money that year.

SIGNIFICANCE

The Astaire-Rogers series began at a time when the techniques for filming screen musicals were changing. Director Mark Sandrich has been credited with formulating the playback method of prerecording the performers' songs with the orchestra and then having the actors lip-

Ginger Rogers and Fred Astaire in a scene from the first true Astaire-Rogers musical, The Gay Divorcee *(1934). (AP/Wide World Photos)*

sync the lyrics during shooting. The advantages of this approach can be seen by comparing any of the Astaire-Rogers films with a musical such as *The Cocoanuts*, an early talkie starring the Marx Brothers. In that film, the usually fast-moving comedians are noticeably more stationary because of their need to hear the off-camera accompaniment and because of the immobile camera and sound apparatus used at the time. By 1935, the playback method had improved and the equipment was lighter, allowing the creation of livelier musical numbers and more ambitious dance sequences.

These dance numbers were enormously effective. More than any other element, they give the Astaire-Rogers films their unique stamp. Dancing became Astaire's way of reshaping the film medium. In the same way that Alfred Hitchcock would shoot his suspense scenes by trying to avoid clichéd situations and by emphasizing the visual and Ernst Lubitsch would find fresh ways to film romantic scenes, Astaire brought innovations that forever changed dance musicals.

This change had both technical and dramatic facets. Astaire insisted that dance numbers be shot and shown as much as possible in one continuous camera take. By minimizing editing, he hoped that the audience would notice that a dance number was not a spliced-together sequence representing the best of numerous takes on the sound stage but rather a single perfect performance captured on film. He opposed cutaways and reaction shots, since they interrupted a scene's fluidity and hinted that camera tricks might be involved (and, indeed, the few reaction shots that remain in the dance numbers are always intrusive). Filming in one unbroken take placed greater demands on Astaire and Rogers, since one wrong step would mean reshooting the entire dance from the beginning. Hermes Pan and Astaire also gave attention to camera placement. To move a dancer toward the camera, for example, tended to lessen the audience's overall impression of movement; moving the camera at times with the performer, however, created more kinetic excitement.

Dramatically, the dances develop character and advance the plot. The first number in *Top Hat*, "No Strings," is an anthem of independence for Astaire's character, Jerry Travers. After he sings about his freedom from emotional ties, he dances with syncopated squirts from a seltzer bottle and slaps on the furniture, using rhythm and objects to emphasize his happiness as a bachelor. The film's second song—Berlin's "Isn't This a Lovely Day (To Be Caught in the Rain)?"—becomes a courtship dance for Astaire and Rogers. Trapped on a deserted bandstand when a cloudburst hits, they stroll about

and cautiously ease into concurrent steps; clearly, they are releasing their inhibitions through music. The visual contrast between the downpour outside and the couple moving in graceful rhythm under the roofed bandstand works well: At the start of the song, she faces him as an antagonist, but by the song's end, they are in love. It is a cinematic courtship that takes place through dance rather than words.

The Astaire-Rogers films may have established and popularized the film musical, but they did not spawn a series of close imitations at other studios. Audiences continually cherished the films not because they are time capsules of an age gone by, since such total stylization—people who always wear dinner jackets and formal dresses, drawing rooms as big as gymnasiums—never existed. In fact, Woody Allen gently satirized such films in *The Purple Rose of Cairo* (1985) and even included a clip from *Top Hat*. Instead, the Astaire-Rogers films depict a cultivated artificiality that provided audiences with a welcome escape from the Depression.

—*Glenn Hopp*

FURTHER READING

Astaire, Fred. *Steps in Time*. 1959. Reprint. New York: Cooper Square Press, 2000. More a series of anecdotes than a thorough autobiography, this work is still an entertaining read.

Bergreen, Laurence. *As Thousands Cheer: The Life of Irving Berlin*. New York: Viking Press, 1990. The most thorough and authoritative biography of the famous composer and the first published after his death. Chapter 14 discusses the making of *Top Hat*.

Carrick, Peter. *A Tribute to Fred Astaire*. Salem, N.H.: Salem House, 1984. Carrick's biography describes *Top Hat* more fully than any other Astaire-Rogers film, seeing it as representative of the very best of the series.

Croce, Arlene. *The Fred Astaire/Ginger Rogers Book*. New York: Vintage Books, 1972. Not merely good on the Astaire-Rogers series, Croce's excellent study is one of the best books ever about film. Thoughtfully written and a pleasure to read, the work also cleverly features two series of still frames printed in page corners, so that by flipping pages, one can see Fred and Ginger dance.

Gallafent, Edward. *Astaire and Rogers*. New York: Columbia University Press, 2002. A solid treatment of Astaire and Rogers's work together and as individuals. Dense, serious, and detailed.

Jewell, Richard B. *The RKO Story*. New York: Crown, 1982. Oversized and filled with photographs, but good for reading as well as for browsing. Covers every film RKO produced year by year and includes useful facts about the costs of productions and the box-office receipts of notable successes and failures.

Mueller, John E. *Astaire Dancing: The Musical Films.* New York: Alfred A. Knopf, 1985. Rich analysis of each of Astaire's dances from every film. Mueller's book is rightfully viewed as one of the best on Astaire and dance musicals.

Rogers, Ginger. *Ginger: My Story.* New York: Harper-Collins, 1991. Somewhat slight and anecdotal, and obviously geared toward a popular audience. Nevertheless, valuable for its first-person—albeit highly selective—view.

Thomas, Bob. *Astaire, the Man, the Dancer: The Life of Fred Astaire.* New York: St. Martin's Press, 1984. A popular biography that includes comments by

Astaire. Readers interested in more of Astaire's point of view should consult his autobiography, *Steps in Time* (1959).

SEE ALSO: Oct. 6, 1927: *The Jazz Singer* Premieres as the First "Talkie"; Dec. 27, 1927: *Show Boat* Is the First American Musical to Emphasize Plot; 1929: *Hallelujah* Is the First Important Black Musical Film; 1930's: Hollywood Enters Its Golden Age; 1930's-1940's: Studio System Dominates Hollywood Filmmaking; 1933: *Forty-Second Street* Defines 1930's Film Musicals; 1934: Lubitsch's *The Merry Widow* Opens New Vistas for Film Musicals; 1934-1938: Production Code Gives Birth to Screwball Comedy; Dec. 1, 1934: Goodman Begins His *Let's Dance* Broadcasts; Aug. 17, 1939: *The Wizard of Oz* Premieres.

October 10, 1935
GERSHWIN'S *PORGY AND BESS* OPENS IN NEW YORK

George Gershwin permanently blurred the distinction between musical theater and opera with Porgy and Bess *and opened the door to other ambitious experiments in form.*

LOCALE: Alvin Theater, New York, New York
CATEGORIES: Theater; music

KEY FIGURES
George Gershwin (1898-1937), American composer
Ira Gershwin (1896-1983), American lyricist
DuBose Heyward (1885-1940), American poet and playwright
Robert Breen (1909-1990), former general director of the American National Theatre and Academy

SUMMARY OF EVENT
On the night of October 10, 1935, after a brief overture, the curtain rose at the Alvin Theater in New York City. The audience heard a solo soprano voice sing a plaintive lullaby, "Summertime." From there, the joys, sorrows, laughter, and tears of *Porgy and Bess* cascaded from the stage. This opening, which today seems so elegant and has seemed so right since 1935, was not the first choice. Like much else in musical theater, the opening went through drastic changes before the work debuted. Prior to the world premiere on September 30 in Boston, it was planned that *Porgy and Bess* would open with a black pi-

ano player playing jazz in a smoky dance hall. The change was based purely on economy—the dance hall would have required another set. Such choices are part of the collaboration common in musical theater, and the story of *Porgy and Bess* is a story of collaboration.

Often referred to as George Gershwin's *Porgy and Bess*, the story about the crippled Porgy and his woman, Bess, had a genesis that was quite removed from the sophisticated composer. In 1924, an insurance salesman named DuBose Heyward decided to become a full-time writer. He had written some poetry as a hobby and had become involved in a summer writers' colony. Heyward set out to write a novel, and he chose for his subject the people of the poor black section of his native Charleston, South Carolina. Specifically, Heyward used as inspiration a crippled man named Sammy Smalls who moved about the poorer sections of Charleston in a cart pulled by a particularly pungent goat. Heyward read a short article in the Charleston *News and Courier* detailing Smalls's arrest for aggravated assault and attempted escape on his cart. Another inspiration was an area of Charleston called "Cabbage Row." It was an area of decay, with a courtyard fronted by vegetable stands. It was a place of poverty, crowds, and numerous calls to the police. Heyward passed it every day as he went to work. In his mind, he transformed it into "Catfish Row."

Heyward took these ideas with him to the MacDowell

1935

Colony, an artists' community, where he met and married a playwright named Dorothy Kuhns. He worked on his novel while she worked on plays and mysteries. Heyward's main character was first called Porgo. Like Smalls, he made his way on a cart pulled by a goat. His wife immediately saw dramatic potential in the unfinished manuscript, but Heyward was hesitant. He wanted to concentrate on his work as a novel. In addition, the mid-1920's was not a time to put a serious treatment of African Americans on the Broadway stage.

The novel was completed in 1925, renamed *Porgy*, and published to a very positive response. In very little time, the former insurance salesman became a literary celebrity. Cecil B. DeMille expressed interest in filming the novel for a group called the Producers Distributing Corporation, with Paul Robeson considered for the lead. Finally, however, the business minds at the corporation ended the project because it would not sell in the South.

Others had higher hopes for Heyward's novel. Dorothy Heyward was still at work, secretly, on a dramatic treatment. In the late summer of 1926, Heyward received a letter from George Gershwin indicating interest in and excitement about the possibility of turning *Porgy* into an opera. DuBose Heyward may have been unfamiliar to Gershwin, but Gershwin was very familiar to Heyward. By 1926, Gershwin's name was quite well known.

Because he was the son of immigrant Jews, Gershwin's name had changed several times. George began as Jacob. His elder brother's name went from Israel to Isadore to Ira. Their last name was Gershovitz in Russia and then became Gershvin, Gershwine, and, finally, Gershwin. George began piano lessons at the age of twelve and was playing in bars at fifteen. Soon, while working for a music publishing house, he became familiar with popular music and show music. By 1916, he had written a song for a revue. In 1919, Broadway saw the first George Gershwin musical, *La La Lucille*. Previously in that year, Al Jolson had sung Gershwin's song "Swanee" in *Sinbad*.

For the 1922 edition of the revue known as George White's Scandals, Gershwin and Buddy DeSylva wrote a twenty-minute "jazz opera" called *Blue Monday*. It dealt with infidelity among African Americans, although the parts were played by white actors in blackface. After opening night, the piece was cut from the show, but it clearly indicated Gershwin's future work with *Porgy*. In 1924, Gershwin made important strides in several directions. Paul Whiteman, the orchestra conductor for *Blue Monday*, had admired the work and approached Gershwin with the idea of composing and performing a serious

George Gershwin. (Library of Congress)

work using jazz idioms. The result was *Rhapsody in Blue*. Later that year, Gershwin opened *Lady, Be Good!* on Broadway. This was his first collaboration with his brother, Ira.

George had worked with other lyricists and he would work with others in the future. Ira also had worked with other composers and he would work with more as well, but there was something special about the brothers working together. Their other shows included *Girl Crazy* (1930), *Strike Up the Band* (1930), and the Pulitzer Prize-winning *Of Thee I Sing* (1931), the first musical to win that award.

This was the reputation George Gershwin had started to build when he wrote to Heyward about turning *Porgy* into an opera. As Heyward considered a partnership with the great Gershwin, Dorothy Heyward confessed that she had been writing a dramatic version of *Porgy*. Both were convinced that the issue was a choice between a play or an opera. It did not occur to either that they could have both. Heyward was drawn to his wife's work not only out of loyalty but also because it was good. He was intrigued by how well she was able to make the story work on stage. Heyward told Gershwin of his decision, assuming that it would put an end to the opera. Gershwin's greater theater experience led him to believe that the two options were not mutually exclusive, however. In fact, Gershwin realized that working from a play would give him a needed structure.

With this news, the Heywards set to work revising the first draft. DuBose was able to make the unique contribution of accurate dialect. Dorothy, however, made the key suggestion of changing the novel's ending to show that Porgy's spirit had not been crushed. The play was produced by the Theatre Guild in October, 1927, under the direction of Rouben Mamoulian. It was a hit and only served to increase Gershwin's determination to create an opera from the material.

Other proposals were made, including a musical by Jerome Kern and Oscar Hammerstein II, to feature Al Jolson in blackface. By 1933, Heyward and Gershwin were committed contractually to the project. George wrote the music, and both Heyward and Ira Gershwin created lyrics. They had very different styles of working. According to Ira Gershwin, it took the poet that Heyward was to create "Summertime," but when it came to up-tempo, rhythmic songs such as "It Ain't Necessarily So," Gershwin would step in. Ira could not read music; he would simply listen to the melody his brother created and work from there. In at least one instance, the three collaborated. It was agreed that Porgy needed a happy song. George played a happy melody for the two lyricists. Ira immediately suggested the line "I got plenty o' nuthin', and nuthin's plenty for me." Heyward took that line and the music and finished the song.

Mamoulian, by this time a noted film director in Hollywood, was brought back to direct the opera, once again produced by the Theatre Guild. By the time of the much anticipated Boston premiere on June 24, 1935, Gershwin had made several cuts in the score. At the suggestion of the producers and the director, he made several more as the show was prepared for its New York opening. Following the New York opening on October 10, 1935, the reviews and the public response were mixed. Many realized the genius of each of the collaborators, but others were unsure as to exactly what had been created. George Gershwin was certain that this was his stage masterpiece. As fate would have it, it was his last major work for the stage. He and his brother worked on several films following *Porgy and Bess* and then, in 1937, he died of a brain tumor.

SIGNIFICANCE

In addition to the obvious contributions of Gershwin's melodies and the story of Porgy told by Heyward and Ira Gershwin, the production of *Porgy and Bess* made several other unique contributions to music and theater. First among these was the use of black actors on stage. Clearly this was not the first time African Americans had been on stage; it was not even the first time black actors had serious singing roles on stage. *Show Boat*, by Jerome Kern and Oscar Hammerstein II, had in 1927 featured a character named Joe, who sang "Ol' Man River." The original stage version of *Porgy* featured serious black actors. For the most part, however, black actors in Broadway musicals were in revues such as *Shuffle Along* (1921) and *From Dixie to Broadway* (1924).

Lack of experienced black actors made casting a challenge, and it meant that the performers who eventually were hired were in many cases in need of coaching. The original Porgy, Todd Duncan, was a music teacher from Washington, D.C. Anne Brown (Bess) and Ruby Elzy (Serena) were both graduates of Juilliard. A vaudeville performer, John W. Bubbles, was hired to play Sportin' Life. The Eva Jessye Choir, a black touring choir, was added to the chorus. As is the case with most productions that open and then tour, *Porgy and Bess* went through many cast changes over the years. The musical afforded unique opportunities for many black performers.

In the early 1950's, Robert Breen, the former general director of the American National Theatre and Academy, began a crusade to revive *Porgy and Bess* and tour it worldwide. Over the next seven years, the show toured with various casts to London, Italy, Germany, and the Soviet Union. It was the first American theatrical production to play in the Soviet Union since the 1917 revolution. There was some hesitation about a production there, as it might communicate a false impression to audiences about how black people lived and acted in the United States. Another view was that *Porgy and Bess* showcased members of a minority who were gifted artists and should be given the opportunity to share their gifts. That view won out. Otto Preminger directed a 1959 film version starring Sidney Poitier and Dorothy Dandridge.

A contradiction existed concerning the show itself. Some critics thought it was an opera, whereas others were sure it was a Broadway musical. The various arguments are clear. It appeared first on the Broadway stage, although it became part of the repertoire of several leading opera companies. It was composed by a "popular" composer, and there are "standard" songs in the score. At the same time, this "popular" composer did work in the classical arena, and the score is filled with recitatives and choruses. Another argument made is that *Porgy and Bess* does not have the kinds of characters usually found in opera—this is basically the same argument used later concerning the status as a tragedy of Arthur Miller's *Death of a Salesman* (pr., pb. 1949).

The debate concerning classification of *Porgy and Bess* is in part a question of attitude. Although *Porgy and Bess* may not be populated with the usual characters of opera, it certainly has opera characteristics. Technically, it has elements of a sung-through score, grand passions, and tragedy. For some, the fact that it is in English—American English, no less—precludes it from consideration as an opera. Others perceive its blending of forms between Broadway and the opera as leading to Frank Loesser's *Most Happy Fella* (1956), Tim Rice and Andrew Lloyd Webber's *Jesus Christ Superstar* (1971) and *Evita* (1979), and other such shows. Whether George Gershwin wrote an opera therefore is debatable, but he certainly wrote a great work of art that led to other great works.

—*William B. Kennedy*

FURTHER READING

Alpert, Hollis. *The Life and Times of Porgy and Bess.* New York: Alfred A. Knopf, 1990. Exceptional study of the show uses research and interviews to re-create the experience, from the newspaper article that gave Heyward his idea to the 1959 film. Focuses as much on the art as on the business. Includes pictures and summary of the original New York production. Useful resource for the layperson as well as the scholar.

Engel, Lehman, with Howard Kissel. *Words with Music: Creating the Broadway Musical Libretto.* Rev. ed. New York: Applause Theatre and Cinema Books, 2006. A serious look at the needs and problems of the libretto in the musical theater by a conductor and theorist of the musical. Includes a helpful discussion of opera and the differences between the opera and the musical. An essential book for serious study of the musical.

Hutchisson, James M. *DuBose Heyward: A Charleston Gentleman and the World of "Porgy and Bess."* Jackson: University Press of Mississippi, 2000. Biography of the originator of the story that became Porgy and Bess places the work's creation in the context of the author's life and times. Chapter 4 addresses the transformation of the story into a work for the stage. Includes index.

Knapp, Raymond. *The American Musical and the Formation of National Identity.* Princeton, N.J.: Princeton University Press, 2004. History of the genre focuses on how themes in American musical theater productions relate to how Americans view themselves. Chapter 8 addresses *Porgy and Bess* within the context of a discussion of race and ethnicity. Includes useful appendixes, notes, bibliography, and index.

Laufe, Abe. *Broadway's Greatest Musicals.* Rev. ed. New York: Funk & Wagnalls, 1977. Standard history gives a good, if basic, chronological overview of the growth of musical theater in the United States. Includes numerous illustrations.

Smith, Cecil, and Glenn Litton. *Musical Comedy in America.* 1981. Reprint. New York: Theatre Arts Books, 1991. Excellent overall history of the musical theater provides photographs and thorough and literate text. Goes beyond the expected chronology and discusses technique. Provides a good explanation of the opera/musical debate concerning *Porgy and Bess.*

SEE ALSO: Feb. 12, 1924: Gershwin's *Rhapsody in Blue* Premieres in New York; Dec. 27, 1927: *Show Boat* Is the First American Musical to Emphasize Plot.

October 11, 1935-July 15, 1936
LEAGUE OF NATIONS APPLIES ECONOMIC SANCTIONS AGAINST ITALY

The League of Nations applied economic sanctions against Italy for invading Ethiopia, establishing economic sanctions as a means to obtain political objectives.

LOCALE: Geneva, Switzerland

CATEGORIES: Diplomacy and international relations; expansion and land acquisition; trade and commerce

KEY FIGURES

Pietro Badoglio (1871-1956), commander of Italian troops in Ethiopia beginning in November, 1935, appointed governor-general and viceroy of Ethiopia in 1936

Anthony Eden (1897-1977), British minister for League of Nations affairs, June-December, 1935, and British foreign secretary, 1935-1938

Sir Samuel John Gurney Hoare (1880-1959), British foreign secretary, June-December, 1935

Pierre Laval (1883-1945), French foreign secretary

Ato Wolde-Mariam (fl. early twentieth century), Ethiopian delegate to the League of Nations

Benito Mussolini (1883-1945), dictator of Italy, 1922-1943, and minister for the armed forces of Italy, 1922-1945

Haile Selassie I (Tafari Makonnen; 1892-1975), emperor of Ethiopia, r. 1931-1936 and 1941-1974

SUMMARY OF EVENT

In the early 1930's, Ethiopia occupied an approximately circular area, five hundred miles in diameter, in the interior of East Africa. It was bounded by the Red Sea, the Gulf of Aden, and the Indian Ocean. Strips of coastal land surrounding Ethiopia had been colonized by the British, the French, and the Italians. Ethiopia was one of a few African nations not controlled by Europeans. The name Ethiopia, preferred by rulers of the nation, was derived from black African sources, whereas Abyssinia, another traditional name, was derived from Arabic sources and refers to the racial mix of the region.

The conflict between Italy and Ethiopia began in the late nineteenth century, when Italy occupied a strip of the Red Sea coast later called Eritrea. In 1887, an Italian army of five hundred soldiers was surprised and completely destroyed by an Ethiopian army of twenty thousand soldiers. Hostility between the nations never disappeared. Then, at 2:00 A.M. on October 3, 1935, Italian

patrols crossed the Mareb River, which served as the border between the Italian colony of Eritrea and the nation of Ethiopia. Those patrols attacked outposts of the Ethiopian army in the Adowa area. Three hours later, Italian aircraft bombed Adowa. As a result of these actions, the League of Nations issued economic sanctions against Italy on October 11, 1935. The sanctions were formally withdrawn on July 15, 1936.

In order to add prestige to his reign, as well as gaining access to oil fields, Italian dictator Benito Mussolini saw the successful invasion of Ethiopia as vital to Italian interests. What he needed was an incident to justify the invasion. A suitable situation developed in the southwest section of Ethiopia near the town of Walwal, an Ethiopian oasis outpost located about one hundred miles from the border of Ethiopia and Italian Somaliland. This outpost had been occupied since 1928 by Italian forces to protect their access to the water of the oasis. Borders were neither precisely marked nor well defined by local residents, and bickering was common. In 1928, Mussolini made his one and only attempt to broker a treaty with Ethiopia. The Treaty of Friendship ceded economic concessions to Italy, but Ethiopia's emperor, Haile Selassie I, feared Italian aggression and was unable to meet his end of the agreement.

Each side viewed the other as a trespasser. The two sides exchanged shots on December 5, 1934. Ethiopia immediately brought the incident to the attention of the League of Nations, as a formal action of notification of an attempt by another nation to disturb the peace. Italians were offended by this action. By December 20, 1934, Mussolini had drawn up an important but secret document, the Directive and Plan of Action for the Resolution of the Italian-Abyssinian Question. This directive essentially established an Italian goal of conducting a war of colonial conquest of Ethiopia during October, 1935. The conquest of Ethiopia was completed in May, 1936, at a cost of 3,600 Italian and Eritrean lives and 275,000 Ethiopian lives. The use of mustard gas by the Italians was a significant factor. Liberation of Ethiopia by the Allies came in the spring of 1941.

Mussolini's position toward Ethiopia was heavily influenced by developments in Europe. Adolf Hitler was elected in 1933, and militarization in Germany began almost immediately. If Italy wanted to establish a presence

1935

2875

in North Africa, Mussolini realized that he needed to act before Germany was fully armed (and therefore ready to move into Austria, territory in which Italy also had an interest). The British and French were carefully watching the Germans, and Mussolini reasoned that they might overlook his move into Ethiopia if they thought it would aid efforts to create a united front against Germany.

In an attempt to avert war between Ethiopia and Italy, the League of Nations had formed several international committees to study the situation and to make recommendations for continuing the peace. Finally, a group called the Committee of Six (Britain, Chile, Denmark, France, Portugal, and Romania) made a report on October 7, 1935, in which they concluded that the Italian government had violated article 12 of the Covenants of the League of Nations. All representatives on the Council, except for the Italian representative, approved the report. The report was endorsed four days later, on October 11, in the Assembly by fifty of the fifty-four members present; Austria, Hungary, Italy, and Albania were against the report. The United States and Germany were not members of the League of Nations, although their opposite influences were strongly felt by members.

Because a violation of article 12 (conducting unlawful war) automatically enacted article 16 (punishments), the next step for the League was to determine what punitive action to take. Although article 16 allowed for military action, that was never considered. Discussions focused on economic restrictions. The term "sanctions" was coined at this time, presumably to avoid the more extreme implications of a term such as "punishments." By tradition, since that time, the term has come to refer to economic restrictions. The task of designing these sanctions fell to a coordinating committee, which appointed a subcommittee to draw up a series of proposals for sanctions. On October 19, 1935, the subcommittee presented its proposals to the coordinating committee, which adopted them on behalf of the League.

The five proposals that were approved and became the official sanctions of the League were as follows: lifting of an arms embargo against Ethiopia, prohibition of loans or credit to Italy by member nations, prohibition

Emperor Haile Selassie addresses his subjects from his palace balcony in July, 1935, a few months before the Italian invasion of Ethiopia began. (Library of Congress)

against importing Italian goods except precious metals, prohibition against exporting goods normally exported by member nations to Italy, and economic support by large member nations for small member nations that depended on Italian trade for livelihood. A significant aspect of these provisions was that there was not a prohibition against the sale of iron, coal, and oil to Italy. Some nations, such as the United States, restricted the sale of these resources to Italy voluntarily, but the overall supply to Italy was not severely affected. Oil was a necessity for short-term military success. Had an immediate ban been placed on oil, the effects of economic sanctions might have been very different. Italy might have been stopped from further military actions, domestic support for Mussolini's ambitions might have dwindled, and the various agreements between Italy and Germany in 1936 (the "Axis Accords") might not have occurred. Perhaps the aggression of Germany in Europe would have been slowed, allowing the Allies to develop their offensive strategies.

Ironically, the provisions of the League of Nations sanctions seemed to have an immediate effect opposite to that intended. Although the sanctions did bring about minor domestic hardships, Italy suffered enormously because of the economic and external political costs of the Ethiopian invasion itself. Mussolini, however, was able to shift the perception of responsibility for the economic consequences of the invasion from himself to the sanctioning nations. He thus obtained greater loyalty and sacrifice from the Italian population. Italians came to believe that desertion by former allies, rather than the costs of invasion, had produced their economic crisis.

Three important ideas concerning the use of economic sanctions to bring about political ends were developed and became part of the general strategy of the use of economic sanctions. First, sanctions must be very broad in terms of goods restrictions and must focus on those goods most directly related to the resource needs of the sanctioned nation. Second, the issuance of sanctions must be independent of other events that could potentially become a substitute point of blame for the actual cause of the nation's problems. Third, based on the long experience of failed economic sanctions not only under the League but also under its successor, the United Nations, sanctions against an authoritarian regime that is unresponsive to its population's suffering will only frustrate the population and leave the wayward regime intact.

The sanctions were not universally enforced by members. Four nations refused to participate at all, and more than 25 percent of the remaining nations refused to apply the sanctions in their entirety. Because some nations did not fully support the sanctions and because Britain and other nations wanted to maintain cordial relations with Italy in the event of a possible war with Germany, alternative proposals were drawn up. One such plan was the Hoare-Laval proposal to divide Ethiopia, giving part to Italy and allowing part to be a sovereign nation. This proposal was the joint work of British foreign secretary Sir Samuel John Gurney Hoare and French foreign secretary Pierre Laval.

During the nine months following the imposition of sanctions, member nations of the League looked on them with increasing disfavor. The Italian conquest was viewed favorably by American business interests, and the U.S. government approved of it in a formal statement on June 22, 1936. This worldwide trend of opinion led to the conclusion that sanctions were not relevant and were essentially inappropriate. The British formally denounced sanctions on June 18, 1936. France, Austria, Canada, Haiti, Honduras, Uruguay, and Belgium did so by June 22, and on June 25 the "neutral nations" of Sweden, Norway, Denmark, Holland, Finland, Switzerland, and Spain followed suit. A speech by Emperor Haile Selassie I of Ethiopia on June 30, 1936, caused a temporary reconsideration of the wisdom of lifting sanctions. Ethiopia submitted two resolutions regarding its plight. They were rejected on July 4, but on the same day the president of the League of Nations made a formal recommendation to lift sanctions against Italy. It was passed by a vote of 44 to 1, with 4 abstentions. On July 6, 1936, the coordinating committee decided to end sanctions. This action came into effect on July 15, 1936.

SIGNIFICANCE

Italy's attack on Ethiopia served to discredit the League of Nations and thus hastened the development of World War II. One crucial outcome was the general conclusion that the Western democracies, especially Great Britain and the United States, were weak and would not pose a threat to international aggression. This made an impression on Adolf Hitler, who in 1936 was still a student of Benito Mussolini. The Rome-Berlin Axis was a direct outcome of the invasion and League sanctions. Mussolini advised his nation to meet sanctions with quiet resolve to do more with less. The Italian population was thus conditioned to endure the hardships of the much longer war to come. A less obvious but far-reaching impact of the invasion and sanctions was that Africans became convinced that the traditional colonial system was of no use to them. Nationalist fervor developed, and the continent would not return to former ways. Self-governance and self-reliance became the only realistic options after the lack of trust that developed.

In economic terms, Ethiopia gained from Italian investments and development in infrastructure, but at a high price in terms of lives and freedom. The use of economic sanctions to achieve political ends, however, was firmly established in spite of failure in this first use. It has been refined and, in combination with other methods, has been used successfully in attempts by nations to limit the aggression of others. As a single solution, however, economic sanctions have never been successful, perhaps because of the failures of 1936. Economic sanctions have become more of an initial tactic rather than a complete strategy. When the income and employment opportunities of nations become restricted, popular sentiment for military adventurism declines quickly. As politicians have recognized for decades, immediate effects on personal and family incomes are of major consequence in determining popularity for various business and government proposals. Economic sanctions that can affect those incomes thus have an important strategic role.

—*Steven K. Paulson*

FURTHER READING

Asante, S. K. B. *Pan-African Protest: West Africa and the Italo-Ethiopian Crisis, 1934-1941.* London: Longman, 1977. The purpose of this book is to examine the effects on, and reactions of, black Africans to the Italian invasion of Ethiopia in 1935. Most analyses are from a European perspective. Extensive bibliography.

Baer, George W. *The Coming of the Italian-Ethiopian War.* Cambridge, Mass.: Harvard University Press, 1967. One of two important volumes on this subject by Baer, this 403-page book begins by describing events of the period 1889-1934 that led up to the Italian invasion of Ethiopia. The majority of the book discusses the nine months preceding the October, 1935, invasion.

_____. *Test Case: Italy, Ethiopia, and the League of Nations.* Stanford, Calif.: Hoover Institution Press, 1976. This 367-page book is an extraordinarily complete reference concerning the response of the League of Nations to the Italian invasion of Ethiopia. Chapter 12, "Ethiopia Is Italian," is a very readable, vivid description of the issuance, and then withdrawal, of sanctions against Italy by the League of Nations.

Barker, A. J. *The Civilizing Mission: A History of the Italo-Ethiopian War of 1935-1936.* New York: Dial Press, 1968. A thorough description of the invasion of Ethiopia by Italy. Takes the point of view that the originating motivation for the invasion was rooted in late nineteenth century attempts by Italy to establish colonies in East Africa and in unexpected defeats by the Africans. Thirty interesting photographs, convenient timetable outline, ten maps, and four helpful appendixes, including one with details concerning the composition of Italian invasion troops.

Clark, Martin. *Modern Italy: 1871-1982.* London: Longman, 1984. This 444-page volume provides a competent history of modern Italy. Of particular interest is chapter 14, which presents a concise discussion of the Ethiopian invasion of 1935 and repulsion in 1941. Insightful discussion of the relationship of the creation of the IRI (Istituto per la Ricostruzione Industriale) and the Ethiopian invasion.

Clough, Shepard B., and Salvatore Saladino. *A History of Modern Italy: Documents, Readings, and Commentary.* New York: Columbia University Press, 1968. This substantial book (657 pages) presents a helpful and concise review of the events of the Italian-Ethiopian war. Of special note are key documents that have been included verbatim (in translated form): "Mussolini's Speech to the Chamber of Deputies, May 25, 1935" and "Mussolini's Speech on the Eve of Hostilities Against Ethiopia, October 2, 1935."

Coffey, Thomas M. *Lion by the Tail: The Story of the Italian-Ethiopian War.* New York: Viking Press, 1974. Presents a thorough history of events leading to the withdrawal, by the League of Nations, of sanctions against Italy. The style of this book is particularly engaging. Eighteen carefully selected photographs.

Del Boca, Angelo. *The Ethiopian War, 1935-1941.* Chicago: University of Chicago Press, 1965. A straightforward account of the war and of the short-lived Italian rule in Ethiopia. Del Boca strongly supports Haile Selassie's efforts to maintain Ethiopian independence.

Dugan, James, and Laurence Lafore. *Days of Emperor and Clown: The Italo-Ethiopian War, 1935-1936.* New York: Doubleday, 1973. The premise of this book, begun by Dugan and completed by Lafore, is that the Italo-Ethiopian war of 1935-1936 was important not only in and of itself but also in giving impetus and direction to World War II. The "Note on Usages and Literature" is very helpful for American or European readers of the history of this event.

Hardie, Frank. *The Abyssinian Crisis.* Hamden, Conn.:

Archon Books, 1974. Presents a concise sequential history and assessment of the Italian invasion of Ethiopia using, lightly, a chess metaphor. Useful appendixes provide principal dates of the Ethiopian crisis and "Notes on Books" used in research for the book.

Macartney, M. H. H., and P. Cremona. *Italy's Foreign and Colonial Policy, 1914-1937*. London: Oxford University Press, 1938. The Ethiopian conquest allowed Italy to sever its traditional relationship with Great Britain and establish closer relations with Hitler's Germany. Even so, the authors argue that Mussolini's foreign policy was consistent with his predecessors.

Marcus, Harold G. *A History of Ethiopia*. Berkeley: University of California Press, 1994. A survey of Ethiopian history from prehistoric times to the present. Marcus's account is supportive of Haile Selassie and his efforts to modernize Ethiopia and to maintain its independence.

Mockler, Anthony. *Haile Selassie's War: The Italian-Ethiopian Campaign, 1935-1941*. Northampton, Mass.: Olive Branch Press, 2002. Includes detailed factual information about Ethiopia. A lengthy "tale of blood and war" which the author hopes is objective and accurate. Covers not only the Italian invasion but also the British invasion in 1941.

Sbacchi, Alberto. *Legacy of Bitterness: Ethiopia and Fascist Italy, 1935-1941*. Trenton, N.J.: Red Sea Press, 1997. Sbacchi places the struggle in a broader global context and pays particular attention to development of black nationalism and its reaction to the war.

Schaefer, Ludwig F., ed. *The Ethiopian Crisis: Touchstone of Appeasement?* Chicago: D. C. Heath, 1961. Collection of essays by well-known statesmen, general historians (including Winston Churchill and Arnold Toynbee), and specialists. Suitable for high school-level readers.

SEE ALSO: 1911-1912: Italy Annexes Libya; Apr. 28, 1919: League of Nations Is Established; 1925-1926: Mussolini Seizes Dictatorial Powers in Italy; June 17, 1925: Geneva Protocol Is Signed; Aug. 27, 1928: Kellogg-Briand Pact; Apr. 2, 1930: Haile Selassie Is Crowned Emperor of Ethiopia; Mar. 7, 1936: German Troops March into the Rhineland; Dec., 1936: Inter-American Conference for the Maintenance of Peace; Sept. 13, 1940: Italy Invades Egypt.

October 23, 1935-November 15, 1948
KING RETURNS TO POWER IN CANADA

William Lyon Mackenzie King returned to office as prime minister of Canada on October 23, 1935, after having served from 1921 to 1930. King enjoyed the lengthiest tenure of any Canadian prime minister and led the nation through the difficult years of World War II. Under his cautious leadership, Canada emerged from the war as a prosperous and confident nation.

LOCALE: Ottawa, Canada

CATEGORIES: Diplomacy and international relations; government and politics

KEY FIGURES

William Lyon Mackenzie King (1874-1950), prime minister of Canada, 1921-1926, 1926-1930, and 1935-1948

Franklin D. Roosevelt (1882-1945), president of the United States, 1933-1945

Winston Churchill (1874-1965), prime minister of Great Britain, 1940-1945

Louis St. Laurent (1882-1973), Liberal Canadian minister of justice, 1941-1946, secretary of state for external affairs, 1946-1948, and prime minister, 1948-1957

SUMMARY OF EVENT

William Lyon Mackenzie King was born in Berlin (later Kitchener), Ontario, on December 17, 1874, and died at Kingsmere, Quebec, on July 22, 1950. King's political career began in 1909, when he became labor minister in Prime Minister Wilfrid Laurier's Liberal government. In 1911, the Liberals were defeated by the Conservatives, and King lost his parliamentary seat. In 1919, King was reelected to Parliament and chosen as leader of the Liberal Party. He led the Liberals to a majority in the 1921 federal election but could muster only a minority government in the 1925 election, and this government soon lost a confidence vote. The Conservatives formed a government that quickly collapsed, forcing another election. King again won a majority, and he governed until 1930,

1935

when the Liberals again lost to the Conservatives. The defeat was a political blessing, as the Conservatives were forced to govern during the worst years of the Great Depression. In the 1935 election, the Liberals, led by King, were reelected and he returned as prime minister, winning three straight federal elections before his retirement in 1948.

The first years of King's third administration (1935-1940) were largely focused on domestic issues created by the Depression's devastating economic impact. His government transformed the Bank of Canada from a private corporation into the nation's central bank and made it responsible for Canada's monetary policy. Under King, the Royal Commission on Dominion-Provincial Relations was created to investigate both the fiscal plight of the provinces and the relations between provinces and the federal government, and King also began to consider the possibility of creating a national insurance plan for the unemployed. In 1939, the Liberals deliberately ran a budget deficit in an attempt to stimulate the economy, but the effects of the Depression lingered. As World War II approached, nearly half a million Canadians remained unemployed.

King maintained a policy of cautious autonomy from Britain, ensuring that Canada's foreign policy interests were determined by Ottawa, not by London. Outside the Commonwealth, King also developed a close relationship with Franklin D. Roosevelt, and the two worked together to expand trade relations and to cooperate on defense issues. King was particularly successful in his negotiations on defense, and when Canada entered World War II in September, 1939, Roosevelt's administration made it clear that it was prepared to defend the continent from any external threat.

King hoped to avoid entering the war, and he skillfully led the nation from 1939 to 1945, although this was arguably the most tumultuous period of his political career. National unity was King's most important goal, and he wished to avoid the profound discord that occurred between English and French Canadians during World War I. In particular, King wanted to avoid conscription, and initially he sought a limited role for the military, one that focused on schemes such as the British Commonwealth Air Training Plan (BCATP), which developed and trained pilots from around the world. Opposition from the provinces led King to call an election in early 1940, and he again asserted his opposition to conscription. His consistency assuaged the French Canadians' concerns, and the Liberals were awarded another majority victory.

Following the rapid German victories in Western Europe and Scandinavia in May and June of 1940, the King government vastly expanded its war effort. The BCATP grew (eventually producing 131,000 crew members), a large navy was raised and played a vital role in protecting the North Atlantic convoys sailing to Britain, and an overseas land army of five divisions was eventually mobilized for service in several of the war's theaters. By 1945, 1.1 million Canadians were serving in the Canadian armed forces, a significant number given that Canada's total population numbered only 11.5 million.

Canada's increased involvement in the war put King's nonconscription promise in jeopardy, and the issue began to threaten party unity. King was able to compromise by amending the National Resources Mobilization Act of June, 1940, which had authorized home-defense conscription for thirty days. This did not, he stressed to Canadians, necessarily entail conscription. Despite Conservative protests, King called for a 1942 plebiscite to release his government from his earlier promise. The government won, although the vast majority of French Canadians voted against it. However, as Canadian casualties mounted in Europe during 1944, a reinforcement crisis developed. King had delayed imposing conscription, using all of his political skills to avoid splitting the country along regional and linguistic lines, but the issue could be avoided no longer. Finally, King opted to send conscripts to Europe. Quebecers were overwhelmingly opposed to conscription, but it was apparent that King had tried to accommodate conflicting national viewpoints. Although King appeared indecisive to many English Canadians, his search for compromise had allowed him to succeed in negotiating the political tempest of conscription and to avoid tearing the country apart.

The close working relationship established among King, British prime minister Winston Churchill, and Roosevelt was one of the cornerstones of the Allied effort. This relationship became especially vital for Canada as the war progressed. Roosevelt had pressed for a defense alliance and King acquiesced, which freed Canadian men and resources for the overseas war effort. King was also able to persuade Roosevelt to solve a deeply worrisome wartime trade deficit that threatened to undermine the Canadian economy.

Before the Hyde Park Declaration of April, 1941, Canada had accumulated huge trade deficits with the United States as a result of wartime purchases. The American lend-lease plan with Britain threatened to exacerbate this problem, particularly if it meant that Canada could lose British business. Under the agreement, the Americans promised to buy as much in Canada, if not more, as Canada was buying in the United States, thereby wiping out the trade deficit.

Fearing social unrest and another economic downturn after the war, King carefully laid the planks of the Canadian welfare state. The Liberals introduced unemployment insurance in 1940 and family allowances in 1944. Large sums were given for new housing, the Department of Health and the Department of Welfare were created, and returning veterans could choose from several programs designed to help them reintegrate into postwar society. Public works projects increased as the war ended, and this decreased postwar unemployment levels.

The government's wartime record was impressive: The new social programs were popular, and the economic transition from wartime to peacetime appeared seamless. Still, Canadians never really warmed to King, and the seventy-one-year-old won a hard-fought victory in 1945. His final years in office were dominated by Cold War strains and pronounced political wariness, and King announced his retirement in January of 1948. He had a remarkable ability to recruit talent, and the Liberal Party made a smooth transition into the government of Louis St. Laurent in 1948. The cautious craft of politics had been King's life, but it had taken a toll, and he died in 1950.

SIGNIFICANCE

King was not an inspiring politician, but he led Canada for twenty-two years (the record among Commonwealth leaders) and successfully navigated his way through half of the Great Depression and World War II. Arguably, it was during the years after 1935 that King made his mark as prime minister. He kept Canada relatively unified during this period with strong, if cautious, leadership, a considerable feat given the fissures that occurred during World War I. Under strict government control, Canada's wartime economy—which had been ravaged by the Depression—was rapidly transformed and tightly controlled.

From 1945 through 1948, Canada continued its robust growth and ushered in an era of prosperity. King borrowed heavily from the left-wing Cooperative Commonwealth Federation Party's platform to create social welfare programs, a move that disarmed his opponents.

These programs were popular, and future governments expanded on them. Globally, King oversaw Canada's emergence as a "middle power" that played an increasingly important international role, and the country maintained active memberships in the United Nations, the North Atlantic Treaty Organization (NATO), and the Commonwealth. King's record of consistently successful political strategies led many historians to suggest that he was Canada's greatest prime minister.

—*Ryan M. Touhey*

FURTHER READING

Bliss, Michael. *Right Honourable Men: The Descent of Canadian Politics from MacDonald to Mulroney*. Toronto: HarperCollins, 1994. Biographical study of Canada's prime ministers presents a highly favorable assessment of King in two well-researched chapters.

Granatstein, J. L. *Canada's War: The Politics of the Mackenzie King Government, 1939-1945*. Toronto: University of Toronto Press, 1974. One of the most thorough studies of King's wartime governments available, although somewhat dated.

Granatstein, J. L., and Norman Hillmer. *Empire to Umpire: Canada and the World to the 1990's*. Toronto: Irwin, 2000. An excellent survey of Canadian foreign relations during the King years.

_____. *Prime Ministers: Ranking Canada's Leaders*. Toronto: HarperCollins, 1999. A thoughtful and balanced general summary of King's political career by two of Canada's leading political historians.

Stacey, C. P. *A Very Double Life: The Private World of Mackenzie King*. Toronto: Macmillan of Canada, 1976. Based on text from King's private diaries, much of which was previously unavailable to the public. Provides an unflattering but fascinating view of King's character.

SEE ALSO: 1911-1920: Borden Leads Canada Through World War I; May 15-June 26, 1919: Winnipeg General Strike; July 10, 1920-Sept., 1926: Meighen Era in Canada; 1921-1948: King Era in Canada; Aug., 1930-1935: Bennett Era in Canada; Sept. 8, 1930: Canada Enacts Depression-Era Relief Legislation; Aug. 1, 1932: Canada's First Major Socialist Movement; Sept. 10, 1939: Canada Enters World War II.

1935

November-December, 1935
EGAS MONIZ DEVELOPS THE PREFRONTAL LOBOTOMY

António Egas Moniz pioneered the surgical treatment of psychiatric disorders, giving impetus to the widespread practice of lobotomy.

LOCALE: Lisbon, Portugal
CATEGORIES: Health and medicine; psychology and psychiatry

KEY FIGURES
António Egas Moniz (1874-1955), Portuguese neurologist
Pedro Almeida Lima (b. 1903), neurosurgeon who performed the first prefrontal lobotomy under Moniz's direction
Walter Jackson Freeman (1895-1972), American neuropathologist and neuropsychiatrist

SUMMARY OF EVENT

In the early twentieth century, no consensus existed in the medical community concerning the treatment of mental illness. In part, this lack of consensus reflected opposition between two broad approaches to human development. One stressed the biological determinants of behavior, whereas the other stressed the role of environment and experience in shaping the psyche. (This division was mimed by the professional rivalry between neurologists and psychiatrists.) More fundamentally, however, this lack of consensus simply reflected a lack of knowledge.

As the number of patients admitted to hospitals for psychiatric treatment steadily increased (by 1938, according to an article in the *New England Journal of Medicine*, there was "one bed for mental disease for each bed for all other diseases in America"), the demand for effective treatment increased proportionately. The issues at stake were not only humanitarian—many psychiatric patients, especially those in state institutions, were condemned to live in utter misery with no hope of relief—but also financial, for the costs of maintaining such patients for years and even decades were enormous. This was the climate that encouraged the development and acceptance, in the 1930's, of such radical therapies as shock treatment (using drugs or electric shock to induce coma or convulsions) and lobotomy.

António Egas Moniz, the pioneer of lobotomy, was an extremely ambitious and multitalented man, with many interests outside his career in neurology. Prior to the development of lobotomy, he was best known for his work in cerebral angiography, which permits the visualization of the blood vessels in the brain after the injection of a radiopaque substance. He had hoped to receive a Nobel Prize for this work, which was done in the late 1920's, and he was very disappointed when it became apparent that such recognition was not forthcoming.

In August, 1935, Egas Moniz traveled to London for the Second International Congress of Neurology. There, he attended a symposium on the frontal lobes of the brain, including a presentation by Yale University researchers John Fulton and Carlyle Jacobsen on the effects of removing much of the frontal lobes of two chimpanzees. Egas Moniz himself later asserted that this presentation was not decisive in the development of lobotomy, which, he said, he had been considering for some time. Contemporary observers, however, noted that Egas Moniz seemed to be deeply impressed by the fact that the surgery had a calming effect on one of the chimpanzees, which had previously been subject to fits of temper and other disturbances.

As Elliot S. Valenstein has shown, Egas Moniz's interpretation of the Fulton-Jacobsen study was selective and deeply flawed, yet this misreading entered medical folklore and was even perpetuated by the Nobel Prize Committee in its citation of Egas Moniz in 1949. Egas Moniz ignored the fact that, although one of the subjects was indeed less agitated after the surgery, the other chimpanzee was affected in the opposite way, becoming much more temperamental and uncooperative postsurgery. This latter result did not accord with the presuppositions that Egas Moniz brought to the London congress. He believed that many psychiatric disorders were caused by "abnormal adhesion" between nerve cells, as a result of which neural impulses "keep following the same path . . . constantly giving rise to the same morbid ideas, which are reproduced over and over again." This hypothesis of "fixed ideas" was sheer speculation, but the lack of evidence did not deter Egas Moniz. He interpreted the Fulton-Jacobsen study as a confirmation of his belief that if the nerve fibers in which the pernicious "fixed ideas" were conducted could be destroyed, the patient might experience significant improvement. Thus, in November, 1935, only three months after the London congress, Egas Moniz made his first attempts at psychosurgery.

Long crippled by gout, Egas Moniz himself did not perform the operations; rather, he directed his younger colleague, the neurosurgeon Pedro Almeida Lima. Initially, Egas Moniz used injections of alcohol to destroy nerve fibers in the frontal lobes. The first operation took place on November 12, 1935. The patient was a sixty-three-year-old woman with a long history of mental illness. Two holes were drilled in the top of her skull and injections were made on both sides of the brain in the prefrontal area. In the following weeks, Egas Moniz and Almeida Lima repeated this procedure with six more patients, steadily increasing the amount of alcohol injected. With his eighth psychosurgical patient, however, Egas Moniz adopted a new method, cutting (or, at first, crushing) the nerve fibers. This surgery, performed on December 27, 1935, may be called the first lobotomy.

Egas Moniz himself did not employ the term "lobotomy," which was first used in 1936 by his American disciple Walter Jackson Freeman and became the standard designation for the operation in the United States. The term that Egas Moniz coined for the operation was "leucotomy," from the Greek word for white (because the nerve fibers are white matter, as opposed to gray

matter, which contains nerve cell bodies); accordingly, the surgical instrument he employed was called the "leucotome." This instrument, the design of which was refined and modified by Egas Moniz and others, contained a retractable wire loop. After the leucotome had been inserted into the brain, this wire loop was extended and the instrument was rotated. In the first leucotomy, one such rotation (or "core," as Egas Moniz termed it) was made on each side of the brain; in subsequent operations, as many as six cores were made on each side of the brain.

In 1936, Egas Moniz published a monograph in which he reported on the outcome of psychosurgery for the first twenty patients he treated (including those treated with the alcohol-injection method). These patients suffered from a variety of disorders, ranging from disabling anxiety and depression to chronic schizophrenia. Egas Moniz reported that of the twenty patients, seven had been cured as a result of the surgery and seven had improved; six were said to be unchanged. Despite the fact that Egas Moniz's claims could not bear scrutiny (he overestimated improvement, underestimated postoperative difficulties, and failed to conduct adequate follow-up, basing most of his analyses on observations made within days of the operation), his monograph was widely hailed as persuasive evidence for the potential benefits of psychosurgery.

SIGNIFICANCE

The impacts of Egas Moniz's radical and well-publicized use of brain surgery to treat psychiatric disorders were both immediate and lasting. Within three months of the publication of Egas Moniz's 1936 monograph, prefrontal lobotomies had been performed as far afield as Italy, Romania, Cuba, and Brazil, as well as in the United States, where the acceptance of lobotomy owed much to Freeman's advocacy.

Freeman, a superb lecturer and a man of seemingly inexhaustible energy, was head of the neurology department at George Washington University when, in 1936, he read Egas Moniz's monograph. Soon thereafter, assisted by a colleague, James Winston Watts, Freeman performed his first lobotomy; by the end of the year, he and Watts had performed twenty lobotomies. In 1942, Freeman and Watts published *Psychosurgery: Intelligence, Emotion, and Social Behavior Following Prefrontal Lobotomy for Mental Disorders*. The book was extremely influential, not only in the United States but also abroad. In the immediate postwar years, there was a dramatic increase in the number of lobotomies per-

António Egas Moniz. (New York Academy of Medicine)

formed worldwide; in the United States, lobotomies increased from approximately five hundred per year in 1946 to five thousand in 1949. When Egas Moniz received the Nobel Prize in Physiology or Medicine in 1949 for the development of the prefrontal lobotomy (he shared the award with Walter Rudolf Hess, a Swiss researcher recognized for his discovery of the function of the middle brain), the credibility of psychosurgery was further enhanced.

Within only a few years, however, by the mid-1950's, the number of lobotomies performed annually began to decline steeply. There were two reasons for this sudden turnabout: First, tranquilizing drugs such as Thorazine had been developed, and their widespread use was sufficient by itself to restrict lobotomy to exceptional cases; second, serious concerns about the validity of lobotomy were being expressed in the medical community. Some physicians had been opposed to lobotomy from the beginning, but as more long-term studies of lobotomized patients became available, it became evident that proponents of lobotomy, like Egas Moniz before them, had not been objective in assessing the consequences of such surgery. Although the operation as performed by Freeman and his colleagues became something quite different from Egas Moniz's early attempts, lobotomy always involved radical injury to the frontal lobes. Lobotomized patients frequently lost their abilities to plan ahead, to think abstractly, and to perform other vital functions. In many cases, particularly in the treatment of patients suffering from schizophrenia, lobotomy was not only excessively costly in psychic terms but also generally ineffective.

In the 1960's and 1970's, growing public awareness of ties between the government and science and a new appreciation of the threat of various kinds of mind control led to the placement of further limitations on the use of psychosurgery, including some legislative restrictions. Psychosurgery is still practiced in the United States on a small scale, with greater precision than ever before, thanks to technological advances and significant improvements in knowledge concerning the brain's circuitry. Despite such advances, resistance to psychosurgery remains high, both within the medical profession and among the general public.

—*John Wilson*

FURTHER READING

El-Hai, Jack. *The Lobotomist: A Maverick Medical Genius and His Tragic Quest to Rid the World of Mental Illness.* New York: John Wiley & Sons, 2005. Biography of Walter Jackson Freeman draws on his writings, including journals and personal correspondence, to place his work in the context of his life and times. Discusses Egas Moniz's development of the lobotomy. Includes bibliography and index.

Freeman, Walter, and James W. Watts. *Psychosurgery: Intelligence, Emotion, and Social Behavior Following Prefrontal Lobotomy for Mental Disorders.* 2d ed. Springfield, Ill.: Charles C Thomas, 1950. Second edition of the 1942 landmark volume—part textbook, part popularizing manifesto, part how-to manual—that had a worldwide influence in promoting lobotomy. Although the book is dedicated to Egas Moniz, Freeman and Watts eschew his flights of speculation and seek to provide a solid rationale for psychosurgery. Heavily illustrated, with copious references; reports the results of 619 lobotomies, compared with 80 reported in the first edition.

Fulton, John F. *Frontal Lobotomy and Affective Behavior: A Neuropsychological Analysis.* New York: W. W. Norton, 1951. Fulton (1899-1960), a leading figure in the American medical establishment of his time, received grants for several major studies of lobotomy. This short book, dedicated to Egas Moniz and Almeida Lima, discusses lobotomies of animals as well as of human subjects and presents a very positive overall assessment of the achievements of and prospects for lobotomy. Includes illustrations and bibliography.

Lippman, Helen. "Lobotomy Enters the Twenty-First Century." *Clinical Psychiatry News* 30 (January 1, 2002). Brief discussion of limbic surgery, which is now the name attached to improved versions of the lobotomy procedure. Notes the arguments for using such surgery in intractable cases of obsessive-compulsive disorder and major depressive disorder.

Sackler, Arthur M., et al., eds. *The Great Physiodynamic Therapies in Psychiatry: An Historical Reappraisal.* New York: Hoeber-Harper Books, 1956. Compilation of articles selected from the *Journal of Clinical and Experimental Psychopathology* and the *Quarterly Review of Psychiatry and Neurology* includes Egas Moniz's article "How I Succeeded in Performing Prefrontal Leukotomy" and a brief biographical sketch of Egas Moniz.

Shutts, David. *Lobotomy: Resort to the Knife.* New York: Van Nostrand Reinhold, 1982. Highly readable popularized survey of the history of lobotomy. Recounts Egas Moniz's development of the lobotomy, but focuses primarily on the life and work of Freeman. Unreliable in detail; should be used only in conjunction with the Valenstein book cited below. Includes illustrations and bibliography.

Valenstein, Elliot S. *Great and Desperate Cures: The Rise and Decline of Psychosurgery and Other Radical Treatments for Mental Illness.* New York: Basic Books, 1986. Excellent treatment of psychosurgery presents lobotomy in its historical context, not as a bizarre aberration but rather as a representative if unusually dramatic case of "uncritical enthusiasm running rampant and causing great harm to desperate patients." Includes illustrations and extensive notes.

See also: Apr., 1938: Cerletti and Bini Use Electroshock to Treat Schizophrenia.

November 5, 1935
Armstrong Demonstrates FM Radio Broadcasting

During the early 1930's, Edwin H. Armstrong invented frequency-modulated radio broadcasting, although he would neither receive credit for it nor see its widespread use in his lifetime.

Locale: New York, New York

Categories: Science and technology; inventions; radio and television; communications and media

Key Figures

Edwin H. Armstrong (1890-1954), American inventor
David Sarnoff (1891-1971), founder of the Radio Corporation of America

Summary of Event

Because the original radio broadcasts used amplitude modulation (AM) to transmit their sounds, they were subject to a sizable amount of interference and static. As amplitude modulation relies on the amount of energy transmitted, energy sources in the atmosphere between the station and the receiver can distort or weaken the original signal. This is particularly irritating when the sound being transmitted is music. Edwin H. Armstrong provided a solution to this technological constraint. A graduate of Columbia University, Armstrong made a significant contribution to the development of radio with his basic inventions for circuits for amplitude-modulated receivers. (Indeed, the money Armstrong made from his earlier inventions financed the development of the frequency modulation, or FM, system.) Armstrong was one among many contributors to AM radio. For FM broadcasting, however, Armstrong must be ranked as the most important inventor.

During the 1920's, Armstrong established his own research laboratory in Alpine, New Jersey, across the Hudson River from New York City. With a small staff of dedicated assistants, he carried out research on radio circuitry and systems for nearly three decades. At that time, Armstrong also began to teach electrical engineering at Columbia University.

From 1928 to 1933, Armstrong worked diligently at his private laboratory at Columbia University to construct a working model of a frequency-modulated radio broadcasting system. With the primitive limitations then imposed by the state of vacuum tube technology, a number of Armstrong's experimental circuits required as many as one hundred tubes. Between July, 1930, and January, 1933, Armstrong filed four basic FM patent applications; all were granted simultaneously on December 26, 1933.

Armstrong sought to perfect FM radio broadcasting, not to offer radio listeners better musical reception but to create an entirely new radio broadcasting system. On November 5, 1935, Armstrong made his first public demonstration of FM radio broadcasting in New York City to an audience of radio engineers. An amateur station owned by Armstrong's friend, Randolph Runyon, based in suburban Yonkers, New York, transmitted these first signals. The scientific world began to consider the advantages and disadvantages of frequency-modulated radio broadcasting. Other laboratories began to craft their own versions of FM radio broadcasting. At the then-dominant Radio Corporation of America (RCA), scientists began to experiment with FM radio broadcasting.

Because Armstrong had no desire to become a manufacturer or broadcaster, he approached David Sarnoff, head of RCA. As owner of the top manufacturer of radio sets and the top radio broadcasting network, Sarnoff was interested in all advances of radio technology. Armstrong first demonstrated FM radio broadcasting for Sarnoff in December, 1933. This was followed by visits from RCA engineers, who were sufficiently impressed to recommend to Sarnoff that the company conduct field tests of the Armstrong system.

1935

Edwin H. Armstrong. (Smithsonian Institution)

In 1934, Armstrong, with the cooperation of RCA, set up a test transmitter at the top of the Empire State Building, sharing facilities with the then experimental RCA television transmitter. From 1934 through 1935, tests were conducted using the Empire State Building facility, to mixed reactions of RCA's best engineers. AM radio broadcasting already had a performance record of nearly two decades. The engineers wondered if this new technology could replace something that had worked so well. This less than enthusiastic evaluation fueled the skepticism of RCA lawyers and salespeople. RCA had too much invested in the AM system, both as the leading manufacturer and as the dominant owner of the major radio network of the time, the National Broadcasting Company (NBC). Sarnoff was in no rush to adopt frequency modulation. Changing systems would endanger the millions of dollars RCA was making as the United States emerged from the Great Depression, and Sarnoff believed the risk was too great.

In 1935, Sarnoff advised Armstrong that RCA would cease any further research and development activity in FM radio broadcasting. (Still, engineers at RCA laboratories continued to work on frequency modulation to protect the corporate patent position.) Sarnoff declared to the press that his company would push the frontiers of broadcasting by concentrating on research and development of radio with pictures—that is, television. As a tangible sign, Sarnoff ordered that Armstrong's FM radio broadcasting tower be removed from the top of the Empire State Building. Armstrong was outraged. By the mid-1930's, the development of FM radio broadcasting had grown into a mission for Armstrong. For the remainder of his life, Armstrong devoted his considerable talents to the promotion of FM radio broadcasting. Armstrong was certain that Sarnoff was simply trying to suppress FM radio broadcasting to preserve RCA's profits.

After the break with Sarnoff, Armstrong proceeded with plans to develop his own FM operation. Allied with two of RCA's biggest manufacturing competitors—Zenith and General Electric—Armstrong pressed ahead. In June of 1936, at a Federal Communications Commission (FCC) hearing, Armstrong proclaimed that FM broadcasting was the only static-free, noise-free, and uniform system—both day and night—available. He argued, correctly, that AM radio broadcasting had none of these qualities.

An FM radio broadcasting transmission tower was built in Alpine, New Jersey, and in 1938, station W2XMN became the first FM station. Armstrong gained backing from the regional radio network and, in cooperation, a transmitter tower was built atop Mount Asnebumskit in Massachusetts. The radio network would invest a quarter of a million dollars in FM radio stations. The central question turned from the technological to the legal: What part of the spectrum should be allocated for frequency modulation? Space on the very high frequency band was set aside, and, in the days before World War II, preliminary licenses were granted for more than fifty stations. In 1941, the FCC decreed that sound for the new television system it had approved should be telecast by FM principles. (It remains so to the present.)

In December, 1941, the United States became involved in World War II. Innovation of frequency modulation was halted, and the infant industry was maintained at an arrested stage of development. Armstrong gave the military permission to use frequency modulation with no compensation, and his patriotic gesture cost him millions when the military soon became all FM. This did, however, expand interest in FM radio broadcasting. World War II had provided a field test of equipment and use.

Armstrong's final battle to institute FM radio broadcasting began in 1948 when he filed a lawsuit charging infringement of patents by RCA. This was a struggle for the claim of invention rather than the possible development of an industry. Armstrong would not live to see his invention of FM radio broadcasting come to mainstream use; on January 31, 1954, he committed suicide. The case was settled shortly thereafter. The court sidestepped the basic question of who had invented FM radio broadcasting but ordered RCA to pay the Armstrong estate $1 million for infringement of patents.

SIGNIFICANCE

It would be three decades before Armstrong's legacy of FM broadcasting had its full impact. When the FCC granted FM radio broadcasting licenses after World War II, most went to successful AM stations. The AM radio stations acquired the FM licenses to ensure that no serious competitors would threaten their market shares.

During the 1950's, a handful of independent FM stations labored at the margins of the radio industry, playing ethnic, classical, jazz, and folk musical programming to small audiences. At that time, a radio receiver that could pick up FM radio broadcasts cost much more than a radio that could pick up the far more popular AM radio broadcasting signals. A particular impediment came with the lack of radios in automobiles that could pick up FM signals. As late as 1966, only one car radio in twenty-five was equipped to receive FM radio broadcasting.

The FCC initiated a change in 1966. To encourage greater diversity in programming, the FCC dictated that FM broadcasting licensees needed to provide at least 50 percent original programming on FM stations. That meant that those who owned an AM and FM station in the same market could no longer simulcast their signals. That is, they could no longer transmit the same signal on both outlets simultaneously. Although this meant hiring more staff and thus less profits in the short run, the disgruntled owners complied rather than lose their FM licenses. At first, there was abuse of the regulation. For example, a number of station owners simply ordered that staff members replay earlier tapes of the AM programming on the FM station. The signals were the same, but not simultaneous. Gradually, risk-taking station owners sought to differentiate their products to see if they could see greater profits in the long run. The first change came with alternative rock; then came all-jazz, all-talk, and all-sports FM stations. Listeners loved the fact that radio sounded as good as their stereo record players.

The result in the 1970's was tremendous growth in FM radio broadcasting. By 1972, one in three radio listeners tuned in an FM station at some time during the day. Advertisers began to use FM radio stations to reach the young and affluent audiences that were turning to FM stations in greater numbers. The advertisers were attracted also by the low rates. Gross revenues soared from about $10 million for 1962 to nearly $85 million a decade later.

By the late 1970's, FM stations were surging past AM radio broadcasts. In 1976, the average FM station began to show a profit. By 1980, nearly half of radio listeners tuned in to FM stations on a regular basis. A decade later, FM radio listening accounted for more than two-thirds of audience time, and regulators and station owners were seeking ways to boost the fortunes of AM radio broadcasting, but FM radio listening dominance persisted into the twenty-first century. Armstrong's predictions that listeners would prefer the clear, static-free sounds offered by FM radio broadcasting had been proven correct by the mid-1980's, nearly fifty years after Armstrong commenced his struggle to make FM broadcasting a part of commercial radio.

—Douglas Gomery

FURTHER READING

Barnouw, Erik. *A History of Broadcasting in the United States.* 3 vols. New York: Oxford University Press, 1966-1970. The standard history of broadcasting in the United States. The development of FM radio broadcasting is covered in the first two of the three volumes.

Bilby, Kenneth. *The General: David Sarnoff and the Rise of the Communications Industry.* New York: Harper & Row, 1986. Presents a detailed history of the activities of RCA and its founder, Sarnoff, in the invention and innovation of FM radio.

Erickson, Don V. *Armstrong's Fight for FM Broadcasting: One Man Versus Big Business and Bureaucracy.* Tuscaloosa: University of Alabama Press, 1973. Attempts to reclaim Armstrong's role in the history of broadcasting by exposing the collaboration between the FCC and the entrenched broadcasting lobby to protect then-dominant AM radio.

Head, Sydney W., Thomas Spann, and Michael A. McGregor. *Broadcasting in America: A Survey of Electronic Media.* 9th ed. Boston: Houghton Mifflin, 2000. The standard introduction to radio and television in the United States. Includes an analysis of the invention of FM radio broadcasting and Armstrong's role.

1935

Inglis, Andrew F. *Behind the Tube: A History of Broadcasting Technology and Business*. Boston: Focal Press, 1990. Offers a contemporary examination of the technological history of the mass media. Chapter 3 provides a fine overview of the history of FM radio, including Armstrong's contributions.

Lessing, Lawrence. *Man of High Fidelity: Edwin Howard Armstrong*. New York: J. B. Lippincott, 1956. Paints a portrait of Armstrong as a great man who, against the odds, was able to convince a nation to adopt FM radio broadcasting.

Lichty, Lawrence W., and Malachi C. Topping, comps. *American Broadcasting: A Source Book on the History of Radio and Television*. New York: Hastings House, 1975. Collection of articles and documents concerning the history of radio and television. Treats the invention and innovation of FM radio transmission in some detail.

Sterling, Christopher H., and John Michael Kittross. *Stay Tuned: A History of American Broadcasting*. 3d ed. Mahwah, N.J.: Lawrence Erlbaum, 2001. The standard one-volume history of radio and television in the United States. Provides particularly strong coverage of the history of FM radio broadcasting.

Whetmore, Edward Jay. *The Magic Medium: An Introduction to Radio in America*. Belmont, Calif.: Wadsworth, 1981. Fine textbook covers all phases of radio, including Armstrong's invention and attempted innovation of FM radio. Places Armstrong's role in the history without the "wronged man" rhetoric found in other accounts.

SEE ALSO: 1920's: Radio Develops as a Mass Broadcast Medium; Aug. 20-Nov. 2, 1920: Radio Broadcasting Begins; Sept. 9, 1926: National Broadcasting Company Is Founded.

November 10, 1935
CONGRESS OF INDUSTRIAL ORGANIZATIONS IS FOUNDED

The Congress of Industrial Organizations, a militant congress of trade unions, organized both skilled and unskilled workers regardless of race or gender.

LOCALE: United States
CATEGORIES: Business and labor; organizations and institutions

KEY FIGURES
John L. Lewis (1880-1969), president of the United Mine Workers
Philip Murray (1886-1952), head of the Steel Workers' Organizing Committee
William Green (1873-1952), president of the American Federation of Labor
David Dubinsky (1892-1982), head of the International Ladies' Garment Workers' Union
William L. Hutcheson (fl. mid-twentieth century), head of the Carpenters' Union
Homer Martin (1901-1968), president of the United Auto Workers
Sidney Hillman (1887-1946), president of the Amalgamated Clothing Workers
Frank Murphy (1890-1949), governor of Michigan, 1936-1938
Myron C. Taylor (1874-1959), chairman of the board of the United States Steel Corporation

Franklin D. Roosevelt (1882-1945), president of the United States, 1933-1945

SUMMARY OF EVENT
The struggle that produced the Congress of Industrial Organizations (CIO) revolved around a disagreement over labor tactics and philosophy. The American Federation of Labor (AFL), founded in 1886, was organized on a craft basis and did not include the skilled and unskilled workers in mass-production industries. By 1934, however, some members of the AFL wanted to form one union for an entire industry to include these mass-production workers. William Green, president of the AFL, and the generally conservative members of that organization's executive council associated industrial unionism with violence and radicalism. Leadership in the move for more militant unionism came primarily from John L. Lewis, president of the United Mine Workers and vice president of the AFL. Lewis criticized the voluntarism preached by Green and argued that it was imperative that the AFL become active in politics and in industrial unionism. Sidney Hillman, president of the Amalgamated Clothing Workers, and David Dubinsky of the International Ladies' Garment Workers' Union were the other leading figures in this insurgency.

At the 1934 convention of the AFL, Lewis and other

industrial union supporters succeeded in receiving an endorsement for the chartering of unions in a number of industries, including auto and rubber. In addition, there had been a promise made to organize the steel industry. However, little was done in the following months to implement the resolution. The next year, the AFL leadership rejected appeals for help in instituting a more active movement among the industrial workers. Lewis addressed the convention, pleading to "organize the unorganized" and thereby make the AFL the "greatest instrumentality . . . to befriend the cause of humanity." His resolution failed by a substantial majority. The frustrated Lewis confronted the head of the Carpenters' Union, William L. Hutcheson, who was quelling dissent among some of the workers, and started a fistfight. Lewis knocked Hutcheson to the floor, disrupting the convention; afterward, a new image became popularized of a "battling Lewis" who fought for industrial organizing.

Rebuffed by the convention, Lewis, Hillman, and others proceeded to meet separately, and on November 10, 1935, they formed what was originally called the Committee for Industrial Organization. Ostensibly this group was working within the AFL to promote organization of the mass-production industries. Green and his executive council, however, quickly concluded that such activity was in disregard of majority AFL sentiment as expressed at the convention and that it could easily lead to dual unionism. The council called on the Committee for Industrial Organization to disband. The unions now involved in this revolt included the United Mine Workers, the United Auto Workers, the Amalgamated Clothing Workers, the United Textile Workers, the International Ladies' Garment Workers' Union, and a number of smaller organizations. They ignored the AFL request, and, in August, 1936, the entire group was suspended. A peace conference between Green and Lewis was arranged, but it collapsed—a result primarily of the latter's uncompromising attitude. In March, 1937, the insurgent group was formally expelled from the AFL. Green also announced that the AFL itself would begin an immediate campaign to organize the mass-production industries. In 1938, Lewis's group changed its name to the Congress of Industrial Organizations (CIO).

SIGNIFICANCE

The decision of the AFL to move into mass-production industry unionism was probably prompted by the remarkable success of the CIO. Initially, the insurgent unions had approximately 1.8 million members, but in seven months the CIO claimed to represent more than 3.7

million workers. This growth resulted from organizational victories in the steel and automobile industries. In 1935, Lewis appointed Philip Murray, vice president of the United Mine Workers, to head the Steel Workers' Organizing Committee. Before Murray could start activities, however, a crisis arose in the automobile industry that demanded attention from the CIO leadership. Under the AFL, the United Auto Workers (UAW) had been losing members, and local leadership was completely intimidated by management. In 1936, Homer Martin, a former minister, took over the union and began to work closely with the CIO. Although Lewis would have preferred to attack steel first, he rushed to the support of the now-militant UAW when on December 28, 1936, the union began a dramatic sit-down strike in the Flint, Michigan, plant of General Motors.

Although the sit-down tactic had been utilized on a limited scale before, the dramatic effect of thousands of men refusing to work but remaining in their plant took the public by surprise. Following normal procedure, General Motors immediately requested government assistance. An injunction was issued by a local judge, but the sheriff refused to serve it and was backed up by Michigan governor Frank Murphy, a Democrat who supported the rights of the workers and strove for a compromise settlement. Management, realizing that little support could be expected from Washington, constantly prodded by Murphy to go to the bargaining table, and faced with a considerable loss of profits, decided to meet with the UAW. On February 11, 1937, a contract was signed providing for the dismissal of the injunction, recognition of the UAW as the sole bargaining unit, and procedures for collective bargaining on wages and hours. The other automaking companies, with the exception of Ford, which held out until 1941, quickly fell into line.

In the meantime, Murray was conducting his campaign to organize the steel industry, although in the end steel was broken from the top down. Myron C. Taylor, chairman of the board of the United States Steel Corporation, desiring to avoid a work stoppage that would jeopardize a lucrative foreign contract and anticipating inevitable union recognition, invited Lewis to private talks that lasted for three months. The result was the signing of a contract on March 2, 1937, that granted union recognition and provided for a 10 percent wage increase, a forty-hour week, and overtime pay. Many other companies followed Taylor's lead, but three of the "Little Steel" companies, under the moral leadership of Tom M. Girdler of Republic Steel, fought unionization successfully, culminating in the so-called Memorial Day

1935

Massacre on May 30, 1937, when police fired on union demonstrators in front of the South Chicago plant of Republic Steel. It was not until World War II that the entire industry was finally "organized."

Nevertheless, within the space of one month, the CIO had achieved a remarkable victory over two huge industries that had long been immune to unionization. The drive of men such as Lewis, Murray, and Martin and the reasonableness of men such as Taylor were important in this advance, but the attitude of the government on both the state and federal levels was also of critical importance. Without the fair-minded attitude and support of Governor Murphy, the UAW would have been driven from the General Motors plant. Although Lewis and President Franklin D. Roosevelt were soon to be enemies, the White House placed considerable pressure on the employers to negotiate. Finally, the work of the National Labor Relations Board and the revelations by a Senate subcommittee, headed by prolabor senator Robert M. La Follette, Jr., of the unsavory antiunion tactics used by employers helped the CIO to consolidate and expand its gains over the next year.

By the end of the 1930's, union membership had increased to 30 percent of all workers. The CIO's commitment and democratic initiatives to bring workers into the union organization regardless of skill, job, race, or sex, as well as a policy of inclusion on the part of the mass-production industries, revolutionized unionization. Although not completely removed from discrimination, hundreds of thousands of African American workers were able to join unions. Women, despite obstacles to their gaining key union leadership roles, nevertheless were instrumental in building the forces of the CIO, especially in cases involving issues specifically relating to women.

—*George Q. Flynn and Marilyn Elizabeth Perry*

FURTHER READING

Babson, Steve. *The Unfinished Struggle: Turning Points in American Labor, 1877-Present*. Lanham, Md.: Rowman & Littlefield, 1999. Concise and comprehensive history of the American labor movement. Includes notes and index.

Barnard, John. *Walter Reuther and the Rise of the Auto Workers*. Boston: Little, Brown, 1983. Fine account written for lay readers provides an important vignette of mid-1930's CIO activity in a major industry. Includes bibliographic essay and index.

Bernstein, Irving. *Turbulent Years: A History of the American Worker, 1933-1941*. Boston: Houghton Mifflin, 1969. Authoritative, clearly written general history of American labor in the era between the world wars. Discusses the development of unionism and collective bargaining in American industry and public policy relating to collective bargaining during the New Deal era. Includes bibliographic notes and index.

Brooks, Thomas R. *Toil and Trouble: A History of American Labor*. 2d ed. New York: Delacorte Press, 1971. Provides good personality sketches and colorful anecdotes. Solid and informative, despite the author's clear prolabor bias. Includes index.

Dubofsky, Melvyn, and Foster Rhea Dulles. *Labor in America: A History*. 7th ed. Arlington Heights, Ill.: Harlan Davidson, 2004. Comprehensive account of American labor and labor movements since colonial days. Devotes substantial discussion to national organization during the 1930's, including the rise of the CIO and the merger of the CIO and the AFL. Features bibliographic notes and index.

Fine, Sidney. *Sit-Down: The General Motors Strike of 1936-1937*. Ann Arbor: University of Michigan Press, 1963. Well-told account presents a clear scholarly view of specific CIO battles with business and the community. Includes notes, bibliography, and index.

Galenson, Walter. *The CIO Challenge to the AFL: A History of the American Labor Movement, 1935-1941*. 1960. Reprint. Cambridge, Mass.: Harvard University Press, 1981. History of the CIO during what the author calls a revolutionary era marked by a radical change in the power structure of American labor.

Green, James R. *The World of the Worker: Labor in Twentieth-Century America*. 1980. Reprint. Champaign: University of Illinois Press, 1998. Focuses on notable labor leaders, including John L. Lewis and Sidney Hillman, emphasizing the relationships between leaders and workers. Provides a valuable description of the conflict over power and authority in the unions. Includes bibliographical essay and index.

Stolberg, Benjamin. *The Story of the CIO*. 1938. Reprint. New York: Arno Press, 1971. Readable journalistic account encapsulates well the atmosphere and personalities that affected the establishment of the CIO. Combines theory and history. Includes index.

Taft, Philip. *The A.F. of L. from the Death of Gompers to the Merger*. New York: Harper & Brothers, 1959. An invaluable study, although at times dense reading. The best work of its kind for understanding the AFL and CIO dissidents. Chapter notes, valuable index.

Zieger, Robert H. *The CIO, 1935-1955*. Chapel Hill:

University of North Carolina Press, 1995. History of the CIO prior to its merger with the AFL draws on archival records and oral histories. Includes endnotes and index.

SEE ALSO: June 27, 1905: Founding of Industrial Workers of the World; Oct. 15, 1914: Labor Unions

Win Exemption from Antitrust Laws; June 28, 1919: International Labor Organization Is Established; May 20, 1926: Railway Labor Act Provides for Mediation of Labor Disputes; Mar. 23, 1932: Norris-La Guardia Act Strengthens Labor Organizations; July 5, 1935: Wagner Act; June 25, 1938: Fair Labor Standards Act.

November 27, 1935
NEW ZEALAND'S FIRST LABOUR PARTY ADMINISTRATION

The New Zealand Labour Party, once considered a fringe socialist group, emerged from the Depression of the 1930's as the party with the most comprehensive support among New Zealanders. The easygoing and compassionate personality of Labour's first elected prime minister, Michael Joseph Savage, helped unify New Zealand as the country experienced economic uncertainty and war, and helped consolidate New Zealand's identity as a society that placed more emphasis on social equality than on free enterprise.

LOCALE: New Zealand

CATEGORIES: Government and politics; social issues and reform

KEY FIGURES

Michael Joseph Savage (1872-1940), New Zealand's first Labour prime minister, 1935-1940

Peter Fraser (1884-1950), deputy and prime minister of New Zealand, 1940-1949

Walter Nash (1882-1968), finance minister under Savage and prime minister of New Zealand, 1957-1960

Adam Hamilton (1880-1952), leader of the opposition National Party during Savage's term

John A. Lee (1891-1982), leftist Labour Party activist who became one of Savage's most virulent opponents

SUMMARY OF EVENT

Michael Joseph Savage, perhaps New Zealand's most important prime minister, did not settle in the country until he was thirty-five years old. He came from the Australian state of Victoria, and many commentators noted that his antiauthoritarian populism had a streak of the larrikinism, or outlaw gallantry, often associated with Victoria and especially with the Irish-Australian bushranger Ned Kelly. Like Kelly, Savage was a Roman Catholic, which was rather unusual for New Zealand,

which (unlike Australia) did not have a large Irish Catholic population and was dominated by an often puritanical Protestantism. Savage's Catholicism was evident in his opposition to conscription during World War I, a cause popular among Catholics in the British dominions, who were anxious about the restive state of the Catholic portions of British-occupied Ireland. Savage's religious beliefs also appeared in his social policies, which had an integralist aspect not far from the policies advocated by Pope Leo XIII in his encyclical *Rerum Novarum* (1891).

Savage drifted into the labor union movement more by chance than by ideological intent. Once involved, however, he became a radical who joined the faction of Red Feds associated with leaders such as Bob Semple. In his early political career, Savage was not content with simply improving the conditions under which workers labored; he wanted to make a fundamental change in society's nature. However, Savage began to move away from his more extreme positions after he was elected a member of Parliament in 1919. After the death of Labour's leader, Harry Holland, Savage worked throughout the 1920's and early 1930's to redefine Labour's image as a party capable of governing. His task was made easier as New Zealand voters looked for new ideas to help them overcome the the economic circumstances created by the Great Depression. The Depression had catastrophic effects around the world, but it had a particularly harsh impact on New Zealand's undiversified, resource-based economy. Prices for wool and lamb plummeted.

When the Labour Party was elected in 1935—with 90.8 percent voter turnout—Savage and an entire generation of leaders, including Peter Fraser and Walter Nash, were brought to power. Fraser, like Savage, had been a laborer; Nash had been a shop clerk and tailor's assistant. All three leaders, however, had what the Italian Marxist theoretician Antonio Gramsci termed an "organic" rela-

1935

tionship to the New Zealand working class; these politicians came from backgrounds very similar to those of their constituents. The three were also united by the fact that, although they had not received much formal schooling, they had both intellectual and instinctive approaches to New Zealand's social problems.

The new Labour government immediately gave unemployed New Zealanders substantial cash payments to supplement preexisting benefits. Housing was a huge problem in Depression-era New Zealand, and many unemployed farmers and factory workers became itinerants who traveled from homestead to homestead with no fixed address. The government committed itself to constructing a large number of new housing units and facilitated access to these units for the dispossessed and impoverished. Savage set minimum prices for dairy and other resources that helped New Zealand place its products in the world market. Members of the conservative opposition, however, such as Adam Hamilton, believed that some of the Savage government's policies deprived workers of freedom of choice.

New Zealand's first Labour government also made significant efforts to improve relations with the Maori, New Zealand's indigenous people, although efforts in this area were often underrated. Unlike Australia, where the Labor Party basically supported the reigning "White Australia" policy and called for assimilation of the Aborigines, the Savage government recognized Maori identity and sought—and largely achieved—a rapprochement with the Ratana movement, a syncretic religious group that espoused both Christian and indigenous Maori beliefs. Ratana essentially became the Maori arm of the Labour Party, as Ratana candidates dominated the allotted Maori seats and gave crucial support to Savage's overall agenda.

Labour won the 1938 election, although Savage's triumph required huge personal sacrifices: Before the campaign, he had learned that he had cancer but did not actively seek medical attention, both because he feared that treatment would take time away from the campaign and because he feared losing the election if his illness became public knowledge. By 1939, Savage was obviously ill, and his opponent John A. Lee was widely criticized for his attacks on the ailing politician. Although people in political circles were widely aware of Savage's illness, the reluctance of newspapers to be candid about the health of political figures in that era meant that Savage's death came as a shock to the New Zealand electorate.

By the time Savage died, World War II had begun. Ironically, the world's second great conflict involved the physical environment around New Zealand less than had the first, in which German South Pacific territories had been involved; during World War II, the Japanese never seriously approached Polynesia. However, if New Zealand had fewer threats to its own security, it made more sacrifices in Europe and the Middle East. Despite their different ideologies, British prime minister Winston Churchill respected Peter Fraser, who succeeded Savage, as an Allied leader and kept him current on military planning efforts.

SIGNIFICANCE

Although Labour prime ministers had served in Britain and Australia before 1935, they never exerted unchallenged authority and often headed coalition governments that diluted their political force. The government headed by Savage was the first Labour government in the English-speaking world to be voted into office by a groundswell of support from the populace, and it was the first to be secure in its ability to legislate its platform. Labour's fate, however, might have been very different were it not for the outbreak of World War II, which cemented the Labour leadership position and swathed it in patriotism.

The precedents established by Savage, Fraser, and Nash formed the basis for Labour's prestige and continued hold on power. Even as many of its economic policies were reversed and its social assumptions began to be seen as outdated, the Savage government still inspired warm feelings on the part of New Zealanders. Indeed, Savage remained one of the most popular of New Zealand's prime ministers. His combination of charisma and idealistic views lent him a status somewhat similar to that of nationalist president Lázaro Cárdenas in Mexico.

Like his fellow World War II leader William Lyon Mackenzie King of Canada, Savage never married and had an interest in mysticism. However, unlike King, who was rather remote, Savage was an unabashed populist. He also had a vulnerability, a humility, and a lack of interest in concealing his own failings that placed him in diametric opposition to the swaggering figures who dominated world politics in the 1930's. In contrast to these administrations, New Zealand's Labour government provided humane, accessible leadership for the island country at a time of worldwide turmoil and ideological upheaval.

—*Nicholas Birns*

FURTHER READING
Bassett, Michael. *The State in New Zealand: Socialism Without Doctrines.* Auckland, New Zealand: Auck-

land University Press, 1998. A negative assessment of Savage's economic policies by a historian committed to free-market ideology.

Belich, James. *Paradise Reforged.* Honolulu: University of Hawaii Press, 2001. Emphasizes Savage's role in the articulation of a distinct New Zealand identity, one based in the working class but sufficiently moderate to appeal across the population.

King, Michael. *The Penguin History of New Zealand.* Auckland, New Zealand: Penguin Books, 2003. Argues that though Labour in the Savage era did not have an ideology that was recognizable in the orthodox Marxist sense, it nonetheless had an articulated intellectual platform.

King, Michael, and Merle van de Klundert. *God's Farthest Outpost: A History of Catholics in New Zealand.*

Auckland, New Zealand: Viking Press, 1997. Depicts Savage as a pioneer for Catholics in New Zealand politics.

Mein-Smith, Phillippa. *A Concise History of New Zealand.* New York: Cambridge University Press, 2005. Provides insight into Savage's Catholicism and the importance of his Australian background; also gives a good general sense of the first Labour government's role in New Zealand history.

SEE ALSO: Jan. 1, 1901: Commonwealth of Australia Is Formed; June 12, 1902: Australia Extends Suffrage to Women; May 14, 1907: Formation of the Plunket Society; July 10, 1912: Massey Is Elected Prime Minister of New Zealand; 1921: First Woman Elected to Australian Parliament; Dec. 11, 1931: Formation of the British Commonwealth of Nations.

1936
LEHMANN DISCOVERS THE EARTH'S INNER CORE

Inge Lehmann's hypothesis that the earth has an inner and outer core led to investigations that confirmed her theory.

LOCALE: Copenhagen, Denmark
CATEGORIES: Science and technology; geology; earth science

KEY FIGURES
Inge Lehmann (1888-1993), Danish seismologist
John Milne (1850-1913), English engineer

SUMMARY OF EVENT
Prior to the development of the seismograph, an instrument that records vibrations of the earth, or earthquakes, very little was known about the composition of the inner parts of the earth. In the late 1800's, a basic knowledge of vibrations generated by a seismic source evolved. It was found that these vibrations, or waves, travel outward through the earth at measurable speeds.

The science of geophysics recognizes two major types of "elastic" waves, which were defined by the British geologist Richard Dixon Oldham. The first type is called a P wave because it causes a "primary" disturbance that deforms the earth by means of alternately lengthening and shortening in the direction of the source of the wave. P waves are also called "compressional waves" because the volume of the earth that is affected is alternately compressed and expanded. The second type

of elastic wave is the S wave, which produces a "secondary" disturbance. The S wave is a transverse body wave that travels through the interior of an elastic medium. S waves do not change the volume of the medium, but they do change its shape; for this reason, they are also called "distortional waves" or "shear waves." Both P waves and S waves pass through the interior of the earth; for this reason, they are called "body waves."

When an earthquake occurs, its waves travel through the body of the earth and are recorded by seismographs at earthquake observatories. These seismic waves carry to the surface information about the material through which they have passed. In 1883, the English engineer John Milne surmised that every large earthquake at any point of the globe could be recorded if there were an instrument designed for that purpose; however, it was not until 1893 that he perfected the first clockwork-powered seismograph.

In later years, when extremely sensitive seismographs had been developed, it was found that some weak P waves actually were penetrating a shadow zone, an area opposite the projected core of the earth. The shadow zone, discovered in the research of the Croatian geophysicist Andrija Mohorovičić, was left unexplained in earlier research conducted by pioneers in the use of seismographs to map the interior. Inge Lehmann postulated the existence of an inner core that could reflect the rays back into the shadow zone.

At the Copenhagen Seismological Observatory, Lehmann had for a number of years been clearly observing, through the core, seismic waves caused by earthquakes in the Pacific Ocean. Among these were the shocks that occurred at Murchison and Hawke's Bay in New Zealand in 1928 and 1931, respectively. It was evident from these records that a P-type wave that should have been within the shadow zone was arriving at seismological stations. This phenomenon could be explained only by the existence of an inner core that was about 1,250 kilometers (roughly 777 miles) in radius and was denser than the outer core.

Lehmann believed that core waves could be classified into three separate types of P wave. The standard explanation for the first two of these wave types was that their rays were refracted at the boundary between the mantle and core and focused toward the antipodes, placed opposite each other on the globe. She explained that waves of the third type were reflections from another sharp discontinuity within the core itself. This family of waves is made up of the core refractions. Beyond about 103 degrees, the direct P wave cannot be recorded because of the shadow effect of the core. Beyond this distance, the first wave to appear on long-period instruments is often a PP wave, which does not penetrate so deeply and therefore is able to avoid the obstacle. Short-period instruments show a refracted wave arising from complexities within the core, but it is not quite as prominent as P when it makes its reappearance at 142 degrees. Because it is deflected from its path and disappears altogether for nearly 40 degrees, it is called a PKP wave (K stands for *Kern*, the German word for "core").

In 1936, after ten years of interpreting seismograms (records made by a seismograph) and using a well-established scientific method, Lehmann was prepared to discover the inner core. Her first step was to calculate a direct problem. She assumed an earth model that was particularly simple. It had constant velocities in the mantle (10 kilometers, or 6.2 miles, per second) and in the core (8 kilometers, or 5 miles, per second). These were reasonable average values for both regions. She then introduced a small central core, which again had a constant velocity. These simplifications enabled her to view the seismic rays as straight lines; therefore, their travel times could be calculated by using elementary trigonometry. She then showed by making successive adjustments that a reasonable velocity and radius of the inner core could be found that predicted a travel-time curve close to the observations of the third type of P wave. In effect, she proved an existence theorem: A plausible three-shell earth structure could be defined that explained the features of the observed waves.

Lehmann's discovery of the inner core was very complicated, but it convinced Beno Gutenberg in the United States and Harold Jeffreys in England that her hypothesis was a viable one. Within two years, they had independently carried out more detailed calculations involving many observed travel times of P waves and calculated by means of an inverse method both the radius of the inner core and the P-velocity distribution in it.

SIGNIFICANCE

After the discovery of the earth's inner core, the measured travel times could be transformed, using inverse theory, into plausible P velocities in the mantle and the outer core. In late

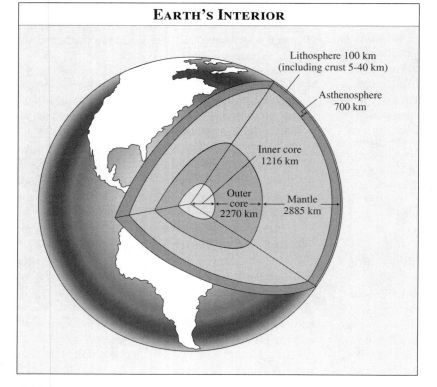

EARTH'S INTERIOR

Lithosphere 100 km
(including crust 5-40 km)

Asthenosphere
700 km

Inner core
1216 km

Outer
core
2270 km

Mantle
2885 km

1938 and 1939, Gutenberg and Jeffreys computed, independently, the average velocity based on thousands of observed travel times of P and S waves. Their agreement was extremely close; in fact, their calculations were so well developed that they have not been seriously altered since.

As a result of the development of sensitive seismographs, an increase in the number of seismographic stations around the world, and the availability of large-capacity computers, a better understanding of the earth has become possible. The core has a role in many geophysical studies, and the way it is affected during great earthquakes is being probed actively. If the physical properties inside the earth were better known, the frequencies and amplitude patterns of the resonant vibrations could be calculated, thereby making it possible to prevent loss of life.

—*Earl G. Hoover*

FURTHER READING

Bolt, Bruce A. *Inside the Earth: Evidence from Earthquakes*. 1982. Reprint. Fairfax, Va.: Techbooks, 1991. An easy-to-read, copiously illustrated introductory textbook covering the evolution of knowledge of the middle earth, types and measurements of earthquake waves, main shells of the earth, structural vibrations densities, elastic properties, and temperatures. Includes a guide to further reading.

Clark, Sydney P., Jr. *Structure of the Earth*. Englewood Cliffs, N.J.: Prentice-Hall, 1971. Brief and very readable introduction to the earth's structure. Areas covered include geologic structures, the earth's magnetic field, plate tectonics, seismology, and heat flow and the earth's temperature. Includes many illustrations and references as well as suggestions for further reading.

Jacobs, I. A. *The Earth's Core*. New York: Academic Press, 1975. Geared for graduate students and research workers in geophysics. Focuses on seismology and geomagnetism; contains many graphs and mathematical computations. Areas covered include the general properties of the earth, the origin of the earth's core, and the thermal regime of the earth's core. Includes both author and subject indexes.

Stein, Seth, and Michael Wysession. *An Introduction to Seismology, Earthquakes, and Earth Structure*. New York: Blackwell Science, 2002. Introductory textbook intended for advanced undergraduate and first-year graduate courses in seismology. Heavily illustrated. Includes suggestions for further reading and index.

Strahler, Arthur N., and Alan H. Strahler. *Environmental Geoscience: Interaction Between Natural Systems and Man*. New York: John Wiley & Sons, 1973. Introductory college textbook weaves the basic principles of geoscience with information on environmental and resource problems. Of particular interest is the discussion of the magnetosphere and the core as the source for the generation of the earth's magnetism. Abundantly illustrated.

Tarbuck, Edward J., and Frederick K. Lutgens. *The Earth: An Introduction to Physical Geology*. 8th ed. Upper Saddle River, N.J.: Prentice Hall, 2004. Introductory-level text offers a very good overview of the earth's interior. Well written and illustrated with color graphics.

SEE ALSO: 1906-1910: Oldham and Mohorovičić Determine the Earth's Interior Structure; 1913: Gutenberg Discovers Earth's Mantle-Outer Core Boundary; Jan., 1935: Richter Develops a Scale for Measuring Earthquake Strength.

1936

1936
MÜLLER INVENTS THE FIELD EMISSION MICROSCOPE

Erwin Wilhelm Müller invented the field emission microscope, the first instrument to depict the crystal structure of metals and the forerunner of the more powerful field ion microscope.

LOCALE: Berlin, Germany
CATEGORIES: Science and technology; physics; inventions

KEY FIGURES
Erwin Wilhelm Müller (1911-1977), German physicist and engineer
Eugen Goldstein (1850-1930), German physicist
Ralph H. Fowler (1889-1944), English physicist
Robert Gomer (b. 1924), American chemist and physicist

SUMMARY OF EVENT

Erwin Wilhelm Müller began to study the physical process that would constitute the basis of the field emission microscope while he was a research physicist in Berlin from 1935 to 1937. Field emission is the emission of electrons, the negatively charged subatomic constituents of all matter, from a metal electrode under the influence of a strong electrical field into a vacuum. The strong field induces the electrons to travel in the direction of the field. In 1876, Eugen Goldstein had demonstrated this effect experimentally. Goldstein projected the image of a small coin onto the fluorescent wall of a vacuum tube by using the coin as the electron-donating electrode, or cathode, of an electrical circuit, and the fluorescent wall of the tube as the electron-receiving electrode, or anode. The resulting electrical field around the metal coin induced electrons to traverse the vacuum tube and strike the fluorescent wall. When the moving electrons struck the fluorescent coating of the tube wall, a blurred, glowing image of the coin appeared.

Müller's research involved electron emission from point sources, not flat sources such as coins. One particular source consisted of a sharply edged tungsten needle. At first, Müller was simply interested in the paths taken by the field emitted electrons. Because Müller was familiar with the work of Goldstein and others, he set out to construct a similar apparatus, replacing the flat coin with his convex metal needles in order to stimulate the electron flow.

Müller's vacuum tubes were more like lightbulbs than tubes, with the hemisphere opposite the needlelike cath-

ode coated with a fluorescent material. In 1936, when Müller applied an electric field of approximately 40 million volts per centimeter to this apparatus, he did not view an image of the needle point analogous to that of Goldstein's coin face. Instead, his images were single, unstable blotches of light and dark that were at first nearly impossible to interpret. He soon recognized that the images of the convex needles produced by the instrument were highly magnified, whereas Goldstein's images offered no magnification at all; they were mere representations. The apparatus was a crude version of the field emission microscope.

In order to overcome the poor image quality, Müller worked to improve the quality of the needle tip through the chemical and electrolytic preparation of fine, heat-treated metal wires. Such procedures allowed Müller to manufacture needles with tips that were no larger than 0.00002 centimeter in diameter. At this size, many of the needles were composed of one nearly perfect crystal of the metal. With such improvements, Müller was able to publish emitted electron images of the surface crystallographic structure of tungsten in the German journal *Zeitschrift für Physik* in 1937. The magnification of these images was so great that it offered the first glimpse of the metallic crystal structure at the level of the atoms making up the crystal lattice. These were the first applications of the new invention, dubbed the field emission, or field electron, microscope. Soon thereafter, Müller obtained similar micrographs of the crystal structures of molybdenum, platinum, nickel, and copper.

Müller realized the importance such an instrument would have on the study of metallic surfaces. Such an instrument could be used to study the adsorption, or the physics of adherence, of contaminating materials onto the very structure of the metal. He also recognized that the instrument would be useless without a firm understanding of the physical process on which it depended—the field emission of electrons. The power of the field emission microscope would depend on the limits that the physical process of field emission imposed on it, for any scientific instrument is limited by the physical system on which it depends in order to operate.

Two of the most important parameters in assessing the power of any microscope are magnification and resolution. The former is a measure of the size of the smallest objects that the microscope can make visible; the latter concerns the size of the objects that it can distinguish, and is thus a measure of accuracy. For example, a microscope that has a magnification of one hundred times will make objects appear one hundred times larger than they are in reality. A microscope with a resolution of two millimeters can distinguish objects that are separated by a distance of two millimeters. Objects that are separated by less than two millimeters will not be seen as distinct objects. The electron emission process influences both these parameters and would ultimately preclude the instrument from depicting the images of individual metal atoms within the crystal lattice.

Müller studied the effect of needle shape on the performance of the microscope throughout much of 1937. He discovered that the magnification of a field emission microscope depends on the ratio of the fluorescent screen radius to the metal emitter radius. This underscores the importance of having a needle-shaped electron emitter. The more precise the tip of a needle is, the smaller its radius will be. The smaller this measure becomes, the larger the ratio of the screen radius to emitter radius becomes, and hence the higher the magnification becomes. The reason Goldstein's apparatus produced an unmagnified image of the coin was that the radius of the screen was approximately equal to that of the coin; because their ratio was approximately equal to one, the apparatus yielded no magnifying power at all. This should not be interpreted as meaning that the needle emitter should be fashioned into the sharpest point possible with a radius approaching zero. Indeed, when Müller showed the instrument to the German physicist Max von Laue in 1937, von Laue maintained that the emitter should have the sharpest point that the particular metal (and its associated crystal structure) would allow. Based on his knowledge of metallic crystal behavior, however, he reasoned that a smooth, hemispherical tip, albeit a very small one, would be the most efficient electron emitter. This was indeed the case.

When the needles had been properly shaped, Müller was able to realize magnifications of up to one million times. This magnification allowed Müller to view what he called "maps" of the atomic crystal structure of metals. Although the magnification may have been great, the resolution of the instrument was severely limited by the physics of emitted electrons, which caused the images Müller obtained to be continually blurred.

Müller was well aware of the contemporary developments in quantum mechanics, especially those resulting from the work of Ralph H. Fowler, which applied these theories to field electron emission. Quantum mechanics is the set of physical theories that describes phenomena at the subatomic level, which states that entities such as electrons behave both as particles and as waves. Given that the electrons have particle-like properties, they would have a particular velocity, like any other moving particle. Given that they also behaved like waves, they would have a particular wavelength, as do sound waves or light waves. The electron velocity was extremely high and uncontrollably random, which caused the blurred micrographic images. In addition, the electrons had an unsatisfactorily high wavelength. When Müller combined these two factors, he was able to determine that, theoretically, the resolution of the field emission microscope would never reach below 20 angstroms. This may seem quite small. In fact, a resolution of 20 angstroms is equal to a resolution of 0.000000002 meter. Müller noted, however, that the atoms in an atomic crystal lattice are separated by only 4 to 5 angstroms. Thus the field emission microscope could never depict single atoms, for it was a physical impossibility for it to distinguish one atom from another.

SIGNIFICANCE

Even with its inherent limitations, the field emission microscope had an enormous impact on two fronts: the field of surface science and Müller's development of the field ion microscope in the early to mid-1950's.

Robert Gomer, an American chemist and physicist, was among the first scientists to put Müller's invention to use in actual scientific investigation. Most other microscopes and magnifying instruments consist of an independent system of lenses that process the image of the specimen under investigation by focusing the reflection of some wavelength of radiation (visible light, X rays, and the like). The field emission microscope does not require such an apparatus, however. The specimen under study—the needle—is an integral part of the instrument, for it is also the electron emitting cathode. Whatever happens physically or chemically to the specimen will affect directly the resulting image. Gomer was attracted to the device because of this simplicity, and it was this simplicity that permitted the types of experiments he conducted.

As size requirements dictated that the needle often consists of only one individual crystal of the metal, Müller realized that the properties of individual crystals could be examined. The most important of these properties was the adsorption of materials onto the needle surface. The instrument offered such a precise map of the crystal structure that a layer as thin as one one-hundredth of an atom would affect the emission quality and hence the resulting image. Gomer used the field emission microscope to study the adsorption and desorption of materials such as barium.

The field of surface science was in its infancy at the time of Müller's invention, and the field emission microscope provided the impetus that allowed this discipline to expand and flourish through the 1940's and 1950's. By the late 1950's, Gomer used the instrument to investigate and study the rate of migration of gases that diffused into the lattice itself. In order to achieve this, Gomer immersed a field emission microscope in a bath of liquid helium, creating an extremely high vacuum within the bulb. This allowed him to introduce gases such as hydrogen and oxygen into the bulb and view their movement through the crystal by viewing the subsequent changes in the emitter image. The studies of diffusion and adsorption allowed Gomer and others to view the gross molecular structure of any material that could be either embedded within or adsorbed onto the emitter surface. Medium-sized molecules of materials such as phthalocyanine have also been observed.

Despite these advances, Müller's studies of the limitations of the microscope eventually led to his development of the more powerful field ion microscope between 1951 and 1956. Rather than imaging the needle tip with emitted electrons, Müller used emitted positive ions. The ions had smaller velocities and shorter wavelengths than the much lighter electrons, and hence the inherent resolution problems of the field emission microscope were overcome at last. By 1956, Müller and his colleagues at the Pennsylvania State University's Field Emission Laboratory reported the first images of individual atoms in metal lattices.

— William J. McKinney

FURTHER READING

Müller, Erwin Wilhelm. "The Field Ion Microscope." *American Scientist* 49 (March, 1961): 88-98. Largely devoted to Müller's work on the field ion microscope, but presents some introductory material concerning the physical limitations of the field emission microscope that eventually led to the later microscope's development.

_____. "Field Ion Microscopy." *Science* 149 (August, 1965): 591-600. Focuses on the later and more powerful field ion microscope, but discusses Müller's realization of the resolving problems of the field ion microscope. Also addresses the ramifications of the fact that the imaging medium and sample are one and the same in both the field emission and field ion microscopes.

_____. "The Imaging Process in Field Ion Microscopy from the FEM to the Atom Probe." In *Chemistry and Physics of Solid Surfaces*, edited by Ralf Vanselow and S. Y. Tong. Cleveland: CRC Press, 1977. Technically concise and accessible account of the development of the field emission microscope. Like most of Müller's work, presented in the context of the later field ion microscope. Traces the history of the field emission microscope and includes illustrations and micrographs from Müller's original German publications, including micrographs of the tungsten crystal and barium adsorbed onto tungsten.

Müller, Erwin Wilhelm, and Tien Tzou Tsong. "Fundamentals of Field Ion Microscopy." In *Field Ion Microscopy: Principles and Applications*. New York: Elsevier, 1969. Müller's most comprehensive account of the application of his inventions in the field of surface science. Focuses mostly on the later field ion microscope, but the introductory chapter gives a concise account of the historical events leading to the development of both instruments.

Oudar, Jacques. "Recent Methods in the Study of Adsorption." In *Physics and Chemistry of Surfaces*. Glasgow: Blackie & Son, 1975. Details the use of both the field emission and the field ion microscopes in surface studies. Adequately illustrated, although sparse in technical content.

SEE ALSO: 1902: Zsigmondy Invents the Ultramicroscope; Apr., 1931: First Electron Microscope Is Constructed.

1936-1946
FRANCE NATIONALIZES ITS BANKING AND INDUSTRIAL SECTORS

Through nationalization of banking and some industrial sectors, France moved toward a mixed economy.

LOCALE: France

CATEGORIES: Government and politics; trade and commerce; business and labor; banking and finance

KEY FIGURES

Léon Blum (1872-1950), premier of France, 1936-1938

Charles de Gaulle (1890-1970), head of the Free French government in exile during World War II

Maurice Thorez (1900-1964), leader of the French Communist Party, 1932-1964

SUMMARY OF EVENT

In the 1930's, faced with economic depression, several Western countries experimented with innovative policies. Governments intervened in the economy in order to promote recovery. Solutions varied, but the concept that national governments should intervene in the economy and exert countercyclical pressures remained, becoming a prominent feature of post-World War II economic policy. Between 1936 and 1946, France chose to enact the nationalization of credit and some industrial sectors to help build a mixed economy that ultimately would become compatible with private business practices.

French leaders considered nationalization to be part of the solution to France's economic woes in the 1930's. The principal advocates of nationalization were the Socialists, the Communists, and the left-wing trade union Confédération Générale du Travail (CGT). All three were influenced by Henri de Man, a Belgian Marxist who called for a mixed economy, one between socialism and capitalism on the political and economic spectrum. De Man and his French followers were not interested so much in government ownership as in governmental control of investment. Through nationalization of credit, the state could provide cheaper and easier credit for small businesses, which could then increase wages and contribute to growth. Small businesses supported nationalization of France's credit structure.

The Left, however, was divided concerning the role nationalization should play. The Socialists, led by Léon Blum, saw nationalization not so much as an instrument to achieve socialism but as a means of promoting greater worker welfare within a capitalist structure. The Socialists envisioned indemnification of private owners upon nationalization. The Communists, led by Maurice Tho-rez, expressed disbelief in the improvement of workers' welfare while a capitalist economy was still in place. They saw nationalization and planning as measures to be taken only after revolution.

In 1936, the Front Populaire (Popular Front), an electoral alliance of Socialists, Communists, and Radicals, took over the government. Its program included nationalization on a limited basis. The Popular Front was far more active in the field of social and labor legislation, enacting a number of social welfare measures, reducing the workweek to forty hours, and granting the right to collective bargaining. These measures alarmed the business community and contributed to considerable capital flight abroad.

Only the Bank of France and the armaments industry were initially directly affected by nationalization. They were followed in 1937 by the railway. Government control of the Bank of France was popular because of the bank's deflationary policies and its proclivity to favor large firms when extending credit. The government stopped short of outright nationalization and instead enacted administrative reform as a means to introduce strong state representation on the bank's executive boards. Further steps were envisioned but never taken, and the bank did not change its policies markedly. Effective nationalization instead hit the armaments industry. This too caused panic in the business community. The Schneider firm, as one case, walled off the newly nationalized armament section of its plant from the remainder of it. It appears, however, that nationalization of armaments improved national defense, government control over mobilization, and production centralization.

There are a number of reasons the Popular Front government led by Blum enacted such a limited nationalization program. The government feared losing the confidence of businesspeople and the middle class at a delicate political juncture, when Europe seemed to be swept by fascism. France did not appear to be immune to that danger. An excessively radical program might have brought economic conflict with Western democracies. Finally, Blum would do nothing to create an efficient state apparatus of economic control if such creation might facilitate formation of a fascist government in the future. These preoccupations reflected growing fears of resurgent Nazi Germany and of possible armed conflict. The latter issue preoccupied the Popular Front far more than did nationalization.

The only other major nationalization of the 1930's concerned the railroad system. The Railway Act of 1937 created a mixed company, Société Nationale de Chemins de Fer Français (SNCF). State intervention in this case was prompted by the sector's huge budget deficit. The existing network of private lines was consolidated, and operations were streamlined. The government retained 51 percent of ownership.

A second nationalization phase took place in 1945 and 1946 and was more extensive. As a result of their active role in the Resistance against Nazi occupation, the Socialists and Communists were popular at the end of World War II and dominated the political agenda. The Left reopened the issue of nationalization, which this time was more popular, supported even by France's conservative leader, General Charles de Gaulle. De Gaulle saw nationalization as a means for the state to acquire sufficient authority to be able to promote recovery and unprecedented growth and in the process reestablish France as a major world power. Several political groups shared de Gaulle's idea that nationalization could put the "levers of command" into the hands of the state. Little opposition to nationalization existed at the end of World War II, except in the business community.

The business community, however, was on the defensive because of widespread perceptions that it had collaborated with the German occupiers. For example, Louis Renault's property was confiscated because he had supplied the Germans with some military materials during the occupation, and Renault became a state company.

After the war, the private sector clearly lacked sufficient capital to fuel rapid recovery unaided. As a consequence, between December, 1945, and April, 1946, nationalization was enacted by large parliamentary majorities. It affected the Bank of France and the four largest deposit banks, electricity, gas, the thirty-four largest insurance companies, and coal. After April of 1946, popular and party support for nationalization slackened considerably, as political tides began to change.

SIGNIFICANCE

The overall impact of nationalization was relatively limited. Nationalization remained confined to a few, though important, sectors of the economy. The political influence of the Socialists, the Christian Democrats, and other moderates ensured that nationalization would not fundamentally alter the market-oriented character of the French economy.

Although after World War II there was widespread agreement that nationalization was necessary to achieve rapid economic recovery and modernization, divisions continued among the major parties about the exact role the nationalized sector should play in the economy. The Socialists conceived of the nationalized sector as a stepping-stone toward socialism. The Communists, to the contrary, still separated the issue of veritable revolution from mere nationalization of some sectors of the economy. To the Communists, nationalization was only a patriotic measure meant to reinforce the French government's control over resources and make the country more independent as a consequence. The Movement Republicain Populaire (MRP) saw nationalization as a means to break the large trusts, but it was no panacea: It should be adopted only when government regulation proved inefficient. It continued to prefer joint public-private ownership and to ascribe a moral mission to the nationalized sector of humanizing working conditions.

Disagreement arose, moreover, concerning institutional and political control of nationalized enterprises. Socialists and Communists disagreed about whether the nationalized sectors should be strongly centralized and about who should hold managing authority. The Socialists favored a decentralized technocratic approach, as they sought efficiency above all. The Communists preferred instead strong centralized control by the government, matched within each nationalized enterprise by tripartite boards composed of state, labor, and consumer representatives. Compromises were adopted whereby the natural gas and electricity industries followed a centralized approach with strong tripartite boards. The coal industry instead was decentralized and bound to technocratic criteria.

The model that emerged was therefore one of compromise. The nationalized sector never had the authority or power to function as a "lever of command" through which the government could direct the economy. A degree of coordination within the nationalized sector was brought about only by the French Modernization and Equipment Plan (PME).

Initially, the business community bitterly criticized the nationalized sector. In the 1930's, nationalization caused widespread capital flight abroad. In 1945-1946, deputies close to business interests sought to obstruct or influence legislation, with little success. Accusations were launched against the nationalized sectors that they were mismanaged, particularly because of the system of tripartite boards that were stacked with left-wing trade union representatives, that they increased the state's budget deficit, and that they created a huge bureaucratic apparatus.

French premier *Léon Blum addresses a crowd in Poissy, France, in 1936.* (NARA)

The first accusation by the business community was well founded. Once the early enthusiasm for nationalization had subsided, Socialists and the MRP managed in the late 1940's to impose a managerial approach in which technocratic criteria prevailed over political ones. The bureaucratic apparatus was also streamlined.

The accusation that nationalized industries operated at a loss and drained state resources was only partially founded. The nationalized sectors had to be rebuilt after six years of war and four years of harsh Nazi occupation. Large deficits during the period of recovery and modernization were therefore inevitable. It has been argued that had the nationalized sectors been left in private hands, and given the scarcity of private capital, it would have been far more difficult to achieve as spectacular and rapid a recovery as the one that in fact took place by the end of 1949.

After 1947, France began to enjoy the fruits of a massive American aid package to Europe, the Marshall Plan. By choosing to participate in the plan, France made a clear pro-Western political choice. French politics moved toward the center, with the Left losing control and influence. As a consequence, business confidence began to return and criticism of the nationalized sector subsided.

Business criticism also diminished because the nationalized sector, by the late 1940's, no longer appeared to be threatening the health of the private sector. To the contrary, private enterprises began to recognize some advantages to them of nationalization. Chief among these was the fact that during the difficult reconstruction period, private businesses could enjoy the low energy costs that only a subsidized national sector could provide. In addition, it became clear that credit practices were not significantly altered in France despite the nationalization of the largest deposit banks. Criteria adopted to extend or deny credit were by and large no different from before. Finally, a positive "personal" factor intervened to modify the negative attitudes of the business community. Very often, public and private enterprise managers were alumni of the same schools, knew one another, and shared the same economic philosophies. Moreover, many managers embarked on mixed careers, accepting executive positions in both private and public businesses, switching from one sector to the other with ease. By the 1950's, the initial animosity against the nationalized sector no longer existed. France emerged as a "mixed economy" insofar as the state owned a share of the means of production and adopted economic planning, but it remained nevertheless an economy ultimately still driven by market imperatives.

—*Chiarella Esposito*

FURTHER READING

Colton, Joel. *Léon Blum: Humanist in Politics.* 1966. Reprint. Durham, N.C.: Duke University Press, 1987. Outstanding political biography of Blum by an American historian. Part 2, "The Years of Responsibility," particularly deals with the Popular Front experience,

1936

Blum's leadership of two cabinets, his economic philosophy, and the so-called French New Deal of the 1930's.

Ehrmann, Henry W. *Organized Business in France.* 1957. Reprint. Westport, Conn.: Greenwood Press, 1981. Thorough and informative book on the French business community from the 1930's to the mid-1950's; one of the best on the topic available in English. Presents a historical survey and then describes the post-World War II structure of French business associations. Concludes with an in-depth analysis of business attitudes and policies in France.

Forsyth, Douglas J., and Ton Notermans, eds. *Regime Changes: Macroeconomic Policy and Financial Regulation in Europe from the 1930s to the 1990s.* New York: Berghahn Books, 1997. Collection of essays by historians, economists, and political scientists includes discussion of the nationalization of France's banking sector.

Horn, Gerd-Rainer. *European Socialists Respond to Fascism: Ideology, Activism, and Contingency in the 1930s.* New York: Oxford University Press, 1996. Study of developments in Europe in the years 1933-1936 provides background for the move toward nationalization in France.

Kuisel, Richard F. *Capitalism and the State in Modern France: Renovation and Economic Management in the Twentieth Century.* Cambridge, England: Cam-

bridge University Press, 1981. Excellent comprehensive study of twentieth century French capitalism. Traces the evolution of French state-capital relations from the late nineteenth century to the early 1950's, explaining how France arrived at its postwar mixed economic model. Information on nationalization appears in chapters 4 and 7.

Lacouture, Jean. *Léon Blum.* Translated by George Holoch. New York: Holmes & Meier, 1982. Provides a thorough account of Blum's political career. Part 2, "The Tests of Power," sets Blum's tenure of power against the backdrop of a mounting fascist threat within France and elsewhere in Europe. Explains Blum's policies as products of an unprecedented and dangerous political environment.

Pinkney, David H. "The French Experiment in Nationalization, 1944-1950." In *Modern France: Problems of the Third and Fourth Republics*, edited by Edward Mead Earle. Princeton, N.J.: Princeton University Press, 1951. Straightforward account of French nationalization after World War II provides all the basic information. Adeptly sets nationalization in the context of the postwar political climate and describes both the advantages and the disadvantages of nationalization.

SEE ALSO: Dec. 29, 1920: Rise of the French Communist Party; Mar. 18, 1938: Mexico Nationalizes Foreign Oil Properties.

January-March, 1936
CONSUMERS UNION OF THE UNITED STATES EMERGES

After industrialization, buyers and sellers in the United States were no longer neighbors or acquaintances. Consumers Union arose to fill the need for tests, standards, and guarantees to protect all consumers.

LOCALE: New York, New York
CATEGORIES: Business and labor; government and politics; organizations and institutions

KEY FIGURES
Arthur Kallet (1902-1972), first director of Consumers Union
Colston Warne (1900-1987), first president of Consumers Union
Dewey Palmer (1898-1971), first technical supervisor of Consumers Union

Frederick John Schlink (1891-1995), coauthor of *Your Money's Worth* (1927), cofounder of Consumers Research, and unwitting catalyst for the beginning of Consumers Union
Stuart Chase (1888-1985), coauthor of *Your Money's Worth* and cofounder of Consumers Research, the predecessor of Consumers Union

SUMMARY OF EVENT
Before the Industrial Revolution, producers and purchasers of food, clothing, and other items were usually neighbors, friends, or even members of the same family. With the rise of factories, however, many common items were no longer produced locally. Instead, they were made by strangers, often in faraway places. The quality of these items varied greatly, and most familiar items

such as soap, shirts, and wagon wheels began to be made by machine. The variety of available products increased, and each manufacturer made claims that might or might not prove to be true. The use of electricity brought many electrical appliances onto the market: lightbulbs, toasters, hair-curling devices, and more.

Consumers could try to judge the quality of a product before purchasing it in two ways: by brand name and by advertising. A brand name, such as Standard Oil, Armour Meat, or Heinz Soup, could be placed on a company's products in hopes of guiding consumers to buy all a company's products if they found that one of them was reliable. Even the most well-known brands, however, often were made under unsanitary conditions or with questionable or inferior ingredients. In many cases, there was no quality control to ensure that the products were not defective.

Advertising, then, became one of producers' most important tools. Advertisers attempted to create a desire for a product in the public's awareness by promising certain results from using it or by getting endorsements of the products from well-known people—movie stars for beauty products or doctors for medicines. Often these claims either were untrue or were unsupported by facts. Another problem was the lack of standardization of items. Not only was quality not guaranteed, but sizes, weights, and measures of items also varied, even with products made by the same manufacturer.

The attitude of many businesses about these problems was *caveat emptor*: "Let the buyer beware." The responsibility was left with the buyer to purchase the right product; if a purchaser got a faulty product, it was not considered to be the producer's problem. In 1927, a book titled *Your Money's Worth* became a best-seller within months after its appearance. The authors were Frederick John Schlink, an engineer, and Stuart Chase, an economist. The book pointed out some of the serious problems that consumers experienced as they tried to guess their way through the maze of products and advertising. Consumers were "so many Alices in the Wonderland of salesmanship." Schlink and Chase pointed out practices of shortweighting, quackery, mislabeling, and uselessness of some products, naming specific products as examples. They proposed scientific research as the antidote and noted that the U.S. government had already begun to do testing and to set standards and specifications for some products.

In response to the hundreds of letters they received requesting information about products, Chase and Schlink began Consumers Research of New York City. Previously a neighborhood consumer club formed by Schlink in 1927, it had done its own home testing and produced a mimeographed list of products—"good values" versus products to avoid—called "Consumer's Club Commodity List." The mimeographed list evolved into the *Consumers Research Bulletin*. It took no financial support of any kind from producers or advertisers and was the first magazine to be established solely to test products for consumers' benefit. Five years after it began, the bulletin had 42,000 subscribers, compared with 565 subscribers in 1927.

Schlink and Chase, with the help of other scientists and writers, published an array of pamphlets, books, and articles in addition to their bulletin. One of these, a book published in 1933 titled *100,000,000 Guinea Pigs: Dangers in Everyday Foods, Drugs, and Cosmetics*, was a tremendous success, and it inspired a wave of investigative writing about consumer-oriented topics. Schlink cowrote *100,000,000 Guinea Pigs* with Arthur Kallet, a young engineer who was also on the board of Consumers Research.

Stuart Chase had left Consumers Research to pursue other interests, but Schlink remained at the helm with a staff of more than fifty and a large number of outside consultants. With the growth in size of the staff, there were differences of opinion about the direction the organization should take. This was especially true of decisions about spending. Should resources be used primarily for educating consumers, for political purposes, or for improving the testing program?

In May, 1933, the organization moved into a large stone building in Washington, New Jersey. In Washington, a small town about a hundred miles outside New York City, Schlink hoped to be able to expand his testing facilities. He was also drawn to the location because of the lower costs; he believed that people who were seriously interested in the consumer movement would come with him. In fact, however, only six of the seventy employees moved from New York to New Jersey with Schlink, and Schlink, his wife, and close friends became the majority on the board of directors. Schlink tried to stay in complete control of the organization. He had a difficult time working with anyone who held differing ideas about what Consumers Research should try to accomplish, and he fired many people who disagreed with him. He also believed that it was a privilege for employees to work for Consumers Research, and so he rejected their appeals for higher wages or shorter working hours. When three employees tried to form a labor union in order to improve working conditions, they were fired.

1936

Forty other employees then left their jobs in a show of support for their colleagues.

Although thousands of workers across the country were also on strike during that time, the strike at Consumers Research was particularly significant. Consumers Research had a stated goal of upgrading the lives of consumers, and the irony of its own workers having to strike for better conditions was considered humorous by the popular press. Liberal leaders were concerned and offered to help the workers and management reach a compromise, but Schlink would accept no such offers. Instead, he used the same strikebreaking tactics used by the big corporations—legal injunctions, strikebreakers, and armed detectives. *Consumers Research Bulletin*'s fifty-five thousand subscribers were caught in the middle of the ruckus.

Arthur Kallet, who had coauthored *100,000,000 Guinea Pigs* with Schlink, had been a rather inactive member of the Consumers Research board of directors. When the strike began, however, he resigned from the board and supported the workers. As 1935 wore on with no end to the strike in sight, he helped to keep the strikers together. The idea began growing among them to start a publication of their own in order to compete with *Consumers Research Bulletin*. The group planned to use its many contacts, financial and academic, with unions, researchers, and sympathetic *Bulletin* subscribers to help with its initial efforts. The new publication—*Consumers Union Reports*—would support the interests of both consumers and workers. The organization itself would be run collectively rather than by a management team.

By March, 1936, New York State had given Consumers Union of the United States its charter as a nonprofit organization. The first issue of *Consumers Union Reports* magazine was published in May of that year. Three years later, it was known simply as *Consumer Reports* and had gained a larger number of subscribers than *Consumers Research Bulletin*. The director of the new organization was Arthur Kallet. Dewey Palmer, formerly technical director of Consumers Research, became the technical supervisor. Colston Warne, a professor at Amherst College, was made president and served in that role for the next forty-four years.

Consumers Union staff members had been politically active: They participated in labor movement picketing, testified at government hearings, and had promotional drives for the poor. Product testing suffered, however, as a result of this focus. Ultimately, the board decided that testing should not be sacrificed, since the scientific rating program was at the foundation of Consumers Union's existence. Thus, in December, 1939, a joint conference

was arranged by Kallet and Warne between the members of Consumers Union and the Cambridge-Boston branch of the American Association of Scientific Workers (AASW) to gain support for Consumers Union among scientists. The conference resulted in AASW's offering to provide advice and assistance not only to Consumers Union but also to consumer organizations in general.

In 1986, the year of its fiftieth anniversary, Consumers Union reported that it had helped many additional consumer organizations get started. These included the American Council on Consumer Interests, the Emergency Care Research Institute, the Washington Center for the Study of Services, the Consumer Federation of America, the Center for Auto Safety, the International Organization of Consumers Unions, and the British Consumers Association. In addition to aiding other consumer groups, Consumers Union directly affected the lives of many Americans by conducting research that led to reforms or legislation in the areas of fallout from nuclear testing, risks of smoking, and automobile safety. It also did pioneering research on air pollution's cost to consumers, unhealthy additives and chemicals in foods, and pesticide dangers in the food chain. During the 1960's and 1970's, these became important issues for reforms.

SIGNIFICANCE

When it began, Consumers Union was considered to be a pioneer in the consumer movement. Colston Warne later reported, "The idea of testing and appraising products by name constituted an overdue scientific mechanism designed to restore rationality to the marketplace." This idea, he stated, was "nothing less than a social invention." To the original four thousand members of Consumers Union, the organization was not only a guide to making better consumer decisions but was also "an *approach* to the choices and problems of our materialistic world," as one charter member wrote fifty years later. Consumers Union's reports helped to bring about improvements in specific products, such as certain electric fans that it reported in 1956 to have dangerously exposed blades. Poor sales of product brands that received bad ratings in *Consumer Reports* caused manufacturers to correct the products' problems. On the other hand, a good product rating in *Consumer Reports* boosted an item's sales. Volkswagen cars and Maytag washers both received superior ratings, and spokespeople credited the ratings for the products' tremendous increases in sales.

The original goals of Consumers Union were to provide scientific information about products and to report on the labor conditions under which those products were produced; ultimately, Consumers Union sought to achieve a decent standard of living for all consumers. For the first several years, a discussion of labor issues was included in the product descriptions but not in the actual criteria for product ratings. As time went on, the labor analysis was dropped in favor of emphasis on objective scientific testing. Although Consumers Union did not pursue its second goal as aggressively as it did its first, the organization has carried on its strong tradition of providing reliable product information for consumers. *Consumer Reports* has over the years appealed for food stamps for the poor, demanded fairer tax laws, argued against harsh methods of debt collecting, pushed for national health insurance, and urged provision of "lifeline" banking services and utility rates.

—Caroline Godwin Larson

FURTHER READING

Bishop, James, Jr., and Henry W. Hubbard. *Let the Seller Beware.* Washington, D.C.: National Press, 1969. Lively and informative history of the consumer movement from the 1800's to the 1960's. Full of specific examples of consumer problems and the people who attacked them and, in many cases, eventually won legislation to correct them. An optimistic look at trends in the consumer movement. Includes index.

Cohen, Lizbeth. *A Consumers' Republic: The Politics of Mass Consumption in Postwar America.* New York: Alfred A. Knopf, 2003. Excellent history of post-Depression American economics. Analysis of the postwar creation of suburbs highlights the difficulties and inequalities faced by women and African Americans as they encountered the opportunities and hurdles created by trends toward mass consumption.

Consumers Union. "Fifty Years Ago." *Consumer Reports* 51 (January/February, 1986): 8-10, 76-79. On the occasion of its fiftieth anniversary, Consumers Union included this two-part narrative in consecutive issues of *Consumer Reports.* A detailed summary of events leading to, and following, the founding of Consumers Union. Provides a summary of many of the organization's activities and achievements up to 1986.

Leach, William R. *Land of Desire: Merchants, Power, and the Rise of a New American Culture.* New York: Vintage, 1994. Nominated for the National Book Award, this readable volume offers an overview of the ways in which manufacturers, banks, and religious and government leaders promoted the creation of a nation of consumers.

Nadel, Mark V. *The Politics of Consumer Protection.* Indianapolis: Bobbs-Merrill, 1971. Looks at governmental policies relating to consumer protection and analyzes the reasons they developed. Includes historical information from the early twentieth century and discussions of Ralph Nader and other consumer advocates of the 1960's. Contains tables, index, and extensive list of references.

Olson, Mancur. *The Logic of Collective Action: Public Goods and the Theory of Groups.* Cambridge, Mass.: Harvard University Press, 1965. This scholarly text looks at various types of groups and their interactions. Chapters on labor unions and pressure groups provide an overview of the history and role in society of unions and collective action groups, including the period during which Consumers Union began. Includes an index and footnotes.

Reid, Margaret G. *Consumers and the Market.* New York: F. S. Crofts, 1938. Work written at the approximate time of Consumers Union's origin provides a fascinating summary of the problems then facing consumers in areas of labeling, quality, advertising, and price setting, with specific examples and historical references. Includes tables and index.

Ryan, Edward W. *In the Words of Adam Smith: The First Consumer Advocate.* Sun Lakes, Ariz.: Thomas Horton & Daughters, 1990. Easily read presentation of the ideas of Adam Smith, the "father of modern economics." Consists mainly of passages from Smith's treatise *An Inquiry into the Nature and Causes of the Wealth of Nations* (1776), with connecting and explanatory comments. Smith's clear prose includes some of the earliest statements of consumer advocacy. Includes index and bibliography.

Silber, Norman Isaac. *Test and Protest: The Influence of Consumers Union.* New York: Holmes & Meier, 1983. Provides thorough coverage of the origin of Consumers Union and the conditions that led to its formation, in addition to coverage of specific Consumers Union research projects, their impacts, and the organization's evolution over time. Includes notes, bibliography, and index.

SEE ALSO: 1903: Scott Publishes *The Theory of Advertising*; Feb., 1906: Sinclair Publishes *The Jungle*; June 30, 1906: Pure Food and Drug Act and Meat Inspection Act; 1927: U.S. Food and Drug Administration Is Established; 1933: Kallet and Schlink Publish *100,000,000 Guinea Pigs*; June 25, 1938: Federal Food, Drug, and Cosmetic Act.

1936

January 1, 1936
FORD FOUNDATION IS ESTABLISHED

Founded by Henry and Edsel Ford as a tax shelter against the Revenue Act of 1935, the Ford Foundation began as a charitable organization that gave millions each year to organizations in the Detroit area. By 1951, the foundation was donating billions of dollars to causes around the world.

LOCALE: Dearborn, Michigan
CATEGORIES: Humanitarianism and philanthropy; organizations and institutions

KEY FIGURES

Henry Ford (1863-1947), founder of the Ford Motor Company

Edsel Ford (1893-1943), Henry Ford's only child, president of the Ford Motor Company, 1919-1943, and cofounder of the Ford Foundation

Clara Bryant Ford (1866-1950), wife of Henry Ford and a significant influence on the Ford Foundation

SUMMARY OF EVENT

Very little has been documented about the actual day the Ford Foundation was incorporated, mainly because the press was not immediately notified, and the neither the Ford family nor its lawyers made any formal public announcement. The public became aware of its existence only after the director of the state of Michigan's corporation and securities division in Lansing informed a reporter that a lawyer from the offices of Bodman, Longley, Bogle, Middleton, and Farley had filed incorporation papers (which consisted of only three pages). The law firm refused to make comments on the foundation, and when asked by reporters, Edsel Ford simply said that the foundation would have a small scope and that he did not expect the scope to increase, a very peculiar statement in light of the foundation's later influence.

The Ford Foundation began with a donation of twenty-five thousand dollars from Edsel Ford and was headquartered at the Ford Engineering Laboratories in Dearborn. Although the paperwork filed with the state of Michigan stated that the foundation was nominally concerned with strengthening scientific, educational, and other charities, it is clear that the Fords used the foundation primarily as a way to pool their funds to assist local Detroit causes with which they were already involved: the Edison Institute (a campus for primary, secondary, and postsecondary education), the Henry Ford Hospital, the Detroit Institute of Arts, the Detroit Symphony, the

Henry Ford Museum, and Greenfield Village (the first outdoor museum in the United States, dedicated to the American traditions of liberty, industry, and innovation). After incorporation and until 1950, the foundation continued to give approximately one million dollars a year to these charities. (This sum rose dramatically after the foundation went international in 1950.) However, it was no coincidence that the foundation became incorporated at nearly the same time the Revenue Act of 1935 went into effect.

The Revenue Act of 1935, part of President Franklin D. Roosevelt's New Deal, raised the estate tax to 69 percent on estates worth twenty million to fifty million dollars and to 70 percent on estates worth more than fifty million dollars. Henry Ford and many others believed that the tax was directed specifically at the Ford Motor Company: The government, Ford believed, wanted to confiscate the family's personal assets and force them into selling Ford stock to pay the tax. In addition to creating immense underwriting costs, the 70 percent tax would have left the Fords with almost nothing and no option but to surrender control and go public with the Ford Motor Company.

In fact, the Fords did face significant pressure to sell stocks. Wall Street, the Bureau of Internal Revenue, and other automobile companies may well have wanted the Ford Motor Company to cease being a family-owned corporation. This prospect appealed to competitors such as General Motors, which was beholden to its voting stockholders and their power to siphon off money that could be used in design and production by demanding more dividends. In contrast, the Fords could use its profits to improve plants, equipment, sales, and other areas as they saw fit.

The Revenue Act diminished the Ford Motor Company's competitive edge, and at the same time it supported the interests of Wall Street, the federal government, and the American public. However, the act contained a loophole: A provision allowed a portion of an estate's assets to be tax-exempt if they were given to charitable, religious, or educational organizations. A charitable foundation operated by the Fords would fit into that category. As a result, even though the Fords lost a vast amount of money to the Revenue Act, this provision allowed them to retain family control of the company, at least temporarily.

The foundation's first administrators—Edsel Ford,

Burt J. Craig, and Clifford B. Longley—effectively functioned as its board of trustees. Craig had previously been the Ford Motor Company's secretary and treasurer, and Longley had served as legal counsel for the company until 1929, when he left to establish a private law practice in Detroit. This board and Clara Bryant Ford, Edsel Ford's mother, left a legacy of donating money to causes that the foundation still champions today. Even before the foundation began, Clara Ford, for example, was very involved with establishing the Berry School, which eventually became a liberal arts college in Georgia known for teacher education and teaching English as a second language. Her influence helped create the Ford Foundation's tradition of championing liberal arts schools, teacher education, teaching English as a second language, and many other education-oriented endeavors.

Although he did not publicly discuss his involvement with the foundation, Henry Ford consistently donated his own money to provide a hands-on secondary and postsecondary educational model to help students learn a trade, and his gifts funded the Edison Institute in Michigan and the Richmond Hill Project in Georgia. The elder

Henry Ford. (Library of Congress)

Ford also believed that education should be used to help people help themselves, a goal exemplified by his creation of several programs in Michigan that taught self-sustaining agricultural and manufacturing techniques to troubled teens and impoverished communities. Furthermore, the Fords designed the Henry Ford Hospital, now the Henry Ford Health System, to provide excellent health care at a price affordable to all citizens. The foundation carried its health- and education-focused mission throughout the United States and the rest of the world to help developing nations provide health care to as many people as possible. In addition, Edsel Ford used a great deal of effort and money to help the Detroit Institute of Arts become a world-class organization, and this endeavor launched the Ford Foundation's tradition of championing art institutions.

SIGNIFICANCE

By 1947, both Henry and Edsel Ford had passed away, and the Ford Motor Company was losing tens of millions of dollars every year. Henry Ford II, Edsel's son, had control of the company, and his family's lawyers and advisers recommended that he sell the family's stock in order to save the company. Profits from the company's sale gave the foundation so much revenue—$474 million—that the foundation became the largest in the nation, and the foundation's board of directors decided to make it an international organization. By 1951, offices were based mostly in New York City, and the organization became an entity separate from the Ford Motor Company and the Ford family.

The eight-member board of independent consultants gave the foundation five primary goals: to promote world peace and a world order of law and justice; to secure and maintain allegiance to the principles of freedom and democracy; to promote stable economies that would facilitate the realization of democratic goals; to improve educational institutions and enable individuals to realize their potential and to promote equality in education; and to increase knowledge of factors that influence human conduct and extend that knowledge to benefit individuals and society.

These goals were inspired by the interests and concerns expressed by Henry, Clara, and Edsel Ford, and the foundation's board interviewed hundreds of consultants from many backgrounds and fields. The wide array of opinions that shaped the foundation's policies extended the organization's revenue, workforce, and influence over almost every part of the world, but the foundation was not without its critics. Left-wing activists criticized

1936

it for championing right-wing ideals, and conservatives chastised it for being too progressive.

— *Troy Place*

FURTHER READING
Greenleaf, William. *From These Beginnings: The Early Philanthropies of Henry and Edsel Ford*. Detroit: Wayne State University Press, 1964. Provides an exhaustive description of these philanthropies. Greenleaf ends the book with a description of the foundation's beginning.
MacDonald, Dwight. *The Ford Foundation: The Men and the Millions*. New York: Reynal, 1956. Provides very specific information on the foundation from 1947 to 1955. Includes discussion of the controversy,

leadership, early direction, and vision, as well as explanations of why and how the foundation went international.
Magat, Richard. *The Ford Foundation at Work: Philanthropic Choices, Methods, and Styles*. New York: Plenum Press, 1979. In 1975, at the request of the board of trustees of the Ford Foundation, Magat provided this self-study of the foundation. Analyzes the foundation's beginnings and possible future directions.

SEE ALSO: Nov. 25, 1910: Carnegie Establishes the Endowment for International Peace; Mar. 1, 1913: Ford Assembly Line Begins Operation; May 14, 1913: Rockefeller Foundation Is Founded; Jan. 5, 1914: Ford Announces a Five-Dollar, Eight-Hour Workday.

January 26, 1936
TUDOR'S *JARDIN AUX LILAS* PREMIERES IN LONDON

With his Jardin aux lilas, *Antony Tudor created a new form of dance, the psychological ballet, which represented a step forward in the evolution of twentieth century ballet.*

LOCALE: London, England
CATEGORY: Dance

KEY FIGURES
Antony Tudor (William Cook; 1908-1987), British choreographer
Marie Rambert (1888-1982), founder of London's Ballet Rambert
Nora Kaye (1920-1987), American ballet dancer
Hugh Laing (1911-1988), British ballet dancer
Agnes de Mille (1905-1993), American choreographer
Richard Pleasant (1906-1961), cofounder of Ballet Theatre
Lucia Chase (1897-1986), cofounder of Ballet Theatre

SUMMARY OF EVENT
When Sergei Diaghilev's Ballets Russes broke up in 1929, the company's dancers and choreographers dispersed throughout the West, taking with them the heritage of Diaghilev's bold experiments with contemporary arts and themes. For those who went to England, there was little opportunity for performance; most English ballet was relegated to the music halls. There were, however, two good dance schools in London; one had been formed in 1920 by Marie Rambert, the other in 1926 by Ninette de Valois. Both women had worked with Dia-

ghilev and would found, respectively, Ballet Rambert and the Royal Ballet.

Marie Rambert was interested in following Diaghilev's lead in developing contemporary ballet, and she had an acute eye for talent. In 1930, she presented her Rambert Dancers (later called the Ballet Club) in the first season of English ballet. One of her students who had come to study dance in 1928 helped with lights, stage management, refreshments, and anything else that needed doing. He was twenty-two years old, and his name was William Cook. Nine years later, he changed his name to Antony Tudor.

After only three years of study, Tudor created his first ballet. According to Rambert, it was not a good piece, but it showed considerable talent. Tudor honed his talents on Rambert's dancers (including himself) for another five years. In 1938, the Ballet Club presented his first major work, *Jardin aux lilas* (later called *Lilac Garden*). *Jardin aux lilas* was unlike anything anyone had seen on the ballet stage. Although he worked in the idiom of classical ballet, Tudor had transformed his technique into a vehicle for exposing the characters' psychological states.

Jardin aux lilas does not have a plot; rather, it depicts a social situation in which the characters are caught with no means of escape. Set in a lilac garden in Edwardian times, it concerns a young woman, Caroline, who is soon to enter a marriage of convenience to a man she does not love. At a farewell party in the lilac garden she must say goodbye to the man she loves, and her fiancée must reaffirm his parting from a former mistress. As Edwardian propriety demanded that personal desires be subjugated to the mandates of society, all four main characters are constrained to accept the situation without overtly expressing their true feelings. Still, Tudor's first audiences saw very clearly the yearning, frustration, and anguish suffered by each.

To depict these emotions, Tudor did not use the customary approach to choreography, which was to design steps that would then be danced with appropriate feelings. Instead, he reversed the process and derived the movement from the feelings. He understood that even the posture of a character reveals a psychological state. Hence Caroline stands with her arms straight to her sides, her back stiff, her body charged with the effort of self-control. Tudor used small, everyday gestures to the same effect. Fingers to the temple, tentative reaches, a head turning back over the shoulder all suggested the fragments of thought and feeling that passed through the characters. He used classical steps to express or intensify emotion; no steps were included merely for the sake of dancing. Tudor's use of the dramatic form differed from the standard balletic treatment. He chose music (in this case, Ernest Chausson's *Poème for Violin and Orchestra*) that did not have easily identifiable beats or measures but that flowed in long phrases. Tudor choreographed along these sweeping phrases and moved the characters from moment to psychological moment, not from dance to dance. There might be duets, solo passages, and group dances, but these erupted from and receded into the general flow of the ballet.

Unusual uses of time, reminiscent of cinematic effects, also appear in *Jardin aux lilas*. Encounters between Caroline and her lover, between the man she must marry and his mistress, are furtive and fleeting close-ups within the fluid picture. Toward the end of the piece, when Caroline realizes the time is near when she will never see her lover again, she swoons into the arms of the man she must marry, and all action stops while the music continues. As the other characters stay frozen, Caroline alone moves toward her lover, reaching. The reach is somnambulistic and devoid of hope. She then moves backward into the swoon, and all the characters resume action. This short sequence, the turning point of the ballet, is highlighted by the use of these cinematic techniques (freeze-frame, slow-motion, and dream-sequence effects). The cumulative effect of these elements of style was one of austere beauty and poignancy.

Jardin aux lilas was immediately recognized as a masterpiece. Within the next three years, Tudor created three more major works in London. The first of these,

Dark Elegies (1937), performed to Gustav Mahler's *Kindertotenlieder*, was an expression, in ritual form, of the grief of a village of parents who have lost their children. The piece, although more abstract than *Jardin aux lilas*, displayed the same potency of feeling beneath its simple, folk-based movements.

Despite his predominant emphasis on the psychological aspects of human difficulty, Tudor had a sense of the comic that came out in the remaining two of his significant London works. *Judgment of Paris* (1938) was a satiric comedy based on the myth of Paris and the Golden Apple. *Gala Performance*, also created in 1938, poked fun at the backstage intrigues of the ballet world and, most particularly, at the pretensions of ballet dancers from the three major schools, Russian, Italian, and French. By 1938, Tudor had left Rambert to form his own company, the London Ballet, for which he produced *Judgment of Paris* and *Gala Performance*. In 1939, however, World War II intervened, and the London theaters were closed. Although he was already a recognized master choreographer, he had no place to work.

During the years when Tudor was developing his craft, American choreographer Agnes de Mille was also in London establishing herself as a ballet recital artist. She was in the original cast of *Dark Elegies* and danced the role of Venus in *Judgment of Paris*. In 1938, de Mille returned to New York. Hearing that the newly formed Ballet Theatre (later American Ballet Theatre) was looking for a choreographer, de Mille urged the company to invite Tudor to the United States. He arrived in New York in 1939.

In its inaugural season in January, 1940, Ballet Theatre presented his *Jardin aux lilas, Dark Elegies*, and *Judgment of Paris*. American audiences and critics alike embraced him as a major new choreographer, and Tudor was to spend most of the remainder of his life in the United States. At the time of Tudor's American debut, the new modern dance was gaining rapid ground. Tudor had seen in Europe the works of German expressionists Mary Wigman, Harold Kreutzberg, and Kurt Jooss. He discovered in them the valuable precept that feeling and its gestural expression originate in the torso. Of his mode of working, he said: "We start from the spine and the torso, and we get to the feet later. In ballet school you usually start with the feet." According to American modern dance pioneer Martha Graham, *Dark Elegies* was "the first ballet to invade modern dance."

In 1942, Tudor created what is universally considered to be one of the great ballets of the twentieth century. Set to the music of Arnold Schoenberg's *Verklärte Nacht*,

1936

Pillar of Fire tells the story of Hagar, a young woman of nineteenth century New England. Facing spinsterhood, Hagar hopes for a match with a friend of the family, but the friend appears to be more interested in her younger sister. In desperation she gives herself to a roué and is subsequently ostracized by her family and the town. The ballet focuses on the dilemma of those who, like Hagar, have passions that run deeper than social codes and roles can tolerate and who therefore often become outcasts.

In addition to using posture, everyday gesture, and a blend of modern and ballet techniques in *Pillar of Fire*, Tudor employs two groups of dancers (the "Lovers in Innocence" and the "Lovers in Experience") to underline Hagar's suspension between society's "good" and "bad." The hip-swinging, free-wheeling movements of the Lovers in Experience are in contrast with the softer, more conventional movements of the Lovers in Innocence, which, in turn, contrast with the stiffer movements of the judgmental townspeople. Tudor worked on *Pillar of Fire* for a solid year. On opening night, the labor was rewarded with thirty curtain calls and, subsequently, the highest critical praise. Hagar was danced by Nora Kaye, who was recognized from then on as a great dramatic ballet dancer. She was eminently capable of expressing the finest emotional nuances within the difficult, highly stylized movements and was for many years the model for aspiring Tudor dancers. Other original cast members who set a standard for future dramatic dancers were Tudor's principal male interpreter and lifelong companion, Hugh Laing, Tudor himself, and Lucia Chase, who eventually became codirector of Ballet Theatre. Following *Pillar of Fire*, Tudor created *The Tragedy of Romeo and Juliet* (1943), *Dim Lustre* (1943), and *Undertow* (1945) for Ballet Theatre, *Shadow of the Wind* (1948) for England's Royal Ballet, and in 1975, his last masterwork (for American Ballet Theatre), *The Leaves Are Fading*, an abstract piece with strong lyric undertones.

SIGNIFICANCE

Tudor's work focused on the experiences of real people rather than on the adventures of the fairy-tale characters, colorful ethnic personalities, or mythic heroes more typical of ballet. Rather than following a narrative about realistic characters, however, he drew portraits of people whose psychological reactions, in combination with their social situations, created the events.

Tudor influenced a whole generation of dancers and choreographers by the way he worked. He was meticulous and would research his subject extensively before beginning a ballet. He derived gestures from the character in the moment, sometimes taking two or three hours to find and work on one movement. This intensive search for the psychological motivation of movement was entirely new to ballet.

Tudor did not necessarily tell his dancers much about the characters or story. Rather, he led them into it by asking questions and by goading them. Indeed, although dancers flocked to his classes and yearned to be in his ballets, they were almost always terrified of being the target of one of his merciless personal barbs. The purpose behind these verbal assaults was to strip away the "ballet persona" that develops early in many young dancers and that often engenders such set reactions to movement that it becomes almost impossible for many dancers to respond to dramatic situations with any spontaneity or truth. There was no doubt that Tudor's ballets brought out unsuspected depths of expression in the dancers who performed them.

At a time when English and American ballet were just getting started, Tudor brought to them both distinction and a progressive leap forward in the evolution of ballet. He was the first to achieve a genuine integration of ballet and modern dance and the first to create what has come to be called the psychological ballet. He directly influenced future choreographers of high stature, such as Great Britain's Walter Gore and America's Agnes de Mille and Jerome Robbins. His work pulled choreographers away from melodrama and superficial acting and taught dancers to work in depth, to search for the real motivations of movement. Tudor's dramatic ballets have been compared to the works of Marcel Proust, Renate Stendhal, and Anton Chekhov for their detailed portraiture of personal inner landscapes. Beginning with *Jardin aux lilas*, Tudor did something no one else thought possible. In the words of dance critic Fernau Hall, "For the first time in the twentieth century a choreographer succeeded in emulating the achievements of good dramatists, novelists and film directors."

—*Catherine Sim*

FURTHER READING

Amberg, George. *Ballet: The Emergence of an American Art*. New York: New American Library, 1949. Begins with a background of classical ballet from the nineteenth century through Diaghilev's Ballets Russes and traces the development of ballet in the United States through the 1940's. A fascinating, exhaustive examination of companies, choreographers, works, dancers, and the evolution of twentieth century American aesthetics as seen in its ballet. Chronology. Repertoire listing of all major American companies of the period. Index.

Chazin-Bennahum, Judith. *The Ballets of Antony Tudor: Studies in Psyche and Satire*. New York: Oxford University Press, 2006. A colleague of Tudor, Chazin-Bennahum deliberately adopted an approach very different from that of Tudor biographer Donna Perlmutter; Chazin-Bennahum focuses more on Tudor's productions than his personality. Essential reading for those interested in Tudor and a valuable contribution to the history of dance.

De Mille, Agnes. *Dance to the Piper*. New York: Little, Brown, 1952. The first volume of De Mille's autobiography. Separate chapters on Marie Rambert, Tudor and Hugh Laing, and Martha Graham. De Mille's brilliant writing makes this a classic of dance biography. Index.

_____. *Speak to Me, Dance with Me*. New York: Little, Brown, 1973. De Mille's letters from her early career years in London. Gives accounts of several trips to the western United States (including one to work for her uncle, Cecil B. DeMille). Includes her time spent with Tudor, Laing, and Rambert and gives a good sense of the struggle experienced by the independent ballet artists of the 1930's. Interesting "what became of" section of major figures mentioned in the book. Index.

Lee, Carol. *Ballet in Western Culture: A History of Its Origins and Evolution*. New York: Routledge, 2002.

A good starting place for any student of ballet. A readable history that traces ballet's evolution from ancient Greece to modern the United States. Index.

Perlmutter, Donna. *Shadowplay*. New York: Viking Press, 1991. A complete biography of Tudor that follows his life and career in clear chronological sequence. Detailed descriptions of the creation of Tudor's major ballets, with emphasis on their development as a reflection of Tudor's life and relationships. Bibliography, source notes, choreographic chronology, and index.

Rambert, Marie. *Quicksilver*. London: Macmillan, 1972. Autobiography contains interesting accounts of Rambert's childhood in Poland (then part of the Russian Empire), her work with Diaghilev's Ballets Russes, her fostering of Tudor's early career, and the evolution of Ballet Rambert. Factual rather than critical, with many anecdotes of theater and dance greats of the 1920's through 1960's. Index.

SEE ALSO: May 19, 1909: Diaghilev's Ballets Russes Astounds Paris; June 2, 1909: Fokine's *Les Sylphides* Introduces Abstract Ballet; June 25, 1910: *The Firebird* Premieres in Paris; May 29, 1912: *L'Après-midi d'un faune* Scandalizes Parisian Audiences; May 29, 1913: *The Rite of Spring* Stuns Audiences; Dec. 6, 1934: Balanchine's *Serenade* Inaugurates American Ballet; Apr. 5, 1938: Ballet Russe de Monte Carlo Debuts.

January 28, 1936
SOVIETS CONDEMN SHOSTAKOVICH'S *LADY MACBETH OF THE MTSENSK DISTRICT*

The condemnation of Dmitri Shostakovich's opera Lady Macbeth of the Mtsensk District *was a landmark in Soviet cultural history, drawing worldwide attention and leading to the oppression of other Soviet artists.*

LOCALE: Moscow, Soviet Union (now Russia)
CATEGORIES: Music; theater

KEY FIGURES
Dmitri Shostakovich (1906-1975), Soviet composer
Joseph Stalin (Joseph Vissarionovich Dzhugashvili; 1878-1953), general secretary of the Communist Party and absolute ruler of the Soviet Union
Nikolai Leskov (1831-1895), Russian author

SUMMARY OF EVENT
In January of 1936, Dmitri Shostakovich was only thirty years old and had already achieved world fame as a leading Soviet composer. At that time, he was in the city of Archangelsk on a concert tour, buoyed by the recent successes of his opera *Ledi Makbet Mtsenskogo uezda* (1930-1932; *Lady Macbeth of the Mtsensk District*). On January 28, he went to the railroad station to buy a copy of *Pravda*, the official newspaper of the Soviet Communist Party. He opened the paper and was shocked to read a scathing editorial condemning his opera. It was a turning point in his life and for the future of Soviet culture as a whole.

1936

2911

Shostakovich was born in 1906 in St. Petersburg. When the Bolsheviks seized power in 1917, he became a child of the new Soviet state, and his hometown was renamed Leningrad. As a boy, Shostakovich exhibited great musical talent and studied at the Leningrad Conservatory. He composed his first symphony at the age of nineteen, and the work was premiered in the West to great acclaim. Shostakovich was the first Soviet composer who came of age after the revolution to become world famous. Symphonies, ballets, film scores, and incidental music followed. His first opera, *Nos* (1927-1928; *The Nose*), was based on a satire of czarist Russia by the novelist Nikolai Gogol.

Shostakovich was an indefatigable worker and versatile composer. By 1929, he had evolved a style that was dazzling, pungent, lyrical, ironic, and haunting—in a word, unique. His musical idols were Ludwig van Beethoven, Modest Mussorgsky, Gustav Mahler, Igor Stravinsky, and innovative Western composers of the 1920's such as Alban Berg.

His fame assured and his individuality seemingly unthreatened, Shostakovich in 1930 began to write a tetralogy of feminist operas about the struggles of Russian women. The tetralogy was modeled on Richard Wagner's *The Ring of the Nibelungs*. The first opera would portray the misery of women under the old regime, the second would present revolutionary women who helped to overthrow the czars, and the third and fourth would celebrate the triumph of the new Soviet heroine of the future.

Only the first opera was to be completed. Shostakovich chose for his story of oppressed Russian womanhood the short nineteenth century novel *Ledi Makbet Mtsenskogo uezda* (1865; *Lady Macbeth of the Mtsensk District*, 1922) by the Russian classical writer Nikolai Leskov. Shostakovich was also inspired by the operatic models of Georges Bizet's *Carmen* (1875) and Alban Berg's expressionist and atonal opera *Wozzeck* (1925). Both explored important social problems and stormy relationships between men and women.

Leskov's novel is somewhat reminiscent of Gustave Flaubert's great work *Madame Bovary* (1857; English translation, 1886) in its exploration of an intelligent, frustrated woman in a narrow provincial society. Katerina Izmaylova is the wife of a boring merchant in a small, provincial Russian town of the 1840's. Stifled by her existence, she takes a young lover, Sergei, poisons her father-in-law after he discovers her unfaithfulness, strangles her husband with the assistance of Sergei, and is sentenced to penal servitude in Siberia along with her lover. When Sergei becomes unfaithful to Katerina in Siberia, Katerina

Dmitri Shostakovich. (Library of Congress)

kills his new mistress and herself, and the story ends.

Shostakovich was captivated and inspired by this theme. He composed his opera from 1930 to 1932 and dedicated it to his future wife, Nina Varzar, with whom he had a stormy romance during that period. Shostakovich wrote a lengthy commentary on the opera in which he spelled out his intentions. He intended the drama to be a "tragic satire," prompting some to liken his musical style to the content of the profound novels of Fyodor Dostoevski retold by the comic actor Charles Chaplin. He also strove to create a Marxist opera in which he would portray Katerina as a victim of a rotten bourgeois society that has corrupted her, leading to her self-destruction and the destruction of others.

Shostakovich played a key role in writing the libretto. He departed from Leskov's story in four major respects. First, the opera was much more a satire on the middle-class, patriarchal society of nineteenth century Russia than the novel had been. Second, Shostakovich incorporated a new episode, a pointed satire on police corruption and arbitrary behavior, into the third act. Third, Katerina was treated sympathetically as a heroic victim of circumstance, despite her adulterous and violent behavior. Finally, the inhuman conditions of penal servitude in Siberia were vividly depicted.

The music and the orchestra were given special prominence to sustain the story line, and the music flowed without interruption. In the manner of the work of expressionist composers, the music indulged in violent contrasts between lyricism and dissonance and employed unusual effects to produce violent contrast, heighten emotions, and create effects of irony, crudity, and realism. Katerina alone was given lyrical solos to heighten her individuality and her tragic plight. The music also daringly attempted to describe the erotic behavior of the principal characters.

Lady Macbeth of the Mtsensk District received its premiere on January 22, 1934, in Leningrad, and was produced later that year in Moscow. It was a resounding success, receiving eighty-three performances in Leningrad and ninety-seven in Moscow in just two seasons. Soviet writers hailed it as a great triumph of Soviet culture and a piercing satire of middle-class society. By 1935, it was introduced to the major cities of Europe and was premiered in Cleveland and New York. On the whole, Western critics viewed the work favorably, although there was some division of opinion. Some called it a masterpiece of true social criticism and dramatic intensity, whereas others were put off by its violence, unusual musical effects, and erotic themes.

The Soviet political and cultural scene, however, was changing rapidly. The relatively free, experimental period of the 1920's in culture and the economy was coming to an abrupt end. From 1929 to 1933, the Soviet Union experienced a "second revolution from above" that took the form of forced collectivization of agriculture, rapid industrialization, and the use of state-sponsored terror and forced labor to ensure obedience and conformity. By 1932, the official doctrine of "Socialist Realism" imposed drab, optimistic formulas in art and literature, and newly organized writers' and composers' unions regimented the arts through the supremacy of Communist bureaucrats.

By 1936, Joseph Stalin had become the absolute dictator of the Soviet Union, personally intervening in all state-supervised areas of Soviet life and imposing his views and his will. When he visited the Bolshoi Theater in Moscow in January of 1936 and heard Shostakovich's *Lady Macbeth of the Mtsensk District*, the fate of Soviet music, and of Soviet culture as a whole, was sealed.

SIGNIFICANCE

Stalin left the Bolshoi Theater in a rage, offended by the dissonance, stark realism, eroticism, and tragic theme of the opera. In addition, he was upset by the satirical attack on the police, which he interpreted as an affront to himself. His control of the police was a vital source of his immense power and a weapon of the terror he was unleashing against Soviet society.

The now-famous vehement editorial in *Pravda* followed the next day, on January 28. The long article was titled "Chaos Instead of Music." It condemned Shostakovich as a bourgeois "formalist" and the opera as filled with "an intentionally ungainly, muddled flood of sounds [that] drown, escape, and drown once more in crashing, gnashing, and screeching." The success of the opera in the West was attributed to its appeal to the depraved tastes of the bourgeoisie. The article warned Shostakovich that things "could end very badly." A week later, a second editorial in *Pravda* condemned Shostakovich's 1935 ballet *The Limpid Stream*. Nevertheless, the first editorial gave Shostakovich an opportunity to redeem himself: *Pravda* recognized his great talent and his ability to express strong and direct emotions in music. The article was unsigned, meaning that it reflected the views of the highest officials in the party. Some scholars think that much of the article was written by Stalin himself.

Shostakovich was shattered. He was certain that he would be arrested, for this was a time when arrests and executions were commonplace. He kept a suitcase at the ready that contained warm underwear and a sturdy pair of shoes. He could not sleep. This frightening episode cast a shadow over the rest of his life. His anxiety was increased by his friendships with other persecuted avant-garde cultural figures.

Shostakovich was shunned. His works were no longer performed, and friends who saw him on the street would cross to the other side to avoid meeting him. Still, he was allowed to continue teaching. He discreetly withdrew his completed Fourth Symphony and started working on his Fifth Symphony, which would rehabilitate him, a work so successful that when it premiered in November, 1937, it received a forty-minute ovation.

Why was Shostakovich not arrested or executed, as were so many other great Soviet cultural figures? First, he was well known in the West as a product of the revolution and a great Soviet artist. Ironically, most Westerners saw him as a committed Communist, although his Communist critics attacked him as a bourgeois formalist. Nevertheless, it could be argued that his notoriety made him even more vulnerable. Second, Shostakovich had written three very popular film scores prior to 1934. Stalin loved films as a form of relaxation and appreciated the potential for propaganda and self-glorification that the medium had to offer. Finally, Stalin might have used Shostakovich as an example of an artist who would recant, a model for others. Subsequently, Stalin heaped both rewards and humiliations on the beleaguered composer.

The major significance of the condemnation of *Lady Macbeth of the Mtsensk District* lay in the powerful warning it sent to all Soviet cultural figures to abandon innovation and to toe the new line of Socialist Realism. The government also seized on the opera to mechanize and regiment Soviet cultural life. Shostakovich thus became a test case and a living example of what could happen to a modernist, experimental artist. The condemnation of Shostakovich was followed by a flood of directives controlling every area of cultural life.

The attack on Shostakovich increased the use of two favorite Soviet code words, "formalism" and "Socialist Realism." "Formalism" denoted abstraction, symbolism, and experimentation. Stalin liked opera as well as film. After attending a performance of *Lady Macbeth of the Mtsensk District*, he formulated certain guidelines to be followed for opera, guidelines that illuminated the meaning of "Socialist Realism." Opera, said Stalin, should be optimistic in content, should be filled with simple folk melodies, and should glorify the Soviet system and even the Russian past.

The impact of the condemnation of Shostakovich on the composer's style is still a matter of debate. Some Western critics have argued that his innovative, dashing style of the 1920's was ruined by the incident and that he retreated into stilted formulas and mannerisms. Until the death of Stalin, Soviet critics argued that Shostakovich's style had matured into serious and disciplined art, although he continued to be taken to task from time to time. Shostakovich's posthumously published memoirs, however, make it apparent that he became a kind of secret dissident, eliminating the blatant themes of modernism but using tragic and satirical themes in a critical musical language, at the same time continuing to write film scores and popular works to placate the regime.

In 1958, during the more liberal period of de-Stalinization, *Lady Macbeth of the Mtsensk District* was revised; the new version was performed in 1963. Shostakovich retitled the opera *Katerina Izmaylova* and slightly revised the score and libretto. This time the somewhat changed conditions in both the Soviet Union and the West enabled the opera to be judged more from a musical and dramatic standpoint than from an ideological one, and critics hailed it as the greatest Russian opera since Peter Ilich Tchaikovsky's *Pikovaya Dama* of 1890. The verdict of 1936 was thus reversed, and, in this instance, art outlived tyranny.

—*Leon Stein*

FURTHER READING

Fay, Laurel E. *Shostakovich: A Life*. New York: Oxford University Press, 2000. Comprehensive biography draws extensively on Shostakovich's correspondence and other primary documents, such as concert programs and reviews. Includes list of works, glossary of names, bibliography, and index.

_____, ed. *Shostakovich and His World*. Princeton, N.J.: Princeton University Press, 2004. Collection of essays on Shostakovich as well as some of his personal correspondence and other documents that shed light on his life and creative process. Includes index.

Leskov, Nikolai. *Lady Macbeth of Mtsensk*. In *Six Great Russian Short Novels*, edited by Randall Jarrell. Garden City, N.Y.: Doubleday, 1970. Useful edition of the short novel on which Shostakovich's opera was based, with a fine introduction by Jarrell. Necessary reading for an understanding of the opera.

MacDonald, Ian. *The New Shostakovich*. Boston: Northeastern University Press, 1990. Excellent volume on Shostakovich's life and work clarifies misconceptions about the composer in the West. Argues that Shostakovich was losing faith in communism at the time he wrote *Lady Macbeth of the Mtsensk District* and afterward adopted strategies to evade censorship while at the same time composing great music to memorialize the sufferings of the Soviet people. Includes photographs and bibliography.

Schwarz, Boris. *Music and Musical Life in Soviet Russia, 1917-1970*. London: Barrie & Jenkins, 1972. Excellent survey of the period, with fine sections on the episode of the condemnation of *Lady Macbeth of the Mtsensk District*. Provides valuable insights into the political and social conditions of the period that affected Shostakovich's music.

Shostakovich, Dmitri, and A. Preis. *Lady Macbeth of Mtsensk: Or, Katerina Izmailova*. Translated by Edward Downe. New York: G. Schirmer, 1983. Clear, attractive translation of the English libretto that captures the essence of the spicy Russian original.

Volkov, Solomon, ed. *Testimony: The Memoirs of Dmitri Shostakovich*. Translated by Antonina W. Bouis. 1979.

THE TWENTIETH CENTURY, 1901-1940

Darling Founds the National Wildlife Federation

Reprint. Pompton Plains, N.J.: Limelight, 2000. Valuable source on the life and work of Shostakovich by a friend who pieced together many of their conversations, mostly from the period 1970-1974. Shostakovich emerges as a secret dissident, outraged by the sufferings caused by the Soviet regime. Posits the interesting theory that Shostakovich was in the tradition of the Russian *yurodivy*, the artist-saints of Russian history who fought tyranny with their spiritual strength. Includes excellent photographs.

SEE ALSO: 1929-1930: *The Bedbug* and *The Bathhouse* Exemplify Revolutionary Theater; Apr. 23, 1932: Stalin Restricts Soviet Composers; Apr. 23, 1932-Aug., 1934: Socialist Realism Is Mandated in Soviet Literature; 1934: Soviet Union Bans Abstract Art.

February 4, 1936

DARLING FOUNDS THE NATIONAL WILDLIFE FEDERATION

Jay Darling founded the National Wildlife Federation, an organization that united local and state wildlife concerns into one association. Since its inception, the National Wildlife Federation has played a key role in the creation of laws controlling the pollution put forth by humans' use of air, water, and hazardous chemicals.

LOCALE: United States
CATEGORIES: Environmental issues; organizations and institutions

KEY FIGURES
Jay Darling (1876-1962), American cartoonist and founder of the National Wildlife Federation
Franklin D. Roosevelt (1882-1945), president of the United States, 1933-1945
Theodore Roosevelt (1858-1919), president of the United States, 1901-1909
Aldo Leopold (1887-1948), American forester who championed a scientific approach to the management of wildlife and other natural resources

SUMMARY OF EVENT
On February 3, 1936, President Franklin D. Roosevelt officially proclaimed the opening of a conference dedicated to organizing all public and private institutions involved with conservation. The conference was the brainchild of nationally acclaimed cartoonist Jay Darling, whose hope was to not only establish a national federation of conservation clubs but also to form strong state conservation organizations where they did not exist or where they were weak. He also encouraged the participation of organizations that already had been working toward conservation of natural resources. Darling hoped that Canada and Mexico would also participate in the new federation and that a spirit of ecological cooperation among the two countries and the United States would be fostered.

Darling was born in 1876 in Norwood, Michigan, where his father was a minister. His father's profession took the family to a number of different areas of the Midwest. This opportunity for travel allowed Darling to get a firsthand view of the region's geographic diversity and to observe the variety of changes that occur on its terrain. As a child, Darling took a great interest in his environment and was an admirer of John James Audubon, Gifford Pinchot, and other conservationists. He also enjoyed sketching, and when he entered college he became the art director of the Beloit College yearbook, where he gained notoriety for the caricatures he fashioned of the Beloit College faculty. Later, he distinguished himself as an artist who caricatured famous legislators and corporate chiefs who did not favor conservation efforts.

In 1900, Darling began his career as a cub reporter for the *Sioux City Journal*. He soon began drawing cartoons, many of which incorporated his hero, Theodore Roosevelt. By 1906, Darling had taken a position with the *Des Moines Register*. His first cartoon for the newspaper depicted a polluted Des Moines, Iowa. He left the *Des Moines Register* in 1911 for a brief stint at the *New York Globe*, but he returned to Des Moines and the *Register* two years later. He enjoyed the autonomy he was afforded at the Iowa paper, and his fans rewarded him with dedication to his work. He became so popular that the *Herald Tribune* syndicate issued Darling an offer that he could not refuse, and so he worked diligently for both papers. It was through his affiliation with the syndicate that Darling was able to gain fame nationwide. He used his popularity to draw cartoons that depicted the despoliation of the landscape as well as the damage caused to wildlife by lack of attention.

Darling's interest in conservation and his love of the outdoors led him to place pressure on the Iowa legislature to enact legislation creating an Iowa Fish and Game

Commission. He became a charter member of this commission and went on to exert his influence nationally as a delegate to the Republican National Convention in 1932. In 1934, President Franklin D. Roosevelt appointed Darling to a seat on a three-member commission whose mission was to study factors that threatened wildlife. The committee was named the Beck Committee in honor of the editor of *Collier's* magazine.

Recognition of the need for human attention to wildlife preservation was apparent and had received its first support in the nineteenth century. In the mid-nineteenth century, the New York State Game Protective Association was formed. At the same time, a number of naturalists began exhorting the public to find legal means to protect wildlife. In 1886, the New York Audubon Society was founded by George Bird Grinnell. The early efforts of the Audubon Society and similar organizations were aimed at hunters whose primary motive was to kill birds and other wildlife for the feathers or furs they yielded for market. In 1900, the first federal law regulating wildlife was passed. This legislation made it a violation to kill game for shipment in interstate commerce. In 1902, the International Association of Game, Fish, and Conservation Commissioners was formed. Toward the end of the nineteenth century, the growth of the wildlife refuge movement began. The first park designated as a refuge was Yellowstone National Park, which served as a haven for the last herd of buffalo residing in the nation. Subsequently, other national parks and forests were established as refuges.

Under President Theodore Roosevelt, the conservation movement began to evolve into a coherent national program. A number of federal bills were passed to regulate wildlife, and all received the overwhelming support of Roosevelt, who was an ardent lover of the outdoors. Roosevelt was instrumental in instituting a system of wildlife refuges. In 1908, he convened a conference of governors which dealt, in part, with preservation issues. This led the governors to go back to their home states and initiate agendas that included the establishment and expansion of state wildlife departments.

By 1911, attention began to be paid to the issue of protection for migratory game birds. In that year, an organization known as the American Game Protective and Propagation Association was formed; its main tasks involved the safeguarding of migratory game birds. This organization was responsible for drafting a number of pieces of federal legislation that were designed to give federal attention to pressing wildlife issues. Among the most important of these legislative concerns was the

1916 Migratory Bird Treaty, which was negotiated by President Woodrow Wilson and a representative from Great Britain. This treaty placed many species of birds under federal protection and banned the killing of sandpipers and shorebirds. It also gave migratory birds federal protection and invested the secretary of agriculture with the authority to regulate the hunting of game birds and gave the federal government authority to enforce the legislation.

During the 1920's, concentration was placed on the prevention of the depletion of the wetlands of waterfowl. This led to the realization that a concentrated effort would have to be made in order to provide safe refuges for waterfowl. Aldo Leopold, one of Jay Darling's co-commissioners on the Beck Committee, articulated the relationship between wildlife and its habitations, and this led to the concept of managed wildlife. As a result, the Upper Mississippi River National Wildlife and Fish Refuge Act was passed in 1924. The bill gave Congress the authority to buy bottomlands that would provide sanctuary to waterfowl. This act was followed in 1929 by the Norbeck-Andresen Act, which established a series of waterfowl refuges.

The Beck Committee met in 1934 in the wake of these accomplishments. The committee made a number of important recommendations, including the proposal to use lands that were considered less than optimal for other purposes as wildlife refuges. The committee also diverted money from other resources and used it to employ workers who performed many vital functions relevant to wildlife preservation. As a result of the work that Darling accomplished on the Beck Committee, Roosevelt asked him to head the Bureau of Biological Survey, which was the precursor to the U.S. Fish and Wildlife Service. Darling had been a critic of the Biological Survey and was ready for the task of reorganizing it. In doing so, he was careful to choose the most qualified researchers rather than naming political appointees. His accomplishments at the helm of the organization were considerable; they included the establishment of limits on the amount of hunting that could take place in certain areas, the elimination of the use of live decoys and other objectionable practices, and the procurement of cash resources for the preservation of wildlife.

Darling was also able to establish the Cooperative Wildlife Research Unit Program, a federal program similar to the one he had successfully established on the state level in Iowa. This project created a program of wildlife research and training for students attending land-grant colleges. Darling gained funding for this project by inviting a group of industrialists to a dinner at the Waldorf Astoria Hotel in New York. The financial backing that the program needed emerged from this monumental meeting, and so did ideas for a number of wildlife organizations, some of which soon materialized. Darling, for example, got the idea for the National Wildlife Federation from a similar organization that existed in Indiana. In that organization, local conservation clubs reported to county associations, which in turn were accountable to a state organization.

The historic North American Wildlife Conference took place in Washington, D.C., from February 3 to February 7, 1936. The delegates to the conference voted unanimously to form the General Wildlife Federation, the name of which was changed to the National Wildlife Federation in 1938. Darling directed this assembly, which included more than one thousand members, and was elected the temporary head of the new organization. The membership decided that the federation would become permanent once federations were established by the individual states. The purposes of the General Wildlife Federation were to assemble into one organization all who had an interest in the conservation and refurbishment of wildlife and other natural resources, to produce a policy designed to promote the conservation of wildlife, and to involve the public in a search for solutions to the problems that existed. The conference was considered an overwhelming success and led to a successful program of wildlife conservation.

The founding of the National Wildlife Federation changed the entire scope of the wildlife conservation movement, and the new group—under Darling's leadership—adopted a bold legislative agenda. Darling stressed to the organization's members that political action was necessary to achieve the goals set forth by the organization's constitution. At the first annual meeting of the organization in 1937, seven resolutions were passed, one of which led to the Pittman-Robertson Act, one of the most important pieces of wildlife legislation in U.S. history. This act served two important functions: It placed a federal excise tax on guns and ammunition and provided the state with funding to promote wildlife management. Among some of the other measures discussed at the annual meeting of the National Wildlife Federation were trapping restrictions, expansion of wildlife research, and national attention to the issue of water pollution. The delegates also voted to set aside one week per year to be known as National Wildlife Restoration Week. This week would bring the subject of wildlife preservation to the attention of the public, would help to educate

them concerning important conservation issues, and would raise money to fund these issues.

SIGNIFICANCE

National Wildlife Federation members have engaged in legislative activities to reach their goals, and their legislative triumphs have been numerous. For example, in 1947 the Federal Insecticide, Fungicide, and Rodenticide Act required the labeling of chemicals to avoid contamination of creatures not targeted by the chemicals. This was the first act to deal with the issue of toxins and their effects on the environment. In 1956, the Water Pollution Control Act stated that the federal government could designate funds to build water treatment plants. The 1963 Clean Air Act authorized the Department of Health, Education, and Welfare and the Environmental Protection Agency to take whatever action they deemed necessary to gain compliance with clean-air standards. In 1966, the Endangered Species Preservation Act set aside as much as $15 million to be used to encourage the breeding of certain endangered wildlife. This act was expanded in 1969. In 1972, the Clean Water Act established strict standards to control pollution of bodies of water in the United States. In 1986, the Superfund Reauthorization Act was passed; it set forth a timetable for the cleanup of toxic materials from accidents caused by human beings. This act also required chemical companies to report to the public any toxic emissions as well as a schedule for the alleviation of the problem of toxic emissions.

Over the years, the National Wildlife Federation has considered the education of the public to be its foremost aspiration and has worked toward that goal in many ways. National Wildlife Week, for example, serves as an educational tool. During that week, the organization distributes educational kits to schools throughout the country. Beginning in 1968, the National Wildlife Federation introduced a new character named Ranger Rick to its educational kit; this character has served an important function in educating children about the environment both through books and through *Ranger Rick's Nature Magazine*, a publication that came to symbolize the organization's recognition that the environmental issues of tomorrow are in the hands of today's children. In 1980, the National Wildlife Federation designed another publication for children who are not yet of reading age, and it continues to publish thousands of documents, books, pamphlets, and films aimed at diverse audiences.

Another important educational function of the National Wildlife Federation is served by the Conservation

1936

Summits, which began in 1970. These summits are educational vacations that provide entire families with the opportunity to learn more about the environment. Each year, hundreds of thousands of people are recipients of the fruits of the work of the National Wildlife Federation, which boasted four million members and supporters throughout the United States as of 2005.

—*Judy Arlis Chesen*

FURTHER READING

Allen, Thomas B. *Guardian of the Wild: The Story of the National Wildlife Federation*. Bloomington: Indiana University Press, 1987. Discusses the organization's founding in great detail, addressing its historical origins as well as the environmental conditions that led to the need for its establishment. Emphasizes the federation's position as an umbrella organization linking local and state conservation organizations.

Clepper, Henry, ed. *Origins of American Conservation*. New York: Ronald Press, 1966. Twelve conservationists trace the evolution of the conservation movement and illustrate the manner in which management of natural resources came about in order to address environmental issues such as wildlife regulation, soil, water, range, park, and aquatic preservation.

Cronon, William, ed. *Uncommon Ground: Rethinking the Human Place in Nature*. New York: W. W. Norton, 1996. Taken from a series of essays presented at the University of California at Irvine in 1994, this interesting volume examines modern conceptions of nature and its role in modern society. Useful for understanding the reasoning behind our views toward the natural world.

Lendt, David L. *Ding: The Life of Jay Norwood Darling*. Ames: Iowa State University Press, 1979. An insightful biography of cartoonist and conservationist Darling. It follows Darling from his boyhood in Michigan and Iowa through his six-decade association with the *Des Moines Register*. The biography successfully integrates Darling's career as a cartoonist with his environmental activities.

Nash, Roderick Frazier. *Wilderness and the American Mind*. 4th ed. New Haven, Conn.: Yale University Press, 2001. Brilliant intellectual history of Americans' relationship with the wilderness begins with the earliest days of European contact.

Norton, Bryan G., ed. *The Preservation of Species: The Value of Biological Diversity*. Princeton, N.J.: Princeton University Press, 1986. Collection of essays presents an interdisciplinary exploration of the reasons for conservation. The contributors go beyond scientific explanations of conservation of vanishing wildlife and delve into the philosophical issues that impact decision making with regard to endangered species.

Street, Philip. *Vanishing Animals: Preserving Nature's Rarities*. New York: E. P. Dutton, 1963. Discusses some of the causes of and solutions to the problem of diminishing species of certain animals throughout the world. Street discusses those varieties of wildlife remaining in the wild as well as those living in captivity.

SEE ALSO: Mar. 14, 1903: First U.S. National Wildlife Refuge Is Established; July 3, 1918: Migratory Bird Treaty Act; Jan., 1922: Izaak Walton League Is Formed; Mar. 16, 1934: Migratory Bird Hunting and Conservation Stamp Act; Oct. 19, 1934: Marshall and Leopold Form the Wilderness Society; Sept. 2, 1937: Pittman-Robertson Act Provides State Wildlife Funding; July 1, 1940: U.S. Fish and Wildlife Service Is Formed.

February 4, 1936
KEYNES PROPOSES GOVERNMENT MANAGEMENT OF THE ECONOMY

John Maynard Keynes revolutionized the field of economics when he proposed active government management of the economy through taxation, borrowing, and spending.

ALSO KNOWN AS: *The General Theory of Employment, Interest, and Money*
LOCALE: London, England
CATEGORIES: Government and politics; economics; publishing and journalism

KEY FIGURES

John Maynard Keynes (1883-1946), British economist
Richard Kahn (1905-1989), British economist who collaborated with Keynes
Joan Robinson (1903-1983), British economist and pupil of Keynes
Paul Samuelson (b. 1915), American economist whose undergraduate textbook was instrumental in spreading Keynes's ideas in the United States
Roy Harrod (1900-1978), British economist who helped Keynes develop the theories that culminated in Keynes's book
Ralph Hawtrey (1879-1975), British economist with whom Keynes discussed his new theory while writing his book
Alvin Hansen (1887-1975), American economist initially critical of the Keynesian revolution who later became one of the leading supporters of Keynes's theory
James Tobin (1918-2002), American economist who developed and refined Keynesian ideas
Milton Friedman (1912-2006), American economist critical of Keynesian economic theory and policy

SUMMARY OF EVENT

In 1936, John Maynard Keynes of the University of Cambridge in England published *The General Theory of Employment, Interest, and Money* (also known simply as *The General Theory*). Undoubtedly the most influential book on economics written in the twentieth century, Keynes's monograph touched off what has come to be called the Keynesian revolution. It provided a new theoretical structure for dealing with the aggregate economy, a structure that revolutionized both economic theory and policy. No other book, not even Adam Smith's *The Wealth of Nations* (1776) or Karl Marx's *Das Kapital* (1867, 1885-1894), had such an impact on economic theory and policy.

The General Theory was published at a critical juncture in the history of Western civilization. In the early 1930's, the world was in the midst of the Great Depression, the most sweeping economic catastrophe of modern times. As the Depression deepened, millions of people were thrown out of work. In the United States, from 1929 through 1932 more than eighty-five thousand businesses failed, more than five thousand banks suspended operations, farm income fell by more than half, manufacturing output decreased by almost half, and the unemployment rate increased to 25 percent. The Depression came at a time when natural resources were still plentiful. Thousands of factories stood idle or operated far below capacity, and workers had the same skills as they had in better times and wanted to put them to work. The U.S. economy and other economies clearly were able to produce, yet millions of people begged, borrowed, stole, and lined up for charity. The widespread social unrest caused by mass unemployment also threatened the viability of democratic institutions. The appeals of communism and fascism gained strength. A totalitarian government took power in Italy, and the National Socialist Party was on its way to taking power in Germany. Many people thought that this was the end of capitalism and that Karl Marx's predictions regarding socialism's inevitability were coming true.

The Depression was a mystery that posed problems that no one knew how to overcome. Conventional economics suggested that further wage cuts were necessary in order to allow more people to be hired, but this approach aggravated the malaise instead of relieving it. Even workers who had jobs barely supported themselves, and because they had low incomes they could not buy things produced by other workers. The appearance of *The General Theory* provided both a revolutionary explanation of the problem and theoretically supported solutions within a democratic framework, thus offering potential solutions to the burning political, economic, and social problems.

The central idea of *The General Theory* is that policy planners cannot rely on free markets to maintain full employment in the economy. The self-correcting features of the system are too weak to do that. Modern capitalist economies may be plagued by unemployment because of a deficiency of aggregate demand (the total of planned spending by consumers, investors, and the government). Some products may remain unsold because no one wants to buy them. Paradoxically, this problem gets worse as a society becomes affluent, because consumers have a tendency to

1936

FROM *THE GENERAL THEORY*

In chapter 12 of The General Theory, *Keynes considers the obstacles faced by the average investor:*

There is one feature in particular which deserves our attention. It might have been supposed that competition between expert professionals, possessing judgment and knowledge beyond that of the average private investor, would correct the vagaries of the ignorant individual left to himself. It happens, however, that the energies and skill of the professional investor and speculator are mainly occupied otherwise. For most of these persons are, in fact, largely concerned, not with making superior long-term forecasts of the probable yield of an investment over its whole life, but with foreseeing changes in the conventional basis of valuation a short time ahead of the general public. They are concerned, not with what an investment is really worth to a man who buys it "for keeps," but with what the market will value it at, under the influence of mass psychology, three months or a year hence. Moreover, this behaviour is not the outcome of a wrong-headed propensity. It is an inevitable result of an investment market organised along the lines described. For it is not sensible to pay 25 for an investment of which you believe the prospective yield to justify a value of 30, if you also believe that the market will value it at 20 three months hence.

Thus the professional investor is forced to concern himself with the anticipation of impending changes, in the news or in the atmosphere, of the kind by which experience shows that the mass psychology of the market is most influenced. This is the inevitable result of investment markets organised with a view to so-called "liquidity." Of the maxims of orthodox finance none, surely, is more anti-social than the fetish of liquidity, the doctrine that it is a positive virtue on the part of investment institutions to concentrate their resources upon the holding of "liquid" securities. It forgets that there is no such thing as liquidity of investment for the community as a whole. The social object of skilled investment should be to defeat the dark forces of time and ignorance which envelop our future. The actual, private object of the most skilled investment today is "to beat the gun," as the Americans so well express it, to outwit the crowd, and to pass the bad, or depreciating, half-crown to the other fellow.

This battle of wits to anticipate the basis of conventional valuation a few months hence, rather than the prospective yield of an investment over a long term of years, does not even require gulls amongst the public to feed the maws of the professional;—it can be played by professionals amongst themselves. Nor is it necessary that anyone should keep his simple faith in the conventional basis of valuation having any genuine long-term validity. For it is, so to speak, a game of Snap, of Old Maid, of Musical Chairs—a pastime in which he is victor who says Snap neither too soon nor too late, who passes the Old Maid to his neighbour before the game is over, who secures a chair for himself when the music stops. These games can be played with zest and enjoyment, though all the players know that it is the Old Maid which is circulating, or that when the music stops some of the players will find themselves unseated.

Source: John Maynard Keynes, *The General Theory of Employment, Interest, and Money* (New York: Harcourt, Brace, 1936).

devote an increasing percentage of their income to saving rather than to consumption. This tendency to save more will not create difficulties as long as savings are channeled, via financial markets, into an equivalent amount of investment spending on factories and equipment. There is no mechanism, however, to guarantee that every dollar saved will be converted to an equivalent amount of investment. Thus, if there is not enough investment spending to absorb the increased saving, the result will be unemployment as firms begin to produce less. An economy can get stuck in such a position, according to *The General Theory.*

Keynes argued that aggregate demand (especially investment) is inherently unstable and that government must pick up the slack when necessary. Thus when business activity falls and there is substantial unemployment, the government should increase its expenditures or reduce taxes (or perhaps both); during periods of prosperity it should do the opposite. Such active intervention offered the possibility of maintaining full employment.

The General Theory was the product of Keynes's involvement in the economic problems of the Western world in the 1920's and 1930's. The roots of his ideas can be traced back to before the 1929 stock market crash that signaled the beginning of the Depression. Keynes's *Indian Currency and Finance* (1913) was a contribution to understanding the functioning of economies with gold exchange standards, but it was his *The Economic Consequences of the Peace* (1919) that brought him international fame. In it, he questioned the widely accepted modes of thought about war reparations and war debt and presented a vivid examination of an extraordinary episode of laissez-faire capitalism. A later book, *A Tract on Monetary Reform* (1923), was written in response to the monetary disorder following World War I, and it was followed by *A Treatise on Money* (1930), which contained a comprehensive exposition of monetary theory and policy.

Keynes's preface to the Japanese edition

of *A Treatise on Money*, dated April 5, 1932, was possibly the first public intimation of the ideas to appear in *The General Theory*. Keynes's correspondence and discussion with economists Joan Robinson, Roy Harrod, Richard Kahn, Ralph Hawtrey, and others give indications that he began writing the book in the summer of 1932. These economists also played crucial roles in the origin and development of the book, as Keynes made extensive revisions based on their feedback and circulated drafts among the group. On October 10, 1932, Keynes began the first of his eight lectures for the fall term. He changed the title of these lectures from "The Pure Theory of Money" to "The Monetary Theory of Production" and in effect announced the beginning of the Keynesian revolution.

In a letter to playwright and philosopher George Bernard Shaw in 1935, Keynes wrote that the book he was then writing on economic theory would revolutionize the way the world thinks about economic problems. His prophecy was amply fulfilled. *The General Theory* is a technical, theoretical book addressed to the economics profession, and economists hotly debated the merits of Keynes's theory and policy prescriptions. Although

John Maynard Keynes. (Library of Congress)

Keynes's ideas did not gain instantaneous acceptance, it was not long before the book became the gospel of an ardent group of followers. Within a short time, the ideas and analytic techniques of *The General Theory* stimulated what came to be called the Keynesian revolution.

The timing of the publication had much to do with the book's acceptance. The protracted unemployment of the 1930's cast doubts on the viability of laissez-faire capitalism, and *The General Theory* offered a theoretically justified plan to retain capitalism, although with significant active government participation. With the outbreak of World War II, unemployment problems began to melt away. Increased government expenditures during the war transformed severe unemployment to shortages of labor. The war experience suggested that Keynes's ideas were correct: A government's wise use of taxation, borrowing, and spending can move an economy to full employment.

The book can be credited with giving intellectual justification to the notion that an economy can be and perhaps should be managed to smooth out fluctuations in output and employment. To Keynes and his followers, a balanced economy is more important than a balanced budget. Specific recommendations to tackle an economic depression were maintenance of low interest rates through central control, redistribution of wealth through taxation, and augmentation of insufficient private investment by government spending. For these policy prescriptions, Keynes was accused of being both a left-wing ideologue as well as a defender of imperialist capitalism. Keynes always claimed that his intention was to save capitalism, not to destroy it.

The publication of *The General Theory* coincided with the development of quantitative economic data on employment, the gross national product and various related income categories, consumer spending, and savings and investment. These data made it possible for analysts to test macroeconomic relationships empirically. The various concepts discussed in *The General Theory* were widely incorporated into the economics profession and created the modern macroeconomics that still forms the basis of what is taught in undergraduate macroeconomics courses throughout the world. Policy implications were widely adopted to provide the tax, expenditure, and debt management agendas of most countries.

Keynesian economics achieved its greatest influence in the United States during the 1960's. One of the longest unbroken economic expansions in American history occurred in the period 1961-1968, during which time the members of the Council of Economic Advisers were

1936

Keynesian almost without exception. They promoted tax cuts that coincided with increased prosperity, as expected by Keynesian logic. During the 1970's, however, Keynesian economics failed to provide a satisfactory answer to the twin problems of high unemployment and high inflation. Keynesian economics has often been criticized for ignoring inflation. Economists such as Milton Friedman generated a counterrevolution in economics in the 1970's, claiming that government is not wise enough to manage the economy along Keynesian lines and recommending that government's influence in the economy should be kept to a minimum. The views of Friedman and other economists (referred to as monetarists) have also become widely accepted. Data do not yet exist to prove either Keynesian or monetarist theory correct; the principles underlying both schools of thought are widely believed and taught. However, the gradual globalization of the international economy and fluid movements of capital by private banks and corporations across national boundaries have inhibited the ability of governments to control the money supply strictly through centralized monetary policy. Supply-side economists have also pointed out that fiscal approaches that seek to control inflationary periods by raising taxes hurt business activity, leading to declining revenue. According to proponents of this school of thought, low and lower taxes are always better for economic growth and generation of government revenue.

SIGNIFICANCE

The General Theory's revolutionary impact on the field of economics and on the general public can be seen in the speed with which the policies advocated in it were incorporated into government planning. Many of the measures instituted during the later years of the New Deal were Keynesian in origin. Franklin D. Roosevelt, by his second presidential term (1937-1941), had come to embrace deficit spending as a necessary condition of prosperity. He recommended resumption of lending to increase aggregate demand. In 1946, the U.S. Congress passed the Employment Act, which legally (although in vague terms) obligated the government to maintain high levels of employment. The president's Council of Economic Advisers and the Joint Economic Committee in Congress were created to fulfill this mandate.

In Great Britain, *The General Theory*'s influence was clearly demonstrated in the 1941 budget and the coalition government's White Paper on Employment (1944), which made a strong commitment to full employment as a public policy. By the end of World War II, Canada,

New Zealand, Australia, Sweden, and South Africa had accepted national responsibility for achieving high levels of employment. Similar concepts of economic management were embodied in the new French constitution of 1946, in the Charter of the United Nations, and in the Treaty of Rome.

Keynesian economics found success because it offered something to almost everyone. Labor liked the government's support during economic depressions, businesses benefited from government contracts, banks found profitable areas for investment in government bonds, and government control gave the banking system liquidity, security, and stability. Reformers and intellectuals enjoyed increased employment in the government services and influence on government policies.

—*Baban Hasnat*

FURTHER READING

Blaug, Mark. *John Maynard Keynes: Life, Ideas, Legacy.* New York: St. Martin's Press, 1990. An excellent book for general readers and beginning students of economics.

Clarke, Peter. *The Keynesian Revolution in the Making, 1924-1936.* New York: Oxford University Press, 2006. Provides a historical account of Keynes's thought leading to publication of *The General Theory.* Good for those interested in economic history.

Hamouda, Omar F., and John N. Smithin, eds. *Economics and Policy.* Vol. 2 in *Keynes and Public Policy After Fifty Years.* New York: New York University Press, 1988. Covers a wide range of topics. Part 1 concerns public policy in Great Britain and the United States, with some discussion of Keynes.

Harrod, Roy F. *The Life of John Maynard Keynes.* New York: St. Martin's Press, 1963. A definitive biography of Keynes. Chapter 11 provides letters written by Keynes and to Keynes on the theory and policy articulated in *The General Theory.*

Kahn, Richard F. *The Making of Keynes' "General Theory."* New York: Cambridge University Press, 1984. Collection of lectures on the book by an economist closely associated with Keynes. Valuable insights into the making of the book are given in lectures four and five; Keynes's relations with other economists are discussed in lecture six.

Lekachman, Robert, ed. *Keynes' "General Theory": Reports of Three Decades.* New York: St. Martin's Press, 1964. Part 1 contains Austin Robinson's excellent discussion of Keynes's life and ideas.

Moggridge, Donald E. *John Maynard Keynes.* New

York: Penguin Books, 1976. Suitable for both economists and noneconomists. Provides a simple exposition of Keynes's ideas, his work, and his influence.

Skidelsky, Robert. *John Maynard Keynes, 1883-1946: Economist, Philosopher, Statesman.* New York: Penguin Books, 2005. Abridged version of Skidelsky's three-volume biography of Keynes. Although biased toward his subject, Skidelsky forcefully argues that

Keynes was a visionary who changed the course of economic theory.

SEE ALSO: Aug. 14, 1935: Roosevelt Signs the Social Security Act; Aug. 23, 1935: Banking Act of 1935 Centralizes U.S. Monetary Control; Aug. 17, 1937: Miller-Tydings Act Legalizes Retail Price Maintenance.

February 17, 1936
CORPORATISM COMES TO PARAGUAY

A regime came to power in Paraguay that offered a program with recognizably corporate elements. Corporatism accorded more power to small, often professional groups, but internal struggles made the experiment short-lived.

LOCALE: Asunción, Paraguay
CATEGORY: Government and politics

KEY FIGURES

Rafael Franco (1896-1973), leader of the Febrerista Party and president, 1936 and 1937

Carlos Antonio López (1790-1862), president of Paraguay, 1844-1862, and father of Francisco Solano López

Francisco Solano López (1827-1870), president of Paraguay, 1862-1870

José Gaspar Rodríguez de Francia (1766-1840), supreme dictator of Paraguay, 1814-1840

José Félix Estigarribia (1888-1940), hero of the Chaco War, ambassador to the United States, and president of Paraguay, 1939 and 1940

Higinio Morínigo (1897-1983), Paraguayan military leader and president, 1940-1948

Juan Stefanich (1889-1976), politician, journalist, novelist, and essayist whose writings provided the ideological base for the Febrerista Party

Bernardino Caballero (1839-1912), founder of the Asociación Nacional Republicana (Colorado Party) and president from 1880 to 1886

SUMMARY OF EVENT

Colonel Rafael Franco's takeover of the Paraguayan government on February 17, 1936, was a response to Paraguay's long history of dictatorial regimes and disregard for the needs of the peasant class. Franco and his Febrerista party represented themselves as nationalist

socialists ready to introduce democratic reforms, and Franco's military coup was a step in the turbulent progression of Paraguayan politics.

When Paraguay emerged as an independent nation in 1811, it was as an isolated buffer state separating Argentina and Brazil. At the time, Paraguay was under the despotic control of one man, José Gaspar Rodríguez de Francia, and it continued to have essentially one-man rule until the last decade of the twentieth century. Francia, called "El Supremo," was the driving force behind both Paraguayan independence and the establishment of Paraguay's political parameters. Francia became indispensable to the governing of the state and ensured that no reasonable alternative to his rule existed. Those few individuals who dared to suggest otherwise found themselves in prison or the cemetery.

As Paraguay's leader, Francia focused the nation's resources on the creation and maintenance of a strong army to defend the borders of his hermit kingdom. The state drafted not only the manpower of the nation but also its economy. The peasants worked as sharecroppers on land leased from the state, state-controlled industries supplied the military and civilian markets, and production and trade were closely regulated. Francia's policies brought a considerable measure of prosperity to Paraguay, but they also denied the people fundamental political freedoms.

El Supremo designated no political heir, but ultimately Carlos Antonio López seized control in 1844, after a period of political chaos following Francia's death in 1840. The political autocracy and state-run socialism initiated by Francia continued, but López did moderate the regime's rigor. After the death of Carlos Antonio López in 1862, the government of Paraguay was entrusted to his son, Francisco Solano López, whose character and intentions remain a subject of historical controversy. He is variously viewed as a barbaric egomaniac who sacrificed his countrymen in pursuit of grandiose schemes and as the quintessential patriot who bravely fell in battle against foreign imperialism.

The true Francisco Solano López is obscure, but the consequences of the war he presided over—and was killed in—are not subject to dispute. The end of the War of the Triple Alliance (1864-1870) found more than half the population of Paraguay dead and the economy in ruins. The struggle between Brazil and Argentina for regional supremacy almost destroyed Paraguay, but the process allowed Paraguay to avoid absorption. Moreover, the government imposed by Brazil and Argentina

was, within a short time, overthrown by Bernardino Caballero's successful appeal to antiforeign sentiments engendered by the postwar occupation.

Unfortunately, General Caballero inherited an empty treasury from his predecessors. He saw little choice but to continue the sale of the extensive state enterprises begun by the occupation governments. Foreign corporations established feudal enclaves (*latifundios*) throughout the nation and subjected the peasantry to merciless exploitation. As a result, the prospects of a broadly based representative political system that surfaced at the end of the war vanished without a trace.

The Chaco War, a boundary dispute with Bolivia, lasted three bloody years (1932-1935), diverted enormous amounts of manpower and resources from Paraguay's economy, and caused significant numbers of casualties. Although the peace treaty confirmed Paraguay's control of twenty thousand square miles of the Chaco, the victory cost the nation two dead per square mile, a casualty rate that many Paraguayans attributed to the failure of the Paraguayan government to adequately prepare for war.

The government was further indicted for its inability to sponsor meaningful reforms in the structure of Paraguayan society. Land reform was first on the list of demands, followed by improvements in the standard of living, the public welfare services, and working conditions, in addition to the reform of an educational system that was probably the poorest in Latin America. As was the case throughout most of Latin America in the period before World War II, the landowning aristocracy reaped the benefits of governmental power, and the middle class was largely nonexistent. Paraguay, in short, was in need of renovation and redemption, if not revolution.

Colonel Rafael Franco, a prominent figure in the Chaco War, organized a group within the Paraguayan military to stage a coup that took place on February 17, 1936. Once in power, the revolutionaries deemed it necessary to present themselves as more than simply another junta of discontented officers. Therefore,

PARAGUAY, 1936

the nation was informed that Paraguay would adopt a more democratic version of the nationalistic socialism of the Francia-López era. A serious attempt to encourage the growth of small and medium-sized landholdings was undertaken, and regional agricultural schools, agricultural experiment farms, and a bank for low-cost agricultural loans were proposed. Equally important, a labor department was created, and a moderately progressive labor code was promulgated.

The official goal of the revolution was a "natural democracy" of peasants and workers, a regime that would identify and utilize the best parts of individualistic democracy, corporatism, and socialism in order to provide benefits to the whole of the Paraguayan people. Colonel Franco repeatedly indicated his opposition to the total transplantation of any foreign system to Paraguay. His Mussolini-like speeches from a balcony in Asunción, however, led some to characterize his government as the first manifestation of fascism in Latin America.

The ideological hero of many in the new regime was Juan Stefanich. Stefanich found little appeal in either laissez-faire capitalism or Marxist socialism. He saw the former as at fault for the worldwide depression and the latter as a path to a totalitarian, Soviet-style state. Like countries as diverse as Portugal, Ireland, and Italy, Stefanich's Paraguay sought salvation in what he termed *democracia solidarista*, which was an attempt to organize the state along corporate models and thereby accord power to professional and occupational groups. Stefanich espoused corporatism, but the Franco regime remained a mixture of political and ideological opposites. These diverse elements (corporatism, socialism, and traditional political partisanship) struggled for control of a revolution that came to power without a central theme, and this internal conflict assisted those who supported a counterrevolution. The Febreristas, as supporters of Colonel Franco were later named, were replaced on August 15, 1937, by a group who gave only lip service to the new governmental programs.

The Febreristas were overthrown for several reasons. They promised land and better social conditions but were unable to undertake anything more than symbolic implementation. Labor was "liberated" through the creation of the National Department of Labor, which defined labor's rights and privileges, but there was only enough time for strikes and turmoil, not the requisite negotiations between the workers and management. A decree authorizing the expropriation of land was promulgated, but the land reform program was only a beginning and was not continued by the new regime. Effective land reform—

indeed, reform of almost any kind—would be difficult as long as the country was dominated by foreign capital in league with an upper class wedded to the status quo. Despite the renewed power of the old order, the promises of the Febreristas continued to attract support, a circumstance that explains the emergence of José Félix Estigarribia. General Estigarribia, a hero of the Chaco War, ran for and won the presidency in 1939. He was a popular candidate whose speeches indicated a decided preference for many of the Febrerista ideas.

SIGNIFICANCE

Traditionally, most Latin Americans insisted that unity, not diversity, was key to political success. Latin American governments thus generally eschewed attempts to balance competing centers of power and attempt to integrate or eliminate them in the name of collective harmony. The idea that two competing ideologies might barter or negotiate for anything less than total victory was anathema.

Paraguay was operating under two vastly different concepts of legitimate government: the Francia-López tradition of autocratic state socialism and the democratic free enterprise liberalism of the postwar decades. Febrerismo attempted to fuse these opposing principles by recourse to corporatism. The objective of the Febreristas was not a totalitarian state but a "perfected" democratic regime. The state was not to serve as a policeman; instead, it would regulate and defend society. The state would intervene to solve political, social, and economic problems, and national interests would take precedence over individual interests. Thus *democracia solidarista* differed from totalitarianism in that the latter places the state first and fits individuals into a pattern that subordinates and even denies their liberties. The Febreristas, however, recognized individual liberties and tried to reconcile them with collective or group rights.

The Febrerista experiment was cut short, but the pressure for reform remained undiminished. Thus the new Estigarribia government scrapped the Constitution of 1870 and replaced it with a new instrument approved by plebiscite on August 4, 1940. The new constitution envisaged a powerful chief executive assisted by an advisory council composed of representatives from business, banking, the church, education, the government, agriculture, processing industries, and the military. The council was designed to oversee an "orderly democracy," in which the government had extensive powers to intervene in the economy. Furthermore, the president might declare a state of siege and thereby acquire virtual dictatorial powers. Corporatism fell into disrepute at the end of

1936

World War II, because it was often confused with fascism. They are, however, very different: The latter involves a leadership principle, a mass political party, and an aggressive foreign policy that are not characteristic of the former. Colonel Franco and those elected in accord with the Constitution of 1940 might have resembled the fascist dictators of the prewar decades, but they owed more to Francia and the Lópezes than to Hitler or Mussolini.

Despite their reverence for ideological accord, some Latin American governments ruled in the name of the whole by integrating diverse interests. Others governed in the name of a privileged part of that whole by excluding or eliminating representatives of the less privileged. The government of Paraguay, despite its corporate pretensions, adhered more to the latter model than to the former. These general patterns of Latin American politics persisted until the last quarter of the twentieth century, when, beginning around 1980, the trend shifted toward the emergence of a more pluralist political life, competitive parties and elections, and the resolution, in Central America, of long-standing civil wars, which permitted the exploration of more stable democratic forms of government. From Mexico to Chile, a more vibrant and competitive party politics emerged, and the old-style authoritarian governments of the past, although not everywhere eclipsed, were no longer the norm. Democratization gradually spread throughout Latin America, as it had during the same period in the world at large. Paraguay was one of the countries that joined this democratic bandwagon, and although it later experienced some political turmoil (including the assassination of its vice president in March of 1999 and the 2003 impeachment of President Luis González Macchi), the country has been able to operate under a democratic constitution and maintain a lively and very competitive multiparty system that demands coalition government.

—*J. K. Sweeney*

FURTHER READING

Alexander, Robert J. *A History of Organized Labor in Uruguay and Paraguay*. Westport, Conn.: Praeger, 2005. A thorough analysis of the historical relationships among labor, political leaders, and the economy in these South American countries.

Kolinski, Charles J. *Historical Dictionary of Paraguay*. Metuchen, N.J.: Scarecrow Press, 1973. The only reference work of this type on Paraguay. It is not encyclopedic in its coverage, but it does contain a useful multilingual bibliography.

_____. *Independence or Death: The Story of the Paraguayan War*. Gainesville: University of Florida Press, 1965. The only work in English on this important event in the history of Paraguay. Essential to any understanding of the country's political history or prospects for the future.

Leuchars, Chris. *Paraguay and the Bitter End: Paraguay and the War of the Triple Alliance*. Westport, Conn.: Greenwood Press, 2005. Focuses on Paraguay's role in the war, its direction under the leadership of Francisco Solano López, and the war's long-term effects on Paraguay's relations with Brazil, Uruguay, and Argentina.

Lewis, Paul. *Paraguay Under Stroessner*. Chapel Hill: University of North Carolina Press, 1980. Although this monograph is primarily concerned with a political analysis of the long regime of Alfredo Stroessner (president from 1954-1989), the author places considerable emphasis on discussion of Paraguayan politics in the decades before Stroessner's rise to power.

_____. *The Politics of Exile*. Chapel Hill: University of North Carolina Press, 1965. A behavioral analysis of the Febrerista party's organization. The only work in English on the topic, it analyzes the workings of the party, its ideology, its formal organization, and the pattern of relationships among the leaders.

Rouguié, Alain. *The Military and the State in Latin America*. Berkeley: University of California Press, 1987. This comparative analysis places Paraguay within the context of the entire continent.

Warren, Harris G. *Paraguay: An Informal History*. Norman: University of Oklahoma Press, 1949. The seminal work in English on the subject. The bibliographic essay is basic.

_____. "Political Aspects of the Paraguayan Revolution, 1936-1940." *Hispanic American Historical Review* 30 (February, 1950): 2-25 . This is the only historical treatment of this event in English. It is heavily footnoted and invaluable, although dated.

Zook, David H. *The Conduct of the Chaco War*. New York: Bookman Associates, 1960. The definitive English monograph on a conflict that influenced twentieth century Paraguay to the same degree as the War of the Triple Alliance affected the previous century.

SEE ALSO: Dec. 2-5, 1902: Founding of the International Sanitary Bureau; Dec. 14, 1922: Oil Is Discovered in Venezuela; June 3-Aug. 28, 1929: Tacna-Arica Compromise; Mar. 4, 1933-1945: Good Neighbor Policy; Dec., 1936: Inter-American Conference for the Maintenance of Peace.

March 7, 1936
GERMAN TROOPS MARCH INTO THE RHINELAND

Having already successfully violated armament provisions of the 1919 Treaty of Versailles, Adolf Hitler embarked on his first great gamble: moving his troops into the Rhineland frontier toward France. The French government, torn by internal debate over how best to respond, was unable to secure backing from Britain in support of intervention against this move and consequently allowed Germany again to flout post-World War I peace accords.

LOCALE: Germany; France; Great Britain
CATEGORIES: Military history; diplomacy and international relations; wars, uprisings, and civil unrest; government and politics; World War II

KEY FIGURES
Adolf Hitler (1889-1945), chancellor of Germany, 1933-1945
Werner von Blomberg (1878-1946), German field marshal and minister of war, 1935-1938
Werner von Fritsch (1880-1939), German general and commander of the German army, 1935-1938
Albert Sarraut (1872-1962), prime minister of France, 1936
Pierre-Étienne Flandin (1889-1958), French foreign minister, 1936
Maurice Gamelin (1872-1958), French general and chief of the general staff, 1935-1940
Winston Churchill (1874-1965), British parliamentarian and advocate of intervention against Germany
Stanley Baldwin (1867-1947), prime minister of Great Britain, 1923-1924, 1924-1929, and 1935-1937
Benito Mussolini (1883-1945), prime minister and dictator of Italy, 1922-1943

SUMMARY OF EVENT
From 1918 to 1930, the German Rhineland was occupied by Allied—mainly French—troops. After this

period, in accordance with the provisions of the Treaty of Versailles of 1919 and the Locarno Treaties of 1925, the area was to be permanently demilitarized. Through his early official foreign policy statements, German chancellor Adolf Hitler indicated support for the Rhineland demilitarization and the settlements at Versailles and Locarno, but his domestic statements to the German people carried a different message. At home, Hitler made no secret of his contempt for the treaties' provisions and of his determination to undo the settlement one provision at a time. Upon gaining power on January 30, 1933, Hitler launched what was at first a clandestine buildup of German military power. As time went on, this became a more overt campaign that clearly violated the military limitations set forth in the Versailles treaty. As Hitler continued to push his boundaries, he encountered no effective opposition from other European powers or from the United States.

THE RHINELAND

German troops enter the demilitarized zone of the Rhineland, breaking the Treaty of Versailles. (Hulton Archive/Getty Images)

Prior to 1936, Hitler had limited himself to internal rearmament, but by March of that year he was poised to embark on a riskier, much more aggressive project: the reoccupation of the Rhineland by German troops. A rift had developed between Italy and its former allies France and Britain over Italian dictator Benito Mussolini's decision to attack Ethiopia in 1935, an action that had been condemned by the French and British governments. Hitler saw an opportunity to profit from this disagreement by making his move at a time when the erstwhile Allies were unlikely to cooperate with one another. Hitler's secret plan for remilitarizing the Rhineland was opposed by Minister of War Werner von Blomberg and Commander General Werner von Fritsch, who argued that the German army was vastly inferior to the French army and that any military intervention by France would have to be met by a quick and humiliating retreat that would probably prove fatal to the Nazi regime.

Although Blomberg and Fritsch might be right, Hitler conceded, he was convinced that the British and French leadership would not intervene because they were desperate to avoid renewing the horrors of trench warfare that had been a hallmark of World War I. Appeasement and national self-interest, he believed, would prevail over any desire to enforce international agreements. Furthermore, Hitler argued, Mussolini was unlikely to mend his relationships with Britain and France.

On March 7, 1936, a small contingent of German troops—estimated at no more than thirty-five thousand—marched across the line of demarcation and began to garrison the Rhineland all the way to the French border. The orders from Blomberg, however, were to retire immediately in the event of any French advance across the German border. Hitler insisted that his intentions were strictly nonaggressive and driven by concerns for German national security. Moreover, he said, recent

French diplomatic overtures to the Soviet Union had violated the Locarno Treaties, and Germany was therefore freed from the terms of those agreements.

Prime Minister Albert Sarraut and Foreign Minister Pierre-Étienne Flandin of France favored an instant and overwhelming military response. However, they were countered by General Maurice Gamelin, who warned that war with the Germans could be perilous, even though the French army numbered 1.5 million soldiers. Gamelin ordered only thirteen divisions and some tanks into a defensive position near the German border. The debate between Sarraut and Gamelin divided and paralyzed the French government, and Flandin was dispatched to London on March 11, where he tried to convince the British to help repel the Germans.

Flandin's diplomatic mission was a total failure; he could garner support only from Winston Churchill, who was adamant that Germany's rearmament and aggressive defiance of the Versailles provisions were threats to future world peace. Churchill argued that Hitler must be stopped before he gained so much strength that another global conflict would be required to prevent him from attaining world control. However, at this time Churchill was a shunned and ignored political figure, even within the ranks of his own Conservative Party. The real power in Britain lay with Prime Minister Stanley Baldwin, who had scant knowledge of (and even less interest in) foreign affairs. Baldwin believed that Britain and the British public were unready for war and did not think that the nation should take even the smallest risk of another conflict like World War I. Diplomatically abandoned, the French government was not willing to make further moves, and Germany's rearmament in the Rhineland was allowed to stand unchallenged.

SIGNIFICANCE

Hitler's assessment of the Allies' war-weary state and their lack of will to enforce the Versailles provisions proved to be shrewd, timely, and accurate. The German army would soon build a formidable network of fortifications known as the Siegfried line, which facilitated German aggression in the region by preventing any Anglo-French efforts to safeguard the integrity of smaller Eastern European states such as Austria and Czechoslovakia. The setback further demoralized the French, who became increasingly defense-oriented and obsessed with dependence on the Maginot line.

Internationally and domestically, Hitler's prestige rose as a result of this triumph, and he was able to secure greater control over Germany's armed forces. Blomberg

and Fritsch were undermined, and they were relieved of their posts in 1938. The Nazi seizure of military control over the Rhineland set into motion a campaign of "racial purity" against the so-called Rhineland bastards (the offspring of German women and African or Southeast Asian soldiers stationed in the area during France's garrisoning of the Rhineland). These children and adolescents were persecuted and in many cases sterilized.

—*Raymond Pierre Hylton*

FURTHER READING

Churchill, Winston S. *Memories of World War II*. Boston: Houghton Mifflin, 1987. In his assessment of the events of 1936, Churchill views the Rhineland occupation as one of the most significant steps to World War II, and he chides his Conservative Party colleagues for failing predict later developments.

Eimerl, Sarel. *Hitler over Europe: The Road to World War II*. Boston: Little, Brown, 1972. The author sees a paranoid fear on the part of the Western Allies as the most significant element behind the success of Hitler's military and diplomatic coup.

Kershaw, Ian. *Hitler, 1889-1945: Hubris*. New York: W. W. Norton, 1999. The Rhineland rearmament is viewed as the triumphant capstone of Hitler's early political career and the springboard for his more aggressive global initiatives.

Redlich, Fritz. *Hitler: Diagnosis of a Destructive Prophet*. New York: Oxford University Press, 1999. Although mainly a behavioral study, this book does focus some attention on the Rhineland reoccupation as a psychological milestone in the Nazi dictator's obsessive quest for power.

Shirer, William L. *The Rise and Fall of the Third Reich: A History of Nazi Germany*. 30th anniversary ed. New York: Ballantine, 1991. Classic account of Hitler's rise and fall; extremely detailed. Credits the success of the Rhineland occupation to Hitler's iron nerve and instinct for bluffing.

SEE ALSO: Jan. 30, 1933: Hitler Comes to Power in Germany; Feb. 27, 1933: Reichstag Fire; June 30-July 2, 1934: Great Blood Purge; Nov. 25, 1936: Germany and Japan Sign the Anti-Comintern Pact; Feb. 12-Apr. 10, 1938: The Anschluss; Sept. 29-30, 1938: Munich Conference; Nov. 9-10, 1938: Kristallnacht; 1939-1945: Nazi Extermination of the Jews; Aug. 23-24, 1939: Nazi-Soviet Pact; Sept. 1, 1939: Germany Invades Poland.

1936

March 11, 1936
BOULDER DAM IS COMPLETED

Completion of Boulder Dam provided irrigation, municipal water, flood control, and abundant power, but it also catalyzed great environmental and economic change.

ALSO KNOWN AS: Hoover Dam
LOCALE: California; Nevada; Arizona
CATEGORIES: Environmental issues; natural resources; engineering; energy

KEY FIGURES

Henry J. Kaiser (1882-1967), American industrialist and leading figure in the Six Companies consortium
Elwood Mead (1858-1936), American commissioner of reclamation
Ray Lyman Wilbur (1875-1949), president of Stanford University and U.S. secretary of the interior
Herbert Hoover (1874-1964), U.S. secretary of commerce and federal representative to the Colorado River Commission
Philip D. Swing (1884-1963), U.S. congressman from California
Oliver M. Wozencraft (1814-1887), physician, promoter, and member of the California Constitutional Convention and the first state legislature
Frank Crowe (1882-1946), civil engineer who was superintendent of construction for Boulder Dam
Arthur Powell Davis (1861-1933), hydrographer and engineer who directed the Reclamation Service in initial stages of development of Boulder Dam
Walker Young (1884-1982), engineer who represented the Bureau of Reclamation on the scene as construction engineer and led preliminary tests of sites in Boulder and Black Canyons

SUMMARY OF EVENT

Boulder Dam (also called Hoover Dam after 1947) was officially accepted by Secretary of the Interior Harold Ickes on March 11, 1936. On completion, the dam was the world's highest and largest, rising 727 feet above bedrock and containing more than 3 million cubic yards of concrete. The Grand Coulee Dam, completed in 1942, surpassed it with more than 10 million cubic yards of concrete, and the Mauvoisin Dam, completed in Switzerland in 1958, was the first higher dam at a height of 777 feet. Lake Mead was formed by Boulder Dam; with a capacity of more than 31 million acre-feet of water, it was

the world's largest reservoir until 1959, when the Kariba Dam on the Zambia-Zimbabwe boundary created a reservoir of 130 million acre-feet capacity. Boulder Dam and Lake Mead, however, remain among the largest structures of their kind.

The Boulder Dam project had its roots in Oliver M. Wozencraft's efforts to promote diversion of Colorado River water to irrigate the Imperial Valley of California. In 1859, at Wozencraft's instigation, the California legislature passed a bill petitioning Congress to cede the Imperial Valley to the state for reclamation purposes. Wozencraft's desert-land bill finally was introduced in Congress in 1862 but failed to pass. Private construction of irrigation works began in 1898, and the first water was diverted in 1901. Severe floods in 1905 and 1906 broke through the levees and canals, bringing Colorado River water to the Salton Depression and creating the Salton Sea. It took two years to bring the flood under control, and the strong possibility remained that the river could break through again. A flood would inundate more than one million acres of irrigated farms. Erosion of the channel also threatened to dry out additional irrigated lands at Yuma, Arizona, and farmland to the north. Furthermore, the 1905-1906 flood and subsequent floods exceeded the financial capacity of private companies and irrigation districts to maintain irrigation systems in the valley. The inability of private organizations to cope with the flood threat and the advent of proposed private hydroelectric power schemes resulted in appeals for governmental intervention.

Conflicting claims by the states of the Colorado basin for river water and the perceived need to regulate public and private power caused Congress, on August 19, 1921, to authorize the states of the Colorado River drainage basin to enter into a compact dividing the basin's waters. The Colorado River Commission, which was composed of representatives of the states as well as the secretary of commerce, was appointed by the president and states. At the commission's first meeting, on January 26, 1922, Herbert Hoover, the U.S. secretary of commerce, was elected chairman. After prolonged controversy, the Colorado River Compact was signed by the commission on November 24, 1922, opening the way for unified development of the Colorado River basin. The means by which that development was achieved, however, remained controversial.

The Colorado River Compact divided the basin into a

Boulder Dam as seen from the Nevada side. (Archive Photos)

lower basin comprising Arizona, California, and Nevada and an upper basin within Utah, New Mexico, Colorado, and Wyoming. Both basins were allocated 7.5 million acre-feet of water and the right to draw an additional one million acre-feet of unallocated water for beneficial consumption if additional water was available. Division of water within the upper and lower basins, however, was not specified, and conflict between Arizona and California remained an obstacle. The water allocated was designated primarily for domestic and agricultural purposes, secondarily for power generation, and thirdly for navigation. Much later, Mexico was allocated 1.5 million acre-feet from the surplus waters. If there was insufficient surplus water to supply the Mexicans, the lower and upper basins were required to surrender equal amounts to fulfill the Mexican quota. Arizona and the upper-basin states immediately objected, because California had already appropriated all, or nearly all, of its share of the water and was prepared to take more. In contrast, the upper-basin states lacked the dams and reservoirs needed for storage and diversion of their share of the water. In addition, conflicts over the role of government and private enterprise

in producing and selling electrical power delayed construction.

After prolonged political maneuvering, the fourth Swing-Johnson bill (named for its primary author, Congressman Philip D. Swing of California), which authorized the Boulder Canyon Project, passed Congress on December 19, 1928. Three previous versions failed to pass in 1922, 1923, and 1925. Under the terms of the act, also known as the Boulder Canyon Project Act, a high dam and reservoir were to be constructed at either Boulder or Black Canyon in order to control floods, improve navigation, regulate the flow of the Colorado River, store water for reclamation and other beneficial purposes exclusively within the United States, and generate electrical energy. Construction of the Imperial Dam and All-American Canal, which were designed to divert water to the Imperial Valley by means of works entirely within the United States, also was authorized in the bill.

Construction of the high dam commenced on May 16, 1931. Because of engineering considerations, the dam was built in Black Canyon instead of in Boulder Canyon. A town, a railroad, a highway, and power lines were built

1936

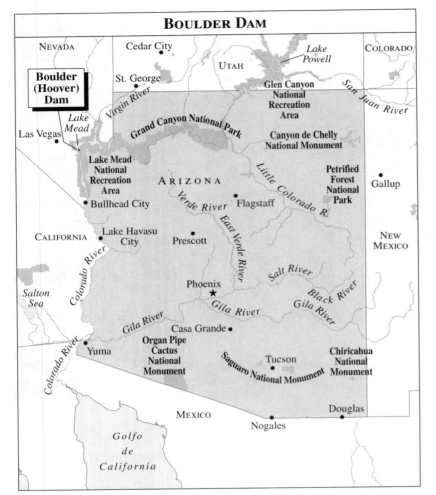

BOULDER DAM

NEVADA · Cedar City · · COLORADO
Lake Powell

Boulder (Hoover) Dam · St. George · UTAH

Virgin River · Glen Canyon National Recreation Area · San Juan River

Las Vegas · Lake Mead · Grand Canyon National Park

Canyon de Chelly National Monument

Lake Mead National Recreation Area · A R I Z O N A · Little Colorado R. · Petrified Forest National Park · Gallup

Bullhead City · Verde River · Flagstaff

CALIFORNIA · Lake Havasu City · Prescott · East Verde River · NEW MEXICO

Colorado River · Salt River · Black River

Phoenix ★ · Gila River

Salton Sea · Gila River · Casa Grande · Gila River

Yuma · Organ Pipe Cactus National Monument · Saguaro National Monument · Tucson · Chiricahua National Monument

Colorado River

Douglas

MEXICO · Nogales

Golfo de California

The dam began regulating Colorado River flow on February 1, 1935. It was dedicated on September 30, 1935, and was accepted by Secretary of the Interior Harold Ickes on March 1, 1936, two years and two months ahead of schedule, at a cost of $51,950,000—essentially the price at which it had been bid. By June, 1937, the power plant was in routine operation, although not all the contemplated turbines and generators were installed until decades later. The dam was renamed Hoover Dam in 1947 to honor Herbert Hoover, who as secretary of commerce and as president of the United States played a large role in the dam's construction.

SIGNIFICANCE

Boulder Dam fulfilled all the purposes for which it was built. Irrigation water was supplied to the Imperial Valley and riverine lands below the dam. Water stored in the reservoir became available to maintain irrigation during droughts. Flooding on the Lower Colorado River occurred only once after completion of the dam, and the great flood of 1953 would have been far more severe without storage of much of the waters in Lake Mead. An installed capacity of 4.33 million kilowatt-hours of electric power was expected upon installation of all planned generators. Additional benefits of the dam's construction included temporary stimulation of the economy in the midst of the Great Depression and creation of a major recreational resource. This resource, the Lake Mead National Recreation Area, preserved a large area of desert environment.

Boulder Dam was the first very large modern dam, and it initiated worldwide expansion of large-scale hydroelectric and irrigation-dam construction. The Tennessee Valley Authority, the Columbia basin system, and the Pick-Slogan program in the Missouri basin were developed in part because of the momentum generated by completion of Boulder Dam. The federal government constructed more than one thousand dams between 1930 and 1980. Construction of the Parker Dam and the Colorado River Aqueduct began immediately after completion of Boul-

---

to allow construction to proceed in the previously isolated, uninhabited area. Four diversion tunnels were driven around the site, and a cofferdam was erected to keep the river out of the dam site. The diversion tunnels became operable in March, 1931, and the upper cofferdam was completed in March, 1933. On June 6, 1933, the first concrete was poured for the dam after the rock abutments had been stripped and the valley floor excavated to bedrock. On March 23, the main body of the dam was completed to crest elevation. The large volume of concrete required cooling to dissipate the heat of curing and to avoid cracking and deforming the dam. For this purpose, refrigerant piping was buried in the concrete, and a substantial refrigeration plant was built to supply internal cold-water circulation. This technique, invented for Boulder Dam's construction, was later used for building other massive concrete structures.

der Dam. Aqueducts to service San Diego and the Coachella Valley were built somewhat later and met California's primary objectives for the Boulder Canyon Project. Efforts to secure use of the upper basin and Arizona's share of the water, however, were unsuccessful.

The Colorado River Storage Project, which was approved by Congress in 1956, authorized construction of ten dams in the upper Colorado River basin. These dams were to store 48.5 million acre-feet of water and to ensure delivery of the upper basin's share of water as stated in the Colorado River Compact. Glen Canyon Dam, completed in 1966, was the largest of those actually built. The Central Arizona Project, authorized in the Colorado River Basin Project Act, signed on September 30, 1968, finally delivered Arizona's share of water allocated under the Colorado River Compact. The Colorado River Basin Act also provided for a domestic water aqueduct to Las Vegas, authorized several upper-basin dams and projects, and assumed responsibility for delivering acceptable water to Mexico.

Although the completed works in the Colorado basin are adequate to deliver the water allocated to the states of the basin and Mexico, most people believe that the river does not supply enough water to meet the quotas. The estimated average annual flow, on which the allocations were based, was determined by available flow rate measurements. These measurements, however, were made during a wetter-than-average climatic cycle. As a consequence, virtually no water reaches the Gulf of California. In addition, irrigation water leaches salts from the soil and returns saline water to the river. This process, as well as the natural increase in salinity as the river crosses the Colorado Plateau and the desert, so degraded the river water at the Mexican boundary that it became unfit for irrigation. Crop damage in Mexico provoked protests from the Mexican government, and these protests culminated in 1973 with a threat to bring the matter before the World Court. This protest has been somewhat quelled by the authorized construction of a $300 million desalination plant to treat water crossing the border and additional salinity-control projects upstream. Water flowing downstream to the Gulf of California is even more highly saline and has greatly altered wetlands on the Colorado River delta. Reduction in flow also has led to saltwater incursion on the delta.

Boulder Dam and Lake Mead remove all sediment from the Colorado River. As a consequence, the clear water below the dam erodes the bed and banks of the river. Also, the delta and the floodplain no longer receive sediment.

Water delivered by the Los Angeles and San Diego aqueducts permitted and stimulated the large population increase in Southern California. Irrigation water was ensured for the Imperial Valley and the districts along the Colorado River. Power from Hoover Dam serviced the pumps on the aqueducts and met a large part of the increased power demands during World War II. A magnesium reduction works at Henderson, Nevada, was the principal source of magnesium for the war effort. Inexpensive power also was sent to the zinc mines at Pioche, Nevada.

The dam's name has been subject to partisan political conflict and has been a source of confusion. The Democratic Swing-Johnson bills authorizing the dam referred to the Boulder Canyon Project and referred to the dam as Boulder Dam. On "driving the silver spike" on the branch line to the site, Ray Lyman Wilbur, Herbert Hoover's Republican secretary of the interior, named the dam Hoover Dam, and this name subsequently was used in congressional bills and appropriations. In May, 1933, the new Democratic secretary of commerce, Harold Ickes, changed the name to Boulder Dam. In 1947, the first Congress elected with a Republican majority since 1932 passed a bill restoring the name Hoover Dam. Democratic President Harry S. Truman signed the bill. This ended the partisan series of name changes, but both names remain in common use.

—Ralph L. Langenheim, Jr.

Further Reading

Berkman, Richard L., and W. Kip Viscusi. *Damming the West*. New York: Grossman, 1973. Excellent volume about the process of damming rivers in the American West. Places the construction of Boulder Dam into a larger context and underscores its catalytic role.

Dunar, Andrew J., and Dennis McBride. *Building Hoover Dam: An Oral History of the Great Depression*. Reno: University of Nevada Press, 2001. A people's history of the dam's construction that focuses on the day-to-day realities experienced by the workers.

Hoover, H. C. *The Memoirs of Herbert Hoover, the Cabinet, and the Presidency, 1920-1933*. New York: Macmillan, 1952. Hoover's own account of his actions, motives, and beliefs regarding the Boulder Canyon Project. Emphasizes his role in the Colorado River Commission and his work to clear the way for the project. Also relates details about the naming and renaming of the dam and about Hoover's exclusion from the dedication ceremonies.

Kleinsorge, Paul Lincoln. *The Boulder Canyon Project:*

1936

Historical and Economic Aspects. Stanford, Calif.: Stanford University Press, 1940. Provides excellent coverage of the legislative battle over the Boulder Canyon Project Act, or Swing-Johnson bill. Addresses how the legislative process works and accurately describes the underside of that process.

_____. *The Boulder Dam Project*. Stanford, Calif.: Stanford University Press, 1941. Describes the Colorado River and the history of navigation, agriculture, flood control, and power development on the lower river. Reviews political action leading to construction of the dam and the financing and construction of the dam. Includes an economic evaluation of the project. Readable and comprehensive through 1940.

McBride, Dennis. *In the Beginning: A History of Boulder City, Nevada*. Boulder City, Nev.: Boulder City Chamber of Commerce, 1981. Discusses the people involved in the project, although in a somewhat romanticized manner. Gives a feeling that through all the trials and tribulations, a sense of community was established. For a wide audience.

Mann, Elizabeth, and Alan Witschonke. *The Hoover Dam: The Story of Tough Times, Tough People, and the Taming of a Wild River*. New York: Mikaya Press, 2001. A very readable account; written for high school students. Includes sidebars with first-person narratives. Fully illustrated.

Moeller, B. S. *Phil Swing and the Boulder Dam*. Berkeley: University of California Press, 1971. Sympathetic political biography describes Swing's dedication to furthering Imperial Valley irrigation. Minimizes Hoover's contributions to the project. Readable and well documented.

Reisner, Marc. *Cadillac Desert*. New York: Viking, 1986. Best seller about water policy in the western United States concludes that water is being overused, that water projects are largely uneconomical, and that desertification awaits. Describes and evaluates the entire Colorado River project.

Stevens, Joseph E. *Hoover Dam: An American Adventure*. Norman: University of Oklahoma Press, 1988. Superb resource on the people who built the dam. Presents an especially strong account of the technical aspects of the construction, but pays little attention to the environmental impacts.

Watkins, T. H., et al. *The Grand Colorado: The Story of a River and Its Canyons*. Palo Alto, Calif.: American West, 1969. The Colorado River is one of the great and majestic rivers in the United States. This volume captures the spirit of that river as it passes through some of the most hostile but beautiful areas if the country.

Woodbury, D. J. *The Colorado Conquest*. New York: Dodd, Mead, 1941. Fictionalized account of events leading to construction of Hoover Dam and the All-American Canal. Asserts that the actions and statements of the historical figures portrayed are factual and that the fictional characters are composites of individuals the author knew as a resident of Brawley, California. Very readable.

SEE ALSO: June 17, 1902: Reclamation Act Promotes Western Agriculture; Dec. 19, 1913: U.S. Congress Approves a Dam in Hetch Hetchy Valley; 1923: Federal Power Commission Disallows Kings River Dams; Mar. 19, 1931: Nevada Legalizes Gambling; May 18, 1933: Tennessee Valley Authority Is Created; Sept. 8, 1933: Work Begins on the Grand Coulee Dam; Mar., 1937: Delaware River Project Begins.

April 15, 1936-1939
GREAT UPRISING OF ARABS IN PALESTINE

Palestinian Arabs united first through a general strike and then through violent resistance to the British mandate and its policy supporting a Jewish homeland. A severe British response left thousands dead, but the Arabs succeeded in curtailing immigration.

LOCALE: Palestine

CATEGORIES: Wars, uprisings, and civil unrest; colonialism and occupation; immigration, emigration, and relocation

KEY FIGURES

Sir Arthur Grenfell Wauchope (1874-1947), British high commissioner of Palestine

First Earl Peel (William Robert Wellesley Peel; 1867-1937), head of the 1936 Peel Commission

Amīn al-Ḥusaynī (c. 1895-1974), mufti of Jerusalem and head of the Supreme Muslim Council

ʿAbd Allā ibn al-Ḥusayn (1882-1951), leader of Transjordan and first ruler of Jordan, 1946-1951, as ʿAbdullah I

Abd al-Qādir al-Ḥusaynī (1907-1948), military commander of Arab forces

Izz al-Dīn al-Qassām (1882-1935), Syrian-born Muslim preacher and militant activist

Fawzī al-Qāwuqjī (1890-1977), leader of Syrian revolt who assisted the Palestinian uprising

Orde Charles Wingate (1903-1944), British military commander

Chaim Weizmann (1874-1952), head of the World Zionist Congress

Jamāl al-Ḥusaynī (1893-1982), chairman of the Arab Higher Committee

SUMMARY OF EVENT

The Shaw Commission, which had investigated the 1929 riots at the Western Wall in Jerusalem, concluded that the major cause of unrest in Palestine was the worsening economic condition of rural Palestinians, and it recommended limitations on Jewish immigration and land purchases. However, British prime minister Ramsay Mac-Donald essentially ignored this report, and conditions grew more perilous for Palestinians. Instead of looking to the Palestinian countryside, the new British high commissioner, Sir Arthur Grenfell Wauchope, recruited European Jewish investors to improve the urban economy.

A younger generation of Arabs, who had been educated under the British mandate, began to direct their hostility at the British occupiers. New parties were formed around the principle of noncompliance, including the pan-Arab Istqlal Party, which was founded in 1932 in the northern towns. At the same time, Khalil al-Budayri, a Jerusalem physician impressed with Gandhi's efforts in India, proposed a strategy of nonviolent resistance. This tactic had proved successful elsewhere in the Arab world: Demonstrations in Damascus in 1935 had led to renegotiations of agreements with the French, and similar demonstrations in Egypt affected British policies.

In 1933, however, thousands of Arabs had taken to the streets of Jaffa to protest British policy. They were met with force, and a dozen Arabs were killed in one day. In response, Sheik Izz al-Dīn al-Qassām, a fundamentalist Syrian Muslim preacher in Haifa, began a wave of militant attacks on Jews and British interests. Although he was killed by the British agents in November of 1935, he quickly became a martyr who inspired further resistance.

On April 15, 1936, the murder of two Jews and the immediate retaliation by Jewish forces triggered an uprising. For the first time, various Arab factions were able to come together to form the Arab Higher Committee, which called for a general strike that lasted from April to November. The strike included a total boycott of Jewish goods and prohibition on the sale of goods to Jews. Paid agricultural workers on Jewish settlements quit their jobs, and many laborers in factories and construction accepted significant sacrifices by refusing to work. Those who had already been living at subsistence levels were stretched to the limit. Government workers continued in their positions in order to retain influence, but they contributed 10 percent of their earnings to aid other strikers. The Jerusalem elite were taxed to support the poor. Bands of young men took it upon themselves to enforce compliance by attacking both Jewish shopkeepers and Arabs suspected of dealings with Jews.

In many ways, the strike was a failure. Vacated jobs were soon taken by Jewish immigrants. The closing of the port of Jaffa led Jews to develop their own port in Tel Aviv. This unified action, however, succeeded in attracting British attention. A commission of inquiry led by the First Earl Peel recommended that Palestine be partitioned into a Jewish state and an Arab state. Jerusalem and a corridor to the port of Jaffa would remain under British authority. The division of territory fell roughly in line with population figures, which meant that Jews would receive only 20 percent of the land. However, the recommendation that the proposed Arab state be joined with Transjordan (now Jordan) under the authority of ʿAbd Allā ibn al-Ḥusayn did not sit well with Arab notables of Jerusalem, who expected self-rule. It was an even greater blow to the 250,000 Arab inhabitants of the northern region who would be expected to cede their fertile land to the proposed Jewish state. These northern Arabs had taken an active role in the uprising's earliest stages with the help of the Istqlal Party and the militant al-Qassām. They rejected the offer and resumed the struggle.

In 1937, the center of the uprising shifted from the cities to the rural areas. The movement was led by figures from within Palestine such as Abd al-Qādir al-Ḥusaynī and by figures from outside, such as Fawzī al-Qāwuqjī. These men had gained military experience in Syria and Iraq, and they helped make the movement increasingly violent. Armed bands mined roads and tried to disrupt transportation, and the railroad was a frequent target. A newly constructed oil pipeline from Iraq to the port of Haifa was sabotaged, and eventually postal service came to a halt.

A number of attacks were made on Jewish settlements. In September, rebels killed a significant number of Jews in Tiberias, and they raided British prisons and set political prisoners free in other cities. At one time, two thousand rebels occupied Jerusalem's Old City for five days, and they wrested control of Jaffa away from the British for several months. Perhaps the blow that hit the British hardest was the September, 1937, murder in Nazareth of Lewis Andrews, the acting commissioner of Galilee. The numbers of British troops increased to twenty thousand, and they came down on the Arabs with an iron fist. Leaders of the Arab Higher Committee were arrested, more than one hundred militants were publicly hanged, and homes that harbored rebels were dynamited. Jerusalem mufti Amīn al-Ḥusaynī, the first head of the Arab Higher Committee, and others were forced into exile.

The British also encouraged retaliation by the Jewish defense force, the Haganah, which by this time numbered around fifteen thousand troops. British military strategist Orde Charles Wingate came from India to organize Jewish forces, and he helped them make night raids on Arab villages. More extremist Jewish military groups emerged, but when one of these groups, Irgun, killed seventy-seven Arabs in a period of three weeks with bombs in Arab marketplaces, the British also publicly hanged one of the Irgun leaders. In its latter stages,

the uprising turned into a civil war: There were reports of Muslims attacking Christian Arabs and the poor attacking the elite. Many Arabs who supported cooperation with the British were killed or sent into exile. By 1939, the once-united Arab resistance was fragmented and exhausted, and by the time order was restored, nearly five thousand Arabs, four hundred Jews, and two hundred Britons had been killed.

SIGNIFICANCE

The uprising of the late 1930's has been described as the event that shaped the Palestinian Arab identity. For the first time, Arabs were able to unite in a sustained push for a common cause, and their efforts changed British policy. The British mandate had been built on the principle of the 1917 Balfour Declaration, which had promised to establish a Jewish homeland in Palestine without fully considering the existing population's needs. Unlimited Jewish immigration and land purchase had been the norm for two decades, but after the 1936-1939 uprising, the British reversed themselves. The 1936 Peel Commission, the Woodhead Commission, and a 1938 white paper demonstrated that partition was not a satisfactory solution, and they led to limits on immigration.

This latter decision was the result of a follow-up diplomatic conference in London in 1939. Instilled with new confidence, the Arabs demanded that they be able to negotiate directly with the British. Meeting separately with Colonial Secretary Malcolm MacDonald, Zionist leader Chaim Weizmann reiterated the need for continued unlimited Jewish immigration, especially with the precarious position of European Jews. Jamāl al-Ḥusaynī, speaking for the Arab delegation, asked for a reconsideration of an independent Arab state promised by the British diplomat Henry McMahon during World War I. In the end, the British agreed with the Arab proposals, and the British government issued another white paper on May 17, 1939, that called for the eventual creation of a single Palestinian state. At the time, the region was about 70 percent Arab and 30 percent Jewish, and the British promised to limit Jewish immigration to ensure an Arab majority. The 1939 white paper reinterpreted the Balfour Declaration's promise of a Jewish homeland, saying that it would be determined by the needs of the existing Arab inhabitants. With Jewish interests now defeated in the diplomatic arena, their struggle shifted to force the British out of Palestine. The extremist military groups Irgun and Stern Gang began to direct terrorist attacks on the British. The well-organized Haganah began to prepare itself for its war of independence after the departure of the

British and the eventual partition of Palestine by the United Nations.

—Fred Strickert

FURTHER READING

Bowden, Tim. "The Politics of Arab Rebellion in Palestine, 1936-1939." *Middle Eastern Studies* 11 (1975): 147-74. Chronicles the difficulties inherent in attempts to organize the rural peasantry and compares this population to the traditional urban political elite.

Kimmerling, Baruch, and Joel S. Migdal. *The Palestinian People: A History.* Cambridge, Mass.: Harvard University Press, 2003. Sees the Arab uprising as the formative event in shaping Palestinian identity.

Morris, Benni. *Righteous Victims: A History of the Zionist-Arab Conflict, 1881-1999.* New York: Alfred A. Knopf, 1999. Reevaluation of the history of the period draws on original sources.

Pappe, Ilan. *A History of Modern Palestine: One Land, Two Peoples.* Cambridge, England: Cambridge University Press, 2004. Concerned that Israelis and Palestinians have separate histories shaped by their own ideologies, Pappe writes an interwoven story that focuses on the lives of the victims, not the powerful.

Segev, Tom. *One Palestine, Complete: Jews and Arabs Under the British Mandate.* Translated by Haim Watzman. New York: Metropolitan Books, 1999. A comprehensive journal drawn from the diaries and letters of three decades of the British mandate.

Smith, Charles D. *Palestine and the Arab-Israeli Conflict.* 2d ed. New York: St. Martin's Press, 1992. Designed as a textbook for undergraduate college classes. It gives a balanced introduction to the conflict.

SEE ALSO: 1909: First Kibbutz Is Established in Palestine; Nov. 2, 1917: Balfour Declaration Supports a Jewish Homeland in Palestine; July 24, 1922: League of Nations Establishes Mandate for Palestine; Aug. 23, 1929: Western Wall Riots.

June 19, 1936
ROBINSON-PATMAN ACT RESTRICTS PRICE DISCRIMINATION

The Robinson-Patman Act amended the Clayton Antitrust Act of 1914 to make it more difficult for firms to charge different prices to different buyers, particularly if the buyers were businesses buying to resell.

ALSO KNOWN AS: Anti-Chain-Store Act; Robinson-Patman Antidiscrimination Act

LOCALE: Washington, D.C.

CATEGORIES: Business and labor; laws, acts, and legal history

KEY FIGURES

Marvel Mills Logan (1874-1939), U.S. senator from Kentucky, 1931-1939

Wright Patman (1893-1976), U.S. congressman from Texas, 1929-1976

Joseph Taylor Robinson (1872-1937), U.S. congressman from Arkansas, 1903-1913, and U.S. senator from Arkansas, 1913-1937

SUMMARY OF EVENT

The Robinson-Patman Act was passed in order to strengthen the price-discrimination provisions of the Clayton Antitrust Act of 1914. Price discrimination occurs when a seller charges different prices to different buyers for the same product or service when there are no comparable differences in the cost of serving the different customers. As examples, barbershops and motion-picture theaters commonly charge children less than they charge adults, and electricity rates are often higher for residential customers than for businesses. Charging different prices to different buyers can often increase profits for the sellers, provided that the seller can separate the markets. By separating the markets, the seller ensures that favored buyers do not resell to the less-favored ones, and that demand is significantly less sensitive to price in one market than in another.

During the notorious "trust movement" of the late nineteenth century, many believed that aggressive and predatory firms such as John D. Rockefeller's Standard Oil Company used price discrimination as a means of harassing rivals. The big trust might offer its product for sale at a very low price in the area served by the smaller and weaker rival, thereby "persuading" the rival firm to enter into collusion with the trust or to sell out to it on favorable terms. At the same time, the trust might be selling at a much higher price in other localities, although the price would be limited by people's ability to buy cheaply in one area and ship for resale into a more expensive area.

Price discrimination's ill repute caused it to be explic-

1936

itly outlawed by section 2 of the Clayton Act of 1914, which forbade it in situations whose effect "may be to substantially lessen competition or tend to create a monopoly in any line of commerce." If price differences reflected differences in grade, quality, quantity, costs of selling, or costs of transportation, they were not discriminatory. Further, a discriminatory price offered "in good faith to meet competition" would not be illegal. The Federal Trade Commission (FTC), created in 1914, was given the principal responsibility for enforcing the act, responding mainly to complaints from injured parties. Not many cases were brought by the FTC, and its efforts to prevent price discrimination met with a number of rebuffs from the courts.

Strong pressure to amend the Clayton Act reflected a shift in focus. During the 1920's, the U.S. economy experienced a large increase in the activity of chain stores such as the A&P grocery chain and mass marketers such as Sears, Roebuck. Because of their size, these firms were often able to gain price concessions from their suppliers, price concessions that worked to the competitive disadvantage of smaller wholesalers and retailers trying to compete with such large operations as A&P or Sears. The FTC completed an exhaustive report on chain stores in 1934 and provided examples of the preferential treatment of large buyers. The FTC also issued a complaint against Goodyear Tire and Rubber Company, alleging that unlawful price discrimination was involved in its contract to sell tires to Sears at cost plus 6 percent. The commission alleged that Sears was gaining an advantage of 29 to 40 percent over its retail competitors by this discriminatory pricing arrangement.

Political efforts to limit chain store activities were undertaken by independent wholesalers and retailers on a number of fronts. A number of states, for example, levied special taxes on chain stores. The lobbying efforts intensified when the Great Depression drove many small firms out of business. The legal counsel for the United States Wholesale Grocers Association drafted a bill to amend the price discrimination law to make it a stronger protection for smaller firms against mass distributors. Senator Joseph Taylor Robinson of Arkansas and Representative Wright Patman of Texas introduced the bill in Congress, where it was commonly known as the Anti-Chain-Store Act. In Senate debate, Senator Marvel Mills Logan of Kentucky presented the major arguments for the bill.

The Robinson-Patman Act was approved on June 19, 1936. The test criterion of illegal discrimination was broadened: Discrimination was now illegal if its effect might be "to injure, destroy, or prevent competition with any person who either grants or knowingly receives the benefit of such discrimination, or with customers of either of them." The thrust of this change was that price discrimination might be illegal if it simply caused injury to some competitor, even if the vigor of competition itself was not impaired and no monopoly was created. The law was also amended to justify quantity discounts only if they made "due allowance" for cost differences; thus firms accused of illegal price discrimination might be required to present data on the costs of handling orders and shipments of different sizes.

Whereas the Clayton Act permitted discriminatory pricing "to meet competition," the Robinson-Patman Act restricted this provision; firms could make price cuts "to meet the equally low price of a competitor" but presumably not to undercut that price. The FTC was given authority to set limits on quantity discounts if it found that "available purchasers in greater quantities are so few as to render differentials on account thereof unjustly discriminatory or promotive of monopoly." In other words, a price reduction might be illegal—even if it could be shown to reflect proportionally lower costs—if it appeared to give monopoly power to one or two very large buyers, such as Sears or A&P. The FTC, however, has never invoked such restrictions.

Large purchasers were often able to dispense with the services of brokers in dealing with suppliers. They would sometimes pressure their suppliers to give them price concessions in lieu of the brokerage charges those suppliers might have paid under different conditions. The 1936 law prohibited such brokerage allowances when no independent broker was involved. Special provisions such as promotional allowances, advertising allowances, and services or facilities provided by sellers were required to be available to all businesses that bought a company's products, on "proportionally equal" terms. If Coca-Cola Company, for example, was willing to subsidize Kroger's advertising of Coke, it had to make similar subsidies available to smaller retail firms, proportional perhaps to their purchases of Coke during the previous year.

In the first twelve years following the Robinson-Patman Act, the FTC issued 186 cease-and-desist orders involving price discrimination. Of these, 104 were based on the prohibitions against paying brokerage allowances where no brokers' services were involved. Immediately after passage of the act, the A&P grocery chain began to insist that its suppliers provide price concessions equal to former brokerage allowances; the concessions were to take the form of quantity discounts. The FTC moved quickly to block this and was upheld in the courts. In some other brokerage allowance cases, prohibitions appear to have been unfairly directed against independent purchasing agencies and cooperative buying agencies serving small firms.

The next most frequent type of complaint concerned promotional allowances, subsidies and services made available to large buyers on a discriminatory basis. The FTC issued 54 such cease-and-desist orders up to the beginning of 1948. For example, Corn Products Refining Company was ordered to stop paying to advertise products of the Curtiss Candy Company, since it was not comparably advertising for smaller customers. The Elizabeth Arden cosmetics firm was ordered to stop its policy of supplying demonstrators to help its large retail customers sell its products, because smaller retailers were not offered similar opportunities.

The FTC also dealt with a number of cases involving quantity discounts. Firms offering discounts on individual orders sometimes successfully showed cost justifications, but price concessions based on cumulative orders over a sustained period were usually banned. Morton Salt, for example, was permitted to sell more cheaply for carload shipments than for less-than-carload shipments, but it was not allowed to offer further discounts based on the number of cases purchased over a twelve-month period. Ironically, there have been very few cases of local price cutting like those attributed to the old predatory trusts. Some such considerations were involved in a case involving the Utah Pie Company, a small local enterprise that lost significant sales in its home territory when major national firms made discriminatory price reductions for sales in Salt Lake City. The Supreme Court found the discrimination illegal in *Utah Pie Company v. Continental Baking Company* (1967) even though Utah Pie continued to be profitable during the price war.

The FTC was able to use the Robinson-Patman Act as the basis for an attack on systems of delivered pricing for certain heavy products such as steel, cement, and corn syrup. These involved the so-called basing-point system, in which customers in a given locality would find all suppliers quoting identical delivered prices, regardless of how close the supplier might be. A seller shipping from a longer distance would realize a smaller net price after paying shipping charges. The pricing system was employed as a way for sellers to avoid direct price competition with one another. A series of cases in 1945 and 1948 found that such pricing systems violated the Robinson-Patman Act.

Enforcement of the Robinson-Patman Act, like that of the original Clayton Act, was primarily the responsibility of the FTC, which was authorized to issue orders to "cease and desist" when it found evidence of illegal price discrimination. These orders carried no direct penalty, and if the firms continued their violations, the FTC had to go to court to enforce its orders. The 1936 law also provided that injured parties could sue for damages. The issue of price discrimination reached the Supreme Court in the 1993 case *Brooke Group v. Brown and Williamson Tobacco*, but the FTC has not had any notable victories in price-discrimination issues since.

SIGNIFICANCE

The Robinson-Patman Act has not been well regarded by economists studying antitrust policy. Firms competing actively for business may often charge different prices to different customers, and such practices need not lead to oppressive monopoly. Wholesale and retail trade, on which much of the litigation has focused, is generally characterized by easy entry for new firms and absence of sizable economies of large-scale operation. Those characteristics make it unlikely that a dangerous monopoly will arise. The A&P grocery chain, which was a primary target of the law, faded into insignificance; apparently, it did not benefit greatly from any monopoly power. A large proportion of FTC orders relating to price discrimination involved the highly competitive food products industry. Critics of the law hold that it had the purpose and effect of reducing the vigor of competition. They argue that the test of illegality has often been whether some competitor was injured by a low price rather than whether the vigor of competition itself was impaired. Competition has the potential to injure competitors, but it is desirable (according to economists) as a way of improving efficiency and securing high-quality products at low prices for consumers.

Defenders of the Robinson-Patman Act argued that large firms have strategic advantages that do not reflect superior quality or efficiency and that it is appropriate to counterbalance these. For example, large firms may be in a better position to lobby for preferential treatment by government units or to engage in costly lawsuits against smaller rivals. Still, only a small minority (approximately 5 percent) of price-discrimination complaints filed with the FTC typically involve firms with more than one hundred million dollars in annual sales. Many relatively small firms face the possibility of being cited for violations, and the law has given rise to a large and confusing body of litigation. The consensus among econo-

1936

mists is that the Robinson-Patman Act is one of many well-intentioned pieces of economic micromanagement that has ended up generating more costs than benefits.

—*Paul B. Trescott*

FURTHER READING

Adelman, Morris A. *A&P: A Study in Price-Cost Behavior and Public Policy.* Cambridge, Mass.: Harvard University Press, 1959. The A&P grocery chain was a major target of the Robinson-Patman Act and other antitrust action. Adelman examines these issues in detail and comes out largely in defense of the company.

Benson, Bruce L., and M. L. Greenhut. "Special Interests, Bureaucrats, and Antitrust: An Explanation of the Antitrust Paradox." In *Antitrust and Regulation*, edited by Ronald E. Grieson. Lexington, Mass.: Lexington Books, 1986. Looks at the competing pressures of special interests on the Federal Trade Commission that led to policies aimed at protecting competitors against competition. Includes interpretation of the Robinson-Patman Act by the FTC.

Blackburn, John D., Elliott I. Klayman, and Martin H. Malin. *The Legal Environment of Business.* 6th ed. Boston: Pearson Custom Publishing, 2003. College-level text presents an up-to-date view of the Robinson-Patman Act, with extensive quotations from court cases.

Blair, Roger D., and David L. Kaserman. *Antitrust Economics.* Homewood, Ill.: Richard D. Irwin, 1985. Textbook treatment explains the economic reasoning behind price discrimination and reviews the law and cases, including relatively recent ones. Critical of the law.

Crews, Wayne. "Reexamining Antitrust: Can 'Anticompetitive' Business Practices Benefit Consumers?" *USA Today* (Society for the Advancement of Education) 130, no. 2862 (March, 2002): 1-28. Advocates a skeptical approach to study of antitrust policy, particularly with regard to modern corporations like AOL/ Time Warner and Microsoft.

Dirlam, Joel B., and Alfred E. Kahn. *Fair Competition: The Law and Economics of Antitrust Policy.* Ithaca, N.Y.: Cornell University Press, 1954. Stylish, opinionated analysis that is very critical of the Federal Trade Commission's presentation of price discrimination cases but praises the law's tendency to restrict the power of dominant firms.

Gellhorn, Ernest, William E. Kovacic, and Stephen Calkins. *Antitrust Law and Economics in a Nutshell.* Series. St. Paul, Minn.: Thomson/West, 2004. Consistently accurate guide to the confusing world of antitrust law gives special attention to the roles of evidence, the granting of immunity, and government intervention.

Patman, Wright. *Complete Guide to the Robinson-Patman Act.* Englewood Cliffs, N.J.: Prentice-Hall, 1963. One of the creators of the law describes its purposes and effects. Biased, but has an interesting chapter titled "Supporters and Opponents of the Act." One appendix lists all the cases brought to date, and another presents the legislative history, with committee reports and debates. A valuable, comprehensive source.

Purdy, Harry L., Martin L. Lindahl, and William A. Carter. *Corporate Concentration and Public Policy.* 2d ed. New York: Prentice-Hall, 1950. This older college text gives a good brief survey of the chief provisions and major early cases involving the Robinson-Patman Act.

Scherer, Frederic M. *Industrial Market Structure and Economic Performance.* 2d ed. Boston: Houghton Mifflin, 1980. The most comprehensive economic examination of the law and its effects. Very critical of the anticompetitive tendencies of the law and its administration by the FTC.

SEE ALSO: 1902: Cement Manufacturers Agree to Cooperate on Pricing; Mar. 14, 1904: U.S. Supreme Court Rules Against Northern Securities; Oct. 15, 1914: Clayton Antitrust Act; June 16, 1933: Roosevelt Signs the National Industrial Recovery Act; Aug. 17, 1937: Miller-Tydings Act Legalizes Retail Price Maintenance.

June 25, 1936
THE DC-3 OPENS A NEW ERA OF AIR TRAVEL

The Douglas DC-3 revolutionized air travel by providing passenger comfort and operating capabilities and by creating profit-making potential in the fledgling airline industry.

LOCALE: United States

CATEGORIES: Transportation; manufacturing and industry; travel and recreation; space and aviation

KEY FIGURES

Donald W. Douglas, Sr. (1892-1981), founder of the Douglas Aircraft Company

Jack Frye (1904-1959), vice president of flight operations for Transcontinental & Western Air Lines

Charles A. Lindbergh (1902-1974), chief technical adviser for Transcontinental & Western Air Lines

W. E. Patterson (1899-1980), president of United Air Lines

Eddie Rickenbacker (1890-1973), president of Eastern Air Lines

C. R. Smith (1899-1990), president of American Airlines

SUMMARY OF EVENT

The Air Mail Act of 1925 authorized the U.S. postmaster general to contract with any individual, firm, or corporation for the carriage of mail by aircraft between points designated by the postmaster general. This legislation signaled the beginning of what would become the airline industry. The Air Mail Act's first amendment (in 1926) changed the basis for payment to these contract mail carriers, but even with this change, which essentially amounted to subsidization, the young airlines frequently had difficulty generating a profit. The carriers came to recognize that earning additional revenue would be easier if aircraft could carry passengers in addition to mail. This demand eventually led to a larger aircraft, suitable for combined mail and passenger service. The first generation of these aircraft could accommodate from two to six passengers, but soon, larger multiengine aircraft became operational. The most popular of these were the all-metal Ford trimotor and Fokker's wood and fabric trimotor, which used laminated plywood as the wing skin. It was this plywood wing that ultimately would lead to Donald W. Douglas's DC series.

In March, 1931, a Fokker trimotor owned by Transcontinental & Western Air Lines (TWA, which became

Trans World Airlines in 1950) crashed while en route from Kansas City to Wichita. One of the passengers aboard was Knute Rockne, the University of Notre Dame's famous and beloved football coach, and his death was mourned around the nation. Public pressure began to mount on the Department of Commerce as the news media became increasingly strident in calling for public release of information on the cause of the accident, particularly because Rockne had been one of the passengers. Ultimately, the Department of Commerce concluded not only that the accident was traceable to the Fokker's wooden wing structure but also that all Fokker F-10's should be grounded temporarily while inspections and structural fixes were made. Publicity surrounding the accident turned public opinion against Fokker's trimotors, forcing TWA to depend solely on its Ford trimotors. The airline's vice president of flight operations, Jack Frye, recognized that a more modern aircraft type was needed as soon as possible.

Frye visited Seattle in an attempt to obtain some of Boeing Aircraft's new B-247 models. The B-247 was a ten-passenger, streamlined, all-metal airplane that Boeing thought would revolutionize air travel. The first sixty B-247's, two years' worth of production, were destined for United Air Lines, an affiliated company then under the Boeing umbrella. Frye and his engineers, with technical advice from aviation pioneer Charles A. Lindbergh, then proceeded to develop a set of specifications for a trimotored transport, and proposals were solicited from a number of aircraft-manufacturing companies, the smallest of which was Donald W. Douglas's company in Santa Monica, California.

Douglas's engineers, after studying TWA's specifications, determined that they could meet the stringent requirements with a twin-engine airplane by using new design applications as well as new, more powerful engines then being developed by both the Wright Aeronautical Company and Pratt & Whitney. A contract was signed on September 20, 1932, for the first airplane, at a cost of $125,000; the contract also included a one-year option for up to sixty additional planes priced at $58,000 each. TWA later admitted to Douglas that obtaining financing for the purchase had been difficult. Bankers, it seems, doubted that an aircraft could be built that would meet all of TWA's specifications. Eleven months after receiving the specifications, Douglas's first version of this new generation of aircraft, the twelve-passenger Douglas

1936

Commercial-1 (DC-1), made its first flight. Even before the plane's delivery to TWA, the airline asked for design changes that would, among other things, increase the DC-1's capacity by two passengers. TWA quickly ordered twenty-five units of this new model, the DC-2. Douglas began work on the new version immediately after flight tests had been completed on the DC-1, and in May, 1934, TWA took delivery of its first DC-2.

The DC-1 first flew on July 1, 1933. It could operate at 180 miles per hour while carrying twelve passengers. On the other hand, United's Boeing B-247, the pride of its fleet, could carry only ten passengers while cruising at 165 miles per hour. At TWA's insistence, Douglas immediately started making refinements to the DC-1, and orders began coming in for this improved model, the DC-2. Within two years, the DC-2 had evolved into the larger and more powerful DC-3, capable of carrying twenty-one passengers at 195 miles per hour. The DC-3 would continue as the workhorse of the world's airlines through World War II and into the early postwar years.

One of the earliest DC-2's was delivered to KLM, the Royal Dutch Airline, and it was almost immediately entered in the MacRobertson Trophy Race, which started in London and ended in Melbourne, Australia. The DC-2's second-place finish to a British twin-engine fighter aircraft—it placed well ahead of a Boeing B-247, even while carrying a few passengers—helped firmly establish the DC-2 in the traveling public's mind as the fastest and most reliable passenger aircraft yet made.

As the number of carriers ordering the DC-2 continued to grow, Douglas's engineers began working with specifications developed by American Airlines for an aircraft with sleeping berths that could provide American's passengers with overnight transcontinental sleeper service. Stretching and enlarging of the DC-2 created a new aircraft, the DC-3. Because of its combination of operating performance, passenger comfort, and operating costs, the DC-3 quickly became the most widely used passenger airplane in the world. C. R. Smith, president of American Airlines, commenting on his company's high regard for the DC-3, said that it was "the first airplane in the world that could make money just by hauling passengers."

In February, 1934, President Franklin D. Roosevelt abruptly canceled all existing airmail contracts and transferred airmail operations to the Army Air Corps. The service, hampered by continuing and worsening budgetary reductions, was anxious to demonstrate its capabilities to Congress and the American public. Tragically, during the Army's four months of airmail opera-

tion, sixty-six crashes took place, with twelve fatalities, three of which occurred as Army pilots were en route to their assigned origination points. As the Army was preparing to fly the mail, the DC-1 was used to demonstrate the capabilities of airlines and their new aircraft. In a highly publicized demonstration flight only hours before the Army was to take over airmail carriage, TWA's Jack Frye and Eastern's Eddie Rickenbacker flew the DC-1 from Burbank Air Terminal near Los Angeles to Newark, New Jersey, in slightly more than thirteen elapsed hours, with two refueling stops, at Kansas City, Missouri, and Columbus, Ohio. The flight's success did much to convince the American public of the efficiency and capability of the nation's airlines.

Although airmail contracts were again awarded to private carriers after June 1, 1934, the Roosevelt administration's change of heart resulted not from the February DC-1 demonstration flight of Frye and Rickenbacker but instead from growing public displeasure with the Army's obvious inability to sustain the airmail operation: Its inexperienced pilots flew virtually obsolete aircraft. Contractually, the airlines had been receiving from 42 to 54 cents per mile for airmail carriage, but the cost to the taxpayer of the Army's operation was put at $2.21 per mile, an unacceptable difference.

In June, with the contract situation resolved and airlines again carrying the mail, TWA began operating DC-2's on its overnight service from Newark to Los Angeles, with intermediate stops at Chicago, Kansas City, and Albuquerque. At the same time, American Airlines, on its overnight transcontinental service, was operating a sleeper version of the Curtiss Condor, a twelve- to fifteen-passenger, twin-engine airplane that was the last bi-wing air transport in commercial service in the United States. After TWA quickly gained a competitive edge with its DC-2's, American began looking for a replacement aircraft for the Condor, one capable of carrying a greater payload at a faster speed and at lower operating costs. American's search began and ended at Douglas Aircraft.

With American's order for an upgraded version of the DC-2 that could accommodate sleeper berths, Douglas realized that this new model, the Douglas Sleeper Transport (DST), would essentially be a new airplane. The fuselage, enlarged to accommodate sleeper berths, could be fitted with twenty-one seats, and this new, larger version's operating performance still handily exceeded that of the two-year-old DC-2's. Although Douglas's development costs for its DC-3 series reached $400,000, prospects for sales of this series were strong enough to assuage most concerns. American Airlines was so pleased by the combination of passenger comfort, performance, and operating costs that over the next few years, at a cost of $110,000 per plane, its aircraft fleet gradually was converted exclusively to DC-3's. This revolutionary airplane's payload capacity, gross weight, and operating performance exceeded those of any other aircraft then in commercial operation.

The DC-3 became an instant success with the airlines and their passengers. Although the DC-2 had proven successful, Douglas decided to terminate further production when it became evident that the DC-3 would outperform its predecessor rather significantly, and at lower operating costs. Up to that point, Douglas had built a total of 191 DC-2's and had recouped all of its development costs with production of the seventy-fifth aircraft. The success of the DC series caused Boeing to terminate its B-247 line after the production of its seventy-fifth aircraft. William Boeing's revolutionary new transport had been in production for less than three years.

In the meantime, a provision of the 1934 Air Mail Act prohibited any interlocking of airlines with aircraft-manufacturing companies, a practice common up to that time. As a result, United Air Lines was freed of dependence on Boeing as its principal aircraft supplier, and

United's new president, W. E. Patterson, immediately contacted Douglas. United's primary transport, the Boeing B-247, could not match the DC-3's carrying capacity, performance, or cost. Patterson realized that he needed to upgrade United's fleet quickly, and as a result, over the next few years United became almost exclusively a DC-3 airline. Eastern Air Lines quickly followed suit. It was becoming obvious to the entire industry that this new Douglas transport was revolutionizing air travel throughout the world.

American Airlines, the first operator of the new DC-3 series, began taking delivery of both versions in mid-1936. It put its first DC-3, a sleeper version, into regular line service on June 25, 1936. Most aviation chroniclers consider that day to have marked the beginning of a new era in air transportation, one that marked an end to airline operations that had been delivering, at best, only marginal profits on an irregular basis. The DC-3 and its predecessor the DC-2 proved so popular with the traveling public that within the first calendar year following the DC-3's introduction and first flight, one million passengers had flown on scheduled airlines in the United States. This total would grow significantly each year; after doubling within two years, it exceeded two million in 1939. Douglas originally had estimated a total sales volume of

A DC-3 in flight in 1959. (Library of Congress)

1936

fifty DC-3's, but because of the airline's popularity with travelers and operators alike, a total of 803 eventually were built. In addition, almost 10,400 military versions of the DC-3—known as the C-47—saw service during World War II.

SIGNIFICANCE

In the years following the Army's around-the-world flight in 1924 with Douglas-built airplanes, the company continued designing and building mostly military aircraft, but TWA's 1931 accident in Kansas had the ironic result of revolutionizing air travel by presenting Douglas with an opportunity to enter the commercial aircraft market. TWA needed a new type of aircraft that could exceed the performance capabilities of the Boeing B-247, which was about to be introduced by its chief competitor, United Air Lines. The B-247 gave United a definite competitive advantage over TWA, with its older and slower trimotors, but that advantage lasted only for little more than one year. On August 22, 1932, Jack Frye, seeking a new and competitive airplane for TWA, solicited proposals by sending letters containing the airline's detailed specifications to six aircraft manufacturing companies. Donald Douglas later would refer to Frye's letter as the "birth certificate of the modern airliner."

The DC-3 revolutionized commercial air travel throughout the world. Its well-deserved reputation for reliability and safety attracted more and more people to air travel. Within two years of the first DC-3 commercial flight, a significant industry milestone was reached when, for the first time, passenger revenues exceeded airmail revenues. From an airline standpoint, the DC-3 offered a virtually unbeatable combination of revenue potential and low operating costs. It is little wonder that by 1939, 90 percent of the world's airlines were using the Douglas DC-3, a plane that unquestionably changed airline travel forever.

—*James D. Matthews*

FURTHER READING

Blistein, Roger E. *Flight in America: From the Wrights to the Astronauts.* Baltimore: The Johns Hopkins University Press, 2001. An excellent first stop for those looking for information about the history of aviation in the United States. Comprehensive and very readable.

Glines, Carroll V., and Wendell F. Moseley. *The DC-3: The Story of a Fabulous Airplane.* Philadelphia: J. B. Lippincott, 1966. An excellent account of the DC-3's

evolution, although much more emphasis is placed on its military service in World War II than on its role in the commercial airline industry.

Holden, Henry M. *The Boeing 247: The First Modern Commercial Airplane.* Blue Ridge Summit, Pa.: TAB Books, 1991. Interesting account of the development of the DC-3's primary competitor, Boeing's B-247, and the DC-3's effect on Boeing and its pride and joy.

Johnson, Robert E. *Airway One.* Chicago: United Air Lines, 1974. Written by a longtime member of United Air Lines' top management, this is one of the better corporate narratives. Includes an interesting look at United's developmental years and its changeover from a Boeing B-247 airline to a DC-3 airline.

Kane, Robert M. *Air Transportation.* 11th ed. Dubuque, Iowa: Kendall/Hunt, 1993. Primarily a college-level aviation textbook. Includes some interesting information on the early airline period and the evolution of the DC-3.

Morrison, Wilbur H. *Donald W. Douglas: A Heart with Wings.* Ames: Iowa State University Press, 1991. An excellent account of the DC-3's development, seen as one of the landmark accomplishments of this aviation pioneer.

Pattillo, Donald M. *Pushing the Envelope: The American Aircraft Industry.* Ann Arbor: University of Michigan Press, 2001. An excellent resource for those looking for a survey history of the American aerospace industry. Makes clear the relationships between the aircraft industry and the military and economic power structures and is careful to avoid overly technical language.

Pisano, Dominick A. "The Crash That Killed Knute Rockne." *Air & Space Smithsonian* 6 (December, 1991): 88. A fascinating narrative of the accident that would lead TWA to request proposals for a new airplane that ultimately would become the revolutionary DC-3.

SEE ALSO: Dec. 17, 1903: Wright Brothers' First Flight; July 25, 1909: First Airplane Flight Across the English Channel; Sept. 8, 1920: U.S. Post Office Begins Transcontinental Airmail Delivery; Feb. 2, 1925: U.S. Congress Authorizes Private Carriers for Airmail; May 20, 1926: Air Commerce Act Creates a Federal Airways System; May 20, 1927: Lindbergh Makes the First Nonstop Transatlantic Flight; May 20-21, 1932: First Transatlantic Solo Flight by a Woman.

July 17, 1936
SPANISH CIVIL WAR BEGINS

The Spanish Civil War began as a military uprising against the Spanish Republic and resulted in a three-year civil conflict that brought Francisco Franco and the Fascist Falange to power.

LOCALE: Spain; Morocco
CATEGORIES: Wars, uprisings, and civil unrest; government and politics

KEY FIGURES

Manuel Azaña y Díaz (1880-1940), president of the Spanish Republic, 1936-1939

José Calvo Sotelo (1893-1936), monarchist leader in the Cortes

Santiago Casares Quiroga (1884-1950), prime minister of the Spanish Republic, May-July, 1936

Francisco Franco (1892-1975), leader of the uprising against the Spanish Republic and later military leader of Spain, 1939-1975

Adolf Hitler (1889-1945), chancellor of Germany, 1933-1945

Francisco Largo Caballero (1869-1946), prime minister of the Spanish Republic, 1936-1937

Benito Mussolini (1883-1945), premier of Italy, 1922-1943

José Antonio Primo de Rivera (1903-1936), leader of the Falange

José Sanjurjo (fl. early twentieth century), one of the leaders of the uprising against the Spanish Republic

SUMMARY OF EVENT

In the spring of 1936, Spain was on the verge of chaos. Five years of Republican government had heightened the tensions of the previous hundred years. A liberal, reform government had been defeated by conservatives in 1933, who began to reverse changes that had benefited workers and supporters of federalism. The elections of February brought the Popular Front government to power, but its varied composition of Liberals and Socialists, with tacit support from the Anarchists, meant that it could not act effectively to curb public and civil disorder caused by the Anarchists and the right-wing Falange.

The Anarchists, impatient with Republican reforms and desiring a revolution immediately, had begun uprisings and takeovers of land after the election. There were many strikes, and economic chaos threatened. The Falange, the Fascist party organized and led by José An-

tonio Primo de Rivera, son of the former dictator of Spain, responded with violence to the Anarchists' actions to show the Republican government's inability to cope with the problem. There were assassinations and gunfights in the streets. In addition, military and right-wing groups were organizing to oppose the newly elected government. Finally, the election victory of the Popular Front polarized both left-wing and right-wing extremes, and the country seemed to be moving inexorably toward violence. Even so, the government of Prime Minister Santiago Casares Quiroga refused to believe reports of military plots, while President Manuel Azaña y Díaz frantically sought a political solution that would not require arming workers against the military.

José Calvo Sotelo, a monarchist deputy in the Cortes (Spain's national legislative assembly), José Antonio Primo de Rivera, and General José Sanjurjo formed a conspiracy to overthrow the government and restore order to Spain. Although they did not commit themselves to a specific form of government, they were able to get the support of the monarchist leaders, who hoped for the restoration of Alfonso XIII, and the Falangists, who wanted to establish a Fascist state. Throughout the spring of 1936, they made plans for an uprising that summer.

In the Cortes, where Calvo Sotelo regularly complained of the civil disorder, the government could not answer the complaints of its critics. President Azaña did little except wait for the situation to improve, for he feared the leftist extremists. Francisco Largo Caballero, leader of the Socialist Party and one of the mainstays of the Republic, staged a march of ten thousand workers in Madrid on May 1, 1936, to demand a workers' government. There was talk about a leftist revolution to prevent a rightist coup and to implement long-desired radical reforms.

On July 13, 1936, Calvo Sotelo was arrested and murdered in revenge for a Falangist assassination of a Liberal policeman. So great was the public's shock at this deed that the military conspirators decided to take advantage of the nation's mood and advanced the date of their planned uprising. On July 17, military garrisons of the Canary Islands, Morocco, and throughout Spain pronounced against the Republican government and began taking over control of local governments. Despite the uprisings, Azaña and the government refused to distribute arms to proletarian organizations and the trade unions.

1936

Nevertheless, workers seized arms and resisted the military. In Madrid and Barcelona, armed workers were responsible for the failure of the insurrection, which had triumphed in about half of Spain.

SIGNIFICANCE

The conflict that began on July 17 settled into a prolonged civil war. The conspirators, called the Nationalists, had the support of the rightist elements—the Church, the landed classes, and many moderates—but, more important, they were able to get military aid and material from the Italian Fascist dictator, Benito Mussolini, and from Adolf Hitler, the German chancellor. Mussolini wanted influence in Spanish affairs, and Hitler wanted to

keep Mussolini embroiled in war so as to draw him away from the Western powers. By October, 1936, General Francisco Franco had emerged as the leader of the Nationalists, and in that month he proclaimed himself *caudillo*, or military leader, of Spain.

On the Republican, or Loyalist, side chaos prevailed. The military uprising allowed the Anarchists to implement a proletarian revolution in several areas of Spain. Workers seized factories and elected committees to oversee operations, while owners were murdered or fled. Azaña and Largo Caballero, who had become prime minister, were powerless to stop Anarchist workers, whose activities, while fulfilling the hopes of many workers, antagonized many moderates

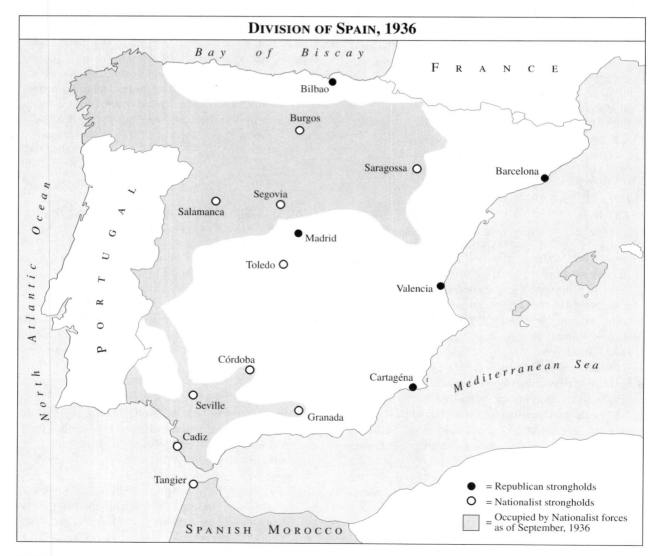

DIVISION OF SPAIN, 1936

● = Republican strongholds
○ = Nationalist strongholds
▫ = Occupied by Nationalist forces as of September, 1936

who came to support the Nationalists. The Republicans' only source
of outside aid was Soviet Russia,
whose leader, Joseph Stalin, sent
supplies and military advisers. With
its control over the distribution of
Russian aid, the Spanish Communist
Party, a relatively small and powerless group before the uprising, became powerful.

The democratic Western powers
stood aside from the conflict, hoping
that it would not spread into a general European war. Throughout
1936 and 1937, the Nationalists
slowly encircled the Republicans,
whose army was largely undisci-
plined. By 1939, the superior military force of the Nationalists had
prevailed, and in April, General
Franco seized Madrid, the last Republican stronghold, and the war
was over.

—*José M. Sánchez and*
James A. Baer

FURTHER READING

Alpert, Michael. *A New International History of the Spanish
Civil War.* 2d ed. New York:
Palgrave Macmillan, 2004. Well-
researched analysis focuses on
the international aspects of the
war, placing it in the context of
other world events. Includes map,
bibliography, and index.

Bolloten, Burnett. *The Spanish Civil War: Revolution
and Counterrevolution.* Chapel Hill: University of
North Carolina Press, 1991. Massive study provides
extensive detail regarding the role of the Communist
Party in undermining the revolution and the efforts of
the Spanish Republic to operate outside of Stalin's
control.

Forrest, Andrew. *The Spanish Civil War.* New York:
Routledge, 2000. Brief text designed for undergraduates covers all aspects of the war, including the roles
played by foreign powers. Features illustrations, selected bibliography, and index.

Hills, George. *The Battle for Madrid.* New York: St.
Martin's Press, 1976. Provides detailed history and

FRANCO'S FASCISM

*In 1936, General Francisco Franco emerged as the leader of the Nationalists
and he proclaimed himself Spain's military leader. He would remain in power
to 1975. Here are some excerpts from Franco's speeches during the Spanish
Civil War:*

- *July 17, 1936, on the eve of the war:* Spaniards! The nation calls to her defense all those of you who hear the holy name of Spain, those in the ranks of
the Army and Navy who have made a profession of faith in the service of the
Motherland, all those who swore to defend her to the death against her enemies. The situation in Spain grows more critical every day; anarchy reigns in
most of the countryside and towns; government-appointed authorities encourage revolts, when they do not actually lead them; murderers use pistols
and machine guns to settle their differences and to treacherously assassinate
innocent people, while the public authorities fail to impose law and order.
Revolutionary strikes of all kinds paralyze the life of the nation, destroying
its sources of wealth and creating hunger, forcing working men to the point
of desperation.
- *November 26, 1937:* I will impose my will by victory and will not enter into
discussion. We open our arms to all Spaniards and offer them the opportunity of helping to form the Spain of tomorrow which will be a land of justice,
mercy, and fraternity. The war is already won on the battlefields as in the
economic, commercial, industrial, and even social spheres. I will only agree
to end it militarily. My troops will advance. The choice for the enemy is fight
or unconditional surrender, nothing else.
- *July 18, 1938:* Our fight is a crusade in which Europe's fate is at stake. . . .
Spain was great when she had a State Executive with a missionary character.
Her ideals decayed when a serious leader was replaced by assemblies of irre-
sponsible men, adopting foreign thought and manners. The nation needs
unity to face modern problems, particularly in Spain after the severest trial
of her history. Separatism and class war must be abolished and justice and
education must be imposed. The new leaders must be characterized by austerity, morality, and industry. Spaniards must adopt the military and religious virtues of discipline and austerity. All elements of discord must be removed.

---

analysis of both the political and the military battle
for Madrid during the Spanish Civil War. Includes
maps and photographs.

Payne, Stanley G. *The Spanish Revolution.* New York:
W. W. Norton, 1970. Thorough account of events in
Spain from the early twentieth century through the
Civil War. Focuses on the revolutionary changes oc-
curring in the Republican Zone. Informative, al-
though clearly biased toward the liberal Republic.

Preston, Paul. *The Spanish Civil War, 1936-1939.* Chicago: Dorsey Press, 1986. Short interpretive work argues that the military uprising under Franco ended a
Republican government that was doing the best it
could for Spain.

1936

Thomas, Hugh. *The Spanish Civil War*. Rev. ed. 1977. Reprint. New York: Modern Library, 2001. Updated, expanded edition of a classic study of the war presents both political and military perspectives. Addresses the war's impacts on both individual lives and nations.

SEE ALSO: Apr. 14, 1931: Second Spanish Republic Is Proclaimed; Aug. 31, 1935-Nov. 4, 1939: Neutrality Acts; Aug. 2-18, 1936: Claretian Martyrs Are Executed in Spain; Jan. 6, 1937: Embargo on Arms to Spain; Apr. 26, 1937: Raids on Guernica; July, 1937: Picasso Exhibits *Guernica*.

August 1-16, 1936
GERMANY HOSTS THE SUMMER OLYMPICS

The Berlin Olympics of 1936, the most controversial Olympic Games of the modern era, were used by the Nazis to showcase their racial ideology and strengthen their regime through carefully staged pageantry and propaganda. The gold medals won by African American athlete Jesse Owens in four events represent one of the most spectacular individual achievements in Olympic history.

ALSO KNOWN AS: Nazi Olympics; Hitler's Games
LOCALE: Berlin and Kiel, Germany
CATEGORIES: Sports; diplomacy and international relations

KEY FIGURES
Avery Brundage (1887-1975), American businessman and head of the American Olympic Committee
Carl Diem (1882-1962), general secretary of the organizing committee in charge of planning and overseeing the Games
Joseph Goebbels (1897-1945), Nazi propaganda minister
Adolf Hitler (1889-1945), chancellor of Germany, 1933-1945,
Jesse Owens (1913-1980), African American athlete who won four gold medals
Leni Riefenstahl (1902-2003), German filmmaker who produced *Olympia*, 1938, a groundbreaking documentary on the 1936 Olympics

SUMMARY OF EVENT
Berlin had been scheduled to host the 1916 Olympic Games, which were canceled because of World War I, and German athletes were not invited to the 1920 and 1924 Olympics as a punishment for Germany's role in the war in an early interjection of politics into the Olympic Games. When they competed in the 1928 Games in Amsterdam, however, German athletes finished second to the Americans in the overall medal count. The selec-

tion of the venue for the 1936 Olympics was made in 1931, when Berlin bested Barcelona, Spain. Olympic practice allowed the host of the Summer Games to do the Winter Games as well, and Germany selected the Bavarian resort of Garmisch-Partenkirchen. Some Germans were not pleased with Germany's hosting the 1936 Olympics, both because Jewish and black athletes would be competing and because of the expense involved in sponsoring the Games during the Great Depression.

Planning for the 1936 Olympics had begun before Adolf Hitler was appointed chancellor. Carl Diem, general secretary of the organizing committee, attended the 1932 Games and took copious notes on the pageantry and handling of the events. With Hitler in power, however, several new issues arose. What was Hitler's attitude toward hosting the Olympics? Would the Nazi government adhere to the Olympic ideals of equal access for all athletes? How would athletes and governments react to an Olympics sponsored by Nazi Germany? After some initial hesitancy—overcome by Joseph Goebbels's strong support for the Games—Hitler authorized full funding of the 1936 Olympics. He saw the Games as a vehicle to promote Nazi ideology, strengthen the government and Germany, and to deflect criticism from the Nazis. Although German sports officials had made a June, 1933, written promise that Jewish athletes would not be excluded from the German Olympic team, Jewish athletes and officials were expelled from German athletic associations, which effectively barred them from the Olympics.

Such actions led to a movement in the United States and Western Europe to move the Games or to boycott the Berlin Olympics if Jewish and black athletes were barred from competing. Avery Brundage, president of the American Olympic Committee, went on a fact-finding tour of Germany in 1934 to investigate matters. He urged that American athletes participate in the Games and condemned the boycott movement as interfering with athletics. Passage of the discriminatory Nazi Nuremberg Racial Laws in 1935 energized the boycott movement, but Brundage was able to outmaneuver boycott supporters at the December, 1935, vote of the American Athletic Union (AAU), which decided to send athletes to the Games. Individual athletes then faced the dilemma of whether to participate. Two Jewish athletes were recalled from abroad to participate for Germany: Rudi Ball played on the hockey team at the Winter Games, and Helene Meyer won a silver medal in fencing at the Summer Games and did the required Hitler salute on the medal platform.

The Winter Games at Garmisch-Partenkirchen, which lasted from February 6 to 16, 1936, attracted athletes from twenty-eight countries. Complaints from high-level Olympic officials caused the Nazis to remove anti-Semitic signs from the roads leading to the site prior to the commencement of the Winter Games. The reoccupation of the Rhineland by German troops on March 7, 1936, led to renewed calls for boycotts in France and Britain, but athletes from both nations competed, and the Nazis removed anti-Semitic signs from Berlin, suspended anti-Jewish activity, and cleaned the city in preparation for the Summer Games. Carl Diem and Joseph Goebbels had created great publicity and propaganda campaigns to advertise the Olympics, which featured both an Olympic exhibition and an Olympic caravan.

The Summer Games opened with tremendous fanfare and pageantry. The famous composer Richard Strauss led a 100-piece orchestra and chorus of 3,000 in the German national anthem, the Nazi Party's anthem (the "Horst Wessel" song), and a special composition to honor the Olympics. The 110,000 spectators saw the culmination of the torch run from Olympia, Greece, and Hitler was presented with an olive branch from Olympia. The Nazis paid careful attention to media coverage by providing print journalists with impressive facilities; shortwave radio was used to broadcast the Games in twenty-eight languages to an esti-

mated 300 million listeners worldwide; and an experimental television network beamed the events to select locations throughout Berlin. Filmmaker Leni Riefenstahl, with secret funding from the Nazis, was able to document the Olympics in her groundbreaking three-and-one-half-hour film, *Olympia* (1938). This work set the standard for sports documentaries but raised questions about Reifenstahl's connection to the Nazi regime and her artistic vision. In general, however, the pageantry and festivities resonated with many excited participants and visitors.

The sailing competitions at Kiel and the other events in Berlin brought together forty-nine nations, about five thousand athletes, and more than three million attendees. German athletes won the most medals—eighty-nine—and the United States was second with fifty-six. These Games, however, were remembered for the tremendous accomplishments of the African American athlete Jesse Owens, who won four gold medals: in the 100-meter and

---

THE HORST WESSEL SONG

The hosting of the 1936 Summer Olympic Games was only part of a large propaganda apparatus designed to showcase the Nazi regime to the world. The Games opened with tremendous fanfare and pageantry, including famous composer Richard Strauss conducting a one-hundred-piece orchestra and three-thousand-voice chorus in the Nazi Party's anthem "Die Fahne hoch" ("The Flag on High"), commonly known as the Horst Wessel song after the storm trooper who wrote the song's lyrics. The anthem was later banned in Germany.

Flag high, ranks closed,
The S.A. marches with silent solid steps.
Comrades shot by the red front and reaction
march in spirit with us in our ranks.

The street free for the brown battalions,
The street free for the Storm Troopers.
Millions, full of hope, look up at the swastika;
The day breaks for freedom and for bread.

For the last time the call will now be blown;
For the struggle now we all stand ready.
Soon will fly Hitler-flags over every street;
Slavery will last only a short time longer.

Flag high, ranks closed,
The S.A. marches with silent solid steps.
Comrades shot by the red front and reaction
march in spirit with us in our ranks.

1936

200-meter dashes, in the broad jump, and in the 4- by 100-meter relay. The relay remained controversial because of the last-minute replacement of two Jewish members of the American team, Martin Glickman and Sam Stoller, with two African American runners, Jesse Owens and Ralph Metcalfe. Questions still remain whether this was done to field the fastest team or to avoid offending the Nazis.

Contrary to popular belief, Hitler did not refuse to shake Owens's hand: On the first day of competition, the head of the International Olympic Committee had insisted that Hitler congratulate either all or none of the victors. Hitler chose to not congratulate any of the participants, but the American media were unaware of the situation and thought that only American athletes were affected.

At the end of the Berlin Games, the site for the 1940 Olympics was announced—Tokyo, Japan—but World War II caused the 1940 and 1944 Games to be canceled. After the closing ceremonies were over, many spectators launched into a series of "Sieg Heils."

SIGNIFICANCE

More than any other Olympics, those of 1936 were linked to the head of state of the host country who was a highly visible spectator and beneficiary of the validation which the Games brought to his regime. The nearly flawless execution of events and festivities, coupled with suspension of anti-Semitic activities during the Olympics, convinced many foreign journalists and visitors that accounts of earlier anti-Semitic actions had been exaggerated. Although a few perceptive observers saw through the propaganda, the Nazis achieved their goals through their politization of the 1936 Olympics.

New innovations and technologies became permanent fixtures at the Olympics: the torch run, the extensive use of radio and the experimental medium of television, and the elaborate pageantry. The boycott movements in the United States and Western Europe set an example that would become a reality during the U.S.-led boycott of the Moscow Games in 1980 and the Soviet Union-led retaliatory boycott of the 1984 Los Angeles Olympics.

The reasons for the success of the German athletes are subject to scholarly disagreement: Some tout nationalistic and ideological motivation, while others focus on the rigorous and scientific training that would soon become standard for world-class and Olympic athletes. In any case, the strong showing by the totalitarian regimes in the medal count—Germany in first place, Italy in third; and Japan in eighth—caused other nations to emulate their

examples for physical education programs for school children and training athletes. Perhaps emboldened by their Olympic successes, Germany, Italy, and Japan drew closer and became more aggressive: Japan invaded China in 1937 and Germany invaded Poland in 1939, and many nations were engulfed in World War II within a few years of the Berlin Games.

—*Mark C. Herman*

FURTHER READING

Bachrach, Susan D. *The Nazi Olympics: Berlin, 1936.* Boston: Little, Brown, 2000. Developed from an exhibit of the U.S. Holocaust Memorial Museum, this concise treatment's strength is the superb photographs that supplement the text.

Hart-Davis, Duff. *Hitler's Games: The 1936 Olympics.* New York: Harper & Row, 1986. This journalistic account examines the 1936 Olympics from the British perspective.

Krüger, Arnd, and William Murray, eds. *The Nazi Olympics: Sport, Politics, and Appeasement in the 1930's.* Urbana: University of Illinois Press, 2003. A valuable collection of eleven scholarly essays covering the 1936 Olympics from the point of view of individual nations.

Mandell, Richard D. *The Nazi Olympics.* 1971. Reprint. Urbana: University of Illinois Press, 1987. Has a new preface. The first scholarly treatment of the 1936 Games highlights the strong connection between Nazi ideology and the propaganda to which the Olympics were subjected.

Schaffer, Kay, and Sidonie Smith, eds. *The Olympics at the Millennium: Power, Politics, and the Games.* New Brunswick, N.J.: Rutgers University Press, 2000. These essays provide an overview of key themes of Olympic history in the twentieth century. Especially valuable is "Jewish Athletes and the 'Nazi Olympics'" by Allen Guttman, et al.

Senn, Alfred E. *Power, Politics, and the Olympic Games.* Champaign, Ill.: Human Kinetics, 1999. A historical overview which explores the relationship between domestic and international politics and the Olympics.

SEE ALSO: May 5-July 27, 1912: Stockholm Hosts the Summer Olympics; 1919-1933: Racist Theories Aid Nazi Rise to Political Power; Jan. 25-Feb. 5, 1924: First Winter Olympic Games; Jan. 30, 1933: Hitler Comes to Power in Germany; Mar. 7, 1936: German Troops March into the Rhineland; Feb. 12-Apr. 10, 1938: The Anschluss; Nov. 9-10, 1938: Kristallnacht.

August 2-18, 1936
CLARETIAN MARTYRS ARE EXECUTED IN SPAIN

Over a period of days, Republican militia executed fifty-one Claretian priests and seminarians in one of the Spanish Civil War's most brutal episodes of anticlerical persecution. Thousands of priests, nuns, and laypeople were ultimately killed during the war.

LOCALE: Barbasto and Madrid, Spain
CATEGORIES: Atrocities and war crimes; wars, uprisings, and civil unrest

KEY FIGURES

Florentino Asensio Barroso (1877-1936), bishop and apostolic administrator of Barbasto, Spain
Felipe de Jesús Munárriz Azcona (1875-1936), rector and father superior of the Barbastro seminary
Faustino Pérez García (1911-1936), cleric who composed a farewell dedicated to the Claretian congregation
Francisco Franco (1892-1975), leader of the uprising against the Spanish Republic and later military leader of Spain, 1939-1975

SUMMARY OF EVENT

The extensive persecution, brutal treatment, and summary executions of Catholic clergy and laypeople during the Spanish Civil War (1936-1939) is one of the conflict's most overlooked elements. The most intense period of killings of innocent clergy and laypeople occurred in the first few months of the civil war, before the so-called international brigades of the Republican cause began arriving in Spain. Nearly 7,000 clergy members were killed, more than half of whom were diocesan bishops. The rest were priests or seminarians, including 283 nuns. The exact number of laypeople killed is difficult to establish, but it certainly numbered several thousand and may have been as high as tens of thousands.

Anticlericalism had been on the rise in Spain since the early nineteenth century, when the fortunes of the Spanish Empire waned, and the country became vulnerable to foreign intervention. As the collapse of Spanish power gave rise to a debate about how to restore the country's former greatness, a small, mostly urban, politically progressive, and anticlerical elite emerged. This group blamed traditional Catholicism as the cause of national decline. On the other hand, a large number of Spaniards, most of whom came from rural areas, continued to cling to the Catholic faith and to more conservative and traditionalist attitudes. Added to these two schools of thought

was another, more complicated set of issues that surrounded regionalist and nationalist or centralist strategies for ruling the country. Centralists tended to be anticlerical, while the clergy tended to rally to the regionalist cause. The Napoleonic invasion of 1808 revealed this division and gave rise to the first anticlerical government in 1810, ushering in a dynastic struggle that persisted through the nineteenth century.

A complicated politics of land expropriations by the government gradually deprived the Church of much of its property and increased its dependence on bourgeois elements in Spanish society. In the class conflict that resulted, the Church largely supported the middle class, which led to a sense of resentment against the clergy by the working classes. The struggle over control of education also pitted clerical and anticlerical parties. Democratic and radical political parties emerged at the turn of the century, and levels of anticlerical sentiment varied among the disparate groups that comprised the left wing of the Spanish populace, which included many Freemasons, atheists, communists, anarchists, and moderate socialists. Many leftists considered the Catholic Church to be helplessly enmeshed in aristocratic and monarchial thinking and part of a Spanish legacy that had to be uprooted for the country to establish a modern democracy. It is equally certain, however, that at least half of the Spanish population continued to be Catholic in sentiment, even if they did not regularly practice the religion.

The deep cultural divisions in the country became even more obvious after World War I, as governmental authority disintegrated. A military coup in 1923 imposed only a semblance of order, and eventually Republican and Socialist parties toppled the monarchy in April 1931. Agreeing on little except the need for anticlerical policies, the Republican-Socialist coalition imposed brazenly antireligious policies that prohibited any public display of religion, including traditional processions and even the simple wearing of crucifixes. Anarchists began another wave of church burnings, driving many lukewarm Catholics otherwise disposed toward reform away from the left-wing coalition. The elections of 1933 and 1936 showed a country almost evenly split, but when the Republican-Socialist bloc took power in 1936 (after conservatives won the popular vote but lost control of Parliament), the Popular Front declared amnesty and anarchists freed from prison went on a rampage of anticlerical violence. In July of 1936, the army rose to oppose the Republican government, and the active phase of the Spanish Civil War began.

Murders of priests, bishops, and other church members occurred in almost every area dominated by Republican forces: Churches, convents, and monasteries were attacked and destroyed, and those members of congregations who did not flee were attacked. In the Madrid region alone, more than 1,100 clerics—about 30 percent of the diocesan clergy—were killed. By far the highest proportion of clergy killed was in Barbastro, where 123 of its 140 clergy were murdered by Republican anarchists. Among those shot to death was Barbastro's bishop, Florentino Asensio Barroso. On July 20, the local Republican committee, which was composed of both Republican sympathizers and anarchists, broke into the Claretian house, arrested its three most senior priests, in-

---

A MARTYR'S LAST LETTER

Seminary student Ramón Illa wrote the following letter on August 10, 1936, shortly before he was martyred.

Dearest Mother, Grandmother and Well-remembered Brothers:

I am writing to you with deep joy of soul, and the Lord knows I'm not lying. I say it before heaven and earth. I'd never rest without letting you know by these lines that the Lord has seen fit to place the palm of martyrdom in my hands. By these lines, too, I'm sending you my only will and testament, namely, that when you receive them you will sing to the Lord for the great and signal gift of martyrdom that He has deigned to grant me.

We've been in this jail since July 20th. The whole community is here: 60 just individuals. Eight days ago they shot our reverend Father Superior and some other Fathers. Happy they, and happy we who will follow them. I wouldn't exchange my jail for the gift of working miracles, nor my martyrdom for the apostolate, which has been my life's dream.

I'm going to be shot for being a religious and a member of the clergy, or if you will, for following the teachings of the Roman Catholic Church.

Thanks be to the Father through our Lord Jesus Christ. Amen.

Ramón Illa, C.M.F. Barbastro

Source: Quoted in Gabriel Campo Villegas, *Claretian Martyrs of Barbastro* (Glenlivet, Scotland: Scalan Association, n.d.).

---

cluding the seminary rector, Felipe de Jesús Munárriz Azcona, and placed them in separate prison cells.

After the arrival of the much more radical and bloodthirsty Catalan Columns on July 25, pressure mounted to begin executions of the detained clergy. The three Claretian superiors were executed, along with other local clergy, on August 2. The fifty remaining Claretians were detained over the next few weeks and subjected to degrading conditions before being killed. The six oldest priests were executed on August 12, and the rest were put to death in groups over the days that followed, with the exception of two Argentine seminarians who were released and later recounted the inhumane and degrading treatment of their classmates as well as the occasional humane acts performed by their captors. The two freed clerics also carried a handwritten farewell address written (on a chocolate wrapper) by Faustino Pérez García in which the doomed priest and his associates forgave their persecutors. The last two Claretians of Barbastro were murdered on August 18. Although executions continued throughout other parts of Republican-held Spain, the Barbastro bloodbath was over as virtually all the priests in the area had been exterminated. The Catalan Columns then moved on to more fertile ground.

SIGNIFICANCE

Although atrocities occurred on both sides of the Spanish Civil War, the concentrated fury against innocent clergy was especially notable in the war's first months, and it pushed many Spaniards, including some of the more moderate Catholics, to support General Francisco Franco, who promised to deliver relief from the anticlerical carnage. As the decades passed and the partisan passions subsided, historians were able to better assess and attain a more balanced understanding of the atrocities committed on all sides of a complicated cauldron of political animosities. Caught in the middle of this tragic violence were many innocent religious people whose heroism was recognized not only by historians but also by the Catholic Church, which began the process of beatification and canonization of many of the Spanish martyrs, including the fifty-one Claretians of Barbastro. The Claretians were beatified by Pope John Paul II on October 25, 1992. The barbarity of the Spanish Civil War sometimes seems to pale in comparison when set against the backdrop of the even more extensive barbarisms of Nazi and Communist regimes in Europe during and after World War II. However, the Spanish atrocities did illustrate the degree to which hatred of religion could lead political regimes that were otherwise dedicated to progressive social programs to debase themselves in patently unjust outbursts of brutality against clearly innocent and harmless religious believers.

—*Robert F. Gorman*

FURTHER READING

Royal, Robert. *The Catholic Martyrs of the Twentieth Century*. New York: Crossroad Publishing, 2000. Contains an excellent summary chapter on anticlerical persecution during the Spanish revolution.

Sánchez, José M. *The Spanish Civil War as a Religious Tragedy*. Notre Dame, Ind.: University of Notre Dame Press, 1985. A scholarly account by an expert on anticlericalism.

Thomas, Hugh. *The Spanish Civil War*. New York: Si-mon & Schuster, 1986. A balanced assessment of this bitter conflict by a respected British historian.

Villegas, Gabriel Campo. *Claretian Martyrs of Barbastro*. Scalan Association, Glenlivet, Scotland. http://www.scalan.co.uk/gordondelsur.htm. One of the most extensive historical reconstructions of the Barbastro incident available, based on collected eyewitness testimony.

SEE ALSO: Jan.-Feb., 1932: El Salvador's Military Massacres Civilians; Aug. 11-13, 1933: Iraqi Army Slaughters Assyrian Christians; July 17, 1936: Spanish Civil War Begins; Jan. 6, 1937: Embargo on Arms to Spain; Apr. 26, 1937: Raids on Guernica; Mar. 2, 1939: Pius XII Becomes Pope.

November, 1936
CARNEGIE REDEFINES SELF-HELP LITERATURE

Dale Carnegie, a farm boy who struggled through adversity to establish a career in public speaking, achieved fame with his practical advice for business and personal success.

ALSO KNOWN AS: *How to Win Friends and Influence People*

LOCALE: New York, New York

CATEGORY: Publishing and journalism

KEY FIGURE

Dale Carnegie (1888-1955), American writer and lecturer

SUMMARY OF EVENT

Dale Carnegie was born into a world undergoing painful social and economic change. For most people in the United States, farms and small communities represented a mythic past; the future was in the cities. New York City, for example, grew from a population of 125,000 in 1820 to more than 5 million by 1910. Many urban inhabitants were immigrants, of whom some 9 million entered the United States in the single decade between 1900 and 1910. Most dreamed of solvency, if not success, but they entered a struggle for mere survival in an increasingly complex industrial world.

Formal education had little to offer, and demand for public education was met only gradually. For example, the United States had fewer than eight hundred high schools in 1878, and that figure increased to only fifty-five hundred during the next twenty years. High school education, if achieved at all, marked the end of formal schooling for most Americans; in 1904, approximately one hundred thousand students were enrolled in U.S. colleges or universities, which, in any case, were more nearly allied to the traditional European studies of Latin, Greek, and rhetoric than to the needs of a newly industrialized age.

An overwhelming demand existed for adult education, and that demand was met in a number of ways. Most successful was the Chautauqua program, which influenced Carnegie in his youth. Founded in 1874, by 1883 this summer camp had expanded to include a winter home-study program. In 1888, New York began offering free lectures for working people, resulting in an attendance of seven million within the first fifteen years. That idea spread, as did public libraries (largely funded by millionaire Andrew Carnegie) and mechanics' institutes.

For most Americans, however, the printed word remained the primary source of information. Although self-help books had long been popular, most still dealt with manners and morals, offering advice on the use of forks and cures for consumption and rabies. Self-help books for men dealt mostly with the vast generalities of writers such as Ralph Waldo Emerson, John Ruskin, and Émile Coué.

Dale Carnegie, like many other Americans, had undergone the experience of being the outsider in a system that rejected him. Born in Maryville, Missouri, he was the son of a devout Methodist mother, a schoolteacher before her marriage, and a farmer father who had completed six years of education. (Until 1916, the family name was Carnegey.) Carnegie's father was unsuccessful; his crops were wiped out by flood and his livestock by disease. The father suffered severe and suicidal depression, overwhelmed with health problems, debts, and threats of bank foreclosure on the farm. The son attended a one-room school.

The family moved to live near Warrensburg so that Dale could live at home and attend the tuition-free college that later became Central Missouri State University. Awkward, self-conscious, and poorly dressed, he was a failure until he trained himself to compete in oratorical and debate contests. Eventually, he began to win, and his success gave him confidence. He left the college in 1908, but he never graduated, having failed in his studies of Latin.

He became for a time a salesman for the International Correspondence School, after which he eked out a living selling meat in small Dakota towns. In 1911, he went to New York to study at the American Academy of Dramatic Arts. The school, founded in 1886, taught a natural acting style that contrasted with the overstated and stylized acting that dominated much of the nineteenth century stage. Carnegie went on the road with an acting company, but he discovered he was not suited for the stage.

In 1912, he was living in a New York slum and attempting to sell cars. Depression and headaches caused him to give up that job, however, and he dreamed of being a writer. (He eventually completed a novel, *The Blizzard*, in 1921, only to have it rejected by publishers and his literary agent.) Deciding to write and teach public speaking, he applied to teach adult courses at Columbia University and New York University but was rejected. At last, he worked out an agreement to teach at the Young Men's Christian Association (YMCA) at 125th Street in Harlem, which was then primarily a white neighborhood. The YMCA doubted the course would prove attractive and offered to pay him only a percentage of profits rather than the two dollars per session he had requested. He was soon earning thirty dollars per session. By the outbreak of World War I, he was able to hire instructors and to write tracts to standardize his methods.

By this time, he had rejected the formal oratorical techniques he had studied in college and had developed techniques similar to those he had studied at the Academy of Dramatic Arts. In 1915, with J. Berg Esenwein, he wrote *The Art of Public Speaking*, which was based on his theories. He followed this with *Public Speaking: A Practical Course for Business Men* (1926), *Little Known Facts About Well Known Men* (1934), and a study of his boyhood hero, *Lincoln the Unknown* (1932).

Carnegie's next book, *How to Win Friends and Influence People*, appealed to a wide audience frightened by economic and urban change and, by 1936, wearied of economic depression. In 1936, only 12.9 percent of high school graduates would enter college, but an urbanized and industrialized society with widespread unemployment demanded more skills than did the community life of the past. By 1936, one American family in four was reported to be on relief; 38 percent of families (11.7 million families) lived below the poverty line. In Europe and the United States, fascists on the political right and socialists and communists on the left wanted to overturn a seemingly failing system, but the majority of Americans simply wanted to survive and, if possible, thrive. To these people, Dale Carnegie offered hope.

SIGNIFICANCE

How to Win Friends and Influence People was, Carnegie wrote, the book he wished he could have read two decades earlier. He was modest about the book and its future, hoping it would sell fifteen or twenty thousand copies. Instead, the book was a sensational success. Its effects were personal and immediate as well as general and far-ranging.

Carnegie's personal success was quickly obvious. The book soon began to sell five thousand copies per week. Despite parodies by humorists such as James Thurber and uncompromising condemnation by academics and intellectuals, the book appeared for two years on *The New York Times* best-seller list. By the time Carnegie's widow, Dorothy, revised the book in 1981, more than fifteen million copies had been sold.

The effect of this success on his courses in public speaking was also immediate; enrollment in the courses increased dramatically. Carnegie was to have problems with these classes during the late 1930's and World War II, but, by 1992, Dale Carnegie training was offered in every U.S. state and in some sixty other countries. Graduates by then numbered 3.5 million. *Life* magazine named Carnegie as one of the one hundred most important Americans of the twentieth century.

Carnegie also revolutionized the genre of self-help literature. Rather than speaking as a specialist, Carnegie addressed his students as a slightly more experienced equal speaking to equals, freely admitting his own mistakes. The roots of his style clearly lie in the Methodist sermons of his youth. His work is heavy with anecdotes about people,

CARNEGIE'S "SIX WAYS TO MAKE PEOPLE LIKE YOU"

Among the topics he addresses in How to Win Friends and Influence People, *Dale Carnegie expounds on how an individual can make others like him or her. He sums up by advising the reader to follow these six basic "principles":*

1. Become genuinely interested in other people.
2. Smile.
3. Remember that a man's name is to him the sweetest and most important sound in any language.
4. Be a good listener. Encourage others to talk about themselves.
5. Talk in terms of the other man's interest.
6. Make the other person feel important—and do it sincerely.

Source: Dale Carnegie, *How to Win Friends and Influence People* (New York: Simon & Schuster, 1936).

both famous and unknown, who have overcome adversity using the techniques Carnegie advocates; he often echoes the rhetoric of a Protestant minister, drawing lessons from the parables and other stories of the Scriptures. Carnegie's tone is informal, conversational, even ungrammatical. His sentences generally are brief, although never condescending, and his words are simple.

If in his style he offered a work consistent with the religious experiences of many, in substance he offered a simple, easily comprehended system that was unlike the heavy-handed philosophizing of earlier self-help literature. His most direct source was American philosopher William James, from whom Carnegie borrowed the idea that emotion follows action, rather than precedes it. Logically, then, the imitation of a mood will produce the desired mood. The emotions he advocated are essentially a secularized version of the biblical Golden Rule: courtesy, sensitivity to others, assertiveness rather than aggression. Understanding the need to motivate others, he advocated a system based on rewards and praise, not punishment. He advocated what would later be called conflict resolution and teamwork to replace the aggressive individualism of the mythic American frontier. Implicit everywhere and frequently explicit was the assumption that financial rewards will follow.

Unlike earlier self-help literature, Carnegie's book was an exhortation to action. He gives instructions on how to use the book and summarizes his points for easy reference. Theories were kept to a minimum; anecdotal accounts were written so that a reader could imitate the behavior described.

Although condemned by critics and academicians, Carnegie's techniques and style, by the late twentieth

century, had spread throughout much business literature as well as self-help literature. In the academically sanctioned *A Passion for Excellence* (1985), for example, authors Tom Peters and Nancy Austin incorporated much of Carnegie's anecdotal approach, gave tips for developing courtesy and sensitivity to others, and echoed Carnegie in their advocacy of motivation based on rewards and praise. Carnegie's influence also is evident in literature produced by entrepreneurs such as Mary Kay Ash, founder of Mary Kay Cosmetics, who directly echoed Carnegie with chapters on "Golden Rule Management" and instructions about how to make others feel a sense of self-worth in *Mary Kay on People Management* (1984). Ash, too, urged motivation through rewards. Carnegie's views were also echoed in some New Age literature, such as Marilyn Ferguson's *The Aquarian Conspiracy: Personal and Social Transformation in the 1980s* (1980), in which abilities to motivate, engender self-esteem, and demonstrate sensitivity were defined as essential qualities in leaders of the future.

Stress reduction was the subject of the second best seller produced by Carnegie as a result of his initial success. *How to Stop Worrying and Start Living* (1948) became perhaps Carnegie's most influential book. *How to Win Friends and Influence People* was written on the assumption that behavior modification is relatively simple: Imitate a feeling, and the feeling will come. In the preface to his next book, however, Carnegie observed that the process is actually more complex because of the intervention of emotional blocks, chief among them anxiety or worry, which would later, as he described them, come to be called "stress." At the heart of these blocks, he noted, are unfocused fears about the future, humorlessness and self-importance, depression, inability to deal with criticism and life's inevitable adversities, and inability to accept oneself.

Carnegie had no access to statistics indicating a relationship between stress and disease, but he inferred this relationship from popular psychiatric literature and from personal observation of his father's depression and of his own tension-related headaches while he was living in New York slums. He found many historical anecdotes to show his readers that, if they were suffering, they were not alone. The book ended with thirty-one stories by in-

1936

dividuals who overcame stress, ranging from relatively unknown businessmen to singing cowboy Gene Autry, baseball star Connie Mack, and boxing champion Jack Dempsey. In effect, Carnegie had produced the first modern work on stress management. Again, he had offered his readers hope with the promise that at least some of their fate was within their control. By 2005, fifteen million copies of *How to Stop Worrying and Start Living* had been sold, and the book's influence had been felt in the writings of many other self-help leaders.

—*Betty Richardson*

FURTHER READING

Carnegie, Dale. *How to Develop Self-Confidence and Influence People by Public Speaking*. New York: Simon & Schuster, 1956. Adaptation of *Public Speaking and Influencing Men in Business* (1926), which was itself an adaptation of *Public Speaking: A Practical Course for Business Men* (1926). Includes chapters on memory development, preparation, and vocabulary development. More a formal textbook than a book of practical hints.

_____. *How to Stop Worrying and Start Living*. Rev. ed. New York: Simon & Schuster, 1984. The original 1948 work with some revisions by Dorothy Carnegie.

_____. *How to Win Friends and Influence People*. Rev. ed. New York: Simon & Schuster, 1981. The original 1936 work with some revisions by Dorothy Carnegie.

Kasson, John F. *Rudeness and Civility: Manners in Nineteenth-Century Urban America*. New York: Hill & Wang, 1990. Makes passing mention of Carnegie and treats his work with contempt as showing the middle classes how to achieve a spurious gentility. Includes much valuable material about the self-help tradition and the emergence of urbanization and industrialization, but facilely categorizes readers of self-help literature and ignores economic motivations.

Kemp, Giles, and Edward Claflin. *Dale Carnegie: The Man Who Influenced Millions*. New York: St. Martin's Press, 1989. Pulls together materials from other sources, including newspaper reports and reviews, to describe Carnegie's influence. Compensates for a scarcity of biographical material with accounts of Carnegie's training sessions.

Meyer, Donald. *The Positive Thinkers: Popular Religious Psychology from Mary Baker Eddy to Norman Vincent Peale and Ronald Reagan*. Rev. ed. Middletown, Conn.: Wesleyan University Press, 1988. Scholarly work surveys self-help writers. Unfortunately lumps together many dissimilar writers and provides only superficial readings of many texts, including Carnegie's.

SEE ALSO: Nov. 28, 1908: *Christian Science Monitor* Is Founded; Feb., 1922: *Reader's Digest* Is Founded; 1926-1927: Mail-Order Clubs Revolutionize Book Sales.

November 2, 1936
BBC AIRS THE FIRST HIGH-DEFINITION TELEVISION PROGRAM

The British Broadcasting Corporation's inauguration of regularly scheduled high-definition television service had enormous impacts on industry, commerce, and popular culture.

LOCALE: Alexandra Palace, London, England
CATEGORIES: Radio and television; communications and media; science and technology; inventions

KEY FIGURES
John Charles Walsham Reith (1889-1971), first director-general of the BBC, 1927-1938
John Logie Baird (1888-1946), Scottish engineer
Alan A. Campbell Swinton (1863-1930), British engineer
Hugh Carleton Greene (1910-1987), director-general of the BBC, 1960-1969

SUMMARY OF EVENT

Television was not the unique invention of a single genius but more a case of an idea whose time had come. Shortly after the development of the telephone and the radio, a number of inventors, scientists, and engineers addressed themselves to the problem of transmitting pictures electronically. Alan A. Campbell Swinton, a British engineer, proposed in 1908 a remarkably accurate theory of how this might be done. On a more practical level, John Logie Baird, a Scottish engineer, began successful experiments with low-definition television in the 1920's. Unfortunately for Baird, he relied on a mechanical scanning system to transmit pictures; an electronic system utilizing the cathode-ray tube would eventually prove superior. Baird was important because he helped to popularize this new form of entertainment. By the early 1930's, experimental demonstrations of television were taking place.

Central to the development of television was the British Broadcasting Corporation (BBC). Founded as a company in 1922, the BBC was transformed into a corporation by royal charter in 1927 and was given a monopoly on the transmission of all programming. It was financed by a license fee on all users of radios (called wireless sets) and was thus free of commercial pressure and of the need to rely on Parliament for funding. This independence ensured that the BBC's programming would be free of government influence. Because radio was growing enormously in popularity, the financial basis of the BBC was secure, and income increased each year. For example, 4.5 million licenses were granted in 1932; six years later, that figure had risen to 8.5 million. The BBC raised additional money from the sale of its publications, such as *Radio Times* and *The Listener*.

No proven guidelines existed to draw upon when it came to harnessing the immense power of radio, then later television. Much of the direction of the BBC was determined by its first director-general, John Charles Walsham Reith. A serious-minded Scottish Presbyterian, Reith could be arrogant, domineering, and self-righteous, and certainly he imposed his strong personality on the corporation. He also had a deep sense of public service and was determined that the BBC would not only entertain but also inform and educate. He had no wish to court vast audiences by producing banal, vulgar, and tawdry programs; the BBC should maintain moral standards and expand the minds and cultural sensitivities of its listeners. Above all, he wanted the BBC to retain its monopoly status and remain independent of both government and business by having its own source of income. Within a short time, the BBC became the most admired radio network in the world, famous for its quality, objectivity, professionalism, and wide variety of programming.

When the television age dawned, Parliament gave the BBC the task of providing this new service. The television industry from the earliest moment thus benefited from the high standards and traditions already established by the BBC in general and Reith in particular. The world's first regularly scheduled high-definition television program was broadcast on November 2, 1936, from Alexandra Palace, London. Germany had begun regular service a year earlier, but it utilized a low-definition system of 180 lines, whereas the BBC transmitted a 405-line picture. (The United States eventually adopted a 525-line system.) Programming was limited to two hours a day,

from 3:00 to 4:00 in the afternoon and from 9:00 to 10:00 in the evening, six days a week. Sunday service and additional hours were added later. Initially, the BBC was unable to decide which television system was the best, that advocated by Baird, utilizing his mechanical scanning system (240 lines), or that of the Marconi-EMI Company, using the cathode-ray system (405 lines). It adopted the peculiar arrangement of alternating the two systems every other week. Within a short time, however, the latter system proved vastly superior. The BBC adopted it exclusively in February, 1937.

From the beginning, certain trends emerged that were to remain a permanent part of the television landscape. Although serious drama was an integral part of BBC programming, the public overwhelmingly preferred light entertainment such as prize fights, boat races, cricket matches, circuses, and popular plays. Women quickly became prominent in front of the camera, serving as presenters or entertainers, although senior administrative staff positions were dominated by men. The public also demonstrated that it was addicted to dramatic national events, such as the coronation of King George VI. About ten thousand viewers watched the event, foreshadowing the enormous audiences that later were to watch inaugurations, coronations, and high-profile sporting events. Opinion polls consistently showed that the public thought the quality of the BBC's service and programming was excellent.

Still, by 1939, television reached only a small audience, mainly in the London area. Although the cost of television sets was falling dramatically, there were only about ten thousand of them in use. The new medium was regarded as essentially a toy of the rich. When World War II broke out, the government ordered the television transmitter at Alexandra Palace shut down, because its signals would have been an excellent detection device by which German bombers could find London. Ironically, the last programming to be shown before the war was a Mickey Mouse cartoon. Service was not resumed until June 7, 1946.

SIGNIFICANCE

After the war, television proved to be immensely popular with the British public. The prosperous 1950's saw a sharp increase in the sale of television licenses. In 1953, about 2.1 million television licenses were issued. Many people were encouraged to buy television sets by the televising of the coronation of Queen Elizabeth II. Sales of licenses increased at the rate of about one million a year. Simultaneously, there was a vigorous debate as to

John Logie Baird, inventor of an early version of television, presents his machine to the Science Museum in London in 1926. (The Granger Collection, New York)

whether the BBC should retain its monopoly. One alternative was to establish a second channel, to be financed by advertising. Opponents of the BBC argued that a second channel was needed for greater variety, that monopoly was inconsistent with a free society, that competition would actually benefit the BBC, and that a channel showing advertisements would provide British industry with a powerful tool in marketing its products.

After much debate, Parliament passed legislation in 1956 creating a new public corporation, the Independent Television Authority, to run commercial broadcasting. Even supporters of commercial television had no wish to introduce American-style television, with its alleged vulgarity, crassness, endless commercial intrusions, and programming catering to the lowest common denominator. A system of controlled competition was set up that imposed certain programming standards and closely regulated commercials. Advertisers could only buy time; they had no control or influence over programming. Moreover, the time allotted to advertising was limited and minimal,

usually working out to only one brief commercial break during a half-hour program. Commercials were not allowed to disrupt the dramatic flow of a program.

Competition initially devastated the BBC. The new channel captured almost 80 percent of the viewing audience, and hundreds of BBC staff members defected to the opposition for higher pay or new challenges. Some of the worst fears of those who opposed commercial television appeared to prove true. It was estimated that the BBC carried about three times more serious programming than did its rival, which soon slipped into a conventional and bland format of programs lest it alienate its huge audience and jeopardize advertising revenue.

The BBC fought back. Much of the corporation's success in the 1960's was directly related to the personality of Hugh Carleton Greene, who served as director-general from 1960 to 1969. Greene is often considered to be the second most influential personality in the history of the BBC, behind Reith. He is generally credited with modernizing the structure and programming of the BBC, as he was forward-looking and made sure the corporation reflected the most modern trends in British society. During his tenure, the BBC brought in enterprising and imaginative writers and took chances on new forms of entertainment. The corporation also began to spend more money on television, at the expense of its radio division.

When Greene became director-general, the corporation had a staff of seventeen thousand and revenue from ten million licenses. By 1969, he had added some seven thousand staff positions, and the number of licenses totaled sixteen million. Programming in the field of comedy became more daring, police dramas reflected the gritty realism of law enforcement, and controversial documentaries both shocked the nation and stimulated debate.

In 1964, the BBC was authorized to set up a second channel, simply called BBC2. A logical division ensued: BBC1 concentrated on high-quality light entertainment and first-rate news and information programs, and BBC2 specialized in serious programming, catered to the needs of minorities such as opera lovers and science buffs, and experimented with new forms of entertainment. Eventually, the BBC won back about half the viewing audience. In 1982, a second commercial channel was created, giving Great Britain four channels equally divided between the BBC and commercial television.

The impact of television on Great Britain in particular and modern society in general has been enormous. To compare it to the invention of the wheel or the written word is probably no exaggeration. It created vast new industries in the field of electronics and dramatically expanded other industries, such as advertising. In the process, it changed the global economic balance of power. The ability to produce quality television sets and related electronic goods played a significant role in the dramatic rise of Japan and the Pacific Rim countries, at the expense of Great Britain and the United States. It encouraged industrial research and produced a string of new products such as color television and video cassette recorders. Business directly benefited from home shopping networks. Television technology allows people in different places to see each other during teleconferences. The television industry itself employs millions of people.

Television wreaked havoc on other sectors, such as daily newspapers and weekly magazines. The film industry benefited from the larger market for films, but theaters suffered. Television had profound social and cultural implications and rearranged the way that families lived and communities operated. The moral and ethical dimensions of television were constantly debated. Television has been accused of promoting promiscuity, en-

couraging violence, and destroying the family. It has been charged with polluting the democratic electoral process. In the United States, for example, a successful candidate for a major office must be telegenic and have access to vast sums of money for political advertisements. In business, cynics claim that the quality of a product matters less than how attractively it is presented in television commercials.

Even the most severe critics concede that at its best, television offers wondrous opportunities. It provides information, knowledge, and entertainment beyond the dreams of previous generations. Television gives people access to news events as they happen and to high-quality documentary programming dealing with history, nature, and society. On a human level, it undoubtedly has enabled millions of people to cope with loneliness, illness, and boredom. Its impact on education has also been considerable. In 1971, the BBC began providing television courses for the Open University, which offered degrees primarily to nontraditional students studying at home. By 1980 these broadcasts were reaching about seventy thousand students; about twenty-one thousand already had been graduated. The Open University has been called the most successful educational experiment in modern British history.

Starting from the most humble beginnings in Alexandra Palace in 1936, television emerged as one of the great industries of the modern epoch. It is difficult to imagine business and commerce operating effectively without television, just as it is difficult to imagine daily life without it. Many observers have noted that television constantly poses new problems to industry and society but never offers solutions. Certainly one of the great ongoing business and ethical challenges for modern society concerns how to harness the immense power of this medium for the benefit of all people while minimizing its potential for misuse.

—*David C. Lukowitz*

FURTHER READING

Black, Peter. *The Mirror in the Corner: People's Television*. London: Hutchinson, 1972. Lively and useful account of how the BBC's television monopoly was ended. Focuses on the debate leading to the creation of the Independent Television Authority and how commercial television affected the BBC.

Boyle, Andrew. *Only the Wind Will Listen: Reith of the BBC*. London: Hutchinson, 1972. Unconventional biography focuses only on Reith's years at the BBC. Adopts a psychological approach, emphasizing the puritanical and depressive side of Reith's personality. Fascinating reading.

Briggs, Asa. *The BBC: The First Fifty Years*. Oxford, England: Oxford University Press, 1985. Excellent introduction to the BBC by a distinguished British scholar. Includes useful list of significant dates and a fine bibliography.

Cain, John. *The BBC: Seventy Years of Broadcasting*. London: British Broadcasting Corporation, 1996. Lively, entertaining, and informative volume provides an ideal introduction to the history of BBC radio and television. Includes numerous photographs, including some depicting early television sets and transmitting apparatus.

Crisell, Andrew. *An Introductory History of British Broadcasting*. 2d ed. New York: Routledge, 2002. Comprehensive history of British radio and television discusses the beginnings of BBC television in chapter 4. Includes time line, bibliography, and index.

Paulu, Burton. *Television and Radio in the United Kingdom*. Minneapolis: University of Minnesota Press,

1981. Scholarly work by a noted authority on European television details the structure of the BBC, including finances, personnel, programming, and legal status.

Pawley, Edward. *BBC Engineering, 1922-1972*. London: British Broadcasting Corporation, 1972. Immensely valuable work on the application of technology to the development of BBC services. Intended for readers with some scientific and technical background.

Smith, Anthony, ed. *Television: An International History*. 2d ed. New York: Oxford University Press, 1998. Collection of essays on the history of television around the world includes discussion of the BBC and its impacts. Features a list of television museums and archives.

SEE ALSO: Dec. 29, 1923: Zworykin Applies for Patent on an Early Type of Television; Jan. 1, 1927: British Broadcasting Corporation Is Chartered; Apr. 30, 1939: American Television Debuts at the World's Fair; Sept. 1, 1940: First Color Television Broadcast.

November 11, 1936
RECIPROCAL TRADE ACT

In 1936, the United States and Canada established their first reciprocal trade agreement since 1854.

LOCALE: United States; Canada
CATEGORIES: Diplomacy and international relations; economics

KEY FIGURES

Cordell Hull (1871-1955), U.S. secretary of state, 1933-1944
William Lyon Mackenzie King (1874-1950), prime minister of Canada, 1921-1926, 1926-1930, 1935-1948
Franklin D. Roosevelt (1882-1945), president of the United States, 1933-1945

SUMMARY OF EVENT

A reciprocal trade agreement between two nations provides for both countries to reduce tariffs on trade goods. Such agreements between the United States and Canada date to 1854. British diplomats had begun negotiations with the U.S. government two years earlier, but they were unable to reach a conclusion at the time because of a dispute over fishing rights off the eastern coast of Can-

ada. Negotiations continued until the fisheries dispute was resolved and a reciprocity treaty was signed on June 6, 1854. This treaty gave fishermen from the United States the right to catch fish in the Atlantic coastal fisheries off Newfoundland, which were then the richest fishing grounds in the world. In turn, British fishing boats were granted permission to operate in U.S. coastal waters off Maine. The agreement also created a list of goods, such as timber, wheat, and corn, that neither country would tax in trade with the other. Trade between the two nations increased rapidly after ratification of this treaty.

In 1866, because of complaints from U.S. farmers, the United States repealed its part of the agreement. The American Civil War had ended a year earlier, and many veterans had resumed farming; they protested loudly against free importation of Canadian grain, so reciprocity was ended. The Canadians wanted a new agreement, however, and in 1871 sent a delegation to Washington, D.C., to open trade talks. Nothing came of the talks, and the 1871 Treaty of Washington barely mentioned reciprocity of trade.

The issue was not raised again until 1911, when Canada's finance minister, William S. Fielding, told the

House of Commons that negotiations with the United States would begin immediately. The goal was to obtain as much free trade as possible, and Fielding suggested that once that was accomplished, the Canadian economy would flourish and unemployment would decline rapidly. Loud protests from workers and industrialists in Ontario indicated that many Canadians did not agree. The protesters argued that reciprocity and free trade would give a tremendous advantage to powerful industries in the United States, such as the steel and textile industries, which would flood Canada with huge amounts of goods, driving Canadian industries into bankruptcy and costing thousands of Canadian jobs. Trade became the major issue in the Canadian election of that year. Conservatives denounced reciprocity in the campaign and won the election, bringing an end to discussions of free trade with the United States.

In 1924, both nations signed a treaty limiting halibut fishing off the coast of Washington and British Columbia, but reciprocity talks failed. Republican administrations in the United States wanted only one thing from the Canadians: an agreement to construct the St. Lawrence Seaway to link the Great Lakes with the Atlantic Ocean. This massive project would make it easier to ship grain from the Midwest to Europe and, it was hoped, greatly improve the prosperity of farmers in the region. By 1932, it seemed as if negotiations on this project were almost completed. President Herbert Hoover signed an agreement in July with the Canadians, but the U.S. Senate was unable to get the two-thirds majority required by the Constitution for ratification. The major opposition came from senators opposed to the seaway's projected high costs. The seaway would not be constructed for another twenty-five years.

Relations between Canada and the United States improved greatly after the inauguration of President Franklin D. Roosevelt in 1933. Roosevelt promoted the Good Neighbor Policy with all nations in the Western Hemisphere, which included support for reciprocal trade agreements. Talks with Canada began in 1934 but were not concluded until two years later. Roosevelt had signed the Trade Agreements Act of 1934, significantly lowering tariffs on many items. This bilateral agreement was not satisfactory, however, to the newly elected Liberal government of Prime Minister William Lyon Mackenzie King. King, a fervent advocate of reciprocal trade agreements, led a delegation to Washington to discuss such an agreement with representatives of the U.S. Department of State.

Secretary of State Cordell Hull headed the U.S. negotiating team. He favored reducing trade restrictions with as many nations as possible, but he faced considerable criticism for his position within his own Democratic Party and especially from conservatives in the Republican Party. He knew it would be difficult to win the two-thirds majority vote needed in the Senate for approval of any bill reducing tariffs. Many conservatives in both parties thought higher tariffs rather than lower presented the best opportunity for protecting jobs. The Great Depression, they argued, made it necessary for countries to protect themselves from competition from outside states by building a high tariff wall.

Hull wanted Canada and the United States to reach an agreement quickly. This, he explained to the Canadians, would demonstrate to the rest of the world, especially the Europeans, that persons of goodwill could still sit down and negotiate peacefully. The Germans, Italians, and Japanese seemed to prefer war or economic suicide to any attempt to discuss seriously the mutual sacrifices required by reciprocal trade treaties. The United States and Canada could show world leaders an alternate course for resolving economic problems. Friendly nations had to show that talking still could produce results, Hull argued. The fact that the King government recently had signed a bilateral agreement with the German Nazis angered him, but he indicated that this would not stand in the way of the current discussions. He hoped that reciprocal trade agreements could reduce conflict in the world and provide an alternative to cutthroat methods of bilateral trading, with each nation looking out only for its own narrow self-interest.

Hull believed that unless freer world trade was provided for, the nations of Europe and the Far East would face continued economic strife and chaos. Economic disaster would affect all countries and bring about an even worse financial collapse than the Great Depression. Only a broad program to remove excessive trade barriers, he told the Canadian delegation, could save the situation. The world needed a policy of equal treatment for all nations and a method to promote and protect fair trade methods and practices. If nations such as the United States and Canada refused to take the first steps in this direction, catastrophic consequences awaited the peoples of the world. Hull's warnings of the terrible consequences of failure encouraged a quick end to negotiations.

SIGNIFICANCE

The final result, the Reciprocal Trade Act of 1936, produced far fewer reductions in trade barriers than had been gained in 1854, but it proved satisfactory to both sides.

1936

The United States agreed to admit limited amounts of cream, cattle, lumber, and potatoes with significantly reduced rates. In return, Canada accepted more manufactured goods from the United States. Members of Canada's Liberal Party hoped that this trade would produce higher incomes for Canadian farmers, loggers, and ranchers. They also predicted it would reduce Canada's economic dependence on the United States. As it turned out, it made little difference. Both policies, the high tariffs favored by Conservatives in the 1920's and the Liberal support for freer trade, had the same result: They increased Canadian economic dependence on the United States.

From 1923 to 1935, the period of the highest tariffs on U.S. manufactured goods, the number of U.S.-owned factories and businesses in Canada increased from 524 to 816. U.S. goods were kept out, but corporations bought the factories or built new ones in Canada rather than pay the increased rates. One Canadian economist observed that it made little difference whether Canadians were buried by U.S. exports or U.S. branch plants—they would lose control of their economy either way.

The 1936 agreement remained in effect until 1948, when both nations signed a general agreement that superseded prior trade treaties. In 1994, Canada joined Mexico and the United States as a member of the North American Free Trade Agreement, which solidified the movement toward free trade that gathered momentum after World War II with the formation of the General Agreement on Tariffs and Trade.

—*Leslie V. Tischauser*

FURTHER READING

Butler, Michael A. *Cautious Visionary: Cordell Hull and Trade Reform, 1933-1937*. Kent, Ohio: Kent State University Press, 1998. Discusses the impacts on U.S. trade policy of Hull's tenure as secretary of state, given his strong views on the importance of fair trade. Includes notes, bibliography, and index.

Corbett, Percy E. *The Settlement of Canadian-American Disputes: A Critical Study of Meetings and Results*. New Haven, Conn.: Yale University Press, 1937. Covers treaty and tariff negotiations from the 1840's to 1936. Provides detailed discussion of the trade policies of both nations.

McInnis, Edgar. *Canada: A Political and Social History*. 4th ed. Toronto: Holt, Rinehart and Winston of Canada, 1982. Contains a useful discussion of Canadian trade policy in the 1930's and a brief discussion of the treaty.

Riendeau, Roger. *A Brief History of Canada*. 2d rev. ed. New York: Facts On File, 2006. Concise history includes discussion of Canada's difficulties during the Great Depression, tariff protections, and reciprocity.

U.S. Department of State. *British Dominions and Canada*. Vol. 1 in *Papers Relating to the Foreign Policy of the United States, 1936*. Washington, D.C.: Government Printing Office, 1951. Contains the complete record of the discussions and negotiations.

Welles, Sumner. *Seven Decisions That Shaped History*. New York: Harper, 1951. Discusses the U.S. secretary of state's views on trade relations and his belief that freer trade would prevent a future war. Written by a participant in the 1936 negotiations with Canada.

SEE ALSO: Sept. 8, 1916: United States Establishes a Permanent Tariff Commission; Oct. 21, 1924: Halibut Treaty; Oct. 29, 1929-1939: Great Depression; June 17, 1930: Hoover Signs the Hawley-Smoot Tariff Act; July 18, 1932: St. Lawrence Seaway Treaty; Oct. 23, 1935-Nov. 15, 1948: King Returns to Power in Canada.

November 23, 1936
FLUORESCENT LIGHTING IS INTRODUCED

Decorative lighting for the one hundredth anniversary celebration of the U.S. Patent Office was provided by fluorescent lamps, setting the stage for the widespread use of this efficient form of lighting.

LOCALE: Washington, D.C.
CATEGORIES: Science and technology; inventions

KEY FIGURES
Vincenzo Cascariolo (1571-1624), Italian alchemist and shoemaker
Francis Hauksbee (c. 1660-1713), English scientist
Heinrich Geissler (1814-1879), German glassblower
George Gabriel Stokes (1819-1903), English physicist and mathematician
Peter Cooper Hewitt (1861-1921), American electrical engineer

SUMMARY OF EVENT
On the night of November 23, 1936, more than one thousand industrialists, patent attorneys, and scientists assembled in the main ballroom of the Mayflower Hotel in Washington, D.C., to celebrate the one hundredth anniversary of the U.S. Patent Office. A transport liner over the city was about to radio the names of the twelve greatest American inventors, as chosen by the Patent Office, and as the distinguished group strained to listen for those names, "the room was flooded for a moment by the most brilliant light yet used to illuminate a space that size." This is how *The New York Times* summarized the commercial introduction of the fluorescent lamp on the day following the event. Among the twelve inventors named as greatest were Thomas Alva Edison, Robert Fulton, Charles Goodyear, Cyrus Hall McCormick, and Samuel F. B. Morse, but the list did not include the name of the inventor of fluorescent lighting. The honor for inventing fluorescent lighting is shared by many who participated in a series of discoveries over a very long period.

The fluorescent lamp operates as a low-pressure, electric discharge inside a phosphor-coated glass tube that contains a droplet of mercury and a rare gas, commonly argon. At room temperature, the droplet gives off a very weak vapor of mercury atoms. Because mercury ionizes more easily than the rare gas atoms, the mercury atoms control the discharge despite the much larger number of rare gas atoms. The inside of the glass tube is coated with fine particles of the phosphor, a material that fluoresces when bathed in the strong ultraviolet radiation

from the mercury atoms in the discharge. The light from a fluorescent lamp is composed mainly of the broad-spectrum, whitish light from the phosphor with a small, but significant, contribution from narrow-spectrum mercury emissions in the violet, blue, green, and yellow. In contrast to an incandescent lamps, a fluorescent lamp gives off light with little heat.

The high light efficiency of the fluorescent lamp is caused by a finely tailored match between the phosphor coating within the lamp and the mercury discharge. Commercial production of the fluorescent lamp followed only after a long sequence of events that instructed scientists on the colorful properties of fluorescent materials and of electrical discharges.

The setting for the introduction of the fluorescent lamp began at the beginning of the 1600's, when Vincenzo Cascariolo, an Italian shoemaker and alchemist, discovered a substance that continued its glow after exposure to strong sunlight. After exposure to the sun, the material gave off a bluish glow in the dark. The fluorescent substance was apparently barium sulfide and was so unusual for that time and so valuable that its formulation was kept secret for a long time. Gradually, however, scholars became aware of the preparation secrets of the substance and studied it and other luminescent materials.

Sir Isaac Newton, who favored the particle theory of light, studied fluorescence and incorrectly attributed the delayed emission of light to the time spent undergoing internal reflections within the grains of the substance. Sir George Gabriel Stokes, who favored the wave theory of light, studied the phenomenon as well. In 1852, he termed the afterglow "fluorescence" and announced a law that summarized the findings on fluorescent substances: The exciting light always has a shorter wavelength than the fluorescing light. For example, short wave violet light can produce longer wave green fluorescence, but green light does not produce violet fluorescence.

It is now known that shorter wavelengths correspond to higher light frequencies and energies, with frequency energies increasing from red, yellow, and green through to violet and ultraviolet. Shorter wavelengths of light thus correspond to higher packets of energy. Stokes's law requires that the exciting light must be more energetic than the emitted fluorescence. Although light does have particle-like properties, the delayed emission is not caused by internal reflections; rather, it is caused by a real delay in emission during which the energy is held within individual atoms, or groups of atoms, inside the fluorescent material.

While these advances were being made on fluorescent substances, other workers were taking the steps needed to bring about practical discharge that could produce energetic light. In 1706, Francis Hauksbee fabricated an electrostatic generator. He then used a vacuum pump produced by Otto von Guericke to evacuate a vessel to a low pressure and tested his electrostatic generator. Therefore, Hauksbee obtained the first human-made electrical glow discharge by capturing lightning in a jar. Later, investigators worked on this novel form of trapped lightning. In 1854, Heinrich Geissler, a glassblower and apparatus maker, opened his shop in Bonn, Germany, to make scientific instruments; in 1855, he produced a vacuum pump that used liquid mercury as an evacuation fluid. That same year, Geissler made the first gaseous conduction lamps while working in collaboration with the German scientist Julius Plücker. Plücker referred to these lamps as "Geissler tubes." Geissler was able to create red light with neon filling a lamp and light of nearly all colors by placing different gases within the lamps, thus giving birth to both the neon sign business and the science of spectroscopy.

A variety of scientists and inventors studied Geissler tubes extensively. At the beginning of the twentieth century, the practical American engineer Peter Cooper Hewitt put these studies to use by marketing the first low-pressure mercury-vapor lamp. The lamp was quite successful, although it required high voltage for operation, shed an eerie blue-green light, and shone only dimly in comparison with its eventual successor, the fluorescent lamp. At about the same time, systematic studies of phosphors had finally begun.

By the 1920's, a number of investigators discovered that the low-pressure mercury-vapor discharge marketed by Hewitt was an extremely efficient method for producing ultraviolet light, if the mercury and rare gas pressures were properly adjusted. With a phosphor to convert the ultraviolet back to visible, the Hewitt lamp made an excellent light source.

Scientists learned that the mercury vapor was proper if the coolest portion on the discharge wall was kept between 40 and 45 degrees Celsius, quite cool for a lamp. Under these conditions, the scientist found that 60 percent of the electrical energy entering the discharge appeared as ultraviolet energy radiating from the mercury atoms in the discharge.

Several commercial European laboratories began development of a practical fluorescent lamp in the early 1930's. Around 1934, laboratories in the United States undertook earnest efforts toward production. A range of durable and efficient phosphors were devised. Sturdy, but inexpensive, electrodes were designed for operation with special metal-oxide coatings that, when heated in the lamp, readily boiled off electrons to supply current to the discharge and so reduced the operating voltage from the high value found in the Hewitt lamp. At the same time, engineers developed the transformer circuitry needed to start the lamp at somewhat elevated voltage and then operate it at the lower voltage available on the electrical lines. Finally, the light coming from the developing fluorescent lamps had to be measured and compared with other light sources. Electrical power is measured in watts; light power is measured in lumens. Invisible powers, such as ultraviolet and infrared light, contain no lumens. The number of lumens per watt of actual power thus must depend on color within the spectrum of visible light. Per watt, violet and red give fewer lumens than green and yellow, which lie near the middle of the spectrum, where the eye is most sensitive. The measurements demonstrated that the fluorescent lamp was quite efficient, at least twice that of an incandescent lamp of similar light output, depending on the phosphor blend chosen for the fluorescent lamp.

Early in 1936, the U.S. Patent Office announced plans for its centennial celebration, and new discoveries were invited for presentation. Fluorescent lighting was chosen to be among the new inventions displayed. On November 23, 1936, fluorescent lighting debuted, and an extraordinary editorial in *The New York Times* on November 24 carried these words: "We must look for the revolutionary inventions to come—engines driven by atomic energy, rocket ships that voyage in interplanetary space, lamps that glow without heat."

SIGNIFICANCE

The revolution of light that glowed without heat took place almost immediately. By 1938, production of fluorescent lamps was well under way. By April, 1938, four sizes of fluorescent lamps in various colors were offered to the public and more than 200,000 lamps were sold. When the United States entered World War II, the demand for efficient factory lighting soared. In 1941, more than 21 million fluorescent lamps were sold.

During 1939 and 1940, two great expositions—the New York World's Fair and the San Francisco International Exposition—helped popularize fluorescent lighting. Thousands of tubular fluorescent lamps formed a great spiral in the "motor display salon," the car show-room, of the General Motors exhibit at the New York World's Fair. Fluorescent lamps lit the Polish Restaurant and hung in vertical clusters on the flag poles along the Avenue of the Flags at the Fair, and upright fluorescent tubes two meters long illuminated buildings at the San Francisco International Exhibition.

Technical advances improved the fluorescent lamp, especially in the area of light efficiency, commonly rated in lumens per watt. Depending on its exact shade, a perfectly efficient white source may yield 200-300 lumens per watt, whereas a common twenty-first century 100-watt incandescent lamp with a normal lifetime of 750 hours of use has a light efficiency of slightly more than 17 lumens per watt. Even in 1938, the common 40-watt fluorescent lamp had an efficiency of about 45 lumens per watt. This efficiency increased to more than 57 lumens per watt by 1948 and to nearly 80 lumens per watt by the mid-1980's. All of this was accompanied by large increases in the useful life of the fluorescent lamp from about 2,000 hours in 1942 to nearly 20,000 hours by the mid-1980's.

The fluorescent lamp did have a number of drawbacks that limited complete acceptance, and some of these persisted. One limitation is the need for a transformer ballast to operate the lamp; this has prevented the widespread use of fluorescent lamps in homes in the United States. It is much simpler to insert an incandescent lamp into a light socket than to replace a fluorescent lamp in a bulky light fixture. Another disadvantage of fluorescent lamps is their relatively poor color rendition in comparison with sunlight and incandescent lamps. In comparison with the color of high-pressure mercury-vapor lamps and sodium-vapor lamps, used for lighting highways and large areas, the color rendition of fluorescent lamps is excellent. The color of fluorescent lamps, however, is not highly uniform across the spectrum, because of the strong blue and green lines of mercury. Also, it is deficient in the red in comparison with sunlight and, especially, in comparison with the incandescent lamp. Because red colors are especially flattering to the skin tones of most people, the use of fluorescent lighting has been severely limited in the home and in mood settings outside the home.

Despite the limitations of the fluorescent lamp, this new form of lighting offered the enormous advantages of high efficiency, long life, and relatively low cost. When it was introduced in 1936, a new industry was born. Within three years after production of the first commercial fluorescent lamps, the industry had reached $100 million in sales. In comparison, the automobile industry took fifteen years after the first cars were produced to reach that sales figure, and the radio industry needed five years.

—*Peter J. Walsh*

FURTHER READING

Bova, Ben. *The Beauty of Light*. New York: John Wiley & Sons, 1988. Provides an excellent, readable account of light: how it is seen, how it is used, and how it affects people. Chapter 14 discusses light sources, including fluorescent lighting and its deficiencies.

Bowers, Brian. *Lengthening the Day: A History of Lighting Technology*. New York: Oxford University Press, 1998. Concise history of lighting technologies, including fluorescent lighting. Discusses both technical aspects of different lighting technologies as well as the societal effects of advances in such technologies. Well illustrated, with exploded diagrams and reproductions of etchings.

Elenbaas, W., ed. *Fluorescent Lamps*. New York: Macmillan, 1959. Collection of articles by experts provides technical details about the fluorescent lamp.

Kane, Raymond, and Heinz Sell, eds. *Revolution in Lamps: A Chronicle of Fifty Years of Progress*. 2d ed. New York: Fairmont Press, 2001. A history of the progress made in lamps and lighting as well as information on new lighting technologies, aimed at designers, engineers, and architects as well as lay readers. Includes a chapter on fluorescent lamps.

Stern, Rudi. *The New Let There Be Neon*. New York: Harry N. Abrams, 1988. An atlas of vivid neon lights. Includes a survey of the historical development of gas-discharge and related types of lamps.

Zwikker, C., ed. *Fluorescent Lighting*. New York: Elsevier Press, 1952. Provides a good mix of technical detail and information on the historical development and practical aspects of fluorescent lamps.

SEE ALSO: 1901: Hewitt Invents the Mercury-Vapor Lamp; Dec. 10, 1901: Röntgen Wins the Nobel Prize for the Discovery of X Rays.

1936

November 23, 1936
LUCE LAUNCHES *LIFE* MAGAZINE

The emergence of Life *marked not only the birth of another American magazine but also the creation of a new genre within the publishing industry, one that precipitated the enormous impact of photography combined with journalism.*

LOCALE: New York, New York
CATEGORIES: Publishing and journalism; photography

KEY FIGURES

Henry R. Luce (1898-1967), creator of *Time* and *Fortune* and editor in chief of *Life*
Clare Boothe Luce (1903-1987), second wife of Henry Luce, journalist, playwright, congresswoman, ambassador, and originator of the *Life* idea
John Shaw Billings (1898-1975), first managing editor of *Life*
Daniel Longwell (1899-1968), first executive editor of *Life*
Margaret Bourke-White (1904-1971), staff photographer and war correspondent for *Life*
Alfred Eisenstaedt (1898-1995), German photojournalist who joined *Life* in 1936

SUMMARY OF EVENT

Henry R. Luce married Clare Boothe Brokaw on November 23, 1935; it was a second marriage for both. The couple returned from a ten-week honeymoon in Cuba in February, 1936, and the announcement of their intent to start a pictorial magazine soon followed. Henry Luce's biographer, John Kobler, writing in 1968, identified Clare Luce as the source of the idea for the magazine, and scholars often point to a pattern for such a magazine she had sketched out for Condé Nast, the publisher of *Vanity Fair*, of which she had been editor.

Clare Boothe Luce, who was thirty-three at the time of her marriage to Luce, had begun her career six years earlier at *Vogue* magazine and went on to write three relatively successful Broadway plays before involvement with World War II took her back into journalism and politics. Henry Luce had been cofounder with Briton Hadden of Time Incorporated and its lead periodical, the successful newsweekly *Time*, from its inception in 1923. In addition, in February of 1930, Luce had created a significant monthly magazine for American business called *Fortune*. In March of 1931 he inaugurated the radio news program *The March of Time*, and in April, 1932, he ac-

quired and then remodeled into a professional exemplar the periodical *Architectural Forum*.

The title of the new pictorial magazine originally was to be *Dime*—its initial newsstand cost. Over the eight months of frantic preparation, a whole series of alternative working titles were tried, including *Parade*, *Scene*, *Seen*, and *Pictures*, while the subtitle remained most descriptive: *The Show-Book of the World*. By midsummer, a mock-up issue of the magazine had been produced. The decision was made to print the magazine on paper measuring ten and one-half inches by fourteen inches, making it somewhat larger than most other magazines of the day; when an issue appeared on the newsstands, its dimensions allowed it to stand out from the other displayed titles competing for the purchaser's attention. By September, a trial mock-up had been created under the name *Rehearsal*. Throughout the preparatory period, the company had to deal with a large number of unknowns, including the location of presses capable of handling the projected print run, the availability of equipment permitting high-quality photographic reproduction on a large scale, and the feasibility of obtaining supplies of coated paper on which high-quality images could be sustained.

In describing his intended pictorial magazine, Luce had written, "To see life; to see the world; to eyewitness great events; . . . to see and to take pleasure in seeing; to see and be amazed; to see and be instructed; thus to see, and to be shown, is now the will and new expectancy of half mankind." The obvious title for the unnamed magazine thus emerged; if "to see life" was the objective, then the medium of the seeing would be called *Life*. Clare Boothe Luce had used this very designation in her original sketch for Condé Nast.

Another *Life*, a humor magazine, had existed since 1883, but it was fading rapidly under the impact of the national economic plight of the Great Depression and its own inability to keep pace with the times and with the competition of such rivals as *The New Yorker*. Luce and company purchased the title for $92,000 in August, and work on the first issue of the new *Life* followed immediately. Bearing the date Monday, November 23, 1936, the new weekly *Life* appeared on the newsstands on the preceding Thursday, November 19. A circulation of 250,000 had been guaranteed to potential advertisers, and the initial printing was of 466,000 copies. These sold out within hours of hitting the stands.

Every page of the inaugural issue had some kind of illustration of greater spatial proportion than text, with the exception of page 3, which featured an essay titled "Introduction to This First Issue of *Life*." On the facing page 2 was a full-page photograph captioned "Life begins"—an infant just after birth in the hands of an attending physician. The first issue's front cover depicted Fort Peck Dam, a Works Progress Administration (WPA) project being built in Montana. The cover photograph was taken by Margaret Bourke-White, whose work also illustrated the lead article on pages 9 through 17. Color was used in the photographs on eleven of the interior pages, although except for a four-page article illustrating the paintings of John Steuart Curry of Kansas, all the color was used in advertisements.

Advertising occupied thirty-three full pages, including three of the covers, plus nine half-page ads and three quarter-page ads. Advertisements were sold at the rate of $1,500 for a full black-and-white page and $2,250 for color. The magazine itself sold for 10 cents. Total revenues for the first issue exceeded $110,000, but this was insufficient to cover printing costs. Loss of money was a regular venture through many years of *Life*'s publication.

Issues were affectionately known by the staff as the "Big Red." Each had a red band at the bottom across the front cover (a feature eliminated with the issue of June 2, 1961). A bold red rectangle with the word "LIFE" in white lettering was set dramatically in the upper-left-hand corner. Only once was this recognition symbol absent: in the issue published April 16, 1937, when it would have interfered with the photo of a rooster's comb. Once, too, the recognition symbol appeared in black—on the issue printed on November 29, 1963, after President John F. Kennedy's assassination.

Life was not intended as a war magazine, as its covers made evident. There was much more to see: *Life* paid special attention to women, who adorned at least one of every three covers, and the magazine's pages included many illustrating fashion and the perennial interest in swimsuits. From its second issue, and for the sixteen years that followed, *Life* had a regular feature called "Movie of the Week," and the magazine made stars' careers by featuring photographs of them. The magazine's greatest love affair was with Elizabeth Taylor, who appeared on its covers a record twelve times.

Yet *Life*'s first decade was dominated by the interactive forces of depression and war. As a result, it became widely known as a war magazine, and this development did not hinder its initial growth. By 1947, circulation had risen to 5,369,000 copies per week, the largest circulation of any magazine. Wartime issues (beginning October 11, 1943) went overseas without advertising. *Time* could be illustrated, but its success was dependent on its ability to create and use the language of mid-twentieth century America. *Life*, on the other hand, was intended to provide images of the midcentury world as seen through the eyes of the United States. Regular features of *Life* thus came to spawn other magazines, including its own international editions (from July 22, 1946) and the Spanish-language *Life en Español* (from January 5, 1953), as well as *Sports Illustrated* (from August 16, 1954) and *People* (from March 4, 1974). In addition, both as composites from issues and as creations from without, *Life* generated whole series of books—magazine journalism in hard covers.

Life could do essays with photographs, but its best pieces were the arresting illustrations with word captions. On the occasion of the celebration of photography's sesquicentennial, Lance Morrow noted that photojournalism is not only "the first impression of history" but also, disturbingly, "history's lasting visual impression." In an article titled "What Is Photojournalism?" Wilson Hicks observed that "*Life* had been projected headlong into its own evolutionary state." The magazine was the laboratory in which the intended art form was accomplished.

Early issues of *Life* show abuses of photographs that were cut to eliminate the unwanted or to fit some aesthetic notion of space. An awareness of the camera gradually emerged, so that what was actually taken—though the images were certainly affected by the photographer's eye and bias—was precisely what appeared in the magazine. *Life*'s photographers provided an average of thirty-five thousand pictures for every ten thousand that were used, but the editorial selection of the approximately two hundred images used per issue—itself an aesthetic act—ensured that the selected images remained inviolate.

SIGNIFICANCE

Henry Luce thought of *Life* as a new kind of magazine. The picture magazine had already appeared in varying degrees: The *Illustrated London News* originated in May, 1842, just after the invention of photography, but it was chiefly illustrated by drawings and engravings into the 1920's. *Harper's Weekly* had incorporated Civil War photographs by Mathew Brady, and Boston of the 1880's had *Gleason's Pictorial Drawing Room Companion*. From the beginning of the new century, photography was

1936

exploited by major illustrated weeklies in Paris, Leipzig, and Berlin. Luce, however, was aiming for something more—a genre not yet created.

Luce had identified films and radio as the magazine's most obvious competitors, but by the time *Life* emerged, television had already been invented. Rather than giving the public what it wanted, Luce elected to offer "what they must have lest they perish." By perfecting the magazine's craftsmanship, Luce thought his brainchild could compete with its electronic rivals. As late as 1965, George P. Hunt, then *Life*'s managing editor, could still observe: "Permanence is what photographs and paintings are. The TV set represents the fleeting moment. You can see the great photos in *Life* forever."

Nevertheless, television was in part destructive of both *Life* and its photojournalistic competitors. *Collier's* and *Woman's Home Companion* both folded in December, 1956; the *Saturday Evening Post* was bought out by Time Inc. and eliminated in February, 1969; *Look* survived until October, 1971. From November 23, 1936, to December 29, 1972, 1,864 regular weekly issues of *Life* appeared. In addition were special editions, including "Israel's Swift Victory" (1967), "The Kennedys" (1968), and "To the Moon and Back" and "Woodstock" (1970). From 1973 to 1977, *Life* produced only two issues per year, one "special" and a year-end "The Year in Pictures." *Life* resumed publication as a monthly between 1978 and 2000 and also put out occasional special issues, remaining as a survivor of the golden age of photojournalism. It resumed a weekly format and as of 2005 was published every Friday and distributed in more than seventy American newspapers each week for a total circulation of twelve million.

—*Clyde Curry Smith*

FURTHER READING

Doss, Erika Lee, ed. *Looking at "Life" Magazine*. Washington, D.C.: Smithsonian Institution Press, 2001. Collection of more than a dozen essays chronicles the magazine's impact on American history. Especially interesting is the discussion of *Life*'s role in shaping American sentiment toward the Vietnam War.

Elson, Robert T. *Time Inc.: The Intimate History of a Publishing Enterprise, 1923-1941*. Edited by Duncan Norton-Taylor. New York: Atheneum, 1968.

_____. *The World of Time Inc.: The Intimate History of a Publishing Enterprise, 1941-1960*. Edited by Duncan Norton-Taylor. New York: Atheneum, 1973.

These two volumes and their sequel, Curtis Prendergast's *The World of Time Inc.: The Intimate History of a Changing Enterprise, 1960-1980* (1986), constitute an official account. The authors had full access to the private papers of those involved in the Time Inc. publishing enterprise. The birth of *Life* is chronicled in the first volume, and its success is discussed in the second. The third volume deals with the magazine's late-1970's revival.

Goldberg, Vicki. *Margaret Bourke-White: A Biography*. New York: Harper, 1986. Informative biography of a principal *Life* photographic contributor.

Henle, Faye. *Au Clare de Luce: Portrait of a Luminous Lady*. New York: S. Daye, 1943. Early biography has the advantage of emphasizing Clare Boothe Luce's own prior editorial success before *Life* was launched.

Hicks, Wilson. *Words and Pictures: An Introduction to Photojournalism*. New York: Harper & Brothers, 1952. Written by an editor of *Life*, this book discusses the history and nature of pictorial journalism. Extensively illustrated with examples from *Life*.

Kobler, John. *Luce: His Time, Life, and Fortune*. Garden City, N.Y.: Doubleday, 1968. Written immediately after the death of Luce. Contains valuable information about the creation of the magazines, including the role of Clare Boothe Luce's memo on the format and character of *Life*. Includes bibliography.

Swanberg, W. A. *Luce and His Empire*. New York: Charles Scribner's Sons, 1972. A political assessment of Luce and the perspective appearing within his publications. Independent of the official history of the company, and thereby lacks sources of information pertinent especially to *Life*. Includes photographs and a thorough index of names.

Time Life Books. *The Best of "Life."* Alexandria, Va.: Author, 1973. A selection of the magazine's highlights, compiled after the demise of the weekly version. Captions alongside each selection and picture credits at the end.

_____. *"Life": The First Fifty Years, 1936-1986*. Boston: Little, Brown, 1986. An official commemorative, with illustrations of every cover, samples from every year, and brief interpretive essays on each decade. The finest all-around introduction to the magazine and its impact.

_____. *"Life" Goes to the Movies*. Alexandria, Va.: Author, 1975. Focuses on a social arena that *Life* regularly appreciated and exploited. Stars, studios, and behind-the-scenes aspects of Hollywood are illustrated and put into perspective.

_____. *"Life": One Hundred Events That Shook Our World*. New York: Author, 2005. Presents some remarkable photographs from the magazine's long history.

SEE ALSO: Nov. 7, 1914: Lippmann Helps to Establish *The New Republic*; Sept. 15, 1917: *Forbes* Magazine Is Founded; Feb., 1922: *Reader's Digest* Is Founded; Mar. 3, 1923: Luce Founds *Time* Magazine; Feb. 21, 1925: Ross Founds *The New Yorker*; Feb., 1930: Luce Founds *Fortune* Magazine.

November 25, 1936
GERMANY AND JAPAN SIGN THE ANTI-COMINTERN PACT

Germany and Japan signed a largely symbolic agreement out of mutual self-interest, signaling a proto-Axis alliance that was conceived as a means of confronting the Soviet Union with a two-front war. Hitler ignored and abrogated the Anti-Comintern Pact in 1939 with the Molotov-Ribbentrop Pact, but Japan showed little interest in being drawn into a European conflict.

LOCALE: Berlin, Germany; Moscow, Soviet Union (now Russia)
CATEGORIES: Diplomacy and international relations; government and politics; laws, acts, and legal history

KEY FIGURES

Adolf Hitler (1889-1945), leader of the Nazi Party and chancellor of Germany, 1933-1945
Neville Chamberlain (1869-1940), prime minister of Great Britain, 1937-1940
Joachim von Ribbentrop (1893-1946), Hitler's foreign minister, 1938-1945
Vyacheslav Mikhailovich Molotov (Vyacheslav Mikhailovich Skryabin; 1890-1986), premier of the Soviet Union, 1930-1941, and foreign minister, 1939-1949 and 1953-1956
Joseph Stalin (Joseph Vissarionovich Dzhugashvili; 1878-1953), general secretary of the Communist Party in Russia and dictator in the Soviet Union, 1929-1953

SUMMARY OF EVENT

On November 25, 1936, Adolf Hitler announced that he had signed an anti-Comintern Pact with Japan. Foreign correspondent William L. Shirer, then in Berlin, recalled that Hitler claimed that the two countries had banded together to defend Western civilization. Meanwhile, Joseph Stalin's Comintern (Communist International) was aiding Communist activities throughout the world, especially in those countries that seemed on the brink of revo-

lution. Exploiting Western fears of Communist subversion, Hitler deflected attention away from his own aggressive actions at home and abroad, and by suggesting that he was helping to isolate the Soviet Union as a rogue nation, Hitler sought to obscure his efforts to promulgate German hegemony in Europe. The success of his efforts was at least partly dependent on whether he could convince the British that it was in their best interests to cooperate with Germany.

The treaty with Japan also had a secret protocol: In the event of a Soviet attack on either country, Germany and Japan would work together to preserve their common interests and do nothing to support Soviet policies, including signing any agreements with the Soviet Union that did not have the approval of both Germany and Japan. Hitler consolidated his alliance of fascist countries when he persuaded Italy's dictator, Benito Mussolini, to sign the Anti-Comintern Pact on November 6, 1937.

Hitler's annexation of Austria in 1938 demonstrated that his rationale for promoting the Anti-Comintern Pact was sound. British prime minister Neville Chamberlain rejected a Soviet request for a conference of nations that would seek to check any further German expansion. Not only was Chamberlain unwilling to use force against Hitler, he was not even willing to exert concerted diplomatic action against Germany's growing power. Hitler correctly calculated that the West's suspicion of Stalin would prevent any significant effort to halt German efforts to dominate Europe. That Hitler already had in hand an axis of powers on his side—Italy and Japan—did not seem to trouble Chamberlain.

As 1938 wore on, Hitler continued to use the Anti-Comintern Pact as a kind of cover for his territorial designs. In the events leading up to his takeover of Czechoslovakia in 1939, he demanded that the Czechs sign the pact, which served as a pretext for his claim that Czechoslovakia was somehow pursuing a foreign policy inimical to both German and Western interests.

1936

By the end of October of 1938, Hitler's foreign minister, Joachim von Ribbentrop, who had been advancing the German claim to the Polish city of Danzig, requested that Poland also sign the Anti-Comintern Pact, which had become a kind of German test of any European country's determination to resist the Third Reich's foreign policy (masked, as always, as an anti-Soviet program). In other words, if the Poles wished to show their good faith and demonstrate their anti-Communist credentials, they had to be willing to join the Anti-Comintern Pact. In return for acceding to an alliance with Germany, the Poles would receive a renewed guarantee that Germany would respect Poland's borders. Poland had fought a war against the Soviet Union in 1920 and was traditionally anti-Russian, and so Hitler could present his demands in the guise of an effort to protect the very country he would soon invade. The Poles, however, refused to sign the Anti-Comintern Pact, which to them would mean acknowledging Germany's preeminence in central Europe.

The more Hitler emphasized the importance of the Anti-Comintern Pact, the harder it was for Western leaders like Chamberlain to include the Soviet Union in any effort to check belligerent German foreign policy. At any rate, for Chamberlain any act in concert with the Soviet Union meant that he would simply be strengthening the ties of the countries that had already signed the Anti-Comintern Pact. That the pact itself was not much more than Hitler's ruse never seems to have occurred to Chamberlain. Indeed, by April of 1939, Hitler's speeches no longer contained his customary anti-Soviet language, although fascist Spain signed the Anti-Comintern Pact on April 5. In fact, in October of 1938, Stalin had opened secret negotiations with Hitler in a reaction against Chamberlain's continued refusal to include the Soviet Union in efforts to check German expansionism.

The minor importance Hitler actually placed on the Anti-Comintern Pact was made apparent when German diplomats did not object to the demands of Soviet Foreign Minister Vyacheslav Mikhailovich Molotov that the German government offer concrete proof of its intention to fundamentally alter its hostile policy toward the Soviet Union. Hitler acceded to the Soviet demand that he sign a nonaggression pact with the Soviet Union, and he signaled this major policy shift by sending Ribbentrop to the Soviet Union to meet with Molotov, a sign of respect that the British had never accorded the Soviets.

Ribbentrop explained to Molotov that the Anti-Comintern Pact had never really been directed against the Soviet Union but rather against the Western democracies. At this meeting of foreign ministers, Stalin seemed to agree with Ribbentrop and with German foreign policy: The Soviet leader said that the pact had in fact intimidated British financiers and shopkeepers, presumably because it showed the weight Germany could bring to world affairs and, more important, foreshadowed the diminution of the British Empire. Ribbentrop then told Stalin that the joke in Berlin was that soon Stalin himself would join the Anti-Comintern Pact. With the signing of the German-Soviet nonaggression pact (known as the Nazi-Soviet Pact or the Molotov-Ribbentrop Pact) in 1939, the Anti-Comintern Pact was effectively abrogated, but the Soviet Union abolished the Comintern in 1943 in an attempt to placate its Western allies.

SIGNIFICANCE

As historian John Lukacs has argued, before the beginning of World War II, Hitler had created an astoundingly successful foreign policy record. Virtually all of his major objectives had been achieved: rearmament, the reoccupation of the Rhineland, the annexation of Austria, and the takeover of Czechoslovakia. The Anti-Comintern Pact was part of Hitler's clever effort to mask his anti-Western foreign policy with a seemingly aggressive stance toward the Soviet Union. In particular, he aimed to dupe Britain into believing that the two countries both opposed Stalin. In fact, to some extent, the two countries did share concerns about the threat of Communist subversion, and Hitler wanted to maintain an alliance with Britain as long as Chamberlain continued to appease him. After a British alliance failed to materialize, however, and after Stalin agreed to the nonaggression pact, the need for the Anti-Comintern Pact evaporated. In the meantime, the Anti-Comintern Pact had served its purpose: It had allowed Hitler to give the impression of being a friend to Western democracy while simultaneously forcing the unification of Germany, Japan, and the fascist powers in Italy and Spain.

—Carl Rollyson

FURTHER READING

Kershaw, Ian. *Hitler, 1936-1945: Nemesis.* New York: W. W. Norton, 2000. The second volume of Kershaw's acclaimed biography of Hitler (the first was *Hitler, 1889-1936: Hubris*). Accords Ribbentrop a central role in strengthening Germany's alliance with Japan, a role that the professionals in the German Foreign Office belittled because they considered Japan a sideshow. In effect, Ribbentrop was establishing an alternative foreign policy that found favor with Hitler.

Lukacs, John. *The Hitler of History.* New York: Alfred A. Knopf, 1997. Although this book does not specifically deal with the Anti-Comintern Pact, it is an indispensable and concise explanation of why Hitler's foreign policy was so successful until the beginning of World War II.

Shirer, William L. *The Rise and Fall of the Third Reich: A History of Nazi Germany*. 30th anniversary ed. New York: Ballantine, 1991. Classic work is still one of the most readable and informative histories of the Third Reich. Although Shirer's research has been superseded in some respects, this remains one of the best introductions to the Nazi era, especially given that the author witnessed many of Hitler's actions while serving as a foreign correspondent in Berlin.

SEE ALSO: Mar. 2-6, 1919: Lenin Establishes the Comintern; Jan. 30, 1933: Hitler Comes to Power in Germany; June 30-July 2, 1934: Great Blood Purge; Mar. 7, 1936: German Troops March into the Rhineland; Feb. 12-Apr. 10, 1938: The Anschluss; Sept. 29-30, 1938: Munich Conference.

December, 1936
INTER-AMERICAN CONFERENCE FOR THE MAINTENANCE OF PEACE

The countries of the Western Hemisphere met in an attempt to formulate strategies for avoiding warfare in the region. The conference set the tone for future relations among North, Central, and South American nations.

LOCALE: Buenos Aires, Argentina

CATEGORIES: Diplomacy and international relations; government and politics

KEY FIGURES

Franklin D. Roosevelt (1882-1945), president of the United States, 1933-1945

Cordell Hull (1871-1955), U.S. secretary of state, 1933-1944

Carlos Saavedra Lamas (1878-1959), foreign minister of Argentina, 1932-1938

SUMMARY OF EVENT

Prospects for world peace diminished during 1936. Imperial Japan had taken over Manchuria in 1931 and threatened to invade China. Italian Fascist dictator Benito Mussolini had sent his army into Ethiopia in order to build Italy's African empire. German chancellor Adolf Hitler hoped to unite Austria, the country of his birth, with Germany, and he also wanted to incorporate western Czechoslovakia into the greater German Reich. Spain's Fascist military leader Francisco Franco and his troops rebelled against the central government and began a civil war that lasted for three years (1936-1939) before Franco defeated the Spanish Republican forces and took power.

In addition to the outbreak of strife in continental Europe, turmoil in the continents of Africa and Asia had also become a serious concern for the countries in the Western Hemisphere. As a group, the Americas were suffering from the continuation of the serious economic depression that had begun in 1929, and an expansion of global unrest during the decade of the 1930's only increased the severity of the depression. The need for the development of strong hemispheric economic program that would meet the needs of all of the countries in the Americas weighed heavily on those responsible for the planning of U.S. foreign policy.

Thousands of Italians and Germans had immigrated to Argentina, Chile, Uruguay, and Brazil in the preceding fifty years. The Argentine army had many officers trained by the Germans and Italians, and German officers actually served with the Argentinians on regular tours of duty in that country. The U.S. State Department and War Department worried about whether the governments of Italy and Germany would attempt to utilize these close connections to influence foreign policy.

President Franklin D. Roosevelt and Secretary of State Cordell Hull were very concerned about the expansionist policies being used by Germany, Japan, and Italy. Could the Western Hemisphere be drawn into global conflict? To answer this question, in 1936 the American leaders called for a conference of the area's independent nations to discuss a plan for preserving peace in the face of any threat from outside the hemisphere. Roosevelt traveled to South America at the conference's opening, a trip that made him only the second American president to travel abroad to open a pan-American conference. He visited Uruguay, Brazil, and Argentina, and he received a tremendous welcome in all three countries. Undoubtedly, the newly reelected president's appearance at heavily attended public gatherings was a successful public relations strategy. Roosevelt took advantage of his popularity and stressed the need for the conference dele-

1936

gates to adopt a Good Neighbor Policy. He announced that the United States was committed to this principle and said that he hoped that the conference's commitment to peaceful discussion of international disputes could serve as a model for the rest of the world.

The Latin American countries did not automatically respond to President Roosevelt's statements. Historically, the United States had not been a good neighbor. In the course of the nineteenth and twentieth centuries, the U.S. government had sent troops into Mexico, Haiti, and Nicaragua, and the Americans had U.S. Marines stationed in Haiti as recently as 1934, although they were recalled in an attempt to demonstrate the commitment of the United States to the Good Neighbor Policy. Earlier in the century, however, President Theodore Roosevelt had fomented a civil war in Colombia's Central American territory that led to the establishment of an independent Panama. He ordered support for the Panamanian rebels solely for the purpose of building the canal that would connect the two oceans and serve U.S. interests in the region. This shortcut greatly enhanced the shipment of trade goods from coast to coast.

Nevertheless, the Inter-American Conference for the Maintenance of Peace was held at Buenos Aires in December of 1936, and out of the conference came the framework for a Western Hemisphere agreement. The main provisions were as follows: All of the members agreed to respect the sovereignty of other members, all members would consult immediately if the peace of the American community of nations was disturbed, no acquisition of territory made through violence would be recognized, intervention by one state in the internal or external affairs of another was condemned, forcible collection of debt was made illegal, and any dispute between American nations had to be settled through conciliation, arbitration, or the operation of international justice. Much of the content of the declaration was designed to convince the Latin American nations that the United States truly intended to be a good neighbor, and the document set the tone for all future hemispheric meetings among the American states.

SIGNIFICANCE

Although the Latin American countries agreed to adopt the concept of the Good Neighbor Policy, Argentine foreign minister Carlos Saavedra Lamas led these countries in insisting that the declarations clearly delineate the concept of equality for all of the conference's members, and the conference set the stage for the maintenance of independence of action for all its participants.

Despite a proposal from the United States for a united front against the fascist dictatorships of Europe, Argentina pursued a policy of neutrality throughout World War II. That country's independent action endorsed the concept that each participant in the Inter-American Conference had the right to formulate its own foreign and domestic positions.

—*Carl Henry Marcoux*

FURTHER READING

Bailey, Thomas Andrew. *A Diplomatic History of the American People.* 10th ed. Englewood Cliffs, N.J.: Prentice Hall, 1980. Presents an overview of American diplomacy since the country's founding.

Gellman, Irwin F. *Good Neighbor Diplomacy: United States Policies in Latin America, 1933-1945.* Baltimore: The Johns Hopkins University Press, 1979. Provides a thorough history of the period.

_____. *Secret Affairs: Franklin Roosevelt, Cordell Hull, and Sumner Welles.* Baltimore: The Johns Hopkins University Press, 1995. An analysis of the three major actors in the development of the Good Neighbor Policy of the United States during the 1930's and 1940's.

Hull, Cordell. *The Memoirs of Cordell Hull.* Vol. 1. New York: Macmillan, 1948. Autobiographical account of the U.S. State Department's pan-American policies during Hull's years as secretary of state.

Woods, Randall Bennett. *The Roosevelt Foreign-Policy Establishment and the "Good Neighbor": The United States and Argentina, 1941-1945.* Lawrence: Regents Press of Kansas, 1979. Discussion provides insights into Argentine neutralism during World War II.

SEE ALSO: Dec. 2-5, 1902: Founding of the International Sanitary Bureau; Nov. 8, 1932: Franklin D. Roosevelt Is Elected U.S. President; Mar. 4, 1933-1945: Good Neighbor Policy; Feb. 17, 1936: Corporatism Comes to Paraguay.

December 10, 1936
EDWARD VIII ABDICATES THE BRITISH THRONE

Edward VIII gave up the British throne in the wake of the public scandal surrounding his romantic involvement with an American divorcée.

LOCALE: Great Britain

CATEGORIES: Government and politics; crime and scandal

KEY FIGURES

Edward VIII (1894-1972), king of Great Britain, January 20-December 11, 1936, later duke of Windsor

Wallis Warfield Simpson (1896-1986), twice-divorced American woman whom Edward VIII wished to marry

Stanley Baldwin (1867-1947), Conservative prime minister of Great Britain, 1935-1937

Winston Churchill (1874-1965), British statesman and author

George Geoffrey Dawson (1874-1944), English journalist and editor of the London *Times*, 1923-1941

William Cosmo Gordon Lang (1864-1945), archbishop of Canterbury, 1928-1942

SUMMARY OF EVENT

Edward VIII was unconventional but popular both as Prince of Wales and as king—popular, perhaps, because he seemed modern and unconventional. His father, George V, had endowed the British monarchy with a comfortable sense of middle-class propriety. His eldest son, however, had a less clear sense of the duties and responsibilities of the monarch. Edward wanted to attune the monarchy to the times and to the people, and he was suspicious of what seemed to him the unimaginative and insensitive leadership of tired old men that characterized British politics in the 1930's.

Because of his intimate relationships with married women and his pro-German sympathies, the Prince of Wales was regarded in many circles with distaste and even suspicion. A constitutional crisis drove him from the throne before he had reigned one year. The king, who at age forty-one was still a bachelor, fell in love with Wallis Warfield Simpson, an American and a commoner. Not only was Mrs. Simpson married at the time to Ernest Simpson, a London stockbroker, but she had a former husband from whom she had been divorced many years before. The intimate friendship between the king and Mrs. Simpson soon became a matter of gossip in London society and of comment in the American press. The British

The duke and duchess of Windsor following their wedding on June 3, 1937. (AP/Wide World Photos)

THE DUKE OF WINDSOR ADDRESSES THE NATION

On December 11, 1936, the day after he abdicated the British throne, the Duke of Windsor addressed his former subjects through a radio broadcast. He began with these words:

At long last I am able to say a few words of my own. I have never wanted to withhold anything, but until now it has not been constitutionally possible for me to speak.

A few hours ago I discharged my last duty as King and Emperor, and now that I have been succeeded by my brother, The Duke of York, my first words must be to declare my allegiance to him. This I do with all my heart.

You all know the reasons which have impelled me to renounce the Throne. But I want you to understand that in making up my mind I did not forget the country or the Empire which as Prince of Wales, and lately as King, I have for twenty-five years tried to serve. But you must believe me when I tell you that I have found it impossible to carry the heavy burden of responsibility and to discharge my duties as King as I would wish to do without the help and support of the woman I love.

press, with its traditional respect for the royal family's privacy, treated Mrs. Simpson as if she did not exist. Stanley Baldwin, the Conservative prime minister, chose to bide his time and wait for the king to make a mistake or come to his senses.

In October of 1936, Mrs. Simpson sought and was awarded a divorce from her husband. This decree freed her to marry again after six months. At this point, the king told Baldwin that he intended to marry Mrs. Simpson. Baldwin and the entire cabinet opposed the marriage. They believed that the king's marrying a twice-divorced woman would violate the principles of the Church of England (of which the king was supreme governor) regarding divorce and remarriage. The archbishop of Canterbury, William Cosmo Gordon Lang, strongly upheld the church's view. Divorce still barred a man from public life in Britain, and it would be an intolerable affront if the king were to marry Mrs. Simpson. The cabinet correctly assumed that public opinion, in Great Britain and in the even more conservative countries of the Commonwealth, would display a similar outrage at what the king wanted to do. The king, the monarchy, and the government would be drawn into the storm of political controversy. There would likely be permanent political damage to the monarchy and all that it represented for the unity of the British people and the solidarity of the Commonwealth.

The king was legally free to marry any woman he wished, but he was constitutionally obliged to accept the advice of the cabinet. If he did not, the cabinet would be justified in resigning, as it now threatened to do. The question of the king's marriage became a constitutional crisis. Baldwin endeavored to convince the king to renounce Mrs. Simpson; otherwise it was his duty to abdicate. For Edward VIII, who apparently had little sense of the duties of the royal family, the choice was simple. He decided to marry the woman he loved. Meanwhile, the British public knew nothing because the secret was so well guarded. Then, suddenly, on December 3, the press broke its self-imposed silence. The nation was shocked and disbelieving. There was some popular support for the king and numerous demonstrations were held. Yet Baldwin and the cabinet had been right; most of the British people disapproved and public sentiment in the Commonwealth against the king also ran high. Most of the British press was against the monarch. Winston Churchill's attempts to stir up support in the House of Commons failed dismally.

The king notified Baldwin on December 5 of his decision to abdicate. Certain conventions had to be honored, and Parliament was not informed until December 10. On December 11, a Declaration of Abdication Bill was introduced in Parliament, passed both houses, and received royal assent. Edward was now a private citizen. The new king, the former duke of York, succeeded as George VI. That evening, Edward broadcast a touching farewell message to the people of Great Britain and the Commonwealth in which he said that he could not continue his life without the help of "the woman I love." Immediately afterward, he went into self-imposed exile in France, where he married Mrs. Simpson the following June. Although Edward was created duke of Windsor, his wife was not accorded the title of royal highness. The British royal family, bitter at how Edward had behaved during the abdication crisis and convinced that Mrs. Simpson was responsible, refused to receive her or acknowledge her as duchess of Windsor. There was some softening of their attitude, however, before the duke of Windsor's death in 1972.

SIGNIFICANCE

Edward VIII's abdication became one of the most controversial episodes in the history of the British monarchy. Modern scholarship now contends that Edward VIII mishandled his personal and public affairs throughout the period that led up to the abdication, and in the process he alienated many members of Parliament. His later expressions of pro-German sentiment in the 1930's and 1940's have also hurt his historical reputation. After his abdication, the duke met with several Nazi Party officials and even had an audience with Adolf Hitler; the Nazis hoped to reinstall the duke on the throne and thereby establish a Nazi presence in England. The plan was not a serious one, however, and in 1945 the duke accepted Churchill's offer of a post as governor in the Bahamas. Fortunately, the duke's departure had proved no more than a minor tremor for the British monarchy, and though Windsor family relations were severely strained, their conflicts were not made as public as some later disagreements. Furthermore, the spotlight quickly turned to the duke's brother, King George VI, who made an excellent monarch. As a result, the abdication controversy passed quickly and was almost as quickly forgotten. Eventually, the duke returned to England for visits and for the funerals of his brother in 1952 and his mother, Queen Mary, in 1953. Fourteen more years would pass before the duke and duchess were formally invited to a royal gathering, although the pair were ultimately buried together at Windsor Castle's Frogmore.

—*James M. Haas and Lewis L. Gould*

FURTHER READING

Bloch, Michael, ed. *Wallis and Edward: Letters, 1931-1937—The Intimate Correspondence of the Duke and Duchess of Windsor*. New York: Summit Books, 1986. A valuable primary source for understanding how King Edward VIII and the woman he loved viewed the constitutional crisis that had changed their lives.

Bradford, Sarah. *The Reluctant King: The Life and Reign of George VI, 1985-1952*. New York: St. Martin's Press, 1989. Looks at the abdication crisis from the point of view of Edward VIII's brother and successor and is critical of the performance of the future duke of Windsor.

Donaldson, Frances. *Edward VIII: A Biography of the Duke of Windsor*. New York: J. B. Lippincott, 1974. The first thorough and critical biography of the duke of Windsor, one that began the reappraisal of his life and the implications of the abdication and its background.

Edward VIII, King of Great Britain. *A King's Story: The Memoirs of H.R.H. the Duke of Windsor*. New York: G. P. Putnam's Sons, 1951. The ghostwritten memoirs of the king illustrate the strengths and weaknesses of his personality and approach to his royal responsibilities.

Williams, Susan. *The People's King: The True Story of the Abdication*. New York: Palgrave Macmillan, 2004. Williams was the first of Edward VIII's biographers to have access to scores of official records and private diaries, and so she is able to argue convincingly that the duke's democratic leanings were just as—and perhaps more—responsible for his ouster than his desire to marry Simpson.

Windsor, Wallis Warfield, Duchess of. *The Heart Has Its Reasons: The Memoirs of the Duchess of Windsor*. New York: David McKay, 1956. The duchess of Windsor offers her account of the abdication crisis, which reveals how little she understood the British monarchy and the political system of the country.

Ziegler, Philip. *King Edward VIII: A Biography*. New York: Alfred A. Knopf, 2001. Excellent modern biography of the king presents a thorough and balanced treatment of the abdication crisis and its aftermath.

SEE ALSO: Jan. 1, 1927: British Broadcasting Corporation Is Chartered; July 2, 1928: Great Britain Lowers the Voting Age for Women; Jan., 1935: Schiaparelli's Boutique Mingles Art and Fashion; Nov. 2, 1936: BBC Airs the First High-Definition Television Program.

1936

1937
DREYFUSS DESIGNS THE BELL 300 TELEPHONE

Henry Dreyfuss's design for the Bell 300 telephone—which remained the standard desk telephone from its introduction in 1937 until 1950—was a milestone for the developing world of industrial design in the United States.

LOCALE: New York, New York
CATEGORIES: Fashion and design; science and technology

KEY FIGURES

Henry Dreyfuss (1904-1972), pioneer of industrial design in the United States
Doris Marks Dreyfuss (1903-1972), one of Dreyfuss's first employees and, after their marriage in 1930, his firm's business manager
Norman Bel Geddes (1893-1958), theatrical designer turned industrial designer
Walter Dorwin Teague (1883-1960), pioneer in the professionalization of industrial design in the United States
Raymond Fernand Loewy (1893-1986), industrial design innovator

SUMMARY OF EVENT

Henry Dreyfuss was born on March 2, 1904, in New York City. He graduated from the Ethical Culture Fine Arts High School in 1922. His father and grandfather had been in the theatrical equipment business, supplying costumes and props, and Dreyfuss followed family tradition by becoming an apprentice to stage designer Norman Bel Geddes in the design of the sets for the 1924 Broadway hit *The Miracle*. Starting in 1923, Dreyfuss worked as a designer for the stage productions of the Strand Theater in New York City. His success at the Strand led to similar work for the nationwide RKO Orpheum chain of vaudeville theaters. "Out of the sheer necessity of producing six new sets weekly for 260 weeks," he recalled in his *Designing for People* (1955), "came an understanding of what people like."

Dreyfuss was first attracted to industrial design in 1927, when an executive at Macy's department store asked him to look into the possibility of redesigning the store's merchandise to boost sales. Dreyfuss turned down the job because he thought that the changes involved would require excessively expensive retooling. He concluded that the way to improve the design of a product was to work directly with the product's manu-

facturer before the manufacturer had made a major investment in machinery and materials. "A fundamental premise was involved in my refusal—one from which I have never retreated," he later explained. "An honest job of design should flow from the inside out, not from the outside in."

Interest in industrial product design first appeared in Europe, climaxing in a 1925 Paris exhibition of designs and decorative arts. Industrial design, however, emerged as a profession first in the United States, where the rise of a consumer culture occurred earlier than in Europe. In the 1920's, demand for mass-market consumer items such as automobiles, sewing machines, refrigerators, radios, and other electric appliances increased enormously, and at the suggestion of their advertising agencies, manufacturers began to give more attention to the appearance of their products. Henry Ford's decision to meet increasing competition by replacing the Model T automobile with the new Model A in 1927 gave other businessmen a high-profile demonstration of the importance of style to sales. The Great Depression further pushed manufacturers into searching for ways to boost sales by making products more attractive and efficient.

The leading philosopher of the emergent profession of industrial design was Dreyfuss's mentor in stage design, Norman Bel Geddes. Geddes's 1932 book *Horizons* did much to popularize what became the dominant American style of the 1930's, streamlining, which emphasized the separation of the outer shell of a product from its internal mechanism. The outer shell typically had a smooth and flowing surface with rounded edges. Streamlining was strongly influenced by research in aerodynamics—the techniques for eliminating the friction of wind resistance to a moving vehicle. Researchers had concluded that the teardrop was the aerodynamically most efficient shape for a moving vehicle. Industrial designers in the 1930's extended the teardrop shape from its use in locomotives and automobiles and began to apply it to stationary objects.

Geddes was a technocratic utopian who envisaged industrial design transforming the world. A similar vision animated Walter Dorwin Teague. Teague had a successful career as an advertising illustrator before he began his second career as an industrial designer by creating (around 1930) several cameras for Eastman Kodak. He would count among his clients such other corporate giants as Ford, Texaco, and Du Pont. Teague and Dreyfuss took the initiative in promoting organization of a professional association for industrial designers; they in turn brought in Raymond Fernand Loewy to constitute the founding triumvirate responsible for the establishment in 1944 of the Society of Industrial Designers.

Loewy came to personify for the lay public the new profession. Loewy—who had been born in Paris in 1893—launched his own independent design firm in New York City the same year that Dreyfuss opened his office. He would go on to become a household name with such designs as the Gestetner stencil duplicating machine (1929), the remodeled Coldspot refrigerator for Sears, Roebuck (1934), the interior of the Pennsylvania Railroad's *Broadway Limited* train (1938), the Chrysler Motors Building at the 1939 New York World's Fair, the red-and-white package for Lucky Strike cigarettes (1941), the Greyhound Scenicruiser bus (1954), and the Studebaker Champion (1947), Starliner (1953), and Avanti (1962) automobiles.

In April, 1929, Dreyfuss opened his own independent design office on New York's Fifth Avenue. One of his first employees was Doris Marks, whom he married in 1930. After their marriage, she remained active in the firm as business manager. During the firm's early years, when clients were few, Dreyfuss kept afloat financially by designing the sets for such Broadway shows as *The Last Mile* (1930) and *The Cat and the Fiddle* (1931). Gradually, however, he built a following among manufacturers. One of his first commissions was his redesigned mason jar, which occupied less space; Dreyfuss achieved the goal by making the jar square with a rounded top. His Toperator washing machine for Sears, Roebuck in 1933 was a runaway sales success. So was his design in 1934 of a refrigerator for General Electric that had its motor unit at the bottom, enclosed in an easy-to-clean cabinet, instead of at the top. Starting in 1930, he worked as a consultant for the Bell Telephone Laboratories to design an improved desk telephone. The result of his collaboration with the Bell engineers, the 300 model—introduced in 1937—confirmed his reputation as a

leader in the new field of industrial design. The 300 model remained the standard desk telephone until 1950, when it was replaced by another Dreyfuss model.

Other Dreyfuss designs included the Big Ben and Baby Ben alarm clocks for Westclox, a vacuum cleaner for Hoover, the Eversharp pen, a Royal typewriter, gas stations for Cities Service, bathroom fixtures for Crane, and farm equipment for John Deere. His influence was strongly felt in magazine publishing via his design of the formats for *McCall's*, *Time*, and *Reader's Digest* magazines. His scale model of the "city of tomorrow" for the interior of the Perisphere at the 1939 New York World's Fair did much to bring his name to popular attention.

Dreyfuss's most publicly visible contributions were in the transportation sphere. The two trains that he planned for the New York Central Railroad—the *Mercury* (1936) and the even more famous *Twentieth Century Limited* (1938)—set a new standard for luxurious rail travel. He designed the interiors of the American Export Lines ships SS *Independence* and SS *Constitution*, along with those of many airplanes. He was proudest, however, of the prosthetic devices he invented for the victims of limb loss during World War II.

By the 1950's, his firm had grown to include two offices (in New York City and South Pasadena, California) headed by six partners, with a staff of fifty specialists and

Model 302 in the Bell Telephone 300 series, designed by Henry Dreyfuss.

office personnel. Dreyfuss himself divided his time between the two offices. His approach to design called for detailed knowledge of all aspects of the manufacturing and selling of the product. Accordingly, he placed heavy emphasis on research and teamwork in the design process, and he limited his clients to approximately fifteen at a time.

SIGNIFICANCE

Dreyfuss lacked the personal flamboyance and flair for self-publicity exhibited by his colleague Raymond Loewy. Dreyfuss's tastes were more plain: Brown was his favorite color, not only for his suits but also for his office decor. However, he shared Loewy's pragmatism. He saw increasing sales for the client as the industrial designer's primary responsibility. He applied to design problems a five-point yardstick: utility and safety, ease of maintenance, cost, sales appeal, and appearance. Although many of his designs reflected the dominant streamline model, he was no rigid devotee of that style. The keystone of his design credo was the maxim that "the most efficient machine is the one that is built around a person."

Dreyfuss's goal was thus to achieve maximum simplicity in fitting a product's form to its function. He was wary about moving too far ahead of popular taste. The industrial designer, Dreyfuss commented in *Designing for People*, "is a businessman as well as a person who makes drawings and models. He is a keen observer of public taste.... He has an understanding of merchandising, how things are made, packed, distributed, and displayed. He accepts the responsibility of his position as a liaison linking management, engineering, and the consumer and cooperates with all three."

Dreyfuss was elected president of the Society of Industrial Designers in 1947. He was a consultant in industrial design at the California Institute of Technology and lectured in engineering at the University of California at Los Angeles. He had privately printed a pictorial record of his designs: *Ten Years of Industrial Design: Henry Dreyfuss, 1929-1939* (1939); *A Record of Industrial Designs, 1929 Through 1947* (1947); *Industrial Design: A Progress Report, 1929-1952* (1952); and *Industrial Design: A Pictorial Accounting, 1929-1957* (1957). His *Designing for People* combined autobiographical reminiscences with a summation of his design philosophy. He presented the data he had accumulated about the physical dimensions of the "average" American in *The Measure of Man: Human Factors in Design* (1960).

—*John Braeman*

FURTHER READING

Bush, Donald J. *The Streamlined Decade*. New York: George Braziller, 1975. An excellent survey, with accompanying extensive illustrations, of the application of streamlining to locomotives, automobiles, ships, airplanes, industrial products, and even buildings during the 1930's.

Dreyfuss, Henry. *Designing for People*. New York: Simon & Schuster, 1955. A handsome volume, all aspects of which (jacket, binding, typography, and page layout) were designed by Dreyfuss himself. The text combines autobiographical reminiscences with a summation of Dreyfuss's design philosophy.

_____. *The Measure of Man: Human Factors in Design*. New York: Whitney Library of Design, 1960. A portfolio containing charts summarizing the data that Dreyfuss compiled on the physical dimensions of the "average" American for the guidance of industrial designers.

Flinchum, Russell. *Henry Dreyfuss, Industrial Designer: The Man in the Brown Suit*. New York: Rizzoli, 1997. Offers clear and concise discussion of Dreyfuss's work. Includes more than two hundred carefully chosen images.

Gorman, Carma, ed. *The Industrial Design Reader*. New York: Allworth Press, 2003. Valuable for its inclusion of dozens of primary-source critiques on individual works rather than just their photos. Features not only essays by the artists but also essays by advertisers, industrialists, academics, and politicians.

Meikle, Jeffrey L. *Twentieth Century Limited: Industrial Design in America, 1925-1939*. Philadelphia: Temple University Press, 1979. A detailed and thoroughly researched account of the formative years of the industrial design profession in the United States. Focuses on the so-called big four of Geddes, Loewy, Teague, and Dreyfuss. Illuminates the assumptions, concepts, and visions influencing, and underlying, their design work.

Pulos, Arthur J. *The American Design Adventure, 1940-1975*. Cambridge, Mass.: MIT Press, 1988. Pulos carries on his history of American industrial design from where his first volume left off, with the same first-rate results.

_____. *American Design Ethic: A History of Industrial Design*. Cambridge, Mass.: MIT Press, 1983. A pioneering survey of American product design from the colonial period to the 1940's. Approximately the last third of the volume is devoted to the post-1920's period, when industrial design began to emerge as a recognized profession. Lavishly illustrated; includes an extensive bibliography.

SEE ALSO: 1902-1913: Tiffany Leads the Art Nouveau Movement in the United States; 1903: Hoffmann and Moser Found the Wiener Werkstätte; Oct., 1907:

Deutscher Werkbund Is Founded; 1917: *De Stijl* Advocates Mondrian's Neoplasticism; 1919: German Artists Found the Bauhaus; Jan. 1, 1925: Bell Labs Is Formed; May-June, 1925: Paris Exhibition Defines Art Deco; 1929: Loewy Pioneers American Industrial Design.

1937
PROUVÉ PIONEERS ARCHITECTURAL PREFABRICATION

Jean Prouvé initiated and refined the total prefabrication of homes and a variety of other structures in an effort to bring building into the industrial age.

LOCALE: France
CATEGORY: Architecture

KEY FIGURES
Jean Prouvé (1901-1984), French metal craftsman, engineer, and designer
Walter Gropius (1883-1969), German architect
Le Corbusier (1887-1965), Swiss-born French architect
Tony Garnier (1869-1948), French architect
Eugène Elie Beaudouin (1898-1983), French architect
Marcel Lods (1891-1978), French architect

SUMMARY OF EVENT
In 1937, near Buc, a French village too small to appear in atlases, construction was completed on the Roland Garros Aeroclub. Almost the entire building, including floors, walls, ramp, and roof—indeed, all the structure's pressed-metal components—were prefabricated. Dismantled by the Germans a few years later during World War II, the Aeroclub nevertheless has subsequently been identified by architectural historians as one of the twentieth century's most interesting and important buildings. Although the Aeroclub was less influential than Antonio Gaudí's Casa Milá flats, Le Corbusier's Villa Savoye, or Alvar Aalto's Villa Mairea, it was in many respects more innovative than any of these architectural milestones. So, too, was another structure built in 1938 in the Paris suburb of Clichy, the Maison du Peuple, a large market and auditorium with floors, walls, and a roof that moved electrically—all within an envelope of stressed-skin panels separated by coil springs. The Maison du Peuple was another novel building that was industrially designed and industrially produced. Moreover, although the designs of

the Aeroclub and the Maison du Peuple engaged the talents of the same two notable architects, Eugène Elie Beaudouin and Marcel Lods, the buildings' distinctive characters were as much the work of Jean Prouvé, a remarkable metal craftsman, engineer, and self-taught architect.

By 1946, barely a decade after erection of the Aeroclub, Prouvé was pioneering not only the total prefabrication of industrial and public buildings but—of equal importance from his perspective—the prefabrication of entire houses and housing units. Prouvé believed that neither architects nor builders had adequately availed themselves of industrial materials or techniques and had therefore failed to recognize the efficiencies and potential afforded by an industrial age. Prouvé's convictions made him one of the leaders of the modern movement in building technology.

The son of Victor Prouvé, a painter prominent in the decorative arts that flourished in Nancy (France) around 1900, Jean was born in Paris in 1901. Nancy—the home to which the Prouvés soon returned—was a manufacturing center lying at the heart of an iron mining region with major ironware and steel industries. Consequently, after his preliminary education, the young Prouvé, under the aegis of master craftsmen in Paris, trained from 1916 to 1923 as a blacksmith and metalworker. Back in Nancy by 1924, he married and, as a qualified engineer, founded his own metal-fittings and furniture establishment. Like many of the century's famed and formally educated architects, such as Walter Gropius, Le Corbusier, Alvar Aalto, Marcel Breuer, and Ludwig Mies van der Rohe, Prouvé came to an understanding of architecture early in his career through the design and manufacture of furnishings.

He rapidly became a master of modern building materials, and his designs and the works of his establishment were avidly sought by the greatest architects. In the early 1930's, for example, Prouvé collaborated with Tony Garnier, producing operating theaters and sliding windows for a Lyon hospital and doors, partitions, and furniture for the Boulogne-Billancourt town hall. In the mid-1930's, too, Prouvé began more than thirty years of intermittent collaboration with Le Corbusier. Prouvé entered this association modestly with the design of a portable toilet for the Paris World's Fair. In the ensuing years, he provided such design and building components as the suspended ceilings for Le Corbusier's Unité d'Habitation as well as the staircases, kitchens, and furnishings for the Cité Radieuse, both major projects of Le Corbusier in Marseille. Over the years, Prouvé did similar business with other notable French architects who had international repute, including Bernard Zehrfuss and Robert Mallet-Stevens. His work was also solicited by leading corporations, banks, hospitals, research institutions, schools, oil companies, hotels, subway systems, and cinema and television chains, as well as by the governments of France and many other European and African nations.

Prouvé's industrialized design and production of prefabricated housing was the result of several factors. First, his own mastery of modern building technology and materials, in addition to his familiarity with the manufacture and installation of nearly every modern structural component, brilliantly equipped him to carry his work into the production of entire dwelling and structural units. Second, France's preparations for and engagement in World War II created huge demands for swiftly constructed housing. Third, Prouvé, along with the great architects with whom he collaborated, believed that the industrialized production of housing more honestly reflected the efficiency, character, and potential of an industrial era than did traditional design.

Prouvé's first experiment with full prefabrication was the creation of eight hundred units in Lorraine for the Ministry of Reconstruction and Town Planning, a project closely followed by the construction of a house in Vesoul; both projects took place in 1944, while Prouvé was still working with the French Resistance. Pressures for housing increased at war's end, and his work began maturing with construction of Nancy's Cité Universitaire student quarters. The following year, he produced the fully prefabricated Portico House for his own workshop as well as boarding facilities for the Apprenticeship Glassworks Center and a more modest private home in Carnac. In 1948, he continued his prefabrication for the ministry, producing demonstration houses in four French towns. In 1949, serving as architect himself, he prefabricated so-called Metropole and Coque housing,

again for the ministry, in Meudon. These were successful ventures, and he repeated construction of the Metropole houses in both Oran and Algiers for local utility companies. Until 1976, Prouvé averaged one commission on fully prefabricated structures per year. Always disdainful of the conservatism of professional architects and builders (not to mention the general public), Prouvé had difficulties with industrialized housing. As a consequence, he continued earning much of his living by supplying others with his superb prefabricated components and furnishings, which always spoke by their excellence of the aesthetic and economic possibilities of industrialized building.

SIGNIFICANCE

By the early twentieth century, prefabrication was an old idea and a frequently utilized construction technique. Many examples existed before Prouvé's work began. The prefabrication of Venetian galleys for Venice's great commercial fleet functioned effectively throughout the fifteenth century. Similarly, on the American and Canadian frontiers during the late nineteenth century, whole towns of individual homes and shops were preassembled, transported westward, and assembled again. More notably, London's spectacular Crystal Palace of 1850— one of the century's architectural landmarks—was premanufactured and, amazingly, assembled within a few days. Quite commonly by the 1880's, whole building facades of premanufactured cast iron distinguished businesses on the Main Streets of American cities.

Until the twentieth century, however, prefabrication generally was definable as the manufacture and assembly of varied building components, not as the design and manufacture of industrialized structures that represented complete industrial products in themselves. For influential schools of architecture such as Germany's Bauhaus as well as for precedent-breaking architects—Gaudí, Garnier, or Le Corbusier, for example—the very objective of designs was to bring building, and lifestyles, into the machine age. These innovators sought to explore and experiment with the qualities (and economies) of modern construction materials such as concrete, steel, aluminum, glass, and plastics and envisioned the "machining" of all sorts of structures. Gropius, for years the leader of the Bauhaus, was profoundly interested in this form of prefabrication; in the early 1930's, before Prouvé's industrialized structures had appeared, Gropius had contracted with the Hirsch Copper Company, a German firm, to manufacture scores of company houses. A few years later, he effected an identical arrangement with another German firm, although in each instance the materials to be employed were largely traditional ones such as wood. Undertakings like these united Gropius, Garnier, and Le Corbusier, among others, in mutual influences and collaborative enterprises.

In the United States, R. Buckminster Fuller had begun experiments with manufactured housing and other buildings in an attempt to provide light, sturdy structures that were easy to erect and that used not only modern materials such as steel, prestressed concrete, and aluminum but also paperboard, plywood, and bamboo. It was not until 1946, however, that Fuller succeeded in completing his famed Dymaxion House and geodesic domes. These and similar twentieth century experiments, although undeniably impressive, were nevertheless architectural "sports" developed beyond the pale of architecture's everyday business of building design and construction.

The steady impetus toward industrialized building came not only from the aesthetics and creative curiosities of a handful of architects but was also stimulated by the immense backlog of housing created by two world wars. In France and the rest of Europe, incentive stemmed more urgently from the requirements of national reconstruction and from the increasing intervention of governments in all areas of national life. Each of these circumstances directly informed Prouvé's expectations and experiments.

Prouvé's work and its analogues had profound consequences in the second half of the twentieth century. The testimonials to his influence stand as familiar parts of urbanized landscapes around the developed world. For industrialized building as a type of architecture, Prouvé set singular and exemplary standards. His sensitivity to the capacities and possibilities of materials and machines opened architects' eyes to new structural vistas for individual homes, housing complexes, towns, offices, and schools.

Nevertheless, it is more common to witness the drab, monotonous expanses of wartime prefabrications, of construction camps, and trailer towns, than it is—as Prouvé complained before his death—to know the whereabouts of factories that produce houses much as other types of factories mass-produce automobiles. Acknowledging by the 1980's that both the principles and practice of what he meant by "prefabrication" had taken root, Prouvé was still aware of the shortfall of his expectations. Architects, he advised, needed to be intimate parts of manufacturing, which as yet they were not. Too much industrialized building, he argued, unnecessarily continued employing new materials in traditional

ways—a fault of both architects and builders. Having designed and manufactured his own products as if nothing had ever been built before, he deplored adaptations of buildings to existing machine processes, many of which he disdained. In the twenty-first century, the general approbation for his industrialized pressed-metal structures—including his exhibition village, at Michel-sur-Orge, his Pierrelatte workshop for France's atomic energy workers, and his Fontainebleau holiday resort for Air France, all built in the 1960's—continues to goad architects and builders to escape confinement in the thinking of the past.

—*Clifton K. Yearley*

FURTHER READING

Arieff, Allison, and Bryan Burkhart. *Prefab*. New York: Gibbs Smith, 2002. Examination of innovative prefabricated structures includes a chapter devoted to the history of prefabricated housing. Features photographs, bibliography, and index.

Lavedan, Pierre. *French Architecture*. London: Scolar Press, 1971. Readable, scholarly survey places Prouvé in a national setting and clarifies the innovativeness of his work and that of other modernists. Very informative. Includes photographs, bibliography, and index.

Newton, Nigel. "Prouvé: Modern Movement Pioneer." *Building Design* 30 (March, 1984): 175-178. Essentially a tribute to Prouvé published shortly after his death. Gives Prouvé his due and touches on his amazingly brilliant collaborations. Includes photographs.

Prouvé, Jean. *Jean Prouvé: Prefabrication, Structures, and Elements*. Translated by Alexander Lieven, edited by Benedikt Huber and Jean-Claude Steinegger. New York: Praeger, 1971. One of the few discussions available on the prefabrication of buildings and of Prouvé's role in the field. Deals with Prouvé's work in context. Includes plates, notes, bibliography, and index.

Rowlands, Penelope. *Jean Prouvé: Compact Design Portfolio*. San Francisco: Chronicle Books, 2002. Focuses on Prouvé's furniture designs, but includes an introductory essay on his life and work in general. Features many illustrations.

Sulzer, Peter. *Jean Prouvé Highlights 1917-1944*. Translated by Gerald B. Binding. Basel, Switzerland: Birkhäuser, 2002. Discusses Prouvé's architectural work during the period covered and his importance to the history of twentieth century design. Includes many illustrations.

"The Work of Jean Prouvé." *Architectural Design* 33
(1963): 511-525. Solidly professional and laudatory
examination of Prouvé's contributions to architecture. Published while Prouvé was at the top of his
form and attracting international attention and honors. Includes photographs.

SEE ALSO: 1910: Gaudí Completes the Casa Milá Apartment House; 1919: German Artists Found the Bauhaus; Spring, 1931: Le Corbusier's Villa Savoye Exemplifies Functionalist Architecture; 1937-1938:
Aalto Designs Villa Mairea.

1937-1938
AALTO DESIGNS VILLA MAIREA

*Alvar Aalto's design of Finland's Villa Mairea, an
architectural masterpiece, confirmed him as one of the
world's leading architects and helped to revolutionize
residential architecture.*

LOCALE: Noormarkku, Finland
CATEGORY: Architecture

KEY FIGURES
Alvar Aalto (1898-1976), Finnish architect
Aino Marsio Aalto (1894-1949), Finnish architect-
designer and Alvar Aalto's first wife
Erik Gunnar Asplund (1885-1940), Swedish architect
and friend of Alvar Aalto
Le Corbusier (1887-1965), Swiss-born French
architect who was an early influence on Alvar Aalto
Walter Gropius (1883-1969), German architect who
was a founder of modern architecture
Frank Lloyd Wright (1867-1959), American architect
who had a humanistic influence on Aalto and Villa
Mairea

SUMMARY OF EVENT
Alvar Aalto's design and construction of Villa Mairea in
Noormarkku, Finland, in 1937 and 1938 produced one of
the masterpieces of modern domestic architecture.
Among architects and architecture critics, the structure
has been accorded rank with Ludwig Mies van der
Rohe's Tugendhat House (1930), Le Corbusier's Villa
Savoye (1931), and Frank Lloyd Wright's Fallingwater
(1936) as a twentieth century landmark. Like many other
impressive artworks, Villa Mairea also represented a
fruitful symbiosis between wealthy, intellectually progressive clients and an inspired architect whose own evolution required opportunity, empathy, and experimental
freedom.

Aalto's patrons and clients were millionaires Henry
Gullichsen and his wife, Maire Ahlström Gullichsen.
Mrs. Gullichsen was heiress to Finland's Ahlström for-

tune, wealth that had been earned over three generations
in lumber, pulp mills, paper products, and furniture.
Upon his marriage to Maire, Henry Gullichsen became
chairman of the board of the Ahlström business. Maire, a
painter by profession as well as a successful executive,
collaborated with Alvar Aalto and his designer-architect
wife, Aino Marsio Aalto, in manufacturing and marketing the Aaltos' unique wood and plywood furniture. Both
Gullichsens were patrons of the arts and, like the Aaltos,
they were social and political liberals who looked forward to contributing to fuller lives for workers and employers alike.

By 1937, Aalto had been a practicing architect for fifteen years. Until then, both his writings about his architectural philosophy and his works clearly indicated the
influence of the earlier works of Walter Gropius, Le
Corbusier, and several of their disciples, including
Aalto's Swedish friend and colleague Sven Markelius
(Jonsson). Aalto's early works and writings thus showed
his adherence to a strict rationalist or functionalist style
known as modern architecture or the International Style.
Aalto, like all functionalists, rejected the older architectural criteria of aestheticism and decorativeness. Instead, he believed that a building should reflect only
its specific needs. Just as an engineer would design a
machine for a definite purpose rather than with an artistic end in mind, the rationalist architect, too, treated
each structure as a discrete product of social, technical,
psychological, and economic organization, with the architect as a presumptive social administrator. The creation of beauty, of course, was not ignored, but it was
asecondary consideration in the design of functionalist
architecture.

Aalto's earlier designs and structures, therefore, display the characteristically spartan, boxlike, and elementary geometric forms that Le Corbusier, himself a painter
as well as author and architect, derived from purist and
cubist painting. There was ample evidence of this bent in

four of Aalto's most important commissions before 1937: the *Turun-Sanomat* newspaper building (1928-1929), the Paimio Tuberculosis Sanatorium (1930-1933), the Viipuri Municipal Library (1933-1935), and the Helsinki Savoy restaurant (1937). The modernist style is also reflected in his (and Aino's) splendidly distinctive functional furniture, which by the mid-1930's had gained international acclaim.

By the late 1930's, however, Aalto's perspectives were changing. There were several explanations for this. To begin with, after Eliel Saarinen's departure for the United States, Aalto aspired to replace him as Finland's dominant national architect. Then, too, during the 1930's, with the broadening of his influential professional contacts in Europe and the United States, Aalto shed much of his remaining provincialism. Morever, the freedom vouchsafed him by the Gullichsens to design their vacation home in Noormarkku allowed him to synthesize the best aspects of his previous designs. Aalto sited Villa Mairea in the hills of western Finland's pine forests on an Ahlström family estate that contained domestic architecture representative of three generations of one of Finland's leading families. The villa was intended to serve as a vacation home for the Gullichsens and their children, as an art studio for Maire, and as a business and entertainment center—or, as need be, a retreat—for both husband and wife. Aalto was to design everything: building, interior decor and furnishings, swimming pool, and sauna.

Completed, the villa established a great sense of privacy yet satisfied all of the Gullichsens' practical and aesthetic requirements. The building was a U-shaped, open structure that nevertheless was subtly divided into living and service areas. Thus, although the ground-floor living spaces were flowing and continuous, they could be broken up for the display or enjoyment of the family's collected art by means of easily movable partitions (in which artworks were also stored), and dining facilities were separate. The ample living room was divided between a private Finnish hearth and, by way of contrast, a substantial, well-planted solarium with large picture windows. Far to the left of the main entrance was a superstructure that served as Maire Gullichsen's studio, which on the second floor gave way to another living room and bedrooms with boldly projecting windows. To the rear, visible directly through back windows of the main living room, ran a covered portico that ended in a right angle containing a sauna—almost Japanese in its motifs—and a kidney-shaped swimming pool. The home's rough "U" was closed by forest.

Aalto's inimitable detailing marked both exterior and interior. Outside, there were venetian blinds, exposed vertical board and batten, columns bound by willow withes, and a natural turf-and-grass roof for the sauna. The inside featured pole space dividers, living room pillars protected by leather wrappings, slatted wood ceilings of Finnish birch, distinctive ventilation through tens of thousands of hand-bored holes in the living room ceiling, daringly ingenious staircases, and, throughout, specially designed Aalto furniture. Villa Mairea, as critic Göran Schildt summarized, embodied "the vernacular tradition, the organic overall conception of Art Nouveau, Neo-Classical humanism, rational Functionalism, Japanese feeling for texture and Aalto's personal susceptibility to the complex interaction of natural forces."

By the late 1930's, Aalto was taking full advantage of his clients' natural environments and designing structures that afforded them the most humane living and working conditions. The Sunila Sulphate Mill, completed in 1939, rises out of its granitic terrain faced by a warm, rough Finnish brick, its horizontal lines softened by a slight arch over the central structure and accented by a tall smokestack. Nearby is the employee and executive housing, initially a small, cellular community that Aalto planned around a communal laundry and steam bath—later expanded to include larger civic and community centers—has been kept to human proportions by using the broken granite moraine to divide dwellings into modest clusters. Furthermore, at Aalto's insistence, few of the houses are identical; in line with the evolution of Finland's ancient village housing, provisions were made for each home to expand as family needs changed. Aalto carefully discriminated between the need for standardized production of construction materials and standardized housing.

Aalto's concern with placing humans more properly in their natural surroundings by the use of rugged, natural materials became even more apparent in his design of the Finnish Pavilion for the 1939 New York World's Fair. A proud nationalist aware of his country's need for good relations with the United States, he built the pavilion of Finnish woods and highlighted the interior with an undulating wooden display wall reminiscent of the northern lights. The pavilion was a warm, inviting structure adjacent to the American exhibition and provided a romantic alternative to the International Style. Aalto's new rationalism had accomplished much the same effect in his stepped multiple housing project at Kauttua, where varied residential structures marched up a hillside as in an Italian hill town and where Aalto's use of vertical poles and metal railings, covered with vines, repeated themes from the surrounding trees and forests.

With the reconstruction required in 1940 after the end of the Russo-Finnish War—one immense consequence of which was the loss of Karelia, Finland's most populous province, and the forced resettlement of a huge population—Aalto even more imaginatively spoke to his desire to clarify relations between humans and nature in his design of the cellular housing project of Rovaniemi. More impressive still was his plan for the Finnish Technical Institute at Otaniemi, on the outskirts of Helsinki, where terrain almost entirely dictated the structure's character. Thereafter, just as Aalto had drawn some inspiration from Frank Lloyd Wright's Fallingwater house in Pennsylvania, so too his own future work was characterized increasingly by his departures from literal rationalism toward a more personal, more humane, architectural expression. The evolution of his style is visible in his later works, such as his design of the Baker House (1946-1949) at the Massachusetts Institute of Technology, where Aalto taught part-time from 1945 to 1951.

SIGNIFICANCE

The completed Villa Mairea marked Aalto's maturation. His background and character, blended through experience with his work, modified, romanticized, and humanized his earlier rationalist ideology and functionalist architecture. Born in 1898, Aalto spent formative years in a rural, heavily forested Finland that, until 1917, was a western province of Imperial Russia untouched by extensive industrialization and urbanization. Even its major resources and their related industries—timber, wood and paper products, mining, and waterpower—required only small, isolated rural communities. The forces and mythologies of nature were part of his environment, as they were for his father, a surveyor, and his grandfather, a forester. Respect for nature, terrain, and environment, qualities that began manifesting themselves in Aalto's designs of the Paimio Sanatorium, the Viipuri Library, and the Finnish Pavilion at the 1937 Paris Exposition, became even more striking after completion of Villa Mairea.

Aalto definitively signaled his presence at Villa Mairea. He was soon viewed as Finland's national architect and as an international figure of the front rank, and some thought him the greatest architect alive. He had reversed the formulas of Gropius and Le Corbusier; his mature view was that nature, not the machine, should be the architect's most important model. In the United

States alone, his humane perspective won him the allegiance of young architects such as Hugh Stebbins, Charles Warren Callister, and Ralph Rapson. Aalto mastered the use of his origins and its vernacular, building within the whole fabric of his environment yet bending modern materials to achieve his purposes. A warm, modest man, he lacked Le Corbusier's capacity for stridency and self-advertisement and did not have others' urge toward monumentality and self-aggrandizement. He was a brilliant innovator, exquisitely sensitive to his local traditions and conditions and yet able to draw on all of architecture's major styles for the benefit of humankind.

—Clifton K. Yearley

FURTHER READING

Aalto, Alvar. *Alvar Aalto*. Edited by Karl Fleig. Zurich: Les Éditions d'Architecture Artemis, 1970. Splendid text and photographs of Aalto's major works. Parallel texts in German, French, and English recite detailed descriptions of Aalto structures, designs, and furnishings. Hundreds of photos and plans, but no other reader aids. Worth careful perusal.

Diaconis, Pamela. *Scandinavian Country*. New York: Friedman/Fairfax, 1999. Provides a basic introduction to modern Scandinavian design. The book's full-color photos make it worth examining.

Donnelly, Marion C. *Architecture in the Scandinavian Countries*. Cambridge, Mass.: MIT Press, 1992. Important in placing Aalto in the specific vernaculars of Scandinavia. An authoritative, easily read survey. Many excellent photographs and annotated texts. Appendixes, chapter notes, fine bibliography, and an excellent index.

Giedion, Siegfried. *Space, Time, and Architecture*. 5th rev. ed. Cambridge, Mass.: Harvard University Press, 1967. A recognized classic and a handmaiden to most architects' recapitulation of their own professional history. Should be read in its entirety, but Giedion clearly understood the importance of Aalto's outlook and work and thus included a full chapter on him before he was widely known. Some illustrative matter, notes, and bibliography, as well as an index. Outstanding, regardless of whether one agrees with the author's critical pronouncements.

Gutheim, Frederick. *Alvar Aalto*. New York: George Braziller, 1960. Five brief, sketchy, and superficial chapters that suffice only for an introduction to Aalto. Should be supplemented with the work of Fleig, Pearson, or Schildt for any real understanding of the man or his works. Many good photographs, plans, a chronology of works, brief select bibliography, and an adequate index.

Lane, Barbara Miller. *National Romanticism and Modern Architecture in Germany and the Scandinavian Countries*. Edited by Richard A. Etlin. New York: Cambridge University Press, 2000. Aalto certainly exhibited Romantic tendencies, and this is arguably the most thorough work ever produced on the relationships among the artistic, literary, and architectural arms of national Romanticism.

Pearson, Paul David. *Alvar Aalto and the International Style*. New York: Whitney Library of Design, 1978. Authoritative and appreciative. Organization is chronological, and the text is detailed and easily read. A fine one-volume review of Aalto's origins, career, achievements, and philosophies. Prominence is accorded to Villa Mairea. Scores of excellent photographs and plans, good chapter notes, useful bibliography—particularly for article materials—and a solid triple-columned index. A crucial volume for laypersons and experts alike.

Schildt, Göran. *Alvar Aalto: The Decisive Years*. New York: Rizzoli, 1986. Enjoyable and indispensable; matchless for intimate, personal perspectives on Aalto's mature years. Schildt was Aalto's favorite critic, and he does a brilliant job of summarizing Aalto's and other functionalists' ideas about a technological utopia. Also discusses changes in Aalto's rationalist beliefs. Contains much material on Villa Mairea. Scores of excellent photographs and plans. Includes a detailed list of Aalto's works from 1928 to 1939 along with drawings and thumbnail descriptions.

SEE ALSO: 1903: Hoffmann and Moser Found the Wiener Werkstätte; 1905: Hoffmann Designs the Palais Stoclet; Oct., 1907: Deutscher Werkbund Is Founded; Oct., 1909: Completion of the AEG Turbine Factory; 1910: Gaudí Completes the Casa Milá Apartment House; 1917: *De Stijl* Advocates Mondrian's Neoplasticism; Spring, 1931: Le Corbusier's Villa Savoye Exemplifies Functionalist Architecture; Oct., 1932: Wright Founds the Taliesin Fellowship.

1937-1939
RENOIR'S FILMS EXPLORE SOCIAL AND POLITICAL THEMES

With such socially conscious films as The Grand Illusion *and* The Rules of the Game, *Jean Renoir established himself as one of the world's premier directors.*

LOCALE: Paris, France
CATEGORY: Motion pictures

KEY FIGURES
Jean Renoir (1894-1979), acclaimed motion-picture director considered by many the world's greatest
Charles Spaak (1903-1975), screenwriter who collaborated with Renoir
Pierre Fresnay (1897-1975), actor who played the role of de Boeldieu in *The Grand Illusion*
Erich von Stroheim (1885-1957), motion-picture director and actor who played the role of von Rauffenstein in *The Grand Illusion*
Marcel Dalio (1900-1983), actor who played the roles of Rosenthal in *The Grand Illusion* and Robert de la Chesnaye in *The Rules of the Game*
Jean Bachelet (b. 1894), photographer who worked with Renoir on many films

SUMMARY OF EVENT
When it premiered on June 4, 1937, at the Marivaux Cinema in Paris, Jean Renoir's film *La Grande Illusion* (*The Grand Illusion*) marked the culmination of Renoir's career as a French motion-picture director who explored social themes, expressed sympathy for workers, and criticized establishment capitalism. Renoir's films before 1937 included *Le Crime de M. Lange* (1936; *The Crime of Monsieur Lange*), about a worker who saves a company and then kills the boss. Earlier, Renoir showed interest in the naturalistic tales of Émile Zola and Maxim Gorky, with a silent film, *Nana*, in 1926 and a talking film, *Les Bas-fonds* (*The Lower Depths*), in 1936. He made *La Vie est à nous* (*The People of France*), blatantly proletarian propaganda, in 1936, but it did not have a public screening in France until 1969. *The Grand Illusion* is a continuation of Renoir's preoccupation with working peoples' struggles against social and political tyranny. Set during World War I, the film sets forth a view of the future that makes heroes of an unlikely team, the mechanic Maréchal and the rich Jew Rosenthal. While a plea for peace, it is not altogether an antiwar

film, because its heroes escape captivity to continue their struggle against their common enemies, the old order of European aristocracy and the German army.

La Règle du jeu (*The Rules of the Game*), released in a cut print in 1939, was hooted by its first audiences, nearly lost when its original negative was destroyed during Allied bombing raids during World War II, and finally restored to something near its original length in 1956. Despite the film's stormy beginning, its reputation grew tremendously over the decades until it became one of the world's most critically acclaimed achievements in motion pictures. In the film, Renoir examines again the relationships of workers and owners, servants and masters, with a dashing hero who is killed by a jealous husband, a wealthy aesthete of Jewish ancestry who is married to a moralistic Austrian, and two complementary poachers—one a failed artist and the other a failed servant.

Both motion pictures were achievements of a distinctive style that has been praised as realistic and democratic. Deep-focus shots were made of scenes in which several events occurred simultaneously, allowing spectators to observe a variety of movements, characters, and complications in a single field of vision. Subjects intermingle, as war and captivity bring together men of contrasting social backgrounds in *The Grand Illusion*, and love throws together men and women of varying social classes in *The Rules of the Game*. Both narratives follow similar patterns: from prison enclosure to pastoral liberation in *The Grand Illusion;* from sophisticated urban hypocrisy to pastoral farce in *The Rules of the Game*. The director casts a cold eye on decaying values, but he also exposes a sympathetic understanding of the trials through which people pass as their values are tested and found wanting.

The Grand Illusion explores the ironies of a war in which the officers of the opposing armies may have more in common with one another than they have with the men who serve under their commands. Von Rauffenstein is a gentleman with training and tastes shared by de Boeldieu; when together, they often speak English, which is the language of the aristocracy and is not understood by the commoners. Von Rauffenstein is the commandant of a gloomy and massive castle used as a prison for French, English, and Russian prisoners of war. He is not happy to be a policeman, but he has little choice, since he is crippled and scarred from battle. Von Rauffenstein is forced, by his code of honor, to shoot de Boeldieu when the French officer helps his men to escape the German prison.

Maréchal and Rosenthal make their escape and nearly die of hunger and exhaustion, but they finally reach an idyllic (although not completely safe) haven in the farm home of a German widow, Elsa, and her little girl. The French soldiers are warmly received by this family of the enemy, and they celebrate Christmas together. Eventually, the Frenchmen continue their escape, despite Maréchal's love for Elsa, and they succeed in crossing the border into Switzerland before a German patrol spots

Jean Renoir. (Hulton Archive/Getty Images)

them. Several borders are crossed in the film's symbolic use of realistic material, including the sexual borders that disappear when the prisoners dress as women to present a musical entertainment and, of course, the social and racial borders that are dissolved when the laborer allies himself with the Jewish bourgeoisie.

When de Boeldieu dies, von Rauffenstein cuts the blossom of his geranium, and by this gesture enhances the symbolic richness of the film. *The Rules of the Game* is full of such details, and it also includes a car wreck, a rabbit and bird hunt on a country estate, and a musical entertainment that concludes in a dance of death. The social texture of life in this motion picture is richly complicated, but moving across the boundaries of class distinctions are two profoundly interesting characters—the game poacher Marceau and the failed artist Octave, who is played by Renoir himself. The film complicates human relationships through the game of love, but it also analyzes the rules governing the game of civilization.

As a political statement, *The Grand Illusion* seemed to challenge militarist solutions to personal and social problems; indeed, some believed the film was highly pacifistic. Such an interpretation, however, has to take into account the sympathetic treatment of the soldiers as men doing their duties, sacrificing personal comforts, and devoting themselves to patriotism. In this respect, then, *The Grand Illusion* is romantic. Certainly, when de Boeldieu diverts German attention to assist the escapes of Maréchal and Rosenthal, de Boeldieu is performing a very romantic act of self-sacrifice.

To describe de Boeldieu's self-sacrifice as a theatrical role in the grand manner would not be an exaggeration. Renoir frequently used the device of theater or musical performance as a visual metaphor within his films. This technique of self-reflection and self-commentary would be taken up with equal sophistication by younger directors, such as François Truffaut and Federico Fellini. Truffaut, certainly, and Fellini perhaps were both students of Renoir's film style, against which they increasingly defined themselves.

It may seem odd to say that the self-reflective technique of theatricality within a motion picture is in a realistic style. The realism lies in the ostentatious claim by art to mirror reality, by drama to show an audience to itself, and by art to abstract the timeless from the temporal. Renoir's theatrical metaphors perform these functions. The soldiers' show in drag, followed by de Boeldieu's grand operatic gestures of self-sacrifice (which he carefully directs and stages for maximum effect), enclosed by von Rauffenstein's stiffly disciplined show of power,

reveal a confidence that play and art reveal essential truths and at the same time can be instruments for individual freedom and personal integrity. Soldiers dressed as women are men expressing their sexual and romantic desires. Grand gestures of sacrifice focus on tragic heroes, allowing romantic ones to escape. Discipline without purpose becomes an iron prison of the spirit.

Mechanical motions, from phonographs to crippled soldiers, occur in counterpoint to organic development in *The Grand Illusion* (ironically presented in von Rauffenstein's cutting the geranium blossom, as well as in the contrast between the massive prison and the idyllic farm). Similar counterpoint occurs in *The Rules of the Game*, but discipline is a source of integrity in that film, in which social order preserves individual identity from the anarchy represented by a thief (Marceau, a rabbit poacher) and an aviator (Jurieux, a solo flier). Although the film's protagonist, Chesnaye, seems to arrange and explain events, he is able to do so largely because of the animating spirit of the artist Octave. The fact that Renoir played this part is surely a reason the film is so intriguingly successful as a self-reflective experience of art. Octave is nearly a victim of misunderstanding, but he is also a figure of animality (symbolized by his wearing of a bear costume), which unites people in an organic way. Octave is a complement to Chesnaye. Their relationship is a warm advance on the destructive one that marked the pairs in *The Grand Illusion*.

Still, audiences did not like what they saw in *The Rules of the Game*, perhaps because it told them they were decadent, without direction, and careless about the value of life. The film ends with Chesnaye excusing a murder and turning back to his lighted chateau after Octave has wearily moved into the darkness of the opposite direction. The ending sometimes left audiences feeling dislocated and torn apart at the center; many have noted that the film tends to separate form from substance and discipline from vitality. This joyless conclusion irritated the Nazis and Fascists condemned by the movie. Others, such as U.S. president Franklin D. Roosevelt, saw something different.

SIGNIFICANCE

The Grand Illusion won several prizes for Renoir, including one in Venice in 1937 for best artistic production and one in New York in 1938 for best foreign film. Most interesting, however, was the vote by an international jury at the Brussels World's Fair in 1958 that ranked the film fifth among the best films of all time. *The Rules of the Game* also earned great respect when it was chosen as the third-greatest film ever made by an international poll of film critics in 1962. The latter film also earned the dubious honor of being hissed by its first audiences in Paris, banned by Nazis and Fascists, and praised by President Roosevelt.

Perhaps the most lasting impact of *The Rules of the Game* is in its portrayal of the triumph of the will to be, to endure, even when the game seems about to end and the rules are shown to be vulnerable to passion and to chance. Chesnaye, like a master of ceremonies, turns away from his audience at the end, and Octave moves into the audience as he moves into the darkness. (Renoir, like Chesnaye, turned away from his European audience and moved, like Octave, into an American one when he migrated to the United States during the war and later became an American citizen.) There is an affirmative consequence from these opposing movements, as the spirit of life disappears into the audience itself, where it can rejuvenate as it hibernates through the long, dark spiritual winter that is expected to follow (and did, in the war years). Such a residue of feeling, a calm beneath the passion spent, is more lasting because it is more realistic for living beings, moving through organic rhythms of light and dark, vigor and rest. Here is the major impact of the film, and of others directed by Renoir: entertainments end, ironies soften, and artists disappear through their art into their audiences.

—Richard D. McGhee

FURTHER READING

Durgnat, Raymond. *Jean Renoir*. Berkeley: University of California Press, 1974. A masterful survey of Renoir's life and work, with analyses of Renoir's films in chronological order. Durgnat presents Renoir as a storyteller with a mind to share. Contains a bibliography, an index, and many photographs, both stills from the films and views of Renoir at home and at work.

Ellis, Jack C. "Golden Age of French Cinema, 1935-1939." In *A History of Film*. 3d ed. Englewood Cliffs, N.J.: Prentice Hall, 1990. Sees Renoir's career as peaking in the era when films by Jacques Feyder, Marcel Pagnol, and Marcel Carné drew on a rich literary, theatrical, and painting tradition. Political turmoil, with escapist tendencies, was reflected in their movies. Includes stills, a list of major films, and a bibliography.

Faulkner, Christopher. *The Social Cinema of Jean Renoir*. Princeton, N.J.: Princeton University Press, 1986. A demanding study of the origins of Renoir's themes in political activity of the 1930's. Faulkner employs techniques of ethnography to analyze many of Renoir's films, including *The Grand Illusion* and *The Rules of the Game*. Contains a bibliography and index.

Leprohon, Pierre. *Jean Renoir*. Translated by Brigid Elson. New York: Crown, 1971. Presents Renoir as a painter's son and a craftsman who matured during the 1930's with three masterworks. The American Renoir is sketched as struggling to please Hollywood but eager to return to his sources. Contains excerpts of interviews, screenplays, essays, anecdotes, filmography, bibliography, and index.

Mast, Gerald. "France Between the Wars." In *A Short History of the Movies*. 3d ed. Indianapolis: Bobbs-Merrill, 1981. French experimental film of the 1920's prepared for the triumphant films of the 1930's. Analyzes *The Crime of Monsieur Lange, The Grand Illusion*, and *The Rules of the Game*. Surveys René Clair, Jean Vigo, Jacques Feyder, Marcel Carné, and Jacques Prévert. Contains an index and a valuable bibliography/filmography.

O'Shaughnessy, Martin. *Jean Renoir*. Manchester, England: Manchester University Press, 2000. Written for the general public, this analysis of Renoir's sound films summarizes the current debate over Renoir's social views and places them in historical and political context.

Pechter, William S. "Radical Freedom: Aspects of Jean Renoir." In *Twenty-Four Times a Second: Films and Film-Makers*. New York: Harper & Row, 1971. Pechter sees a continuity of theme over thirty years of Renoir's work. Failure to resolve conflicts between individual freedom and social commitments results in sadness.

Renoir, Jean. *My Life and My Films*. 1974. Reprint. Cambridge, Mass.: Da Capo Press, 2000. Renoir's autobiography is highly acclaimed as a model in the genre, and the director's energy and spirit radiate through every page.

SEE ALSO: Dec. 4, 1924: Von Stroheim's Silent Masterpiece *Greed* Premieres; 1925: Eisenstein's *Potemkin* Introduces New Film Editing Techniques; 1925-1927: Gance's *Napoléon* Revolutionizes Filmmaking Techniques; 1927: Kuleshov and Pudovkin Introduce Montage to Filmmaking; 1927: Lang Expands the Limits of Filmmaking with *Metropolis*; 1928: Buñuel and Dalí Champion Surrealism in *An Andalusian Dog*; 1934-1935: Hitchcock Becomes Synonymous with Suspense.

January-September, 1937
SEGRÈ IDENTIFIES THE FIRST ARTIFICIAL ELEMENT

Emilio Gino Segrè positively identified and characterized the first human-made chemical element, technetium, atomic number 43.

LOCALE: Palermo, Italy
CATEGORIES: Science and technology; physics

KEY FIGURES
Emilio Gino Segrè (1905-1989), Italian-born American physicist
Enrico Fermi (1901-1954), Italian physicist
Ernest Orlando Lawrence (1901-1958), American physicist

SUMMARY OF EVENT

The periodic table of chemical elements is an ordered array of the elements positioned to reflect the similarities and trends among the different discrete substances that compose matter. When the table was first created in the mid-1800's, controversy arose regarding placement of the limited number of chemical elements known at that time. The Russian chemist Dmitry Ivanovich Mendeleyev is credited with the foresight to leave voids within the framework of his representation of the periodic table, predicting that as-yet-undiscovered elements would fill these voids. In the years following his prediction, the majority of these missing elements were discovered and properly placed within the framework of the modern periodic table, with some notable exceptions. Even after scientists gained a more thorough understanding of atomic structure, as developed in the early 1900's, and with the work of Henry Moseley, who utilized X-ray spectral data to ascertain the atomic numbers of the elements available to him—thus providing experimental support to the periodic array previously based solely on similarities of chemical and physical properties and trends—voids remained.

The periodic table is arranged in order of increasing atomic number—that is, the number of protons within the nucleus of each atom of an element. There were no reports of discovery in the scientific literature on the isolation and identification of elements with atomic numbers 43, 61, and 85. The search for these elements among the rocks and minerals of the world was intense. Searching was not altogether random. The element 43 in particular, because of its reserved location in the framework of the periodic table, would have properties similar to those of manganese. Mendeleyev had tentatively named the element ekamanganese and predicted some of its chemical and physical properties. Scientists concentrated their search on ores and minerals known to contain those elements whose chemical behavior would be close to that of the missing element.

Several claims were made for the discovery of element atomic number 43 (which was later named technetium), the earliest of which was in 1887. All claims, however, were subsequently proved false until 1925, when Walter Noddack, Ida Tacke, and Otto Berg, based on unobserved X-ray spectral lines, reported a new element identified as atomic number 43. Each chemical element emits, under proper experimental treatment, X rays uniquely characteristic of that element. The emissions of known elements had been studied thoroughly and their wavelengths and relative intensities tabulated. Given, for example, an unknown substance, one could generate the X-ray spectrum of the sample, match it to the tabulated values, and identify its composition. Recognition of a previously unreported X-ray spectrum warranted the claim that a new element had been discovered. Following Noddack, Tacke, and Berg's initial claim of discovery, in which they named their element masurium, they attempted to isolate a pure sample of the element from the mineral columbite, the source material of their newly defined X-ray spectrum. Because they were unable to do this and without a pure sample to support their claim, their discovery was rejected.

During the period when the search for the natural occurrence of atomic number 43 was taking place, another seemingly unrelated series of scientific investigations was under way. Natural radioactivity had been observed first at the beginning of the twentieth century. Certain naturally occurring substances sent out emissions spontaneously; that is, they were radioactive. Notable among these was uranium. The study of radioactivity, the identification of radioactive emissions (now recognized as corning from the nucleus of the emitting atom), and potential implications of this phenomenon for humanity were beginning to be recognized. Among the early pioneers in the study of radioactivity and the structure of that atom was Enrico Fermi, an Italian physicist. Fermi received the Nobel Prize in Physics in 1938 for his work on the production of artificial radioactive elements. Upon bombardment of a stable chemical element with nuclear particles, frequently new and often unstable isotopes are formed. Artificial radioisotopes are of enormous interest not only for the information they provide regarding the structure of matter but also for their practical applications in industry, medicine, and other areas.

Emilio Gino Segrè was the first of many graduate students to receive a Ph.D. degree in physics under Fermi's guidance. He later received the 1959 Nobel Prize in Physics with colleague Owen Chamberlain for their discovery of the subatomic particle the antiproton. Segrè collaborated with Fermi on several studies pertaining to the interactions of particles with matter. These studies provided him with considerable insight into various nuclear processes. While serving as director of the physics laboratory at the University of Palermo, Italy, he received a sample of irradiated molybdenum sent to him by Ernest Orlando Lawrence. Lawrence had developed the cyclotron, a huge device weighing hundreds of tons and costing millions of dollars, which is capable of propelling nuclear particles to great energies. When these high-energy particles strike a target, they interact with the target material, producing artificial radioactive isotopes. Study of these isotopes and their decay contributed greatly to the understanding of matter and to the applications of radioisotopes for both peacetime and military use. The Lawrence Radiation Laboratory at the University of California at Berkeley was and remains today a leading center for the study of nuclear processes.

In December, 1939, Lawrence sent Segrè the molybdenum metal sample that had been bombarded by deuterium nuclei for several months in the cyclotron. Segrè and his research group undertook to study the effects of this bombardment and to isolate and identify the artificial radioisotopes produced. Separation of radioisotopes by chemical means—the only means available in 1937— was not an easy task. The transmuted products are many and are themselves undergoing radioactive decay forming further substances. Often, the quantity of each transmuted element is negligibly small, too small to be weighed by ordinary means. The presence of these products is generally ascertained indirectly through the measurement of their characteristic radio or X-ray emissions. Because these emissions are frequently very similar, prior chemical separations are mandatory if one is to say with certainty that a particular radionuclide is present. The slightest contamination of one component by another as complete chemical separation is seldom if ever achieved; it clouds the observed emissions.

It had been predicted from theoretical considerations that technetium could be one of the radioactive products formed from bombardment of molybdenum with deuterons. Segrè and his group were prepared to observe among the several predicted products (including isotopes of zirconium, niobium, and molybdenum) previously unreported emissions that might be attributed to technetium. Following lengthy chemical separations involving fusion, precipitation, filtration, and volatilization, an emission activity was observed that could not be assigned to any known element. This activity was attributed to atomic number 43, and Segrè first reported the results in a coauthored paper in the *Journal of Chemical Physics* in September, 1937. A series of papers by Segrè and his associates followed this initial notice and further characterized technetium by identifying several of its isotopes and studying its chemical and radiochemical properties. In 1947, Segrè reported formation of technetium from uranium fission rather than bombardment of molybdenum. The first significant quantity of the element, gram amounts, was prepared by others in 1952 from uranium fission products. Because of the availability of fissionable uranium from nuclear reactors, it is this source from which technetium is now prepared in commercially available quantities. The radiochemical data of Segrè's group could not be disputed, and the name technetium (symbol Tc) was given to atomic number 43.

Scientists ask whether or not technetium occurs naturally. The half-life of the longest technetium isotope, Tc-97, is 2.6×10^6 years. The term "half-life" refers to the time interval for one-half of any newly formed radioactive substance to decompose by emission of radioactive particles or rays. In the second half-life interval, half of the remaining amount decomposes. It is estimated that radioisotopes with half-lives of less than 1.5×10^8 years would be virtually undetectable considering the time interval between the present and when the earth was formed. Because of natural radioactive fission of uranium from interaction with cosmic radiation, however, it is suggested that some, albeit a small amount of, Tc can be found naturally. It has been estimated that this amount is on the order of 10^{-13} gram per gram of uranium ore and that this amount was sufficient to produce the X-ray emissions reported by Noddack, Tacke, and Berg in 1925.

SIGNIFICANCE

With the identification of technetium and later astatine by Segrè and his colleagues, the missing gaps in the periodic table of the elements were filled. Although some questioned whether human-made elements should be recognized as true chemical forms, their complaints were quickly dispelled; credit for the discovery of technetium was given to Segrè and his research group. As with other

the kidneys, bones, lungs, heart, liver, brain, and thyroid. Although other radionuclides are used in nuclear medicine, of the millions of diagnostic imaging procedures conducted each year, over 80 percent involve the use of ^{99m}Tc." The metastable technetium isotope ^{99m}Tc emits a 0.143 million electronvolt gamma radiation with a half-life of 6.0 hours, transforming itself into the more stable ^{99}Tc isotope. Combining ^{99m}Tc into compounds uniquely essential for various body organs and functions allows one (by monitoring the emitted gamma radiation) to determine the extent and duration necessary for incorporating these compounds into various bodily functions. If in monitoring this incorporation, one finds deviation from the expected normal body utilization of these materials, an abnormality is indicated and appropriate medical treatment can be started. Because of its short half-life, the ^{99m}Tc-containing compound rapidly loses its radioactivity, causing little if any long-term damage to the patient.

Technetium, with its numerous chemical oxidation states, forms a variety of chemical compounds, in particular those incorporating organic molecules similar to or identical to those found in body organs. Technetium is taken up easily in these organs and suited for a specific organ whose normal function is suspect. Studies on other animal species and on various plant functions also incorporate technetium containing radionuclides.

Scientists have amassed considerable information regarding the hazards of technetium and its proper and careful handling. As is true of all substances, technetium-containing compounds pose a potential danger both to humankind and to the environment if they are carelessly used.

—Gordon A. Parker

Emilio Gino Segrè. (AP/Wide World Photos)

radionuclides—both natural and artificial—studies of their properties have enhanced the understanding of matter and its composition and decomposition. Technetium, through its spectral emissions, has been identified on distant stars. Given existing knowledge concerning the half-lives of the various technetium isotopes, these data provide evidence regarding the time origin and composition of these stars.

Elemental technetium alone and in various alloys exhibits the property of superconductivity; that is, it passes an electric current with negligible resistance. As with all superconducting materials, this property is exhibited only at temperatures approaching absolute zero, yet as developments in this field advance, technetium may find a role in the manufacture of superconducting magnets.

The greatest use of technetium is in the field of medicine as a radiochemical tracer. In 1985, Thomas C. Pinkerton and his coauthors noted in the *Journal of Chemical Education* that "a wide variety of tissues can be visualized with ^{99m}Tc radiopharmaceuticals, including

FURTHER READING

Barr, Robert Q. "Technetium." In *Van Nostrand's Scientific Encyclopedia*, edited by Glenn D. Considine. 9th ed. Vol. 2. New York: Van Nostrand Reinhold, 2002. Brief summary of technetium traces its history, isolation, chemistry, and applications to industry and medicine.

Boyd, G. E. "Technetium and Promethium." *Journal of Chemical Education* 36 (January, 1959): 3-14. Detailed account of the discovery, chemistry, and uses of these two radioactive elements.

Deutsch, Edward, Karen Libon, and Silvia Jurisson. "Technetium Chemistry and Technetium Radiopharmaceuticals." In *Progress in Inorganic Chemistry*, edited by Stephen J. Lippard. Vol. 30. New York: John Wiley & Sons, 1983. Review of technetium includes information on its chemical reactions, electro-chemistry, and chromatographic separation techniques. Briefly discusses radiopharmaceuticals.

Holden, Norman E. "The Delayed Discovery of Nuclear Fission." *Chemistry International* 12 (September/October, 1990): 177-185. A very personal account of the activities of those associated with the events leading to the discovery of nuclear fission.

Kotegov, K. V., O. N. Pavlov, and V. P. Shvedov. "Technetium." In *Advances in Inorganic Chemistry and Radiochemistry*, edited by H. J. Eméleus and A. G. Sharpe. Vol. 11. New York: Academic Press, 1968. Overview of technetium traces its history, nuclear and chemical properties, separation procedures, and uses.

Krebs, Robert E. *The History and Use of Our Earth's Chemical Elements*. 2d ed. Westport, Conn.: Greenwood Press, 2006. Introductory text explains the importance of an understanding of the chemical elements and examines individual elements within their groups. Presents information on the discovery, history, and uses of each element.

Paneth, F. A. "The Making of the Missing Chemical Elements." *Nature* 159 (January, 1947): 8-10. A discussion on the search for atomic numbers 43, 61, 85, and 93. Urges the discoverers of artificial elements to name their discoveries.

Pinkerton, Thomas C., et al. "Bioinorganic Activity of Technetium Radiopharmaceuticals." *Journal of Chemical Education* 62 (November, 1985): 965-973. Detailed discussion of technetium imaging for studying functions in the thyroid, brain, kidney, liver, bone, and heart.

SEE ALSO: 1906: Barkla Discovers the Characteristic X Rays of the Elements; Jan. 2, 1931: Lawrence Develops the Cyclotron; 1933-1934: First Artificial Radioactive Element Is Developed; 1934: Discovery of the Cherenkov Effect.

January, 1937-February, 1940
ADAMS LOBBIES CONGRESS TO PRESERVE KINGS CANYON

Ansel Adams, photographer and Sierra Club director, used his photographs to lobby the U.S. Congress to create the Kings Canyon National Park.

LOCALE: Washington, D.C.; San Francisco, California
CATEGORIES: Environmental issues; natural resources; photography

KEY FIGURES

Ansel Adams (1902-1984), American photographer and conservationist
Harold Ickes (1874-1952), U.S. secretary of the interior, 1933-1946
Bertrand Wesley Gearhart (1890-1955), U.S. congressman from California
John Muir (1838-1914), American explorer, naturalist, and conservationist

SUMMARY OF EVENT

On March 4, 1940, the U.S. Congress enacted the legislation necessary for the establishment of Kings Canyon National Park in east-central California. The passage into law of the proposed legislation marked the successful conclusion of a long battle to protect these lands from commercial development, protection first sought by the preservationist John Muir nearly forty-nine years earlier.

During his initial exploratory trip into the Kings Canyon area in 1875, Muir recognized the unique scenic beauty of the region. Even at that early date, however, Muir encountered signs indicating attempts to establish livestock rights in the canyons and the initial stages of environmental degradation.

In December, 1881, Senator John F. Miller of California introduced a bill in Congress that would have established an enormous national park in the Sierra Nevada that would have included the Kings River area. This attempt failed. Ten years later, on his fourth visit to the canyons of the Kings River, Muir found the surroundings suffering from the ever-increasing activities of loggers and sheepherders. Muir had just successfully completed the campaign that led to the establishment of Yosemite National Park, barely one hundred miles to the northeast. The signs of commercial and agricultural encroachment in the Kings area spurred Muir to make a public request for park status for this region as well. Commercial interests were already well established in the area, however.

In the end, national forest status was conferred on the region, and it was placed under the jurisdiction of the U.S. Forest Service. Afterward, although repeated attempts were made to introduce legislation in Congress that would transfer the status of the area from national forest to that of national park, Forest Service lobbies successfully defeated all proposals. National park status would have placed the Kings Canyon forests under the direction of the Federal Park Service, a division of the Department of the Interior, and the lands would have been managed in the interest of preservation and recreation, without commercial interest. In the meantime, the Forest Service, as part of the Department of Agriculture, encouraged active management of the land and allowed hunting, logging, and mining to take place. During the previous year, in 1890, Sequoia National Park had been established, but without Kings Canyon. In the same year the General Grant National Park was established to preserve the General Grant grove of sequoia trees.

The efforts of Muir and others were resisted by stockmen, lumbermen, and those in Los Angeles who feared restrictions on waterpower development. The Federal Water Power Act of 1920 was amended in 1921 to exclude existing national parks from future water projects, but not national parks established after that date. The Kings Canyon had tremendous potential for waterpower development. The city of Los Angeles was seeking six sites in the region, thereby making any battle for park status that much more difficult. Between the years 1916 and 1926, bills were sent before each session of Congress calling for the enlargement of Sequoia National Park so that it included the Kings and Kern River canyons and the Mount Whitney area. Partial success was attained in 1926 when the latter two parcels were added to Sequoia National Park.

In 1935, the threat of greater and greater commercial development in the territories of the Kings River took on a new urgency among park constituents when the New Deal public works program proposed constructing a major highway into the area to spur private development of the region. The threat of a new road into the remote countryside reinvigorated conservationists' efforts to preserve the area as a public park. Leading the movement was the Sierra Club, a recreational and environmental organization cofounded in 1892 by John Muir, who served as its first president until his death in 1914.

Ansel Adams had joined the Sierra Club in 1919 and had been a member of the organization's board of directors for two years when in 1936 he was assigned the task of assisting the club's congressional lobby. The Sierra Club's lobbyists were promoting the preservation of much of the Kings Canyon as originally proposed by Muir, land that had been repeatedly left out of Sequoia National Park. Included in the lobbyists' bid was the Redwood Mountain Sequoia Grove, one of the largest

stands of big trees outside of the national parks. This grove had been under the protection of private owners, but as a result of a tax sale, it had become available for purchase.

The club's directors believed that the best means of achieving their goal was for Adams to present his photographs, as visual surrogates, to those lawmakers who were unable to experience the beauties of this region personally. Previously, photographs had had a positive effect in establishing Yosemite Park in 1864 and Yellowstone Park in 1872.

Adams had visited the Kings Canyon region in 1925 and again in 1926. The photos he would present in Washington, however, were taken long before he became a part of the efforts to establish the park; these images were not special products designed for propagandizing the club's cause. Adams's approach to photography was known as straight photography, because his photos were artistically achieved without retouching. Furthermore, as Adams would later explain, the subject was of secondary importance in his work. Adams's first objective was achieving a print that accurately recorded the artist's feelings or emotions visualized at the moment of exposure. Adams's photos were therefore particularly well suited to the Sierra Club's endeavor.

In November, 1936, Adams traveled to New York for the opening of his solo exhibition of fifty photos sponsored by Alfred Stieglitz's gallery, An American Place. Stieglitz was honoring the young photographer with a one-man show, something that he had allowed only once before with the work of noted American photographer Paul Strand.

Adams departed New York for Washington, D.C., during the second week of January, and after visiting congressmen with his portfolio of photographs under his arm, he was invited to address the congressional commission conducting park hearings. Afterward he spent two days in the capital with congressmen from districts abutting the Kings River territory.

On his return to California there was no indication of the bill's impending doom. Without further active support, however, the bill for a Kings Canyon Park failed in the 1937-1938 session of Congress. Nearly three more years elapsed before the Kings Canyon project passed into law.

During this interim, Secretary of the Interior Harold Ickes, whom Adams had encountered in Washington, visited San Francisco, where he met with Sierra Club directors. The meeting resulted in a compromise between Ickes, who promised to protect the wilderness values of

One of the photographs that Ansel Adams took with him to Washington, D.C., to lobby for the preservation of Kings Canyon. (NARA)

Kings Canyon with special provisions in a new park bill, and the club, which promised to support a smaller park area. Another part of Ickes's strategy was to accept a proposal from other park advocates and append the name of John Muir to the proposed bill, thereby assuring Sierra Club support.

Ickes convinced the club that this bill contained the idea for a new type of park, one that would not allow Yosemite-like luxury accommodations. The secretary of the interior envisioned a park for fishermen and hikers or mountaineers, where wildlife could be restored, a park serviced by a minimum of roads and horse or foot trails. Permanent improvements such as hotels and roads would be prohibited. At Ickes's request, a bill for a John Muir-Kings Canyon Park was introduced in Congress by Representative Bertrand Wesley Gearhart of California early in 1939. The title honoring Muir was later changed

while the bill was in committee because it was not a custom to assign individuals' names to national parks.

Prior to the submission of this successful legislation, Adams sent a complimentary copy of his book *Sierra Nevada: The John Muir Trail* (1938) to the National Park Service, which forwarded it to Ickes in early January, 1939. This work contained many of the pictures of the Kings Canyon region Adams had taken to Washington, D.C., three years before. Ickes was enthusiastic about Adams's book and presented his copy to President Franklin D. Roosevelt, who consequently lobbied in favor of the bill's passage. The Kings Canyon National Park bill passed the House that summer and the Senate in February, 1940.

Sierra Nevada: The John Muir Trail obtained the desired response and brought Adams compliments on the persuasive effectiveness of his photography. Adams often argued, however, that he was not willing to produce propaganda. Speaking later about his Kings Canyon folio, he insisted that he had adhered first of all to his own artistry.

SIGNIFICANCE

General Grant National Park was abolished in 1940 and became a part of the 460,123 acres set aside for Kings Canyon National Park. This and other groves in the Kings park area contain some of the largest living trees in the world. Following the establishment of the new park, visitors could enjoy not only the giant sequoia trees but also the spectacular contrasts between some of the highest peaks in the Sierra Nevada and the canyons formed by the middle and south forks of the Kings River rising in the High Sierra north of the border of Sequoia National Park.

The Kings Canyon National Park bill represented a significant and early move toward wilderness visions advocating preservation of natural environments rather than unlimited recreational use of the same areas. The creation of Kings Canyon National park was the culmination of the Sierra Club's most important conservation campaign of the 1930's. As of the end of the twentieth century, the park remained nearly roadless, closed to hunting, and accessible only to hikers or horseback riders.

Another result of Adams's work on the Kings Canyon Park project was the commission he received from Ickes in 1941 for a landscape photomural to hang in the Interior Department's Washington, D.C., offices. Adams's artistry continued to be instrumental in the preservation of many regions throughout the United States, including Three Sisters Park in Oregon's Cascades and Golden Gate Recreation Area near his own home. In 1958, Adams began collaboration with Nancy Newhall on the production of *This Is the American Earth* (1960), a book based on a photographic exhibit first organized in 1956. *This Is the American Earth* is only one of many of Adams's publications that focuses on the American wilderness environment.

Adams's environmental concerns went far beyond the artistic recording of nature. For example, in the late 1950's and early 1960's, the National Park Service initiated the "Mission 66" program, promoting automobile travel and thereby necessitating more park accommodations for the increasingly larger numbers of visitors to national parks. Part of the Mission 66 proposal included the remaking of the Tioga Road through the Yosemite high country, the construction of which would destroy a part of the Tenaya Lake area. Adams and others proposed alternative routes so that the road would avoid Tenaya Lake. In addition, Adams offered his resignation to the Sierra Club to protest the club's lack of action as well as the government's construction policy. Although Adams's actions gained some media attention, particularly his telegram to the heads of the National Park Service and the secretary of commerce in 1958, the road design changed little.

Adams also actively worked for the preservation of Alaskan lands; he was a member of the preservationist groups Americans for Alaska and the Wilderness Society, in addition to serving as president of the Trustees for Conservation, established in 1954 as an adjunct lobbying group in support of conservationist organizations.

Adams was tireless in his efforts to protect the nation's wilderness areas at the highest levels of national government. In 1965, he joined the environmental task force created by President Lyndon B. Johnson, and he later presented President Gerald R. Ford with a copy of his memorandum listing *New Initiatives for the National Parks*. In 1980, President Jimmy Carter recognized Adams's artistic and environmental achievements when he awarded the photographer the National Medal of Freedom, the nation's highest civilian honor. Adams's portrait of President Carter, the first official photographic presidential portrait, hangs in the National Portrait Gallery in Washington, D.C. Adams continued to challenge the federal government regarding care of the nation's environmental resources under the Ronald Reagan administration when he called for the resignation of Interior Secretary James Watt, whose federal land policy he opposed.

The name, artwork, and environmental achievements of Ansel Adams will always be inseparable from the American conservationist movement. Adams's photographs continue to give artistic tangibility to a specifically American vision of a people's relationship with its parks and wilderness.

—*William B. Folkestad*

FURTHER READING

Adams, Ansel. Interview by David Sheff and Victoria Sheff. *Playboy*, May, 1983, 5-6, 67-73, 76, 81-82, 84, 87, 226. Good source for a frank discussion of Adams's objections to the policies of Interior Secretary James Watt.

Adams, Ansel, and Mary Street Alinder. *Ansel Adams: An Autobiography*. 1985. Reprint. New York: Bulfinch, 1996. Provides insights into the artist's personal history and viewpoint. Very readable.

Cohen, Michael P. *The History of the Sierra Club, 1892-1970*. San Francisco: Sierra Club Books, 1988. Carefully written, well-researched study sheds light on the context in which Ansel Adams's artwork was nurtured, endorsed, and publicized.

Fox, Stephen. *John Muir and His Legacy: The American Conservation Movement*. Boston: Little, Brown, 1981. Very useful, well-written guide to the myriad personal, political, and philosophical influences that contributed to the environmental movement in the United States in the nineteenth century.

Nash, Roderick Frazier. *Wilderness and the American Mind*. 4th ed. New Haven, Conn.: Yale University Press, 2001. Intellectual history of Americans' relationship with the wilderness begins with the earliest days of European contact. Includes bibliography and index.

Newhall, Nancy. *Ansel Adams: The Eloquent Light*. San Francisco: Sierra Club Books, 1964. Well-illustrated topical treatment of Adams's photographic work.

Runte, Alfred. *National Parks: The American Experience*. 3d ed. Lincoln: University of Nebraska Press, 1997. History of national parks in the United States discusses the various motivations, political constraints, and other factors that have affected the establishment and maintenance of the park system. Includes maps, illustrations, and index.

Strong, Douglas Hillman. *Trees—or Timber? The Story of Sequoia and Kings Canyon National Parks*. Three Rivers, Calif.: Sequoia National History Association, 1967. Provides sound historical treatment of the forestry issues surrounding the establishment of the two parks.

SEE ALSO: May, 1903: Roosevelt and Muir Visit Yosemite; Jan. 11, 1908: Roosevelt Withdraws the Grand Canyon from Mining Claims; Aug. 25, 1916: National Park Service Is Created; Feb. 26, 1917: Mount McKinley National Park Is Created; May, 1927: Indiana Dunes Are Preserved as a State Park; Oct. 19, 1934: Marshall and Leopold Form the Wilderness Society; Feb. 4, 1936: Darling Founds the National Wildlife Federation; 1938: John Muir Trail Is Completed.

January 6, 1937
EMBARGO ON ARMS TO SPAIN

The United States adopted a noninterventionist approach in dealing with the Spanish Civil War.

LOCALE: United States
CATEGORIES: Diplomacy and international relations; wars, uprisings, and civil unrest

KEY FIGURES
Manuel Azaña y Díaz (1880-1940), president of the Spanish Republic
Francisco Franco (1892-1975), leader of the Nationalist forces rebelling against the Spanish Republic
Cordell Hull (1871-1955), U.S. secretary of state, 1933-1944
Franklin D. Roosevelt (1882-1945), president of the United States, 1933-1945

SUMMARY OF EVENT
As the Great Depression of the 1930's deepened and economic hardship increased, most people in the United States, including President Franklin D. Roosevelt, placed major emphasis on domestic problems. In 1935, the U.S. government passed a neutrality law that provided for a mandatory embargo of U.S. arms shipments to all belligerents. Despite most Americans' desires, however, international events were developing in a way that eventually would frustrate any hopes of noninvolvement. In Europe, Adolf Hitler had begun his career in Germany and Benito Mussolini was elaborating the fascist system that he had established for Italy in 1922. As the decade unfolded, it had become apparent that these nations were on the move, dissatisfied with the results of World War I and dedicated to changing the status quo. The two main champions of the Treaty of Versailles, the settlement that had concluded the war, were England and France, both of which, because of numerous factors such as internal economic problems, were willing to accept limited expansion on the part of both Germany and Italy as the best means of preserving peace.

It was in such a historical setting that the Spanish Civil War began in 1936. Seldom has an event represented the culmination of so many complex and long-range forces as did the decision of General Francisco Franco and his Nationalist forces to revolt against the Spanish Republic, led by President Manuel Azaña y Díaz, in July, 1936. Spain had become a republic in April, 1931, and was torn by dissension from the very beginning. In broad terms, by 1936, the Spanish Republic had come to represent the liberal, anticlerical forces of the nation and was dedicated to agrarian reform and disestablishment of the Roman Catholic Church, against which more than one act of violence had been directed by Republican sympathizers. However, large segments of the population, represented by the army and monarchists on the right and by the Anarcho-Syndicalists on the left, rejected this Republican government and by spring, 1936, civil disorder was widespread.

The immediate reaction of England and France to the civil war was the fear that it might spread into a general European conflict. To avoid this threat, France sponsored a British-authored plan for the establishment of a Non-Intervention Committee to see that the struggle in Spain remained localized. This solution soon developed into a farce, as Germany, Italy, and Russia—all members of the committee—began extending aid to different parties of the civil war. That England and France were unwilling to acknowledge or to prevent this aid can be explained by several factors: concerns that a leftist revolutionary Spain might open the door to social revolution and Soviet involvement in Western Europe, a desire not to permit relations with fascist Italy to deteriorate further, and the haunting fear of a local war leading to a general European conflagration.

In the United States, events had once more demonstrated the futility of trying to legislate for all contingencies in international affairs. The Neutrality Act in force at that time made no mention of civil wars, and the Spanish Republic (Loyalists) immediately requested military aid from the United States. Even before England and France decided on their Non-Intervention Committee, President Roosevelt and Secretary of State Cordell Hull had agreed that noninvolvement would be the best course for the United States to follow. Supporting this decision, the Department of State was strictly neutralist, as were William Bullitt, the ambassador to France, and Joseph P. Kennedy in London, two heavy contributors to Roosevelt's electoral campaign. Urging support for the Loyalists was Ambassador Claude Bowers in Madrid, who warned that a fascist state in Spain could have a fascist "domino effect" in Latin America. Bowers's input into policy formulation was largely ignored by Roosevelt and Hull. The administration announced that, although not legally binding, the arms embargo should be considered as extending to the Spanish situation.

Roosevelt and Hull had many reasons for this action. This seemed an opportunity whereby the United States could act in unity with England and France to preserve the peace by promoting noninterference in Spain and at the same time serve the cause of noninvolvement, the dominant attitude of Congress, the American people, and the administration. It would permit continuance of the policy of complete disengagement from situations involving foreign wars. This initial decision met with almost universal approval by the American people. Unfortunately, the unofficial embargo proved inadequate to the situation. The desire for profit led one entrepreneur to export more than $2.7 million worth of aircraft equipment to the Loyalists despite the disapproval of President Roosevelt, and it appeared that others were eager to follow this example. This situation forced the administration into requesting from Congress a special amendment to the existing Neutrality Act that would legalize the embargo on arms to Spain. Passed on January 6, 1937, by overwhelming majorities in both houses, the joint resolution soon became the focal point for a vigorous national debate, as the tide of battle turned decidedly in favor of the Axis-supported Nationalists under Franco.

SIGNIFICANCE

On January 9, 1937, *The Nation*, a liberal weekly, printed an editorial condemning the embargo resolution as "profascist neutrality." This particular line of reasoning was soon adopted by the elite segment of the American public, representing in most cases the liberal, professional, and well-educated classes. Ranged on the other side of the controversy were many who felt the embargo was a good assurance of U.S. noninvolvement and a minority who were anxious for a Franco victory. Numerous U.S. public opinion polls during the period indicated that most Americans favored the Loyalists in the civil war, but an even larger majority favored noninvolvement. Of those groups most vigorous in support of retaining the embargo, an especially large number were Roman Catholics.

During 1937 and 1938, the debate on the wisdom of the administration's policy continued. Liberal weeklies such as *The Nation* and *The New Republic* consistently debated the question with Catholic periodicals. A concerted lobbying campaign was undertaken in the spring of 1938 to end the arms embargo. Twenty-eight hundred volunteers from the United States went to Spain to aid the Republic, most serving in the Lincoln and Washington Brigades. Some were African Americans, such as Abraham Lincoln Brigade commander Oliver Law. About nine hundred Americans, including Law, died in Spain for the Republican cause. The embargo was never lifted, however, and by March, 1939, Franco was in complete control of Spain.

Many different theories have been advanced to explain why President Roosevelt decided not to initiate a change in the embargo policy toward Spain. Some scholars have asserted that Roosevelt retained the embargo because he feared the alienation of Roman Catholic Democrats, a bulwark of the party. Others have pointed to a divided cabinet and Roosevelt's ignorance about Spanish affairs. Still others have emphasized that the president desired to cooperate with the noninvolvement policy of France and England. U.S. military aid to one side in the Spanish Civil War would have flouted the international Non-Intervention Committee and placed the United States in the company of Germany, Italy, and Russia. Some scholars have asserted that retention of the embargo was simply another reflection of the predominant attitude of isolationism that controlled U.S. opinion during the 1930's. The policy clearly was not isolationist, however, but noninterventionist, as the seriousness with which the issue was debated indicated a lively concern about how best to respond to a very nasty and complicated civil war. To adopt neutrality was to choose among a range of possible responses.

—*George Q. Flynn and Irwin Halfond*

FURTHER READING

Alpert, Michael. *A New International History of the Spanish Civil War.* 2d ed. New York: Palgrave Macmillan, 2004. Well-researched analysis of foreign policy formulation in the era of the Spanish Civil War. Includes map, bibliography, and index.

Bolloten, Burnett. *The Spanish Civil War: Revolution and Counterrevolution.* Chapel Hill: University of North Carolina Press, 1991. Comprehensive and extensively documented study draws on previously unavailable materials from the Spanish archives. Includes maps, bibliography, and index.

Falcoff, Mark, and F. Pike, eds. *The Spanish Civil War, 1936-1939: American Hemispheric Perspectives.* Lincoln: University of Nebraska Press, 1982. Collection of scholarly analyses of reactions to the Spanish Civil War in the United States and major Latin American nations.

Forrest, Andrew. *The Spanish Civil War.* New York: Routledge, 2000. Brief text designed for undergraduates covers all aspects of the war, including the roles of foreign powers and the noninterventionist stance of the United States. Features illustrations, selected bibliography, and index.

Little, Douglas. *Malevolent Neutrality: The United States, Great Britain, and the Origins of the Spanish Civil War.* Ithaca, N.Y.: Cornell University Press, 1985. Provides an in-depth, critical evaluation of motivations underlying U.S. foreign policy objectives during the Spanish Civil War.

Thomas, Hugh. *The Spanish Civil War.* Rev. ed. 1977. Reprint. New York: Modern Library, 2001. Updated, expanded version of a highly readable seminal study of the war and its impacts on both individual lives and nations.

Traina, Richard. *American Diplomacy and the Spanish Civil War.* 1968. Reprint. Westport, Conn.: Greenwood Press, 1980. Standard work on U.S. policy concerning the war remains indispensable to any research on the subject.

SEE ALSO: July 17, 1936: Spanish Civil War Begins; Aug. 2-18, 1936: Claretian Martyrs Are Executed in Spain; Apr. 26, 1937: Raids on Guernica; July, 1937: Picasso Exhibits *Guernica.*